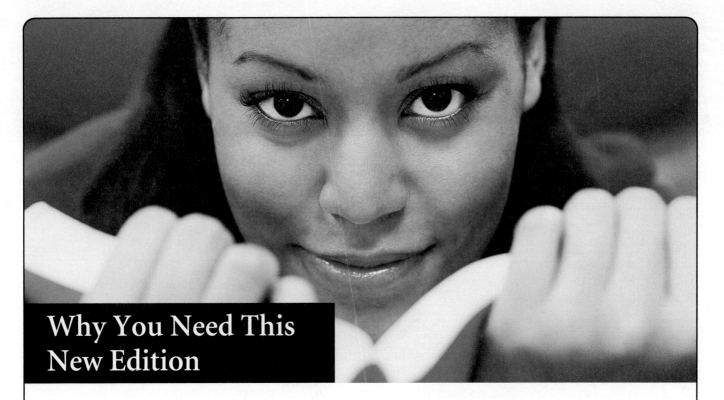

Why You Need This New Edition

The second edition of *Family Life Now* incorporates a significant number of changes that reflect more inclusion and attention to diversity and multicultural experiences, as well as new information about emerging areas of study in family life. Several topics have either been added or given significantly expanded coverage and discussion in this edition:

- The **racial/ethnic compositions and experiences of families**
- **Forgiveness**
- The agents of **gender socialization**
- The differences in **intimacy experiences in collectivist and individualistic cultures**
- **Dating** (heterosexual and homosexual), **breaking up, jealousy,** and **stalking**
- The advantages and disadvantages of **cohabitation**
- An **entirely revised sexuality chapter** that focuses less on sexual response, and more on sexual experiences; this includes an enhanced discussion about cheating, with the addition of information about online relationships and infidelity
- The conflict that occurs during the **transition to parenthood**, and an added discussion about heterosexual and homosexual decisions to become parents

- **Family size and family size trends**, and a new discussion about adoption
- **Motherhood, fatherhood, and co-parenting**; a new section about the best practices of parenting
- How children learn about their **racial/ethnic identities**
- The growing trend of **grandparents as parents**
- **Contraception and abortion**
- A new chapter about **balancing family life and work**, which includes discussions about diversity in the workforce, debt (including a section on student loan debt), and military families
- The **racial and ethnic differences in the experience of divorce**, as well as divorce and military service
- How to **avoid divorce**
- How **divorced moms and dads** differ in their experiences of divorce, and a new section about **living and loving in post-divorce families**
- 2010 Census Update--The inclusion of data from the 2010 Census throughout is an exciting opportunity for you to explore the history, methods, and application of one of the largest and longest-running sociological studies ever conducted

Family Life Now

Census Update

Second Edition

Kelly J. Welch

Kansas State University

Allyn & Bacon

Boston   Columbus   Indianapolis   New York   San Francisco   Upper Saddle River
Amsterdam   Cape Town   Dubai   London   Madrid   Milan   Munich   Paris   Montreal   Toronto
Delhi   Mexico City   Sao Paulo   Sydney   Hong Kong   Seoul   Singapore   Taipei   Tokyo

Publisher: Karen Hanson
Development Editor: Jessica Carlisle, Deb Hanlon and Maggie Barbieri
Editorial Assistant: Christine Dore
Executive Marketing Manager: Kelly May
Marketing Assistant: Janeli Bitor
Production Editor: Claudine Bellanton
Manufacturing Buyer: Debbie Rossi
Cover Administrator/Designer: Kristina Mose-Libon
Editorial Production and Composition Service: PreMediaGlobal
Interior Design: Mark Bergeron, Publishers' Design and Production Services, Inc.
Photo Researcher: Kate Cebik

Credits appear on page 632, which constitutes an extension of the copyright page.

Library of Congress Cataloging-in-Publication Data

Catalog-in-Publishing data unavailable at press time

10 9 8 7 6 5 4 3 2 1   CRK   15 14 13 12 11

Allyn & Bacon
is an imprint of

www.pearsonhighered.com

ISBN: 10: 0-205-00683-3
ISBN: 13: 978-0-205-00683-0

This book is dedicated to my father, Jim Shea.

Unconditional. Love.

Dad, Daddy, Pop—you were our first family life educator.
I love you forever and always.

—*Chickie*

Brief Contents

Contents

5 Intimacy: Developing and Experiencing Affectionate Bonds   139

7 The Path to Commitment: Attraction, Dating, Partnering, and Cohabitation 205

8 Coupling: From Singlehood to Marriage   241

13 Uncoupling: Relationship Deterioration and Divorce   423

Preface

A Note to the Student

Oftentimes, students ask me what leads me to teach, research, and write about marriages, families, and intimate relationships—and it's always a tough question to answer because there are so many reasons why! I suppose the short answer to "why" I do what I do is because, to me, our families and our intimate partners are our foundation: They are our source for being nurtured and loved, and they are of the utmost importance in our lives. While it is safe to say that all families are far from perfect and have room for improvement (mine included!), our families are usually there for us when the rest of the world is not. And, however each of us experiences family and intimate relationships, most of us want to be supportive, active participants.

But our families also serve as models for learning to love and to be intimate. In many, many ways, the family that a person is raised in sets the stage for a person's relational future. How *do* we learn to love? To communicate? To resolve conflict? To be sexual? And, if our family life isn't/wasn't healthy, are we doomed to failure in our future relationships? I am passionate about what I do because I want to empower and equip you to "do" family and intimate relationships to the best of your capabilities. I consider it an *honor* and a *privilege* to be able to help you learn about this important area of study—a subject that affects your everyday life.

There are so many issues that intimate partners and families face today. Before I began to write this second edition, I spent a lot of time talking to students and reading their emails so I could get to the heart of what *students really want to know*. Having loved ones deployed to Iraq and Afghanistan, seeing parents experience bankruptcy or the loss of the family home because of the economic downturn, dealing with the past and present effects of intimate partner violence, and a myriad of questions about sex were the starting points for this edition. Not only have I included a lot of personal stories and stories from students, but I've worked really hard to bring you the most current, up-to-date research to guide you through your exploration of intimate and family life. And, because college life is so demanding today, I've also shortened the length of the chapters to make your study a bit easier. I think you'll find that this textbook is just what you are looking for—it's real, it's transparent, and it's *relevant* to your life.

As you work your way through this text, you may have questions or opinions you'd like to share with me. Please feel free to email me your thoughts at kwelch@ksu.edu. You can also chat with me on my website, http://www.drkellywelch.com or follow me on Twitter. I look forward to hearing from you!

It is my deepest hope that with this book and with your professor's or instructor's guidance and instruction, you will come away with the knowledge that allows you to enjoy rich and satisfying intimate and family relationships. Now, let's roll up our sleeves and get busy!

A Note to the Instructor

It's been said that if knowledge is power, then enthusiasm pulls the switch—and I bring this second edition of *Family Life Now* to you with much enthusiasm!

As I began to research and write this second edition, I spent a great deal of time talking with students, colleagues, and even friends, to try to get to the heart of what people *want* and what they *need* today in a book that addresses marriage, family, and intimate relationship experiences. Then, in the midst of this revision, my father suffered a serious and rapid decline in his health. There I was—suddenly finding myself navigating an experience (providing elder-care and being tapped as an official member of the sandwich generation) that I read about, write about, and teach about for a living. But despite this knowledge base, I still at times felt lost and helpless when trying to care for Dad and at the same time balance all my other responsibilities. Too many times to count, I felt like I was making up the script and the rules as I went along. Often during these past few months my siblings have said, "What do people do who don't have a background in this? Where do they turn? How do they even know where to start?" Through these experiences, I have been reminded that what we do as family practitioners and educators *really is life changing*—and greatly needed in our hectic, stress-filled society today. As difficult as these past few months have been, the experiences have deepened the passion I have to educate and to inform others about how to "do" family to the best of their capabilities. And I have brought that passion to this textbook.

Having taught over 20,000 undergraduate students in human development, sexuality, and marriage and family classes, I know from personal experience that teaching is a demanding and often daunting task, because in our field we are confronted with the difficulty that much of what we teach is value-laden and sometimes politically polarizing. From heterosexuality and homosexuality, to sex inside and outside of marriage, to dating and cohabitation, to marriage and divorce, as instructors we need to find ways to teach the material with balanced viewpoints so that we don't alienate our students, and so they can come away with the "best of the best." Adding to this challenge, our students today must often simultaneously cope with the demands of school and unprecedented stressors, such as having a parent, spouse, or loved one deployed to Iraq or Afghanistan, or experiencing the loss of a family home or the inability to get financial aid because of the recent economic downturn experienced in the United States. So, how do we best reach and teach them?

As you thumb through the pages of this book, I think you'll find a voice that is simultaneously informative and rigorous, humorous and entertaining, and always compassionate and heartfelt. I bring you and your students the most current, relevant information about the social and emotional aspects of relational and intimate living, and present a candid, sensitive, inclusive, nonjudgmental, balance of theory and "real life." The contemporary research in this book is accompanied by practical, minds-on, hearts-on activities that make your students feel comfortable and safe talking about everything from dating, to sex, to intimate partner violence. It is my hope that you find this to be a natural partner to your course, and that your students discover a resource to help them make informed decisions about their personal and family relationships.

As students begin their process of discovery, they will notice a prominent theme woven throughout this text: We are all, as relational people, products of our intergenerational families of origin. Indeed, we do not develop our relationship capacities in isolation! From love, to intimacy, to communication, to our experiences of sexuality, even to the experiences of divorce, this text shows students how we affect and are affected by those in our environments—both at family and societal levels.

This book follows the Family Life Education framework to examine marriages, families, and intimate relationships. Throughout the text, theories from the fields of sociology, family studies, psychology, lifespan human development, and other social sciences are integrated, making this text applicable to students' everyday lives.

Instructor's Transition Guide

Content Changes by Chapter

Family Life Now provides students with a realistic, engaging, personally relevant, and academically informative introduction to the study of intimate relationships, marriage, and families. The second edition builds on the success of the first edition and maintains many of its original features, such as its conversational tone and the *Family Life Now, Own It!, Healthy Selves/Healthy Families, The Family Table,* and *Taking Sides* feature boxes. Global changes in the second edition include new and expanded numbers of informative graphics and photos, more attention to diversity and multicultural issues, and significantly updated research, with hundreds of new research studies and demographic trends reported. Further, chapter lengths have been streamlined and condensed where possible.

I am also pleased with the addition of Chapter 12, "Family Life and Work: A Balancing Act." This chapter addresses the struggles couples and families face when trying to balance work with relational life. Some highlights include the economic downturn experienced in the United States in 2008 and its effects on families, as well as practical advice on such things as how to manage student loan debt. To this end, the material from Chapters 1 and 2 was combined/condensed.

There is no question that the fields of intimate relationships, marriage, and family are in a continuous state of change, and it is my sincere hope that my hard work on this revision helps instructors and students alike stay on the leading edge of these changes.

Chapter 1: Family Life Now This chapter presents an in-depth look at the landscape of contemporary experiences of marriages and families. With updated sources and demographic trends, changes in the second edition include

- expanded coverage of racial/ethnic compositions of families.
- new discussion about *Native American/Alaska Native families.*
- expanded discussions about the significance of collectivist and individualistic cultures, and how these social identities shape family experiences.
- *Bronfenbrenner's Ecological Model* (moved from Chapter 2 to Chapter 1).
- revised discussion about *Family Life Education* to include information about practicing as a family life educator.
- six new figures, including a time line of Family Life Education.
- **Added Research Studies** (selected)
  - "Acculturation and the sexual reproductive health of Latino youth in the United States" (Afable-Munsuz & Brindis, 2006).
  - "Between religion and desire: Being Muslim and gay in Indonesia" (Boellstorff, 2005).
  - "Sexuality in Islam" (Bouhdiba, 2001).
  - "Getting past our myths and stereotypes about Native Americans" (Fleming, 2007).
  - "Environmental, social, and personal correlates of having ever had sexual intercourse among American Indian youths" (Hellerstedt et al., 2006).
  - "Great Mysteries: Native North American religions and participatory visions" (Makes Marks, 2007).
  - "Cohabitation and marital dissolution" (Manning & Jones, 2006).

- "The sources of gender role attitudes among Christian and Muslim Arab-American women" (Read, 2003).
- "Contested meanings of the veil and political ideologies of Iranian regimes" (Zahedi, 2007).

Chapter 2: Understanding Families through Research and Theory It has been my experience that students *dread* learning about research and theory. By explaining the social science research process from start to finish, along with common social science research methodologies, I hope to not only minimize students' fears about research but also help them become excited about the research they will learn about in this text. I want them to come away knowing that if we, as professionals, want to enrich (and perhaps improve) the intimate and relational lives of the populations we educate and serve, we must understand how to undertake social science research. The distinguishing feature of this chapter is that it teaches students how to be *consumers* of the literature, and how to better tell the difference between peer-reviewed science and "pop" science, which is often presented on such television shows as *Dr. Phil* and *Oprah*. Students are also introduced to some of the theoretical foundations for understanding family life. In this edition, changes include

- definitions of *quantitative* and *qualitative;* expanded discussion about these two concepts.
- a condensed *Family Life Cycle*, which is presented in table form.
- updated trends (U.S. Bureau of Labor Statistics, 2008).
- a new feature box on animal research in social science and a new time line featuring the human life cycle.
- **Added Research Studies** (selected)
  - "Marital happiness and psychological well-being across the life course" (Kamp et al., 2008).

Chapter 3: Family Communication, Conflict, and Forgiveness Unlike other texts that jump right into "how to communicate" (with the assumption that we all have the same notion about what communication *is*), *Family Life Now* first includes a discussion about communication as an ongoing, ever-changing process that develops and changes over time; the fact that *all* communication is the result of multigenerational and cultural influences is woven throughout this chapter. We then examine two primary communication theories, which are essential to students' understanding of all aspects of their sexuality and sexual experiences: Family Systems theory and Symbolic Interaction theory. The chapter also focuses on those types of communication that contribute to couple satisfaction, such as understanding relational and nonrelational messages, the creation of private couple meanings, and the development of a relational culture. Conflict is also discussed. Changes to this edition include

- new discussion about communication between men and women, and different ways in which the sexes communicate.
- new discussion and a reading about the role of forgiveness in family and intimate relationships.
- **Added Research Studies** (selected)
  - "Forgiveness in marriage: Current status and future directions" (Fincham et al., 2006).
  - "Responses to interpersonal transgressions in families: forgivingness, forgivability, and relationship-specific effects" (Hoyt et al., 2005).
  - "Attitudinal ambivalence, rumination, and Forgiveness of partner transgressions in marriage" (Kachadourian et al., 2005).
  - "Forgiveness and its associations with prosocial thinking, feelings, and doing beyond the relationship with the offender" (Karremans et al., 2005).
  - "Validating the developmental pathway of forgiveness" (Knutson et al., 2008).
  - "Unraveling the role of forgiveness in family relationships" (Maio et al., 2008).
  - "Forgiveness in marriage: Putting the benefits into context" (McNulty, 2008).
  - "Communicating forgiveness in friendships and dating relationships" (Merolla, 2008).
  - "Dispositional forgiveness of self, others, and situations" (Thompson et al., 2005).

Chapter 4: Gender in Today's Society This chapter emphasizes the importance of gender in intimate and family relationships. Following an in-depth examination of the sociocultural influences of gender is a discussion about the paradigms of socialization: Learning theory, Social Learning theory, Cognitive Development theory, and Kohlberg's concept of childhood gender development. Updated coverage about the influences of media is included, as well as

- a new chapter opener vignette.
- streamlined discussion of the biological foundations of gender.
- new thoughts about masculinity, femininity, and gender inequality, which includes discussions about the glass ceiling, the wage gap, and the confidence gap, with updated data and trends from the U.S. Census Bureau.
- a new discussion about the agents of socialization. This section includes discussions about learning gender from parents, play, peers, and the media; it also includes an updated discussion about gay and lesbian parents.
- three new figures and five new tables.
- **Added Research Studies** (selected)
  - "Acculturation and the sexual reproductive health of Latino youth in the United States" (Afable-Munsuz & Brindis, 2006).
  - "Intercultural dimensions of communicating masculinities" (Jandt & Hundley, 2007).
  - "The Femininity Ideology Scale" (Levant et al., 2007).
  - "Confucianism and women: A philosophical interpretation" (Rosenlee, 2006).
  - "The gender gap in college" (Sax, 2008).
  - "Wrestling with masculinity: Messages about manhood in the WWE" (Soulliere, 2006).
  - "Counseling the culturally different: Theory and practice" (Sue & Sue, 2003).
  - "African American men, gender role conflict, and psychological distress: The role of racial identity" (Wester et al., 2006).
  - "Culture, masculinity, and psychological well-being in Punjab, India" (Yim & Mahalingam, 2006).

Chapter 5: Intimacy: Developing and Experiencing Affectionate Bonds Chapter 5 is unlike any chapter in other marriage and family texts as it explores intimacy as a process that develops from birth through adulthood. While other books discuss intimacy and love as interchangeable terms and experiences, the purpose of this chapter is for students to understand that who we are as intimates, as relational people, is shaped from birth and takes place within our families of origin. This chapter also presents the ways in which a culture's social identity influences intimacy experiences. The chapter concludes with a discussion about common obstacles to intimacy. Changes in the second edition include

- a new presentation on the differences in intimacy experiences in collectivist and individualistic cultures.
- a streamlined discussion about the psychosocial development of children, adolescents, and young adults, with emphasis placed on the significance of peer groups during these developmental stages.
- a new figure on same-group friendships among college students.
- **New Research Studies** (selected)
  - "Does campus diversity promote friendship diversity?" (Fisher, 2008).
  - "Cross-sex friendships: Who has more?" (Lenton & Webber, 2006).
  - "Cultural differences in intimacy: The influence of gender-role ideology and individualism-collectivism" (Marshall, 2008).
  - "A meta-analytic test of intergroup contact theory" (Pettigrew & Tropp, 2006).
  - "How do we decide whom our friends are?" (Rybak & McAndrew, 2006).
  - "How do friendships form?" (Sacerdote & Marmaros, 2005).

Chapter 6: Love and Loving In this chapter we turn our attention to the experiences of love and loving. We first examine love as a cultural experience, then look at the differences between passionate love and companionate love. This discussion is followed by a review of the prominent theories of love and again includes a cross-cultural, inclusive perspective. Embedded within the coverage of love and loving is the lifespan perspective of the development of attachment bonds. This chapter concludes with a thoughtful segment about the relationship between love and sex. New to the second edition is coverage of all of those factors that make love and loving so complex, such as

- a streamlined discussion about the history of love and romance.
- an updated discussion about the influence of culture on passionate love experiences.
- a new section titled "The Negative Sides of Love," which includes sections about stalking and jealousy.
- a new table explaining the passionate love scale and new time line chronicling love experiences across the lifespan
- **Added Research Studies** (selected)
  - "Jealousy and the threatened self: Getting to the heart of the green-eyed monster" (DeSteno et al., 2006).
  - "Passionate love and sexual desire" (Hatfiled & Rapson, 2007).
  - "College men and jealousy" (Knox et al., 2007).
  - "A Swedish adaptation of the Emotional Contagion Scale" (Lundqvist, 2006).
  - "Love and elopement in northern Pakistan" (Marsden, 2007).
  - "Perceived attitudes towards romanticism: A cross-cultural study of American, Asian-Indian, and Turkish young adults" (Medor et al., 2002).
  - "How does culture influence the degree of romantic loneliness and closeness?" (Seepersad et al., 2008).

Chapter 7: The Path to Commitment: Attraction, Dating, Partnering, and Cohabitation Frisky business! This chapter explores three influential theories of mate selection in a condensed format from the previous edition: the Evolutionary theory of physical attraction, the Social Exchange theory, and the Filter Theory of Mate Selection. Knapp's Relationship Model and Duck's Relationship Filtering Model help students understand the multiple processes associated with relationship development. This chapter concludes with a thorough and balanced discussion about nonmarital cohabitation. Changes in the second edition include

- updated research studies and data trends throughout.
- a new section, "The Dating Game," which includes discussions about dating scripts, heterosexual dating scripts, and same-sex dating scripts.
- a new section, "Breaking Up."
- updated cohabitation information, with new discussions about the advantages and disadvantages of cohabitation.
- three new tables and four new figures.
- **Added Research Studies** (selected)
  - "Relational quality and communicative responses following hurtful events in dating relationships" (Bachman & Guerrero, 2006).
  - "Getting it on(line)" (Barraket & Henry-Waring, 2008).
  - "The dating game: Similarities and differences in dating scripts among college students" (Bartoli & Clark, 2006).
  - "The economics of lesbian and gay families" (Black et al., 2007).
  - "Gay and lesbian partnership: Evidence from California" (Carpenter & Gates, 2008).
  - "Risk factors and consequences of unwanted sex among university students: Hooking up, alcohol, and stress response" (Flack et al., 2008).
  - "University students' experiences of nonmarital breakups: A grounded theory" (Hebert & Popadink, 2008).
  - "Cohabitation and marital dissolution" (Manning & Jones, 2006).

- "Overview of cohabitation research" (Olson & Olson-Sigg, 2007).
- "The close relationships of lesbians and gay men" (Peplau & Fingerhut, 2007).
- "Trends in marriage and cohabitation in culturally diverse families" (Trask & Koivunen, 2006).
- "Shacked up: A demographic profile of non-marital cohabitation" (Wu, 2007).

Chapter 8: Coupling: From Singlehood to Marriage This chapter begins with a discussion about Peter Stein's different types of singlehood, followed by a thorough exploration of today's singles, including never-married singles, gay and lesbian singles, and divorced and widowed singles. A discussion of *urban tribes*, the contemporary social structure that serves as temporary families for singles, is included. The chapter then turns its focus to the social functions of marriage, the legal dimensions of marriage, the rights and privileges of marriage, and the benefits of marriage. By discussing the processes associated with forming a new family system through marriage, students learn why the transition to married life is so tough. Interfaith and interracial marriages are included in this discussion. The chapter concludes with a discussion about those factors that contribute to satisfying marriages. Changes to the second edition include:

- updated coverage throughout.
- expanded and updated "Gay and Lesbian Never-Marrieds" section.
- enhanced discussion about the reasons people marry.
- up-to-date discussion about sexual orientation and marriage laws.
- updated and enhanced discussion about the Defense of Marriage Act (DOMA).
- seven new figures, including a time line illustrating the age of first marriage by gender
- **Added Research Studies** (selected)
  - "The deinstitutionalization of American Marriage" (Cherlin, 2004).
  - "Same-sex couples and the gay, lesbian, bisexual population" (Gates, 2006).

Chapter 9: You, Sex, and Your Sexuality Students always seem to make it to class for this lecture, don't they? This chapter explores the cultural contributions to sexuality, including family, racial, and ethnic influences. Particular attention is given to the different experiences of sex and sexuality in collectivist and individualistic cultures. Sex in marriage is explored, including a discussion about extramarital sexuality. Nonmarital sex, such as sex in cohabiting couples and gay and lesbian couples, is also covered. The discussion in this chapter is candid and frank. Coverage in the second edition now includes

- updated coverage throughout.
- new definitions of *heterosexual, homosexual, bisexual,* and *asexual.*
- an added "Cultural Scenarios: Parents as Sexuality Educators" section.
- an added "Racial/Ethnic Differences in Parent-Child Communication" section.
- an added "Cultural Scenarios: Race and Ethnicity" section, which includes discussions about Latino, African American, Asian, Native American, and Arab American cultures' views on sexuality and sex.
- streamlined discussion about sexual arousal and response (now summarized in a table).
- updated and enhanced discussion about sexual scripts.
- an added "Consequences of Adolescent Sexual Behaviors" section.
- a discussion about "Sexually Transmitted Infections" (moved from Chapter 11); updated trends are discussed.
- an expanded discussion in the "Sexual Frequency in Intimate Relationships," section, with updated studies included that address orgasmic response in women.
- an enhanced/updated section titled "Cheating: Sex Outside the Relationship."
- a new discussion in "The Connection between Love and Sex," which includes "Is Sex Better if We Love Our Partner?" and "Are There Differences in How Men and Women View Sex?"

- an enhanced discussion about sexual dysfunctions in women and men.
- four new tables and six new figures.
- **Added Research Studies** (selected)
  - "Oral Sex: Varied behaviors and perceptions in a college population" (Chambers, 2007).
  - "Protective factors associated with American Indian adolescents' safer sexual patterns" (Chewning et al., 2001).
  - "Female sexual dysfunction in lower Egypt" (Elnashar et al., 2006).
  - "Marital and sexual satisfaction in Chinese families" (Guo & Huang, 2005).
  - "Environmental, social, and personal correlates of having ever had sexual intercourse among American Indian youths" (Hellerstedt et al., 2006).
  - "What's love got to do with it? Sexual behaviors of opposite-sex couples through emerging adulthood" (Kaestle & Tucker, 2007).
  - "University student beliefs about sex: Men vs. women" (Knox et al., 2008).
  - "What makes women experience desire?" (Laan & Both, 2008).
  - "Prevalence and correlates of heterosexual anal and oral sex in adolescents and adults in the United States" (Leichliter et al., 2007).
  - "Personal and family factors associated with virginity among African American male and female high school students" (Lindley et al., 2007).
  - "Heterosexual risk behaviors among urban young adolescents" (O'Donnell et al., 2006).
  - "Recovering from an extramarital relationship from a non-systemic approach" (Oppenheimer, 2007).
  - "Sexual expression: Its emotional context in heterosexual, gay, and lesbian couples" (Ridley et al., 2008).
  - "Prevalence of and risk factors for erectile dysfunction in U.S. men" (Selvin et al., 2007).
  - "American sexual behavior" (Smith, 2006).
  - "Teaching about human sexuality and family: A skills-based approach" (Weinstein & Rosen, 2006).
  - "We met on the Net" (Wildermuth & Vogl-Bauer, 2007).
  - "Patterns of sexuality communication between preadolescents and their mothers and fathers" (Wyckoff et al., 2008).
  - "Contested meanings of the veil and political ideologies of Iranian regimes" (Zahedi, 2007).
  - "Parent-adolescent sex communication in China" (Zhang et al., 2007).

Chapter 10: Becoming Parents: Choices and Challenges We first look at the current childbearing trends in the United States, including the rapidly changing trends in teenage pregnancy and in interventions for adolescent parents. We turn our attention to the decision to have children among heterosexual and homosexual parents, and the increasing trend of couples choosing to remain childfree. This chapter also includes an examination of infertility and the impact of infertility on a couple's relationship. Unlike other textbooks, this book looks at the emotional and relationship changes associated with pregnancy, trimester by trimester. New material about the conflict that occurs during the transition to parenthood is included in the second edition. Unexpected outcomes, such as having a physically challenged baby and pregnancy loss are examined. Additional changes in this revision include

- a new chapter opener vignette.
- updated resources and demographic data/trends throughout.
- a new section, "Having Children: Now, Later, or Never?" This discussion includes "The Perceived Value of Children," "The Appeal of Parenthood," and the factors that gay and lesbians consider when they desire to have children.
- an added section, "Family Size: Lots of Tots?," which addresses growing trends, the Quiverfull movement and the Resource Dilution Hypothesis.
- a new section, "Adoption: By Circumstance or Choice," which includes a discussion about the adoption process and gay/lesbian adoptions.
- the addition of a new section titled "Contraception and Abortion."

- four new tables and two new figures, including a month-by-month pregnancy time line.
- **Added Research Studies** (selected)
  - "Gay men: Negotiating procreative, father, and family identities" (Berkowitz & Marsiglio, 2007).
  - "Which factors determine the sexual function 1 year after childbirth?" (Brummen et al., 2006).
  - "Partner relationships during the transition to parenthood" (Figueiredo et al., 2008).
  - "Pathways to childlessness" (Hagestad & Call, 2007).
  - "Religiosity and fertility in the United States: The role of fertility intentions" (Hayford & Morgan, 2008).
  - "Conflict frequency and relationship quality across the transition to parenthood" (Kluwer & Johnson 2007).
  - "Gay and lesbian families: What we know and where to go from here" (Lambert, 2005).
  - "Couples share similar changes in depressive symptoms and marital satisfaction anticipating the birth of a child" (Salmela-Aro et al., 2006).
  - "Parenting as a dynamic process" (Strohschein et al., 2008).
  - "The long-term phenomena of women's postabortion experiences" (Trybulski, 2005).

Chapter 11: Parenting Life Now The experiences of parenting are fluid. This chapter discusses parenting as a process, and introduces students to the different parenting styles conceptualized by Diana Baumrind. In addition, the Psychoanalytic, Behaviorism, Cognitive, and Sociocultural theories of child development are discussed. Single parenting, and gay and lesbian parenting are given significant attention with updated and expanded coverage. In this revised edition, changes include

- an enhanced chapter-opener vignette.
- updated resources and demographic trends/data throughout.
- a new section, "Motherhood," discusses the social construction of motherhood.
- a new section, "Fatherhood," discusses the social construction of fatherhood.
- a new section, "Co-parenting: Go Team!," discusses the importance to team parenting to children's overall development and well-being.
- "Ethnic Group Differences in Parenting," another new section, describes the differences in parenting styles among racial/ethnic groups.
- an enhanced section titled "Motherhood and Fatherhood: Adjusting to New Family Roles."
- a new section, "Grandparents as Parents: A Growing Phenomenon," describes the trends associated with grandparents as primary caregivers to their grandchildren.
- a new section, "How Do Children Learn about Their Racial/Ethnic Identity?," discusses the ways in which families teach children about the social meanings of their race/ethnicity.
- "Parenting 101: Best Practices for Parenting," yet another new section, describes four parenting practices that promote children's development and well-being.
- a new table on coparenting styles and a new time line of racial/ethnic identity development.
- a new *Healthy Selves, Healthy Families* feature box titled "It's Just No Fun Anymore: Leisure Time and Parenthood."
- **Added Research Studies** (selected)
  - "Lifecourse transitions and housework" (Baxter et al., 2008).
  - "Child, parent, and situational correlates of familial ethnic/race socialization" (Brown et al., 2007).
  - "Neighborhood context, SES, and parenting: Including a focus on acculturation among Latina mothers" (Ceballo & Hurd, 2008).
  - "Beyond socio-economic: Explaining ethnic group differences in parenting through cultural and immigration processes" (Chao & Kanatsu, 2008).
  - "No fun anymore: Leisure and marital quality across the transition to parenthood" (Claxton & Perry-Jenkins, 2008).
  - "Considering culturally relevant parenting practices in intervention development and adaptation" (Coard et al., 2007).

- "First-time mothers' expectations of parenthood: What happens when optimistic expectations are not matched by later experiences?" (Harwood et al., 2007).
- "Excavating culture: Ethnicity and context as predictors of parenting behavior" (Hill & Tyson, 2008).
- "Parents' ethnic-racial socialization practices" (Hughes et al., 2006).
- "Ethnic socialization and the academic adjustment of adolescents from Mexican, Chinese, and European backgrounds" (Huynh & Fuligni, 2008).
- "Marital satisfaction across the transition to parenthood" (Lawrence et al., 2008).
- "Disentangling ethnicity and context as predictors of parenting within rural African American families" (Murry et al., 2008).
- "Children of lesbian and gay parents" (Patterson, 2006).
- "Disentangling ethnic and contextual influences among parents raising youth in high-risk communities" (Pinderhughes et al., 2008).
- "Kinship care and the situation for grandparents" (Raphel, 2008).
- "Variations in parenting and adolescent outcomes among African American and Latino families living in low-income, urban areas" (Roche et al., 2007).
- "Delinquency, victimization, and substance use among adolescents with female same-sex parents" (Wainright & Patterson, 2006).

Chapter 12: Family Life and Work: A Balancing Act This is a new addition to the second edition! We begin our discussion by exploring the contemporary landscape of working families. This up-to-date discussion includes an exploration of today's dual-earner couples, and includes comprehensive coverage of a new section, "Service Men and Women," and the unique financial challenges they face when deployed. Coverage is also devoted to "Single Parents in the Workforce," and the challenges they face. We then take a realistic look at the demands of juggling work and family life, such as daycare and household chores, and explore the challenges associated with unemployment, a reality for many in America today. We examine the government's role in family finances as we take a look at social policies for working families. We conclude with a discussion about marriage and money, and deal with practical issues such as repaying student loan debt. This new chapter includes

- a new table, nine new figures, and five new feature boxes.
- **Added Research Studies** (selected)
    - "The cost of the Iraq, Afghanistan, and other global War on Terror operations since 9/11" (Congressional Research Service, 2007).
    - "Implications of shift work for parent-adolescent relationships in dual-earner families" (Davis et al., 2006).
    - "Two sides of the same coin? The differing roles of assets and consumer debt in marriage" (Dew, 2007).
    - "Debt change and marital satisfaction change in recently married couples" (Dew, 2008).
    - "Military families under stress: Implications for family life education" (Drummet et al., 2003).
    - "Balancing work and family" (Eyre & Eyre, 2008).
    - "The triangular theory of balancing work and family" (Harris, 2008).
    - "The gender wage gap" (Institute for Women's Policy Research, 2008).
    - "What we need to get by" (Lin & Bernstein, 2008).
    - "Balancing shiftwork and life outside work" (Loudon, 2008).
    - "Motherhood in the 21st century" (Medina & Magnuson, 2009).
    - "For richer, for poorer: Money as a topic of marital conflict in the home" (Papp et al., 2009).

Chapter 13: Uncoupling: Relationship Deterioration and Divorce Although the primary focus of this chapter is divorce, it is important to note that much attention is given to the processes associated with *relationship decline*. This distinguishing pedagogy recognizes that *all* relationships face the possibility of deterioration and termination—cohabiting relationships, gay and lesbian relationships, intimate friendships, as well as marriages. This chapter provides a careful review of the most current data as they relate to divorce trends. The correlates and causes of divorce are explored, and attention is given to racial and ethnic differences in divorce. The chapter concludes with a thorough discussion about legally ending a marriage, including property settlement, child support, child custody, and divorce mediation. Second edition revisions include

- updated sources and trends/demographics throughout.
- an expanded "Racial and Ethnic Differences in Divorce" section.
- a new coverage of "Structural Factors" and "Cultural Factors."
- "Divorce and Military Service," another new section.
- a new section, "Avoiding Divorce: Getting a Marriage Back on Track." This discussion includes "Where to Find Help for Troubled Marriages" and "Healing Marital Relationships."
- a new table and seven new figures.
- **Added Research Studies** (selected)
    - "Religiosity and marital stability among Black American and White American couples" (Brown et al., 2008).
    - "Race-ethnic differences in marital quality and divorce" (Bulanda & Brown, 2007).
    - "Marital therapy, retreats, and books: The who, what, when, and why of relationship help-seeking" (Doss et al., 2009).
    - "Divorce, race, and military service: More than equal pay and equal opportunity" (Teachman & Tedrow, 2008).
    - "Military divorce rates" (US Department of Defense, 2008).

Chapter 14: Rebuilding: Family Life Following Divorce Family living following divorce includes many transitions, from establishing a binuclear family, to negotiating ex-spouse relationships, to the effects of divorce on children and adolescents and their post-divorce adaptation. The challenges for single, divorced parents—household finances, changes in residence, changes in boundaries, changes in the emotional climate of the family, and dating—are examined. Significant coverage is given to the transitions associated with remarriage and stepfamily living. In this edition, changes include

- new sections, "Divorced Moms" and "Divorced Dads." These sections address the unique challenges women and men face when they are parents and then divorce.
- A new section, "Living, Loving, and Parenting in Post-Divorce Families," explores emerging findings that divorce does not have to be a negative experience for ex-spouses and children.
- an updated and expanded section about the challenges for post-divorce single parents.
- two new tables and a new figure.
- **Added Research Studies** (selected)
    - "Family ties after divorce" (Ahrons, 2007).
    - "Adult children of parental alienation syndrome" (Baker, 2007).
    - "Post divorce paternal disengagement" (Baum, 2006).
    - "You want to know how it affected me? Young adults' perceptions of the impact of parental divorce" (Cartwright, 2006).
    - "Effects of the Dads for Life intervention on interparental conflict and co-parenting in the two years after divorce" (Cookston et al., 2007).
    - "Custodial mothers and fathers and their child support" (Grall, 2007).
    - "Fathers' experiences after separation and divorce" (Hallman & Deinhart, 2007).
    - "Mothers' cooperation in coparental relationships" (Markham et al., 2007).
    - "Are married parents really better for children?" (Parke, 2007).
    - "Father post-divorce well-being" (Stone, 2007).
    - "Noncustodial parents' participation in their children's lives" (U.S. Department of Health and Human Services, 2009).
    - "Changes in family financial circumstances and the physical health of married and recently divorced mothers" (Wickrama et al., 2006).
    - "Divorce and adult psychological well-being" (Williams & Dunne-Bryant, 2006).

Chapter 15: Family Change: Stress, Crisis, and Transition None of us is immune from stress or crisis, and no family escapes stress, change, or crisis. We first begin our study by looking at family development stress, stress that occurs because of changes in family structure, family roles, or family rules. Because of the interconnectivity of family members, we examine how the experiences of *individual* stress reverberate throughout the entire family system—what happens to one family member is eventually experienced by the entire family. Hill's Family Crisis Model explains those factors that help families navigate the stressors of individual and family life, such as their perception of the stressor event and the resources they have available to help them cope. Family adaptive tasks are also discussed. The crisis of family violence is covered extensively, including discussions about the battered and characteristics of batterers. The chapter ends with a careful examination of those things that family members can do to increase family coping skills and resilience. In this second edition, changes include

- a condensed discussion of the ABC-X Crisis Model.
- updated and extended coverage of the crisis of family violence.
- a new *The Family Table* box on young families and stress management.
- four new figures.

Chapter 16: Family Life and Aging After a close examination of aging and the aged in the United States, we turn our attention to family ties through aging. We explore in-depth marital satisfaction, sexuality, divorce, and remarriage among the aged. Extensive discussion is provided about intergenerational ties, such as parent–child relationships in midlife and in late adulthood, as well as the experiences of grandparenting. Changes toward the end of life, including retirement and family caregiving, are explored. The chapter concludes with a comprehensive discussion about dying, the transition from life. Changes in the second edition include

- updated trends and demographic data.
- three new tables, including a retirement time line, and three new figures.
- **Added Research Studies** (selected)
  - "Secular trends in self-reported sexual activity and satisfaction in Swedish 70 year olds" (Bechman et al., 2008).
  - "A study of sexuality and health among older adults in the United States" (Lindau et al., 2007).

Census Update

- 2010 Census Update - Features fully updated data throughout the text–including all charts and graphs–to reflect the results of the 2010 Census.
- A Short Introduction to the U.S. Census - A brief seven-chapter overview of the Census, including important information about the Constitutional mandate, research methods, who is affected by the Census, and how data is used. Additionally, the primer explores key contemporary topics such as race and ethnicity, the family, and poverty. The primer can be packaged at no additional cost, and is also available online in MySeachLab, as a part of MyFamilyLab.
- A Short Introduction to the U.S. Census Instructor's Manual with Test Bank - Includes explanations of what has been updated, in-class activities, homework activities, discussion questions for the primer, and test questions related to the primer.
- MyFamilyLab2010 Census Update gives students the opportunity to explore 2010 Census methods and data and apply Census results in a dynamic interactive online environment. It includes a series of activities using 2010 Census results , video clips explaining and exploring the Census , primary source readings relevant to the Census, and an online version of the 2010 Census Update Primer.

Supplements

Pearson Education is pleased to offer the following supplements to qualified adopters.

Instructor's Manual and Test Bank (ISBN 0-205-75087-7): This essential instructor tool includes detailed learning objectives, chapter summary, chapter outline, key terms and concepts, lecture launchers, discussion topics, class activities, suggested readings, and Web links. Also included is the test bank that contains over 1,000 questions in multiple-choice, true/false, and essay formats. All multiple-choice and true/false questions are page referenced to the text and classified by the degree of difficulty.

MyTest (ISBN 0-205-75075-3): This online, computerized software allows instructors to create their own personalized exams, to edit any or all of the existing test questions, and to add new questions. Other special features of this program include random generation of test questions, creation of alternative versions of the same test, scrambling question sequence, and test preview before printing.

PowerPoint® Presentations (ISBN 0-205-75076-1): You have the option in every chapter of choosing from any of the following types of slides: Lecture, Clicker Response System, and/or Special Topics PowerPoints. Lecture PowerPoints follow the chapter outline and feature images from the textbook integrated with the text. The Clicker Response System allows you to get immediate feedback from your students regardless of class size. The Special Topic Power-Points allow you to integrate rich and exciting primary source material into your course with minimal amount of preparation time. Additionally, all of the PowerPoints are uniquely designed to provide students with a clear visual of succinct points for each concept. They are available to adopters at www.pearsonhighered.com.

MyFamilyLab (ISBN 0-205-75994-7): MyFamilyLab is an easy-to-use online resource that allows instructors to assess student progress and adapt course material to meet the specific needs of the class. This resource enables students to diagnose their progress by completing an online self-assessment test. Based on the results of this test, each student is provided with a customized study plan, including a variety of tools to help him or her fully master the material. MyFamilyLab then reports the self-assessment results to the instructor, as individual student grades and as an aggregate report of class progress. Based on these reports, the instructor can adapt course material to suit the needs of individual students or the class as a whole. Contact your local Pearson Education representative for ordering information, or visit www.myfamilylab .com.

Acknowledgments

Recently, I overheard one of my son's phone conversations. He had been asked by a friend if we could all go out to dinner, and I heard him reply, "No, we're writing the second edition of my mom's book." *We're* writing—truer words have never been spoken, because I certainly didn't accomplish this on my own! There are many people who deserve to be recognized—and praised!—for their roles in helping to launch this fantastic second edition.

Second Edition Reviewers

Oftentimes, reviewers are the last group to be thanked in the writing process. I acknowledge them first, because *without them, this book would not exist.* Although I have never met them, I owe them a *tremendous* amount of gratitude and many, many thanks for the insight, direction, and suggestions they provided. Their comments gave me clear direction and focus, and guided me in making sure that all students who holds this book in their hands see themselves and their experiences somewhere in the pages. Thank you Rebecca Adams, Ball State University; Tiffany Aholou, University of Georgia; Margaret Bader, Nunez Community College; Anita Glee Bertram, University of Central Oklahoma; Leslie Bessellieu, University of South Carolina; Denise Bodman, Arizona State University; Wendy Boivin, University of Rhode Island; Jeremy Boyle, Kansas State University; Rhonda R. Buckley, Texas Women's University; Joi W. Bulls, University of North Carolina–Greensboro; Sidney Craig Campbell, Weber State University; Sandra L. Caron, University of Maine; Kim Cragun, Snow College; Elaine Eshbaugh, University of Northern Iowa; Victor Harris, Utah State University; Jeanne M. Hilton, University of Nevada–Reno; Joy Jacobs, Michigan State University; Matt Johnsen, Worcester State College; Kari Morgan, University of Wyoming; Jean Ann Moylan, California State University–Sacramento; Romana Pires, San Bernardino Valley College; Margaret Preble, Thomas Nelson Community College; Kris Ramassini, Indiana University of Pennsylvania; Christina Robert, University of Minnesota; Carrie Sillito, University of Utah–Salt Lake; Joanne Sommers, Bowling Green State University; Janie Jones Sowers, East Carolina University; Alan Taylor, East Carolina University; Carlos Valiente, Arizona State University; Brad van Eeden-Moorefield, Central Michigan University; Heather Von Bank, Minnesota State University–Mankato; Tamara Jo Whitten, East Carolina University; and Erica Yeager, West Virginia University.

First Edition Reviewers

You got us off the ground! Thank you Arfa Aflatooni, Linn-Benton College; Sylvia Asay, University of Nebraska; Richard Ball, Ferris State University; Larry Barlow, Florida State University; Janet Borst, Emporia State University; Kelley Brigman, Minnesota State University; Tiffany Brown-Griffin, Montclair State University; Norma Burgess, Syracuse University; Helena Carrasquillo, Capitol Community College; Joyce Change, Central Missouri State University; Wanda Clark, South Plains College; Susan Cody, La Grange College; John Coggins, Purdue University; William Cross, Illinois College; Beverly Curry, University of Nebraska; Jana Daniels, South Plains College; Mary Doyle, Arizona State University; Catherine Felton, Central Piedmont Community College; Eugene Folden, Ohio State University; Jean Gerard, Bowling Green State University; Scott S. Hall, Ball State Univeristy; Terry Hatkoff, California

State University–Northridge; Charles B. Hennon, Miami University; Greg Kennedy, Central Missouri State University; Kris Koehne, University of Tennessee; Lori Maida, Westchester Community College; Anne Marenco, College of the Canyons; Margaret E. Matyastik Baier, Baylor University; Jacqueline Oertel, State University of New York–Plattsburgh; Karen Schmid, Indiana State University; Ronaele Ruth Whittington, University of Hawaii; Ani Yazedjjan, Texas State University–San Marcos; and Betty Young, Minnesota State University.

I also wish to thank Maxine Effenson Chuck, my first developmental editor for this book. Max, your vision got us started and you're still a champion for the cause. Although our paths seldom cross anymore, know that you are frequently in my thoughts.

Colleagues Worth Their Weight in Gold

I first and foremost need to give a heartfelt thank you to Dr. Victor W. Harris, Lecturer and Coordinator/Advisor of the Family Life Studies program, Utah State University. Dr. Harris's contributions to the new Chapter 12 were invaluable. Vic, I turned to you not only because you are a treasure-trove of research experience and information when it comes to balancing work and family life but also because you share my passion and commitment to families and their health and well-being. It was a true pleasure to work with you!

I am also very appreciative and grateful for colleagues "behind the scenes," people who don't even know I admire them and their work from a distance: Dr. Arminta Jacobson, Professor in the Department of Counseling and Higher Education, University of North Texas; Dr. Carol Darling, Professor at Florida State University and 2008 recipient of the Margaret E. Arcus Outstanding Family Life Educator award; Drs. Sharon Ballard and Kevin Gross (extraordinary educators and mentors!), East Carolina University; and Dawn Cassidy, CFLE Education Director, NCFR. You inspire me through your research and your unparalleled dedication to the people we serve.

I am so incredibly grateful to my colleagues at Kansas State University:

- Dr. Ginny Moxley, Dean of the College of Human Ecology
- Dr. Bill Meredith, past Chair, School of Family Studies & Human Services
- Dr. Emily Lehning, Assistant Vice President for Student Life
- Dr. Pat Bosco, Vice President for Student Life

Without your support, guidance, flexibility, and frequent you-can-do-this words of encouragement, this book would not have been possible. I can't even begin to count how many coffee dates I broke with you. Coffee's on me—for about the next two years! Go 'Cats!

The Folks at Pearson Education

I can't imagine a kinder group of people to work with! I don't know how to thank Jeff Lasser, Executive Editor for Sociology. Jeff, it was your vision and your unwavering confidence in me that brought this book to reality, and for that I am eternally grateful. You are, and will always be, a friend. I also whole-heartedly thank Karen Hanson, Publisher, who jumped in and calmly guided this ball of nerves to the finish line! Karen, you are an absolute delight to work with, and I look forward to many successful projects in the future. Sharon Geary, Director of Development, encouraged me five years ago to focus on the words, the meanings, the pedagogy, and the learning. Sharon, your e-mail is framed and now has a permanent place on the wall above my computer. Thank you for helping me to always keep my focus. I am also grateful to Deb Hanlon, Development Editor (Psychology), who took care of all of the last-minute details to make sure the book stayed on schedule; to Courtney Shea and Lauren Macey, Editorial Assistants, who worked so diligently in preparing the manuscript for production and finding reviewers (and a special thank you to Lauren for keeping me in my oh-so-necessary supply of felt-tip pens!); to Claudine Bellanton, Production Editor, who shepherded this book through the production process; to Mark Bergeron, PD&PS design team, whose design for this book is beyond what I could have imagined (!); to Kate Cebik—Photo Researcher *extraordinaire;* and to Lynda Griffiths, project manager and copyeditor. I also want to thank Kelly May, Executive Marketing Manager (Sociology), who works her creative magic to make sure that *Family Life Now* is a best-seller. You folks are the best!

Jessica Carlisle, Senior Development Editor . . . wow, Jess, how can I even begin to put into words what you've done for this book, for me? To say that you're an extremely talented and gifted editor is an understatement. To say that you've further developed me as a writer is an even greater understatement. You are the force behind this edition, and I look forward to many years of working together. You. Are. Amazing.

Finally, I owe a world of gratitude to Nancy Forsyth, President of Pearson Teacher Education and Student Success. Nancy, you forever changed my life and the lives of my husband and children. Thank you.

To Those Closer to Home

First I have to thank my students. *You* are the reason I do this every day. You breathe life and energy into me with your emails and phone calls. You make me look forward to coming to class every week. You laugh at my stupid jokes and encourage the frustrated comedian within me. You put up with my crazy schedule as I prepared this manuscript. You found a path around the stacks of research on my floor. And always, always, you turn my day around when you smile and say, "Hey Dr. Dub, what's up?!" I hope you know how much I truly love you.

Finally, I could not have written this book without my family and friends. They alone know the countless sacrifices they made:

- My husband, Dave. Thirty-two years hasn't been nearly enough time with you. The beach is calling.
- My Guys and Gals: Eric and Gretchen, Shawn, Danny and Kateland, and Kyle. Educators. Mentors. Missionaries. Entrepreneurs. Adventurers. Always remember to buckle up and enjoy the ride! But promise me one thing: If you adopt our family's summer rule of "Don't come inside unless one of you is bleeding or needs an ambulance," make sure to tell your children that "needing an ambulance" *does* include if a sibling falls from a tree and is knocked unconscious. Clarifying this rule ensures that your children won't leave a sibling lying there like you did your brother, while debating whether "unconscious" falls into the needing-an-ambulance category, because it certainly didn't fall into the "bleeding" category! And at last—we have uncovered the 20-year-old mystery of who wrote "Dad is a bute hed" on the side of the house.
- My father, Jim. Daddy, you've always been my real-life hero.
- My siblings and their spouses: Terri and Pete, Tim and Michele, and Dan and Roxanne. We could never have predicted what we'd be up against these past few months. Although the grief was gut-wrenchingly painful at times, and although the confusion and fear engulfed us and sometimes left us paralyzed, we did what Mom and Dad taught us to do best—we were there for each other and loved each other, no matter what, through it all. I love and cherish you all.
- My niece, Molly. Gurl, what would I have done if you weren't here for the every-day-at-4:00 delivery of my popcorn and diet orange pop?! I also can't thank you enough for your meticulous attention to making sure all of the references were accounted for! I learned more from you than you'll ever know. I luvs ya!
- Aaron Duff, my Undergraduate Peer Educator. Thank you for tying up all the loose ends and for writing the end-of-chapter quizzes! You possess strength of character and integrity—it is a privilege to have you on my staff and to call you friend.
- Jay Peters, my Teaching Assistant. Jay, without your organization, I would still be buried!! La Fie's on me, forever.
- Joe Knopp, a quiet voice of reason and strength in the midst of a battering storm. You got us through.

- Dr. Ryan Darrow (Mesa Community College) and Dr. Ryan Peterson (University of Central Missouri)—be ready to take the torch!
- Pastor Ed and Angela Walker, and our community of church friends. All I can say is *Thank you!!*

Again, I sincerely hope that you enjoy reading and teaching from this book. I've worked so diligently to try to incorporate everything on your wish lists, and have given my best to ensure that issues facing us all today are included. At the end of the day, I hope that students are presented a realistic picture of intimate and family life today, and that they hold in their hands a book that is relevant to their lives. My very best to you!

Kelly

Family Life Now

1

It has been nearly 30 years (and still counting!) since my wedding day, and I remember it as if it happened yesterday—the dusting of snow on the ground, friends I knew I would never lose touch with, the tears in my mother's eyes, my husband-to-be's locked gaze on mine. And my father's words have stayed with me, spoken just seconds before we took that first step toward my chosen life mate: "When you take your first step down this aisle, you must do so as if the word 'divorce' does not exist—you must enter this marriage knowing that divorce is a possibility, but something that should be your very last resort. Because after today, I can guarantee you that along with the happiness and joy you are feeling at this very moment, marriage will bring with it sorrow. There will be heartbreak, there will be tragedy, there will be financial difficulties. Before I walk you down the aisle, you must know in your heart that marriage—and everything that comes with it—is truly what you want."

Source: Author's files

WILL this couple divorce? While it is impossible to prepare for the "everything" that comes with intimate partner life, we can better understand the processes associated with family living and lessen our vulnerability to divorce.

Characterizing marriage and family life is a tall order. My youngest son once asked me, "Mom, why do you need to teach a class about families? Doesn't everyone have one?" He had no idea how complicated and lengthy my response would be! Marriage, family, and intimate relationships are a complex web of interwoven influences: intimacy, gender roles, sex, childbearing and parenting, family conflict, divorce and remarriage, family stress, family distress, family communication patterns, dual careers, work/family conflicts, finances, and a wide array of realistic and not-so-realistic expectations. In addition to this potentially endless list of influences, we all experience family life from a different perspective: Each of us is an expert in our own interpretations and experiences of "family" and other intimate relationships. Because of these experiences, we often take our first steps into a serious intimate relationship thinking we *know* everything that comes with a commitment to a life partner.

But realistically speaking, none of us is equipped to tackle the "everything" that comes with marriage and other intimate relationships. Parents may argue; they may experience financial hardship or the loss of a pregnancy, parents or children may become ill; sex may be less than ideal; and in-laws may be a point of contention. Couples may disagree about who should get the children off to school or daycare, or have difficulty getting used to each other's sometimes-annoying habits. In the course of a relationship, we may experience infidelity or family or partner violence. Events outside of our control, such as the terrorist attacks on September 11, 2001, the destruction caused by Hurricane Katrina in August 2005, being deployed to Iraq or Afghanistan, or falling victim to the economic crisis that began to sweep the United States in 2008, may forever shake up our sense of reality. We change. Families change. We grow. And the "everything" we expected in our relationships is different from what we expected.

What Is Marriage? What Is Family?

Our intimate relationships, marriages, family, and individual lives within the context of family are integral facets of who we are. Most of us don't need a course in family life to allow us to be active family members. Some students taking this course do so because they hope to pursue careers in family services or policy, family therapy, ministry, or family education. Other students take this course because they want to deepen their understanding in the workings of family so that they may someday enjoy fulfilling, gratifying, and rewarding relationships of their own. Is it really possible to prepare for family life? Is it possible, for example, to "divorce-proof" a marriage, or to understand how and why people communicate the way they do? If it seems our parents' relationship is in crisis, or if a sibling is causing parents undue stress, does our understanding of family life make a difference?

Your instructor and I are privileged to help you gain an understanding of how you affect and are affected by the intimate relationships in your life, and to help you better understand the dynamics of your family life. By pointing you toward a path along which you make your own discoveries, you will gain insight into the intricacies of family life and intimate life. We begin our intriguing study of contemporary family life and intimate relationships by first gaining an understanding of the different facets of marriage. This discussion is followed by examining the composition of today's families.

UNDERSTANDING MARRIAGE

Marriage includes religious, legal, and social aspects, and people worldwide experience marriage and family differently. To some, marriage is believed to be a *social union,* wherein the

Intimate Relationships, Marriage, and Family Life

Own It!

Although marriage and family relationships can often be quite complex, it is possible to gain a better understanding of how we affect and are affected by the relationships in our lives.

Quickly jot down five things you hope to learn about intimate relationships, marriage, and family life over the course of our study.

1. Why did you choose these particular five areas?
2. What is it that makes these issues or process more important to you than others?

partners declare a commitment to one another. To others, marriage is a *religious*, holy, consecrated act. Let's take a look at the experiences of marriage, both in the United States and around the world.

Marriage as a Social and Legal Union A **social union**—often referred to as a **civil union**—is a legal term that speaks to the commitment, or the marriage contract, made by the partners. In the United States, marriage is a union that is legally allowed only between heterosexual couples, with the exception of the states of Massachusetts, Connecticut, Iowa, Vermont, Maine, and New Hampshire (beginning January 1, 2010), which sanction legal marriage between homosexual couples. This social/civil union carries with it binding, legal obligations. Although today the term *civil union* is more commonly associated with unions between same-sex partners who desire to socially declare their commitment to one another, the term *civil union* is still used worldwide to acknowledge the legal status of marriages.

Students often ask me why couples need a piece of paper (a marriage license) in order for their state to recognize their union. According to the U.S. Supreme Court (1888), American marriage is defined as a *legally* recognized social union—a *legal* and binding civil contract that is thought to be permanent—between a woman and a man who meet the specified, *legal* age requirements, and who are not otherwise *legally* married to another individual. And a marriage is not considered *legal* unless the couple obtains a government-issued marriage license. Thus, couples need a marriage license because, within the United States, marriage is a *legal commitment*, not a private bond between the couple.

Marriage is also a legal contract between the couple and the state in which the couple resides. The instant the couple says "I do," and the wedding officiate pronounces them to be husband and wife, their relationship acquires legal status. As the

WHILE in Western culture we typically select a life mate based on our feelings of love, in many cultures across the world marriage partners are selected by the bride and groom's parents. How would you feel if your parents selected your life mate? Would you trust your parents' choice?

IN Colonial America, the definition of "family" was broad and inclusive. In the 1600s and 1700s, family consisted of not only the mother, father, and children, but it also included anyone else over whom the patriarch (the father) had authority. This included servants, slaves, apprentices, and other dependents, such as his parents or his wife's parents, aunts, uncles, or cousins. (North Wind Picture Archives)

Supreme Court observed in 1888, "The relation once formed, the law steps in and holds the parties to various obligations and liabilities." In 1996, President Bill Clinton signed into law the **Defense of Marriage Act (DOMA)**, which confirms that marriage is a legal union of one man and one woman as husband and wife. We visit DOMA legislation in Chapter 8.

Many of you may someday choose a marriage partner based on love and intimacy, your shared values and principles, and a desire for a similar lifestyle. Or, perhaps after completion of your studies, you will return to your home country where your life mate will be (or has already been) chosen for you. As you begin your study of marriage and family life, it is important to keep in mind that marriages across cultures do not necessarily follow the Western format of selecting a life mate. In parts of the world still today, for instance, child brides, charity marriages *(sadaqa)*, and forced marriages are commonplace social unions (Saad, 2002). In Egypt, young, adolescent girls are given in marriage around the age of 12 to 15, typically to a cousin. The Amhara people of Ethiopia negotiate marriages between two families, with a civil ceremony following to seal the contract. In Somalia, a man becomes engaged to the woman before she is even born. The man makes the arrangements with the expectant parents, to whom gifts are given to seal the marital rights. And in the United States, people often choose their future mates based on love or other interpersonal attraction reasons, without necessarily seeking their parents' approval.

Social and Economic Aspects of Marriage Marriage is an important *social institution*, or structure, and serves society on several levels. The structure of the seventeenth-century American family in Colonial Williamsburg protected the aristocratic family's wealth and political power; at the same time, the common family structure provided efficient production units for lower-class families, such as planters (farmers) and shopkeepers. It was within the family that children were educated and received religious instruction. It was also within the family that the elderly and disabled were cared for. Thus, the family was *the* basic political, religious, social, and economic unit of colonial living. Even today in contemporary America, the family is foundational to many levels of society. David Popenoe and Barbara Dafoe Whitehead, co-directors of the National Marriage Project, maintain that the marital union between a man and a woman is the "social glue," the "fundamental social institution that contributes to the physical, emotional, and economic health of men, women, and children—and thus to the nation as a whole" (2002, p. 4).

In addition to forming a social union, many couples form an *economic* partnership as well by sharing economic resources such as bank and investment accounts, property, and cars. Each time a marriage takes place, the new social unit takes on certain financial responsibilities that are necessary for the society's survival, such as rearing and socializing children either born or brought into the relationships (such as by foster parenting or adoption). We explore the economics of marriage at length in Chapter 12.

Marriage as a Religious Act In the Christian, Jewish, Hindu dharma, and Islamic religions, marriage is considered to be divinely ordained, a sacred, religious act not to be entered into lightly. In these religions, marriage is viewed as a lifelong commitment between a woman and a man. Within these religious communities, the *sacrament* or act of marriage is believed to be the strongest of all social bonds around which the rest of society is organized. This bond, in turn, "initiates the new generations into the culture and traditions and facilitates further evolution of their civilization. It is the link that joins the past with the present and with the future in such a way that social transition and change can take place through a healthy and stable process" (Saad, 2002, p. 13). In Chapter 8, we'll examine the aspects of marriage as a religious commitment and sacred act.

Across the world, marriage is experienced as a civil union, a sacred act, a legal partnership, or a social and/or economic union. There are also variations in marital types—*monogamy* and *polygamy*.

Marital Types Marriages across the world are typically classified as either monogamous or polygamous. **Monogamy**, the legal structure of marriage recognized in the United States and in other Western civilizations, is a dyadic (two-person) form of marriage that involves the practice of having one sexual partner. The sex partner reciprocates this exclusivity to his or her marital partner. Monogamy itself refers solely to sexual exclusivity to one partner, but in the context of marriage there is also an expectation of exclusivity of emotional fidelity and love. **Monogamism** is the belief that monogamy is the only true morally and socially appropriate type of marriage or love relationship.

In some non-Western cultures, exclusivity is not a right of marriage. Today, **polygamy**, the practice of having more than one marriage partner, is the more widely practiced form of marriage across the world, particularly in those regions where the Islamic or Muslim faiths dominate the culture. Generally, polygamy is a form of *plural marriage* wherein either multiple wives or multiple husbands exist. The practice is usually passed down from generation to generation, and has existed throughout the recordings of history. In the biblical Old Testament, for instance, Abraham, David, and Solomon (who had 700 wives and 300 concubines) practiced polygamy. Likewise, in the 1500s, Martin Luther tolerated polygamy in instances where he believed the practice would "ensure the success of the Reformation" (Stack, 1998, p. 2).

Polygyny is one form of polygamy or plural marriage, and involves the practice of a man having multiple wives at the same time. In the Islamic and Muslim faiths, polygyny is permitted by the Quran (Koran), and its practice is commonplace, with certain limitations. Along with small pockets of nonconformist Mormons who practice polygamy in the United States, many Native American tribes allow the practice of polygyny. In his essay on the practical aspects of polygamy, polygamist Samuel Chapman denotes the benefits of plural marriages for women, citing, among other things, the availability of automatic childcare, the lack of pressure that husbands may feel to commit adultery, and the availability of a female friend for life.

Why would a woman choose to live in a relationship where multiple wives exist? Why would a woman choose to share her husband with other women? Mary Ben David (2005) notes the many benefits of her polygamous marriage, particularly in the areas of shared housekeeping, cooking, and childcare. She further notes that with several women in her home, her identity "cannot be wrapped up in her husband's identity."

Polyandry is another form of polygamy in which women have multiple husbands at the same time. These husbands are typically brothers. In polyandrous relationships, the woman mates with more than one male. This is a rare sexual mating system, even in the animal kingdom. Polyandry is a common practice among families in Tibet, where it is considered a wealth-conserving kinship mechanism (Goldstein, 1987/2002). According to anthropologist

ALTHOUGH the practice of having more than one marriage partner was banned by the Mormon church in the late 1800s, today some non-conformist segments of the church still practice polygamy. Warren Jeffs was a leader of the Fundamentalist Church of Jesus Christ of Latter Day Saints (FLDS); this church still practices polygamy. If the United States changes its legal definition of marriage to include gay and lesbian couples, do you think this will affect existing polygamy laws? Why or why not?

Melvin Goldstein, polyandry is practiced as a means of preventing or prohibiting the family's estate from being divided too many ways and thereby diminishing the family's overall wealth. When brothers share a wife, it is seen as the means by which the family's quality of life is sustained and the way to maximize economic advantage, generation to generation.

Cenogamy is a form of marriage often referred to as *group marriage.* In this type of marital community, every man and every woman is married to each other at the same time. This form of marriage allows casual, indiscriminate sexual activity among all its members. Today, the practice of cenogamy is most often found in communal living—a commune where collective living takes place—such as in tribal cultures. This form of marriage is not legal in the United States.

Just as there are differences in how we can experience marriage, there are also differences in how each of us defines and experiences family.

UNDERSTANDING FAMILY

What is "family"? How do you define it? In all likelihood, your definition may be entirely different from the federal government's definition, or from mine. The reason for these differences is that my definition and your definition of family are based on our *unique experiences within our own families.* Throughout this book, I will be sharing some of my family life experiences with you as I ask you to explore aspects of your family life that have helped shape who you are. Your professor may also share stories of family life, as may your classmates. As you exchange stories, you might find that you share similar family experiences. Most likely, you will have some experiences that are vastly different from any you have heard or read about.

According to the United States Census Bureau (2005), the federal organization responsible for collecting data about the nation, its people, and the economy, a **family** "consists of two or more people related by birth, marriage, or adoption residing in the same unit." On the other hand, a **household** "consists of all people who occupy a housing unit regardless of a relationship" (U.S. Census Bureau, 2005a). Thus, according to the federal government, a married couple and their children are considered to be a family, whereas intimate couples who live together who are not married make up a household. In nearly all societies the world over, the family is the social unit that is responsible for nurturing, protecting, educating, and socializing children (Barbour, Barbour, & Scully, 2005). Figure 1.1 illustrates for us the types of households in the United States (U.S. Census Bureau, 2008a). As you can see, half of all households today are married-couple families, but there is also great diversity in family forms.

The question arises, then, Is it possible to arrive at a one-size-fits-all definition of "family," as the U.S. Census Bureau describes? Probably not, for there exist as many definitions or descriptions of "family" as there are students who are reading this textbook, and beyond. The concept of family is, indeed, a subjective notion.

Each of us begins our relational journeys in our family of origin, or family of orientation. Our **family of origin** is the family into which we are born or brought into by adoption. It is the family in which we are raised and socialized to adhere to the customs and norms of the culture in which we live. And, just as importantly, it is within the family of origin we learn how to love and to be intimate with others. The **family of procreation** is the family unit that is formed when we marry and produce children. As we explore the nature of today's families, we use statistics to help us identify current patterns and trends. Although it is sometimes tempting to skip over statistics when reading, numbers are necessary because they present overall trends and provide us with an instant snapshot of U.S. families.

FIGURE 1.1 Types of Households in the United States

Today, there is no such thing as a "traditional" family form in the United States. There is great diversity in the configurations of households.

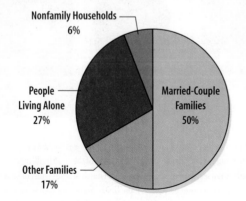

- Nonfamily Households 6%
- People Living Alone 27%
- Married-Couple Families 50%
- Other Families 17%

Source: U.S. Census Bureau (2010).

NUCLEAR AND EXTENDED FAMILIES

Today, it is essential that students of family life know the differing family arrangements of families, because this understanding allows human service providers and other family professionals to more effectively support, value, and work with diverse families (Banks & McGee Banks, 2002).

In essence, **diversity** refers to the broad spectrum of demographic and philosophical differences among groups of people within a culture. When we talk about being **diverse**, or about diversity in the United States, we are referring to people's differences in age, gender, race, ethnicity, cultures, sexual orientation, and religion. When we study people from a diversity perspective, it not only furthers our knowledge base about the variances in marriage and family experiences but it also helps us value individuals and groups, free from bias. This, then, fosters a climate of equity and mutual respect. In the sections that follow, we'll first take a look at *nuclear* and *extended* family forms. We'll then examine the expanding family landscape in our culture today.

Nuclear Family The **nuclear** family consists of a biological father, a biological mother, and their biological or adopted children. In the truest sense of the definition, nuclear families consist of first-time married parents, their biological or adopted children, and no other family members living in the home. In 2010, the "typical" nuclear family form was found in about 22 percent of the 117.5 million households (U.S. Census Bureau, 2008b). Figure 1.2 illustrates the family configurations in which children in the United States live today. Notice that although the majority of children live in nuclear families, other family forms show the complexity of contemporary family living.

Often, the nuclear family is referred to as the *traditional* family. This term carries with it a conventional depiction of the family form and the accompanying family values and traditions. *Family values* is a term that is commonly used today by politicians and TV news reporters, although it may mean different things to different people. Most often, **family values** refers to a society's paradigm or viewpoint that expects its members to adhere to perceived proper social roles, such as marrying and having children, remaining monogamous and faithful to the

FIGURE 1.2 U.S. Household Configurations

Children live in a variety of household types today.

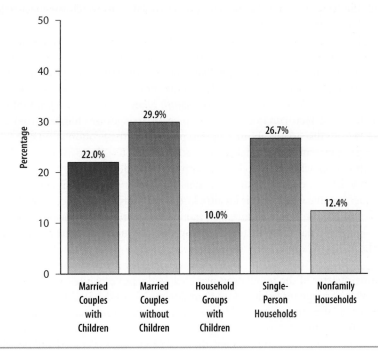

Source: U.S. Census Bureau (2010).

IN the 1950s, the television and media portrayed an idealized image of the American family: the breadwinning dad, the breadmaker mom, and the practically perfect children who all live in their always-perfectly kept home. Divorce, infidelity, children's problems, teen problems, substance use, and stepfamilies were never discussed. Some contend that this idealized family form never really existed.

marriage partner, and opposing same-sex relationships, marriages, and parenting by gay or lesbian partners. The family values viewpoint also frowns on births to women outside of marriage. It evokes a certain set of ascribed gender roles; for example, the women fulfill homemaker and mothering responsibilities (the breadmaker role), and the men fulfill the role of primary wage earner (the breadwinner role). This particular family form is also considered a *patriarchy*, wherein the male is dominant and is in charge of most decision making in the family.

Historian and author Peter McWilliams (1998) offers insight into the roots of the traditional family. He notes that the modern concept of two adults rearing their children under a single roof grew out of necessity during the Middle Ages, when the minimum number of people required to own and maintain a plot of land was two. In order to multiply their wealth, it was necessary to have others work the land; children were free labor. Thus, in order to have the free labor provided by children, it was economically necessary that one of the adults was a man and the other was a woman—and they were thus paired until death. According to McWilliams, love had nothing to do with the pairing. "Even if a husband and a wife hated each other, all they had to do was wait a little while—with disease, war, childbirth, and an average lifespan of about 35, most marriages lasted less than five years. The departed partner was immediately replaced, and the system continued." Men and older children worked the land and the women tended to the livestock, the crops near the home, and the younger children. Because the system worked so well, the church eventually got involved and, over time, the one-man/one-woman for life theology emerged.

If we were to identify a specific period in American history that the traditional family form was in vogue, we would look at the period of the 1950s in the United States (McWilliams, 1998). The high postwar marriage and birth rates, coupled with a prosperous economy in which a single wage earner could support a family, led to a national perception of the period as a "golden era" for families (McWilliams, 1998).

Through the television and the media, families tuned in to watch the idealized image of the American family: the wise, reassuring father who came home from a hard day at the office; the apron-clad homemaker mother (wearing pearls) who offered comfort and support to her hard-working husband and perfect children; the clutter-free, immaculate home; and the homogeneous neighborhood. Notes McWilliams (1998), the family life portrayed in the 1950s media was wholesome: There were no single parents (unless the father was a widower, such as with the fathers in *My Three Sons, The Andy Griffith Show,* and *Bonanza*), no infidelities, no divorce, no abuse, no teen runaways, and no prior marriages or children from prior marriages. There was no discussion about religion, politics, or the economy; no one lost his job; there was no gang violence in the neighborhood, no drug usage, no racism, no high school dropouts, no homosexuality, and no babies born out of wedlock.

Despite TV Land's depiction of the American family during this era, like *Leave It to Beaver*, it is questionable whether this idealized image of family really ever existed. Author and professor of comparative family history, Stephanie Coontz, notes the discrepancies of the idealized 1950s "good old days" family form portrayed in the media and the reality of family living during the 1950s (Coontz, 1992; 1999):

- About one-quarter of the population lived below the poverty line.
- The number of pregnant brides more than doubled from the 1940s.
- From 1944 to 1955, the number of babies born outside of marriage and placed for adoption rose 80 percent.
- Juvenile delinquency was so prevalent that in 1955 Congress considered nearly 200 bills to address the problem.

As Coontz notes, the 1950s were a dismal time for women, minorities, homosexuals, and any other social group that did not "fit in" with the images typified on the television screen.

The traditional, nuclear family is no longer predominant in the United States. In the new century, 1950s television shows like *I Love Lucy* and *Leave It to Beaver* have been replaced by shows such as *The Simpsons, Family Guy, Two and a Half Men,* and *Brothers and Sisters,* which perhaps better reflect the diversity found in today's families.

Is the American Family Deteriorating?

FAMILY LIFE NOW

So prominent are the changes in the structures and experiences of the American family over the past 40 years that great debate erupted during many political campaigns in the 2008 Presidential race about the "family values" of America. Is the American family deteriorating?

YES: Founder of the National Marriage Project, author David Popenoe asserts that the American family is in a state of deterioration. "It is well known that there has been a weakening of marriage and the nuclear family in advanced, industrialized societies, especially since the 1960s" (Popenoe & Whitehead, 2005). According to the National Marriage Project research findings (2005), the trends associated with family deterioration are:

- Increased number of divorces
- Increased number of couples opting to live together before marriage, or instead of marriage
- Increased number of out-of-wedlock births
- Increased number of women in the workforce
- Increased number of children living in nonnculear families

A National Issues Forum (NIF) research study also supports the belief that the American family is in trouble. They noted that all of the trends seen in today's family structure—"the breakdown of family and the erosion of family values"—affect children significantly (1996). These impacts are seen in the increased incidences of teen violence, teen pregnancy, and teen substance abuse.

NO: Other scholars believe that the family is in a continuous state of change, as it always has been, in order to adapt to societal influences. For example, the first settlers in America experienced extended family forms in order to adjust to their harsh environmental conditions; as life improved, family structures reflected this change. Scientist for the Institute for Social and Behavioral Research, Rand Conger (Conger & Conger, 2002) studied today's emerging family systems and made these conclusions:

- The *quality* of parenting—not the experience of nuclear adult relationships—teaches children and adolescents how to behave in marital relationships.
- The *quality* of the parents' relationship *did not* directly influence how young adults experience their own adult relationships.
- The *quality* of parenting (nurturing and affectionate versus harsh and angry) influences whether children/adolescents use drugs, become teen parents, or engage in teen violence—not whether the child is reared in a single-parent home or stepfamily.

And some contend that the American family is not deteriorating, but is adapting to the social changes brought by diversity of races, ethnicities, genders, and sexual orientations.

WHAT DO YOU THINK?

1. Are the trends we see in today's families a result of change or deterioration?
2. Where do you see the American family in the year 2020? 2050?

Sources: National Issues Forum (1996); Popenoe and Whitehead (2005); Conger and Conger (2002).

Extended Family The *extended family* is typically defined as a family unit where two or more generations of close family relatives live together in one household. There are three common extended family configurations (Barbour, Barbour, & Scully, 2005):

1. A mother and father with children (may be married or not), with one or more grandparents
2. A mother and father with children (may be married or not), with at least one unmarried sibling of the parents, or another relative, such as a cousin
3. A divorced, separated, or never-married single parent with children, in addition to a grandparent, sibling, or other relative.

This type of extended or multigenerational family structure was the basic element of slave life in the nineteenth century, and remains today an integral part in the lives of many families, particularly in families of color. For example, families with African roots often experience close-knit, multigenerational family groups—in addition to parents and children, family members may be grandparents, aunts, uncles, and cousins. Today, about 23% Black of African American/Black Caribbean children live in an extended family configuration (Pew Research Center, March 18, 2010: The Return of the Multi-Generational Family Household). Similarly, Mexican American and Asian American families are often characterized by an extended family form that consists of several generations; 22% Hispanic 25% Asian one-fourth of Hispanic and Asian American children live in an extended family, as compared to about 13% of white children (Pew Research Center, March 18, 2010: The Return of the Multi-Generational Family Household). In 2008, the U.S. Census Bureau indicated that 10% of U.S. households included grandparents or other relatives and children under the age of 18 living in the same home. No data exist to determine how many extended family members live nearby (not necessarily with) other family members, but we know that multigenerational family members can provide much emotional and economic support, along with the richness of family legacy and heritage.

THE EXPANDING FAMILY LANDSCAPE

In the United States today, there is no such thing as a "traditional" or "typical" family configuration. In order to better serve today's families and to help them reach their full potentials, we need to understand the changing compositions of contemporary families, as well as the racial and ethnic compositions of these families.

Single-Parent Family **Single-parent** family types can be the result of the choice of the parent or by circumstance; they can result either from divorce, the death of a spouse, or unmarried parenthood. Trends indicate that single-parent households are on the increase in the American family.

Although the majority of the nation's 72 million children live with two parents (either their biological parents, stepparents, or others), the dawn of the new millennium saw an increase in parenting households where there is no spouse. Today, it is estimated that 14% of families are single-parent families (U.S. Census Bureau, 2006a). Over 85% of all single-parent households are headed by females (U.S. Census Bureau, 2010). Slightly over 14 percent of single-parent households are headed by males. There are also racial and ethnic differences among single-parents families. For example, over one-half of all African American/Black Caribbean children live with their mother only, whereas only about one-fourth of Hispanic children live only with their mother; among all races, only about 5 percent of children live only with their fathers (Child Trends, 2008). Understanding these trends in single-parenting experiences is important, because as our study will show us in just a bit, single parents oftentimes live in poverty—which, in turn, affects their children's development.

Childless/Childfree Family On average, Americans have been having fewer children than in decades past. Couples may consider themselves **childless** if they are unable to conceive or bear children of their own or adopt children. Some couples today prefer to remain **childfree** as a conscious choice. Currently, 19 percent of women between the ages of 40 and 44 do not have children; 47 percent of all women ages 15 to 44 are childless (U.S. Census Bureau, 2010). The U.S. Census Bureau measures the presence of children primarily by comparing **fertility rates** (how many children a woman bears) and the percentage of households with children. Today, U.S. households have, on average, 1.88 children, down from 2.4 in 1972 (U.S. Census Bureau, 1955 To Present).

It is important to note, however, that this is not the first generation of people who are deciding not to have children. Notes Philip Morgan, professor of sociology at Duke University, "Childlessness is not new, [but] in the past it was more closely connected with non-marriage than now. During the depression, many Americans also chose not to have children because they could not afford them. Childlessness levels now are not higher than those in the 1930s" (*Chicago Tribune*, 2005). Morgan adds that there are many factors involved in couples' decisions to remain childfree today.

Family practitioners and social scientists differ in their opinions about today's trends in childfree couples. For example, directors of the National Marriage Project, David Popenoe and Barbara Dafoe Whitehead (2002), maintain that the decline in the number of children in U.S. households indicates a loss of "child centeredness" in the nation, and that "neighborhoods are less likely to contain children, and that children are less likely to be a consideration in daily life." They attribute this decline to the fact that "the needs and concerns of children—especially young children—gradually may be receding from our consciousness" (p. 24). On the other hand, authors and founders of the Alternatives to Marriage Project, Dorian Solot and Marshall Miller (2004), counter these claims, noting that today we recognize and embrace family diversity and the range of family forms, and thereby accept couples' choices to remain childfree.

Stepfamily A **stepfamily** (or reconstituted family) is formed when, after death or divorce, a parent marries again. A stepfamily is also formed when a never-married parent marries and children from different biological families end up living within the new marriage for part of the time. In short, the presence of a stepparent, stepsibling, or half sibling designates a family as a stepfamily (U.S. Census Bureau, 2008c).

The U.S. Census Bureau recently stopped providing data related to marriage, divorce, and remarriage, so it is difficult to obtain accurate statistics about stepfamilies. But census experts today estimate that two of five Americans—about 42 percent—is now either a stepparent, a stepchild, a stepsibling, or some other member of a stepfamily (Pew Research Center Released: January 13, 2011 A Portrait of Stepfamilies). Although the popular sitcom 1970s television show *The Brady Bunch* portrayed stepfamily living as an emotionally cohesive, trouble-free, happily adjusted family, this idealized concept of the stepfamily form is simply not the norm. (Because of the complexities of stepfamily living, an entire segment of a chapter is devoted to this family form in Chapter 14.)

Cohabiting Family Unmarried partners who live together in a single household are referred to as **cohabiting** couples. Although once considered a scandalous, uncommon alternative lifestyle, cohabiting before marriage (or instead of marriage) is now the prevailing living arrangement of intimate partners—the next step following serious dating. In 2010, there were 7.5 million unmarried heterosexual partner households (over 15 million people) (U.S. Census Bureau, 2010). Data from the National Survey of Family Growth (NSFG) show that over 60 percent of women ages 25 to 39 have cohabited at least once, nearly doubling the rate from just seven years earlier (U.S. Department of Health and Human Services, 2006). Further, since 1995, more than two-thirds of men and women who marry for the first time cohabited beforehand (Manning & Jones, 2006). Many of these couples have no plans for eventual marriage. Indeed, some 53 percent of women's first marriages are preceded by cohabitation (Manning & Smock, 2003). Census bureau statistics indicate that about 4 percent of all children in the United States live with two cohabiting parents (U.S. Census Bureau,

FIGURE 1.3 Percentage of Children Living with a Cohabiting Parent by Race

Cohabitation is the prevailing living arrangement of intimate partners before (or instead of) marriage. A number of cohabiting partners have children.

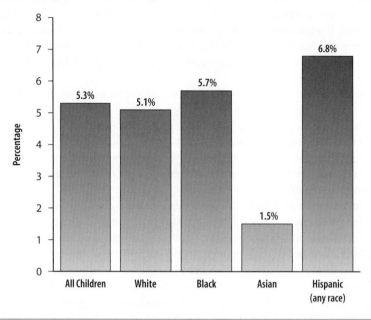

Source: U.S. Census Bureau (2008c).

TODAY in America, there are over three-quarters of a million same-sex households.

2010). The rates of cohabiting parents vary by race; these data are presented in Figure 1.3. The U.S. Census Bureau currently estimates that in the United States about 11 million people live with their unmarried partner; approximately 10 million of these households consist of unmarried, different-sex partners, whereas the remaining estimated one million households comprise same-sex couples (U.S. Census Bureau, 2008c).

Gay and Lesbian Families Lesbian and gay families consist of same-sex partners who live together in the same household, and may include either natural-born or adopted children. In the United States today, there are 780,000 same-sex households representing over a 300 percent increase in same-sex households since 1990 (U.S. Census Bureau, 2008d U.S. Census Bureau News July 21, 2008). Census Bureau statisticians point out, however, that this increase reflects the fact that same-sex families were previously uncounted, undercounted, or underreported, and not that the numbers of gay or lesbian families have increased significantly (Smith & Gates, 2001). Same-sex family forms may or may not resemble traditional marriage roles, but they often do (with the exception of the legal status granted by the state in which they reside). Today, many same-sex couples pledge a commitment to each other in a public ceremony. Like legally married couples, they share property, expect sexual fidelity, and share joint responsibility in child rearing.

Obtaining accurate demographic trends regarding same-sex partner households has been difficult in past years. The Obama administration has addressed the issue and has ordered the United States Census Bureau to count same-sex marriages in the 2010 census.

Our study so far has shown us that in this new century it is hard to encapsulate or sum up the "typical" American family—it simply doesn't exist today in our complex, multifaceted, ever-changing, global society. To get the full grasp of intimate, marriage, and family relationships, we now need to examine the racial and ethnic characteristics of contemporary families.

Contemporary Families

Is the American family in a state of decline, or is it in a state of change? As we have seen so far, the "traditional" family form is no longer the norm in American culture, and today's families are experiencing a number of changes. The family structures, values, and attitudes we observe today are a result of changes that have evolved over the past four or five decades.

As the United States moved into the second half of the twentieth century, a number of social and cultural, economic, and political changes occurred that continue to have an impact on today's twenty-first–century families and family living: *social and cultural factors,* such as lowered birth rates and an increase in nonmarital cohabitation; *economic factors* that include the influx of women into the workforce; and *political factors,* such as legalized abortion in 1973 and the Civil Rights legislation of 1965 which bans racial, ethnic, and sexual discrimination.

All of these factors worked in tandem to change the traditional family in this century. Experts in the field of marriage and family living, however, view the changes occurring during the last half of the twentieth century differently. Those with more conventional, conservative, or religious outlooks are concerned about what they perceive to be a moral decline in family life—that is, the increase in nonmarital cohabitation and same-sex relationships and in the number of births outside of wedlock. These groups prescribe a return to more conventional, long-held family values as a way to reverse the trends (Popenoe & Whitehead, 2004). Those with a more contemporary outlook hold that these trends represent both flexibility and adaptability in today's families and in the society at large (Solot & Miller, 2004). In spite of increasing relational and economic stresses faced by today's families, marriage represents the most frequently chosen family form, with approximately 90 percent of the population choosing marriage at least once (U.S. Census Bureau, 2010).

In the United States, there is more diversity now than ever before. Families today are complex and diverse, ranging from traditional two-biological-parent family structures, to single-parent homes, to extended family forms, to households headed by gay or lesbian adults or same-sex couples. There is also greater diversity of racial, ethnic, economic, and religious composition, and so social workers, family life educators, psychologists, sociologists, and health and mental health professionals must be aware of the full range of diversity in families today (see Figure 1.4 on page 14).

As we just saw, when researchers use the terms *diverse* or *diversity,* they are often referring to the racial and/or ethnic attributes of a given population. **Race** refers to a group of people who are distinguished from another group of people, typically by their skin color, ancestry, or genetics. **Ethnicity** refers to a social construction that is used to identify groups of people (commonly, races) who share common cultural traits, such as religion, customs, language, and dress. Furthermore, in the United States today there is an increasing trend in interracial diversity—2 percent of the U.S. population (about 7.5 million people) is multiracial (U.S. Census Bureau, 2009). **Multiracial** individuals can be any combination of races (White, African American, Black Caribbean, Asian, Native American, Alaska Native, Pacific Islander, Hispanic, and any other race) and ethnicities.

FIGURE 1.4 **Racial and Ethnic Composition of American Families: Projected Population by Race, 2000–2050**

The racial and ethnic family composition of American families continues to be diverse.

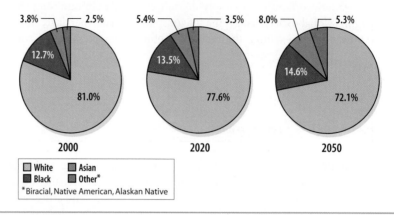

Source: U.S. Census Bureau (2004a).

Knowing the racial and ethnic composition of U.S. families is important because it aids in our understanding of the complex, changing nature of family living. Here, we briefly examine the racial and ethnic compositions of families so that you have a firm understanding of the diversity within the United States.

AFRICAN AMERICAN/BLACK CARIBBEAN FAMILIES

Historically, African American/Black Caribbean families assumed the traditional married-couple family structure, with children born inside the marital union. Today, it is common for black children to be born to a single mother. As Figure 1.5 illustrates, nearly 70 percent of the births to black women of all ages are to unmarried women (Child Trends, 2008). In comparison to white families, where nearly one-fourth of children live with a single parent (most likely a mother), over one-half of black children live in a single-parent home (U.S. Census Bureau, 2008c). Three-fourths of black children eventually reside in two-parent homes, but many of these families are formed with a child who was born outside of the marriage (U.S. Census Bureau, 2008b; Barbarin & McCandies, 2003).

Multigenerational, extended family ties are common among black families. Census bureau data estimate that about 9 percent of African American/Black Caribbean children live in some type of extended family (Child Trends, 2008). According to a study by Robert Taylor (2000), characteristics of African American/Black Caribbean extended kin include:

- Strong commitment to family and family obligation
- Willingness to allow relatives and close nonrelatives to move into the family home
- Family interactions and get-togethers
- Close system of mutual aid and support

Because of the large numbers of female-headed households among African American/Black Caribbeans, some research suggests that the childrearing and economic support of extended kin is necessary, because it is within the extended family networks of grandmothers, grandfathers, aunts, uncles, and cousins that children are cared for, socialized, educated, and have their emotional needs met (Taylor, 2000). About one in three black families is headed by an elderly family member (Smith & Drew, 2002). Of all racial and ethnic groups in the United States, African American/Black Caribbean families suffer the highest levels of unemployment

FIGURE 1.5   Percentage of Births to Unmarried Women by Race: 2006

The percentage of births to unmarried women varies by race.

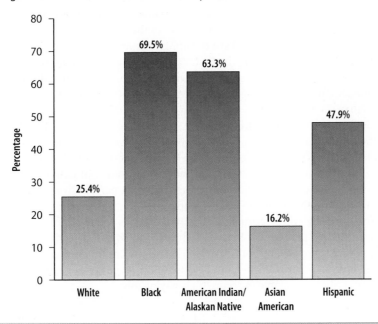

Source: Child Trends (2008).

and poverty and the lowest median family income—slightly over $30,000 annually (U.S. Census Bureau, 2006b).

LATINO FAMILIES

Today, Latino Americans account for 16 percent of the total U.S. population; this figure does not include the nearly 4 million residents of the U.S. territory, Puerto Rico (U.S. Census Bureau, 2009, 1-Year Estimates). The fastest-growing population in the United States because of the large proportion of Latina women of childbearing age, by the year 2020, Latinos are expected to account for nearly one-half percent of the nation's population growth (Afable-Munsuz & Brindis, 2006).

Latinos place a high value on *familism,* which emphasizes the importance of family life, and close, interdependent relationships among the person, the family, and the community. Typically, familism also stresses the importance of extended family; thus, Latino families are also composed of extended kinship networks (grandparents, aunts, uncles, and cousins). Within this family dynamic, family members are provided clothing, shelter, food, education, and emotional support. Latino families further extend family relationships to **fictive,** or nonrelated, **kin,** such as godparents and close friends. Within Latino communities, the well-being of the family takes precedence over the well-being of the individual.

LATINO families enjoy the rich, multigenerational relationships of extended family members and nonrelated members who become as close as blood relatives. Latino families embrace familism, where the best interests of the family are placed ahead of the interests of the individual family member.

In the United States, about 16 million Latino children reside within families in which at least one parent is an **immigrant**—foreign-born—or who are themselves foreign-born (Kids Count Data Snapshot, 2007). Today, one out of five U.S. children is living in an immigrant family (Kids Count Data Snapshot, 2007). If current immigration levels continue, children in Latino immigrant families will constitute 30 percent of the nation's school population in 2015 (Kids Count Data Snapshot, 2007). Latino immigrants and their children commonly live within extended family forms during the first 10 years following immigration (Carranza and others, 2002). Even as immigrants establish their own households, they do so nearby their families' homes. Second- and third-generation Mexican Americans have even larger extended kin networks than do immigrants (Carranza and others, 2002).

About 66 percent of Latino children live within two-parent families (Child Trends, 2008). Similar to the experiences of African American/Black Caribbean women, births to unmarried Latina women have increased since the 1970s. Nearly one-half of all Latino births are to unmarried women (Child Trends, 2008). Currently, one-fourth of Latino children live in a household with their mothers and have no father present; 4 percent live in a household with their father with no mother present (Child Trends, 2008).

One of the poorest ethnic groups in the United States today, Latino families earn, on average, about $40,000 per year (U.S. Census Bureau, 2009, 1-Year Estimates). The reasons for the high poverty rates among Latinos are varied. Many Latino immigrants may have professional degrees from other countries, but because of the language barrier when they arrive in the United States, they are unable to secure high-paying jobs.

The FAMILY Table

Talking with Children about Diversity

Because we live in a world that is not free from bias and discrimination, as parents, guardians, and teachers, we impart to children that *everyone* has the right to feel included. It is important to teach children that hate hurts and leaves emotional scars that can affect not only a person's self-worth but also every aspect of a person's life. Because a child develops his or her self-concept and beliefs about others well before he or she enters kindergarten, anti-bias and antidiscrimination education must begin early in the home and in school. Parents, guardians, and teachers need to model attitudes and behaviors that help young children appreciate and value the differences in others. To avoid prejudice and discrimination, we must:

- Model the values, attitudes, and behaviors we want our children to develop. This requires being aware of our own conscious and unconscious stereotypes and behaviors.
- Expose children to people and experiences from other cultures.
- Encourage children to see that relationships with people who are different from themselves can be rich and rewarding experiences.
- Talk with children about the similarities and differences between themselves and others. Help them to see that being "different" from someone does not mean the person is "worse" than someone else.
- Integrate diversity information and communication into conversations and activities.
- Teach children to be sensitive, critical thinkers, so that through examining and questioning they can better understand any issue.
- Adopt a "zero tolerance" policy about racism, prejudice, bias, and discrimination. Teach them that words *do hurt*.

ASIAN AMERICAN FAMILIES

Asian American families come to the United States from countries including Korea, Japan, China, Taiwan, Vietnam, Cambodia, Sri Lanka, and Indonesia. Each Asian country has a unique culture unto itself, which accounts for the vast cultural and ethnic differences within this racial group. Like Latino families, Asian American families place greater emphasis on extended kinship ties and the needs of the entire family, rather than on the needs of the individual. About 84 percent of all Asian American children live with both biological parents; only 10 percent live in mother-only families, and about 4 percent live in father-only families (Child Trends, 2008). Today, about 16 percent of Asian women give birth outside of marriage (Child Trends, 2008). With an annual income of almost $69,000 per year, Asian American families have the highest median household income of all racial groups in the United States (U.S. Census Bureau, 2009, 1-Year Estimates). This is perhaps because Asian Americans have the highest educational qualifications of all ethnic groups in the United States—nearly one-half of all Asian American adults have attained at least a bachelor's degree (U.S. Census Bureau, 2007b).

Asian families are childcentric. Within the Asian family structure a greater emphasis is placed on the parent–child relationship than on the husband–wife relationship. In exchange for the undivided loyalty and for sacrifices parents make for their children, Asian American parents expect respect and obedience from their children. Guilt and shame, rather than physical discipline, are used to reinforce the expected behavior of the children (Fong, 2002).

NATIVE AMERICAN/ALASKA NATIVE FAMILIES

The terms *Native American, American Indian, Alaska Native*, and *Indian* are often used interchangeably. Here, we use the term **Native American/Alaska Native (NA/AN)** to refer to aboriginal peoples of the United States and their descendants, and who maintain tribal affiliation or community attachment. Today, about 2 percent of the total U.S. population reports that they are Native American or Alaska Native (U.S. Census Bureau, 2010). About one-fourth of the total U.S. population is under the age of 18, but among NA/AN, 31 percent of the population is under the age of 18, making this a young ethnic group (U.S. Census Bureau, 2009). As with other racial and ethnic groups in the United States, NA/AN communities are culturally diverse with 594 federally recognized Native entities, and an additional 365 state-recognized American Indian tribes (U.S. Census Bureau, 2007b). Native Americans prefer to be identified by tribal names, such as *Wampanoag, Lakota*, and *Kickapoo* (Fleming, 2007); our discussion here is generalized.

In order for us to accurately understand Native American marriage and family experiences, we must be aware of the unique qualities associated with this race. Unfortunately, comparatively little research has been conducted on Native American family life, and especially on Native American marriage. Despite this gap in the empirical literature, however, the census data do give us insight into some characteristics of Natives. For instance, 38% of all Native American households are married couple households (see Figure 1.6 on page 18). Interestingly, nearly 30 percent of households are nonfamily households; this means that a significant number of Native American families are headed by someone other than a parent, such as a grandparent, or even by nonfictive kin. The median income for NA/AN is just over $35,000 per year (U.S. Census Bureau, 2009, 1-Year Estimates).

The predominance of extended family/nonfictive kin households among NA/AN is a reflection of the cultural roots of this racial group. Native American/Alaska Natives embrace a social identity that stresses

NATIVE Americans/Alaska Natives embrace rich cultural heritages and an identity that stresses the importance of intergenerational family ties. Indians' spiritual and religious beliefs are numerous and diverse, and the beliefs often shape their attitudes toward marriage and family life.

FIGURE 1.6 Characteristics of Native American/Alaska Native Households, 2006

Native American/Alaska Native populations are diverse, with 594 federally recoganized Native entities.

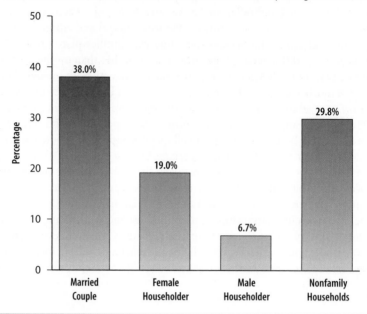

Source: U.S. Census Bureau (2009).

the importance of family ties. For example, when they introduce themselves to other Indians, they do so by telling them their maternal heritage, clans, and homelands (Makes Marks, 2007). In contrast to patriarchal societies where people's lineage is determined along *patrilineal* lines (the father's heritage), the roots of NA/AN social and clan relationships are by and large *matrilineal*; that is to say, these societies trace their heritage from a female ancestor to a descendent of either sex. This is also referred to as a *uterine descent*. Within these societies, women are not given power per se because they are women—they are given power because of their status of mother, the power of female as mother.

Indians' spiritual traditions and religious beliefs are also numerous and diverse, and as such, the depth and dynamics of Native Americans' religious experiences are difficult to categorize or classify. Even so, there is an underlying or essential principal belief that informs most Indians' spiritual practices: the belief in the existence of unseen powers, that something exists beyond them that is sacred and mysterious (Makes Marks, 2007). Within this belief are embedded tradition, respect, and reverence. But how these religious beliefs shape marital and family attitudes, norms, and behaviors is unknown, because NA/AI are among the most misunderstood and understudied ethnic group in our culture; this is because they are commonly culturally isolated (Hellerstedt, Peterson-Hickey, Rhodes, & Garwick, 2006).

ARAB AMERICAN FAMILIES

Very little empirical information exists about Arab American families, although their population is increasing in the United States. Coming from countries such as Afghanistan, Israel, Iran, Iraq, Kuwait, Palestine, Saudi Arabia, Syria, and Turkey, the term *Arab American* does not refer necessarily to a racial group as much as it does geographic location and religion, which among Middle Eastern families is very diverse. Arab Americans make up just slightly over 0.5 percent of the U.S. population, reflecting 8 Arab countries (U.S. Census Bureau, 2009).

Although there is a common perception that most Arab Americans adhere to the Muslim faith, this is not so; about two-thirds of Arab Americans practice the Christian faith, about one-fourth practice the Muslim faith, and the remaining adhere to another faith or have no religious affiliation (Arab American Institute, 2007). This is important to understand, because cultural typecasts of Arab American women tend to lump religion (Muslim) and ethnicity into one-and-the-same components of culture, portraying them as veiled Islamic traditionalists who are submissive, secluded in the home, and uneducated (Zahedi, 2007).

But, as sociology professor and researcher Jen'nan Ghazel Read of the University of California points out, understanding Arab American culture is complicated (2003). On the one hand, as a group, Arab Americans are more highly educated and earn higher incomes than any other ethnic or racial group in the United States (Arab American Institute, 2007). On the other hand, Arab religious and cultural customs and rituals reinforce traditional gender roles wherein women raise and nurture the children, and men protect and provide for the family. As a result, many Arab Americans' marital and family experiences are strongly shaped by traditional Arab views of honor, modesty, and gender, as well as by the historical values of Islam (Davis & Davis, 1993). For instance, the Islamic faith is a sex-positive religion, wherein sex and sexuality are viewed as gifts from God, or Allah; sexuality is thought to be the right of every person (Boellstorff, 2005). Marriage, then, is the social institution that organizes and controls sexuality. Further, within the Islamic faith anything that "violates the order of the world"—in this instance, marriage as an organizer of sexuality—is considered to be a source of evil and anarchy (Bouhdiba, 2001, p. 30). As a result of these tenets of Islam, heterosexual marriages and nuclear families are expected of devout Muslims (Boellstorff, 2005).

Without a doubt, there is great variation and diversity in our upbringing and our individual experiences with family and family living. It is virtually impossible in contemporary society to rely on the U.S. Census Bureau's rigid definition of *family* consisting of "two or more persons living together and related by blood, marriage, or adoption."

Despite the fact that today's families are diverse in structure, income level, and racial and ethnic composition, and despite the fact that today's families experience family living in diverse ways, one particular theorist has been able to organize the different cultural contexts of family life so we can see the level of influence each context has on us. With this in mind, in the section that follows we'll take a look at *Bronfenbrenner's Ecological Model*, a model noted for grouping the various contexts that surround us and influence our individual and family development.

Families in Cultural Contexts

John Donne in his *Meditation*, reminds us that who we are is influenced by factors outside of ourselves and beyond our control. He says, *"No man is an island entire of itself; every man is a piece of the continent, a part of the main."* Each of us has needs for sustenance, clothing, shelter, security, intimacy, and emotional support. Because of these needs, we find ourselves interacting with others in some capacity throughout our lives.

As we begin our study of marriage, family, and intimate relationships, it is necessary to understand and embrace the idea that we do not develop in isolation. Who we are as human beings—every emotion, fear, thought, and behavior—is somehow linked to the family in which we were raised, both genetically and environmentally. It is also important to understand that there are many areas of family life that are affected and influenced by the broader culture in which we live, by the many facets of society that surround us. Often these influences are overlooked in the study of both individual development and the processes associated with family life.

SOCIAL IDENTITY: ALL FOR ONE AND ONE FOR ALL?

How individuals understand and practice their intimate and family relationships is influenced by the culture in which they live. It is important to understand that family life experiences are determined in large part by how a culture defines its **social identity,** or whether societal goals emphasize the advancement of the group's interests or individual interests. Particularly

COLLECTIVIST cultures value strong relationships with their families. Their values, belief systems, and relationships reflect the goals of their cultures—not their individual goals.

important is whether the culture defines itself as a *collectivist* culture or an *individualistic* culture, because culturally approved beliefs influence our expectations, experiences, attitudes, and behaviors (Neto, 2007). It profoundly affects the ways we behave and respond to the world.

Collectivist Cultures In **collectivist cultures,** individuals define their identity in terms of the relationships they hold with others. For instance, if asked the question, Who are you?, a collectivist is likely to respond by giving the family's name or the region from which he or she originates (Triandis & Suh, 2002). The goals of the *collective*—the whole society—are given priority over individual needs, and group membership is important (Myers, 2008). In these cultures, members strive to be equal, contributing, beneficial members of the society, and their personal behavior is driven by a feeling of obligation and duty to the society (Triandis & Suh, 2002; Johnson and others, 2005). Collectivist cultures promote the well-being and goals of the collective *group*, rather than the well-being and goals of the *individual*. Because of the desire to maintain harmony within the group, collectivist cultures stress harmony, cooperation, and promoting feelings of closeness (Kupperbusch and others, 1999).

Latinos, for example, value strong interdependent relationships with their families and they value the opinions of close friends (who, in many cases, are treated as family members); this, in turn, influences how they select mates and display and experience emotions, such as love and intimacy (Casta-eda, 1993; Fernandez-Dols, 1999). Asians, too, accentuate the importance of the collective whole and they therefore emphasize family bonds in their experiences of love, including extended family members. People's self-concepts, personal goals, mate selection, sexual attitudes, expectations of family members, family experiences, and the larger society are inseparable in collectivist societies (Johnson and others, 2005).

Individualistic Cultures In **individualistic cultures,** where individual goals are promoted over group goals, people define their identity or sense of self in terms of personal attributes, such as wealth, social status, education level, and marital status (Myers, 2008). Unlike in collectivist cultures, *individualists* view themselves as truly independent entities from the society in which they live, and their personal needs and rights guide their behavior, rather than the needs of the society (Johnson and others 2005). Individualistic cultures, such as those of the

United States and Europe, promote the idea of autonomy and individuation from the family; in turn, this autonomy promotes the practice of people selecting partners based on individual reasons (such as attraction, love, sex, money, security, etc.), rather than collective reasons (such as prearranged marriages in China and India) that might benefit the culture as a whole. Along these lines, when cultures promote the autonomy and independence of individuals (as seen in much of Western civilization), this autonomy, in turn, affects relationship satisfaction, the ease with which intimacy is established, and "love" as a basis for marriage (Dion & Dion, 1993). Relationship partners are free, by society's standards, to choose a partner that best suits their needs; it is thought that this freedom of choice enhances relationship satisfaction and the experiences of love, intimacy, and sex.

As you saw earlier in this chapter, a culture's social identity shapes and directs the attitudes, norms, and behaviors of its members, such as how extended family members are important to Latino and Asian families—these behaviors are the result of how collectivist ideals shape families. But there are other cultural factors that significantly influence and shape intimate and family life experiences. The **social ecology** perspective recognizes that individual family members' experiences, along with outside social factors and policies, significantly affect the quality and the nature of their relationships (Alberts, 2002). In the section that follows, we examine the ways in which families are affected by the variety of contexts that surround them as we study the Ecological Model and the various contexts within that model: the *microsystem, mesosystem, exosystem, macrosystem,* and *chronosystem.*

THE ECOLOGICAL MODEL: CULTURALLY SPECIFIC INFLUENCES THAT AFFECT FAMILY LIFE

To understand the multiple areas of individual and family development, we turn our attention to the **Ecological Model** developed by Uri Bronfenbrenner (1979). Central to this model is the concept that people develop in a variety of interacting contexts. **Contexts** refer to areas of individual and family development that play a role in the relationship between people and their environments. These multiple environments surround individuals from birth and play a significant interactive role in development. In order to truly understand individual relationship behaviors (such as communication) and the development of family life, we must first understand the interactive relationships *between* and among the different factors within the various contexts of development (Huitt, 2003). For example, if we want to study the effects of divorce on a child's development, we can study the child separately, but we can also introduce or take away various factors within a certain context to better determine which has the greatest impact on the child's development. Similarly, if we want to better understand a couple's difficulty with sexual arousal and response, we can look at contextual factors such as the stressors associated with employment, to see if they are exerting negative influences on the couple.

Figure 1.7 (on page 22) presents the Ecological Model. Notice that the person is located in the center of five concentric, nested circles that expand outward, similar to ripples on the surface of water. Each of those circles represents a different layer of societal interactions and influences external to the individual, which affects his or her development. The circles nearest the individual have more immediate impacts on us, and those farther out are more distant. Perhaps what makes this model so useful is that Bronfenbrenner recognized that the impact on relationships is *bi-directional.* Not only does the environment influence the individual but also the individual influences the environment. For example, a new baby in a family has an impact on the parents just as much as the parents have an impact on the baby. When a couple goes through a divorce, both spouses are affected, but their children and other extended family members and friends are also affected. And, even though the individual or the family may not directly interact with various levels of society (such as the different levels of government), as you will see later in our study this term, these social influences have an impact on family functioning and health.

As we examine each context in the model, it is important to bear in mind the positioning of the context to better understand the degree of influence on the individual. To help guide

FIGURE 1.7   Bronfenbrenner's Ecological Model

People and families develop in a variety of interacting contexts, or ecosystems, which surround the person from birth and play a significant role in both individual and family development.

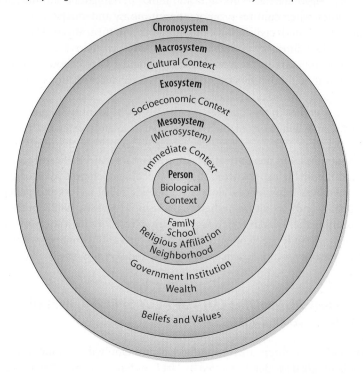

Source: Bronfenbrenner (1979).

this process, we will discuss each context, or **ecosystem**, within the Ecological Model. Those contexts nearest the individual carry the greatest influence on her or his development.

The Person   At the center of this model is the person. Bronfenbrenner recognized that a person's development is not simply a matter of biology, cognition, or social interaction. Development is instead an intricate intertwining of *all three* of these components. Individual influences include, but are not limited to, race, ethnicity, genetics, health, nutrition, and physiological abilities or disabilities. The contexts that surround us can affect, for example, our overall health.

The Microsystem   The **microsystem** is the developmental context nearest the individual and represents those interactions in which people are directly involved. The elements that make up this ecosystem are the individuals, groups, and agencies that have the earliest and most immediate influences on the individual. These include:

■ *The family of origin.* The family in which we are raised is the most influential on our development. The family structure (single-parent family or two-parent family), socioeconomic status (wealthy, middle class, or low income), race and ethnicity (strong influences on family educational and income levels), parenting styles (Are the parents warm and supportive? Do they abuse or use substances?), and parental involvement all play important roles in who children become.

■ *Daycare/schools.* Because children spend on average seven hours a day in daycare or in a classroom, Bronfenbrenner believed them to be a key influence on development. For example, the location of the school is important; students in small or rural communities or small suburbs tend to score higher on standardized tests than children from larger schools (Huitt, 2003).

■ *The community.* Many of us have heard the saying, "It takes a village to raise a child." Neighbors, neighborhoods, peer groups, and workplaces make up a community. The greater the community's involvement in the child's life, the greater the child's success and achievement throughout life (Niemiec, Sikorski, & Walberg, 1999). Community involvement may include literacy programs, nutritional programs, recreational opportunities, or teen mentoring programs.

■ *The church, synagogue, or mosque.* Religious institutions influence the development of a person's character and ethical and moral development (Nord & Haynes, 1998).

We individuals also have an impact on our environment: as we comply or rebel, agree or disagree, or express our views, hopes, ambitions, we exert influence on the elements with which we interact.

The Mesosystem In the **mesosystem,** Bronfenbrenner retains all of the elements that are present in the microsystem, but now focuses on the interaction *between* the various elements rather than on the individual. For instance, how does the school affect the family? How does the church or temple affect the family? Does the school affect the neighborhood? Consider a school district that tries to establish a sex education program that offers condom distribution and referrals to health clinics for abortion in a community that has a strong fundamental religious belief system. Is it likely that a conservative community would endorse these practices? Likewise, consider the influence of a church or temple that creates an after-school athletic and academic program for children located in a neighborhood that has a large gang presence, or a neighborhood watch organization that creates a network of "safe" houses that children can run to if a stranger attempts to approach them on the way home from school. These scenarios illustrate how elements within the microsystem interact with each other rather than directly with an individual and his or her family.

The Exosystem The **exosystem** consists of the fabrics of society in which policies are made and influenced that ultimately have an impact on the elements of the microsystem and the individual. Social policies are beneficial to families when they foster and support the major functions of a family, such as childrearing, economic support, and caring for family members (Alberts, 2002). As Figure 1.7 illustrates, the exosystem serves as an umbrella for all of the "systems" in a society.

Consider the state board of education, which establishes policies and selects curricula that are used in each of the local school districts. At the same time, the hierarchies of various

Hurricane Katrina: Families in the Context of Society

In the summer of 2005, Hurricane Katrina left hundreds of miles of devastation in her wake. Hundreds of thousands of people were displaced from their homes and businesses in the days immediately following the storm, and nearly 350,000 were still refugees in the weeks and months following this unprecedented tragedy. Rebuilding New Orleans and the other communities devastated in the Gulf Coast region by Hurricane Katrina has not been an easy task, as the damage estimates are in the tens of billions of dollars and the estimates of rebuilding the infrastructure, business, and homes in New Orleans alone top $100 billion.

1. Is it the responsibility of those not affected by the natural disaster to help foot the bill for rebuilding the affected areas through federal tax increases? Who do you believe should be responsible?

2. Do you, as a member of the "greater whole" of society, feel an obligation to assist others when tragedy strikes? Why or why not?

religious denominations determine the central tenets of their faith, which include and determine what behaviors are deemed to be appropriate or inappropriate according to those tenets. In turn, those religious beliefs in large part determine what is taught in the public schools. As a result of this influence, a public school education may be vastly different in one state compared to another, depending on the components of the exosystem. In Kansas public schools, teachers are permitted to teach the tenets of evolution, but they are also required to teach creation by intelligent design. The theory of *intelligent design (ID)* maintains that the universe is best explained by creation by an intelligent cause, rather than by the evolution of species. Further, in 2005, battles raged in the Kansas legislature as state representatives moved to no longer require sex education in the public schools. The state's current policy provides an *opt-out* option, where parents can have their children removed from the sex education class; at

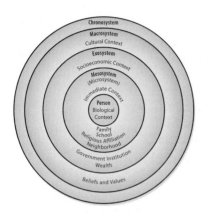

issue in the current debate is to make sex classes *opt-in* curricula, where parents would have to approve any and all discussions concerning sexuality. The issue remains undecided. The broader point here is that because Kansas is in the center of the "Bible Belt" in the United States, many curricula decisions are centered on the religious hierarchy of the state.

The media are another element within the exosystem. Some news outlets are thought to have either liberal or conservative bias in the way that they report news information, consequently influencing how certain policies and perspectives are viewed. In movies and through television programming, we also see changes in how families and family life are portrayed. Whether these changes are simply representations of historical changes in families over time, or are attempts to change perceptions about what family life should be, is not always clear. How these movies and TV shows are perceived may depend, to some extent, on a person's life experiences and the influences that have shaped their development to this point.

The Macrosystem The **macrosystem** represents the next layer in Bronfenbrenner's model. It recognizes that a society has a set of overarching cultural values and beliefs that affect individual development by establishing either implicit or explicit rules about what is or is not acceptable behavior. In a population as diverse as that of the United States, there are hundreds of different religious, racial, and ethnic groups. Each may have specific cultural norms that do not conform to a broader set of values. Additionally, not all groups that fall within a general ethnic category will be the same. For instance, not all Hispanics share the same belief system. Mexican Americans may have cultural values and expectations different from those of Cuban Americans. Jews have different values than do Islamics or Buddhists. And liberals have different values than do conservatives. The cultural values of parents who are first-generation immigrants to the United States may be vastly different from those of their children who have been acculturated in American values through their interactions with peers at school and the media.

The Chronosystem The **chronosystem**, the next, and outermost, layer, reflects changes that happen over time. It accounts for the collective historical precursors of current social debates over, for example, social and economic discrimination, women's rights to reproductive choice, and the long-held definition of marriage, such as whether marriage should be solely between one man and one woman, or whether it should include the union of same-sex couples (Dutton, 1998).

Bronfenbrenner's framework allows us to grasp both the nature of the main interacting influences on our lives and to examine the role that each plays. With the Ecological Model we can explore and better understand marriage, intimate relationships, and family life in various contexts. Throughout our study together, we'll explore certain areas of Bronfenbrenner's model, such as the *economic, religious,* and *government contexts*, and how they shape and affect the experiences of intimate partners and families today.

Up to this point, our study has highlighted the fact that the United States is a blend of races, ethnicities, and religions from all over the world. Often, though, we tend to focus on our own families, failing to realize the vastness of the human race. Many of us fall into the trap of thinking that how *we* experienced family and intimate relationships is the *only* way to experience these aspects of life. In order to gain a truer insight into the workings of the family, intimate relations, and marriage, we must step back from our cultural norms and stereotypes and enlarge our scope, so that we may see and take in more—and so far, our study has given us this opportunity.

But this wonderful medley of race, ethnicity, culture, and ways of life is not embraced by all. With this in mind, Dorian Solot and Marshall Miller (2004), founders and directors of the Alternatives to Marriage Project, put forth the following affirmation of family diversity:

> We believe that all families should be valued, that the well-being of children is critical to our nation's future, and that people who care for one another should be supported in their efforts to build happy, healthy relationships. One of America's strengths is its diversity, which includes not only a wide range of races, ethnicities, creeds, abilities, genders, and sexual orientations, but also a range of family forms.

Now that you have a knowledge base in the forms and functions of marriages and families, before we conclude this chapter let's take a brief look at one of the central ways in which we'll explore family life throughout our course of study: the *family life education* perspective.

THE 1960s ushered in rapid change within American society, as young adults began to rebel against the long-held, established beliefs about marriage, sexuality, gender roles, and politics.

Family Life Education: The Study of Families through a Family Lens

The central concept of this book is to examine family and intimate relations by using a family life education approach as a central theme. Borrowing and adapting theoretical frameworks from the fields of sociology and psychology, the **family life education** perspective unveils the inadequacies families feel when they are faced with change, and then provides organized, programmatic education to help strengthen families. Some approaches (such as family therapy) first look to *intervention* instead of education; however, this text's approach acknowledges that intervention often comes too late to be effective in fully developing the potential of individuals and families. Family life education is a tool used to explore family and intimate relationships, but it is not a "theory." Instead, it is a *lens* through which we can study the family.

UNDERSTANDING FAMILIES' NEEDS AND DEVELOPING THEIR POTENTIALS

As early as the 1960s, when U.S. culture experienced much social upheaval, people who had concerns for the "staggering list of social ills" that had an impact on family life began to conceive and organize education for family living (Smith, 1968). With young adults' newfound emphasis on sex, drugs, and rock and roll, the country was ripe for a family education concept. These early efforts to educate families centered on a **dealing-with-problems focus** (Arcus, Schvaneveldt, & Moss, 1993). Society was rapidly changing. The Vietnam War provoked cries from young adults against the "establishment"—those who promoted long-held, established societal beliefs and norms about marriage, sexuality, gender roles, childbearing, childrearing, and politics.

A concept that went hand in hand with the dealing-with-problems focus to educate families was the **preventing-the-problems focus**. Family life education professor and parent educator Richard Kerckhoff (1964) maintained that families faced with radical societal changes only needed to be shown how to do the correct things. According to Kerckhoff, if families could somehow be pointed in the right direction, then "the divorce rate would drop, children would be reared properly, and the institution of family would be saved" (p. 898). Problem prevention remains a prevalent theme in family life education today. As renowned family life educator and professor of human sciences Carol Darling noted, efforts to educate families in family living is "the foremost preventive measure for the avoidance of family problems" (1987, p. 816). The **developing-family-potentials focus** also arose out of the societal turmoil of the 1960s. Promoting goals ranging from building on family strengths to developing healthy, fulfilling, and responsible interpersonal relationships, family life education efforts were—and are still today—intended to build on positive aspects of family life and bring about human capabilities that improve and enhance personal life and family living (Arcus, Schvaneveldt, & Moss, 1993).

The definitions of *family life education* have changed and progressed over time, as the time line in Figure 1.8 shows us. But what has remained consistent over the decades is that the family life education perspective takes into consideration *individual development* and lifecourse experiences, and how our interpersonal relationship skills and interaction patterns are shaped within the context of *family living*. To understand the aspects of sexuality within the context of relationships, for example, we first must have an understanding of our sexual development. Similarly, in order to understand why we love the people we do, we first have to acquire an understanding of how these capacities develop and are maintained within the context of family living. So, as we work our way through our course of study, we will focus on our development into relational people as we examine areas of family living and family development. Finally, the family life education perspective also provides a coherent system of family-oriented services that strengthen families and family living (Arcus, Schvaneveldt, & Moss, 1993; Weiss, 1990).

FIGURE 1.8   Time Line of Family Life Education

Early 1960s:
Education was primarily found in public schools, where educators taught students to be effective present and future family members. Traditional gender roles were reinforced.

Mid-1960s:
Coinciding with the Civil Rights Movement in 1964, family life education efforts involved teaching students and families facts, attitudes, and skills associated with relationships. Dating, marriage, and parenthood were emphasized, as were the relationships between parent–child and husband–wife.

Late 1960s:
Family life education scholars began to study family members' behaviors, functioning, values, and attitudes. It was a planned and programmed learning program within the community (not just schools) geared toward developing people's relational potentials.

Early 1970s:
Family life education programs centered on interactions between family members, individual characteristics, and imparting information about family relationships so that people gained a greater understanding of how they affect and are affected by their families. Taught in schools, religious settings, colleges, and within the community.

PRACTICING FAMILY LIFE EDUCATION

Today, an increasing number of professionals are family life educators because family studies is *multidisciplinary*. For example, psychologists, sociologists, and social workers may also simultaneously practice as family life educators. A **Certified Family Life Educator (CFLE)** is someone who has demonstrated knowledge (gained through work experience and college coursework) in the content areas displayed in Table 1.1. As you can see, the family life education perspective addresses every area of marital, intimate, and family living, including diversity and family policy. Family life education is also *multiprofessional* in its scope—pastors, rabbis, priests, health professionals, mental health professionals, and researchers may be family life educators.

Today, the *National Council on Family Relations (NCFR)* sponsors the only international program that certifies family life educators; such certification recognizes a professional's proven background, understanding, and knowledge of the content areas. And, while a CFLE may concentrate his or her expertise in one discipline, such as sexuality education, competencies in the multiple areas reflect the understanding that today's families face a wide range of issues that affect their ability to "do" family well. Thus, the awareness of and knowledge in the content areas also enables CFLEs to be more effective in their educational work with individuals and families (NCFR, 2009).

Now, armed with an understanding of the many aspects of family life education, as well as the diversity in families today, it's time to roll up our sleeves and begin our exploration of contemporary family life. The next step is to help you gain an appreciation of how you affect and are affected by the intimate relationships in your life. Although each of us accomplishes

Mid-1970s:
Family life education programs focused on providing instruction for families so they could understand the physical, mental, emotional, social, and economic aspects of family life.

Early 1980s:
Planned and programmatic information about life issues was offered to individuals of all ages.

Late 1980s:
Family life education became concerned with preserving and improving the quality of human life by studying individuals and families as they interacted with their many environments.

1990s–Current:
Family life education enables adults to reach their full personal potential in daily living, relating to others, and coping with life's events, such as the effects of the Iraq war on family and intimate life.

TABLE 1.1   Key Content Areas in Family Life Education

- **Families in Society** includes varying family forms; cross-cultural and diverse families and family values; and social and cultural variations (ethnicity, race, religion).

- **Family Dynamics** focuses on family communication patterns, conflict resolution, coping strategies, families in crisis/stress and distress, and families with special needs (military, step-, foster, adoptive families, etc.).

- **Human Growth and Development** explores human development across our lifespan.

- **Human Sexuality** presents sexual anatomy and physiology, reproduction, the emotional aspects of sexuality, sexual response and dysfunction, and our sexual values.

- **Interpersonal Relationships** focuses on love, human intimacy, and relational skills.

- **Family Resource Management** focuses on family financial goals and planning, and money decisions.

- **Parent Education** looks at the choice and challenges of parenthood, including the rights and responsibilities of parents, parental roles, and variations in parenting practices and styles.

- **Family Law and Public Policy** focuses on laws relating to marriage, divorce, cohabitation, child custody, child protection and the rights of children, and public policy (civil rights, social security) as it affects the family.

- **Ethics** concerns the diversity of human values and the complexity of how values are shaped in contemporary society.

Source: Adapted in part from HANDBOOK OF FAMILY LIFE EDUCATION by S. R. Czaplewski and S. R. Jorgensen. Copyright 1993 by Sage Publications Inc Books. Reproduced with permission of Sage Publications Inc Books in the format Textbook via Copyright Clearance Center.

many developmental milestones in our individual lifespan development, we do so within the context of family living. Every phase of our individual development across our human life cycle intersects with the development of the family throughout its developmental cycle, ultimately shaping who we are as relational people. In the next chapter, we'll examine how a people's families of origin shape their individual development, and in turn, shape their capacity to love and to be loved later in life.

Family Life Education

All of the diversity seen today in the United States contributes to a unique, distinct social fabric that adds a deep richness to our culture. But along with diversity comes substantial differences in family structure, family living, and family experiences. Although the "traditional" family has long been held as the "ideal" standard in childrearing and family life, we are no longer a society composed primarily of married couples raising their biological or adopted children. Today, there really is no such thing as a homogenized American family composed of a breadwinning male who provides for all of the family's needs and a breadmaking female who tends to the family's needs. While some family practitioners maintain that the changes we see in family structures today is a negative experience, others argue that the changes simply reflect more acceptance of diversity in our culture. You may also have a strong feeling or opinion about the changes seen in today's families; throughout our course of study together, you will gain not only a deeper understanding of family life today but also a deeper appreciation for these differences.

As diverse and distinct as U.S. families are today, though, they are all a part of the whole. We do not develop in isolation! Just as important, we do not experience family living and family life separately from our surrounding environments—and we do not experience family life in isolation from other families, no matter how different they may be from our own.

Is the Family of Origin Really That Important?

As couples prepare to enter into a serious relationship or into marriage, it is important that they are able to negotiate every kind of issue. But their past experiences in their families of origin greatly influence how they deal with things that crop up in their relational life. Given the importance of the family of origin, is it important that couples share similar family experiences in their backgrounds?

Her Side: I come from a family that has faced a lot of issues. My mom and dad were divorced when I was about 10, and my dad is now on his third marriage (and who knows how long that one will last?). My entire childhood was filled with nothing but my mom and dad arguing—even after they got divorced. Even though my dad is in my life (I mean, I see him regularly), it's not like he's ever lived up to anything he's ever promised . . . he didn't even come to my high school graduation. So I don't know. I love my fiancé, but his parents' marriage is so different from my experience with my parents and their marriage. I only know certain ways to act, certain ways to handle conflict (I tend to clam up and not say anything, whereas my fiancé wants to talk it all out). My mom is remarried now, but it's like she can't fully trust him because in the back of her mind she thinks he'll leave her like my dad did. So when you talk about the importance of the family of origin, I have to question whether it's wise to marry someone with vastly different experiences from mine.

His Side: I have given our differences a lot of thought. On my first trip home to meet her family I noticed right away that her family is pretty different from mine. Like, in my family it's a pretty happy, laid back house most of the time, whereas in her family it's like there's just this thick tension that's always just below the surface—and you just don't know when someone's going to blow up or get [ticked off] at someone else. And, they do seem to fight and argue quite a bit . . . a lot of times over nothing really, but they just fight. But having said that, I have to admit that [my fiancé] is *not* like her family. She really does see that all families aren't like how she grew up, and that just because that's her family of origin doesn't mean she *has* to repeat those same behaviors in our relationship. I think being aware of the differences in our families is what is most important—being aware of the differences and vowing not to fall into those destructive behaviors.

Your Side: Take into consideration what you have learned in this chapter, along with your personal life experiences.

1. Do you believe couples who have opposing families of origin should marry? Why or why not?
2. What potential difficulties do you foresee in this couple's marital future? In what ways can their discrepant backgrounds strengthen their marital relationship?
3. Before you read the information about the influences the family of origin exerts in our future relationships, had you given much thought to this area of family living? Why or why not? Is similar family background an important mate selection factor for you?

Because "family" and intimate relationships transcend race, religion, ethnicity, and sexual orientation, you will see yourself somewhere among the pages of this book. *Together*—you the student, your classmates, I the author/teacher, and your professor or instructor—using this text as our guide, we will examine and understand the complexities and intricacies of family life. I hope that this book will help you gain a solid, practical understanding of family and intimate relationships and equip you and empower you with the education to help you develop your full potential in your professional, personal, and family life. In this pursuit, I hope to engage your entire essence—your intellect, your emotions, and your heart.

Summary

What Is Marriage? What Is Family?

- There are differing cultural, religious, legal, and social aspects of marriage worldwide. To some, marriage is a social union; to others, it is a religious act and a strong social bond around which the rest of society is organized.

- Marriage is an important social structure that serves society on political, religious, social, and economic levels.

- Marriages across the world are typically classified as either monogamous or polygamous. *Monogamy* is the legal structure of marriage recognized in the United States and in other Western civilizations. *Polygamy* is the more widely practiced form of marriage across the world.

- The concept of family is a subjective experience, and "real-world" definitions are infinitely varied. Your family of origin (or family of orientation) is the family into which you were born or brought into by adoption and where you learn cultural norms. The family of procreation is the family unit that is formed when you marry and produce children. Sociocultural, economic, and political changes in the United States have influenced the family form and family life, giving way to a more complex and diverse definition of family.

- To help families reach their full potential, those who study family life education attempt to understand the changing compositions of contemporary families by using statistics to help them identify current patterns and trends. Students of family life understand that the new family landscape includes a wide array of family forms: nuclear, extended, single-parent, childless/childfree, stepfamily, cohabiting family, and gay/lesbian families.

Contemporary Families

- Students of family life understand that contemporary families are racially and ethnically diverse. They study the ever-changing racial and ethnic composition of U.S. families to further their understanding of the complex, changing nature of family health and family living.

Families in Cultural Contexts

- No human being develops in isolation—every emotion, every fear, every thought, and every behavior is linked to the family in which we were raised, either by genetics or by the family environment. In addition, many areas of family life are influenced by the economic, religious, and political systems that make up the broader culture in which we live.

- Family experiences are largely shaped by the culture's social identity—whether it adopts a collectivist or individualistic identity. Collectivists work together for the good of the group, while individualists do what they believe to be in their best personal interests.

- In his Ecological Model, Uri Bronfenbrenner theorized that people develop within developmental contexts, with the individual at the center of five ecosystems, or outside influences on the individual or family. The individual is influenced by the environment and also influences the environment.

  Microsystem This is the developmental context nearest to the individual and includes environments to which people are directly exposed, such as the family of origin, schools, the community, and religious affiliation.

  Mesosystem This describes the interaction between the various elements (for instance, How does the school have impact on the family? How does the religious institution?)

Exosystem This is the context in which policies are made and influenced, which ultimately have an impact on the elements of the microsystem and the individual. This context of development can be seen as an umbrella for all of the systems in a society (educational, religious, economic, etc.).

Macrosystem The recognition that a society has a set of overarching cultural values and beliefs that also affects development by giving its members either implicit or explicit rules about what is or is not acceptable behavior.

Chronosystem This system reflects the changes that happen over time.

Family Life Education: The Study of Families through a Family Lens

■ Borrowing and adapting theoretical frameworks from the fields of sociology, psychology, and other theories, the family life education perspective unveils the inadequacies families feel when they are faced with change, and then provides organized, programmatic education to help strengthen families. These theories, as well as statistics, help us understand and recognize family trends and experiences, but a student of marriage and family life should look beyond the numbers to see what they are really telling us.

■ Family life education is multidisciplinary and multiprofessional in its scope, examining theories and frameworks that are foundational to the understanding of human behavior and family relationship patterns. Family life education is a lens through which we can study family processes.

Key Terms and Concepts

Suggested Reading

Coontz, S. (1997). *The way we never were.* New York: Basic Books.

Olson, D. H., & Olson, A. K. (2000). *Empowering couples: Building on your strengths.* Minneapolis, MN: Life Innovations.

Pulido-Tobiassen, D., & Gonzalez-Mena, J. (2005). *A place to begin: Working with parents on issues of diversity.* Oakland, CA: California Tomorrow.

Zweig, M. (2004) *What's class got to do with it? American society in the 21st century.* New York: Cornell University Press.

Multiple-Choice Questions

1. The _____ of 1996 confirms that marriage is a legal union of one man and one woman as husband and wife.
   a. Correctness of Marriage Act (COMA)
   b. Defense of Marriage Act (DOMA)
   c. Sanctity of Marriage Act (SMA)
   d. Marriage Preservation Act (MPA)

2. _____ is a dyadic (two-person) form of marriage that involves the practice of having one sexual partner and is commonly recognized in the United States and other Western civilizations.
   a. Monogamy
   b. Polygamy
   c. Polygyny
   d. Polyandry

3. The _____ is the family unit formed when we marry and produce children.
   a. family of origin
   b. family of orientation
   c. family of procreation
   d. civil union family

4. Latino families further extend family relationships to _____ , or nonrelated, kin, such as godparents and close friends.
   a. indirect
   b. related
   c. normative
   d. fictive

5. Family life experiences are determined in large part by how a culture defines its _____ , or whether societal goals emphasize the advancement of the group's interests or individual interests.
   a. social identity
   b. attitude
   c. expectations
   d. social ecology

6. In _____ individuals define their identity in terms of the relationships they hold with others.
   a. communal cultures
   b. collectivist cultures
   c. group cultures
   d. tribal cultures

7. The contexts within the Ecological Model include the microsystem, mesosystem, _____ , macrosystem, and chronosystem.

   a. ecosystem

   b. metasystem

   c. exosystem

   d. thermosystem

8. The _____ is the context or ecosystem that forms the outermost layer of the Ecological Model and reflects changes that happen over time.

   a. exosystem

   b. microsystem

   c. macrosystem

   d. chronosystem

Answers: 1. b; 2. a; 3. c; 4. d; 5. a; 6. b; 7. c; 8. d

Understanding Families through Research and Theory

2

I am a 21-year-old college student from Kentucky. Like many newly-weds, I couldn't wait to set up our first home. Everything was perfectly planned. Our five-year goals were in place: He would join the Army, I would finish my degree, he would finish his four-year stint in the service, finish his degree, and we would then begin to start our family. Because of his service in the military, our student loans would be minimal, and we would be in a position to buy our first home. It was a perfect plan.

I have been married for nine months, and nothing has gone like we thought it would. Two weeks before our wedding, my husband was called up to serve in the war in Iraq. Our wedding went off without a hitch, but we had to cut our honeymoon short because of his deployment to the war. We were transferred to a military base in the Midwest! I didn't know anyone, I had no family, no friends. I felt like I was dropped off alongside the highway and expected to make the best of it. But we survived his first tour of duty. I thought to myself, "Finally, we can start our marriage." We both felt that if we could survive the separation so early in our marriage, we could survive anything. He was home for about three months and everything changed again—he was deployed again to Iraq.

To be honest, I'm scared. I'm scared every day that he won't come back to me, that something will happen to him. I feel so cheated—I didn't bargain for this! I have to wonder, what will happen to our marriage? Can we make it through these separations? How many more separations will there be over the next three years? How do couples get through this?

Source: Author's files

Science is humankind's exploration of how the world works. Religion, philosophy, art, mythology, and literature have also historically attempted to quench the insatiable thirst of human inquiry, but science is distinguished from these other modes of exploration—and explanation—by the methods used to discover and to know (Babbie, 2006; Pedhazur & Schmelkin, 1991; Sellitz, Wrightsman, & Cook, 1976). The exploration to discover and understand often begins with a simple inquiry, such as the question posed by the newlywed in the opening vignette: How are marriages and families affected when a loved one serves his or her country overseas, for extended periods of time? When examining social and individual processes by engaging in and using methods beyond logic, common sense, intuition, or reason alone, we engage in scientific inquiry—in the practice of social science research.

Understanding Families through Research

Many students feel alienated from the research process. They have a hard time understanding how facts and figures help us understand the "big picture." This alienation, in fact, has been an obstacle for many would-be social science practitioners over the years. A colleague of mine, for example, told me that for as long as she could remember, she had wanted to be a psychologist. She majored in psychology as an undergraduate—that is, until it was time to begin coursework in research methods and statistics. Because she had a fear of and an aversion to statistics, her advisor suggested that she change her major to English. I must confess I had a similar fear of the research process. I remember thinking, *"But I'm not a statistician—that's why I'm studying the family, not numbers!"* As it happened, I was luckier than my colleague. Because of a dynamic research methods professor who was able to show the relevance and importance of theories and research, I was able to replace my fear with excitement about the research process. And it was while I was taking that course that the research bug bit me.

THE research process helps family practitioners and family scientists better understand the complex issues that face today's families, such as young couples who are separated by military service

The research process is an integral and critical part of your study of marriage and family. Research is important because it enables social scientists, family practitioners, psychologists, and sociologists to develop family theories and family education programs, create family policies that strengthen and serve today's families, and better understand societal trends, such as the demographic trends of contemporary families, as you saw earlier. Indeed, research is neither boring nor insignificant, because it has an impact on the daily lives of today's families. It is through research and these theories that we come to a deeper understanding of family functioning and family process.

SOCIAL SCIENCE RESEARCH

The term **research** means to study thoroughly through the process of scholarly or scientific inquiry. **Social science research** is the scholarly discipline used to examine human society and relationships. When conducting research in the social sciences, researchers examine behaviors, emotions, and relationships—all of which cannot be easily quantified or examined within neat, tidy categories. I like to refer to social research as "the other side of the microscope"—in other words, social scientists are not concerned with what the results are under the microscope as are biologists, but instead, they are concerned with factors that cannot be seen microscopically; they are concerned with people.

Researching family life allows us to explore intimate relationships within the context of marriage and family. Family research provides information that allows family practitioners—such as family life educators, social workers, teachers, members of the clergy, therapists, and psychologists—to develop, implement, and evaluate programs that may enhance family life and family growth. Understanding the problems that face today's family and finding explanations and answers to those problems would not be possible without the practice of social science inquiry through research.

As nineteenth-century American humorist Artemus Ward once noted, "It ain't the things we don't know that gets us in trouble. It's the things we know that ain't so" (Sellitz, Wrightsman, & Cook, 1976). This tongue-in-cheek statement has an element of truth. We often believe we "know" something to be true or factual because it seems to be the logical, commonsense conclusion. Take, for example, the following statements:

- Children reared by same-sex parents experience harmful outcomes.
- A couple who cohabits before marriage increases their chances that their marriage will last, since they will work out all of their difficulties before going down the aisle.
- Married couples who frequently argue have lower levels of marital satisfaction than couples who experience few conflicts.

What is your logical, commonsense response to these statements?

Relying on logic or common sense frequently "limits us to the familiar" (Sellitz, Wrightsman, & Cook, 1976, p. 4). If you agree with the previous statements, you are using your intuition or existing beliefs, your life experiences, and your expectations to draw those conclusions. You are reasoning about what might be a plausible or the most likely outcome, and drawing your conclusions based on your interpretation of circumstances. Are your conclusions accurate?

The problem with using our common sense and logic is that everyone sees things differently based on different value systems, political beliefs, religious beliefs—the very values and beliefs that provide the lens through which we view our social environments. Because of our differences in values and beliefs, how can we "know" that, for example, children reared by same-sex couples really do (or really do not) experience negative developmental outcomes? What aspects of our belief system would lead us to believe that couples who live together before marriage have a higher (or lower) success rate than couples who do not? How can we "know" how marital separation, such as in the opening vignette, impacts marital happiness or satisfaction? We "know" when we conduct research that supports or does not support our suppositions. We look at the numbers, we draw conclusions, and we apply theories, all of which gives us insight and helps us know and understand the truth.

THE RESEARCH METHOD: START TO FINISH

In his 1911 work, *The Grammar of Science*, statistician Karl Pearson maintained, "There is no shortcut to truth, no way to gain a knowledge of the universe except through the gateway of scientific method" (p. 17). The **scientific method** is a process by which social science researchers formulate questions concerning social and individual phenomena and seek out answers. Using the scientific method, researchers design a process from start to finish that details the sequential, interrelated investigative steps the researcher will follow. Much like building a house, a solid investigative design plan moves researchers systematically through each step as they look for answers to their initial questions.

From Start to Finish If you have a well-conceived research design and a sound, logical plan, your plan is more likely to yield valuable results. Figure 2.1 (on page 38) illustrates the starting point of a research design, either through interest in a topic, an idea, or a desire to explore a theory. This design can be used for both quantitative research and qualitative research. **Quantitative research** uses statistical methods to count and measure outcomes from a study; it is a systematic attempt to define, measure, and report on the relationships between elements that are being studied. **Qualitative research** involves detailed verbal or written descriptions of characteristics under investigation; this research typically involves observation

FIGURE 2.1 The Research Process from Start to Finish

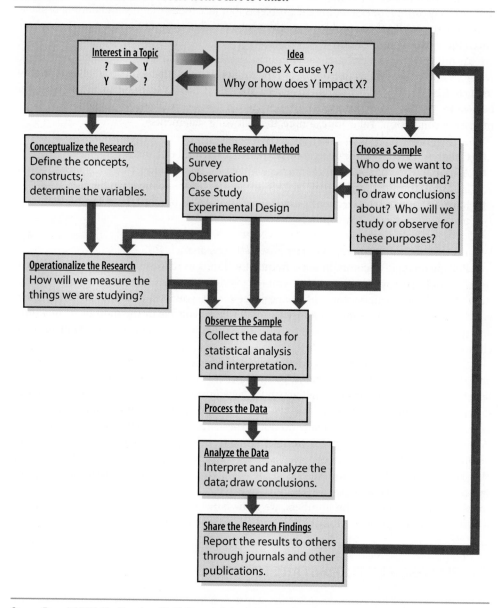

Source: From BABBIE. *The Practice of Social Research (with CD-ROM and Info Trac)* 11th edition. © 2006 Wadsworth, a part of Cengage Learning, Inc. Reproduced by permission. www.cengage.com/permissions.

and interviews to collect data. To aid in your understanding of the research process, we'll follow a research design plan that examined marital satisfaction among deployed members of the U.S. Army (Schumm, Bell, & Gade, 2000).

Choosing the Research Topic (Step 1) Intimacy, jealousy, the effects of divorce on children, sexuality, gender identity and gender roles, family communication and conflict—the choice of potential research topics is virtually limitless, and investigators choose to examine topics for a variety of reasons. Some may select a research topic because of a concern with a social issue or problem, such as the effects of peacetime and war deployment on military families, as illustrated in the opening vignette; some may have a great interest in a particular area of behavior; others may choose to examine the validity of a certain theory; still others may select a topic because of financial or professional incentives to do so (Sellitz, Wrightsman, & Cook, 1976).

Once a research topic is chosen, the investigator needs to determine which variables to study. A **variable** is a characteristic that is measured in a study. It is called a variable because the *value* or degree of the characteristic varies among the people or group of people being studied.

In the military study, for example, the examiners wanted to assess changes in marital satisfaction over time among soldiers who were on a peacekeeping mission overseas. They wanted to better understand if long-term separation reduced marital satisfaction, and to see if satisfaction became elevated once the soldiers returned home (Schumm, Bell, & Gade, 2000). A few of the variables for this investigation included soldiers' assessments of their marital satisfaction pre-deployment, mid-deployment, and post-deployment. Another variable was marital stability, or how stable the soldiers' marriages were before, during, and after deployment.

Creating the Research Question (Step 2) At the core of any valid research is the **research question**, or the **research hypothesis**. Before researchers pose a research question or hypothesis, they must first have a clear understanding of the problem and a clear vision of their objective. In the military study, the research question was *What impact do long overseas deployments have on the families of soldiers?* Because initial research hypotheses may involve many unknowns at the outset, researchers often need to refine their investigation by doing an exhaustive search of the existing research studies related to their topic of inquiry. This is referred to as a **literature review**. This process allows researchers to get a better grasp on the scope of the problem and all aspects related to the research topic.

After the researcher has a solid understanding of the problem he or she wants to investigate, a research hypothesis is formed. A **hypothesis** is a speculative statement about a variable or the relationship between variables in a study. In a sense, hypotheses are predictions about the variables that will be measured in the study (Agresti & Finlay, 2008). In the sequential research process, statistical **hypotheses testing** takes place at a later point in the investigation. A hypothesis is never accepted or confirmed; based on the evidence gathered, a researcher can either *reject* a hypothesis or *fail to reject* a hypothesis.

Conceptualizing the Research (Step 3) Once a researcher has generated an idea or interest in a topic area, has formulated a research question, and has selected the variables to be studied, the next step in planning the design of the research study is conceptualization. **Conceptualization** is the process through which the researcher specifically denotes or indicates all of the concepts—or constructs—under investigation. A concept, or **construct**, refers to intangibles. For example, if I asked you to define *sexual response, marital satisfaction,* and *positive parenting,* we would soon discover that definitions for these terms are as numerous as the number of students reading this textbook. As research methodologists Elazur Pedhazur and Liora Schmelkin put it, "Even for people who speak the same language, words have different meanings, depending on, among other things, who speaks, to whom, in what context, at what time, and with what purpose. Words . . . are loaded with connotations" (1991, p. 164). Thus, a construct is a "mental creation" (Babbie, 2006) that allows individuals to communicate in concrete terms about abstract ideas that have no single, unwavering meaning—such as love. If we pause just a moment to think about Earl Babbie's description of a construct, then we quickly come to the conclusion that just about everything examined in the social sciences is a construct.

Using Operational/Empirical Definitions (Step 4) Because constructs are mental creations and words may have different connotations, it is important that researchers come to a workable definition for the constructs under investigation. For example, how can I be sure that when you are reading my research you, in your mental creation, are referring to "marital satisfaction" in the same capacity that I am? In the past, *marital satisfaction* has been operationally defined by some researchers as a set of desirable characteristics of the ideal marriage, such as maintaining feelings of mutual love and respect, equitable sharing of duties and responsibilities, making decisions together, mutual sharing of interests, and mutual agreement on important issues (Fowers & Olson, 1993). Today, other researchers define marital satisfaction by using global evaluations of a couple's behaviors and feelings, such as the amount of

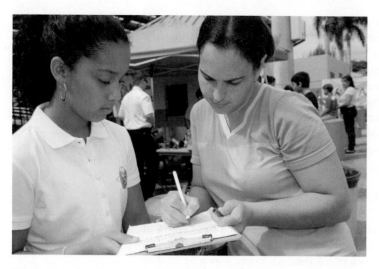

THE survey research method is the most widely used technique that social scientists use to gather data about intimate relationships and family. Have you ever participated in a survey of some kind? If so, did you find it difficult to provide information about your feelings and behaviors? Why or why not?

conflict between the couple or whether the couple would marry his or her spouse again if they had it to do over (Kamp, Dush, Taylor, & Kroeger, 2008). So you see, the definition of a construct can change depending on who the researcher is, and the purpose of the study.

To avoid confusion, *at the outset of the research*, researchers create **operational definitions** that describe or characterize the constructs (concepts) that are being studied. As the research progresses, the empirical (scientific) definitions may need to be refined. Whether a consumer of the research agrees with empirically defined terms is not important.

Choosing the Research Method (Step 5)

The next step in the research process involves selecting which research method (or the combination of research methods) to use when pursuing the investigation. In order to represent in a statistical format human behaviors and patterns of behavior, empirical data must be gathered. Deciding the best method for studying the family, marriage, and other interpersonal relationships largely depends on the purpose of the research—whether it is exploration, description, or explanation. To study families, family scientists typically use four primary research methods to collect data: the survey, observational research, the case study, and experimental design.

Surveys For three decades, influential social and economics science researcher Don Dillman has helped social scientists effectively plan and conduct survey research with his landmark book, *Mail and Internet Surveys: The Tailored Design Method* (1978). The **survey** research method, a structured questionnaire, is the most popular technique for gathering data when studying families and interpersonal relationships (Dillman, 1978/1999). Standardized questionnaires are an excellent method for determining trends and behavioral patterns, and for gathering original data about a certain population. By collecting survey responses from a group of people, a **sample**, researchers can sometimes infer conclusions based on study data and extend them to the larger population.

We will discuss methods of sampling later in this chapter. For now, understand that in order for a questionnaire or survey to yield valuable information that reflects the characteristics of the population being studied, it must be well constructed and well designed. According to Don Dillman (1978/1999), a well-constructed survey is unbiased and easily understood by study respondents. The questions in a good survey should also be carefully worded and nonobjectionable.

There are many different types of surveys and questionnaires. Some are mailed or e-mailed to potential respondents, some are Web-based, and others are carried out by telephone or face-to-face interviews. Whatever the method, each has its strengths and weaknesses. And the success of any survey research is measured by the response rate of the study subjects.

Response rates The **response rate** is the percentage of the study subjects who respond to the survey. Perhaps one of the most questionable response rates was obtained by Shere Hite, author of the well-known human sexuality study, *The Hite Reports*. Hite indicated she sent out 100,000 sexuality questionnaires to women, but only about 4,500 women responded to the survey, or a 4.5 percent response rate. This low response rate was a red flag for social scientists. Because the response rate to a survey or questionnaire indicates how representative the study sample is (to what extent it accurately reflects the characteristics) of the larger population, very low response rates such as Hite's show that those who *did not* respond to the survey differed from those who *did* respond. How high a response rate is high enough? Universally, a response rate of 50 percent is considered to be adequate for analyzing data; 60 percent is good; and a 70 percent response rate is very good (Babbie, 2006).

Survey drawbacks Despite the fact that surveys and questionnaires are the most common means of obtaining social science data, there are some inherent problems with their use. In the physical sciences, the units of measurement are very precise, but in social science research, we must depend on human beings to provide information—which is subjective—on their feelings and behaviors.

Take the example of a teenage male filling out a survey that assesses how sexually active he is—while sitting beside his very sexually experienced buddy. To impress his friend, the adolescent may overreport his sexual encounters. Conversely, if his friend is an active member of a church youth group that frowns on premarital sex, it is possible the teen male might underreport his sexual activity. Because survey research is dependent on human beings providing human responses to their past and current experiences, there is an inherent risk of overreporting or underreporting certain behaviors. This is referred to as **response bias**, a flaw that may occur when researchers rely on individuals' self-reports.

Another area of concern lies in how reliable assessments are of human behavior, attitudes, and experiences. These may be difficult to assess by rigid, standardized questions. For example, how can research measure "commitment" or "love"? It is quite possible that when responding to a survey, the respondents may want to delve deeper into their responses—which would provide much greater insight into their behavior and feelings—but there is no provision on the survey or questionnaire to do so. Thus, researchers are left with an incomplete understanding of the context of the respondent's life situation.

As we discussed earlier, much of what researchers examine in social science inquiry are constructs. For this reason researchers must take care when empirically defining these concepts to ensure that responses are valid. **Validity** speaks to the extent that a researcher is able to provide an empirical definition that reflects the true meaning of what is being studied. For example, if we wanted to study marital satisfaction, do we want to study the amount of conflict in the couple's relationship or do we want to study the couple's mutual love and respect for each other? We have to make sure that our measurements accurately assess what we want them to assess.

The validity of survey research is often criticized because the questions may not really measure what the researchers claim they are measuring. In a sense, what happens is the researcher strains to provide an empirical definition that (ideally) accurately represents a construct, and then the research participant is asked to fit that behavior or emotion to a predetermined scale that may or may not reflect how the respondent wants to answer. In Babbie's (2006) view, very seldom do our opinions neatly fall into categories of "always," "sometimes," "never," "strongly agree," "somewhat agree," and the like. When people are asked to approximate their behavior to fit within a standardized scale, validity is put in jeopardy.

Observational Research Our observations help us understand and make sense of our world. Each of us continuously observes the behavior of others, whether we are craning our necks to see who is going into whose dorm room, or whether we're driving slowly by a vehicle accident. More recently, our media-savvy society allows us to peer into the lives of the rich and fabulous twenty-somethings in *The Hills*, stranded castaways on *Survivor*, *Big Brother* house members, and bachelors and

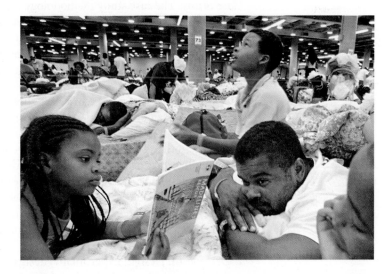

OBSERVING the behaviors and experiences of families who were displaced after Hurricane Katrina provided valuable information to researchers that can be used to develop programs to help similar victims in the future.

bachelorettes seeking "true love" through reality TV programming. The problem with reality TV, however, is that it is part reality and part entertainment, and what we ultimately observe is not "real" at all. Social science inquiry requires a much more systematic method of observation.

The **observational research method** is a systematic process in that (1) the observation is systematically planned, (2) the data are gathered and recorded in a systematic format, and (3) systematic checks and balances assess the reliability and validity of the observations (Sellitz, Wrightsman, & Cook, 1976). Observational research can take place either in a laboratory-like setting, such as a married couple in a counseling session being observed behind a one-way glass, or the more natural setting that we call **field research**. In both cases, investigators want to objectively record and describe the behavior that is being observed.

Researchers Sellitz, Wrightsman, and Cook (1976) described three purposes of using observational research:

1. *Observational research may be performed for purposes of description*, such as describing how children respond immediately after viewing a violent video clip or how infants respond when their parents leave them unattended.
2. *This research method is used when the subject matter does not lend itself to other methods.* For example, near ground zero of the World Trade Center catastrophe in 2001, children were in their school classrooms when the tragedy took place. If researchers were present at this site, they could have more accurately recorded the immediate reactions and responses of the children, directly assessed the impact of the tragedy on these students, and ultimately created educational or counseling programs that truly met and reflected the needs of the children.
3. *Observational research is appropriate when other research methods are inaccurate.* When trying, for example, to ascertain information about behaviors, experiences, and attitudes, observational research may allow researchers to observe and record accurate descriptions of behavior that other methods would not permit. The results of such studies may, in some cases, be representative of the larger population, and not just relevant to the sample studied. For instance, if we wanted to better understand the effects of the long-term displacement of families following Hurricane Katrina in 2005, observing their behaviors and experiences would yield much more valuable information than a survey, which might not be able to fully capture the feelings and attitudes of the flood victims. These observational experiences could then be used to formulate policies and educational programs that promote family health, home relocation/replacement, and job relocation following other natural disasters in the future.

Case Study The **case study** methodology involves study of either a single person or a small group of people. Case studies are often used to obtain an in-depth understanding of emotional and/or behavioral patterns by providing detailed descriptions of either an individual case or a group of case studies related to one another. When a comprehensive (almost biographical) description is needed or desired, researchers turn to the use of case studies. Sometimes an area of interest is so new that one-by-one case studies are the means by which the data are gathered and new theories are subsequently generated; other times the area under investigation is an uncommon or rare occurrence, such as our examples of the World Trade Center tragedy and Hurricane Katrina.

Aside from the drawback of being time consuming to the researcher, case study methodology findings may be limited in that they are not typically generalizable—applicable—to the larger population. For example, although the case studies of the children from ground zero in the September 11 attacks provide very valuable information about the effects of the trauma on the children, researchers cannot assume that these effects could be generalized to children in war-torn Iraq. Case studies do not allow us to see cause-and-effect relationships.

Experimental Design **Experimental design** is used to determine causal relationships among variables. Conducting experimental design research requires researchers to control the experimental procedure—controlling or holding constant the variables being studied in order to determine which variable is indeed effecting the change in the other variable.

FIGURE 2.2   The Experimental Design Research Method

Population (N = Sample Size)	Groups (R = Random Selection)	Pre-Test	Experimental Treatment (X)	Post-Test	Differences
N (number in sample)	R—Experimental Group	The group's characteristics before the treatment or program.	X—One group gets the treatment or program.	The group's characteristics after the treatment or program.	Change?
N (number in sample)	R—Control Group	The group's characteristics at the start of the study.	No treatment or program.	The group's characteristics at the end of the study.	Change?

An experimental design comprises two groups: the **experimental group** is the group that is exposed to the independent variables under question; the **control group** is treated exactly the same as the experimental group, except they are not exposed to the independent variable (see Figure 2.2).

A limitation of experimental research is that the laboratory is an artificial environment in which to study human response. Consider, for example, the reality MTV show, *The Hills*. When Lauren and Jason got back together, or when Audrina had the dramatic breakup with Justin in front of millions of viewers, were these relationships and emotions authentic? Would these people be acting the way they are or saying what they do if the cameras were not on them? The answer is no. In other words, we have to consider how much the presence of the camera is influencing their behavior. In this same vein, how much does the knowledge of an experiment alter an individual's behavior?

Selecting a Population and Sampling (Step 6) After a researcher has conceptualized the research, empirically defined all constructs/concepts under investigation, and chosen the type of research method to be used, the next step in the research process involves selecting a population or sample to be studied. In the military research, the examiners wanted to study the effect of separation on marital satisfaction among service members. The researcher could not possibly locate all the service men and women in that **population** (the entire group of people who shared this experience); to overcome this, a researcher selects a sample from the population under investigation.

In the social sciences, our investigation of people's behavior and emotional states must take into account people's differences. For this reason we have to be very precise and deliberate in our selection of whom we study via sampling. There are two types of sampling: *probability sampling* and *nonprobability sampling* (see Figure 2.3 on page 44).

Probability sampling is necessary because not every person in every population shares exact characteristics. In a **probability** (random) **sample**, each person has the same likelihood (probability) of being selected for the study. In probability sampling, the notion of **representativeness**, or the degree to which the characteristics of the population are represented by the sample, is key. The **sample size** also affects the degree to which the sample is considered to be representative. Statistics gathered based on probability samples are used to draw conclusions about the sample, because researchers can reasonably assess the amount of sampling (expected) error that will take place.

Nonprobability samples are not selected randomly, but are used when the use of probability samples is impossible. For example, when the investigators decided to study U.S. service members, it was not feasible for the researcher to select a probability sample from the

FIGURE 2.3   Research Samples

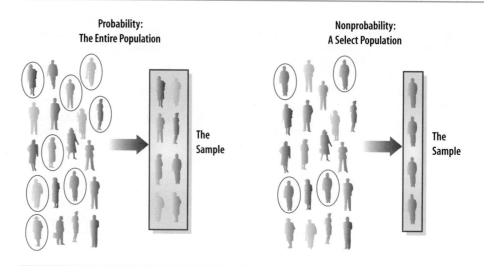

Source: From BABBIE. *The Practice of Social Research (with CD-ROM and Info Trac)* 11th edition. © 2006 Wadsworth, a part of Cengage Learning, Inc. Reproduced by permission. www.cengage.com/permissions.

population at large (what would their chances be that their sample would include people who had served overseas?); they instead used a nonprobability sample.

Collecting, Processing, and Analyzing Data (Step 7) Only after careful methodological planning of the total research design is the social scientist ready to collect, process, and analyze the data. These processes are beyond the scope of our discussion here, but it is vitally important for novice researchers to understand the relevance and necessity of each step in the design process. Although inexperienced researchers may be eager to collect data in an area that is of great interest to them, and even though it might be tempting for experienced researchers to become lax and complacent in research design, less-than-desirable results are almost assured. Remember, these steps are not necessarily sequential; the overlap among the design elements is continuous throughout the entire investigative procedure. A poor research design almost always produces poor research results.

Applying Research Findings (Step 8) Once a researcher collects, processes, and analyzes the data generated from the research, the findings of the study are usually presented in some type of format (such as a journal or professional conference) for scholars, researchers, policy makers, or other users to apply. Some may choose to use their findings to support and bring about societal change through the creation of family policy. Other researchers may elect to have their study reviewed by colleagues and then publish the research process and findings in a journal devoted to a given area of study, such as the *Journal of Marriage and Family*, the *Journal of Sex Research*, the *Journal of Men's Studies*, and *Family Relations*, to name a few. Still other researchers may use their research findings and research skills to design, implement, and evaluate family life education programs that promote the health and functioning of today's families.

MAKING SENSE OF IT ALL: HOW TO READ SOCIAL SCIENCE LITERATURE

How do we separate truth from untruth, fact from fiction? Through the process of research. Despite its inherent flaws, social science research is the only method by which we can gain a deeper understanding and appreciation of family and family life. Now that you understand the research design process, we will focus on how to get the most out of research, and how to distinguish well-written, valid research from poorly designed research that yields invalid or

What's All the Fuss about Research?

S tudents commonly have fears or apprehensions about research methods and statistics.

1. What are your greatest apprehensions about the research process? Are your hesitations specific worries or fears related to designing the research plan? Or are your apprehensions related to using statistical methods to analyze and interpret your research findings?
2. Take a moment to jot down three apprehensions you have about research and theory. After you read this chapter, see if any of your attitudes changed.

insignificant results. A colleague of mine who teaches graduate-level social science research methods courses makes the point that those interested in family and family life need to become *consumers* of the literature. By making the time to separate the wheat from the chaff, so to speak, you will be better able to draw meaningful conclusions as you read (consume) the social science literature.

Learn to Discern Many readers in search of information tend to skip over the results section of a research article and jump directly to the more engaging, accessible discussion section where authors take the liberty to interpret the results of their study. Most authors include within the discussion a section devoted to the limitations of the current study. Many novice consumers of the literature, however, are also novices when it comes to interpreting what they are reading, and mistakenly assume the discussion section portrays a precise interpretation of the results section. Unfortunately, this is not always the case.

Throughout this book, you will notice numerous research citations that substantiate the information that is conveyed. These citations or references refer to research or findings presented by an author or several authors. As you read research, consider the following questions to ensure that it is valid and reliable.

- *Are the purposes of the research and/or the hypotheses clearly stated?*

  Be wary of research that does not specifically state the intended purpose of the research or present a clearly stated research hypothesis at the outset. There is an expression, "Anyone can make any research say anything." Although educated consumers of the literature will avoid this pitfall, to a certain extent this statement is true. **Data churning**, or "fishing," refers to the practice of devising the purposes of the research or formulating a research hypothesis after the data are gathered and analyzed. Data churning reduces the value of statistical findings because, sooner or later, something that appears to be statistically significant will turn out that way simply because of random chance.

- *What is the method by which the data are collected?*

  Researchers obtain data by asking carefully constructed questions or through the direct observation of behavior. Because surveys and questionnaires are the means by which the majority of social science information is gathered, it is important to examine the survey instrument (a questionnaire, for example) and the survey process.

  The content of surveys and/or questionnaires largely depends on the purpose of the study (exploration, description, or explanation) and the type of information the researcher is hoping to gather. Types of question content areas may include (Sellitz, Wrightsman, & Cook, 1976):

  1. Content aimed at ascertaining facts
  2. Content aimed at ascertaining beliefs about the facts
  3. Content aimed at ascertaining feelings

4. Content aimed at discovering standards of action
5. Content aimed at past or present behavior
6. Content designed to discover beliefs, feelings, and behavior

When scrutinizing surveys, look at how demanding the questions are. Are they asking people to articulate, recall, and express detailed information? Are the questions written in a biased format to elicit desired statements, or are they unbiased and open? For instance, if a survey posed the question, "Why did President Bush make the wrong decision in deciding to go to war with Iraq?," it would be asking a biased question because the way this question is constructed presupposes a value on his decision (the word *wrong*). As a careful reader, consider what questions skew the results of the study. Are the questions too vague? Too precise? Has the researcher assumed too much about the respondents' behavior? Has the researcher assumed too much about the respondents' knowledge base?

■ *How was the study sample selected? Is the sample representative?*
What constitutes a "good" study sample? In order for a study sample to represent a desired population under investigation, a probability sample is the research method of choice. By employing randomization—a sample that ensures everyone has an equal chance of being selected—the researcher minimizes the possibility of misleading results. Does the study sample have enough participants from the population under inquiry so that statistical approximations can be made to it? Or is the sample, instead, a **convenience sample,** or a volunteer sample? A sample that is not scientifically selected calls even the most well-intended research into question.

■ *What is the response rate?*
In order to fully interpret the meaning of statistical data, it is imperative that consumers of the literature understand the composition of the study participants. To determine the applicability of survey findings, the response rate must be sizable. Recall from our earlier discussion that in social science research, a response rate of 50 percent is considered a "good" response rate. Why is this an important measure? The response rate is an indicator of how representative the survey or questionnaire is; the higher the response rate, the more likely it is that the survey responses reflect the population under investigation. For example, in the military group under study, of the 200 married service personnel, 113 responded to the survey— or about 57 percent of the population under investigation. Of these 113 soldiers, 70 percent provided data throughout the length of the study.

Investigators must also understand the makeup of the population. Are the respondents' characteristics more heavily concentrated in one area than another? (This may or may not pose a problem, depending on the intended purpose of the research.) Equally important is the consideration of who did not respond.

■ *What is the weight of the evidence for conclusions?*
Always be wary of claims that cite "most" or "many" or "several," if the sample size is not known. Ask yourself: Most, many, or several of what number? When viewing data that are represented by percentages, immediately ask, *X* percentage of how many? In other words, is the percentage reflected 33.3 percent of a sample of *three*, or of *three hundred thousand*? Whether data are presented in graphic form, such as a bar graph, or in tables that present percentages, keep the percentages in perspective. Always know the sample size and response rate before trusting the percentages.

TO obtain valid, reliable research results, social scientists must make sure that their research sample is representative of the population they are investigating. If researchers obtain a high response rate (at least 50 percent), it is likely the survey or the questionnaire represents the study population.

- *Do confounding (rival) factors exist?*

Confounding, or **rival**, **variables** are variables that are unrelated, unconnected, or not pertinent to the variables under investigation, which can skew or affect the results of the study. Results are often influenced by these extraneous factors. My college statistics professor gave an example of confounding variables in a study that sought to determine who had the greater incidence of cancer, individuals who ate oatmeal or individuals who consumed Kellogg's Frosted Flakes. The researchers found that individuals who ate oatmeal had higher rates of cancer than those who ate Frosted Flakes. The confounding variable? Those who ate oatmeal were older than those who ate Frosted Flakes—*age* was the contributing factor to incidence of cancer, not what was consumed for breakfast!

Whether you are preparing to become a social worker, an educator, a family life educator, a member of the clergy, a child life specialist, or any type of human services provider, the very nature of your profession calls on you to make judgments and assessments about the reliability and validity of research results.

It is the researcher's ethical responsibility to present information in a forthright and honest manner, but it is also the consumer's responsibility to determine the sufficiency of the research process and the dependability of the results. It is together in the researcher/consumer enterprise that reliable, repeatable, useful information is obtained through social science investigation.

Research with Animals in Social Science

Although most research in the social sciences uses people as subjects, research with animal subjects continues to be essential for answering some questions regarding human behavior, such as understanding the biological significance of certain behaviors. For instance, if we want to understand the connection between stress and disease, we can better create psychological interventions for coping with stress more effectively if we know the biological mechanisms that are triggered by stress. Animal research has been particularly helpful for social scientists to better understand how the central nervous system works, and it has been a significant contributor to our understanding of such problems as mental illness, memory disorders, and drug addiction.

Today, about 7 to 8 percent of psychological research involves the use of animals. Every research facility is required to maintain an Institutional Animal Care and Use Committee (IACUC), which is the governing committee responsible for the ethical treatment of research animals (similar to the IRB for human subjects). Many government safeguards exist to assure that animals are treated humanely, and that the research causes as little suffering to animals as possible. There are "three Rs" that are the guiding principles for the use of animals in research:

- **Reduction** refers to research methods that allow researchers to obtain comparable levels of information from fewer animals, or to obtain more information from the same number of animals.
- **Replacement** refers to the preferred use of nonanimal research methods whenever it is possible to achieve the same scientific aim.
- **Refinement** refers to research methods that alleviate or minimize potential pain, suffering, or distress, and to enhance animal welfare for the animals used for scientific purposes.

Through research with animals, scientists have gained essential information that contributes not only to our understanding of people but also to advancing people's welfare and well-being.

Source: American Psychological Association. (2008). *APA Board of Scientific Affairs: Committee on Animal Research and Ethics.* Available www.apa.org/science/animal2/html [2008, September 13].

RESEARCH ETHICS AND INTEGRITY

The practice of social science research is an endeavor that requires responsible conduct on the part of the researcher, particularly in light of the fact that human subjects are the object of study. The federal government sets procedural guidelines to ensure that researchers conduct their research ethically and with integrity.

In general, **ethics** refers to the principals or standards of people's conduct, or the principals of right and good. In the realm of social science research, ethics refers to the rules and standards that govern researchers' conduct as they examine human behaviors, feelings, and attitudes (National Academy of Sciences [NAS], 1995). Following research procedural guidelines set forth by the federal government, and to ensure the ethical treatment of research subjects, academic institutions and other research institutions have established research review committees, or **The Institutional Review Board (IRB)**. Often, IRBs are referred to as *human subjects committees*. Before pursuing a research plan, scientists must first gain the approval of their institution's IRB. These committees are concerned with the study participants' safety and well-being, ensuring that all participants have been fully informed of the true nature of the research, and the assurance of privacy and confidentiality.

Scientific endeavors are based on trust: IRBs trust researchers to abide by the ethical guidelines that are set in place to ensure the protection of research subjects; study subjects trust researchers to treat them with care and concern; academic and medical communities trust that the results reported by researchers are accurate and valid; and society trusts that research results are accurate and not biased (National Academy of Sciences, 1995).

Whereas research ethics is concerned with the relationship between the researcher and the research subjects, **research integrity** is concerned with the relationship between researchers and the truth in reporting their findings (Pimple, 2001). In other words, is it good, reliable science? Research integrity involves:

- A competent research design plan
- No manipulation of the data to construe the results one way or another
- Sound statistical methods
- No falsification of the results
- No fabrication of the results
- Sharing the results with the academic and/or medical world
- Giving credit where credit is due (citing research sources used in the gathering and publishing of research findings)

As you can see, the process of social science research is a carefully crafted balance of research design, research ethics, and research integrity. Discovering ways through research to strengthen families and the quality of family life is a tedious yet exhilarating experience. Within the social sciences, it is especially rewarding to know that our research efforts have direct impact on the populations we care deeply and passionately about. It is through research that family practitioners and social scientists create educational programs and family polices that serve humankind. Research also promotes the creation of family theories.

Understanding Families through Theory

Because we all consider ourselves knowledgeable about family life, it can be quite tempting to make assertions about a form of family behavior we consider to be "right" or "wrong" based on our personal experience. But "family life" extends well beyond our personal worlds. One way to understand and envision "family" beyond our own worlds is to expand our knowledge through theories.

Strongly held beliefs about what constitutes "family" have molded, and at times, dominated, services available to families and family policy. Yet, in order to move beyond these commonly held assumptions and common beliefs about family, family life theorists cannot rely on widely held suppositions about family; rather, they must study the family empirically.

A solid, foundational knowledge base in *Family theory* is essential for students of and professionals interested in the field of family life. Throughout our study, we will examine several *theories* and *frameworks* that are fundamental to the understanding of human behavior and family relationship patterns. In the family sciences, a **theory** is a general principle that is used to understand or to explain certain events or family experiences, such as family communication or family crisis. A **framework** is a systematic structure for classifying families, their behaviors, or their experiences. Theories profoundly affect what we know about families, because they provide structure for how we think about families, what we observe, how we interpret what we observe, and how we use this information to create programs and introduce policies that affect and enhance family life (Smith, 1995). In short, a theory allows us to move beyond our everyday, common beliefs about family and move toward an objective, scientific understanding of family and family processes.

AN INTRODUCTION TO FAMILY THEORIES

We do not develop in a vacuum. The most significant influence on both our individual development and our ability to relate to others, by far, is our family of origin. Our family is the base from which we venture out and learn to share ourselves in close and intimate relationships. The ability to share ourselves is a complicated, elaborate mixture of our own individual development and our family experiences (whatever they might be). Our family history also plays a significant role, as generations before produced our grandparents and parents—those who have influenced us the most.

Today, many theories exist that attempt to explain the workings of family, and each have made numerous contributions to the field of family studies. James White and David Klein, authors of *Family Theories: An Introduction* (2008), describe today's prevailing family theories.

1. *Ecological theory* is concerned with the many social and cultural contexts that affect family living. As you learned in Chapter 1, these contexts include factors that exert immediate influences on the family, such as schools, churches or temples, and neighborhoods. Other contexts include the government, educational systems, the political system, and the overarching value system of a given society.

2. *Family Development theory* divides the experiences of family into phases, or stages, of normative changes associated with family growth and development, such as the birth of children and the launching of these children into early adulthood. This theory is concerned with understanding the changes in family structures and the roles of family members across each stage of family development. According to this theory, healthy families are able to adapt to these changes across time.

3. *Conflict theory* maintains that society shapes individual and family behavior. At the core of this theory is the notion that conflict is normal and expected in families and in society. Thus, to understand families, Conflict theory maintains that we need to understand the sources of conflict and the sources of power.

4. *Family Systems theory* concentrates on the interactions between family members, and it views the family as an interconnected group of individual members whose behaviors affect and are affected by other family members' behaviors. What happens to one family member, such as an illness or a loss of a job, affects every family member. (Chapter 3 provides an indepth discussion about Family Systems theory.)

5. *Symbolic Interaction theory* concerns itself with how people form and share meanings in their communication efforts. Its primary focus is the use of symbols to convey meaning through verbal and nonverbal communication. (We examine this theory at length in Chapter 3.)

6. *Social Exchange theory* (discussed in Chapter 7) focuses on the costs and rewards associated with our human behaviors. In short, this theory maintains that people weigh costs and rewards

ACCORDING to Structural-Functionalist theory, males adopt instrumental roles such as providing for the family, while females adopt expressive roles, such as nurturing the husband and children.

before they decide to act—we engage in behavior that brings us maximum rewards and minimum costs. According to this theory, we form relationships with other people if we expect that the relationship will be rewarding. It is human nature to avoid relationships that we perceive will be costly to us.

Because of the family life education approach of this textbook, and because of this book's topical nature, as we work our way through our study we will focus on the foundations of various family theories and how they help us understand the intricacies of our interpersonal relationships. We will examine the theories throughout the coming chapters as they relate to certain topics. We begin by looking at what is recognized by many family specialists and sociologists as the "grandfather of Family theory": Structural Functionalism.

STRUCTURAL FUNCTIONALISM

Perhaps the most influential contributor to the study of family and family life is Talcott Parsons (1902–1979). Out of his passion to investigate the wide range of problems concerning American values, social structure, social problems, and patterns of institutional change, Parsons devised the **Structural-Functionalist perspective** of the family (Fox, Lidz, & Bershady, 2005). This theory has continued to influence Family theory for 30 years.

Parsons's functionalist view of the family maintained that gender-based role specialization was necessary in order to promote family (and hence, societal) equilibrium. **Instrumental roles** were assigned to the husband-father, who, as the task-oriented mate, was assigned responsibility for being the primary breadwinner and protector against imbalance or disequilibrium. To complement the male, the wife-mother was assigned **expressive roles**, the people-oriented mate responsible for enhancing emotional relationships among the members of the family (Boss, Doherty, LaRossa, Schumm, & Steinmetz, 1993). According to Parsons, then, the 1950s heterosexual, nuclear breadwinner–homemaker family represented the most functional of all family forms (Parsons, 1951). To be sure, Parsonian thought heralded the belief that if men and women abided by their gender-specific roles, not only would the family unit be ensured stability and solidity but also society at large would similarly benefit.

Although some of the original ideas of this theory have been discarded because of their patriarchal nature (such as the belief that the "correct" family form is that of a man, woman, and child), many of the theory's assumptions are still in use today. Much of what you will see in other family theories in this text are clear descendents of functionalism.

Key Concepts of Structural Functionalism At the heart of Structural Functionalism rests the notion that society is considered to be a whole that is made up of separate, interconnected parts, and that this whole (social system) seeks maintenance and stability in order for it to persist and endure. Functionalism also holds that each subsystem (or social unit) seeks balance, or *homeostasis;* a change in one unit effects a change in the other units in order for balance to be maintained. The core of Structural Functionalism is that each member of the social system conforms to a certain set of clearly defined rules or beliefs that exist for the sole purpose of advancing the greater good and continued existence of the society to which the individual belongs. In other words, the whole social system must survive, and it cannot survive without individual members working together toward its continued existence by way of *certain functional requirements* (Boss and others, 1993, p. 196), such as sexual reproduction, economic reproduction, education, and religion (Bernardes, 2000). This theory derives its name in part because of the function of each subsystem—the contribution—to the survival of the whole societal system. A subsystem's function can contribute either in a positive fashion (functional) or a negative fashion (dysfunctional) to the society.

In order for functions to contribute to the overall good of the society, they must adhere to **structures**, or patterns of role arrangement. For example, the family is thought to be a key subsystem because it promotes the survival of the societal system by providing new members through procreation, and by socializing children to conform to societal beliefs, norms, and ways of life (Boss and others, 1993). According to structural functionalists, the traditional nuclear family has historically been thought to best promote the needs of the larger society. A *nuclear family* is defined as the "socially sanctioned cohabitation [marriage] of a man and a woman who have preferential or exclusive enjoyment of economic and sexual rights over one another and are committed to raise the children brought to life by the woman" (Pitts, 1964). This definition clearly delineates social organization and properties of the family system, as the following conditions illustrate:

1. The marital couple assumes the responsibility of childrearing, and such specialized roles increase the functionality of the system.
2. The man and the woman have exclusive economic and sexual rights over one another. According to Boss and colleagues, such clearly outlined marital roles establish well-defined rights and obligations to one another—and thus, to the society at large.
3. With the clearly specified roles that foster exclusive economic and sexual rights over one another, in addition to bearing and rearing children within the socially sanctioned form of cohabitation, these types of role specialization underscore the most significant property of a system—its ability to maintain homeostasis or balance. When family balance is enhanced, the overall equilibrium of the society is reinforced, as well. (Boss and others, 1993)

Structural Functionalism dominated sociological theory from the early 1940s through the 1960s, then fell out of the theoretical limelight; however, despite being considered obsolete by some scholars, particularly feminist scholars, other academics believe that Structural Functionalism still governs much of today's study of family sociology and family life (Boss and others, 1993; Smith, 1993).

Structural Functionalism and the Family Structural Functionalism emphasizes the traditional, heterosexual nuclear family and highlights two primary functions of the family in society: the socialization of children to society's culture and norms, and the stabilization of adult personalities. This view revolves around the idea that the family is organized and governed by unchangeable, fixed, irreversible role configurations—and that these gender-specific family functions operate in order to benefit the family itself as well as to promote the greater good of the society. With these functions and family structures in mind, let's take a look at

Is Parsons's Theory Relevant Today?

Talcott Parsons believed that the family form most functional and beneficial to society is a heterosexual marriage in which men assume breadwinner/protector roles, and women assume homemaker/nurturer roles.

1. Based on your family experiences, would you agree or disagree with Parsons's assumption that men take on instrumental roles in marriage, and that women take on expressive roles?
2. In today's complex, ever-changing society, do you think Parsons's theory is outdated or still relevant? What makes his theory outdated? What makes his theory relevant to today's families?
3. If you could change one thing about Parsons's theory, what would it be?

Own It!

research that addresses the increasing occurrence of same-sex couples bearing or adopting children.

In 2002, the American Academy of Pediatrics supported legislation permitting lesbian partners to co-parent children born to one partner or adopted by the couple. The Academy maintained that children reared in lesbian families "can have the same advantages and the same expectations . . . for adjustment, and development" as those children reared in heterosexual families (p. 339). Similar findings suggest that no substantial differences exist between lesbian and heterosexual parents in affective development or areas of self-concept, happiness, and overall adjustment (Allen & Burrell, 1996; Millbank, 2003; Patterson, 2002). Dr. Susan Golombok (1983, 1999), founder of the Family and Child Psychology Research Centre at City University, London, further maintains that children of lesbian mother families do not appear to demonstrate greater instances of psychological disorders, difficulties in peer relationships, or atypical gender development. As for sexual orientation, Golombok notes that most children reared in lesbian families identified with heterosexuality.

If we were to apply Parsons's Structural-Functionalist theoretical framework to this research, the *male* husband-(always)father and the *female* wife-(always)mother, we see the theory calls into question the normalcy of same-sex couples. Recall, too, that these specialized gender roles allow the family to successfully carry out its chief function of socializing the children to the predominant beliefs and norms of the culture.

If we compare Parsons's assigned roles to roles depicted in contemporary research on lesbian parenting, where there exist two family members—both *female* wife-mothers—what happens to family stability? When two women rear children and do not abide by clearly outlined, specialized gender roles, what happens to the family structure? By Parsonian assumption, the lesbian parenting family form deviates from the ideal family form, and as such should turn out children who are nonconforming to societal norms. But is this what studies of lesbian parenting suggest? On the contrary, the studies indicate that children born into and/or reared by lesbian parents show no significant negative or harmful effects in the children's emotional development, self-concepts, or overall adjustment. In fact, there appear to be no differences between children of lesbian parents and children of heterosexual parents. According to current research, then, the gender of the parents doesn't affect children's sexual orientation, as long as the children are being cared for in a nurturing environment. One could perhaps argue, however, that one lesbian parent assumed the instrumental role and the other assumed the expressive role and that as long as each of the roles were filled, one's gender doesn't matter.

While Structural Functionalism may be considered the grandfather of Family theories, many more theories have been created to shed new perspectives on family life today.

CONFLICT THEORY

Similar to Structural Functionalism, **Conflict theory** concentrates primarily on social structures and their interrelationships. Like Structural Functionalism, Conflict theory supports the notion that society has some bearing on and to some degree shapes individual behavior. This paradigm differs, however, in its basic theme that human beings are prone to conflict—that conflict between members of the human race is expected, natural, and inevitable.

Why is there conflict? According to the conflict perspective, inequality is a defining trait built into any society or culture. Dominant and subordinate groups and classes within society are always in competition for the society's limited resources and for whatever the society deems important. It is the competition for resources—with the "haves" competing to keep what they possess, and the "have nots" trying to gain what they do not have—that produces conflict. For example, there is economic inequality in nearly every society. Some society members will always have more economic resources than others, while some will always have less.

Because of these inequalities, some society members inherently have more power and control than others. According to Conflict theory, then, friction, discord, disputes, tensions, and antagonism are normal and natural societal experiences.

The big question in Conflict theory is, Who benefits at whose expense? Nineteenth-century social theorist and political activist Karl Marx sought to answer this question.

Karl Marx and Class Struggle Karl Marx (1818–1883) was a German economist who viewed the world through the perspective that every aspect of human life is based on economics and economic relationships. Indeed, Marx believed that the economic system was the driving force, the real foundation, of any society. His viewpoint revolutionized the ways in which people think about social arrangements and human society.

Marx observed that during the Industrial Revolution (the late eighteenth and early nineteenth centuries) in Europe, there appeared to be two fundamental, distinct classes of people. The owners or ruling class—the *capitalists*—possessed the land, businesses, and factories. The working class—the *proletariat*—was subordinate to the demands of the ruling class. Their value was based on how much they could produce as a result of their labor. Class was determined by means of one's production and one's productivity. Marx was outraged at the cruel and vicious treatment that factory workers and their families endured at the hands of the ruling class and concluded that owners exploited workers by paying them far less than their work was worth, in order to gain economic (and hence, societal) power. The economic exploitation of the working class led to oppression. Further, Marx believed that the ruling class used its economic power to gain more control of the society, such as using police power to protect its property. Marxian theory supports the notion that the function of every social institution (such as the educational system, religious institutions, and even marriage and the family) is to support the society's class structure.

This exploitative economic composition of capitalism—the *class struggle*—is the root of all conflict because the two classes have opposing interests and unequal balance of power. And it is because of this unequal balance of power that conflict is an inherent part of human existence and human relationships. Who benefits at whose expense? The capitalists can only pursue their individual needs, goals, and resources at the expense of the proletariat. Thus, Marxian theory holds that because of the inequality of power, the working class would organize and begin a revolution to establish a classless society wherein the society's wealth, resources, and power would be evenly distributed among the members. But what does social inequality have to do with marriage and the family?

Conflict Theory and the Family Conflict theorists view the family as a social institution composed of varying relationships. These relationships benefit some family members more than others. Throughout history, women and children were considered to be the property of men. Consequently, in relationships between men and women, one class (men) exploited and oppressed the other class (women) in order to gain resources and power. In fact, according to conflict theorists, the entire reason marriage evolved as a legal contract was to protect the property of men.

As Marxian theory illustrates, property owners wielded power. In most societies, the power possessed by men is endorsed by social norms. In other words, because society approves of men attaining higher educational levels and employment opportunities or capitalist endeavors than women, men are able to pursue particular self-interests that afford them more power than the women who are relegated to the home to provide unpaid labor and childcare. Conflict theory suggests that men do not do housework despite the fact that 48 percent of today's workforce is comprised of women (U.S. Department of Labor, 2008) because it is not profitable for them to do so. Thus, the family as a social structure perpetuates or maintains the inequalities and imbalance of power in male–female relationships. This inequality is reinforced as children are socialized according to the same male-dominant paradigm. This, then, perpetuates social norms that contribute to the class system.

Throughout your course of study, you will see discussed at length in subsequent chapters a number of social conflicts that some sociologists and family scientists would argue are a direct result of the

FEMINIST movements and organizations, such as the National Organization of Women (NOW), focus their efforts on experiences that are unique to women, such as reproductive rights and violence that is perpetrated against women.

inequalities of power in family structures: family violence, the feminization of poverty, divorce, single motherhood, and violence against the elderly. Although Conflict theory is not frequently used in family studies to shed light on marriage and family life, its application is of great value when examining the inequalities in human relationships and factors such as gender, ethnicity, race, and socioeconomic class. Conflict theory survives today in its contemporary form—Feminist theory.

WOMEN'S STUDIES: FEMINIST THEORY

Feminist theory embraces the conflict approach to understanding and analyzing the roles of marriage and family in perpetuating inequalities in male–female relationships. Because most societies the world over promote male domination in the home and in the workplace, feminism, or Feminist theory, focuses on the plight of women.

There is no single Feminist theory; rather, there are a number of feminist perspectives that apply to sociological and family studies that help us better understand human behavior. A theory is deemed Feminist theory if it (1) centers on the experiences specific to women, (2) views experiences from a woman's vantage point, and (3) advocates on behalf of women (Lengermann & Brantley, 1988). Types of Feminist theory, outlined by authors MaryAnn Schwartz and Barbara Scott (2003), include:

- *Marxist Feminist theory*, similar to Marx's theory, maintains that the inequality and oppression that women experience is a result of the women's subordinate class position.
- *Radical Feminist theory* states that the universal oppression that women experience is a result of patriarchy (male-dominated society). Violence against women is another consequence of patriarchy.
- *Liberal Feminist theory* views the inequality and oppression of women as a result of sexism—the belief that men are superior and women are inferior. Liberal feminists focus their efforts on issues of equal opportunity, such as in the workplace and in education.
- *Lesbian Feminist theory* focuses primarily on the predominance of heterosexuality in patriarchal (male-dominated) societies. Adherents to this theory believe that in order to fully understand women's inequality, attention must be given to the oppression of lesbians.
- *Women-of-Color Feminist theory*, along with sexism and classism, focuses its attention on forms of racism—the belief that women of color are inferior to white men and women. According to this perspective, women do not share common experiences; instead, they are thought to be molded by their unique experiences of race, class, and societal and cultural influences.

These different types of Feminist theory indicate there are a number of ways in which the feminist perspective can be applied to study family and intimate relationships. Many researchers use these theories to acknowledge that there is great diversity not just between men and women, but among women. These perspectives help them explain individual experiences within the contexts these theories provide.

Do men and women engage in power struggles in today's marriages? If so, what is it about contemporary society that accounts for this conflict in marriages? Do gender differences affect the day-to-day lives of today's families? If so, what generates or perpetuates these gender differences and how are they expressed? Are gender differences necessarily a bad thing—or a good thing?

For Feminist theorists, the aim of family research is to determine why and how gender inequality and power differences develop and are sustained and maintained in family life. Feminist theorists may question, for example, whether women's oppression is inherent because of the predominance of the patriarchal family structure seen throughout the world. Or instead, they may question whether these differences, perpetuated through the processes of marriage and family living, affect the way children are socialized. Are these behaviors and interaction patterns then repeated when these children mature, marry, and start families of their own? Throughout this course of study, you will see how much of what we learn as infants and children through our family of origin is reinforced in subsequent interpersonal relationships throughout our lives.

MEN'S STUDIES

We've just discussed how male–female inequality causes conflict, antagonism, and tension. In this section, we will view gender differences from another perspective: that of "being male." Women's studies courses and degree programs have been offered at U.S. universities and colleges for the past 30 years, but men's studies have not.

Sam McCready is the co-director of the Center for Young Men's Studies at the University of Ulster, Northern Ireland. He and his colleagues maintain that with the ushering in of the feminist movement and the influence of feminist studies, and because of the significant cultural changes seen in the past three decades with the dawn of women's studies (and the resultant changes in roles and responsibilities for men), the study of men with a particular lens is necessary (McCready, Harland, & Beattie, 2006). Since the 1990s, organizations that examine issues specific to men's lives have emerged, such as the American Men's Studies Association (AMSA) and the National Coalition of Free Men. Empirical journals and print media, such as the *Journal of Men's Studies* and the *Allyn & Bacon Catalog: Men's Studies*, devote their scholarship to important areas of men's lives, such as defining gender roles and exploring shifting definitions of masculinity. The primary objectives in men's studies has been to encourage scholarship in an effort to generate theory specific to the study of masculinity, as well as to shun all forms of oppression—sexism, racism, homophobia, and classism.

Empirical research in men's lives has been prompted by the fact that, as one professor of a university men's studies program observes, men are victims of sexism and sexist norms in society; men, similar to women, also exist under oppression because of their social conditioning (Laughlin, 2005). In other words, because of their social learning and conditioning, men are limited in their emotional capacities and in how they can express their personalities. This social conditioning, may, in fact, limit men's career choices. As a result of these socially imposed limitations, men may feel oppressed. It is the basic assumption of men's studies, then, that sexism and gender affect men's lives as significantly as they do the lives of women (McCready, Harland, & Beattie, 2006).

Like women's and feminist studies, **men's studies** investigate the multiple social and cultural forces and issues that affect men. It is an umbrella term that encompasses a number of issues specific to men's lives, such as men's and father's rights, family violence, sexuality, and war and trauma.

This area of study is not to be confused with the number of men's movements seen in the 1980s and 1990s, such as Promise Keepers, National Center for Fathers, and the Alliance for Noncustodial Parents. It is instead a specific area of academic study that looks at the ways in which men are oppressed by their socialization and societal or cultural expectations. John Laughlin (2005), professor of men's studies at Akamai University, Hilo, Hawaii, suggests that men's studies programs are designed to equip students with "the capabilities needed to effectively manage the resulting changes in men's roles and responsibilities." Men's studies combine theory and practice to effect social policy and to build a broad knowledge base in the study and research of both genders. In this manner, both women's and men's studies seek to better understand the ways in which gender affects both men's and women's individual and family experiences. Having a parallel body of academic work that examines issues specific to men affirms the idea that social, cultural, political, economic, educational, and family structures are equally important to both genders.

Today, no single portrait portrays the essence of "manhood" or "fatherhood," because men and their roles in society and the family are multifaceted, complex, and ever-changing. Because of the cultural evolution taking place in Western society, social and family scientists are now shifting their focus to men's roles. Of particular interest to social science researchers and family practitioners is the role of fatherhood.

TODAY, scholars are paying increasing attention to the socialization and cultural expectations of men, such as how their roles are changing to include the nurturing and care of children.

In the 1980s, research began to focus on the fact that men were playing more active roles in childrearing as demonstrated by their ability, and willingness, to change their babies' diapers. Since that time, empirical study in the roles and lives of fathers has been gaining momentum. For instance, contemporary studies are seeking to better understand the unique characteristics of fathers of various cultural and religious heritages. They are also investigating different fathering styles in the wide array of family arrangements, such as single-parent fathers, fathers in two-parent homes, fathers who are men of color, and fathers who are gay. Subsequent chapters in this textbook present information about social trends that affect the lives of men, such as questions pertaining to how much time fathers devote to their role as caregivers in these various family forms.

Researchers are also looking at how involved fathers are in the lives of their children. They are looking at whether the father's role today is still utilitarian (useful, practical), or whether men are adopting women's emotional/expressive roles to better accommodate the multiple roles of the working woman. How do factors such as age, occupation, education, and sexual orientation affect the experiences of fathering? Of what significance is grandfathering in an individual's lifespan? And a question that remains unanswered in empirical study today is: How does the experience of fathering affect and influence the lives of men?

Now that you have a knowledge base in the forms and functions of marriage and family and the basic concepts of Family theory, it is necessary that you understand how you affect and are affected by the intimate relationships in your life. Next, we build on our knowledge base as we explore individual and family development.

Family Interactions and You

Each of us accomplishes many developmental milestones in our individual lifespan development, and we do so within the context of family living. Every phase of our individual development across our human life cycle intersects with the development of the family throughout its developmental cycle, ultimately shaping who we are as relational people. In this section, we take a close look at the *human life cycle* and the *family life cycle*.

THE HUMAN LIFE CYCLE

All human development is a complex, dynamic, and multifaceted process. As we grow and change, we accomplish what developmentalists, psychologists, and therapists term **developmental tasks**. These entail achieving certain biological, physical, cognitive/intellectual, social, emotional, and spiritual tasks across the lifecourse. It is important to be aware of these developmental milestones, because every point in our life cycle interconnects with the developmental stages of the family (Carter & McGoldrick, 2005). A son who becomes chronically ill during his college experience, for example, may disrupt a parent's plans to retire early because of the added health expenses. Conversely, a dying parent might delay a student's college experience because she feels she needs to be with her family through her parent's illness.

The developmental tasks that most of us experience are considered to be **normative**—they come at relatively predictable points in our lives and are generally expected. These events are often referred to as **on-time events** because of their relative predictability across the lifespan. For example, we expect an adolescent to undergo physical changes somewhere between

10 and 16 years of age. Along with these physical changes, we expect them to begin to desire more and more independence and freedom from their family of origin. Even though certain developmental tasks may be normative, they may nevertheless cause disruptions in the family's interactions. Additionally, sometimes events occur at atypical points in the lifespan, such as when a young adolescent gives birth. This is referred to as an **off-time event** because it does not take place at the more typical point in the person's life.

Non-normative life events are those that we do not anticipate, and that we cannot predict, but that do have an impact on our developmental lifecourse. It is not expected that both parents who are in the military will be called to serve in a war oceans away, for example, leaving the children to be reared by grandparents, aunts, uncles, or friends. We don't anticipate or expect that our son or daughter will have a severe reading disability. Nor do we expect that a parent will lose his or her job, or that a natural disaster such as Hurricane Katrina in 2005 will destroy a major U.S. city. Whatever the situation or circumstance, the nuances of our individual development affect the family and its development.

NON-NORMATIVE life events are those that we do not anticipate, such as the devastating cyclone that destroyed Myanmar in 2008. Tens of thousands of people were killed, and countless were left homeless.

Although human development is complex, it is important to gain a fundamental understanding of what developmental tasks take place over the lifecourse. This allows us to grasp the significance of how the members of our family affect us and each other through each stage of our development. For our purposes of more fully understanding the intricacies of human relationships, our discussion focuses on the **psychosocial** (social and emotional) aspects of development. What follows is a brief synopsis, adapted in part from renowned and influential family life educators, Betty Carter and Monica McGoldrick (2005).

Infancy (0–2 years) From infancy to about 2 years of age, babies learn to walk, talk, and trust their caregivers. Every time a baby cries, the baby is sending out a signal of distress or need. Every time a caregiver responds to the baby's signals of distress or need and meets those needs with comfort and love, the baby learns that the world is a secure place and begins to form the foundation of trust that will be central—in fact crucial—to his or her future intimate relations.

Early Childhood: The Play Years (2–6 years) During this period of growth, children are eager and able to learn new skills—including social and emotional skills. In this phase, children begin to learn empathy and show concern for others' feelings; they will comfort someone who appears to be sad or in need. Children of this age begin to form relationships with peers, learn to obey rules, control their emotions, and delay the need for immediate gratification—all essential stepping stones to future, "grown-up" relationships.

Middle Childhood: The School Years (7–12 years) This phase of development brings with it a growth in moral development and what is termed by some researchers as "heart logic" (Carter & McGoldrick, 2005). As friendships become increasingly important, so does the importance of being able to express feelings and emotions in an appropriate fashion and of being able to respect the rights and needs of others. As children's capacity for empathy and understanding develops, so too does their tolerance for diversity, such as differences in gender, race, and ethnicity, unless parents and those in authority over them instruct them differently. During the school years, a child's sexual development and sexual identity also begin to intensify. All of these developmental leaps add to "who" the child will be someday in her or his intimate partnerships.

Adolescence (13–21 years) With rapid body changes also comes an increase in the adolescent's capacity for moral understanding; an increase in the understanding of self in relation

FIGURE 2.4   **Time Line of the Human Life Cycle**

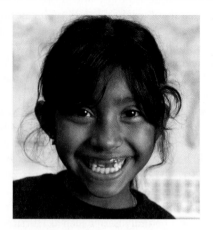

Infancy (0–2 years):
Infants show unique
personality traits and
temperaments. They begin to
form emotional bonds with
their caregivers.

Early Childhood (2–6 years):
Children begin to develop
morality, their sense of gender
and their sense of
race/ethnicity. Self-concept,
self-worth, and self-esteem
develop. As children become
more interactive while playing
with others, social skills
emerge. Peer relationships
become more important, and
children form friendships
based on trust. They begin to
feel and show empathy.

Middle Childhood (7–12 years):
Sense of self, self-esteem, and
self-worth become well
established, and morality
continues to develop. The
understanding of differences
in race and ethnicity solidifies.
Children compare themselves
to other children in order to
understand themselves. Their
friendships become very
important, and through their
friendships they gain an
understanding of social
respect and social rules.

Adolescence (13–21 years):
Self-esteem continues to
solidify, self-concept reflects
others' opinions of them. The
central developmental task for
teens is to form an identity
separate from their family of
origin. Teens define
themselves and their roles
based on the opinions of their
peers, and these peer
relationships dominate their
time.

to peers, family, and the community; and an increased awareness of his or her sexual identity (Carter & McGoldrick, 2005). As their ability to understand the world and relationships increases, adolescents become better equipped to tackle intimate social relationships.

Early Adulthood (22–34 years) As young adults, men and women during this developmental phase develop the ability—based on the relational foundations laid throughout all of infancy and childhood—to form and engage in emotionally mature intimate relationships. Throughout this phase of life they continue to master their abilities to negotiate the complexities of marriage, family, and intimate relationships. At this phase, they learn to steer the course in interdependence, mutuality, and reciprocity in relationships, and open themselves up to those they trust (see more about this in Chapter 5). At this juncture, they seek someone to share their lives with.

Middle Adulthood (35–60 years) Adults in their middle adulthood years are typically actively involved in raising and caring for their children. Adults look beyond themselves and focus their energies and attentions on the next generation and on others, such as their aging parents.

Late Middle Age (60–74 years) Although adults at this age deal with and manage declines in their physical and intellectual abilities, they begin to take steps to "pass the torch" to the next generation (Carter & McGoldrick, 2005). They feel a responsibility to future generations and will reach out in an attempt to make connections with them. My father, for example, a veteran of the Vietnam war, faced and endured such difficulties during his year in combat that

Early Adulthood (22–34 years):
Forming intimate relationships dominates this period. Couples may cohabit or marry, and childbearing typically begins. Changes associated with careers, marriage, and parenting are stressful. The ability to form lasting, intimate relationships is highly dependent upon the emotional bonds formed in early life.

Middle Adulthood (35–60 years):
Adults begin to develop an awareness of their own mortality and are reflective about their lives. Marital satisfaction is typically high, and other family relationships are rewarding.

Late Middle Age (61–74):
Those in late middle age feel a responsibility to future generations. For this reason, aging adults review their lives with others, share, and connect with them.

Late Adulthood (75+ years):
"Life review" begins where adults reflect upon their lifespans. They begin to accept their mortality and the deaths of their spouse, family, and friends.

he never shared them with his family. Now, though, as he begins to near the end of his own lifecourse, he is beginning to share his experiences with his children and grandchildren; in doing so, he is connecting us to his past.

Late Adulthood (75 and older) Grief, loss, retrospection, and growth are the benchmarks of this developmental phase (Carter & McGoldrick, 2005). As adults age and start to think about the end of life, they begin to reflect on their lives and come to grips with the legacy they will leave to future generations. At the same time, they must accept the deaths of family and friends and their spouse or life partner—and they must accept the inevitability of their own mortality and death's eventuality. Not only do they need to accept death and dying but they must also accept the lives that they lived.

As you can see, our early life experiences—from the moment of birth—have an impact on our development of our relational skills and abilities.

THE FAMILY LIFE CYCLE

What perhaps best distinguishes a family life education approach in the study of marriage, family, and intimate relations from other disciplines is the focus on and application of the family life cycle. Although some fields such as psychology, sociology, and feminist studies might disagree with the tenets of the family life cycle, Carter and McGoldrick perhaps best sum up the efficacy of its inclusion in the examination of family when they note, "We strongly believe that individual development takes place only in the context of significant emotional relationships and that most significant emotional relationships are family relationships, whether by blood, adoption, marriage, or commitment" (1999, p. 5).

There are experiences throughout our lives that establish a foundation for our ability to love and relate to others. Integral to these experiences is our family of origin. As you have learned throughout our study so far, we do not develop in isolation! Every phase of our development is affected by, intersected by, and overlapped with the developmental cycle of our family, and our family development is influenced by the multiple cultural contexts that surround it, as Bronfenbrenner's model illustrated for us in Chapter 1. The **family life cycle** comprises multiple entrances and exits from the family of origin. For example, a young adult leaving for college is an exit, whereas the formation of a new family of origin as children marry is an entry. Families with young children experience multiple entries with their new family members, but families in later life experience multiple exits, such as when family members die. Along with the changes in the *structure* of the family come certain *emotional transitions* and *related changes* in the family status that are needed to move on developmentally.

This cycle of family growth and transition is depicted for us in Table 2.1. As you can see, in each stage there are challenges in family life that cause us to develop or gain certain rela-

TABLE 2.1 The Family Life Cycle: Phases, Tasks, and Issues

Phase	Task	Issue
Pairing/Marriage	Fusion as couple	Leaving family of origin Readiness for intimacy Establishing goals, roles, values as new couple
Childbearing	Creation	Sharing each other with children Role ambiguity—wife, woman, mother?
School-age children	Nurturing	Providing security (emotional and environmental) Learning how to parent Simultaneously spouse and parent Increasing parenting demands Increasing work demands
Family with adolescent children	Boundary-testing	Control versus freedom Power struggle and rebellion Separation from family of origin Social and sexual exploration
Family as "launching ground"	Leaving/letting go	Changing roles of children still at home The empty nest—loss or opportunity? Parents rediscover each other Latent marital conflict may surface
Middle years	Reviewing/reappraising	Mid-life crisis? Fulfillment/disappointment Accepting limitations Changing self-image Death of parents Anticipating retirement
Aging	Facing mortality	Aging, illness, death Religion and philosophy Isolation/dependency Bereavement

Source: Adapted from Neighbour, R. H. The Family Life Cycle. *Journal of the Royal Society of Medicine,* (1985); 78(Suppl 8): 11–15. Reproduced by permission of the Royal Society of Medicine Press.

tional skills. Developing these skills helps us work through the changes associated with family life; at the same time, we develop relational skills we will someday carry into our own intimate relationships. Of course, few make these transitions seamlessly; sometimes families' relationships are painfully stretched as they experience job loss or financial problems, severe illness, or the death of a loved one.

Throughout our study, we will examine a number of family processes (such as communication, gender roles, love, intimacy, and sexuality) and how they are developed over time within the family of origin. You will come to see that family development is, certainly, a multifaceted molding process as change occurs both inside and between family members. Whether you are a parent or child, brother or sister, bonded by blood or love, your experiences through the family life cycle affect who you are and who you become.

It is important to note, however, that there are criticisms of the family life cycle. Specifically, the family life cycle has been criticized because it ignores the varying family constellations we discussed in Chapter 1 (such as families of color, gay/lesbian families, or intergenerational/extended families). In short, any deviations or differences from a "traditional" family is ignored by the family life cycle. It also assumes that *all* families of origin share a common group identity, ignoring the fact that many today have departed from the previously common progression of family life. Finally, the model has been criticized because it is child-centric—it assumes that all families have children.

Prominent family life educators Betty Carter and Monica McGoldrick address these inadequacies of the family life cycle in their book, *The Expanded Family Life Cycle* (2005). They note that today students of family and intimate life need to think about human development and the life cycle in a way that reflects society's shifts to a more diverse and inclusive definition of the family. Without question, as Chapter 1 showed us, today there is no prototype of an American family.

Family Life Education

Although we are a diverse people, we all have in common that we were born into or brought into a family, and each of us has experienced some degree of family life. But because of the enormous differences that exist in families today (Single-parent or two-parent? Absent father or present father? Divorced or married? Single-earner couple or dual-earner couple? Children or no children? Cohabiting or married? Same-sex partners/parents or heterosexual partners/parents?), the study of family presents difficult challenges to sociologists, family life practitioners, and researchers.

The study of marriage, family, and intimate relationships is fascinating. By using a solid research methodology that provides researchers and consumers with reliable scholarship, we can look beyond our own family experiences, intuition, logic, and instinct to examine and understand the impact of our family members on our lives. By using the many theoretical frameworks provided by sociological and family studies, we have a lens through which we can view and better understand marriage and family relationships. By employing the practice of social science research and theoretical frameworks, we can explore, explain, and develop a far deeper understanding of family. In essence, we can "know" family and family life.

Summary

Understanding Families through Research

- Social science research uses the tools of scientific inquiry to examine human society and relationships (logic or common sense is not effective because everyone sees things differently based on different value systems, political beliefs, religious beliefs, etc.). Family research provides information that allows professionals to develop, implement, and evaluate programs that seek to enhance family life and family growth. Understanding the problems that face today's family and finding explanations and answers to those problems would not be possible without the practice of social science inquiry through research.

- The scientific method is a process by which social science researchers formulate questions concerning social and individual phenomena and seek out answers. Using the scientific method, researchers design a process from start to finish that details the sequential, inter-related investigative steps the researcher will follow. These steps include choosing the research topic; creating the research question and hypothesis; conceptualizing the research; using operational/empirical definitions; choosing a research method; selecting a population and sampling; collecting, processing, and analyzing the data; and, finally, applying research findings.

- In order to get the most out of research, and learn how to distinguish well-written, valid research from poorly designed research that yields invalid or insignificant results, those interested in family and family life need to become consumers of social science literature by asking demanding questions of the literature.

- Because human subjects are the object of study, the practice of social science research is an endeavor that requires responsible conduct on the part of the researcher. To ensure the ethical treatment of research subjects, academic institutions and other research institutions establish research review committees, or Institutional Review Boards (IRBs).

Understanding Families through Theory

- Family theories allow us to move beyond our everyday, common beliefs about family and move toward an objective, scientific understanding of family and family process. Today, many theories exist that attempt to explain the workings of family, and each has made numerous contributions to the field of family studies, among them Ecological theory, Family Development theory, Conflict theory, Family Systems theory, Symbolic Interaction theory, and Social Exchange theory.

- Considered the "grandfather of Family theory," Structural Functionalism (Talcott Parsons) maintains that gender-based role specialization is a necessary function in order to promote family (and hence, societal) equilibrium. Instrumental roles are assigned to the husband-father, and the wife-mother is assigned expressive roles.

- Structural Functionalism revolves around the idea that the family is organized and governed by unchangeable, fixed, irreversible role configurations. These gender-specific family functions operate in order to benefit the family itself as well as to promote the greater good of the society. Research suggests, however, that no substantial differences exist between lesbian and heterosexual parents in affective development or in areas of self-concept, happiness, and overall adjustment.

- Conflict theory states that competition for resources is built into every society and that the struggle for these resources leads to inequality and conflict. Because of these inequalities, some society members inherently have more power and control than others.

- Feminist theory centers on the experiences specific to women, views experiences from a woman's vantage point, and advocates on behalf of women in an effort to understand and analyze the roles of marriage and family in perpetuating inequalities in the male–female relationships. Although there is no one Feminist theory, there are a number of feminist perspectives that apply to sociological and family studies that help us better understand human behavior.

- The influence of feminist studies and significant cultural changes in the past three decades (and the resultant changes in roles and responsibilities for men) has created a need for specialized men's studies. Men's studies explore important areas of men's lives, such as defining gender roles and shifting definitions of masculinity. Men's studies also strive to generate theory specific to the study of masculinity, as well as to shun all forms of oppression—sexism, racism, homophobia, and classism.

Family Interactions and You

- All human development is a complex, dynamic, and multifaceted process. During our lifecourse, we accomplish developmental tasks, which include biological, physical, intellectual, social, emotional, and spiritual growth.

- Most developmental tasks we experience are normative—coming at relatively predictable points in our lives. Non-normative life events are unanticipated and also affect our development.

- Understanding what psychosocial (social and emotional) developmental tasks take place over the lifecourse allows family life educators to understand how members of a family affect each other through each stage of development.

- Because every phase of our development is integrated with the developmental cycle of our family, family practitioners use the family life cycle to study marriage, family, and intimate relationships.

Key Terms and Concepts

research, p. 36

social science research, p. 36

scientific method, p. 37

quantitative research, p. 37

qualitative research, p. 37

variable, p. 39

research question, p. 39

research hypothesis, p. 39

literature review, p. 39

hypothesis, p. 39

hypotheses testing, p. 39

conceptualization, p. 39

construct, p. 39

operational definition, p. 40

survey, p. 40

sample, p. 40

response rate, p. 40

response bias, p. 41

validity, p. 41

observational research method, p. 42

field research, p. 42

case study, p. 42

experimental design, p. 42

experimental group, p. 43

control group, p. 43

population, p. 43

probability sample, p. 43

representativeness, p. 43

sample size, p. 43

nonprobability samples, p. 43

data churning, p. 45

convenience sample, p. 46

confounding (rival) variable, p. 47

reduction, p. 47

replacement, p. 47

refinement, p. 47

ethics, p. 48

The Institutional Review Board (IRB), p. 48

research integrity, p. 48

theory, p. 49

framework, p. 49

Structural-Functionalist perspective, p. 50

instrumental roles, p. 50

expressive roles, p. 50

structures, p. 51

Conflict theory, p. 52

Feminist theory, p. 54

men's studies, p. 55

developmental tasks, p. 56

normative, p. 56

on-time events, p. 56

off-time events, p. 57

non-normative, p. 57

psychosocial, p. 57

family life cycle, p. 60

Suggested Readings

Babbie, E. (2006). *The practice of social research*. Belmont, CA: Wadsworth Publishing.

Carter, B., & McGoldrick, M. (2005). *The expanded family life cycle*. Boston: Allyn & Bacon.

Slater, S. (1999). *The lesbian family life cycle*. Champaign: University of Illinois Press.

Multiple-Choice Questions

1. _____ involves detailed verbal or written descriptions of characteristics under investigation; this research typically involves observation and interviews to collect data.

   a. Quantitative research

   b. Qualitative research

   c. Scientific research

   d. Literature research

2. By collecting survey responses from a group of people, known as a _____ , researchers can sometimes infer conclusions based on study data and extend them to the larger population.

   a. sample

   b. hypothesis

   c. survey

   d. case study

3. The _____ is not exposed to the independent variable; the _____ is the group that is exposed to the independent variables under question.

   a. experimental group/control group

   b. control group/experimental group

   c. experimental group/population

   d. control group/sample

4. _____ , or rival, variables are variables that are unrelated, unconnected, or not pertinent to the variables under investigation, which can skew or affect the results of the study.

   a. Conflicting

   b. Interrelated

   c. Clashing

   d. Confounding

5. _____ is a speculative statement about a variable or the relationship between variables in a study.

   a. A hypothesis

   b. A variable

   c. A sample statement

   d. A construct

6. According to Structural-Functionalist theory, _____ are assigned to the husband-father, and the wife-mother is assigned to _____ .

   a. expressive roles/instrumental roles

   b. impressive roles/fundamental roles

   c. instrumental roles/expressive roles

   d. fundamental roles/impressive roles

7. The _____ claims that the universal oppression that women experience is a result of patriarchy (male-dominated society). Violence against women is another consequence of patriarchy.

   a. Lesbian Feminist theory

   b. Marxist Feminist theory

   c. Liberal Feminist theory

   d. Radical Feminist theory

8. Often referred to as *on-time events*, the developmental tasks that come at relatively predictable points in our lives and are generally expected are considered to be _____ life events.

   a. non-normative

   b. common

   c. normative

   d. predictive

Answers: 1. b; 2. a; 3. b; 4. d; 5. a; 6. c; 7. d; 8. c

Family Communication, Conflict, and Forgiveness

3

My mother's sister was only in her 30s when she learned that her cancer had metastasized to her rib cage. Her condition was considered terminal, and other than medical treatment to ease her pain, there was nothing that could be done. Although we lived in the Midwest and she and her family lived in California, my mom and my aunt talked almost daily until about two or three days before Aunt Jean died. My aunt was honest with my mother about her illness, and my parents were, in turn, honest with my siblings and me. We knew our aunt was dying. We began our mourning and began to say our good-byes to this person who would be so greatly missed.

But there was a secret—Aunt Jean's children did not know she was ill. They did not know that she had had surgery for her cancer about four years earlier. They did not know she was dying. Her children, ages 12 and 15, were not told of their mother's imminent death. They were brought to the hospital only as she approached the last hours of her life and only then were they able to express their love and say good-bye.

Although I was only in the eighth grade when these events unfolded, I couldn't believe how unfair it was to the children that they did not know their mother was dying. How could anyone keep this devastating and life-altering news from someone they loved? Why all the secrecy?

In my frustration with the situation I yelled at my parents, *"Who makes up these rules about when we can say things in our families and when we can't?"*

Source: Author's files

At one time or another in our families we have probably either said or heard:

- "That's not what I said!"
- "You never listen to me!"
- "That's not what I mean."
- "Let me finish!"

Not too much time elapsed in my relationship with my husband before I realized that there were potentially rough seas ahead as we moved in and through the uncharted waters of interpersonal communication. With differing views of "too much" (such as, "It costs too much"), "not enough" (such as, "Not enough sex each week"), or "a few" of anything ("I'll be home in a few minutes," "Let's just spend a few days with my parents"), we quickly discovered that although we *thought* we were communicating, we were far from it.

Our parents or guardians spend the first 2 years of our lives teaching us to walk and to talk—and the next 16 years teaching us to sit down and be quiet. We all have been "communicating" in one form or another since the moment of birth and have been using words to convey our needs, wants, hopes, and feelings since about the first year of life, so why is it that so many of us have such difficulty conveying what we *mean?* Why is it that our mate or other family members have such difficulty in *accurately receiving* the messages we send? And who does make up the rules as far as when and what we can or cannot say in our families?

The Communication Process

Communication is best thought of as a *process. Process* implies progression, development, and change over time. All interpersonal relationships involve change, and communication is no exception. As our intimate relationships grow, change, and develop over time, so too do our communication patterns and behaviors. The communication process is such a critical aspect of our lives that it shapes the family and gives it its distinct identity (Galvin, Bylund, & Brommel, 2008).

When we communicate, whether in interpersonal or social interactions, we have a joint or reciprocal impact on each other in our exchanges. This dynamic is a **transactional** process in which we *simultaneously affect and are affected by our intimate relations.* When we discuss communication in this context, the focus of the interaction is not on the *words* individual family members speak, but instead on the *interconnectedness* of the relationship. To fully understand the communication process, we first need to explore two theoretical frameworks that are a foundation of family studies: the Family Systems theory and the Symbolic Interaction theory.

FAMILY SYSTEMS THEORY: THE FAMILY AS AN INTERCONNECTED SYSTEM

The family as a system of interrelated components is a contemporary framework for examining family interactions. Developed by psychiatrist and theorist Murray Bowen (1913–1990), the **Family Systems theory (FST)** views families as a whole entity made up of interconnected parts that seek to maintain balance. In recent years, this theoretical approach has become so popular among family researchers and family practitioners that an expanding array of family topics have been examined through this lens, including youth suicide, cancer treatments, family grief, and spiritual development. The popularity of its use is due, in part, to a central concept that all of us maintain *interdependent* relationships with others on a day-to-day basis. Within family life, FST acknowledges that the family is made of interconnected parts that affect each other.

The Family as a System Encompassing areas of study from economics to biology to the intricacies of family life, **General Systems theory (GST)** is a worldview or a paradigm that puts forth the notion that objects do not exist in isolation, but instead are interconnected to parts of a larger whole (Boss and others, 1993). The term **system** means "to place together" or to connect one entity to another (Rosenblatt, 1994).

Consider the human body—as a whole, living, breathing, ever-changing organism. But as a *system*, it comprises numerous interdependent yet separate entities, such as the nervous system, the circulatory system, the digestive system, the reproductive system, and so forth. In short, the human body is a complex network of many subsystems that are organized into a single whole. Just as the human body illustrates how a system works, a **family system** is also a living, ever-changing, dynamic entity that consists of various individuals and

ALL communication is multigenerational and cultural. When we communicate with others, we draw on the ways we have learned to speak. We rely on verbal communication—our languages we speak—and our nonverbal communication.

their interconnected, intergenerational patterns of interactions. In this context, a system's primary function is to bring together and arrange the various interrelated parts into a whole, organized entity (Rosenblatt, 1994).

The Family Systems theory provides a framework for those who work with families and allows them to gain insight into the relational patterns and interactions among the separate individuals, or **subsystems**. Prior to the 1950s, the treatment of psychological and behavioral problems and emotional distress focused on the internal world—the internal dysfunction—of the individual patient. However, that treatment model failed to take into consideration the reciprocal, interactive nature of interpersonal relationships (Nichols & Schwartz, 2009). As the concepts of the General Systems theory gained widespread acceptance across disciplines, family practitioners, social workers, and family therapists began to view and understand individual psychological problems in a new way—that these problems *were developed and maintained within the context of the family.*

Key Concepts: Applying the Systems Framework to the Family There are several key concepts and metaphors used to convey the thoughts and ideas central to Family Systems theory. The core assumptions of this family framework hold that every part of the system is interconnected, and that we can understand only by viewing the whole (White & Klein, 2008).

Interconnecting To get a better handle on these assumptions, let's return to the example of the human body. Suppose that through laboratory diagnosis you are found to have diabetes; if left untreated, will the disease remain in its initial state or will it eventually spread to and affect other systems in the body? You probably assumed correctly that, indeed, if left untreated, the diabetes would eventually spread throughout the multiple body systems, causing blindness and even loss of a limb because of the interrelated, interdependent relationship between the various body systems.

The family as a system of interconnected subsystems is no different. Family members affect and are affected by each other—what happens to one family member eventually affects (or happens to) others within the family unit. Thus, the Family Systems theory is concerned with the *interactions* and *interrelations* between the various pieces of the whole and their effect on each other.

Consider what happens to a mobile or wind chime when anything disrupts it or causes it to move. What disrupts one piece of the mobile, for example, disrupts and affects all of the other pieces on the mobile. The same holds true in family life (see Figure 3.1 on page 70).

FIGURE 3.1 Virginia Satir's Concept of the Family as a Mobile

Virginia Satir was the first to describe the family as a mobile. Similar to a mobile, the family is a *system* comprising multiple interconnected parts that hang in balance. When something disturbs one piece of the mobile, the entire system reacts to the disturbance and reverberates.

Expected or not, joyous or tragic, such events impact and have an effect on every family member (subsystem) within the family system.

Looking at the Whole A second key assumption of Family Systems theory is the idea that the only way we can understand an individual family member's behavior and communication patterns is by looking not just at the individual member, but by *looking at the whole*, the entire family system. Because we affect and are affected by each member in our families, it is impossible for us to understand each other's behavior and communication patterns without knowing more about the families in which we were reared—our **family of origin**.

In your family, have you ever been able to finish another family member's sentence? Have you ever been able to predict, almost to the minute, how long your parents' argument will last, and what it is about? Most of us know what behavior or communication pattern will elicit certain responses from our siblings or parents in many situations. Similarly, we recognize patterns in our family members such as what might lead to an argument or praise. The communication patterns that exist in our families come about as a result of this concept of wholeness. As interconnected pieces, we create our family's own reality, and that reality is distinct and separate from any other family (Galvin and others, 2008).

Establishing Boundaries Every system, whether it is an educational system, political system, or family system, has some type of border or **boundary** between it and its environment. In a family—and particularly in a discussion about family communication—boundaries serve the purpose of affecting the flow of information within the system. Boundaries are essential, because they are what separate and make us distinct from our environment or from other family members.

Boundaries fall along a continuum. On one end are **closed boundaries**, where no information comes in or goes out; on the other end, there are **open boundaries** where the transfer of information is so unobstructed that family members within the systems lose their identity. A family system's health is categorized by the degree to which the boundaries are permeable (White & Klein, 2008). In Figure 3.2, note how in the closed boundary system the borders are so tightly closed that little or no information is allowed in or out of the family system. This type of a closed boundary is often seen in families where abuse occurs. The amount of information that leaves the family system is quite limited (such as family members not discussing publicly what takes place privately in the home). In the same way, information or interference from outside of the family system is limited or prohibited (such as the abusive partner dictating who can visit or phone family members).

FIGURE 3.2 Types of Boundaries

Boundaries affect the flow of information within a family system and make us distinct from other family members. A family's health and well-being is categorized by how open or closed the boundaries are.

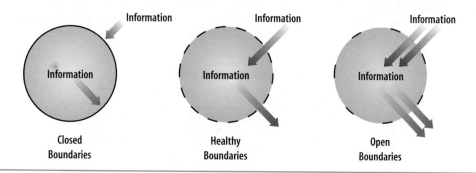

Conversely, notice in open systems that information is allowed to freely come in and exit the family system. A certain level of open boundaries is necessary for the health and well-being of families. However, when boundaries are too open—when too much information flows between the subsystems—members in the family system lose their distinct identity. For example, if parents continually share pieces of their parental subsystem with their children (such as their marital problems, their financial problems, or their work-related problems), the boundaries become blurred and the children lose their distinct identity as children.

Maintaining Balance When an infection enters your body, various systems work together to bring your body back into **balance**, or **homeostasis**. According to Family Systems theory, every family has the same goal, which is to maintain its balance or homeostasis when it experiences any departure from its usual state of balance (the family's state of "normal"). Regardless of the system type, it will act to reduce any source of disruption or disturbance (Boss and others, 1993). The disruption can be of internal origin, such as a teenager who suffers from an eating disorder, or it can be of external origin, such as a parent who loses his or her job. Whether from within the family or outside the family, the system will do whatever it takes to bring it back to balance—and this includes arguing, disagreeing, and family conflict.

To restore equilibrium in a family system, we most often use established, habitual communication interactions and behaviors. Sometimes our communication strategies are healthy and adaptive; sometimes they are dysfunctional, unhealthy, and maladaptive. The *Circumplex Model* is a tool family therapists and family practitioners use to understand the boundaries of families, and hence to better understand families' health and level of functioning.

The Circumplex Model Those who study and work with family systems are particularly interested in what constitutes behavioral, relational, and communication interaction patterns. In an effort to provide a means by which to assess a family's level of functioning and health, the **Circumplex Model of Marital and Family Systems** was created to address family cohesion, adaptability, and communication (Olson, Sprenkel, & Russell, 1979).

David Olson, an influential family therapist and professor, posited that families whose cohesion, adaptability, and communication patterns place them more toward the center of the model exhibit balance, as illustrated in Figure 3.3 (page 72). Consequently, these families function more sufficiently and effectively over time than those families whose interaction patterns place them on the outer edges of the model. Because a family's position on the model may be on the outer edges rather than toward the center does not necessarily indicate a level of dysfunction; this placement may just reflect current circumstances. For example, a family in the midst of crisis or stress may exhibit lower than usual levels of cohesion, adaptability, and communication. Additionally, although some families may fall on the extreme outer levels on the model, satisfactory levels of family function may still exist if those levels represent usual, normative family members' expectations (Boss and others, 1993).

FIGURE 3.3 Olson's Circumplex Model of Family Functioning

The Circumplex Model focuses on two primary dimensions necessary for family health: cohesion and flexibility. Families that are balanced (toward the center) tend to be more functional than unbalanced families (toward the edge). *Cohesion* refers to the family's emotional bonding. This ranges from *disengaged* (very low) to *connected* (moderate) to *enmeshed* (very high). *Flexibility* refers to how families balance change in roles and relationships. This ranges from *rigid* (very low) to *structured* (moderate) to *chaotic* (very high).

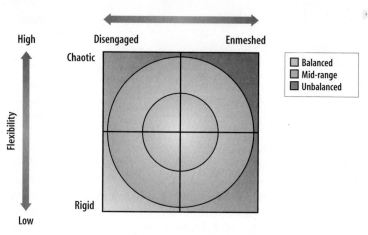

Source: Olson, Sprenkil, & Russell (1979).

Creating Rules This chapter's opening vignette reminds us that some families have secrets. These secrets may range anywhere from a college student's substance abuse to Aunt Betty's eating disorder to child maltreatment or financial difficulties. In many cases, families with secrets appear fully functional, cohesive, and adaptable, but perhaps within these families, the family members recognize that this is far from the truth. All families have rules for how they communicate with each other and how and what information is shared (or not shared) with those outside of the family system. There are communication **rules** that govern what family members can and cannot discuss or share and how they are to interact with their own family members.

Who *does* make the rules concerning what family members can and cannot say within their families, and how do these rules come about? The *family of origin*—with its cultural, ethnic, and multigenerational influences—creates an individual family's rules of communication. For example, you may have only been "shsssh'd" once or twice before you learned that it was not okay to talk with your friends or other relatives about how your parents seem to constantly argue about money. You may have discovered after an attempt or two or three that your parents were not comfortable talking about sex with you. Through repeated interactions such as these, over time you learned what is acceptable to talk about, either within or outside of the home.

Professors of communication studies Kathleen Galvin, Carma Bylund, and Bernard Brommel (2008) provide some categories of rules for communication:

- *What we can and cannot talk about.* Every family has different values and contexts that dictate how they communicate about sex, health issues, salaries, bills, or a family member who is deceased.
- *Feelings that are allowed to be shared.* In some family cultures, feelings are masked by accepted behaviors. In other family settings, expressing anger, fear, sadness, and rage is encouraged. Culture, ethnicity, values, and family history come into play when establishing rules for dealing with feelings and emotions.
- *Decision making.* Each family has its own set of rules for decision making. Are decision-making responsibilities shared? Divided? Dictated by the head of household? Can decisions be challenged? Families may run the gamut on how decisions are made.

- *How we can talk about it.* Can you talk about a situation openly, or do you have to somehow dance around the real issue? Is Mom really just "under the weather," with a cold or the flu, or does she have a more serious illness?
- *Communication strategy.* Each family has rules that govern its communication strategies. Do you talk about a situation only when everyone has calmed down? For example, in some families there is the timing-is-everything strategy. Family members learn *when* they can

Family Diversity and Communication

Because our first experiences with interpersonal relationships occur within our families of origin, our understanding of how families communicate and of family life is often narrow (Turner & West, 2006), so we need to widen our knowledge of communication behaviors within a broad range of family types. Do family structures differ in the issues that challenge them?

Communication within Nuclear Families

Issues important in today's contemporary families center on communicating about the division of household chores, the effects of work life on family life, and the involvement of men in their children's lives. Men in contemporary nuclear families have increased the amount of time they spend with their children as well as doing household chores. But spillover—when the stresses associated with work affect home life—tends to increase levels of conflict at home.

Communication in Gay and Lesbian Families

In some respects, gay and lesbian partners and parents struggle with relationship issues (such as conflict) and parenting issues (such as child care) just as heterosexual parents do. But gay fathers tend to receive more support from their families of origin than do lesbian mothers, although self-disclosure of their sexual identity is a difficult communication subject for many.

Communication within Stepfamilies

Family communication within stepfamily structures most often centers on negotiating roles, communication rules, and the unique family subsystems that are formed when two families merge to form a stepfamily. Families who understand that it takes time for families to "blend" see less family conflict than those families who challenge or resist the process of merging the two families.

Communication within Single-Parent Families

In families where *collectivism* is endorsed (as in African American families and Hispanic or Mexican American families), single parents receive a great deal of support, protection, and emotional reinforcement. In cultures where *individualism* is embraced, as in white families, the family of origin may communicate blame and guilt to the single parent.

Communication within Heterosexual Cohabiting Families

Unique to cohabiting couples is a lack of communication role models for this specific family configuration. Cohabiting couples face greater demands in the areas of roles and support of their family structure.

TALK ABOUT IT

1. Do family structures differ in the issues that confront them? What surprised you most about communication within differing family types?
2. What benefits does our culture gain from having so many family configurations?
3. What about challenges?

Source: Turner & West (2006).

The FAMILY *Table*

approach a parent for advice or ask for something special. Some families also strategize *with whom* they can share certain information (such as, Don't tell dad, he'll get upset!).

Such communication rules are not easily broken. Even if we know that our family's communication rules do not work or are not effective, we tend to remain loyal to them (Kellogg, 1990). We are less likely to try to challenge or change the rules if our family is not flexible or adaptable to change. Well-adjusted families allow some rules to be renegotiated as the family passes through the various developmental stages in the family's life cycle (Galvin and others, 2008).

Putting Family Systems Theory into Action: Family Wholeness and Interconnection To continue our examination of the interconnectedness of families and the concept of wholeness in family communication, let's take a look at a hypothetical family situation (Natenshon, 1999).

It was quite obvious to Amybeth's parents that some sort of medical intervention was needed for their daughter. She was becoming dangerously thinner, and her eating disorder was now all-consuming. But Amybeth wasn't the only one suffering—everyone in the family home was suffering along with her.

Because Amybeth only picked at her food, family meals had become a battleground with tempers flaring and emotions running high. Her brother often retreated to his bedroom in the heat of the arguments. Her mother, Terri, usually ended up in tears, and her father, Peter, usually ended up yelling at no one in particular. Even though her parents did not feel that they were the base cause of their daughter's disordered eating, they did experience feelings of confusion, inadequacy, and overwhelming guilt—and they transferred their feelings to everyone in the family. They knew their reactions to Amybeth's disordered eating were contributing to the deterioration of the family.

Peter explored the treatment options for Amybeth by speaking with their family doctor and by searching the Internet. He found that most eating disorder treatment plans excluded the parents and siblings, relying instead on individual psychoanalysis for the individual patient. This puzzled him, because not only was it obvious that the entire family was affected by Amybeth's illness but it would also be instrumental in her recovery process. The family doctor referred him to a licensed family therapist who specialized in the treatment of eating disorders in children and adolescents.

During the initial consultation with Amybeth and her parents, the therapist noted that family therapy would be a very effective way to treat not just Amybeth's individual needs but also to treat every family member's needs. The therapist outlined a treatment program of facilitated changes that would aid her recovery. The treatment plan also allowed the family to make its own parallel changes that would accommodate Amybeth's changing needs, as well as the needs of their family system.

In our hypothetical example, Amybeth's parents came to understand through family therapy their daughter's patterns of disordered eating and learned how to help her. They also understood that they must lead a joint effort between the various components of the family system so the family could work together to help Amybeth—and in doing so, help the entire family. The family-centered therapeutic treatment they selected recognized and respected the power of the family system to help eradicate the disease Amybeth was fighting (Natenshon, 1999). The family system had

WHAT affects one family member affects the entire family, as is the case when a teen girl deals with an eating disorder. Have you ever experienced a situation in your personal life that affected your whole family? Has someone in your family experienced a situation that affected or impacted you?

the potential to either bring about a positive, healing change, or continue family behaviors and communication/interaction patterns that sustained Amybeth's eating disorder.

Unlike conventional psychological theories (such as psychoanalysis) that focus on the individual person and his or her behavioral problems or emotional distress, Family Systems theory encourages the examination and the inclusion of the entire family system in the medical or psychological treatment of one family member. Understanding the interconnection of family members is important, because it is within the family system that communication patterns and behaviors are acquired (from the family of origin), and it is within the family system that *every* family member plays a part in the family's health and functioning.

And herein lies the dilemma that each new couple faces: Each partner brings to the relationship the established and familiar boundary types, balance, and rules from his or her own family of origin. Each member of the couple acts on his or her own subjective *meanings* of what family life is and what it is not. In our everyday interactions with one another, then, how do we communicate these meanings? How do we understand one another? What determines if our communication efforts are successful? Symbolic Interaction theory, a foundation of family studies, seeks to answer these questions.

HEALTHY or unhealthy, well functioning or not, each of us brings established ways of interacting and communication patterns into our intimate relationships. Is it any wonder that conflict can easily erupt?

MEANINGS: THE SYMBOLIC INTERACTION FRAMEWORK

We all have probably viewed a play or movie when we had to stifle laughter because the acting was so awful. And we all have been brought to sobs and tears or side-splitting laughter because the actors on stage were *so* believable, so realistic, and authentic in their character portrayal. Why is it that some actors are able to convey their meanings and their messages—their *roles*—so skillfully and credibly that we are drawn into the very center of their agony or humor, whereas others clearly didn't pay attention in acting class? The ability to effectively communicate meanings between actors is essential not just in the theater but in family life, too.

In our daily interactions, most of us have said, often in frustration, "That's not what I mean!" The **Symbolic Interaction theory** revolves around the notion that human behavior is a continuous dialogue where people watch the behaviors of other people and then react to those behaviors. All human behavior is social behavior, where there is an exchange of messages and symbolic meanings between actors. This is much more complex than it appears at first glance, because in order to understand the exchange of these messages/meanings, we also have to gain an understanding of *how* we acquire the meaning in the first place.

Communication Rules

Take a moment and reflect on the unique communication rules that exist within your own family. Specifically, write down your responses to the following questions:

1. Within your family of origin, are there issues, topics, relatives, or feelings that you are not allowed to talk about? If so, how did you learn that you were not to discuss these things within your family, or with other people?

2. Are there any particular strategies you use to communicate with your family members? For instance, do you use different strategies to communicate with your mother than you do when you communicate with your father?

3. In your present or future family, are there communication rules that you have abandoned or will abandon? Are there communication rules that you have kept or will keep?

Own It!

Key Concepts: Conveyors and Interpreters of Meaning Fundamental to Symbolic Interaction theory is that people react based on the meanings they find in any situation. According to Symbolic Interaction theory, the goal of human interaction is to create shared meanings and to understand the meanings that are communicated between people.

Symbols In an attempt to share meanings, each culture uses **symbols**, or codes. Some symbols are universal behaviors, such as the kiss, which represents affection, love, or a greeting. All cultures use language as a means to anchor meanings to each symbol.

We live in a world that is full of symbols, and knowingly or not, we communicate using these *shared codes* or *shared meanings*. From the moment a newborn baby takes its first breath, communication between the baby and its caregivers is based on the sharing of symbols; from birth and throughout life, we attach meanings to symbols, define symbols, and interpret symbols in our individual environments. For example, a smile can be a symbol of reassurance, compassion, understanding, or greeting. Or it can be a symbol of contempt or condescension.

Our socialization within our culture and how we socially interact aid in our acquisition and interpretation of the meanings of symbols. For example, children in the United States are taught to maintain eye contact with adults while they are spoken to, but children from Latino and Asian cultures avoid eye contact with authority figures as a symbol of respect. Similarly, Native American children are taught that direct eye contact with a teacher is "showing off" (Torres, 1993).

Culture also affects attitudes about symbols of affection, such as a hug or a handshake. In European and Asian cultures, hand-holding or casual embraces by members of the same sex is culturally acceptable. Americans, however, may not share these symbols of friendship and may feel uncomfortable by this display (Torres, 1993). Physical distance during a conversation is a symbol of respect in some cultures. For instance, in the Middle East and South America, people stand closely while conversing, whereas European Americans and African Americans prefer more distance. Being sensitive to cultural communication practices enhances our communication skills. Table 3.1 provides guidelines to consider when communicating among diverse cultures.

Although we spend a lifetime sharing and interpreting symbols, we run into difficulty in our interpersonal and family relationships when we operate on the assumption that we all are on "the same page," that we all share the exact, precise meanings of symbols.

As an example of this, when walking across campus one day with an emeritus professor, much older than I am, a student passed by and called out, "Hey, Dr. Dawg, wassup?" Knowing the student, I stopped and engaged in conversation for a moment or two. As the professor and I continued our walk, she was visibly shaken and upset, "Dog? What does he mean, *dog*? Dog? Students are now calling professors *dog*?" I spent several minutes trying to convince her that when the student used the term, it really was a term of endearment and affection. This example illustrates that all social and intimate relationships depend on our ability to nurture a culture of shared **meanings** (White & Klein, 2008). We must, as individual actors, ensure that we are on common ground—or be able to recognize when we are not on common ground—and share the same connotation in our communication efforts.

Roles Another key concept in Symbolic Interaction theory is the idea of **role**, which Boss and colleagues (1993) call a "system of meanings" (p. 147). We all have different roles in our families and in our circles outside our families. Sometimes one role takes priority over another, but that does not negate or minimize the other roles we have either taken on or have been assigned. For example, I simultaneously have the roles of wife, mother, daughter, sister, aunt, friend, professor, volunteer, researcher, patient, and author. In each of my roles, I take on the role of actor and I follow the rules—the *expectations*—assigned to that role (like it or not). As audience members during a play or a movie, we have certain expectations of the actors on stage or on screen. This is different from being a theatrical actor; taking on or being assigned a role carries with it certain expectations from not just oneself but from others as well (Mead, 1934). These role expectations allow us to anticipate the behavior of others (Boss and others, 1993). When a person takes on or is assigned too many roles, role strain and role conflict may

TABLE 3.1   Cultural Competence: Enhancing Cultural Communication Skills

Cultural competence refers to accepting and respecting cultural differences, being aware of the dynamics of these differences, and continually expanding cultural knowledge (Torres, 1993). Being sensitive to cultural beliefs and practices not only conveys respect for the diverse people in contemporary U.S. society but it also minimizes cultural stereotyping.

1. *Cultural awareness* refers to the process of becoming sensitive to another culture's beliefs, practices, and lifestyles. It also includes appreciating our own culture and becoming aware of biases or prejudices we may hold toward others.
2. *Cultural knowledge* refers to understanding the worldviews from which others operate.
3. *Cultural skill* involves being able to accurately interpret other's cultural ways of interacting.
4. *Cultural encounter* refers to directly engaging in cross-cultural interactions in order to gain a culture-specific understanding of someone.

When communicating with a person from another culture, keep the following in mind:

African Americans

■ Address a person formally; do not use a first name. This is especially important to older adults and the elderly.
■ Make direct eye contact.

Chinese/Chinese Americans

■ People from China are more formal in their communication than Americans.
■ Ask how to pronounce the person's last name; be aware that the last name is often presented first (not last, as in American culture). Husbands and wives do not always have the same last name.
■ Assertive behavior or aggressiveness is considered rude.
■ A nod of the head can mean "yes" or "no." The nod of the head more likely indicates that the person heard you rather than agrees with you.

Japanese/Japanese Americans

■ Children and adults alike avoid eye contact with authority figures.
■ Avoid aggressive, outgoing gestures, as these are interpreted that you have been poorly socialized in social interactions.
■ Often elderly people are not comfortable verbalizing their emotions. It is important to pay attention to their nonverbal behaviors. Nonverbal communication such as respect, empathy, sympathy, and kindness are appreciated.

Source: Torres (1993).

result. **Role strain** occurs when there are competing demands from multiple roles. **Role conflict** is the psychological stress and tension that result when people undertake multiple roles that are incompatible. (See Chapter 4 for an in-depth discussion about role conflict and role strain.)

Putting Symbolic Interaction into Action: Assigning and Sharing Meanings The Symbolic Interaction framework has been used to examine a number of family issues. These issues include father involvement following divorce, the study of the cultural influences of ethnicity, shared grief work following the death of a loved one, the shared meanings associated with sexuality, and gender role attitudes between mothers and daughters. Family communication interactions lend themselves to the use of Symbolic Interaction theory because the central themes of this theory are concerned with how meanings are formed, assessed, sustained, and transformed through culturally and socially defined processes (Blumer, 1969). Although not specifically related to family communication, the following research example gives us insight

Should Children Be Used as Language Brokers?

In the United States, nearly 20 percent of the children speak a non-English language at home (Crawford, 2005). Because many of the adults in these families do not speak the English language, their children are called on to be mediators and to speak or read for the adults, since in most cases the children are the first to acquire competence in a new language. This mediating activity is called **child language brokering**.

Child language brokering is typically an informal social interaction where children are asked to act as the go-between for their parents or other family members and an English-speaking person, such as a teacher, a postal worker, or a store clerk. Child language brokers fulfill an important role in their families. But does child language brokering positively contribute to the child's development?

YES: According to language broker researcher Linda Halgunseth (as presented in Coleman & Ganong, 2003), the experiences of the child language broker positively shape the child's development in the following areas:

- *Cognitively.* Because child language brokers are called on to mediate communication between parents and various members of the community, these children acquire vocabularies and word lists that enhance their school performance.
- *Interpersonally.* Language brokering develops children's communication and social skills because children learn to adapt them to the situation. According to Halgunseth, these skills help children develop strong feelings of self-worth, value, and usefulness.
- *Emotionally.* Enhanced self-esteem, feelings of independence and autonomy, confidence, and feelings of maturity and importance result when children feel they fulfill the important function of communicator in their families.

NO: Child language brokering does not necessarily positively shape the development of children. It can instead be a stressful experience for immigrant children in the following areas (Umaña-Taylor, as presented in Coleman & Ganong, 2003):

- *Role reversals.* Child language brokering almost always involves a bilingual child who is under the authority of the beneficiary. Because of this, unequal power exists, and parents become dependent on their children.
- *Increased anxiety.* During the brokering process, children often learn or are asked to convey confidential information about their parents. Because situations such as these are typically not developmentally appropriate for children, it may be stressful for them.
- *Inhibited identity formation.* A central developmental task of all children as they mature is to establish an identity that is separate and distinct from that of their parents. Child language brokers are continually called on by their parents to fulfill adult tasks, and this in turn limits their opportunities to explore their own identity.

WHAT DO YOU THINK?

1. Is child language brokering a positive or a negative life experience for bilingual children?
2. Have you acted in the capacity of a language broker for your family? If so, were you embarrassed to share private health or financial information? If you have not acted as a child language broker, would you have felt comfortable performing this role for your family?

Sources: Crawford (2005); Halgunseth (2003); Umaña-Taylor & Fine (2003).

into the meanings people assign to behaviors, such as abusive behaviors. For some of you, the discussion may be difficult to read because it addresses incestuous relationships between parents and their children. If this content is difficult for you, please move forward to the next section, "Communication between Men and Women."

Incestuous relationships are sexual relationships between people to whom marriage is prohibited, such as a father and a daughter or a mother and a son, or culturally frowned on, such as between a stepfather and a stepdaughter. The study of incestuous relationships involves examining variables such as the type of sexual activity, incidence patterns (such as the regularity of incestuous encounters and the duration of these encounters), and whether substance abuse problems existed with the perpetrator.

One researcher who examines child maltreatment issues sought to examine fathers' and daughters' *descriptions* of the sexual activity in addition to their *interpretations* of what occurred (Phelan, 1995). Using the Symbolic Interaction framework to structure her study of 42 families, Phelan posited that in order to understand incestuous relationships more fully (and thus, to develop and implement education and support groups for victims of such relationships), the meanings and the interpretations of the events to those involved must be considered. She wanted to determine the ways in which the perpetrator and the victim conceived, reflected on, and interpreted the circumstances of their sexual encounters and the actions by each party.

The researcher found that although the fathers' and daughters' reports of the circumstances surrounding the initiation of the sexual activity were quite similar (back rubs, watching television, wrestling, reading in bed), *interpretation* of the incestuous events were in stark contrast to one another. For example, most of the study participants indicated that there was very little verbal interaction during the acts of incest; daughters reported (interpreted) that the silence was because of confusion, fear, and disbelief, while over half of the fathers or stepfathers interpreted the daughters' silence as acceptance.

> *Stepfather:* (The child was sick and watching TV on the sofa with her stepfather.) She was complaining about being hot and I asked her if she would like me to put lotion on her. She said, "Yes," so I did. It started out frankly as a very innocent thing and ended up just exploring as much as I could explore. I just kept going and going and she didn't stop me. She didn't say no, don't do that, or anything else.

> *Stepdaughter:* I just—I didn't know what it was but I just knew it wasn't right. I didn't put any words to it. (Phelan, 1995, p. 18)

More than half of the fathers or stepfathers in the study reported that they interpreted their daughters' behavior as that of enjoying what was taking place. The daughters reported that clearly this was not the case. Contrary to what the children reported, 12 fathers reported that their daughters initiated the incestuous activities—not they.

> *Stepfather:* She was really enjoying it. She accepted it. She thought it was a game— enjoying it as a game but nothing serious.

> *Stepdaughter:* I was ignorant. I didn't know what he was doing. I didn't know what it was called so I wasn't brave enough to [say] what he was doing or tell anybody what it was. (Phelan, 1995, pp. 17–18)

Although more than three-fourths of the men in the study reported that they knew their actions toward their daughters were inappropriate (and illegal), the men indicated that they felt that they had "rights" to their daughters because of their position as father. Surprisingly, these stepfathers and biological fathers voiced that sexual relations with a child other than their own child was a "much graver offense."

The Symbolic Interaction approach to examining family and family communication revolves around an exchange process of messages and shared symbolic meanings and interpretations between actors. In this research example, the actors are the step- or biological fathers and their step- or biological daughters. It is clear that while both the fathers and the daughters experienced the same incestuous events, each attached opposing meanings and interpretations. As Phelan (1995) concludes, "The *meanings* people attach to incestuous events are central to understanding the phenomena and further, that meanings arise, in part, through the defining activities of fathers and daughters as they interact" (p. 8).

This lack of shared meanings and inaccurate interpretations cause frustrations and misunderstandings in all forms of human interactions—especially in family and intimate relationships. Some researchers argue that these frustrations would be greatly minimized if we understood the differences between how men and women acquire and share language meanings.

Communication between Men and Women

I admit it—I am technology challenged! I was quite proud of myself when I recently learned how to create graphs and bar charts in PowerPoint, and I was even more proud of myself when I figured out how to text message. Consider this phone conversation I had with my son, a computer engineer:

> *Me:* "Help!"
>
> *Son:* "What's wrong *this* time?"
>
> *Me:* "I think I killed my laptop!"
>
> *Son:* "Did you plug it in to recharge the battery?"

I begin to explain the problem as I see it ("stupid computer," or words to that effect).

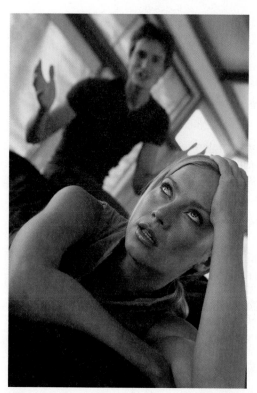

"**YOU** don't understand!!" Are men and women on the same page when it comes to communication? Deborah Tannen, a linguistics professor, believes that they are not, and that this is why there are so many misunderstandings in heterosexual intimate relationships.

> *Son* (politely interrupting me)*:* "Well, what you need to do is [technical term], [very technical term], and [even more very technical term]. And that will fix the problem."
>
> *Me:* "What??"
>
> *Son:* "It's really simple, Mom. Put Dad on the phone and I'll explain it to him."

I thought about this conversation for quite awhile. Did I really have that much trouble following my son's instructions to fix my computer? Were we just not on the same page because I'm not familiar with technology lingo? Or was there a fundamental gender difference in how we communicate? Would a woman have differently explained how to fix the computer?

The study of gender differences in interpersonal communication is a topic that generated great interest in the 1990s. In fact, a number of books were written on the subject, such as the popular *Men Are from Mars, Women Are from Venus* (Gray, 1992). In her best-selling book, *You Just Don't Understand: Women and Men in Conversation*, professor of linguistics Deborah Tannen proposed a framework that maintains that men and women interpret communication messages in fundamentally different ways (Tannen, 1990).

We will explore gender at length in the next chapter, but for now it's necessary to understand that as we grow up, we are taught how to be a "boy" or a "girl," or a "man" or a "woman" in a number of different ways. We receive countless messages from society on a daily basis that reinforce these *gender cues*. It's no different with communication—we are taught, by examples in our environment, how to communicate as a boy and how to communicate as a girl. And as we have seen so far in this chapter, we then carry these patterns of communicating and relating into our future relationships.

According to Tannen (1990), boys and girls grow up and learn entirely different—yet equally valid—communication meanings and symbols. She asserts that men and women are so different in how they communicate and interpret relational messages, and in what they focus on while communicating, that their communication is, in essence, akin to differences we might expect to see between people from different cultures. Tannen thus refers to the man–woman communication differences as *genderlects,* or *cross-sex* communication styles (p. 42). She proposed that these gender differences can lead to problems, misunderstandings, and tensions in all kinds of communication between men and women.

In the sections that follow, we'll briefly examine what the empirical evidence has to say about how men and women communicate; we'll pay particular attention to Tannen's (1990) *difference framework* of gender communication.

MR. Fix It. Men's underlying communication context is that of helping and fixing the problem at hand. This is why they offer advice so quickly when someone approaches them with relational or other problems.

MEN'S COMMUNICATION: OFFERING ADVICE

In all human behavior and communication, there are two levels of meaning that are conveyed. First there is the **message**, which is the obvious meaning of the communication. If we return to the example of my son assisting me with my computer problems, the clear-cut message was that I was helpless to fix the problem. The second level of meaning is what Tannen (1990) refers to as the metamessage. A **metamessage** is the underlying context in which the communication takes place—it is the information about the relationship between the parties communicating (in this case, mother and son) and the attitudes toward each other. Tannen's gender difference linguistic research shows that men attune to the metamessage of *helping* and *fixing problems*. That is to say, the underlying context of men's communication is to be a problem solver and an advice giver (Tannen, 1990). In the case of my computer woes, this is precisely what took place: I had a problem, and my son immediately jumped to the solution, rather than listen to me describe the problem in detail. Tannen asserted that men's communication behaviors are focused on control and dominance, and that this is why men are problem solvers in dialogues with women.

Tannen (1990) also suggested that when men are confronted with **trouble talk**, or talking about emotional and relationship problems, they are much more likely than women to give advice, tell jokes, change the subject, or remain silent (to avoid emotional expression). Thus, Tannen asserts that when men engage in trouble talk and women offer sympathy to them, men feel that they are being looked down on, put in a lower status, or being condescended to (Michaud & Warner, 1997).

WOMEN'S COMMUNICATION: CONNECTING WITH OTHERS

Let's suppose that I had a daughter who was a computer engineer, and she answered the phone when I had difficulties with my computer:

Me: "Help!"

Daughter: "What's wrong *this* time, Mom?"

Me: "I think I killed it!"

Daughter: "Oh, I'm so sorry you're having so many troubles. I know how busy you are. Don't worry; we'll figure this out."

I begin to explain the problem as I see it ("stupid computer," or words to that effect).

Daughter (who politely lets me describe the problem): "Well, what you need to do is—okay, do you see that little slot on the back? Okay, now twist that to the left and that will pop out your battery. Okay, now put the battery back and try to turn it on."

Me: "It's working! Thanks!" And we continue on in our conversation—that has nothing to do with the computer.

According to Tannen's research, women attune to the metamessage of *empathy* and *understanding*. In trouble talk, then, women tend to openly express sympathy for and care about the situation; this shows that they align with or show solidarity with the other person. The hypothetical situation with my "daughter" handling the computer problem illustrates Tannen's assertions that when women communicate, they desire to connect with others, to build relationships, give support, and show cooperation (Tannen, 1990).

MISS Congeniality. Women's underlying communication context is to show empathy and understanding. This might be why girls never seem to be able to go to the restroom without their circle of friends, and why they often give support en masse when one of their friends is hurting.

AND HEREIN LIES THE PROBLEM

When we communicate, there are a number of possible emotional responses to receiving messages, and we often expect the same emotional response that we would give in a similar situation (Michaud & Warner, 1997). For instance, when a woman conveys sympathy in trouble talk, she anticipates that she will receive sympathy in response to her trouble talk (Michaud & Warner, 1997; Edwards & Hamilton, 2004). When a man gives advice or suggestions for solving a problem, he expects that he will receive advice in response to his trouble talk. But when he offers *advice* when she is expecting *sympathy*, she feels that her feelings are invalidated or that her problems are being trivialized. When she offers *sympathy* when he needs or wants *advice*, he feels that she is putting him down (Michaud & Warner, 1997). She may feel that his joke-telling is making fun of her situation; he may feel that her comforting is treating him like a child. Thus, it is not the *words* that are the underlying source of communication differences between men and women—it is the tendency for women and men to *interpret messages in systematically different ways* that is at issue (Edwards & Hamilton, 2004).

Tannen (1990) puts forth the idea that if men and women stop blaming one another for their communication difficulties, differences, and frustrations, and instead begin to communicate across gender cultures, then marriages and other intimate relationships would become strengthened. When men and women enhance their understanding of gender differences in communication, they are less likely to say to their intimate partner, "You don't understand!"

Although there has been widespread acceptance of different communication cultures both in academics and in popular culture, it is important to point out that recent studies do not support Tannen's gender differences framework. For instance, one recent study showed that there was no evidence that men were more unresponsive than women when talking to friends about problems; in fact, they did not differ in their expressions of sympathy or minimize the other's problem (MacGeorge, Graves, Feng, & Gillihan 2004). Another study found that the use of humor by men is a means of support for distressed friends—not a *lack* of support as Tannen asserted (Bippus, 2000). Indeed, as one study concluded, "Both men and women view the provision of support as a central element of close personal relationships; both value the supportive communication skills of their friends, lovers, and family members; both make similar judgments about what counts as sensitive, helpful support; and both respond quite similarly to various support efforts" (MacGeorge and others, 2004, p. 172).

Now that you have a firm understanding of communication as a transactional process, a knowledge base about how we acquire/share meanings, and the significance of these meanings in gendered communication, it is time to explore two more fundamental topics of communication: *verbal* and *nonverbal* communication.

Types of Communication

Any interpersonal or social interaction provides us with a wealth of information. But why is it that today's divorce courts commonly hear that husbands and wives are "failing" to communicate (Gottman, 1999; Gottman, Ryan, Carrere, & Erlye, 2002)?

How we communicate in our families influences the quality and the content of our relationships. Because we develop all of our interpersonal (social and relational) communication skills within our family of origin, this is where we build our foundation (whether in healthy ways or unhealthy ways) for communicating to resolve conflict, share intimacy, and express our needs, wants, fears, hopes, frustrations, anger, or desires. When we discuss marital and family communication, we are referring not just to the talk that takes place among couples, but also to the entire array of communication transactions.

Broadly stated, **communication** is the process of making and sharing meanings. Professors and researchers of communication studies, Lynn Turner and Richard West (2006) summarize the general concepts of communication that we have learned so far:

ALL human behavior is social behavior where there is an exchange of messages and symbolic meanings between actors. Do you think this mother and daughter share the same symbolic meanings for the daughter's clothing? Why or why not?

- *Communication is a transaction.* Communication is a transactional process where parties act simultaneously as senders or receivers of messages. All human behavior is a continuous dialogue.
- *Communication is a process.* Communication is dynamic and ever-changing. Viewed in this way, emphasis is placed on the *process* of meaning-making, rather than on the *outcome* of the exchanges. Each family undertakes the process of meaning-making differently; culture and ethnicity are key in the process of meaning-making.
- *Communication involves co-construction of meanings.* Each person in a relationship speaks a unique language that was acquired from his or her family of origin. The process of communication thus consists of learning the meaning of things—*constructing definitions*—between family members.
- *Communication involves symbols.* In order to construct meanings or definitions of things, people rely on *symbols* or *codes*. Across cultures, the codes that are used for communication are *verbal* and *nonverbal*. These two broad categories are used to describe how we convey meanings to one another, both in our interpersonal and social relationships.

VERBAL COMMUNICATION

The role of communication receives a lot of attention when talking about marriage and intimate relationships, and for good reason: The presence of or absence of effective communication skills plays a key part in whether a marriage succeeds or fails (Gottman, 1999). Our ability to effectively send and receive messages to a large extent predicts or is associated with marital satisfaction in couples (Markman, 1984; Gottman, 1999; Gottman and others, 2002).

Verbal communication refers to exchanges of thoughts, messages, or information through the spoken word. It includes the content and substance of the words being spoken, the tone and the expression, as well as the structure and organization of the words. All verbal communication takes place within the context of a specific environment. It is the language we speak. Despite the information communicators exchange, though, exclamations of "You don't understand!" and "That's not what I mean!" echo throughout the hallways of our homes.

In the twentieth century, empirical marital and family communication studies were conducted to examine the significance of effective verbal communication skills and how these skills affect overall marital satisfaction. For example, one study looked at couples whose marriages were not in distress, couples who were in marital therapy, and couples in the process of divorce (Christensen & Shenk, 1991). The researchers found that those couples who were not in distress showed more effective verbal communication styles in their day-to-day communication efforts than did those couples engaged in marital therapy and those couples divorcing. In addition, the couples in therapy and the divorcing couples exhibited lower levels of verbal communication skills than the nondistressed couples did.

Barbara Okun (2002), a professor of counseling psychology, also examined verbal communication skills as they relate to marital satisfaction. She notes that the majority of the problems found in marriages and families stem from ineffective communication. When role expectations and desires are not fulfilled, frustration and anger result. Okun further adds that when couples seek professional help with their verbal communication inadequacies, these couples consistently have trouble recognizing and communicating their problems or concerns to the spousal partner. Training couples in the area of verbal communication skills is becoming an increasingly popular and important component in approaches to marital counseling (O'Donohue & Crouch, 1996). Psychologist William Shadish (1993) and his colleagues maintain that the reason troubled couples rarely have positive outcomes is because each member of the couple lacks effective communication skills.

There are four fundamental verbal communication processes or skills that Brant Burleson (1992), professor of communication studies at Purdue University, lists that affect how we send and receive messages. These are summarized in Table 3.2. As you can see, these skills range from accurately conveying our messages, to accurately anticipating how our words will affect the other person, to how we process social information we receive from our environment. But conveying meanings through the spoken word is not the only means of communication. When people communicate, they use symbols and behaviors other than words to express and exchange their thoughts, feelings, and information. This is referred to as *nonverbal communication*.

NONVERBAL COMMUNICATION

Our emotions are almost always accompanied by overt physical displays. **Nonverbal communication** occurs with or without the spoken word. It includes facial expressions, motions of the body, eye contact, patterns of touch, expressive movements, hand gestures, the spatial arrangements in the physical environment, and displayed emotions. Emotions provide invaluable information as we attempt to interpret the messages conveyed by the sender. The physical gestures and movements that convey our emotions are most often referred to as nonverbal communication, or **emotional communication** (Senecal and others, 2003). Although we all

TABLE 3.2 Verbal Communication Processes

- **Communication effectiveness.** This skill requires us to convey messages accurately; it is the ability to send messages with the intended meaning. This is a fundamental skill in communication.
- **Perceptual accuracy.** Being able to deliver messages so they are received in the manner we *intend* is another critical skill.
- **Predictive accuracy.** This skill requires us to be able to accurately anticipate how our words will affect the other person. Usually when we speak, we know before the words leave our mouths what impact those words will have on the person we are speaking to.
- **Interpersonal cognitive complexity.** This area of communication skills deals more with our ability to process social information we receive from our environments than from person-to-person communication. Burleson (1997) refers to this skill as a *social perception* skill.

may have difficulty in accurately interpreting the meaning of words that we hear, interpreting nonverbal/emotional communication can present an even greater challenge. Emotional communication is conveyed and interpreted in a number of different ways.

Relational and Nonrelational Messages Of particular interest to communication studies researchers Ascan Koerner and Mary Anne Fitzpatrick (2002a) is the idea that **relational messages**, which refer to those messages that have something to do with the partner or the relationship, differ from **nonrelational messages**, or those issues or topics that have to do with things outside of the relationship. Specifically, the researchers hold that most often, relational information is not communicated with words; instead, when we wish to discuss something that concerns our partner or the state of the relationship, these relational messages are almost always communicated in nonverbal or emotional behaviors. For example, if a partner feels insecure or rejected by the other partner, rather than say the words, "I feel really insecure and rejected when you have long phone conversations with your ex," a person may instead pout, pull away from a hug or a touch, or give glaring, dirty looks. And herein lies a secret to effective, well-adjusted marital, family, and couple relationships—a secret about how to successfully navigate relational communication—increase your ability to accurately decode your partner's emotional communication.

Decoding How we **decode** or interpret the unspoken exchanges that take place in the many nuances of "couple talk" greatly affects marital adjustment and marital satisfaction (Tannen, 1990). In fact, research since the 1970s consistently indicates that couples who are well adjusted relationally decode the emotional/nonverbal communication of their mates better than those couples who are less well adjusted (Carton, Kessler, & Pape, 1999; Lindlof & Taylor, 2002; Koerner & Fitzpatrick, 2002a; Noller, 1993). In other words, couples who have stronger marriages are better able to read their partner's nonverbal behaviors than are those couples who are relationally not as strong.

In a study that investigated how married couples decode messages and the impact this has on marital satisfaction, Koerner and Fitzpatrick (2002b) describe their findings in terms of three specific emotional messages as they relate to nonverbal communication. For example, *positive emotional messages* are experienced as love, pleasure, and affection. *Negative emotional messages* are experienced in the form of anger and irritation, and are often the result of being injured, harmed, or mistreated in interpersonal interactions. *Neutral emotional messages* are often hard to interpret, because the person delivering the message either gives no specific cues or gives ambiguous cues. This type of nonspecific emotional communication, unfortunately, leads to many misunderstandings (and hurt feelings).

Koerner and Fitzpatrick (2002a) maintain that being able to recognize or decode messages so we can recognize whether emotional communication is due to relational or nonrelational factors is crucial for overall relationship satisfaction. The danger lies in how we decode messages. There are times we may *think* a partner's behavior concerns the relationship, when, in fact, it does not. For example, there may be a situation in which a partner seldom comes home from work in time for dinner. At the same time, perhaps a partner always comes home to a messy house. If we decode the nonverbal information as something that pertains to the relationship—if we *personalize* it—when it does not, these misinterpretations over time can lead to the dissolution of the marriage or the couple.

Private Couple Meanings Couples represent special, unique pairs of interaction and have specific rules of communication. In their effort to study partners' predictions and judgments about each other's emotional communication behaviors, nonverbal communication researcher Sacha Senecal and colleagues (2003) discovered that married couples in particular are quite astute at predicting their partner's reaction to certain situations. These researchers attribute this ability to the fact that couples generally have a lot of information about each other that no one else has. This, in turn, influences the dynamics of interpersonal interactions.

For example, if college student Molly is going back and forth to her home to help care for an ill parent or assist her family during a difficult time, her partner will take this information

Own It!

Family Stories

Storying is one of the most fundamental ways families create meanings and thus their unique family identity. Growing up, how many times did you hear family stories like "When you were a baby, you . . ." or "Ask Shawn to tell you about the time he drove the car through the garage door when he was 4 years old." Family stories tell us how our family came to be, how the family stands behind its members, how the family handles diversity, and what it means to be a Welch, a Carlisle, or a Garcia. Family stories are what give meaning to everyday family life, allowing families to reflect upon their collective experiences (Galvin and others, 2008).

1. Is there a particular holiday, family vacation, or other family event that stands out in your memory? What makes this occasion more memorable than another?

2. Have your memories of this event changed over time?

3. What do you think a nonfamily member would learn about your family from this story?

Sources: Galvin and others (2008); International Reading Association (2005); McLaughlin (2005); Wells (1986).

into consideration if she snaps at him or is unusually quiet. But a clerk at a store or a waiter who does not know Molly's contextual information might assume that she is being rude or impolite in a social interaction. Because of this additional "inside" knowledge, couples develop private communication systems (Gottman, 1979; Gottman & Porterfield, 1981) that allow them to form couple-specific interpretations of verbal and nonverbal information (Senecal and others 2003).

Cornerstones of Communication

Why is it that some couples have such deep trust and intimacy in their relationships while others find it difficult to discuss even day-to-day issues such as bill paying, childrearing, or grocery shopping? Why is it that some families stay tightly knit across multiple generations and others are emotionally distant or torn apart? Maybe in your family of origin the sole form of communication is **functional communication**—the type that addresses only the ins and outs of daily life—which leaves you feeling as though something is lacking in your family connections. Or, conversely, perhaps your family experiences deeper levels of **nurturing communication**, which translates into interactions that convey intimacy, caring, recognition, and validation of family members (Galvin and others, 2008).

To better understand nurturing communication in marital and family settings, it helps to know what forms the basis for effective communication patterns and behaviors. Kathleen Galvin and her colleagues (2008) offer insight into concepts that provide families rewarding and satisfying communication across the developmental life of the family. From their research they outline the key concepts of family-strengthening communication.

DEVELOP RELATIONAL CULTURES

Intimacy is the foundation of every aspect of satisfying, successful interpersonal relationships, whether they are friendships, romantic relationships, or family. Communication that takes place in intimate relationships can be thought of as a relational culture. **Relational culture** refs to a framework of understandings—a private, unique, distinct language—that couples construct in private. These understandings serve to coordinate the attitudes, actions, and identities of the couple and of the family members. Relational cultures among couples and families are important examples of communication dynamics, for interpersonal relationships "are created out of communication, maintained and altered in communication, and dissolved through communication" (Galvin and others, 2008, p. 75).

As newly formed couples attempt to share and interpret meanings of their private language, most will struggle to coordinate these meanings as they transfer them from each of their families of origin to their new relationship. It is not uncommon for newlyweds or those couples newly cohabiting to discover that they argue and disagree much, much more than they did before they lived together. Misunderstandings, arguments, disagreements, and hurt feelings are common (and perhaps even necessary) as couples form their own, unique relational culture and shared meanings.

USE CONFIRMING MESSAGES AND RESPONSES

Confirming messages/responses validate those with whom we are communicating. These types of communication are characterized by recognition of the other person, relevant dialogue, and acceptance; all of these show a willingness to be involved in the relationship (Sieburg, 1973). When we use confirming messages and responses, not only do we acknowledge the other person's presence but we also suggest we are willing to become involved with that person.

There are two key aspects of confirming messages or responses: recognition and acceptance. *Recognition* essentially consists of confirming or acknowledging—either verbally or nonverbally—another's presence and validates the person as a significant, contributing member of the relationship. Such confirmation is an absolute must for intimate marital and family relationships. Confirming messages such as "It was so sweet of you to run that errand for me today—it really freed up my afternoon," or "Thank you so much for unplugging the phone so I could sleep in this morning!" imply acceptance of the other. On the other hand, rejecting responses such as "You're so stupid," or "Oh shut up, you don't know what you're talking about!" serve only to invalidate or reject the family member or mate (Canary, Cody, & Manusov, 2000). Over time, the individual feels rejected and that he or she is of little importance to the family system.

Acceptance simply means that every family member has the sense that they are "all right" (Galvin and others, 2008). On the surface, this seems reasonable and easy to achieve. But ethnic and cultural differences affect how we react and respond to those with whom we are communicating. In some cultures, families talk openly and are affectionate, but in other cultures, family members are reserved and formal. To illustrate, I was reared in a very warm, affectionate southern family; my husband was reared in a family where affection was not displayed physically or verbally. When I first ventured to say "I love you" to him and he replied, "Thanks," I interpreted his reply as rejection. At the time, I didn't recognize how he had been raised. Only as we became a couple, then a family, did our communication intimacy grow deeper. As our relationship grew, only then did we each feel the other's acceptance and recognition. Our experiences are not unique. For everyone, the growth of interpersonal relationships depends on messages that reflect each person's investment in the relationship (Galvin and others, 2008). To communicate in confirming and meaningful ways, it is necessary to self-disclose.

SELF-DISCLOSE

Self-disclosure is voluntarily sharing something personal or private with someone else. This is a *two-way* process because it means that when we send a message, we take a risk that the person receiving the message will accept what we are sharing. Self-disclosure requires a high

WHEN we share our deepest thoughts, fears, hopes, dreams, and goals with our partner, we are increasing our relational intimacy. Do you struggle with self-disclosure, or does it come easily to you? Why do you think this is?

degree of trust, which Galvin and associates (2008) refer to as **emotional safety**. In general, self-disclosure

- Increases as relational intimacy increases
- Tends to be reciprocal (mutual)
- Increases relational satisfaction (relational satisfaction appears to be greatest when moderate levels of disclosure take place)

Disclosure is also affected by gender and socialization; it is particularly related to family of origin, cultural, and ethnic backgrounds. Empirical study, for example, found that married men self-disclose less frequently to their male friends than married women do to their female friends (Omarzu, 2000; Tschann, 1988). The broader point here is that each couple and each family has its own unique opportunities for self-disclosure, yet this can only take place if family members take advantage of these opportunities and communicate often.

COMMUNICATE OFTEN

Students in my family relationships and gender roles class hear me state repeatedly throughout the semester, "A hectic, chaotic lifestyle supports a hectic, chaotic relationship." Family and marital intimacy can either be enhanced or hindered by the time devoted to—committed to—nurturing the process of communication. According to the Pew Research Forum (2008), 75 percent of the respondents indicated that a lack of time with family was a greater family problem than a lack of money, despite the economic crisis in the United States in 2008. Simply stated, if you are not ever together as a couple, then precious little time exists to nurture the relationship, and this includes the fundamental element of family—communication. It helps if couples and families periodically take an inventory of what is happening in each other's lives and open the lines of communication when taking stock of communication patterns and behaviors. **Family meetings** or weekly family discussions (whether they are formal or informal) provide structure and organization to the family system and allow for meaningful conversation. It is up to the parents to ensure that a safe, trusting atmosphere exists within the home to foster an environment that encourages open, honest communication between parents and the children.

LISTEN ACTIVELY

Communication is most effective when **active listening** takes place. When we actively listen, we *hear* what the other person is saying. We are interacting with someone who is important to us. This process is considered an art that connects us to another so we understand not only what others are saying but what they are feeling, too (Lindgren, 1998). When active listening does not take place, the effects of poor listening can be quite detrimental to a family's communication patterns. Family scientist Herbert Lindgren (1998) describes several styles of poor listening in Table 3.3. Notice that the primary reasons behind poor listening styles tend to be *self*-centered rather than *other*-centered. And herein lies a base skill in effective, meaningful communication: accurately hearing and receiving the words, meanings, attitudes, feelings, and emotions of the person sending the messages.

TABLE 3.3   Poor Listening Styles

To truly listen to others involves the art of connecting in such a way that you fully understand not only what they are saying but also what they are feeling. Indeed, active listening is a vital, essential skill that is needed in marriages, families, and intimate relationships. Family scientist and practitioner, Herbert Lindgren, notes that ineffective or poor listening often is the result of bad listening habits or styles:

- **The Faker.** Fakers pretend to listen but don't. Their minds wander in and out of the conversation, but they may nod their head or smile as if they are listening.
- **The Interrupter.** Interrupters are more concerned about their own thoughts and feelings than they are with those of others. They seldom allow the other person to finish, or they immediately respond without pausing for much reflection or consideration of what the other has said. They seldom offer an understanding ear.
- **The Intellectual Listener.** Rather than listen relationally, intellectual listeners attend only to the actual spoken words. They ignore nonverbal communication cues and approach the conversation in a rational, logical way, rather than relying on their feelings or emotions.
- **The Self-Conscious Listener.** These listeners are more concerned with their own status and impressing someone than they are with the thoughts, ideas, or feelings of the other. Because they are trying to impress people with whom they are communicating, they do not listen with understanding. Instead, while the other is talking, the self-conscious listener is already forming his or her reply.
- **The Judge and Jury Listener.** These listeners judge the ideas and behaviors of others, letting others know how wrong or incorrect their thoughts and feelings are. In doing so, they do not hear what the other is saying.

Communication is a two-way, transactional process. Both the listener and the speaker have responsibility to make sure the message is understood.

Source: Lindgren (1998).

Another form of attentive listening is **reflective listening**, when we pay close attention to a person's verbal and emotional (nonverbal) messages, and respectfully acknowledge their perspective. During the course of the communication exchange, we should occasionally seek clarification from family members by saying things such as, "When you said _____, did you mean _____? I want to make sure I understand," or "Am I understanding you correctly when you say _____?" By taking time to *repeat in our own words* what we think the message is, we are both clarifying and validating the message we are receiving. Although reflective listening exchanges such as these will sometimes result in a family member saying, "You're still not listening; that is not what I mean!," we need to keep in mind that reflective listening is not necessarily aimed at reaching an agreement as much as it is aimed at trying to come to understanding the message.

Another effective strategy in resolving conflict is to **reframe** an issue, which means looking at the issue from another perspective. Reframing allows you to see the issue while standing in the shoes of another. Reflective listening and reframing together foster an open, trusting, and caring communication environment.

USE HUMOR: A LITTLE LAUGH GOES A LONG WAY

When I was seriously ill, my husband and I found ourselves talking about those things we hoped we would not have to address at such an early point in our marriage—what would happen if I died. It was a tough conversation, and there came the time when we began to discuss funeral arrangements. In the midst of this emotion-packed conversation, I quickly added, "I know what I want on my tombstone. I want it to say *I told you I was sick!*" It took several minutes for our laughter to subside, and at that point my husband indicated that he, too, knew what he wanted inscribed on his tombstone: *She told me she was fine!* It was at that moment that we both knew that no matter what the outcome of my illness, everything would eventually be okay.

There are several reasons why humor and laughter aid family communication and contribute to overall marital and family satisfaction. First of all, when we laugh our bodies produce *endorphins*, a feel-good, natural pain-reliever. These chemicals are released not only while we are laughing but also after exercise, after sexual encounters, after eating, while holding a baby—all of those things relax and calm us. When our bodies are flooded with endorphins, they lower the level of *cortisol* that our body produces when under stress (Lindgren, 1998). Humor also brings people together and helps to keep things in perspective, sometimes protecting us from focusing too intently on what is immediately before us.

Despite our blue-ribbon efforts, however, sometimes our communication efforts are ineffective or they fail. When this happens, couples and families experience conflict, or instances of stress or disagreements (Anderson & Sabatelli, 2007). Sometimes the conflict is chronic or ongoing.

Conflict in Relationships

Every couple fights. Every family fights. Due to the complex, interrelated nature of interpersonal relationships, conflict is inevitable. In all facets of intimacy, love, sexual encounters, parenting, childrearing, communication, and communication patterns, there are opportunities for quarrels and differences of opinion that may lead to arguments, conflict, and all-out shouting matches. Because of the interactive, systemic nature of family and intimate relationships, conflict can quickly spill into every area of family life. When this occurs, strained relationships lead to a stressful living environment.

Although the experience of conflict is unique to each family, when looking at empirical studies that examine conflict there appear to be common themes of marital and family conflict. Family interaction authors Stephen Anderson and Robert Sabatelli (2007) provide an overview of the current scientific studies as they relate to these areas of marital conflict.

- *Money matters.* Who makes it? Who spends it and how? Who manages the family finances?
- *Division of household labor.* Who does what and when and how often? Is there role equity within the home? Is equality important in this context? Who decides?
- *Sex.* How frequently does each partner want to have sex? How long should it last? Who does what and when? What are each partner's sexual scripts and are these scripts flexible enough to accommodate the partner's desires?

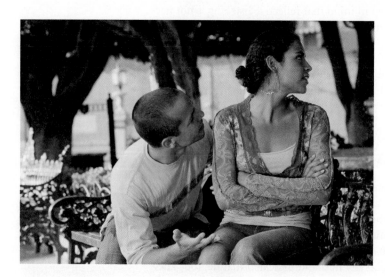

NOT all conflict in a relationship is bad. Constructive conflict can help deepen a couple's intimacy and commitment. The key is to make sure that there are more positive exchanges than negative exchanges. Do you shy away from conflict? If so, why do you think you do?

- *"Tremendous trifles."* This category is a catch-all for a wide array of disputes that emerge over *personal habits* such as snoring, not picking up after oneself, and consistently being late; *personal preferences*, such as preferring to watch television reruns and figure skating competitions over golf, baseball, and action adventure movies; and *day-to-day living*, such as who picks up the kids from school, who takes the kids to soccer, who picks up the dry cleaning, and who does the grocery shopping.

The issue at hand, then, is not whether conflict will erupt—it will. The question is what kind of conflict will it be? Just because conflict exists does not mean that there is a problem with the relationship. John Gottman (1994b), the most influential researcher in the areas of marital happiness/marital satisfaction and conflict management, points out that the basic difference between functional and dysfunctional families is the way in which families process—or *use*—conflict.

Next, we will have a look at the process of conflict and those factors associated with family conflict, as well as the nuances of *destructive, constructive,* and *unresolved conflict.*

WHAT'S ALL THE FUSS? THE SOURCES OF CONFLICT

Conflict typically occurs when family members believe that their desires and goals are not compatible with those of one or more members in the family (Galvin and others, 2008). Many newly formed couples or families try to avoid conflict, but if they manage it properly, conflict can actually be quite beneficial to the relationship and foster growth within the family system. As with any other aspect of marriage and family life, learning about the sources of conflict allows us to better navigate our personal relationships, and helps us help others to use conflict to foster stronger relationships.

There are so many things we can argue about when it comes to family living: where to go to eat, whether a once-used towel is clean or not and needs to be thrown into the laundry hamper, what time the children should be home—the list is virtually endless! Anderson and Sabatelli (2007) provide a comprehensive discussion concerning marital and family conflict and the underlying sources of conflict in marriage: *conflicting role expectations; conflicting needs for connection and autonomy;* and *conflicts in fairness and equity.*

When Role Expectations Conflict We establish relationships, and when we marry we bring with us a ready set of expectations based on how each of us has been socialized. When our expectations are not met, conflict results. For example, women who have been socialized to accept more traditional gender roles may expect to be the primary caretakers and disciplinarians for the children. They may also expect to be primarily responsible for household tasks and expect their husbands to manage the household finances. These women may also expect their husbands to initiate sexual activities. Conversely, men who have been reared according to more contemporary gender roles may expect to be equal partners and have equal say in how the children are reared. They may also assume that household tasks and household finances will be divided equally between the spouses. They may expect sex to be initiated by either partner. When expectations such as those just described are not fulfilled, conflict erupts.

Anderson and Sabatelli note an impressive body of research that speaks to role conflict and differences in role expectations as major sources of marital strain, friction, opposition, and hostility (among others, Bagarozzi & Anderson, 1989; Sabatelli, 1988). When spouses have opposing expectations, and when couples do not discuss their expectations or periodically align them, fertile ground exists for discontent to take root.

When Connection and Autonomy Conflict The interdependent nature of marital and family relationships essentially guarantees that conflict is inevitable due to a human need to be intimately connected and yet separate (autonomous) at the same time. According to Anderson and Sabatelli, as long as one partner's needs do not conflict with the other's, the couple peacefully coexists. But when one partner's need to be alone competes with the other partner's need to be together, the potential for conflict arises.

When Fairness and Equity Are in Question When we enter into a marital partnership, we do so with our own unique perceptions of what constitutes a fair and equitable relationship. For instance, many people enter into committed partnerships and marital relationships expecting that the relationship will always be 50-50. Perhaps the relationship would remain relatively conflict-free if these expectations were consistently met. But how realistic are these expectations? Anderson and Sabatelli (2007) point out that any infringement, breach, or abuse of these norms—our perceptions—becomes the underlying source of conflict within our interpersonal relationships.

As you will see in Chapter 7, intimate relationships can be viewed in terms of cost versus benefit. In assessing the concepts of equity and fairness, we tend to believe that the relationship is *fair* if the benefits we receive are comparative to the costs. In other words, if we get as much out of the relationship as we put into it, then it is fair. An *equitable* relationship exists when each partner gains similar benefits for being in the relationship. When there is perceived

Are You Controlling Anger or Is It Controlling You?

The innate, natural way to respond to anger is through aggression, because anger is the body's way of responding to something that we perceive to be threatening. Some people exhibit more anger than others, perhaps because they are genetically wired to be irritable. Others learn from their families of origin to have a low tolerance for frustration and don't take things in stride. Often these individuals come from family backgrounds that are disruptive and chaotic, and from families with low verbal and nonverbal communication skills.

There are three primary ways in which people deal with their anger.

1. **Expressing angry feelings.** Expressing feelings of anger in assertive or firm ways—without aggression—is the healthiest way. Being assertive means to be able to convey to others in a confident, self-assured manner what your needs are without hurting the other person. Assertive expression of anger does not mean being demanding or difficult.

2. **Suppressing angry feelings.** People who suppress their anger often try to think of a more positive thought in an attempt to keep the angry feelings at bay or convert the anger into more positive feelings. Although this anger management technique is acceptable for mild frustrations, it is not healthy over the long run. Some people who consistently suppress their anger redirect it to other people, becoming cynical or hostile.

3. **Calming angry feelings.** Try to calm the feelings that anger arouses. Not only does this mean calming and controlling external behaviors such as yelling but also internal responses such as breathing slower to control the heart rate and blood pressure. Some people use *self-talk* techniques to calm themselves, such as, "He's not late on purpose just to ruin my day. Traffic jams happen."

For healthy selves and healthy families, keep anger at bay by learning those things that trigger anger among family members. Also, develop coping strategies, such as:

- **Relaxing.** Take a moment to step back, to take a few deep breaths, or to count to 10. Discuss the situation only after the immediate tensions and sensations subside.
- **Reframing/restructuring.** Change the way you think about the situation. Logic defeats anger because it prevents us from becoming irrational when we are upset and keeping a balanced perspective.
- **Planning.** Not all problems have a solution, but planning ahead or anticipating that anger will crop up in family relationships provides families with proactive coping techniques.
- **Listening.** When a family member is upset or angry, it helps to listen to the emotions behind the words. For example, he might be angry because she did not call to say she was going to be home late from work, but in actuality he is angry because he is afraid something happened to her on her way home.

Source: American Psychological Association (2005).

unfairness or perceived inequity, conflict results (Anderson & Sabatelli, 2007). When couples work at resolving the conflict, the result is a change in how the couple interacts.

TYPES OF CONFLICT

Relationship conflict usually occurs because of miscommunication, poor communication, or misperception. Sometimes it is the result of negative behaviors. We generally think of conflict as something we need to avoid because the term implies that conflict is harmful to a relationship. But conflict can be beneficial and strengthen the relationship and initiate growth if dealt with properly. Conflict can be either *constructive* or *destructive* to the marital relationship. Additionally, couples vary in their conflict styles.

Constructive Conflict   While in the midst of a heated argument it might be difficult to think that any good can come out of it; however, **constructive conflict** serves to build relationships and foster loyalty, commitment, and intimacy.

John Gottman has consistently found that the manner in which couples handle conflict ultimately determines whether they divorce. In a study that sought to determine the differences in communication patterns of those couples who sought marital counseling and those who did not, Gottman and his colleagues found that the more happily married couples avoided negative comments (such as hurling insults at one another during a disagreement or a heated battle) and instead affirmed the value and worth of the other partner, in spite of their disagreements (Gottman, Markham, & Notarius, 1977).

In a landmark empirical study, Gottman (1994b) found that how couples communicated about their differences determined marital longevity: Even though some of the arguments the couples experienced were all-out shouting matches or openly verbally combative, couples with high marital satisfaction maintained a ratio of *five* positive comments to every *one* negative comment. In his work, *Why Marriages Succeed or Fail* (1994b), Gottman explored his idea that conflict management styles distinguish troubled from nontroubled couples. Through his study, he found there are two specific marriage types: *regulated* and *nonregulated.*

Regulated couples use communication patterns and interpersonal behaviors that promote closeness and intimacy, such as using more positive comments than negative comments during times of tension. According to Gottman (1994b), there are three types of regulated couples: the *validating* couple, the *volatile* couple, and the *conflict-minimizing* couple.

- *The validating couple.* This type of couple uses a constructive conflict management style. They tend to be empathic and supportive of one another, and try to gauge each other's emotions. These couples listen actively and respectfully and validate that what their partner is feeling is important. Validating couples seldom express negative emotions toward one another. They tend to be happy but not necessarily passionate.
- *The volatile couple.* Unlike the validating couple, the volatile couple type is charged with intense emotion, passion, and romance, and it is this emotion and passion that spills over into every area of marital and family life, including conflict. But despite the intense, emotional disputes, fights, and shouting matches that take place, these couples remain genuinely and intimately connected to one another.
- *The conflict-minimizing couple.* These couples ignore or avoid conflict, or minimize the significance of the trouble. Despite the fact that the conflict-minimizing couple reduces or lessens the conflict that exists—and hence, live with unresolved issues just below the surface—these couples manage to keep the discontentment and unresolved problems from spilling over into other areas of their relationship. According to Gottman, they still manage to use positive language rather than negative, distancing language, which ultimately promotes a closer level of intimacy.

How can a volatile couple with explosive emotions or a couple who totally ignores or avoids the conflict be considered constructive in their conflict management? When Gottman proposed that successful, satisfied married couples maintain a five-to-one ratio of positive comments to negative comments, he illustrated the importance of balance and affirmation. When couples are able to balance positives and negatives constructively, the end result is an effective relationship that withstands and grows from conflict.

Destructive Conflict We have all had our share of disputes and arguments with family members. The dispute or conflict may have been successfully resolved so that the relationship was able to change, adjust to the stress, and subsequently deepen loyalty, commitment, and intimacy levels. At other times, however, many of us have experienced conflict that resulted in greater hurt, anger, confusion, and pain. **Destructive conflict** can be either *overt*, which refers to obvious conflict, or *covert*, which is more subtle but nonetheless hurtful. Whether it is overt or covert, destructive conflict is unhelpful, and at its very worst, deadly (as in the case of physical violence that escalates).

According to Galvin and her colleagues (2008), covert destructive conflict falls within five specific categories:

1. *Denial* is exhibited when a person's words do not align with his or her nonverbal behavior—for example, when someone shouts, "Nothing is wrong!" as he storms out the room.
2. *Disqualification* occurs when a person attempts to cover up an expressed emotion—for example, she might say, "I'm sorry I'm so upset with you, but it's been a horrible day at work."
3. *Displacement* refers to a situation in which someone takes out his or her frustration on someone who is not the original object of anger. An example of this displacement is **scapegoating**, which occurs when anger and hostility are directed at one family member in particular, who always bears the brunt of everyone's frustration. A child who is always blamed for instigating trouble in the family, for example, is known as the family's scapegoat.
4. *Disengaged* couples or family members have little or no emotional closeness. These family members act out their anger or hostility through their lack of interaction with one another.
5. *Pseudomutuality*, the fifth type of destructive conflict, refers to pseudo (fake or false) mutuality (getting along). Pseudomutual families may appear to be close with no indication that conflict exists, yet anger and hostility are always just beneath the surface.

Overt destructive conflict is often verbal, and is characterized by the use of negative, hurtful language, such as "idiot," "stupid," or "jerk." Verbal assaults may or may not involve screaming or yelling (Galvin and others, 2008). When couples and families engage in this type of destructive conflict, they often resort to language that will inflict the most harm possible.

Another type of verbal conflict is **gunnysacking**, which is also destructive. This describes when a spouse or a family member holds in resentment, hurt, anger, frustration, and bitter feelings until that "last straw"—finally unloading all of the pent-up feelings in the midst of an argument.

According to Gottman (1994b), **nonregulated couples** are those who have a difficult time bouncing back from arguments and disputes because the way they handle the conflict only compounds the issues at hand. Even day-to-day disagreements erupt into full-fledged arguments. Nonregulated couples are distinguished from regulated couples in that their interactions tend to be far more negative than regulated couples, and they have a substantially lower ratio of positive-to-negative exchanges. According to Gottman, there are four ways in which nonregulated couples handle conflict. He characterized these as the "Four Horsemen of the Apocalypse":

1. *Criticism.* Criticism almost always involves the word *you*. You never . . . You always . . . You are so . . . You are such a . . . Almost without exception, criticism involves an attack on the *person*, rather than a complaint against the family member's *behavior*. In other words, the comments are meant to hurt, and usually they do.

2. *Defensiveness.* It is human nature to defend ourselves if we perceive that we are being attacked, be it physically, verbally, or emotionally. Recall from our previous discussion that often the way we perceive a message is not the way that the sender intended it to be received; however, often someone speaks words deliberately aimed to hurt. The criticism/defense/criticism/defense interaction pattern becomes a vicious cycle of negativity.

3. *Contempt.* Contempt can be characterized as disrespect, scorn, or all-out hatred for one another, and it is most often the result of constant critical interactions. This pattern of criticisms and defensiveness breeds deeper levels of disdain in a marriage. Over time, the mutual contempt becomes so pervasive and all-encompassing that it erodes all other areas of the marriage to the point where the couple eventually focuses only on the negative behaviors of the other spouse.

4. *Stonewalling.* According to Gottman (1994a), **stonewalling** takes place when communication between marital partners completely shuts down. In these instances, either one or both spouses distance themselves by refusing to communicate, ignoring and becoming remote from the other. Marital separation or dissolution is a likely outcome when this negativity process becomes the standard.

Nonregulated couples' inability to constructively manage their conflict ultimately causes a downward spiral in the marriage. As the negativity increases and intensifies, over time nonregulated couples eventually reframe their perception of their marriage and *focus only on the negative aspects of one another's behavior and the relationship.*

Conflict in family and marital life is normal and is to be expected. Marital partners and families who deal with conflict in constructive, positive ways and avoid negative interactions with their mates further increase their intimacy, loyalty, and commitment. On the other hand, spouses and family members who engage in destructive communication and experience frequent negative interactions increase the likelihood of relationship deterioration and divorce.

The Role of Forgiveness in Family and Intimate Relationships

Betrayal. Aggression. Just plain insensitivity. People can, and do, hurt us in countless ways, whether it's being cut off in traffic, being backstabbed by a co-worker, or being yelled at by a loved one.

When someone—a family member, a friend, or a dating partner—hurts you or offends you, do you let the hurtful comments or actions go and get back to the business of the relationship, or do you tend to hold a grudge and silently vow to "get even" somehow? Although the concept of *forgiveness* has received a lot of attention from philosophers, theologians, and Biblical scholars for decades, only as recently as the past decade has forgiveness as a family process emerged as an area of interest in the social sciences (Rusbult, 2002). For instance, what motivates someone to forgive? Or not to forgive and hold the trespass against someone? And why is it so hard to forgive, even if we want to?

WHAT IS FORGIVENESS?

A Campaign for Forgiveness Research (2008) is a foundation that supports scientific studies that deepen our understanding of forgiveness and how reconciliation takes place. It seeks to answer questions such as, How does forgiveness improve the human condition? How do we choose to forgive? What are the effects of holding grudges and seeking revenge? In the social science literature, **forgiveness** is described as a deliberate process that transforms a strong

MANY marriages can survive even the deepest of emotional hurt, such as infidelity. There is no question that forgiveness aids in the longevity and health of family and intimate relationships. It is one of the most underutilized tools we have to strengthen the relationships with those we love and care about.

desire for revenge into a positive response (Maio, Thomas, Fincham, & Carnelley, 2008). In other words, forgiveness is a process where the forgiver intentionally moves from negative thoughts, feelings, and behaviors associated with the event to more positive ones (Maio and others, 2008). It is not condoning, excusing, or forgetting what happened. Forgiveness occurs at two different levels: at an *individual* level and at a *relationship* level (Thompson and others, 2005).

Forgiving: The Individual Level All too frequently, the people we love the most are the people who we hurt and are hurt by (Fincham, Beach, & Davila, 2004). But how can we move past this inevitable hurt—what motivates us to forgive someone? Why do some people put more effort into forgiveness than others?

When discussing forgiveness at the individual, or *intrapersonal*, level, we first need to recognize that the concept of forgiveness is an internal process—it is primarily for the individual who was hurt, not for the offender. When we forgive someone, we free ourselves from the control of the person who hurt us.

We also need to understand that forgiveness is subjective. As our study in this chapter has shown us, each of us comes into our intimate relationships with different beliefs and family experiences—and forgiveness is no exception. We are each taught in our families of origin what behaviors demonstrate or convey forgiveness and unforgiveness; the concept of forgiveness is defined in each home to serve the needs of those particular family members. For example, each semester I pose this question to my class: If your partner had sex with another person while committed to you, would you leave that partner and end the relationship? Overwhelmingly, the class responds that yes, they would leave their partner. But every now and then a student will indicate that one of their parents had been cheated on, yet chose to stay in the marriage and work things out. By their example, the couple taught their children that forgiveness is an option in this situation.

Certainly, subjective notions of forgiveness vary from person to person, and from culture to culture. In fact, this has been one of the looming hurdles for investigators who desire to examine the application of forgiveness to certain relationship problems (Silberman, 1995). In addition to the intrapersonal level, forgiveness can be applied differently to situations within the same relationship.

Forgiving: The Relationship Level The reality of intimate relationships is that everyone fights! In order for a relationship to succeed, then, it is important for us to grasp the concept that forgiveness is essential in our relational lives because it can break patterns that would otherwise interfere with—or even destroy—the relationship. When we discuss forgiveness at the relationship level, we are referring to the *interpersonal* level.

Forgiving spouses report more positive outcomes in their relationships, because forgiveness is linked to tendencies to behave more positively in the marriage (Fincham and others, 2004; Fincham and others, 2006). For instance, in one study that examined forgiveness among 72 newly married couples, the researcher found that spouses who were forgiving reported being happier in their marriages than those who did not report high levels of forgiveness (McNulty, 2008). The research also revealed that forgiveness was associated with having less severe marital problems, as well as spouses who behaved less negatively (such as bickering, arguing, stonewalling) with each other.

Emerging scholarship suggests that there are a number of factors associated with the interpersonal level of forgiveness. These include conflict-resolution skills and the willingness to forgive, overall relationship satisfaction, and the commitment to the relationship (Fincham and others, 2004; Kachadourian, Fincham, & Davila, 2004; Younger, Piferi, Jobe, & Lawler, 2004). The rapidly expanding body of forgiveness research shows us that people forgive others both at the intrapersonal and interpersonal levels. But we still must determine *how* people forgive.

COMMUNICATING FORGIVENESS: A FAMILY PROCESS

Forgiveness is an essential family process that is necessary to help family members deal with and heal from the inevitable offenses, hurts, or traumas that take place in relationships (Wade, Bailey, & Schaffer, 2005). If we don't forgive, emotional and relational wounds fester and cause anger, fear, and rage to develop—just as our earlier exploration of Gottman's research showed us. But how do families and individuals develop the capacity to forgive?

There are many different pathways to forgiveness, and researchers have begun to better understand models of relational forgiveness. For example, Dr. Fred Luskin, a researcher from Stanford University, put forth a model of forgiveness in which people pinpoint their rage, realize that harboring anger is unhealthy, and look at their situation differently so it's not as problematic as they first thought (Luskin, 2003). A recent study found that people contemplate their situation and go through a series of thoughts before considering forgiveness as an option (Knutson, Enright, & Garbers, 2008). Table 3.4 presents the 82 study participants' responses, in order of importance. As you can see, forgiveness is a process that begins with admitting to ourselves that someone hurt us. As we move through the process, we acknowledge that our resentment is consuming us and changing us, and that we have to consider forgiving the offender before the anger can leave us.

Other contemporary research reveals that there are three ways in which we communicate forgiveness: *directly, indirectly,* and *conditionally* (Kelley, 1998).

- *Direct forgiveness.* With **direct forgiveness,** family members or intimate partners clearly, plainly, and directly tell the offender that she or he is forgiven. Forgivers use statements such as, "We talked about the situation and I told her she was forgiven," and "I let him know that by saying I forgave him so he has no doubts about it" (Merolla, 2008). When using direct forgiveness, people typically use strategies that include discussing the offense and the issues surrounding it, and the forgiver telling the person that he or she understands (Kelley, 1998).

- *Indirect forgiveness.* Family members or intimate partners communicate **indirect forgiveness** by nonverbal displays (such as a hug, a smile, or eye contact) and by acting as though the transgression never happened—by getting back to normal (Kelley, 1998). Forgivers indicate, "I forgave him by acting the way we did before the event took place" (Merolla, 2008).

- *Conditional forgiveness.* The third way people forgive is with conditions attached to the forgiveness, which is why it's referred to as **conditional forgiveness.** This type of forgiveness is used when people want relational repair, but they want to make it very clear that repeating certain behaviors will not be tolerated (Merolla, 2008). For instance, a forgiver might say, "I'll forgive you, but you have to stay off the booze," or "If you promise never to do it again, I'll forgive you" (Merolla, 2008).

TABLE 3.4 Rank Ordering of the Forgiveness Process by Study Participants

1. I admitted to myself that the person hurt me.
2. I became aware of my anger.
3. I admitted to myself that I felt shamed or humiliated by what the person did.
4. I lost my energy by staying resentful.
5. I thought over and over about what happened.
6. I compared my unfortunate state with my offender's more fortunate state.
7. I realized that I may have been permanently changed by the offense.
8. I began to think that people in general—not just my offender—were bad and selfish.
9. I realized that my ways of handling the problem were not working.
10. I was willing to consider forgiveness as an option.
11. I committed to forgive the person who hurt me.
12. I thought of the person who offended me in broader and more positive terms.
13. The anger left me.

Source: Knutson, Enright, & Garbers (2008).

Clearly, forgiveness is not a process in which the forgiver condones, excuses, or forgets what happened to him or her (Knutson, Enright, & Garbers, 2008). For example, it is certainly possible to forgive an absent father, an abuser, or a cheating partner without reconciling with the person. As one group of researchers observes, "When forgiveness is properly understood, it occurs from a position of strength, not weakness, because the forgiver recognizes the injustice and labels it for what it is" (Knutson and others, 2008, p. 193).

Finally, forgiveness needs to be understood just as any other process in family living. That is to say, the traits associated with forgiveness change as individuals progress through their lifespans, and as families progress through the family life cycle (Maio and others, 2008).

BARRIERS AND BENEFITS

The most common roadblocks to forgiveness in intimate relationships center on pride (Baumeister, 2002). First, those people who believe that they are entitled to, or deserve, only the good things in life view forgiveness as too risky and unfair to them (Baumeister, 2002). These people are referred to as having a strong sense of **narcissistic entitlement.** This is an important finding, because as another researcher notes, if someone possesses a sense of entitlement and thus believes that she or he is above forgiving or asking for forgiveness, how can a relationship survive? (Exline, Baumeister, Bushman, Campbell, & Finkel, 2004). As Gottman's research showed us, unresolved conflict eventually leads to a breakdown in the relationship.

Another form of a pride-related barrier to forgiveness is **self-righteousness**, where a person can't see his or her own potential for doing wrong or hurting another person. Roy Baumeister (2002), a researcher with Florida State University, found in a series of studies that when people have a sense of self-righteousness, they tend to be less willing to forgive others and are harsher in their judgments of others. Baumeister observed that following the national tragedy of September 11, 2001, people reported they had less vengeful, unforgiving feelings if they believed the United States had committed similar serious acts on other countries in the past. In other words, low levels of self-righteousness allow people to see that they themselves are capable of committing such acts; as such, they are quicker to forgive or ask for forgiveness.

Finally, some people are afraid to forgive because they think it opens them up to or sets them up for being hurt again (Baumeister, 2002). Although researchers have found very little evidence that forgiving someone increases the chance of being hurt again by the same person, Baumeister's findings suggest that people still worry about the possibility.

Forgiveness is one of the most underutilized family processes that people can use to maintain healthy intimate and family relationships and friendships. Outside of love, forgiveness is perhaps the most important tool available for the longevity of relationships.

Family Life Education

If we reflect on the opening story of this chapter, we can begin to recognize the destructive and potentially damaging long-term effects certain communication patterns can have on us. When my family members involved in keeping "the secret" were doing what they felt was best, they did not anticipate that eventually this very secret would significantly damage people's abilities to trust, self-disclose, and form their own relational cultures. The story should remind us that although we all need to communicate—to give or receive information—the communication process involves much more than the sharing or withholding of information.

With divorce courts backed up with marriages that failed because couples believe they are not communicating, communication is not in fact the reason for the dissolution of the marriages. Couples *are* communicating—by every spoken word, every form of nonverbal or emotional behavior. The trouble is that they are not communicating effectively. As we discussed, effective, healthy communication means listening and hearing *beyond the words*. Sometimes it means hearing with our hearts—listening compassionately—and not with our ears. Productive and healthy communication also involves a basic understanding that everything we say or do in a family affects us, as we simultaneously affect others. And sometimes it means forgiving someone who has offended us or deeply wounded us, even though it can be a challenge—and a lot of individual and relational work—to do so.

Who makes the rules about what we can or cannot say in a family? *We* make the communication rules. *We* enforce these communication rules over time, through repeated interactions, even if they prove to be ineffective or destructive. To create a relational culture that is

Why Are Men So Analytical? Why Do Women Talk So Much?

There have been many attempts over the years to determine and explain the differences in communication between men and women. Geneticist Anne Moir and coauthor David Jessel (1991) contend that the areas of the brain that are essential to communication are programmed in the early stages of pregnancy by the presence or the absence of testosterone. According to their work, male and female brains are structured differently—wired differently—and thus they process information differently. This accounts for the differences in communication. Moir and Jessel claim the innate, biological differences appear to be:

High-Testosterone People (Male Brains) Prefer	Low-Testosterone People (Female Brains) Prefer
facts, logic	feelings, senses
power/status	relationships
winning	sharing
analyzing	"knowing"
intellectual understanding	empathizing
sex	intimacy
thinking	feeling
reports/information	rapport/bonding

Whether communication differences between the genders are due to genetics or environmental influences, these contrasting language practices can create discord and become fertile ground for conflict.

Her Side: Sometimes he seems so distant, so insensitive. He doesn't want to talk about real things, like how he's feeling about something or what he thinks about a certain topic. If I share a problem with him, he immediately has a solution for the problem or has a suggestion about how to "fix" it. He doesn't try to understand my *feelings*. When I ask him about how his day went, he gives me an item-by-item report. I don't want to hear a list of facts—I want him to talk to me.

His Side: She talks all the time! *Everything* is an important topic to her, and she shares every detail. And to top it off, she always wants to talk about our relationship. I think our relationship is fine. If I don't want to talk about it, she gets offended and will say something like, "You see, our relationship is in trouble!" It's very confusing and frustrating to me.

Your Side: In your opinion, do you think there are gender differences in men's and women's communication styles? Consider the following questions:

1. Do you agree or disagree with the "male brain" list and the "female brain" list the researchers compiled? What leads you to your conclusion?
2. In your opinion, are the differences in communication between the genders determined genetically or are they due to the influences of socialization?

Source: A. Moir & Jessel (1991).

rich and rewarding to each family member, confirming your family members and/or your partners by recognizing and accepting their messages is essential. One of the greatest gifts a couple can give their children is to create an environment where each child is valued as a contributing member to the family system, as a contributor to family communication, an environment where communication aids in self-disclosure and the creation of intimacy, where family members communicate often. Active, reflective listening, too, fosters self-disclosure and intimacy. Finally, remember that humor goes a long way to bring family and partners together.

Summary

The Communication Process

- Communication is a transactional process in which we affect and are affected by our intimate relations. When we discuss communication in this context, the focus of the interaction is not on the words individual family members speak, but on the interconnectedness of the relationship.

- Family Systems theory (FST) is a General Systems theory (GST) that sees the family as an interconnected system—a whole entity comprising interconnected parts that seek balance.

- Family Systems theory concerns *interactions* and *interrelations*. This includes study of both normative (expected) and nonnormative (not expected) life events that affect all members within the family unit.

- We can understand an individual family member's behavior and communication patterns only by looking at the entire family system and a person's family of origin.

- Every family system has some type of border or boundary, from closed to open, between it and its environment that affects the flow of information within the system and separates us from our environment or from other family members. Boundaries fall along a continuum that ranges from closed (no information comes in or goes out) to open (the transfer of information is so unobstructed that family members within the systems lose their identity). A family system's health is categorized by the degree to which the boundaries are permeable.

- According to Family Systems theory, every family's goal is to maintain its balance when confronted with any departure from the family's usual state of "normal." To restore equilibrium, families most often use established, habitual communication interactions and behaviors, which may be healthy or unhealthy.

- Olson's Circumplex Model is a tool that was created to address family cohesion, adaptability, and communication, and to assess a family's level of functioning and health.

- The family of origin creates an individual family's rules of communication. They include what things may be talked about and how.

- Symbolic Interaction theory proposes that all human behavior is a continuous dialogue where there is an exchange of messages and symbolic meanings. People assign learned symbolic meanings to others' behavior.

- To share meanings, each culture uses symbols (codes) and uses language to anchor meanings to each symbol. These meanings are indicated by communication symbols acquired and developed throughout life, and, knowingly or not, we communicate using these *shared codes* or *shared meanings*.

- All people are assigned or take on roles (systems of meanings) within their families and society, and these roles carry with them certain expectations. When a person takes on or is assigned too many roles, role strain and role conflict may result.

Communication between Men and Women

- As we are growing up, we are bombarded with cultural messages about what it is to be a "boy" or a "girl" in our society. These messages are referred to as *gender cues*.

- Linguist researcher Deborah Tannen discovered that in all human communication, there are two levels of meaning: the message and the metamessage.

- Men are attuned to the metamessages of helping and fixing problems. The underlying context of men's communication is to be a problem solver and an advice giver.

- Women are attuned to the metamessages of empathy and understanding. The underlying context of women's communication is to show sympathy and empathy for the situation.

- When men and women communicate, they need to be aware that genders may convey and interpret messages in systematically different ways.

Types of Communication

- Communication is the process of making and sharing meanings. The process is a dynamic transaction involving shared definitions of symbols or codes.

- Verbal forms of communication refer to exchanges of thoughts, messages, or information through the spoken word. They include the content and substance of the words being spoken, the tone and the expression, as well as the structure and organization of the words. All verbal communication takes place within the context of a specific environment.

- Nonverbal communication occurs with or without the spoken word and includes facial expressions, motions of the body, eye contact, patterns of touch, expressive movements, hand gestures, the spatial arrangements in the physical environment, and emotions.

- Relational messages refer to those messages that have something to do with the partner or the relationship. Nonrelational messages refer to issues outside of the relationship. Relational messages are almost always communicated by nonverbal or emotional behaviors. A couple's skill in decoding, or interpreting, unspoken exchanges greatly affects marital adjustment and satisfaction.

- Armed with "inside" knowledge about each partner that no one else has, many couples can predict their partners' reactions to certain situations and develop private communication systems and private couple meanings.

Cornerstones of Communication

- Couples and families that communicate effectively learn to send verbal and emotional messages more clearly, and also how to interpret received messages. They are able to move beyond mere functional communication toward nurturing communication.

Conflict in Relationships

- Conflict normally occurs in family life, typically when family members believe that their desires and goals are not compatible with one or more members in the family. Typical sources of conflict include conflicting role expectations, degrees of independence, and issues of fairness and equity.

- Constructive conflict builds relationships and is typical of regulated couples who use communication patterns and interpersonal behaviors that promote closeness and intimacy. Nonregulated couples have difficulty recovering from arguments because their interactions tend to be far more negative, compounding the issues at hand.

- Destructive conflict—conflict that results in greater hurt, anger, confusion, and pain—can be either overt (obvious) or covert (more subtle). Destructive conflict is typically manifested through "gunnysacking," denial, disqualification, displacement, disengagement, or pseudomutuality.

The Role of Forgiveness in Family and Intimate Relationships

- Forgiveness is a deliberate intrapersonal process that transforms a person's strong desire for revenge into positive thoughts, feelings, and behaviors toward the offender. Forgiveness is for the person who was hurt, not for the person who hurts.

- Forgiveness first occurs at the individual, or intrapersonal, level. There are a number of variables linked to whether we forgive someone, such as level of empathy, high levels of emotional stability, how agreeable a person is, and how able someone is to forgive herself or himself.

- Forgiveness also occurs at the relationship, or interpersonal, level. People who forgive their spouses report more positive outcomes in their marriages than those who do not. Factors associated with interpersonal forgiveness include conflict resolution skills, overall relationship satisfaction, and commitment to the relationship.

- Forgiveness is a family process that undergoes change over time. There are three types of forgiveness: direct, indirect, and conditional.

- There are a number of barriers and benefits to forgiveness. Ultimately, forgiveness aids in the longevity of family and intimate relationships by opening doors for emotional and psychological healing. There are also physical benefits to forgiveness.

Key Terms and Concepts

transactional, p. 68

Family Systems theory (FST), p. 68

General Systems theory (GST), p. 69

system, p. 69

family system, p. 69

subsystems, p. 69

family of origin, p. 69

boundary, p. 70

closed boundaries, p. 70

open boundaries, p. 70

balance/homeostasis, p. 71

Circumplex Model of Marital and
Family Systems, p. 71

rules, p. 72

Symbolic Interaction theory, p. 75

symbols, p. 76

meanings, p. 76

role, p. 76

role strain, p. 77

role conflict, p. 77

child language brokering, p. 78

message, p. 81

metamessage, p. 81

trouble talk, p. 81

communication, p. 83

verbal communication, p. 83

nonverbal communication, p. 84

emotional communication, p. 84

relational messages, p. 85

nonrelational messages, p. 85

decode, p. 85

functional communication, p. 86

nurturing communication, p. 86

relational culture, p. 86

confirming messages/responses,
p. 87

self-disclosure, p. 88

emotional safety, p. 88

family meetings, p. 88

active listening, p. 88

reflective listening, p. 89

reframe, p. 89

constructive conflict, p. 93

regulated couples, p. 93

destructive conflict, p. 94

scapegoating, p. 94

gunnysacking, p. 94

nonregulated couples, p. 94

stonewalling, p. 95

forgiveness, p. 95

direct forgiveness, p. 97

indirect forgiveness, p. 97

conditional forgiveness, p. 97

narcissistic entitlement, p. 98

self-righteousness, p. 98

Suggested Readings

Luskin, F. (2003). *Forgive for good: A proven prescription for health and happiness.* San Francisco: Harper San Francisco.

Moir, A., & Jessel, D. (1991). *Brain sex: The real difference between men and women.* New York: Doubleday.

Tannen, D. (1990). *You just don't understand: Women and men in conversation.* New York: Ballantine.

Multiple-Choice Questions

1. The _____ revolves around the notion that human behavior is a continuous dialogue where people watch the behaviors of people and then react to these behaviors.
   a. Family Systems theory
   b. Entity Systems theory
   c. Symbolic Interaction theory
   d. Family Entity theory

2. _____ is the psychological stress and tension that result when people undertake multiple roles that are incompatible. _____ occurs when there are competing demands from multiple roles.
   a. Role conflict/Role strain
   b. Role strain/Role conflict
   c. Conflict strain/Relational pressure
   d. Relational pressure/Conflict strain

3. Tannen's gender difference linguistic research shows that men attune to the _____ of helping and fixing problems.
   a. message
   b. metamessage
   c. necessity
   d. solution

4. Broadly stated, communication is _____ .
   a. talking
   b. listening
   c. the process of delivering information
   d. the process of making and sharing meanings

5. _____ translates into interactions that convey intimacy, caring, recognition, and validation of family members.
   a. Functional communication
   b. Emotional communication
   c. Nurturing communication
   d. Relational communication

6. Thought of as a two-way process, _____ is voluntarily sharing something personal or private with someone else.
   a. emotional safety
   b. self-disclosure
   c. communication
   d. functional communication

7. Known as a _____ , this type of couple uses a constructive conflict management style.
   a. conflict-minimizing couple
   b. volatile couple
   c. validating couple
   d. regulated couple

8. According to Gottman, which of the follwing is NOT one of the four ways in which nonregulated couples handle conflict?
   a. gunnysacking
   b. criticism
   c. stonewalling
   d. defensiveness

Answers: 1. c; 2. a; 3. b; 4. d; 5. c; 6. b; 7. c; 8. a

Gender in Today's Society

4

There's not really a typical [transgender] story. A lot of people will say that they have always felt they were trapped in the wrong body, that their body was wrong, or that their gender identity was at odds with what their genitals said they should be. [I was born a male in 1955] . . . when I look back, I think I remember that I wouldn't have minded being a girl . . . but in my early 20s it became clearer to me that I wanted to express my gender differently from how I was expressing it [as a male]. While I was expressing it in the "traditional" way at that time, I remember wishing I could express more femininity. . . . I knew all along I ideally wanted to express myself differently, but at the time there wasn't much [information] about being transgender.

I thought of myself as being in the middle [somewhere between "male" and "female"] for quite awhile, and that's where I identified. I think maybe that was just safer for me. Then I began to make tiny, tiny little changes over time . . . from crop pants, to earrings, to wearing a skirt in public. Being a woman is complicated and multidimensional, but I finally thought, "I can feel comfortable there." I wasn't sure I wanted to do the physical changes, but eventually I did. . . . I think I finally just threw in the towel on trying to be intergender, in-between . . . it just didn't feel OK. But now, being transgender is a hard place to be. People just don't get it. Gender is a social construction, and people respond to us differently . . . despite the fact that we're doing a gender and we present to others that this is our gender, and that we convey to others this is our identity . . . but what do they give us? It leaves you in this weird space because no one can make sense of you. Unless my body looks "this way," people won't get me. But I've told myself that I would do this for myself. . . . I'm experiencing gender my own way, on my own terms . . . internally and externally. I think I will always be "male" in some sense—and maybe that's OK. Given the choices [between male or female], I'm different and that's OK.

Can we as a culture learn to respond to other gender cues? I don't know, but we should give it a try. I don't want to keep waiting for society to change. . . . Whether a person is transgender or not, we're all just trying to find comfort being who we are.

Source: Author's files

Abraham Lincoln once posed the following question to a group of intellectuals: "If you call the tail of a donkey a leg, how many legs does the donkey then have?" The group replied, "Well, Sir, of course it would have five legs." Lincoln replied, "No, Gentlemen. Simply calling it a leg does not make it a leg." Could the same hold true in a discussion about gender? In other words, does the presence of certain anatomy make someone a "male" or the absence of certain anatomy make someone a "female"?

Scientific literature strives to understand the processes by which we "become" male or female, and how the varying roles associated with "male" and "female" evolve and help society achieve its goals. With this in mind, it is not surprising that the study of *gender* has typically been, and still is, interdisciplinary and multidisciplinary in its scope, comprising sociological, anthropological, political, and relational inquiry (Muehlenhard, Peterson, Karwoski, Bryan, & Lee, 2003). To more fully understand the intricacies involved in human relationships, this chapter examines the **nature** influences of gender (the influences of biology) and the **nurture** influences of gender (environmental influences).

It Matters: The Biology of Gender

When I had my children in the 1980s, the now routine prenatal ultrasound examinations that are used today to determine the age, sex, and health of the developing fetus were not commonly performed unless a problem arose during pregnancy. As each of my children inched his way into the world, intense anticipation filled my heart as I waited to discover the gender of my baby. When my husband and I were minutes away from the delivery of our fourth child—*a fourth son?*—my obstetrician quipped, "Boy, girl, what does it matter?"

SEX IS NOT GENDER

We begin our study of *gender* and *gendered behavior* here, because biology is the basis of all social and cultural influences that ultimately have impact on gender roles and gender identity—and subsequently our experiences in and with interpersonal relationships. There has been much debate over the years about which comes first: Do boys act "boyish" (active, aggressive) and do girls act "girlish" (cuddly, early to jabber) because of innate drives to do so, because of "boy" or "girl" inborn personality traits? Or does the presence or absence of a penis at birth carry with it certain parental and societal expectations and thus reinforcement of certain socially created, expected—maybe even anticipated—gender behaviors?

Sex and *gender* are two distinct terms, although in our culture the words are used interchangeably. **Sex** refers to biological traits that distinguish males from females, such as the internal and external reproductive anatomy, chromosomes, hormones, and other physiological characteristics. Sex, then, describes *biologically* determined characteristics. Without complicated surgical procedures and artificial hormone supplements, sex cannot be changed. Gender is more than a social label ascribed to us on our birth certificates. In essence, **gender** can be thought of as the sum of our developmental and lifecourse experiences and it encompasses a number of characteristics, which we will explore at length throughout this chapter.

WHICH infants are male? Which infants are female? From the moment of birth, social messages shape "gender."

Biological Sex: The Foundation of Gender A person's sex is determined the moment the sperm and ovum fuse together in the process of fertilization. The developing person receives either two X sex chromosomes (one from the mother and one from the father) or one X and one Y sex chromosome (an X from the mother and a Y from the father). The **XX sex chromosome** combination results in a "female" genetic blueprint for the developing embryo, and the **XY sex chromosome** combination results in a "male" genetic blueprint. It is the coupling of the XX or XY chromosomes, then, that determines a fetus's sex characteristics (Ovaries or testes? Clitoris or penis?), both internally and externally.

Male and Female When a Y sex chromosome is present, tissue begins to develop into the testes in the male. The testes then begin to produce **androgens** (testosterone), the masculinizing **sex hormones**. These increasing levels of testosterone then direct the development of the *internal male reproductive organs*, which include the seminal vesicles, vas deferens, and testes. Sometime during the third month of pregnancy, the *external male genitalia*, the penis and scrotum, form under the direction of the androgens, primarily **testosterone**.

It was once believed that, without hormonal influences, the overall pattern for prenatal sexual development is female (Pinel, 1997). Today, we know that when a Y sex chromosome is not present and thus testosterone is not produced, the tissue continues to develop into the *internal female reproductive organs*, which include the ovaries, uterus, Fallopian tubes, and vagina. So, it is not the *presence* of **estrogen**, the feminizing sex hormone, that produces the biological sex, female—it is the *absence of the testosterone* that ultimately results in the creation of a female. By around the third month of prenatal development, the *external female genitalia* begin to develop. As you can see from Figure 4.1 (page 108), females and males are more biologically similar than many people think.

For the most part, nature works the way it is programmed to, but sometimes children are born with genitalia that are not distinguishable as male or female. When a child's genitalia are ambiguous or indistinguishable, a child is termed *intersexed*.

SOMEWHERE BETWEEN "MALE" AND "FEMALE"

At the moment of birth we are branded, or labeled, to be *one* genetic sex *or* the other; we are then raised in the gender brand of our assigned sex. For 98 percent of babies born in the United States, this either/or sex assignment accurately describes their biologic sex (Evans, 2004); that is to say, the outward appearance (the genitals) match up with the sex-linked brand of "male" or "female." But what happens when the genetic sex of a child is just not that clear? Is that child "male" or "female"—or somewhere between? And, just as importantly, does it matter?

Intersex An **intersex** person, or an **intersexual**, is someone who is anatomically somewhere along the continuum between male and female. While there are different types of intersex conditions, the root is always genetic. These genetic anomalies or irregularities can occur due to either varying degrees of a person acquiring both male and female anatomical structures and/or sex chromosomes, or because of ambiguous (not easily distinguishable as male or female) genitalia. It is currently estimated that as many as 2 percent of the total U.S. population is affected by an intersex condition (Evans, 2004). The average number of intersex births in the United States is approximately 2 births out of every 100 live births.

There are a number of other genetic anomalies or irregularities that can occur, resulting in other types of intersex conditions. Although a detailed discussion of these syndromes is beyond the scope of our discussion here, a basic understanding of them is necessary because they are not necessarily rare occurrences: You, your intimate partner, or your child may be affected by one of these types of intersex syndromes:

- **Androgen Insensitivity Syndrome (AIS)** affects an estimated 1 in 100 live births (Evans, 2004). The disorder is characterized by an abnormality of the X sex chromosomes that

FIGURE 4.1   Sex Differentiation of Males and Females

Males and females are more biologically similar than most people think. Notice the similarity of the undifferentiated tissue.

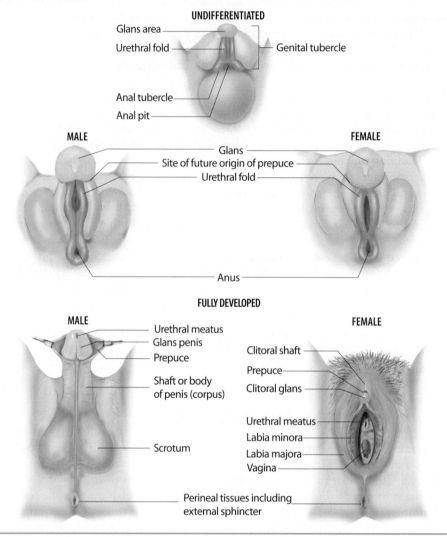

results in prenatal development that continues as if no androgen at all were present. A baby affected with AIS is born with external genitalia that appear to be female—and in all likelihood will be raised as a "girl."

■ **Turner's Syndrome** occurs when one of the two X sex chromosomes is completely or partially absent. This disorder affects females only. Current estimates show this condition affecting about 1 in 2,000 to 2,500 live births (Turner's Syndrome Society, 2009). Because of the "dropped" chromosome, the developing fetus does not develop ovaries; this renders her infertile and incapable of producing estrogen.

■ **Klinefelter's Syndrome** is a genetic disorder in which an extra X chromosome is present, resulting in an XXY chromosomal pattern. This disorder is considered to be one of the most common of all genetic abnormalities and affects about 1 in 500 live male births (National Institutes of Health, 2005). The internal reproductive organs and external genitalia develop normally, but a male affected by Klinefelter's Syndrome will have smaller-than-normal testes and will not produce sperm.

Although certainly intersex conditions are not medical emergencies that threaten a child's overall health or well-being, often the intersex newborn is seen as a "social emergency." This

Should Parents Be Able to Select the Sex of Their Child?

Own It!

Thanks to the advances in technology, companies such as MicroSort are becoming increasingly popular among hoping-to-become-pregnant couples. Used for the purposes of genetic disease prevention (such as in hemophilia or forms of muscular dystrophy) and family balancing (referred to as "gender variety" in offspring), sperm-sorting technology allows couples today the option of selecting the sex of their children. While there are currently no laws in the United States that ban sex selection, potential concerns arise, such as sex ratio imbalances in the future, which already exist in China and India.

Take a moment to jot down your opinions on the following questions:

1. Does sex selection create a climate where sex discrimination can flourish?

2. If as a society we begin to choose embryos based on particular, desirable traits, will society make the move to discard embryos based on less desirable traits—will society begin to push for "designer" babies?

3. Would you choose sex selection? Would your parents?

implies that since intersexual children do not fit neatly into either the "male" or "female" brand, there is the general social perception that something must be done to "fix" them.

Medical Management: One Body, One Gender As commonly as some of the chromosomal irregularities and prenatal hormonal imbalances occur, why have the majority of cultures the world over settled into an *either-or* categorization of male/female? What do we—a two-sex-categories-only culture—"do" when a child is born with ambiguous, indistinguishable genitalia, when a child is born intersex, or when a child is born with other chromosomal anomalies that make it difficult to determine the "sex"?

The typical medical treatment of intersex infants and infants with ambiguous genitalia throughout the twentieth century was to "match" their socialization to the outward signs of "gender." If surgery was required to "fix" genitalia to appear more "normalized," then surgery was performed very early on in the infant's life; supplemental hormones later in child and adolescent development sustained the surgically assigned "gender." But since the formation in 1993 of the Intersex Society of North America and the testimony of adults who underwent sex reassignment surgery since the 1970s, earlier medical practices are now being criticized. Today, the medical field understands more and more the complexities and intricacies in the formation of gender, and understands that it takes more than external genitalia alone to constitute gender. An extensive review of the literature, however (see, for example, Diamond & Sigmundson, 1997; Dreger, 1998; Fausto-Sterling, 2000; Hendren & Atala, 1995; and Kipilis & Diamond, 1998), reveals that despite this knowledge base about the development of gender, the standard of care is slow to change. Current medical protocol in the medical management of ambiguous genitalia or intersexed children is that

- Genetic females [XX sex chromosomes] should always be raised as females, preserving reproductive potential, regardless of how severely the patients are [masculinized].

- In genetic males, the gender of assignment is based on the infant's anatomy, predominantly the size of the [penis]. (Donahue, 1991, p. 527)

As Alley, the voice in the opening vignette of this chapter, observes, "If we [as a culture] truly acknowledged the complexity of [sex], we would understand that biologically there are more than just the two choices society offers. While most of us acknowledge racial, ethnic, religious, and other types of diversity, [our culture] is blind to sex diversity because we continue to live in this either-or world."

Earlier I posed the question: By labeling someone as "male" or "female," does this make him or her so? As you have seen in our study of gender so far, the presence or absence of a penis does necessarily make someone a boy or a girl. Gender is much more complex than that, because it is an intricate interaction of *both* biology (physiological characteristics) and environment. In the case of gender, it's not nature *or* nurture—it's nature *and* nurture. Indeed, gender is as much a social and cultural process as it is a biological process.

It Matters: The Culture of Gender

The concept of gender is significantly more complex than biological attributes alone. Those who study social interactions have, in a number of different ways, defined gender as

- "the socially constructed roles associated with each sex" (Rosenblum & Travis, 2003, p. 23).
- "what culture makes out of the 'raw material' of biological sex" (Crawford & Unger, 2000, p. 21).
- "the culturally and historically specific acting out of 'masculinity' and 'femininity'" (Rosenblum & Travis, 2003, p. 23).

From these varying definitions one central theme emerges. While "sex" refers to the biological attributes of male and female, "gender" refers to the *socially* or *culturally* determined traits, characteristics, and expectations of male and female—it is a social conceptualization, culturally specific, experienced differently in different cultures.

GENDER ROLES: THE MAKING OF MALE OR FEMALE, MASCULINE OR FEMININE

Gender is multidimensional and it is *created* by people's culture. It includes the following characteristics:

- **Gender role** refers to behaviors, attitudes, beliefs, and values that culture deems appropriate for males and females.
- **Gender identity** refers to how a person accepts the culture's prescribed gender roles; how an individual adapts the expected gender to role to his or her identity. Gender identity is subjective to the individual.
- **Gender presentation** refers to how an individual presents his or her gender identity through personality, habits, and behaviors.
- **Gender stereotypes** encompass the cultural beliefs about "what" gender roles are and "how" these roles should be enacted. It tends to reflect culture's belief about the ways in which men and women behave.
- **Gender attribution** is the process by which we encounter someone and reach an opinion of what his or her gender is.

Each individual society orchestrates, directs, and dictates its expected gender roles, gender presentations, and gender stereotypes of male and female. From these, gender identity is shaped. In essence, we *learn* what it means to be male and female, masculine and feminine, from cultural cues. Societal roles are therefore *gendered*, meaning that differences are assigned to each biological sex.

From the moment of birth (or a prenatal diagnostic test that reveals the sex of a baby), we are repeatedly exposed to culturally driven beliefs, ideas, perceptions, and opinions about the differences between genders. Because this continuous flow of cultural information informs us of what is "appropriate" behavior and what is "inappropriate" behavior, we eventually internalize (make part of ourselves) these prototypes for behavior and adopt them: We are *taught* from our culture how to be "male" or "female" (Bem, 1981; Bussey & Bandura, 1999). We then use these models to organize and categorize all social information, including relationships. **Gender socialization** refers to the specific messages and practices we receive from our culture concerning the nature of being a male or a female, of being feminine or masculine.

Societal expectations establish criteria to which its members are to adhere to ensure the longevity and the continuation of that society. From industrialized societies such as the United States, Canada, and Europe, to the most remote tribal cultures such as the Honeymen, the Shenko people in western Ethiopia or the Hamar and Karo, southern Ethiopian tribes, these societal expectations are broken down along gender lines. *Gender roles* are the cultural norms for male and female attitudes and behaviors;

SOCIETAL roles are assigned to each biological sex. These culturally specific roles direct the behaviors and expressions of males and females.

these roles delineate what is considered to be appropriate for people of a particular sex.

These gender roles, then, are the explicitly expressed and implicitly implied behaviors, feelings, attributes, and traits that society expects of the male or the female. Women are typically thought to possess more nurturing tendencies than males. Because of this gender-ascribed *characteristic*, the gender *role* of childcare responsibilities typically fall to the women. Similarly, because men are thought to be stronger and possess more protective capabilities than women, the primary gender role of responsibility and provision for the family unit typically falls to the male. Essentially, gender roles are referred to as either masculine or feminine. When we refer to *masculinity* or *femininity*, we are talking about the configurations of how we practice our biological sex.

MASCULINITY: "DOING" MALE

The term *male* can be used to describe the genetic sex of any species, but **masculinity** is a socially/culturally constructed set of beliefs, values, and opinions that shape manly character, or manliness—it prescribes and defines how men should act and feel. Every culture also has an ideal, dominant standard of masculinity to which men are to aim. This is referred to as **hegemonic** (pronounced heh-jeh-MON-íck) **masculinity** (Connell, 1987). Although hegemonic masculinity isn't necessarily the most prevalent form of manliness found in a culture, it is the most socially endorsed and desired; this standard changes over time. For example, in the 1950s and 1960s, the normative, desired way of being masculine was represented in movies by the actors John Wayne and Elvis Presley. Today in the United States, images of hegemonic masculinity abound in popular culture media representations, such as *American Gladiators* and *WWE Wrestling*. These presentations of masculinity are consistent with an earlier landmark study that described seven areas of masculinity that are commonly found in most Western societies (Saltzman Chafetz, 1975). This study found that "ideal" men are physically strong, sexually aggressive and experienced, and dominating leaders.

Throughout their lives, boys learn and acquire these masculine characteristics and traits through language, the toys they play with, certain behaviors that are rewarded or discouraged, and occupations they are encouraged to pursue (Jandt & Hundley, 2007). For example, by age 3, boys engage in more competitive games, wrestling, and play fighting than girls do, and fathers encourage these types of behaviors in their sons (Geary, 1998; Jhally, 2002). We'll look at the various gender socializing agents at length later in this chapter.

Black Masculinities Of course, one problem with this characterization of masculinity is that it most often describes *white*, middle-class conceptions of what being a "man" is supposed to act or look like. Most of the existing empirical science tends to overlook men of color and their construction of masculinity (Wester, Vogel, Wei, & McLain, 2006).

Euro American masculinity stresses *individual* success and economic achievement, often excluding collaborative or group efforts (Wester and others, 2006). Conversely, within traditional black cultures, cooperation and the promotion of the collective good are promoted, as is *group* success. Because of these conflicting masculine gender expectations, many men of color in the United States have had to adopt *both* the Euro American ideal of "success through competition" while at the same time expressing their black cultural beliefs that highlight support, community, and the importance of interpersonal relationships (Wester and others, 2006). This blending of two cultural masculinities among African Americans and Afro-Caribbeans has resulted in a new, exaggerated version of masculinity for them. Referred to as **cool pose**, black masculinity "presents a powerful face to the world" while at the same time entails the expected cooperative behaviors of black culture (see Canales, 2000; Wester and others, 2006).

Intercultural Masculinities Because of the global nature of our society today, researchers have recently begun to argue that there is an increasing need to recognize the integral role of culture in shaping masculinity beliefs (Yim & Mahalingam, 2006). Prior studies, for example, have identified features of masculinity across cultures; these include sexual prowess, the ability to protect women and one's family, and the ability to provide for family (Gilmore, 1990; Malhotra, 2002). Societies that emphasize hegemonic masculinity (such as the United States, Australia, Japan, and Latin American cultures) are characterized by high degrees of male dominance, independence, aggression, achievement, and endurance (Williams & Best, 1990). These types of cultures are referred to as *masculine cultures.*

There is perhaps no better example of masculine cultures than Latin America, such as Mexico, Central and South America, Puerto Rico, and the Caribbean, which are collectivist societies. Embedded within these cultures are deeply held traditions that influence gender behaviors and attitudes. One such attitude is that of machismo.

Machismo refers to the idea that men are superior to women, and that men are socially and physically dominating. The adjective *machista* is a derivative of the word *machismo*, and it means "sexist." Machismo is not necessarily an act per se, but it is more of an attitude that can range from a sense of sexual power, to masculinity, to male superiority. This machismo cultural attitude translates to many areas of interpersonal relationships, including choosing whom to date and to marry, and the role of power to decide birth control and/or contraceptive behaviors during sex (Afable-Munsuz & Brindis, 2006; Villarruel & Rodriguez, 2003). In just a bit we'll look at the opposite of machismo in Latin America, the female culture of *marianismo.*

Another example of a masculine culture is that of India. In India, honor, or *izzat,* is the dominant masculinity theme that governs the lives of men (Gilmore, 1990). Within this culture, a man's primary duty is to be a defender of women's purity, his family, and his family's position in the society. Thus, much value is placed on a man's ability to protect (Gilmore, 1990). Asian

MACHISMO refers to Latino cultures' belief that men have sexual power and are strong and virile. This attitude directs many relationship patterns and behaviors among Latino men and women.

American men tend to adopt gender roles such as a strong obligation to family, the authority figure in the home, and restricting displays of emotions (Sue & Sue, 2003).

Psychologists and other social scientists have been interested in whether there are negative outcomes associated with masculine gender roles. They are particularly interested in determining if masculinity is associated with additional stressors.

Pressures Associated with Masculinity Since the 1970s, women have broadened and overlapped their roles with men's roles. For example, women today are free to enter into occupations traditionally held by males, such as firefighting, architecture, and engineering. Indeed, women even serve as military personnel on the front lines in the Iraq and Afghanistan wars today. But while women's gender roles have expanded, men have not been given the same freedom to take on roles that have traditionally been held by women, such as childcare providers and maternity nurses (McCreary, Newcomb, & Sadava, 1998). Men have also been prohibited by cultures to adopt certain characteristics associated with femininity, such as being emotionally expressive (Yim & Mahalingam, 2006). This rigid confinement to traditional gender roles, sometimes referred to as "the hazards of being male," is associated with increased pressures and stress (Goldberg, 1976).

Masculine Gender Role Stress theory (MGRS) maintains that there are stressors that may result from a man's fear that he is not measuring up to or meeting societal expectations for masculinity (Eisler & Skidmore, 1987). Using a survey that they administered to male and female college students, these researchers wanted to measure the amounts of stress men experienced in certain areas, such as being in situations that required emotional expression and feeling physically inadequate. As the investigators expected, men were significantly more likely than their female counterparts to describe these situations as stressful and pressure inducing (Eisler & Skidmore, 1987). Follow-up research also found in a study of 220 college students that men scored higher than women on MGRS measures such as anxiety, depression, and hostility (McCreary and others, 1998).

> All of these findings speak to the importance of realizing that today, masculine gender role socialization is not always compatible with situational demands. In other words, today's concept of "masculinity" often conflicts with nontraditional behaviors, such as striking a balance between the demands of work with the responsibilities of parenting or being a loving, supportive spouse (Wester and others, 2006).

FEMININITY: "DOING" FEMALE

Distinct from the biological sex classification of *female*, **femininity** refers to qualities, behaviors, and attitudes that are deemed by a particular culture to be ideally appropriate for girls and women. Femininity, or womanliness, is most often associated with nurturing, life-giving attributes such as kindness, gentleness, and patience.

For the past decade, social and family scientists have attempted to design survey instruments to measure the degree to which study participants agree with or adhere to "traditional" femininity values, ideas, and opinions—how women *should* act and feel. The Femininity Ideology Scale (FIS) survey contains 45 statements to which research participants indicate their agreement or disagreement (original unpublished work, Philpot; Lehman, 2000). With statements such as, "Women should have soft voices," "A woman's natural role should be the caregiver of the family," and "Women discuss their feelings with others," recent researchers attempted to identify five categories of femininity attributes: (1) Images and Activities, (2) Dependency/Deference, (3) Purity, (4) Caretaking, and (5) Emotionality (Levant, Richmond, Cook, House, & Aupont, 2007).

Overall, the participants did not agree with the traditional beliefs and attitudes associated with the five areas of femininity under investigation, and the women indicated they held less traditional views than the men did. However, both women and men strongly endorsed *Caretaking* as a feminine characteristic or attribute (such as women should try to soothe hurt feelings of others; women should be gentle; women should be the caretaker of the family;

women are responsible for making/organizing family plans) (Levant and others, 2007). Caretaking was followed by *Purity, Emotionality, Images and Activities,* and *Dependency/Deference.*

Intercultural Femininities Just as with men, there are racial and ethnic differences in how cultures define and socialize "femininity." In Hispanic cultures, for example, the female equivalent of machismo is *marianismo,* the essence of Latina femininity. Based on the Catholic religion's belief that Mary gave birth to Jesus and is thus the mother of God, **marianismo** teaches that women are semi-divine and are morally superior to and spiritually stronger than men (Faulkner, 2003; Noland, 2006). The Latino male thus wants a "Maria" (Mary) for a wife—a wife who is observant of religious laws and who is emotional, kind, instinctive, passive, compliant, and unassertive.

In white, westernized cultures, gender roles are largely delineated by divisions of labor based on a person's biological sex—there are separate spheres of labor for men (protection and provision) and women (nurturing and caregiving). However, for more than 200 years, black women functioned in similar capacities to their male counterparts (Buckley & Carter, 2005). That is to say, as a necessary means of survival, black women traditionally had to adopt both masculine and feminine gender roles, such as hard work, self-reliance, resistance, and perseverance (masculine) and care and nurturance (feminine) (Collins, 2004). Today, black men and women still tend to adopt more flexible and less restrictive gender roles. For example, one study found that black adolescent girls today take on both masculine and feminine gender roles in that they assume roles of worker, independence, and assertiveness, as well as that of mother and caregiver (Buckley & Carter, 2005). The researchers observed that adolescent girls today continue to adopt these more traditional black gender roles, because the roles—and the characteristics associated with them—are consistent with their cultural histories and teachings (Buckley & Carter, 2005).

In many Far East Asian countries (such as China, Japan, Korea, Taiwan, Thailand, and Vietnam), Confucian philosophy dominates, influences, and shapes societal attitudes regarding relationships and gender (Oldstone-Moore, 2002). Confucius believed that the society—which is *the family*—is based on unequal, hierarchical relationships, and that each individual has his or her responsibility to carry out certain functions within these relationships (Phuong-Mai, Terlouw, & Pilot, 2005). To be masculine is to be an active, dominant provider who continues his ancestors' traditions and behaves appropriately according to cultural expectations. Conversely, to be feminine is to be a passive, subordinate, submissive, obedient, nurturing caretaker who models these behaviors to her subordinate, submissive children (Bi & D'agostino, 2004). In Chinese culture, the *yin-yang* comparison is used to describe the hierarchical nature gender (see Figure 4.2)—one is different from the other, but one gender cannot live without the other.

Examining the role of gender in a study of marital, family, and intimate relationships is important because gender carries with it socially sanctioned, approved, and endorsed prescribed *life roles* (housewife or provider?), *occupations* (flight attendant or pilot?), *relationships* (heterosexual marriage or same-sex union?), and *abilities* (verbal or mathematical?) (Bussey & Bandura, 1999; Howard & Hollander, 1997). It is these commonly held beliefs that lead to *gender stereotypes,* or long-held assumptions or labels about male and female capabilities and limitations. Consider for a moment the arrogant antagonist "Dr. Gregory House" from the hit television show, *House.* If you were ever to see him in a different television or movie role, such as playing a tender, loving, compassionate, reverent pastor or priest, would it be difficult for you to see him portraying such a role? If so, it is because you have typecast him, or assigned to him a stereotype of what role he can portray. When we or society pigeonhole gender characteristics and gender roles, it is very difficult to move toward change.

Being a Girl or a Woman: Does It Mean a Lower Status? In her work that examined the difficulty for societies to make the transition away from traditional

FIGURE 4.2 Yin-Yang of Relationships

For many Asian Americans, the Chinese concept of Yin and Yang is an important concept. When referring to gender, yin/yang means that men and women are interconnected, yet independent, complete opposites within a greater whole.

Yin
moon, female, wife, passive, nature, shady

Yang
sun, male, husband, active, human, sunny

Source: Rosenlee (2006).

The FAMILY Table

Gender Role Conflict in Family Life

Today, more and more couples struggle to meet the demands of their multiple roles, such as the roles of husband and wife, parent, employee, and caregiver of an aging parent. Role conflict results when people undertake multiple roles that are incompatible. Understanding and discussing role conflict in contemporary families is important because high levels can result in harmful outcomes for the individual (anxiety, depression, poor physical health, and dissatisfaction with life), for family relationships (increased levels of conflict, poor communication, emotional separation, and divorce), and for the workplace (increased absenteeism). Because much of a person's family and employment roles and behavioral expectations are in large part culturally determined and fall along gender lines, it is important for family members to communicate about what is expected of them.

In family living, there are three primary types of role conflict:

- **Time-based.** The pressures from multiple roles demand and compete for the person's time; for example, a meeting at work that runs late makes it difficult to pick up a child from daycare or make it to the child's ball game or music recital.
- **Strain-based.** Role strain in one area of life interferes with the performance of role expectations in another area of life. For instance, a husband who has a critically ill wife may not be able to meet the expectations of his workload in the workplace.
- **Behavior-based.** This type of role conflict stems from competing roles. For example, a police officer is expected to be unemotional on the job, but if he or she displays these same behaviors at home, conflict will likely ensue.

TALK ABOUT IT

1. How does gender function as a dimension of family living?
2. What can be done in families to reduce the tension experienced as a result of gender-divided household tasks and chores?
3. In family living, does gender matter?

Source: Greenhaus & Beutell (1985).

gender stereotypes and gender roles, gender activist Joyce Banda (2004) concurs with the gender researchers just cited that throughout the world, life opportunities are gender-based. She notes specifically, "Nearly every society throughout history has traditionally ascribed a lower status for women, and therefore, ascribed to control the lives of women in society" (p. 1).

The status of women in Afghanistan during the rule of the Taliban provides an example that substantiates Banda's perspective. The Taliban was a political and military movement that ruled Afghanistan for a five-year period from about 1996 to 2001. The fundamentalist Islamist sect sharply restricted the daily lives of women, including prohibiting them from working and receiving medical care, a complete ban on education for females of any age, and the requirement that women wear a long veil that fully covered their faces and bodies. So restricted were the lives of women that former President Bill Clinton called Afghanistan "perhaps the most difficult place in the world for women."

Banda's work concludes with comments about the ongoing, tremendous gender-related changes that are taking place across the world, and notes that in order for the advancement and progress to continue in countries where women are undervalued, "it is necessary to incorporate the interests of *both* men and women effectively within society's vision for progress" (p. 2).

This discussion leads us to another concept about masculinity and femininity that we haven't yet looked at: *gender polarization*.

GENDER POLARIZATION: COMPLEMENTARY OPPOSITES— OR INEQUALITY?

Rather than emphasize the *similarities* between men and women, cultural viewpoints almost always emphasize the *differences* between men and women. This "opposite" model is referred to as **gender polarization**, or **bipolar gender** (Bem, 1993).

Many problems crop up when cultures polarize gender. For instance, when we emphasize masculine/feminine differences and categorize them as total opposites, if a person deviates from the "typical" cultural characteristics, she or he is then seen as belonging to the *other* category (Bem, 1993). For example, if a man freely expresses his emotions, he is not only seen as less masculine but also more feminine. Similarly, if a woman shows aggression, she is seen as less feminine and more masculine.

Gender polarization is also problematic because there are individuals who are somewhere "in between" on this continuum, as Alley's story in the opening vignette showed us. This view also poses difficulties because traditional views of masculinity and femininity as opposites can cause a number of different types of *inequality* or *gaps*, such as inequality in societal status (such as what happened when the Taliban was in rule), wages, education, employment opportunities and advancement, and social and intimate relationships.

Society's division of gender into either-or categories leads to **gender inequality,** which can be obvious or hidden disparities or discrimination in opportunities or advancements among individuals; these differences are based solely on a person's gender. Inequality between the sexes is often referred to as *sexism.* **Sexism** is defined in a number of different ways:

- A prejudice or discrimination based on biological sex
- A belief system that assumes a hierarchy of human worth based on the social construction of the differences between the sexes
- An ideology of male supremacy, superiority, authority, and beliefs/behaviors that support and sustain this ideology

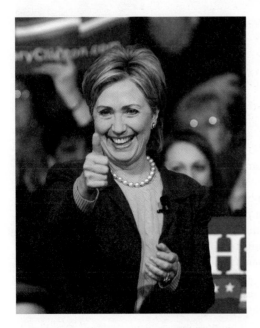

REFERRING to the presidency as the highest glass ceiling in America, presidential candidate Hillary Clinton, upon conceding the Democratic nomination to Barack Obama, said, "Although we weren't able to shatter the highest, hardest glass ceiling this time, it's got about 18 million cracks [votes] in it. And the light is shining through those cracks [for women], filling us all with the hope that the path will be a little easier next time."

Sexism, then, supports the belief that people of one sex (typically, males) are inherently superior to people of the other sex. These attitudes and beliefs lead to the unfair treatment or discrimination of the "weaker" sex (typically, females)—the cultural dominance of one sex over the other leads to disadvantages and/or unequal opportunities. In short, people are treated differently because of their biological sex. For example, during the 2008 U.S. presidential election, vice presidential candidate, Sarah Palin, was photographed through her legs, from behind. Would this same type of photo have been taken of her rival, Joe Biden? If so, would the photos have elicited the same response? Further, her wardrobe and the cost of her wardrobe were discussed extensively by the media. However, the media failed to mention the cost of the male candidates' tailor-made suits. This type of treatment is referred to as **sexist,** because the V.P. candidate was treated differently throughout the presidential campaign because of her sex.

These types of inequalities and differences in how a person is treated can be manifest in a number of dimensions in a person's daily life, but today in the United States it is still seen particularly in the work and education arenas.

The Glass Ceiling The term **glass ceiling** refers to situations where the advancement of a qualified person within the hierarchy of an organization is stopped at a lower level due to of some form of discrimination, such as sexism (Hesse-Biber & Carter, 2005). *Glass ceiling* is often associated with women and their ability to advance in their careers. The term *ceiling* is used because it represents her block to upward advance-

TABLE 4.1 Gender Differences in Annual Median Income, by Education

	High School	Some College	Bachelor's Degree	Master's Degree	PhD	Professional Degree
Male	$31,237	$39,125	$57,714	$67,123	$78,324	$78,582
Female	$20,861	$26,937	$39,263	$45,730	$54,666	$52,150

Sources: U.S. Census Bureau (2006a, 2009).

ment; the term *glass* is used because limitations to advancement aren't apparent—often, these limitations are "unofficial, unspoken policy" (Hesse-Biber & Carter, 2005).

A good example of the effects of the glass ceiling was played out in front of American voters in the 2008 presidential election. Many sociologists, political authorities, and critics believed that Hillary Clinton, the presidential nominee for the Democratic party, faced a glass ceiling throughout her campaign. Not only did they believe that she was a victim of sexism (such as, she couldn't be "aggressive" in political debates because she would appear to be "unfeminine" and "demeaning") but they also believed that there are still invisible gender barriers in the United States that impeded her success. Indeed, while campaigning Clinton herself noted numerous times that the presidency is the "highest glass ceiling in America." Many sociologists and social scientists believed that there are still prevailing gender attitudes in the United States that aren't compatible with having a woman as president of the United States.

The Wage Gap The United States also still struggles with equality in the workforce, particularly in wages. This inequality in wages is referred to as the **wage gap.** On average, a woman today earns about 77 cents for every dollar a man earns (U.S. Department of Labor, 2008). Even the highest levels of education don't necessarily mean a higher income for women, as the data in Table 4.1 show us. As you can see, whether a woman has a high school diploma, a college bachelor's degree, a master's degree or doctorate, or a professional degree, she still earns less than a man. There are also racial differences in women's wages, as Figure 4.3 illustrates.

The reasons for this discrepancy in income are difficult to determine. For instance, is it because girls are socialized to nurture others, and because of this they choose "helping" careers (such as teaching or nursing), which typically pay less than professional careers (such as

FIGURE 4.3A Median U.S. Income by Gender, 1953–2000

FIGURE 4.3B U.S. Income by Race, 2005

In 2005, median income levels were highest among Asian and white males and lowest among females of all races.

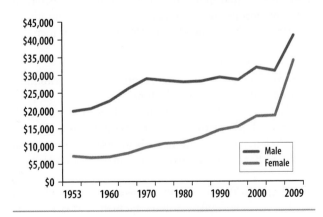

Source: ACS 2009 (1 Year Estimates).

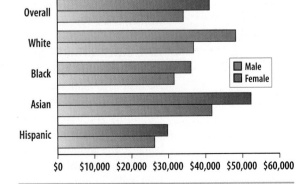

Source: ACS 2009 (1 Year Estimates).

engineering or architecture)? Or is it because throughout elementary school and high school they came to believe that they didn't have the abilities to succeed in professional careers?

The Confidence Gap Linda J. Sax, an associate professor of education at the University of California at Los Angeles, believes it's time to get a better understanding of the gender issues facing men and women on college campuses (Sax, 2008). Using data gathered from millions of college students nationwide in a freshman survey, Sax found that men and women have different confidence levels in their academic abilities. In every area other than writing ability, freshmen women have less confidence than men do. These are very interesting findings, because women's self-ratings aren't consistent with data that showed that they actually do better academically than men do. So, it's not that men *perform* better than women do in these areas—they don't. Instead, it's that men have *much more confidence* in their academic abilities than women do. Sax (2008) refers to this new phenomenon as the **confidence gap**. Of particular concern to Sax is that women have difficulty believing that they are "as competent as their performance would suggest." Unfortunately, the confidence gap appears to grow and widen throughout college.

These findings are so new that no other social or family scientists have had an opportunity to further research the confidence gap: How does it form? What reinforces it? Why is it so prevailing? Do lower confidence levels influence the college majors/career choices of women? Much more research needs to be conducted in this area so that we have a more complete understanding of those issues that may create and perpetuate the glass ceiling and the wage gap.

GENDER SCHEMAS: PERCEIVING MALE OR FEMALE, MASCULINE OR FEMININE

The ways we internalize and incorporate specific gendered behaviors and expectations are called **gender schemas**. A *schema* is a mental representation or a set of specific symbols or images we hold about something. These cognitive frameworks organize and guide a person's perceptions; in this case, the schemas guide an individual's perception about what it is to be male or female, masculine or feminine (Bem, 1981). These self-schemas allow us to organize and categorize social information and to "organize the way individuals think about themselves in social interactions" (Belansky & Boggiano, 1994, p. 647).

Perhaps some of the earliest research designed to distinguish between masculine and feminine characteristics and traits is attributed to Gough's Masculinity–Femininity Scale (1957). Sandra Bem's (1974) later work—considered to be one of the primary works concerning gender schemas—was based on her assumption that there appear to be characteristics that are more socially desirable for men than for women, and characteristics that are more socially desirable for women than for men. Because of the implied cultural mandate to adhere to specifically assigned gender roles, Bem suggests that individuals will suppress "any behavior that might be considered undesirable or inappropriate for his sex" (p. 155). She notes that a person who has "internalized"—made a mental schema of—"desirable" behavior for men and women is sex-typed.

Instrumental and Expressive Schemas **Instrumental schemas** are associated with masculinity focus on task-oriented behaviors and "getting the job done" (Bem, 1974, p. 156). According to Bem, masculine behavior is thought to be task-oriented and includes traits such as ambition, competitiveness, and acting as a leader. **Expressive schemas** are associated with femininity and have an interpersonal or relational orientation. As Bem notes, those with an expressive schema are concerned for the welfare of other people, and include such traits as being gentle and loyal.

The lists in Table 4.2 drive home an important point. Are any changes noted since 1974 in how males in our culture are socialized to become "male"? Still today, men in Western civilization are socialized—taught—to be independent, strong, assertive, aggressive, responsible

TABLE 4.2 Instrumental and Expressive Schemas

Instrumental Schemas (Masculinity)	Expressive Schemas (Femininity)
Acting as a leader	Affection
Aggression	Compassion
Ambition	Gentleness
Assertiveness	Loyalty
Competitiveness	Understanding
Dominance	Sensitivity
Independence	Sympathy
Self-reliance	
Willingness to take risks	

Source: Bem (1974).

leaders. Take a look at the list of expressive traits thought to characterize women. Are any changes noted in how females in our culture are socialized to be "female"? Despite the efforts of the feminist movement in the twentieth century, it appears that women are still being socialized to be relationally oriented—to be affectionate, nurturing, empathic, sensitive, compassionate, and dependent.

The experience of maleness or femaleness is socially and culturally driven. What happens in the instances where a person displays *both* male and female traits?

Androgynous When referring to the concept of **androgyny**, we mean that something either has no gender value assigned to it, or that a person possesses traits, behaviors, or characteristics that are typically associated with the opposite gender. It occurs as a result of the two primary concepts associated with gender: the biological influences of gender and the social influences of gender.

There are three types of androgyny. The first is *physiological androgyny*, which deals with physical or biological traits, such as occurs in the cases of intersex individuals. The second is *behavioral androgyny*, which involves the blending of masculine and feminine traits; an androgynous person might display traits and behaviors that are typically associated with male and female—not one or the other. The third type of androgyny is *psychological androgyny*, which involves the individual's gender identity.

Some cultures are **androgynous**. This means that there are no rigid gender roles guiding men and women's behaviors. The Hijras of India, Pakistan, and Bangladesh are often described, for example, as "neither male nor female." In her book, *Neither Man nor Woman*, Serena Nanda (1990) discusses the fascinating lives of the Hijras. Raised as boys, the ritualistic removal of the genitals takes place between the ages of 10 and 15. The Hijras have a separate social category—they are not male, they are not female. The social role of Hijras is to dress and act as women and perform at weddings and religious ceremonies after the birth of a boy. Hijras are feared and revered in Hindu society, as they are thought to ward off both impotence and infertility.

About her friendship with a Hijra, British photographer Dayanita Singh writes, "When I once asked her about her [anatomy], she told me, 'You really don't understand. I am the third sex, not a man trying

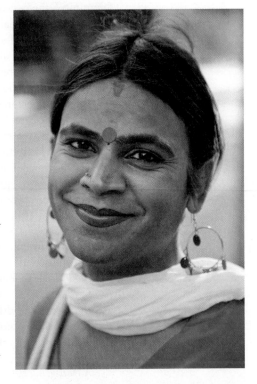

THE Hijras in India, Pakistan, and Bangladesh are often described as "neither male nor female." Feared and revered in Hindu society, Hijras perform rituals for religious ceremonies.

to be a woman. It is your society's problem that you only recognize two sexes'" (2001). So commonplace are Hijras in Indian society that in 2005, Indian passport application forms were updated and now include three gender options: M (male), F (female), and E (eunuch).

This discussion leads us to an unanswered question: What happens if our internal, mental schemas and our cognitive conception of our gender constancy do not line up with what our family or society says our mental schemas *should* be, as Alley talks about in the opening vignette of this chapter?

GENDER IDENTITY: "BEING" MALE OR FEMALE, MASCULINE OR FEMININE

While gender roles have more to do with what society expects of its males and females, *gender identity* refers to our intuitive sense of our maleness or our femaleness (White, 2003), our internal feelings of what it is to be a man or a woman. Gender identity speaks to how a person settles in to society's assigned gender roles. In other words, it is a *subjective*, continuous, persistent sense of who we are as a male or a female.

Gender identity does not refer to sexual orientation. **Sexual orientation** refers to the focus of a person's erotic desires or fantasies, or a person's affectionate or romantic feelings toward a particular gender. This is the term most often used by family practitioners, therapists, and the medical community because the word *orientation* implies that one's gender preference is biologically predetermined. Those who believe that sexuality is fluid and is more a matter of choice than biology use the alternate term, **sexual preference**.

Gender identity and sexual orientation are often confused. In an exploratory study of early childhood teachers' attitudes toward gender roles, for example, the researchers observed that the preschool teachers had a difficult time differentiating gender identity from sexual orientation. The researchers note, "When a child's behavior (such as a boy wanting to play with dolls or who easily cries; a girl who is rough-and-tumble) calls into question [masculinity and femininity], the issue of the child's *sexual* identity was raised" (Cahill & Adams, 1997, p. 518, italics mine). Cahill and Adams comment that because of this assumed relationship between gender identity and sexual orientation in young children, parents, teachers, and society at large have a fear of allowing greater gender latitude, in fear of "making" a child become a homosexual. Their research concludes that when preschool teachers limit gender expression to society's expectations, "it is related to homophobia" (p. 528).

Usually a person's gender identity matches his or her assigned biological sex, but this is not always the case. Coined by gender activist Virginia Prince in the 1970s, **transgender**, an umbrella term, refers to people who feel that their biologically assigned gender is a false or incomplete description of themselves.

The National Transgender Advocacy Coalition (NTAC) describes a transgender person as "someone whose gender display at least sometimes runs contrary to what other people in the same culture would normally expect." The NTAC delineates several types of transgender individuals:

- *FTM* (female to male) are people who were born female but see themselves as partly to fully masculine.
- *MTF* (male to female) are people who were born male but see themselves as partly to fully feminine.
- *Intersexuals*, as discussed earlier in this chapter, are born with some combination of male and female physiology (similar to hermaphrodite), who may accept as natural their mixed gender.

A *transgenderist* is a person who lives as a gender opposite to his or her biological sex. For example, in 2008, Thomas Beatie (a female-to-male transgender) became known as the world's first "pregnant man." After having his breasts removed and undergoing years of testosterone hormone therapy, Mr. Beatie legally changed his gender from female to male, and he lived for several years as a man. However, he kept his female internal reproductive organs so that he could someday bear children. Great debates erupted across the nation, as some people argued that Mr. Beatie was not "really a man" since he still had a uterus, while others argued that if he identified as a man, he was a man, despite the fact that he had a uterus.

People often confuse a transgender person with a transsexual. A **transsexual** is a person whose sexual identity is opposite to the one assigned at birth. This phenomenon is stereotypically described as a woman feeling that she is "trapped inside a man's body," or vice versa. Transsexual men and women work toward transition from the gender of their birth to a permanent identity of the opposite gender through a complex process called *gender reassignment*. The gender transitioning process is complex and involves medical and mental health professionals. In most cases, gender reassignment involves psychological counseling, hormonal supplements, and **sex reassignment surgery** (**SRS**), where a surgical alteration to the body is performed. This is also called *genital surgery*. Most people considering SRS are required to make a gradual transition to their preferred gender over a period of several months.

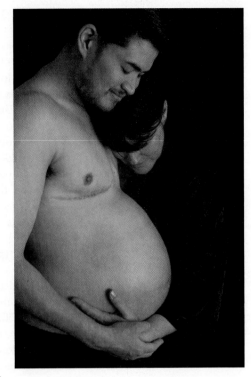

IN 2008, Thomas Beatie, a female-to-male transgender, gave birth. Do you believe he was a pregnant man? Why or why not?

Unlike transsexuals who seek a permanent gender change, transvestites do not. Broadly speaking, a **transvestite** dresses and acts in the manner of a person of the gender opposite from their own. Popular culture refers to transvestites as *cross-dressers*. The sexual orientation of transvestites varies.

As we have discussed throughout this chapter, gender is not a case of either-or. As NTAC notes, ultimately "gender is a mix-and-match mode of self-expression . . . it is best to think of [gender roles, gender behavior, and] gender identity as varying along a continuous spectrum of self-expression, rather than in just one of two or three ways." According to NTAC, transgender individuals identify themselves in a number of ways, using terms such as *drag queen, butch, femme, drag king, intersexual, transvestite, cross-dresser*, and *transsexual*. "Gender" is as much a social and intrapersonal construction as it is a biological construction. We are not the first to debate whether nature (biology) is the dominant influence or whether it is nurture (society, culture, and the environment). Plato thought that we already have inborn "male" or "female" structures and ways of thinking, while Aristotle thought that we construct our ideas of "maleness" and "femaleness" from our life experiences.

But another important question remains to be answered: By what processes do we "become" male or female, androgynous or transgender?

The Theories of Gender Development

A student of mine, Sarah, once shared with me an interesting story involving her 3-year-old son, Ethan. As a never-married single mom, Sarah's life revolved around her full-time college student status and the two jobs she worked in order to support and provide for her son, leaving little time for dating or much else. Because there was no male influence in her son's life, Sarah was concerned that Ethan would not "learn" how to be a "boy." But an all-too-infrequent trip to the city park one Saturday afternoon seemed to calm her anxieties.

As they were making their third lap around the park, the young boy noticed that a manhole cover near the curb of the street was missing. Seemingly out of nowhere Ethan remarked, "Mommy, look at that big hole." "Umhm," replied his mom, "That is very dangerous, Ethan. Don't ever go near things like that."

The precocious 3-year-old responded, "Mommy, a big, strong man needs to come here and lift that and put that back on the hole to make it safe again." Sarah was stunned. "Ethan, can't Mommy fix that?" He retorted, "No, Mommy! Only someone big and strong can fix that and mommies aren't big and strong."

She later asked me, "Where did he learn that from, where did he pick up that only a big, strong man could fix the problem to make things safe again?" Perhaps he was influenced by books, television, Disney movies, or billboards. Gender influences are found everywhere.

"If there was no such thing as gender, if we had no expectations of children biased by their sexual label, would gender-specific behavior disappear?" asks researcher J. Bland (1998, p. 2). In other words—if there were no such thing as gender, what expectations would Sarah have of Ethan? In order to answer Bland's question, we need to consider some theories that attempt to explain the process by which we are socialized to adhere to gender-specific behaviors.

LEARNING THEORY

Psychologists David Perry and Kay Bussey define *gender role development* as "the process whereby children come to acquire the behaviors, attitudes, interests, and emotional reactions that are culturally defined as appropriate for members of their sex" (1984, p. 262). Implicit to this definition, then, is the notion that we are not *born* with gendered behaviors, attitudes, interests, and the like, but take them on through the daily stream of incoming information from our environment. Such is the nature of **Learning theory**: Traits and behaviors are not inborn—we learn them.

Early behaviorists such as B. F. Skinner, Ivan Pavlov, and John Watson attempted to explain all human behaviors through learning theories, with the notion that all behavior is learned. The basic learning theories were predicated on the belief that we are born as "blank slates" waiting to be filled by the social instruction of our parents, teachers, the media, and society. Strict behaviorists maintained that a given stimulus (S) would produce a given response (R). Schematically, the theory would look something like this:

$$S \rightarrow R$$

By applying the concepts of reward and punishment, behaviorists contend that all behaviors—including gendered behaviors—are *learned responses*. If, for example, a little girl in a party dress is rewarded for sitting daintily in a chair with her ankles crossed, she is likely to repeat that behavior. And if the girl is punished for sitting or acting not so ladylike or acting tomboyish, she is less likely to repeat that behavior. Similarly, if a little boy desires to play with a Barbie doll and is punished, he is more likely to choose his fire truck out of the toybox the next time. By repeated "rewards" and "punishments" throughout infancy, early childhood, childhood, adolescence, and adulthood, specific gender behaviors are either *reinforced* (and thus, more likely to occur again and again) or *extinguished* (less likely to occur).

SOCIAL LEARNING THEORY

Social Learning theory (SLT) is an offshoot of traditional Behaviorism theory. While SLT does address the roles of reward and punishment, it goes a step further to include an individual's realm of *cognition*—the role of observation—in the process of learning.

Children make countless day-to-day observations that ultimately shape their gender-related thinking, understanding, and behavior. These daily social and environmental cues are quite specific to males and females. Albert Bandura is an academic psychologist who has made an enormous impact on personality theory and therapy techniques. He placed an emphasis on observational learning, and is the theorist most associated with SLT. Bandura (1977) maintained that individuals learn behaviors via observation in three different ways:

- *By imitating observed behaviors in their environment.* Children learn gendered behaviors by observing and then imitating the behavior of a model, someone who demonstrates a particular behavior.
- *By observing the punishments or rewards based on others' behaviors.* Bandura did not believe that a person had to actually experience the rewards and punishments themselves. Simply watching the consequences of others is enough to "teach"—we learn by watching what happens to others. Because the learning doesn't necessarily have to happen directly to us, Bandura thought that much of learning was vicarious.
- *By exposure to another's thinking.* Exposure to many different models is particularly useful in changing traditional stereotypes (Rutledge, 2000). For example, exposing someone to an intersexual child might serve to break down long-held beliefs.

Indeed, Bandura's research highlighted the role of cognition or observational learning in the acquisition of gender. He maintained that there are three reciprocal, interacting components in acquiring any human behavior:

- You, the **P**erson—your genetics, race, ethnicity, age, biological sex
- Your **B**ehavior—the choices and decisions you make, your responses and reactions to the incoming information in your daily life
- Your **E**nvironment—your parents, school, peers, neighborhood, the media, the religious hierarchy, and the political structure of the culture in which you live (similar to Bronfenbrenner's Ecological Model, discussed in Chapter 1)

These three interwoven components—**P, B, E**—are dynamic, in a continuous state of change. Rather than the seemingly straightforward approach to learning represented as **S → R** put forth by earlier learning theorists, Bandura added the element of cognition (thought) and put forth the notion that cognition then acts as a *filter* of sorts between the stimulus and the response. As the **P**erson, **B**ehavior, and **E**nvironment all interact, countless messages, cues, and forces (stimuli) from the social environment are filtered through the process of cognition (observation); ultimately, certain behaviors are accepted and thus acted out, and certain behaviors are rejected (response). A schematic drawing of Bandura's Social Learning theory would look something like Figure 4.4 (page 124).

Bandura's (1986) work also addresses the many social factors that contribute to gendered behavior. In particular, he paid attention to the influences of media in the shaping, molding, and directing of gendered behaviors. Bandura best sums up the impact of social and cultural influences on gender development when he comments that from the moment of birth, we are continuously exposed to clearcut environmental and social cues that dictate our gender behaviors. Specifically, Bandura notes that these gender cues are experienced "in the home, in school, in readers and storybooks, and in representations of society on the television screens of every household" (p. 93). Indeed, the environmental cues are many and they are what ultimately transform the basic fundamental biological attributes of sex into a socially and culturally determined "gender."

COGNITIVE DEVELOPMENT THEORY

As a developmental psychologist and professor for many years at Harvard University, Lawrence Kohlberg popularized his theory of moral development through research studies at Harvard's Center for Moral Education. In 1966, Kohlberg proposed the **Cognitive Development theory** of gender, which holds that children could not be influenced by outside experiences until they developed cognitively. In other words, the Cognitive Development theory maintains that before social and environmental forces can influence a child's concept of

FIGURE 4.4 The Social Cognitive Filter

As the person, behavior, and environment interact, innumerable messages, cues, and stimuli from the environment are filtered through a social cognitive filter. An individual may choose to accept certain messages and act on them, or reject them entirely.

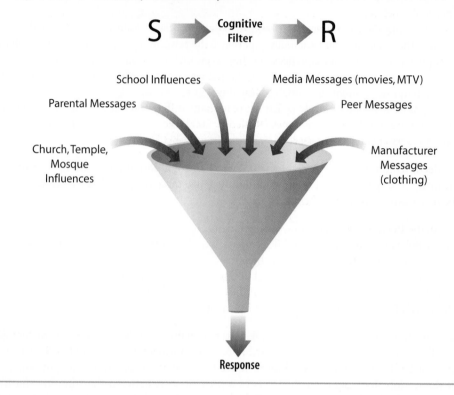

gender (as maintained by behaviorists and Social Learning theory, for example), the child must first gain a certain awareness or understanding about gender (Helwig, 1998). Ultimately, though, Kohlberg believed that children develop stereotypes of gender based on what surrounds them in their social world. To this end, Kohlberg suggested that children's conception of gender changes as their cognitive development progresses. He thus delineated three phases of gender understanding:

■ *Gender identity.* Around the age of 3, children become keenly aware that they biologically are male or female. Around the same age, they are able to label others as "girls" or "boys" or "mommies" or "daddies."
■ *Gender stability.* Sometime between the ages of 4 and 6, children reach the realization that their gender will always be the same—that they were a boy or a girl as a baby and will be a boy or a girl when they grow up. This is referred to as **gender stability**.
■ *Gender constancy.* Sometime around the age of 6, children reach the understanding that no matter what they might change in how they dress or how they play or what they play with, they are still a boy or a girl. It is only after children consistently think of themselves as an unchangeable boy or girl that they begin to take on both family and socially expected gendered behaviors.

Kohlberg believed that **gender constancy** is achieved when children cognitively reach the understanding that biological "sex is a permanent attribute" (Bussey & Bandura, 1999, p. 4) that is associated with certain anatomical characteristics that cannot be changed. This understanding ultimately leads to what Kohlberg defined as a *stable gender identity*. In short, children come to realize that gender is constant across age and time.

Kohlberg's research has come under fire and been hotly debated in the past two decades, particularly by Carol Gilligan (1982), a gender studies professor at Harvard University. Gilligan was a former of student of Kohlberg, but believed that Kohlberg's concepts of moral development and gender identity development are biased against women because women develop their moral codes differently than men. Other empirical studies have also found limited support for Kohlberg's theory as well (among many, many others, Bussey & Bandura, 1984, 1992; O'Keefe & Hyde, 1983; Franken, 1983; Huston, 1983; Nelson, 1978).

Gender identity is a lifelong process and involves a delicate, complicated interaction between biological and cultural forces. As these gender theories help us to understand, gender, gender behavior, and gender thinking are constantly influenced by the environment in which we live. In the following section, we take a deeper look at the different socializing agents in our contemporary culture: the influence of *parents*, *peers*, and the *media*.

It Matters: The Agents of Socialization

As we have discovered throughout this chapter, gender and gender roles—and to a large extent, perhaps even gender identity—are learned from exposure to a number of sources across an individual's lifespan, from parents and other family members, to the schoolroom, from sports icons to toys, from peers to books.

LEARNING GENDER FROM PARENTS

Because of the immediate and consistent influences of the newborn's family, it is not surprising that parents infuse gender messages into their children, knowingly or unknowingly. Think about it—from encouraging certain behaviors and discouraging other behaviors (*big boys don't cry*), to parents exhibiting certain overt gender behaviors (*boys take out the trash, girls don't*) and making covert suggestions (*is that any way to act like a lady?*), to the activities and opportunities that parents expose their children to, children are in a constant state of being gender socialized (Witt, 1997).

The various theories of gender socialization show us that as children are exposed to cultural-specific expectations of gender and culturally defined gender roles, they internalize, and ultimately act out, what is expected and what is appropriate for each biological sex—boys act and think one way, girls act and think in different ways. Parents socialize children through a number of ways, but most especially through modeling particular gendered behaviors, such as mothers assuming the lion's share of nurturing the children and housekeeping tasks, and fathers assuming the physical tasks, such as home repair and maintenance and protection/provider for the family (Boyd & Bee, 2009).

Play and Gender Messages Parents also send gender messages by the ways in which they encourage their children to play. A number of empirical studies have found that parents encourage their children to engage in certain sex-typed activities, such as encouraging their daughters to play with dolls instead of trucks, and to take ballet lessons or play soccer instead of playing football (among many others, Campenni, 1999). Not surprisingly, other research has discovered that the toys children prefer

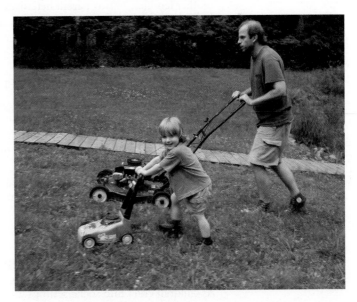

IN our daily lives, we are exposed to countless gender messages, messages that tell us what duties boys are supposed to perform and what duties girls are supposed to perform. If you have children, will you socialize them to adhere to traditional gender roles? Why or why not?

RESEARCH shows that boys raised by lesbian mothers are no different in their gendered behaviors than boys who have fathers. Do these results surprise you?

to play with are related to how parents sex-type their children (Wood, Desmarais, & Gugula, 2002). All of these messages with play and toys send clear-cut messages to children that girls are to play and to assume future roles that are nurturing and geared toward childrearing and housekeeping, while boys are taught to play and to assume future roles that are more along the lines of providing and protecting (Campenni, 1999). However, these studies all examined children who were reared by heterosexual parents. Do children who are reared by gay or lesbian parents assume traditional gender roles?

Learning Gender from Gay or Lesbian Parents Although it should not be expected that children growing up in lesbian-mother households would fare worse than children who are raised by heterosexual parents with similar parenting styles (such as warm, responsive, communicative parenting), some segments of American society and other cultures expect that children who are raised in a lesbian-mother family will have psychological or gender role identity problems—in particular, there is a prevalent belief that children of gay or lesbian parents will have difficulty constructing "appropriate" gender schemas and gender roles (Stacey & Biblarz, 2001; Golombok and others, 2003). To date, emerging social science research has failed to bear out these concerns (among many others, Golombok & Hines, 2002; Patterson, 2000, 2004). To the contrary, current research suggests that gendered behavior, gender roles, and gender identity develop in similar ways among all children, whether they are raised by heterosexual parents or lesbian parents (Patterson, 2004).

Susan Golombok is a professor at City University in London whose research efforts focus on outcomes for children growing up in nontraditional family forms. She and her colleagues (2003) undertook a study that sought to understand the quality of parent–child relationships and gender development of children with lesbian parents. A sample that included 39 lesbian-mother families, 74 two-parent heterosexual families, and 60 families headed by single heterosexual mothers were compared in areas such as parent–child relationships (such as, warmth, emotional involvement, levels of conflict, and parenting quality), and children's social and emotional development (including emotional health, gender role/gender identity development, and peer relationships).

Among all family forms, Golombok and associates (2003) found no significant differences in the ways children draw/write/read, the shows they watched on television, or their rough-and-tumble play. In short, boys and girls raised in lesbian-mother families did not differ from those children raised in heterosexual families in their gender-typed behavior—sexual orientation of mothers was not a major or significant influence on children's gender development.

Of course, we don't learn gender expectations just from our families of origin. Throughout our lives we receive numerous other gender cues from our environments, particularly from our friends.

LEARNING GENDER FROM PEERS

As children enter into social settings in the early years, and subsequently throughout the rest of childhood during their school years, a child's gender identity is further reinforced through play and within the classroom setting.

Gender, Emotion, and Family Living

Understanding stereotyped gender roles is important to a person's emotional and physical health because sometimes these culture-specific roles are personally limiting or socially divisive. Often, if a person does not conform to society's gender expectations, the person feels that his or her behavior is wrong or unacceptable; these feelings become internalized and affect well-being and overall health, leading to depression, eating disorders, anxiety, and thoughts of self-harm or suicide.

Females, for example, are socialized to suppress their anger because it is unfeminine for them to express it; conversely, they are taught to openly express their feelings and experience the full range of emotions (such as sadness, fear, disappointment, hurt, etc.). On the other hand, males are socialized to hide or suppress their vulnerable emotions and to express their anger and frustration. Women are socialized to cooperate, men are socialized to believe that power, winning, success, and achievement are essential to their self-worth. Whether it is in the bedroom or in the boardroom, it is not always socially acceptable for a woman to have power, experience, knowledge, or expertise.

The broader point here is that any time one trait is deemed more valuable than another trait, inequality exists—whether it is in the professional domain or in the home. Socialized behaviors and expectations limit *both* men and women by confining them to rigid, stereotyped gendered roles and rules for living.

Too often in family life socialized behavior causes misunderstandings, hurt feelings, disappointment, frustration, and anger. I can recall expressing great frustration to my husband once because all of *his* household tasks and chores were limited to mowing the lawn, taking out the garbage, cleaning out the garage, bringing in firewood, cleaning the pool—and *seasonal!* In family interactions, women often become disappointed when their male partners are hesitant to self-disclose, share intimacy, or show vulnerability; men become frustrated when their wives or female companions seem uninteresting. In both of these instances, what is often overlooked is that the women and men are simply behaving and interacting in the ways in which they were socialized.

For healthy families and healthy selves, minimize gender role stereotypes in family living:

- *Discuss bothersome issues.* For example, if a family member does not like always being the one to do the dishes or take out the trash, he or she should express those concerns and work toward a solution that is beneficial to the family.
- *Alternate* performing household tasks and chores that are typically specific to one gender or the other.
- *Challenge stereotypical gender roles.* If the wife desires to support the family financially and the father desires to stay home and care for the children, disregard socialized roles and do what is in the best interest of the family.
- *Do not allow* demeaning, sexist language or actions as acceptable family behaviors.
- *Respect* the different values and opinions of every family member.

Children exhibit a preference for same-sex playmates, referred to as **homosocial play**, from about the age of 3, until about the age of early adolescence (age 11 or 12) (Boyd & Bee, 2009). As children interact with their same-sex peers, established gender roles continue to be reinforced. As an example, boys prefer to engage in rough and aggressive types of play, and girls prefer to engage in fantasy, imaginary, and relational play (Boyd & Bee, 2009). Because of these differing play styles, children often choose playmates of their same sex, because they, too, enjoy that particular brand of play. While engaging in play, the gender differences are made more concrete.

In recent years, significant strides have been made in both policy and practice in early childhood programs. In efforts to value the importance of children as active participants in their own gender development, early childhood educators are attempting to de-feminize the preschool culture. In general, early childhood centers (and to a large extent, school settings in general) are *feminized cultures*; that is, the staff is predominately female, who nurture and provide care in stereotypical gendered fashion (Skelton & Hall, 2001). Essentially, there is no presence of men within early childhood centers, which can potentially transmit the message that only women are capable of caring for young children.

Christine Skelton and Elaine Hall (2001), early childhood education professors in the United Kingdom, were commissioned by the Equal Opportunities Commission to investigate the development of gender in young children. Their two-prong purpose was to re-create early childhood programs that would challenge stereotypes and encourage diversity, and to create guidance materials for instructors that encouraged examples of how to achieve gender equity. To achieve these ends, Skelton and Hall (2001) suggest that early childhood educators should:

FAMILY LIFE NOW

Is It Possible to Raise Gender-Neutral Children?

While most people adhere to the socially and culturally determined gender roles ascribed to them, today more and more individuals are filling nontraditional gender roles. This flexibility and fluidity between the genders has some researchers questioning whether it is possible to raise gender-neutral children in contemporary society. Is it possible to raise children where there are no clear-cut lines between "male" and "female"?

YES: Psychologist and researcher Sandra Lipsitz Bem contends that it is possible to raise gender-neutral children, and she uses her own children as examples in her scholarly writings. Bem and her husband sought to retard the stereotypical gender messages in their children's environments.

Intent on exposing their children to nontraditional gender roles, Bem and her husband did all they could to eliminate the common correlations between a person's biological sex and day-to-day tasks. For example, the Bems took turns doing certain household tasks, caring for the children, and driving the car. They went out of their way to show their children men and women engaging in nontraditional occupations, such as driving by a construction site every day so their children would see the female construction worker. So gender neutral were they in their parenting that their son referred to individuals as "heorshe," implying there were not two genders, but one.

Throughout childhood and adolescence, the Bems

- encouraged their children to be skeptical of conventional cultural messages about gender by emphasizing diversity;
- provided their children with nongendered ways of observing traditional messages about gender (by saying such things as, "Yes, boys like to play baseball, but so do a lot of girls"); and
- helped them understand that all gender messages are created by culture and society.

NO: Sociologists Denise Segura and Jennifer Pierce (1993) maintain that gender identity and gender roles are very closely tied to family and cultural expectations; because of this, they contend that gender-specific role fulfillment is critically vital to certain cultures. To support their claim, they examine the Chicana/o culture of Mexico where the role of women as mothers is central to both gender identity formation and group or ethnic identity formation.

Central to the development of gendered personality of the Chicana/o are the family and cultural influences; of particular interest is the unique constellation of features that define these

- Be aware of and understand their own subconscious gender stereotypings, such as, *Do I expect children to act differently because they are boys or girls? Do I have different expectations for a child's performance based on whether the child is a boy or a girl?*
- Be aware of what images of "male" and "female" children bring with them into the class-room setting, such as, *What are children's favorite games, toys, and books? What do these tell children about the "correct" way of being a boy or a girl?*
- Pay attention to the messages given to children in day-to-day routines, such as, *Am I aware that "girls" and "boys" are not always homogeneous groups—that sometimes girls will act aggressively and boys will play cooperatively?*

In sum, Skelton and Hall put forth the notion that teachers should provide children in their care with a nonsexist, nontraditional, nonstereotypical environment. An interesting question is brought to the surface here: Given all that you have learned so far in your study of the construction of gender, do you believe is it really possible (or necessary?) to socialize children to behave in gender neutral ways? Taking a glance at "Family Life Now" may help you to better decide.

FAMILY LIFE NOW

families. The constellation of Chicana/o family types include *familism* (where a strong value is placed on family unity and the presence of multigenerational ties), *compardrazgo* (a high level of interaction with close nonfamily), and *nonexclusive mothering* (mothering by other trusted individuals through extensive family networks, such as grandmothers and aunts).

All of these features of the Chicana/o family types have significant implications in the development of masculine or feminine personalities, because gender identities in this culture are closely blended or intertwined with community and society. Unlike European American mothers, Chicana mothers rear their children to act communally, or to think and act in ways that benefit the family and the community. Sons and daughters in Mexican cultures are raised to believe that they are extensions not of their parents but of their culture. Consider how females are reared in this culture:

- With multiple mother figures, daughters' gender identification centers on Mexican cultural practices and beliefs, such as appropriate mothering roles; knowledge of cultural traditions, behaviors, and values; and honoring other kin ties. The Chicana believe that these roles compliment the role of men, which is to be the provider for the family.

Consider how males are reared in the Mexican culture:

- Because of the presence of several female role models in the sons' lives, the transmission of culture and gender expectations is accomplished by a process known as "becoming masculine." Chicana women repeat the centuries-old Mexican saying, "*feo, fuerte y formal.*" Roughly translated, the young boy is to be rugged and strong, to be a man who is steadfast and responsible, and to be a good provider for his family. Young Chicano boys learn how to be a male by *not* being a female.

In the Mexican culture, the role of women is emphasized, yet it is these unique family constellation features that ultimately contribute to the acquisition of gender identity—a gender identity that is nearly inseparable from group, ethnic, and cultural identity.

WHAT DO YOU THINK?

1. Is it possible to raise gender-neutral children in societies where gender messages abound?
2. Is it necessary to raise gender-neutral children?
3. What are the advantages of a gender-neutral society? What are the disadvantages?

Sources: Bem (1998); Segura & Pierce (1993).

As children move through their middle childhood and adolescent years, peers become increasingly important. This change in peer involvement brings with it increasing pressure for children to feel that they "fit in" (Carver, Yunger, & Perry, 2003). Gender identity has as much to do with people's perceptions of how they fit in as it does with how they feel internally about their biological gender assignment and their ascribed gender roles. Carver and her colleagues (2003) found that during the preadolescent years of human development, feelings of gender typicality and gender contentedness increase with age; feelings of intergroup bias and gender conformity decrease with age. In other words, as children move toward adolescence, feeling the need to conform to gender stereotypes decreases and contentedness with their assigned biological sex increases, thus allowing children to "be" who they are, male or female, or who they desire to be.

Gender, gender roles, and gender identity are learned from exposure to a number of sources across an individual's lifespan. Still, we need to examine one more influence on gender development and gender behavior in contemporary society: the role of the media.

LEARNING GENDER FROM THE MEDIA

When examining the influences of popular culture and the media on gender, a decades-old debate emerges: Does the media influence societal patterns? Or is the media merely a reflection of the existing cultural values and norms? The question has perplexed communication experts, social science researchers, and social analysts for decades. That gender roles and stereotypes are *determined* and *formed* by the media would be a difficult case to make. But it is clear that gender roles are *supported* and *reinforced* by media. To better understand how the media reinforces gender and gender behaviors, here we examine the portrayal of gender in television and film, and advertising.

Television and Film Children's conceptions of gender are based primarily on what they see and hear (Bandura & Bussey, 1999). Television cartoons and movies play a powerful role in gender stereotyping, in part because they are so popular among children of all ages. Beginning in early childhood, movie viewers are exposed to numerous images of masculine and feminine "ideals." Consider the Walt Disney compilation of the ideal woman:

> Snow White possesses fair, flawless skin, and dark hair; she is shapely, pleasant, and patient; and she has a soprano singing voice. She is waiting for her prince to bring her to life.

> Cinderella possesses fair, flawless skin, and blonde hair; she is shapely, pleasant, and patient (even in the most degrading situations); and she has a soprano singing voice. She is waiting for her prince to save her.

> Belle *(Beauty and the Beast)* has fair skin, has flowing brown hair, and is shapely. She has a lilting soprano voice, and falls in love with a wolfish-looking beast—who turns out to be a prince.

Even as the cultural form of Disney's heroine has evolved, certain physiological and behavioral traits continue to linger. Consider the Native American motif of Pocahontas. Although her skin tones are darker, the thin, shapely body and soprano singing voice are still present. Films with characters such as these reinforce the socially and culturally driven concept of the "ideal" woman: She is always thin; has curves in all the right places; is pretty; has long, luxurious hair; is pleasant and cheery; has a sing-song voice; and is very dependent on the strong handsome prince (who, some would argue, is prone to wearing puffy sleeves).

Once a person outgrows Disney movies and turns his or her attention to other forms of media, the gender stereotypes are still present; societal expectations still prevail where women are seen for their nurturing abilities and beauty, and men for their strength and intellect. Media trends tracked by women's groups such as the National Organization for Women (NOW) indicate that women in the media are commonly portrayed as young, attractive, nurturing, married (or romantically involved), and employed in traditional female occupations, such as nursing. Conversely, men are portrayed as heads of government, as lead criminal investigators and crime specialists, and in dominant positions in hospitals.

Media Watch, a volunteer-based feminist organization, was established in 1981 in an effort to change the media's portrayal and treatment of women. Their analysis of prime-time television found that over 140 television female stars are Miley Cyrus *(Hannah Montana)* look-alikes: They are thin, white, and beautiful. They are not women of color, lesbian, overweight, single (for long), or impoverished (Media Watch, 2008). On the other hand (and similar to real life), men in television typically hold positions of power—and it does not necessarily matter if they possess drop-dead good looks (Media Watch, 2008). These are troubling trends, indeed, because such traditional representations of women and men influence society's definition and perception of gender roles and the expectations for those roles.

Media Watch further identifies the pervasive gender trends in film and television media:

IS Walt Disney guilty of typecasting the "ideal" image of boy and girl? *High School Musical* stars Zac Efron and Vanessa Hudgens portray Disney's image of high school students. How realistic are they?

- *Irrelevant sexualization* uses women's bodies in sexual ways in an attempt to attract attention or to use a woman's or man's sexuality to sell products, such as is common with Abercrombie & Fitch advertising campaigns.
- *Infantilization* presents women as childish, coy, silly, passive, or vulnerable. This is in contrast to men who are commonly portrayed as strong, confident, assertive, and serious.
- *Domestication* defines women in relationship to their husbands, boyfriends, or the man to whom they are attracted. Even if the female TV character works outside of the home environment, she is typically shown interacting in her home relationships and not in her work environment.
- *Distortion of female body image* is seen in the increasingly thinner and thinner females portrayed in prime-time television, such as the lead actresses in the ABC hit series, *Desperate Housewives.*
- *Victimization* portrays women as victims of violent acts or as victims of female and male brutality.

Shari Graydon (2003), educator, past president of Media Watch, and a columnist for the *Vancouver Sun,* maintains that distorted imagery of women in the media worsens or aggravates sexist attitudes, discriminatory conditions, and behaviors. Graydon notes that teenagers are especially vulnerable to the effects of these media messages because they are at a particularly vulnerable stage in their developmental process. This vulnerability makes them more sensitive to "impossible-to-attain" messages about the feminine ideal, expected sexual availability, and limited career opportunities for women.

Advertising Television shows and movies aren't the only way boys and girls are socialized by the media today. They are also exposed to advertising. For example, the typical North American child views some 40,000 advertisements each year (Graydon, 2003), and the messages they receive about gender are clear: Men are dominant and strong. Women are submissive and weak. Men are aggressive and intelligent. Women are passive and intuitive. These are the traits deemed appropriate by society, and advertising in the media does much to strengthen them (Macdonald, 2003). Typically, men are featured in autonomous settings displaying numerous occupations and skills. Women in advertisements usually are in a domestic setting, most often playing girlfriends and wives, homemakers and mothers (Macdonald, 2003). The commercial voiceover—the "expert" of the ad, the "trusted" person—is most often male. In fact, some advertising

GENDER issues shape our daily lives. In the 21st century, gender roles are changing for women. Should women engage in armed combat? What factors shape your decision?

experts estimate as many as 94 percent of ads use a male voice-over (Chandler, 2005).

As little girls and little boys develop into adolescents, and then into women and men, they are continuously exposed to countless hours of media influences. For instance, teenagers today drive the consumption and development of new video platforms, such as playing videos on their cell phones and iPods, and accessing streaming video on the Internet with YouTube (Nielsen Media, 2008). With children spending an average of four hours a day in front of a television screen (Boyse, 2008), gender representation in media will certainly play a profound role in shaping the ideals of gender and gender identity.

As we have discussed throughout this chapter, we all have different conceptions of what it is to be a man or a woman in contemporary society, and we came to these understandings through multiple biological, cultural, and psychosocial forces that are continuously at work in our lives. Whether on a big screen, the television screen, in magazines, in music, or on the Internet, the representation of gender roles in media are clearly reinforcing cultural understandings of manhood and womanhood.

It Matters: Gender and Contemporary Issues

Professors of law Catherine Mackinnon (2001) and William Eskridge and Nan Hunter (1997) compiled a comprehensive, extensive review of case law as it applies to gender and sexuality. The *equal protection doctrine* (part of the Fourteenth Amendment to the United States Constitution) provides that "no state shall . . . deny to any person . . . the equal protection of its laws." In essence, this clause of the Constitution addresses the proposition that "all men are created equal," and should be treated as such. As the law professors suggest, a broad survey of gender as it relates to the law is an important area of study, because the equal protection doctrine is shaped by gender issues in our daily lives. In today's political, economical, and home environments, issues of gender are front and center, with concerns such as women in combat, adoption of children by gays and lesbians, and an expanding right to marry. For example, with the exception of only a few states, current marriage laws prohibit people of the same sex to marry; this leads Mackinnon, Eskridge, and Hunter to maintain that marriage between same-sex couples is a *gender* issue and a *civil rights* issue, because same-sex couples are being denied their equal protection rights. In Chapter 8, we'll look at this issue in depth when we discuss the Defense of Marriage Act (DOMA), which forbids federal recognition of same-sex marriages.

Even though the Fourteenth Amendment to the U.S. Constitution was passed in 1868 in an effort to "eliminate legalized racism" (Mackinnon, 2001, p. 13), still some 100 years later racial equality was far from realized in the United States. The Civil Rights Act of 1964 was passed by Congress to prohibit discrimination in the workplace on the basis of race, color, religion, sex, or national origin. But as Mackinnon notes, "Equality in human societies is commonly affirmed, but rarely practiced. Few lives are lived in equality, even in democracies. As a fact, social equality is hard to find anywhere" (p. 2). Beyond a form of justice to ensure the rights of all U.S. citizens, the Civil Rights Act has changed and still contributes to the changing experiences of American family and family life.

The Civil Rights Act of 1964, for example, expressly prohibits any form of sexual discrimination. In short, **sexual harassment** is any unwelcome sexual or physical conduct by either gender, directed to either gender. The Equal Employment Opportunity Commission (2004) states that "unwelcome sexual advances, requests for sexual favors, and other verbal or physical conduct of a sexual nature constitutes sexual harassment when submission to or rejection of this conduct explicitly or implicitly affects an individual's employment, unreasonably interferes with an individual's work performance, or creates an intimidating, hostile, or offensive work environment." Sexual harassment is an issue wherein gender and authority are the central components. It involves the unfair use of power that one person exerts over another. It can occur in a work setting such as when a boss holds a good performance evaluation over the head of an employee by requesting sexual favors. It can also occur in academic setting, as in the following examples:

- A university freshman seeks help from his female teaching assistant. After going over the coursework, she suggests they go out to grab a bite to eat, indicating that his grades might improve if he got to know her better.
- A female worker having a bad day at work is told by her male co-worker that maybe she is in a bad mood because she just needs to have more sex.

In some of the situations the harassment is obvious, in other cases it is more subtle. Many people, *regardless of their gender,* who experience unwanted sexual comments or advances report feeling powerless to stop a situation. Many fear retaliation if the incidents are reported (such as receiving a lower grade or consequences at work), and as a result they may feel the need to change their major or drop a course, or they begin to have physical symptoms of stress. Mental health experts advise victims of sexual harassment not to ignore the behavior. College campuses and workplaces alike have an Affirmative Action office where the victim can file a complaint. Universities and colleges also have student counseling services. They emphasize that the victim hasn't done anything wrong and that the offending behavior was not just a joke. Such behavior is not just a "guy/gal kind of thing." Sexual harassment has nothing to do with the intent of the offender ("I didn't mean it, it was only a joke!")—it has everything to do with its effect on the victim. If the behavior is unwanted, it is sexual harassment.

Family Life Education

In the words of my obstetrician, "Boy, girl, what does it matter?" As the opening vignette demonstrates, the issue of gender does matter to those individuals who feel they don't conform to society's gender expectations.

The simple truth is: Gender matters! It matters in our examination of marital, family, and intimate relationships because the socially sanctioned, approved, and endorsed gendered behaviors affect life roles, occupations, and every aspect of our interpersonal relationships. It matters in some parts of the world where adherence to gender roles and behaviors literally means life or death, such as in Afghanistan. It matters because of the countless social and environmental gender cues that surround us from the moment we are born. It matters because sometimes "boy" or "girl" isn't always a clear-cut determination. It matters because sometimes the outward signs of the biological sex are not congruent with how someone feels internally about his or her gender, as Alley's experiences show us. It matters because sometimes being a particular gender does not grant permission to those of the opposite gender to behave in a sexually offensive manner or perpetrate crimes against them. It matters because many gender-centered legal battles have shaped and continue to shape the fabric of the American family. It matters.

Should Boys Play with Dolls? Should Girls Be Allowed to Play in Male-Dominated Sports, Such as Football?

Meredith is a 14-year-old freshman in high school. A gifted, talented athlete, she excels in every sport she plays, from volleyball to softball, from soccer to track, and from basketball to football. She began playing football in elementary school and played on flag football teams for a number of years. Now that Meredith is in high school, she wants to continue playing football. This issue has started a heated battle between her parents.

Mom's Side: We have always taught Meredith that she can do anything she puts her mind to, whether it is in sports, in academics, or in her career some day. I think it's fine for Meredith to continue to play football. She is extremely talented in sports, and football is no exception to that. She excels in the sport and even has aspirations of playing Division I college football some day. No, we don't see female running backs in collegiate football. Who's to say Meredith won't be the one to change that some day? I fully embrace her decision to play high school football.

Dad's Side: I was okay when Meredith wanted to play football in elementary school and junior high school, but I cannot endorse her decision to play high school football or college football. In the lower grades, Meredith's physical stature was similar to boys'—one gender was not necessarily more muscular or taller than the other. But in high school those same boys are now becoming men. It is not about "gender" to me—it is about her getting hurt. Some of those young men will weigh over 300 pounds; Meredith barely weighs 130 pounds. I played high school football, I know where people get hit and I know how hard those hits are. Can a developing woman's body take those kinds of impacts? I don't know.

Your Side: If you were Meredith's parents, would you allow her to play high school football? In your decision-making process, consider the following questions:

1. Can young women physically compete against young men?
2. Is football socially constructed? In other words, has society defined the roles of the actors in football—that women are to be on the sidelines as cheerleaders or dancers and men are to be on the field as coaches, players, and referees?
3. Do existing beliefs about gender differences affect your decision? If so, how?

Summary

The Biology of Gender

- Because men and women constitute the social, economic, and political reality of every society, it's important to understand both the nature influences of gender (the influences of biology) and the nurture influences of gender (environmental influences).

- Sex and gender are not interchangeable terms. *Sex* describes biologically determined characteristics, anatomical, hormonal, physiological. *Gender* encompasses society's expectations, such as how we behave and how we present ourselves.

- During fertilization, the coupling of the XX or XY chromosomes (inherited from the sperm and ovum) determines a person's sex characteristics. The XX sex chromosome combination results in a "female" genetic blueprint, and the XY sex chromosome combination results in a "male" genetic blueprint.

- Rare cases of genetic anomalies can result in an intersexed condition such as hermaphrodism or Androgen Insensitivity Syndrome or other genetic conditions like Turner's Syndrome or Klinefelter's Syndrome. Genetic irregularities have presented tremendous medical management challenges, and although advances have been made, the standard of care for intersexed persons is slow to change.

The Culture of Gender

- Sociocultural gender assumptions assign prototypical male and female behaviors and traits.

- *Gender roles* are the explicitly expressed and implicitly implied behaviors, feelings, attributes, and traits that society expects of the male or the female.

- *Masculinity* and *femininity* are defined differently within cultures.

- *Gender polarization* refers to the concept that masculinity and femininity are on opposites ends of a continuum. Inherent to gender polarization is the emphasis of the differences between the genders. This emphasis leads to inequality, particularly in women's career advancements, earnings, and education.

- *Gender stereotypes* are long-held assumptions about gender capabilities.

- *Gender schemas* are mental constructs of how a person internalizes specific gendered behaviors and expectations. Three such schemas are the *instrumental* schema ("getting the job done"), the *expressive* schema (relational-oriented), and the concept of *androgyny*, where an individual can be both (or neither) masculine and feminine, but not one or the other.

- A transgender person is someone whose gender identity does not line up with his or her biological sex.

The Theories of Gender Development

- The paradigms of socialization attempt to explain the process by which we are socialized to adhere to gender-specific behaviors. They include Learning theory, Social Learning theory, and Cognitive Development theory.

The Agents of Socialization

- Children learn to "do" masculine or feminine from their parents (heterosexual or homosexual), children's first and primary agents of socialization. They also learn what is appropriate for their gender through play.

- Peers reinforce stereotypical gender roles that children learn at home.

- Children's conceptions of gender are based primarily on what they see and hear, and beginning in early childhood, movie and television viewers are exposed to numerous images of masculine and feminine "ideals." The social impact of distorted portrayals of women and men exacerbate and reinforce existing gender attitudes.

Gender and Contemporary Issues

- The Bill of Gender Rights asserts a person's right to assume and freely express any gender role and the right to make his or her body congruent with that gender role.

- Gender issues play a significant role in legal and public policy.

Key Terms and Concepts

Suggested Readings

Abrahams, G., and Ahlbrand, S. (2002), *Boy v. girl: How gender shapes who we are, what we want, and how we get along*. Minneapolis, MN: Free Spirit Publishing.

Clark, B. L., and Higonnet, M. R. (Eds.). (1999). *Girls, boys, books, toys: Gender in children's literature and culture*. Baltimore: Johns Hopkins University Press.

Sommers, C. H. (2001). *The war against boys: How misguided feminism is harming our young men*. Kent, UK: Touchstone Books.

Multiple-Choice Questions

1. In the process of fertilization, the _____ sex chromosome combination results in a "female" genetic blueprint for the developing conceptus, while the _____ sex chromosome combination results in a "male" genetic blueprint for the developing conceptus.
   a. XY/XX
   b. XO/YY
   c. XY/YY
   d. XX/XY

2. Which of the following is NOT a type of intersex syndrome?
   a. Turner's Syndrome
   b. Androgen Insensitivity Syndrome
   c. Asperger Syndrome
   d. Klinefelter's Syndrome

3. The ways we internalize and incorporate specific gendered behaviors and expectations are called _____ .

   a. gender norms
   b. gender schemas
   c. gender roles
   d. gender stereotypes

4. A(n) _____ is a person whose sexual identity is opposite to the one assigned at birth.
   a. transgenderist
   b. transsexual
   c. intersexual
   d. transvestite

5. _____ holds that before social and environmental forces can influence a child's concept of gender, the child must first acquire certain awareness and understanding about gender.
   a. Social Learning theory
   b. Learning theory
   c. Cognitive Development theory
   d. Biological Development theory

6. The concept of _____ refers to something that either has no gender value assigned to it, or that a person possesses traits, behaviors, or characteristics that are typically associated with the opposite gender.

   a. androgyny

   b. instrumental schemas

   c. expressive schemas

   d. gender identity

7. _____ are associated with masculinity focus on task-oriented behaviors and "getting the job done."

   a. Expressive schemas

   b. Gender schemas

   c. Androgens

   d. Instrumental schemas

8. _____ teaches that women are semi-divine, and are morally superior to and spiritually stronger than men.

   a. Machismo

   b. Femininity

   c. Marianismo

   d. Masculinity

Answers: 1.d; 2.c; 3.b; 4.b; 5.c; 6.a; 7.d; 8.c

Intimacy: Developing and Experiencing Affectionate Bonds

5

Brad Pitt: I know all these things are supposed to seem important to us—the car, the condo, our version of success—but if that's the case, why is the general feeling out there reflecting more impotence and isolation and desperation and loneliness? If you ask me, I say toss all this—we gotta find something else. Because all I know is that at this point in time, we are heading for a dead-end, a numbing of the soul, a complete atrophy of the [human] being. And I don't want that.

Rolling Stone: So if we're heading toward this kind of . . . dead-end in society, what do you think should happen?

Brad Pitt: Hey, man, I don't have those answers yet. [My] emphasis now is on success and personal gain. I'm sitting in [success and wealth], and I'm telling you, that's not it. I'm the guy who's got everything. I know. But I'm telling you, once you've got everything, then you're just left with yourself. I've said it before and I'll say it again: it doesn't help you sleep any better, and you don't wake up any better because of it.

Source: Excerpted from "The Unbearable Bradness of Being" by Chris Heath from *Rolling Stone* 824, October 1999 © Rolling Stone LLC 1999. All Rights Reserved. Reprinted by Permission.

HUMAN nature requires that each of us desires to be emotionally close to another person.

Although Brad Pitt possesses great looks, has enjoyed a successful acting career, and has achieved what many would consider tremendous success, the "guy who has everything" recognizes that great fame and wealth beyond what you and I can probably comprehend are not what brings happiness and contentment, not what brings a sense of richness and satisfaction in life. In his interview with *Rolling Stone* magazine, this popular, American cultural icon identified what he believes is perhaps an atrophy, a wasting away of a basic, necessary human need in our society—intimacy.

Much of what you learn throughout this academic term in your study of marriage and the family is interconnected. You will notice as you make your way through your course, for example, that sex and intimacy are as much interrelated as are intimacy and love, love and family communication, and family communication and parenting, circling back to parenting and intimacy, and so on. In fact, it is difficult to disentangle or separate one aspect of marriage and family from another. This is the complex task of yesterday's and today's family scientists and family practitioners.

As we begin our in-depth examination of marital, family, and intimate relationships, it is important for you to keep in mind that I have broken the topics down into chapters for ease of study and discussion, but this in no way implies that they are separate areas of study. Remember, each and every chapter you read ties into and relates to the other chapters. As you read the chapters that follow this one, you may find yourself thinking, "Wait a minute . . . this sounds a lot like what we were studying in the love chapter," or "This area is very similar to the communication chapter." When you find yourself synthesizing and weaving together the material from one chapter to the next, then you will know that learning is taking place.

To understand the nature of intimate relationships among those people who are close to us, we must have a solid understanding of why we need to relate to others, how intimacy develops, and what happens to relationships when there are obstacles to the development of intimacy.

Intimacy: Do We Have a Need to Relate to Others?

Man is by nature a social animal . . . anyone who either cannot lead the common life or is so self-sufficient as to not need to, and therefore does not partake of society, is either a beast or a god. (Aristotle, 384–322 B.C.E.)

Aristotle penned these words centuries ago. While our cultural experiences of marriage and family life have changed since then, human nature has remained the same. As Aristotle recognized, the human race is a social people. We are *relational creatures* who seek—either by design or evolutionary drives—to be with another or to be with others. That's human nature.

We all want to belong to someone, to share with someone, to be intimate with someone. To be human carries with it almost a requirement of sorts that we relate to or relate with another human being, that we share intimacy with someone. Derived from the Latin word *intimus*, intimacy means inner or internal, or to come from within the individual. In personal relationships, intimacy is often conceptualized as a reciprocal trust between the partners, emotional closeness, and comfortable levels of self-disclosure in which partners can openly share their thoughts and feelings (Timmerman, 1991). It is a process of relating that promotes closeness, bondedness, and connectedness (Heller & Wood, 2000). Intimacy is thought to also include **responsiveness**, which is the verbal and/or nonverbal behavior that conveys support and affection to a partner (Miller, Berg, & Archer, 1983). Recall also from Chapter 3 that the multiple processes in interpersonal relationships are *transactional* and *interconnected*, which means that we simultaneously affect and are affected by our interpersonal relationships. So, if we weave together these concepts, we see that **intimacy** is the feelings of closeness that result from a transactional process between partners' self-disclosures and responsiveness (Marshall, 2008). In other words, as we self-disclose and share, and as our partner responds to these disclosures, our emotional bond to one another is strengthened and deepened. Although the meaning of intimacy varies from relationship to relationship, physical closeness is not necessarily a component of intimacy.

Some sociologists and anthropologists believe that intimacy is the **need for affiliation**, or the need to have relationships in our lives, and that this is a universal, innate drive. They believe that this may explain why intimate, interpersonal bonds are found the world over, across all ethnic and cultural boundaries (Erber & Erber, 2001). This drive for interpersonal relations is thought to fulfill important psychological needs. *Need fulfillment* was at one time considered as perhaps *the* primary purpose and function of intimacy in marriage and family relationships (Clinebell & Clinebell, 1970).

FULFILLING PSYCHOLOGICAL NEEDS

Empirical investigation in the 1970s, 1980s, and much of the 1990s virtually ignored the concept of relationship intimacy as a contributor to psychological need fulfillment. Karen Prager, one of the definitive researchers in the area of marital and relational intimacy, and her colleague Duane Buhrmester (1998) sought to determine whether the presumed links between need fulfillment and intimacy would promote a better understanding of the link between couple intimacy and individual well-being. The primary goals of this study were to see if and in what ways intimate couple communication and various intimacy components contributed to the overall well-being of the individuals and how these also contributed to need fulfillment. Prager and Buhrmester's work concluded that relational intimacy, measured by a couple's daily interactions, positively correlates with individual need fulfillment. They found that through frequent, intimate communication in which partners' communications consist of a positive tone, daily personal sharing with the partner, listening, and understanding, *individual* psychological needs are met by way of the *couple*. Other bodies of research substantiate that high levels of intimacy in relationships enhance the psychological, physical, and relational well-being of each partner, as well as lower risk of divorce (Hassebrauck & Fehr, 2002; Firestone & Firestone, 2004; Schneller & Arditti, 2004).

The universality of human relationships and the global drive of humans to connect to others can be explained in the survival needs that are met, such as safety, shelter, and provisional needs. But psychological needs must also be met. Sociologist Robert Weiss's (1969) discussion of sociability or friendliness suggests that when people form close interpersonal relationships, five essential psychological needs are met that cannot be met in other forms of impersonal human contact:

1. *Intimacy* is a basic, universal psychological need that drives us to share our innermost feelings with another or others.
2. *Social integration* is the innate need to belong to a social group. These needs propel us to vent our worries, fears, and anxieties with others.
3. We all have an internal desire *to nurture and to be nurtured*, to care for another and be taken care of.
4. At times we need *assistance* from others. Interpersonal relationships provide this.
5. *Reassurance* that we have worth, and that we are wanted, needed, and loved comes from intimacy with another person.

Through our intimate relationships, our basic psychological needs and our basic relationship needs are met. These healthy intimate relationships, in turn, contribute to the overall well-being of each partner (Kirby, Baucom, & Peterman, 2005).

THE ROLE OF INTIMACY IN RELATIONSHIPS

Intimacy is experienced differently from relationship to relationship. Its meaning varies not only from couple to couple but over time as well. For some couples, the experience of intimacy has to do with sharing moments of emotional closeness. For other couples, intimacy is linked with sex or physical closeness. For still others, intimacy is a spiritual or religious experience. However couples define and experience intimacy, it is necessary to meaningful relationships. Multifaceted and multidimensional, intimacy's components vary from culture to culture, ethnicity to ethnicity, and person to person.

EACH couple and family experience intimacy in different ways. Factors specific to the family's cultural background affect their attitudes and beliefs about intimacy, such as their willingness to self-disclose and their emotional reactions to intimacy.

Intimacy Is Multicontextual As Prager (1999) notes, each couple experiences intimacy and intimate relating in unique ways because of the many contextual factors that influence, impinge on, and nurture the couple's relationship. Figure 5.1 illustrates the multicontextual factors of intimacy.

According to Prager (1999), there are five different levels of intimacy contexts, which are shown in the model. At the very center, the **immediate context** refers to factors that influence the couple's interaction, such as the physical setting (is it quiet, relatively free of interruptions, private?), the couple's mood during the intimate interaction, and the couple's reason for talking.

The **personal context** includes factors specific to each person, such as personality traits, attitudes and beliefs about the overall status of the relationship; emotional reactions to intimacy; willingness to self-disclose; and each partner's intimacy needs, goals, and motives. The level of a partner's individual development of intimacy influences how we experience intimacy; it will be different at different stages of our relationship development.

The **relational context** refers to characteristics of the relationship and how the couple defines it. Factors such as companionship, trust, level of commitment, each partner's intimacy needs, and the presence of or type of conflict are all part of the relational context. For example, if a couple has underlying conflict in their relationship, such as unresolved problems with the

FIGURE 5.1   The Many Contexts of Intimacy

According to Karen Prager (1999), there are five different levels of intimacy contexts. Intimate interactions can occur *between* aspects of each context as well as *among* all other contexts.

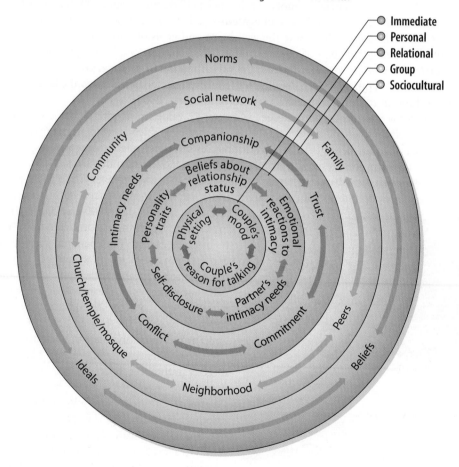

Source: 1999 from *The Intimate Couple* by J. Carlson and L. Sperry (Eds.). Adapted by permission of Routledge/Taylor & Francis Group, LLC.

in-laws, this conflict is always in the background of the couple's relationship. Much like background noise that can interrupt or interfere with our concentration on reading, unresolved conflict can ultimately interfere with how each partner experiences elements associated with intimacy, such as trust and/or commitment.

The **group context** includes the couple's social network, including each partner's family, peer relationships, neighborhood, and the community in which the couple lives. As Prager reminds us, social networks are important because they provide couples with instrumental support, such as advice, assistance with needs, guidance, and emotional support. This support, in turn, supports intimacy levels within the couple's relationship. (In Chapter 14, when we turn our attention to family crisis, you will see how these group context resources aid families in navigating the difficult twists and turns of family life.)

The **sociocultural context** is the overarching umbrella that contains such factors as the norms, beliefs, and ideals of the culture and subcultures in which couples live and relate. This context shapes each person's expectations about intimacy in her or his interpersonal relationships. Prager points out that it is society and culture that determine, or *prescribe*, how we are to intimately relate to another. In large part, it is the culture's **social identity** that emphasizes either the group's interests or the individual's interests. Particularly important is whether the culture defines itself as a collectivist culture or an individualistic culture.

In **collectivist cultures,** individuals define their identity in terms of the relationships they hold with others. For instance, if asked the question, "Who are you?," a collectivist is likely to respond by giving the family's name or region from which they originate (Triandis & Suh, 2002). The goals of the *collective*—the whole society—are given priority over individual needs, and group membership is important (Myers, 2005). In these cultures, members strive to be equal, contributing, beneficial members of the society (Triandis & Suh, 2002), and their personal behavior is driven by a feeling of obligation and duty to the society (Johnson and others, 2005). Collectivist cultures promote the well-being and goals of the collective group, rather than the well-being and goals of the individual. These cultures emphasize interdependence, interpersonal harmony, cooperation, and the subordination of personal goals to group goals (Kupperbusch and others, 1999). People's self-concepts, personal goals, and the larger society are inseparable in collectivist societies (Johnson and others, 2005).

Latinos, for example (as you will see in Chapter 7), value strong interdependent relationships with their families and they value the opinions of close friends (who, in many cases, are treated as family members); this, in turn, influences how they select mates and display and experience family processes such as intimacy (Castaeda, 1993; Fernandez-Dols, 1999).

In **individualistic cultures,** where individual goals are promoted over group goals, people define their identity in terms of personal attributes, such as wealth, social status, education level, and marital status (Myers, 2005). Unlike in collectivist cultures, *individualists* view themselves as truly independent, self-reliant entities from the society in which they live, and their personal needs and rights guide their behavior rather than the needs of the society (Johnson and others, 2005). Most Western societies, such as the United States, Canada, and Europe, are individualistic societies.

Social identity is important because it directly influences how we experience intimacy. For example, within individualistic (Western) cultures, *both* self-disclosure and responsiveness are important to the experience of a couple's intimacy, which ultimately determines to a large extent overall relationship satisfaction (Laurenceau, Barrett, & Rovine, 2005). But does this hold true for other cultures? In East Asian cultures, such as China,

IN collectivist cultures, people place emphasis on relationships with family and friends. Intimacy is experienced on an individual level, but these experiences are prescribed by the culture.

some research has discovered that *responsiveness* is a very necessary component of intimacy, and that it heightens relationship satisfaction (Heine, 2001). Other research has shown that *self-disclosure* is less significant (Chen, 1995). In other words, in some collectivist cultures both components are not necessary for the experience of intimacy—only responsiveness is.

There is also emerging evidence that gender roles are significantly influenced and shaped by the culture's social identity, and that these gender roles then influence the experiences of intimacy. In China, for instance, traditional gender roles are emphasized. In these roles, wives are subordinate to husbands and are more likely to assume household and mothering roles, while their husbands are more likely to work (Marshall, 2008). Gender role traditionalism is associated with lower levels of self-disclosure in relationships because, as you saw in the previous chapter, men are not encouraged to reveal their feelings. Today, there is emerging evidence that some Chinese men influence the levels of intimacy experienced within the relationship because of gender role traditionalism that inhibits self-disclosure (Marshall, 2008). Due to the transactional nature of intimacy, as Chinese men restrain self-disclosure, Chinese women reciprocate these low disclosures by lower levels of responsiveness, resulting in low levels of intimacy. This isn't to say, however, that there are lower levels of relationship satisfaction. Since the culture is a collectivist one and doesn't emphasize personal needs and wants, the lower levels of intimacy may not result in relationship dissatisfaction, as it would in individualistic cultures. The broader point to consider here is that cultural groups outside of the United States define and experience intimacy differently, and that lower levels of intimacy may not be a negative influence on relationships.

Prager's (1995) multitiered model of the many contexts of intimacy is important in our discussion of intimacy because it provides a visual reference of those factors that influence how intimacy is shaped, expressed, and experienced. In Figure 5.1 (page 143), note the interactions that occur *between* aspects of each distinct context; note the interactions that occur *among* each of the different contexts. Without question, these many contexts of intimacy determine and drive the extent to which intimacy is enhanced or hindered in our personal lives.

Intimacy Is an Emotional Attachment Although the aspects of intimacy may vary from one person to another, intimacy in committed relationships can best be thought of as an emotional attachment to another person (Openshaw, 2004). **Emotional attachment** is at the core of all love relationships, and it is characterized by feelings that promote a sense of closeness, bonding with one another, and connection (Heller & Wood, 1998). These feelings of closeness and bonding promote the well-being of another. According to Prager (1995), intimacy can be thought of as a three-pronged process that involves (1) disclosing things that are personal and private to ourselves, (2) experiencing positive feelings about ourselves and the other person(s) involved in the relationship, and (3) having interpersonal interactions that serve to advance or reflect partners' understanding of each other. For instance, as a couple shares, over time, private things about themselves with one another, they negotiate the differences in the way they think, feel, and behave. This sharing leads to the couple's "speaking the same language," which, in turn, strengthens the couple's common bond and their emotional attachment to one another (Heller & Wood, 2000). It is this emotional attachment that distinguishes their relationship from any other couple relationship.

Intimacy Is a Process Developing intimacy is a process, as it is dynamic and ever-changing. The term *process* implies *change* and *progression* over time. Just as we grow, change, and develop over time, so too do the contexts of our relational experiences. Intimacy is not a static or unchanging aspect of a relationship. The intimacy we share with our partners and family today will not be the same intimacy levels we share with them 5, 10, or even 20 years from now. As we get to know another person and as we begin to self-disclose our thoughts and feelings, personal sharing often leads to deepened levels of trust. This trust, in turn, facilitates greater self-disclosure and greater sharing of personal vulnerabilities, which even further deepens the level of trust (Heller & Wood, 1998). Over time, these interactions strengthen the intimate bonds couples and families share.

COMPONENTS OF INTIMACY

What constitutes intimate relationships? Family researchers have attempted to answer this question through empirical study. From his research of intimacy among married couples, marriage therapist Edward Waring (1984) describes eight components of intimacy:

1. *Conflict resolution.* This component addresses how couples manage the inevitable conflict that occurs within the relationship, and how they resolve differences of opinion. Effectively managing conflict optimizes high levels of intimacy.
2. *Affection.* How partners express affection and show feelings of emotional closeness is an important aspect of intimacy and affects the degree to which partners self-disclose, and the degree to which each reciprocates by sharing feelings and emotions.
3. *Cohesion.* This component looks at the degree to which the marriage relationship is valued, not only the level of commitment to the marriage but also each partner's sense of the other's level of commitment. A cohesive relationship fosters trust.
4. *Sexuality.* Not only is it important that each partner is able to communicate sexual needs, wants, and desires, but it is also important that each partner's sexual needs, wants, and desires are fulfilled by the marriage. This aspect of intimacy is considered the most intense togetherness a couple can experience.
5. *Identity.* Maintaining partners' individual identities is another aspect of intimacy that is important in order for both partners to be self-confident and have a high level of self-esteem. It is important that each partner's *individual* identity is not lost in the identity of the couple.
6. *Compatibility.* This component speaks to how partners relate to each other, work together, and play together. When intimacy exists, couples have a sense of comfort when they are together; they mutually fulfill the other's needs.
7. *Expressiveness.* The degree to which partners allow each other to know their most personal thoughts, beliefs, and feelings are strong indicators of intimacy.
8. *Autonomy.* Independence from a person's family of origin provides the emotional freedom a person needs to develop, nurture, and sustain intimacy with a partner.

Psychologist Bernard Schulman and his colleague have also determined, through scientific study, the relational components of intimacy (Peven & Shulman, 1999). Their work resulted in similar findings to Waring's. They too found that couples' ability to express themselves sexually, to resolve conflict, and to trust their partners influence and enhance marital intimacy. The researchers also found respect and the management of anger and warfare (times of conflict) to be components of intimacy. Social workers Mackey, Diemer, and O'Brien (2000) list personal disclosure, companionship, mutual appreciation, nonverbal communication, equity (mutuality in decision making), physical closeness (both sexual and nonsexual contact), and warmth as components of intimacy. And still other theorists have determined that love, affection, trust, and personal validation are components of intimacy (Berscheid, 1985; Hatfield & Rapson, 1993). There is no doubt that "intimacy" is a concept that means different things to different people.

Finally, other researchers have found spirituality and shared religious faith to be the foundation of all other components of intimacy. For example, shared religious and ethnic heritages provide couples with a useful resource and a

FOR many couples, spirituality is a bond that brings the couple closer together on emotional and other levels.

strong foundation from which they can navigate and negotiate their differences (Heller & Wood, 2000). The shared religious beliefs provide common ground (the "glue") to the marital couple. Others also found spirituality and faith to be a foundation for marital intimacy. They note that sharing and self-disclosing of a person's spiritual life and self-disclosing through moments of shared prayer are "probably the strongest knot that binds a couple" (Morgan & Kuykendall, 2000, p. 60). Through the sharing of faith and religious customs such as prayer, maintain both Heller and Wood (2000) and Morgan and Kuykendall (2000), intimacy is intensified.

There are also sex differences in how people define and experience intimacy. For example, earlier studies suggested that women initiate *verbal* intimacy with their husbands more than their husbands do with them, and they tend to define intimacy as "being" together with someone (Tannen, 1990). This finding shows us that, in general, women try to get closer to people by engaging in discussions with them; they also express more concern in their relationships than men do. Conversely, men have what is referred to as a "doing" orientation. That is to say, men prefer to engage in activities with their partners to show togetherness, rather than just "being" together. According to this body of research, then, women define and experience intimacy as "being," whereas men express "doing" characteristics of intimacy (Tannen, 1990).

In more recent research, investigators examined the attitudes and beliefs of nearly 400 undergraduate college students, and found that there are sex differences in the experiences of intimacy (Hook, Gerstein, Detterich, & Gridley, 2003). In this study, women scored higher than men on the intimacy factors of love and affection, and personal validation. These findings suggest that women place more emphasis on love, affection, emotional sharing, and the expression of tenderness (such as warm feelings) more than men do. A surprising finding was that women and men did not significantly differ in their responses about trust as it relates to intimacy; both men and women expressed that they were comfortable with giving and receiving emotional support in relationships.

Certainly, it is difficult to assess and define intimacy because of its multidimensional components and characteristics, but an understanding of this relationship process as a separate experience from love is important: If any component (however a couple defines it) is missing, relationship satisfaction will be negatively impacted (Hook and others, 2003). On the other hand, if couples work to discover—at the outset of their relationships—what factors of intimacy are important to them and in what ways they experience intimacy differently, then the gendered experiences and expressions of intimacy would no longer be an obstacle to relationship satisfaction (Hook and others, 2003).

TYPES OF INTIMATES

Not only have family researchers over the years attempted to identify those components that make up intimacy, researchers and family practitioners have also attempted to define the different types of intimates. These typologies are categorized according to attributes that reflect an individual's capacity for intimacy.

Basing their work on Erikson's (1963) classic theory of intimacy development in young adulthood (which we will explore in depth a bit later in this chapter), psychologist Jacob Orlofsky and his colleagues (1973) developed specific types of intimates. Using a framework that has as its foundation *commitment*, the degree to which each partner in the couple is dedicated to the relationship, and *depth*, the closeness and involvement in the relationship, Orlofsky, Marcia, and Lesser (1973) identified **intimacy status**.

- The first intimacy status is the **intimate**. The intimate is capable of experiencing closeness, forming an emotional attachment to another, and is committed to depth in a relationship, which fosters long-term, enduring relationships. Intimates can be any age, and this intimacy status can be found in many types of relationships, such as marriage, same-sex partnerships, and even friendships. The distinguishing characteristic of intimates is that they possess the capacity to express their innermost feelings and thoughts with another person—this leads to deeper levels of commitment and closeness.

Intimacy Inventory

High levels of intimacy in personal, intimate relationships are associated with positive mental health and emotional well-being for couples and families. As you have learned, experiences of intimacy in partner and marital relationships are crucial determinants of relationship satisfaction. However, all forms of intimacy develop over time. Establishing and maintaining intimacy requires nurturing attention to the relationship. Take time to examine your individual intimacy needs by completing the intimacy inventory below.

Intimacy Inventory

When we are emotionally close, I feel _____.

I would describe our intellectual closeness as _____.

As far as intimacy in our relationship is concerned, I am most satisfied when _____.

I am least comfortable about our relationship when _____.

When you express your emotions and feelings, it makes me _____.

When you express physical closeness, it makes me _____.

Spiritual closeness is _____.

When I experience intimacy with you, I feel _____.

When I am with you, my individuality is _____.

Intimacy leads to good feelings and bad feelings. Knowing this makes me feel _____.

Some people resist intimacy. This makes me think _____.

When I reveal my innermost thoughts, feelings, emotions, and fears, I expect _____.

When my partner/friend reveals his or her innermost thoughts, feelings, emotions, and fears, it makes me _____.

Intimately relating with another carries with it a risk of rejection. The possibility of rejection makes me feel _____.

In general, I am trusting of others. This makes me _____.

In general, I am not trusting of others. This makes me _____.

If I were to sum up the role of intimacy in my life, I would characterize it as _____.

- A **pseudointimate** appears to be intimate on the surface but lacks depth. Pseudointimate relationships may never progress beyond friendship, or the pseudointimate may experience only superficial levels of emotional closeness in a dating, cohabiting, or marital relationship. Some pseudointimates bounce from one seemingly intimate relationship to another, but because of their inability to develop emotional closeness—and thus, their inability to fully commit to another person—these relationships are doomed from the outset.
- **Preintimates** are capable of intimacy, and may even desire it, but they lack the ability to make the commitment necessary to sustain long-term, or perhaps long-distance, relationships. For instance, education or career demands, or a military deployment may impede on someone being able to fully commit to his or her partner until the individual's circumstances change. Some clergy, such as nuns and priests, may also be considered to be preintimates, because their statuses preclude them from being able to share commitment and depth in a couple relationship.

- **Stereotyped relationships** are those in which an individual has any number of casual relationships; however, these relationships are devoid of depth and commitment. Unlike pseudointimates where there is a superficial appearance that relationships are intimate even though they are not, in stereotyped relationships there is no representation of commitment or depth.
- **Isolates** are people who are socially withdrawn and have no apparent need for either social or close interpersonal interactions. For example, Ted Kaczynski is the infamous "Unibomber," a domestic terrorist in the United States from the 1970s through much of the 1990s. Until he was captured in 1996, Kaczynski lived in isolation and seclusion, away from human contact, for nearly 20 years.

Other intimacy researchers expanded the intimacy statuses developed by Orlofsky and colleagues to include the **merger status** (Whitbourne & Weinstock, 1979). These researchers contend that the intimate status requires partners in a relationship to experience an equal balance of power, or equity. When there is an imbalance of power, with one partner dominating, the partner being dominated feels a subsequent loss of autonomy and sense of individual identity. Because of this imbalance of power, a relationship may appear to have depth and commitment, yet it cannot reach the full status of intimate.

Developing Intimacy

Although we are just at the start of our study of marriage, family, and intimate relationships, you have already discovered that much of our ability to relate to others in a meaningful way takes place during the very early years of life. While each of us develops the capacity to love and be intimate with others throughout infancy, childhood, adolescence, and early adulthood, it is the very early stages of life that establish the foundation of the ability to love and share intimacy. In a very real sense, the relationships experienced from the moment of birth help shape and mold a person's "intimate" self, because each relationship formed during the first 20 years or so serve as first-of-a-kind interactions upon which later interpersonal interactions and intimate relationships are built.

Recall from Chapter 1 that we do not develop in isolation; rather, our individual development takes place in the context of significant emotional relationships, particularly in our family of origin. This is true of the development of intimacy as well. The moment a baby is born, a mutual, interdependent relationship exists between the newborn and his or her caregivers. It is within the family context, in combination with the environment and other outside factors, that intimacy develops—in essence, we learn to be intimate (Cardillo, 2005). We have already established that intimacy is a universal human need. If this is the case, then do we really need to *learn* to be intimate, shaped to be intimate, as Cardillo suggests? Erik Erikson's (1902–1994) theory of social and emotional development provides insight into this question. In the section that follows, we'll take a brief look at Erikson's theory because it allows us to see how our capacity to be intimate with another person develops over our lifespan.

THE PSYCHOSOCIAL DEVELOPMENT OF CHILDREN

Similar to the foundation of a house that is built, floor by floor, so too is the foundation of our ability to be intimate with another built on developmental stage by developmental stage. In the 1950s, psychologist Erik Erikson provided a lifespan approach for **psychosocial development**, which is the social and emotional development of an individual. Essentially, Erikson's **Eight Stages of Man** were formulated to put forth the notion that our social and emotional development is a lifelong process; that what happens or does not happen at one stage will eventually affect our psychosocial development during later stages of life. Table 5.1 (page 150) outlines Erikson's eight developmental stages, which encompass what developmentalists refer

TABLE 5.1 Erikson's Developmental Stages

Influential psychologist Erik Erikson formulated the Eight Stages of Man developmental theory. According to Erikson, a person is in a continuous state of development from the cradle to the grave.

Erikson's Theory of Psychosocial Development

Stage	Age	Developmental Task
Trust vs. Mistrust	Infancy, 0–24 months	Child develops a belief that his or her caregivers will provide a secure and trustful environment.
Autonomy vs. Shame and Doubt	Toddlerhood, 2–4 years	Child develops a sense of independence and free will; feels shame if he or she doesn't use the free will appropriately.
Initiative vs. Guilt	Early Childhood, 4–6 years	"The Age of Acquiring": Child learns to explore his or her environment and acquires a newfound set of skills; feels a newfound sense of initiative and accomplishment.
Industry vs. Inferiority	Middle Childhood, 7–12 years	"The Age of Mastery": Child masters the skills acquired during early childhood.
Identity vs. Role Confusion	Adolescence, 13–21 years	Teen develops a sense of who he or she is in comparison to others (sense of "self"); develops a keen sense of role expectations.
Intimacy vs. Isolation	Young Adult, 22–35 years	Develops ability to give and receive love; begins to consider long-term relationships, marriage, and parenting as realistic options.
Generativity vs. Stagnation	Middle Adulthood, 36–65 years	Develops interest in giving of himself or herself to younger generations by helping them lead meaningful lives and by caring for them.
Integrity vs. Despair	Older Adulthood, 65+ years	Desires to find meaningful and personal gratification with the life he or she has lived.

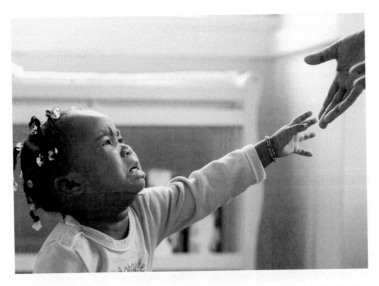

ALTHOUGH some parents may be concerned that picking up a baby when he or she is crying may spoil the child, researchers have discovered that doing so establishes a sense of trust in the infant. This trust is the foundation on which all other forms of intimacy are built throughout life.

to as a *cradle-to-grave* approach to understanding individual psychosocial development. We begin our study of intimacy formation by examining the early experiences in life, from infancy through the school years.

Learning to Trust The fundamental developmental task of infancy (0 to 2 years) is learning to *trust* our primary caregivers. During this time, if the child is nurtured, loved, and receives affection, he or she will develop a sense of trust and security. Every time a parent or caregiver responds to a baby's cries of distress or needs for attention, the adult sends resounding signals to the baby that the world is a safe place to be in. If, on the other hand, a parent or primary caregiver does not respond to the needs of the baby, or if the baby's distress signals are ignored or neglected, the baby will become insecure and mistrustful of others. It is during this time the child's initial capacity for intimate and loving relationships begins to take shape—and the foundation for *current and future intimacy* and loving relationships is laid.

Consider the following scenario. When my sons were younger, I took them to the city swimming pool one afternoon. While there, I saw a friend who had recently adopted a son. The child was about 3 years old at the time of his adoption; he had been removed from his birth mother's home because of neglect and physical abuse. The adoptive father and I engaged in conversation while his son played in the "kiddie" pool. He relayed to me how the child appeared to be withdrawn. He explained that his son would not snuggle or cuddle with them, and would not respond to any displays of affection. A woman approached us and said, "Excuse me, but is that your little boy?" My friend looked up to see that his child had fallen and seriously cut his forehead. We might expect a 3-year-old who has banged his head to scream and cry or run over to a parent for emotional and physical comfort, but this little boy, cut and bleeding, did not cry. He did not come to his father for help. Instead, he got out of the swimming pool, lay down on the concrete, and put his head in his arms.

This story illustrates the significance of early relationships and their significance to relational intimacy in later life stages. Because this child received little or no nurturing and affection from his first intimate relationship—the mother–child relationship—he did not develop a sense of trust in his caregivers, as most children do. And because of this lack of trust, he did not turn to his father when he was hurt. Without a doubt, having security and comfort needs met in the early years of life plays a significant role in shaping intimate relationships (McAdams, 1989). In a very real sense, early intimate relationships provide a "crystal ball" that allows us to look into the future of a child's relational and intimacy abilities. This child's early experiences don't necessarily spell relational doom for him, however; there are many opportunities for him to form healthy attachments in his lifespan. (In Chapter 6 we more closely examine the development of trust and emotional attachment.)

Developing Independence Through early childhood (ages 2 through about 6) children develop independence, or *autonomy*, in their social and emotional capacities. This is important to the foundation of intimacy, because it is this capacity that allows children to explore their environments with confidence and surety. This, in turn, helps children learn to get along and cooperate with others, as well as learn to relate to other family members and peers—all necessary components in the giving and receiving of intimacy later in life.

As children's sense of autonomy heightens during the preschool years, this drive for independence affects their relationships with peers. Their relationship with peers, however, is influenced by and embedded in their intimate relationships with their parents or primary caregivers. Research also indicates that children in this early stage of life are capable of expressing sensitivity and empathy in peer interactions; these abilities are key elements in intimate relationships when we are older (Prager, 1995; Prager & Buhrmester, 1998; Cardillo, 2005).

Consider the interaction and relational patterns between you and your parent(s) or primary caregiver. Did these experiences allow you to feel that you were worthy of affection and love? Or instead, did your early parent–child experiences cause you to feel shame, guilt, and doubt, resulting in fear of intimacy, fear of abandonment, betrayal, and rejection in your adult relationships?

Developing and Mastering Friendships The elementary school years present a tremendous opportunity for social and emotional growth. For children in about first grade through sixth grade, the initiation and formation of peer groups increases, as does the significance of these relationships to the child's developing sense of self. As children move through elementary school, more and more of their time is spent interacting with same-sex peers. Be it a whispered secret during recess, a quick pickup game of basketball after school, or helping with the drudgeries of long division in a school hallway, childhood

CHILDHOOD and adolescent friendships provide children companionship and support for their emerging self-concepts and sense of identity. Think back to your childhood and adolescent friendships. In what ways did these friendships promote your intimacy capacities? In what ways did these friendships hinder your intimacy capacities?

How Does the Family Environment Affect Intimacy?

Past family experiences are very much a part of present relationships. Family scientist Danielle Sjoberg (2002) sought to understand parent–adolescent relationships and how they relate to intimacy formation.

The relationship adolescent boys have with their fathers, for example, has more impact on intimacy formation than does their relationship with their mothers. Good communication with fathers was linked to close, personal relationships in adolescent boys. These boys had more close friends, longer friendships, and higher self-esteem. The significance of the boys' relationships with their fathers cuts across ethnic and racial differences, although white and Hispanic youth tend to experience greater intimacy with their fathers and friends than do African American youth. Sjoberg posits that perhaps meaningful relationships with fathers helps adolescent males achieve close, personal, and enjoyable relationships with their peers.

In addition, Sjoberg's review of studies indicates that adolescent girls from single-parent homes headed by mothers are more likely to become teen single mothers, engage in high levels of sexual activity, and experience poorer interpersonal relationships with the opposite sex. Father-absent females tend to experience less intimacy in their marriages than father-present females.

In her review, Sjoberg notes that children raised in same-sex parent households experience little or no differences in the kinds and levels of intimacy compared to those children reared in opposite-sex parent homes. Sjoberg concludes that it is not the family structure, per se, that influences the development of a healthy sense of intimacy, but that the adolescent feels closeness and trust with influential adult figures.

TALK ABOUT IT

1. How does parenting function as a dimension of intimacy formation?
2. What can be done in families, regardless of their structure, to positively influence the development and experience of intimacy?

Source: Sjoberg (2002).

---

friendships provide children great companionship and an opportunity to disclose their innermost secrets, wishes, and fears. In addition, childhood peer relationships afford children a "safety net" that allows them to practice and rehearse their new relational roles.

The formation of peer groups is a multistep process. An academic who studied the formation of friendships, D. C. Dunphy (1963) in a classic study examined adolescent friendship development in urban areas. The earlier stages of friendship development described by Dunphy are found during the school years:

■ **Stage One: Pre-Crowd Stage**. From about kindergarten through fifth grade, during this stage of friendship development, isolated unisex peer groups exist in the form of *cliques*, small groups of four to nine members. Spontaneous, shared activities provide the opportunity to relate personally. Boys tend to join larger groups and enjoy doing activities together, whereas girls tend to join smaller, more intimate groups. These peer group types dominate the school years. It is not uncommon to see these types of peer groups on a school playground, where boys are excluding girls from their pickup football game at recess, or where girls forbid boys to listen in on their "girl talk." Members are attracted to one another on the basis of similar interests, neighborhoods, schools, or religions. Boys' groups are often larger and more stable than girls' groups (Atwater, 1992).

■ **Stage Two: Beginning of the Crowd**. Still same-sex in nature, peer groups toward the end of sixth grade or beginning of seventh grade begin to shift to *crowds*, which consist of 10 or more members. Crowds are essentially a collection of cliques—membership in cliques is required to belong to the crowd (Atwater, 1992). Crowd activities such as after-school dances and sporting events provide preadolescents the chance to "practice" interacting with the opposite sex, alleviating the uneasiness that often comes with opposite-sex relationships. For instance, Katie may have a crush on Danny, yet she flirts with all the other boys in her friendship crowd. In this way, she practices her newfound intimacy skills on others, without the risk of being rejected by Danny if she flirts with only him.

■ **Stage Three: Crowd in Transition.** During the end of junior high (eighth or ninth grade) and throughout high school, peer groups are seen as in transition. During this time, smaller cliques are formed within the larger crowd. The pairing off of male and female couples, typically seen sooner in early maturing boys and girls, drives the crowd into transition. While the crowd may still hang out together for certain events, such as going to a movie or to a school basketball game, they more frequently begin to prefer to interact with the smaller group of friends, and begin to exclude others from the emerging smaller clique.

■ **Stage Four: Fully Developed Crowd.** The fully developed crowd is composed entirely of opposite-sex cliques; no longer are the same-sex friendship affiliations dominant as they were throughout elementary school and the early years of junior high. Peer groups during this stage exist only long enough for members to learn or to be socialized into those characteristics needed for adult relationships, such as sharing intimate thoughts and feelings, and interdependence.

■ **Stage Five: Crowd Disintegration.** As adolescents mature into adulthood and take on adult responsibilities, such as a job or pursuing a college degree, and as they become involved in serious intimate relationships, crowd-type friendship groups begin to disintegrate. Often the support of friends is replaced by an intimate partner with whom young adults now share and disclose, and with whom they are perhaps sexually involved. Friendship groups consequently become more loosely associated. Over time, many find their spouse or life mate to be their "best" friend, although they still hold on to one or two close friends.

Other researchers have since found peer group formation to be similar to Dunphy's original 1960s study of peer group formation (Atwater, 1992; Paul & White, 1990).

What is it that makes friendship so special or so different from other kinds of relationships in our lives? Recent research has shown that friendships, unlike family relationships, provide us more feelings of freedom, closeness, and pleasure; we are also able to experience higher levels of self-disclosure with our friends than we do with our families (Mendelson & Kay, 2003; Rybak & McAndrew, 2006). Furthermore, friendships are often quite emotionally rewarding because the sharing that takes place between friends fosters the growth and development of empathy. **Empathy** is the capacity to understand another's circumstances or situation, and the ability to feel or express emotional concern for another person. It is believed that the experiences of empathy are what lead to a greater sensitivity—and emotional bond—to each other, both in friendships and any other intimate relationship (Rybak & McAndrew, 2006).

PEER group formation goes through several stages. These relationships are essential in our lives because they allow us to develop, practice, and maintain our relational skills. Can you trace your friendships through the various stages of your development? How closely do they align with Dunphy's stages of peer formation?

As you can see from Dunphy's study, as children grow through childhood and enter adolescence, their dependence on their parents for intimacy lessens and they turn to "chumships" for support. It is also interesting to note how the changes in friendships are associated with life transitions. Some researchers have discovered that maintaining and adapting friendships throughout these life changes help buffer the stress associated with major transitions, such as going away to college or getting married (Brooks, 2002; Oswald & Clark, 2003). It is important to understand these developmental changes in peer groups structures and the significance of friendships, because each type of friendship group (intimate relationships) throughout life affects a person's psychosocial development in all subsequent stages of life. During adolescence, intimate friendships contribute to the adolescent's *identity formation*, and the establishment of their *autonomy, intimacy,* and *sexuality*.

ADOLESCENTS' AND YOUNG ADULTS' PSYCHOSOCIAL DEVELOPMENT

The adolescent period of human growth and development is a time of many transitions for the teen. According to adolescent intimacy researcher D. Kim Openshaw (1999), the biological, cognitive, and psychosocial changes that occur through adolescence trigger a change in teens' *need* for intimacy. These changes, in turn, create a change in teens' *capacity to experience* intimate relationships, and the *extent* to which and the *way* in which intimacy is expressed.

Along with the physical changes that take place during puberty come changes in teens' cognitive capabilities, as well as growth and change in the social and emotional areas. Family practitioner and professor of child development, Angela Huebner (2000) provides a thorough discussion of these psychosocial changes. The following key points highlight her findings.

Establishing an Identity, Autonomy, and Intimacy In order to experience healthy intimate relationships in later stages of adult development, an individual must first have a strong sense of **identity**, or the sense of "who" he or she is (Erikson, 1963). Friendships play a key role in the adolescent's social, emotional, and relational development.

The questions "Who am I?" and "Why am I on Earth?" occupy an adolescent's thoughts, and over the course of the adolescent developmental period, teens incorporate their beliefs, values, and opinions of influential others (parents, peers, teachers) into their own identity. At the same time, adolescents begin the process of **individuation**—that is, forming an identity that is separate from that of their family of origin.

This developmental process of individuation affects the development of intimacy, because as teens open up and disclose with their peers, it helps them clarify their own thoughts and emotions, and thus helps them better define their own uniqueness (German, 2002). As teens share with their peers and the significant others in their lives, they develop a deeper understanding of not only themselves but also of others. Intimate friendships are more common during adolescence because teens feel that it's safer to reveal their thoughts and feelings to friends rather than to family (Berndt & Savin-Williams, 1990). In essence, teens feel that since others their same age are going through similar experiences, they are better able to relate. The outcome of this process is that as adolescents approach the transition to early adulthood, they have a clearer sense of their values, beliefs, and relationship expectations. This enhanced sense of identity promotes intimacy.

Teens must also develop **autonomy**, which refers to not only establishing a sense of independence but also becoming a self-governing person within the context of relationships. Adolescents must begin to take responsibility for their actions and decisions that affect themselves and, in many cases, those around them. For instance, if an adolescent chooses to have unprotected sex, he or she must realize that this decision may carry associated risks, such as acquiring a sexually transmitted infection or resulting in an unwanted pregnancy, and that these risks don't just affect them but their partner and families, as well.

As we discussed earlier in this chapter, the capacity for intimacy is acquired from the moment of birth, from our very first intimate relationship with our parent(s) or primary caregiver. As we develop throughout our early childhood and our school years, our peers become increasingly important to us, and also to the formation of our capacity for intimacy. Perhaps more than at any other time in our lifecourse development, it is during adolescence that friends are most significant. Through friendships we learn to be open and honest, to self-disclose, to share empathy, and to trust. These are the foundations of intimacy.

During adolescence, friends provide advice, counsel, comfort, ego strokes, and a sense of belonging. As we progress through adolescence and approach early adulthood, our friendships move from same-sex group interaction, to mixed-sex interactions, to coupling or pairing off, to eventually having only a select, few friends.

Establishing Comfort with Sexuality We are all sexual beings. Our capacity to engage with another person on a sexually intimate level is a process that begins during the prenatal period. The discovery process begins for adolescents, however, as they experience the biological, cognitive, and psychosocial changes that we have just discussed. These changes lead adolescents to explore who they are sexually, perpetuating the desire to become sexually intimate with another.

As the adolescent experiences the changes in cognition and thought processes, his or her *need for intimacy* changes—there is much to make sense of in this world, and reaching out to another who is experiencing the world similar to an adolescent helps teens navigate these changes. As adolescents individuate, find their own identity, and are given more freedom, their *capacity to have intimate relationships* changes. This, too, is seen in the formation and maintenance of peer relationships. As adolescents undergo the physiological changes associated with puberty, they have a new way in which to be *intimate* with others—sexual intimacy is now possible. Of course, there is much, much more to being sexually intimate than the sex act itself (such as being comfortable with our sexual skin or being comfortable expressing our sexuality). We will examine sexual intimacy in great detail in the sexuality chapter later in this text.

It is important to note that there are differences between male intimacy experiences and female intimacy experiences. There are also cultural differences.

Experiencing Gender Differences in Friendships How do male friendships differ from female friendships? As you saw from Dunphy's (1963) study, as children mature, their peer groups shift in gender preference. As the shifts in gender preference occur, other discrepancies between males and females emerge:

- Females attach more emotional importance to their friends than do males (Lempers & Clark-Lempers, 1993).
- Men are less expressive and supportive toward friends than women are (Bank & Hansford, 2000; Burleson, 2003).
- Men are less likely to turn to their friends in time of trouble than women are (Rubin, 1986).
- Females more strongly emphasize mutual understanding, security, and mutual exploration of interests than do males (Kuttler, LaGreca, & Prinstein, 1999).
- More so than males, females discuss family problems and activities, personal dreams, fears, personal problems, and secrets (Johnson & Airies, 1983).
- Males emphasize activity and achievement in their group friendships; they show less interest in reciprocity/mutuality, and support/caring than do girls (Thorne, 1986).
- Males discuss sports and hobbies more so than females (Johnson & Airies, 1983).

Researchers believe that the differences found between male and female friendship experiences are due to socialization patterns, or **gender typing** (Johnson & Aries, 1983; Kuttler, LaGreca, & Prinstein, 1999). As you learned in Chapter 4, male socialization tends to emphasize the establishment and maintenance of achievement, whereas female socialization tends to emphasize the importance of the establishment and maintenance of interpersonal relationships. Recent empirical study has revealed that gender typing affects the type of communication between friends (Basow & Rubenfeld, 2003). For example, women are more likely to try to resolve a problem, offer sympathy, and share a similar story as a response to a friend with a problem, whereas men are more likely to try to resolve the problem, tell the friend not to worry, or change the subject in a similar circumstance (Basow & Rubenfeld, 2003). There are also gender differences in feelings and emotions in response to being given advice from a friend—women are more likely to feel comforted and grateful when advice is offered by a friend, whereas men are more likely to feel angry and hurt.

Emerging research suggests that there is still much to learn about friendships, particularly in the area of cross-sex friendships. **Cross-sex friendships (CSFs)** are friendships between opposite-sex peers. For many decades, CSFs were viewed by researchers as potential romantic attractions between partners, and not as friendships (Bleske-Rechek & Buss, 2001). Today, however, empirical study is beginning to view CSFs as qualitatively different from both romantic relationships and friendships in four distinct areas: defining the relationship, managing sexual attraction, establishing equality, and managing the interference of other friends and family (such as pushing the cross-sex friends to pursue dating) (Lenton & Webber, 2006).

A number of recent studies show us that

- Men have more CSFs than women do (Reeder, 2003). This may be because men view the friendship as a potential gateway to sexual interaction; it may also be because men are more comfortable sharing their thoughts and feelings with a woman and not a man.
- Men may gain intimacy from their female friends (West, Anderson, & Duck, 1996).
- Women may gain protection from their male friends (Bleske-Rechek & Buss, 2000).
- Cross-sex friendships may be a mate acquisition strategy for women (Bleske-Rechek & Buss, 2001).
- Some men and women may use CSF as a way to become exposed to more opposite-sex people, thus increasing their chances of meeting a romantic partner (Monsour, 2002).
- More single people have CSFs than married people (Lenton & Webber, 2006).
- "Feminine" people (both men and women) report having more female than male friends; "masculine" people (both men and women) report having more male friends (Reeder, 2003).

All of these recent findings are interesting because they point to potential societal changes in how and why we select the friends that we do, and to changes in how we select potential mates. Much more study needs to be done to understand the multiple factors associated with CSFs, and to understand the benefits of these relationships to the development of intimacy.

So far we have discovered that there are differences between male intimacy experiences and female intimacy experiences. Considering the intrinsic diversity within contemporary society, another question remains to be answered: How do cultural differences influence adolescent friendships and intimacy?

RESEARCH shows that interracial relationships provide richness to college students' university experiences.

Culture/Ethnicity and Friendship Despite the fact that the United States is rich in cultural diversity, scant research exists that examines the influences of culture and/or ethnicity on friendship formation.

In a recent study of the formation of adolescent friendships, researcher Caryn Dolich (2005) examined three cultures in an attempt to determine whether cultural differences affect males' and females' friendships. She compared the differences in aspects of friendship among Moroccan, European, and American adolescents. Dolich found that within all of the cultures, females reported higher ratings of the importance of intimacy and companionship than did males. In addition, she found that among the cultures, females discussed personal and daily events/trivial issues more frequently than males did. Consistent with prior research (such as Johnson & Airies, 1983), females among the three cultures in Dolich's study developed more intimate and personal relationships than males did. However, unlike the results found in previous research, the males in Dolich's study did report that they discuss with some frequency such things as intimacy, family relationships, dating, and sex with

Interracial Intimacy

Interracial dating, intimate partnering, and marriage are on the rise in the United States. **Interracial** relationships comprise romantic or marriage partners of different races. **Miscegenation** refers to those of different races, ethnicities, or religions who produce children together. Given the increase in the numbers of couples choosing to date or marry outside their race or ethnicity, it is important to consider whether these relationships promote family health and well-being.

YES: Interracial families possess many strengths. These strengths include (Burrello, 2005):

- **The richness of living in culturally diverse neighborhoods.** This helps eliminate racial boundaries and racial stereotypes.
- **The preservation of customs, rituals, and languages of both cultures represented in the family home.** Children are privileged to experience all sides of their multiple heritages.
- **The firsthand experience of understanding diversity and accepting differences.** Children of interracial families learn to respect and appreciate differences among people. Interracial families tend to exhibit more patience and understanding about others' differences.

NO: Some opponents to interracial dating, marriage, and parenting believe that those who date or marry outside their race or ethnicity betray their families, as well as abandon their cultural heritage. African American attorney Lawrence Otis Graham notes that children of interracial couples do not have sufficient black role models who help them understand their racial identity. In a recent study that examined interracial couples, the researcher found social and psychological implications associated with interracial intimacy (Killian, 2001). These include:

- **Reduced social support.** Many of the couples in Killian's study limited their contact with their family and friends; they also reported an extensive disruption or loss in their family support networks.
- **Social resistance.** Several interracial couples reported overt experiences of racism, including subtle public avoidance, exclusion from conversations, people staring, and discrimination in housing.
- **Silenced family histories.** Creating a couple identity from two distinct ethnic/cultural backgrounds proved difficult for the interracial couples in Killian's study. Most couples indicated they had to de-emphasize their individual family histories and rituals and create their own.

WHAT DO YOU THINK?

1. What is your opinion of interracial dating and/or marriage? What is your opinion based on?
2. After reviewing the studies just described, what do you think is most positive about interracial dating or marriage? The most negative?
3. If you chose to marry someone from another race, what kind of family support and social support do you think you would receive?

Sources: Burrello, (2005); Lee & Edmonston (2005); Killian (2001).

opposite-sex friends. Dolich's study did not determine whether culture ultimately influences the experience of friendship during adolescence.

The **contact hypothesis** maintains that the idea that negative stereotypes (prejudices) about other groups exist because of the lack of contact and interaction between racial groups (Allport, 1958). Given that college and university campuses are often the most racially and ethnically diverse environments that most students have experienced, does this mean that the college environment translates into a more diverse friendship network? Some studies have shown that greater diversity in junior high and high school does foster the development of relationships across racial and ethnic lines, and that intergroup contact leads to improved racial attitudes (Duncan, Boisjoly, Levy, Kremer, & Eccles, 2003; Quillian & Campbell, 2003; Sacerdote & Marmaros, 2005). This intergroup contact, in turn, leads to fewer negative stereotypes (Pettigrew & Tropp, 2006). Unfortunately, to date little research exists about interracial/ethnic friendships in college, but one recent study gives us insight into these friendship experiences.

In a study of nearly 4,000 white, black, Hispanic, and Asian first-time college students in the United States, the investigator sought to determine friendship diversity on college campuses (Fischer, 2008). As Figure 5.2 shows us, white and black students reported that most of their friends belong to the same racial/ethnic group as they do; there are few cross-group friendships. Asian and Hispanic students reported fewer same-group friendships. Furthermore, students who had more diverse friendship networks in high school were more likely to report having cross-group friends in college. These new findings about diversity in friendships are important because past research has shown that interracial friendships are rewarding experiences.

In a University of Michigan study that examined interracial friendships, the researcher found that college students reported that their interracial/ethnic friendships were positive, and that these friendships increased in number throughout their four years of college (Gurin, 1999). Figure 5.3 denotes the percentages of college students who grew to be even more positive over their four-year college experience. It is important to note, however, that Gurin's study has been criticized because factors such as racial tensions, conflict, and polarization were ignored by the researcher (for example, see the National Association of Scholars, 2001).

As you can see from our discussion, there are differences in how each gender experiences intimate relationships with others. Cultural and ethnic differences also appear to enrich the

FIGURE 5.2   Percentage of College Students Who Have Same-Group Friendships

Some college students belong to the same racial group as their friends do.

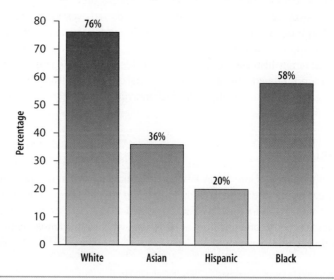

Source: Fischer (2008).

FIGURE 5.3 Positive Feelings toward Different Races: First Year in College Compared to Fourth Year in College

College students indicate that their relationships with students from different racial/ethnic groups than their own are positive, enriching life experiences. As the data indicate, when responding to the statement, "My relationships with students from different racial/ethnic groups at the University have been positive," most groups indicated an increase in positive feelings over their four-year college experience.

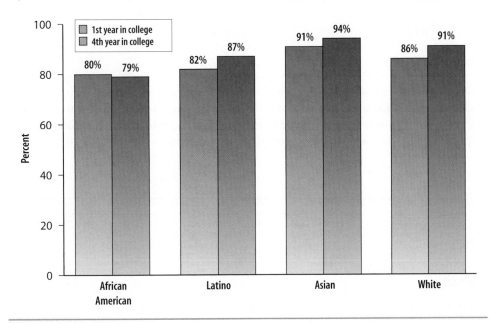

Source: Gurin (1999).

adolescent and young adult developmental periods. Within these friendships, adolescents establish their unique identities and intimacy.

Forming Deeper Bonds Each time I attend a high school graduation ceremony, I can't help but smile as graduate after graduate crosses the platform. As the adolescent crosses the platform to receive the high school diploma and tries to remember which hand to shake with, so much more is taking place than is visible to the casual observer. This ceremony represents a bridge between adolescence and early adulthood, taking most adolescents from total dependence on their family of origin to more independent emotional, moral, and financial responsibility. The platform on which the diploma is received seems to be launching the adolescent into a new phase of development. So it seems appropriate that early adulthood is often referred to as the *bridge years*.

During the years between adolescence and middle adulthood, young men and women find themselves accepting both the rewards and challenges of independence and the responsibility that accompanies autonomy. Along with this independence, young adults begin examining those qualities they find desirable in a life partner or spouse and begin to contemplate the commitment of marital and life-partnering relationships. The notion of bearing children also becomes more appealing and more realistic.

Social and emotional development during early adulthood is marked with the formation of deeper intimacy in interpersonal relationships. These intimate relations differ from childhood and adolescent friendships in that they involve a greater level of mutuality, respect, reciprocity, and self-sacrifice. Erikson suggested that these intimate relationships are essential to healthy development and without such, developing adults are at risk for an isolation-filled life (1986). More attention will be given to adult (early, middle, and late) development throughout this textbook.

We saw earlier how the process of intimacy development unfolds from the moment of our birth, as we experience our first intimate relationship with our parents or primary caregiver, and continues throughout infancy, early childhood, childhood, the teen years, and early adulthood. Our intimacy capacity does not develop in one isolated period in our lifespan; rather, it is a *continuous* process that is built on as we make our way through the lifecourse. It is the relationships that we are born into, are surrounded by, and surround ourselves with that ultimately shape our intimate selves. The Miller Social Intimacy Scale (MSIS) helps people assess their levels of intimacy (see Table 5.2).

TABLE 5.2   Miller Social Intimacy Scale (MSIS)

The Miller Social Intimacy Scale was developed to assess people's levels of intimacy. The 17-item scale requires participants to assess, among other things, their displays of affection and their levels of self-disclosure. Scores can range from 17 (the lowest level of intimacy) to 85 (the highest level of intimacy). The scale is used by social and family scientists to examine couple and family intimacy, but it is also used by some social workers and other mental health professionals to assess intimacy levels of those who commit crimes such as child molestation.

	Very Rarely		Some of the Time		Almost Always
1. When you have leisure time, how often do you choose to spend it with him/her alone?	1	2	3	4	5
2. How often do you keep very personal information to yourself and do not share it with him/her?	1	2	3	4	5
3. How often do you show him/her affection?	1	2	3	4	5
4. How often do you confide very personal information to him/her?	1	2	3	4	5
5. How often are you able to understand his/her feelings?	1	2	3	4	5
6. How often do you feel close to him/her?	1	2	3	4	5
7. How much do you like to spend time alone with him/her?	1	2	3	4	5
8. How much do you feel like being encouraging and supportive to him/her when he/she is unhappy?	1	2	3	4	5
9. How close do you feel to him/her most of the time?	1	2	3	4	5
10. How important is it to you to listen to his/her personal disclosures?	1	2	3	4	5
11. How affectionate do you feel toward him/her?	1	2	3	4	5
12. How important is it to you that he/she understands your feelings?	1	2	3	4	5
13. How much damage is caused by a typical disagreement in your relationship with him/her?	1	2	3	4	5
14. How important is it to you that he/she be encouraging and supportive to you when you are unhappy?	1	2	3	4	5
15. How important is it to you that he/she shows you affection?	1	2	3	4	5
16. How important is your relationship with him/her in your life?	1	2	3	4	5
17. How satisfying is your relationship with him/her?	1	2	3	4	5

Total Score: _____

Source: Adapted from Miller and Lefcourt (1982).

Obstacles to Intimacy

Because we each have different needs and capacities for intimacy, we may find that our need for intimacy is not the same as that of our partner or significant other. Similarly, we may find that the needs of our family members may be different from our own. Thus, we can think of intimacy as a continuum; at one end is total isolation with no need for intimacy, and at the other end there exists total enmeshment, where partner or family intimacy needs so overlap that it is difficult to distinguish whose need is whose. Neither extreme is healthy. Such differences may lead to significant levels of relationship discord.

BARRIERS TO DEVELOPING INTIMACY

Intimacy is achieved as we build trust with another person and as we disclose our innermost feelings and thoughts. There are many reasons why some relationships experience poor levels of intimacy, including lack of communication, work-related pressures, and financial difficulties. Every close relationship experiences lapses in intimacy from time to time; however, researchers have found the *family environment* and the family's *past experiences* to be essential components in establishing intimacy.

Our Family Environment Family environment is a key player in people's capacity to experience and express intimacy. As you saw in Chapter 3, different families and different cultures relate and communicate in different ways. For example, each culture has its own standards about nonverbal communication, such as how much distance between the communicators is acceptable or how much eye contact can be made. Each culture also has its own rules about emotional expression or the expression of intimacy, such as what kind and how much. In Asian cultures, for instance, emotional reserve is not only expected, it is cherished (Prince & Hoppe, 2000). On the other hand, in Italian and Greek cultures, feelings are freely expressed, often loudly (Prince & Hoppe, 2000).

Consider your own family. If your family of origin encouraged you and your siblings to express feelings for one another, it is likely that you will enjoy emotional closeness with another (or others) when you establish friendships and a family of your own someday. It is also likely that you will not have difficulty in experiencing and expressing intimacy. But sometimes a family can be too emotionally close—too intimate—where no boundaries exist between family members. Then intimacy can be smothering and intrusive. When children from this kind of family engage in new relationships, they may be wary if their partner is too emotionally demanding. They may push the other away by causing an argument or trying to create distance in some other way (Maleki, 2000). Conversely, some family environments do not encourage the expression of intimacy or emotions. Children whose parents are ill at ease expressing their feelings may require excessive attention when starting new relationships. They may seem overly demanding in having their intimacy needs met (Maleki, 2000).

INTERGENERATIONAL Family theory suggests that the ways we experience and express intimacy are influenced by our family of origin and by multigenerational influences. As you intimately relate to your friends and family members, do you find yourself repeating relational patterns of your parents? Which intimacy patterns from your family of origin do you desire to keep? To change?

Past Families and Past Experiences Researchers have found some evidence that indicates the experience and expression of intimacy are influenced not just by our immediate family of origin but by multigenerational influences as well (Lawson & Brossart, 2001). **Intergenerational Family theory** suggests that patterns of relational functioning (including intimacy) are passed down from generation to generation. The theory's basic premise is that our parents acquired their family relational patterns from their parents, who acquired them from their parents, and so on. Consequently, the way we relate to and interact with others is a product of not just our parents' influence on our lives but also the relational patterns that were passed down to them. In turn, our intimacy patterns with our parents (and their parents) are replicated some day with our own spouses, children, friends, and significant others.

To illustrate this concept, consider the following example. As a child, Molly was brought up in a family where her mother and father's relationship was more platonic than romantic. It was companionable, friendly, and nonphysical. Soon, though, the friendship faded and they eventually divorced. As Molly looked back into her mother's childhood, she learned that her mother was reared in a physically abusive, secret-filled home. Rather than risk more hurt, her mother closed herself off emotionally to others—including her husband and her children. Her mother then carried her fear of intimacy to her marriage and to her parenting. Molly recently found herself repeating the relational patterns of her parents (particularly those of her mother). After dating someone for nearly a year and a half, she felt that the relationship was not progressing beyond the friendship stage, even though on the surface it seemed that both partners desired the relationship to deepen. She realized that she was replicating her parents' relationship, platonic and devoid of intimacy. In an attempt to break an unhealthy relational cycle she saw in her family and in herself, she entered into therapy to better recognize and correct the destructive relationship patterns passed down to her.

Sometimes trusting others and revealing ourselves to others is difficult—maybe even impossible—because of some trauma we suffered and endured during the early years of our development. If we have been hurt, violated, attacked, bullied, or relentlessly teased, it can be difficult to allow ourselves to open up to another, as this could leave us vulnerable. Individuals who have been sexually abused often find it difficult to trust others and may have difficulty making a commitment. They may also expect that their intimate partner will leave them, and therefore not allow their partner to become too emotionally close (Burney, 2002). We'll examine the effects of sexual trauma and other forms of violence on interpersonal relationships later in this text. For now, it's important to understand that the family environment and family experiences help shape our capacity to be intimate. The past is very much a part of our present relationships.

BARRIERS TO ESTABLISHING AND MAINTAINING INTIMACY

Some people put up barriers to establishing intimacy. There are many reasons for this, such as jealousy and deception (Galvin and others, 2008). However, the fear of intimacy is often a primary barrier to establishing a relational environment that allows couples to share their vulnerabilities, a wide range of feelings, and their hurts and fears.

Fear of Intimacy "Our fear of intimacy . . . inspires ingenious ways of avoiding it" (Barbor, 2001, p. 1). Because intimacy with another requires that we unmask ourselves and thus become vulnerable in doing so, many people have a fear of intimacy. Many of these people may not even be aware that they possess these fears. People afraid to establish and maintain intimate relationships put up walls, or form barriers, that prevent anyone from getting in; this, in turn,

ESTABLISHING and maintaining intimacy requires mutual self-disclosure and mutual sharing in all areas of relating— emotionally, intellectually, physically, and spiritually.

prevents them from getting hurt. For example, some people may form many friendships rather than one close, intimate relationship; others may become overly involved in work or volunteer activities to avoid interacting more personally with others; others shut themselves off from others completely, becoming isolated.

Fear of intimacy comes in many forms and may manifest itself in any of the following ways, according to intimacy researchers Robert Firestone and Joyce Catlett (2000):

- A fear of *failure*—What if this relationship doesn't work out?
- A fear of being *vulnerable*—Is it worth subjecting myself to hurt and emotional pain?
- A fear of *rejection*—Should I risk opening myself up without knowing if the other person will reciprocate?
- A fear of being *smothered* in a relationship—What if I lose my identity?
- A fear of *sex*—What if we end up having sex and he/she doesn't really love me? What if he/she disapproves of my body?
- A fear of *losing someone we love*—What happens if I fall in love or become intimate and this person breaks up with me or dies? How will I ever recover from the loss?
- A fear to take a *risk*—I can only go with the "sure thing" in my life. I don't have time to invest in someone if it isn't going to work out.
- A fear to *accept the responsibility* of an intimate relationship—Relationships are hard work; I just don't have the time or desire to invest that kind of energy.
- A fear of experiencing *anger* or *hostility* in the relationship—My father [mother] is a very angry person. I just can't risk being immersed in all of that hostility again.
- A fear of *abandonment*—What he if she/he leaves me?
- A fear of being "*found out*"—What if someone finds out who I "really am"?

The Glendon Association (2005), a teaching and research organization dedicated to enhancing mental health, notes that fear in personal relationships sets up barriers to becoming truly intimate with another person. The organization notes that most of what goes wrong in an intimate relationship comes from fear; because we bring these fears into our relationships from our family experiences, we become guarded so as not to become hurt. In turn, we stop disclosing, confiding, and trusting in our significant other—and subsequently set up walls to guard our emotions.

Is It Possible to Sustain Intimacy in Long-Distance Relationships?

Own It!

Today, about 33 percent of dating relationships in college or university settings are long-distance in nature. Often, these couples use e-mail, instant messaging, and cell phones to stay in touch. If finances allow, some couples plan regular visits with their partners. Most of these couples view their separation as necessary and temporary, and as an investment in their future. Can partners in long-distance relationships (LDRs) who communicate frequently or have frequent affectionate contact with one another sustain intimacy in long-distance relationships?

Take a moment to jot down or journal your opinions about the following questions:

1. Have you ever been a part of a long-distance relationship? If not, would you be? Why or why not?

2. If you have had a long-distance relationship, was it successful? If it ended, was it due to the difficulties of being apart?

3. What can be done to sustain intimacy in long-distance relationships?

Communication According to the American Psychological Association (2005), an ideal intimate relationship is one in which openness, honesty, respect, and integrity exists. To foster the growth of intimacy, and to maintain intimacy, meaningful communication is essential. So crucial is the communication process of personal sharing to intimate relationships that marital and familial intimacy is not possible without effective communication strategies in place. It is difficult to examine intimacy without taking into account communication, and it is difficult to examine communication without taking into account intimacy.

Recall from Chapter 3 that there is an interconnectedness of the family. This family systems framework provides an understanding of the boundaries with which we establish and maintain in our family, verbal and nonverbal communication skills, decoding our partner's messages, and self-disclosure. Marital/partner and family intimacy requires communication that promotes acceptance and worth of the individuals in the family. It also requires private, personal self-disclosure that promotes a reciprocal, mutual sharing on a number of levels (emotional, intellectual, spiritual, physical). The capacity to experience intimacy within a marriage or life partnership and within family requires effective, meaningful communication. Healthy communication thus serves to encourage and promote intimacy within the marriage and the family.

Family Life Education

Whether intimacy is an innate, driving force that binds together social, relational beings or whether being intimate with another fulfills our basic, individual psychological needs, this family process is necessary for healthy, happy, fulfilling, and satisfying relationships. Not only is it a critical component in our lives; our intimate relationships establish interaction patterns for generations that follow.

Some of you may experience intimacy on a cognitive or intellectual level where you share ideas and thoughts and enjoy expressing your differences of opinions. Some of you may enjoy a type of experiential closeness where you actively involve yourselves with each other whenever you are together. Although you might not share many of your innermost thoughts and feelings, you take pleasure in mutual activities. And some of you may experience an emotional bond whereby you comfortably share your feelings and are aware of your partner's emotional needs. This type of intimate relationship often leads to physical or sexual intimacy.

As you have discovered, intimacy is many things to many different people—and it is different things to the same people at different times. Each relationship you have, from your first intimate relationship with your parent(s) or primary caregiver through old age, will build on the previous relationships. Each of these relationships creates who you are as an intimate. Your culture, ethnicity, family environment, intergenerational experiences, and the multicontextual aspects of intimacy, all play an important role in how you experience it.

Intimacy does not always come easily to everyone. In fact, most of the time establishing and maintaining a close personal relationship with another requires hard work because it is a process that unfolds and changes over time. With this in mind, it is important to remember that if you find yourself having to work at your relationship, it does not necessarily mean that something is wrong or that your partner is the wrong partner. If you desire someone to openly, honestly, and completely share with you, you must be willing to be open and honest about your needs and desires. And you must also be willing to reciprocate the personal sharing and empathy shown by your partner. Only then will the seeds of intimacy have a chance to flourish and thrive.

And maybe this kind of intimacy is what Brad Pitt was referring to in his interview with *Rolling Stone* magazine. Knowingly or unknowingly, Pitt is speaking to a perpetual sense of meaninglessness in our success/consumer/power-driven society—to the notion that our relationships today are less and less grounded in purpose and in meaning.

In the drive for "the car, the condo, and our version of success," we are what the actor calls a society of desperate and lonely people. As you turn your attention back to the opening vignette in this chapter, you see that Pitt refers to this feeling of meaninglessness as a sense of impotence in our society—a sense of weakness, inability, or an incapacity. An incapacity for what? Relating? Belonging? Human connection?

As you take that step that brings you to reveal, share, and disclose your innermost personal thoughts and feelings, as you lower the barriers and allow another person to really know you, you begin the process of intimacy. As your partner reciprocates, this mutual sharing, co-created process unfolds. Thus, intimacy not only allows you to know and understand your partner but it also helps you to be known and to be understood by your partner. And it is this process of mutuality and reciprocating in human interactions that not only fulfills our psychological needs, but helps us to successfully navigate expected and unexpected family experiences.

Even the Lone Ranger wasn't alone!

Can a Relationship Work When There Are Differing Intimacy Needs?

How do couples sustain pleasure, contentment, and happiness in intimate relationships when there are differing intimacy needs? For many partners, one person needs more or less intimacy than the other. This can be frustrating and upsetting when one person desires or needs more intimacy than the other person is willing to give or is capable of providing. Most of the time, for the person whose intimacy needs are not met, hurt and feelings of neglect mount. In the following case, what can be done so that each partner enjoys a satisfactory and comfortable level of intimacy?

Her Side: He knows that I love him, but why can't he just give me some space? I feel like when I allow him into my personal thoughts more, when I share more or when I open up more, he just wants more of me—no matter how much I share, it's not enough. When he's like this, I feel totally smothered and I pull away. Sometimes I start an argument on purpose just so he will back off a little bit. Why can't he understand that sometimes I just need a little distance? It doesn't mean I don't love him anymore—it just means that I feel like I'm losing who I am when he gets too close. I try to tell him how I feel, but he just doesn't seem to understand. I know he wants to understand.

His Side: From our first date, I have always felt like the pursuer in the relationship. I feel like I'm the only one who wants this relationship, the one who is chasing her. This is crazy—we're living together, and I feel like I still have to chase her to keep her! The closer I move to her, the more distance she seems to create. I'm the pursuer, she's the distancer. Sometimes we'll have very close periods of intimacy, and then just as suddenly, she'll pull away again. This you-can-have-me-but-only-at-a-distance relationship has to end. I love her, but it hurts too much. One of these days she is going to push me away and it will be the last time. The last time.

Your Side: Each partner in this relationship expects the other to show her or his intimacy in a way that is different from the current pattern. What can be done so that each partner enjoys a satisfactory and comfortable level of intimacy? Consider:

1. Is change in the way the couple expresses and shares intimacy a realistic expectation? Is it possible?
2. What ways can this couple build the intimacy in their relationship?
3. Does either partner have fears about intimacy? What can be done when a partner or a friend has intimacy fears?

Source: Although the case scenario is hypothetical, information about intimacy pursuers was adapted for use from Gordon (2001).

Summary

Intimacy: Do We Have a Need to Relate to Others?

- Humans are *relational creatures* who seek—either by design or evolutionary drives—to be with another or to be with others.

- *Intimacy* is the need for affiliation and refers to reciprocity of trust between the partners, emotional (not just physical) closeness, and comfortable levels of self-disclosure.

- The drive for interpersonal relations is thought to fulfill important psychological needs, or *need fulfillment*.

- Researchers Prager and Buhrmester (1998) found that through frequent, intimate, and positive communication, *individual* psychological needs are met by the *couple*.

- The global drive of humans to connect to others is motivated not only by survival needs, such as safety, shelter, and sustenance, but also by the psychological need for intimacy, social integration, nurture and nurturing, assistance, and reassurance.

- Intimacy is experienced differently from relationship to relationship. Although its meaning may vary, intimacy is a necessary component in meaningful relationships.

- Each couple's experience of intimacy is unique because of the many factors that influence, impinge on, and nurture the couple's relationship. There are five different levels of intimacy contexts: the immediate, the personal, the relational, the group, and the sociocultural.

- In *collectivist cultures,* the goals of the entire society are important, and this is reflected in experiences of intimacy. In *individualistic cultures,* the goals of the individual are emphasized, causing people to strive for higher levels of intimacy.

- *Emotional attachment* is at the core of all love relationships and is characterized by feelings that promote a sense of closeness, bonding, and connection that promote the well-being of another.

- Intimacy can be thought of as a three-pronged process that involves (1) disclosing things that are personal and private to ourselves, (2) experiencing positive feelings about ourselves and the other person(s) involved in the relationship, and (3) having interpersonal interactions that serve to advance or reflect partners' understanding of each other.

- Researchers describe eight components of intimate relationships: conflict resolution, affection, cohesion, sexuality, identity, compatibility, expressiveness, and autonomy. Researchers have also found that respect and the management of anger, self-disclosure, companionship, mutual appreciation, nonverbal communication, equity in decision making, physical closeness (both sexual and nonsexual contact), warmth and spirituality, and shared religious faith are significant components of intimacy.

- With a foundation of *commitment* and *depth,* Orlofsky and colleagues (1973) identified five intimacy statuses: the intimate, the pseudointimate, the preintimate, stereotyped relationships, and isolates.

Developing Intimacy

- While each of us develops the capacity to love and be intimate with others throughout infancy, childhood, adolescence, and early adulthood, it is the very early stages of life that establish the foundation of the ability to love and to share intimacy.

- Psychosocial development is the social and emotional development of an individual over his or her life span.

- Erikson's *Eight Stages of Man* were formulated to assert that our social and emotional development is a lifelong process.

- Development of need and capacity for intimacy revolves around biological, cognitive, and psychosocial changes that occur throughout adolescence.

- Adolescence marks the processes of individuation and the establishment of autonomy, of intimacy, and the exploration of sexuality.

- We learn the foundations of intimacy through adolescent friendships. There are significant differences between male intimacy experiences and female intimacy experiences, as well as cultural differences.

- In early adulthood—the bridge years—young adults contemplate deeper intimacy in interpersonal relationships. These intimate relationships are essential to healthy development; without such, developing adults are at risk for an isolation-filled life.

Obstacles to Intimacy

- Researchers have found the *family environment* and the *family's past experiences* are essential to establishing intimacy. *Intergenerational Family* theory suggests that patterns of relational functioning (including intimacy) are passed down from generation to generation.

- Because intimacy with another requires that we unmask ourselves and thus become vulnerable, many people fear intimacy. The fear may manifest itself in any number of ways.

- Marital and familial intimacy is not possible without effective communication strategies. Marital/partner and family intimacy not only requires communication that promotes acceptance and worth of the individuals in the family but also self-disclosure that promotes mutual sharing, on emotional, intellectual, spiritual, and physical levels.

Key Concepts and Terms

responsiveness, p. 141

intimacy, p. 141

need for affiliation, p. 143

immediate context, p. 143

personal context, p. 143

relational context, p. 143

group context, p. 144

sociocultural context, p. 144

social identity, p. 144

collectivist cultures, p. 144

individualistic cultures, p. 144

emotional attachment, p. 145

intimacy status, p. 145

intimate, p. 147

pseudointimate, p. 148

preintimate, p. 148

stereotyped relationships, p. 149

isolates, p. 149

merger status, p. 149

psychosocial development, p. 149

Eight Stages of Man, p. 149

Pre-Crowd stage, p. 152

Beginning of the Crowd, p. 153

Crowd in Transition, p. 153

Fully Developed Crowd, p. 153

Crowd Disintegration, p. 153

empathy, p. 153

identity, p. 154

individuation, p. 154

autonomy, p. 154

gender typing, p. 155

cross-sex friendships (CSFs), p. 156

interracial, p. 157

miscegenation, p. 157

contact hypothesis, p. 158

Intergenerational Family theory, p. 162

Suggested Readings

Lerner, Harriet. (1990). *The dance of intimacy*. New York: Harper & Row.

Moran, Rachel. (2003). *Interracial intimacy: The regulation of race and romance*. Chicago: University of Chicago Press.

Savage, Elayne. (2003). *Breathing room: Creating space to be a couple*. Oakland, CA: New Harbinger Publications.

Multiple-Choice Questions

1. Although the meaning of intimacy varies from relationship to relationship, _____ is not necessarily a component of intimacy.

   a. trust between partners

   b. emotional closeness

   c. comfortable levels of self-disclosure

   d. physical closeness

2. Among the five different levels of intimacy contexts, the _____ includes factors specific to each person, such as personality traits; attitudes and beliefs about the overall status of the relationship; emotional reactions to intimacy; willingness to self-disclose; and each partner's intimacy needs, goals, and motives.

   a. relational context

   b. personal context

   c. immediate context

   d. group context

3. A(n) _____ appears to be intimate on the surface, but lacks depth and often has relationships that may never progress beyond friendship, or may experience only superficial levels of emotional closeness in a dating, cohabiting, or marital relationships.

   a. pseudointimate

   b. preintimate

   c. isolate

   d. intimate

4. _____ refers not only to establishing a sense of independence but also becoming a self-governing person within the context of relationships.

   a. Individuation

   b. Identity

   c. Autonomy

   d. Empathy

5. Which of the following was NOT included in a number of recent studies?

   a. "Feminine" people (both men and women) report having more male friends.

   b. Men have more CSFs than women do.

   c. More single people have CSFs than married people.

   d. Men may gain intimacy from their female friends.

6. Adolescents begin the process of _____ , forming an identity that is separate from that of their family of origin.

   a. autonomy

   b. individuation

   c. intimacy status

   d. identity formation

7. _____ suggests that patterns of relational functioning (including intimacy) are passed down from generation to generation.

   a. Fear of intimacy

   b. Individuation theory

   c. Family of Origin theory

   d. Intergenerational Family theory

8. The _____ contends that the intimate status requires partners in a relationship to experience an equal balance of power, or equity.

   a. eight stages of man

   b. merger status

   c. psychosocial development

   d. need for affiliation

Love and Loving

6

I stand by the bed where a young woman lies, her face postoperative, her mouth twisted in palsy, clownish. A tiny twig of the facial nerve, the one to the muscles of her mouth, has been severed. She will be thus from now on. The surgeon had followed with religious fervor the curve of her flesh; I promise you that. Nevertheless, to remove the tumor in her cheek, I had to cut the little nerve. Her young husband is in the room. He stands on the opposite side of the bed and together they seem to dwell in the evening lamplight, isolated from me, private. Who are they, I ask myself, he and this wry mouth I have made, who gaze at and touch each other so generously, greedily?

The young woman speaks. "Will my mouth always be like this?" she asks.

"Yes," I say, "it will. It is because the nerve was cut."

She nods and is silent. But the young man smiles. "I like it," he says, "It's kind of cute." Unmindful, he bends to kiss her crooked mouth and I am so close I can see how he twists his own lips to accommodate to hers, to show her that their kiss still works.

Source: Selzer (1978, pp. 45–46)

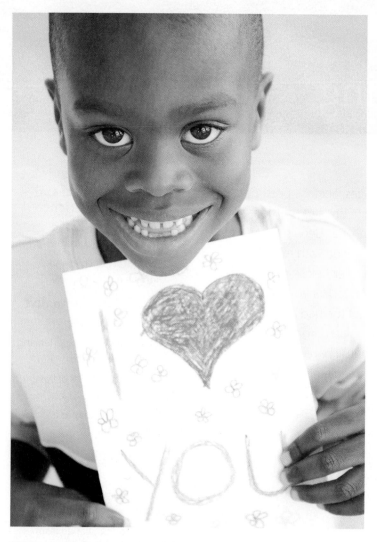

LOVE is a very difficult relational process to define and to describe because it is experienced in a lot of different ways. Also, we can love the same partner in different ways across the life of the relationship.

I have a favorite place in this 110-year-old farmhouse my husband and I have renovated and have made our home for 20 years. The favorite place is not a particular room in our home or anywhere on the land that surrounds it, but a well-worn cupboard door near the back entrance of the house. Scribbled in permanent red marker in my son's 5-year-old handwriting, the words "I love you" stand out in stark contrast against the white. Even though the cupboards have been painted several times, I cannot bring myself to paint over those three words.

Love is a tough subject to tackle in one chapter, but it is a necessary discussion as we consider intimate relationships among friends, lovers, and family. But what is *love?* Even among researchers in the social and family sciences, "love" has been a difficult concept to define because different people experience it in ways that are unique to them. Depending on who they are "loving" and their past experiences of love, no two people experience or express their love in precisely the same way because the concept of love has such a vast, diverse, tremendous range in its meaning. Is it a husband's unconditional acceptance of a young bride with permanent twisted and crooked facial features who conforms his own lips to hers, to assure her the "kiss still works"? Is it the scrawling, scribbling handwriting of a kindergartner in permanent red ink? Is it a pounding heart and a nervous stomach every time a certain person is near? Is it a sense of calm and comfort—or anger, hurt, and jealousy?

Love Is a Cultural and Historical Experience

Several researchers have studied love as it is defined among different cultures of the world. Social psychologists Anne Beall and Robert Sternberg's (1995) research concludes that the experience and definition of love are culturally determined. Psychologists and researchers Elaine Hatfield and Richard Rapson's (1993) work appears to support the notion that "love" and "loving" experiences are driven by the culture in which we live. Their particular body of research found, for instance, that culture plays a key role in how individuals display emotions as well as how they react to the emotions and feelings of others. Is the culture in which a person lives a culture that accepts public demonstrations of affection toward another (such as in Italy), for example, or is the culture more reserved in the display of affection (such as in England)?

It is important to understand that "love" and "loving" are determined in large part by how a culture defines its social identity. As you saw in the previous chapter in our discussion about intimacy, when examining various processes found in interpersonal relationships, it is particularly useful to understand whether a culture defines itself as a collectivist culture or an individualistic culture.

LOVE IN COLLECTIVIST AND INDIVIDUALISTIC CULTURES

Recall that in collectivist cultures the goals of the collective, or the whole society, are emphasized over a person's individual needs or wants, which are emphasized in individualistic cultures. Because of this desire to promote harmony within the cultural group, collectivists approach love differently than individualistic cultures do.

In the United States, Canada, and Europe, the idea of autonomy and individuation from the family is promoted; in turn, this autonomy encourages the practice of people selecting partners based on *individual* reasons (such as attraction, love, money, security, and so on), rather than *collective* reasons (such as prearranged marriages in China) that might benefit the culture as a whole. Individualistic cultures also promote strong levels of desire for romantic relationships compared with collectivist cultures (Medora, Larson, Hortacsu, & Dave, 2002). Furthermore, the importance of love for choosing a marriage mate is much more prevalent in individualistic cultures than in collectivist cultures such as Japan and India.

When cultures promote the autonomy and independence of individuals (as seen in much of Western civilization), this autonomy then affects relationship satisfaction, the ease with which intimacy is established, and "love" as a basis for marriage (Dion & Dion, 1993). Relationship partners are free, by society's standards, to choose a partner that best suits their needs and with whom they are "in love"; it is thought that this freedom of choice enhances relationship satisfaction and the experiences of love and intimacy. A recent study helps to explain how and why relationship satisfaction is enhanced. In a study that examined emotional closeness and loneliness in 271 American and Korean college students, the researchers found that American students have a greater degree of closeness in their romantic relationships than Korean students do because of two interacting reasons: (1) they have an individualistic cultural desire to have a romantic relationship and therefore invest more into their love relationships and (2) they have idealized romantic notions that magnify the feelings found in romantic relationships (Seepersad, Choi, & Shin, 2008). The researchers also discovered that Korean students do not necessarily identify their feelings as "loneliness" or a lack of emotional closeness, because they don't view romantic relationships with the same degree of importance as a source of love and psychological intimacy as American students do.

Most of us are familiar with the societal expectations of love and loving in our individualistic culture in the United States, but we often have questions about love in other cultures. For example, is love as important a family process in collectivist cultures, such as Pakistan, as it is in U.S. culture?

In Muslim societies, romantic love is the source of much discussion today, particularly because love experiences in collectivist cultures have been seldom documented in the scholarly literature (Marsden, 2007). Among these people groups, "love" means many things—there is a clear distinction in love between family, friends, romantic partners, and physical attraction, and different words are used to describe these various experiences. More recently, however, researchers are examining the various experiences of love and

IN Southeast Asia, such as in Pakistan, marriages are typically prearranged by the parents of the bride and groom. Parents believe that joining certain blood lines through marriage are beneficial to the good of the society, or to the collective. Today, though, more and more couples are eloping in secret marriages, marrying someone they love.

loving in these societies, particularly among Muslims in South Asia, because individualistic, Western attitudes of romantic love are making inroads into Muslim societies.

Where traditionally many marriages are prearranged in these South Asian collectivist societies, a contemporary sweeping trend is **elopement**, or secret marriages between love partners, that takes place without parental approval and/or knowledge. In some villages in Pakistan, elopement marriages are viewed as an act of resistance against collectivist Muslim society traditionalism, and as rebellion against arranged marriages (Marsden, 2007). This is an important trend to understand because it speaks to a gradual shift in this particular society's social identity—a potential shift away from collectivism and to individualism. Young couples' relationships are becoming injected with a recognition that there are emotional and physical elements associated with love that are rewarding and pleasurable (Marsden, 2007).

The experience of love is driven by not only culture but by the period in history in which the relationship exists, as well (Beall & Sternberg, 1995). A glimpse of the past can help us understand how and why we view and experience love today, and how our experiences of love have evolved over the centuries.

THE HISTORY OF LOVE AND ROMANCE

Throughout history, perhaps no topic has generated as much attention as the topic of love. Philosophers, poets, writers, scholars, and lyricists have all sought to provide an account of love and its mysteries. In keeping with the theme of this book, the study of marriage and family, our focus will be on various experiences of love as recorded throughout history. This journey into the past, outlined by historian Morton Hunt (1959), illustrates how the historical influences of love affect how we experience love in our contemporary society.

Love and Romance throughout History Adam and Eve fell in love first, although some have commented that they probably didn't have much choice in the matter! Fast-forward several thousand years: In the first century, love was thought of as bittersweet emotion, an ambivalent feeling; in the third century, love was experienced as a somber, guilt-ridden experience intertwined with the act of sex; by the sixteenth century, marriage was viewed as a physical and financial union—love was not the foundation, or even a significant part of the marriage. But as the British came to New England during the sixteenth and seventeenth centuries, the Puritans and Pilgrims showed themselves to be romantically sentimental—and thoroughly enjoyed sex within the confines of marriage. As a result of this new relationship dynamic, romance and sex became hallmarks of love. But these love experiences were short-lived as eighteenth-century Puritans gave way to the oppressive, stuffy, formality of the Victorians—in love, romance, and sexual practices.

During the Victorian era (1837–1901), the virginal, shy, virtuous woman was the epitome of the attitude toward sexuality and the role of women. Although attitudes toward sexuality were prim and stuffy, the Victorian ideal of love, for the first time in history, perpetuated a sense of *couple togetherness*. When not at work, men during the Victorian era were expected to be at home, enjoying the company of their wives and family. Relative to the scope of love throughout history, the Victorian era was short-lived and quickly gave way to the emergence of the concept of romantic love in the early twentieth century.

Romantic Love The early decades of the twentieth century saw rapid social changes: Family planning activist Margaret Sanger (1914) claimed that lovemaking and procreation were two entirely different experiences, and she gained national attention when she claimed that women had the right to control their own fertility. At the same time, the nation ushered in the *emancipation* of women and experienced the rise in capitalism and industrialization. And, for the first time in the annals of history, *both* men and women sought out romantic love relationships that combined sexuality, affection, intimacy, and togetherness—and discovered that all of these relational elements could be found in one relationship.

Is Love the Basis for Marriage?

Is love a prerequisite for marital bliss and happiness? While people from *collectivist cultures* may marry someone based on what is considered to be good for the entire group, people from *individualistic cultures,* like the United States, typically marry someone who fulfills their personal, individual goals, such as being in love. Is love the basis for marriage?

YES: Marriage and family therapist Henry Grunebaum (2003) notes that "love" contains unique characteristics that are unlike any other emotion or feeling experienced by human beings, and that true love rarely occurs. He believes people consider love to be a precious and enduring experience, and claims the elements needed to foster an enduring relationship of any kind are needed to foster a strong, enduring love relationship: intimacy, communication, kindness, and an active interest in the other person. Grunebaum points out that loveless marriages are difficult to repair. In his clinical experience, "When romantic love is lost, it is almost always gone for good."

NO: Marriage and family therapist Joseph Silverman (2003) contends that the feelings associated with love are mainly nervousness associated with the excited feelings produced by the chemicals in the brain when we are attracted to another person. While in this excited state, couples make lifelong commitments to one another—and set themselves up for disappointment. According to Silverman, there are problems with linking love as a basis for marriage:

- People overestimate the significance of the importance of love, and they feel deprived or empty if the excitement wanes. Other aspects of the relationship—such as compatibility, sharing experiences, or similar family goals—are equally important as feelings of love.
- There is no such thing as a "perfect partner"; anyone who is reasonably tolerant and flexible can successfully marry nearly anyone.
- The most important relationship in any person's life—marriage—cannot fulfill every desire of both partners.

In Silverman's view, "not every marriage has to be violins and roses." Marriages of convenience and marriages where love does not exist have a place.

WHAT DO YOU THINK?

1. Do you agree with Grunebaum's statement that romantic love occurs rarely? Why or why not?
2. Do you agree with Silverman's statement that a person can "successfully marry nearly anyone"? Why or why not?
3. Is love a prerequisite for marriage for you?

Sources: Grunebaum (2003) and Silverman (2003).

By the 1930s, romantic attraction to another became *the* acceptable form of choosing a life mate. The way many of us experience love today came into being within the past century. In a true sense, the concept of romantic love is in its infancy, a twentieth-century phenomenon (Luhmann, 1986). Yet, this form of partnering based on love and affection, and tenderness and care, is still today a goal for many.

What Is Love, Actually?

Today, *love* is perhaps the most overused four-letter word in the English language. I "love" buttered movie popcorn. I "love" the sound of a newborn baby's cry. I "love" spring. I "love" the prairie. I really "love" collegiate football. I "love" my husband and my children, and my family and friends. I "love" teaching. This crazy little thing called love has been assigned over 20 definitions in the dictionary as well as in the thesaurus, and includes such descriptions as:

- feeling affection for
- adoration
- worship
- devotion
- fondness
- passion
- feeling a weakness for

A problem with the dictionary and thesaurus definitions still remains, though. As you can see, we can "have a weakness for" pizza; we can be "fond of" pizza; we may even be "devoted to" or "adore" pizza! In today's society, we tend use the word *love* when we really mean we *prefer* something or *enjoy* something or *like* to be in someone's company.

The ancient Greeks recognized this dilemma and distinguished between the different key qualities of or types of love. For example, the term **eros** was used to describe the sexual, physical components of love (this is the root word of the term *erotic*). **Philos**, or brotherly love, was used to describe the affectionate feelings shared between friends and family (hence the name Philadelphia, the "city of brotherly love"). **Agape** was thought to be a self-sacrificing, spiritual love that looked out for the interests and well-being of others. Today in North America, we still have only one word to express our love. One researcher, Beverley Fehr (1988), paid particular attention to how individuals assess or appraise the essential aspects of love, or what she termed *love prototypes*.

LOVE AS A PROTOTYPE

Fehr (1988) decided to take a somewhat different approach to her scientific quest in an effort to understand the definitions people attach to the concept of love. Fehr started with the premise that each of us acquires a model in our own families of origin of what love is and what it is not. In her research, she asked her study sample to freewrite (unedited, uninhibited writing) various features or attributes they assigned to "love." The list the study sample provided was thought to be their **prototype** or model of love. A different sample group later ranked the features in order of importance. Table 6.1 shows the top 12 central features of love identified by Fehr's research. It is important to note that if any group of individuals, such as a group of students, were given the task of creating attributes they assigned to "love," each person would generate a love prototype list of attributes or characteristics that is unique to them. The list a person generates is important because it represents his or her own *definition of love*. As Fehr notes, the aspects a person lists are central to and ultimately *characterizes* his or her love relationships. If any of the key attributes of love are dishonored, violated, or lost at any time during the relationship, the love relationship is threatened and may end.

Similar to Fehr's concept of love prototypes is world-famous sexologist John Money's (2003) concept of **love maps**. A love map is a mental blueprint of sorts that we carry internally. According to Money, love maps present an image of the "ideal" love relationship that is shaped by our experiences with love in infancy and early childhood. It is also informed by the attitudes of love and sexuality of our parents or primary caregivers.

While each of us has a love prototype or love map when we first begin to question whether we are "in love" with another person, it is often difficult to determine whether our

TABLE 6.1 Fehr's Twelve Central Features of Love

The top 12 central features of love, according to Fehr's research, by order of importance, are:

1. Trust
2. Care
3. Honesty
4. Friendship
5. Respect
6. Desire to promote the well-being of the other
7. Loyalty
8. Commitment
9. Accepting the other without wanting to change the other
10. Support
11. A desire to be in the other's company
12. Consideration of and interest in the other

Does your love prototype list include attributes or characteristics of love that Fehr's list does not? If so, why do you think that is?

feelings are feelings of *infatuation,* or whether they are feelings that will lead to an enduring, *committed* love relationship.

PASSIONATE LOVE: EXPERIENCING LOVE AS INFATUATION

Infatuation refers to an intense, extravagant, and often short-lived passion for another person, and many times these feelings are confused for love. Most of us have had a "crush" on someone or we have suffered through "puppy love" at some point in our early teens or younger. These crushes are referred to as **simple infatuation**, a physical attraction that is often accompanied by emotion-filled daydreams and fantasies about someone—perhaps an actor/actress, a pop star or singing idol, or even a teacher. In the 1970s, the object of my infatuation was Donny Osmond (my choices were slim—I had the options of Donny or Greg Brady of *The Brady Bunch*). Today, common objects of daydreams and fantasies are *High School Musical* stars Zac Efron and Vanessa Hudgens, and the 2008 "Two Davids" *American Idol* contestants, David Cook and David Archuleta. Objects of infatuation can also be classmates.

What's Your Love Prototype?

Take a few minutes to jot down 10 key attributes that you consider central or necessary for a committed love relationship to thrive (such as, trust, respect, sex, humor, etc.). Because love is a unique experience, your list will likely differ from your classmates' lists. After you have your list, follow these instructions:

1. Rank the order of importance of your chosen attributes, with 1 being the most important and 10 being the least important. For example, which is more important, humor or sex?

2. How does your list compare to Fehr's research findings?

Own It!

These and similar first love experiences, often during junior high school or the early high school years, are actually simple infatuation. Although parents, social workers, clergy, educators, and other providers of human services understand this love is not the "real," committed love that marriages are made of, it is important that they recognize that the feelings experienced are no less intense than those adults experience.

Infatuation as Romance **Romantic infatuation** is often referred to as *romantic love*. Defined in the *American Heritage Dictionary* as "a foolish, unreasoning, or extravagant passion or attraction," and "an object of extravagant short-lived passion," romantic infatuation involves a complicated, often overpowering blend of emotion and sexuality.

Empirical studies appear to support the dictionary's definition. Notably, Elaine Hatfield and her colleagues (1988, 1989, 1998) distinguish between two different types of love: *passionate* and *companionate* (to be discussed later in this chapter). The researchers describe **passionate love** as a wildly powerful emotion that is experienced as intense longing for the selected love object, along with profound sexual arousal and confused feelings. Passionate love can either be a blissful experience if the love is reciprocated, or a painful experience if the love is ignored. Other research shows that romantic love involves a mix of intense emotional and physical characteristics, such as a pounding heart, a choking sensation in the throat, sweating palms, and/or a constricting sensation in the chest (Rice, 1993). The emotional manifestations of romantic love include idealizing the romantic partner; intense sexual attraction; a surge of self-confidence; adoration of the love interest; and an all-consuming, selfless desire to promote the well-being of the partner (Rice, 1993). In short, it's the love-struck stuff that the relationships on reality TV dating shows (*The Bachelor, The Bachelorette, Elimidate*) are made of—but not what long-lasting marriages are made of.

Are you in love with someone now, or have you been in love? The Passionate Love Scale was developed by Elaine Hatfield to assess the cognitive, physiological, and behavioral indicants of passionate love (1986). As you can see from Table 6.2, this scale measures attitudes associated with passionate love. To date, this scale been translated into a number of languages, including Farsi, German, Indian, Indonesian, Korean, Peruvian, Spanish, and Swedish (Kim & Hatfield, 2004; Lundqvist, 2006). And today, a number of anthropologists believe that passionate love is a universal experience that transcends culture (Fischer, 2004).

PASSIONATE love is a wildly powerful emotion that is fueled, in part, by chemicals in the brain and by hormones. The intense sexual attraction and the all-consuming desire for the other person are what reality TV dating shows are made of—but not what long-lasting relationships are made of.

Social psychologist Z. Rubin (1973) studied romantic love/infatuation and how the attachment to the love interest develops, both physically and psychologically. Akin to what happens on the reality TV dating shows, Rubin found that infatuation tends to start very quickly and often leads to what people think of as "love at first sight." Romantic infatuation occurs as the result of an attraction, probably to some physical trait, such as an appealing body part, her captivating smile, or his bedroom eyes. Physical attraction is an important element in emotionally mature love relationships, but it is not one of the *primary* factors in relationship satisfaction and longevity. With romantic love, however, there are relatively few factors beyond the physical traits that attract us to the other; thus, such attraction doesn't lead to loving someone else, but only loving or being attracted to a certain part of the person. It should come as no surprise that as the attraction to a particular trait begins to wane, so too does the "love." **Fatuous** (infatuation) relationships tend to end as quickly as they begin.

Like Rice, Rubin found that romantic infatuation carries with it an urge to assist or aid the lover in whatever capacity needed, to promote the lover's well-being. I often comment to my students that the popular *Judge Judy* courtroom television show would not exist if it were not for jilted, once-infatuated lovers attempting to

TABLE 6.2 The Passionate Love Scale

Think of the person whom you love most passionately right now. If you are not in love, please think of the last person you loved. If you have never been in love, think of the person you came closest to caring for in that way. Try to describe the way you felt when your feelings were most intense. Answers range from (1) *Not at all true* to (9) *Definitely true*.

	Not at all true							Definitely true
I would feel deep despair if _____ left me.	1	2	3	4	5	6	7	8	9
Sometimes I feel I can't control my thoughts; they are obsessively on _____.	1	2	3	4	5	6	7	8	9
I feel happy when I'm doing something to make _____ happy.	1	2	3	4	5	6	7	8	9
I would rather be with _____ than anyone else.	1	2	3	4	5	6	7	8	9
I'd get jealous if I thought _____ was falling in love with someone else.	1	2	3	4	5	6	7	8	9
I yearn to know all about _____.	1	2	3	4	5	6	7	8	9
I have an endless appetite for affection from _____.	1	2	3	4	5	6	7	8	9
For me, _____ is the perfect romantic partner.	1	2	3	4	5	6	7	8	9
I sense my body responding when _____ touches me.	1	2	3	4	5	6	7	8	9
_____ always seems to be on my mind.	1	2	3	4	5	6	7	8	9
I want _____ to know me—my thoughts, fears, and my hopes.	1	2	3	4	5	6	7	8	9
I eagerly look for signs indicating _____'s desire for me.	1	2	3	4	5	6	7	8	9
I possess a powerful attraction for _____.	1	2	3	4	5	6	7	8	9
I get extremely depressed when things don't go right in my relationship with _____.	1	2	3	4	5	6	7	8	9

Passionate Love Scale Scores

Extremely passionate: 106–135 points *You are wildly and recklessly in love!*

Passionate: 86–105 points *You are passionate, but with less intensity.*

Average: 66–85 points *You have occasional bursts of passion.*

Cool: 45–65 points *Your passion is lukewarm and infrequent.*

Extremely cool: 15–44 points *Sorry baby, but the thrill is gone.*

Sources: Hatfield & Sprecher (1986); Fehr (1988); Hendrick & Hendrick (1989).

reclaim property that they gave away during the course of a romantic infatuation relationship. Cries of "But your Honor, I *had* to pay his tuition or he couldn't finish school," or "But your Honor, she *needed* to use my cell phone so she could apply for a job," or "But your Honor, I *had* to buy him the car so he could get a job so we could afford rent so we could live together" flood the popular judge's courtroom.

Another characteristic of romantic infatuation relationships was documented by Elaine Hatfield (1988). She found that when couples are in relationships consumed by romantic infatuation, both partners become completely absorbed with each other and exclude friends and family. Family, friends, academics, sports, work, and anything else that was once important lose their priority in life. Because of the exclusive nature of the relationship, family and friends may disapprove of the relationship because they are being neglected and ignored by the couple. In fact, if parents, family, and friends voice concern about the exclusivity of the relationship, it is perhaps an indication that the relationship is not "real love."

Passionate Love: The Influences of Culture As we saw earlier, whether a culture defines itself as collectivist or individualistic has a profound effect on how people experience and define "love." Given this, it stands to reason that social identity would also have an effect on how passionate love is experienced. Unexpectedly, though, passionate love is a more common global experience than researchers anticipated (Hatfield & Rapson, 2007). For example, in a study of 1,667 college-aged men and women from the United States, Russia, and Japan, the investigators found no evidence that the individualistic cultures (the United States and Russia) had more experiences of passionate love than those from the collectivist culture, Japan (Sprecher, Sullivan, & Hatfield, 1994). Another study using the Passionate Love Scale found that young adults from European, Filipino, and Japanese ethnicities appeared to love their partners as passionately as young adults from the United States do (Hatfield & Rapson, 1987).

Conversely, Dan Landis and William O'Shea (2000), researchers from the University of Mississippi, found that the experience of passionate love/infatuation is influenced by cultural attitudes and social identity. Landis and O'Shea's (2000) elaborate multicultural research concludes that the experience and expression of fatuous love is multifaceted and is "uniquely defined within each culture" (p. 752). Studying nearly 2,000 participants from the United States (consisting of Caucasians as well as Japanese Americans and Chinese Americans), Denmark, England, Canada, and Israel, Landis and O'Shea asked respondents to complete a sexual behavior and sexual attitudes questionnaire and to rate how strongly they agreed with statements such as:

- Sometimes my body trembles with excitement at the sight of him/her.
- I want him/her physically, emotionally, mentally.
- I yearn to know all about him/her.
- No one else could ever love him/her like I do (would).
- Sometimes I feel I can't control my thoughts; they are obsessively on him/her.
- I would get jealous if I thought he/she were falling in love with someone else.

Each culture under investigation provided culture-specific responses. For example, Canadian males were characterized as more excited about their love object, whereas males from the United Kingdom were characterized as more melancholy on the same measures. The researchers found that, overall, those cultures that were characterized as relatively feminine (such as Denmark) showed differences in their passionate love experiences in terms of security and commitment; masculine cultures, such as Israel, appeared to foster more "self-centered" relationships.

The physical and emotional exhilaration, the fever-pitched excitement, and the sexually charged atmosphere that accompanies infatuation may be more the work of the not very romantic-sounding neurotransmitters and hormones than the work of rational decision making. These *neurotransmitters* and *hormones* may, in fact, be the primary influence on relationship junkies. (See the feature box "Healthy Selves/Healthy Families" for an explanation of these biochemical processes.)

Unfortunately, there is also a negative side of infatuation: *stalking*.

THE NEGATIVE SIDES OF LOVE

In February 2007, NASA astronaut Lisa Nowak was arrested and charged with the attempted murder of the woman she believed was her romantic rival for a space shuttle pilot's affections. So obsessed was Nowak in finding her rival, she drove from Texas to Florida wearing adult diapers so she would not have to stop along the way. When arrested, Nowak noted that she was not stalking her victim, and that she only wanted to scare her victim into talking with her. Prior to her arrest, Nowak had persistently harassed her victim, via cell phone and text messages, for over two months. We discuss intimate partner violence at length in Chapter 15, but here it is necessary to understand that there is a negative side to passionate love and infatuation: stalking.

I Can't Help Falling in Love: The Science of Love

Healthy SELVES Healthy FAMILIES

What is love, actually? What is the basis of the giddy, walking-on-air feelings we experience when we fall in love? Recent advances in science may reveal the answer.

The initial feelings of love don't have much to do with romance, but instead have more to do with functions of the brain. Information between brain neurons is communicated by the movement of certain chemicals—neurotransmitters—across areas of the brain. When we begin to fall in love, the "high" we experience is the result of the release of these neurotransmitters. When two people are attracted to one another, the brain becomes flooded with a gush of neurotransmitters that mimic *amphetamines* (commonly referred to as "uppers"). The neurotransmitter culprits are *dopamine,* which make us feel good, *norepinephrine,* which causes pounding hearts and racing pulses, and *PEA (phenylethylamine),* which causes feelings of excitement and euphoria. Because chocolate contains PEA, it has long been rumored to promote infatuation between lovers (however, it is probably more the result of the large amounts of caffeine and sugar found in chocolate).

The neurotransmitters then signal the *pituitary gland* (located in the region of the brain known as the hypothalamus) to release a multitude of hormones that rapidly flood the bloodstream. The sex glands, in turn, release even more hormones into the bloodstream. It is the combination of the flood of neurotransmitters in the brain and the subsequent release of the hormones into the bloodstream that allow new lovers to make love all night or talk for hours on end. When these chemicals are produced over a period of time, people interpret the physical sensations as "falling in love." Love, actually, is a cocktail of neurochemicals.

Source: Aron, Mashek, Fisher, Li, & Brown (2005).

Stalking: An Obsessive Following **Stalking** is the obsessive following, observing, or contacting of another person, or the obsessive attempt to engage in any of these activities. It can be done in person, or online; online stalking is referred to as **cyber-stalking**. The U.S. Department of Justice (2007) provides us some relevant statistics regarding stalking:

- Each year, over 1 million women are stalked, and over 370,000 men are stalked.
- 1 in 12 women and 1 in 45 men will be stalked in their lifetime.
- Most victims know their stalker.
- 81 percent of women who are stalked have also been physically assaulted by that partner.
- The average duration of stalking is 1.8 years, and two-thirds of stalkers attempt to contact their victim at least daily, by the use of many methods.

Stalking can also be a problem on college campuses, with 3 in 10 college women reporting being emotionally, psychologically, or physically harmed from being stalked; 80 percent knew their stalker. In 2007, over one-half of stalked women took some type of self-protective measure, and 11 percent had

REFERRED to by the media as an "astronut," NASA astronaut Lisa Nowak stalked her romantic rival for months.

to relocate; over one-fourth of stalking victims lost time from work as a result of emotional turmoil caused by stalking.

Stalking exists in many forms, and sometimes victims don't even realize that it is happening because it can be subtle. In general, there are five types of stalkers (Mullen, Pathe, & Purcell, 2000):

1. **Rejected stalkers** want to reverse, correct, or avenge rejection of their affections, infatuation, or love. This type of stalking either begins as the perpetrator senses the relationship is about to end, or after the couple has separated and/or terminated the relationship.
2. **Intimacy seekers** desire to establish an intimate, loving relationship with their victim. They believe that their victim is their one-and-only soul mate, and that fate has brought them together.
3. **Incompetent suitors** commonly have poor social and emotional skills, and have difficulty expressing themselves. They develop a fixation on someone they feel romantically attracted to. In most cases, however, the victim is already in a relationship with someone else.
4. **Resentful stalkers** are out for vengeance because they believe they were wronged by their victim. This type of stalking is motivated primarily by the desire to frighten the victim and cause her or him distress.
5. **Predatory stalkers** spy on the victim in order to plan a sexual attack.

Online and offline stalking are federal crimes under the laws of all 50 states. It is also considered to be a crime in Canada, Japan, and the United Kingdom. We'll explore the multiple mental, emotional, and physiological health effects of stalking later in this text.

Jealousy: A Perceived Threat "Heaven has no rage like love to hatred turned, Nor hell a fury like a woman scorned." These infamous words, penned by William Congreve in 1697, refer to a woman's jealousy in a love-gone-bad relationship. We don't know the relational experiences that led Congreve to write this passage, but we can come to a pretty quick conclusion that he experienced the wrath and anger of a jealous woman! A popular theme in movies such as *Closer* and *Unfaithful*, jealousy is a component of love for most of us.

Jealousy is an emotional reaction to the perception that a valued relationship is threatened because of a third party (Knox, Breed, & Zusman, 2007). This perceived threat can be real or imaginary. Typically, jealousy is aroused when one person believes that someone is getting what the person wishes to have for himself or herself, such as attention, love, or affection. It is an emotion that can be manifest in several ways, including anger, fear, hurt, betrayal, anxiety, sadness, paranoia, depression, feelings of powerlessness, or inadequacy (Brem, 1992). It can be experienced in a number of different relationships: Children can be jealous of siblings who get the attention of parents; friends can be jealous of other friends in the peer group; and workers can be jealous of co-workers (DeSteno, 2004). The central theme to jealousy is that a valued relationship is endangered and may be taken over by a rival (DeSteno, 2004).

Whatever we feel when we are jealous, the central emotion behind jealousy is *fear*—fear about change, fear about the future of the relationship, fear of abandonment, or fear of losing power in the relationship. At the very least, jealousy causes hurt feelings; at its worse, it can result in family violence (see Chapter 15) or lead to a murderous rage (White, 1981). "Enraged jealousy" was the motivation for murder suggested by the prosecution team during the O. J. Simpson trial; indeed, jealousy was a likely contributing factor in about 40 percent of female homicides in 2000 (Knox and others, 2007; U.S. Department of Justice, 2003).

Some theories, such as Social Learning theory and Evolutionary theory (see Chapter 7) maintain that jealousy serves a useful, adaptive function in relationships. We established in the previous chapter that we all have an innate, intrinsic drive to be involved in an intimate relationship with someone, and that intimacy fulfills both psychological and physiological needs. To protect intimacy, theorists believe that a specific emotion designed to protect relationships—jealousy—has evolved over time (DeSteno, Valdesolo, & Bartlett, 2006). Given that jealousy is a global experience, found in cultures all over the world, it stands to reason

The **FAMILY** *Table*

Seeing Green: Recognizing and Managing Jealousy

Commonly referred to as the *green-eyed-monster,* feelings of jealousy are an indicator of underlying fear—we may feel insecure and threatened that someone or something will take our lover away from us. Although some jealousy can be unhealthy and dangerous, such as in the case of controlling and/or abusive partners, for the most part it is a common component of our love relationships. To overcome—or at least dilute it a bit—here are some suggestions:

- **Don't compare yourself to anyone else.** *Everyone* is unique and *everyone* has something to bring to a relationship. When you compare yourself to other people, you only sabotage your own uniqueness and individuality—and the relationship.
- **Know your own strengths.** What do you bring to the relationship? Just remember: You have the advantage, because you are the one that is currently in the relationship—not your rival!
- **Use jealousy to your advantage.** Okay, so you're jealous of someone else's attributes. Use this energy as the fuel to help you accomplish your goals and to grow!
- **Affirm the other person.** Look at the rival for who he or she really is. What are his or her good qualities? Try to see the other person for who he or she really is, not just as a threat to your relationship.
- **Get rid of the toxicity.** If someone in your circle of friends is toxic to you and to your relationship, remove yourself from their presence. And, if necessary for your emotional well-being and health, remove yourself permanently.

Remember, there will always be someone who is more talented, more beautiful, more successful, and wealthier than you. So what?

Source: Adapted in part from Sorgen (2008).

that this emotion has evolved as an adaptive response, triggered by fear of rejection, to safeguard relationships. None of us is immune to the experiences and emotions associated with jealousy.

Research reveals there are four stages of jealousy (White, 1981):

1. *Suspecting the threat.* Some people look for signs of relationship deterioration or relationship threat where there are none, while others overlook obvious signals. In general, women are more likely to admit feeling jealous. Typically, women are jealous over a mate's emotional attachment to another person. Conversely, men are more likely to deny feelings of jealousy. Men typically become jealous of sex, and they accept the belief that "jealousy shows love" (Knox and others, 2007). Sadly, men are more likely to be abusive when they feel they can no longer control their partner's feelings for them (Sagarin and others, 2003).

2. *Emotionally reacting.* Emotional reactions to threats of our love relationships can range from clinging dependency (more often by women but by men as well), to violent rage (mostly by men), to depression with thoughts of suicide (mostly by women). While men respond more intensely to jealousy, women take longer to get over it.

3. *Coping.* In general, when coping with jealousy, women often cry, plead, or blame themselves for the problems in the relationship. They also tend to eat to cope with their jealous feelings (Knox and others, 2007). They also confide more often in their friends about jealous feelings than men do. Men attempt to bolster their egos by becoming competitive (this may involve becoming sexually involved with a different, more attractive partner). They also tend

to drink alcohol when they feel jealous (Knox and others, 2007). Women tend to delay entering into another relationship.

4. *Moving on.* If feelings of jealousy erupt, it is important to discuss these feelings of vulnerability openly with the partner and then find a creative way to deal with these feelings. For example, some couples create a private code word to use in social gatherings to indicate that they are feeling insecure or jealous. Above all, it's important to validate and respect the partner's feelings.

Of course, there are a number of things that determine how we experience jealousy, such as family of origin experiences, past relationship experiences, sexual attitudes and beliefs (for instance, some people are more sexually permissive than others), and gender role attitudes (Russell & Harton, 2005). Jealousy is a complex emotion that has many sides to it, and because of this, it has been difficult for scientists to measure. But given its purposes of protecting intimate and family relationships, and given its consequences to our psychological and physical well-being, more research needs to be conducted so we can better understand its forms, functions, and outcomes.

So far, our study has shown us that love can be experienced as a romantic infatuation, which involves a complicated, overpowering blend of emotion and sex. There are also negative sides of romantic love, which include stalking and jealousy (although jealousy can be experienced in any type of relationship). But unlike passionate love, where feelings may wax and wane, *companionate* love is characterized by deep, mature, affectionate attachment bonds.

COMPANIONATE LOVE: EXPERIENCING LOVE AS A COMMITMENT

There's love . . . and there's love that lasts. It is not uncommon for us to question whether our experiences with love are "real love" or "true love." With such a flood of biochemicals in the brain and the surge of hormones in the bloodstream when we become attracted to someone, it is little wonder that it is difficult to determine if what we are feeling is the real, lasting thing or a fleeting fling. Unlike infatuation, *companionate love* leads to committed, perhaps even lifelong, love relationships.

Companionate Love It is not uncommon for relationships to move from the have-to-be-intimate-24-hours-a-day phase (passionate love) to a phase of love that is less dominated by lust. Much in the same way ravenous binge eating must eventually come to an end, so too must the ravenous passionate/infatuated love come to an end. (If the love remained at the sexually and emotionally charged state, we would be too worn out to accomplish much else!) If the romantic love experience is to endure, it must at some point be combined with or transition into a calmer, more tender, more affectionate type of love. While passionate/romantic love is a rapid-fire frenzy of emotion, sexual arousal, anxiousness, and life that revolves around the two-person world, companionate love is distinctly different. **Companionate love** refers to deep, tender, mature, affectionate attachment bonds shared between two people; companionate love may or may not include feelings of physical arousal.

Passionate love happens quickly; companionate love grows gradually over time. Contrary to "love at first sight" relationships or "love [hormone] connections" observed in passionate love relationships, companionate love develops between partners who have known each other long enough to have acknowledged and accepted all of the failings, faults, shortcomings, oddities, and quirks of each partner—and still *like* the partner.

Liking is a necessary ingredient in companionate love. It is impossible to arrive at companionate love without liking each other. Why? Liking develops as a result of consistent, repeated **rewards**, such as nurture, care, appreciation, trust, and making/seeing the other person happy. Essentially, whatever attributes people have on their love prototype list are their perceived rewards in the relationship. Building the rewards takes time and patience—both fundamental components of companionate love. Passionate love relationships typically do not want to devote the time necessary to build up rewards, because the very nature of these relationships contradicts spending time on anything.

Expression of Love To further our understanding of the distinctions among the experiences of liking, infatuation, and committed love, Robert Sternberg (1986, 1988) developed his **Triangular Theory of Love**, which conceptualizes eight different types of love relationships. These relationships take into account that each individual will experience many types of love throughout life. Recognizing that love is a *process* that undergoes change, Sternberg proposed that love relationships consist of three interconnected components: intimacy, commitment, and passion. As you can see in Figure 6.1, each of these interlocking components corresponds to one side of the love triangle; because love is not a fixed or static experience, the three components of love will not always be in perfect balance. Indeed, all three components may not necessarily be present at the same time. For this reason, we may experience different types of loving, even within the same relationship, over a period of time.

Intimacy According to Sternberg (1986), **intimacy** refers to loving relationships characterized by feelings of closeness, connectedness, and bondedness. Recall from Chapter 5 that intimacy involves an emotional attachment (we can think of intimacy as the *emotional component* in a love relationship) and includes many components such as self-disclosure of personal and private aspects of our lives, respect, trust, affection, warmth, mutuality, and spirituality. As with companionate love, intimacy builds slowly and gradually over time and is a prominent feature of a love relationship.

Commitment Sternberg (1986) defines *commitment* as a decision to love someone else and as a decision to maintain that love over time. **Commitment** refers to loving another person as a conscious act of will—it is a deliberate choice. Commitment can thus be thought of as the *cognitive component* in a love relationship. It includes such things as being loyal to another person, being responsible and reliable, being trustworthy and trusting, and putting forth our best effort in a relationship (Fehr, 1988).

FIGURE 6.1   Sternberg's Triangular Theory of Love

Robert Sternberg conceptualized love as a process that undergoes change throughout a person's life, with three interconnected components: intimacy, commitment, and passion. Because love is not a fixed experience, the three components are not always in perfect balance.

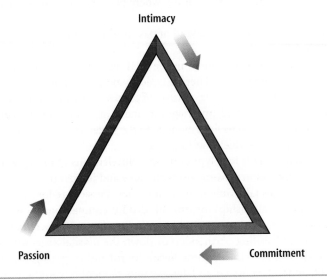

Sternberg observed that the process of commitment occurs gradually, with the levels of commitment to the partner increasing somewhat slowly at first. Commitment—just as in the instances of loving and liking—is possible only after several rewards are reciprocated between the partners. After commitment begins to increase in a relationship, these levels accelerate and then gradually find a leveling-off point. If at any time during the relationship any of the key attributes of commitment are dishonored, violated, or lost, the love relationship becomes threatened or may even end.

COMPANIONATE love is a deep, tender, emotionally mature affectionate attachment shared between two people. It grows slowly, gradually over time, and accepts all of the shortcomings and faults of each partner.

Passion The passion element of Sternberg's triangle of love refers to many of the facets discussed earlier in our coverage of passionate/infatuation love relationships. **Passion**, in this instance, refers to the physical attraction and romantic feelings that initially draw us to another person. According to Sternberg, passion is the driving force of romance, physical attraction, and sexual consummation. It is important to note, however, that passion can still exist in a relationship whether sexual intercourse is a part of the relationship or not.

Of the three components of Sternberg's theory, passion is the most intense and immediate. Passion peaks quickly. Over time, however, the initial excitement levels of passion reduce to a stable level; at the same time, liking and intimacy levels continue to rise, giving way to companionate love. While some couples fear that they have "fallen out of love" when the passion begins to fade, others become comfortable with the calm stabilization of their love relationship. Sternberg notes that if a relationship is ended, an individual may experience feelings of loss. If this occurs, a person's capacity for passion may be negative for a time until the sense of loss abates.

Sternberg's Love Types Recall that Sternberg's theory acknowledges that each individual experiences many types of love throughout life, and that love is a *process* that undergoes change. Notice in Figure 6.2 that each of the eight types of love represents a combination of any of the three components of love, but only one includes all three. As you view the varying types of love, keep in mind that a single relationship may experience each type of love, as described by Sternberg. The eight types of love include:

1. **Nonlove.** The absence of intimacy, commitment, and passion characterizes this type of love. Nonlove may exist in a relationship where physical, emotional, or sexual violence is present.
2. **Empty love.** This type of love is devoid of passion and intimacy. *Commitment* is the only element in the relationship.
3. **Liking.** *Intimacy* is the sole element in the relationship and is the stuff that great, long-lasting friendships are made of. There is typically no passion or commitment.
4. **Infatuated love.** This type of love consists of *passion* only; this is the stuff that television dating shows and "Hollywood" marriages are made of, but not long-term marriages. Sudden and explosive physical feelings along with the idealizing of the love object, infatuated love relationships end as quickly as they begin.
5. **Companionate love.** This love type combines the elements of *intimacy* and *commitment*. Companionate love often starts as romantic love and is then transformed into companionate love as couples take time to build intimacy. Passionate love junkies probably will not give romantic relationships the time needed for companionate love to grow.
6. **Fatuous love.** Combining *passion* and *commitment*, fatuous love relationships result in a sprint toward a cohabiting partnership or down the marital aisle. But because the relationship lacks intimacy and the time necessary for intimacy to grow and develop, and because passion will fade sooner or later, the only element remaining is commitment. The

FIGURE 6.2 Sternberg's Love Types

Each of the eight types of love proposed by Sternberg represents a combination of the three components of love. As a relationship grows and changes, it may experience each type of love. The solid lines represent the components that are present in the different types of love. The dots represent the missing components (such as empty love has commitment but not intimacy or passion).

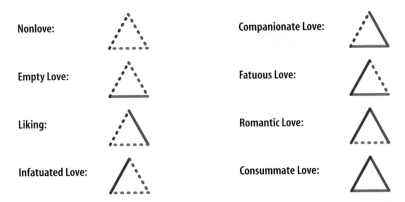

commitment is not the type that has been nurtured through the ups and downs of relational life; the commitment thus fades in time.

7. **Romantic love**. *Intimacy* and *passion* are the elements that make up romantic love. Because of the physical and/or sexual attraction and arousal that accompanies romantic love, it is thought to be a more intense form of love than liking.

8. **Consummate love.** Sternberg considers consummate love to be total, whole, absolute, and all-inclusive. This type of love combines all three elements of love—*intimacy, commitment,* and *passion.* Some may attain this type of relationship, but not without nurturing and working to maintain the relationship.

Developing Love

The ability and capacity to love *are not totally inherited*—they are nurtured from our first experiences of love. The development of love is a complex interaction of heredity, such as personality traits; the environment in which we are reared; our family of origin; and the myriad of events, incidents, and situations we experience in family life. Interactions and love experiences we have with people across our lifespan, as well as our educational background, all contribute to how love develops in our lives.

FIRST EXPERIENCES OF LOVE

The first love relationship many of us experience is the parent–infant relationship. Thrust into an unfamiliar, foreign environment, we begin our relational lives as dependent creatures, fully reliant on our parents and caregivers for our most basic survival needs (nourishment, shelter, warmth, and touch). It is this very dependency on others that propels us to form emotional bonds in which we give and receive love. Likewise, it is from the experiences of the earliest of all love relationships that all of our later-in-life love relationships take shape.

The early love bond that parents form toward their child is **altruistic love**, an unselfish, giving kind of love in which they seek to provide for the needs of their child. Altruistic love promotes the well-being of another with no expectation of reciprocity or return, and it is difficult to specifically pinpoint the rewards or benefits such a love relationship provides.

Indeed, the rewards of altruistic love are **intrinsic rewards** (such as joy, satisfaction, contentment, pleasure, gratification, etc.) derived from the relationships. Most of us do not feel the need for altruistic love to be reciprocated because the rewards obtained are pleasurable in and of themselves.

Perhaps the key concept that differentiates adult–infant love from adult–adult love is the concept of *reciprocity*. Certainly, parents and caregivers cannot realistically expect the return of love from a baby, but adults do expect their love to be reciprocated by their friends and love partners. The ability for people to be dependent and have someone depend on them is referred to as **interdependent love.** Unlike **dependent love** as seen in the adult–infant pair bond where an adult immediately meets and gratifies the needs of an infant, interdependent love is expressed between emotionally mature adults who recognize that love is a give-and-take process. Adults recognize that there are times when one partner may have to give more than the other, such as in the case of illness or times of extreme stress or distress. Emotionally mature adults understand that interdependent love requires that, at times, some wants and needs may have to be delayed in order to promote the well-being of a partner or the couple.

The growth from dependent love to interdependent love is a process that takes place over many developmental phases of life, from infancy, through childhood and adolescence, through the transition to early adulthood to the end of life (see Figure 6.3). As in the case of intimacy, the capacity to love others develops throughout the lifespan. As you have learned, relationships we form during the early years of life serve as template interactions on which subsequent interpersonal intimate and love relationships are built.

The development of our capacity and ability to love takes place in the context of early emotional relationships, particularly within our family of origin. In the next section, we take a closer look at the emotional bond that significantly impacts our ability to give and receive love throughout our lives: attachment.

ATTACHMENT: AN EMOTIONAL BOND

Attachment is best described as an emotional or affectional bond that ties or binds the child to the parent or primary caregiver (Bowlby, 1988). In order to describe enduring, lasting pat-

FIGURE 6.3   Time Line of Love Experiences

Our first experiences of love are experienced because we have our survival needs met by our parents. Babies are not capable of reciprocating the love.

As babies age, they become independent. This independence continues throughout childhood and adolescence. Through family relationships and friendships, children and teens learn how to give and receive love.

terns of interpersonal relationships from the cradle to the grave, John Bowlby developed the **Attachment theory** based on his observations of parent–child interactions (1969/1973/1980). With the premise that all infants need nurturance in order to survive, Bowlby asserted that in the process of providing for these survival needs, newborns form a type of bond—an *attachment*—with their caregivers (typically the mother and/or father). Bowlby's Attachment theory posits that it is from this close affectional and emotional bond that children derive a sense of security, a trusting sense that the world, and the interpersonal relationships we encounter along the way, is a safe place to be.

Because of the importance of these early human relationships, Bowlby, along with prominent researcher Mary Ainsworth and her associates, asserted that the attachment behaviors that take place throughout infancy ultimately direct, shape, and mold our personality. Consequently, these behaviors significantly direct, shape, and mold the interpersonal attachment relationships we experience later on as children, adolescents, and adults (Ainsworth, Belhar, Waters, & Wall, 1978). Some researchers believe that attachment may begin even earlier. They suggest that the emotional and affectional bonds actually begin during pregnancy, well before birth takes place (Klaus, Kennell, & Klaus, 1995). Although researchers may not all agree on the exact time attachment occurs, they do agree that the ability to form and experience an emotional attachment to a parent(s) or caregiver in the earliest days of life is, in effect, a predictor of an individual's ability to form interpersonal (and love) relationships in the future (see Chapter 5).

Attachment and Its Significance to Love Attachment theory serves as a useful foundation for viewing how emotional bonds are formed and for looking at infants' reactions to parents and caregivers, but there is research that goes beyond Bowlby's theory. Using the same concepts and principles associated with attachment to more fully understand the concept of adult experiences of love, researchers have gathered an abundance of empirical evidence that speaks to the importance and significance of the quality of attachment during infancy and the subsequent impact of this attachment quality to relationships later in life, throughout childhood, adolescence, and adulthood (such as Allen & Land, 1999; Elliot & Reis, 2003; Furukawa, Yokouchi, Hirai, Kitamura, & Takahashi, 1999; Howe, Brandon, Hinings, & Scofield, 1999; Markeiwicz, Doyle, & Brendgen, 2001; Seiffge-Krenke, 1993; Weiss, 1982).

The capacity to love moves from an independent kind of love to an interdependent type of love. This love is said to be emotionally mature love, because it is capable of giving and receiving love, and of delaying the gratification of needs for the benefit of the other person. When we reach emotional maturity, we then have the capacity to allow a baby to be fully dependent on us—thus starting the cycle over again.

An equally abundant body of research exists that examines adults' secure or insecure attachment to their own parents and their subsequent responsiveness and sensitivity in their parenting behaviors toward their own children (among others, Geiger, 1996; Field, 1996; Bartholomew, 1990; Crittenden, Partridge, & Claussen, 1991; Main & Hesse, 1990). For example, Marinus van Ijzendoorn (1995), a developmentalist who studies intergenerational aspects of childrearing and attachment, sought to understand the extent to which parents transmit their own attachment experiences to their children. He found in his study of 59 mother–infant pairs that about three-fourths of the pairs were identical in their attachment behaviors. There is even some evidence that attachment behaviors and patterns span multiple generations (Benoit & Parker, 1994). According to researchers Clyde Hendrick and Susan Hendrick (1992), attachment is a developmental phase that we never outgrow.

Attachment Types One study in particular is quite helpful in our quest to gain insight into the development of our ability to love others. Based on Ainsworth and colleagues' (1978) descriptive categories of attachment styles observed in infants, psychologists Cindy Hazan and Phillip Shaver's (1987) research supports the notion that patterns of attachment early in life influence adult love relationships. In their examination of adult love relationships conceptualized as an attachment process, Hazan and Shaver classified adult love relationships in the following way.

- **Secure attachment types.** Secure adults, like securely attached infants, have little difficulty seeking or maintaining closeness (physical, emotional, affectional) with another. They don't fear being abandoned or losing their partner. Secure adults allow others to get close to them and depend on them. These adults report enduring, happy, warm, trusting relationships that promote self-esteem.
- **Avoidant attachment types.** Avoidant types report that they seldom find "real" love. Hazan and Shaver described these adults as being uncomfortable when too emotionally or physically close to another person. Avoidant attachment types show discomfort with intimacy and are hesitant to trust others (Feeney & Noller, 1991). They find it difficult to allow themselves to depend on others. Avoidant types commonly report that they experienced separation from their mothers (emotional and/or physical separation).
- **Anxious/ambivalent attachment types.** Insecurity is the hallmark of this adult attachment type. When an adult shows this type of attachment, it is not a matter of *if* a romantic partner leaves them, but *when*. With the constant fear or worry that the partner isn't really in love with them, anxious/ambivalent adults cling to their partner and push for commitment (Feeney & Noller, 1991)—and in doing so, often push the partner completely out of the picture. Poor attachment in adulthood can prohibit people from getting too emotionally close to attachment figures, causing them to withdraw and pull away before they get rejected (Pickover, 2002).

As a student told me,

My experiences leave me very distrustful of others . . . although it has been very difficult to undergo counseling, I have become aware of the many areas in which I need to heal. I have to totally re-learn to relate to people. I am learning that I don't have to feel guilty when I am not punished for doing or saying the wrong thing . . . I am learning that I don't have to constantly apologize for things I have no control over . . . I don't have to earn people's kindness or love! I do still, though, feel extreme guilt in knowing I am— and might always be—an emotionally high-need person. Eventually I will have to take the risk of telling another person what happened to me and letting him decide if he is willing to deal with me while I deal with the past. (Author's files)

The empirical evidence is clear—our experiences with early attachment relationships to our parent(s) or primary caregiver become the foundation on which all future love relationships are built.

THERE'S more to this intergenerational family than we can see at the surface. Each of us learns our relational behaviors—including how we give and receive love—from our parents, and they received those love models from their parents. How we love is an intergenerational experience!

LOVE STORIES: SHAPED FROM GENERATION TO GENERATION

As recipes and cooking may be passed down from generation to generation, so too are the origins of our capacity to love and to be loved. It is these family influences that ultimately shape our **love stories**—our unique, personal experiences with love. There is a story that surfaced several years ago about a newly married couple. It makes a strong point concerning the development of love within the family of origin.

In preparation for their first big dinner with both sets of parents and grandparents, the new husband was puzzled as he watched his new bride put the ham in the oven. He inquired of her, "Honey, why did you cut the ham in half and then put it in the pan?"

She replied, "Oh, I don't know . . . I suppose because that's how Mom always did it. It must help it cook faster or something."

At dinner that evening the bride asked her mother, "Mom, why do you cut the ham in half before you bake it?"

The mother, baffled by her daughter's question, thoughtfully replied, "I suppose it's because that's always how my mom did it." All eyes in the room turned on the bride's grandmother. The grandmother, quite amused, chuckled and replied, "When I was first married I didn't have a pan large enough for the ham to fit in—so I always cut it into two halves and just kept doing it that way. I guess I just got accustomed to doing it that way."

As this story illustrates, so often we do things and interact in certain established ways because we have become accustomed to doing things in these ways. So it is with much of what makes up family life, including how we love others and how we allow others to love us. Thus far in your study of family and intimate relations you have come to understand the nature of family process. You have learned to recognize that our actions influence and are influenced by our family of origin.

Murray Bowen (1974), a central figure in an **intergenerational approach to family therapy**, sought to understand the transmission of relational behaviors from one generation to the next. Indeed, as marriage and family therapists Michael Nichols and Richard Schwartz point out, "The family remains with us wherever we go" (p. 119).

According to Nichols and Schwartz (2004), Bowen believed that when examining the family, it is not enough to say that past experiences influence present experiences; he also wanted to look at the relationships within the family and explore the path that guided the emotional processes from generation to generation. And it is from this theory the use of *genograms* was born.

Bowen created **genograms**, which are diagrams with various figures that serve to illustrate relationships between family members. These relationships can be drawn to illustrate simply the immediate family, or, in greater detail, it may include extended family relationships and multigenerational relationships. Whether using a genogram to trace certain medical histories such a cancer or heart disease, to create family trees, or to gain a clearer understanding of the family processes and emotional behaviors and patterns passed down through the generations as Bowen did, genograms give us an instant snapshot of relationship history within a given family.

In Figure 6.4a, squares are used to represent males; females are represented by circles. Notice that each of the figures is assigned an age. A solid horizontal line indicates marriage and the marriage date, while the vertical lines link parents and children. To denote a family member who has died, an "×" is placed through the square or the circle. Figure 6.4b illustrates other symbols used to indicate relationship dynamics. These dynamics speak in large part to the emotional connection of the family members.

Genograms are most commonly used for therapeutic purposes. When an individual family member or a family seeks family therapy, the marriage and family therapist may use the genogram in order to map out family dynamics. So, one family's genogram may resemble something similar to Figure 6.4b. Notice how this illustration shows that the relationship between all of the siblings is either distant or estranged, as is the relationship between the husband and the wife. Only the mother and daughter appear to have emotional closeness. A therapist can use this information to help the family establish healthier boundaries, and thus, improve the family's health and functioning.

FIGURE 6.4A   Basic Genogram Symbols

In the family genogram, squares represent males and circles represent females. The solid horizontal line indicates marriage and the marriage date, while the vertical lines link parents and children.

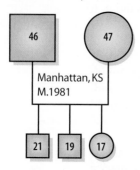

Source: Nichols, M. P. & Schwartz, R. C. *Family Therapy Concepts and Methods,* 6e. Published by Allyn and Bacon, Boston, MA. Copyright © 2004 by Pearson Education. Reprinted by permission of the Publisher.

FIGURE 6.4B   Genogram Symbols for Relationship Dynamics

Genograms are useful tools used by therapists to map out family dynamics, particularly the emotional connections between family members.

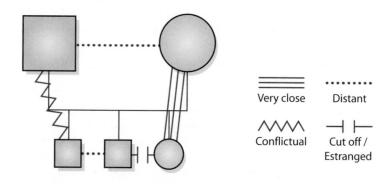

Source: Nichols, M. P. & Schwartz, R. C. *Family Therapy Concepts and Methods,* 6e. Published by Allyn and Bacon, Boston, MA. Copyright © 2004 by Pearson Education. Reprinted by permission of the Publisher.

Create a Family Genogram

To understand more clearly how your capacity to love and to be loved develops across the generations in your family, let's adapt Bowen's theoretical concept of the genogram and create a "love map" of sorts. Using the family genogram as your template, take the time to sketch out your family and indicate with a plus (+) or minus (–) symbol those family members who influenced your "love" capacities and abilities in either positive or negative ways. For example, perhaps a parent or a sibling consistently demonstrated unconditional love to you; place a (+) symbol in that family member's square or circle. On the other hand, maybe a family member remains emotionally distant from you, or perhaps you experienced abuse by that family member; denote this by placing a (–) symbol in that family member's square or circle.

1. Did you notice in your love genogram any consistent patterns that have been passed down to you from previous generations?

2. If so, are these patterns something you want to repeat in your interpersonal relationships or something that you wish to change?

Theories of Love and Loving

We have already taken a look at one prominent theory, Sternberg's Triangular Theory of Love, and we have devoted significant time to Attachment theory. Let me now turn your attention to other conceptualizations of love. Two additional theories, Lee's Six Types of Love Styles and Reiss's Wheel Theory of Love, have received much attention and consideration. Another theory, Love Economic Model, is just emerging on the social science scene.

LEE'S SIX TYPES OF LOVE STYLES

As noted earlier in this chapter, the Greeks solved the problem of using only one word—*love*—for perhaps the most complex emotion known to humankind. Canadian sociologist John Alan Lee (1973) conceptualized love in a manner similar to that of the Greeks in that he proposed six different love styles. Recognizing the theoretical richness and multidimensionality of Lee's work, Hendrick and Hendrick (1986) then built on Lee's work to create instruments with which to measure the varying types of love (Neto, 2001).

1. *Eros: Passionate and Tantalizing.* The Greeks used the term **eros** to refer to a type of sensual or sexual love. Lee noted that **erotic lovers** are passionate and romantic and seek out passionately expressive lovers. They thrive on the tantalizing nature of love and sex. They have an "ideal mate" in their mind's eye and believe there is only one "true love" in the world for them. Sexual activity usually occurs early on in the relationship, and the sex is hot, passionate, exciting, and insatiable all at once. Once sexual activity takes place, the eros lover is usually monogamous.

2. *Ludus: Flirtatious and Fun.* **Ludus** refers to love that is playful, flirtatious, carefree, and casual. **Ludic lovers** don't care as much about commitment as they do about playing the sport or the game of love. For the ludic lover, variety is truly the spice of life—the more partners, the better. Because ludic lovers don't share intimacy, love with a ludic person is fun and easygoing, nonchalant and unconcerned about tomorrow.

3. *Storge: Affectionate and Constant.* **Storge** (pronounced STOR-gay) love can best be conceptualized as friendship love, or a type of affectionate love between companions. **Storgic lovers** typically come to love each other over time, as opposed to the instantaneous type of love found with eros lovers. Neto (2001) notes that this type of love engenders shared interests, trust, and acceptance, all of which develop over time.

4. *Manic: Frenzied and Chaotic.* Jealousy, envy, protectiveness, and exclusivity are the hallmark traits of **manic lovers.** Manic love is frenzied, agitated, hectic, and chaotic all at the same time. The highs are very high, the lows are very low—making the relationship very much a roller-coaster ride of emotions. When a love relationship ends, a manic lover has difficulty thinking of anyone or anything else except the lost love.

5. *Pragma: Practical and Careful.* Practicality and logic guide the *pragmatic* lover. With **pragma love,** the costs and benefits associated with love are carefully weighed and considered before entering into a relationship. If the "perfect mate" items on the pragmatic lover's list are fulfilled—suitability of education, family background, socioeconomic status, religion, and so on—the love candidate has a good chance of becoming a mate or life partner.

6. *Agape: Selfless and Patient.* Lee describes **agape love** (pronounced uh-gah-PAY) as a selfless, enduring, other-centered type of love. Taken from the Latin word *caritas,* which means "charity," the Greeks used the term *agape* love to refer to unconditional, willful, "I-love-you-because-I-choose-to" kind of love. It is a love type that provides intrinsic (rewarding in and of itself) satisfaction, with no reciprocity expected or demanded. Inherent to agape love is patience, kindness, and permanence.

Cross-Cultural and Gender Influences Felix Neto, from the University of Porto, Portugal (2000), focused his research on the question of whether everyone experiences love, worldwide, in the same way (see Neto and others, 2000). His previous work (1993, 1994) indicated that Lee's love styles, characteristic of American students, were also found to be relevant to students in Portugal. In Neto and his colleagues' more recent work (2000), the love typologies were found across multiple cultures, including Africa, Asia, South America, and Europe, although they did find some cross-cultural differences. Specifically, those love typologies that involved "strong emotional feelings," such as *mania, eros,* and *agape,* were nearly free of cultural influences—in other words, across cultures people tend to experience these love typologies in very similar ways. Those love typologies that involved "strict social rules," such as *pragma, storge,* and *ludus,* were quite dependent on cultural values.

According to Hendrick and Hendrick (1983), an individual's love style is not static and fixed, but can change over the course of a lifetime, or even during a relationship. Neto's (2001) work that investigated the love styles held by three generations of women (college students, their mothers, and their maternal grandmothers) seems to support this notion. The goal of Neto's study was to determine the similarities and differences in love styles among the three generations, and to explore whether experiences of love styles change over time. Each of the 144 study participants from 48 families was given a questionnaire that assessed their love styles. Results of this study indicate that there was very little similarity in the experiences of love styles among the three generations of women. In

INHERENT to any love relationship is the fact that sometimes unimaginable, unforeseeable things happen that will serve to rattle even the most solid of all relationships, as in the case of the young couple in the opening vignette of this chapter. What kind of love is really strong enough to withstand an unexpected turn of events? Is it possible that a love relationship can survive tragic circumstances—and, if so, how can that type of love be fostered?

fact, Neto found significant differences between the women in the eros, storge, pragma, and agape love styles.

Finally, one body of research suggests that some love styles are considered to be more socially desirable among men and some more socially desirable among women (Davies, 2001). Primarily, *eros* and *ludus* were found to be associated with social desirability in men but not in women. *Agape* love was found to be associated with social desirability in women, but not in men. As you learned in Chapter 4, many experiences in intimate and family relationships are influenced by how men and women are socialized. The experiences of love are no different; this research supports the notion that how a person is taught to be male or female helps determine love styles.

REISS'S WHEEL THEORY OF LOVE

Sociologist Ira Reiss (1960, 1971) described love as a developmental process, a process that unfolds over time. **Reiss's Wheel Theory of Love** (Figure 6.5) suggests four stages or processes of love: *rapport, self-revelation, mutual dependency,* and *personality need fulfillment*. Similar to a rolling wheel, these stages of love may be experienced many times, and, in turn, deepen the love bonds between partners. The four processes of love include:

1. *Rapport.* **Rapport** refers to a connection or bond we feel toward another person. Most often, we establish rapport with someone who is similar to us in our cultural background, social class, religious beliefs, educational background, or upbringing. According to Reiss, we are typically more comfortable with someone who is most like us. These similarities allow us to pursue our initial interests in another person.
2. *Self-revelation.* When we feel comfortable in another person's presence, we feel more comfortable self-disclosing our personal hopes, dreams, fears, and goals. **Self-revelation** refers to self-disclosure; as you learned in Chapter 5, self-disclosure deepens a couple's relationship.
3. *Mutual dependency.* As a couple self-discloses, the intimacy levels deepen in their relationship. The couple begins to spend more time together, and they enjoy sharing activities and pursing shared interests. **Mutual dependency** refers to the couple's reliance on one another for need fulfillment, such as social needs and sexual needs.
4. *Personality need fulfillment.* During the fourth and final stage, partners experience **personality need fulfillment,** which is an established pattern of mutual exchanges of

FIGURE 6.5   Reiss's Wheel Theory of Love

Sociologist Ira Reiss described love as a developmental process that unfolds over time, in four stages. Similar to a rolling wheel, these stages of love may be experienced many times within the same relationship, deepening the love bonds between partners. If the wheel stops turning, the love relationship may end.

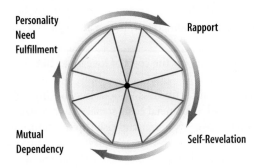

Source: Reiss (1960, 1971).

support, sympathy, and decision making. Each person also satisfies a partner's deeper needs, such as emotional needs and sexual needs.

Reiss suggests that as long as the wheel continues to move forward, a deep and lasting relationship is formed and maintained. If, however, the wheel stops turning—if the processes diminish—the love relationship may come to an end.

The love theories we have explored so far have received much attention and consideration among family life educators, sociologists, psychologists, and family practitioners. A new theory of love is emerging on the social science scene: *Love Economic Model*.

LOVE ECONOMIC MODEL

It was bound to happen sooner or later. With the premise that no one, single source answers eras-old questions such as "How do I find love?," "Why do I fall in love?," and "How do I get out of love?," researcher Chau Vuong (2003) conceptualized a theoretical framework in which he uses mathematical equations to examine "love." He contends that his mathematical, economic model of love provides a means to predict and explain all human behavior pertaining to love.

Vuong's **Love Economic Model** is based on the primary assumptions that people are rational decision makers who are able to tally up both the benefits and costs of falling in love and being in love. In addition, Vuong contends, "Sex and commitment are the only differences between friendship and love" (p. 12). The Love Economic Model is based on several core variables.

The Benefits of Love The equation for the benefits of love looks like this:

Benefits of love = emotional needs + entertainment needs + materialistic needs

1. **Emotional needs** include esteem needs, social needs, spiritual needs, and safety needs. *Esteem needs* refer to obtaining those things that make us happy and content, such as a family. *Social needs* refer to the need for social acceptance, prestige, and access to certain people, events, and resources. *Spiritual needs* include feeling connected to a higher power than ourselves, and *safety needs* include the size and quality of and access to our support network of family and friends.
2. **Entertainment needs** are considered by Vuong to be, by and large, social aspects of day-to-day living and family life. Needs variables include hobbies, interests, and experiences that serve to provide *automatic* partners. By engaging in these activities, we are bound to meet potential love partners.
3. **Materialistic needs** refer to those *primary needs* required for survival and happiness, including food, water, shelter, and transportation. Vuong also considers *sexual needs* to be a materialistic need. *Materialistic desires* are those things not necessarily needed for survival or happiness, but that make life more enjoyable. Vuong terms these "the finer things in life," and contends that if a person cannot satisfy these materialistic desires personally, she or he will seek out someone who can and will.

The Costs of Love The equation for the costs of love looks like this:

Costs of love = search cost (attractiveness + social networking skills + search time cost [free time × selectiveness] + financial cost [social network size × selectiveness]) + rejection costs + maintenance costs + breakup risk (lover's future net benefit with you + lover's net benefit with another love + lover's current breakup cost) + breakup costs (breakup emotional cost + breakup financial cost + replacement cost for another love + previous friendship loss)

TABLE 6.3   Love Economics Translations

According to Vuong's Love Economic Model, when a partner says one thing, it really translates into Love Economics.

English	Love Economics
You are funny.	You are fulfilling my entertainment needs.
I don't care about money.	I have already fulfilled my primary and materialistic needs.
You are picky.	Your selectiveness coefficient is very small.
I am falling for you.	Your net benefit is at sufficient levels for me to reciprocate my love.
We are in love.	Our net benefits exchange is at equilibrium.

Whew! Let's break it down:

1. **Search cost** includes our *attractiveness,* or our ability to attract potential partners, along with *social networking skills.* The author of the Love Economic Model posits "love is a numbers game" (p. 22)—the more people we date, the better our odds of finding someone to love. In what Vuong defines as the "soulmate criteria for a picky person," he calculates how many opposite-sexed people a finicky dater would have to meet in order to find a life mate: 2,604,167!
2. **Rejection costs** include, among other things, *rejection sensitivity* (anxiety, lowered self-esteem), *immunity to rejection* (frequency of past rejections), and the *emotional cost* of the rejection.
3. **Maintenance costs** are delineated as emotional costs and time costs involved in finding the right person. Consequently, those who have relatively little free time have no time for relationships and are less susceptible to falling in love. *Financial costs* are those costs associated with pursuing the relationship (for example, if he or she wants children, children cost money and the financial costs are elevated if the relationship is pursued).
4. **Breakup risk** is a relationship cost that includes determining the lover's future overall benefit with the individual, the lover's future net benefit with another lover, and the lover's current breakup cost. If these costs are considered high, the risk of being "dumped" is relatively low.
5. **Breakup costs** include *emotional* costs, *financial* costs, and the *search* cost necessary to find another love.

Table 6.3 depicts Vuong's conceptualization of "love economics" translations (p. 62). Vuong's framework is complex (and at times difficult to understand if a person is as mathematically challenged as I am!), but nonetheless intriguing. This is the first theoretical framework that examines love by the numbers.

Family Life Education

Love is perhaps the strongest emotion known to humankind and no two people experience it in the same way. It can keep us up all night because of a fiery-hot, erotic/ludic/manic attraction to another, or it can keep us up all night because of a child who is fiery-hot with fever. The world over and across all racial, ethnic, and cultural lines, it can be experienced as a sudden romantic infatuation or an enduring, committed love.

Each of us carries with us an internal prototype of love, a "list" of those components of our unique definitions and characterizations of love. The way we love is indeed complex; it is a compilation of our family of origin and the multitude of events, incidents, and situations we experience in our family life, in tandem with the interpersonal interactions and love relationships we experience throughout our lifespan. But it is from the earliest of all relationships—our parent–infant relationship and the ensuing attachment that takes place—that our ability and capacity to love others (and allow others to love us) is shaped and molded.

Inherent to any love relationship is the fact that sometimes unimaginable, unforeseeable things happen, things that will serve to rattle even the most solid of all relationships, as in the case of the young couple in the opening vignette of this chapter. But as we look back to the story of the young woman, we see that the real-life story contains within it all the elements of an enduring, long-lasting love relationship that Sternberg described in his love types theory.

As the author pulls us near the postoperative bedside of the young woman, we envision the couple's situation. We picture her forever-deformed facial features and wonder what we might do in that situation—would our love really be strong enough to withstand this unexpected turn of events? Notice in the vignette the first element essential to love relationships, that of *passion*. Sternberg maintained that passion does not necessarily refer to sexual intercourse; rather, it refers to that drive, that physical attraction between lovers. Despite her now "clownish" appearance and twisted mouth, the husband went out of his way to assure her that their kiss would always still work—that the passion would always remain.

The *intimacy* element of their relationship is demonstrated in the couple's closeness, connectedness, and bondedness they share as they dwell in each other's presence. To be sure, the type of intimacy that survives a tragic accident is the kind that develops slowly over time and is the bedrock of a long-lasting relationship.

Sternberg defined *commitment* as "the decision that one loves someone else . . . and the [decision] to maintain that love." In other words, it's the commitment to the commitment, a conscious act of our will to remain committed to our partner, regardless of life's circumstances. As the husband bent over to kiss his wife, he assured his wife he would be there for the long haul.

True passion. True intimacy. True commitment. That's the stuff that lasting partnerships are made of—that's real love.

Are There Gender Differences in Emotional and Affection Needs?

Love is a developmental process that unfolds over time. After we establish rapport with someone we find similar to us, we begin to self-disclose our most personal hopes, dreams, fears, and ambitions. In doing so, the intimacy levels deepen within the relationship—so much so that over time, couples become mutually dependent and reliant on each other for the fulfillment of their intimacy and love needs. In the beginning stages of the love experience, couples are eager to care for one another; they are highly motivated to satisfy each other's emotional needs and to nurture one another's love needs. When emotional needs are met, a person feels happy and content. When these needs are not met, a person is left feeling frustrated, unsatisfied, and unfulfilled. Because men and women do not prioritize needs in the same manner, it is likely that at some point emotional needs will be unmet. Compounding this discrepancy, we tend to try to meet our partner's needs based on *our* needs—not what our *partner* needs. If left unattended, the relationship begins to suffer.

The question then arises: How do we know what our partner's love needs/emotional needs are? Are there gender differences in emotional and affection needs? Psychologist and marriage counselor Willard Harley (2001) denotes the 10 most commonly cited emotional needs of men and women:

1. Admiration
2. Affection
3. Conversation
4. Sexual fulfillment
5. Family commitment
6. Honesty/openness
7. Physical attraction
8. Recreational companionship
9. Domestic support
10. Financial support

Her Side: In Harley's research and practice, he observes that women's top five emotional needs are affection, conversation, family commitment, domestic support, and honesty/openness.

His Side: Men's top five emotional needs are admiration, sexual fulfillment, physical attraction, recreational companionship, and honesty.

Your Side: Harley notes that everyone's emotional needs are different, and he also states that emotional needs change over time. In considering his research and his findings from his marriage counseling practice,

1. Do you agree or disagree with Harley's categories of emotional needs?
2. To what extent do you believe these emotional needs, as suggested by Harley, are socialized (that is, shaped by our environment)? What led you to your conclusion?
3. In a love relationship, is it realistic to expect that your partner can meet *all* of your emotional needs?

Source: Harley (2001).

Summary

Love Is a Cultural and Historical Experience

- "Love" and "loving" are determined largely by how a culture defines its social identity, whether as collectivist (society's goals take priority over individual needs) or individualistic (individual goals are promoted over group goals).

- The experience of "love" is also driven by the period in history in which the relationship exists. From "somber, joyless, guilt-ridden experience intertwined with the act of sex" to love relationships that combine sexuality, affection, and togetherness, each expression of love is as distinct as the society and time period in which it was formed.

What Is Love, Actually?

- An individual's love *prototype*, or model of love, will ultimately *characterize* an individual's love relationships. Similarly, *love maps*, or mental blueprints, shaped by our experiences with love in infancy and early childhood, present images of our "ideal" love relationship.

- *Infatuation*, an intense, extravagant, and often short-lived passion for another person, is often confused with love. *Romantic infatuation*, or *romantic love*, involves a complicated, often overpowering blend of emotion and sex. Couples in relationships consumed by romantic infatuation often become completely absorbed with each other to the exclusion of friends and family. The experience of passionate love/infatuation is multifaceted and culturally determined.

- *Stalking* and *jealousy* are negative components of love.

- *Companionate love* refers to deep, tender, mature, affectionate attachment bonds shared between two people and may or may not include feelings of physical arousal. *Liking,* which develops over time as a result of consistent, repeated rewards, is essential to companionate love.

- Robert Sternberg proposed that love relationships are expressed through three interconnected components—passion, intimacy, and commitment. His *Triangular Theory of Love* conceptualizes eight different types of love relationships that each individual may experience throughout his or her life.

Developing Love

- The ability and capacity to love *are not inherited*—they are nurtured. One's first experiences of love develop as a result of the interaction of heredity, environment, family of origin, educational background, and the interactions and love experience one has with people across his or her lifespan.

- The first love relationship many of us experience—the *dependent* parent–infant relationship—propels us to form emotional bonds in which we give and receive love. This relationship has additional importance in that it is from the experiences of the earliest of all love relationships that all of our later-in-life love relationships take shape. Parental love toward infants is typically altruistic love and reaps intrinsic rewards.

- The key difference between adult–infant love and adult–adult love is *reciprocity:* Adults experience *interdependent* love and expect their love to be reciprocated by their friends and love partners.

- *Attachment* is best described as an emotional or *affectional* bond that ties or binds the child to the parent or primary caregiver. *Attachment theory* asserts that newborns form an attachment with their caregivers and that it is from this close affectional bond that children derive a sense of security. The attachment behaviors that take place throughout infancy shape our personality and these behaviors in turn shape the interpersonal attachment relationships we experience later on as children, adolescents, and adults.

- The concept of attachment and Attachment theory is important to the study of love because research has shown that the quality of attachment during infancy significantly affects the quality of attachments (and love) throughout childhood, adolescence, and adulthood. Research has also shown a direct correlation between adults' secure or insecure attachment to their own parents and their subsequent responsiveness and sensitivity in their parenting behaviors toward their own children. Attachment behaviors and patterns may even span multiple generations. There are three attachment types in adult love relationships: secure attachment types, avoidant attachment types, and anxious/ambivalent attachment types.

- Family influences ultimately shape our personal experiences with love. *Genograms* can illustrate relationships between family members, providing family therapists with a snapshot of relationship history within a given family.

Theories of Love and Loving

- Researchers continue to develop theories to explain the complex contexts of love. Drawing from the ancient Greek's multifaceted view of love, sociologist John Alan Lee developed six types of love styles: *eros, ludus, storge, manic, pragma,* and *agape.*

- Research shows that although Lee's love typologies are found across multiple cultures, there are cultural differences: All people tend to experience the love typologies of mania, eros, and agape, but the love typologies of pragma, storge, and ludus are quite dependent on culture. Additional research suggests that an individual's love style is not static and fixed and may change over the course of a lifetime (or even during a relationship). And the social desirability of some love styles may be different for women and men.

- Sociologist Ira Reiss's *Wheel Theory of Love* describes love as a four-staged developmental process: rapport, self-revelation, mutual dependency, and personality need fulfillment. Similar to a rolling wheel, these stages of love may be experienced many times; as long as the wheel continues to move forward, a deep and lasting relationship is formed and maintained. If, however, the wheel stops turning, the love relationship may come to an end.

- Vuong's *Love Economic Model* is an equation that attempts to calculate the benefits of love. Its basic assumption is that people are rational decision makers who are able to tally up both the benefits and costs of falling in love and being in love.

Key Terms and Concepts

Suggested Readings

Gottman, John, & De Claire, Jean. *The relationship cure: A 5-step guide to strengthening your marriage, family, and friendships*. New York: Three Rivers Press, 2001.

Harley, Willard F. *His needs, her needs: Building an affair-proof marriage*. Grand Rapids, MI: Fleming H. Revell, 2001.

Swindler, Ann. *Talk of love: How culture matters*. Chicago: University of Chicago Press, 2001.

Multiple-Choice Questions

1. _____ , or brotherly love, was used to describe the affectionate feelings shared between friends and family.
   a. Agape
   b. Eros
   c. Philos
   d. Ludus

2. A _____ is a mental blueprint that presents images of the "ideal" love relationship and is shaped by our experiences with love in infancy and early childhood.
   a. "love ideal"
   b. "love map"
   c. "perfect plan"
   d. "model map"

3. _____ is a wildly powerful emotion that is experienced as intense longing for the selected love object, along with profound sexual arousal and confused feelings.
   a. Romantic love
   b. Infatuation
   c. Passionate love
   d. Companionate love

4. Of the five types of stalkers, _____ commonly have poor social and emotional skills, and have difficulty expressing themselves.
   a. incompetent suitors
   b. rejected stalkers
   c. intimacy seekers
   d. resentful stalkers

5. _____ refers to deep, tender, mature, affectionate attachment bonds shared between two people and may or may not include feelings of physical arousal.
   a. Passionate love
   b. Infatuation
   c. Storge love
   d. Companionate love

6. _____ is seen in the adult–infant pair bond where an adult immediately meets and gratifies the needs of an infant; interdependent love is expressed between emotionally mature adults who recognize that love is a give-and-take process. The ability for people to be dependent and have someone depend on them is referred to as _____ .
   a. Dependent love/interdependent love
   b. Interdependent love/dependent love
   c. Dependent love/companionate love
   d. Interdependent love/passionate love

7. _____ love can best be conceptualized as friendship love, or a type of affectionate love between companions.
   a. Erotic
   b. Storge
   c. Ludic
   d. Manic

8. _____ describe(s) love as a four-staged developmental process: rapport, self-revelation, mutual dependency, and personality need fulfillment.
   a. Attachment theory
   b. Sternberg's Triangular Theory of Love
   c. Wheel Theory of Love
   d. Lee's Types of Love Styles

Answers: 1. c; 2. b; 3. c; 4. a; 5. d; 6. a; 7. b; 8. c

The Path to Commitment: Attraction, Dating, Partnering, and Cohabitation

7

[I am] a heterosexual female in the 21st century. I pride myself on the fact that I take people at more than face value, that I appreciate human beings for their character rather than their looks. Why do I find myself making conversations with physically attractive males while blowing off [others]?

Why does my head whip around when I see man in a Porsche? Why do my male friends all have the same prerequisites for the perfect female despite race and ethnicity [differences]: perky breasts, slim waist, and full hips? Despite most people's lofty notions of equality, and beauty being in the eye of the beholder, we are all susceptible to certain physical and material traits that make some human beings more "desirable" than others.

Source: Fernandez (2002)

We are an odd pair, my husband and I. He is over six feet tall; I am about five feet tall on a good day. I love opera, but he prefers to listen to original heavy metal music by Led Zeppelin or Steppenwolf. He is calm, cool, and collected and seldom raises his voice; I have a fiery temper and occasionally enjoy a good argument. We are polar opposites in the truest sense. How, then, did we come together as partners in life? Why didn't these dissimilarities drive a wedge between us rather than pull us together?

The study of interpersonal attraction and the pathways to partnering are important in our examination of marital and intimate relationships, because dating, courtship, and partnering practices map out different courses to marriage and other lifelong couple relationships, such as civil unions between gays or lesbians. In this chapter we explore the theories and realities associated with interpersonal attraction, dating, and mate selection in contemporary society. Just as the college student in the opening vignette asks herself, Why are we attracted to one person and not another? If we're straight, do we choose intimate partners differently than if we're gay or bisexual? We begin by examining the theories that address why we are attracted to certain people but not others. You will notice that some theories specifically address heterosexual attraction, while other theories are more general, and thus account for heterosexual, homosexual, or bisexual attraction.

"Frisky Business": Interpersonal Attraction Theories

Every society the world over has some type or form of socially approved union between couples (Erber & Erber, 2001). Whether we are referring to a technologically advanced society, such as the United States, or to a tribal culture, such as the Zoe in the state of Para, Northern Brazil, all societies have certain beliefs and expectations when it comes to selecting a mate. Since all societies place such emphasis and importance on the process of selecting a mate, it seems logical to assume that choosing the most suitable mate is essential to the longevity of a society or culture. For instance, if a person continually chooses an unsuitable mate, the consequences of such decisions would ultimately be the failure to reproduce; if poor mate selection continued, at some point the longevity of the society would be jeopardized. Perhaps the next logical assumption could then be that throughout history, mate selection has had an evolutionary purpose to ensure the continuation, longevity, and survival of a culture or society. Although we cannot answer here the age-old question, "How do I know if he (she) is the right one for me?," we can investigate how and why we have been socialized to think the way we do about certain physical characteristics and qualities in those to whom we are attracted as we take a look at three influential interpersonal attraction theories: *Evolutionary theory, Social Exchange theory,* and *Filter theory.*

EVOLUTIONARY THEORY: THE EVOLUTION OF PHYSICAL ATTRACTION

British scientist and environmentalist Charles Darwin (1809–1882) became famous for his theories about evolution and **natural selection**, the belief that nature selects the best adapted varieties of species to survive and reproduce. **Sexual selection** occurs in two ways. In the first, members of one sex compete among themselves for opportunities to mate—the pool of potential mating candidates is limited. The "winners" reproduce more than the other competitors and natural selection occurs. In the second type of sexual selection, a sex chooses to mate with a specific person (or people)—some people are more preferable to mate with than others. Thus, the **Evolutionary theory** for mate selection purports that we choose mates for the sole purpose of maximizing and enhancing our reproductive efforts, to ensure reproductive success—and the success of the species and society (Needham, 1999; Singh, 2002, 2004; Sprecher and others, 1994; Symons, 1979).

Mate selection evolutionist-based theories, then, maintain that there are two specific biological goals—one for *male sexual selection* and one for *female sexual selection*—that must be achieved when selecting a mate.

What Men Want: Reproductive Promise The primary evolutionary biological goal of males in mate selection is the need to impregnate as many women as possible (Needham, 1999). According to evolutionists, *men are concerned with quantity*—mating is a numbers game, and the more mates the better to ensure numerous offspring are produced. Interpersonal attraction empirical research findings conclude that this is perhaps why men engage in more casual sex than women do, and why men have more sexual partners across their lifespan than do women (Schmitt & Buss, 2001; Schmitt, Shackelford, Duntley, Tooke, & Buss, 2001). When seeking mates, then, men will select women who possess certain **fertility cues**, such as youth and curves (full breasts, small waist, curvy hips), because men associate these traits with successful fertility (Feingold, 1992).

What Women Want: Protectors and Providers Charles Darwin (1871) reasoned that because childbearing (pregnancy, labor, birth, and breastfeeding) is riskier for women than for men, women are more selective when it comes to finding a mate. A man produces literally millions of

CHARLES Darwin (1809–1882) is famous for his belief that nature selects the best-adapted species—including humans—to reproduce.

sperm each day and therefore has seemingly limitless supplies of his genetic material, but the female is very limited in her ability to reproduce. Thus, while men may be concerned with the number of children they produce, women are concerned with the *quality of the children* they produce. Consequently, they look for someone who can contribute not only positive genetic traits and characteristics but they also tend to seek out a mate who possesses **protector/provider cues**, such as intelligence, physical strength, industry (a hard worker), and ambition (Feingold, 1992; Buss & Schmitt, 1993; Buss, 1994).

When it comes to body shape and size, women find average-size men more attractive than muscular men (Cunningham, 1986). Personality traits and behavior characteristics are also important factors for women in choosing a marriage mate. Characteristics such as kindness, warmth, openness, and commitment are key influences in women's selection of a mate (among many others, Buss & Angleitner, 1989; Doosje, Rojahn, & Fischer, 1999; Hatfield & Sprecher, 1995; Li, Bailey, Kenrick, & Linsenmeier, 2002). Recent research indicates that women rate emotional stability and the commitment to marriage and family (*family orientation*) more highly than do men (Oda, 2001; Waynforth, 2001).

What Makes Your Head Whip Around?

Charles Darwin reasoned that men and women select mates based on certain interpersonal attraction cues that ensure successful reproduction of the human species. From your experiences with dating, hooking up, or partnering, respond to the following questions:

1. Without giving it much thought, quickly jot down 10 things that attract you to another person. On your list, are there those things that the Evolutionary theory asserts that draw us to another person, such as curves or the ability to provide or protect? What surprises you the most about your list?

2. Have you ever given much thought to why you're attracted to one person and not to another? Have you ever *wanted* to be attracted to another, but found that something was missing? If so, what was that "something"?

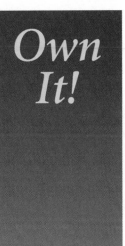

Own It!

Now that you have an understanding of why men and women are attracted to certain physical traits and certain personality characteristics, we turn our attention to two other theoretical frameworks that seek to explain why we choose the marriage mate or lifelong partner that we do. Here we examine the Social Exchange theory and the Filter Theory of Mate Selection.

SOCIAL EXCHANGE THEORY: THE REWARDS AND COSTS OF ATTRACTION

Let's suppose you exchanged phone numbers with someone you met at a bar, and a few days later your cell phone rings—with that certain person's number showing on the caller ID. At the first ring, a scenario like the one that follows may play out in your mind (or even aloud!), and within a couple of ticks on the clock you have a certain conversation with yourself that goes something like this:

> *Phone:* Ring!
>
> *You:* Who could that possibly be? Don't they know I've got a Chem test in an hour?
>
> *Phone:* Ring!!
>
> *You [glancing at caller ID]:* Wow! It's so-and-so from the bar! Do I answer the phone or not? Was I only interested in him/her because I had a few too many drinks? Or do I really want to invest the time in getting to know this person? (You weigh the rewards of answering the phone. You weigh the costs. You perceive that answering the phone may result in greater benefits or rewards than not answering the phone. You answer the phone.)

This example illustrates the essence of the **Social Exchange theory**. Very broadly stated, the Social Exchange theory centers on the exchange of people's resources; the resources can be material or symbolic. This theory asserts that individuals are thought to act out of self-interest in ways to enlarge and make the most of the resources they possess. It also helps explain what *motivates* individuals to act (White & Klein, 2008).

Key Concepts of Social Exchange Theory Susan Sprecher (1998), a social psychologist who studies personal relationships, outlines the key concepts of the Social Exchange theory:

1. All social behavior is a series of varying exchanges.
2. Within these social exchanges, all individuals attempt to maximize their *rewards* (exchanged resources that are rewarding and satisfying) and minimize their *costs* (missed opportunities or exchanged resources that result in loss or punishment).
3. When rewards are received from others, the benefactor or the receiver feels obligated to reciprocate.
4. Reward minus cost equals the outcome of the interpersonal exchange.

Rewards are the benefits (the payback, profits, or compensations) that are exchanged in social relationships (Boss and others, 1993). Family theory authors James White and David Klein (2008) note that a reward is *anything* considered beneficial to an individual. The role of rewards in a relationship is the probability that a behavior will continue—as long as the perceived rewards are greater than the perceived costs of a given behavior, the behavior will continue. A **cost** increases the likelihood or probability that a person will *not* take part in a given behavior. Costs can be experienced as punishments (lost rewards) because individuals may engage in one behavior over another (Boss and others, 1993). For example, an unmarried woman may cohabit with her alcoholic, abusive partner. Although her partner gets drunk and physically abuses her (the *costs*), she may consider his paycheck, her home, and her financial security (the perceived *rewards*) to be greater than the costs of his drinking and abusive behavior. If there is no reward that results from a behavior, the individual will act in a way that will result in the least cost. For instance, while there may be no rewards in staying in the abusive relationship, if she tries to leave the relationship he may harm her. She may therefore conclude that staying in the cohabiting relationship is the least costly to her.

The Social Exchange theory presents the notion that when you (Actor) are presented with a situation in your interpersonal or family relationships, you sensibly and judiciously analyze the ratio of the rewards to the costs, and you then make a decision that results in the greatest reward (White & Klein, 2008). Because of the assumption that all Actors are rational when making decisions, the theory presumes that Actors' behaviors in like situations are interchangeable. In other words, given the same situation with the same potential rewards and costs, *you* would make the exact same decision that *I* would make.

ALTHOUGH we probably don't exchange money back and forth when we choose a mate, we are calculating the rewards and costs of getting into a relationship with that particular person.

Several examples illustrate this point. If I decided to seek a divorce because my husband and I drifted apart, I could assume that you would seek a divorce under like circumstances. I could assume that you would respond to a crisis by reaching out to others as I would in a crisis. These comparisons may seem rational and logical, but they don't take into account individual differences.

You may think, "Wait a minute! How do you know what I consider to be rewarding or what I consider to be costly?" Precisely! Let's suppose that you are in a new relationship and you view the increased time you spend together as a couple as rewarding. Your partner, on the other hand, may feel like he or she has less time, less freedom, and less independence because of the increased time spent together as a couple, and sees the time commitment as a cost. Thus, when examining interpersonal and family relationships, we need to have an understanding of the significance or importance (the weight) that *each* Actor assigns to each reward and to each cost.

Just as the Social Exchange theory's name implies, human interaction of any kind has a built-in requirement of some type of reciprocity or exchange. Thibaut and Kelley (1959) were the first scholars to suggest that the behaviors of Actors in relationships are interdependent or reciprocal in nature. In a dating relationship even though one partner (as an *individual* relationship member) seeks to make the most of personal rewards and minimize costs, that individual must also consider what rewards and costs will occur for the other partner. For example, one dating partner may be eager to propose marriage (reward), but may have to delay his or her proposal so the other dating partner can finish a college degree (potential cost if the degree is not completed). Even though a couple represents a collection of individuals (White & Klein, 2008) who are seeking to maximize their own rewards, Thibaut and Kelley held that they are *mutually reliant on one another* for rewarding results.

Putting Social Exchange Theory into Action: Partner Selection We can use the Social Exchange theory and apply it to interpersonal attraction and human sexuality. In an extensive, comprehensive research article that addresses the use of exchange theories to the understanding of human interpersonal and sexual interactions, Sprecher (1998) used the Social Exchange theory to better understand sexual and relational interactions with regard to partner selection, the negotiation of the onset of sex, the evaluation of sexual satisfaction, and the initiation and refusal of sex.

Sprecher found that most researchers who use the Social Exchange theory in their study of interpersonal attraction equate mate/partner selection to a competitive *marketplace* (such as a marketplace of available men and women) that has rewards and costs. The **matching**

hypothesis refers to the fact that most of us want a "socially desirable person regardless of his or her own level of social desirability" (Sprecher, 1998). To put it another way, people who possess socially desirable characteristics (such as beauty, wealth, status, and education) tend to partner with people who also possess these same desirable characteristics—their resources are equally matched. With regard to Social Exchange theory, when we select dating or sexual partners, we calculate and weigh the perceived rewards (partnering with someone who is socially desirable) against the perceived costs (partnering with someone who does not possess socially desirable characteristics).

As we examine the intricacies of relationship development and family life throughout this text, you will see time and again how relationships and family life take place in a series of interdependent relationships. White and Klein (2008) suggest that because the Social Exchange theory focuses on cost-benefit analysis, tenets of this framework are helpful in aiding those working with families and individual family members to employ intervention and prevention strategies that focus on increasing positive/rewarding behaviors and decreasing negative/costly behavioral interactions.

FILTER THEORY OF MATE SELECTION

Earlier in the chapter I pondered how my husband and I came to be marriage partners, given the fact that our personality traits and physical characteristics are such polar opposites. The **Filter Theory of Mate Selection** may provide an explanation; it suggests that individuals use a filtering mechanism that helps them sort out a potential mate from the vast **pool of candidates**, or eligible partners. Figure 7.1 illustrates how this theory draws on tenets from the evolutionary perspective as well as the Social Exchange theory. The variables we use to filter potential mates include propinquity, homogamy, heterogamy, physical attraction, and reciprocity.

You will more than likely marry someone who comes from the same geographic region as you. **Propinquity** refers to *geographic closeness*. Simply stated, you can't get to know someone or interact with someone if you are not in the same general location. Like their heterosexual counterparts, gay men and lesbians indicate that they meet their potential dates/mates in "conventional" ways, such as through friends, at work, at a bar, or at a social event (Bryant & Demian, 1994). In addition to proximity, we tend to marry someone with whom we share things in common. **Homogamy** refers to partnering with someone who is similar to you in ethnic and racial background, religious upbringing, age, education level, political ideology, socioeconomic status, and values and beliefs. For example, although my husband I possess quite different personality traits, we are very similar in our social backgrounds and our belief system. According to the Filter theory, this explains why our relationship works.

Because gay and lesbian interpersonal attraction and dating are fairly empirically unexplored processes, little is known about how gay and lesbian relationships develop and progress (Kurdek, 2005). However, a few studies have looked at the qualities that lesbians and gay men seek in romantic partners. These studies reveal that regardless of sexual orientation, most people value certain things in a mate, such as affection

FIGURE 7.1   The Filter Theory of Mate Selection

According to the Filter theory, we narrow the pool of all eligible partner candidates to select someone who is most similar to us. Through our filter, we consider such things as geographic closeness, age, race, religious beliefs, physical attraction, and whether we think that person will reciprocate our feelings. From here, we eventually select Mr. or Ms. Right.

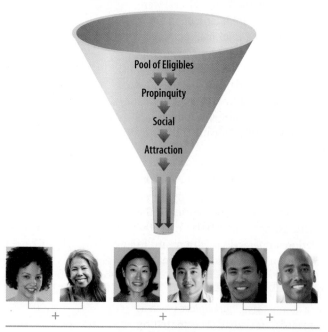

and dependability. Just as with heterosexuals, homosexuals also tend to partner with someone who is similar to them, and they place importance on things such as shared interests and similarity of religious beliefs (for a review, see Peplau & Fingerhut, 2007). Further, lesbians and gays are more likely than heterosexuals to begin as friendships that develop into a love relationship, and eventually a sexual relationship (Rose, Zand, & Cini, 1993, cited in Peplau & Fingerhut, 2007).

As you saw in Chapter 1, certain cultural rules and norms define who we can and cannot marry. **Exogamy** means that we must marry outside of a particular group. In the United States, for example, we cannot marry a sibling or a first cousin. **Endogamy** refers to the notion that certain groups marry within that same group, such as Muslims marrying Muslims or Asians marrying Asians. Conversely, **heterogamy** refers to partners who are of different races, religions, and ethnicities. It also refers to partners of different ages. While in today's diverse society more and more people are choosing heterogamous lifelong partners, they often face difficulties. Chapter 8 explores in detail interracial and interfaith marriages.

Each of us has our own ideal of what we find physically attractive in a potential mate, and we filter potential mates based on these culturally socialized internalized standards of physical attractiveness. Unlike Evolution theory, Filter theory isn't necessarily as concerned with *why* or *how* we are attracted to someone as it is with the notion that we just *are*—and physical attraction is one filtering mechanism. Regardless of sexual orientation, men are more likely than women to emphasize the importance of their partner's physical attraction; women, regardless of sexual orientation, assign greater importance to personality characteristics (Peplau & Spalding, 2000).

The balance sheet filter refers to *reciprocity*. When all is said done and we have exhausted all propinquity, social, and physical attractiveness filters, we look at what someone can offer us that we cannot find in anyone else. Ultimately, the balance sheet filter must reflect a mutual, reciprocal commitment to the relationship in order for a mate to be considered "the one."

Now that we have looked at the various theories of how and why we select a particular mate over another, let's examine the pathway to committed relationships that may or may not result in marriage.

ALTHOUGH *endogamy* is still the prevailing norm in mate selection across cultures, today interracial, interethnic, and interfaith relationships are increasingly becoming more common.

The Path to Commitment

Although the customs and rituals may vary across racial, cultural, ethnic, economic, and religious boundaries, people come together to form **pair bonds**, or couples. For example, the Surma people of a remote region of southwest Ethiopia engage in an annual courtship ritual where hundreds of men join together to fight for the available women. To woo a potential bride, the men engage in a mock display of violence, wielding and wildly swinging large sticks.

Wodaabe nomad men of Niger participate in a males-only beauty pageant where they parade before unmarried women who select their lovers from the parading pageant "contestants." The men spend countless hours painting elaborate patterns on their bodies in the hope of turning a young woman's eye. Although Western civilization's interpersonal attraction rituals may pale in comparison to other

SPENDING countless hours decorating their bodies with elaborate patterns, the Wodaabe nomad men of Niger participate in a beauty pageant of sorts in hopes of getting the attention of an unmarried woman.

worldwide mate selection customs, all serve the same purpose—to form a bond that will lead to marriage.

COURTSHIP: MARRIAGE IS THE GOAL

While not all Americans follow the same path to marriage or committed partner relationships, when asked what causes young adults and adolescents the most stress, issues surrounding dating and mate selection were at the top of the list (Myers, 2004). In a culturally, ethnically, and religiously diverse nation such as the United States, the path to commitment varies greatly. Not all of us will be in a committed relationship, nor will all of us marry. Certainly, some people are single by choice or by happenstance, and we'll discuss singlehood at length in the next chapter. Here, our purpose is to explore how couples go from being attracted to one another to committed relationships.

In 1828, *Webster's* defined *courting and courtship* as "the act of soliciting favor. The act of wooing in love. Solicitation of a woman to marriage. Civility, elegance of manners." **Courting** and **courtship** are practices that groom young adults for marriage, practices that are socially prescribed forms of conduct that guide men and women toward matrimony (Kass, 1997). The following example better illustrates the concept of courting.

My grandmother, Neva, was born in 1904. It was she who first taught me the difference between courtship and dating when she described how she and my grandfather came to be married. Her parents were of French origin and in that culture they viewed the notion of wooing a potential mate as a true art form. On the other hand, my grandfather, George, was the son of an Irish immigrant and aspired to become a professional baseball player—not quite polished, refined, sophisticated, or a match for a French American girl. Despite the fact that his manners and etiquette were sub-par for the era, he pursued my grandmother for *eight years.* (I suspect the time period would have been shorter had he shown a little more finesse!) There was nothing casual about their times together. The strict rules of the era mandated that the woman and her mother set the conditions of the interactions, and that if he was truly serious about her, then their relationship was pursued with nothing short of a view to marriage.

Although the practices and rituals associated with couple formation have changed dramatically in Western societies over the past 60 years, there are still members of these cultures who adhere today to the practices of courting and courtship. For example, in Japan there is a type of courtship called *omiai,* which is formal courting with the intention of pursuing a marriage partner. This is still commonly practiced among Japanese and Japanese Americans who have acculturated to America.

Although courtship may seem outdated and quaint for contemporary society, it is making a rebound in certain religious sectors of the United States. For example, in Islamic American cultures, premarital, one-on-one intimate relationships with the opposite sex are strictly forbidden. According to Islam, the choice of a marriage partner is considered to be life's most important decision, and it should therefore not be taken lightly or left to hormones to decide. When a young adult is ready to marry, the decision is made with his or her

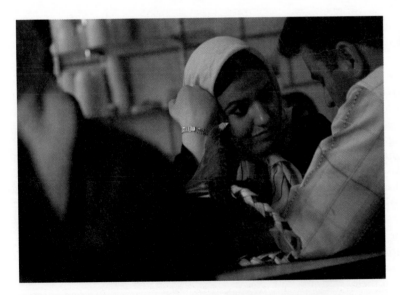

COURTSHIP is making somewhat of a comeback among some groups in the United States, but in Muslim cultures courting is the culturally approved form of mate selection.

family's involvement. In Islamic cultures, the process of courtship is viewed as an assurance that the marriage will be a strong, enduring relationship because it draws on others' wisdom and guidance, not on erotic or romantic feelings of young adults.

In other mainstream religious denominations, the concept of courtship is seen as religious commentator and psychologist James Dobson (2005) notes, "[Young people] are being taught to go from one relationship to another. Wouldn't they then be more inclined later to bail out on a marriage partner when bored or frustrated?" Some religious contemporaries maintain that courting or courtship charts the course for a committed marital relationship with the probable husband or wife. The customs and rituals of courting help the couple navigate the complexities of physical attraction, sexual attraction, falling in love, and committing to a lifelong partnership (Cere, 2001).

THE DATING GAME

Dating is a relatively new concept that became increasingly popular in Western culture during the mid-twentieth century. Prior to today's dating rituals, *courtship* was the common path to marital commitment. In contemporary Western societies, **dating** is an occasion where people get together socially for any number of reasons, such as a means of relaxation and escape from everyday responsibilities ("hanging out"), pursuing a relationship to determine whether the partner is a potential spouse or a partner for a lifelong relationship ("going out"), or getting together sexually with no strings attached ("hooking up").

There are several distinctions between *dating* and *courting*, but perhaps the primary distinction is that courtship is viewed as preparation for and anticipation of marriage. Dating, on the other hand, is considered more recreational and fun. It is a way for people to get to know each other and determine whether there are commonalities beyond their initial physical attraction that might lead them to a long-term, committed relationship such as marriage. When we go out on dates, we tend to follow culturally determined dating scripts.

Dating Scripts Script theory is one avenue that helps us understand dating practices among heterosexual couples and homosexual couples. According to **Script theory,** each of us uses *scripts* that help us organize the information in our environments. Scripts typically provide information about expected, stereotypical actions; because of this, they help us predict the behaviors of people, and help guide our decisions about how to act and interact with others (Klinkenberg & Rose, 1994). In essence, scripts are guidelines, or an internalized "how-to" manual for social behavior. There are three different general types of scripts (Simon & Gagnon, 1986):

1. **Cultural scripts** are common guidelines that provide instructions about what behaviors and emotions are expected in certain situations. For example, is it okay to have sex with someone on the first date? To a large extent, culture dictates these behaviors and emotions, and for the most part we tend to stick to these cultural scripts.
2. **Intrapsychic scripts** are personal and individualized, and represent our private wishes, hopes, desires, and dreams. These scripts may contain sexual or relational fantasies, or personal expectations for another person's behavior. In these scripts, for instance, a woman may expect that her dating partner pay for everything on every date.
3. **Interpersonal scripts** are highly personalized and detailed, and are a combination of a person's cultural and intrapsychic scripts. For instance, a common American cultural script for a first date includes going to a movie (Bartoli & Clark, 2006), whereas a person's intrapsychic script may specify engaging in a shared interest, such as playing a round of golf together. In order to have a successful date, it's important that each dating partner shares with the other what he or she believes to be an "ideal" date, so that each person's interpersonal script is followed.

WHAT do your dating scripts include? Do you prefer to go out with a group of people so you can get to know your dating partner, or do you prefer to be alone? Who influenced your dating scripts the most?

If we put all of these scripts together, we come up with scripts that relate specifically to dating. These are referred to as **dating scripts**, and these models guide our dating interactions.

Heterosexual Dating Scripts For a number of years, social scientists have examined the behaviors of dating couples. These studies are important because they help us better understand how relationships develop and are maintained. Among college students, for example, we know that dating scripts for heterosexual couples include role differentiation that is often stereotypically gender-based. Past studies have revealed that the man is initiator of the date, the planner, and the one who pays for the date, while the woman is the one who nurtures the conversation during the date (Levinger, 1982). Other research compared people's perceptions of an "ideal" first date (initiating the date, meeting, engaging in activities, ending a date, and concluding the date) with the experiences of the "actual" first date. All of the studies found one thing in common: Dating scripts reflected traditional gender roles, with the man being the *active* partner (the initiator and the planner), and the woman being the *reactive* partner (accepting the invitation, rejecting sexual activity) (Rose & Frieze, 1989, 1993; Laner & Ventrone, 1998). But do college students today still adhere to these stereotypical dating scripts?

In a study of 182 college students, investigators looked at men's and women's dating scripts for a "typical date" (Bartoli & Clark, 2006). The study participants were given dating scenes and were asked to report what activities and events usually took place on a typical date in these scenes. Table 7.1 shows us dating scripts of first-year college students. For example, both men and women tend to initiate dates by meeting in class or at a party/bar, talking with their partner, and going to a movie and dinner is a common dating activity. Dating conclusions included goodnight kisses, or going to a partner's house for a drink or talking. Traditional gender roles were seen in that women were the sexual "gatekeepers" (they limited sexual activity), and that men had higher expectations for nonsexual intercourse sexual activities than women did. Overall, the study found that if the dating scenario was "typical," men and women held similar dating scripts, or expectations.

Of course, not all dating couples are heterosexual couples. This leads to some interesting questions. For example, since we are all socialized by our cultures to follow certain dating scripts—scripts that assume heterosexual coupling—what dating scripts do gay men and lesbian couples follow? And how do they come by them?

Same-Sex Dating Scripts Studies that address relationship initiation and formation among homosexual couples are scant. Most studies that do exist focus on the later stages of long-term relationships, such as commitment (Klinkenberg & Rose, 1994).

What we do know is that gays and lesbians do incorporate some traditional gender roles in their dating scripts, but they also appear to have more opportunities to develop their own unique, interpersonal scripts. For example, just as with straight men, early on in relationships gay men are likely to stress the physical and sexual attraction to their dating partners over the emotional aspects (see Sergios & Cody, 1985). Similarly, lesbians, like heterosexual women, tend to emphasize personality traits in their partners, rather than sexual attraction (Deaux & Hanna, 1984). But unlike straight women, emotional intimacy is a valued aspect of lesbian dating (Klinkenberg & Rose, 1994). They engage in deep levels of self-disclosure and emo-

TABLE 7.1 Scripted Events for a Typical Date

First Year Women's Dating Scripts	First Year Men's Dating Scripts
Initiation	**Initiation**
Talking	Talking
Meeting in Public	Meeting in Public
Shared Interest	Shared Interest
Meeting in Group	Man Picks up Date
Man Picks up Date	Call
Meet in Common Place	Casual Interaction
Casual Interaction	
Activities	**Activities**
Movies	Movies
Dinner	Dinner
Talking	Shared Interest
Shared Interest	
Outcomes	**Outcomes**
Talking	Talking
Watching TV	Go Back to the House
Go Back to the House	Kiss Goodnight
Kiss Goodnight	Go Home
Go Home	Relationship Development
Relationship Development	Take Date Home

Source: Bartoli & Clark (2006).

tional sharing on their first dates, and they are much more likely to establish a close friendship with someone before dating them (Zand & Rose, 1992).

In a study that looked at dating scripts of 96 gays and lesbians, the researchers examined hypothetical versus actual dating scripts (similar to the study that explored heterosexual dating scripts); the results are presented in Table 7.2 on page 216 (Klinkenberg & Rose, 1994). The findings about initiating a date, preparing for a date, interactions with a date partner, and date closing behaviors are very interesting because they show us that the cultural/interpersonal dating scripts for same-sex partners mirror those of heterosexual partners. It appears that when it comes to going out on a date, it doesn't necessarily matter if we're gay or straight—we tend to follow culturally determined dating scripts regardless of our sexual orientation.

Contemporary dating can take the form of more traditional dating that eventually leads to cohabitation or marriage, or it can take more casual forms, such as speed dating, online dating, and hooking up.

Speed Dating **Speed dating** allows people to meet each other face-to-face to decide if they share mutual interests and if they are interested in another, more extended, date. Speed dating was established by Rabbi Yaacov Deyo in 1999, and it is based on a Jewish tradition of supervised social gatherings of young Jewish singles. Its popularity quickly caught

DATING script templates for gays and lesbians combine some scripts that are traditionally adopted by straight couples, but they also venture from traditional gender roles. If you are gay or lesbian, what or who influenced your dating scripts the most?

TABLE 7.2 Scripts for Hypothetical and Actual First Dates for Gay Men and Lesbians

Hypothetical Date		Actual Date	
Gay Men	Lesbians	Gay Men	Lesbians
Discuss plans	Discuss plans	Discussed plans	Discussed plans
Groom/dress	Tell friends about date	Was nervous	Was nervous
Prepare (clean apartment)	Groom/dress	Groom/dress	Groom/dress
Meet date at location	Meet date at location	Picked up date	Prepared (clean apartment)
Get to know by talking	Leave for another location	Left for another location	Picked up date
Talk/laugh/joke	Get to know by talking	Evaluated date	Got to know date
Go to movie/show	Talk/laugh/joke	Went to movie/show	Talked/laughed/joked
Eat/drink (nonalcohol)	Go to a movie/show	Ate/drank (nonalcohol)	Went to movie
Initiate physical contact	Eat/drink (non-alcohol)	Drank alcohol	Positive feelings
Make out	Initiate physical contact	Made out	Kissed/hugged
Make plans for another date	Make plans for another date	Had sex	Took date home
Take date home	Kiss/hug goodnight	Stayed over	Went home
	Go home	Made plans for another date	
		Went home	

Source: Klinkenberg & Rose (1994).

on, and now through organizations such as 8MinuteDating, HurryDate, and FastImpressions, heterosexuals, homosexuals, and a variety of religious and ethnic groups are provided the opportunity to have quick, one-on-one dates with a roomful of eligible singles who share common interests.

Online Dating The development of computer technology has introduced new dynamics into the twenty-first-century process of finding a mate. Internet chatrooms are quickly replacing barrooms as a place for meeting available singles. Organizations such as Match.com, eHarmony.com, Facebook.com, MySpace.com, and Xanga.com provide a virtual space in which people can place personal ads, *blog* daily journals of their life happenings, and place personal photos. People can engage in synchronous communication (such as IMing), or asynchronous communication (like e-mail). Today, many people Skype (Web-cam) to enhance their interactions. Online sites generate opportunities to initially interact with someone, and then move to face-to-face relationships if they desire to pursue the friendship or relationship. These electronic liaisons allow people to remain anonymous or to fully self-disclose personal information.

Today, some sites are getting the entire family involved in the matchmaking process. The social networking site, Engage.com, invites family and friends to engage in choosing potential partners for their loved ones (Barraket & Henry-Waring, 2008).

A $1 billion industry in the United States, currently there are about 3 million registered **online dating** users; in 2006, 1 in 10 Internet users indicated they had gone to a website so they could meet people online, and nearly one-third of all American adults say they know someone who has used a dating website (Madden & Lenhart, 2006). Looking across age groups, the youngest age cohort (18 to 29 years old) had the largest percentage of online daters within it, with 18 percent reporting visiting an online dating site (Madden & Lenhart, 2006). In one survey of over 4,500 Internet users, respondents aged 18 to 24 indicated that they met an average

INSTEAD of barrooms, students today often opt for Internet chatrooms and blog sites to meet eligible mates. Have you ever met someone on the Internet and agreed to meet in person? What are some advantages to this contemporary way of meeting someone?

of 10 dating partners in online chatrooms (Hollander, 2003). People engage in various dating-related activities online; these are illustrated in Figure 7.2. As you can see, individuals use the Internet in a number of ways, from flirting to breaking up.

Recent research reveals some benefits to online dating, some of which challenge our existing understanding of relationship formation. For example, earlier we discussed the importance of *propinquity,* or geographic closeness, in selecting a potential mate. With online dating, physical proximity is de-emphasized as a necessary feature of relationship formation—individuals are free to interact with people from across the globe (Barraket & Henry-Waring, 2008).

Another benefit of Internet dating is that it frees people to meet others outside of their existing social networks (Barraket & Henry-Waring, 2008). As one 25-year-old male observed, "It elevates you out of your social circle, and you're sort of broadcast to a broad bunch of people, and if you're fairly open-ended in your profile, and not so descriptive about what you do or don't do, then you get the opportunity to meet lots of different people that you would never know" (p. 157). For some, being able to go beyond their current social network allows them the freedom to explore and express their sexuality in different ways, or to experience deeper levels of self-disclosure (it's easier for some people to disclose over the Internet than it is for face-to-face disclosure). For others, the increased freedom gives them the opportunity to take chances on relationships they might not venture to try in their "real" lives, because if the

FIGURE 7.2 **Dating-Related Activities Online**

There are a number of factors that affect who visits online dating sites.

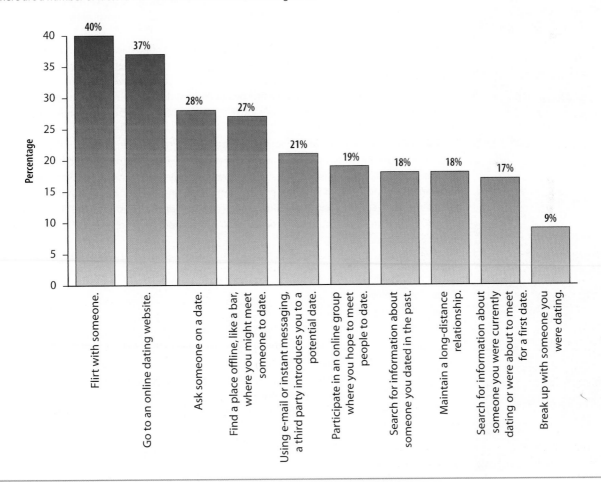

Source: Pew Internet & American Life Project Tracking Survey (see Madden & Lenhart, 2006).

relationship doesn't work out they don't have to see them everyday. One female noted, "I think the fact that you never have to see them again is wonderful. You know, if it's friends or work or whatever, and it doesn't work out, then you've got all the awkwardness . . . that carries into your life" (Barraket & Henry-Waring, 2008, p. 157).

Others indicate that being able to have high levels of control over the "pace and place" of electronic communication is a benefit (Barraket & Henry-Waring, 2008). What may be surprising to some people is that online dating etiquette seems to mimic offline dating norms. Traditionally gendered patterns of interaction are practiced in online dating, with male users "making the first move" in contacting their prospective partners online (Barraket & Henry-Waring, 2008).

There is a hazardous side to cyber-dating, however. While you may be looking for love, the person on the other end of the mouse may be looking for a quick sexual encounter or may have even more dangerous intentions (Madden & Lenhart, 2006). For example, in 2005, 17-year-old college coed Taylor Behl formed an Internet relationship with a 38-year-old man

Healthy SELVES Healthy FAMILIES

Dating Violence and Date Rape

Dating violence is the perpetration or the threat of an act of violence against a person, straight or gay, involved in a dating or courting relationship. Violence includes any type of sexual assault (including rape) or physical violence, and any form of verbal or emotional abuse. Both males and females inflict and are victims of dating violence; however, women and girls are twice as likely to be victims of coercion and violence in dating relationships than are men and boys.

Date rape (sexual assault) is the act of forcing sex on a date or a partner who has not consented, and it happens every two minutes across North America. Date rape involves a victim and an offender who know one another, either because they have an established relationship, are friends, or they are on a first or subsequent date. Of the rapes that occur on college campuses across the United States, 80 to 95 percent are carried out by someone the victim knows.

Date rape is not typically as physically violent as rape by a stranger, but under the law it is still rape: *Any sexual activity committed against the will of the victim* is considered to be an act of sexual assault. Date rape is often the result of mixed messages between dating partners—not listening to one another, and wishful thinking. There is a high correlation between the use of alcohol and date rape because of the diminished capacities of one or both parties. The sexual act or acts *do not need to conclude with penetration* in order for the aggression to be considered rape or a sexual assault.

Protect yourself against date rape:

- Avoid secluded places until you fully trust your partner.
- Stay sober.
- Never leave your drink unattended.
- Never accept open drinks (alcoholic or nonalcoholic) from people you do not know; only accept drinks in closed containers to avoid falling prey to date rape drugs ("club drugs") such as Rohypnol and GHB.
- Never spend time alone with someone who makes you feel uneasy or uncomfortable—trust your instincts!
- Say *No!* Say *No* loudly, clearly, and often. NO ALWAYS MEANS NO.

Sources: Witmer, D. (2005). *Dating violence.* Retrieved October 29, 2005 from www.parentingteens.about .com/cs/daterape; Russo, L. (2000). *Date rape: A hidden crime.* Australian Institute of Criminology, ISSN 0817-8542, Number 157.

who portrayed himself on the Internet as a photographic artist. After meeting the man face-to-face and having a brief sexual encounter with him, Behl tried to sever the relationship. She was murdered a short time later.

To minimize risk to a person's safety and well-being, some guidelines to Internet dating have been proposed (Starling, 2000):

1. *Practice common sense.* Don't give out personal information such as phone numbers, e-mail addresses, or home addresses. If you do decide to meet, meet in a public place.
2. *Pay attention.* Liars, exploiters, and predators abound on the Internet.
3. *Research.* Before getting too involved in an online relationship or before agreeing to meet face-to-face, research phone numbers, places of work, and e-mail addresses to make sure the person is who he or she says. Ask for references and *check them.*
4. *Know what you want.* Before getting too involved in an Internet relationship, make sure you know your intentions. Do you want a casual fling or a long-term friend? Make sure your intentions are made clear to your Internet dating partner.

If approached with caution and care, Internet dating is another alternative to meeting people of like interests.

Hooking Up **Hooking up** refers to physical interactions (usually sexual) with the absence of commitment or affection. As one of my students described it, "It's awesome—there are literally no expectations from each other, no strings attached."

Today on college campuses students are frequently opting to hook up, and college fraternities, sororities, and dorms commonly host hooking-up parties (England & Thomas, 2007). Gaining widespread popularity among adolescents and young adults, with as many as 40 percent of college students reporting that they have hooked up, the latest trend in physical attraction involves sexual encounters and includes anything from kissing, to mutual masturbation, to oral or anal sex, to sexual intercourse (Glenn & Marquardt, 2001).

The practice of hooking up is not as ambiguous as it might appear. Across college and university campuses, hookups are shaped by culturally shared rules that include sexual behaviors without the expectation of a committed relationship. In a study of dating and courtship

Friends with Benefits: Are There Benefits to Hooking Up?

Why hook up? Some college students lack time for an emotionally committed relationship, some have recently ended a long-term relationship and are not ready to get into another one. Still others may lack interest in their hookup partner, and others simply prefer a no-strings-attached get-together.

But are there benefits of having "friends with benefits"? Or is hooking up risky business? Take a few moments to jot down your opinions to the following questions:

1. Will you be able to remain friends without complication once you engage sexually with your hookup buddy? How will the friendship change after you become sexual partners? Will the friendship become strained? Uncomfortable?
2. Do you want more from the hookup than just the benefits—the sex?
3. Are you able to remain emotionally unattached from someone after you sexually interact? Do you have feelings for your hookup partner that will make the situation more confusing?
4. Can you and your hookup buddy communicate about safer sex?

Own It!

attitudes of contemporary college women, researchers found a distinction between whites and blacks when describing hooking up. When white college women describe hooking up, there is always a clear sexual connotation to the term. On the other hand, black college women describe hooking up as ranging from getting someone's phone number, to meeting up with someone after class, to going on a date, to a sexual fling (Glenn & Marquardt, 2001).

How often do hookups know one another? There are random hookups, where the students who get together do not know one another before they hook up (about 14 percent) (England & Thomas, 2007). However, more than half of those college students surveyed indicated that they knew their hookup partner moderately or very well; over half of those who reported a recent hookup indicated that they had previously hooked up with the same person. A **friend with benefits** or **booty call** are examples of terms used to describe one who has regular sex with another, but does not relate to that person as a boyfriend or girlfriend. Multiple hookups with the same person sometimes lead to an exclusive relationship.

In a recent study that surveyed over 600 West Coast college students, researchers found that nearly half of all hookups start at a party or hanging out at a bar or a dorm, and about 25 percent of those who have hooked up had one to four hookups. About 20 percent experienced 5 to 10 hookups, and over one-third had hooked up more than 10 times (England & Thomas, 2007). In this study, hookups were categorized by how far things went sexually. Figure 7.3 depicts the percentages of those college students who participated in certain sexual acts in their hookup encounters (such as kissing, touching, mutual masturbation, oral sex, and sexual intercourse).

Hooking up commonly follows a lot of drinking, with men averaging five drinks before hooking up and women averaging three drinks (England and Thomas, 2007). Because alcohol lowers people's inhibitions, it plays a significant role in hooking up. College students indicated that drinking allows them to do sexual things they are too self-conscious to do while sober (Glenn & Marquardt, 2001; England & Thomas, 2007). A few of the college students reported

FIGURE 7.3   Sexual Acts in College Hookups

Across college campuses today, hookups involve a number of different sexual acts.

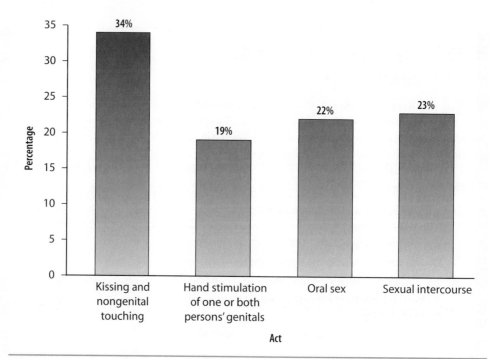

Source: England & Thomas (2007).

that alcohol played a role in their going further sexually than they normally would. Other disadvantages of hooking up include feelings of insecurity after the sexual encounter, feeling exploited, or being confused about whether the guy would call back (Glenn & Marquardt, 2001).

Although hooking up is not yet well understood, women report that their worst hooking up experiences involved being pressured or forced by their male partner to engage in unwanted sexual behavior. For example, in a study that examined unwanted sexual behaviors among 178 college students, over three-fourths of the female study participants indicated that their unwanted vaginal, anal, and/or oral sexual intercourse experiences (sexual assault) took place within the context of a hookup (Flack and others, 2008). This research reveals a lot, because it first shows us that hooking-up relationships may be sexually dangerous for women and may be ripe situations for sexual assault to occur. It also shows us that hooking up is no time to be ambiguous about expectations—partners need to be very clear about how far they're willing to go *before* the hookup encounter takes place. But given the amount of alcohol that is typically consumed prior to hooking up, set boundaries may not be adhered to.

HOOKING up frequently occurs after a lot of drinking. College students report that drinking allows them to do things they might be too self-conscious to do while they are sober. Girls report that drinking allows them to be more sexual. Do these behaviors increase the risk of date rape and other types of sexual assault?

Is hooking up a negative experience in the lives of young adults? Perhaps a concern on a developmental level is that hooking-up experiences do not allow adults in a transition phase of their lives to learn how to form and maintain mature, committed relationships. More common than not, long-term committed relationships do not result from hookups, although some college students indicate they became a committed couple after several hookup encounters.

The ways in which people come together to form intimate couple bonds has changed significantly in the United States. From the eras-past practice of courtship under the watchful eye of a parent, to today's Internet dating, speed dating, and hooking up, couples have always found ways to be intimate with one another. Now let's look at how these relationships develop.

RELATIONSHIP DEVELOPMENT

The pathways to commitment are different from culture to culture. In some parts of the world today, forced marriages, child marriages, and arranged marriages are still practiced (see Chapter 8). In some of these cultures, it is the parents' responsibility—particularly the father's—to choose their child's life mate. In other industrialized, individualistic cultures, such as America, however, most couples marry for romantic love (see Chapter 6). How couples move beyond the initial physical attraction and form committed relationships is explored through two models: Knapp's Relationship Escalation Model and Duck's Relationship Filtering Model.

Knapp's Relationship Escalation Model Mark Knapp, communication studies author, studied interpersonal relationships to better determine how they develop. His work is often referred to as the Relationship Escalation Model because it describes how relationships are initially formed and how they progress over time (1984):

- *Initiation.* The initiation into a relationship can occur in just a few seconds. This is the point at which individuals present their "public selves" by using common pleasantries and everyday greetings such as "Hi, how are you?" It is this stage in the relationship where people initially observe the traits or characteristics of another person, while they are also being judged.

- *Experimenting/Exploration.* This stage can be thought of as the information-gathering stage of a relationship. Individuals still have not spent a lot of time together, but it is at this point that they gather enough information, through casual conversation, to determine if either party desires to continue the relationship.

- *Intensification.* As individuals spend more time together, their formal interactions give way to less formal and more spontaneous conversation. The level of self-disclosure increases, as might the level of physical contact. During this stage, the parameters of the relationship are set and individuals begin to state their levels of commitment.

- *Integrating.* This is when the two individuals become a "couple" and are identified as a couple among their friends and family. Each shares their relational identity.

The Essentials of a Great Relationship

More and more couples today are skipping steps in (or eliminating all together) the traditional pathways to commitment and long-term relationships. Meeting in bars or on college campuses in fraternities, sororities, or dorm rooms, the hookup is quickly becoming a normal experience among young adults. It is questionable whether the experiences provide opportunities for people to develop relationship skills essential to the success of any future long-term committed partnership such as marriage.

In the long run, the elements essential to any satisfying or enjoyable sexual relationship are the same ones that are essential to the success of any love relationship:

- **Communication**. Talking about things, from the really mundane things in life (Who's taking the dog to the vet?), to the really important things in life (How are we going to work through our differences in how we spend money?) is fundamental to any interpersonal relationship. Without communication, we can never really know our partner. Without communication, there is no understanding.

- **Understanding**. Being considerate, supportive, and perceptive of one another's needs and wants allows the initial spark of physical attraction to develop into a mature, stable love. Out of communication and understanding grows acceptance.

- **Acceptance**. Recognizing the diversity, strengths, and weaknesses that each partner brings to the relationship deepens the richness of the relationship and further strengthens the couple's bond. Without communication, understanding, and acceptance, there is no respect.

- **Respect**. Valuing and admiring the other person work in tandem with communication, understanding, and acceptance to form the foundation of a love relationship.

TALK ABOUT IT

1. Does hooking up provide opportunities for young men and women to develop relationship skills necessary for long-term partnerships?
2. Can a relationship exist without some of the elements discussed above? Which element(s), in your opinion, can be missing in a relationship without affecting the quality of the relationship?
3. Do the different pathways to relationships and commitment in contemporary society support the development of the above relationship elements?

Source: Tooman (1970). It goes to bed with you, no matter what you are. *Marriage,* April 1970, pp. 28–31.

- *Bonding/Intimacy.* During this stage, the couple reaches a shared level of interdependence. Knapp notes that during this relationship stage, some type of formal, official announcement is made of the couple's commitment to one another (such as an engagement or marriage).

Duck's Relationship Filtering Model Similar to the filter model of mate selection we discussed earlier in this chapter, Stephen Duck (1985) proposed that when deciding whether to enter into or continue an interpersonal relationship—or what type of relationship—we sort information through a set of filters.

According to Duck, we use different types of cues to sort interpersonal relationship information. The first filter is the **sociological** or **incidental cue**, which relates to the restrictions and limitations placed on our ability to meet people. These cues speak to a person's *sociological* location or position, or the places where we live and work. **Preinteraction cues** provide at-a-glance information that helps us decide whether we would even consider wanting a date with a certain person. For example, from outward appearances someone might be physically attractive to you and you might determine right away whether the person is your type or not.

Interaction cues allow us to make assessments about whether we want to get to know a person better. For example, most of us at some time have had a crush on someone we barely knew. While our crush may be based on physical attraction, the attraction may end when he or she begins to talk. Through this interaction we learn more about one another. If we do find we want to spend more time with someone, we rely on **cognitive cues**, which tell us more about a person beyond a superficial, casual level. We get to know another's personality traits, beliefs, goals, and aspirations, as well as the roles they play in life. From these cues we determine whether any of them match with who we are and what we need or desire in a life partner. At this point, after much self-disclosure and time, we decide to try to take the relationship to a deeper level and enter into a committed partnership.

COMMITMENT

The process of moving from a causal dating or sexual relationship to a committed relationship occurs over time. Increasingly today, young adults and older adults alike choose singlehood as a lifestyle instead of marriage or lifelong partnership. (In Chapter 8, we examine in depth the experiences of singlehood in the United States.)

Like love and intimacy, *commitment* is difficult to define because it can mean different things to different people. For many, **commitment** is the until-death-do-us-part component of a couple's relationship. It speaks to relationship longevity, stability, quality, and satisfaction. According to relationship psychologist Eli J. Finkel and his colleagues (2002), the growth of commitment in a relationship is the result of three factors:

1. Growing satisfaction with each other's ability to meet and gratify important needs
2. Decreasing reliance on friends and family to meet needs that members of a couple provide each other
3. Increasing investments in the relationship, such as time, material resources, and emotional/personal investment

When these factors are present in a relationship, it indicates that partners have made a commitment, a *long-term orientation* (Rusbult & Buunk, 1993). As a college student, for example, you may be committed to your relationships with your siblings and your parents and you may be committed to your studies at your university. Commitment involves the viewpoint that no matter the costs (such as in the social exchange perspective), a person is in it for the long haul—and that the long haul will undoubtedly involve difficulties and hardships at some (or many!) points along the way.

Family and social psychologist Michael P. Johnson identified three different types of commitment. For example, **personal commitment** refers to the feelings, thoughts, and beliefs we have about a spouse, life mate, or significant other. This type of commitment is reflected in the sense of connection, liking, fondness, affection, tenderness, warmth, and love that couples feel for each other. Empirical research suggests that people who are committed to a spouse as a *person*—not just in terms of their commitment to the relationship—report less marital distress and fewer marital problems, as well as higher levels of marital happiness and marital satisfaction (Swenson & Trahuag, 1985). Those who exhibit personal commitment also express more love to their partners.

Moral commitment refers to each person's value and belief systems. Before committing to or ending a relationship, individuals consciously weigh what is right and what is wrong. They are guided by their value/belief/religious framework. **Structural commitment** refers to those commitments bound by institutions such as marriage. Although many individuals who have personal commitments also have structural commitments, having a structural commitment to the marital union does not necessarily mean that the partners are committed to one another on a personal level, or that there is love or affection present in the relationship. In fact, Swenson and Trahaug's research concludes that marital happiness and marital satisfaction are lower in those couples who display only structural commitment.

Same-sex couples face unique challenges in constructing committed relationships, because they have to create scripts that are different from the typical heterosexual commitment scripts (Rostosky, Riggle, Dudley, & Wright, 2006). In a study that explored commitment in 90 same-sex couples, the researchers found that these couples perceived relationship commitment as involving:

- *Investments in their partners.* Emotional and physical investment as well as investments of personal resources
- *Rewards.* Companionship (significant for lesbians but not gay men), sexual satisfaction and fulfillment
- *Costs.* Limits of personal freedom, legal constraints (such as not being able to legally marry), and stress/conflict associated with disclosing the relationship to family and friends
- *Personal values and ideals.* Desire for sexual and emotional intimacy, communication, and overall high relationship quality.

Many of these may seem similar to those relationship components found in committed heterosexual relationships, but each of these factors can have different meanings or levels of importance for same-sex couples (Rostosky and others, 2006). In addition, other factors, such as moving in together, social disclosure of the relationship, and actively making plans for the future as a couple, signify relationship commitment for gay and lesbian couples (Rostosky and others, 2006).

Like love, intimacy, communication, or any other area of family life, commitment is a *process* that progresses over time. As with any other area of family life, commitment requires an active, practical effort from both members of the couple to ensure its success. Left untended or ignored for too long, it will wane—and breaking up is more than likely to occur.

BREAKING UP

It seems as though the people who love us the most—family, friends, or romantic partners—are the people who hurt us the most. This is because feeling hurt is almost always the result of interpersonal relationships (not the result of words or actions). The nature of relationships is that hurt is always possible because someone said or did something—or didn't say or do something. Sometimes we let the hurt stay under the surface and allow it to fester. This unresolved conflict almost always becomes the "background" of the relationship, and it's always present no matter how hard we try to make the relationship work. Other times it seems as though all we do is fight with our partner, over big things, small things, and things that don't really matter at all.

There are a number of relational transgressions that cause hurt. It would be impossible to discuss all of them here, because as you learned in Chapter 3 about symbolic interaction, each us of acquires and assigns different meanings to behaviors—what is hurtful to you may not be hurtful to another person. Generally speaking, however, **relational transgressions** are hurtful words or actions that communicate a devaluation of the partner or the relationship (Bachman & Guerrero, 2006). Some examples of relational transgressions include deceit, unfaithfulness, criticism, blaming, and betrayals of self-disclosure (Bachman & Guerrero, 2006). At the very least, these hurtful comments or actions may increase uncertainty about the relationship and may create temporary problems for the couple. For many,

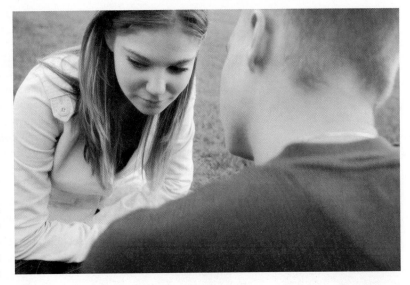

THERE'S no doubt about it: Breaking up is almost always hard to do! For most of us, it's tough to repair a relationship if we have been deeply hurt by our partner.

the ultimate consequence of relational transgressions is a breakup. Although some people do stay in relationships and work out even the most serious violations of trust (Roloff, Soule, & Carey, 2001), people who are deeply hurt by their partner's actions are likely to dissolve the relationship (Vangelisti & Young, 2000).

Breaking up is tough for most people, and it is associated with a number of negative physical and emotional responses, from anxiety and depression, to loneliness, to the suppression of the immune system due to stress (Davis, Shaver, & Vernon, 2003). In a study of nearly 5,300 participants (mostly in their teens and 20s), the researchers observed a range of reactions to breaking up; these are presented in Table 7.3. As the table shows us, there are two types of breakup reactions: *distress* and *protest*. **Distress reactions** include such things as physical and emotional pain, loss of interest in sex, and guilt; **protest reactions** are behaviors and feelings that attempt to reestablish the relationship, such as trying to reinvolve the ex-partner in sexual relations (Davis and others, 2003). The researchers also found that those who did not initiate

TABLE 7.3   Distress/Protest Reactions to Breaking Up

Distress reactions

Physical/emotional distress

Lost interest in sex

Self-blame

Guilt

Partner blame

Protest reactions

Want/try to get back together

Sexual arousal

Anger/hostility/revenge

Physically hurt

Preoccupation

Exploration/interference

Source: Davis, Shaver, & Vernon (2003).

Unmarried to Each Other: Is Cohabitation a Trial Marriage or Playing Commitment?

The reasons people live together vary. Some, like same-sex couples, live together because they have no other options for the legal recognition of their love and commitment for one another. Some divorced people may be hesitant to marry again and choose instead to cohabit. Still others would rather drive over a cliff than walk down the marital aisle and have a piece of paper define their relationship. The question arises, then, Does living together before marriage serve as a trial marriage?

YES: According to cohabitation advocates and authors Dorian Solot and Marshall Miller, living together before marriage serves as a trial to marriage in the following ways:

■ It provides each member of the couple time to examine why she or he desires to be together as a couple and to form clear expectations of each other and of the relationship.
■ It helps couples keep reasonable expectations for each other and the relationship.
■ It allows cohabiting partners to see the "real" partner. "If you don't like what you see in an unmarried significant other, you definitely won't like it in a spouse."
■ Negotiating roles, finances, the sexual relationship, and property provide opportunities for conversations that help clarify the couple's expectations and help strengthen the relationship. It is a good reality check.

NO: If living together serves as a trial or a test of what the marital relationship will be like, doom lies ahead. The *cohabitation effect* is the effect that cohabitation has on first marriages, and it posits a negative relationship between premarital cohabitation and marriage. Those who cohabit before marriage and later marry experience:

■ Higher divorce rates (Binstock, 2003; Teachman, 2003)
■ Lower levels of happiness (Waite & Gallagher, 2000)
■ An erosion in the belief that marriage is permanent (Teachman, 2003)
■ Less satisfying sexual relationships (Waite & Gallagher, 2000)

WHAT DO YOU THINK?

1. Is cohabitation good preparation for marriage—a good trial of marriage?
2. What are good reasons to live together before marriage? What are good reasons not to live together before marriage? Are your reasons based on your personal opinions or are they based on the research findings?
3. In your opinion, is nonmarital cohabitation a positive or a negative life experience? Support your answer.

the breakup felt a lost sense of identity, and were more likely to jump immediately into a replacement relationship. Some also turned to alcohol and/or drugs to help them cope with the breakup.

Clearly, the end of a relationship sometimes means that we'll go through a period of mourning and loss. There appear to be three phases that follow ending a relationship, particularly in breakups that involve college students: (1) *Experiencing a loss*, which includes emotionally processing the loss and realizing its implications; (2) *Pulling apart*, which involves separating emotionally, physically, and symbolically from the partner; and (3) *Moving beyond*, which encompasses not only a reduction in distress but also an ability to grow from the experiences (Hebert & Popadiuk, 2008). College students in this study went from devastation

("This wasn't a breakup—it was a smash up") to coping ("I'm sad, but I'm trying to use my sadness in the most constructive ways possible; I'm letting it motivate me to do better in school and go to the gym"), to healing and resolution ("Breaking up is the best divorce you can have before you get married—you learn *a lot* from it").

There are a number of how-to-survive-a-breakup sites on the Internet. Many of these sites contain good advice, such as taking time to examine what really happened and why; thinking through things thoroughly, but not excessively; dealing effectively with the hate phase, such as talking to friends or writing your feelings down in a journal; staying active; and making a conscious decision to let go of the hatred and realizing that harboring hate only hurts you, not your ex. If, after a breakup, you find that your sleeping and eating patterns are changing, that you can't focus, that you have low energy or are irritable, or if you feel a continued, general sense of sadness, it's best to talk to a healthcare professional on campus. Being single doesn't mean you have to be alone.

Nonmarital Cohabitation: Living Together

Traditionally, the initial route to commitment for heterosexual couples has been attraction, courtship/dating, and then marriage; in recent years, however, a detour of sorts has appeared on the relationship scene—cohabitation. Increasingly in Western civilizations across the world, cohabitation is viewed as the next step following dating and preceding marriage.

Cohabitation is a term used to describe the living arrangements of unmarried, intimate partners who typically have a sexual relationship; these relationships often resemble a marriage. A cohabiting relationship can be a short-term arrangement or a long-term union with the shared economic and parenting responsibilities found in marriage (Trask & Koivunen, 2006). A **common law marriage** is a relationship comprised of cohabiting heterosexual partners, but no legal marriage ceremony has taken place; however, the couple holds themselves out to the world that they are husband and wife. After the couple has been living together for a certain length of time (the time varies by state), they are considered to be legally wed. In Canada, cohabitation is referred to as *common-law status*.

Cohabiters can be straight or gay, never-before-married or divorced-and-now-single. They can be young parents or 68-year-old widows and widowers. Studying cohabitation is important to our understanding of sex and sexuality because this social phenomenon corresponds to a dramatic shift in the social and demographic behaviors through which intimate and sexual relationships, as well as families, are formed, organized, and dissolved (Wu, 2007).

Once considered a scandalous, uncommon alternative lifestyle, cohabiting before marriage (or instead of marriage) is now the prevailing living arrangement of intimate partners—the next step following serious dating. In fact, data show that there were 7.5 million unmarried heterosexual partner households (over 15 million people) in the year 2009 (U.S. Census Bureau, 2009). When gay couples are included in the numbers of those cohabiting, the figure increases to nearly 6 million people (Simmons & O'Connell, 2003).

CHARACTERISTICS OF COHABITATION

Cohabitation has become a normal part of the lifecourse for many Americans, young and old alike. Consider the following trends of nonmarital cohabitation in the United States (Black, Sanders, & Taylor, 2007; Kennedy & Bumpass, 2007):

- Almost one-half of adults in their 20s and 30s live together before marriage.
- The current rate of cohabitation before marriage is nearly 70 percent. This means that for 70 percent of young adults, their first couple experience is cohabitation rather than marriage.
- Of the cohabiting couples that recently married, 58 percent lived with their partner before marriage; 14 percent had also lived with someone else other than the person they married.

- Among self-identified gays and lesbians nationwide, cohabiting estimates for gay men and lesbians are about 50 and 63 percent, respectively.

Several factors contribute to whether a person chooses to live with an intimate partner and forego the traditional path of marriage. The rates of cohabitation vary between *different regions* in the United States, *religion, age, among races, social class,* and levels of *educational attainment.*

Factors that Affect Cohabitation As presented in Figure 7.4, nonmarital cohabitation is higher in the Northeast than it is in the South or the Midwest (Simmons & O'Connell, 2003). In those states where religion is a predominant part of the culture (such as the Church of Latter Day Saints in Utah, and throughout the "Bible Belt"—the South and the Midwest), cohabitation rates are lower. Nearly 45 percent of those who cohabit before marriage have no religious affiliation, whereas those who attend church or other religious services on a weekly basis are twice as likely not to cohabit before marriage (Jones, 2002).

The Pew Research Center is a nonpartisan "fact tank" that provides information on the issues, attitudes, and trends that shape America and the world. Their recent random telephone survey of over 2,000 respondents in the United States queried whether living together without getting married or before marriage is a good thing for society, a bad thing, or a new trend that doesn't make much difference (Pew Research Center, 2007); see Figure 7.5. Their research revealed a number of differences in attitudes about cohabitation.

For example, those who attend church or temple frequently (weekly or more) tend to believe that living together instead of marriage is a bad thing for society, whereas those who attend church or temple less frequently (monthly or less) tend to look more favorably on cohabitation. Similarly, those who hold to more moderate or liberal political beliefs tend to view cohabitation more favorably than those who do not. Figure 7.5 shows us that overall,

FIGURE 7.4 Percentages of Persons of the Opposite Sex Sharing Living Quarters across Regions of the United States

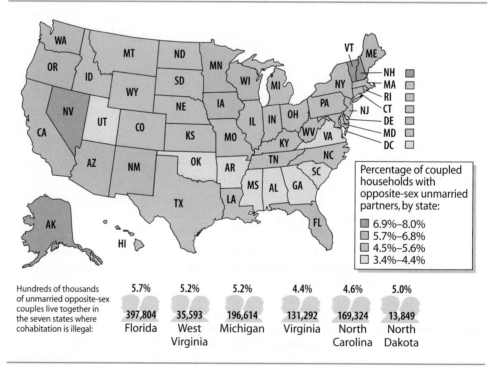

Source: U.S. Census Bureau (2003).

FIGURE 7.5 Living Together without Getting Married

Is this trend a good thing for society, a bad thing for society, or does it make much difference?

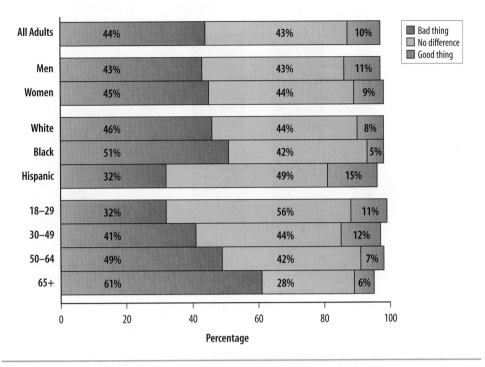

Legend:
- Bad thing
- No difference
- Good thing

Group	Bad thing	No difference	Good thing
All Adults	44%	43%	10%
Men	43%	43%	11%
Women	45%	44%	9%
White	46%	44%	8%
Black	51%	42%	5%
Hispanic	32%	49%	15%
18–29	32%	56%	11%
30–49	41%	44%	12%
50–64	49%	42%	7%
65+	61%	28%	6%

Source: Pew Research Center (2007).

men and women are fairly equal in their beliefs about whether cohabitation is a good thing, a bad thing, or something that doesn't much difference to them.

In general, women who cohabit tend to be younger than cohabiting men. For college-age students, 24 percent of the women and 16 percent of the men are under age 25 (Fields, 2004). However, college students do not represent the largest group of cohabiters; rather, most unmarried partners are in their 30s and 40s (Simmons & O'Connell, 2003). About three-fourths of cohabiting women expect to marry their partners, but only about one-third of those living together eventually marry (Trask & Koivunen, 2006).

Race is also a key factor in cohabitation, and it is especially common among disadvantaged minority groups such as blacks and Hispanics (Brown, Van Hook, & Glick, 2005). Figure 7.6 illustrates the rates of nonmarital cohabitation by race. As you can see, African Americans and American Indian/Native Alaskans have nearly equal rates of cohabitation; Asian Americans have the lowest rate of nonmarital cohabitation (Simmons & O'Connell, 2003). Further, as depicted in Figure 7.7, among Hispanics, blacks, and whites, the birth of a couple's first child occurred during cohabitation in anywhere from 12 to 32 percent of couples (Centers for Disease Control, 2008).

Marriage is a more likely outcome of cohabiting relationships for whites than it is for blacks and Hispanics, and if a pregnancy occurs during the cohabiting period, whites are much more likely to marry than blacks and Hispanics are (Smock & Manning, 2004). Employment also plays a key role in whether a cohabiting couple eventually marries. Among blacks, if both partners are working, they are more likely to marry; however, among white couples, if a woman is not working, the couple is less likely to wed (Smock & Manning, 2004). It is very important to note, however, that even though nonmarital cohabitation is seen among all groups, it still continues to be a trend seen in those who are economically disadvantaged (Smock, Manning, & Porter, 2005).

FIGURE 7.6 Rates of Cohabitation by Race

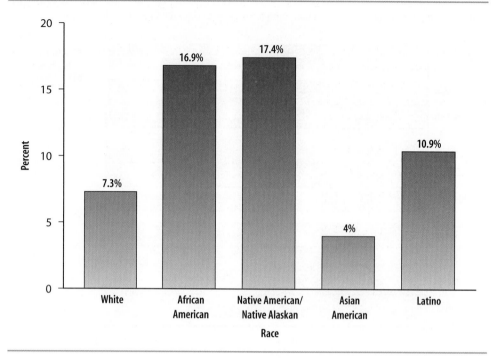

Source: Simmons & O'Connell (2003).

FIGURE 7.7 Percentage of Parents Who Were Married or Cohabiting at the Birth of Their First Child, by Race/Ethnicity and Sex

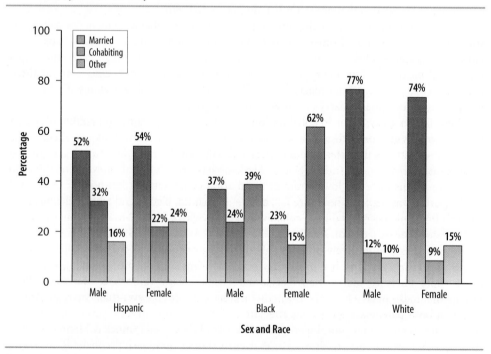

Source: Centers for Disease Control (2006).

Among Puerto Ricans, cohabitation unions usually begin informally, and these relationships are unlikely to be legalized through marriage (Brown and others, 2005). However, unlike blacks and whites who cohabit, Puerto Ricans' live-together relationships are similar to their married counterparts in terms of education, employment, and childbearing (Brown and others, 2005). In one study, most Puerto Rican women described their cohabiting relationships as a form of marriage (Brown and others, 2005).

All of these findings are important because they help us see that cohabitation has different meanings for different racial groups. Among whites, for example, cohabitation is often a steppingstone to marriage, a transitional phase between dating and a potentially lifelong commitment. For blacks, cohabitation functions as a substitute for marriage (Trask & Koivunen, 2006). Some sociologists speculate that blacks cohabit instead of marrying because they lack the economic stability they consider to be a necessary must for marriage (Brown and others, 2005).

When explaining cohabitation rates, it is important to note that social class and education levels interact with race as a determining factor in who cohabits and who does not. For example, high school dropouts are twice as likely to cohabit as those who finish high school. Similarly, 41 percent without a high school degree cohabit, compared to 26 percent of those with college degrees (Bumpass & Lu, 2000). The Pew Research Center's recent findings indicate that these trends are changing, however. For instance, among those surveyed, nearly one-third of college graduates and one-third of those with a high school education or less indicate that cohabiting is a favorable life choice, while 43 percent of those with some college education believe it is a favorable life choice (Pew Research Center, 2007). If education levels and income levels are low, men are more likely to cohabit, particularly African American men (Manning & Smock, 2003).

Cohabitation among Gay Men and Lesbians The availability of social science data concerning cohabitation experiences of gay men and lesbians is quite limited. Earlier we noted that the prevalence of cohabiting is about 63 percent for lesbian couples and about 50 percent for gay men (Black and others, 2007). Other demographic characteristics reveal that gay male cohabiters are more likely to be white, are more highly educated, and are less likely to have children in their household compared to nonpartnered gay men (Black and others, 2007). Lesbians in cohabiting relationships tend to be older (about age 39), are more likely to be white and to have been in a prior legal heterosexual marriage, more likely to have children in their household, and are more highly educated than nonpartnered lesbians (Black and others, 2007).

Cohabitation in Other Cultures Nonmarital cohabitation is not a trend that is seen only in the United States. Cohabitation appears to be increasing in prevalence all over the Western world. Figure 7.8 (page 232) presents the percentages of all couples who cohabit in countries throughout Europe, in the Near and Middle East, and in Asia. As you can see from the data, Scandinavian countries have the highest levels of cohabitation in Europe. At the other extreme are the southern European countries, together with Ireland. The rest of Europe falls in between (Bernhardt, 2004).

In other countries, such as Asia, and in Near and Middle East countries, cohabitation is a rare occurrence. Although we know essentially nothing about cohabitation among Asians and Asian Americans, the available data suggest that their cohabitation rates are among the lowest of all ethnic groups (Brown and others, 2005). These low rates are because of the taboo on premarital sex in Asian cultures. This taboo on premarital sex is also found among those of Jewish ethnicity, particularly because sex before marriage is considered to be a sin within the Jewish faith. Among Islamic countries, cohabitation is virtually nonexistent because it is forbidden by the Islamic law and the Muslim faith.

A live-together arrangement between intimate partners is the contemporary "next step" in relationship development. But are these arrangements a *substitute* for marriage or viewed among the couples as a *trial* marriage? And what reasons do couples give for cohabiting?

FIGURE 7.8 Proportion of Couples Who Cohabit Before or Instead of Marriage, by Country

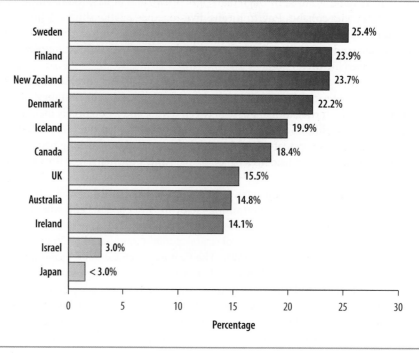

Source: Wu (2007).

WHY DO COUPLES COHABIT?

With the increasing number of years that most young adults are single, and the growing trend in cohabitation, couples report several common reasons for cohabiting. David H. Olson created the PREPARE/ENRICH Couple Program for couples who want to better prepare for marriage or enrich their existing marriages. In this program, couples complete inventories that assess couples' relationship types, as well as characteristics of each couple member's family of origin. In a recent survey of over 50,000 respondents, Olson and Olson-Sigg (2007) found these contemporary reasons that couples live together before marriage:

- Economic advantages
- Time together
- Increased intimacy
- Less complication dissolution of relationship if it doesn't work out
- "Testing" compatibility
- Trial marriage

Data gathered by the Pew Research Center (2007) give us further insight into why couples live together before marriage or instead of marriage. Nearly one-fourth of those survey respondents who cohabit did so to test the relationship, to make sure that the partner is the right one.

But what is cohabitation like behind the numbers? In an effort to go beyond the raw numbers, over 100 black, Hispanic, and white young adult cohabiters were interviewed to better understand how nonmarital cohabitation relationships begin and end, as well as their living arrangements and the language used to refer to their partners (Manning & Smock, 2003). The extensive, in-depth interviews reveal much about the beginnings and endings of cohabiting relationships: "In a way it did just kind of just happen. . . . I would come over and stay with him at night and one night led into two nights, two nights leading into three nights and then next thing you know I have clothes over there and I'm cooking dinner for him" (black female, computer services, age 28, pp. 14–15).

When called on to describe their relationship with their live-in, intimate partner, many cohabiters are at a loss: "It wasn't 'roommate' and I realize . . . there is no term for somebody who is in between girlfriend and wife" (white male, office worker, age 33, p. 20).

Unlike marital relationships, there is much ambiguity with cohabiting relationships. As the researchers note, there are really no defining moments that signal the beginning or end of the cohabiting arrangements (Manning & Smock, 2003). In many instances, there is a gradual transition, with most couples drifting in and out of these arrangements. The researchers contend that living together before marriage does not appear to be a substitute marriage (a long-term commitment between intimate partners that does not involve legal marriage) or a trial marriage (living together to see what marriage would be like). Cohabitation, instead, is seen as an alternative to being single.

There also appears to be ambiguity in what to call one's partner, because those who participated in the research felt that the term *unmarried partners* did not fully capture the essence of their relationships—it didn't convey how the intimate partners actually felt about one another (Manning & Smock, 2003). As one black female concludes, "[The term *unmarried partner*] . . . to me [sounds like] just a person I'm having sex with" (p. 23).

BUT DOES COHABITATION WORK?

In certain regions of the United States, there are few more hotly or intensely debated topics in family life than the issue of whether or not couples should cohabit before marriage. Aside from whether cohabitation is a moral life choice is the issue of whether cohabitation has advantages or disadvantages.

Advantages of Cohabitation   Our study so far has shown us that nonmarital cohabitation is an increasingly common living arrangement for intimate partners both in the United States and other cultures. Given the current trends in living together, many are curious as to what advantages are associated with cohabiting. The literature is virtually silent on the potential positive outcomes associated with cohabiting, but what little empirical evidence that does exist suggests that couples do experience a few advantages if they cohabit before or instead of marriage:

- Couples who cohabit have more personal autonomy than those who are married (Bernhardt, 2004).
- Cohabiters have more personal individual freedom than married partners do (Waite & Gallagher, 2001).
- Those who live together have more individual financial freedom than married partners do (Waite & Gallagher, 2001).
- Cohabiters have greater gender equity, less traditional gender roles, and share household chores more than married couples do (Bernhardt, 2004).
- Couples who cohabit have greater flexibility in their commitments to their relationships (Bernhardt, 2004).

Given the unique, individualized nature of intimate relationships, some might argue that these points are disadvantages, rather than advantages, of nonmarital cohabitation.

Disadvantages of Cohabitation   There is little information available regarding the advantages of cohabitation, but the research is consistently clear regarding its disadvantages: Cohabitation before marriage or in place of marriage is by and large a negative relationship experience. Specifically:

- Couples who live together have the lowest level of premarital satisfaction when compared to other living arrangements (Olson & Olson-Sigg, 2007).
- Marriages preceded by cohabitation are more likely to end in divorce (among many others, Waite & Gallagher, 2001).

- Married couples that cohabited before marriage have poorer communication skills in discussing problems than those couples who did not live together (Cohan & Kleinbaum, 2002).
- Cohabitation before marriage carries with it an increased risk of violence against women and children (see especially Fagan & Hanks, 1997). In cohabiting relationships, there is more verbal aggression, anger, and attempts to control the partner's feelings than exists in married relationships (Cohan & Kleinbaum, 2002). (Chapter 15 provides an in-depth look at family violence.)

You may be asking yourself, "Why is it, if cohabitation is thought of as a trial marriage for some, that there are such negative consequences associated with this living arrangement?" Olson and Olson-Sigg (2007) note, "One explanation is that while the basis for marriage is a strong ethic of commitment, cohabiting couples are much more oriented toward their own personal autonomy and are more willing to terminate the relationship. It is easy to speculate that once this *low-commitment/high-autonomy pattern* of relating is learned, it becomes hard to change. Cohabitation reflects uncertainty" (p. 3). To answer the question posed earlier, "Does cohabitation work?," the answer from empirical research suggests that no, it does not.

While it is clear from the skyrocketing increase in the numbers of those who cohabit before marriage that public opinion approves of this relational pathway, family life specialists and researchers are not so sure this relationship course is the best route. As noted by the Australian Family Association,

> The sharp rise in unmarried cohabitation is perhaps one of the most alarming trends of the . . . family this century. Living together prior to or instead of marriage may seem like a progressive approach to intimate relationships . . . [but] among other things, unmarried cohabiting couples express less commitment to an ideal of relationship permanence. [Cohabitation] is, for the most part, not a relationship with a future, but one that lasts for a period of time and then ends. [It] does not improve the choice of marital partners, nor does it offer an enriched courtship where partners can get to know each other and gain experience with matters related to marriage. Unmarried cohabitation's only advantage over marriage is that it guarantees free entry, free exit, no commitment, and no responsibility. (www.northernlife.com/au).

Despite the increasing numbers of singles today, despite the noticeable trend of couples delaying marriage for longer periods of time, and despite the increased trends in nonmarital cohabitation, most Americans still marry at least once in their lifetime.

Family Life Education

I vividly recall when I suspected my husband was "the one" I wanted to marry (Spring Break, 1979, South Padre Island). Our relationship took a somewhat traditional path (for the time) from casual acquaintance, to casual dating, to more serious dating, to engagement, to marriage. I have to wonder, however, if we were to meet each other for the first time today, would our path to commitment be the same? Would we skip any steps? Would we add any steps, such as cohabitation?

The study of interpersonal attraction and the pathways to partnering are important in our examination of marital and intimate relationships because dating, courtship, and partnering practices map out different courses to marriage and other lifelong couple relationships. Today, some looking for love still choose a traditional route to finding someone they hope to spend the rest of their life with, while others choose a present-day dot-com approach and use the Internet.

Relationally, as a society we are living in uncharted and unprecedented times. How did we move from the tradition of courting under the eye of a parent, to free-for-all, transient sexual hookups? If we look at the past 50 to 60 years, the way people develop interpersonal partnerships has undergone extraordinary changes, from parent-directed and parent-approved courtship with the intention of marriage, to speed and Internet dating, to no-strings-attached sexual hookups, and to trial sexual and economic live-together unions. We wonder what other types of changes might be in store.

Who Determines Society's "Ideal Body" Standard—Men or Women?

Who determines society's "ideal body" standard—men or women? One researcher tried to answer this question by doing his own content analysis of *Vogue* magazine models (to assess the female standard of ideal body shape), *Playboy* centerfold models (to assess the male standard of ideal body shape), and Miss America winners (a sort of catch-all to assess both female and male standards of ideal body shape) (Barber, 1998). He posed two questions:

1. Is a male's standard of women's attractiveness curvier than the female's standard?
2. Do women or men determine the "ideal body" standard?

According to Barber (p. 3), "American women's standard for female bodily attractiveness differs greatly from that of men." From 1978 to 1986, the *Vogue* models' bustlines were significantly smaller than the *Playboy* models' bustlines or the winners of the Miss America beauty pageant. In fact, the *Vogue* standard for physical attractiveness did not predict the *Playboy* or Miss America standard of "ideal" body shape! Barber's analysis also determined that the bust–waist ratios for *Playboy* models and Miss America winners were not significantly different; in other words, the bust and the waist measurements of *Playboy* models and Miss America contestants were virtually the same. Barber subsequently concluded from this research that the female body standard, over time, has converged with the male ideal body standard—curves.

Wondering how students today would respond to Barber's research questions and findings, I posed them to my marriage and family class. The students responded:

Her Side: "I just don't get it. I mean, as women we are bombarded day after day after day with images in print and electronic media that tell us we are never thin enough. We're urged to purge, we're urged to get rid of curves—and now we find out that men actually *like* curves? If that's the case, then why is a woman over a size 6 considered 'fat'? Why do women's magazines constantly insist on pushing their impossible-to-achieve version of 'beautiful' on us?"

"Why should *men* get to decide the standard of beauty?!"

His Side: "But I don't think that the images in *Playboy* are fair to women, either. That magazine sends the message that all women have to be perfectly proportioned to be attractive and beautiful, and that's not true. I think if you asked most guys they would say that women are attractive if they are healthy."

"Hey, don't blame the guys! Every man knows that women don't dress to please men, they dress and diet to please other women!"

Your Side: From your casual observations,

1. Do you think men or women determine the ideal body standard for women in today's society?
2. From looking at women's magazine covers, what is the woman's ideal body standard? From looking at men's magazine covers, what is the male's ideal body standard for women? Do you agree with the images that are advertised as "ideal"?
3. Do you think the ideal body standard for women will change over time?

Source: Barber (1998).

Summary

"Frisky Business": Interpersonal Attraction Theories

- Evolutionary theory for mate selection purports that we choose mates solely to further our reproduction. Since every society has some form of socially approved union between men and women, sociologists and anthropologists have sought to determine the mechanisms by which men and women are attracted to one another.

- Mate selection evolutionist-based theories maintain that there are two specific biological goals—male sexual selection goals and female sexual selection goals—that must be achieved when selecting a mate. According to evolutionists, men are concerned with quantity: To impregnate as many women as possible, males must select females who are able to bear children and will select women who possess certain fertility cues, such as youth, attractiveness, body shape, and permissiveness. Women are concerned with the quality of the children they produce and search for provider/protector cues such as intelligence, dominance, physical strength and prowess, and ambition.

- Social Exchange theory explains what *motivates* individuals to act and asserts that individuals act out of self-interest in ways to maximize their rewards and minimize their costs. Although each individual in a relationship may seek personal rewards with minimal costs according to researchers Thibaut and Kelley, both individuals are mutually reliant on one another for rewarding results.

- The Filter Theory of Mate Selection suggests that individuals use a filtering mechanism (based on propinquity, homogamy, heterogamy, physical attraction, or reciprocity) that helps individuals sort out a potential mate from the vast pool of candidates, or eligible partners.

The Path to Commitment

- Courting and courtship are socially prescribed forms of conduct that guide men and women toward matrimony. Dating is an occasion where people get together socially for various reasons, such as for relaxation or to determine whether the partner is a potential spouse or lifelong partner, a lifelong relationship, or a sexual encounter with no strings attached.

- Knapp's Relationship Model describes how relationships are initially formed and how they progress over time through the stages of initiation, experimenting/ exploration, intensification, integrating, and bonding/intimacy. Duck's Relationship Filtering Model asserts that we use different types of cues or filters to sort interpersonal relationship information: sociological/incidental cues, preinteraction cues, interaction cues, and cognitive cues.

- The growth of commitment (personal, moral, or structural) in a relationship is the result of (1) growing satisfaction with each other's ability to meet and gratify important needs; (2) decreasing reliance on friends and family to meet needs that a partner provides; and (3) increasing investments in the relationship, such as time, material resources, and emotional involvement. When these are present, partners have made a commitment, or long-term orientation.

Nonmarital Cohabitation: Living Together

- *Cohabitation*—the term that is used to describe the living arrangements of unmarried, intimate partners who typically have a sexual relationship—is the prevailing living arrangement of intimate partners and the step following serious dating. Religion, age, race, social class, and levels of education all affect the rate of cohabitation among different regions in the United States.

- Public opinion suggests that cohabitation is the next logical step after serious dating, yet research consistently makes clear that cohabitation before marriage or in place of marriage is by and large a negative relationship experience. Cohabitation before marriage not only correlates with higher relationship dissatisfaction and higher risk of divorce in the event of marriage but it also carries with it an increased risk of violence against women and children.

Key Terms and Concepts

natural selection, p. 206

sexual selection, p. 206

Evolutionary theory, p. 206

fertility cues, p. 207

protector/provider cues, p. 207

Social Exchange theory, p. 208

reward, p. 208

cost, p. 208

matching hypothesis, p. 209

Filter Theory of Mate Selection, p. 210

pool of candidates, p. 210

propinquity, p. 210

homogamy, p. 210

exogamy, p. 211

endogamy, p. 211

heterogamy, p. 211

pair bonds, p. 211

courting/courtship, p. 212

dating, p. 213

Script theory, p. 213

cultural scripts, p. 213

intrapsychic scripts, p. 213

interpersonal scripts, p. 213

dating scripts, p. 214

speed dating, p. 215

online dating, p. 216

hooking up, p. 219

friends with benefits/booty call, p. 220

Knapp's Relationship Escalation Model, p. 221

Duck's Relationship Filtering Model, p. 223

sociological/incidental cue, p. 223

preinteraction cue, p. 223

interaction cue, p. 223

cognitive cue, p. 223

commitment, p. 223

personal commitment, p. 223

moral commitment, p. 224

structural commitment, p. 224

relational transgressions, p. 225

distress reactions, p. 225

protest reactions, p. 225

cohabitation, p. 227

common law marriage, p. 227

Suggested Readings

Gibson, Valerie. *Cougar: A guide for older women dating younger men.* (Firefly Books, 2002).

Harris, Joshua. *I kissed dating goodbye: A new attitude toward romance and relationships.* Sisters, OR: Multnomah Publishers, 2003.

Sherman, Alexa Joy, & Toantins, Nicole. *The happy hook-up: A single girl's guide to casual sex.* Berkeley, CA: Ten Speed Press, 2004.

Solot, Dorian, & Miller, Marshall. *Unmarried to each other: The essential guide to living together as an unmarried couple* (2002). New York: Marlowe & Company/Publishers Group West.

Multiple-Choice Questions

1. Intelligence, physical strength, industriousness (a hard worker), and ambition are examples of _____ .

   a. protector/provider cues

   b. fertility cues

   c. matching hypothesis

   d. Social Exchange theory

2. _____ suggests that individuals use a filtering mechanism that helps them sort out a potential mate from the vast pool of candidates, or eligible partners.

   a. Social Exchange theory

   b. Evolutionary theory

   c. Filter Theory of Mate Selection

   d. Cohabitation theory

3. Which word refers to partners who are of different races, religions, and ethnicities?

   a. exogamy

   b. heterogamy

   c. endogamy

   d. homogamy

4. _____ are personal and individualized, and represent our private wishes, hopes, desires, and dreams.

   a. Interpersonal scripts

   b. Cultural scripts

   c. Dating scripts

   d. Intrapsychic scripts

5. In Knapp's Relationship Escalation Model, _____ is when individuals spend more time together, and their formal interactions give way to less formal and more spontaneous conversation.

   a. intensification

   b. experimenting/exploration

   c. integrating

   d. initiation

6. If we find we want to spend more time with someone, we rely on _____ , which tell us more about a person beyond a superficial, casual level.

a. interaction cues

b. incidental cues

c. cognitive cues

d. preinteraction cues

7. _____ are behaviors and feelings that attempt to re-establish a relationship, such as trying to re-involve the ex-partner in sexual relations.

a. Distress reactions

b. Protest reactions

c. Relational transgressions

d. Interaction cues

8. Which of the following is NOT true about cohabitation?

a. Marriages preceded by cohabitation are more likely to end in divorce.

b. Couples who live together have the lowest level of premarital satisfaction when compared to other living arrangements.

c. Married couples that cohabited before marriage have poorer communication skills in discussing problems than those couples who did not live together.

d. Cohabitation before marriage carries with it a decreased risk of violence against women and children.

Answers: 1. a; 2. c; 3. b; 4. d; 5. a; 6. c; 7. b; 8. d

Coupling: From Singlehood to Marriage

8

The pastor asked of the young couple, "Eric and Gretchen, will you have one another, to be one flesh with you? Will you love one another, care for one another, honor one another, respect one another, and protect one another, in every situation of life? Will you prefer each other above all others and forsaking all others, be faithful as long as you both shall live?"

Gretchen and Eric nervously held each other's hands, and answered the pastor's questions in unison by vowing to each other:

"Gretchen/Eric, I ask you to come with me and be my wife/ husband. I promise to love you as no one else can. I will give you my strength and will accept yours in return. In happy times, or in sad times, when life is stormy or quiet. I will love you when we are together, I will love you when we are apart. From the depths of my heart I will always be open and honest with you. Your happiness will be my happiness, and my strength will be your protection, my tenderness and care will be your comfort. I will make your goals and dreams my goals and dreams. Together we will build a home where love abides. I give myself to you."

Source: Author's files

The past few years my husband and I have attended so many wedding ceremonies, and recently we've experienced the indescribable joy of seeing two of our sons marry. At each of their weddings, we sat in the surreal moment, smiling and crying from the inside out (where *did* the time go?), remarked that the brides have never looked more beautiful (our new *daughters!*), and that our sons (no longer boys, but *men*) had never looked more nervous. As soon as the wedding official asked the marrying couples of their intentions toward one another and they each, in turn, replied "I do," my husband I exchanged a knowing glance. If they only knew!

If they only knew that their promises to love one another, care for one another, respect one another, and protect one another will be tested time and time again—sometimes to the breaking point. *If they only knew* that it's not always easy to be open and honest, and that it's not always easy to be happy for their partner or share their partner's sorrow. *If they only knew* that, while they today pledge that they will be "one," that oneness in purpose and goals and dreams is much easier said than done. Even though most young married couples know that their marital union will be a journey fraught with ups and downs and unexpected joys and sorrows, few know at the outset the complexities of being married. And as current divorce statistics indicate, few are adequately prepared and equipped to negotiate their new roles and to navigate these complexities.

In our examination of intimate relationships we must obviously consider marriage; however, discussing all of the nuances associated with marriage is an arduous and demanding task. To complicate matters further, the subject is greatly influenced by our own family of origin experiences—for example, Are your parents divorced or have they been married for some time? Were you raised by a single-parent mother or a single-parent father? Have you ever witnessed marital violence between your parents? Compound your family experiences of marriage with your cultural and ethnic background and your religious upbringing, and you can see how our perceptions of marriage are influenced by many factors.

Our family studies framework is an applied approach to examining marriage and marital life, and because of this integration of application and theory, the following discussion may be quite unlike other textbooks you may have read that focus on sociological and anthropological aspects of marriage. In this approach we might think of marriage as a compass to provide direction, rather than as a road map. A road map provides the details a journey can take. A compass helps you learn where you are—and which direction to take. Neither a text nor an instructor can provide a map for marital bliss, but we can become oriented and directed by some landmarks along the way.

Before we examine marriage, we will first discuss being single, which is an increasing trend among America's young adults. We will then look at marriage in a variety of contexts, such as how marriage is both a relational and legal reality, as well as the ever-evolving status of gay and lesbian marriages and civil unions. We'll study the rights, privileges, and benefits of marriage, as well as the pitfalls that might trap some couples in marital dissatisfaction. Finally, we will examine the keys to a successful marriage—marital expectations.

Being Single

In Chapter 7, we looked at the contemporary trends in dating in the United States. As you discovered, dating and courtship are practices that typically lead to the selection of a marriage partner, or a life mate. In U.S. culture, and in cultures around the world, marriage is assumed to be the next stage in a person's life following adolescence and early adulthood. But not everyone who dates necessarily has marriage on his or her mind. American culture today is seeing increasing numbers of singles, and singlehood is becoming a popular trend among the young and old as well. This trend is due, in part, to the *individualistic* nature of American society; that is, individual needs and wants, such as self-fulfillment, educational attainment, and the fulfillment of career goals, are promoted over the *collective* needs of the society. For the most part, Western societies readily accept young adults' pursuits of their goals and dreams. This current trend in the large and increasing numbers of singles is also partly because numbers of young adults are delaying marriage. Today, the average age of marriage for men is 27.5 years; for women it is 25.5 years (Smock, Casper, & Wyse, 2008). Figure 8.1 shows the average age of marriage for men and women from 1890 to 2008. As you can see, the age at which people marry fluctuates over time; these fluctuations mirror society's attitudes toward marriage and singlehood.

Historically, U.S. culture viewed singlehood as a transitional stage that preceded marriage and parenting; being single was not viewed as a lifestyle that adults purposely chose, but as a stepping stone to the eventual, expected adult roles of spouse and parent. Today, marriage still remains the normative life course for most Americans, with 90 to 95 percent of adults eventually marrying (Smock and others, 2008), but in contemporary society there is an increasing number of adults who are single. In 2006, for example, over 59 million U.S. family households—slightly over one-half—were headed by single men and women (U.S. Census Bureau, 2006). Almost 15 million of these households were headed by single women, another 5 million by single men, with another 39 million belonging to a category described as *nonfamily households*, a term that demographers use to describe gay/lesbian households and heterosexual couples who cohabit without marrying. By comparison, the number of households comprised of married couples stood at more than 58 million, or just under 50 percent of all U.S. households (U.S. Census Bureau, 2010). These trends are significant because they represent a dramatic shift from the year 2000, when married couples made up over 52 percent of American households.

The experience of being single is not universal. Singles are a complex and diverse group, and there are differences in how people experience singlehood. For instance, people may be single because they have never married, because they are divorced, because they are widowed, or because they are lesbians or gay men who are not legally allowed to wed. We'll explore the characteristics of these singles types a bit later on in this discussion, but first we begin by gaining an understanding of the broad categories of singlehood.

FIGURE 8.1   Average Age of Marriage for Men and Women, 1890–2008

Source: U.S. Census Bureau (2008).

TYPES OF SINGLEHOOD

Sociologist Peter Stein (1981) developed a typology of singlehood. According to this classification, there are various categories of single people: voluntary temporary, voluntary permanent, involuntary temporary, and involuntary permanent.

- **Voluntary temporary singles.** Singles in this category include those who have never married, as well as those who were previously married and are now divorced or widowed. Voluntary singles are not opposed to marriage; rather, they are not currently looking for a mate because it is not a priority.
- **Voluntary permanent singles.** This category of singles includes those who have chosen deliberately to remain unmarried. The choice to remain single is stable and permanent over time. Voluntary permanent singles include never-marrieds, those who have divorced and have no intention of remarrying, cohabiting individuals, gay and lesbian couples, and certain members of the clergy, such as priests and nuns.
- **Involuntary temporary singles.** Among this category are singles who want to be married and who are actively seeking a marriage mate. This group of singles includes people who have never married, as well as those who were previously married and are now divorced or widowed.
- **Involuntary permanent singles.** In this category are those singles who wanted to marry but did not find a marriage mate. These singles may be never married, divorced, or widowed. Over time, they come to accept their unmarried status.

Stein's typology shows us that being single is a fluid, changeable state. In other words, there will always be people who are single for a certain period of time, and there will always be people who remain single throughout their lives—either by choice or by circumstance.

EXPERIENCING SINGLEHOOD

As you saw in Chapter 7, for some people dating is a way to have fun, relax, and get to know other people. For others, dating or courting is a pathway for people to find a life mate (Sheehan, 2003). Most of us, at some point in our lives, will find ourselves single—whether it's because we haven't found Mr. or Ms. Right, because we just ended a relationship, or because a spouse has died. Being single means that someone is not married; however, there are different experiences of unmarried people.

Never-Married Singles **Never-married singles** are those individuals who have not married, but they may or may not live alone and they may or may not have an intimate partner. Never-married people are gay or straight, young or old, cohabiters or live-alones.

As you saw earlier, the United States is experiencing an increasing number of singles. It is important to note, however, that there are different racial/ethnic trends among never-marrieds. As Figure 8.2 shows us, nearly two-thirds of African Americans/Black Carribeans are not married; this racial group has the highest percentage of not-married singles (National Center for Health Statistics, 2008). Note also that among Native Americans/Alaska Natives the percentage of those who are married is similar to those who are unmarried. Asian Americans experience the highest percentage of marriage with over two-thirds who are married, and have the lowest rate of non-married singles.

Why do we have an increasing number of singles in United States? There are several reasons why young adults are delaying or forgoing marriage. The trend toward delaying marriage has emerged over several decades as financial and social forces, such as the 2008 U.S. economic crisis and skyrocketing unemployment rates, have made it more difficult for those in their 20s to reach independence from their parents (Campbell, 2002; Waite & Joyner, 2001). In the past, those who delayed marriage or chose singlehood were frowned on by society; after all, taking on spousal and parenting roles was expected, considered to be *the* only appropriate gender roles (Campbell, 2002). Today, however, being single is more socially acceptable than

FIGURE 8.2 Singlehood and Marriage by Race and Ethnicity

There are different trends in singlehood among races.

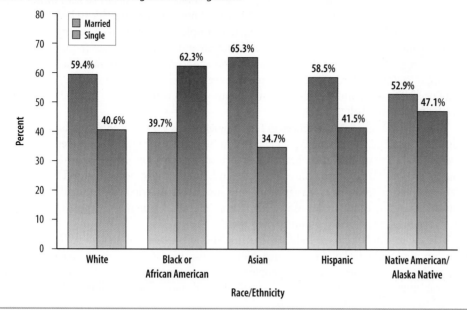

Source: National Center for Health Statistics (2008).

it was in the past, particularly if a young adult is pursuing higher education or career goals. Other social factors, such as society's acceptance of premarital or nonmarital sexual behavior and nonmarital cohabitation, also contribute to the increasing number of never-married singles (Waite & Joyner, 2001). Demographers speculate that other social factors are also at work: Today, there are more highly educated women who have fewer highly educated men of comparable age to partner with. In addition, there are more relationship and career choices open to women today than in decades past—women no longer need to depend on men for their financial and/or relationship security (Smock and others, 2008).

It is also increasingly more common for young adults to remain financially dependent on their family of origin longer than young adults did in the past (Barrett, 1999; Campbell, 2002). If parents and other caregivers continue to help with college expenses and living expenses, it is financially advantageous for a young adult to remain single.

Single and Lovin' It?

While being single may be perfectly acceptable and comfortable for some 20-somethings, they still may have a tough time explaining to their parents (for the umpteenth time) that they are quite content with their single status and that they're in no hurry to tie the knot. Others may struggle with being single because they've come to believe that they need a partner to be truly happy in life.

Are you single and lovin' it—or single and loathing it?

1. If you are single and lovin' it: If your parents constantly ask you about your dating status, have you ever made up an imaginary partner, just to quiet their concerns? If so, how did that tactic work?

2. If you are single and loathing it: What is it about your single status that concerns you the most? Have you ever found yourself falling in love, just so you could be "in love"?

Own It!

Social and Emotional Characteristics The social, emotional, and health experiences of never-marrieds vary from those of other unmarried people. Overall, never-married people report high satisfaction in areas of friendship, general health, and personal economic status (Barrett, 1999; Campbell, 2002). For example, overall life satisfaction tends to be high among never-married people, and it is similar to married couples' life satisfaction (Campbell, 2002); however, some research indicates that the satisfaction and happiness of never-married singles has more to do with the fact that their social and economic needs are met than because of their single status (Bedard, 1992). In general, never-married people experience rich, active social lives with family and friends, and enjoy relationships with dating or cohabiting partners (Barrett, 1999; Campbell, 2002).

There are also gender differences in how singlehood is experienced. For example, young unmarried men and women are typically well educated and have high-status careers and jobs; 85 percent of all never-marrieds have a high school diploma, and 23 percent have at least a bachelor's degree (U.S. Census Bureau, 2009). And, interestingly, never-married men tend to experience poorer health rates than married men, but never-married women tend to have better health than any other group of women. Never-married women also tend to better organize and manage their lives than unmarried men.

Existing research seems to indicate that singlehood is a positive, satisfying experience for many—not a lonely, isolated experience. Nevertheless, in a society that reveres marriage of heterosexual couples, never-married people are often victims of cultural stereotypes. Unmarried women may be referred to as "spinsters" or "old maids," and unmarried men may be referred to as "confirmed bachelors" (Gordon, 2003).

Urban Tribes Given that the traditional social institutions of marriage and family are presumed to provide social and emotional support, an interesting question arises when considering the increasing number of never-marrieds: Who becomes the primary institution or system of support between the years of living in a family of origin and a family of choice? With new trends comes new terminology, and to describe the phenomenon of the increasing numbers of young singles, author and social science researcher Evan Waters (2004) coined the term *urban tribe*.

Urban tribe refers to mixed-gender circles of friends (typically in their 20s and 30s) who are the primary social support system for singles. Similar to the peer groups portrayed in popular television shows such as *How I Met Your Mother*, urban tribes are redefining family and commitment. Typically, urban tribes begin as a group of friends who socialize together every now and then, but over a period of five years or so, each individual within the tribe assumes certain roles, much like in a family. Similar also to families, urban tribes share rituals, such as holiday celebrations, stories and, over time, histories. As you saw in Chapter 3, shared stories and shared histories create unique group meanings, and a group history deepens the bond between family members, or in this case, between tribe members. Urban tribe members feel a mutual obligation to support each other and to care for one another. As Waters observed it appears that today these circles of friends are becoming substitutes for spouses. He believes that in our current complex society, it is these emerging support systems that let marriage wait. Because these friendships are emotionally satisfying—and sometimes sexually satisfying, as hookups are not uncommon among these urban friendships—young adults do not feel the need to rush into marriage. Is the urban tribe an emerging developmental phase in the lives of young adults?

WHO needs marriage? Increasing numbers of young adults today lean on their circle of friends—their urban tribes—to meet their emotional, physical, and sometimes sexual, needs.

Gay and Lesbian Never-Marrieds Because gay men and lesbians do not have the legal privilege of marriage, researchers often view them as never-married singles. In fact, it was not until the 1990 census by the U.S. Census Bureau that demographers provided a distinct category for gays and lesbians who lived together as a couple (U.S. Census Bureau, 2001). That was not to say, however, that legal homosexual marriages would be counted or recognized. Although gay marriage is legal in the states of Massachusetts, Connecticut, Iowa, Vermont, and Maine (as of 2009), U.S. Census Bureau officials in 2008 indicated that same-sex partners who listed themselves as spouses would be recorded as "unmarried partners" in the 2010 census (O'Connell & Lofquist, 2009). However, in June 2009, the Obama administration reversed the previous administration's earlier decision and ruled that married same-sex couples will be counted as such in the 2010 national tally.

Other recent changes make it somewhat easier to ascertain the changing family living arrangements in the United States. For example, unlike the decennial (every 10 years) Census, which aims to count every person in the United States, census demographers are now beginning to use data gathered from the *American Community Survey (ACS)* to assess various family structures. Unlike the U.S. Census, the ACS is an *ongoing* survey that is conducted every year, and it samples about 2.5 percent of the total U.S. population. By 2010, it will replace the decades-old Census long form.

In the 2005, the ACS (the first to be conducted nationwide) sampled about 1.5 million households in the United States. Gary Gates, senior research fellow at the Williams Institutes on Sexual Orientation, Law, and Public Policy at UCLA, analyzed the data obtained from the 2005 ACS. Gates's (2006) analysis revealed the following:

- About 4.1 percent of U.S adults (about 9 million) identify as a sexual minority (gay, lesbian, or bisexual).
- The number of same-sex couples who lived together as intimate partners in the United States grew from 600,000 in 2000 to 777,000 in 2005. This growth represents an increase of more than 30 percent.
- Fifty-three percent of same-sex couples were gay men, while 47 percent of same-sex couples were lesbian women.

FIGURE 8.3 Increase in Same-Sex Couples, 2000–2005

The number of same-sex couples who lived together as intimate partners grew by more than 30 percent in a five-year period.

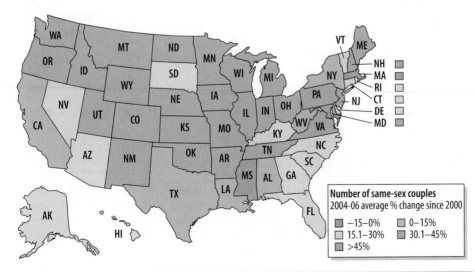

Source: Gary J. Gates, "Same-Sex Couples and the Gay, Lesbian, and Bisexual Population: New Estimates from the American Community Survey" (October 1, 2006). The Williams Institute. Paper gates_8. http://repositories.cdlib.org/uclalaw/williams/gates_8.

- While increases of 41 to 81 percent in same-sex couples were seen in all states, California, Florida, New York, Texas, Illinois, and the District of Columbia have the largest sexual-minority populations, and, as such, have the largest number of same-sex couples (see Figure 8.3 on page 247).

How do we explain these increases seen between 2000 and 2005? It may be possible that more and more same-sex couples are beginning to live together in committed relationships, but Gates (2006) suggests that the magnitude of growth in same-sex couples documented in the ACS is probably because more gay and lesbian couples are reporting their relationships to U.S. demographers. He also suggests that today's same-sex couples may be more willing to come out of the closet because there is a decline in the stigma attached to homosexuality, or that some same-sex couples are taking a stand against anti-gay groups. Although we have this information, empirical science is just now beginning to learn about the experiences of gay and lesbian singles, so the research is still virtually silent about their relational and family lives.

Divorced Singles A small percentage of America's singles are divorced men and women. Although divorce rates escalated in the 1970s and remained high through the 1990s, they appear to have stabilized somewhat (Heaton, 2002). Figure 8.4 illustrates for us that there are gender differences seen in divorced singles, and there are also racial/ethnic differences. A number of other variables, such as age, affect divorce rates; we will discuss these in depth in Chapter 14. For our discussion here, it is important to understand that most divorced people will experience life as a single person at least for some period of time following the end of their marriages.

The Widowed Women are much more likely to outlive their husbands. There is a greater percentage of single *widows* (women) than single *widowers* (men), among all races. In addition to their shorter life expectancies, men are also more likely than women to remarry following the death of a spouse, thus reducing the numbers of single widowers (Lemme, 2005). Additionally, retirement pensions and Social Security benefits allow older adults to live independently for longer periods of time (Lemme, 2005). The experiences of widowhood are discussed in Chapter 16.

FIGURE 8.4 Marital Status of the Population by Sex and Race

Most people will experience being single for a period of time following divorce. Men tend to marry sooner after a divorce than women do.

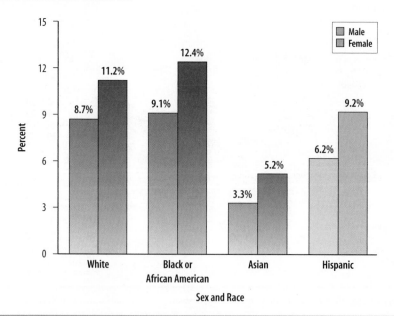

Source: U.S. Census Bureau (2006).

As the current trends in singlehood show us, marriage exerts less influence over how U.S. adults experience their intimate relationships today. Despite the increasing number of singles today, and despite the noticeable trend of couples delaying marriage for longer periods of time, most Americans still marry at least once in their lifetime.

The Act of Marriage

In most cultures throughout the world, there is an expectation that when a person reaches adulthood (ages of adulthood vary among cultures) marriage should soon follow. In the United States alone, each month upwards of 168,000 couples wed, vowing to love, honor, and respect their chosen life mates until death parts them (National Vital Statistics Reports, 2006). The expectation is deeply engrained.

However, the social functions, purposes, and relevance of marriage are rapidly changing in contemporary society, making them less clear-cut than they have been throughout history. For instance, in a Pew Research Center (2007) random polling of over 2,000 individuals, fewer than half of all of the adults polled indicated that if a man and a woman plan to spend the rest of their lives together as a couple, it was important that they legally marry (see Figure 8.5).

Those of us who choose to marry have specific reasons why we decide to marry the person we do. There is a common desire, however, in our Western, individualistic culture: We tend to marry for reasons that benefit ourselves, rather than for reasons that benefit the society at large, such as found in collectivist cultures. Research in Western cultures has found, for example, that the number-one reason people cite for marrying is to signify a lifelong commitment to someone they love (Australian Relationships Survey, 2006). However, this reason is not the only response to why people wed—today, people get married for reasons of commitment, security, and personal belief systems. The Pew Research Center's recent findings suggest that the main reasons people get married are for mutual happiness and commitment, and bearing and raising children (Pew Research Center, 2007). As the data from this survey show us in Figure 8.6 on page 250, there are racial/ethnic, age, and religious differences in what people consider to be the main purposes of getting married.

THE SOCIAL DIMENSIONS OF MARRIAGE

As a family life educator and a professor in the study of marriage and the family, a semester doesn't pass without a student or two seriously (and sincerely) questioning me as to why couples in love need a piece of paper (a marriage license) to validate or give recognition to their love relationship. "If we declare our love and commitment before one another, why do we need

FIGURE 8.5 Importance of Legal Marriage

Although more and more couples are opting to cohabit, Americans indicate that it is important that the couples legally marry if they are going to be life partners.

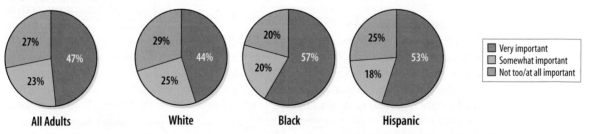

Very important
Somewhat important
Not too/at all important

Source: © 2007. Pew Social and Demographic Trends project. Generation Gap in Values, Behaviors as Marriage and Parenthood Drift Apart, Public is Concerned about Social Impact. http://pewsocialtrends.org/assets/pdf/Marriage.pdf.

FIGURE 8.6　Reasons People Marry, by Race/Ethnicity, Age, and Religious Beliefs

Racial and ethnic differences exist in the reasons people marry.

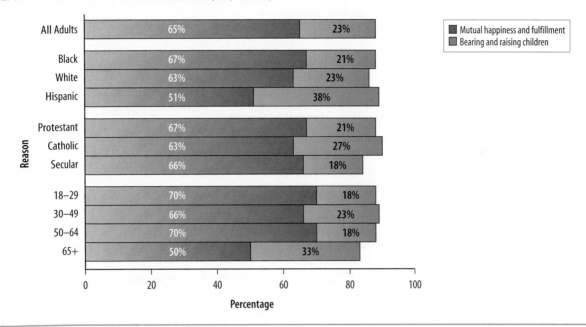

Source: © 2007. Pew Social and Demographic Trends project. Generation Gap in Values, Behaviors as Marriage and Parenthood Drift Apart, Public is Concerned about Social Impact. http://pewsocialtrends.org/assets/pdf/Marriage.pdf

a marriage license or a piece of paper? Why do we even need someone to 'marry us,' or a wedding ceremony? What's the big deal? *Why does marriage matter?*"

Marriage matters for several reasons. First, the act of marriage matters because it defines the couple as having a **pair bond**—two people emotionally bonded to one another—and it characterizes the couple's union. Ultimately, it provides a new identity for a couple and the subsequent roles they will play in their marriage and in the society at large.

From a Necessary Foundation to Deinstitutionalization　In her testimony before the U.S. Senate concerning the importance of marriage to society, Barbara Dafoe Whitehead (2004), codirector of the National Marriage Project (a nonpartisan, nonsectarian, interdisciplinary initiative located at Rutgers University), commented on the purposes of marriage. She observed that marriage, found in all types of cultures the world over, performs a number of key functions in every known society. These functions include things such as establishing family identities, regulating sexual behavior, providing and caring for children, and channeling the flow of economic resources. Whitehead's comments raise an important question: If marriage plays such a crucial role, why is this social institution undergoing such change?

Don Browning, director of the Religion, Culture and Family Project at the University of Chicago (2004), contends that marriage has undergone a shift throughout history, even as recently as during the past 25 years. In centuries past, both collectivist and individualistic cultures embraced **institutional marriage**, which not only encompasses the responsibilities of socializing children to the culture's norms but it also includes the adherence to the idea that marriage is sexually exclusive (monogamous) and permanent (Cherlin, 2004).

The institution of marriage is also typically associated with *patriarchal authority*, where the husband is acknowledged as the leader of and provider for the family. As you learned in Chapter 1, families of the past were economic partnerships—people didn't necessarily marry for romantic reasons (love), but instead they married so they could purchase land. They then had children out of necessity, to help them cultivate and farm their crops; for some, children were nothing more than property. Today, state and federal income tax policies still benefit

Before You Say "I Do"

In Western cultures, most people marry because they are in love. Having realistic expectations about marriage—what each partner expects of a spouse and the marital relationship—significantly affects overall marital satisfaction and happiness. Because each partner comes into a marriage with different family-of-origin experiences and models, couples often have different goals and expectations. By discussing these expectations before they trek down the marriage aisle, couples have a chance to align their ideas and attitudes about what marriage will—and won't—be. Discussing expectations about marriage also gives couples the opportunity to strengthen their communication skills, a key component in successful marriage.

Before you say "I do," there are many issues to consider. First, you should consider *why* (other than being in love) you want to get married. The aim of this discussion is for each partner to fully understand and appreciate each one's reasons for marrying.

As you and your partner consider your reasons for getting married, check off each item that applies to you.

- Because it's the next logical step in our relationship.
- Because I want to show my commitment to him/her.
- I'm tired of being single.
- I want more independence in my life.
- My religion mandates marriage before we can be sexually intimate with one another.
- I want security.
- I'm ready to have children.
- I need his/her friendship and companionship.
- I'm not getting any younger.
- I'm a single parent and I want two parents in my child's life.

1. Did you and your partner come to a general agreement on the reasons why you want to marry? Are your expectations for marriage realistic in comparison to your partner's expectations?
2. Do you see significant discrepancies in your reasons for marrying? If there are some, do you believe these are potential trouble spots in your marriage?

Source: Quilliam (2005).

Healthy SELVES Healthy FAMILIES

those couples who are married and have children. For instance, gays and lesbians who cohabit with their intimate partners are required by law to pay taxes under the *single taxpayer* category; on average, they pay $1,069 more each year in federal taxes than their married counterparts, who receive tax breaks when they file under the *married, filing jointly taxpayer* category (Human Rights Campaign, 2008).

Thus, although marriage was once the social institution considered to be *the* social foundation responsible for the procreation and the socialization of children, as well as the structure for economic security of its members, it is being replaced today by pair bonds that meet individual needs, such as cohabitation. This change is referred to as the **deinstitutionalization of marriage** (Cherlin, 2004). To this end, Browning suggests that in Western, individualistic cultures such as in the United States, people pursue relationships that meet their private, intimate, emotional, and sexual needs. Consequently, the notion that marriage serves an essential *social* function is rapidly losing ground.

According to Browning, determining the cultural and intellectual purposes of marriage in today's culture is less definitive, and he argues that this may be the reason contemporary marital trends are on the decline, reaching historical lows. In order to better understand marriage as a social institution, Browning outlines five specific social dimensions of marriage.

1. Marriage as an organizer of natural desires. The ancient Greeks viewed the marital union as a way to organize natural sex drives of men and women and their urges to bear children. The Greeks also viewed marriage as a vehicle for ensuring that other natural, daily needs—such as safety and security needs, needs for shelter, and needs for food—were met through the division of labor pair that bonding provides. They believed that this need of meeting and sustaining natural desires and daily needs brought a man and a woman together, which in turn, led to marriage.

2. Marriage as a social good. Browning's second dimension of marriage concerns its contribution to the overall good of the culture. This dimension reflects the ideas associated with collectivist cultures wherein the needs of society are put before individual needs. In this context, healthy marriages and healthy families are a vital, necessary, and essential component of a healthy, productive society. According to Browning (2004), Martin Luther in 1522 asserted that marriage is ordained by God for the good and beneficial gain of the married couple, their children, and the culture and society in which they live. This concept is the impetus or driving force behind the concept of **covenant marriages** (see Dimension 4).

3. Marriage as a communicative reality. Browning asserts that marriage should not be thought of as a union where marital lives run parallel to one another, but instead as a communicative reality—the nature of contemporary marriage is a bond where lives are meant to intersect for the purposes of mutual support and mutual comfort, or "oneness." This dimension of marriage is a relatively new occurrence in society, particularly in Western, individualistic societies where people marry for romantic love, Browning observes. Because the emphasis of marriage today is more an individualistic rather than a collectivist need, contemporary marriage places greater emphasis on the *emotional* and *communication* aspects of the relationship. According to Browning, in order to achieve equity and satisfaction in marriage, married couples must develop both communication and interpersonal relationship skills and nurture them throughout the life course of the marriage.

4. Marriage as sacrament and covenant. Many people view marriage as something bound together by more than legal ties or a personal, intimate commitment to one another. The Christian, Jewish, Hindu dharma, and Islamic religions consider marriage to be divinely ordered and ordained; thus, no marriage should be entered into without much thought and consideration; the **sacrament of marriage** is deemed a sacred act. In most religions, marriage is a union between one man and one woman that can be severed only by the death of one partner. An estimated 75 percent of all first-time marriages in the United States take place within a church, temple, or mosque (Evangel, 2004). In light of this statistic, the majority of marriages are officiated by a pastor, minister, priest, rabbi, chaplain, or other clergy. For those couples married in a place of worship and by clergy, marriage is more than a legal state—it is a religious state as well.

Marriage as a Religious Covenant In an effort to curb the escalating divorce rates in the United States, to date more than 20 states have actively considered implementing some form of legislation that would more adequately prepare couples for married life. The legislation would also attempt to preserve marriages through mandated divorce counseling or by delaying divorce.

The Marriage Covenant Act, for example, adopted in Arizona, Arkansas, and Louisiana in the late 1990s, are pieces of marriage legislation that couples jointly agree to abide by. This legally binding agreement spells out the couple's intent to obtain premarital education and/or counseling, clearly delineates the couple's commitment to preserving the marital union and/or a commitment to marriage counseling, if needed, and provides the grounds for divorce.

An example of a marriage covenant agreement is the Louisiana Marriage Covenant Act (see Figure 8.7), which outlines specific provisions.

FIGURE 8.7 Sample Covenant Marriage Agreement

LOUISIANA COVENANT MARRIAGE ACT

Contracting a Covenant Marriage

The couple who chooses to enter into a Covenant Marriage agrees to be bound by two serious limitations on obtaining a divorce or separation. These limitations, that do not apply to other couples married in Louisiana, are as follows:

1. The couple legally agrees to seek marital counseling if problems develop during the marriage; and
2. The couple can only seek a divorce or legal separation for limited reasons, as explained herein.

Declaration of Intent

In order to enter into a Covenant Marriage, the couple must sign a recitation that provides:

- A marriage is an agreement to live together as husband and wife forever;
- The parties have chosen each other carefully and disclosed to each other "everything which could adversely affect" the decision to marry;
- The parties have received premarital counseling;
- A commitment that if the parties experience marital difficulties they commit to take all reasonable efforts to preserve their marriage, including marital counseling; and
- The couple must also obtain premarital counseling from a priest, minister, rabbi, or similar clergyperson of any religious sect or a marriage counselor.

After discussing the meaning of a Covenant Marriage with the counselor, the couple must also sign, together with an attestation by the counselor, a notarized affidavit to the effect that the counselor has discussed with them:

- The seriousness of a Covenant Marriage;
- The commitment to the marriage is for life;
- The obligation of the couple to seek marital counseling if problems arise in their marriage; and
- The exclusive grounds for divorce or legal separation.

The two documents which comprise the Declaration of Intent—the recitation and the affidavit with attestation—must be presented to the official who issues the marriage license with the couple's application for a marriage license.

Divorce in a Covenant Marriage

A marriage that is not a Covenant Marriage may be ended by divorce more easily than a Covenant Marriage. In a marriage that is not a Covenant Marriage, a spouse may get a divorce for adultery by the other spouse, conviction of a felony by the other spouse and his or her imprisonment at hard labor or death, or by proof that the spouses have lived separate and apart for six months before or after filling for divorce.

In a Covenant Marriage a spouse may get a divorce only after receiving counseling and may only get a divorce for the following reasons:

- Adultery by the other spouse;
- Commission of a felony by the other spouse and sentence of imprisonment at hard labor or death;
- Abandonment by the other spouse for one year;
- Physical or sexual abuse of the spouse or of a child of either spouse;
- The spouses have lived separate and apart for two years; or
- The spouses are judicially or legally separated and have lived separate and apart since the legal separation for:
    a. One year and six months if there is a minor child or children of the marriage;
    b. One year if the separation was granted for abuse of a child or either spouse;
    c. One year in all other cases.

Covenant marriage agreements are legally binding contracts between marriage partners that spell out conditions under which couples can divorce or separate.

Source: Reprinted from *Family Case Law: Cases, Materials, and Problems*, 2nd ed., with permission. Copyright 1998 Matthew Bender & Company, Inc., a member of the LexisNexis Group. All rights reserved.

Signing a Covenant Marriage In order to enter into a covenant marriage, the couple is bound by two conditions if they wish to divorce or separate: They must agree to participate in marriage and family counseling, and they must agree to separate or divorce according to the reasons specified in the state's Marriage Covenant legislation.

Declaration of Intent The Declaration of Intent is a legally binding sworn statement indicating that the couple views marriage as a lifelong commitment and union.

Legal Separation Legal separation from a spouse can take place only after the couple undergoes joint marital counseling. In addition, one or more parties must *prove* that the spouse has engaged in certain breeches of trust or dangerous behaviors, such as committing adultery, abusing drugs or alcohol, or being the perpetrator of domestic violence or sexual abuse.

Divorce in a Covenant Marriage In a covenant marriage, divorce is much more difficult to obtain than it is with traditional marriages and marriage licenses. The conditions for divorce are quite similar to those conditions that must exist in order to obtain a legal separation. Just as in the case of separation, the marital parties must participate in joint marital counseling before they are able to proceed with their intentions to divorce.

The covenant form of marriage is not exclusive to newly engaged couples; couples who are already married may file for a covenant marriage by signing a Declaration of Intent and a sworn statement, and by receiving marital education/counseling. Since the covenant form of marriage is a relatively new phenomenon in this country—in existence since only the late 1990s—data do not currently exist that would show whether this form of marriage results in its intended purpose of lowering divorce rates or making divorce more difficult to obtain.

5. **Marriage as a legal contract.** Whether a couple marries in a tribal ritual or in an elaborate church or temple ceremony, marriage across cultures is considered a contractual agreement between parties, whether an arrangement between the bride and groom's families where betrothal took place perhaps before the child was even born, or the conventional contractual agreement made between today's bride and groom.

Although marriage means different things to different people, Browning's (2004) discussion about marriage as a social institution helps us see that marriage is more than simply a piece of paper that legalizes a commitment or an intimate bond between two people. Marriage is an act that serves society on many levels, including areas of health and productivity, religiously, and legally. It is perhaps the legal dimensions of marriage that distinguish it from all other forms of coupling.

THE LEGAL DIMENSIONS OF MARRIAGE

The way we experience intimacy, love, romance, dating/courtship, and mate selection differs depending on our regions of the world, as well as our race, ethnicity, and religious beliefs. The same factors influence how different people experience marriage.

In the United States, marriage is considered foremost as a legal contract. While a couple's union is a private, intimate, special bond, when they say "I do" before an official, whether with much fanfare and expense or in a subdued personal setting, their union acquires a legal status. The union becomes a legally binding, contractual, state and federally regulated agreement between the two parties. For instance, marriage laws specifically delineate the boundaries of the marital union, such as restrictions on age or kinship. Although marriage laws vary from state to state, all states follow the same general legal parameters.

What the Law Requires Every state requires couples intending to marry to receive a *marriage license* issued by a town, county, state, or similar authority at least one month before the wedding. When applying for a marriage license, couples must provide *proof of age;* the legal age to get married is 18 in the United States. If an applicant does not meet the legal age of

Should Same-Sex Couples Be Allowed to Marry?

If marriage is a civil union, is it then also a civil right? Across the nation, same-sex couples are challenging long-held marriage laws that only sanction (legally recognize) marriage between heterosexuals. Human rights advocates believe that gay and lesbian couples, as U.S. citizens, should have the same rights and privileges as heterosexual couples—including the right to legally marry the person they choose—whatever gender. Those who oppose same-sex marriages believe that marriage is a social institution that should be protected, and that allowing same-sex couples to marry would further erode the family.

Should same-sex couples be allowed to marry?

YES: The Human Rights Campaign (HRC) is America's largest civil rights activist organization that works to achieve gay, lesbian, bisexual, and transgender equality and to end discrimination. According to the HRC (2004), giving gay and lesbian couples the legal right to marry enhances and strengthens the social institution of marriage and American families. The HRC contends that same-sex marriages address the true, diverse needs of today's families, and if gay and lesbian married couples shared the same rights and privileges enjoyed by married heterosexual couples, families would benefit. Further, denying same-sex couples the right to marry denies them certain civil rights, which include:

- **Hospital visitation.** Same-sex couples do not have the automatic right to visit their partner or to make medical decisions for them, as heterosexual couples do.
- **Health insurance.** If healthcare coverage is provided by an employer for a gay/lesbian partner, the employee must pay taxes on the value of the insurance.
- **Family leave.** Gay and lesbian partners are not entitled to unpaid leave from their jobs to care for an ill spouse.
- **Pensions.** Same-sex couples cannot receive pension benefits.
- **Nursing homes.** Gay and lesbian aging partners cannot live together in retirement or long-term care facilities.

NO: According to Peter Sprigg of the activist organization, the Family Research Council (2004), legal marital unions between homosexual couples will have negative consequences on the institutions of marriage and family. Specifically, Sprigg contends that:

- **Gays and lesbians are not denied the right to marry.** The right to marry extends to *individuals,* not to *couples.* Every individual is free to marry within certain parameters.
- **Same-sex marriage would change the concept of marriage and family.** If gay and lesbian couples are allowed to marry, they would be able to more easily adopt children, perpetuating the negative consequences of growing up without a mother *and* a father.
- **Same-sex couples can easily have the rights of married heterosexual couples.** By simple legal documents, such as a will or a medical power of attorney, same-sex couples can provide for their partner after a death or care for them while they are ill.

Should same-sex couples be allowed to marry?

WHAT DO YOU THINK?

1. Is marriage a *civil* right, or is it a *human* right?
2. If you were to summarize the basis of the HRC's position, what would it be? What is the basis of Sprigg's argument? Do you agree with one position more than the other? Why?
3. What are the advantages to the institutions of marriage and the family by allowing gays and lesbians to marry? What are the disadvantages?

Sources: Human Rights Campaign Foundation (2004); Sprigg (2004).

adulthood, she or he must have notarized, written consent from both living parents or legal guardians. Additionally, marriage laws *prohibit marrying close kin*, which can result in devastating birth defects to offspring. Nationwide, laws mandate that siblings or half-siblings cannot marry; about half of the states will not allow first cousins to marry.

Furthermore, all individuals intending to marry *must be single*. There is no place in the United States where a person who is currently married can marry another person. Finally, some states require that *blood tests* are performed in order to discover any potential genetic disorders that might afflict future offspring, such as testing for HIV/AIDS.

Gender: Sexual Orientation and Marriage Laws   When discussing gender as it relates to marriage, gender is not the issue—*sexual orientation* is. While the social, political, religious, and individual issues surrounding the hot-button topic of marriage between same-sex partners continue to make headlines, the existing laws banning same-sex marriages probably exist because of the long-held, overarching societal belief (based on the nation's Judeo-Christian heritage) that marriage is an essential social institution that exists solely for the procreation, legitimizing, and socialization of children. In 2001, Holland expanded its definition of marriage to include same-sex couples; in 2003, Belgium did the same, followed by Canada (British Columbia and Ontario); Taiwan began drafting similar legislation in 2003, although as of 2009, the plans have not been implemented.

Parts of the United States are beginning to follow suit. In 2004, San Francisco issued marriage licenses to gay and lesbian couples who wished to marry, even though the state of California did not legally recognize these unions. In mid-2008, however, the California Supreme Court struck down the state's ban on same-sex marriages, making it legal for these couples to wed. Hundreds of homosexual couples got married in California following the court's ruling. But during the 2008 election cycle, Californians decided on *Proposition 8*, a ballot proposition that changed the state Constitution to restrict the definition of marriage to "a union between a man and a woman." The passing of this ballot measure by voters now eliminates the right of same-sex couples to marry. It is still not known whether those who married prior to the decision on Proposition 8 are *legally* married. In April 2009, the Iowa Supreme Court ruled that the ban on same-sex marriages was unconstitutional, and it paved the way for same-sex couples to legally wed. In May 2004, Massachusetts was the first state to legally sanction and approve marriage between same-sex couples, thus granting them the same rights, privileges, and benefits as heterosexual couples.

As you can see, the legislation that addresses same-sex couples' rights to marry changes quickly, and it can be difficult to keep up with it! Here are some quick facts about same-sex marriages:

- **Issues marriage licenses to same-sex couples:** Massachusetts, Connecticut, Iowa, Vermont, New Hampshire
- **Recognizes same-sex marriages that take place in other states:** Rhode Island, New York, Washington, DC
- **Allows civil unions that provide state-level spousal rights to same-sex couples:** Connecticut, Vermont, New Jersey, New Hampshire
- **Provides some state-level spousal rights to unmarried same-sex couples:** Hawaii, Maine, District of Columbia, Washington, Maryland

Despite these changes, though, the fight to legalize same-sex marriages is proving arduous: In July 2004, the U.S. Senate blocked a measure to amend the Constitution to allow a ban on same-sex marriages.

So far, we have examined why marriage matters because of the number of social functions it serves. Beyond the legal responsibilities and requirements associated with the act of marriage, there are certain rights, privileges, and benefits of marriage, too. It is these rights and benefits that distinguish the marital union from any other intimate pair bond relationship, such as cohabitation or civil unions between same-sex couples. In the following section, we'll examine other reasons why marriage matters: the rights and privileges of marriage as well as the benefits of marriage to adults and children.

THE RIGHTS AND PRIVILEGES OF MARRIAGE

The U.S. government sanctions marriage and provides the boundaries of the prevailing marriage laws, but it also grants each state the ability to determine the rights, privileges, benefits, and responsibilities associated with marriage. These state-generated and state-regulated laws specifically define the privileges of marriage. These privileges may or may not be applicable in other states.

Consider the following. Suppose that because of your academic path, you reside in a different state than your "home" state. During the summer months, you and your fiancé marry in your home state, and then return to school in a different state. Perhaps the state in which you marry has different marriage and family laws than the state in which you later reside. Once you move to another state, your marriage is subject to the laws of the state that you now live in.

The most relevant example that illustrates the impact of state-by-state regulation of marriage is the cases of same-sex couples that marry in Massachusetts or Connecticut then move to a different state. Under current federal and state marriage laws, marriage must be recognized by all other states. When these current federal and state laws were enacted, however, lawmakers did not anticipate the possibility of same-sex unions, and those same laws conflict with laws in some states that prohibit same-sex marriage. For example, while the residents of Massachusetts may approve of same-sex marriages, the residents of a more conservative state might not. Because marriage and family laws are left in the hands of individual states, same-sex marriages most likely will not be recognized

THERE are a number of rights and privileges associated with marriage that gay men and lesbian partners desire to have as well, such as being allowed to care for or visit their lifemate in the hospital in situations where only "family members" are allowed.

in other states. This has far-reaching ramifications with regard to rights and privileges allowed for married couples. The **Defense of Marriage Act (DOMA)** allows states to choose whether they recognize same-sex marriages as legal unions. This legislation, signed by President Clinton in 1996, forbids federal recognition of same-sex marriages (such as Medicare benefits, Social Security benefits, and income tax benefits that are extended to married couples) (Eskridge & Hunter, 1997). Currently, 38 states recognize DOMA legislation.

Several implied rights and privileges accompany marriage. The following are recognized (although perhaps at varying levels) by all states:

- The right to visit a spouse in the hospital
- The right to make medical decisions on behalf of a spouse in the event that he or she is unable to do so
- The right to joint custody of children
- The right to privileged and confidential communication between spouses
- The right to rear children in a manner the couple deems appropriate (i.e., religious training, education, discipline)
- The right to terminate a marriage according to the laws of the state

Federal and state legislation also provide additional legal benefits to married couples:

- Lower federal income tax rates
- Social Security and Medicare benefits
- Health insurance benefits that cover spouses
- Lower home and auto insurance rates
- Legal protection from domestic violence and abuse

- State-specific inheritance and death benefits for spouses
- The rights associated with the Federal Family Medical Leave Act
- State-specific rights afforded in instances of divorce

THE BENEFITS OF MARRIAGE

In recent years, because of what some Americans perceive as a decline in the moral health of the family and its status in U.S. society, there has been renewed interest in researchers' attempts to discover what accounts for successful marriage and family living. Taken as a whole, the countless empirical studies of marriage indicate that marriage is a beneficial institution across all areas of well-being—in the social and emotional areas, in the cognitive area, and in the physical area of living.

Economic Benefits The adage, "Two can live as cheaply as one," is often true of married couples. For example, married couples often save money by filing federal and state taxes jointly, and owning one house or renting one apartment is cheaper than owning or renting two dwellings.

Professor of economics at George Washington University, David Ribar (2003) cites a substantial body of research that consistently demonstrates that the average annual incomes and financial assets are greater among married couple households than for unmarried adults or for nonmarried cohabitation couples. In his article, "What Do Social Scientists Know about the Benefits of Marriage?," Ribar also suggests additional reasons that married people fare better economically than single adults.

- Marriage allows for **specialization**, in which each spouse can take on tasks and concentrate on those things they do well (for example, he may like to do light carpentry while she may like to do yard work).
- Marriage allows for **instrumental support**, in which husband and wife both boost the well-being, productivity, and career of their spouse. For example, in some families, a husband may willingly take over the lion's share of parenting, household chores, and meal preparation while his wife works at her executive-level position at a bank. His pitching in increases her productivity because she does not have to stop and tend to the other details of their lives. As another example, if one spouse becomes ill, the other spouse steps in and takes on the roles and responsibilities of the spouse who is ill. In both examples, the benefits to the spouses are reciprocal.
- The life commitment of marriage provides **stability**—especially for men. According to Ribar, this stability allows men to mature, making them more likely to find a job and think toward the future instead of engaging in risk-taking behaviors, such as drug and alcohol abuse. Marriage results in a feeling of interdependent financial responsibility to one another. Thus, married men and women are more likely to accept and maintain jobs that may not be all that personally rewarding, but are in the best interest of the couple/family in the way of economic rewards.
- Marriage provides **status**. Because many employers today are "traditional" in their beliefs, they tend to pay married men and women at a higher rate than single men and women. According to Ribar, this discrimination toward unmarried men allows for great economic gain and greater economic opportunities for married men, thereby affording them and their families a certain status unmarried individuals do not have.

Health Benefits Married people are also healthier than nonmarried individuals (Ribar, 2003). Research studies have found, for example, that marriage appears to prolong mental acuity and functioning and is associated with more vitality in women over age 60 (Michael, Berkman, Colditz, & Kawachi, 2001). Also, married men tend to be healthier than unmarried men. Some research suggests that married men are healthier because their wives nurture them and provide "tender loving care" for them (Maushart, 2002).

Children's Benefits Children from homes with married parents fare better in their overall health and well-being, behavior, emotions, and school success (including reading scores and math achievement) than children living in non-marital cohabiting homes, formerly married parents, stepfamilies, or single-parent homes (Cherlin and others, 1995; Dawson, 1991; Ehrle, Kortenkamp, & Stagner, 2003; Ginther & Pollak, 2003; Mauldon, 1992). Researchers also found that regarding poverty and the availability of and access to material goods, children living in nonmarital cohabiting homes, with single parents, or with foster parents or legal guardians, fare worse than children who live in a home where parents are married (Lerman, 2002a, 2002b).

Note that not every married couple will end up with happy, well-adjusted children nor will all children end up in poverty because they're being raised by single parents. Research does not present an all-inclusive picture; it does, however, present indicators. And research suggests that marriage is not simply a private bond made between two people who love and care for one another, but it also is a matter of great interest to federal and state governments—because *marriage matters* to adults, children, and society.

The Transition to Marriage: Why It's So Tough

Marriage is hard work! Although we may start our marriages vowing "I do," most married people will tell you that very soon, those words are replaced with "I won't," or "I can't," or "You do it!," or "Are you kidding?!"

The very nature of marriage requires that the relationship be continuously negotiated. While meeting the needs of their spouses, people often need to meet the needs of their children and employers. In the midst of meeting everyone's needs, many spouses forget to have their own needs met. While everyone may have the best of intentions when they marry, sooner or later, juggling everything conspires against even the most stable couples and competes for their already-divided attention. Even without the different responsibilities and stresses that accompany marriage, newlywed couples soon find out (often before the bills for the ceremony are paid) that they must establish strategies for negotiating and navigating marital life.

TIMES of disagreement are common as couples transition to married life. Do you think conflict is inevitable? Do you think conflict is healthy?

FORMING A NEW FAMILY SYSTEM

Before we discuss the transitions that are inherent in adapting to married life, let's revisit two key concepts presented in previous chapters. Recall from Chapter 1 that the *Family Life Cycle* is a paradigm that allows us to view the multiple entrances and exits that individuals make within the family of origin, such as young adults leaving home for college, or, as it pertains to our discussion here, forming a new family of origin as young adults marry. This paradigm helps depict not only the changes in the *structure* of the family but also certain insights into *emotional transitions* and other related changes in the family status.

Along with the family life cycle paradigm, consider the *family systems* theoretical model discussed in Chapter 3. Recall that in order to truly understand the interactions that take place in marriage and in family life, we must consider the concept of wholeness—the concept of *interconnection* that speaks to how we affect and are affected by each member of the family. Using this paradigm, we need instead to view marriage as a newly formed system (the joined couple).

The paradigm is helpful on two counts. First, it allows us to think about marriage in a broader context, beyond its traditional meaning of procreation and socialization. Specifically, it allows us to consider same-sex couples who pledge a long-term commitment to each other, and it allows us to take into account other family forms, such as stable, committed cohabiting relationships (Anderson & Sabatelli, 2007). We also use this paradigm to examine all of the components and relationship processes that make up the new subsystem (regardless of relationship type or sexual orientation). For example, consider two people from two different families of origin with two distinct experiences with marriage. These two people have distinct ways of communicating and resolving conflict. They also have two very different sets of expectations about what the relationship will provide them. Given these dissimilarities, consider what needs to be accomplished in order for the new family subsystem to be incorporated into the other existing family systems (each member of the couple's family of origin) (see Figure 8.8).

By integrating the Family Life Cycle and the Family Systems theories, we have before us a working model of why the transition to marriage (and married life, for that matter) is a difficult road for many young couples. As you will see in the following discussion, there are developmental tasks associated with forming a new family system. These include establishing marital roles, establishing marital boundaries, managing the house and money, and fostering a marital emotional climate.

DEVELOPMENTAL TASKS IN THE NEW FAMILY SYSTEM

In Chapter 3, we discussed the family as a dynamic system that undergoes growth throughout its lifecourse. Just as an individual has experiences throughout his or her lifespan that both meet and fail to meet expectations, so, too, does a family system. For example, during the developmental phase of young adulthood, most young men and women accomplish the developmental task of learning to nurture not just themselves but also the emotional and physical needs of their friends, family, and those whom they love. At this point in lifespan development, most young men and women also experience interdependence, mutuality, and reciprocity in mature relationships. Many of them marry. These newly married couples must then navigate their way through a new phase of the Family Life Cycle as they negotiate the developmental tasks of their newly formed family. Marriage and family practitioners and researchers, Stephen Anderson and Ronald Sabatelli (2007) describe the number of transitions that newly married couples must negotiate.

FIGURE 8.8   A Newly Formed Subsystem

When a couple marries and forms a family of choice, they bring with them to their new marriage interaction patterns and ways of relating to their new system, their family of choice.

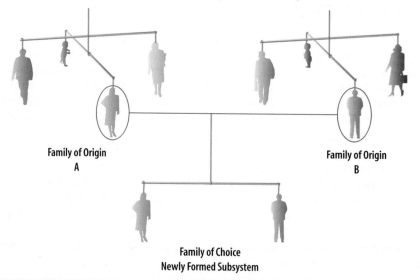

Family of Origin
A

Family of Origin
B

Family of Choice
Newly Formed Subsystem

Establishing Marital Roles Recall from earlier discussions that within our families of origin and within our daily lives, each of us has roles we play. When we take on a role, we take on the rules or expectations that society assigns to that role. When we join together in a marriage or other lifelong committed relationship, we tend to take on the roles society dictates. A **conjugal role** is a culturally defined, culturally assigned set of behaviors (for instance, behaviors related to housekeeping, childrearing, and work outside the home) each spouse is expected to carry out.

As we grow up, our own family of origin shapes and plays a large part in the roles we will take on in our intimate relationships. For instance, imagine a woman reared in a home where the father goes to work each day while the mother stays home to care for the children, clean the house, and prepare meals. A woman raised in this environment may, from a very young age, want nothing more in her adult life than to be a mother and a wife. She would marry with a preconceived, ready-set of expectations of her roles and her husband's roles. If her husband was reared in a similar background, then their expectations of marriage would initially reinforce how they felt about each other and their relationship. When marital roles (reality) match our predetermined notions (expectations), the early years of marriage may be relatively uncomplicated. But, when the reality of conjugal roles does not line up with socialized expectations, a rocky road lies ahead. For this reason those intending to marry or make a lifelong commitment should know from the start what roles they expect their partner to fulfill, and what roles they intend to fulfill in that relationship. Anderson and Sabatelli (2007) suggest that same-sex couples experience greater stress during their transition to a lifelong partnership because of ambiguity or uncertainty about conjugal roles.

Establishing Marital Boundaries Recall from Chapter 3 that all systems must maintain boundaries in order to distinguish them from other systems and from their environment. Marriage is one of these systems. Anderson and Sabatelli (2007) explain that when people marry, they expect to be the primary recipient of their partner's loyalty and devotion. To secure this relationship, some sort of boundary structure must be put into place that incorporates family and friends each partner brings into the relationship. To establish these boundaries, couples must negotiate such things as how often they should get together for dinner or other activities with parents, friends, and other family members. They also need to discuss whether it is acceptable to discuss intimate, personal details about married life with family and friends.

With most couples, each spouse has different expectations, which often depend on how each is socialized within his or her family of origin. For instance, the wife's family may not gather for every major (and minor) holiday, and they may not disclose as much as the husband is accustomed to. The husband's family, on the other hand, may gather for meals every Sunday. If the wife has different expectations and isn't used to so much contact, this behavior may cause conflict.

Managing the House and the Money Determining who takes on which household responsibilities is an important negotiation that should take place early in the marriage—and be revisited as the needs of the family change. According to Anderson and Sabatelli (2007), this issue boils down to three primary factors:

1. *Gender socialization.* Recall from Chapter 4 our discussion about how males and females are socialized to perform different tasks within society. Typically, spouses' ideas of what men's household tasks should be and what women do tend to fall along traditionally held beliefs. Women take care of the cleaning, cooking, and childrearing, while men take care of the lawn, taking out the trash, and household and automotive repairs.
2. *Abilities and expertise.* Whether or not my husband would be willing to do the laundry is not important; what is important is that he is not allowed to be anywhere near the laundry room! While early in the marriage he had the best intentions and was sincere in his efforts to do this household task, only a few ruined loads of laundry were folded before we mutually decided he did not possess the ability to perform this chore. Similarly, while I

Peer Marriages

Is there a way to make love last? According to Pepper Schwartz (1994, 2001), professor of sociology at the University of Washington, prolific author, and international speaker on relationship topics, today's couples are changing the rules about traditional marriage. Schwartz calls this increasingly popular couple type among married couples **peer marriages**.

Unlike traditional couples where the man and woman live by traditionally socialized gender behaviors (and thus, according to Schwartz, live separate but parallel lives), peer couples collaborate, not only in their love relationships but also in day-to-day household tasks, parenting, and managing family finances. According to Schwartz, by "reshuffling" gender relations and behaviors, peer partners foster profound intimacy, closeness, and respect within their marriage. With peer marriages, each partner feels the relationship is fair, and that it supports the emotional needs of both. Indeed, hallmarks of peer marriages are the concepts of *equity* and *fairness:* Each partner is thought to be vital to the relationship. It is this collaboration from which deep friendship and companionship grow.

There are four characteristics of peer marriages that distinguish them from traditional marriages, where men dominate decision-making and women assume childrearing responsibilities (Schwartz, 1994, 2001):

1. Marriage is not always 50-50. Peer marriage partners do not believe that marriages have to have an equal split of responsibilities; instead, as Schwartz found, couples ask themselves, "What wouldn't get done if I didn't do it?"—and they do it without getting angry or resenting the other spouse for not pitching in.
2. When it comes to important decisions (such as major financial decisions or relocating for career opportunities), both partners believe the other has an equal say, an equal influence.
3. Both partners know they have equal control of the family's budget, and both partners have equal access to the family's earnings. Schwartz contends that comments such as, "I'll do that if he'll let me" or "I don't know if she'll let me" are red flags and indicate equal control is not given.
4. Each partner's work is given equal weight in the couple's life plans—one person's work isn't automatically sacrificed for the other person's. Furthermore, the person who works the least hours outside of the home or who earns the lesser amount isn't necessarily the one who takes on the most household tasks or child-care responsibilities.

have great interest in our family's financial picture, I do not have the expertise that he does when it comes to managing the monthly budget or investments.

3. *Power and control.* In many marriages, one spouse may exert more power and control than the other. In these cases, the spouse with the most power will hand over "low-status" tasks (such as cleaning out the litter box or doing the dishes) to the other partner.

Fostering a Healthy Emotional Climate When couples marry, most expect their emotional and physical needs to be met by a spouse. But do spouses realize that they must also meet the needs of their partner? A difficult developmental task for newlywed couples is finding a balance between meeting their own needs as well as those of their spouse. As they learn to juggle these needs, they learn to foster and maintain intimacy and love as they develop a sexual identity (this is referred to as a *sexual script*), communication patterns, and conflict management strategies.

The magnitude of the transition into married life is far-reaching. The multiple, complex processes of marriage (intimacy, finances, sexuality, juggling the responsibilities of work and

The FAMILY Table

Near peers are couples or marriage partners who believe in equality, though when children are born, or to maximize the family's finances, the male often assumes less responsibility for the children.

But if peer marriages are so wonderful, why doesn't everyone have one—or, at the very least, why doesn't every couple strive to be a peer couple? Schwartz looks at the costs and benefits. Yes, peer marriages are rewarding in that they provide a unique intimacy for couples. But there are also costs:

1. There is often little validation and social support for peer marriages. Society (family, friends, co-workers, outsiders) questions the couple's marriage role philosophy.
2. Peer couples have to redefine "successful" marriage, because traditional marriage defines successful marriage along traditional male/female gender roles.
3. Other couples frequently feel resentful of peer marriages. Because peer couples tend to be dedicated to their marriage and to parenting their children, they oftentimes will not engage in spouse "put-downs" with their family and friends. This makes others feel excluded.
4. The sexual dynamics of peer marriages are quite different from those in traditional marriages. Peer couples experience much intimacy on a day-to-day basis. Schwartz contends that because of this everyday intimacy, they have to work harder to find eroticism in their relationship.
5. There is no template for peer marriages, so all of their experiences are by trial and error.

TALK ABOUT IT

1. Of the three couple types—traditional, near peer, or peer—which one will you and your partner/spouse most likely adopt? Why?
2. Do you see potential rewards associated with peer marriages that Schwartz did not address? If so, what? Do you see potential costs associated with peer marriage that Schwartz did not address?
3. In your opinion, what is the future landscape of marriage: Do you think more and more couples will continue to strive for and achieve peer marriages, or do you think that couples will continue to adopt traditional marital roles?

Sources: Schwartz (1994, 2001).

home, communication, etc.) indicate how difficult the transition to marriage is (McGoldrick & Carter, 1999).

THE CHALLENGES OF BLENDING CULTURE AND RELIGION IN MARRIAGE

Our concepts of family and marriage are undergoing many quick-paced changes. An indicator of the rapid changes occurring in the structure of marriage and other intimate pair bond relationships is the increase in **heterogamous** interpersonal relationships—partnering with someone who is dissimilar to you in one or more dimensions, such as race, religious background, age, or values systems and beliefs. In this section, we examine some of the changes that are giving marriage a new face and a new set of circumstances to negotiate over time.

Interracial Marriage In an **interracial** couple, the partners are of different races. More often than not, racial differences go hand-in-hand with cultural and ethnic differences, so couples of different races face potential struggles on three fronts. Xuanning Fu, Heather Tora, and Jessika Kendall (2001), social science researchers from Brigham Young University, define culture as a "learned orientation of 'way of life,'" and a "social heritage that includes values, norms, [and] institutions . . . that are passed from generation to generation" (p. 47). The authors note that interracial/intercultural/interethnic marriages are also inherently accompanied by these distinct racial traditions, attitudes, and behaviors.

Historically, interracial unions were viewed as a threat to the continuation of a society because of the "racial impurity" that would result if children were produced within a racially mixed union. *Miscegenation* is a term used in the mid-1800s to describe the "mixed race" offspring produced by interracial couples. In 1967, the U.S. Supreme Court ruled that miscegenation laws violated the civil rights of U.S. citizens and were unconstitutional. For the first time in U.S. history, couples of different races were legally allowed to wed.

Since the 1967 U.S. Supreme Court's ruling that annulled miscegenation laws, over 2.5 million interracial couples have wed. This number accounts for approximately 7.5 percent of all marriages in the United States; it is up from 2.6 percent in 2000 (U.S. Census Bureau, 2010). Table 8.1 shows us the number of white, African American/Black Caribbean, and Asian interracial couples in the United States. When viewing these numbers, it is important to note a couple of important factors. First, these statistics do not take into account ethnic groups within the same broad categories. For example, a marriage involving a person of Japanese origin and a person of Korean origin would not be considered an interracial marriage. Also, Hispanic status is not considered.

Researchers theorize that because today's youth have grown up with an ideology that supports racial integration, they are "more color-blind than their elders when it comes to matters of the heart" (Padgett & Sikora, 2003). It is therefore likely that the number of interracial unions will continue to rise. There are a number of factors that influence the trends in interracial/intercultural/interethnic marriages.

Who Intermarries? Sociologist Zhenchao Qian (1999) believes that the increase in interracial marriages indicates a decline in racism. Interracial marriages are highest among Latina, Asian, and American women, and among African American and Caucasian men (Kenney, 2002). According to Qian (1999), several factors affect those who intermarry:

- **Educational attainment.** According to Qian, when people share the same level of educational attainment, they are more likely to intermarry.
- **Immigration status.** Those who are born outside the United States and then immigrate here are less likely to intermarry than those who are of different racial, ethnic, or cultural backgrounds who are born here.
- **Region of residence.** Those who live in the West or the Northeast of the United States are more likely to intermarry than those in the South or the Midwest. Coupled with the more conservative leanings in the South and Midwest and the more liberal leanings in the Northeast and Northwest is the fact that these regions of the country have fewer minorities residing there, lessening the opportunity to meet someone of a different race.

TABLE 8.1 Married Couples in the United States, 2006, by Race

	White Wife	Black Wife	Hispanic Wife	Other Wife
White Husband	42.6	0.15	1.0	0.9
Black Husband	0.4	3.9	0.09	0.1
Hispanic Husband	1.0	0.04	6.2	0.09
Other Husband	0.6	0.03	0.07	3.2

Source: U.S. Census Bureau Table FG4: Married Couple Family Groups, by Presence of Own Children/1 In Specific Age Groups, and Age, Earnings, Education, and Race and Hispanic Origin/2 of Both Spouses: 2010.

Challenges for Contemporary Interracial Couples Interracial couples face the same marital challenges and stresses as couples of the same race, with one significant difference: Mixed-race couples must deal with how others perceive their union (Kenney, 2002). Key to interracial couples' marital happiness is the degree to which the couple receives social support for their relationship. For the marriage to be successful, each couple must be aware, before they marry, of how their marriage may be perceived by others with regard to racial issues (Kenney, 2002). Even with this in mind, by and large the research evidence suggests that interracial marriage is more difficult than same-race marriage every step of the way because of the limited social support—and often limited family support—these couples receive.

Fu and colleagues' (2001) examination of interracial marriages, for example, found strong evidence that racial differences have a negative effect on marital happiness. Specifically, the authors maintain that it is not the cultural differences per se that affect marital happiness. Rather, they believe the marriages appear to be affected *domestically* on two counts: cultural lifestyle and the spouses' expectations of marital life formed throughout childhood and adolescence. Kristen Goodman (1991), interfaith marriage researcher, also found that in regard to racial and ethnic differences, understanding and responding to a spouse's expectations for the marriage are key factors in overall marital happiness and satisfaction, and that similarity of cultural backgrounds affects expectations for marriage. Goodman differs from Fu and colleagues, though, in her contention that cultural differences *do* affect marital happiness; she maintains that marital expectations are based on socialization to marriage that takes place through childhood.

Because we live in a largely race-based society, it is important for educators, social workers, family life practitioners, clergy, mental health professionals, and other providers of human services to understand the heritages of the families they serve, to avoid uninformed characterizations of biracial families and children. By seeking to understand the diversity among the populations we serve, we can better transcend negative attitudes and conceptualizations about biracial families and children (Glass & Wallace, 1996). Biracial children form their identities through the multiple influences of family and community (recall Bronfenbrenner's Ecological Model of human development from Chapter 1), and because of this, human service providers should support them in ways that allow them to feel a sense of pride, and to embrace all of their heritages (Chiong, 1998).

Interfaith Marriage When people of different religious faiths marry (for example, when a Christian marries a Hindu), their union is called an **interfaith marriage**. **Intrafaith marriages** are those in which individuals adhere to the same religion but may have different beliefs or follow different traditions within that faith (such as a Baptist who marries a Presbyterian).

Throughout history and in most societies, marrying outside of a person's religion was strictly forbidden. Although some contemporary societies no longer forbid interfaith marriages, some research indicates that marrying outside of a person's religion sometimes carries with it consequences such as being ostracized from the family and/or church community, disinheritance, or both (Ross & Ross, 2004). In contemporary America, however, with its increasingly diverse population and with a growing acceptance of others' differences, more couples are moving beyond the pre-established social norm of marrying only within their own religion. Finding even an approximate number of those with interfaith marriages is difficult, because in many instances, one marriage partner will convert to the faith of the other partner, either before marriage or when children are born into the marriage. As of the 1990 Jewish Population Survey, the rate of intermarriage among the Jewish faith was 52 percent. Ross and Ross estimate that at least 60 percent of Catholics today are married to non-Catholics.

Potential Difficulties Despite the promise of these limited findings and evidence that among today's college students four out of five wholeheartedly support interfaith unions

A couple who shares different faith beliefs faces a number of potential difficulties in their marriage, but there are many ways for these couples to strengthen their relationships.

(Knox, 2002), there are potential difficulties that interfaith couples may encounter. In some instances, when couples are first in love, it is easy to gloss over religious differences. Some find that as they near the wedding ceremony, which may bring to light some immediate differences in beliefs and values, the challenge begins. One woman in a Christian-Hindu marriage provides for us a glimpse into the difficulties faced in her relationship:

> Each family wants its own religious [wedding] rite . . . what normally marks the coming together of two families can become the first sign of division . . . Would I fit into [their religious] culture? Was I willing to accept the joint family and the loss of self it entailed? How would I cope in this community? . . . Practice of my own religion was in question . . . Would I have to play down my own familiar religious celebrations? Would this [marriage] affect my religious affiliation? (Gajuwala, 2004)

As this woman illustrates, combining faiths presents yet one more challenge that a couple must explore and resolve together. Forming a new religious identity while making the joint transition to marriage may also require individual soul-searching and discovery.

Strengthening Interfaith Marriages Although the challenges are many and potentially great, there are suggestions to help interfaith couples strengthen their marital unions:

- Understand both the traditions of your faith as well as those of your partner's faith (Gruzen, 1990).
- Do not try to push your spouse into converting to your faith; a noncoercive, nonmanipulative family environment is important (Gruzen, 1990).
- Be sensitive to cross-cultural issues by encouraging a relationship between the two religious communities (Mayer, 1987).
- Recognize that a spouse's religion is not just something he or she participates in, but it is something that is a part of him or her (Mayer, 1987).
- Before marriage, discuss how children will be reared in a religion (Gruzen, 1990; Mayer, 1987).

Marriages built on love, shared interests, and mutual respect are destined to become stronger and deeper with time. Regardless of the challenges, if couples work together, they greatly improve their chances for a long and enduring life together.

Satisfying Marriages

In preparation for writing and teaching about marriage, I did a bit of my own impromptu research; I purchased several bridal magazines to try to get a glimpse into how the media portray marriage today. While the purpose of these magazines is, indeed, to "sell" *weddings*, there is little content that addresses how to enter *marriage*. Consider, for example, the titles of the articles dealing with marriage (what one magazine called the "Heart to Heart" section):

- "Real Love: Planning your Big Day"
- "Honeymoon How-To's"
- "The Newlywed Rulebook"—with helpful marriage tips such as "humor us while we play matchmaker for your single friends"

With the articles' emphasis on the fairytale event and the romantic getaway that follows, it is understandable how and why people today spend many months and thousands upon thousands of dollars planning for a one-day celebration of love, but not nearly the same investment in preparation for their actual *marriage*. What the magazines don't tell you is that sooner or later the honeymoon must come to an end, and when the reality of marriage kicks into full gear many couples find they are unprepared. The question then becomes: Is it really possible to plan for the perfect marriage? How can we *predict* beforehand those marriages that will be successful?

PREMARITAL COUPLE TYPES

As early as the 1930s, social scientists and family practitioners have tried to determine what factors were associated with successful marriage (Fowers, Montel, & Olson, 1996). These efforts continue today as researchers seek to find ways to curb the high incidence of divorce. A host of investigations into marital process repeatedly demonstrates that the quality of couples' premarital relationship is predictive of marital satisfaction and stability (Fowers & Olson, 1986; Larsen & Olson, 1989). By knowing and better understanding those factors that contribute to or detract from marital adjustment and marital satisfaction, family scientists and family practitioners are able to develop premarital educational and counseling programs to enhance couples' relationships—and ameliorate the current trends in divorce.

In studying the correlation between premarital relationships and subsequent marital outcomes, family practitioner and marriage therapist Blaine Fowers and his colleagues (1996) developed typologies of premarital couples in order to assess premarital relationship quality. According to Fowers, their study suggested that when relationship difficulties were identified before marriage, high-risk couples might "reconsider their marriage plans." Fowers' typologies comprise several types of couples.

- *Vitalized couples.* These couples are characterized by high levels of overall relationship satisfaction, self-disclosing, and sharing feelings. They also have high levels of expressing affection and sexuality. They have equal roles and often emphasize religion in their marriages.
- *Harmonious couples.* These couples experience moderate levels of relationship satisfaction, and have the ability to resolve conflict. They feel comfortable with their levels of self-disclosure.

Marriage Models

Marriage models are marriages we have seen or have experienced that influence and deeply affect our way of thinking about marriage (Quilliam, 2005). Marriage models are those of our parents, relatives, friends, co-workers, community members, or perhaps a previous marriage of our own.

From your experiences with marriage models,

1. Are there marriage models that you will replicate someday in your own committed relationship? If so, why did you choose this/these marriage models? What characteristics do these marriage models have that you wish to someday have?

2. Are there marriage models that you will *not* replicate someday? If so, what characteristics do these marriage models have that you hope to someday avoid in your own committed relationship?

- *Traditional couples.* Among these couples there is strength in decision making and planning, but there is a bit of dissatisfaction with a partner's personality and habits. There are moderate levels of relationship dissatisfaction.
- *Conflicted couples.* These couples are characterized by communication problems and difficulties in their sexual relationship. They also experience difficulties in relating to a partner's family and friends, and in participating in joint activities.

In a follow-up group studied by Fowers and his colleagues, conflicted couples made up almost one-half of the separated or divorced couples. Conflicted couples were also three times more likely to break off their engagements and cancel the wedding as were vitalized couples. Harmonious couples divorced or separated twice as often as traditional couples. Vitalized couples had the highest overall marital satisfaction.

MARITAL COUPLE TYPES

Just as researchers developed premarital typologies to better understand marital adjustment factors for the purpose of developing education programs, researchers have also developed marital couple typologies with a similar goal—to determine marital satisfaction.

Couple Types Mary Anne Fitzpatrick, recognized as a leading scholar in family and marital communication, has done extensive research in the area of different couple types. Fitzpatrick's findings revealed that some types of married couples consistently report higher levels of marital satisfaction than other couple types. Some of the differences among couple types revolved around their levels of self-disclosure, the way they communicate their emotions and feelings to one another, the manner in which they handle conflict, and whether their expectations of the relationship are fulfilled.

Traditional Couples **Traditional couple** types adhere to conventional beliefs about marriage. These couples are interdependent in their relationship and prefer to be less independent and self-sufficient than the other marital types. Traditional couples place emphasis on self-disclosing and sharing, and often convey their positive feelings about each other and their relationship more than the other couple types. Although these couples tend not to be assertive, they do deal with conflict as it arises in the relationship because of the high value they place on relationship stability. Of all the couple typologies, traditional couples report the highest level of marital satisfaction (Fitzpatrick, 1988; Fitzpatrick & Best, 1979; Kelley, 1999).

Independents Like traditional couples, **independent couple** types value closeness, companionship, sharing, and self-disclosure (although they do not disclose quite as much as traditional couples). Unlike traditionals, independent couples are not as conventional in their beliefs about marriage. Perhaps one thing that best distinguishes independents from traditional couples is their competitiveness, or the need for "one-upmanship" (outdoing the other or controlling the other). This couple typology reports lower levels of marital satisfaction than traditional couple types do.

Separates Individuals in **separate couple** types are less willing to relinquish their autonomy than those in traditional and independent couple types. This couple type reports lower levels of self-disclosure and sharing, and as a result, experiences psychological distance. Separate couples do not share the levels of companionship as the other two couple types, and they tend to share less positive feelings about their spouse and about their relationship than the other couple types do. This couple type avoids conflict. According to Fitzpatrick, this couple type scores the lowest in marital satisfaction among all couple types.

Mixed In a **mixed couple** type, the spouses differ in their marital types. For example, one spouse may have the expectations and characteristics of a traditional couple, whereas the other spouse may have expectations typical of an individual couple type. Overall, mixed couple types place importance on affection within the marriage and will compromise when necessary. If the mixed couple type is the common traditional/separate type, marital satisfaction is similar to that found in traditional couples.

Examining marital couple types and the correlation between couple types and marital satisfaction helps researchers predict which types of marriages are more likely to end in divorce and which are more likely to succeed. For example, researchers have found that in couple types where the man is pessimistic and has negative feelings and emotions (common in traditional and conflicted premarital types), marital satisfaction is much lower—and divorce is much higher (Gee, Scott, Castellani, & Cordova, 2002). Fowers and his colleagues (1996) perhaps best sum up the importance as they conclude,

> Divorce has become a crucial social problem with serious consequences for the physical and mental well-being of spouses and children. Marriage and family therapists cannot afford to focus solely on alleviating the discomfort of distressed couples or members of divorced families. It is important . . . to work proactively to help couples build strong and lasting relationships. And by understanding those factors and those couple types more prone to divorce, this goal is better accomplished.

Marital Satisfaction and Happiness How do marital satisfaction and happiness change over time? This area of family life has been studied since the 1920s, and many decades of research since then has shown us that the quality of marriages tends to decline over time (among many, Anderson, Russell, & Schumm, 1983; Karney & Bradbury, 1997; Orbuch, House, Mero, & Webster, 1996; Sternberg, 1986). If we were to quickly sketch out a graph of the level of marital satisfaction and happiness across the lifespan of a marriage, it would look like a U-shaped curve. If we use the U-shaped curve as a guide, we can see how the lifespan of marriage follows a pattern. For example, first marriages tend to begin with peak levels of satisfaction, happiness, and positive outlooks (Karney & Bradbury, 1997). After the honeymoon, when the realities of marriage begin to set in and the euphoria associated with the wedding day and honeymoon wanes, when passionate love begins to give way to companionate love, we see levels of marital satisfaction, happiness, and positive outlooks begin to decline (Sternberg, 1986). This does not mean that one spouse is no longer in love with the other spouse; it simply means that the realities of day-to-day living make it impossible to continue on with a "mountaintop" marital existence.

One body of research suggests that the decline in marital happiness is quite steep during the first several years of marriage, particularly during the first seven years or so (Kovacs, 1983). Similar research also found that marital satisfaction rapidly declines during the first four years of marriage; it then stabilizes for a time, then declines again steeply through the eighth year of marriage (Kurdek, 1999). One family theorist, Wesley Burr (1970), examined couples' satisfaction with different aspects of marriage over the lifecourse and found that marital happiness, marital satisfaction, and overall marital quality are at their lowest level when children begin to arrive. These levels stay relatively low until the children enter adolescence and are "launched" (move away). One body of research (Belsky, Woodworth, & Crnic, 1996) notes that the decline in marital quality during the parenting years is due to the stressors associated with the demands on parents' time, energy, and money. Recent research tends to support prior studies, but only to a certain extent. Results from a survey of over 700 married study participants show that, over time, marital quality tends to decline, rebounds a bit, then tapers off again—the steep upward trend is not seen as in previous research (Anderson, Doherty, & Van Ryzin, 2008).

It is important to point out, however, that most of the research about marital satisfaction is tied to the Family Life Cycle paradigm, and the research conclusions may not necessarily be representative of all families. For example, divorced couples are not included in marital satisfaction research; because of this, marital satisfaction levels go up because the curve is only representing those couples who are still married and more satisfied (Miller, 2001). In addition to the lack of inclusion of divorced families, the Family Life Cycle paradigm does not consider the variations in today's complex families, such as childless couples, single parents, and cohabitors; it also doesn't account for differences in couples' religious beliefs, remarriage, economic status, education, attitudes toward marriage, and racial and ethnic differences (Anderson and others, 2008). When taking all of these factors into consideration, recent research suggests that there are actually five different marital quality trajectories: Some couples experience high levels of marital satisfaction and maintain that over time; others start high and experience the common U-shaped decline; others start low and remain fairly steady; and others start somewhat low and further decline (Anderson and others, 2008). Many other aspects of family living, such as the couple's involvement with their extended family, and physical and emotional changes in the marriage partners are all ignored by the Family Life Cycle as potential contributors to marital satisfaction. Because of this, the Family Life Cycle alone cannot be used to explain why there are changes in marital satisfaction over the lifespan of the marriage (Miller, 2001).

At this point you might be thinking, "What's the use? If the research says we're going to be so miserable after we marry and have children, why marry—or why have children?" All hope is not lost; Burr's (1970, 1973) research revealed that as children enter into adolescence, marital quality begins to climb and continues to do so as each child leaves the nest. As the couple enters late middle adulthood and late adulthood, levels of marital quality and marital satisfaction reach levels that nearly rival the peak levels at which marriage begins.

The consistency of the research findings brings into focus what all couples, married or contemplating marriage, need to know: "Marriage is not a single life event but . . . a set of stages" (Kurdek, 1999, pp. 1283–1284). In other words, although marriage may begin with peaks of happiness, satisfaction, and positive feelings toward a spouse, these levels of marital quality *will* change. In all likelihood, the first seven or eight years of marriage *will* bring a decline in marital happiness; children *will* bring different stressors to marriages, and while they live at home, marital interaction *will* change. There are periods of parenting when marital happiness stabilizes, but overall levels of marital satisfaction typically *will not* begin to increase until they children grow older and eventually leave home. Kurdek concludes that "instances of marital distress might be mitigated by spouses' *expecting and being prepared for* 'normal' periods of decline in marital quality." Stated another way: Marriage should be entered into with realistic expectations.

REALISTIC EXPECTATIONS

When entering into a marital relationship, perhaps wedding vows should reflect the reality of hassled, day-to-day married life rather than the idealized, traditional vows that were exchanged by the couple in the opening vignette of this chapter. In the 1980s movie, *She's Having a Baby*, the nervous groom thinks he hears the priest reciting these vows:

> Will thou, Jefferson, have this woman to be thou wedded wife? Will thou comfort her and keep her, in sickness and in health? Will thou provide her with credit cards, and a four bedroom/two and one-half bath home with central air conditioning and professional decorating, and two weeks in the Bahamas every spring? Will thou try to remember the little things that mean so much, like flowers on your anniversary, a kind word when she's had a bad day, and an occasional "Gee honey, you look pretty today"? . . . Will thou listen to stories about kids' colds, kitchen tile . . . and check-book covers?

Those who are married could add a litany of things to these "wedding vows" that speak to the *reality* of married life. We've mentioned the importance of entering a marriage with realistic expectations. But what should those expectations be? How do these expectations help a couple achieve better marital satisfaction?

If you choose to marry, what will your priorities be? Perhaps companionship or friendship? Do you anticipate a marriage with children? A marriage partner who shares your dreams and life goals? And a marriage that is united in purpose and direction?

When any couple enters into marriage, they inevitably have **relational expectancies**—key factors in marital satisfaction and longevity of their marriage. These expectations that couples have for their marriage and their spouses develop throughout the course of their lives.

Throughout this book, we have seen how our family of origin influences who we are. In the same way, our experiences with our parents' marital history and our own past relational experiences impact and influence our expectancies. Lifespan psychologist Mary Levitt (1991) developed the **Social Expectations Model**, which illustrates how spouses' expectations of marital relationships are based on past relationship interactions with the spouse. This model also takes into account the influence of societal norms (such as women being caregivers and men being providers) on spousal expectations. Both factors help shape our expectancies for married life.

The degree to which relational expectancies are met or violated affects marital satisfaction. Levitt's model examines the link between expectations and marital satisfaction. Her model takes into account the fact that because we are human, expectations are set and expectations are going to be tested within a marriage. Levitt found that when (not *if*) relational expectancies are tested, one of three outcomes will occur:

1. When a spouse's *expectations are confirmed*, the relationship will remain stable. For example, everyone enters into marriage expecting a spouse to be faithful and loyal. Suppose a wife is on a business trip with an attractive, single man. The spouse's expectation is that his wife will not cheat. Once the expectation is tested and confirmed, the marriage remains stable.
2. When a spouse's *expectations are violated*, it has a negative effect on the relationship. Consider the same example of a spouse's loyalty or faithfulness. Assume that when the expectation was tested, the spouse did cheat and have an affair. This violation will destabilize the relationship.
3. When the relationship *expectations are tested* and the spouse's expectations are exceeded, the highest levels of marital satisfaction are reached.

In a study that examined Mary Fitzpatrick's couple types and relational expectancy, traditional couples had the highest level of marital satisfaction because they had the highest levels of met and exceeded relational expectations (Kelley, 1999). Conversely, separate couple types had the highest level of unmet expectations, and hence, lower marital satisfaction.

Expectations *set* versus expectations *met*—can a partner realistically meet the relational expectations that have been set? This appears to be a pivotal issue in marital satisfaction and overall relationship satisfaction.

Family Life Education

Although marriage is a universal experience and sanctioned by all societies the world over, no two couples experience marriage the same way. The marriage experience is influenced and affected by our individual experiences within our families of origin. The experience of marriage is also influenced by our racial, ethnic, cultural, and religious backgrounds. A relational process that undergoes change across time, and a relationship that has a distinct lifecourse of its own, marriage can be experienced as a legal contract, a social contract, a sacred act, or a covenant. Many of you will someday vow to love, honor, and cherish your partner until death parts you, and many of you will someday vow to stick by your partner for "better or worse" or in "sickness and in health," but the divorce trends in the United States indicate that these promises are much easier made than kept.

Empirical evidence indicates that marriage is tougher than most of us anticipate because of the developmental tasks associated with the transition to marital life. Spousal roles must be established and continuously negotiated; marital boundaries need to be created and maintained; along with nurturing a marital emotional climate and countless needs of children, we must also manage the house, bills, and work, as well as a multitude of other daily tasks.

Given the overscheduled nature of contemporary marriages, it is necessary for each partner to enter into the marriage with realistic expectations. The research bears out the notion that, in the end, successful marriages are those marriages where the expectations set and the expectations met are in alignment. While reciting marriage vows, couples acknowledge from the outset that marriage will be anything but a carefree existence. Wedding promises speak to the either/ors in life—either things will be good or they will be bad; either someone will be healthy or someone will be sick; either the bills will be paid or they won't.

But as you will find when you make a lifelong commitment to another, a marital partnership is not about just the good days or the bad days. It's about all the days in between. Some days just *are*—they're not good, they're not bad, they're not great, they're not horrible. They just *are*. When the honeymoon excitement fades to the activities of daily living; when the pressures of daily living tempt us to attack one another instead of attacking the problem; and when it's easier to throw in the towel than to stick to the marital commitment, marital partners need to take a close look at their expectations and determine whether they are asking their spouse to do the impossible.

This is the point where everything we have studied in this book comes together: the experiences of family living, family communication, intimacy, love, experiences of gender, dating, and the other pathways to a committed, lifelong relationship. Each of you has unique, individual experiences within all areas of family life and will probably merge your experiences with another person whose experiences are vastly different. As you enter into a relationship and perhaps marriage, you will have to somehow negotiate and find your way to an interdependent bond that works and is satisfactory and fulfilling for you and your partner.

Hard work? Without a doubt!

Marriage Models

We frequently carry interaction patterns and behaviors from our family of origin to our family of choice when we marry. At times, continuing these behaviors is a deliberate choice; other times, we may not want to interact in ways similar to our parents, but because these patterns are so deeply ingrained in our way of thinking, we carry them into our own marriages. When contemplating marriage, couples must consider the marriage models in their lives and how these have shaped their own attitudes and ideas about marriage.

Her Side: For the most part, the marriage models in my life have been quite positive. My parents have been married for over 25 years, and still today they are warm and affectionate toward each other. My grandparents were married for over 50 years before my grandma died. My parents frequently talk things over, and many times it seems as though they communicate without saying a single word to each other. Of course they've argued—quite passionately at times. But I always get the feeling that they really *enjoy* being married. Divorce? No way. Our religion really frowns on divorce . . . I have a feeling that if they had a bad marriage, they would stay married because of their religious beliefs. I've never given it much thought, but as I look across my family background, there is no divorce in the family tree. I've always wanted a marriage like my parents have. To me, theirs is an "ideal" marriage. I am concerned, because I feel that my fiancé's parents' marriage is a very empty marriage, and void of these things I see in my marriage models.

His Side: My parents' marriage was sometimes good, sometimes bad. I suppose this is how *all* marriages are. Unlike my fiancé's parents, my parents are more independent of one another in their marriage; they do things together, but they are just as content doing things separately from one another. And unlike her side of the family, my side of the family typically doesn't interact a lot with extended family. For example, we seldom have family reunions or celebrate holidays together with them. Yes, there is divorce in our family tree. My fiancé is concerned about this. She thinks that since it has been an acceptable way of handling marital distress in my family background (my sister recently divorced), it might be easier for me to divorce her if things don't work out. It would be fruitless for me to argue that the marriage models in my life have not influenced me. I believe that it is my *choice* whether I adopt their behaviors or not, and that I will not necessarily repeat these behaviors in my own marriage.

Your Side: In your opinion, how will this couple's marriage models influence their marriage? In reaching your decision, consider the following questions:

1. In what ways does each of these partners' marriage models differ? Specifically, what are her marriage model influences? What are his marriage model influences?

2. Do you foresee any potential marital distress ahead for this couple? Why? What areas of their marriage may have difficulty, and why did you choose these specific areas?

3. In your opinion, what things should this couple focus on before they wed?

Summary

Being Single

- Today, there is an increasing number of singles in the United States, and singlehood is becoming a popular trend among the young and the old alike. This contemporary trend is due to the individualistic nature of Western society that embraces pursuing individual goals, such as education, and to the number of young adults who delay marriage. The average age at which people marry fluctuates over time. Today, 90 to 95 percent of adults eventually marry.

- Peter Stein developed a typology of singlehood that comprises four categories. His model acknowledges that some people are single by choice, while others are single for the time being, or are unintentionally single. Stein's four categories of singles are voluntary temporary, voluntary permanent, involuntary temporary, and involuntary permanent.

- Never-married singles are those people who have not married; they may or may not live alone, or may or may not have an intimate partner. African American men and women make up the highest percentage of never-married singles; whites and Hispanics have higher rates of marriage than nonmarriage. In general, the existing research seems to indicate that singlehood is a positive, satisfying experience for many.

- Urban tribes are mixed-gender circles of friends who are the primary social support system for singles. Each individual within the tribe assumes certain roles, much like in a family. Urban tribe members feel a mutual obligation to support each other and care for one another.

- Demographic surveys of gay men and lesbians indicate that between 45 and 80 percent are in a steady or long-term cohabiting relationship.

- A small percentage of America's singles are divorced men and women. Most divorced people will experience life as a single person at least for some period of time following the end of their marriages.

- An even smaller percentage of America's singles are widows and widowers, or people who have lost a spouse to death. Men are more likely than women to remarry following the death of a spouse.

The Act of Marriage

- In most cultures people are expected to marry when they reach adulthood. Although empirical evidence seems to indicate that people marry for many personal, individual reasons, marriage serves society on several levels. The act of marriage also defines the pair bond and provides a new identity for a couple and the subsequent roles they will play in their marriage and in the society at large.

- Marriage was once considered to be the social foundation responsible for the procreation and the socialization of children but is now being replaced by pair bonds that meet individual needs. This change is referred to as the *deinstitutionalism of marriage*. Browning outlined five specific dimensions of marriage: as organizer of natural desires, as a social good, as a communicative reality, as a legal contract, and as a sacrament or covenant.

- In the United States, marriage is foremost a state and federally regulated legal contract. Every state requires a marriage license. Factors limiting marriage vary from state to state, but may include the age, kinship, or sexual orientation of couples intending to marry. The privileges that come with marriage may also vary by state.

- Marriage tends to benefit all areas of well-being. Measurable benefits include economic benefits (including higher average annual incomes and financial assets), health benefits to each partner, and children's benefits (living standards, better health, and better developmental outcomes).

- In many cultures, marriage is a sacred act, and many measures are undertaken to ensure its protection. To curb escalating divorce rates in the United States, many states have considered implementing legislation that forces couples to prepare for married life and some have adopted Marriage Covenant Acts—legally binding agreements that spell out the couple's intent to obtain premarital education and/or counseling, clearly delineate the couple's commitment to preserving the marital union, and provide the grounds for divorce.

The Transition to Marriage: Why It's So Tough

- There are often difficulties associated with the transition to married life. By using the Family Life Cycle paradigm, family life educators can track the changes in the structure of the family as well as emotional transitions and other related changes in the family status. Through the Family Systems theoretical model, researchers better understand the interactions that take place in marriage and in family life. Viewed in this light, marriage is best seen as a newly formed system of the family and of society.

■ Newly married couples must negotiate the developmental tasks of their newly formed family. This includes establishing marital roles and boundaries, managing the house and the money, and fostering a healthy emotional climate.

■ Concepts of family and marriage in the United States are undergoing many changes, including an increase in heterogamous interpersonal relationships. Couples in heterogamous relationships—including interracial and interfaith marriages—face difficulties in addition to the normal transitional challenges all newlyweds face.

Satisfying Marriages

■ Since the 1930s, family life educators have tried to determine factors associated with successful marriage. By learning how they contribute to or detract from marital adjustment and marital satisfaction, family and social scientists and family practitioners are able to develop premarital educational and counseling programs to enhance couples' relationships.

■ Researchers developed typologies of premarital couples in order to assess premarital relationship quality in order to understand the correlation between premarital relationships and subsequent marital outcomes. These premarital couple types include vitalized couples, harmonious couples, traditional couples, and conflicted couples.

■ Researchers also developed marital couple typologies to determine marital satisfaction. These include traditional couple types, independent couple types, separate couple types, and the mixed couple types.

■ The lifecourse of marriage typically follows a pattern: marriages begin with peak levels of satisfaction; marital satisfaction wanes when the realities of marriage set in and the couple has children; satisfaction levels stay low until the children enter adolescence and move away; and as children enter into adolescence, marital quality begins to climb and continues to do so as each child leaves the nest.

■ As the couple enters late middle adulthood and late adulthood, levels of marital quality and marital satisfaction reach levels that nearly rival the peak levels at which marriage begins.

■ Couples entering marriage have expectations for their marriage and their spouses that have been developed throughout the course of their lives. The Social Expectations Model illustrates how spouses' expectations are based on past relationship interactions with the spouse. This model also takes into account the influence of societal norms (such as women being caregivers and men being providers) on spousal expectations.

Key Terms and Concepts

Suggested Readings

Furstenberg, Frank. *The fading dream: Prospects for marriage in the inner city,* in Elijah Anderson and Douglas Massey, (Eds.), *Problems of the century.* New York: Russell Sage Foundation, 2001.

Gottman, Joan, & DeClair, John. *The relationship cure.* New York: Crown Publishers, 2001.

Gottman, John. *Why marriages succeed or fail.* New York: Simon & Schuster, 1994.

Paul, Pamela. *The starter marriage and the future of matrimony.* New York: Villard, 2002.

Multiple-Choice Questions

1. _____ refers to mixed-gender circles of friends (typically in their 20s and 30s) who are the primary social support system for singles.
   a. Near peers
   b. Urban tribe
   c. Never-married singles
   d. Clique

2. Marriage is being replaced today by pair bonds that meet individual needs, such as cohabitation. This change is referred to as the _____ .
   a. deinstitutionalization of marriage
   b. conjugal role
   c. relational expectancy
   d. sacrament of marriage

3. _____ is a legally binding sworn statement indicating that the couple views marriage as a lifelong commitment and union.
   a. Covenant marriage
   b. Legal separation
   c. Marriage as a legal contract
   d. Declaration of Intent

4. These three states issue marriage licenses to same-sex couples: Connecticut, Vermont, and _____ .
   a. Rhode Island
   b. Massachusetts
   c. New Hampshire
   d. Delaware

5. The life commitment of marriage provides stability, especially for _____ .
   a. women
   b. children
   c. the couple
   d. men

6. A _____ is a culturally defined, culturally assigned set of behaviors each spouse is expected to carry out.
   a. conjugal role
   b. predetermined notion
   c. gender socialization
   d. spouse script

7. _____ interpersonal relationships are those that involve partnering with someone who is dissimilar to you in one or more dimensions, such as race, ethnic, and religious backgrounds, or differences in age, political ideology, socioeconomic status, and values and beliefs.

   a. Heterosexual

   b. Homosexual

   c. Heterogamous

   d. Heterogenous

8. _____ marriages are those in which individuals adhere to the same religion but may have different beliefs or follow different traditions within that faith (such as a Baptist who marries a Presbyterian).

   a. Extra-faith

   b. Interfaith

   c. Intrafaith

   d. Super-faith

Answers: 1. b; 2. a; 3. d; 4. b; 5. d; 6. a; 7. c; 8. c

You, Sex, and Your Sexuality

9

Though unspoken, they both knew that after 38 years of marriage their time together would soon draw to an end. Despite the valiant war she waged, the cancer had overtaken every aspect of her being and we all knew she would not be with us when the morning came. We moved her into the family room as she requested, so she could be among her children and grandchildren, not tucked far away from them in a corner bedroom.

My father knelt beside her. Thinking he was simply bathing her (a task I myself had performed every day over the course of that week), I stayed in the kitchen nearby. He raised her left hand and kissed her wedding band. He began to bathe her hand, her arm, her shoulder. He stroked her hair, over and over. She was much calmer, and her breathing that had been so labored in the previous minutes seemed to become less difficult. She turned her face so they were only inches apart from one another. They did not speak; their gaze locked onto one another. His hand lingered over her shoulder, then moved toward her chest. Through her entire illness, I had never seen her shed one tear, until now. His hand did not move. I could only imagine what each of them was thinking. Were they remembering, were they longing, yearning? Were they aching in anticipation of separation? Was he trying to memorize her?

It suddenly dawned on me what was taking place just a few feet away from me. I hurriedly left the room, allowing them to be alone for the last time. To the casual observer, the scene unfolding may have appeared to be a sponge bath from a caregiver for a dying woman—but it was so much more than that. What I was witnessing was a most tender act of lovemaking.

Source: Author's files

Learning Sexuality: Cultural Contributions

- Sexual Scripts
- Cultural Scenarios: Parents as Sexuality Educators
- Cultural Scenarios: Race and Ethnicity

Our Sexual Selves

- Sizzle and Sigh: Sexual Arousal and Desire
- Other Kinds of Sex
- Sexuality in Adolescence and Early Adulthood

Sexually Transmitted Infections

- Gonorrhea
- Chlamydia
- Syphilis
- Herpes
- Human Papillomavirus (HPV)
- Viral Hepatitis

Relationships and Sex

- Sexual Relationship Satisfaction and Marital Satisfaction
- Nonmarital Sex
- Cheating: Sex Outside the Relationship
- The Connection between Love and Sex

Experiencing Sexual Difficulties

- Sexual Dysfunctions in Women
- Sexual Dysfunctions in Men

Family Life Education

1970S or 2007? Socially driven attitudes and beliefs determine how we express our sexuality.

The year 1977 marked the freshman year of my university experience. Abortion had been legal for about four years and was relatively easy and inexpensive to obtain; cohabitation before marriage was becoming more common; the more serious sexually transmitted infections could be treated with a dose of penicillin; the AIDS epidemic was still a few years away. But despite all the sexual freedom my generation was enjoying, *Playboy* magazine was still displayed in brown paper wrappers on magazine stands. In fact, even at colleges and universities, usually among the more open-minded communities, sex was still a controversial subject. The first human sexuality course I took at the university is a case in point. Although the course was available, it was offered in a cloud of secrecy—it was not listed in the course offerings schedules printed each semester! Students knew about it by word of mouth; parents did not. The course was wrapped in "brown paper." Today on college campuses across the country, sexuality courses are taught in filled-to-capacity rooms.

What exactly is sexuality? Too often we mistake *sex* and *sexuality* for the same thing, but they are two distinct, separate entities. While **sex** refers to acts associated with sexual inter-

FIGURE 9.1   Sexual Development across the Lifespan

Infancy (Birth to 2 years): Newborns possess the ability for sexual response. In newborns as young as 24 hours, males have erections and females experience vaginal lubrication.

Early Childhood (2 to 6 years): Children develop a keen sense of their "maleness" and "femaleness," and they begin to engage in sex play at about age 3, such as playing "doctor." Parents shouldn't overreact to these behaviors or scold them, as it is a part of normal childhood development.

Middle Childhood (7 to 11 years): Curiosity about their own genitals increases, as does their curiosity about others' genitals; masturbation is not uncommon. Children experience their first sexual attraction to others, as well as their first sexual fantasies. Sex play and experimentation with peers increases.

course, sociologist Ira Reiss (1989) defined **sexuality** as "the erotic arousal and genital responses resulting from following *sexual scripts* of that society." To better understand how we develop these sexual scripts and what influences them, in this chapter we will explore the significant cultural contributions to our sexuality and sexual experiences in adolescence and early adulthood. We'll then view sexuality through the lens of relationships—marital sexuality, extramarital sexuality, and nonmarital sexuality—as well as what happens when partners experience sexual dysfunction.

At the very foundation of our sexuality are biological contributions, and as you learned in Chapter 4, the biological aspects of our sexual development and sexual maturity begin in the womb and continue until the end of our lives. Based on their extensive research and review of the sexual development literature, sex scientists and sociologists John DeLamater and William Friedrich (2002) developed a progression of benchmarks in sexual development from birth through adulthood. Although beyond the scope of our discussion here, this information is summarized in Figure 9.1 as a reminder that our sexuality is a continuous progression across the lifespan.

Learning Sexuality: Cultural Contributions

You don't *become* sexual at a certain point in your lifespan such as in adolescence or early adulthood; more correctly, you *are continuously becoming* a sexual being. From your very earliest days of life, well into very old age, who you are as a sexual being is shaped by many interrelated factors that include biological influences, your family of origin, the different intimate relationships you may have, life experiences, and other cultural influences (such as the media, as you learned in Chapter 4). Through these influences and contributions, you also develop

Adolescence (12 to 21 years):
Puberty occurs in males and females. These biological changes trigger an increased interest in sex; the physical changes give adoelscents a new capacity to experience their sexuality.

Middle Adulthood (30 to 65 years):
Both men and women experience decreases in their sex hormone levels; these lower levels may account for the decreased interest in sex. Older people commonly enjoy varying, healthy, and active sexual expression.

Late Adulthood (65 years and older):
Use it or lose it! Elderly adults who nurture their sex lives are still capable of having great sex, and many do well into old age. A healthy lifestyle in the younger years is essential to a person's sex life in the later years, as health status is a major contributor to a healthy sex life.

your *sexual identity*, your awareness of yourself as a sexual male or sexual female. Let's explore how we learn to be sexual through the influences of sexual scripts.

SEXUAL SCRIPTS

If we are raised in the same culture, do we differ in how we experience the feelings, behaviors, and attitudes associated with sex? If we do, why? How do we ultimately arrive at what *sex* and *sexuality* mean to us?

John Gagnon and his colleague, William Simon, were sociologists and sexologists in the 1970s who pioneered the ideas that people learn how to be sexual as a function of being raised in a particular culture, and that sexuality is ultimately created by the culture in which we live (Gagnon & Simon, 1973). They put forth the idea of *sexual scripts* as an explanation for how we internalize—make a part of ourselves—our culture's unique expectations for sexual attitudes and behaviors.

The **sexual scripting framework** proposes that societal and cultural processes ultimately determine and prescribe what we perceive as "sexual" and how we behave sexually (Laumann, Gagnon, Michael, & Michaels, 1994). **Sexual scripts** are shared, gender-specific social and cultural expectations that guide our beliefs, attitudes, and values about sex, such as our beliefs about appropriate sexual partners, sexual behaviors, and sexual conduct (Bowleg, Lucas, & Tschann, 2004). Embedded within our sexual scripts is our **sexual orientation**, which is the enduring emotional, romantic, sexual, or affectional attraction we feel toward others. There are four general types of sexual orientation:

- **Heterosexual**, which characterizes the sexual and emotional relationships between people of opposite sexes
- **Homosexual**, which are the sexual and emotional relationships with persons of the same sex
- **Bisexual**, which is the sexual and/or romantic attraction toward members of both sexes
- **Asexual**, which describes individuals who experience no sexual attraction to others

From the moment we are born, and throughout our entire lives, we are bombarded with parental, peer, school, spiritual, media, and other cultural messages. These messages write our sexual scripts and ultimately prescribe our sexuality. Our sexual scripts determine, among other things (DeLamater & Hyde, 1998):

- *With whom* we can engage in sexual relations (age, relationship to self, gender)
- *How* we engage in sex (anal sex, oral sex, "legal" sexual positions)
- *How often* we engage in sexual relations (for instance, it is expected that younger couples have sex more frequently than older couples)

My Sex Scripts

Sex scripts define our sexuality. When you think about your sex scripts,

1. Do you agree with the sex scripts society has assigned you? Why or why not? What would you change if you could?

2. Have you ever had to compromise what you truly desired sexually because of your assigned cultural scenarios?

3. Have you ever had an intimate relationship with someone who had sex scripts that were very different from your own? Did this impact your sexual relationship?

- *When* we have sex (timing parameters such as age at first intercourse or when the children are not present)
- *Where* we have sex (other than the bedroom)
- *Why* we have sexual relations (love, lust, anger, fun, play, boredom, jealousy)

Sexual scripts serve two primary functions. First, they provide us a framework for what is considered normative and expected sexual behavior within a given culture. For instance, in the West, the frequency of sexual intercourse in married or committed couples ranges from less than once per week to twice per week. In other societies that are not as developed, such as the Lepchas in the Himalayas, sexual intercourse is practiced at least once a night; the Chaga people from Tanzania engage in sexual intercourse at least three times a night (Ubillos, Paez, & Gonzalez, 2000). Second, sexual scripts provide a road map of sorts for us—they give us directions as to how we should feel, think, and act in certain sexual situations (Wiederman, 2005). In America, for example, traditional sex scripts prescribe that females should put their own sexual desires aside in order to please their male partners, to be aware of the dangers of sex and to protect themselves, and should only engage in sex if they are involved in an emotionally committed relationship (Holland and others, 1990; Hynie and others, 1998; Wiederman, 2005). Males, on the other hand, are sexually scripted to be independent, assertive, goal directed, and divorced from an emotional commitment to their sexual partner (Wiederman, 2005).

Specifically, the sexual scripting approach delineates three different levels of sexual scripts: (1) **cultural scenarios** that recognize influences such as our families of origin, our communities, mass media, the educational system, and religious beliefs (as shown in Chapter 1); (2) **interpersonal scripts** that recognize how different people interact and relate to each other within specific social situations; and (3) **intrapsychic scripts** (intrapersonal) that account for individual desires, fantasies, emotions, and intensions while at the same time considering the interpersonal responses of others (Simon & Gagnon, 1984). All three levels of these cognitive representations of sex are important in the creation of our sexual identity and how we experience sex and sexuality, and, as with all areas of human development, these changes and development occur simultaneously with our physical and cognitive development.

CULTURAL SCENARIOS: PARENTS AS SEXUALITY EDUCATORS

Most parents, sexuality educators, and even adolescents believe that parents should be the primary providers of sexuality and health education to their children (Byers and others, 2003). Today, parents remain influential regarding their teens' decisions and attitudes about sex, as Figure 9.2 (page 284) shows us. When asked, "When it comes to your decisions about sex, who is the most influential?," about half of high schoolers surveyed reported that their parents influenced them the most; less than one-fourth indicated that their friends were the most influential (Albert, 2007). That's not to say, however, that parents and teens are satisfied with the quality of their sexual communication, or the amount of it (Byers, Sears, & Weaver, 2008).

How did you learn about sex? Did your parents have "The Talk" with you? If so, was it a well-planned, one-time, uncomfortable conversation, or was it laid back, informal, and frequent? There are several factors that play into sexual communication within a family. For example, there is a large body of science that indicates that parents will commonly provide the same level of sex education to their children that they received from their parents (for a complete review, see Byers and others, 2008). Parent–child sexual communication is also influenced by parents'

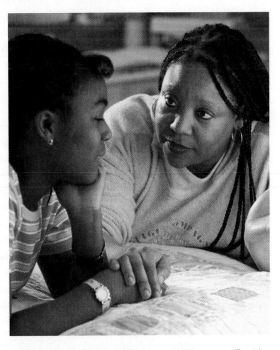

WHAT was your "sex talk" like with your parent(s)? Or are you still waiting for them to have "The Talk" with you? Although many parents are uncomfortable discussing sex with their children, parents are children's first and best sex educators.

FIGURE 9.2 Parents' Influences on Children's Sexuality

Despite the number of cultural influences on our sexuality, children and teens today indicate that their parents are the most influential when it comes to their decisions about sex.

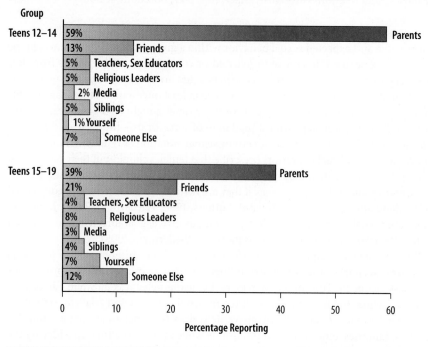

Source: Albert (2007).

perceptions of their own sexual knowledge, and the comfort level they have when discussing sexual topics with their children. In fact, one study found that when mothers did not discuss sexual issues with their daughters it was related to their self-perceived low levels of sexual knowledge and their discomfort with the topic (Jaccard, Dittus, & Gordon, 2000). The mothers were not only embarrassed to approach the subject but they were also afraid that they would be asked something they didn't know the answer(s) to. On the other hand, parents who feel that they have an adequate background in sexuality education, who feel knowledgeable, and who are comfortable with sexuality topics and issues are much more likely to communicate about sex often with their children (Jaccard and others, 2000). Also, mothers are much more involved in the sexuality and health education of their children than fathers are; parents are also more likely to talk about sex with their adolescent daughters than they are their adolescent sons (Meschke, Bartholomae, & Zentall, 2002; Raffaelli, Bogenschneider, & Flood, 1998).

In general, there are five components that affect parent–child sexual communication: the *communication source* (the parent or the child?); the *communication recipient* (the parent or the child?); the *communication itself* (what is the content?); the *family context* (under what circumstances did the communication take place?); and *how the message is communicated* (is it done to promote knowledge—or fear?) (Jaccard, Dodge, & Dittus, 2002). Sandra Byers is a professor of sexuality at the University of New Brunswick, and her influential research is concentrated in the areas of sexual satisfaction, sexuality education, and sexual communication. In her recent work that studied nearly 4,000 parents and youth, she wanted to better understand how the sexual communication factors listed above affect sexual communication with children in kindergarten to about grade 8. She especially wanted to see how often parents talked to their children about 10 sexuality topics: personal safety, correct names for genitalia, puberty, reproduction, sexual coercion and assault, STDs, abstinence, birth control, sexual decision making, and sexual pleasure/enjoyment (Byers and others, 2008). In general, she and her colleagues found that the characteristics of the parent, the characteristics of the child, and

Should Abstinence-Until-Marriage Be the Only Sex Education?

FAMILY LIFE NOW

Is it great to wait? At issue is whether such educational programs keep preteens and teens from having sex until marriage, or whether a lack of education and information serves only to put teens at greater risk for not only unwanted pregnancies but sexually transmitted infections and HIV/AIDS as well. Should abstinence-until-marriage be the only sex education youth and teens receive?

YES: Three million teens—one-fourth of all sexually active teens in America—have a sexually transmitted disease. In addition, teenage moms are more likely to live under the constraints of poverty because 41 percent will drop out of school. Their poverty and limited education have a profound effect on *their* children, who are more likely to have lower grades, be abused, and drop out from school themselves.

But can *Abstinence-Only Programs (AOP)* reduce such sobering statistics? In the late 1990s, the Georgia State Board of Education requested a study be done on "Choosing the Best," an AOP adopted for use in all eighth-grade classes in Columbus, Georgia, over a period of four years. The results?

- There was a 38 percent drop in pregnancies among middle school students between 1997 and 1999.
- In other school districts that did not provide AOPs, there was a 6 percent drop in pregnancies among middle school students during the same timeframe.
- Teens who take virginity pledges—avowing that they will remain virgins until they are married—are 34 percent less likely to engage in sexual activity.

As the old axiom goes, "Abstinence is the only method proven to work every time."

NO: Sue Alford (2001), Director of Public Information Services at Advocates for Youth, believes that Abstinence-Only Programs are dangerous to America's youth. "Federally mandated abstinence-only-until-marriage education jeopardizes the health and lives of young people," Alford argues, "by denying them information that can prevent unintended pregnancy and infection with sexually transmitted diseases, including HIV." Supporters of sex education maintain that AOPs:

- Provide fear-based education that tries to scare adolescents into sexual abstinence
- Are unrealistic—adolescents will have sex, they should protect their health
- Omit critical information, such as options for birth control, including the use of condoms
- Risk alienating bisexuals, gays, lesbians, single moms, and other sexually active teens

Advocates of sex education note that although some teens claim they are virgins, accounts of mutual masturbation, oral sex, and anal sex abound among "abstaining" teens. Abstinence-based programs give one answer to a complex issue. Comprehensive Sex Education (CSE) teaches young people *how* to think through and process sexual choices, all the while providing many tools for engaging in safer activities.

WHAT DO YOU THINK?

1. Are Abstinence-Only Programs effective in reducing the numbers of preteens and teens who have sex before marriage?
2. Do Abstinence-Only Programs put adolescents at risk for unwanted consequences of sex, such as pregnancy and sexually transmitted infections?
3. In your opinion, what is the most effective sex education: abstinence only, birth control/prevention only, or a combination of both programs? Why did you reach this decision?

Sources: Alford (2001); Maher (2004); National Guidelines Task Force (2004).

the content of the communication were all associated with the quality and quantity of parent–child sexual communication. Overall, the study found that parents who were supportive of comprehensive sexuality and health education (both in the home and at school) were more likely to engage in sexual communication with their children, to engage in it more frequently, and to encourage their children to ask questions—no topic was "off limits." It's necessary to point out, though, that this study looked at a white population. Are there racial or ethnic differences in sexual communication within families?

Racial/Ethnic Differences in Parent–Child Sexual Communication In a study of 135 African American/Black Caribbean parent–co-parent–child triads, researchers wanted to determine what types of sexuality and health topics were discussed, and if parents communicated differently with their daughters than they did their sons (Wyckoff and others, 2008). Table 9.1 presents the findings of this study, and the data show us that parents of color are sexuality educators for their children. As you can see, the parents are not at all hesitant to discuss risky behaviors with their kids, such as drug and alcohol use. And although parents of color commonly and easily talk about puberty, reproduction, and dating with their children, they are a little more reluctant to converse about what sex is and abstinence, and about sexual risk prevention (HIV/AIDS and the use of condoms). Contrary to the findings of the study we previously discussed that examined a predominantly white population, parent–child sexual communication with preadolescents is common among blacks in this study. These findings are very important to our understanding of human sexuality among African Americans/Black Caribbeans because, as you will learn a bit later in this chapter, this population is at the greatest risk for acquiring sexually transmitted disease and HIV/AIDS; they are also at the greatest risk for premarital pregnancies.

Little attention has been given to sexual communication among Chinese. This is because talking about sex in public, or between people of different generations, is culturally forbidden in Chinese culture because of its private and sensitive nature (Zhang, Li, Shah, Baldwin, & Stanton, 2007). Due to this taboo, many parents today (even among Asian Americans) still believe that it is inappropriate to provide sexuality and health education/information for their children. But are these attitudes changing?

TABLE 9.1 Percentage of African American/Black Caribbean Parent–Child Pairs Discussing Each Sexuality Topic

	Sons' Report of Discussion with:		Daughters' Report of Discussion with:	
	Mother	Father	Mother	Father
Risk Factor				
Alcohol	79%	77%	87%	72%
Drugs	80%	77%	90%	75%
Sexuality Education				
Puberty	71%	66%	88%	42%
Menstruation	41%	25%	84%	31%
Reproduction	67%	58%	75%	41%
Dating	63%	63%	79%	57%
What sex is	59%	55%	75%	39%
Abstinence	45%	39%	66%	35%
Sexual Risk Prevention Reduction				
Condoms	27%	23%	29%	16%
HIV/AIDS	49%	52%	46%	24%

Source: Wyckoff and others (2008).

In a recent study of 1,319 Chinese men and women (ages 15 to 24) who reside in China, study participants were asked questions about the quality of sex communication with their parents on general topics (Zhang and others, 2007). About one-fourth of the survey respondents reported that it was easy to talk about sex with their fathers, and about one-third of them indicated it was easy to communicate with their mothers. Overall, however, the results of this study showed that parent–adolescent sex communication was less frequent in China than in Western countries, such as the United States—less than one-third of the study participants had *ever* discussed sex-related issues with their parents. But, consistent with the studies we discussed earlier and with other prior research, both male and female adolescents are more comfortable talking with their moms about sex than they are with their dads. There may be less frequent communication, but one of the most important findings of this study is that parents *are* talking to their children about sex. Just what is the best way to have a conversation about sex with a child?

Sexual Communication: How to Talk to Kids about Sex While it does take some planning (and some courage), parents can be accurate, trustworthy, and safe sources of sex education. Planned Parenthood (2006) suggests parents do the following when talking to their kids about sex:

- *Be clear about the family's values and expectations.* It is important for parents to emphasize their faith traditions and what their values are. Parents should explain to children how their values and beliefs agree or disagree with other forms of sex education their children may be exposed to.
- *Talk about facts versus beliefs.* Parents should make sure that they present accurate, factual information, even if it challenges a personal value or religious belief they may have.
- *Don't preach.* Parents should be careful to talk *with* their children—not *at* them. They should take time to listen to their children, and find out what they think and feel about sex and sexuality.
- *Keep the conversation going.* As a popular television commercial reminds us, children have to be reminded several times a week to make their beds, brush their teeth, do their homework, or take out the trash. All too often, parents have "The Talk" with their children, rather than use "teachable moments" and casual conversations to convey information about sex.

CULTURAL SCENARIOS: RACE AND ETHNICITY

Race and ethnicity are cultural scenarios that shape sexual scripts, and these sexual scripts in turn affect our sexual attitudes and beliefs, the types of sexual behaviors we engage in, and our sexual health practices. These cultural scripts are briefly discussed in the sections that follow.

Latino Cultures Because of the *marianismo* cultural mindset (see Chapter 4), Latina women are taught to assume submissive roles in their sexual relationships, allowing the men to direct the sexual encounters. In an attempt to understand Latinas' definitions of sex and sexual relationships, sociologist Sandra Faulkner (2003) interviewed young Latinas from Puerto Rico, the Dominican Republic, and Cuba. She found that, despite influences of twenty-first-century culture and the increasing freedom of expression of sexuality across cultures, her study respondents indicated that they desired to be seen as sexually moral. They did not want to dress or behave in ways that suggested they were flirts but, instead, they wanted their behaviors to indicate that they were "good Latinas."

This marianismo, "good Latina" philosophy may also be why using hormonal contraception and/or using a condom is not practiced by a significant percentage of Latina women (Gurman & Borzekowski, 2004).

THE marianismo cultural norm is an integral part of Latinas' sexual scripts. This cultural expectation is a defining influence in how Latina women experience and practice their sexuality.

Further, *machismo* cultural values among Latino men include the role of power to decide contraceptive behavior, and machismo has been associated with unprotected sexual behavior and multiple sexual partners (Villarruel & Rodriguez, 2003; Hodges Leavy, Swift, & Gold, 1992). This may explain why Latinos use condoms less than whites or African Americans/Black Caribbeans, as Figure 9.3 shows.

Black Cultures Certain populations, such as African Americans/Black Caribbeans, are in a particularly high-risk category, because they tend to initiate sexual intercourse at early ages (Dilorio and others, 2001).

On the whole, blacks become sexually active at much younger ages, have more sexual partners over their lifetime, have more casual sexual partners, are less likely to marry or to have long-term, stable marriages, and have many more children born outside of marriage than other racial/ethnic groups do (Smith, 2006; The Kinsey Institute, 2007). One recent study examined the sexual behaviors and attitudes of 744 black high schoolers, and found several personal and family factors that shaped their sexual scripts, and were associated with the age at which they first had sex. These factors included such things as cultural perceptions of risky sexual behaviors and perceived cultural norms as to when it is "acceptable" to have sex or whether it is "okay" to have sex (Lindley, Joshi, & Vincent, 2007). To the extent that the study participants experienced parental involvement and communication, and to the extent that adolescents held the sexual attitudes that it was socially acceptable to delay sexual intercourse, adolescents were more likely to delay having sex.

Researchers have also discovered that female African American study participants hold to traditional sex scripts prescribed by their culture—that is, being submissive in their heterosexual relationships (Bowleg, Lucas, & Tschann, 2004). This prevailing cultural scenario encourages women to assume a passive role in their sexual relationships, despite the fact that this passive role may put them at greater risk for acquiring a sexually transmitted infection or HIV.

Asian Cultures Within traditional Asian culture, sexual behaviors and expressions outside of marriage are considered to be inappropriate and a violation of their strict moral conduct; thus, modesty and restrained sexuality are highly valued. Because of the taboo nature of sexu-

FIGURE 9.3 Condom Use by Race/Ethnicity

Condom use varies among different racial and ethnic groups. Cultural norms, values, and beliefs shape, in large part, our attitudes about contraception.

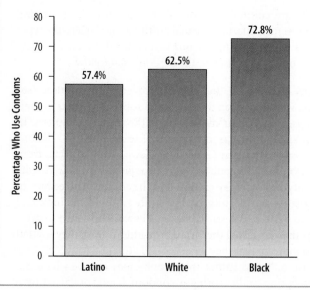

Source: Gurman and Borzekowski (2004).

ality in this culture, it is often difficult to study this racial group, but available data suggest that Asian Americans show conservatism in their sexual scripts. For instance, they hold later sexual timetables for initiating all types of sexual behavior in comparison to other ethnic groups, and they are less likely than any racial/ethnic group to have had sex as an adolescent (Okazaki, 2002). Similar patterns are seen among Asian American college students.

Native American Cultures In all aspects of their lives, Native Americans' beliefs, attitudes, and behaviors are deeply embedded within their religious traditions that emphasize respect and reverence. But how these beliefs shape their sexual scripts is unknown, because Native Americans are among the most misunderstood and understudied ethnic groups in our culture due to their relative cultural isolation (Hellerstedt, Peterson-Hickey, Rhodes, & Garwick, 2006). However, we do know from the available research that the family is the primary influence on Native Americans' sexual scripts. For instance, one body of research found that involvement with family and family support, and the family's scholastic values, were associated with safer sexual behaviors (Chewning and others, 2001). Another recent study found that the strongest influence of positive sexual scripts among Native Americans was having a father present in the home (Hellerstedt and others, 2006).

Arab American Cultures Not all Arab Americans adhere to the Muslim faith, as you saw in Chapter 1; here, though, it is necessary to discuss Islam because these beliefs significantly influence the sexual scripts of those who practice this religion.

Within Islamic faith, religious and cultural customs and rituals reinforce traditional gender roles wherein women raise and nurture the children, and men protect and provide for the family. As a result, many Arab Americans' sexuality is strongly shaped by traditional Arab views of honor and modesty, as well as by the values of Islam (Davis & Davis, 1993). Perhaps one of the best examples of modesty is the veil, or the *hijab*, that Muslim women wear in public. Many Arab Americans believe that the *hijab* is a religious mandate because, according to Muslim religious tenets, a woman's hair is to be covered since it's the very essence of her sensuality and sexuality (Zahedi, 2007).

The Islamic religion is sex-positive and because of this attitude, sex and sexuality are viewed as gifts from God, or Allah; sexuality is thought to be the right of every person, and sexual pleasure is seen as an essential part of human life (Boellstorff, 2005). Marriage is the social institution that is believed to organize and control sexuality, so this culture's sex scripts are very strict about sex outside of marriage for women (such as adultery, premarital sex, and prostitution).

Our sexual behaviors and sexual decisions are guided and directed by the society and culture in which we are raised. While sometimes it can seem tedious (and perhaps boring) to explore the demographics and characteristics associated with different cultural groups, doing so is very important. Aside from needing to understand the general trends so you have a solid knowledge base in the formation and maintenance of sexual scripts, doing so is necessary on a relational level. As you saw in the previous chapter, interracial and interfaith relationships are on the increase in the United States and in many other Western cultures. Given that many of you may someday enter into an interracial or interfaith relationship, it is important that you understand the influences your culture has not only on *your* sexuality but also on *your partner's*. With this understanding, you can each better appreciate—and enjoy—your sexuality and your sexual relationship.

The influences of parents and other cultural factors on our sexual scripts lessen as we get older, although these influences will always be at least a part of "who" we are as a sexual person. Other important aspects of sexual scripts are the biological contributions that include sexual arousal and desire, and response.

IN some muslim cultures, the hijab is a religious mandate for women because it covers her hair—her very essence of being a sexual person.

Our Sexual Selves

The media are screaming "sex, sex, and more sex" to today's adolescents and young adults, yet she often doesn't understand or accept her body; he often feels that he doesn't measure up to her sexual expectations (or to his own)—and the act of sex becomes a proving ground. Certainly, it is clear that today's young men and women are barraged with images of sexuality at an early age, but they are not taught how their bodies respond to sexual stimulation—or why. Each semester when I teach the sexuality information in my marriage and family classes, there is never enough time to answer all the questions my students have about sex. They want to know such things as, "How important a role does the clitoris really play in my girlfriend's sexual response?" "Is it okay to have anal sex?" "Why is it that my boyfriend can become sexually excited so much quicker than I can?" and "Why is it that I can have an orgasm when I masturbate, but not when I have sex with my fiancé?"

In the following section, we'll examine human sexual response. Having a good understanding of sexual arousal and desire, and of sexual response, allows us to comprehend not only *how* our bodies work but *why* we respond the way we do. It also allows us to appreciate how and why our partners respond the way they do. Knowing and understanding our bodies increases our sexual pleasure and satisfaction as well as enhances our sexual relationships.

SIZZLE AND SIGH: SEXUAL AROUSAL AND DESIRE

Do women want sex as much as men do? Are men more easily sexually aroused than women? What are sexual turn-ons for men and women? Do women get turned on by viewing erotic materials—or are they offended by such pictures or movies? What makes us sizzle, sigh, and curl our toes? These are common questions students ask, and they speak to our need as human beings to understand a relationship process that is vitally important to most couples—the act of sex.

Despite popular belief that there is a huge gap between men's and women's sexual arousal and desire, empirical evidence shows us that healthy men and women easily become sexually aroused by "[any] sexually meaningful stimulus" (Laan & Both, 2008, p. 510). Without a sexual stimulus, there is no sexual desire. You may be asking, "So what is a sexual stimulus?" The answer is simple: It depends.

For most of us, our sexual scripts are largely responsible for what sexually stimulates us. For example, what is your cultural background? Your religious background? Who were your *sex models* as you were growing up—were your parents affectionate (holding hands, patting bottoms) in front of you, or did they seldom show affection for one another in front of the children? Are you comfortable in your own skin, or do you struggle with your body image? Other than research that examines how people respond to erotic books, photos, and movies, there are no scientific studies that address what men and women find to be sexually stimulating; this is probably because the potential sex stimuli are potentially endless, given the individual nature of them. There are physical things we can do that are sexually stimulating, such as kissing and touching, and there are also emotional turn-ons, such as having a strong body image or self-esteem. As sexual arousal begins, we begin the four phases of sexual response, which are presented in Table 9.2. But ultimately, great sex isn't just about knowing each other's hot spots. To have great sex, partners need to have great communication. Being able to tell our sexual partners what feels good and what doesn't feel good, and what works and what doesn't work not only helps us to become better lovers but it also deepens the intimacy bonds.

OTHER KINDS OF SEX

Sex encompasses many other behaviors besides sexual intercourse. These behaviors are termed **noncoital**, and include masturbation, oral-genital sex, and anal sex.

Self-stimulation of the genitals, or **masturbation**, was damned by theologians in the past as a weakness of the flesh and a sin against nature. But by the 1990s, not only was masturbation accepted, but it became the topic of television shows, such as a popular episode of *Seinfeld* in which there was a contest among the main characters to see who could refrain from masturbating the longest and remain the "master of [his or her] domain."

In the Janus Report on Sexual Behavior (Janus & Janus, 1993), two-thirds of male respondents agreed with the survey statement, "Masturbation is a natural part of life and continues on in marriage." Using data from 18- to 20-year-old college males, another body of research discovered that 67 percent of those study participants had masturbated by age 15 (Leitenberg, Detzer, & Srebnik, 1993). Sex researcher Carolyn Halpern and her colleagues (2000), in their examination of adolescent males' willingness to report masturbation, similarly found that the majority of the study participants had engaged in solitary sexual practices. Given that the data from these studies were generated via self-report mechanisms, how accurate are the numbers? As a sex therapist colleague of mine remarked, "About 95 percent of men indicate that they masturbate—and the other 5 percent lie."

IN 1998, President Bill Clinton polarized public opinion when he declared he did not engage in sex with his young intern. Public and private conversations centered on a hot-button topic: Is oral sex sex?

Janus and Janus (1993) found that 88 percent of married women reported that they masturbated. That women masturbate is not simply a function of today's more liberating practices for female sexuality.

"I did not have sexual relations with that woman!" declared President Bill Clinton in an address to the nation on January 26, 1998, in response to Clinton's well-publicized extramarital relationship with a twenty-something White House intern. The nation was brought to polarity in opinions as the question of the decade presented itself to the American people: Is oral sex, sex?

Cunnilingus involves the erotic oral stimulation of the woman's external sex organs; **fellatio** is the oral stimulation of the male's external sex organs. **Oral-genital sex (oral sex)** is practiced by all couple types: heterosexual, gay, lesbian, cohabiting, and bisexuals, and it is typically engaged in more by white middle-class individuals than by black or Hispanic individuals (Leichliter, Chandra, Kiddon, Fenton, & Aral, 2007). Additionally, the practice is becoming more acceptable and common among today's youth. In fact, children as young as age 11 reported engaging in oral sex (Booth, 2001). According to Dr. Jonathan Trager (2009), "They think they can participate in an intense sexual act while staying a virgin" (p. 1). College students apparently agree. In a study that focused on gender differences in beliefs held by

TABLE 9.2   The Phases of Sexual Response

Physician William Masters and psychologist Virginia Johnson scientifically measured human sexual response in men and women. They determined that women and men experience four distinct phases of sexual response.

The Phases of Sexual Response

- **Excitement phase.** Within the very first few seconds of this phase, a man's penis becomes erect. Women experience vaginal lubrication, which is a "sweating" on the vaginal walls.
- **Plateau phase.** Both men and women experience an increase in heart rate, blood pressure, and rate of breathing. Involuntary muscle tension occurs; this is what gives us the "toe curling" feelings of muscle intensity during sex.
- **Orgasm Phase.** This phase involves the sudden release of the muscle tension and blood engorgement that has occurred in the penis (males) and labia (females). The intensity of orgasms varies from one sex act to another, and is influenced by how recent and how often intercourse or masturbation has taken place.
- **Resolution.** In both men and women, the heart rate, blood pressure, and respiration return to pre-excitement levels. The penis returns to its flaccid state. Men experience a refractory period, when they are incapable of achieving an erection. The length of the **refractory period** is directly associated with age and other factors such as health and lifestyle habits. Women do not experience refractory periods and are capable of multiple orgasms if they are effectively stimulated.

Testicular Cancer: Did You Know?

Did you know that **testicular cancer**—cancer in one or both of the testes—is the most common form of cancer in men ages 15 to 34 (American Cancer Society, 2008)? According to the American Cancer Society, each year in the United States about 8,400 men are diagnosed with testicular cancer, and nearly 400 will die from this disease. Early detection is key for survival—in those men who are diagnosed early, survival rates are 95 percent. With a simple monthly self-exam, men can detect early growths.

Testicular Self Exam (TSE)

The American Cancer Society suggests that adolescents and men do monthly testicular self-exams to detect any growths. These examinations are best performed while in the shower, because heat relaxes the scrotum and makes it easier to examine. Once a month, follow these steps:

- Standing in front of a mirror, check to see if the skin on the scrotum is swollen.
- Roll the testicle between your thumbs and fingers (it's normal for one testicle to be larger than the other).
- Check for painless lumps (usually pea size) or swelling.
- Is there any pain or discomfort in a testicle or in the scrotum?
- Is there any enlargement in the testicle?
- Is there a feeling of heaviness in the scrotum?
- Do you feel a collection of fluid in the scrotum?

If You Feel a Lump

If you feel a lump or notice any other changes, contact your physician immediately. If the tests indicate that the lump is potentially cancerous, your physician will perform a biopsy. This surgical procedure allows the doctor to remove a tissue sample from the affected testicle; the tissue is examined under a microscope to determine whether it is cancerous. Treatment options vary depending on how advanced the cancer is. In nearly all cases, the affected testicle is surgically removed, because this prevents the cancer from spreading. Depending on how advanced the cancer is, some men will also need to receive other treatments, such as radiation and chemotherapy.

Sex after Testicular Cancer

Understandably, most men are concerned about their sexual function and fertility following the removal of a testicle due to testicular cancer. From a physiological standpoint, sexual function and fertility are not impaired if a man loses a testicle to cancer. With only one testicle, a man is still able to have an erection and produce sperm. If it appears that fertility may become jeopardized, men have the option of storing their sperm in sperm banks for future use. Today, for cosmetic reasons, many men opt to have a testicular implant (an artificial testicle) placed in the scrotum following the removal of the unhealthy testicle.

By taking a couple of minutes, once per month, men can protect their sexual and reproductive health.

Source: American Cancer Society (2008).

university students about sexuality, both men and women agreed with the statement, "Oral sex is not sex" (Knox, Zusman, & McNeely, 2008).

Anal intercourse is the sexual activity of the male placing his penis into his partner's anus and rectum; **anal eroticism** can include anal intercourse, as well as oral stimulation of the anus, manually stroking the outside of the anus, and inserting one or more fingers into the anus. Stimulating the anus is very erotic for most people because it contains a vast supply of nerve endings.

Anal intercourse and anal eroticism are an integral aspect of sexual pleasure among gay men (Blumstein & Schwartz, 1983; Leichliter and others, 2007), but many people incorrectly believe that anal intercourse/stimulation/eroticism is practiced only by homosexual men. In actuality, data from a recent U.S. study of over 12,000 men and women, ages 15 to 44, reveal that nearly one-third of those surveyed indicated they had engaged in anal sex as a sexual behavior (Liechliter and others, 2007); additionally, 1 in 10 female and male adolescents have engaged in heterosexual anal sex.

As we age and experience different relationships with others, whether they are friendships, casual sexual hookups, or serious intimate relationships (that may or may not include sex), we incorporate these new experiences into our sexual scripts. Your sex scripts are not fixed by a certain age; instead, like any other process associated with intimate relationships (such as love, intimacy, and communication), sexual scripts change over time—you continually affect and are affected by your relationships and other cultural/environmental influences.

SEXUALITY IN ADOLESCENCE AND EARLY ADULTHOOD

Puberty encompasses skeletal, muscular, and reproductive maturation, but we commonly tend to associate this universal developmental stage as the time when sexual maturation occurs, the time when we are "awakened" sexually. Although some children may experience their first heterosexual or homosexual interpersonal attraction around the age of 10 (Harrison, 2003), and though they may begin masturbation as early as the first or second grade (Weinstein & Rosen, 2006), most of us become more aware of our sexuality—and desire to act on these new feelings and sensations—during early adolescence.

Adolescents and Sex: What the Numbers Say Young people are engaging in sexual activity—and their attitudes about sexuality and sexual expression are becoming increasingly open-minded. Adolescent sex and sexuality are of great interest to social science researchers and demographers, because often the behaviors put adolescents at risk for a number of health concerns, such as unwanted pregnancies, violence, and sexually transmitted diseases (O'Donnell and others, 2006).

At what age are adolescents losing their virginity today? In her book, *The Real Truth about Teens and Sex,* author and researcher Sabrina Weill (2005) gathered data from 1,000 adolescents, in cooperation with the National Campaign to Prevent Teen Pregnancy. She found that:

- 32.9 percent of ninth-graders have had sex.
- 44.1 percent of tenth-graders have had sex.
- 53.2 percent of eleventh-graders have had sex.
- 61.6 percent of twelfth-graders have had sex.

There is an encouraging downward trend in the number of students who report having sex before the age of 13. For example, recent research reports that sexual intercourse among preadolescents has declined from about 10 percent in 1991 to about 7 percent in 2003 (O'Donnell and others, 2006). However, African American/Black Caribbeans and Latino youth remain at the highest risk for early sexual intercourse. As Figure 9.4 (page 294) shows us, both Black and Latino males and females report having sex before the age of 13 more than white preteens do (SIECUS, 2004). Teens in the United States have sex at much younger ages than those in other countries do, as the map in Figure 9.5 (page 295) shows us.

FIGURE 9.4 High School Students Who Had Sexual Intercourse before Age 13

Age of first sexual experiences vary by race and ethnicity. African American/Black Caribbeans and Latinos are at risk for having sexual intercourse before the age of 13.

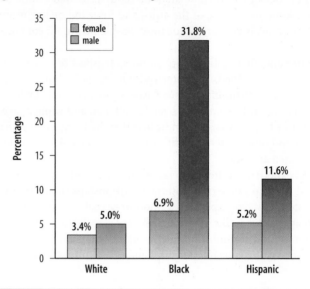

Source: SIECUS (2004).

Consequences of Adolescent Sexual Behaviors While there are obvious consequences of sexual behaviors for any age group, such as acquiring an STD or experiencing an unwanted pregnancy, there are other consequences that also affect this age group. In a recent study that wanted to identify the physical, social, and emotional consequences of 275 high schoolers (all about age 14) who engaged in oral and/or vaginal sex for the first time, students reported on a number of items, such as, "I got in trouble with my parents after I had sex," "I got a bad reputation," and "I feel bad about myself" (Brady & Halpern-Felsher, 2007). Table 9.3 shows the percentages of adolescents who reported various positive and negative consequences of sexual behavior. General findings of this study include:

- Students believe that oral sex is associated with fewer negative consequences than vaginal sex.
- Students who had only oral sex were less likely to feel guilty or used, feel their relationship got worse, and get in trouble with their parents.
- Girls were twice as likely as boys to report feeling bad about themselves following a sex act, and almost three times as likely to report feeling used.
- Boys were twice as likely to report an increase in their popularity after reporting their sexual activities to friends.

It is clear that there are significant medical and social consequences of adolescent sex, but as this study shows us, teenagers do feel that there are some positive consequences of having sex. These are somewhat concerning findings, because experiencing positive outcomes, such as an increase in popularity, may encourage sexual behavior—convincing teens (particularly boys) that there is a negative side with potential life-changing outcomes may be difficult (Brady & Halpern-Felsher, 2007).

Many of you reading this text are in the developmental stage of early adulthood, and many of you may feel that you are in the "prime" of your lives with regard to your social lives and your sex lives. You are still discovering *who* you are sexually and how your sexuality coexists with your partner's. As you saw in Chapter 7, many young adults explore and experience their sexuality through dating relationships, cohabiting relationships, and hooking up.

FIGURE 9.5 Global Trends: Average Age of Virginity Loss

Teens in the United States have sex earlier than teens in other countries do. What cultural factors do you believe encourage this trend?

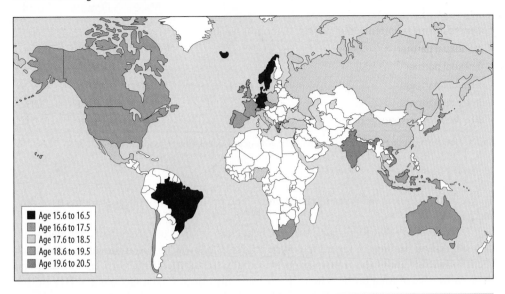

Age 15.6 to 16.5
Age 16.6 to 17.5
Age 17.6 to 18.5
Age 18.6 to 19.5
Age 19.6 to 20.5

Source: Durex (2007).

Doing It: Sexuality in Early Adulthood Is everyone doing it on college campuses? The National College Health Assessment (NCHA, 2008) provides a glimpse into the sex and health behaviors of America's college students. In their recent national survey of 80,121 college students, the NCHA found that nearly 30 percent of the study participants had not had sex within the past 12 months. Table 9.4 (page 296) shows the percentages of college students who had sex within the past 12 months. Table 9.5 (page 296) presents the percentages of college students who had oral sex, vaginal sex, and anal sex within the past 30 days. (In Chapter

TABLE 9.3 Percentages of Reported Consequences of Teen Sexual Behaviors

	Oral Sex	Vaginal Sex	Both
Positive Consequences			
Experienced pleasure	55.1%	76.1%	96.5%
Became popular	7.6%	11.6%	25.9%
Relationship got better	31.1%	44.2%	75.2%
Felt good about self	65.1%	65.5%	83.3%
Negative Consequences			
Got in trouble with parents	4.2%	18.6%	21.6%
Had a bad reputation	12.6%	7.0%	9.7%
Relationship got worse	10.1%	19.0%	31.9%
Felt guilty	19.8%	41.7%	45.5%
Felt bad about self	41.2%	34.5%	48.2%
Felt regret	37.0%	33.3%	52.8%
Felt used	25.0%	37.9%	54.0%
Pregnancy resulted	0.8%	9.3%	14.0%
Contracted STD	1.7%	4.7%	13.0%

Source: Brady & Halpern-Felsher (2007).

TABLE 9.4   Percentage of College Students Who Had Sex in the Past 12 Months

	Percent		
	Male	Female	Total
College students reported within the last 12 months having:			
No sexual partner	31.0%	29.3%	29.9%
1 sexual partner	42.0%	48.8%	46.4%
2 sexual partners	10.6%	11.0%	10.9%
3 sexual partners	6.5%	5.4%	5.8%
4 or more sexual partners	9.9%	5.4%	7.0%

Source: National College Health Assessment (2008); American College Health Association (n.d.).

10, we'll take a look at the types of birth control and protection the college students used during sex.)

A recent study that focused on oral sex behaviors among college students revealed some very interesting findings in regard to college students' knowledge about the safety of oral sex, their knowledge about the transmission of sexually transmitted infections via oral sex, and their knowledge of what protects them against sexually transmitted infections and HIV during oral sex (Chambers, 2007). For instance, although the majority of all the 2,100 research participants were aware of the risks associated with oral sex (such as acquiring an STD), women were less knowledgeable than men when it came to protecting themselves during oral sex—up to nearly three-fourths of the students were not aware of the ways to practice safe oral sex, such as males using condoms or women making dental dams from condoms.

The findings of this study give us insight into sexual behaviors of young adults. What is particularly interesting is that women give more oral sex than men do, and men indicate that they receive oral sex more than women do (Chambers, 2007). Does this mean that women use oral sex more frequently as a means to please their male sex partner? Or does this mean they are less receptive to receiving oral sex? More research is needed in this area. Also, oral sex is no

TABLE 9.5   College Students and Sex

	Percent		
	Male	Female	Total
Oral Sex within the Past 30 Days			
Never did this sexual act	27.8%	28.8%	28.5%
Have not done this the past 30 days	27.8%	26.8%	27.2%
Did this one or more times	44.4%	44.3%	44.3%
Vaginal Sex within the Past 30 Days			
Never did this sexual act	32.8%	30.7%	31.4%
Have not done this the past 30 days	22.1%	18.3%	19.7%
Did this one or more times	45.1%	51.0%	48.9%
Anal Sex within the Past 30 Days			
Never did this sexual act	70.6%	77.3%	74.9%
Have not done this the past 30 days	23.1%	18.9%	22.4%
Did this one or more times	6.3%	3.8%	4.7%

Source: National College Health Assessment (2008).

longer considered to be just a prelude to sexual inter-course; instead, it is something college students partici-pate in for the act itself.

Spring Break and Sex Alcohol and sex are a danger-ous combination for college women. In a recent study of 644 college women by the American Medical Associ-ation (AMA, 2006), Spring Break binge drinking lead to unsafe and unwanted sex, sexually transmitted infec-tions, blackouts, and violence. Key findings of this rele-vant study reveal that among study participants:

- 83 percent drank every night while on Spring Break, or had friends who did.
- 74 percent believed that drinking is an excuse to engage in outrageous behaviors.
- 86 percent believed that these outrageous behaviors contributed to dangerous behaviors by males toward females.
- 57 percent agreed that being sexually promiscuous was a way to fit in with the crowd.
- 92 percent said that it was very easy to obtain alcohol.
- 59 percent knew friends who had sex with more than one partner during the week of Spring Break.
- 3 out of every 5 respondents had friends who had unprotected sex during Spring Break.
- 1 in 5 women regretted the sexual activity they engaged in during Spring Break.
- 12 percent felt forced to have sex.

ALCOHOL and sex can be a bad combination for college students, particularly college women. It's important to know that if a woman says "no" to sex, it always means "no"—even if she's had something (or a lot) to drink.

The combination of alcohol and sex is treacherous. The American Medical Association notes that each spring in Cancun, Mexico, a popular Spring Break destination, there is a sig-nificant increase in the numbers of deaths, rapes, and assaults reported, and all are related to drinking. In 2005 during Spring Break in Daytona, Florida, another popular beach destina-tion, twice as many rape cases were reported than in any other month of the year. As a matter of safety and well-being for college students, the AMA contends that universities and colleges need to change their current policies, requiring Spring Break tour promoters to restrict ads that promote cheap and free alcohol, or to offer Spring Break alternatives that do not include alcohol.

You are beginning to understand that your sexuality does not develop in isolation. Throughout your lifespan, your sexual development is multifaceted, shaped, and reshaped by many interacting influences. Who you are as a sexual person and how you came to be the sex-ual person you are is a complex tapestry woven together from biological, developmental, and cultural influences. And who you will be as an older sexual person is no exception. We will explore many facets of sexuality development during middle and late adulthood in Chap-ter 16.

Sexually Transmitted Infections

Sexually transmitted infections (STIs) are diseases that are transmitted between partners through sexual contact, such as vaginal intercourse, oral sex, nonpenetrative genital contact, or anal sex, and they remain one of our nation's greatest health challenges. Today, two-thirds of all sexually transmitted infections are found in young adults under the age of 25 (Centers for Disease Control, 2009), and almost half of the 19 million diagnosed cases of STIs each year in the United States are among young men and women aged 15 to 24 (Centers for Disease Control, 2009). Because of these data, it is necessary to have an understanding of the trends, treatments, and prevention of common sexually transmitted infections. By gaining an understanding of STIs, young men and women can both protect their sexual and reproductive health, and they can better enjoy their sexuality. In addition to the burden on youth and young adults, women are also severely affected because their physiology places them at greater risk than men for the severe consequences of STIs (Centers for Disease Control, 2009).

There are two broad categories of sexually transmitted illnesses. *Bacterial infections* include gonorrhea, chlamydia, and syphilis. Caused by certain micro-organisms, bacterial infections can be treated by the use of antibiotics. *Viral infections* include herpes, human papillomavirus (HPV), and viral hepatitis. These diseases cannot be treated by antibiotics, although there are medications that help alleviate or lessen the symptoms. Unless otherwise noted, all data trends are gathered from the Centers for Disease Control and Prevention (2009).

GONORRHEA

Sometimes referred to as the *clap* or *drip*, **gonorrhea** is the second-most common STI reported in the United States. On average, 700,000 people are diagnosed with gonorrhea each year. Racial disparities in gonorrhea rates are severe—the rate among African Americans is 19 times greater than that of whites (663 cases per 100,000 for blacks, compared to 35 cases per 100,00 for whites), and in 2007, 70 percent of all gonorrhea cases occurred among blacks. Figure 9.6 shows the racial differences in gonorrhea rates, by race.

Gonorrhea is caused by a bacterium that survives in the mucous membranes of the body, such as the eyes, throat, mouth, cervix, rectum, and urethra. It is transmitted through intercourse, oral sex, and anal sex, and it can also be transmitted from the mother to her baby dur-

FIGURE 9.6   Gonorrhea: Rates per 100,000 Population by Race/Ethnicity, 2007

Gonorrhea is the second-most common STI that occurs in the United States. There are racial and ethnic differences in the occurrences of gonorrhea.

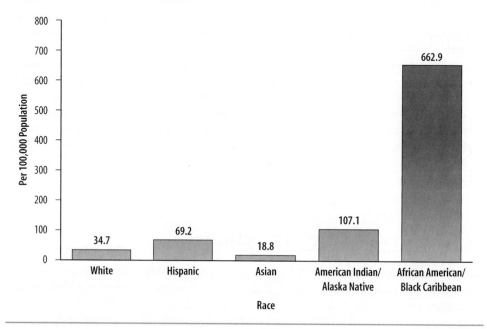

Source: Centers for Disease Control and Prevention (2009).

ing birth; ejaculation does not have to occur for gonorrhea to be transmitted or acquired. In most cases, there are no symptoms of gonorrhea: 80 percent of women and 10 percent of men with the STI show no symptoms. Most people do not know that they are infected; nevertheless, they are still able to infect their sex partners.

Because gonorrhea is a bacterial infection, it responds to antibiotics, such as penicillin. There is a wide range of antibiotics used today to treat gonorrhea; however, the disease is becoming more resistant to the standard treatments. Left untreated, this STI can cause *pelvic inflammatory disease* in women, causing infertility.

CHLAMYDIA

Chlamydia is the most common bacterial STI reported in the United States, with over 1.1 million cases reported in 2007; however, demographers believe that the majority of chlamydia cases are unreported, with at least 2.8 million cases that went unreported in 2007. As with other STIs, African Americans, American Indians/Alaska Natives, and Hispanics are disproportionately affected, and approximately one-half of all chlamydia cases occur among blacks. Figure 9.7 presents chlamydia rates, by race. The disease is transmitted through vaginal and anal intercourse, and from a mother to her baby during birth.

Three-fourths of women and half of men experience no symptoms of chlamydia. If symptoms do occur, they may begin as early as 5 to 10 days after infection; however, if symptoms occur, most experience them within 1 to 3 weeks after they have become infected (Johnsen, 2005). Chlamydia is very easy to treat with antibiotics. In fact, one treatment is given in only one dose. Commonly, the antibiotics are taken over the course of 7 days. To avoid the risk of re-infection, both partners are typically treated and are advised to be tested again after treatment before they resume sexual activity.

FIGURE 9.7   Chlamydia: Rates per 100,000 Population by Race/Ethnicity, 2007

Chlamydia is the most common STI in the United States.

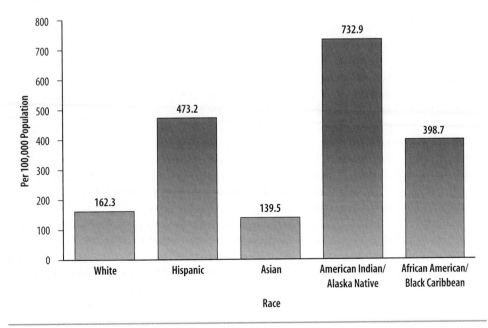

Source: Centers for Disease Control and Prevention (2009).

SYPHILIS

Syphilis is a bacterial infection that is spread through direct contact with a syphilis sore, which typically occurs on the external genitals, vagina, or anus. These sores can also develop on the lips, tongue, or mouth. This STI is transmitted through vaginal, oral, and anal sex, as well as from the mother to her unborn baby during birth. If a mother is untreated, her unborn baby has a 70 percent chance of being infected with syphilis during birth; over 40 percent of babies are stillborn if the mother is untreated. The syphilis rate among blacks is 7 times higher than that of whites (rates are per 100,000):

- African Americans/Black Caribbeans: 14.0
- Hispanics: 4.3
- American Indians/Alaska Natives: 3.4
- Whites: 2.0
- Asians: 1.2

There are three stages of syphilis:

1. During the *primary stage,* the first sore, or *chancre* (SHANK-ker), appears at the site of the infection. This usually occurs 10 days to 3 months after contact; the site of the infection is often internal and not visible to the eye. During this stage, there are no other symptoms.
2. About 3 to 6 weeks after the chancre appears, a rash develops over some or all of the body. This is called the *secondary stage.* During this stage, an infected person may also experience headaches, fever, fatigue, sore throat, and enlarged lymph nodes. These symptoms disappear without treatment.
3. Even left untreated, syphilis goes into a *latent period,* where the infected person is no longer contagious. During this stage, however, about one-third will experience damage to the heart, brain, eyes, and nervous system. Untreated, this can result in mental illness, even death.

Can syphilis be treated? Yes. Even during the latent stage of the disease, patients can be treated and cured, although the damage that occurs is irreversible. The drug of choice since the 1940s is penicillin.

HERPES

Herpes is a *viral* infection. It is caused when the herpes simplex virus (HSV) enters the body. Once a virus enters the body, it has the capability of reproducing itself—it cannot be destroyed by antibiotics like bacterial infections can be. Consequently, once a person becomes infected with a viral sexually transmitted infection, he or she will have it for the rest of his or her life. When the viral infection occurs on or near the mouth, it is called *oral herpes;* when it occurs on or near the genitals, it is called *genital herpes.* Each year, nearly 1 million people are infected with genital herpes, and nationwide, at least 45 million people over the age of 12 have had genital HSV—this represents 1 out of 5 adolescents/adults. Today, about 1 in every 4 women and 1 out of 8 men has herpes.

The virus is transmitted through touching and kissing, and through vaginal, anal, or oral sex. Generally, transmission occurs from an infected partner who is not aware that he or she has the virus. Most people are not aware that they are infected with genital herpes. Those that have symptoms notice the development of a herpes sore, usually within 2 weeks after the person is infected. The blister-like sores will open and "weep," and then scab over and heal in 2 to 4 weeks. It is important to note that most people with herpes will not develop these blisters, and if they do, the blisters may be so mild that they are mistaken for a bug bite or skin rash.

After the first outbreak or episode of genital herpes, most people will have four or five additional outbreaks within the first year. There is no cure for genital herpes. Usually, over a period of 5 or 6 years, the outbreaks of the sores become less frequent and weaker, gradually disappearing all together. If a person experiences more than six outbreaks in a 1-year period, there are medications that can help reduce the frequency and the symptoms of the virus. These types of treatment are called *suppressive therapy*, because while they do not cure the infection, they alleviate the symptoms.

HUMAN PAPILLOMAVIRUS (HPV)

The **human papillomavirus (HPV)** infected 20 million people in 2007. Although it is not the most common STI, experts estimate that three out of four sexually active men and women will be infected with HPV at some point. In its more severe form, *high-risk* HPV can lead to certain cancers, such as cancer of the cervix, vagina, anus, and penis. Other types of the virus, *low risk*, can cause genital warts. This STI is spread through vaginal, oral, and anal intercourse, as well as through skin-to-skin contact, such as during sex play and body rubbing.

In most cases of HPV, there are no symptoms. The virus lives, undetected, in the skin or mucous membranes of the body. Sometimes a symptom of the virus is the appearance of *genital warts,* which are soft, moist, pink/flesh-colored growths found on the vulva, vagina, anus, cervix, penis, scrotum, groin, or thigh. These warts may appear anywhere from 6 weeks to 9 months after infection, or not at all. Most people learn of their infection upon visual diagnosis of a wart or cluster of warts. Women are typically diagnosed by a *PAP test,* which is a routine cancer-screening tool.

The human papillomavirus can be treated, but not cured. But because most of the cases of HPV are low-risk cases and go away by themselves, HPV is considered to be relatively harmless. To keep the warts from growing and multiplying, doctors have several treatment options, including:

- Applying chemical solutions that destroy the warts
- Removing the warts by freezing them with liquid nitrogen (cyrotherapy)
- Removing the warts with surgery or lasers

There is now a vaccine that is highly effective against the types of genital HPV that cause most cases of cervical cancer and genital warts. The vaccine, *Gardasil*, is given in three shots over a six-month period. It is routinely recommended for 11- and 12-year-old girls, and for girls and women ages 13 through 26 who have not yet been vaccinated. If you are sexually active and have not yet had the vaccination, your healthcare provider on campus will be able to give you helpful information.

VIRAL HEPATITIS

In general, **viral hepatitis** refers to inflammation of the liver, causing impairments in liver function. There are three types of viral hepatitis:

1. *Hepatitis A (HAV)*, which is spread through infected fecal matter that is found in water and in food. This type of hepatitis is usually transmitted when people do not wash their hands after using the bathroom.
2. *Hepatitis B (HBV)*, which is transmitted through bodily fluids during sexual contact, such as through semen, vaginal fluids, saliva, blood, and urine.
3. *Hepatitis C (HCV)*, which is typically spread through illegal drug use (infected needles), and unscreened blood transfusions.

Hepatitis B is the most common type of hepatitis. Each year in the United States, 78,000 people are infected with hepatitis B; about 1 in 20 Americans will become infected with HBV at some point during their lives. Because hepatitis is a viral infection, it cannot be treated by the use of antibiotics.

Understanding and protecting your sexual health is essential. Not only is it crucial to your overall health during your reproductive years, and to having a child or avoiding an unwanted pregnancy, but it also affects the health of the next generation—the children you may bear. But the importance of sexual health goes beyond your childbearing years. It directly contributes to your intimate relationships in many areas, including sexual fulfillment, and the physical and emotional comfort and closeness you share with your partner.

Relationships and Sex

None of us simply become "sexual" once we make the transition from adolescence into early adulthood or enter into a life partnership with someone we love—our sexual selves are in a continuous state of growth and change. Yet to fully develop our sexuality and sexual potential, we need an intimate partnership because sexual expression most often occurs in the context of interpersonal relationships (Ridley, Ogolsky, Payne, Totenhagen, & Cate, 2008).

Simon Montefiore (1993), in his qualitative study of "not-thirtysomething" sex (sex in our 30s, 40s, and beyond) noted, "Many of the married couples I spoke to have fantastic sex lives—even if none of them have sex as much as they did when they were single—and are blissfully happy" (p. 66). In his study, one couple married for 10 years noted, "You won't believe this, but we simply don't have sex anymore. On holidays we do, but we really have to convince each other. We're very happy, but a real chunk of my life that used to be important to me is dead. Maybe it's the cost of being happy" (p. 69).

Not as much sex as when they were single? They don't have sex anymore? Sex only on holidays? After only 10 years of marriage? You might be thinking, "How can you have less sex and still be 'blissfully happy'?!"

Throughout the 1990s, the scientific study of interpersonal relationships intensified with an increased emphasis placed on the *relational* aspects of sexuality. As marriage is still the most socially recognizable and socially approved coupling for the expression of sexuality, we first turn our attention to marital sexuality. Yet what makes a sexually satisfying marital relationship depends on a number of factors, which we'll explore, such as sexual frequency, orgasmic response, and extramarital sexuality.

SEXUAL RELATIONSHIP SATISFACTION AND MARITAL SATISFACTION

What makes a great sex life? A rich, committed, communicative marriage? Or, does a great sex life make a great marriage? Is it possible to have a great marriage without a great sexual relationship? Is it possible to have a great sexual relationship without a caring, committed, rich marital partnership? Although researchers have attempted to find answers to these questions, it has been much like the chicken and the egg debate—which comes first, sexual satisfaction or marital satisfaction? Can these issues be disentangled?

As early as the 1960s, researchers explored the roles of sexual satisfaction as a contributor to overall marital satisfaction. According to community health professor Kelli-Ann Lawrance and her colleague, psychologist Sandra Byers (1995), who specialize in marital and sexual satisfaction, sexual satisfaction in long-term heterosexual relationships depends on the partners' perceptions of the relationship. These perceptions include expectations, hopes, desires, and anticipation. All of us enter into relationships with these perceptions and expectations, whether they are spoken or unspoken, realistic or unrealistic.

In a study that examined sexual practices in the United States, one body of research found that, overall, married couples are enjoying sex (Laumann and others 1994). The majority of

My Sexual Inventory

When I am physically close with someone, I feel _____ _____.

I describe sex as _____ _____.

To me, virginity is _____ _____.

My sex scripts include _____ _____.

My sex scripts encourage _____ _____.

My sex scripts discourage _____ _____.

The strengths of our sexual relationship are _____ _____.

We do have weaknesses in our sexual relationship. They are _____ _____.

When we talk about sex, it makes me feel _____ _____.

When we have sex, I like it best when you/we _____ _____.

When we have sex, I like it least when you/we _____ _____.

I am most easily aroused when _____ _____.

Big turn-offs for me are _____ _____.

Sexually, I am most afraid when _____ _____.

If there is one thing our sexual relationship is missing, it is _____ _____.

individuals, around 88 percent, indicated that their sexual relationships were either extremely or very physically pleasing, and these relationships tended to be high in physical affection. Of all couple types who responded to the survey, including married people, cohabitants, gays and lesbians, monogamous married couples reported the highest level of sexual satisfaction. An abundance of other research also indicates that married couples have high levels of sexual satisfaction within their marital relationships (among many others, Edwards & Booth, 1994; Haavio-Mannila & Kontula, 1997; Janus & Janus, 1993; Lawrance & Byers, 1994; Purnine, Carey, & Jorgensen, 1997). Researchers discovered that the quality of the couple's intimate communication—particularly self-disclosure—leads to greater relationship satisfaction, which, in turn, leads to greater sexual satisfaction (MacNeil & Byers, 2005).

Researchers have sought to determine how sexual scripts influence marital relationship and sexual satisfaction. Sociologist Susan Sprecher (2002) found that among women, increased relationship satisfaction leads to increased sexual satisfaction, and among men, increased sexual satisfaction leads to increased relationship satisfaction. Sprecher attributed her findings to the fact that women's sex scripts socialize them to enjoy sex only in committed, fulfilling relationships, while men's sex scripts socialize them to be motivated by sex. Other research confirmed Sprecher's ideas about sex scripts and relationship/sexual satisfaction in marriages (Byers, 2005; Vohs, Cantonese, & Baumeister, 2004).

In a rare study that sought to determine sexual and relationship satisfaction of married couples in mainland China, researchers found that Chinese men and women are moderately satisfied with their marital sexual relationships (Renaud, Byers, & Pan, 1997). The more affection and sexual behavior in the relationship, the greater the sexual and marital relationship satisfaction. These conclusions are consistent with U.S. and Canadian research where husbands' and wives' ratings of sexual satisfaction are associated with increased marital relationship satisfaction (Henderson-King & Veroff, 1994; Lawrance & Byers, 1995; Oggins, Leber, & Veroff, 1993; Schenk, Pfrang, & Rausche, 1983; Young, Young, & Luquis, 2000).

So, what makes great marital lives and great sex lives? Perhaps Hunt sums it up best: "The husband and wife who have a free and intensely pleasurable sexual relationship are much more likely to be emotionally close than the husband and wife who do not, and the close marriage is more likely to involve a genuinely liberated marital sex than the distant one" (1974, p. 232).

Sexual Frequency in Intimate Relationships Frequency of intercourse and overall satisfaction with the marital sexual relationship have received a great deal of scientific inquiry and attention, although it's difficult to find data that address sexual frequency in different couple types. However, in a nonscientific global sex survey funded by Durex (the largest condom manufacturer in the world), statisticians found that, worldwide, married couples have sex an average of 127 times a year (about 10 times per month). Americans were low on the frequency list, at 98 times per year (about 8 times per month). The countries with the lowest frequency of sex were Japan (37 times per year), Malaysia (62 times per year), and China (69 times per year); about 4 percent of Americans claimed they have sex every day (Durex, 2007).

We do know from research that age is often negatively associated with sexual frequency and sexual satisfaction. Married couples tend to have sex less frequently and to feel less sexually satisfied as they age; this finding is also true among Chinese societies (Chevret, Jaudinot, Sullivan, Marrel, & De Gendre, 2004; Mazur, Mueller, Krause, & Booth, 2002; Guo & Huang, 2005).

Orgasmic Response The ubiquitous orgasm. Songs have been written about it ("Oh, sweet mystery of life at last I've found you!"). Men's and women's magazines proudly boast the latest "how to" when it comes to achieving better and more frequent orgasms. Merely mentioning the word to young, inexperienced sexual couples or to those who have not had an orgasm or even to long-term couples adds pressure—she experiences the pressure to "achieve an orgasm," and he feels the pressure to "bring her" to (supposedly) ultimate sexual fulfillment.

In heterosexual encounters, women are less likely to reach orgasm than men; this delay or absence of orgasm is referred to as **anorgasmia** (Richters, de Visser, Rissel, & Smith, 2006). In a recent study of over 19,000 male and female participants, ages 16 to 59, the investigators found that 69 percent of the female respondents had an orgasm during their most recent sexual encounter (such as vaginal intercourse, intercourse with manual stimulation of the clitoris, or intercourse with manual and oral stimulation of the clitoris) (Richters and others, 2006). This is in comparison to 95 percent of males who had an orgasm in their most recent sexual encounter. A previous study found that nearly two-thirds of the female study participants did not experience orgasm in their recent sexual encounters (Seeber & Gorrell, 2001).

Why is it that so many women have difficulties with orgasm, in comparison to men? A number of factors are known to influence orgasmic response in women, such as upbringing, attitudes, religion, anxiety, and previous sexually traumatic experiences (Davidson & Darling,

1989; Andersen & Cyranowski, 1995). Recent studies have revealed other factors associated with women's orgasm experiences (Wade, Kremer & Brown, 2005; Richters and others, 2006):

- *Age.* There appears to be a "learning effect" associated with orgasm. Men and women under the age of 20 and men with less than 3 years of sexual experience are less likely to have an orgasm. Women aged 16 to 19 are least likely to have an orgasm. Older women, ages 50 to 59, are also less likely to experience an orgasm; this may be due to hormonal decreases.
- *Partner type.* Both men and women are less likely to have an orgasm if the sexual encounter was with an occasional or casual sex partner rather than a steady partner; they are more likely to have an orgasm if they have been with their partner for at least one year.
- *Sexual behavior.* Men and women are more likely to experience an orgasm if they engage in a variety of sexual behaviors during the encounter. Women are more likely to have an orgasm when oral and manual stimulation of the clitoris are added to vaginal intercourse (70 percent versus 50 percent whose only reported practice is vaginal intercourse).
- *Knowledge of the clitoris.* In general, men's knowledge about the clitoris is equivalent to women's; however, this knowledge does not translate into orgasm for women. Women's self-exploration and masturbation appear to be associated with higher rates of orgasm.
- *Partner's technique.* Hitting the "hot spots" doesn't happen without practice, practice, practice. Partners' clitoral stimulation techniques increase the likelihood that a woman will have an orgasm.

There is a prevailing North American cultural belief that orgasmic response during the sex act is the be-all and end-all of sexual response. But it is possible that sexual satisfaction and orgasmic response/consistency are two different things.

In support of this notion, sexologist Suiming Pan's (1993) study of Chinese women found that 54 percent experienced low orgasmic response, yet felt that this was perfectly fine and acceptable. In fact, 11 percent of the women surveyed felt that their orgasmic responses were too high! While this study illustrates possible cultural differences in how women view their sexuality, it also indicates that there is a difference between *goal-oriented* sexual activity ("achieving," "reaching," "attaining" orgasmic response) and *pleasure-oriented* sexual activity ("I may not be having an orgasm, but this feels really good and I'm having a great time!").

NONMARITAL SEX

Throughout this text, deliberate effort has been made to refer to sexual couples as "partners" rather than as spouse or husband and wife. This is important to point out because much of what we have previously discussed can be applied to any type of *sexual dyad* (a two-person sexual relationship), whether the couple is married, cohabiting, gay, lesbian, or bisexual. For example, the information concerning sexual dysfunctions and problems can be applied to all couple types. Although the overall trends may be different than for marital sexual partners, nonmarital sexual couples are, by and large, also concerned about relationship satisfaction, sexual frequency, and sexual relationships outside of their committed relationships.

Cohabiting Couples Despite the tenfold increase in cohabiting relationships since the sexual revolution of the 1960s, surprisingly scant attention has been given to the sexual and relational aspects of this dyad type. The 1983 study by Blumstein and Schwartz of American couple types is perhaps the most extensive study to date. In their research, the authors found differences in sexual expression between cohabiting and married couples. The findings suggest that cohabiting couples were more likely to have sexual intercourse more frequently than married couples (three times per week compared to once per week), and were not only more likely to have sex outside of the cohabiting relationship but were also less secretive than married couples about the outside sexual activities. In cohabitant relationships, the female was more likely to initiate sexual acts than were married women. Men in cohabiting relationships tended to be more committed to the relationship if the partner was "attractive."

EMPIRICAL studies about the sexual behaviors of gay men and lesbians are scant, but existing research shows that gays and lesbians have distinct ways they sexually interact with their partners.

In a study that examined sexual satisfaction in premarital cohabitating relationships, Sprecher (2002) found that the respondents indicated overall sexual satisfaction within the cohabiting relationship, and that sexual satisfaction was also positively correlated with relationship satisfaction, love for partner, and the level of commitment to the relationship.

Gay and Lesbian Couples Information concerning sexual relationships of committed same-sex couples indicates that sexuality is quite similar to that of heterosexual couples. For instance, in one study that explored sexual satisfaction, no differences in sexual satisfaction were found among gay, lesbian, heterosexual cohabitants, and heterosexual married couples (Kurdek, 1991). As the discussion of marital relationship satisfaction revealed, overall relationship satisfaction corresponds with sexual satisfaction. Similar to Blumstein and Schwartz's study (1983), other research found that lesbian couples engage in sexual intercourse less frequently than heterosexual married women (Kurdek, 1991; Lever, 1995; Leichliter, Chandra, Kiddon, Fenton, & Aral, 2007). Gay couples, on the other hand, have sexual intercourse more frequently than any other couple type, although as the duration of the relationship increases, sexual intercourse tends to decrease, as in the case of married heterosexual couples. According to Blumstein and Schwartz (1983), gay men exhibit the highest rate of accepted extra-relationship (nonmonogamy) sex than any other couple type.

In 2002, *The Advocate,* a magazine marketed to the gay, lesbian, bisexual, and transgender populations, conducted a poll intended to survey feelings about sexual relationships. Respondents to this nonscientific poll indicated that, overall, they are quite satisfied with their sexual relationships. For example, 88 percent of the males and 79 percent of the women noted that they are quite happy in their same-sex sexual relationships and have no intention of "converting" to heterosexuality. Of the gay/bisexual men surveyed, 22 percent indicated that for them, kissing is the most important part of sex; conversely, 16 percent of the lesbian/bisexual women indicated this to be true. For both sexes (64 percent of women and 57 percent of men) "foreplay" is considered the most important part of the sex act. When asked, "When is sex the best for you?," 67 percent of the men and 87 percent of the women indicated that "building intimacy with a single partner" makes for the best sex.

CHEATING: SEX OUTSIDE THE RELATIONSHIP

Infidelity, or **cheating**, is a breach of faith that occurs when there is a violation of the couple's mutually agreed-on rules or boundaries of a relationship. Oftentimes infidelity is referred to as *extramarital affairs* or *extramarital experiences.* Extramarital experiences can occur when one marital partner ventures outside the relationship and becomes emotionally and/or sexually involved with another person. What constitutes an act of infidelity varies between and within cultures, as well as within individual relationships. Almost always, these types of extramarital experiences result in a breakdown of trust within the relationship. When one partner ventures outside the relationship without the other's knowledge or permission, it is said to be an **involuntary extramarital experience**.

Involuntary Experiences As our study of intimate relationships and sex has shown us so far, intimate relationships—be they dating, cohabiting, gay/lesbian, or marriages—involve behaviors and emotions that are generally expected to be restricted to the relationship. When any behavior oversteps the expectations of exclusivity and expectations of monogamy, it is considered to be an **extra relationship involvement (ERI)** (Banfield & McCabe, 2001). There are three types of ERI (Thompson, 1984):

1. *Sexual ERI.* This type of behavior involves a wide range of behaviors, from flirting, to mutual masturbation, to oral and anal sex, to sexual intercourse.
2. *Emotional ERI.* Emotional extra relationship involvement also includes a range of behaviors and includes a close friendship (with much self-disclosure) rather than being "in love."
3. *Combination of sexual and emotional ERI.* As the term implies, in this category a person can engage in a wide variety of behaviors that encompass both emotional and sexual areas of a relationship.

Extramarital sex (EMS) occurs when a married person has a sexual relationship with anyone other than her or his spouse. Just as with ERI, there are different types of EMS. These include (Clayton, 1997):

- *Clandestine.* In this type of EMS, the participating members do not believe either of their spouses (if the partner is married) knows about the sexual relationship, nor do they believe their spouse(s) would approve.
- *Ambiguous.* In these relationships, the role of the nonparticipating spouse is crucial. The nonparticipating spouse may know about the EMS but cannot prove it; the nonparticipating spouse may choose to tolerate it rather than seek divorce; the nonparticipating spouse may have at one time endorsed the EMS but later disapproved; or he or she may approve of the EMS but does not want details.
- *Consensual.* In this type of relationship, the nonparticipating spouse both knows and approves of the EMS; each spouse may have a consensual relationship outside the boundaries of marriage (we discuss these types of relationships in just a bit).

It is very difficult to acquire data on just how many spouses cheat on their partners, and what data are available are probably outdated. One study suggested that nearly 40 percent of married men and 20 percent of married women have been involved in ERI/EMS at least once during their marriage (Laumann and others, 1994). A more recent study had similar findings, that about 44 percent of men and 24 percent of women had at least one ERI/EMS experience in their marriages (Banfield & McCabe, 2001).

Given the devastating effect cheating has on marital relationships and the difficulty in repairing marriages that have been impacted by extramarital relationships (Oppenheimer, 2007), why do people cheat on their spouses?

Are You a Cheater?

Internet pornography, chatrooms, texting, and IMing may be harmless to some, but others may consider it to be disloyal and believe it violates the trust in their relationship. How do you know if you're an online cheater? Ask yourself these questions:

1. If my partner were standing behind me and looking over my shoulder, would I engage in the same behavior? Are my behaviors intruding in my relationship?
2. Am I seeking things/fulfilling needs from other sources that aren't being met in my relationship? If so, how can I change this?
3. Have I asked my partner how he or she feels about my online activities? How does he or she feel? Are my activities more important than my relationship?

Own It!

Why Do People Cheat? Research has revealed a number of factors that are associated with an increased risk of engaging in ERI/EMS. These include:

- *Gender.* Men are more likely to have extramarital relationships than women are (Atkins, Jacobson, & Baucom, 2001).
- *Age.* Younger married people experience higher rates of extramarital activity than older married people (Kimuna & Kjamba, 2005).
- *Personality traits.* Some personality traits, such as narcissism and low levels of conscientiousness, are associated with cheating (Atkins and others, 2001).
- *Marital satisfaction.* Lower levels of relationship satisfaction are linked to increased rates of extramarital behaviors for both men and women (Wiederman, 1997).
- *Length of marriage.* The longer the duration of the marriage, the less likely a man or a woman is to cheat on the spouse (Liu, 2000).
- *Opportunity.* Some people have more opportunities to cheat, such as jobs that take them away from their spouses (Atkins and others, 2001).

Past research claimed that men and women have different ideas about sex and love. For instance, one study found that men believe women must be in love to have sex, whereas women think that men may have sex without being in love (Harris & Christenfeld, 1996). Other research has similarly found that women do not tend to become sexually involved in the absence of emotional commitment (love), but men can (Townsend, 1995). This research is interesting because it suggests that women may be more likely to engage in emotional ERI, whereas men are more likely to engage in EMS. This leads us to another important question that needs to be addressed: Is an Internet relationship "cheating"?

Are Internet Relationships "Cheating"? This is a common question that my students ask. In some respects it is a difficult question to answer because research into this ever-evolving area subsumes romantic relationships, friendships, and sexual partnerships under the general category of online relationships (McQuillen, 2003). In addition to this, it is difficult to determine the meaning people attach to these relationships—is it just for fun because an Internet user is bored? Is it for sexual pleasure/gratification? Is it "innocent" flirting?

In a study of over 500 online users, researchers found several themes in online relationships. When it came to the question as to whether online relationships constituted extramarital affairs, views were mixed among study participants. Several indicated that they participated in Internet affairs because they were unhappy in their real-life marriages—they stressed that their pre-existing marriage problems caused them to seek an affair. Other participants noted that the online affairs were just as painful a betrayal as real-life affairs, and just as devastating. Noted one participant, "The effect on a husband when he discovers his wife has been having cyber-sex is sheer hell. I now have a deep distrust of my wife and a feeling of constant paranoia. The effects on my marriage [of her online affair] have been disastrous" (Wildermuth & Vogl-Bauer, 2007, p. 219).

Extramarital affairs or sexual relationships outside of committed relationships cause much emotional pain, devastation, and torment for the victimized partner, and include reactions such as rage, feelings of shame, depression, overwhelming powerlessness, and abandonment, along with a prolonged disruption in daily functioning (Gordon, Baucom, & Snyder, 2004). So traumatic are the effects of extramarital affairs, marriage therapist Douglas Snyder (Snyder, Gordon, & Baucom, 2004) maintains that sexual infidelity is the most difficult relationship issue to treat.

THE CONNECTION BETWEEN LOVE AND SEX

Certainly we can love someone without experiencing sex, and certainly we can experience sex without loving the sexual partner, such as in hookups (see Chapter 7). Is there a connection between love and sex? Some researchers argue that the link between love and sex is forged by natural sex selection (Buss, 1985; Frey & Hojjat, 1998). Sex is important, of course, because it transfers genes from one generation to the next and ensures the longevity of the culture. But love is just as important as sex because it binds together family units that serve to nurture and protect the helpless, defenseless offspring; just like sex, love is a necessary mechanism to perpetuate the species. Thus, sex and love are inextricably linked to survival (Frey & Hojjat, 1998).

Newer research suggests that being in love is what actually drives someone to want to have sex with his or her love object. Neuroscientist Arthur Aron and his team of anthropology and social psychology colleagues (2005) used brain scans to study the brains of 17 young men and women who were "newly" or "madly" in love. This study is particularly relevant to our discussion here because the researchers wanted to answer the historic question of whether love and sex are really the same thing. More specifically, the researchers wanted to know if the feelings we have in our early love relationships are, in actuality, just warmed-over feelings of sexual arousal. The results of the brain scans indicated that the early, intense feelings associated with passionate/romantic love have more to do with motivation and reward than with the sex drive. The researchers found that romantic love is a highly motivated, goal-oriented state— and this state is what makes us want to pursue sex with our lovers, and to protect our lovers and the relationship. According to this research, romantic love is more powerful than the human sex drive, and sex and romantic love involve quite different brain systems.

You may be wondering on a more practical level about the connection between love and sex. For instance, is sex better if we love our partner?

Is Sex Better if We Love Our Sex Partner? Love can be an important motivational force for the participation in sexual activities (Kaestle & Tucker-Halpern, 2007; Aron and others, 2005). But is sex actually better if we love our partner?

How we experience sex, and the sense of enjoyment or satisfaction we get from sex is highly personal (Davidson, Darling, & Norton, 1995). There are, of course, a number of characteristics, behaviors, emotions, relationship background factors, and social background factors that contribute to sexual satisfaction, as our study of sexual scripts has shown us (Sprecher & McKinney, 1993). But a wide body of empirical evidence indicates that there is an association between sexual satisfaction and relationship satisfaction (among many, Bartels & Zeki, 2000; Regan, 2000; Christopher & Sprecher, 2000; Sprecher, 2002; Aron and others, 2005; Kaestle & Tucker-Halpern, 2007). For example, one study of 101 college-age dating couples found that men and women who are most sexually satisfied tended also to report high levels of love and commitment; couples who reported lower levels of sexual satisfaction were more likely to report lower levels of love and commitment (Sprecher, 2002).

The most recent investigation of 6,421 young adults, ages 18 to 26, revealed that study participants who were in love reported higher levels of sexual satisfaction (Kaestle & Tucker-Halpern, 2007). For instance, study respondents who reported high levels of love for their partner and who reported that their partner felt high levels of love for them, engaged in a greater variety of sexual activities than those who reported lower levels of love. For both males and females, participating in a particular sexual activity was associated with the love pattern within the relationship. In this study, for example, males were twice as likely to have received oral sex when the partners loved each other; similarly, females were more likely to have received oral sex when the partners loved each other a lot, and when she felt that her partner loved her. Also, if partners indicated they loved each other a lot, they were more likely to engage in anal sex than when neither partner loved the other a lot. Overall, the

THERE'S no doubt about it: Couples in love have better sex than couples who are not in love!

research findings supported the researchers' notion that higher levels of love are associated with greater sexual variety within the relationship, leading to higher levels of relationship satisfaction. Previous studies have also demonstrated that sexual satisfaction is positively associated with other indicators of relationship quality, including love and commitment (Waite & Joyner, 2001; Christopher & Sprecher, 2000; Sprecher & Regan, 2000; Sprecher, 2002). The research certainly tends to support the idea that sex is better if we love our sex partner.

Are There Differences in How Men and Women View Love and Sex? Are men and women really that different when it comes to how they view love and sex? There is some evidence that it is easier for men to have sex with little or no emotional attachment or commitment to the sex partner than it is for women; it is also easier for men to have sex just for pleasure than it is for women (Buss, 1999). There is also empirical evidence that indicates men are more likely than women to want sex early on in the relationship (perhaps within hours!) (Knox, Sturidivant, & Zusman, 2001). Interestingly, although men are more likely to engage in sex without an emotional attachment to their partner, they tend to express their love first and have higher levels of romantic beliefs than do women (Sharp & Ganong, 2000).

A recent study of 147 college undergraduates showed that men are significantly more likely than females to say "I love you" sooner in the relationship—but they have a sexual agenda for doing so (Brantley, Knox, & Zusman, 2002). In this study, the sociology researchers wanted to understand the timing and meaning of saying "I love you" to a new partner. Analysis of their findings showed two interesting results:

1. *Men tend to say "I love you" first.* Men reported that in relationships where both partners mutually loved each other, men disclosed their love first.
2. *Men tend to say "I love you" for sex.* If men thought that saying "I love you" would increase the chance that their partners would have sex with them, they did so.

The authors of the study suggest that men say "I love you" because their past sexual encounters reinforced that declaring their love is associated with women being more willing to have sex. The authors even go a step further and explain that males have adopted this particular sex script as a way to ensure their reproductive success with as many women as possible (see the Evolutionary theory discussion in Chapter 7). Whatever the reason, this study clearly showed that within this study sample, men used love to get sex. As the researchers note, "Students now have empirical verification that hearing 'I love you' may mean little more than 'I am saying this just so . . . you will have sex with me'" (Knox & Zusman, 2002, p. 615).

Experiencing Sexual Difficulties

Let's face it—at some time in our relational careers, our sex parts may fail to meet our expectations or our partner's expectations. While this failure to meet expectations has often been made fun of in television and film comedies, the fact is, sexual difficulties can be emotionally agonizing and negatively affect relationships.

Sexuality is a complex process. It includes the involvement of a number of biological factors, such as the neurological, vascular, and endocrine systems, in addition to a number of societal influences, such as family of origin influences, cultural contexts, and religious beliefs (Bachmann & Phillips, 1998). It also encompasses individual influences, such as relationship quality, needs, and moods. Our sexuality is also altered as we age, or with a decline in health status. A breakdown in any one or more of these areas may lead to or directly cause sexual dysfunction (Phillips, 2000).

Broadly speaking, **sexual dysfunction** is the inability to fully enjoy sex. Sexual dysfunction can begin early in a person's life, or it may gradually develop after a person has previously experienced satisfying and pleasurable sex. For convenience and ease of study, we'll organize our discussion into two categories: women and men.

SEXUAL DYSFUNCTIONS IN WOMEN

Sexual dysfunctions in women are common occurrences, affecting as many as 25 percent—47 million—U.S. women (Gordon, 2002). Specifically, sexual dysfunctions include disorders that result in inadequate sexual functioning in sexual arousal and response; it also includes sexual pain, referred to as **dyspareunia**.

Having too little sexual desire is the most common sexual issue that women encounter, reported by anywhere from 10 to 51 percent of multiethnic women in sexual studies; this low level of desire is commonly accompanied by low levels of sexual excitement and infrequent orgasms in women (Mercer and others, 2003; Matthiesen & Wenn, 2004; Laumann and others, 2005; Basson, 2006; Elnashar, Ibrahim, El-Desoky, Ali, & Hasson, 2006). Rosemary Basson has extensively studied the topic of female sexual desire. In her studies, she has found several inter-related factors that are relevant to difficulties in female sexual desire (Basson, 2005, 2006):

- *Interpersonal and contextual factors.* The two strongest predictors of distress about sex are the emotional relationship with the partner and general emotional well-being. Feeling emotionally close to a partner during sexual activity and having good emotional health are correlated with higher levels of sexual desire.
- *Personal psychological factors.* Sometimes a woman's sexual desire is affected by distractions, such as daily-life distractions (bills, children, schedules, worry, anxiety) or sexual distractions (worrying about becoming pregnant, STIs, not becoming sufficiently aroused, reaching orgasm, body image, or a partner's lack of orgasm or premature ejaculation). This category also includes memories of past sexual experiences, such as rape, abuse, or negative expectations that "this time" will be just like "last time" (such as experiencing physical pain during sex).
- *Biological factors.* A number of biological factors may diminish women's sexual desire, including depression, the use of antidepressants, directly after the birth of a child, hormonal imbalances due to surgical removal of the ovaries or the aging process (menopause), and other illnesses such as diabetes, heart disease, and cancer. We discuss these illnesses, as well as the option of *hormone replacement therapy* (*HRT*), in the next chapter.

Of course, it's understandable that at times we all experience low sexual desire. "Life" sometimes causes us to be too tired or just too stressed to get in the mood. To be better able to determine if we or our partners are experiencing a sexual desire disorder, it is important to become familiar with what our "normal" levels of sexual desire are, so we can then compare this with situations that may cause us to lose interest in sex. Given time and attention, low sexual desire is often reversible.

SEXUAL DYSFUNCTIONS IN MEN

Male sexual dysfunction is one of the most common health problems that affects men (Parmet, 2004). Just as with women, male sexual difficulties can be caused by physical problems, psychological problems, or a combination of both.

Often referred to as *impotence,* **erectile dysfunction (ED)** is the inability of a man to develop and/or maintain a firm erection long enough to have satisfactory sex. This problem can occur at any age, and most men experience it from time to time. It is thought to be a concern if it persists over a period of 3 months (Parmet, 2004). Erectile dysfunction is the most common sexual problem for men, affecting more than 18 million men in the United States over the age of 20 (Selvin, Burnett, & Platz, 2007). In a recent study of 3,400 heterosexual and gay men, for example, the researchers found that from one-third to nearly one-half of the study participants experience ED at least occasionally (Bancroft, Carnes, Janssen, & Long, 2005). Another study revealed that over one-half of the nearly 400 male participants had experienced ED at least periodically (Feldman and others, 2000). The study also demonstrated that ED is increasingly prevalent with age. For instance, at age 40, approximately 40 percent of the study participants experienced either mild, moderate, or complete ED; this rate increased to nearly 70 percent by age 70.

Rapid ejaculation (RE), also referred to as **premature ejaculation**, is ejaculation that occurs before, on, or shortly after penetration with minimal sexual stimulation (American Urological Association, 2008). Rapid ejaculation is the most common sexual dysfunction among men. It's not enough to diagnose the problem, because any one problem can cause a domino effect—premature ejaculation can be addressed, but aspects of the couple's relationship may yet need to be addressed, depression may need to be treated, past traumas may need to be addressed, medication may need to be prescribed, and couples may need to learn or re-learn different ways of thinking and sexual behaviors (Basson, 2005). Any sexual problem that persists for more than a few weeks is worth a visit to a healthcare provider, counselor, or sex therapist.

Family Life Education

The couple portrayed in the opening page of this chapter is my mother and father. From as early as I can remember, my parents were always demonstrative in their feelings toward one another, and quite open in the expression of their sexuality—holding hands, sitting on one another's laps, patting each other on the rear end, kissing, and nuzzling each other. Their final act of intimacy, then, was simply an extension of what I had witnessed as my own sexuality grew, changed, and evolved across my lifespan. Their final act of intimacy was a reminder to me that we are born sexual, and we die sexual.

Their experiences were the foundations of my sexual scripts and today contribute significantly to my own sexuality. The expression of their marital sexuality throughout their marriage was an expression of the richness of their marital union, an expression of pleasure and play, an expression of the mutual comfort and help they provided one another, an expression of the commitment to their relationship, and, in my mother's final moments, an expression of agony and separation. Their corporate sexuality was a compilation of individual development and shared experiences, and of individual and societal expectations—not unlike our own sexuality.

You see, real sex isn't about explosive, perfectly timed orgasms (every time, no less). It's not about two beautiful, perfect bodies performing in perfect, rhythmic sync. Real sex isn't about an affair where suddenly every emotional and physical need of yours is met by someone you don't even know the last name of.

Real sex is so much more than our sex-saturated society portrays. It is so much more than what the academic numbers tell us it is. Yes, frequency of sex is important to marital satisfaction; yes, orgasm consistency is related to sexual satisfaction and thus, marital satisfaction. These data are important in our overall understanding of sexuality.

But real sex also means that sometimes you don't feel like sex, and your partner understands. It means telling your partner what you want and what you need and your partner respecting those wants and needs. Real sex means the "hot spots" are there because *you* put them there: Your partner is beautiful and sexy and sensual and "hot" because that's how you see him or her—and you treat him or her that way.

Real sex means being interrupted, perhaps even at the moment of climax, because your child just threw up in the bedroom next door or the UPS truck pulled up in the driveway. And sometimes it means you can't get aroused because there are too many bills to think about or you have too much work to do. Real sex means reaching out to your partner out of anger or disappointment, exhilaration or desperation, loneliness or celebration. It means clinging helplessly to your partner as if you were on a life raft in the middle of a swollen ocean because you just received word of your father's death, or your child's death. Real sex means navigating around the tubes and the innumerable stitches in her chest because the cancer wouldn't let go. It means aging and finding out that sometimes the emotional connection is just as intense as the physical connection was in earlier years. And, like the couple in the opening page of this chapter, real sex means longing for, aching for, and memorizing your terminally ill partner's body. The pain was real because the sex was real.

"He wants it all the time, at least three times a week."
"I hardly want it at all, only three times a week."

A common theme runs through families today: too many demands, too many pressures, and too little time for couples to connect and feel a part of each other's lives. Often, hectic lives lead to hectic relationships, and rather than talk about hurt feelings and pent-up sexual frustrations, the couple rolls over in bed away from each other, and the hurt intensifies.

Her Side: It's not that I don't love him. I do love him, and I know he tries so hard to make me happy. It's just that I'm *so tired* all the time. With my job, the kids and all of their activities, plus all the things that need to be done around the house all the time . . . I'm just too tired to have sex. And I don't think he even notices what I do in a day, or that I even exist until he wants to have sex. Plus, I don't get a whole lot out of it. I mean, it's great for him, but I never feel like he's in it for me. He just doesn't understand that I can't get in the mood as quickly as he can, and then he gets upset because he thinks I don't need him like he needs me. It's just not worth the trouble—I'm tired of not feeling satisfied, he's tired of me pushing him away.

His Side: I try to be understanding. I mean, I know it's hard for her to have to be a "single parent" all the time with my work schedule and all. I know it's not fair for her to have to do everything for the kids and around the house, plus her job, but I wish she would understand the tremendous pressure I feel at work—and the pressure to succeed and give her the things she deserves. I feel like I give her so much! Not just material things—I'm constantly trying to surprise her with romantic things I know she likes, but she thinks I'm doing those things just so we can have sex. These things aren't just to get her in the mood. I really do want her to be happy. But when we have sex, she just seems so distant. I never know if she's enjoying it or not.

Your Side: Typical of many today, this couple's sex life is beginning to suffer the effects of too much to do, too little time. In your opinion,

1. What are three main issues that are affecting this couple?
2. If you were a marriage and family therapist or counselor, what would you recommend for this couple?

Summary

Learning Sexuality: Cultural Contributions

- Sexual identity is the awareness of oneself as a sexual male or sexual female. Family of origin, family of choice, life experiences, and other cultural influences help shape sexuality.

- Societal norms and expectations dictate the gender-specific public and private expression of our sexuality and help form sexual scripts—shared, gender-specific social and cultural expectations that guide our beliefs about sex, such as our beliefs about appropriate sexual partners and sexual behaviors. There are three levels of sexual scripts: cultural scenarios, interpersonal scripts, and intrapsychic scripts.

- Parents are their children's first and best sex educators. Parents are influential regarding their teens' decisions and attitudes about sex. Mothers are typically more involved in communicating about sex and sexual health to their children than fathers are.

- There are racial/ethnic differences in how parents communicate with their children about sex.

Our Sexual Selves

- Adolescents and young adults are besieged with images of sexuality at an early age without being taught how and why their bodies respond to sexual stimulation. Knowing and understanding our bodies not only increases our sexual pleasure and satisfaction but it also enhances our sexual relationships.

- Sex encompasses many other behaviors besides sexual intercourse. These behaviors are termed *noncoital*, and include masturbation, oral-genital sex, and anal sex.

- Research also indicates that the average age of a person's first experience with sexual intercourse is influenced by race or ethnicity.

- Recent studies show that the majority of college students are sexually active. Of concern to medical health professionals and family practitioners are the risky behaviors that often lead to unsafe or unwanted sex.

- Because Spring Break binge drinking has been shown to lead to unsafe and unwanted sex, sexually transmitted diseases, blackouts, and violence, the American Medical Association (AMA) contends that universities and colleges should stop Spring Break tour promoters from promoting alcohol, or offer Spring Break alternatives that do not include alcohol.

Sexually Transmitted Infections

- Sexually transmitted infections (STIs) are diseases that are transmitted between partners through sexual contact.

- Bacterial infections include gonorrhea, syphilis, and chlamydia. These can be treated by the use of antibiotics.

- Viral infections include herpes, human papillomavirus (HPV), and viral hepatitis. These cannot be treated by antibiotics.

Relationships and Sex

- Research has found that, overall, married couples are enjoying sex. Among several couple types (married, cohabitants, gay men, and lesbians), monogamous married couples reported the highest level of sexual satisfaction.

- Sexual satisfaction in long-term heterosexual relationships depends on the partners' perceptions—expectations, hopes, and desires—of the relationship. Additionally, sexual scripts influence marital relationship and sexual satisfaction.

- While orgasmic consistency and the ability to have an orgasm have long been used as a yardstick of sexual satisfaction, recent studies suggest that sexual satisfaction and orgasmic response/consistency are two completely different things, that there is a difference between *goal-oriented* sexual activity and *pleasure-oriented* sexual activity.

- Extramarital sexuality is a sexual relationship with someone other than a spouse; it may be clandestine, ambiguous, or consensual. Extramarital affairs or sexual relationships outside of committed relationships cause much emotional pain for the victimized partner, and sexual infidelity is considered the most difficult relationship issue to treat. People cheat for different reasons.

- We can love someone without having sex, and we can have sex without being in love. Newer research suggests that for some, being in love is what drives someone to want to have sex.

- Couples who are in love report higher levels of sexual satisfaction in their relationships than people who are not in love.

- It's easier for men to have sex without being in love than it is for women. Some men say "I love you" as part of a sexual agenda.

Experiencing Sexual Difficulties

- Sexual dysfunction covers a wide array of sexual problems or difficulties, but can essentially be broken down into two categories: female sexual dysfunction and male sexual dysfunction. One type of female sexual dysfunction is female sexual arousal disorder, and is said to occur when a woman cannot maintain arousal and lubrication during intercourse, is unable to reach orgasm, or has no desire for sexual intercourse. Types of male sexual dysfunction include erectile dysfunction and rapid ejaculation.

Key Terms and Concepts

Suggested Readings

Anderson, Kristen. (2001). *The truth about sex by high school senior girls*. Self-published.

Banks, Ian. 2004. *The sex-manual: The practical step-by-step guide to sexual health and enjoyment*. (United Kingdom: Haynes Publishing Group, 2004).

Davis, Michel. *The sex-starved marriage: A couple's guide to boosting their marriage libido*. New York: Simon & Schuster, 2004.

Multiple-Choice Questions

1. Shared, gender-specific social and cultural expectations that guide our beliefs, attitudes, and values about sex, such as our beliefs about appropriate sexual partners, sexual behaviors, and sexual conduct, are known as

   _____.

   a. sexual scripts
   b. sexual mores
   c. gender identity frameworks
   d. psychosocial scripts

2. _____ is the oral stimulation of the male's external sex organs.

   a. Cunnilingus
   b. Fellatio
   c. Oral-genital sex
   d. Dyspareunia

3. In the _____ type of extramarital affair, the nonparticipating spouse may choose to tolerate the affair rather than seek divorce.

   a. clandestine
   b. ambiguous
   c. consensual
   d. permissive

4. According to author and researcher Sabrina Weill, 61.6 percent of _____ have had sex.

   a. students in college
   b. eighth-graders
   c. tenth-graders
   d. twelfth-graders

5. Sometimes referred to as the *clap* or *drip*, _____ is the second most common STI reported in the United States.

   a. chlamydia
   b. syphilis
   c. gonorrhea
   d. herpes

6. This type of behavior involves a wide range of behaviors, from flirting, to mutual masturbation, to oral and anal sex, to sexual intercourse.

   a. Emotional ERI
   b. Combination of sexual and emotional ERI
   c. Sexual ERI
   d. Physical ERI

7. According to Blumstein and Schwartz (1983), _____ exhibit the highest rate of accepted extra-relationship (nonmonogamy) sex than any other couple type.

   a. gay men
   b. lesbians
   c. heterosexuals
   d. bisexuals

8. _____ is spread through infected fecal matter that is found in water and in food. This type of hepatitis is usually transmitted when people do not wash their hands after using the bathroom.

   a. Hepatitis D
   b. Hepatitis C
   c. Hepatitis B
   d. Hepatitis A

Answers: 1. a; 2. b; 3. b; 4. d; 5. c; 6. c; 7. a; 8. d

Becoming Parents: Choices and Challenges

10

After four years of marriage, my husband and I were in a place in our lives where we decided it was time to start a family. A year and a half later, I was nowhere near being pregnant. So began the journey for answers and help in becoming parents as we began infertility testing and treatment.

At first it was difficult, the not knowing. During this time of trying, hoping, and praying, many friends around me began to start their families, too. And with each phone call to tell me of their pregnancies I found myself there again, trying to hold back my sadness and tears as I congratulated them on their happiness. . . . Why me?

A year of testing and treatment began for us. Then month after month, the hope of becoming pregnant started to fade. And with each failed attempt to get pregnant with all the technology and medical assistance, I again could not stop the tears. . . . Why me?

But at some point, after living with an exhausted heart for so long, a shift in our thoughts began: What is it you want? What is it you really want? The answer: To become PARENTS. Then we realized that for us, the way to become parents was not through pregnancy, but through adoption. HOPE! So began the second leg of our journey, our journey to make a family.

Many months went by as we went through the process of getting on the adoption list . . . selecting an agency, doing the home study, preparing our home for that someone. And then came The Wait.

Two and a half years go by, and then one October morning it happened—The Call! "You have a son!" For years I questioned, "Why me?" But then suddenly I knew why. . . . Our son was always supposed to be ours, but we just had to wait on him to get here. And oh, he was so worth the wait!

Source: American Adoptions (2008).

Childbearing Trends: Who's Having Babies?
- Who Are America's Parents?
- Teenage Pregnancy

Having Children: Now, Later, or Never?
- Why Do People Want Children?
- Ready or Not? The "Right Time" to Have Children
- Childfree by Choice
- Delayed Childbearing
- Family Size: Lots of Tots?

Being Pregnant and Giving Birth
- Pregnancy: Emotional and Relationship Changes
- Conflict and the Transition to Parenthood
- Sexual and Relationship Satisfaction after Childbirth

Unexpected Outcomes
- When Conception Fails: Infertility
- The Physically Challenged Baby
- Pregnancy Loss

Adoption: By Circumstance or Choice
- The Adoption Process
- Gay and Lesbian Adoption

Contraception and Abortion
- Contraception
- Abortion and Other Methods

Family Life Education

EACH time a baby is born, a family is born, too.

Pregnancy always intrigued me, and newborns always took me captive. So it did not come as a surprise to anyone who knew me when I became a childbirth educator and a **doula**, a professional provider of labor support (emotional, physical, and informational) to women and their companions. Many years and countless births later, I am still intrigued with the mystery of how a single cell zygote is knit together in the secrecy of the mother's womb into a 10-trillion-celled person.

The birth of a baby is life-altering. Each time a child is born, or added to a family through adoption or fostering, a family is born as well. People can grow their families in a number of ways. In this chapter, we begin our study of becoming parents by taking a look at the historical reasons people had children, and how some of these influences still linger in our society today. We then get a good picture of the current childbearing trends in the United States, which includes examining teen pregnancy and parenthood, as well as pathways to gay and lesbian parenting. We look at how people decide to have children and how they determine their family sizes, the emotional and relationship changes that are brought about by pregnancy, and the process of giving birth. We'll conclude our discussion by looking at ways to prevent pregnancy.

Childbearing Trends: Who's Having Babies?

Parents and family life are the foundations that influence a child's development and well-being from birth into early adulthood; both play instrumental roles in stimulating and shaping a child's cognitive, social, and emotional development (Solomon-Fears, 2008). Because of the tremendous influences parents and the home environment exert on a child's development, we begin our study of the pathways to parenting by gaining an understanding of the childbearing trends in the United States today: Who's having babies, and how old are America's parents?

WHO ARE AMERICA'S PARENTS?

Each year, the population in the United States increases by the addition of slightly more than 4 million babies (Centers for Disease Control and Prevention, 2005c). The **crude birth rate** is the number of childbirths per 1,000 women, per year. These figures are tracked worldwide; in general, the crude birth rate in economically disadvantaged countries is higher than in more economically advantaged countries. In less economically developed countries, such as Niger, Uganda, Kenya, and Pakistan, the crude birth rate is significantly higher than in richer countries. In 2007, the crude birth rate in the United States was 14.2 (per 1,000 women) (National Vital Statistics Report, 2008).

The **fertility rate** is the average number of live births per woman, in a given population, per year. The U.S. fertility rate in 2005 was 2.08 (Centers for Disease Control and Prevention, 2005c). Similar to crude birth rates, countries that are less economically advantaged tend to have higher fertility rates. It is important to note, however, that fertility rates also indicate religious, cultural, and ethnic norms. For example, because of their collectivist cultural beliefs and their strong ties to families, Latinos tend to have more children than individualistic cultures such as the United States and the United Kingdom. The one-child policy in China—a practice that encourages late marriages and late childbirths, and mandates only one child per couple in urban areas—is a cultural norm that accounts for China's and Taiwan's low fertility rates. For any given country, a fertility rate of 2.1 is considered to be the *replacement level* of fertility. By tracking the crude birth rate from year to year, as well as the fertility rates, demographers are able to see certain childbearing trends, such as the age of birth mothers.

What is the current teen birth rate? Are women waiting until they are older to have children? Are there more babies born to single women than there are to married women? Answers to these questions can be found by looking at birth certificate data—the registered births. How many teens are giving birth?

Trends among Teenagers In 2007, the Academy Award winning film, *Juno,* took the nation by surprise. In this film, high school junior Juno is faced with an unplanned pregnancy. Fresh, frank, and funny, this movie illustrated the struggles teens confront when they become pregnant. How many teens are giving birth?

In 2004, the birth rates for teenaged mothers reached a historic low. With a decrease of 33 percent since 1991, the overall rate of teen births in 2004 was 41.2 births per 1,000 women aged 15 to 19 (Centers for Disease Control and Prevention, 2005). These trends were encouraging because they indicated that teens were either adhering to abstinence pledges, or that they were practicing safer methods of sex. Sadly, the teenage birth rate in the United States rose in 2006 for the first time since 2001. Between 2005 and 2006, the birth rate for teens (aged 15 to 19) rose 3 percent, from about 41 births per 1,000 to nearly 42 births per 1,000 (Centers for Disease Control and Prevention, 2008). The largest increases were seen among African American/Black Caribbean teens, who experienced an increase of 5 percent. Hispanic teens saw a 2 percent rate increase, white teens experienced a 3 percent rate increase, and American Indian/Alaska Native teens had a 4 percent increase (Centers for Disease Control and Prevention, 2008). Although it is too early to determine if these data indicate that a new trend in teen childbearing is on the horizon, it is concerning to see these notable changes after 15 years of decreasing childbearing trends.

Furthermore, since 2004, the United States has experienced a similar increase in births to adolescent mothers in all population subgroups. Table 10.1 shows the birth rates to teens among racial groups. As you can see, across all groups, the rate of pregnancy among America's teens is increasing (National Center for Health Statistics, 2007).

Trends among Unmarried Parents Nonmarital births are widespread, and they touch families of all different races and ethnicities, income class, religious groups, and demographic

TABLE 10.1   Teen Birth Rates by Race (per 1,000 Women), 1980–2006

Age	1980	1985	1990	2000	2002	2004	2006
All Races							
15–19 years	53.0	51.0	59.9	47.7	43.0	41.2	41.9
White							
15–19 years	41.2	—	50.8	43.2	39.4	37.8	—
African American							
15–19 years	97.8	95.4	112.8	77.4	66.6	62.9	63.7
American Indian							
15–19 years	82.2	79.2	81.1	58.3	53.8	52.5	54.7
Asian/Pacific Islander							
15–19 years	26.2	23.8	26.4	20.5	18.3	17.4	16.7
Hispanic							
15–19 years	82.2	—	100.3	87.8	83.4	82.6	83.0

Source: Centers for Disease Control, National Center for Health Statistics (2007).

areas. In 2006, a record 38.5 percent of all U.S. births were nonmarital births (Solomon-Fears, 2008). Births to unmarried partners can be first births or subsequent births; they can occur to a woman who has never been married, as well as to divorced or widowed women. Further, a woman with children may have had one or more within marriage, and other births outside of marriage. And, because U.S. demographers do not consider gay or lesbian partnerships to be "marriages," births to these couples are considered to be "nonmarital" births. As you learned in Chapter 1, African American families are typically formed when an unmarried mother gives birth to a child; the recent data confirm that nearly three-fourths of African American/Black Caribbean births were nonmarital births.

A number of factors are associated with the unprecedented rates of births that occur outside of marriage. These include (Solomon-Fears, 2008):

- Marriage postponement—there is an increase in the median age at first marriage
- Childfree movement—there is decreased childbearing among married couples
- Increased divorce rates
- Increased numbers of cohabiting couples
- Increased sexual activity outside of marriage
- Improper use/lack of use of contraceptive methods
- Participation in risky behaviors that often lead to sex, such as alcohol and drug use

When considering all of these factors, the trend of births to unmarried partners may very well continue, and may even further increase. Certainly, these trends will continue to reshape the landscape of American family life and experiences.

Pregnancy at Different Ages In the past, women in their 20s were thought to be at the peak of their childbearing years and have historically accounted for the most births. What are today's trends? In 2008, among women aged 20 to 24, the birth rate dipped to an all-time low, with 85.1 births per 1,000 women (U.S. Census Bureau, 2008). These data may reflect the overall trend of women who delay childbearing to pursue educational endeavors. In line with historical trends, in 2006, among women aged 25 to 29, the birth rate was the highest of any age group, with 105.8 births per 1,000 women. These data appear to support the idea that women in their 20s are in their peak childbearing years. (See Figure 10.1.)

FIGURE 10.1   Birth Rates among All Age Groups, 2008

Historically, women in their 20s were considered to be in their peak childbearing years. Although more and more older women are bearing children today, women in their 20s still account for the largest percentages of births.

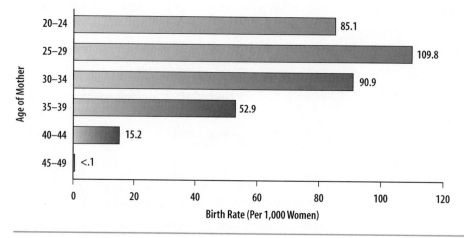

Source: Centers for Disease Control and Prevention, Division of Vital Statistics (2005c).

Birth rates among women in their 30s and 40s increased steadily from 1975 to 1990. Each of those years had approximately a 3 percent increase (Centers for Disease Control and Prevention, 2005c). This trend appears to be continuing into the twenty-first century. In 2004, births to older women were on the rise. Among women aged 30 to 34, for example, the birth rate was 95.5; among women aged 35 to 39, the birth rate was 45.4; and among women in their 40s, the birth rate was 9.0 (Centers for Disease Control and Prevention, 2005c).

Childbearing trends have been evolving throughout the twentieth and into the twenty-first centuries. As the data show, many women are delaying childbearing—perhaps due to education and career opportunities, or perhaps due to relationship circumstances. Later we'll explore in depth why some women and couples delay—or defer all together—childbearing.

Now that you have a good understanding of the birth trends in the United States, let's take a more in-depth look at two groups of parents that have become an increasing focus of family and social scientists: teenage mothers and gay and lesbian parents.

TEENAGE PREGNANCY

During the next 12 months, 1 million teenagers will become pregnant and nearly 500,000 will give birth—about one every minute (The Alan Guttmacher Institute, 2004). Totaling to one-fourth of all unintended pregnancies each year in this nation, adolescent birth rates continue to remain higher than similar birth rates in other Western or developed countries. The Alan Guttmacher Institute, a nonprofit organization that focuses on sexual and reproductive health research, notes that although the United States has seen substantial declines in teen pregnancy rates over the past 10 years, adolescent birth and abortion rates are twice as high as those found in Great Britain and Canada, and five times higher than those rates found in Sweden and France.

In our study of family life and intimate relationships, it is important to understand the incidences of teen pregnancy because births to teen moms are linked to a host of critical issues in our society today: poverty, overall child health and well-being, births to unmarried women, responsible fatherhood, sexuality and health concerns, education/school failure, child abuse and neglect, and other risky behaviors, such as drug and alcohol use and abuse, and crime (National Campaign to Prevent Teen Pregnancy, 2008). Without question, teen mothers face a range of developmental risks.

Impacts of Teen Pregnancy on the Mom Teen parents and their babies start out with many disadvantages. When the head of the family is an adolescent girl, both the teen parent and her child are at increased risk for medical, psychological, developmental, and social-emotional problems.

COMMUNITY programs for teenage moms and dads help enhance their parenting skills and support their unique needs.

- *Medical/Psychological.* The medical risks for adolescent mothers and their babies are significant, especially for younger adolescent mothers (10- to 14-year-olds). For example, their risk of dying during labor and birth is two to four times higher for women at age 17 than it is for women who have children in their 20s (The Allan Guttmacher Institute, 2004).
- *Developmental.* Research consistently shows that adolescent mothers struggle when trying to form and maintain stable interpersonal relationships and family life (Lehrman, 2001; Larson, 2004; Quinlivan, Tan, Steele, & Balck, 2004). Many of these teen parents continue their

dependence on family members rather than shifting to more independence and autonomy (Hanson, 1992).

■ *Socioeconomic.* About half of all teen moms, and over three-fourths of all unmarried teenage mothers, receive welfare within five years of the birth of their first baby; about 80 percent of teen parents eventually depend on welfare for their economic support (Klerman, 2004; The Allan Guttmacher Institute, 2004). Teenage moms are also more likely to drop out of high school than their nonpregnant counterparts

Interventions for Adolescent Parents The National Organization on Adolescent Pregnancy, Parenting, and Prevention (2008) has stated, "[Given that] all children need healthy, nurturing, stable relationships and to experience the protective factors during early childhood . . . [and] given the competing dynamics of adolescence and the demand of parenthood, it is incumbent upon families, communities, and society to provide supportive [structures] to teen parents to ensure their children grow healthy and safe and reach school ready to learn." To this end, a national campaign to reduce teen pregnancy should include the following:

■ *Comprehensive school-based programs* designed to keep the pregnant and/or parenting adolescent in school and on track to complete her degree
■ *Comprehensive family support services* designed to help parents of the pregnant and/or parenting teen to develop parenting skills and coping skills
■ *Expansion of government programs* designed to improve the medical and psychosocial health and well-being of pregnant and parenting teens and their offspring
■ *Comprehensive community programs* designed to enhance adolescents' parenting skills and support the unique needs of teen mothers and fathers and to provide early education for at-risk infants and children

In 2007, then-U.S. presidential candidate, Senator Barack Obama (D-IL), introduced a bill to reduce teen pregnancies in minority communities. The *Communities of Color Teen Pregnancy Prevention Act of 2007* seeks to strengthen community-based intervention efforts for teen pregnancy services, and to establish a comprehensive national database to provide culturally and linguistically sensitive information on teen pregnancy reduction. Then-Senator Obama noted, "Teen pregnancy can derail the plans of students with dreams of achieving professional success, and it's hitting minority communities particularly hard. Pregnancies in African American and Latino communities remain inexcusably high. We must develop innovative approaches to strengthen our community support networks and services to educate our teens about pregnancy and provide them with every chance to succeed in school and beyond."

Having Children: Now, Later, or Never?

Do you want children? At what age did you come to your decision—have you wanted to have children/not have children for as long as you can remember, or have you only recently come to this decision, as you have acquired more relationship and life experiences? And when is the "right time" to have children?

WHY DO PEOPLE WANT CHILDREN?

The decision to become a parent is a very complex issue because it includes a number of interrelated components. For instance, do we have a child because of the subjective value societies place on them, or because of personal, intrinsic reasons—or both? Do we have children because society *expects* us to?

Since the 1970s, researchers have attempted to document the various needs that children fulfill for adults; they have also tried to better understand how adults perceive the value of children (see Hoffman & Hoffman, 1973). Over the past three decades, researchers have discovered that people most often desire to have children because of the psychological satisfactions they offer to parents, the social ties children offer as adults age, and their economic value (such as tax breaks) (for a complete review, see Lawson, 2004). On the other hand, the lack of desire to become a parent has been associated with adults who place a greater importance on self-fulfillment, leisure time, relationship quality, career advancement, and greater financial freedom (Seccombe, 1991).

Two main approaches have been taken by social science researchers to understand the attitudes and motivations associated with becoming a parent: the perceived value of children and the appeal of parenthood.

The Perceived Value of Children Most studies and theories about the motivation to become a parent center on the perspective that there are perceived rewards and costs associated with parenthood (Lawson, 2004). As you learned in Chapter 7, many of us engage in a cost-benefit analysis when we choose our life partners; we also do the same when we decide whether to have children. For example, some research suggests that one of the rewards of having children is that they meet some of our basic psychological needs (such as love and affection), and this is what motivates peoples' desires to have children (Al-Fadhli & Smith, 1996; Yamaguchi & Fergusson, 1995). Some adults may evaluate the costs (such as substantial decreases in personal time and freedom, and substantial increases in financial responsibilities) and decide against having children. If prospective parents believe that the net value of having children is greater than the costs associated with having children, they will be motivated to have children (Lawson, 2004). On the other hand, if they judge that the costs outweigh the benefits, they will forgo the Mommy/Daddy track and seek other sources to meet their needs, such as turning to nieces and nephews for psychological need fulfillment not met by having their own children.

Table 10.2 (page 324) shows us the Perceptions of Parenting Inventory, which helps people determine the rewards and costs they associate with having children (Lawson, 2004). As you can see, this inventory assesses the rewards of parenting, which include *enrichment* and *continuity*, as well as the costs, which include *isolation, instrumental costs,* and *commitment.* As you look through the table, which items do you most strongly agree with? Most strongly disagree with? It's important to note that your answers may change across time. For example, you may not want to have a child at this time because of the financial and emotional costs; however, when your circumstances change, you might decide that the benefits of having children outweigh these particular costs.

The Appeal of Parenthood Probably all of us have had experiences where we see children having a temper tantrum at the grocery store and go limp as a wet noodle when an exasperated parent tries to pick the child up to get him or her out of the store as fast as possible. And under our breath, we have probably said, "I will *never* have children!" Certainly, there are times when having children doesn't seem like a very appealing thought! Despite the fact that all of us have probably not wanted children at one time or another, there is some evidence that there are certain psychosocial factors that are related to the appeal of parenting, particularly that of early childhood experiences.

A number of studies have attempted to show that our early experiences with our parents, such as parental nurturance, discipline, and attention, are significantly related to the motivation to parent. For example, some research has demonstrated that bad memories of our childhood experiences have accounted for unique variances in why some men and women choose to have children, and others do not (Gerson, 1980, 1985, 1986). These experiences underlie what is known as the **family projection process** (Bowen, 1966). This process stresses that the appeal of having children is the result of finding a way to satisfy our individual unmet needs from childhood. Stated another way, people who become parents do so because they feel that they were not given enough love, attention, or support as a child. Their own children, then, serve to enact their internalized unsatisfactory childhood experiences—parents have children to give them what they themselves never had as a child. It's important to note, however, that other research has shown that as individuals enter their 30s, they feel less dependent on

TABLE 10.2 Perceptions of Parenting Inventory: Factors People Consider before Becoming Parents

Enrichment

Caring for the child would bring me happiness.

Parenting the child would be rewarding.

My spouse/partner and I would grow closer together through the experience.

Parenting the child would make me a better person.

Isolation

I would have less time to spend doing what I enjoy.

Caring for the child would interfere with the time I want to spend with my spouse.

Commitment

Parenting the child would be a never-ending responsibility.

The child would be dependent on me.

Instrumental Costs

Raising the child would be financially expensive.

Parenting the child would be emotionally exhausting.

Caring for the child would be physically exhausting.

Continuity

I would look forward to being a grandparent in the future.

Our relationship would change over the years from parent to friend.

The child would carry on my family name.

Perceived Support

My friends and family would help me care for the child.

My family and friends would provide social support.

Source: Lawson (2004).

---

childhood memories in making important life choices, such as having children (Gerson, Posner, & Morris, 1991).

Gay Men and Lesbians: Deciding to Have Children Although the number of planned families by gay men and lesbian women has been steadily growing in recent years, little research has been undertaken to understand the motivations of gays and lesbians to become parents (Bos, van Balen, & van den Boom, 2004). While certainly the existing research concerning the perceived value of children and the appeal of parenthood applies to homosexual parents as well to heterosexual parents, some have ventured to try to determine if gays and lesbians have additional, different motivations to become parents.

In a study of 178 lesbian families and 100 heterosexual families in the Netherlands, the researchers discovered a number of findings when comparing the two groups (Bos and others, 2004):

- *Experience of parenthood.* There were no significant differences between lesbian biological mothers and heterosexual mothers on parental competence, feeling parental burdens (stress), and the desires to become parents.
- *Quality of the couple's relationship.* Overall, there was no significant difference between lesbian and straight couples' relationship satisfaction. However, lesbian mothers were more satisfied with their partners as co-parents than heterosexual mothers were with their husbands as co-parents. In comparison to heterosexual fathers, lesbian co-parents were significantly more satisfied with their couple relationship.

- *Justification of parenting.* Lesbian mothers, more so than heterosexual mothers, felt a greater need to justify the quality of their parenting to others.
- *Synchronicity.* Lesbian couples were more likely than straight couples to share childcare responsibilities and household duties; this synchronicity may account for the higher levels of relationship satisfaction.

The emergence of planned gay fatherhood and lesbian motherhood is indicative of broad social change that is taking place in our society, and societies around the world. Regardless of their sexual orientation, people are questioning existing parenting norms and are finding ways to create families (Berkowitz & Marsiglio, 2007). Examining the experiences of gay men and lesbians gives us an important opportunity to accept them into the parenting mainstream.

The decision to have a child or forego childbearing is a crucial—and irrevocable—decision that warrants careful and thoughtful attention. And, although many of you may know that you desire to have children, the timing of parenthood is also an issue that needs to be considered. Just when is the "right time" to have children in the lifespan of a couple's relationship?

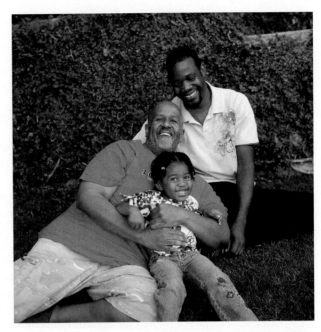

IT is difficult to ascertain how many gay and lesbian parents there are, but it is estimated that upwards of 14 million children have gay/lesbian parents.

READY OR NOT? THE "RIGHT TIME" TO HAVE CHILDREN

You learned in Chapter 1 that families experience a common lifecourse pattern, referred to as the *Family Life Cycle;* for many families, this lifecourse includes having children. Within psychology and family studies, a **life transition** (such as the decision to become a parent) is considered to be a point at which people take on new roles and obligations (Hagestad & Call, 2007). A **turning point** is a transition that entails a permanent, lasting shift in the direction of the lifecourse of a person's relationship. Often, this term is used in connection with the transition to parenthood (Hagestad & Call, 2007). **Timing** refers to the age at which a transition takes place. Thus, when considering the decision to become a parent, the timing of parenthood is given much attention because it speaks to the significance of this transition/turning point in a person's life.

Across life, the majority of individuals follow and relatively adhere to socially approved and shaped pathways, such as the "right" time to get married and the "right" time to have children. These proper times are referred to as **age-related norms.** In the United States, for example, the age-related norm of a woman giving birth for the first time is 25 years old (Centers for Disease Control and Prevention, 2008). As sociologists Gunhild Hagestad and Vaughn Call observe, unlike men who can produce children well into old age, "biology presents a woman with nonnegotiable deadlines [for becoming pregnant]," because after a certain point in her lifespan she no longer has the ability to produce eggs (Hagestad & Call, 2007, p. 1342). Thus, a woman's "window of opportunity" to become pregnant is essentially limited to her teens, 20s, and 30s. Women who pass these age norms are often subjected to informal chastising with comments such as, "Having a baby at *your* age?" (Hagestad & Call, 2007). Society also structures the sequence of life transitions. For instance, many societies condone childbearing only after a couple is married. However, as you saw earlier, nearly 40 percent of all childbirths in this country are to unmarried women; it is clear that the childbearing sequence is undergoing change in Western cultures.

So, when is the "right" time to have children? There is no research that helps us understand parenthood timing from a practical viewpoint, but there are a number of questions a woman or a couple might ask themselves before becoming pregnant or deciding to bring a child into the relationship through adoption. These include:

- *Do I have the parenting skills necessary to raise a child?* Parenting skills include things such as patience; being able to stay calm in the midst of turmoil; being able to control your anger; understanding how to effectively discipline a child in age-appropriate ways; being able to communicate expectations, warmth, and nurturance; and being an effective role model.
- *How strong is your relationship?* The way a couple treats each other teaches children about love, intimacy, relationships, trust, and respect. Do you have a solid foundation on which to raise a family?
- *Do you and your partner have similar beliefs?* It is imperative that parents in relationships share similar beliefs about discipline, education, childcare, and what child behaviors are or are not acceptable. This is especially important if you have an interracial or interfaith relationship.
- *Where are you financially?* Not only must you be able to provide for your child's basic needs (food, shelter, clothing) but you also need to consider saving for their future education needs, as well as your own.
- *Why do you want children?* Rarely does a child bring a couple closer together. Be sure to examine the true motivations for wanting a child.

As most parents will attest, children are wonderful, and worth the sleep deprivation, arguments about how to/not to raise them, and overdue credit card bills. But in each family, there are many personal factors involved in deciding when to have children. It's not a simple decision, because having children *will* change your life. Are you up to the challenge?

CHILDFREE BY CHOICE

The **childfree-by-choice** trend is certainly nothing new as a quick glance at A-list celebrities shows: Kim Cattrall, Stockard Channing, Jay Leno, Steve Martin, George Clooney, and Oprah Winfrey all have opted to remain childfree. Even Dr. Seuss, the infamous children's book author, was childfree by choice. But the "no kids, no thanks" trend is moving beyond the borders of Hollywood and extending to mainstream USA. In 2006, U.S. Census Bureau data showed that the level of childlessness was 18.8 percent—twice the level as 1976 (Current Population Reports, 2008). In the last 30 years, the number of women ages 40 to 44 with no children has almost doubled to 18.8 percent (U.S. Census Bureau, Current Population Survey, 2010). This no-kids trend is not isolated to the United States. One body of research from Australia estimated that one in five women in the childbearing years opted to not have children (Merlo & Rowland, 2000).

To date, there has been little empirical research in family studies, sociology, or psychology that examines the motives of women and men who are voluntarily childless; however, there are a few studies that help us understand why people opt to remain childfree. For example, one body of research found that there are certain categories or groups among those who elect not to become parents. These groups include those who are certain they do not want children, those who are certain they do not

COUPLES may adopt the no-kids/no-thanks track so they can pursue other endeavors, such as volunteering for Habitat for Humanity.

Are Childfree-by-Choice Couples Selfish?

Recently in Britain, senior Anglican Bishop of Rochester, Rev. Michael Nazir-Ali, condemned couples that chose to not have children as "self-indulgent." The bishop asserted that the basic good of marriage is having children, and that not to have children would doom a marriage to failure. He further asserted that couples who opt out of having children have abandoned the societal and cultural duty of all married people—to ensure that the society continues by reproducing. Finally, the reverend stated the those who do not have children are "following the religion of the new 'me,'" are selfish, and have excessive self-regard.

Our study in this chapter has shown us that childfree-by-choice couples are an emerging demographic in our society.

1. Have you decided that children won't fit into your married life? If so, why? If not, why not?

2. Do you believe that children are part and parcel of the whole concept of "marriage"?

3. Why do you think that the decision to remain childfree is met with such criticism?

want children at this point in their lives, those who are ambivalent to having children, and those who feel the decision was made for them due to health reasons or lack of a partner (Cartwright, 1999).

The reasons people remain childfree are as many and varying as those reasons people opt to become parents. Rathus and Nevid (1992) found in their study of hundreds of couples that there are various reasons why individuals and couples opt for the no-kids track: more time with one another, freedom from the responsibility of raising children, financial freedom, able to devote more time to careers, and concerns about worldwide overpopulation.

Other research found that beyond individual factors ("micro" factors), social factors ("macro" factors"), such as the increase in women's education levels and their participation in the job market, "compete with raising children" (Weston & Qu, 2001). Changing social values, decreasing importance of religion, access to legal abortion, and effective contraceptives also alter childbearing. These research findings indicated that those who choose to be childless do so because of their dislike of children, choice of lifestyle, lack of interest in children and parenting, or a belief that the world is too dangerous for children.

Similar to Rathus and Nevid, other studies similarly found that financial security and job security are also factors closely linked to an individual's decision to become a parent (MacKay, 1994; McDonald, 2000; Wooden, 1999). An additional study appears to confirm the findings from prior research. Sociologist Kristin Park (2005) analyzed the motives of 23 childless men and women. Through in-depth interviews, she found that women believed parenting would conflict with their careers and/or leisure activities. The women also indicated that they lacked a "maternal instinct," or they were generally uninterested in children. Men, more than women, believed that parenting required too many sacrifices, including great financial expense. Both men and women indicated that they felt their personalities were not suited to parenting.

Other research into childlessness categorizes childless women in the following groups (Baum, 1999):

- *Hedonists.* These women are not willing to, nor do they have a desire to, sacrifice money, energy, time, or themselves in rearing children.
- *Emotional.* Some women who choose not to become mothers have no "maternal instincts"; these women report that they have no emotional connection or feelings toward babies or children.

- *Idealistic.* These women indicate that they feel the world is not a safe place to bring a child into. They also feel that the world's resources are limited and they raise environmental concerns in their decision not to have children.
- *Practical.* Women in this category desire to remain childfree for practical reasons, such as educational or career goals.

Although to some it may appear that women remain childfree for selfish reasons, this is not necessarily the case. Couples must be honest when assessing whether or not to become parents. Some people feel their lives are complete and full without children. Others choose to be childfree because of unfortunate circumstances, and in these instances, the decision can be a painful one. For instance, a close friend of mine desperately desired to be a mother but because she is a genetic carrier of an always-fatal type of muscular dystrophy, she opted to remain childless. Other couples may not consciously decide not to have children—they simply fall into childlessness.

DELAYED CHILDBEARING

While some couples remain childfree by choice and other couples are childless for medical or physiological reasons that prohibit them from becoming pregnant, some couples have perhaps every intention of becoming parents but for one reason or another parenthood eludes them. As Marcia, a colleague of mine explains,

> Before we became engaged, Richard and I knew we wanted children—it was something we held in common. He comes from a very large family, and I come from a family with three other siblings. Our plan was to have our first child by the age of 30, but our business was really taking off and we thought we had plenty of time. We began trying [to conceive] when we were 35 or so and found out we had infertility problems. We tried fertility treatments for a few years with no success . . . so now we find ourselves in our mid-40s without children. Totally not planned. But even though it's not what we planned, we're very content with our lives right now.

Sociology professor Jean Veevers (1980) sought to determine how couples like Marcia and Richard become a childless couple. This study defined four specific stages involved in delayed childbearing decision-making:

1. *Postponing childbearing for a definite period of time.* Couples in this first stage intentionally delay childbearing in order to achieve certain goals they have set for themselves, such as meeting educational goals. Like Marcia and Richard, perhaps they want to devote their attention to their careers or give their new business time to get established.
2. *Postponing childbearing for an indefinite period of time.* "We'll eventually get around to having children." In this stage of decision making, couples' reasons for not having children become more and more unclear and perhaps indefinable even to themselves. For whatever reasons, they feel that the timing is "just not right."
3. *Weighing the pros and cons of being parents.* During this stage of decision making, couples deliberate the costs and benefits associated with parenthood.
4. *Coming to terms with being childless.* It is at this point that couples realize they have become childless by default. Like Marcia and Richard, many couples may have intended to become parents, but numerous postponements in their decision making essentially made the decision for them.

While subsequent infertility and significantly increased risks of negative outcomes for the baby are associated with delayed childbearing in women, there are several bodies of empirical research that suggest childbearing among older parents is advantageous to children. For example, University of Maryland sociology professor Steve Martin (2002) found through his review of the literature that both economic and psychosocial (social and emotional) benefits for the child are associated with delayed childbearing. He cites a number of studies that indicate that the older a woman is when she has her first child, the greater the economic benefit to both herself and her baby. Findings further indicate that women who postpone childbearing are more likely to stay in the workforce throughout retirement eligibility, and, as a result, they have distinctively higher earning potential than early childbearers. Women who postpone childbearing are also better able to find quality childcare because of their earnings. Quality childcare in turn increases the woman's work productivity, and earnings potential greatly reduces "lost career time." In addition to being born into a higher income bracket, children born to older parents have better access to education opportunities. Children of older parents also suffer fewer financial consequences if their parents divorce.

Children of older parents also experience psychosocial benefits. For instance, older parents have stronger and more reliable social support networks than younger parents, providing more stability for the entire family to cope with the inevitable stressors that accompany child-rearing (Martin, 2002). The quality of the mother–child relationship is higher compared to mother–child relationships of younger mothers. For example, older mothers tend to be more positive about parenting and show less anger and frustration in parenting, while older fathers tend to be very involved in their children's lives, although they are not as physically active in play as are younger fathers. Older fathers are also more likely than younger fathers to share household tasks following the birth of a baby. And finally, because they have already experienced many significant life experiences, older parents are less likely than younger parents to experience depression, loss of self-esteem, or feelings of incompetence in parenting. Martin concludes that although older parents may experience fatigue and a lack of energy, their increased maturity seems to outweigh these negative psychosocial outcomes.

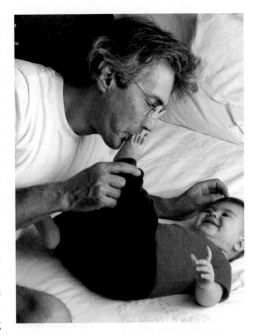

ALTHOUGH the age-related norm of having children in this country is somewhere in the 20s or early 30s, many parents opt to delay childbearing until they are financially secure. Children of older parents experience a number of benefits, such as greater financial security and enhanced time with their parents.

FAMILY SIZE: LOTS OF TOTS?

So, you've made the decision to have children. The next question is: How many children do you desire to have? A recent Gallup Poll (2007) of 1,000 U.S. adults revealed that slightly over half of those surveyed indicated that 2 children is the "ideal" family size; about one-fourth said that 3 children were ideal (see Figure 10.2). The ideal family size trends change over time, and reflect cultural and societal changes. For instance, there is a sharp decline in the perceptions of ideal family size between the 1960s and the 1970s. This trend may reflect the advent of the birth control pill in the 1960s, which gave women more control over their fertility; this increased control may have, in turn, shaped attitudes about ideal family size.

In many ways, the United States is considered to be a pronatalist society. **Pronatalism**, or **natalism**, is an ideology that embraces childbearing. Pronatalist attitudes and beliefs are prevalent in the United States (Watkins,

FIGURE 10.2 "Ideal" Family Size

A recent Gallup Poll asked Americans what they think the "ideal" number of children for a family to have is. Researchers found that, on average, Americans believe that two children is the "ideal" number.

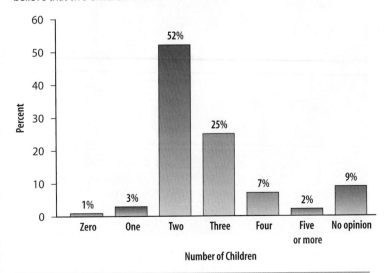

Source: Carroll (2007).

2008). For instance, when a woman or a couple gives birth to just one child and says, "no more," when she or they decide to forego having children altogether, sometimes people aren't sure how to respond. Is she infertile? Are they selfish? **Antinatalist** countries discourage childbearing. An example of this would be China, where each couple is allowed to have only one child.

Do parents have only so much to give to their kids? One theory maintains that some parents' resources are limited and become depleted when additional children are added to the family.

Draining Mom and Dad: The Resource Dilution Hypothesis Parental time, energy, and resources are limited, and the **resource dilution hypothesis** theory contends that parents' finite resources become diluted when spread over a larger number of children (Blake, 1981). A number of studies in the 1980s and 1990s seemed to support this theory when the researchers discovered that a child in a large household receives less attention than a child in a smaller household, and this lack of attention later affected the educational level the child attained (see Strohschein, Gauthier, Campbell, & Kleparchuk, 2008, for a complete review). Other studies have similarly shown that maternal attention is greatest for firstborn children, and less for subsequent siblings, and that mothers reduce positive interactions with their older children following the birth of another. With these results in mind, you may be thinking, "Wow, family size *does* matter—I really should only have one child!" But new research may contradict these prior findings.

Researchers from Canada recently surveyed over 13,000 parents and found that, because the relationship of a parent to each child is unique, effects of family size need to be studied differently than they were in the past (Strohschien and others, 2008). In their current study, the investigators looked at two different areas of parenting: positive interaction (the extent to which parents are responsive to their children's needs) and consistent parenting (the frequency with which parents set boundaries and establish standards for appropriate behavior). Using these two factors, they wanted to determine how parenting practices change when new children are added to the family system. In their long-term study, the researchers discovered that "parents do not so much *dilute* their resources when a new child is added . . . [rather,] they act to deploy their resources differently" (Strohschein and others, 2008, p. 681). Instead of draining resources away from other children, as prior studies suggested, this new body of research indicates that when new siblings are added to the family, parents employ a "managerial approach" to parenting—they shift, reallocate, and reorganize their resources to ensure that every family member's needs are met.

It's impossible to determine the "ideal" family size because it is a uniquely personal decision that is affected by many factors. Today, there is an emerging trend that needs to be addressed when discussing family size: the Quiverfull movement.

The Quiverfull movement: "Don't You Know What Causes That?" Large families are considered unusual in the United States (Arnold, 2005). Although rather common in the past, families with more than 6 children are so rare today that the census no longer tracks these data (Hartill, 2001). But with the Quiverfull movement, today an increasing numbers of parents are having as many as 20 children.

The **Quiverfull movement** is a pronatalist belief that is practiced among some evangelical Protestant Christian couples in the United States, as well as some Catholics and Mormons, and also has some adherents in Canada, Australia, New Zealand, and England. Foregoing all forms of birth control as a matter of principle and personal choice, a "QF" couple is motivated to have many children because of a desire to be obedient to what they

JIM Bob and Michelle Duggar, of Tontitown, Arkansas, are adherents to the Quiverfull movement. They have 18 children—and counting. How do you feel about couples who have this many children? Would you consider having a "large" family? Why or why not?

believe are commands in the Bible. Citing biblical passages such as "be fruitful and multiply" and "blessed is the person who has a quiver full of children," adherents to the Quiverfull movement maintain an "open willingness" to joyfully receive and not thwart however many children are bestowed upon them (Campbell, 2003).

But how does religion affect a person's fertility? Some earlier research suggested that there are three conditions that produce religious effects on fertility: (1) the religion promotes norms about fertility-related behaviors, such as the use of birth control; (2) the organization is able to enforce conformity to these norms (either through social influence or through sanctions); and (3) the religion is a very important part of a person's individual identity (McQuillan, 2004). A recent study of 7,600 nationally representative subjects to identify what determines differences in rates of fertility among some religious groups confirms the earlier research (Hayford & Morgan, 2008). The researchers found that women for whom religion is an important facet in daily life have higher fertility intentions, compared to nonreligious women.

Although some may disagree with QF couples' choices to have large numbers of children, it is important to consider whether they—just as other diverse family forms—should be afforded the same social support as other families are.

Being Pregnant and Giving Birth

Just as with other events associated with family life, pregnancy and childbirth are processes that change over time, and the experiences encompass a number of sequential stages (conception, pregnancy, childbirth, and caring for the baby); these emotional and physical changes in the pregnant woman are associated with changes in spousal well-being and marital satisfaction, and are illustrated across the bottom of pages 332 and 333 for you (Cowan & Cowan, 2000).

In the sections that follow, we'll explore the common emotional and relationship changes that occur during pregnancy, and how these changes affect a couple's relationship, from conflict, to sexuality, to the early days of transitioning to parenthood and incorporating another member into the family system. Having realistic expectations when you are about to become a parent can make the transition to parenthood much smoother, because there's a lot to consider—and to worry about—when a woman or a couple is expecting a baby.

Having a baby and raising it to the age of 18, for example, is a costly endeavor! Table 10.3 shows the estimated annual costs of raising a child; the data are based on a survey by the U.S.

TABLE 10.3   The Cost of Raising a Child to the Age of 18

Housing	Food	Transportation	Clothing	Health	Childcare/ Education	Misc.
Dual-Parent Family (up to $39,000 annual income)						
$41,520	$24,600	$17,610	$8,970	$9,390	$9,990	$12,720
Dual-Parent Family ($39,100–$65,800 annual income)						
$57,360	$29,550	$24,510	$10,470	$12,180	$17,430	$18,960
Dual-Parent Family ($65,800 and up annual income)						
$93,180	$36,780	$33,000	$13,530	$13,980	$27,960	$30,750
Single-Parent Family (up to $39,000 annual income)						
$46,380	$24,600	$12,690	$9,150	$7,410	$8,730	$9,630
Single-Parent Family ($39,100 and up annual income)						
$92,850	$37,110	$39,060	$12,480	$14,790	$22,770	$31,200

Source: U.S. Department of Agriculture (2008).

Department of Agriculture (2008), and show costs based on a family with two children, on a per-child basis. These figures do not include any estimates for sending a child to college, or any costs associated with a child who lives in the home after the age of 18. Each baby brought into a family system (through birth or adoption) is anywhere from a 100 thousand-dollar to a quarter of a million-dollar investment. As soon as a pregnancy is confirmed or the adoption is finalized, parents should sit down together and work out a *realistic* budget—from maternity clothes, baby gear, the baby's nursery, and medical costs associated with having a baby, to perhaps going from two incomes to one—it all adds up quickly. Talking about these anticipated changes early on helps parents better manage their finances, and it also helps reduce conflicts that arise because of money issues.

Aside from the money concerns, couples have other things they must negotiate as they start their journeys to become parents. In particular, the mother will experience emotional and physical changes that will affect the couple's relationship.

PREGNANCY: EMOTIONAL AND RELATIONSHIP CHANGES

The birth of a child is a demanding family life situation, and the transition to parenthood is a very difficult adjustment for most couples (Salmela-Aro, Aunola, Saisto, Halmesmaki, & Nurmi, 2006). What follows are the emotional and relationship changes associated with certain stages in pregnancy (see Figure 10.3).

FIGURE 10.3   A Month-by-Month Guide to Pregnancy

Month 1

Congratulations, you're going to be a parent! Believe it or not, now's the time to start planning a realistic budget for the changes that are going to take place in your family.

Month 2

She may be experiencing quite a bit of fatigue, nausea, and vomiting, so it may be tough to feel very bonded as a couple. Partners could find ways to make things easier for her, like pitching in to help around the house. Follow her lead about sex—her breasts may seem very inviting, but she may have enforced a "No Touching" policy. Her irritability is temporary.

Month 3

Never, ever use the words *fat, big, wide, round*, or *Buddha* to describe her growing belly—she may be quite sensitive to her changing shape. Be sure to keep lines of communication open, and engage in open, honest dialogue about your feelings. There are lots of changes taking place—in her and in your relationship.

Months 4–6

She's probably feeling better, so now's a good time to take a trip together on a mini-vacation. The investment in one another and in your relationship is the most important gift you can give your child. Sex is not off limits unless the doctor says so. Experiment with different positions, and keep your sense of humor.

The First Three Months Due mostly to the hormonal changes that occur in pregnancy, in the early weeks a woman's emotions are often unstable, resulting in mood swings, and it is not uncommon for her to feel depressed. Even if the pregnancy was planned and hoped for, she may cry—often for no apparent reason. Frequently, these emotional changes are unsettling for her husband or partner, and the partner may feel inadequate or incapable of meeting her needs. It is not uncommon for both partners to be concerned about the family's finances, and the additional costs associated with rearing a child.

Studies that explore couple relationships during pregnancy are rare, but in one study, the researcher found that couple relationships are more stable than unstable during pregnancy, despite the hormonal changes that take place in the woman (Richardson, 1981). The researcher also found that, overall, women rate their relationships with their partners as more satisfactory than unsatisfactory during pregnancy. Newer studies have shown that women are particularly sensitive to their husband's negative attitude/mood while they are pregnant, and these emotions from men may cause depressive symptoms in women (Buehlman, Gottman, & Katz, 1992; Notarius, Benson, Sloane, Vanzetti, & Hornyak, 1989); these depressive symptoms are thought to lead to increased levels of conflict in the couple's relationship (Salmela-Aro and others, 2006). Other studies have found that pregnancy can result in decreased levels of closeness and communication in couples, and this leads to increased conflict between the two (Florsheim and others, 2003).

As you learned in the previous chapter, human sexuality is reactive to our daily circumstances, and a couple's sex life changes as they encounter altered circumstances—certainly, pregnancy is a time of "altered" circumstances! Couples are often concerned that having sex during the early weeks of pregnancy may harm the baby or the mother, but these concerns are

Month 7

You're two-thirds of the way there! Now's the time to step up the preparations for the baby's arrival, and to begin childbirth education and parenting classes. Don't forget to continue to nurture your relationship. Plan date nights at least once a week, and stick to it even after the baby arrives. If she's going back to work, finalize preparations for childcare now.

Month 8

She's probably starting to get very uncomfortable and may have difficulty sleeping. Capitalize on these sleepless nights and engage in pillow talk. This not only increases your intimacy, but it may help her to sleep better (it might also lead to sex). Anticipate her needs and help her around the house.

Month 9

That went fast, didn't it?! Aside from practicing getting to the hospital, installing the car seat, and stocking up on baby supplies, take this time to be alone as a couple, just one more time. For some women, sex is uncomfortable and off limits, yet other women still desire to have sex this close to the due date. It's an individual choice, unless the doctor has said no sex.

The Baby's Here!

Once the baby arrives, make sure you carefully guard the time you have with one another and your new family member. While it's understandable that others are excited and want to share in your joy, you can never regain these first few days of being a new family. Make sure to set aside "couple only" time each week after the baby is born, so you continue to nurture your relationship.

typically unwarranted. Unless her physician indicates otherwise, sexual activity is permissible throughout pregnancy. However, both the woman and her partner should remember that, because of the early changes associated with pregnancy (such as breast tenderness), she may not be in the mood for any kind of touch because she is reacting to the changes in her body. Couples need to keep in mind that the woman is not rejecting her *partner*—just the *thought of/act of sex*. It's best for a partner to follow the woman's lead about sex throughout pregnancy.

The Next Three Months The second trimester brings changes in the woman's emotions, too. Most women understand that weight gain is a normal and necessary part of pregnancy, but some women—particularly those who struggle with eating disorders—may become dismayed at their ever-increasing weight. Some women may feel overwhelmed with the responsibilities of parenting or frustrated because their expanding abdomen prevents them from performing job tasks; some may even find that pregnancy interferes with educational or career plans. Worries about finances may affect decisions regarding if and when to return to work after the baby's birth, and, in turn, may affect the couple's relationship. While many women feel attractive and sexy during pregnancy, some feel awkward and unappealing. Most women, however, indicate this as a time of great sexual pleasure. A lot of partners worry that they will "hit" the baby during sexual intercourse, but this concern is unwarranted. The baby is way out of reach, tucked securely in the uterus. Some positions can be uncomfortable for the woman, though, so couples often have to get creative in finding sexual positions, such as side-lying positions. The key to sexuality in pregnancy is the same as during any other point in a couple's communication—open and honest communication. It's also important that the couple continues to nurture their relationship by going out on dates together or having special nights at home with no interruptions from family and friends. The best parents are parents who make their relationship a priority and foster intimacy.

The Last Three Months Coupled with the physiological changes that occur as the big day nears are multiple relational and emotional changes. By the ninth month, many women feel overwhelmed and, frankly, tired of being pregnant! Many women (and their partners) may lose interest in sex, not only because of exhaustion but also because finding a comfortable sexual position is at times an exercise of futility and hilarity. With baby showers being given for the parents-to-be and final preparations being made in anticipation of bringing the baby home, fears, anxieties, and worries about labor and birth become very real and very intense for mothers and their partners. Women may worry that they will not be able to tolerate the pain or that they will appear foolish; the birth partners may worry that they will not be able to meet their partner's physical and emotional needs during the birth process. It is not uncommon for birth partners to worry that the expectant mother will turn to someone else for support; they worry that they will be inadequate. Sometimes a woman may feel that the baby is taking over not only her body but also her entire being. Sometimes a birth partner feels that the mother-to-be is no longer interested in him (or her)—that she will turn all of her attention to the baby. Financial worries may escalate during this time, as well.

CONFLICT AND THE TRANSITION TO PARENTHOOD

The transition to parenthood is difficult for most people. In the past, researchers have concentrated on the *individual* factors that may lead to conflict in relationships during pregnancy, and have ignored the importance of the *relational dynamics* of marital dissatisfaction and symptoms of depression (Salmela-Aro and others, 2006). Thus, results of such studies concluded that the changes in the couple's relationship following pregnancy and during the transition to parenthood were due to such things as a woman's depressed mood, rather than due to the systems nature of their relationship (for example, see Campbell and others, 1992).

To illustrate the importance of examining the couple's relationship, and not just the individual, researchers from Finland studied the experiences of 320 women and their partners through pregnancy and into the early months of parenthood (Salmela-Aro and others, 2006). They discovered that, in those couples who reported high levels of conflict, the struggles and disagreements that were present during the transition to becoming parents were already a part of the couple's relationship. In other words, depressive symptoms and marital dissatisfaction during pregnancy were common to the couple's relationship during pregnancy—these characteristics didn't suddenly appear as the couple became parents, as earlier studies suggested.

The researchers also found a decrease in marital satisfaction during the transition to parenthood among couples who reported high levels of marital satisfaction during early pregnancy. The investigators speculated that this is because pre-pregnancy "happy" couples have taken time to nurture their relationships, and that as pregnancy/parenting demands increase over time, their attention shifts from their relationship to the baby.

Other research that examined 293 Dutch couples explored relationship quality during pregnancy and the early months of pregnancy (Kluwer & Johnson, 2007). Based on the assumption that adding a new member to the family system is accompanied by drastic and dramatic changes in a couple's relationship, this study looked at conflict frequency during pregnancy. This study found:

- More frequent conflict during pregnancy was related to lower levels of relationship quality across the transition to parenthood.
- Lower levels of relationship quality during pregnancy were linked with more conflict during pregnancy.
- Frequent conflict is likely to determine declines in relationship quality during the early months of parenthood.

Labor and Birth

Healthy SELVES Healthy FAMILIES

Labor is divided into four stages, and each stage has one or more phases. Medical science does not know for certain what causes a woman to begin the birth process when she does.

STAGE 1 The opening to the uterus, the cervix, becomes thinner and begins to open. Typically about the thickness of the space between your eyebrows, and about as firm as the tip of your nose, the cervix thins to about the thickness of the small piece of skin

ALTHOUGH the hours of labor are challenging, many couples experience great closeness and intimacy as they work together to bring their child into the world.

between your thumb and forefinger; by the time the baby is born it is as soft as the inside of your cheek. This stage is divided into three phases: *early labor, active labor,* and *transition.*

STAGE 2 Although the journey through the vagina is only about 5 inches, it may take a first-time mother about 2 hours to push her baby out. During the uterine contractions, as the mother bears down, the force of the contraction holds the baby down, helping the opening to stretch. As the intensity of the contraction lessens, the baby retreats upward. Thus, pushing is somewhat of a 3-steps-forward-2-steps-backward process. Once the baby's head is visible, the baby no longer retreats after a contraction.

STAGE 3 During this phase, the placenta (the baby's life support system throughout pregnancy) is delivered. This typically occurs within 5 to 30 minutes after the delivery of the baby.

STAGE 4 Stage 4 is often overlooked by many when discussing the processes of labor and birth, but is no less important. This stages involves the first 2 to 3 hours after birth through the first 24 months after labor and delivery. Because of the tremendous fluctuations that a woman's hormones undergo during the nine months of pregnancy, labor, and birth, it takes time for her body to return to its pre-pregnant state.

These findings are very important to our understanding of intimate and family life because they show us that the couples' marital discord and distress stemmed from problems that *existed during pregnancy*—not necessarily because of the *transition to parenthood*. It may very well be that the first childbirth isn't what elicits marriage troubles, but instead, that the troubles have always been there and are just highlighted once the baby arrives. Some couples may be more vulnerable to a difficult transition to parenthood than others (Kluwer & Johnson, 2007).

Finally, other evidence suggests that couples who do not live together, who are unhappy with their partner, or who perceive their relationship to be a negative experience, experience increased anxiety and depression during pregnancy and the early months of parenting (Figueiredo and others, 2008). All the empirical findings are important, for they suggest that *both* members of the couple need to be supported during pregnancy in order to prevent or decrease the stressors associated with the transition to parenting.

SEXUAL AND RELATIONSHIP SATISFACTION AFTER CHILDBIRTH

As a childbirth educator, perhaps one of the most common questions I am asked by my students in this unit is: How soon after childbirth can we have sex? According to the American College of Obstetrics and Gynecology (ACOG), couples are encouraged to wait six weeks before resuming intercourse (2006). This waiting period allows the woman to heal after her birth and labor experiences, which are discussed in the "Healthy Selves/Healthy Families" feature box on page 335. A general rule of thumb is best to wait to resume sexual intercourse until after the initial post-birth checkup; at this point, couples can also discuss birth control options available to them. Nevertheless, most couples resume sexual activity when they feel comfortable doing so. A recent study indicates that most couples resume sexual activity within six weeks of delivery, although women may not experience an orgasm until about three months after delivery (Connolly and others, 2005). As one body of research confirmed, if both partners enjoy a rich sex life throughout pregnancy, they tend to evaluate their levels of tenderness and communication higher in the first six months following delivery (von Sydow, 1999).

Generally, couples' sex lives will undergo change after they become parents. In particular, sexual desire appears to be lower for mothers than it is for fathers in about the first year following birth (Ahlborg, Dahlof, & Strandmark, 2000; Ahlborg, Lars-Gosta, & Hallberg, 2005). Aside from lower sexual desire, there are also physical changes in the experience of sex after childbirth. A study that examined 480 postpartum women found among new mothers that over 50 percent experienced pain during first intercourse following delivery; this pain continued somewhat for six months (Barrett and others, 2000). Another examined over 500 women and their partners to evaluate which factors determined sexual activity and satisfaction with their sexual relationships one year after a first birth (Brummen, Bruinse, van de Pol, Heintz, & van der Vaart, 2006). By three months following the birth of their babies, over 80 percent of the couples had had sex; by one year after birth, about 94 percent had. The most significant finding in this study was that the researchers found a predictive factor for no sexual intercourse one year following birth: Women who were not sexually active when they were three months pregnant had an 11 times higher chance of not being sexually active one year after giving birth (Brummen and others, 2006).

These changes in the sexual relationship, in turn, cause stress and tension between the couple, and compound the transition to assuming the new roles of parents. If new parents are able to communicate openly about their sexual desires and the stressors associated with becoming parents, and if they confirm each other emotionally and sexually, they experience better adjustment—and have more sex (Ahlborg and others, 2000; Ahlborg and others, 2005). Indeed, a recent study of 820 postpartum couples found that, by the time the babies were about 6 months old, most of the parents indicated that they were "very happy" in their relationships (Ahlborg and others, 2005). Factors contributing to their relationship happiness were a strong social support network and having someone to provide relief so the couple could spend some time away from the baby. Among those who indicated that they were unhappy, factors included economic problems, having a partner who was away from home too much (which led to less closeness), and frustration with the partner's lack of help or sharing responsibility.

Unexpected Outcomes

During each of my pregnancies, I experienced the common fears and worries about the health and well-being of my babies. I went through all of the "what ifs" I could possibly think of, yet there were admittedly some things I dared not think about, such as delivering an unhealthy, physically impaired or physically challenged baby, or even the death of the baby. Many couples experience unexpected outcomes when they are unable to become pregnant. For some couples, becoming pregnant represents grueling work and becomes a difficult and heart-wrenching challenge.

WHEN CONCEPTION FAILS: INFERTILITY

In the United States today, approximately 6.1 million women and over 2 million married couples are unable to conceive (Centers for Disease Control and Prevention, 2005c). **Sterility** refers to the absolute inability to reproduce, either because the woman has no uterus or ovaries, or the male has no testes or sperm production. No amount of medical intervention can help a sterile person reproduce. **Infertility** is the inability to conceive a baby after trying for a period of one year.

Women and Infertility Approximately one-third of the problems associated with infertility are due to women's reproductive systems (American Society of Reproductive Medicine, 2006). Specifically, problems with the monthly release of an ovum from the ovary (ovulation) are responsible for most female infertility. Lack of ovulation may be due to *hormonal imbalances,* which refers to a decline in or an absence of the hormones estrogen and progesterone,

Eggs for Sale!

Across college campuses, classified ads are seeking eggs—egg donors, that is. Calling for physically attractive women under the age of 29, fertility agencies are paying big bucks for eggs. Compensation for egg harvesting typically starts at $5,000, and skyrockets when high I.Q. and high SAT scores are combined with good looks and good personality traits. It is not uncommon for some fertility agencies to pay up to $20,000 when a donor has the right stuff. Compensation is even higher—up to $25,000—for Jewish and Asian donors, whose genetic material is high in demand. In the United States, it's illegal to be paid for body parts, but fertility experts claim that they are not compensating women for their eggs, per se, but for their time, effort, and discomfort.

Once approved for donation, the donor self-administers by injection synthetic hormones that cause the woman's ovaries to produce many eggs—as many as a few dozen, instead of one, which is typical. Once the eggs are mature, ovulation is triggered by medication, and a needle through the vagina retrieves the eggs. The entire process can span up to six months.

1. In your opinion, should the harvesting and sale of human eggs be legal? Why or why not?

2. Do you think it's fair that only beautiful and intelligent women are sought after?

3. Would you, or anyone you know, sell your eggs for profit? Why or why not?

which are necessary for pregnancy. Other causes for infertility may be a pituitary gland tumor (quite rare), or lifestyle habits such as poor nutrition (as in the case of anorexia or bulimia), stress, or even intense athletic training (U.S. Department of Health and Human Services, 2003). Once a woman reaches the age of 35, her ovaries' ability to produce eggs diminishes.

Even when women successfully ovulate, the fertilized ovum may have difficulty reaching the uterus due to blocked or scarred fallopian tubes. This disorder, called **pelvic inflammatory disease (PID)**, is primarily caused by untreated sexually transmitted infections (such as gonorrhea and chlamydia). PID renders 150,000 women per year infertile—making it the leading cause of infertility in young women (Centers for Disease Control, 2009). **Endometriosis**, a disease characterized by the buildup or migration of uterine tissue to other parts of the body (such as the ovaries or fallopian tubes), may also prevent the fertilized ovum from traveling through the fallopian tube to the uterus, or may prevent the fertilized ovum from becoming embedded in the uterine lining.

Men and Infertility About one-third of fertility difficulties are due to male reproductive problems (American Society of Reproductive Medicine, 2006). Healthy, robust sperm are necessary in order for fertilization of the ovum to take place. There are two primary forms of infertility in men: *azoospermia*, which means that no sperm cells are produced, and *oligospermia*, which means that few sperm cells are produced. Sometimes these conditions are the result of a genetic disease, such as cystic fibrosis; sometimes they are the result of poor reproductive health. To produce an adequate number (at least 20 million sperm per milliliter of semen), the male must be healthy and lead a healthy lifestyle.

The American Society of Reproductive Medicine (ASRM) is an internationally recognized nonprofit medical organization that disseminates information, education, and standards in the field of reproductive health. According to the ASRM (2006), to improve fertility, men should consult with a physician about the proper vitamins and minerals that improve sperm function. In addition, men should limit alcohol intake and stop smoking, as alcohol lowers testosterone levels and smoking may cause the production of malformed, slow-moving sperm. Finally, men should keep their cool. For healthy sperm production, the testes must be cooler than the rest of the body—this is why nature designed the male's testicles to hang outside of the body. Males considering parenthood may want to avoid hot tubs, saunas, steam rooms, very hot baths, and placing laptop computers on their laps. Although folklore suggests men should wear boxers rather than briefs to promote the production of healthy sperm, to date no empirical evidence has been found to support such claims.

Treating Infertility In 2003, 9.3 million American women received infertility medical treatments of some kind (Centers for Disease Control and Prevention, 2006). There are a variety of treatment options available, ranging from medication (fertility drugs to enhance ovulation) to surgery. Less invasive medical treatments include fertility drugs and donor insemination, often referred to as *artificial insemination*. In women, fertility drugs increase egg production. When fertility drugs are used, sometimes more than one egg is produced, which leads to multiple births, as in the case of this country's first set of septuplets. **Artificial insemination**, a popular fertility treatment used by both heterosexual and homosexual couples, is the medical process in which donor sperm is placed into the woman's vagina, cervix, or uterus by a syringe. Sperm are collected (through masturbation of the donor) and stored by medical facilities called **sperm banks**. Sperm donors are typically paid $30.00 to $50.00 per specimen; a vial of sperm from a sperm bank costs about $350.00.

If these treatment options fail, there are other more invasive (and more costly) treatment options. The following are descriptions of **Assisted Reproductive Technology (ART)**, which are treatments that involve fertilization through the hands-on manipulation of the woman's ova and the male's sperm. In 2006, more than 50,000 babies were born in the United States as a result of ART (ASRM, 2008).

■ **In vitro fertilization (IVF).** In infertile couples where a woman has blocked or absent fallopian tubes, or where a man has a low sperm count, IVF is typically used to help the couple conceive. In vitro fertilization is a process whereby a woman's eggs are surgically removed from her ovary and mixed with a man's sperm in a laboratory culture dish. After about 40 hours in the culture dish, the eggs are examined to see if they were fertilized, and if they were, to see if cell division is taking place. If the balls of cells appear to be growing at a normal rate, the eggs (embryos) are placed within the uterus. This process bypasses the fallopian tubes. The average cost of IVF is $12,400 per attempt (ASRM, 2008).

■ **Gamete intrafallopian transfer (GIFT)**. This ART process also involves manually manipulating the sperm and eggs, but instead of fertilizing the eggs in a dish, the unfertilized eggs and the male's sperm are placed in the woman's fallopian tubes. This is designed to foster natural fertilization within the woman's fallopian tubes. The average cost of GIFT is approximately $10,000 per attempt (ASRM, 2008).

■ **Zygote intrafallopian transfer (ZIFT)**. Like IVF, this process requires the woman's eggs to be fertilized by the man's sperm in a laboratory culture dish. The fertilized egg is then placed immediately in the woman's fallopian tubes, rather than in her uterus (as in IVF), allowing the conceptus to travel naturally to the uterus and implant. The average cost of ZIFT is $10,000 per attempt (ASRM, 2008).

■ **Surrogacy**. A woman may desire to have a biological child, but for medical reasons she cannot sustain a pregnancy. For these women, IVF is performed; rather than having the embryos implanted into her uterus, however, the embryos are implanted into a **surrogate mother**, who carries the pregnancy to term. Upon birth, the baby is given to the biological parents.

The Psychological Impact of Infertility Infertility is distressing, frustrating, and depressing. Hoping, longing, and wishing month after month after month for a positive pregnancy test only to find out that the efforts failed yet again constitutes a life crisis for couples. The stress on finances and the stress on the marriage can lead to a breakdown of the couple's relationship. Fortunately, many support groups and infertility counseling organizations exist to help infertile women and couples navigate through the physical and emotional challenges infertility brings. Groups such as the National Infertility Association and the International Council on Infertility Information Dissemination offer psychological, psychosocial, and informational support for those experiencing infertility.

THE PHYSICALLY CHALLENGED BABY

While we all long for a healthy baby, not all of us will have the perfect "Gerber" baby. Birth defects and anomalies can range from barely noticeable, to life-threatening, to fatal. No matter how severe the defect, parents of infants with birth defects and physically challenged babies mourn the loss of the healthy child they imagined they'd deliver. At the Parents Encouraging Parents Conference, Roger and Ann Figard (1992, personal communication) presented the Loss and Grief Cycle for parents of physically challenged children (see Figure 10.4 on page 340).

PREGNANCY LOSS

Most pregnancies proceed without many complications. Even when complications do occur, Western medical science provides women with treatment for nearly every complication related to pregnancy. Complications can range from skin rashes, to excessive vomiting, to high blood pressure, to anemia, to vaginal bleeding or cramping, to the loss of the pregnancy.

Miscarriage Any loss of a fetus or embryo before the fourth month of pregnancy is termed a spontaneous abortion, or **miscarriage** (Merck Manual, 2003). *Early miscarriage* occurs with the loss of a fetus before the 12th week of pregnancy; *late miscarriage* occurs with the loss of a fetus between the 12th and 20th weeks of pregnancy. Approximately one-fourth to one-third of pregnant women experience some type of bleeding or cramping during the first 20 weeks of

FIGURE 10.4   Loss and Grief Cycle for Parents of Physically Challenged Children

When parents lose a child to death, or when they have a baby born with birth defects, they experience a cycle of grief and loss.

Pregnancy In pregnancy, the unknowns about the baby encourage a parent to hope and dream and fantasize about what the baby will be like.

The Fantasized, Hoped-For Child Often, the parents develop an idea or mental picture of the perfect child-to-be. This can include the sex of the child, talents, or other characteristics important to the parents.

Birth of a Challenged Child The parent is faced with the reality that the hoped-for child and the real child are not the same child.

Ideational Object Loss Unconsciously, the parent's mind recognizes the death of the dream of the hoped-for child and this moves the parent into a cycle of grief ... letting go of the hoped-for child and accepting the real child.

Shock and Panic
The first stage of grief is one of disbelief and disorientation. The parent often responds in the same manner that he/she always reacts in panic—withdrawal, eating, hysteria, talking, etc.

Searching
After the shock, the parent begins to search for the hoped-for child. This may be done through denial, searching for a diagnosis, or placing blame.

GRIEF CYCLE

Maintenance
The parent reaches a relatively stable state of equilibrium. He/she has found internal and external coping mechanisms to help deal with each new hurdle or obstacle. The parent realizes true resolution cannot occur as long as the child is alive—the grieving cycle can and does start all over again when they are reminded that their child is disabled or malformed.

Experience of Nothingness
This is often a time of strong emotions as the parent realizes the child cannot be "fixed" and the parent must face the reality of the child's disability. At this time the parent is asking why this happened to him/her. Anger, guilt, depression, and rage are some of the emotions felt at this time.

Recovery
The parent takes the intense emotions and begins to resolve them in positive ways. He/she integrates the hoped-for child with the real child—seeing the child's assets along with the disability. Values, goals, and family life are restructured to include the impaired child. The child is now loved for who he or she is.

Source: Roger and Ann Figard (1992), personal communication.

pregnancy; of those, about half of the pregnancies result in pregnancy loss. Merck (2003) estimates that about 85 percent of all miscarriages take place before the first 12 weeks of pregnancy; these pregnancy losses usually take place because of abnormalities in the embryo or fetus. The other 15 percent miscarry from the 13th to the 20th weeks of pregnancy. In two-thirds of these miscarriages, the pregnancy loss can be linked to the mother's health or lifestyle, and in one-third, no cause is known. Known causes of miscarriage include abnormalities within the embryo or fetus resulting from illnesses or disorders such as diabetes, infections, injury, hypothyroidism, or from lifestyle choices such as using cocaine, especially crack (Merck, 2003).

Stillbirth Even though society at large may not recognize the emotional and physical impact of any pregnancy loss, the impact on the parents is life-altering. **Stillbirth** refers to the death of a fetus after the 20th week (fourth months) of pregnancy, and occurs in approximately one in every 115 births, or about 26,000 per year (March of Dimes, 2006). Only about 14 percent of the fetuses die during the labor and birth process; the remaining 86 percent die before labor has begun (March of Dimes, 2006). In developing countries or less economically advantaged countries, the stillbirth rates are much higher because medical care is not as readily available.

Unexpected Outcomes

When preparing for childbirth, most books and childbirth preparation classes skim over—or ignore altogether—the possibility that a baby may be born with a birth defect. Birth defects may vary from mild to severe, but they include abnormalities in the structure, function, or body chemistry that require medical treatment (March of Dimes, 2006). Sometimes birth defects can affect a child's development.

When parents have a baby born with a birth defect they are often overwhelmed by fears and emotions. Human service providers, social workers, healthcare providers, and clergy encourage parents to:

- **Acknowledge their emotions.** As you learned in this chapter, expectant parents have an image of a hoped-for child. When a baby is born with birth defects, parents need time to mourn the loss of this hoped-for child. Shock, denial, and grief are common emotions.
- **Seek support.** Joining support groups or talking with someone who has had similar experiences, or seeking help from a psychologist, clergy member, or social worker is helpful for parents.
- **Seek information.** Parents should educate themselves about their child's condition. Sources of information include the baby's physician, books, the March of Dimes, the National Information Center for Children and Youth with Disabilities, and various support groups. There are also resources (state and local) that assist parents in paying for costs associated with certain birth defects. Hospital social workers can help direct parents to appropriate information resources.
- **Use a team approach.** For the most part, children born with birth defects need a team made up of doctors, child life specialists or developmentalists, and social workers to treat them. Some children's hospitals have such teams already in place. Parents need to play an active role in their child's treatment plan.

TALK ABOUT IT

1. If you are studying to be a human service provider or a medical professional, would you consider being a part of a professional support team to assist parents with children who have birth defects? Why or why not?
2. What scares you most about having a child with a birth defect?
3. In your opinion, what challenges would a couple's relationship face if they had a child who was physically challenged?

Most women find the labor and birth experiences of stillborns to be rewarding and satisfying. Despite the fact that the woman and her partner did not receive the outcome they had hoped for, the birth process is a time of quiet reflection and recognition that the baby was, is, and will always be a significant part of their lives and in the lives of their family. Although it may seem morbid, after the birth of the baby, physicians encourage parents and family to hold, bathe, dress, cuddle, and sing to their infant in order to bond with the baby. Parents and families of stillborn babies are typically given several hours to bond with the baby because this bonding experience is crucial in their grieving and mourning.

In instances of stillbirth, greeting the baby also means saying good-bye. Although parting with anyone we love is devastating, parents who suffer the pre-natal or post-natal loss of a baby carry the loss for the rest of their lives. Whether or not the baby ever took a breath—the life had meaning and significance to the parents and their families. The intense, overwhelming feelings of grief are simply an affirmation that the baby's life was real. Moving through the grief and mourning to a place of healing takes time. Sometimes outside resources are necessary to help parents cope with their devastating loss. In time, the loss is integrated into their marriage, their relationship, and their lives.

Unexpected outcomes are just that—something we do not anticipate. When preparing for the birth of a baby, I strongly encourage you to make your own "what if" list. What if I don't want to be a parent or I'm not ready to be a parent? What if my partner doesn't find me attractive? What if I wanted a nonmedicated birth and I have to use pain medications? What if I have a premature baby? What if my baby has birth defects? What if I can't look at my baby because of the defect? What if my baby is stillborn? What if my baby dies? While we certainly cannot anticipate every possible result associated with pregnancy and childbirth, coming to terms with the fact that sometimes the pregnancy and childbirth experience doesn't yield our desired outcomes is an essential and necessary step in becoming a parent.

Adoption: By Circumstance or Choice

Having a baby is something that seems so easy. But each year, over 6 million couples in the United States face difficulties becoming pregnant; hundreds of others desire to become parents, but for numerous reasons they wish to adopt rather than to become pregnant (American Adoptions, 2009). For those who have hoped to become pregnant, infertility represents an invisible and very painful loss. Once a family decides to grow their family through adoption, a standard process is put into place.

THE ADOPTION PROCESS

Each adoption agency may have its own policies and procedures, but generally there are five steps to adoption. The process may take months, or a few years, depending on whether the couple or individual desires to adopt a newborn baby, or if they are waiting for a specific race/ethnicity.

Step 1: Initial information. To begin, each prospective adoptive parent must select an agency or a private organization through which to adopt. Couples may choose to adopt *domestically* (from the United States), or *internationally* (from abroad). For example, Angelina Jolie and Madonna chose to adopt their children from other countries. Many people believe that international adoptions cost far less than domestic adoptions, but this is not the case. According to the National Council for Adoption (2008), domestic and intercountry adoptions can range from $8,000 to $40,000; typically, adoptions fall in the $15,000 to $25,000 range. In the United States, the majority of international adoptions are from China (National Council for Adoption, 2008). Wait times also vary, depending on the country from which a couple adopts. In the United States, the average wait time is 1 to 18 months; the average wait for a baby from China is 1 year, and most Russian adoptions take 6 to 12 months. For 2006, the U.S. Department of Citizenship and Immigration Services reported that slightly over one-half of the children adopted from China were 1 to 4 years old; over two-thirds of the children adopted from Russia were 1 to 4 years old.

Step 2: Preparation. To be eligible for adoption, prospective parents must undergo a home study. The home study helps to ensure that the child is going to be placed in a loving, caring, nurturing home. During the study, a social worker interviews the couple and assesses such things as their relationship stability, their feelings about and readiness for becoming parents, and aspects about their daily lives. The social worker also checks the parents' health and income status; parents undergo a scrutinizing background check as well. Many adoption agencies and placement agencies are assigned a specialist who helps them through each stage of the adoption process.

Step 3: The family-in-waiting. After the adoptive family has successfully completed all required documentation and the home study, they are considered to be a family-in-waiting—they enter a somewhat unknown waiting period until a match occurs that results in a successful adoptive placement. This time frame varies for every adoptive family.

Step 4: The placement. After the couple is matched with a birthmother/couple, the adoptive couple works with the specialist until the baby is born or an older child is found. Placement typically occurs immediately after all the paperwork is completed and filed. Perhaps one of the most intensely felt fears of adoptive parents is that the birthmother will change her mind; in reality, however, very few birthmothers decide to raise their babies after initiating the adoption process, but it is their right to do so. It is very important that a birthmom is not forced into her decision by others. Women who do change their minds about placing their children for adoption are typically under the age of 17, have no future plans, live with their parents, and have mothers who oppose the adoption (Adamec, 2004).

Step 5: It's final! After the specified time frame has passed (this varies from state to state), and all of the documentation has been completed and filed with the court, a final court hearing is held and the adoption decree is awarded to the parents.

GAY AND LESBIAN ADOPTION

The landscape of gay and lesbian adoption continues to undergo rapid change. Currently, over 20 states in the United States allow gay and lesbian parents to legally adopt the biological child of their partner. Further, some states allow individual gays or lesbians to adopt, but they do not allow same-sex couples to adopt.

Generally, when considering any gay/lesbian adoption, today's courts are primarily focused on "the best interest of the child," and beliefs that lesbian and gay adults are not fit parents have no empirical foundation (among many others, Anderssen, Amlie, & Ytteroy, 2002; Patterson, 2000; Perrin, 2002). As such, a person's sexual orientation cannot be used as a factor in determining whether a homosexual individual or couple can adopt or foster parent a child. Three states—Arkansas, New Hampshire, and Florida—prohibit gay and lesbian individuals and couples from being adoptive or foster parents. The American Civil Liberties Union (ACLU), a nonprofit, nonpartisan group that monitors the individual civil liberties of Americans spelled out in the Constitution, maintains that this is because these states adhere to "stereotypical" views that gays and lesbians are unfit to be parents.

Those opposed to the concept of same-sex adoption may believe that a female role model and a male role model are necessary in children's lives. Others claim that children who are reared by gay or lesbian parents might themselves grow up to be homosexual, or that gay men might molest their children. Others are concerned that children of gay and lesbian parents will be teased ruthlessly and relentlessly by their classmates. Issues at the forefront of this discussion address gender identity and sexual orientation, as well as children's overall well-being:

- *Gender identity.* In response to whether children need both a mother and a father in order to establish a solid gender identity, studies show that few differences in gender

TODAY, more and more states are loosening their restrictions on same-sex couples being allowed to adopt children. Although some believe that both male and female role models are necessary for optimal child development, to date research does not bear out these concerns. Are you in favor of or opposed to same-sex adoption? Why or why not?

identity exist between children reared by same-sex parents and heterosexual parents (Golombok, Spencer, & Rutter, 1983; Green, 1978; Green, Mandel, Hotvedt, Gray, & Smith, 1986; Hoeffer, 1981).

- *Sexual orientation.* Empirical studies reveal that being raised by homosexual parents does not increase the likelihood that the child will be gay or lesbian (Bailey, Bobrow, Wolfe, & Mikach, 1995; Bigner & Jacobson, 1989; Green, 1978).
- *Children's well-being.* Having gay or lesbian parents is less an indicator of the quality of the parent–child relationship than parenting styles are. Ultimately, it is the quality of parenting, not sexual orientation, that determines how children of same-sex parents fare (Lott-Whitehead & Tully, 1992; McCandish, 1987; Pennington, 1987).
- *Shared parenting.* Lesbian and gay parents tend to divide childcare tasks and responsibilities relatively evenly, and report higher levels of satisfaction in their couple relationships than heterosexual couples do (Bos and others, 2004; Johnson & O'Conner, 2002; Ciano-Boyce & Shelley-Sireci, 2002).
- *Parenting.* Gay and lesbian parents possess better parenting skills than heterosexual couples do; this is reportedly due to greater levels of parent–child interaction, and lower levels of physical punishment (Flaks, Ficher, Masterpasqua, & Joseph 1995; Brewaeys & Van Hall, 1997).

Perhaps Sara Bonkowski (2003) best sums up the experience of same-sex adoption when she explains,

Remember that a child needs the love and support of both parents. If one parent is gay or lesbian, in time the child will know and come to understand. Many of the concerns and worries that may be raised about homosexuality are concerns of adults; the concerns of a child are much simpler. If a gay or lesbian parent forms a caring paternal or maternal bond with his or her young child, by the time the child is old enough to understand homosexuality the child will know the parent and appreciate that Mom or Dad is, in every respect, a "good parent."

Contraception and Abortion

When considering pathways to parenting, it is also important to consider methods of protection against unwanted pregnancy. The forms and methods of birth control are wide and varied, as are the effectiveness rates and complications. Deciding which birth control method is right for you often depends on individual needs and circumstances. In general, there are three categories of contraceptives: barrier methods, hormone methods, and other methods.

CONTRACEPTION

Barrier contraceptive methods provide a chemical or physical barrier between the sperm and the ovum. These methods are often not invasive and will usually not affect lifelong fertility (see Table 10.4). They are typically inexpensive and available over the counter (OTC) without a doctor's prescription.

Just as the name implies, **hormone contraceptive methods** use artificial hormones to prevent ovulation as well as thicken the cervical mucus, which inhibits sperm from traveling into the uterus. Because each method uses the same basic principle (the mode of delivery is usually the biggest difference), the pros and cons of each method are similar. The convenience of hormonal methods makes them very desirable, but because the hormones essentially alter the body's chemistry, side effects are common. Hormonal methods are used by women.

Emergency contraception (EC), also referred to as the **morning after pill** or **Plan B**, is made of the same hormones found in birth control pills. These hormones work by keeping a woman's ovaries from releasing an egg, and also by thickening a woman's cervical mucous

TABLE 10.4 Barrier Contraceptive Methods

Method	Ups	Downs	Failure Rate (rated by the FDA)
Condom	Available OTC, inexpensive, STD protection	Lack of sensitivity, interruption of "the moment"	11%
Female Condom	Available OTC, STD protection	Cumbersome, interruption of "the moment"	21%
Diaphragm	Can be inserted hours before sex, does not impede sensitivity	Available only by prescription, often messy, no STD protection	17%*
Cervical Cap	Can be used for multiple acts of sex, convenient	Prescription-only, often messy, no STD protection	17–23%*
Cervical Shield	Can be used for multiple acts of sex, convenient	Prescription-only, often messy, no STD protection	15%*
Contraceptive Sponge	Can be used for multiple acts of sex, available OTC	Messy (requires spermicide), possible health side effects, no STD protection	14–28%*
Intra-Uterine Device (IUD)	Can remain in place for 10 years, very convenient	Must be placed by a healthcare professional, no STD protection	<1%
Spermicides	Inexpensive, available OTC	Messy, no STD protection, not as reliable when used alone	20–50%

*When used with spermicide

(the mucous blocks sperm and keeps it from joining an egg). The morning after pill is *not* an abortion pill. As you'll see in our discussion a bit later, abortion pills empty the uterus of an already-fertilized egg, but the morning after pill prevents pregnancy by interrupting the release of an egg. If taken within 72 hours of an "oops" sexual experience (the condom broke or slipped off, a woman forgets to take her birth control pills, he didn't pull out in time, etc.), EC reduces the risk of pregnancy by 89 percent (Planned Parenthood, 2009); it can be obtained by seeing a healthcare provider on campus, or in your local community.

ABORTION AND OTHER METHODS

Many couples faced with matters of personal preference and/or religious conviction may choose a birth control method that involves neither barriers nor chemicals. Others are faced with an unwanted pregnancy and opt to terminate the pregnancy through abortion.

There are two types of abortion: the abortion pill and the in-clinic abortion. A woman or a couple has many decisions to make when considering abortion. A decision to terminate a pregnancy is a highly personal, individual one, and for most women, it is an agonizing one. Depending on her circumstances and how far along she is in her pregnancy, she may decide to use a medication that ends an early pregnancy.

The Abortion Pill (Medication Abortion) Generally speaking, the abortion pill *(mifepristone)* can be used up to 63 days after the first day of a woman's last menstrual period (Planned Parenthood, 2008). This medication abortion involves three steps:

1. *The abortion pill.* At the clinic, the healthcare provider will give the woman the abortion pill. The pill works by blocking the hormone progesterone—without this hormone, the lining of the uterus breaks down and pregnancy cannot continue. The woman is also given an antibiotic to prevent infection.
2. *Misoprostol.* The second pill is taken at the woman's convenience, up to three days after taking the abortion pill. This pill causes cramps and bleeding, usually within a few hours

of taking it. It causes the uterus to empty. It is common for a woman to have bleeding and cramping for up to four weeks after the abortion.

3. *Follow-up.* A follow-up appointment is made with the healthcare provider to ensure that the abortion is complete and that the woman is well.

Should States Have the Right to Make Their Own Abortion Laws?

In 1970, an unmarried pregnant woman in Texas (given the fictitious name of Jane Roe to protect her identity) sought legal action to have the Texas anti-abortion statute overturned. She claimed that the state's abortion laws violated her constitutional right to privacy. The battle ended up in the United States Supreme Court, and in 1973, the Court ruled that state abortion laws across the nation violated women's rights to privacy. One of the most politically polarizing decisions in U.S. history, the Court's decision overturned every state law that outlawed or restricted the elective termination of a pregnancy. For over 30 years, the Supreme Court has not been directly challenged on state abortion laws—that is, until now.

In March 2006, South Dakota Governor Mike Rounds signed a bill that banned abortions in his state, except in instances where the procedure is needed to save the life of the mother. This new legislation is in direct conflict with the U.S. Supreme Court's 1973 decision. The state senate in Tennessee has also passed a similar proposal to amend its state constitution so a woman's right to abortion is no longer guaranteed. Other states are poised to follow in the footsteps of South Dakota and Tennessee: Alabama, Georgia, Indiana, Kentucky, Louisiana, Michigan, Mississippi, Missouri, Ohio, Oklahoma, and West Virginia.

Do you think states should have the right to determine their own abortion laws?

YES: Anti-abortion organizations, such as the National Right to Life campaign, contend that states should have the right to enact their own abortion legislation. They maintain that:

- Representatives are elected by people in their state to set policy and make laws that reflect the people they are serving; thus, if states outlaw abortion, it is because the state's constituents desire the legislation.
- If put to a popular vote, most Americans would vote that abortion should be made illegal.
- Most abortions are for matters of convenience, not because of rape, incest, or the mother's life being endangered.

NO: Pro-choice organizations, such as Planned Parenthood of America (2006), contend that every woman in every state should have the same and equal access to abortion services, should they need to or desire to terminate a pregnancy. They maintain that giving states individual control over abortion laws:

- Puts the health, safety, and personal well-being of women at risk
- Makes women turn to unsafe, unsanitary methods of terminating pregnancies that put their lives in jeopardy
- Violates a woman's constitutional right to privacy, and jeopardizes her right to manage her own reproductive health

WHAT DO YOU THINK?

1. Should the federal government or individual states determine access to abortion services?
2. In your opinion, do you expect the Supreme Court's 1973 decision to be overturned? Why or why not?

Sources: Planned Parenthood (2006); National Right to Life Compaign, "Abortion in Healthcare Bills," www.nrlc.org.

Women choose this option because it can be done early in the pregnancy and it is very private. The abortion pill is safe for most women, but some risks include an allergic reaction, an incomplete abortion, infection, and very heavy bleeding.

In-Clinic Abortion There are several different kinds of abortions that are done by healthcare providers within medical clinics or hospitals. During these procedures, the woman is medicated with numbing medications, pain medications, or certain types of sedation to make her more comfortable. The uterus is emptied by *aspiration* (a suction device) or by *D&E* (the use of suction and other devices). There are risks associated with any medical procedure, and abortion is no exception. Risks for in-clinic abortions range from blood clots, injury to the cervix or other organs, and very heavy bleeding; death can occur, but this is a very rare complication.

Feelings after an Abortion Deciding to terminate a pregnancy is traumatic for most women, and it's not unusual for women to have a wide range of feelings following an abortion. Little to no empirical evidence exists that addresses the long-term emotional, physical, and psychological consequences of abortion procedures. Some organizations, such as Planned Parenthood, note that immediately after the abortion it is common for women to experience anger, regret, guilt, sadness, or depression; some feel relief (Planned Parenthood, 2008). Earlier research studies that explored whether women experienced depression, regret, anxiety, guilt, mental changes, and changes in emotional health suggested that there are few psychological effects in post-abortion women (Cohen & Roth, 1984; Major and others, 2000; Russo & Zierk, 1992).

Other studies, however, demonstrated that abortion is problematic, leading to prolonged grief, problems with intimacy and sexuality, and prolonged guilt (Angelo, 1994; Lewis, 1997; Williams, 2000). One recent study, undertaken by professor of nursing, JoAnn Trybulski (2005), found in her interview of post-abortive women that abortion is not a one-time experience; rather, abortion is a process that unfolds over time, and one that "may not be time limited in its effects and influences" (Trybulski , 2005, p. 573). Interviewing the women who had abortions at least 15 years prior to the study, the investigator discovered that emotional and psychological problems were intermittent over the years, and were present sometimes years after the termination. All of the women interviewed knew how old their child would have been "today" had it not been aborted.

Family Life Education

It's been said before that you can't really understand the changes in your life that children will bring until you've actually become a parent. Our course of study together has shown us that even good changes that occur in a family system can be very challenging, and becoming parents is no exception to that. Certainly, though, there are rewards that accompany the challenges.

We've covered a lot in this chapter, from gaining an understanding of the current trends in childbearing, to the factors that go into the decision to have children, to the emotional and relationship changes that take place during pregnancy, and the unexpected outcomes that unfortunately occur for some parents. We've also explored ways to protect your reproductive health by examining ways to prevent pregnancy. All of these issues are very important for a fundamental understanding of the choices and challenges people encounter as they begin their journey to parenthood—this period in a couple's relationship is a crucial time for them to enhance, nurture, and fortify their relationship so they are better equipped to handle the stressors associated with parenthood.

Expectant and adoptive parents spend many months preparing for the arrival of their baby. By the time they bring their baby home, they've probably taken birthing classes, attended a few parenting classes, read articles about their newborn baby, and completed the nursery. But even with all of this preparation, the reality is, many parents don't know just how much their day-to-day lives are about to change. The transition to parenthood is one of the greatest stressors a couple or an individual will encounter. To survive and to thrive, preparation needs to go beyond welcoming the baby home. In the next chapter, we explore the ups and downs of parenting.

Childbearing and Intimate Partner Violence

For many women, pregnancy is not a time of joy—in fact, for 324,000 women each year in this nation, pregnancy is the most dangerous time of their lives because of violence they suffer from their partners. Intimate partner violence includes physical, emotional, and sexual abuse. (See also "The Crisis of Family Violence" in Chapter 15.) Murder by an intimate partner is the most common cause of death among pregnant women (Family Violence Prevention, 2006).

Her Side: My fiancé is not violent. He's just feeling insecure about our relationship, worried that the baby is going to take up so much of my time that I won't have time for him. He's very moody right now, and he does get in my face and yell a lot, but that's my fault—I'm so moody and teary right now because of all of these hormones, and he doesn't know how to react to that. He has pushed me a couple of times, and he has hit me, but that was only one time. He was never like this before I got pregnant, so I'm sure that his reactions are temporary. Once the baby gets here, he'll be fine.

His Side: This is not my fault. I may have pushed her around a couple of times, but it's only because I was drunk. I won't go as far as to say she deserved it, but she did keep the fight going until I just lost it. I don't see what the big deal is.

Your Side: There are signs that intimate partner violence is taking place in this couple's relationship, although some of them might be subtle.

1. What are the signs of intimate partner violence?
2. If you were this woman's healthcare provider, what would you recommend she do?
3. Why do you believe that pregnancy is such a dangerous time for women—why do you think violence escalates?

Source: Family Violence Prevention (2006).

Summary

Childbearing Trends: Who's Having Babies?

- Each year, the population in the United States increases by the addition of slightly more than 4 million babies. In 2008, the crude birth rate—the number of childbirths per 1,000 women, per year—in the United States was 14.2. In less economically developed countries the crude birth rate is significantly higher than in richer countries.

- The U.S. fertility rate—the average number of live births per woman, in a given population, per year—in 2005 was 2.08. Countries that are less economically advantaged tend to have higher fertility rates. Fertility rates may be influenced by religious, cultural, and ethnic norms.

- Since 1991, in the United States, the rate of pregnancy among America's teens had steadily declined to a historic low in 2004, but began to rise again in 2005 and 2006. The largest increases in birth rates were seen among African American, Hispanic, and American Indian/Alaska Native teens.

- Childbearing by unmarried women (of all ages) reached a record high in 2006 and childbearing among women aged 25 to 29 was the highest of any age group. Birth rates among women in their 30s and 40s has increased steadily from 1975 to today, perhaps reflecting the cultural trend of women who delay childbearing to establish their careers.

- Teenage mothers face a number of medical, psychological, developmental, and socioeconomic challenges. Their babies also face a number of challenges, including low birth weight, recurrent respiratory infections, and increased risks of having learning disabilities. A number of programs exist that intervene to assist teenage parents.

- It is estimated there are between 6 and 14 million children who have gay or lesbian parents; about 10 million are raised in gay or lesbian households. The issues surrounding same-sex parenting are complex.

Having Children: Now, Later, or Never?

- Most studies and theories about the desire to become parents focus on the perspective that there are perceived rewards and costs associated with parenthood; people tend to engage in a cost-benefit analysis when considering parenthood.

- The perceived value of children and the appeal of parenthood also help to determine whether an individual or couple decides to become a parent(s).

- There are few studies that examine planned families by gay men and lesbian women, but the emergence of planned parenthood by same-sex individuals and couples is indicative of broad social change that is taking place in our society.

- Many couples struggle in determining when the "right" time to have a child is. The lifecourse of each family includes life transitions and turning points, and these influence timing; these all influence when someone decides to become a parent. Age-related norms are socially approved and shaped pathways that somewhat dictate when the "right time" to have a child is.

- Some couples prefer to remain childfree by choice, while others delay childbearing for reasons that are unique to them.

- Americans who were polled believe that the "ideal" family size is 2 children. However, the Quiverfull movement believes that parents should have as many children as possible, and they do not try to prevent conception. The resource dilution hypothesis maintains that parents' energy, time, and resources are drained with each subsequent child.

Being Pregnant and Giving Birth

- Children are costly endeavors!

- A number of emotional and relationship changes occur throughout the nine months of pregnancy. Human sexuality is reactive to our daily circumstances; thus, a couple's sex life undergoes many changes throughout pregnancy.

- The transition to parenthood is difficult for most people, and conflict is common among pregnant couples. Recent research shows that it's not the transition to parenthood per se that is stressful; rather, the struggles and disagreements that were present during the transition to becoming parents was already a part of the couple's relationship, before the baby was born.

- A couple's sex life undergoes changes after they become parents. Sexual desire appears to be lower for mothers than it is for fathers in about the first year following birth.

Unexpected Outcomes

- Infertility is the inability to conceive a baby after the couple has tried for a period of one year. About one-third of the problems associated with infertility are due to women's reproductive systems; about one-third are due to men's reproductive problems.

- There are a number of medical treatments available for infertility. These include artificial insemination, in vitro fertilization, gamete intrafallopian transfer, zygote intrafallopian transfer, and surrogacy.

- Birth defects and anomalies can range from barely noticeable, to life threatening, to fatal. No matter how severe the defect, parents of infants with birth defects and physically challenged babies mourn the loss of the healthy child they imagined they'd deliver. Parents tend to follow similar patterns in dealing with the birth of a physically challenged child, articulated in The Loss and Grief Cycle for parents of physically challenged children.

- Any loss of a fetus or embryo before the 20th week of pregnancy is termed a miscarriage, and about 85 percent of all miscarriages take place within the first 12 weeks of pregnancy. Known causes include abnormalities within the embryo or fetus resulting from illnesses or disorders such as diabetes, infections, injury, hypothyroidism, or from lifestyle choices such as using cocaine, especially crack.

- Stillbirth refers to the death of a fetus after the 20th week of pregnancy and occurs in approximately one in every 115 births, or about 26,000 per year. In developing countries or less economically advantaged countries, the stillbirth rates are much higher because medical care is not as readily available.

Adoption: By Circumstance or Choice

- Once a family decides to grow their family through adoption, a standard process unfolds that includes several steps: Initial Information, Preparation, The Family-in-Waiting, The Placement, and It's Final!

- Many people believe that gay and lesbians are not fit to become parents, but there is no empirical evidence to support this belief.

- Issues at the forefront of gay/lesbian adopting focus on the child's gender identity, sexual orientation, and overall well-being; shared parenting; and parenting styles.

Contraception and Abortion

■ The forms and methods of birth control are wide and varied, as are the effectiveness rates and complications.

■ Contraception is a personal choice and it falls within three primary categories: barrier methods, hormone methods, and other methods.

■ Emergency contraception, taken within 72 hours of a pregnancy scare, is nearly 90 percent effective in preventing an unwanted pregnancy.

■ The two types of abortion, medication and in-clinic, terminate an unwanted pregnancy. Deciding to end a pregnancy is difficult and traumatic for most women.

■ Conflicting evidence exists as to the long-term consequences of abortion. Some studies show that there is long-term grief, depression, sadness, anger, regret, and guilt, whereas other studies show that these are only temporary.

Key Terms and Concepts

Suggested Readings

Goer, Henci. *Obstetric myths versus research realties: A guide to the medical literature.* (Westport CT: Bergin & Garvey, 1995).

Kitzinger, Sheila. *The politics of birth* (Edinburgh: Butterworth, 2005).

Lauersen, Niels. *Childbirth with love: A complete guide to fertility, pregnancy, and childbirth for caring couples* (New York: Putnam, 1983).

Swire-Falker, Elizabeth. *Infertility survival handbook* (New York: Berkley, 2004).

Multiple-Choice Questions

1. The crude birth rate is the number of childbirths per _____ women, per year.

   a. 500

   b. 1,000

   c. 2,000

   d. 5,000

2. According to a study done in the Netherlands of heterosexual and lesbian couples, there were _____ differences between lesbian biological mothers and heterosexual mothers on parental competence, feeling parental burdens (stress), and the desires to become parents.

   a. no significant

   b. minor

   c. major

   d. some

3. A(n) _____ is a transition that entails a permanent, lasting shift in the direction of the lifecourse of a person's relationship.

   a. life transition

   b. age-related norm

   c. turning point

   d. life decision

4. _____ women indicate that they feel the world is not a safe place to bring a child into. They also feel that the world's resources are limited and they raise environmental concerns in their decision not to have children.

   a. Idealistic

   b. Emotional

   c. Hedonists

   d. Practical

5. According to the American College of Obstetrics and Gynecology (ACOG), couples are encouraged to wait for _____ before resuming intercourse after childbirth.

   a. 3 weeks

   b. 4 weeks

   c. 5 weeks

   d. 6 weeks

6. There are two primary forms of infertility in men: _____ , which means that no sperm cells are produced, and _____ , which means that few sperm cells are produced.

   a. oligospermia/azoospermia

   b. azoospermia/oligospermia

   c. oligospermia/endometriosis

   d. endometriosis/oligospermia

7. This ART process involves manually manipulating the sperm and eggs, but instead of fertilizing the eggs in a dish, the unfertilized eggs and the male's sperm are placed in the woman's fallopian tubes.

   a. In vitro fertilization

   b. Zygote intrafallopian transfer

   c. Gamete intrafallopian transfer

   d. Surrogacy

8. Any loss of a fetus or embryo before the fourth month of pregnancy is termed a _____ .

   a. miscarriage

   b. fetal demise

   c. stillborn

   d. neonatal death

Answers: 1. b; 2. a; 3. c; 4. a; 5. d; 6. b; 7. c; 8. a

Parenting Life Now

"You know, when I was nineteen, Grandpa took me on a roller coaster. Up, down. Up, down. Oh, what a ride! It was just interesting to me that a ride could make me so frightened, so scared, so sick . . . so excited and so thrilled all together. Some didn't like it. They went on the merry-go-round. That just goes around. Nothing. I like the roller coaster.

"You get more out of it."

The movie, *Parenthood*, depicts families' everyday struggles while the parents try to balance parenting responsibilities with marital roles and careers. At his wits' end with his parenting frustrations, his marriage, and his failing career, Steve Martin's character, Gil, declares that as a male in this society, unlike women, he has no choices about marriage, parenting, or work. He laments, "My whole life is have-to's." At this point, his very elderly grandmother relays her story about the roller coaster—and in doing so humorously compares it with parenthood.

Parenthood is fraught with ups and downs, choices and challenges, and elation and disappointment. For parents, a "good day" may hinge on whether a child passes a spelling test or wins a blue ribbon at the science fair, or whether a son or a daughter receives a university scholarship. A bad day may be one in which parents discover that their child is victim of a school bully. My husband and I have seen the fear on the faces of our friends as they engaged in a war for their four-year-old daughter's life as she fought (and lost) her battle with leukemia. We have seen the hopeless, helpless, and lost looks on the faces of our friends as they confronted the sudden death of their 14-year-old son in a skiing accident. Parenting is a daunting task—and sometimes frightening.

Source: Parenthood; Author's Files

Change Over Time: Parenting Is a Process
- Motherhood
- Fatherhood
- Co-Parenting: Go Team!

The Styles of Parenting
- Uninvolved Parenting
- Permissive Parenting
- Authori*tarian* Parenting
- Authori*tative* Parenting
- Ethnic Group Differences in Parenting

From Partners to Parents: Making the Transition
- Motherhood and Fatherhood: Adjusting to New Family Roles
- Theories of Child Development
- Bringing Up Baby (or Babies)
- Juggling Parenting and Household Chores

Today's Parents
- Single Parents
- Grandparents as Parents: A Growing Phenomenon
- Gay and Lesbian Parents
- How Do Children Learn about Their Racial/Ethnic Identity?

Parenting 101: Best Practices for Parenting
- Be a Leader
- Be a Teacher
- Be a Disciplinarian—But Be Patient
- Be a Realist

Family Life Education

IN past eras, children were viewed as economic assets because of their free manual labor. For this reason, it was common for families in the past to have many children.

Across the pages of time and history, children were considered a vital, necessary segment of society because they were needed to ensure the survival of the culture or race—they were viewed as necessary economic assets for society's continuation and as the manual labor needed to bring about that continuation. Although the challenges of parenting today are vastly different from those of parenting many years ago, contemporary parents still face unique demands as they raise their children.

Children the world over represent their culture's future, and because of this, society expects parents to do a good job, to create healthy, productive citizens (Lerner, Noh, & Wilson, 2004). To be sure, having a child is a monumental task. Sometimes a pregnancy is planned, sometimes a pregnancy comes as a surprise. Either way, bringing a child into this world is perhaps the biggest decision a couple or a woman will ever make. As you saw in the previous chapters, the transition to parenthood is undeniably one of the greatest challenges a marriage or intimate relationship will encounter. In this chapter, we will explore what it means to become a mother or a father and to parent. We'll also take a look at current issues that today's parents face, such as discipline practices and childcare, and juggling parenting with other responsibilities, such as household chores. As with other areas of family and intimate living, knowing what to expect about parenting and equipping ourselves with knowledge and expertise prepares and equips us to rise to the challenges.

Change Over Time: Parenting Is a Process

For those who are to become parents, there are no words to convey the excitement they will feel the first time they hear the baby's heartbeat, or hear their baby's first cries and first words. When a parent sees a baby's first smile, the sense of love, responsibility, and commitment is palpable. But the thrills move beyond infancy. Watching children grow, learn, and discover and uncover this world at every stage of their development is both entertaining and exciting (except for driver's education—that would fall into the "frightening and scary" category!). To watch them move from the rambunctious, rough-and-tumble years of childhood to the young men and women they become fills parents with a sense of pride, and at times apprehension, as they enter the real world on their own. But that growth from infancy to manhood or womanhood involves a tremendous process of not only individual growth and change but also growth and change in the parents and in their relationship.

Richard Lerner and his colleagues (1995) suggest that parenting is a *process,* a course of events that evolve and change over time. As you saw in the previous chapter, the early days of parenting bring new challenges, experiences, and trials into the family system. As children grow, parents grow, too. This parenting process meets both the biological needs of the children and, at the same time, the needs of the society in which children are socialized. Indeed, two of the base goals of parenting are to meet the **survival needs** of infants, which include the provision of food, shelter, safety, security, and love; and to meet the **socialization needs** of children, which encompasses ensuring they become productive, contributing members to society. Parent educator and author Chris Theisen (2004) notes that there are eight essential parenting responsibilities:

1. Providing a safe environment
2. Providing basic needs
3. Providing self-esteem
4. Teaching children morals and values
5. Developing mutual respect
6. Providing effective and age-appropriate discipline
7. Being involved in the child's education
8. Knowing the child by communicating with him or her

FOR most people, parenthood is fraught with ups and downs as parents balance parenting responsibilities with the ressponsibilities of careers and marriages or other intimate relationships.

Everything you have learned so far in this book about relationships now begins to come together—our intimacy patterns, the way we love, how we communicate, the way we express and feel about our gender, how we find a partner for life, and our sexual identity. All of our interrelationship patterns and behaviors are learned over a period of years from our parents or family of origin. Given the sheer importance of parenting, then, it is of little wonder that so much attention has been focused on this area of family life and intimate relationships. Family practitioner, Virginia Satir, once observed, "Parents teach in the toughest school in the world—the school for making people."

MOTHERHOOD

Our study in the previous chapter showed us that in societies across the globe, women are expected to become mothers by certain culturally determined ages, and this expectation creates pressures for them to bear children. Thus, becoming a mother is considered to be a normative developmental stage for women in all cultures. In the broadest sense, **mothering** is defined as a process whereby someone performs the relational and logistical work of caring for others (Arendell, 2000). With this definition, we can see how someone—a woman or a man—could "mother" someone who is not a child, such as an aging parent or a sibling who has a disability; we can also "mother" a friend or a loved one who is in need. However, in most societies women are expected not only to be the bearers of children but also to nurture, care for, and socialize them as well—mothers are expected to "mother" the children in society (Arendell, 2000).

Our study in Chapter 4 showed us that girls and boys are socialized to fulfill roles that are determined and defined by their cultures; although each society's roles are unique, motherhood is one of the few roles assigned to women that appears to be universal, and the experience of

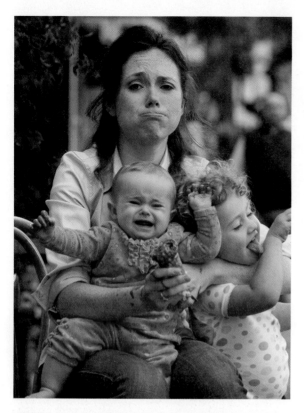

NOTHING left to give? The Western cultural standard of intensive mothering asserts that mothers are to give of themselves unconditionally, and that their children's needs should be met before their own. Do you agree or disagree with this ideology? Is this type of sacrificial mothering good for children, or not?

motherhood today remains a central part of many women's identities (Arendell, 2000). For example, in a study of 1,200 parents, women identified themselves as mothers more often than they identified themselves by their occupation or career, or their marital status; on the other hand, fathers identified themselves by their occupation, and not by their status as fathers (Rogers & White, 1998). Even though today women fill multiple roles, such as provider and caregiver to aging parents, they are also expected to simultaneously "nurture, schedule, taxi, and feed their families"—and to do it all well (Medina & Magnuson, 2009). Because of these multiple demands and expectations, some researchers believe that the standards for "good mothering" are escalating (Douglas & Michaels, 2004, cited in Medina & Magnuson, 2009).

Professor of sociology and women's and gender studies, Sharon Hays, examined the social construction of motherhood in the latter part of the twentieth century. From her scholarly works, she coined the term **intensive mothering** to reflect the mothering roles and expectations that have been evolving since the 1980s, when women flooded the workplace (Hays, 1996). **Intensive mothering ideology** is the Western cultural belief that a mother should give of herself unconditionally, and focus all of her time, energy, money, love, support, and every other resource she has, on raising her children. If she works outside of the home, she is expected to make up the time with her children that is "lost" at work. Furthermore, intensive mothering is expected of mothers even if a father is present in the home, if he is employed, and if they share equally in household and childrearing tasks. As this ideology shows us, the cultural expectation of mothers today is clear: The well-being of children is the responsibility of the mother, and she is to respond to their needs before those of her own or of her husband (or partner). Of course, this means that women who fall short of this cultural ideal do not fit today's social construction of "good mothers" (Medina & Magnuson, 2009). In Chapter 12, we'll explore the stressors associated with mothers' multiple roles and the pressures they feel in trying to adhere to the intensive mothering standard.

The transition to motherhood is a major developmental life event for most women, because it requires women to restructure their goals, behaviors, and responsibilities (Mercer, 2004). The **theory of Maternal Role Attainment (MRA)** speaks to the fluid, continual, fluctuating processes associated with becoming a mother (Rubin, 1967). According to this theory, women actually begin adopting roles associated with motherhood during their pregnancies, such as bonding emotionally with the growing fetus. While pregnant, a woman also begins to observe the behaviors of mother models she has in her environment (such as her own mother, grandmothers, and friends); as her pregnancy continues, she adopts those behaviors she believes would be ideal for her and her child, and she rejects behaviors she judges as inappropriate for herself. Through pregnancy, and after the birth of her child, she continues to construct an "ideal" image of herself as mother; she then adopts roles that support this ideal image.

There are a number of factors that influence MRA. These include (Mercer, 1986):

- Age of the mother
- Socioeconomic background
- Social stress and support
- Temperament
- Self-concept
- Childrearing beliefs and attitudes

- Role strain
- Perception of the infant

Particularly important to MRA is the woman's relationship with her own mother. For example, one body of research demonstrated that young mothers' current relationships with their mothers were re-created in their relationships with their infants (Kretchmar & Jacobvitz, 2002). Other research found that pregnant mothers' attitudes and memories about their mothers influenced their prenatal attachment to their babies, and that young mothers' memories of how accepting or rejecting their own mothers were also influenced their ability to adopt motherhood roles (Priel & Besser, 2001; Crockenberg & Leerkes, 2003).

"Motherhood" is a developmental process that is influenced by many factors, and one that unfolds over time—the new mother affects and is affected by her child, by her spouse or partner, by her past experiences in her own childhood, and by her relationship with her mother.

FATHERHOOD

Like motherhood, the social construction of fatherhood continues to change over time. Among America's first families in Colonial Williamsburg in the seventeenth century, for example, British immigrants brought the traditional patriarchal family structure to Virginia. The **patriarchal family structure** included the father figure, who was considered to be the authority over his entire household—wife, children, dependent kin, servants, slaves, and apprentices. This family structure served to preserve the wealth and power of the patriarch's household and the family's lineage. When fathers died, they willed their land and property to their sons, ensuring that the family's wealth remained within the family. Daughters typically inherited servants and livestock, rather than land or money. Within this family structure, fathers were all-powerful and served as the unquestioned, oftentimes uncaring, ruler (Lamb, 1987). In this era, men were charged with the responsibility of their children's moral and spiritual development, and because of this, discipline was their responsibility. The early father–child relationship was typically emotionally distant and correctional; it also lacked warmth, nurturing, and affection, because these behaviors were associated with parental indulgence that was thought to ruin the character of the children (Pleck & Pleck, 1997). Patriarchal parenting continued in the United States until the mid-eighteenth century.

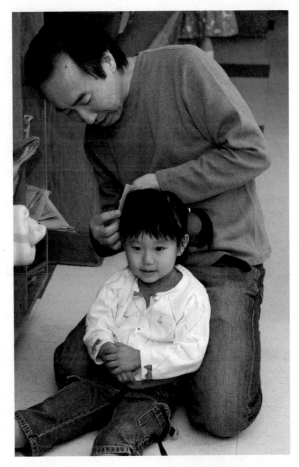

With the rise of industrialism and urbanization in Western cultures, the social construction of fatherhood began to change. As fathers moved their work into factories and away from the home, mothers' roles expanded to include moral teacher and disciplinarian (Pleck & Pleck, 1997). Historians note that the separation of the workplace from the home life created two opposing trends that are still in existence today: *father-absence* and *father-involvement* (Rotundo, 1993). Some men, for instance, withdraw emotionally, psychologically, and physically from their children because their work requires that they are absent from their families; on the other hand, the decline of patriarchy has given men "permission" to display more warmth, nurturing, and intimacy with their children, allowing them to be more involved.

WHILE mothers still spend more time with their children than fathers do, today more fathers are actively involved in the nurturing and rearing of their children.

The **FAMILY** *Table*

Wanted: Fathers!

Whether people are discussing divorce laws in suburbia or crime rates in the inner city, the issue of fathering takes an active, often political, role in the ongoing dialogue over the status of the American family. There is a wide spectrum of thought concerning the importance of fathers in the United States. For some, fathers are merely a perk for children, adding interesting yet nonessential elements to a child's development. To others, the mere presence of a father is enough to cure all of society's ills. Politics aside, the research does seem to suggest that fathers are a valuable part of a child's healthy upbringing.

Consequences of Absent Fathers

Research shows that fatherlessness is linked to several social ills:

- Young children living without their father in the home are 10 times more likely to be extremely poor.
- According to the U.S. Department of Health and Human Services, fatherless children are more prone to drug and alcohol abuse.
- Children from single-parent homes have more instances of physical and mental health problems than those from two-parent homes. Children without fathers are 20 times more likely to have behavioral disorders than are children with father involvement.
- Of all high school dropouts, 71 percent have no father involvement.
- Children from single-mother families are more likely to commit crime. Those with no father involvement are 20 times more likely to end up in prison.
- In homes where there is no father, children and adolescents are 32 times more likely to run away from home than children who have a father present.
- The suicide rate is 5 times higher among those with no father involvement.

Dads as Playmates

In one study of cognitive development in children, the intellectual and social development a child gains through the mother's verbal expressions and educational activities are also learned and reinforced through physical play with the father. Mothers do play with their kids, but children generally respond more to play with their fathers. Fathers are usually more lenient with children when it comes to exploration and adventure, which helps develop cognitive skills and encourages independence.

Decreased Behavioral Problems

As fathers take a more active role in the lives of their children, behavioral issues are positively affected. Eating meals at the table, helping with homework, working on projects together, and informal, spontaneous moments are linked to fewer behavioral issues with children. Children show greater prowess at school when both parents are actively involved, but the level of *fatherly* involvement has been shown to be a more important predictor of scholarly success.

TALK
ABOUT IT

1. Were you at all surprised by the statistics shown regarding fathering? Why or why not?
2. How has the relationship (or lack of one) between you and your father influenced your life? Based on that, would you say that fathers are important?
3. What challenges exist today that might prevent a workable solution to the problem of absent fathers?

Sources: Parke & Brott (2003); Lang & Zagorsky (2001); and Teachman, Tedrow, & Crowder (2000).

Today, modern fathers tend to fall somewhere between these two opposing fatherhood types, even though they are still not quite as involved as mothers in the lives of their children. In one study, researchers discovered that fathers spend about 1.5 hours on a weekday and about 3 hours on a weekend day with their children who are under the age of 13, whereas an earlier study demonstrated that fathers have shown levels of engagement ranging from 2 to 2.8 hours per day (Yeung, Sandberg, Davis-Kean, & Hofferth, 2001; Pleck, 1997). Despite the amount of time spent with children, though, few fathers take primary responsibility for their children's nurturing and other needs; however, in comparison with mother-involvement, father-involvement (time spent with the family) increased to 67 percent of the time mothers spent with the family on

CHILDREN receive far greater benefits if their parents work together in childrearing tasks.

weekdays, and to 87 percent of the time mothers spent with the family on weekends (Hofferth, 2001; Yeung and others, 2001). Among contemporary parenting, involved fathering is a distinguishing feature of parents from fathers in the historical past. There are racial and ethnic differences in fathering experiences, and we'll discuss those in just a bit.

If we use a family systems approach to understanding parenting, we can see that mothers and fathers together create a subsystem in the family—the parent subsystem. Every day, parents are faced with decisions and challenges about how to bring up their children and how to most effectively parent them. When fathers and mothers share parenting responsibilities and when they agree on parenting decisions—when they co-parent—all family members benefit.

CO-PARENTING: GO TEAM!

How parents negotiate their childrearing beliefs and share in everyday parenting responsibilities is referred to as **co-parenting**; in essence, it is the support parents provide to one another in the raising of their children (Gable, Crnic, & Belsky, 1994). Joint parenting is important to children's well-being because it creates a home environment that fosters their growth and development. Although most research concentrates on heterosexual parents who are married or divorced, co-parenting also applies to others who are jointly raising children, such as grandparents, gay men, and lesbians.

Co-parenting can best be thought of as an alliance between parents (Gable and others, 1994). It is a significant component of parenthood because partners can turn to one another for support when they are faced with the stressors and demands of raising children. In a very real way, co-parenting is an extension of the couple's relationship, and it is just as important a process in family living as is communication, love, intimacy, or sex. That's not to say that co-parenting is easy to achieve, however. When a new baby or a child arrives on the scene, partners have to find ways to expand their interactions to include the new addition—but at the same time, they have to set limits on these interactions so as to maintain a healthy couple relationship. In other words, they have to remember that their role as a couple is just as important (if not more so) as their roles of parents. This is sometimes easier said than done! In general, there are three types of co-parenting: supportive, unsupportive, and mixed (Belsky, 1990). These are presented in Table 11.1 (page 360). As you can see, there is a wide range in ways in which parents work to raise their children.

Co-parenting strategies are important to a child's overall development and well-being because they provide predictability and stability in family rules, practices, and discipline for children. For example, numerous studies have linked positive co-parenting to children's

TABLE 11.1　Co-Parenting Styles

Supportive co-parenting.　Parents directly or indirectly agree with each other by promoting the same general message to the child (such as sticking to the agreed-on curfew and not changing it without consent of the other parent). It also occurs when one parent directly asks the other for assistance with an issue that involves the child (such as helping with discipline).

Unsupportive co-parenting.　This occurs when one parent subtly—or not so subtly—undermines the other parent's efforts (such as changing curfew without consulting with the other parent). It also takes place when one parent interrupts the interactions of the other parent and child (such as following a divorce), when one parent is openly critical of the other's parenting styles or parenting activity, or when a parent ignores the other parent's request for assistance with a child's needs.

Mixed co-parenting.　In this type of co-parenting, one or both parents' responses are mixed—sometimes they support one another, sometimes they don't.

emotional well-being and academic success (among others, Schoppe, Mangelsdorf, & Frosch, 2001; McHale, Rao, & Krasnow, 2000). Supportive co-parenting has also been associated with older children's well-developed self-regulatory abilities (Brody, Flor, & Neubaum, 1998). While many of the studies of co-parenting in the United States have focused on white, middle-class samples, research on urban Chinese families and Japanese families has demonstrated that both parents' involvement in daily, meaningful caregiving was linked to academic success and greater child empathy; when parents have conflict in their co-parenting, children are more likely to act out and to display anxious behaviors (McHale and others, 2000; Ogata & Miyashita, 2000).

Despite what family and social scientists currently understand about co-parenting, much still needs to be learned about the relationship between effective and ineffective shared parenting and its impact on children. There are also other factors that have been found to be strong predictors of children's overall well-being: parenting styles.

The Styles of Parenting

Parenting or parenthood is not a single behavior. Professor of family studies and family life educator Carol Darling and her colleague (1993) describe parenting as multiple behaviors that, together, shape children's outcomes. Research psychologist Diana Baumrind asserts that normal parenting centers on the issue of control and that parents' primary roles are to influence, teach, and control their children. Based on her observations of parent–child interactions, Baumrind believes that there are two specific dimensions of childrearing: parental warmth or responsiveness/affection/supportiveness toward the child, and parental control or how demanding or restrictive the parents are toward their child (also referred to as *behavioral control*). In examining these two dimensions, Baumrind (1991) identifies four parenting styles, which we discuss here. Each of these parenting styles reflects different patterns of parental values, practices, and behaviors.

UNINVOLVED PARENTING

Uninvolved parents are typically low in responsiveness, warmth, and affection, and they are low in parental control or demands. Parents may both reject and neglect their children. Not all parents who are uninvolved are neglectful or rejecting; some are simply detached and uninterested in their children's lives. For example, some parents, although they may meet their child's basic needs (shelter, clothing, education, food), may not offer praise for a child's efforts or compliment the child's accomplishments. In essence, there are few meaningful and inclusive family interactions.

There are a number of negative consequences of uninvolved or disengaged parenting for children and adolescent well-being. Across all racial and ethnic groups, for example, there are reports of increased substance use and abuse, higher rates of delinquency, poorer school performance, and negative psychological well-being (Pittman & Chase-Landsdale, 2001; Samaniego & Gonzales, 1999; Steinberg, Lamborn, Darling, Mounts, & Dornbusch, 1994; Steinberg, Mounts, Lamborn, & Dornbusch 1991).

Recent research further suggests that disengaged parenting styles, when combined with families who live in dangerous or socially disorganized neighborhoods, are linked with increased adolescent delinquency in African American and Latino boys (Roche, Ensminger, & Cherlin, 2007). There was also an association of uninvolved/disengaged parenting with increased school problem behavior and depression among African American youth, particularly when mothers are not involved in their children's parenting. This evidence is clear and convincing: The stakes of uninvolved or detached parenting are profound among African Americans, particularly among adolescent males.

PERMISSIVE PARENTING

Also referred to as *indulgent* parents, **permissive parents** demonstrate high levels of warmth, affection, and responsiveness toward their children, and also show adequate to high levels of parent–child communication. This parenting style does not place high demands on children, nor do parents attempt to control their children's behavior; children's behavior is mostly self-regulated. Baumrind (1991) refers to these parents as *lenient* and *nontraditional*.

Similar to uninvolved or disengaged parenting, children and adolescents of parents who set no boundaries and who do not provide behavioral regulations experience higher levels of depression, poorer school performance, poorer psychological adjustment and well-being, and greater use of substances (Pittman & Chase-Landsdale, 2001; Samaniego & Gonzales, 1999; Steinberg and others, 1994; Steinberg and others, 1991). Parents who engage in **autonomy granting** might allow their children to set their own curfews and do not monitor the children's free time. This can evolve into putting their children at risk for elevated depression; this is particularly true for Asian females and African American males (Radziszewska, Richardson, Dent, & Flay, 1996). In high-risk (low income/low education), dangerous neighborhoods and communities, permissive parenting was associated with increased adolescent delinquency, school problem behavior, and poor school performance, particularly among adolescent African American males (Roche and others, 2007).

AUTHORI*TARIAN* PARENTING

According to Baumrind, **authoritarian parents** are "obedience- and status-oriented, and expect their orders to be obeyed without explanation" (1991, p. 62). To put it another way, authoritarian parents are very demanding and controlling with their children, but at the same time not very responsive, warm, or affectionate toward their children. This type of parenting style is characterized by rigid rules of behavior, which children are expected to follow with no questions asked; it is often referred to as *punitive* parenting. Parent–child communication is very low, and there is no room for compromise. Power is the key player.

Across all racial and ethnic groups, this type of restrictive, punitive parenting is associated with increased emotional problems (such as anxiety), psychological problems (such as depression), and increased behavioral problems (Eamon & Mulder, 2005; Grogan-Kaylor, 2005; McLeod & Nonnemaker, 2000). When parents use corporal punishment (spanking or hitting), children and adolescents exhibit more incidences of problem behaviors; however, this is found more among whites and Latinos than it is among African Americans (Lansford, Deater-Deckard, Dodge, Bates, & Pettit 2004). Corporal punishment also appears to be more strongly associated with behavior problems in boys than it is in girls (Grogan-Kaylor, 2005). Interestingly, punitive/restrictive parenting is associated with *increases* in depression, delinquencies, and problem behaviors for African American males who live in safe neighborhoods/communities, but it is linked with *decreases* in these maladies for blacks who live in dangerous neighborhoods. We'll discuss the possible reasons for these findings a bit later.

AUTHORI*TATIVE* PARENTING

With this parenting style, parents are responsive while demanding certain behavioral standards. This style of parenting does not use shame, withdrawal of love, or guilt (as might authoritarian parents) to control behavior. **Authoritative parents** set clear boundaries for their children's behavior, but they are flexible and will change these boundaries if the situation warrants. For example, a teen's regular curfew may be at midnight, but on prom night, she may be allowed to stay out much later. Authoritative parents are warm and responsive, and they encourage parent–child communication. Children are expected to follow the rules of the house but are still allowed to be autonomous. With this style, parents use a balance of power and reason.

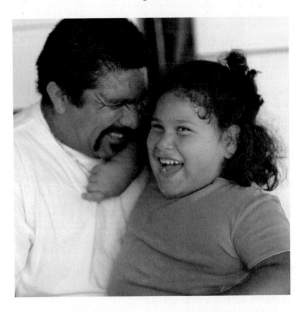

OF the many styles of parenting, research shows that *authoritative* parenting yields the best outcome for children's health and well-being.

Of all of Baumrind's parenting styles, authoritative parenting provides children with a balance of control and warmth, which yields the best outcome for children's health and well-being in the areas of social competence and psychosocial development. A number of research studies consistently demonstrate that

- Children reared by authoritative parents exhibit more social competence than do other children (Amato & Fowler, 2002; McClunn & Merrell, 1998; Steinberg & Morris, 2001).
- Both boys and girls reared by authoritative parents exhibit lower levels of problem behavior across all stages of the lifespan, across all ethnic groups (Jackson, Henriksen, & Foshee, 1998; Kim, Hetherington, & Reiss, 1999).
- Children reared by authoritative parents are better able to balance the demands of conforming to others' expectations with their own needs for uniqueness and autonomy (Durbin, Diclemente, Siegel, Krasnovsky, Lazarus, & Camacho, 1993; Shucksmith, Leo, Hendry, & Glendinning, 1995).

- Both boys and girls tend to perform better in school if they are reared by authoritative parents—this higher level of performance is seen from preschool throughout early adulthood (Brooks-Gunn & Markman, 2005; Chen & Kaplan, 2001).
- Effective parenting skills further the growth of children's social and communication skills, as well as their ability to concentrate on tasks and at school (Connell & Prinz, 2002; Lamb-Parker, Boak, Griffin, Ripple, & Peay, 1999).
- Authoritative parents of adolescents allow their teens to have autonomy, but they simultaneously define clear boundaries and articulate their concerns about safety and well-being (Smetana, 1995).

When parents are warm, sensitive, and responsive to their child's needs, they foster a wide range of interpersonal development in children, from the development of a healthy sense of self, to a sense of belonging and well-being, to high levels of self-esteem (Harvard Family Research Project, 2006).

ETHNIC GROUP DIFFERENCES IN PARENTING

Research demonstrates that race and ethnicity influence parenting styles. In a landmark, large-scale study of approximately 10,000 adolescents representing four ethnic groups (African American, white, Hispanic, and Asian American), the researchers found that the *authoritative* parenting style was the most common among white families and least common among Asian Americans; it was also more common among married biological parents than it was among single-parent or stepfamilies (Steinberg and others, 1991). The study also showed that parenting styles differ by social class. Authoritative parenting was more common among middle-class parents than among working-class parents, with the exception of Asian American parents, who demonstrated authoritarian parenting styles.

Interestingly, this study also demonstrated that there was a strong correlation between *authoritative* parenting and positive outcomes for whites and Hispanics, but Asian American and African American teens had better social and school performance outcomes when their parents used the *authoritarian* parenting style. Subsequent research has found that *parenting goals*, such as raising children so they will succeed in college and in their careers, are tied to parenting styles (Cheah & Rubin, 2004). Parenting goals are influenced by the parents' cultural values. For example, Asian American parents may raise their children with the authoritarian parenting style because they believe it helps to maintain their cultural identity; African American parents may do so because they are "keenly aware of the degree to which social forces such as racism may impede their children's achievement of educational, economic, and social success. . . . They [believe] that adopting an authoritarian parenting style will enhance their children's potential for success" (Boyd & Bee, 2009, p. 224). The link between this parenting style and child outcome variables such as self-control suggest that it is effective for African Americans (Broman, Reckase, & Freedman-Doan, 2006). It is important to note, however, that not *all* African American parents adopt this parenting style—parenting styles are as unique as each individual.

These studies show us that there are *culturally specific* processes that underlie parents' behaviors and communication. The reality of parenting is that it is an experience comprised of interconnected, multiple processes that are affected by the parents' race/ethnicity, cultural beliefs, income level,

PARENTING behaviors and communication are culturally specific—what works well in one culture to raise confident children will not necessarily work well in another culture.

and living environment. Much more work needs to be done to fully understand the interplay of cultural contexts and parenting; these studies can serve as a launching pad for family life education programs and public policies to strengthen family life (Ceballo and others, 2008).

Consider the interaction and relational patterns between you and your parent(s) or primary caregiver. Did these experiences allow you to feel that you were worthy of affection and love? Or instead, did your early parent–child experiences cause you to feel shame, guilt, and doubt, resulting in fear of intimacy, fear of abandonment, betrayal, and rejection in your adult relationships? As we are growing up, our parent and family interactions convey to us our worth—our purpose—as individuals, and this perception influences our ability to relate to others on an intimate level the remainder of our lifespan.

It is indisputable that the manner in which parents interact with and guide their children influences their development in more ways than are immediately visible (such as behavior and school performance). Children's abilities to love, to be loved by another, to feel secure and accepted, and to form attachment bonds with others—the very bonds that will later allow children to enter into love relationships of their own—are also shaped by their parents' parenting style.

Given the ups and downs of parenting and the inherent adjustments that must be made as a result of children's demands, given its uncertainty, given the fact that no two children are alike, and given the fact that no two people (or parent) experience parenting in the same way, is it really possible to prepare for what one developmentalist (Carter & McGoldrick, 1999) describes as "one of the most definitive stages of life"? Probably not. Nevertheless, we can address those contemporary issues that affect parenting and the stressors associated with the transition into parenthood and parenting. Although the experience of parenthood is without a doubt unpredictable, many parents, though not all, find it to be the most rewarding life experience.

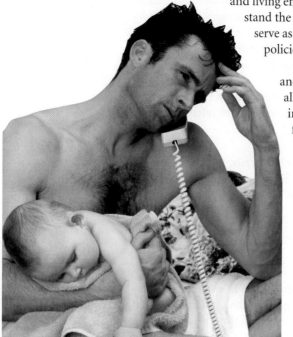

THE transition to parenthood requires adjusting to the demands and changes of new roles associated with the responsibilities of caring for a child.

From Partners to Parents: Making the Transition

When a new baby or child joins a couple, thus creating a new family form, all of the couple's established ways of interacting and relating, their patterns of behavior, and their marital and gender roles have to be adjusted to accommodate the addition to the family system. Whether it's baby number one or baby number seven, transitioning to life with the new family member presents challenges. In this section, we'll examine those challenges that new families face, including adjusting to their new roles, the responsibilities of bringing up baby, juggling parenting and household chores, and the day-to-day decisions parents must face, such as disciplining their children.

MOTHERHOOD AND FATHERHOOD: ADJUSTING TO NEW FAMILY ROLES

Most new parents expect a period of transition after the birth of a baby, but they tend to underestimate the demands and changes that accompany parenting. Part of new parents' disillusionment stems from the unrealistic expectations that come from cultural myths that paint an idyllic picture of parenting (Gilliam, 1981). While there are special, tender, and precious times when parenting seems idyllic, there are more times that dispel these myths, such as when the baby cries through the night, fusses all day, or won't touch his or her food but enjoys eating the pet's food. There is always something to attend to. And it is the new parents' responsibility to learn how to care for, nurture, and love the baby. Meanwhile, parents still have to figure out who they are in their new roles and who their spouse is in their new family system. No longer is the couple simply "husband" and "wife"—they are also a mother or a father and all that goes along with this redefined, multifaceted position. Suddenly, the mom or dad becomes a child development specialist, behavior expert, communications director, therapist, financial wizard/estate planner, nurse, head of safety and health administration, dispute and arbitration authority, labor boss, teacher, sex educator, spiritual advisor, and funeral director/grief counselor (to date, my family has buried two dogs, three cats, three hamsters, one bunny, one squirrel, and about 100 goldfish).

To understand the transition and stressors associated with bringing a baby or a child into the family, we need to recall our study of Family Systems theory from Chapter 3. Remember that the family can be likened to a mobile—any time we add or take away a member from the mobile (the family system) an imbalance is temporarily created. (See Figure 11.1.) This imbalance is felt and experienced as stress and conflict. Even though bringing home a new baby or adopting a child is a joyous occasion for most couples, the happy nature of the event doesn't minimize the fact that a new subsystem has been added to the family system, calling for a shifting of family roles, family balance, and family boundaries; all of these factors are what account for the stressful transition when baby makes three (or four, or five, or . . .).

In general, research has looked at the transition to parenthood in two different ways. In the first, new parents are seen as making an abrupt shift that results in persistent change, and this transition to parenthood is thought to cause negative changes in a couple's relationship dynamics (Lawrence, Rothman, Cobb, Rothman, & Bradbury 2008). The second predominant perspective views the transition to parenthood as a significant—yet temporary—stage in a couple's marriage and family development. According to this paradigm, the changes associated with new parenting roles are anticipated, short-lived, and small in magnitude, normative changes, and different couple types adapt to these challenges in varying ways (Lawrence and others, 2008). Over many years, research into the changes associated with parenthood, be it through birth, adoption, or the formation of stepfamilies, has centered on four primary areas (for a comprehensive review, see Ceballo and others, 2004):

1. *Psychological well-being.* Among biological parents, the transition to parenthood has been associated with increased levels of depression for both mothers and fathers, and these in turn affect marital satisfaction. Because of the stressors associated with adopting a child (such as the drawn-out adoption process and perhaps prolonged periods of infertility), the transition to parenthood for adoptive parents is typically associated with overall positive quality of life

FIGURE 11.1 Revisiting Virginia Satir's Mobile from Chapter 3

Although having a baby or adopting a child is a wonderful, exciting experience for most families, bringing another person into the family system creates imbalance and a need for family members to readjust their roles. These realignments/readjustments cause the stress that is often experienced when couples add to their families.

and high marital satisfaction. Among stepfamilies who are gaining a stepchild, the transition to stepparenthood has been associated with increased levels of depression.

2. *Marital quality.* Following the birth of a child, marital relationships are often characterized by negative interactions, declines in marital satisfaction and sexual intimacy, increased levels of conflict, and drops in leisure time spent as a couple. Most research, however, indicates that these declines persist for only about one year, and that they are modest. In a majority of the studies, parents indicated that the rewards of parenting outweighed the initial negative experiences. Adoptive parents may experience these same declines, but to a lesser extent than biological parents do; creating a stepfamily with children creates a difficult transition for most couples.

3. *Family relations and social support.* For some families, the birth of a child enhances family relationships, and oftentimes relatives help new parents adjust to their roles of mother and father by providing practical and emotional support; some parents experience higher levels of depression and distress if their extended family does not offer such support. Among adoptive parents, studies to date show that the emotional and practical support from family members exceeded their expectations, and this support was related to positive family experiences.

4. *Roles.* After the birth or adoption of a child, roles significantly change for mothers and fathers. Some research suggests that adults indicate that the "parent" role is greater than the "partner" role. Among men, the "worker" role remains stable, but women report sharp declines in that role and relate more to the "mother" role.

As you can see, for several decades family life educators and family practitioners have characterized the transition to parenthood as a challenging, and often difficult, lifecourse stage where couples are faced with unanticipated realities of limited time, energy, and resources. But as emerging research shows us, if prospective parents hold realistic expectations going into parenting, becoming parents is less stressful to them and to their relationship (Harwood, McLean, & Durkin, 2007). Of course, just when parents believe they have figured out the ins and outs of parenting, the child passes into a new phase of growth and development (with its own uncharted territory) or another baby is added to the family.

THEORIES OF CHILD DEVELOPMENT

There are several theories that seek to explain and understand child development. In general, there are four theories of child development—psychoanalytic, learning, cognitive, and sociocultural. Each theory offers its own unique contribution to our understanding of how and why children develop the way that they do. (See also Table 11.2.)

Psychoanalytic Theories The "grandfather of psychology," Sigmund Freud (1856–1939), developed his **psychoanalytic theory**, which focused on the personality development of children. In his view, development takes place through a series of **psychosexual stages**, in which sensual energy or satisfaction is focused on one particular part of the body. For example, during the **oral stage** (from birth to about age 1), the focus of sensual energy is the mouth and the tongue; the emphasis for personality development is thus centered on breastfeeding. In the **anal stage** (ages 1 to 3), the focus of the sensual energy is associated with potty training, particularly with respect to the anus. In the **phallic stage** (ages 3 to 6), Freud believed children were intensely interested in the physical differences between men and women. He also maintained that the focus of the sensual energy during this stage was the genitals, and believed that children engaged in self-stimulation of their genitals to derive pleasure. In the **latency phase** (ages 7 to 11), according to psychoanalytic theory, the sensual energies subside for a time, and during the final, or **genital stage** (ages 12 and beyond), people developed mature sexual interests in the opposite sex. The experiences through these stages—particularly through age 5—shaped a child's personality for an entire lifetime. Freud's psychoanalytic theory also

TABLE 11.2 Ages and Stages of Child Development

Age	Cognitive Stage	Social and Emotional Stage
0–1	Cries to signal needs; vocalizes, babbles, coos; says first words; interested in picture books	Recognizes family members; shows anxiety when separated from parents; fearful of strangers; likes to be tickled and touched; wants parents in sight
1–2	Has vocabulary of 8 to 20 words; identifies objects in books; makes animal sounds	Can play alone with toys; likes to be read to; will comfort others in distress; enjoys pretend play; shows affection
2	Uses 2- to 3-word sentences; sings; names toys, animals, people; enjoys stories and rhymes; enjoys simple make-believe	Possessive of parents' attention; can show beginning of independence; shy around/doesn't share with others
3	Uses 5- to 8-word sentences; listens actively to stories/songs; pretends to read; names colors; counts to 2 or 3	Seeks adult attention; helps with chores; engages in solitary play, but with others nearby; doesn't share; likes to laugh and be silly
4	Is imaginative, loves to make believe; uses complex sentences; counts to 10 or higher; understands categories (small, big, tall); very inquisitive and curious	Likes to engage in cooperative play with others; shares; cooperates; obeys simple instructions; loves to love others
5	Uses complex sentences of 10 or more words; enjoys storytelling, tracing, drawing, writing, coloring; counts; has good attention span; can memorize	Seeks adults' approval; embarrassed by own mistakes; understands relationships among people; likes to give to others; shares and takes turns; enjoys playing with friends
6–8	Reads; understands time of day and days of week; increased attention span; problem-solving capabilities increase; begins logical thinking	Friends become very important; wants to do everything well; easily hurt by criticism; still self-centered, but begins to see others' points of view; gender-centric
9–11	Reads; daydreams about future; logic becomes solidified; begins abstract thinking; begins to think about justice and ethics	Friendships become very important, consuming as much as 40 percent of their time; empathy toward others continues
12–14	Engages in abstract thought; able to think about hypothetical situations; able to think about the future	More mature friendships; friendship groups become larger and now include friends of opposite sex; embarrassed by parents

emphasized the role of the unconscious and held that most of people's actions, behaviors, and emotions are the result of these drives that lie below a person's level of awareness.

Erik Erikson (1902–1994) developed his own psychoanalytic theory based on Freud's original work. (We learned about Erikson's theory in Chapter 5.) Unlike Freud's theory, Erikson developed eight stages that spanned a person's entire lifetime. He also believed that, although early childhood experiences are crucial in shaping a person's personality, later events in life could alter the influence of the earlier experiences.

Learning Theories In general, **learning theories** emphasize the role of the environment— such as the home, school, community, and peers—in shaping a child's development. In other words, all behavior is learned from environmental influences. According to learning theories, parents play a significant role in who their children ultimately become. There are several learning theorists.

B. F. Skinner (1904–1990) believed that children learn behaviors through a series of rewards and punishments, and this series is called **operant conditioning**. **Rewards** reinforce behavior, and increase the likelihood that the behavior will occur again. For example, if a child is praised for making his bed, it is likely that he will repeat that behavior. If, on the other hand, a child is criticized because he didn't do a good job or make his bed perfectly, it is not likely that he will repeat the behavior. **Punishments** decrease the likelihood that a behavior will be repeated. According to Skinner, operant conditioning is the way that parents guide, shape, and mold the behaviors they desire of their children.

John B. Watson (1878–1958) promoted his theory of **classical conditioning,** which proposes that people make associations between two events. For example, babies open their mouths and smack their lips when their parent puts them in a highchair, or when their parent opens the jar of baby food. Conditioning (opening their mouths or smacking their lips) has taken place because the babies make the association between one event (being put in a highchair) and the other event (hearing their food source being opened). Similarly, some children (and college students!) cringe, become panicked, or get sick to their stomachs when an exam is handed out.

Have you ever been told that you sound just like your mother or father? Or that one of your behaviors is just like that of your mother or father, or another family member? Albert Bandura's (1925–) **Social Learning theory** focused on how children acquire behaviors. He believed that the acquisition of behaviors and personality traits are the result of observing others, and that we then imitate the behaviors we observe. For example, parents model certain gender roles, their children observe these modeled behaviors, and they subsequently acquire the same or similar behaviors. As Bandura once noted, "Of the many cues that influence behavior, at any point in time, none is more common than the actions of others."

Cognitive Theories **Cognitive theories** focus on how children think and how they understand their world. The focus of childhood development is not centered on personality development but on children's thinking and reasoning. A 4-year-old will comprehend and reason about his parents' divorce differently than will his 10-year-old brother; a 10-year-old will comprehend and reason about his parents' divorce differently than will his 15-year-old sister. Jean Piaget (1896–1980) advanced the most widely recognized cognitive development theory, which comprised four sequential stages.

Piaget maintained that as children progressed from stage to stage, they applied their current thinking and reasoning capabilities to new experiences. Unlike behaviorist theorists, who believed that children were passive learners, Piaget believed that children actively seek to understand their environment.

Sociocultural Theories Unlike the previously mentioned theories that stated that children proceed from one stage of development through the next, **sociocultural theories** propose that children do not progress through any stages. Instead, children's development is thought to occur as a result of direct interaction with their culture—that the values, goals, and expectations of their culture significantly shape and mold them. Thus, "development" means different things to different children in different cultures; what is considered developmentally appropriate for a child in one culture may not be considered so in another culture. The pioneer of Sociocultural theory is Russian-born psychologist, Lev Vygotsky (1896–1934), who believed that parents are children's primary teachers. According to Vygotsky, parents who are sensitive to their child's development can sense when the child is ready to learn new tasks and skills, and they engage their children in different activities to help their child develop these new skills. For example, whether it is a Mayan mother teaching her daughter to make tortillas, or an American mother teaching her son to measure flour and sugar to make cookies, each parent is teaching her child new skills—and cultural values at the same time.

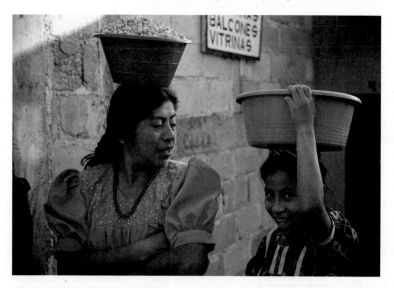

WHEN parents teach a skill to a child, they are also instilling cultural values at the same time.

Studying children and their development is a fascinating field of study. Each theory has a different explanation of how and why children develop the way they do, but each one helps us better understand the complexities of children's development.

BRINGING UP BABY (OR BABIES)

Historically—and *still today*—much of the responsibility for caregiving and childrearing rests on the mother's shoulders, a pattern seen in industrialized and nonindustrialized societies alike. Traditional gender roles in Western culture are based on the belief that mothers (or women in general) have an innate ability that allows them to nurture and care for infants and children better than men do. From diapers to discipline, from empty bottles to emotional support, from daycare to dating dilemmas, mothers seem to be the predominant advisors and guides. They are also the ones doing the laundry, the cleaning, the grocery shopping, and the daily scheduling. In many households, mothers put in twice as much time as fathers when it comes to childrearing (among many, Bianchi, 2000; Cohen, 1993; Deutsch, Lozy, & Saxon, 1993; McBride & Mills, 1993; Pleck, 1997).

Even couples who have an egalitarian (equal) relationship (see Chapter 8) prior to the arrival of a baby tend to fall back into traditional roles once the new baby arrives. Sociologist and researcher of women's issues, Melissa Milkie and her associates (Milkie, Bianchi, Mattingly, & Robinson 2002), examined 234 married couples about their attitudes toward conjugal roles (see Chapter 8) and childrearing. They found that although the parents asserted that both should be equally responsible and equally involved in parenting, caregiving, and childrearing, mothers consistently reported higher levels of involvement for themselves than did their husbands. In particular, mothers expressed significantly higher levels of involvement in the areas of child discipline and providing emotional support for their children. Fathers perceived their involvement in parenting (discipline, emotional support, play, monitoring, caregiving) at much higher levels than the mothers reported, resulting in what the researchers term an **ideal–actual gap**. When mothers viewed the fathers' parenting involvement as less-than-ideal (not equal to their own involvement), their relationships were found to have higher levels of stress. When women felt that discrepancies existed between their roles as disciplinarians and those same roles of their husbands—when they felt they were more involved than their husbands—they reported higher levels of dissatisfaction due to perceived unfairness. Similarly, child and adolescent psychologist and childrearing expert Ron Taffel (1994) discovered that although his study participants reported a fairly equal divide over childrearing tasks, when lists were compared the division was more along the lines of the woman doing about four times more than her husband.

Studies such as these speak to a broader point: Despite the efforts in the twentieth and twenty-first centuries to more actively involve fathers in childcare and childrearing, we cannot escape the ways we have been socialized. Several research studies investigating the division of family work and parental responsibilities showed that women's socialization—and the inherent cultural notion that she will always be the better parent—makes it difficult for the mother to relinquish her traditional role (for a comprehensive review, see Baxter, Hewitt, & Haynes, 2008). This is described as **maternal gatekeeping**.

Women and men today may anticipate and expect their parenting involvement to be equal, but socialization and established ways of thinking make it very easy to fall into traditional gender roles once the first baby arrives. Suddenly, this egalitarian relationship no longer exists, challenging pre-set expectations, raising stress levels, and giving rise to feelings of unfairness. As a result, conflict ensues and marital satisfaction plummets.

JUGGLING PARENTING AND HOUSEHOLD CHORES

During the 1990s, more than 200 research articles addressed the many nuances of the division of household labor. Couples may marry with the intent to share household chores just as they

It's Just No Fun Anymore: Leisure Time and Parenthood

Parenting books, magazines, advice columns, and Internet sites have inordinate information about how to keep relationships stable and satisfying during a couple's parenting years, but perhaps the best advice offered by these sources is that parents find ways to continue to spend time with each other, without the kids. Despite this advice, however, substantial bodies of research show that, as individuals get married and start families, leisure time is set aside—often at the expense of the couple's relationship satisfaction and happiness.

The majority of parents recognize their need to have "alone time" and to put some excitement into their lives, but most have difficulty doing so. Having healthy families, however, requires that parents are emotionally, spiritually, and physically connected to one another. Making time for themselves is the best gift a couple can give to their children, because it increases their relationship satisfaction—and enhances their parenting.

Shared leisure has enduring, positive effects on marriage, and it is particularly beneficial when new couples establish these practices before parenthood. But instead of just a weekly dinner date, couples appear to greatly benefit when they keep the excitement in their relationships. With this in mind, couples can:

- **Take a class together.** Learn Italian. Take ballroom dancing lessons. Learn to deep sea fish. Join a cooking class. The possibilities are endless!
- **Plan an adventure.** Planning a dream-come-true vacation or adventure isn't as important as the actual event, but what really matters is the time the couple spends together planning and preparing for it.
- **Get sweaty together.** It'll feel less like a chore and more like a we're-in-this-together moment when you help each other get your hearts pumping and cheer each other along while you're working out. Or try couples yoga: Twisting your body into pretzel poses will bring you closer together in every way.
- **Romance each other.** Use your imagination!

The whole idea about leisure time for parents is to keep the excitement in their relationship, to remember what it's like to have fun together, and to laugh together. While life can become routine, parents need to work hard to ensure that their relationship does not.

Sources: Claxton & Perry-Jenkins (2008); Lowrey (2009).

intend to share childrearing. But when children enter into the family system, these intentions often do not become reality. Often, discrepancies between who does what becomes a source of recurring conflict. With the majority of mothers today working at least 30 hours a week outside the home, the expectation that they are still responsible for the lion's share of running the household and performing household tasks can become a source of resentment. Sociologist Arlie Hochschild (1989) referred to this burden of taking on the duel responsibilities of wage-earner and housekeeper as the **second shift**.

During this second shift, women spend three times as much time performing household tasks as men do, consuming 32 hours compared to men's 10 hours (Coltrane, 2000). These tasks include house cleaning, meal preparation, grocery shopping, cleanup after meals, and laundry (Blair & Lichter, 1991). Coltrane (2000) refers to these essential tasks as **routine housework** but maintains that "this family work or social reproductive labor is just as important to the maintenance of society as the productive work that occurs in the formal market economy" (p. 1209), and that these tasks keep the household, the family, and society going.

Coltrane cites numerous studies that indicate that, for the most part, neither women nor men enjoy performing routine household chores. They tend to find occasional **residual tasks**, such as bill paying, yard work, and chauffeuring children to be more flexible in nature and more enjoyable to carry out.

Like parenting roles, the division of household duties tends to fall along traditional gender roles once a child is born, even if such tasks were previously handled fairly equally (Baxter and others, 2008). For example, in a study of 2,231 married and cohabiting new parents, the researchers found that the birth of a first child resulted in a dramatic increase in women's housework time—about six additional hours a week on average; having additional children continued to increase women's time on household chores. There was no corresponding change in men's housework hours after the arrival of a child (Baxter and others, 2008). Another excellent example of this happened in my own marital relationship when I was very seriously ill and bedridden for several weeks. I saw the disarray the upstairs was in—I couldn't even bring myself to imagine what the downstairs looked like. In discussing my concerns with my husband, he said to me, "You have your

IN today's families, women still tend to do the lion's share of the work around the house.

way of doing things and I have my way of doing things. My way may not be just like yours, but it still gets the job done. You have to give me permission to do things my way." I conceded and agreed that as long as the kids were being fed, their homework was being done, and they got to school on time wearing clean underwear, then other things could temporarily slide. (Although I did add, "But my way is still the better way!")

Coltrane (2000) identifies several factors that contribute to the division of household chores:

- *Women's employment.* When there are two wage earners in the family, these couples tend to share household tasks more than those couples where only one spouse works.
- *Men's employment.* Men who work fewer hours outside the home tend to pitch in more around the house and with childrearing responsibilities.
- *Earnings.* Women who earn more money benefit from more shared divisions of household tasks.
- *Education.* In households in which one or both spouses have high education levels (a college degree or a postgraduate degree), women tend to perform fewer household tasks and are more likely to hire outside help to render services such as house cleaning. Men with high education levels tend to engage in more household labor.
- *Presence of children.* When children enter the marriage (and change the family dynamic), household labor is less frequently shared evenly between the marital partners, and the woman assumes the majority of housework, along with the responsibilities of childrearing.

While gender appears to be an important factor that dictates generally who does what housework and how often, the research does seem to indicate that the division of labor along traditional gender roles is slowly giving way to changing roles of men and women in contemporary society. This is a "ray of hope" for those who struggle with balancing marital and parenting roles, because, as Coltrane (2000) concludes, "We now know that when men perform more of the routine household work, employed women feel that the division of labor is fairer, are less depressed, and enjoy higher levels of marital satisfaction" (p. 1226).

The challenges of childrearing go far beyond the stereotypical jokes about changing diapers and getting up in the middle of the night. Childrearing not only demands a realignment of roles within a family but it also insists that parents learn how to avoid the potential who-does-what-around-the-house conflicts that may arise. It requires that parents learn how to juggle careers and parenting responsibilities while remaining attentive to the emotional needs of partners and maintaining a strong marriage. Challenging? You bet.

Today's Parents

What makes a father? What makes a mother? What makes a "parent"? Just as the challenges associated with parenting have changed over the past 20 years, so have the faces of today's parents:

- Today, data confirmed for 2010 of children under the age of 18 live in single parent homes.
- Since 1978, the number of babies born to unmarried women each year took a dramatic leap—from 500,000 per year to today more than 1.5 million per year.
- About one-third of all lesbian households in this country have children and, in the United States, there are an estimated 6 to 10 million children who have gay, lesbian, or bisexual parents.
- Today, over 2.5 million fathers are the primary caregivers of their children.
- Some 3.7 million grandparents are helping to raise 7.5 million children.
- Each year, over 100,000 children are adopted in America. (U.S. Census Bureau, 2008b)

Whether a baby is born because of an unintended adolescent or nonmarital pregnancy, an intended marital or nonmarital pregnancy, or by choice (such as with adoption, gay and lesbian parenting, or parenting by grandparents), the shifting boundaries of parenthood in contemporary society are evident.

SINGLE PARENTS

Single parenthood is not a new phenomenon. Throughout history, widows and widowers have reared children alone. But since 1970, the proportion of households made up of married couples with children has decreased while the proportion of households with single parents has increased. According to U.S. Census Bureau demographers (2006), approximately 38 percent of families in the United States are single-parent families. Over 79 percent of all single-parent households are headed by females; about 20 percent of single-parent households are headed by males (U.S. Census Bureau, 2010). In Chapter 1, we saw the racial and ethnic differences among single parents, and in our study in the previous chapter we discovered that there are a number of reasons why the United States is seeing increasing numbers of single parents, such as women getting married later in life, the growth in divorce rates, and an increasing acceptance by society of unmarried childbearing.

Single-Family Models Along with the shift in demographic and societal trends, the way researchers are viewing single parenting is changing, too. Throughout the past three decades, two models of single-parent families have been used predominately.

Family Deficit Model The **Family Deficit Model** dates back to the 1970s, when single-parent families were far less

WELL over one-third of mothers today are single parents. Many are juggling parenting with work and school.

common than they are today. This model promoted the idea that single-parent households were negative experiences for children for the sole reason that the *family structure was not nuclear* (Marsh, 1990). With the base assumption that one-parent families are not the ideal family situation for children, much of the research yielded while using this theory supported this basic assumption (Donahoo, 2004).

Risk and Protective Factor Model Unlike the Family Deficit Model, which assumes at the outset that the only "ideal" family structure is the traditional nuclear family, the **Risk and Protective Factor Model** does not assume at its base that single-parent families are out of the norm (Seifer, Sameroff, Baldwin, & Baldwin, 1992). This model assumes that *every* family form has strengths, or protective factors. According to Seifer and his colleagues, *protective factors* are those factors that positively influence children and lessen the influence and/or impact of any existing risk factors. *Risk factors* are, in essence, the weaknesses in the family system that can have a potentially negative impact on families and children. For example, a family member's employment status, mental health, poverty, educational level, mother's age at first birth, or number of siblings are all factors. Depending on which factors come into play, when risk factors outweigh protective factors, the result most likely will be a negative experience for children; conversely, when protective factors outweigh risk factors, the result will most likely be a positive family experience for children. Although single parenting can be a risk factor for children's overall well-being, it is not *the sole predictor* of negative outcomes as suggested by the Family Deficit Model.

Women as Single Parents As of 2010 approximately 13.5 percent of all households in the United States were headed by single parents (U.S. Census Bureau, 2010 of the nearly 20 million children living with single parents, over 85 percent are living with their mothers. Census Bureau demographers estimate that about 43 percent of the women rearing children by themselves have never been married, and nearly one-third of these families live below the poverty line (Kreider & Fields, 2005). Divorced single mothers seem to fare better economically than do never-married single mothers. Racial differences among single mothers reveal different outcomes. White single mothers are more likely to be divorced, whereas African American single mothers are more likely to have never been married.

Men as Single Parents According to Census Bureau data, of the approximate 15.9 million single-parent families in America today, about 3.3 million are headed by men (U.S. Census Bureau, 2008b). Though these family forms are increasing in number, very little research exists to shed more light on the unique characteristics of these families. Kirk Bloir (2005) asserts that more fathers are rearing children by themselves as a result of four social factors:

1. Current divorce laws and "gender-neutral criteria" for rearing children have made it easier for fathers to gain custody of their children following divorce than in years past.
2. To allow themselves the opportunity to pursue career or personal goals, mothers may choose to grant the father custody of the children.
3. Divorce courts have a more favorable view of the role of fathers in childrearing, resulting in an increase in joint custody arrangements following divorce.
4. There has been an increase in fathers' willingness to take a more active role in parenting than in years past.

Bloir (2005) also notes characteristics that differentiate single fathers from single mothers. These include:

- Single fathers are less likely to live at or below the poverty line (although they tend to be poorer than married fathers).
- They are more likely to be employed.
- They tend to be younger than married fathers, but older than single mothers.
- Single fathers do not have as many children as married fathers, but have more than single mothers.

GRANDPARENTS raising their grandchildren is a rapidly growing trend in the United States. What are the benefits of living arrangements for these children? What are the disadvantages?

- They are more likely to live with other relatives in the household.
- Very few single fathers receive child support from the mother, whereas many mothers receive child support from fathers.
- Single fathers tend to suffer more from work–family role conflicts such as being late, childcare, missing work, leaving early, or work-related travel concerns than married fathers or single mothers.

Just as single fathers are evidence of parenthood in transition, grandparents raising their grandchildren, and gays and lesbians desiring to form a family by choice are also changing the face of today's families.

GRANDPARENTS AS PARENTS: A GROWING PHENOMENON

Today, about 4 in 10 grandparents who live with grandchildren are responsible for raising their grandchildren (U.S. Census Bureau, 2009). Referred to as **kinship care**, grandparents provide a living environment for their grandchildren for a number of reasons, but particularly because the parents struggle with substance abuse, mental illness, economic hardship, divorce, domestic violence, and incarceration (Raphel, 2008). Most of these living arrangements are informal, private, and voluntary—the court system and/or the Social Welfare System are typically not involved in these arrangements. Parents commonly retain legal custody and can make decisions regarding their children, although in some cases the grandparents share legal custody. Although not common, some grandparents adopt the grandchildren, and the rights of the parents are legally terminated.

The role of grandparents as parents is classified into four categories (Reynolds, Wright, & Beale, 2003):

1. *Limited caretaking.* Grandparents have limited contact with their grandchildren, and parents have primary responsibility.
2. *Participatory caretaking.* In these situations, grandparents are engaged and involved in their grandchildren's lives, such as taking an active interest in the children's education and their activities. Care may be provided for grandchildren while the parents are at work, but parents have primary responsibility for them.
3. *Voluntary caretaking.* Grandparents assume the parental role and responsibilities for raising their grandchildren. Although situations vary, typically these types of caregivers assume the role of grandparents as parents to make sure their grandchildren are in a safe, stable environment in the absence of their parents.
4. *Involuntary caretaking.* These grandparents are full-time caregivers of their grandchildren, and most often they have little to no warning; many times, it is not the grandparents' preference—the situation was more or less thrust on them. These types of arrangements are often difficult for children because of the unexpected shift in environments and caregivers.

Many grandparents welcome the opportunity to care for their grandchildren, but others experience financial, social, and emotional intrusions, as well as an increase in health problems. As one body of research suggests, for many grandparents the role of second parenthood limits their independence and their personal development in mid- to later adulthood (Glass & Hunneycutt, 2002). However, other research suggests that there are rewards, such as getting a chance to raise a child differently, to nurture family relationships, and to receive love and companionship from their grandchildren (Burton, Dilworth-Anderson, & Merriwether-de-Vries, 1995).

Grandparents raising their grandchildren is a growing phenomenon in the United States, and much more study needs to be done so family practitioners understand the unique needs of the grandparents and the children they are parenting. With this knowledge, human service providers, such as teachers, social workers, ministers, and mental health workers can begin to successfully implement parenting classes and other resources for caregiving grandparents in order to equip them with the necessary skills to best raise their grandchildren.

GAY AND LESBIAN PARENTS

Until recently, the majority of gay and lesbian parents were people who entered into a heterosexual relationship and had children prior to coming out of the closet (Patterson & Chan, 1996). However, many same-sex couples today are entering into planned parenthood through adoption, surrogacy, or fertilization techniques, as Chapter 10 showed us.

Despite the increasing number of gay and lesbian parents, research demonstrates that some heterosexual adults hold negative attitudes toward them as parents. For instance, some people are concerned that gay male parents are more likely to sexually abuse their children than straight parents are. Research shows, however, that gay men are no more likely to do so than heterosexual men are, and that girls are at far greater risk to be abused by their heterosexual fathers than their gay fathers (Jenny, Roesler, & Poyer, 1994). Gay and lesbian parents are also more likely to be well-educated and affluent, in comparison to heterosexual parents (Patterson, 1996). Other benefits have been documented for children of lesbian parents: They learn respect, empathy, and acceptance of diversity, and are more assertive in challenging traditional gender roles in their relationships (Allen, 1997; Savin-Williams & Esterberg, 2000). More recent research indicates that there are few differences between adolescents living with same-sex parents and those living with heterosexual parents (Wainright & Patterson, 2006). For instance, in this study the investigators looked at the responses of 44 junior high and high schoolers who lived with their same-sex parents who were matched with a similar group of adolescents who lived with their opposite-sex parents. The study revealed that there were no significant differences in the teens' psychological well-being (self-esteem and anxiety), school outcomes (grades and trouble in school), or family relationships (parental warmth and care).

Although much more research needs to take place in this area of family living, to date the empirical evidence seems to indicate that children of gay and lesbian parents do not experience physical, emotional, psychological, or developmental disadvantages. As with any child, it appears to the be *quality of the parent–child relationship* that is the most important to a child's health and well-being—*not* the parents' sexual orientations or their genders (Wainright & Patterson, 2006).

ALTHOUGH some people have concerns about gays and lesbians as parents, research shows that it's the quality of the parent–child relationship that is the most important factor in the well-being of children—not the sexual orientation or gender of the parents.

Own It!

The Case for and against Gay and Lesbian Adoption

Today, New Hampshire, Arkansas, and Florida ban adoption by single homosexuals or same-sex couples. Although numerous states ban adoptions by single gay men or lesbians, they don't ban the adoptions for single straight men and women. Gay and lesbian advocates claim that such bans only hurt the children waiting to be loved. Those opposed to homosexual adoption claim that children are better off in homes where they are raised by a mother and a father.

1. Why do you think that some states consider gay/lesbian adoption to be harmful to children's development and well-being?

2. In your opinion, is it more important in a child's life to have loving parents, regardless of their gender, or loving parents of each gender?

3. Does it matter to you if gays and lesbians adopt children? Why or why not?

HOW DO CHILDREN LEARN ABOUT THEIR RACIAL/ETHNIC IDENTITY?

As our earlier discussion about parenting styles showed us, there are racial/ethnic differences in the strategies parents employ to raise their children. Emerging research is beginning to shed even more light on these differences, especially in the distinct parenting challenges with which people of color are faced.

African American/Black Caribbeans, Hispanics, Native Americans, Asian Americans, and Arab Americans in this country often experience racism. **Racism** is a belief system which holds that race accounts for differences in human character and/or ability; it results in discrimination and prejudice based on someone's race or ethnic background. Because of the historical disparaging and marginalizing views of people of color, and because of historical racial barriers in equal opportunities, racial and ethnic minority parents are faced with the challenges of insulating their children from the negative consequences of racism. They deal with these

FIGURE 11.2 The Development of Racial and Ethnic Identity

Racial/ethnic socilization is a process that unfolds across a number of years. How are children taught to "be" their race/ethnicity and what are the social meanings attached to being a member of a racial or ethnic group?

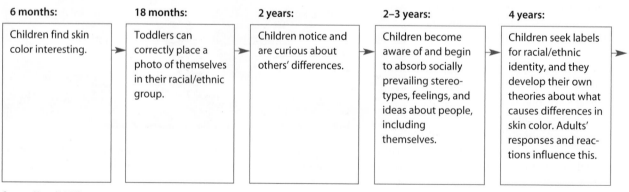

6 months:	18 months:	2 years:	2–3 years:	4 years:
Children find skin color interesting.	Toddlers can correctly place a photo of themselves in their racial/ethnic group.	Children notice and are curious about others' differences.	Children become aware of and begin to absorb socially prevailing stereotypes, feelings, and ideas about people, including themselves.	Children seek labels for racial/ethnic identity, and they develop their own theories about what causes differences in skin color. Adults' responses and reactions influence this.

Source: Katz (1982).

challenges by teaching their children how to "navigate and negotiate" the racism terrain through a process referred to as racial/ethnic socialization (Coard, Foy-Watson, Zimmer, & Wallace, 2007).

Racial/ethnic socialization is the way in which families teach children about the social meanings of their race/ethnicity: What does it mean to "be" black, Hispanic, Asian, Native American, or of Arab descent? Oftentimes, this socialization also includes teaching children the consequences of ethnicity and race, such as racism (Brown, Tanner-Smith, Lesane-Brown, & Ezell, 2007). Throughout the socialization process, which is presented in Figure 11.2, children learn about the similarities and differences between races/ethnicities, as well as prejudice and discrimination that some people face. Through intergenerational discussions (which often include story-telling of ancestors' histories), conversations with parents, observations, and modeling, cultural knowledge is transmitted and children learn to "perform" race (Brown and others, 2007). Racial socialization not only teaches children the values and norms associated with their race/ethnicity, but it also shapes attitudes that help them to cope with race-related barriers (Coard and others, 2007). Typically, many white parents don't place importance on discussing racial or ethnic differences with their children (Brown and others, 2007).

Racial/ethnic socialization practices have been linked to a number of positive outcomes in minority children and adolescents, as shown here. For a comprehensive review of the literature, see Coard and colleages (2007), Hughes and colleagues (2006), Huynh and Fuligni (2008).

- *Well-developed racial identity.* Children embrace racial and ethnic pride, history, and cultural traditions.
- *Heightened self-esteem.* Children's and adolescents' self-esteem is sensitive to the racial/ethnic messages they receive from their parents. Children who are taught to "blend" with mainstream culture have lower levels of self-esteem because they in some ways deny their heritage.
- *Higher academic functioning.* Positive ethnic identity and high self-esteem are associated with better academic outcomes and higher levels of motivation among children and adolescents.
- *Decreased levels of depression and anger.* The practice of cultural socialization is protective against racial discrimination because children and adolescents develop coping and problem-solving strategies to help buffer racism and deal with prejudice.

Racial/ethnic socialization among minority families is an emerging field of family and social science studies. It is a very complex issue and we have much to learn about the multiple processes associated with this type of socialization, as well as how what children are taught about race influences their lives.

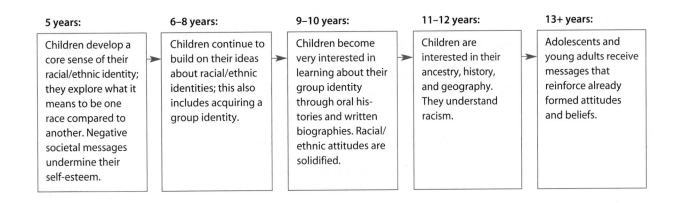

5 years:
Children develop a core sense of their racial/ethnic identity; they explore what it means to be one race compared to another. Negative societal messages undermine their self-esteem.

6–8 years:
Children continue to build on their ideas about racial/ethnic identities; this also includes acquiring a group identity.

9–10 years:
Children become very interested in learning about their group identity through oral histories and written biographies. Racial/ethnic attitudes are solidified.

11–12 years:
Children are interested in their ancestry, history, and geography. They understand racism.

13+ years:
Adolescents and young adults receive messages that reinforce already formed attitudes and beliefs.

Parenting 101: Best Practices for Parenting

There's no doubt about it—parenting is a tough job. Although children do not come with instruction manuals, there are some best practices parents can use to help them bring up their children effectively and lovingly. Some parents are "naturals" and seem to be born with these skills, while others learn along the way. And, for many parents, some situations that arise force them to gain a new skill—in a hurry!

BE A LEADER

It's been said before that values, beliefs, and behaviors aren't *taught* by parents, but that they are *caught* by children. That is to say, children aren't taught the differences between right and wrong, to be moral, to be responsible, and to be kind and sensitive toward others—more accurately, they mimic the behaviors of their parents: Children are honest because parents stress and model honesty, children are forgiving because their parents value forgiveness, children are open in their communication because their parents embrace openness, and so forth (Olson, 2004). Parents who are leaders have goals for their family, and they communicate these goals through their values and their beliefs. For example, is promoting the greater good of society important to a family? If so, parents could model this behavior to their children by volunteering at soup kitchens or homeless shelters, or by exposing their children to the needs of others and encouraging them to serve on mission trips to inner cities or to impoverished areas. These behaviors reflect those they want their kids to emulate. In short, parents who are leaders don't tell their children what to value and what to believe—they show them through words and actions (Olson, 2004). Finally, being a leader also means being an effective communicator—it means talking *with* children, not *at* them.

BE A TEACHER

Parents are their children's first and best educators. Every skill you have today—from walking to talking to writing to driving to using your debit card—was learned, and these skills were probably learned from your parents.

Effective parents take an active role in their children's education, both formal and informal. They provide a rich environment at home, and they willingly engage in their children's schooling, attending parent–teacher conferences, volunteering to be field trip sponsors, helping gather insects for bug collections, going to ball games and sporting events. They give praise when praise is due, but equally important, they know that sometimes the best kind of education comes from the school of hard knocks—they don't rescue their children from consequences when homework is forgotten or trumpets are left on the bus. They're not quick to find solutions for all of their kids' problems, but instead they allow the child to find her or his own successful ways to deal with a problem or a difficulty, while providing a safety net of unconditional love just in case the solution doesn't work.

Being a teacher also requires that parents understand how children develop emotionally, psychologically, cognitively, and biologically. As teachers of children, skilled parents help them build on existing skills, and provide direction when it is needed—they know just how far to push them without frustrating or discouraging them. Skill by skill, ability by ability, children learn their way to maturity.

BE A DISCIPLINARIAN—BUT BE PATIENT

It's tough work to grow people, and being patient is perhaps the greatest parenting skill of all. Children learn by trial and error, and this means too-many-to-count messes and mishaps.

Should Parents Spank Their Children?

FAMILY **LIFE** NOW

Good parents sometimes struggle to maintain the balance between *effective* discipline and *appropriate* response. Then comes the question: Should we spank our kids? Is it ever appropriate to spank a child?

YES: All experts agree that child abuse is wrong. Just what constitutes abuse and where the line between abuse and spanking is crossed are still up for debate. Robert Larzelere, a professor of human development at Oklahoma State University, and his colleague maintain that *how* parents use spanking is more important than *whether* they use it.

- **Spanking is not abuse.** All rational people are outraged when a child is abused, and we should do all we can to prevent such behavior.
- **Spanking is effective if it is appropriately used.** Mild spanking (a couple of swats on the child's bottom) should be an option to parents who wish to shape the behavior of their children. To be appropriate, spanking should never be done when a parent is angry, and should be used in conjunction with other disciplinary tools (time-outs, grounding, etc.).
- **Spanking is not harmful.** When studies separate mild spanking from abusive contact, the results show time and again that appropriately administered spanking is not harmful, especially among children between the ages of 2 and 6.

NO: In 2002, U.S. researcher Elizabeth Gershoff published one of the most thorough reviews to date of spanking research, analyzing 82 studies that covered 62 years of data. Her review found that spanking is linked to a wide range of negative outcomes for children:

- **Children are adversely affected.** Frequent spanking is regularly associated with delinquent children who are prone to cheating, violence, and destructive behavior.
- **Spanking fosters low self-esteem.** Some insist that spanking should be administered appropriately with love and not out of anger, but spanking always contributes to lowered self-esteem.
- **There are effective alternatives.** Parents can employ behavioral techniques and other tools to modify the behavior of their children.

WHAT DO YOU THINK?

1. Were you spanked as a child? How do you remember it making you feel then? How do you feel about it now?
2. Is physical force ever appropriate for adults? When or why not?
3. Will you employ spanking when disciplining your own children? If so, how do you think it should be done? If not, what alternatives will you use?

Sources: Larzelere & Kuhn (2005); Gershoff (2002).

Children can be frustrating, and often it is difficult for parents to discipline them in love, and not out of anger.

For many parents, the word *discipline* refers to some type of punishment, such as spanking a child or having the child sit in "time out" for a period of time. Though the type of child discipline parents use is a highly personal decision adults must make, there is no disputing that there is value in instructing children through disciplinary techniques. However, when

Parenting 101: Best Practices for Parenting ■ 379

correcting children, parents must make sure that their intention is to stop the unwanted behavior—not to *harm* the child because a parent is angry. The overall quality of the parent–child relationship is crucial for healthy discipline, and research shows that parental nurturance is the most critical aspect of this relationship (Chamberlain & Patterson, 1995).

To enhance a child's moral and behavioral development, psychologists and developmentalists note that children's responses to discipline are more effective when parents *consistently* communicate love toward the child. This is accomplished by (Chamberlain & Patterson, 1995):

- Positive involvement
- Using verbal and nonverbal expressions of love, concern, pride, and gratitude
- Praising and encouraging appropriate behavior
- Using calm responses to problem behaviors, disobedience, and conflict

Proactive discipline involves using techniques that encourage appropriate behavior and that discourage inappropriate behaviors from occurring. For example, "catch them being good" is an aspect of this type of discipline. With this technique, parents praise children for good behavior (such as not insisting on getting a new toy during the trip to Wal-Mart). As one researcher noted, "Every time a parent misses an opportunity to catch a child being good, they miss a chance to teach that child appropriate behavior" (Christophersen, 1988).

While discipline is tough and can cause conflict between parents, successful parents balance patience and love with setting necessary limits and boundaries. In this way, they avoid becoming permissive parents.

BE A REALIST

Often, as adults we have unrealistic expectations for our children. These typically come from our own childhood and family of origin—when we become parents, we turn to the expectations our own parents had for us (Hudson, 2009). Similarly, we may have childhood needs or desires that were unmet by our parents, and we then strive to ensure that our children have these things, whether they want them or not!

PARENTING isn't a job for the faint of heart! Although the realities of parenting can mean rough seas ahead, many parents find that the rewards of having children far outweigh the difficulties.

Unrealistic expectations of our children may also originate from cultural viewpoints of how children are "supposed" to behave, and too frequently parents have a tough time letting go of what other people think. For example, when you see a child having a temper tantrum in the store, do you instantly assume the child is misbehaving and that the parent should be able to control the child? Or do you recognize that the tantrum is a way the child is asserting his or her independence, or that he or she is in need of a nap? While most of us would acknowledge that these kinds of tantrums are normal behaviors for young children, why we do cringe and get embarrassed when it happens to *us?* The answer is simple—we're worried that someone may judge us to be an ineffective parent.

When raising children, it's important to examine our expectations. As parent educator Mimi Hudson notes, "Where did the expectations come from? What is their purpose? Whose needs are they based on—mine or my child's? And, do these expectations fit with my child's temperament, age, and developmental stage? Expectations are powerful motivators—but as parents we must be careful not to damage the parent–child relationship by setting unrealistic expectations" (Hudson, 2009).

When it comes to successful parenting, our job as adults is to nourish an unconditional, strong, safe, nurturing relationship with our children. No matter what, we need to consistently convey the message that our kids are great—just the way they are.

Family Life Education

Carter and McGoldrick (1999) echo the sentiments illustrated in the opening vignette and shed some light on why parenting is, at once, frightening and exciting at the same time:

> Once there is a child, life will never be the same again, for better and for worse. It is certainly true that most parents fall passionately in love with their new babies and consider them fascinating, delightful, and unique additions to the family. However, the roller coaster of the early months and years still comes as a shock to almost all new parents: sleep deprivation, shredded schedules, endless chores, worry about the baby's development or one's own competence, and the need for ceaseless diligence. This sudden threat of chaos puts enormous stress on new parents and on their relationship. (p. 249)

Whether or not to have a child is perhaps one of life's most difficult decisions. While most individuals and couples know the decision carries with it life-altering implications, most underestimate how significantly marital relationships are affected after a child is born.

How we parent our children significantly impacts *who* they become. In addition, the changing landscape of "who" can parent—married couples, single mothers, single fathers, grandparents, and gay and lesbian parents—further requires that today's family professional fully recognizes the responsibility associated with parenthood. It follows then that in studying marriage, family, and other intimate relationships, it is important to gain an understanding of those factors and stressors associated with childrearing—what accounts for the "roller coaster" ride.

Parenting is a choice for most, and there are many factors to weigh when deciding whether or not to have children. Couples must consider how this will affect their lifestyle and their needs, and they must realize that family roles have to be realigned to make room for baby. They need to understand that the family system *will* be out of balance for a while, and that the strains associated with household tasks *are inevitable*. The responsibilities of parenthood *will* restrict the couple's freedom and marital satisfaction *will* change (more than likely, it *will decline*).

These are the realities of parenting. If you choose to have children, you will be tired. You may find you have quite a bit of month left at the end of the money. At least in the early years, there will be many times when you must place your own needs aside in order to meet the needs of your children. You will be pulled in more directions than you thought possible. And you will make mistakes.

But those drawbacks, difficulties, snags, and snares associated with parenting and those things that can potentially affect marital satisfaction, many of these negative outcomes can be greatly reduced—if not entirely eliminated—by becoming aware of and understanding the realities of parenthood (Belsky & Pensky, 1988).

And remember—parenting isn't about the destination, it's about the journey. Enjoy the ride!

Don't Call Me Mr. Mom!

In contemporary America, increasingly more and more fathers are staying at home full time with their children, while their wives head off to work each day. In 2006, 1.9 million kids were cared for by their fathers while their mothers were at work (U.S. Census Bureau, 2007). However, this figure is expected to dramatically increase due to the U.S. economic crisis that began in 2008. How do wives and husbands really feel about stay-at-home dads?

Her Side: It's hard to put into words how I feel about me working full-time and him staying home with the kids. I always wanted to be able to stay home with them, but truthfully, I make more money than my husband does. We both agree that we don't want our kids spending their days in daycare, so the only logical option was for him to stay at home. I have mixed feelings—in some ways I feel relieved and happy that he gets to care for them and watch them grow. How many dads are given this opportunity? But on the other hand, it saddens me that I'm not the one that is home. Often, I feel guilty and frustrated, and I regret our decision. I don't like it that we have just abandoned our traditional roles. Doesn't he feel the need to provide for us? How will this ultimately affect him? I think the biggest thing in our favor is that we have a shared goal: We want what's best for our kids, and for us, that means one of us staying home with them.

His Side: I'm not saying that the transition has been an easy one. But what we have found is that instead of ditching the roles we had before, we've had to expand them. And let me tell you, that doesn't happen overnight. We've had to be very open and honest with each other, and we've had to make sure we discuss what our expectations are of each other. The biggest problem so far? She's had a really hard time of letting me do things my way—she tends to want to micromanage the house, the kids, the bills. Plus, there aren't really any role models out there for dads like me, and there's not a lot of social support for people in our situation. Sometimes that makes me feel like I'm not supporting my family, that I'm failing them or letting them down. That's my biggest frustration with our situation.

Your Side: In considering the recent trends of stay-at-home dads in America, do you think these couples face greater challenges than traditional couples? In your answer to this question, consider the following:

1. What are the specific role challenges for this couple?
2. In cases of stay-at-home dads, who do you think makes the most sacrifices: moms or dads? On what do you base your decision?
3. In your own life, would you consider being a stay-at-home dad, or having your spouse or partner be a stay-at-home dad? Why or why not?

Summary

Parenting Is a Process: Change Over Time

- Parenting is a process that addresses the biological, emotional, and socialization needs of children while it addresses the needs of the society in which children are raised.

- Women are expected to become mothers by certain culturally determined ages. Mothering is the process of

performing the logistical aspects of caring for someone, as well as tending to and nurturing the relationship.

- Intensive mothering reflects today's mothers who simultaneously manage several roles, including their roles in the workplace. The intensive mothering ideology promotes the notion that women should give their sacrificial all to their children. Maternal Role Attainment

(MRA) speaks to how women assume the "mother" role over time.

- In eras past, the patriarchal family structure embraced the father as the headship and authority over the family. This was done to ensure that land and money were inherited by his children.

- Today, there are two opposing forces that fathers contend with: father-absence and father-involvement. Contemporary fathers tend to fall somewhere in the middle of these polar opposite types.

- Co-parenting is an alliance that parents form to best raise and support their children. There are three types of co-parenting: supportive, unsupportive, and mixed. It is vitally important that parents co-parent because this parenting strategy provides predictability and stability for children.

The Styles of Parenting

- Regarding two important childrearing dimensions—parental warmth/responsiveness/affection and parental control—research psychologist Diana Baumrind constructed four parenting styles: uninvolved parenting, permissive parenting, authoritarian parenting, and authoritative parenting.

- Of all of Baumrind's parenting styles, authoritative parenting yields the best outcome for children's health and well-being in the areas of social competence and psychosocial development.

- Uninvolved parenting and permissive parenting yield negative outcomes for children, such as increased rates of substance use, higher rates of delinquency, poorer school performance, and negative psychological well-being.

- Authoritarian parents are very demanding and controlling, and this parenting style is associated with increased emotional and behavioral problems in children.

From Partners to Parents: Making the Transition

- When a new baby joins a couple, a new family form is created. All of the couple's established ways of interacting and relating, their patterns of behavior, and their marital/gender roles must be adjusted to accommodate the addition to the family system.

- In general, the changes associated with parenthood affect four primary areas in the couple's life: their psychological well-being, their marital quality, their family relations and social support, and their roles.

- There are a number of theories that explore child development. These include psychoanalytic theories, learning theories, cognitive theories, and sociocultural theories.

- In industrialized and nonindustrialized societies alike, the mother bears most of the responsibility for caregiving and childrearing. Even couples who have an egalitarian relationship tend to fall back into traditional roles once the new baby arrives.

- Research has shown that when mothers view the fathers' parenting involvement as less-than-ideal (not equal to their own involvement), their relationships have higher levels of stress. When women feel that discrepancies exist between their roles as disciplinarians and those same roles of their husbands (more involved than their husbands), they report higher levels of dissatisfaction due to perceived unfairness.

- Working women are still often expected to do the majority of housekeeping tasks. Sociologist Arlie Hochschild referred to this burden of taking on the dual responsibilities of wage-earner and housekeeper as "the second shift."

Today's Parents

- The boundaries of parenthood in contemporary society are currently shifting, evidenced by an increase in childbearing/childrearing through nonmarital pregnancies, parenting by grandparents, and gay men and lesbian parents.

- As parenting demographics shift, the way in which researchers study parenting shifts, too. Throughout the past three decades, two models of single-parent families have been used predominately. The Family Deficit Model promotes the idea that single-parent households were negative experiences for children for the sole reason that the family structure was not nuclear. Alternatively, the Risk and Protective Factor Model assumes that every family form has strengths, or protective factors, which lessen the influence risk factors. While single parenting can be a risk factor for children's overall well-being, it is not the sole predictor of negative outcomes as suggested by the Family Deficit Model.

- Single fathers are rearing children by themselves as a result of four social factors: current divorce laws and "gender-neutral criteria"; mothers granting the fathers custody of the children so that the mothers may pursue career or personal goals; divorce courts' more favorable view of the role of fathers in childrearing; and an increase in fathers' willingness to take a more active role in parenting than in years past.

- Many states allow gay and lesbian parents to legally adopt the biological child of their partner, but many do not. Research suggests that the quality of the parent–child relationship is more important to a child's health and well-being that having parents that are opposite-sexed.

- Racial/ethnic socialization is the process by which parents transmit messages to their children about the significance and meaning of race and ethnicity. This socialization is associated with a number of positive outcomes for minority children.

Parenting 101: Best Practices for Parenting

- There are a number of skills parents need to be effective parents.

- Parents should model the values and beliefs they hope to instill in their children.

- Skilled parents teach with patience and provide rich learning opportunities for their children, both formally and informally.

- Discipline is a necessary part of parenting, and parents should know that there are a number of effective parenting techniques that serve to develop children's moral development.

- It is essential that parents have realistic expectations when it comes to parenting.

Key Terms and Concepts

survival needs, p. 355

socialization needs, p. 355

mothering, p. 355

intensive mothering, p. 356

intensive mothering ideology, p. 356

theory of Maternal Role Attainment (MRA), p. 356

patriarchal family structure, p. 357

co-parenting, p. 359

supportive co-parenting, p. 360

unsupportive co-parenting, p. 360

mixed co-parenting, p. 360

uninvolved parents, p. 360

permissive parents, p. 361

autonomy granting, p. 361

authoritarian parents, p. 362

authoritative parents, p. 362

psychoanalytic theory, p. 366

psychosexual stages, p. 366

oral stage, p. 366

anal stage, p. 366

phallic stage, p. 366

latency stage, p. 366

genital stage, p. 366

learning theories, p. 367

operant conditioning, p. 367

rewards, p. 367

punishments, p. 367

classical conditioning, p. 368

Social Learning theory, p. 368

cognitive theories, p. 368

sociocultural theories, p. 368

ideal–actual gap, p. 369

maternal gatekeeping, p. 369

second shift, p. 370

routine housework, p. 370

residual tasks, p. 371

Family Deficit Model, p. 372

Risk and Protective Factor Model, p. 373

kinship care, p. 374

racism, p. 376

racial/ethnic socialization, p. 377

proactive discipline, p. 380

Suggested Reading

Lev, Arlene Istar. *The complete lesbian and gay parenting guide* (New York: Berkley, 2004).

Melskins, P., & Whalley, P. *Putting work in its place: A quiet revolution* (Ithaca, NY: Cornell University Press, 2002).

Nielson, L. *Embracing your father: Creating the relationship you want with your dad* (New York: McGraw Hill, 2004).

Orange, Cynthia. *Sing your own song: A guide for single moms* (Center City, MN: Hazelden, 2001).

Multiple-Choice Questions

1. Which of the following is NOT one of the eight essential parenting responsibilities?
   a. Providing self-esteem
   b. Developing mutual respect
   c. Providing effective and age-appropriate discipline
   d. Assigning weekly chores

2. This parenting style is typically low in responsiveness, warmth, and affection, and low in parental control or demands.
   a. Permissive parenting
   b. Uninvolved parenting
   c. Authoritarian parenting
   d. Authoritative parenting

3. In the _____ (ages 3 to 6), Freud believed children were intensely interested in the physical differences between men and women.
   a. anal stage
   b. oral stage
   c. phallic stage
   d. latency stage

4. _____ focus on how children think and how they understand their world.
   a. Cognitive theories
   b. Learning theories
   c. Social learning theories
   d. Sociocultural theories

5. About _____ of all lesbian households in this country have children.

   a. half
   b. one-third
   c. two-thirds
   d. one-fifth

6. _____ decrease(s) the likelihood that a behavior will be repeated.
   a. Punishments
   b. Rewards
   c. Operant conditioning
   d. Residual tasks

7. _____ demonstrate high levels of warmth, affection, and responsiveness toward their children, and also show adequate to high levels of parent–child communication.
   a. Uninvolved parents
   b. Authoritarian parents
   c. Permissive parents
   d. Authoritative parents

8. The _____ promoted the idea that single-parent households were negative experiences for children for the sole reason that the *family structure was not nuclear* (Marsh, 1990).
   a. Single Family Model
   b. Risk and Protective Factor Model
   c. Family Deficit Model
   d. Nuclear Model

Answers: 1. d; 2. b; 3. c; 4. a; 5. b; 6. a; 7. c; 8. c

DUPLEX
CALL JEFF BULLERT
218-310-0277

Help-U-Sell
REAL ESTATE

Help-U-Sell
Woodridge Realty
218-722-7010
www.HelpUSell.com
EACH OFFICE INDEPENDENTLY OWNED & OPERATED

FORECLOSURE

Family Life and Work: A Balancing Act

12

I know my life stopped being my life a long time ago. When you get married and have kids, that's part of the deal, I know that. But when you're sitting there and you're figuring out, "Okay, can we afford to have a kid? Can we afford to buy a house? A second car?" you work it out, and it all looks good on paper. On your little worksheet.

But there's nowhere on the worksheet for the other stuff. There's no entry for "Daughter needs therapy." Or, "Mom's really sick, fly home three or four times in one month." Or, "Wife goes through cancer scare." There's always something and we never get a chance to breathe. And you look up and, like, twenty years have passed and this is how you've lived. Not hand-to-mouth anymore, like when we were a young couple, but never really a chance to get any momentum going. And it just wears on me. I mean, my wife doesn't know this, but this is the stuff that rocks me out of sleep at two in the morning, you know, a couple of times a week at least, and you just lay there, thinking about everything that has to get done. And so I'm tired all day, and then I act like a jerk because I'm tired and THAT upsets my wife and then something else happens and it's just this big pile of angst that never goes away. And at the bottom of that pile, it's always about money.

I mean, dig into any issue, and there it is. Money.

Source: Author's files

Working Families: The Transformation of American Homes
- Women Enter the Workforce
- A Portrait of Contemporary Dual-Earner Couples
- Service Men and Women
- Single Parents in the Workforce

Couples and Work: Just Trying to Make Ends Meet
- Dual-Earner Couples and Family Well-Being
- Work Hours and Family Life: Shift Work
- Opting Out: Stay-at-Home Moms
- Leaving the Workforce: Stay-at-Home Dads

The Balancing Act: Juggling Family Life and Work
- Conflicting Demands: Heart-strings versus Purse Strings
- Who Does What and When? Dividing Household Chores
- Childcare
- Ten Strategies for Family and Work Balance

The Government's Role: Policies for Working Families
- Poverty
- Health and Healthcare
- Social Welfare

Marriage and Money
- Money as an Emotional Issue
- Dealing with Debt

Family Life Education

EVERY day, families in the U.S. struggle to balance family life with the responsibilities of work. Some families manage the stressors well, but many families find that their relationships are on the verge of collapse. Is it really possible to juggle it all?

Today, work and family play major roles in the lives of adults. Most Americans come face to face on a daily basis with the demands and challenges of trying to balance work and family life—far too often, there are negative effects when work responsibilities spill over into family life. Married and intimate life brings with it things we can't predict or plan for: Spouses get sick, parents get sick, children need medical care, and money becomes the focus of our every thought. Other things happen that also cause financial worry. For example, the global financial crisis that began in the latter part of 2008 with the failures of large financial institutions in the United States rapidly evolved into a crisis for many Americans—adults experienced job losses by the hundreds of thousands, cars were repossessed, families were forced into bankruptcy, and an unprecedented number of homes were lost because families couldn't afford to pay their house payments. What does a family do in these situations? And what happens to their relationships when they experience such stressors?

Research indicates that money is a major source of relationship concerns for couples today, and that there are potentially serious implications for couples when money issues crop up (Papp, Cummings, & Goeke-Morey, 2009; Dew, 2007). For these reasons, in this chapter we will begin our study of work and family by looking at the landscape of dual-earner couples, including the demands faced by military families when a loved one is deployed to Iraq or Afghanistan, as well as the challenges single parents encounter when they try to balance work and family. We'll then shift our attention to the types of strain and stress families face when they try to juggle work with family life. To best equip you with tools for your own intimate and family relationships, we'll conclude by exploring the skills that effective working families use in their daily lives, and how best to manage your money.

Working Families: The Transformation of American Homes

Economic stability and the ability of families to meet their daily needs is an important measure of family health and well-being (Allegretto, 2005). The **socioeconomic status (SES)** of a family is the government's measure of the family's relative economic and social ranking within a community (Krieger, 2001). Measures of SES typically include the adults' occupation, education level, community/group associations, and income. Other measures may include location of residence and certain home amenities such as a television, computer, telephone, books, and so forth. *Attained SES* refers to the parents' socioeconomic status, and *SES of origin* is the term used when describing a child's family's SES (Krieger, 2001).

We learned in Chapter 1 that as our nation moved into the second half of the twentieth century, a number of sociocultural, economic, and political changes occurred that changed the face of families in the United States. These changes include lowered birth rates and delays in marriage, women's abilities to control their fertility through contraceptives, the legalization of abortion in 1973 and the adoption of no-fault divorce laws, and Civil Rights legislation in 1965 that banned discrimination. All of the factors worked in tandem not only to change how we experience family life but also to change America's workforce as many of these social and cultural factors propelled women into the workplace.

WOMEN ENTER THE WORKFORCE

The 1960s ushered in many changes that helped to shape our conceptions and experiences of women in the workplace today. A new-wave feminist movement, referred to as **Women's Liberation**, put forth the idea that women suffered oppression in patriarchal, male-dominated cultures such as the United States. Equality in the job place and economic equality were primary goals of feminist organizations (such as the National Organization for Women) throughout the 1960s and 1970s. This was referred to as **gender equality**, and in 1964 a last-minute addition to Civil Rights legislation mandated that discrimination based on a person's gender was illegal.

This is not to say, however, that women have achieved equality. In the ensuing decades since the passage of the Civil Rights Act, women continue to fight against bias, prejudice, discrimination, and sexual harassment as they attempt to break down barriers and stereotypes, and as they enter occupations traditionally held by males. The term **glass ceiling** refers to discrimination against women in the workplace, specifically in situations where advancement in an organization is stopped because of **occupational sexism**, or beliefs that the male gender is more capable of certain work-related tasks and professions than women are. Types of glass ceiling barriers include different pay for comparable work, sexual discrimination in the workplace, and lack of family-friendly work policies (Thomas-Hunt & Phillips, 2004). For example, in 2009, the U.S. Census Bureau estimated that women make 77.6 cents on the dollar compared to men (Institute for Women's Policy Research, 2008). This disparity in earnings is referred to as the **gender wage gap**. As Figure 12.1 (page 390) illustrates for us, the gender earnings gap has fluctuated since the 1950s; women's policy groups note, however, that the progress in closing this gap has slowed considerably since the 1990s (Institute for Women's Policy Research, 2008).

Identifying and challenging wage discrimination in the workplace has been an uphill battle, despite the passage of the Equal Pay Act of 1963. For example, in 2004 the case known as *Dukes v. Wal-Mart* became the largest class action lawsuit in history—approximately 1.5 million women were parties to the lawsuit, and claimed that they received less pay and promotion opportunities than their fellow male coworkers. Additionally, in what is now a historic case, Lilly Ledbetter, a former employee of the

SERVING since August 2009, Assistant Justice of the U.S. Supreme Court, Sonia Sotomayor, is the 111th Justice—but only the third female Justice. In some areas, gender equality has been a slow process.

FIGURE 12.1 The Gender Earnings Ratio, 1955–2008, Full-Time Workers

The gender wage gap has fluctuated over time, and it has been a slow process to close this gap.

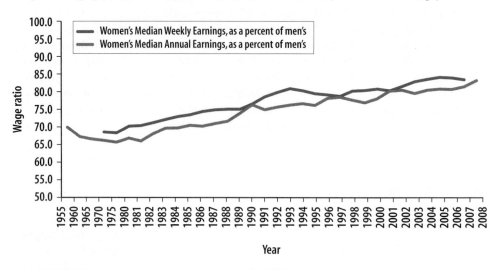

Source: Institute for Women's Policy Research (2008).

Goodyear Tire and Rubber Company, sued the company to receive back pay and damages. After her retirement from the company, she discovered that for years she was paid at significantly lower rates in comparison to her male counterparts. Although she was awarded back pay from a lower court, the U.S. Supreme Court overturned the lower court's decision in 2007. However, in 2009, in his first week in office, President Barack Obama signed into law the *Lilly Ledbetter Fair Pay Act*. While this law removes the legal obstacles for women seeking equal pay in the workforce, it is also a tool to combat workplace discrimination in all forms. As President Obama observed at the signing of the law,

> Ultimately, equal pay isn't just an economic issue for millions of Americans and their families, it's a question of who we are—and whether we're truly living up to our fundamental ideals; whether we'll do our part, as generations before us, to ensure those words put on paper some 200 years ago really mean something—to breathe new life into them with a more enlightened understanding that is appropriate for our time. That is what Lilly Ledbetter challenged us to do.

When comparing women with other women in the workforce, the earnings gap is associated with ethnicity. As Figure 12.2 shows us, Asian workers of both sexes earned more than their white, black, and Hispanic counterparts in 2007 (U.S. Bureau of Labor Statistics, 2008). While men still earn more than women in all racial/ethnic groups, Asian and white women make more on a weekly basis than black or Hispanic women do. In addition, among women, whites earned 86 percent as much as Asians, whereas blacks earned 73 percent, and Hispanics earned 65 percent. For comparison, consider that while white women make about $31,000 per year, black women make $27,000, and Hispanic women make $22,000.

SIGNED into law by President Obama in 2009, the *Lilly Ledbetter Fair Pay Act* helps women receive equal pay in the workforce.

Deborah Chalfie, senior counsel of the National Women's Law Center observes, "One of the problems that women and women of color face in the work force is that female-dominated and jobs dominated by women of color are undervalued and underpaid" (Sullivan, 2009, p. 1). That is to say, women tend to be concentrated in certain occupational categories—this is referred to as the **pink-collar phenomenon.** For example, in 2000, two-thirds of all U.S. working women were still crowded into 21 of the 500 occupational categories (Wage Project, 2009). And, frequently, these jobs are generally rated as deserving less pay than more "masculine" occupations.

This shift from one-earner families to dual-earner families has not only advanced women's opportunities in society but it also dramatically changed the face of American families and how they experience family living today.

A PORTRAIT OF CONTEMPORARY DUAL-EARNER COUPLES

Dual-earner couples is defined as marriages or relationships in which both partners work. Workforce participation varies among dual-earner couples. For example, more than half of married couples in the United States today are dual-earners (U.S. Department of Labor, 2007). In many such couples, one partner works full time while the other partner works part time; in other families, both partners work full time. Many factors influence labor force participation and earnings among dual-earner couples, such as education level, urban living, unemployment, and discrimination. There are also racial and ethnic differences in dual-earner couples.

White couples are highly involved in the workforce, and only Asian couples are more likely to be involved in the workforce than whites. One reason for white couples' high participation in the workforce is that they tend to have higher levels of education, which are strongly associated with higher levels of employment. As a result, whites generally earn more than black and Hispanic men and women, even within the same occupation; fortunately, this wage gap is diminishing, especially among women (U.S. Bureau of Labor Statistics, 2008). The median annual income of white families and these higher earnings are associated with enhanced marital quality among whites (we discuss marital quality later in the chapter) (U.S. Census Bureau, 2008e; Amato, Johnson, Booth, & Rogers, 2003).

Educational attainment is a key factor in employment and earnings for black couples. African American/Black Caribbean men are the least likely to be employed among each of the ethnic groups, whereas black women are the most likely to be employed. In fact, African

FIGURE 12.2 Median Weekly Earnings of Full-Time Wage and Salary Workers, by Sex, 2007

Black and Hispanic women earn less than white and Asian women.

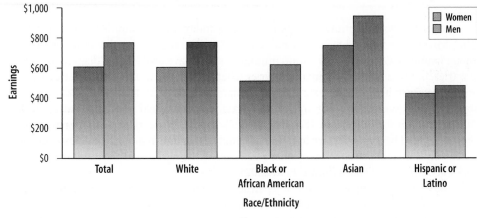

Source: U.S. Bureau of Labor Statistics (2008).

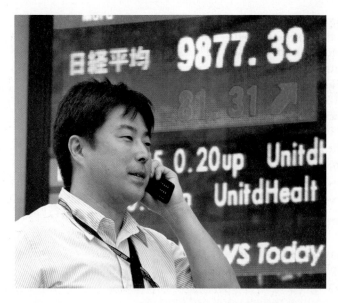

ASIAN American men and women are more likely than any other ethnic group to have high education attainment. For this reason, they have the highest annual salary of all racial and ethnic groups.

American/Black Caribbean men are more than twice as likely to be unemployed than whites. Both black men and women are typically **blue-collar workers**, which means they are highly represented in the service sector (such as sales, office, production, and transportation); as a result, their earnings are generally lower than those employed in **white-collar professional occupations** (such as attorneys, bankers, and doctors) (U.S. Bureau of Labor Statistics, 2008). Of all racial and ethnic groups in the United States, African American/Black Caribbean families suffer the highest levels of unemployment and poverty and the lowest median family income—roughly $33,500 annually (U.S. Census Bureau, 2009, 1-Year Estimates).

Asian men and women are more likely than any of the other ethnic groups to be employed in professional positions (U.S. Bureau of Labor Statistics, 2008). Low divorce rates, high education levels, a strong work ethic, self-sufficiency, familism, and high participation in the labor force have led to the "model minority" status for many Asian couples (Taylor, 2002). With an annual income of almost $69,000 per year, Asian American families have the highest median household income of all racial groups in the United States (U.S. Census Bureau, 2009, 1-Year Estimates). This is perhaps because Asian Americans have the highest educational qualifications of all ethnic groups in the United States—nearly one-half of all Asian American adults have attained at least a bachelor's degree (U.S. Census Bureau, 2009).

Influenced by Confucian ideology, Asian households are typically patriarchal with well-defined roles. Their cultural traditions and roles tend to provide them with order and stability between work life and family life. Additionally, their collectivist perspective has led to a willingness of on the part of many Asian Americans to sacrifice personal needs in order for their families and employees to be successful.

Hispanic couples are similar to Asian couples in that they tend to be patriarchal, familistic, and traditional in their views of men's and women's work roles. Hispanic men are generally highly employed, while Hispanic women tend to have lower employment rates than each of the other ethnic groups (U.S. Bureau of Labor Statistics, 2008). While Hispanic couples are becoming more educated and, therefore, more represented in professional occupations, they are less likely to have completed high school than each of the other ethnic groups; as a result, they are still highly employed in the service sector, resulting in lower earnings than those employed as professionals (U.S. Bureau of Labor Statistics, 2008; Monthly Labor Review, 2004).

One of the poorest ethnic groups in America today, Latino families earn, on average, about $40,000 per year (U.S. Census Bureau, 2008e). The reasons for the high poverty rates among Latinos are varied. Many Latino immigrants may have professional degrees from other countries, but because of the language barrier when they arrive in the United States, they are unable to secure high-paying jobs. Many immigrants today also face discrimination in the workplace; for example, it is not uncommon in California for field workers to earn as little as $300 per month for their labor (Schlosser, 2002). Furthermore, the transnational (families who are divided because they live in different countries) and bi-national (families whose legal citizenship is mixed) status of many Hispanic families has challenged their ability to manage work and family roles (Baca Zinn & Pok, 2002).

Arab American couples are typically patriarchal and traditional—men are often the family's providers, and women are homemakers and raise the children. Arab American men and women tend to be highly educated and are, therefore, well represented in the professional labor force with higher earnings than the national average. In the United States, Arab Americans with at least a high school diploma number 85 percent (Arab American Institute, 2007). Also, more than 4 out of 10 Americans of Arab heritage have a bachelor's degree or higher; 17 percent have a post-graduate degree. Today, over two-thirds of Arab American adults are in the labor force, and are employed in a wide array of occupations (see Figure 12.3). Their median annual income is $47,000, but in comparison to overall U.S. workers, more Arab Americans have higher salary ranges (such as incomes of $75,000 per year).

Limited education, high unemployment, divorce, single-mother families, and substance abuse rates have contributed to labor force participation among Native Americans that is varied and sporadic. About 3 out of 4 married Native Americans are employed, while only about one-half of single female-headed households are employed; this results in higher earnings for those who are married (Taylor, Yellowbird, & Snipp, 2002).

In recent years, families in the United States have been challenged in new ways as service men and women have been deployed overseas due to military engagements in Iraq and Afghanistan. The challenges are many, and all affect the portrait of wage earners in America.

SERVICE MEN AND WOMEN

The United States military, which comprises the Army, Navy, Air Force, Coast Guard, and Marines, deployed as many as 150,000 to 200,000 military personnel in 2007 (Congressional Research Service, 2007). While military families deal with stressors that are common to all families, such as parenting concerns, childcare, juggling work with family, and career decisions, they are also subject to unique stressors because of the separation from family members (Drummet, Coleman, & Cable, 2003).

Preparing for Deployment Until recently, most military personnel had a period of one to two years between deployments. Recently, however, deployments can often occur in quick succession or tours of duty are extended for prolonged periods of time. For example, during the Gulf War in the early 1990s, single parents and dual-career couples were mobilized so quickly that these families had only a few hours to find childcare for their children—both immediate childcare, and extended childcare while the parent was deployed overseas (Drummet and others, 2003).

FIGURE 12.3   Arab Americans in the Workforce

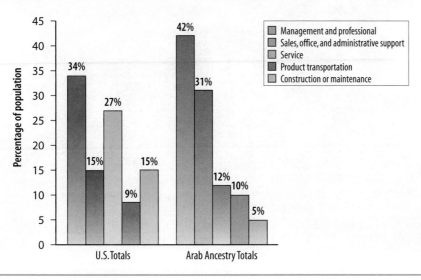

Source: Arab American Institute (2009).

Financial worries are of particular concern to deployed military families. What makes the financial picture much worse for so many military families today is that about 8 percent are young and are receiving paychecks for the first time (Varcoe, Emper, & Lees, 2002). Because of this, young couples have not yet learned effective money management skills, and this puts them at significantly higher risk for money troubles during deployment.

Financial Difficulties for Deployed Families Today, there are increasing incidents of burgeoning financial difficulties among service families because separations due to deployment often catch families financially unprepared. In fact, one study of Army families revealed that almost two-thirds (64.3 percent) of Army spouses work just to cover basic monthly expenses, such as food and housing (Survey of Army Families IV, 2001).

Among those family practitioners who work with military families to improve their financial well-being, current programs are used that focus on financial situations that are unique to the military. Financial programs for military personnel, such as *Money Sense* and *Financial Fitness*, are preventive educational programs that provide information to service members and their spouses/significant others about ways to manage their financial resources. These types of curricula, especially tailored to the needs of military men and women, teach money management skills and include such things as learning how to budget, keep financial records, develop healthy spending habits, establish realistic savings habits, and manage credit card debt. Research demonstrates that financial education as a part of deployment readiness reduces the frequency of families' money problems (Varcoe and others, 2004).

There are, of course, numerous other issues military families face, and we'll explore those a bit later in this chapter when we look at what it takes for all families to juggle work and family life. Here, it's important to recognize the unique financial situations military families experience, and that family life educators and other family practitioners can provide invaluable resources to these families to assist them during these stressful work-related situations.

WHILE military families face the same day-to-day struggles and stressors that all working couples face, they also face unique financial situations when they are deployed to the wars in Iraq and Afghanistan.

SINGLE PARENTS IN THE WORKFORCE

There is great diversity among single-parent households. For example, households headed by single parents include impoverished, never-married ethnic minority women or teenaged mothers, gay and lesbian parents whose unions are not legally recognized, wealthy never-married women who have adopted or borne a child, widows and widowers, and women and men who find themselves single after a marital breakup (Gottfried & Gottfried, 1994). Additionally, many families instantly become single parent families when a spouse is called to war, or when a spouse dies in combat.

Regardless of its makeup, each single parent family has its own unique starting point and its own unique developmental history (Anderson & Sabatelli, 2007). Because mothers with children compose the largest segment of single-parent households—over three-fourths of all single-parent households are headed by females—our discussion begins with looking at work/money issues and challenges faced by single mothers (U.S. Census Bureau, 2008c).

Single-Parent Mothers A large majority of single women with children of all ages work outside the home in the paid labor force. Employment rates among single female parents have significantly increased since the 1990s, where 44 percent of single mothers worked; in 2003, 54 percent of all single mothers were in the workforce (U.S. Department of Health and Human Services, 2006).

Clearly, single parenting affects the economic well-being of women and children. According to the U.S. Census Bureau (2007), a significant number of all households with children headed by mothers live in poverty. Figure 12.4 shows us that nearly one-half of all single-mother families live in economic despair. Black single mothers fare worse than any other group, with a poverty rate of 50 percent. Further, in a review of the characteristics of over 13 million single mothers, the demographers discovered that 40 percent make less than $10,000 per year (Congressional Caucus on Women's Issues, 2005). Importantly, any spousal support, child support, or public

BEING a single parent often carries with it economic disadvantages for both the parent and his or her child(ren). For many single mothers, it's tough to pull themselves out of poverty because many have no more than a high school education.

FIGURE 12.4 Percentage of Children in Poverty, by Family Structures and Race

Single parenting impacts the economic well-being of the family.

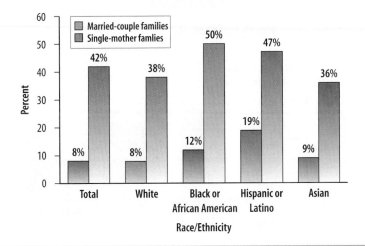

Source: U.S. Census Bureau (2007).

assistance (welfare) the woman receives typically does not come close to offsetting the differences in income between single-mother parents and married parents. A bit later in this chapter, we'll explore poverty at length as we discuss the government's potential roles in creating effective policies for today's working families.

A study sponsored by the Congressional Caucus on Women's Issues (2005) revealed that "single mothers find themselves on a downward slide in their struggle to establish secure and solid footing in the workforce" (Corbett, 2005, p. 2). Other key data from the report reveal that

- Single mothers are "poor" or "near poor," despite the fact that they work, many of them full time.
- Those who are employed work in low-paying jobs; more often than not, these jobs do not include benefits such as health insurance.
- More than half of the single mothers did not have education beyond high school.

In this examination of over 13 million single mothers, the Congressional Caucus found that educational attainment is associated with poverty and children's overall well-being. As Figure 12.5 shows us, nearly two-thirds of single mothers have not completed high school, or they have no further education after high school. In addition, single mothers are much like many other mothers—they work in low-paying jobs that have few benefits and few opportunities for advancement.

As the Congressional Caucus notes, local, state, and federal policy makers must begin to develop programs that better serve single mothers (2005). Women's access to educational training, job training, and support programs that provide skills such as life management and work readiness will contribute to women's successes in the workforce.

Single-Parent Fathers There is an abundance of literature about single mothers, their income levels, their educational attainment, and their occupation status, but virtually none exists about single fathers as household heads. That's not to say, however, that there are not increased incidences in single-dad households. Although most single parents are females, the proportion of families headed by single fathers is increasing in the United States, as well as in many other developed countries.

Family and social scientists attribute the increased numbers of single-father households to a variety of reasons. For instance, more judges are awarding custody to fathers in divorce cases, more women are opting to pursue careers rather than seek custody of their children in divorce cases, and today more fathers are seeking joint custody arrangements (this arrangement reduces their monthly child support payments). Still, single-father households consti-

FIGURE 12.5 Single Mothers' Educational Attainment

Most single mothers have not completed high school.

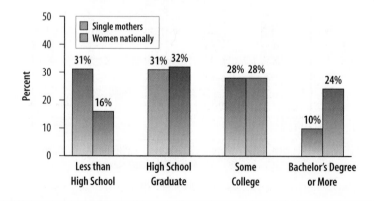

Source: Congressional Caucus on Women's Issues (2005).

tute only a small percentage of the overall picture of single-parent homes. Poverty rates are higher among single-father households than they are among married-couple households.

For children, family structure affects every aspect of their development and well-being. As the recent economic downturn in the United States continues to squeeze parents, millions more children will suffer without sufficient economic resources. A family's economic well-being and health are so essential to family living that the issues took center stage during the 2008 U.S. presidential election, where candidates John McCain and Barack Obama each took on finding ways to ease the lives of struggling middle-class Americans. A bit later we'll take a look at the government's role in shaping and implementing family policies, and how these policies influence family life. Today, a significant number of American families are struggling just to make ends meet.

Couples and Work: Just Trying to Make Ends Meet

Economic stability and the ability of families to meet their daily needs is an important measure of family well-being (Allegretto, 2005). **Basic budgets,** or the amount of money families need to manage at the most basic level, must cover costs associated with housing, food, transportation, childcare, health care, clothing, personal care items, school materials, and taxes. However, a significant number of Americans today have difficulty meeting their family's economic needs.

The picture of today's working family is the United States looks something like this (Lazarovici, 2005):

- The average U.S. employee works 1,978 hours each year; this figure represents a 36-hour increase (nearly a full week) since 1990.

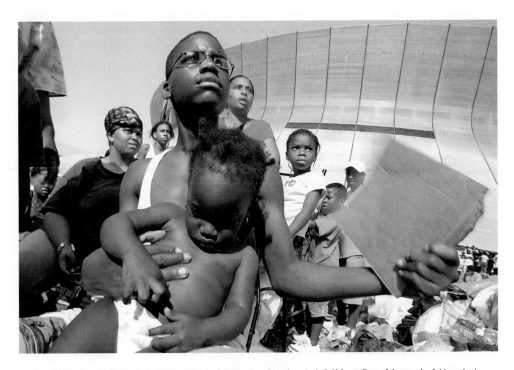

IN 2005, Hurricane Katrina left a path of devastation and destruction along America's Gulf Coast. Tens of thousands of this nation's impoverished people—mostly African Americans—were unable to flee the city because they did not have the financial means to do so. Tragically, countless people lost their lives, many because they did not have the money for a tank of gasoline.

- About 65 million women are in the workforce, including three-fourths of mothers of children younger than age 18.
- More than one-fourth of working women spend at least some time of their nights or weekends at work.
- About three-fourths of all employees say they have little or no control over their work schedules.
- One-half of all women who are married or who share a household with someone else work different schedules from those of their spouses or partners.
- One-half of working families have childcare expenses; two-income families spend about 16 percent of their earnings on childcare, while single-parent families spend about 19 percent of their earnings on childcare.
- Over 54 million adult employees provide some degree of care for an aging, disabled, or ill family member.

What does it cost for families to make ends meet today? On average nationwide, working families with two parents and two children require an income of $48,778 to meet a basic family budget (Lin & Bernstein, 2008). But, as Figure 12.6 illustrates, budgets for four-person families vary widely by geographic location.

Today, a significant number of American families earn less than the family budget average of $48,778. Table 12.1 shows today's share of families who make less than the average budget. In the United States, nearly 30 percent of all families make incomes below the family budget level. As the table also illustrates, there are significant racial/ethnic differences in those families who make less than $48,000 per year—over one-half of African American and Hispanic households fall below the family budget level. In many parts of the country, families must be supported by two incomes.

DUAL-EARNER COUPLES AND FAMILY WELL-BEING

For both men and women, job status, job complexity, job autonomy, and the number of hours worked are some of the important variables that influence child and family well-being (Perry-Jenkins, Repetti, & Crouter, 2001). **Job status** refers to a type or kind of job that offers some kind of prestige in an organization or community (such as managers or executive officers). **Job complexity** occurs when jobs are at the same time challenging and stimulating, and

FIGURE 12.6 Family Budgets for Four-Person Families in Selected Areas

Budgets vary by geographic location.

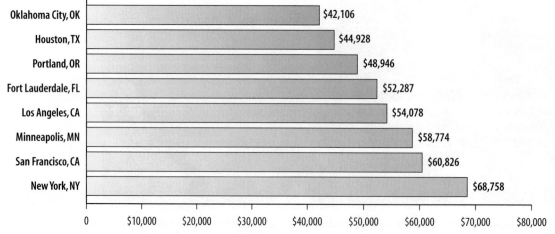

Source: Lin & Bernstein (2008).

TABLE 12.1   Share of Families with Income Less than Family Budget, 2008

	Percentage of Families Below Family Budget Level of $48,778
All	29.8%
Race/ethnicity	
White	20.4%
African American	53.0%
Hispanic	57.4%
Other	22.2%
Education	
Less than high school degree	71.9%
High school degree only	43.7%
Some college	30.8%
College degree	8.9%
Age	
18–30	48.1%
31–45	20.9%
46+	22.3%
Work status	
Full-time, full-year	23.1%
Less than full-time	42.3%
Family type	
1 adult, 1 child	59.7%
1 adult, 2 children	74.7%
1 adult, 3 children	92.0%
2 adults, 1 child	18.1%
2 adults, 2 children	20.3%
2 adults, 3 children	37.9%
Region	
Northeast	30.9%
Midwest	25.1%
South	30.9%
West	32.2%

Source: Lin & Bernstein (2008).

job autonomy happens when employees are allowed a high degree of independence and self-direction. Maureen Perry-Jenkins and her colleagues' (2001) decade review of couples who juggle work with family revealed that when fathers' and mothers' jobs have a high degree of complexity and autonomy, they are more apt to create a positive home environment and show greater warmth in parenting. Job complexity and autonomy are also linked with child outcomes such as enhanced verbal and reading skills and decreases in problem behaviors.

Interestingly, most studies about couples and work focus on the well-being of the *couple*, not well-being at the *family* level (Behnke & MacDermid, 2004). But because of the systems nature of family living—when one family struggles, all others are affected—it is essential that we gain an understanding of how work affects the lives of families. Generally speaking, **family well-being** includes (Behnke & MacDermid, 2004):

- Psychological health, such as low levels of depression and anxiety, and high levels of life satisfaction
- High levels of self-esteem, sense of power, and internal locus of control
- Good physical health
- Low behavior/conduct problems, such as alcohol abuse
- Good social support, such as friendships and contact with extended family
- High marital quality
- High marital stability
- Good parent–child relationships

If a family member is struggling at work, or if work conditions are not conducive to a quality family life, then every family member eventually suffers—a family member's occupational well-being is directly related to a good, healthy, comfortable state for the family. Given the importance of family health and functioning in our lives, it is essential to have an awareness and understanding of the interrelated nature of the workplace and the home. Toward the end of this chapter, we'll explore at length those factors necessary for couples to balance work life with family life to promote the family's health and well-being.

WORK HOURS AND FAMILY LIFE: SHIFT WORK

Researchers and family practitioners are interested not only in the total number of work hours that couples put in each week but they're also interested in how those hours are structured throughout the week (Grosswald, 2004). In many dual-earner families today, one partner works on a schedule that is different from the typical 8:00 to 5:00 schedule, and 57 percent of dual-earner couples—over 15 million—have at least one spouse who works nonstandard hours (Davis, Crouter, & McHale, 2006; Presser, 2003). **Shift work** can mean that a partner works nonstandard hours, such as working from 6:00 in the morning until 2:00 in the afternoon, or it could mean working a schedule other than the typical workweek (Monday through Friday in the United States) (Grosswald, 2004). For example, contemporary couples may have a partner that works 12-hours shifts, four times a week, which are common shifts for nurses, emergency personnel, and firefighters.

A number of advantages and disadvantages are associated with shift work schedules. Potential positive effects of these work schedules include such things as working fewer days each week, having more family time, and getting more time to be away from the job (for a complete review, see Loudoun, 2008).

However, there are negative impacts of shift work on families. For example, although shift workers may physically have more time to be with their families than standard-shift workers do, researchers believe the *quality* of these interactions is significantly less. This is because of the fatigue that intensifies throughout the shift week—some research has revealed that after a shift worker comes home from work and sleeps, he or she has less than two hours a day to attend to family duties, do household tasks, and prepare for the next workday. Other studies have demonstrated that shift work significantly impacts family relationships (for a full review, see Davis and others, 2006):

- *Parental involvement.* There is a "mismatch" in parents' shift schedules and time for children. Overall, studies show that shift workers spend less time with their children than standard, daytime workers do.
- *Marital conflict.* Sometimes, high stress and work demands associated with shift work lead to increased levels of marital conflict.

With the evolving global economy and the increase in shift work within different industries, much more needs to be understood about the effects of nonstandard work hours on family life. As some family practitioners note, these types of hours make it difficult for parents to create routines, rituals, and family activities—the very things that help to knit family members together and provide the foundation for family closeness (Davis and others, 2006).

The Demands of Overtime Organizations typically define **overtime** as the hours a person works beyond her or his normal 40-hour per week schedule (Baird & Beccia, 1980). Working overtime often leads us to feel overworked, burned out—and just plain cranky. But given the systems nature of family living, it's important to keep in mind that these feelings of "enough is enough!" not only influence working moms and dads but they also impact their families.

Decades of research have shown that long work hours increase workers' perceptions that their jobs interfere with their emotional states, and these, in turn, increase marital tension between spouses (for a complete review, see Crouter, Bumpus, Head, & McHale, 2001). Other studies have demonstrated that when fathers are pressured or stressed at work, they tend to have more conflict with their adolescent children (Crouter, 1995). Finally, research has revealed that wives' overtime work (46+ hours per week) decreases marital interaction and happiness, and increases the potential of divorce (Amato and others, 2003).

Working overtime can be successfully managed in the short term, but for many couples it is challenging to manage and balance their family relationships over the long haul due to the limited amount of time they can time spend with one another. That's not to say, however, that families can't make it work. As one family practitioner observed, quality time in great quantity is a staple of creating strong family relationships (Defrain, 2000).

Coping with Unemployment In the latter part of 2008 and the start of 2009, a rapidly growing number of Americans experienced job loss due to the U.S. economic crisis, the recession, downsizing, and business restructuring. As Figure 12.7 illustrates for us, the economic picture was bleak for millions of Americans in 2008. Job loss and financial hardship rank among the more severe stressors that families can encounter.

Unemployment is a traumatic situation for families to deal with, and aside from the obvious financial constraints it puts on a family, there are a number of other negative impacts on the family's emotional and physical health. These include (Furstenberg, 1974; Hanisch, 1999; Voydanoff, 1983):

- Family instability
- Decreased family interactions
- Increased levels of family violence
- Increased mental hospital admissions

Some research further suggests that being married and having children seems to buffer against the negative impacts of unemployment for women, but tends to have the reverse effect for men (Artazcoz, Benach, Borrell, & Cortes, 2004). This may be because when women are unemployed, frequently they still have their basic economic needs met by their husbands; periods of job loss also lessen women's multiple demands and allow them greater involvement in family life. The risks of poor mental health for men may be higher than it is for women because of the pressures of traditional patriarchal gender roles that dictate that men are to protect and provide for their families. Certainly, job loss may make them feel that they are not living up to their prescribed role of breadwinner. And, because men are traditionally less involved in the care and nurturing of children, the researchers speculated that these activities can't successfully replace their jobs, as they do with women.

FIGURE 12.7 Unemployment Rates by Race, 2009

The economic crisis in 2008–2009 left many Americans unemployed.

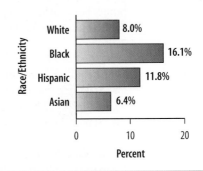

Source: U.S. Census Bureau (2009, 1-Year Estimates).

Coping with Unemployment

In many ways, the stress associated with unemployment is similar to other transitions some families have to weather, such as divorce, acquiring a disability, or losing a home—and it can be as disrupting to a family's balance and health. But research has shown that people can cope well with unemployment and maintain mental health and well-being if they employ certain strategies. If faced with the loss of a job, healthy families should (Fetsch, 2009):

- Allow themselves to grieve, to feel anger, and be depressed or anxious.
- Adopt the attitude, "We're a strong family. We *can* bounce back from this setback!"
- Maintain consistent daily and weekly routines that provide structure and stability for the family.
- Seek emotional support from friends, relatives, and neighbors.
- Assess personal strengths, skills, and values. Often, new directions emerge after doing so.
- If signs of depression emerge, immediately seek counseling either from a professional source or from a pastor, priest, or rabbi.
- Communicate often and honestly with family members.

Unemployment is often a traumatic situation for families to deal with. But if couples tackle the problem as a team and remain supportive of one another, they can take steps that promote their adaptability and emotional closeness—they can "struggle well."

OPTING OUT: STAY-AT-HOME MOMS

Some mothers have decided that staying at home with their children is how they can best experience personal, partner, and family needs with their partner's work responsibilities. These mothers have opted out of the workforce and choose instead to stay at home and nurture their children; this is referred to **household work.** Of the millions of mothers in the U.S. today, it is estimated that 10.9 million stay at home and do not participate in the paid workforce (U.S. Census Bureau, 2009).

The fact that household work is still a critical component of a successful home for dual-earner couples has led some economists to try to place a value on household work. The **opportunity cost method** asks the question, *What would a person be paid in wage labor for one hour of household work?* Because what people earn in wage labor varies, this method can tend to skew the real value of household work. An alternative method is the **market alternative cost method**, which estimates the value of household labor by looking at what it would cost in the current market to pay someone to do the household labor the mother performs, such as preparing three meals a day, doing the laundry, caring for the children, and taking care of the home. For example, a group that tracks salaries and wages conducted a recent survey of over 7,000 Internet users. This group evaluated a stay-at-home-mom's job and found (Salary.com, 2006)

- If paid, stay-at-home-moms would earn $134,121 annually.
- Stay-at-home moms work 49.8 hours per week taking care of children and home responsibilities (22 hours are given to household tasks).
- Stay-at-home moms sleep about 6 hours per night.

Senior Vice President of the company, Bill Coleman, noted that this study "is an eye opener for many people when they see the real market value of the work moms perform."

TODAY, increasingly more and more dads are leaving the workforce and are staying home to raise the kids and to care for household tasks. How do you feel about this shift in traditional gender roles, from the male being the breadwinner to that of breadmaker? If you are male, can you see yourself being a stay-at-home dad? If you are female, would you be comfortable with your husband staying at home and taking on less traditional roles?

Of course, moms aren't the only ones who opt to stay at home and care for the children and the home. Today, an increasing number of fathers are doing the same.

LEAVING THE WORKFORCE: STAY-AT-HOME DADS

A growing number of men have decided to stay at home. **Stay-at-home-dads** are those who have remained out of the labor force for at least one year primarily so they can care for their children while their wives work outside of the home. In 2009, there were an estimated 290,000 stay-at-home fathers in the United States; 60 percent have two or more children (U.S. Census Bureau, 2007, 2009). For most of these dads, the wife has the better, higher-paying job and the couple believes that it is in the best interest of the family if the father stays home while the wife

Enough Is Enough!

In today's fast-paced, hectic society, more and more families are experiencing competing demands for their time. But married people aren't the only ones who have trouble balancing their numerous responsibilities—young adults do, as well. As a college student, it is likely that you have multiple roles, and it is likely that you sometimes feel that there is too much to do in too little time.

1. Do you ever experience times when one role, such as the role of student, interferes with or conflicts with another role, such as being a son or a daughter, a boyfriend or a girlfriend? Are you able to successfully manage these conflicts?

2. What are your coping strategies for dealing with the daily demands of your multiple roles? For instance, do you smoke, do you go out with your friends for a time of escape, do you shop, do you go for a run? Are your coping strategies healthy?

Own It!

works. This is a good example of how each individual and every family must make a choice that is good, better, or best for them in order to balance work and family successfully.

In today's economic environment, there appear to be three social circumstances that are contributing to the increasing numbers of dads who stay home to care for their children. First, among married fathers, the family's economic considerations make it more appealing for him to stay home than they do for her to do so. Second, today's increased divorce rates have resulted in some fathers becoming their children's primary caregiver; because some fathers have economic security, they may opt to stay at home and care for their children, rather than place the children in childcare. Finally, a number of stay-at-home-dads today are gay men whose partners work outside of the home, while they care for the children and assume household tasks. The prevalence of dads staying at home and opting out of the paid workforce will likely increase as this movement continues, and as social acceptance becomes more widespread and attitudes change.

The Balancing Act: Juggling Family Life and Work

"Come on, we're late!" "Let's *go!*" "Do you have your (backpack, briefcase, trumpet, book report, science project)?" "Where are my car keys?" Balancing work and family is nothing new. Since the women's movement in the 1960s and the surging flood of women into the workplace the past few decades, working families across the United States engage in similar morning rituals in their dash to get the kids off to school and parents off to work.

After the birth or the adoption of a child, dual-earner families must make numerous adjustments to accommodate the schedules and needs of both spouses and the children. Unlike the traditional homemaker/breadwinner family configurations found in the 1950s, once a baby arrives, contemporary couples must not only incorporate sleepless nights into their daily lives but they must also find a way to juggle the responsibilities, stressors, and struggles associated with managing the multiple roles of mother/father, employee, and wife/husband.

CONFLICTING DEMANDS: HEARTSTRINGS VERSUS PURSE STRINGS

Sometimes our obligations to our jobs come into direct conflict with the needs of our families. When we take on (or have assigned to us) many roles simultaneously—for example, when the family role demands are incompatible with or conflict with the stresses from the work role—**interrole conflict** occurs (Hammer & Thompson, 2003). Such conflict can result in increased work absenteeism, intentions to leave the work force, decreased job satisfaction, decreased family satisfaction, decreased life satisfaction, negative mental and physical health, strain associated with dependent care responsibilities (both childcare and elder care), and increased interpersonal conflict or divorce.

Something's Gotta Give: Work–Family Conflict Work–family conflict falls into three specific areas and is bi-directional—the conflict goes both ways (Greenhaus & Beutell, 1985):

1. **Time-based conflict** takes place when demands from the work domain and the family domain vie for a parent's time and attention. This is the most common type of role conflict found in working families. For instance, a meeting that runs late at work might make Mom late for coaching her son's soccer game. A last-minute business call might make Dad late for a parent–teacher conference.
2. **Strain-based conflict** occurs when the demands in one domain make it difficult to carry out effective role performance in another domain. For example, consider a mother who finds it difficult to concentrate on her job or complete her job tasks on time because she is also caring for her elderly ill father.

In recognition of the multiple roles with which most American families must now cope, in 1993, the federal government enacted the **Family and Medical Leave Act (FMLA).** Under the FMLA, federal and state employees and those who work for employers with 50 or more employees are able to take up to 12 weeks of unpaid leave in order to care for an ill child, parent, or spouse, or for one's own serious illness, without fear of losing their job, benefits, or status. Unpaid leave can also be taken for the birth or adoption of a child, or when placing a child for adoption or foster care. Both working men and women are protected by this legislation.

3. **Behavior-based conflict** occurs when incompatibilities exist between the demands of the work role and the demands of the family role. For example, on the job, police officers may need to be aggressive, forceful, emotionally detached, and uncompromising. Airline pilots need to be task oriented, detail oriented, hard driving, and singleminded in their purpose. Although these behavior traits may help these professionals be successful in their careers, bringing home these same behaviors to family life may not settle well with the spouse and the children.

Family life is a balancing act. Deciding who will work, who will care for the children, when and how to coordinate schedules, and determining who will transport the children to and from events and activities undoubtedly leads to role conflicts. Commonly, the partner with more flexibility in work schedules is called on to "pick up the slack" when it comes to trying to balance work and family. Oftentimes, though, this leads to frustration and a feeling of being "used" and "unappreciated." Consider, for example, a mother who is frequently frustrated with her husband after the birth of their first child. Because they both work full time, she feels that he should shoulder more of the childrearing responsibilities. Sleep deprivation for both partners is a daily reality and, unfortunately, can result in a cycle of escalating conflict: He feels she should appreciate his efforts more and she believes that she shouldn't have to express appreciation because he was just doing his duty as a father. Good communication and a willingness to avoid criticism, contempt, defensiveness, and stonewalling are important keys to negotiating work–family role conflicts effectively (Gottman, 1994b). When conflicts do arise, learning to calm down, speak without causing defensiveness, and to validate our partner can help us reduce the possibility that these conflicts will harm the successful balancing of our work and family relationships (see also Gottman, 1999b).

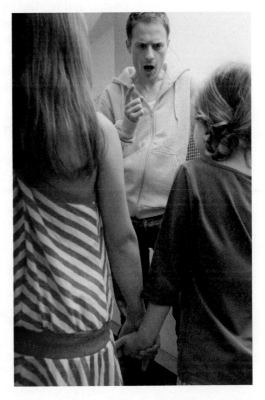

Work–Family Spillover/Crossover Research psychologist Patricia Roehling and her colleague, professor and sociologist Phyllis Moen (2003), conclude that dual-earner couples are vulnerable to work–family conflict, as well as **work–family spillover/crossover,** which occurs when a spouse brings the emotional events and tensions of one environment to the other. This spillover/crossover can occur from *family-to-work*; for example, if a parent has an argument with a teenager before leaving for work, it can lead to poor concentration at work. In the case of *work-to-family* conflict, a "bad day at the office" for either parent may end up being a bad day for everyone else at home. Work–family spillover/crossover can also have positive individual and family outcomes. Roehling and Moen note that good relationships at home energize people, which in turn improves a person's productivity at work; a great day at work can translate to a great day for everyone else at home. The researchers also note that much scientific study shows that couples who combine work, married life, and family report

- Levels of well-being are higher for both men and women.
- Women experience less anxiety and depression.
- Women report better physical health and higher self-esteem.

MANY times a bad day at work translates into a bad night at home, because often it's difficult not to let work spill over into family life.

- Husbands are more involved with the children.
- Children have a stronger network of social support and social relationships.
- Two wages allow the couple to more adequately provide for their children.
- Marital satisfaction is high when the woman's employment is consistent with the husband's and wife's gender role beliefs.

Current economic trends indicate that dual-career marriages are here to stay, but there are things couples can do to better handle the challenges associated with juggling work and family. In addition to promoting the physical well-being and the health of the children through shared caregiving, and in addition to ensuring the economic survival of the family, parents are also charged with the tremendous responsibility of fostering their children's optimal growth.

Balancing It All When our lives are in balance, life just seems better, doesn't it? When it comes to work and family, **balance** can be thought of as the positive psychological state we achieve through regularly meeting our own, others' and work-related needs. It is the state of equilibrium we feel when these needs—and their accompanying responsibilities—are fulfilled to improve our own well-being, and the well-being of those we love (Harris, 2008).

Perhaps we can think about balance in another way by using the *Triangular Theory of Balancing Work and Family*, presented in Figure 12.8 (Harris, 2008). This theory maintains that the interaction of our personal needs, others' needs, and work responsibilities creates ever-changing situations that cause either balance or imbalance in a family. Individuals can choose and change how their needs and responsibilities interact to create greater balance in their relationships and improve subsequent happiness and well-being. In other words, we have a choice in how we attempt to balance our work and family relationships while, at the same time, try to meet our own personal needs. When we are out of balance in any of the three areas (personal needs, others' needs, and work needs/responsibilities), we intuitively sense that a change needs to occur; how we approach these changes makes all the difference in how happy and satisfied we are in our relationships. Other research recently demonstrated that family health and **family cohesion**—the extent to which family members feel emotionally close and bonded to one another—are influenced by how well working couples are able to integrate the demands of work and family life (Stevens, Kiger, & Riley, 2006). One of the biggest challenges working couples face is who is going to do the tasks necessary to keep the house running, and when?

WHO DOES WHAT AND WHEN? DIVIDING HOUSEHOLD CHORES

Couples may marry with the intent to share household chores just as they intend to share childrearing. But when children enter into the family system, these intentions often do not become reality. Discrepancies between who does what often becomes a source of recurring conflict. With the majority of mothers today working at least 30 hours a week outside the home, the expectation that they are still responsible for the lion's share of running the house-

FIGURE 12.8 The Triangular Theory of Balancing Work and Family

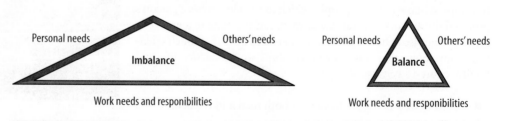

Source: © V. W. Harris (2008).

Household chores are a fact of life, but it's still a hot-button topic for most couples. In many studies couples note that aside from money issues, who does what and when around the house is a primary source of conflict. In your relationship, or in your family of origin,

1. Are/were there instances where household tasks were not shared equally? If so, who did the lion's share of work around the house?

2. Are/were grudges held against a partner or a family member because of unfair workloads? Did the grudges have an impact on the relationship? If so, how?

hold and performing household tasks can become a source of resentment. Sociologist Arlie Hochschild (1989) referred to this burden of taking on the duel responsibilities of wage-earner and housekeeper as the **second shift**.

During this second shift, women spend three times as much time performing household tasks as men do, spending 32 hours compared to men's 10 hours (Coltrane, 2000). These tasks include house cleaning, meal preparation, grocery shopping, cleanup after meals, and laundry (Blair & Lichter, 1991). Coltrane (2000) refers to these essential tasks as "routine housework" but maintains that "this family work or social reproductive labor is just as important to the maintenance of society as the productive work that occurs in the formal market economy" (p. 1209), and that these tasks keep the household, the family, and society going. The author cites numerous studies that indicate that, for the most part, neither women nor men enjoy performing routine household chores. They tend to find occasional **residual tasks**, such as bill paying, yard work, and chauffeuring children to be more flexible in nature and more enjoyable to carry out.

Like parenting roles, the division of household duties tends to fall along traditional gender roles once a child is born, even if such tasks were previously handled fairly equally (Baxter, 1993).

Coltrane (2000) identifies several factors that contribute to the division of household chores. These factors include *women's employment* (the more hours a woman works outside the home, the more men share in household tasks); *men's employment* (men who work fewer hours outside the home tend to pitch in more around the house and with childrearing); *earnings* (women who earn more hire someone to perform household chores); *education* (men with higher education levels tend to engage in more household labor); and the *presence of children* (when children enter the picture, women assume the majority of housework).

Although gender appears to be an important factor that dictates generally who does what housework and how often, the research does seem to indicate that the division of labor along traditional gender roles is slowly giving way to changing roles of men and women in contemporary society. This is a "ray of hope" for those who struggle with balancing marital and parenting roles, because, as Coltrane (2000) concludes, "We now know that when men perform more of the routine household work, employed women feel that the division of labor is fairer, are less depressed, and enjoy higher levels of marital satisfaction" (p. 1226).

CHILDCARE

In 1940, only 10 percent of children in the United States lived in a home in which the mother worked outside the home. By 2004, nearly three-fourths of America's children lived in a home in which the mother worked in the paid labor force (U.S. Bureau of Labor Statistics, 2005). With both parents working, parents must weigh options regarding childcare. Some spouses try to work different shifts so that their children spend less time in a childcare setting.

Is Daycare Harmful to a Child's Development?

Over the past 20 to 30 years, much intense empirical research has focused on the effects of daycare on children's health, development, and overall well-being. While researchers have found that parents are the first and most important influence on their child's development, nonparental care also affects children's health and well-being. Is daycare harmful to a child's development? Researchers disagree.

YES: A number of studies indicate that there are negative developmental effects associated with children who spend their days in paid childcare settings:

- When mothers return to work shortly after giving birth, their children may exhibit slower emotional development. As the child enters into adolescence, the delay in emotional development manifests in lower educational attainments (Ermisch & Francesconi, 2003).
- Children who are in childcare outside of the home from infancy tend to be less compliant and more aggressive. Children who experience 10 or more hours per week of nonparental childcare are more likely to experience more behavioral problems than those children who are cared for by their parents at home (Belsky, 2001).
- Children who receive extensive and early childcare receive the lowest teacher and parental ratings for peer relationships, compliance, work habits, and emotional health by age 8 (Vandell & Corsaniti, 1990).
- Long hours in the daycare setting and couples with stressful parent–child interactions at home are associated with angry, aggressive preschool children (Early Child Care Research Network, 2003).

NO: Whether or not children suffer negative effects from their daycare or childcare experiences depends largely on the relationship with their parents and the parents' ability to provide sensitive, nurturing, intimate, and patient care at home. The daycare experience can have positive influences on a child's development and well-being:

- Daycare and childcare settings allow children the increased opportunity for peer interaction and to learn rules of getting along with others and social interaction (Hartup & Moore, 1990).
- Nearly all children benefit from some level of cognitive enrichment from daycare and childcare experiences (Lamb, 2000).
- Quality daycare/childcare providers and smaller childcare groups or classes lead to improved cognitive skills (McCartney & Haas, 2002).
- Low-income children who are given access to early childhood education and quality daycare/childcare programs have higher reading and math grades from elementary school to adulthood, are more likely to go to college, are older when their first child is born, have enhanced language skills, and have higher educational employment and educational status compared to those children who did not participate in the program (Campbell and others 2002).

WHAT DO YOU THINK?

1. Do you think daycare is beneficial or harmful to a child's development? What is the basis of your decision?
2. What is the parents' role in ensuring children experience positive, beneficial outcomes from the daycare experience?

Consequently, the parents have less time to spend together developing and nurturing their own relationship. Other families have extended family members who are willing to provide childcare. When this option is available, many parents view it as a way for children to receive loving care with trusted family members at a reduced cost. A third option is a childcare center or preschool. Today, many parents are opting for **shared care**, a childcare arrangement in which parents share a babysitter or nanny.

TEN STRATEGIES FOR FAMILY AND WORK BALANCE

Although money doesn't buy happiness, it can definitely provide opportunities for more comfortable daily living and better educational opportunities, health care, family vacations, marriage getaways, and other leisure activities. It can also reduce many of the stressors and strains that those who lack economic advantage inevitably endure (Dyk, 2004). Although the demands of balancing work and family can sometimes be draining on a family, research suggests that most employed women and men believe that there are strong benefits to combining work and family, and that the benefits far outweigh the costs (Barnett & Rivers, 1996). Though it takes some effort, it is possible for families to successfully blend and manage these two most important domains in their lives.

In a study that examines the work/family lives of 47 married couples who appear to successfully manage both spheres, the data revealed that these couples structured their lives around 10 major strategies (Haddock, Zimmerman, Ziemba, & Current, 2001). We discuss these in the sections that follow.

Value Family Dual-earner couples who make their relationship and their children a priority experience greater satisfaction and well-being in their family relationships (Eyre & Eyre, 2008). Through words and actions, couples who do well at balancing work and family work hard to keep their family as their number-one priority, and all of their decisions reflect this priority. Couples can proactively create opportunities for family time and couple time, and during these times can create family rituals and routines—special family times—that are unique to them. Above all, couples need to remember to nurture their relationship: *Strong couples make stronger parents!* Successful couples also emphasize family happiness and well-being over professional responsibilities.

Strive for Partnership Stressing equality and partnership in the marital relationship is critical to working couples' success. While certainly there are varying degrees of equality among couples, and while there is no doubt that some situations call for greater degrees of partnership than others, partners who possess an overall high degree of equality fare better than those who do not. There appear to be three principal areas where equality is a must: the division of household labor, making decisions together as a couple, and having a "team" mentality. As one partner noted, "If I win and she loses, then we both lose. If she wins and I lose, then we both lose. [This belief] has probably made all the difference . . . because you just can't live your life trying to always win. The couple will lose, period."

Derive Meaning from Work Even if it's not always possible to love their jobs, couples who are successful at balancing work and family note that being able to derive meaning out of what they do is important. For these couples, experiencing enjoyment and purpose from their jobs brings energy, enthusiasm, and excitement to their lives; it also seems to buffer them against work-related fatigue and burnout.

Maintain Work Boundaries If couples are able to keep their families as their top priority, it's easier for them to maintain clear—and immovable—boundaries between their home life and their work life. As researchers note, couples who are committed to not allowing work to dictate the pace of their lives are better able to compartmentalize their lives, and prevent overlap between their personal and professional lives. As one study participant said, "I think the

FAMILIES who are effective at juggling work and family life know that having fun when they're not at work is essential to their health and well-being. A little laugh goes a long way!

biggest [strategy] is: When you're at home, you're at home; and when you're at work, you're at work. There's not the crossover. You don't get to think about work unless there's a huge problem."

Be Focused and Productive at Work Many couples talked about the importance of being productive while at work. They observed that even though they set boundaries, their employers tended to better support their commitment to family if they were efficient while they were on the job.

Prioritize Family Fun You gotta have fun! Successful working families make a point to enjoy a lot of fun time together as a family. Not only is family fun a way to relax and de-stress, it's also a way that families build emotional connections and create family rituals. Family time together doesn't have to be a costly trip to Disneyworld—it can be an every-Friday-night board game or movie and popcorn night, a spontaneous bike ride on a Saturday, or a quick toss of the Frisbee in the backyard. Of course, a sense of humor goes a long way in buffering the stressors associated with the demands of balancing work and family. Successful families strive to make laughter and humor the general atmosphere in the family.

Take Pride in Dual Earning Although the reality of family life for many today means that both partners are in the paid labor force, some women today still feel that there are negative societal messages about them working instead of staying home with the children. Couples who successfully balance work and home life adopt the attitude that dual earning is positive for every member of their family, and they refuse to accept negative comments from family or friends. Overall, these couples do not struggle with feelings of guilt, and they don't fret over not spending every spare minute with their children—if they had to sit down to pay the bills, they did so in lieu of playing with the kids. As one parent noted, "I think it's a big benefit for [my son] to have a working mom. . . . He's going to grow up understanding that women and men share equally in what's going on, and he's growing up expecting that he's going to share what happens in [his house.]"

Live Simply A number of successful couples have learned to simplify their lives. For example, rather than allowing their children to be involved in as many activities as they wanted to, parents limit each child to one or two activities that they really enjoy doing. Limiting activities in this way helps minimize the chaos of family living. Couples also note the importance of controlling their finances and living within their budgets as a way to simplify their lives. They also find creative time-saving strategies that make family life more efficient and less complicated. For example, one family helps their children line up their clothes for the entire week; this minimizes the "Where's my other Nike?" and "Where'd you put my belt?" last-minute disorder and confusion in the mornings.

Learn to Say "No" Keeping a clear sense of priorities helps couples make decisions that are in the best interest of their marriage, children, families, and careers. Successful couples don't allow the pace of their lives to dictate their schedules—their schedules dictate the pace. As one husband noted, "I view it as my choice. I have control over what I'm going to do. Rather than, 'This schedule is driving me crazy this week!' I remind myself, 'If it's crazy, then I need to make some other choices—I need to say no.'" Couples who balance family life and work well also note the importance of consistent and frequent communication so they can stay on top of their priorities and always keep the big picture in mind; this keeps them from getting off track by focusing on things that aren't important.

Value Time Couples realize that their time together and time with their families is a valuable commodity and a resource to be spent with great care. They are protective of their family time and seldom allow others or other things to get in the way of the time they've carved out for each other. They carefully determine how their time will be best utilized. Couples also find ways to do things together, such as learning to play golf, so that when their kids are grown they have shared interests.

All too often, families struggle with work–family balance, and frequently these difficulties can begin to erode the couple's relationship. These adaptive strategies, individualized to each family's needs, can significantly help couples' abilities to become active participants in creating a successful balance of family and work. The government has also created family policies that help undergird working families.

The Government's Role: Policies for Working Families

Recall from Chapter 1 that of particular interest to Bronfenbrenner were the social forces that have impact on people and their families, such as being able to afford adequate housing, access to affordable healthcare and quality childcare, access to quality education, being able to work, or living in or above poverty. Broadly speaking, *family policy* refers to governmental goals and/or programs that seek to support and strengthen families. These programs focus on current social factors that often face contemporary families, such as work, health, education, or the community. Family policies address, for example,

- School readiness and literacy
- After-school programs aimed at keeping children safe
- Parenting and childrearing
- Childcare
- Care of the elderly
- Substance abuse/use awareness programs geared toward youth
- Equal housing opportunities

Making Work Work for Families

Work and family are central to our lives, but finding ways to balance the two is not always easy. How important is it for people to manage work so that they can still enjoy marriage, children, and recreation?

Many corporations are finding out that it is *very* important, so important that some employers are finding ways to provide workers with tools and benefits aiding family life and living. Lancaster Laboratories, a company specializing in laboratory services for the environmental and pharmaceutical industry, was one of the first in a wave of companies to offer family-friendly benefits for employees.

In the mid-1980s, executives at Lancaster Laboratories noticed a continuing theme in the needs assessments of its employees, 60 percent of whom were women: When women were absent from work, it was typically due to problems with daycare. With the number of employees at Lancaster who currently had a family or planned on having one in the near future, the $50 million company knew it had to find a way to retain its workers and to reduce absenteeism.

In August 1986, Lancaster Laboratories Child Care Center opened its doors. The first-of-its-kind on-site daycare had 29 openings, which were quickly filled. Parents soon took advantage of daycare just a few feet away from their job site. Today, the childcare center serves 161 children from infancy to school-age, and even offers summer daycare and kindergarten programs.

The programs are great for working parents, but aside from a spot on *Working Mother's* "Top 100 Companies for Working Mothers" list for 11 years, is it beneficial for employers? Human resources executives at Lancaster Laboratories seem to think so. Turnover remains at around 8 percent companywide, employees skip fewer days of work, and 96 percent of new mothers return to their posts in three months.

Creative benefits programs today are not just for working parents. Taking a job with a company used to mean the standard insurance/company car/401(k) package. But today, more and more companies are offering extras such as on-site fitness centers, concert and sporting event tickets, concierge services, and flex-scheduling. Employers are seeing great value in making sure their employees balance good living and hard working. Having happy workers means keeping a healthy bottom line.

Source: Powers (2004).

Today, federal, state, and local agencies promote social policies that relate to families and communities. The mission of these agencies is to create and distribute research-based educational programs and polices that support families. Centers for family policy are especially crucial today because more and more frequently the welfare and the care of families is moving from the federal to the state level. Thus, family policies seek to strengthen families through research, education, and civic involvement. In the section that follows, we examine social forces that affect today's working families, and the family policies that exist to offer assistance: *poverty, health/healthcare,* and *social welfare.*

POVERTY

What does it mean to be poor, or to live in poverty? Defining poverty is difficult because it is a complex social issue and because there are different degrees of poverty. Nevertheless, knowing about poverty in the United States is important, for those affected by poverty are at risk for hunger, disease, and increased mortality rates. Additionally, poverty among children is associated with lower cognitive abilities and difficulty in school, impaired health and development, and other risks such as increased exposure to environmental toxins, poor nutrition, parental substance abuse, and trauma/abuse (Webster & Bishaw, 2007).

The **poverty rate** reflects the percentage of people with incomes below the federal government's published **poverty line**. It is necessary to be knowledgeable of poverty trends because these are an indicator of a nation's well-being, and in large part shape many governmental policies. Figure 12.9 shows us percentages of children who live in poverty, and household poverty rates for different racial/ethnic groups in the United States. When comparing male and female heads of households by ethnicity, female householders had the highest percentage of poverty across all ethnic groups, whereas white male householders had the lowest poverty rates. Female-headed households are particularly vulnerable to poverty—the high rates of female headship among American Indian/Alaskan Native, Hispanic, and African American/ Black Caribbean families is why so many children and youth in this country are poor. In 2009, roughly 14.3 percent of the U.S. population lived in poverty (U.S. Census Bureau, 2008f). Census data reflect that 15.8 million of America's children live in poverty, roughly 21 percent (U.S. Census Bureau, 2010).

The term, **working poor**, refers to people who are working but who continue to remain below the poverty line for their family size. High gas prices, food prices, and healthcare costs often require the working poor to choose between using their income for food or for paying bills, such as their mortgage or rent. As a young married student of mine noted, "Every month is a struggle to make ends meet. I often skip meals for myself, or skip taking my medicine so I can put food on our table or buy medicine for my son's cough."

We need to know about the issues surrounding poverty because the numbers of those living in poverty—and, thus, their quality of life—depend on how equally or unequally income is distributed across a society's population. For example, as SES decreases, physical illness, mental health illness, disability, and mortality increase (Hayen, Lincoln, Moore, & Thomas, 2002). Additionally, SES significantly impacts children's abilities to read and to succeed in school. Families with low SES typically lack many resources, including educational and medical resources that families of higher SES enjoy.

HEALTH AND HEALTHCARE

Married couples generally have higher levels of income than unmarried individuals, and with higher incomes there is more disposable income available for health insurance, doctor visits, and better treatment options. As you saw earlier, poverty has been associated with decreased

FIGURE 12.9 Children and Families in Poverty, by Race

Poverty rates vary by race and ethnicity.

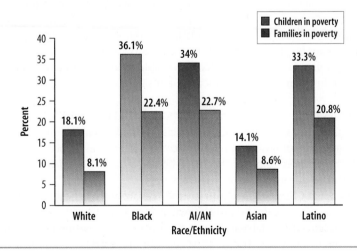

Source: Annie E. Casey Foundation (2009); U.S. Census Bureau (2008; 2008k).

life expectancy, higher rates of infant mortality, and higher rates of infectious diseases, disability, and mortality. These afflictions can be caused by some combination of factors, including the inability to afford doctor visits or necessary medical treatment, and working at jobs that expose individuals to environmental risks and physical danger.

As of 2007, more than 75 million adults—42 percent of all adults ages 19 to 64—were either uninsured during the year or underinsured; this is up from 35 percent in 2003 (The Commonwealth Fund Commission, 2008). In addition, more than one-third (37 percent) of all U.S. adults reported going without needed care because of costs. In contrast, there are many other industrialized nations that provide **universal healthcare**, or guaranteed access to medical treatment, for all citizens, without regard to their ability to pay. Some examples include Germany and Japan who have a higher overall health status than the United States, while they spend half as much as the United States as a percentage of gross national product (Commonwealth Fund Commission, 2008).

Because there is no universal health coverage in the United States, socioeconomic status is a primary determinant of the ability to access appropriate healthcare and attain the highest level of health. Further, those in poverty are restricted to care provided by Medicaid (government-assisted healthcare), which may limit their treatment options, and those working poor who have no insurance or who are underinsured risk bankruptcy in the face of even moderate health procedures. Two of five U.S. adults (41 percent) report that they have significant medical debt or problems with medical bills, despite having health insurance (Commonwealth Fund Commission, 2008).

SOCIAL WELFARE

In 1964, President Lyndon B. Johnson delivered a message to congress that became known as the *War on Poverty*. In this address, he acknowledged the impact of poverty on families throughout the United States. To fight poverty, President Johnson proposed federal legislation that would require federal and state resources to fund a number of social programs and social policies, all in an effort to improve the living quality of the poor. Today, these programs are often referred to as **social welfare**. By highlighting poverty and making it a national concern, numerous welfare programs were established, all of which exist today:

- *Head Start.* This federal program focuses on educating and assisting preschool children of low-income families so they are better prepared for school.
- *Medicare.* This national healthcare insurance program provides medical benefits for people over the age of 65. People with certain disabilities or major health problems are also eligible for Medicare benefits, regardless of their age.
- *Medicaid.* Medicaid is a federally funded medical benefits program for those who live below the poverty level.
- *Food stamps.* Food stamps are coupons issued by the state welfare agency to low-income people or families for the purchase of certain grocery items.
- *Housing assistance.* Housing assistance is available to low- to moderate-income families to assist them in finding safe and affordable housing.

President Johnson's programs worked to reduce poverty and improve life for poor Americans. However, over time, the established welfare policies created an environment of irresponsibility, and even family pathology, in which reliance on welfare was passed from generation to generation. In short, fewer impoverished able-bodied people elected to work, and instead became dependent on governmental assistance.

In 1996, President Clinton signed into law the Welfare and Medicaid Reform Act of 1996, and today needy families receive what is known as *Temporary Assistance for Needy Families (TANF)*. Although governmental assistance is still provided to low-income families, it is limited to a maximum of five years. Today, assistance is more restrictive, requiring that heads of households work and receive job training and job education. These changes in the social welfare policy provide families the help that they need, but are designed to limit assistance so the recipients become less dependent on the government.

But given the severity of the economic crisis in the United States, those at the poverty level aren't the only ones struggling to keep their heads above water. Today, a significant number of American couples are drowning in debt—and it's affecting nearly every aspect of their family and relational lives.

Marriage and Money

Most couples undergo some degree of financial culture shock when they begin to merge their finances. According to family financial expert Alena Johnson (2008), spending styles are directly related to financial personality styles, and these personality styles develop through past experiences with money. Answering questions such as *Was money readily available or pretty tight growing up in your home?* and *What do you like to spend money on?* and *What kinds of things have you saved money for in the past?* are just a few of the questions that help us identify whether we are a spender or a saver, a worrier about or an avoider of money issues, and a risk-inclined or risk-averse financial personality type (see also Mellan, 1994). For example, complete this sentence: If I had a lot more money, I would _____. Would you pay off your student loans? Or would you go to Vegas? In most cases when our financial personalities are not in sync, conflict occurs.

Interestingly, it is common that one partner possesses a dominant financial personality, and this personality overrides the other partner's. In some cases, the dominant partner is able to persuade the more submissive partner to become more like his or her own financial personality profile (Johnson, 2008). What often happens, though, is that the submissive partner becomes even more entrenched in his or her own financial personality style. According to Johnson, this "can create an opposite spending style." When this happens, conflict over money is sure to occur.

Johnson also asserts that financial issues are usually more of a catalyst to revealing underlying, hidden, or deeper couple issues than the actual financial problems are themselves. In other words, couples may fight about finances, but often the financial issues are symptomatic of a couple's communication, intimacy, loyalty, or commitment problems. And oftentimes money is an emotional issue.

MONEY AS AN EMOTIONAL ISSUE

Whether rich or poor, middle class or low income, money is intricately connected with emotion. Have you ever

- worried yourself sick over a bill you couldn't pay?
- felt fantastic because you loaned your friend in need some money to get by until payday?
- splurged on something and felt excited—until the reality of the cost hit you and then you became upset for spending that much?

There is no question that each of us has felt an array of emotions when it comes to money: The lack of it can cause stress and strain, while the abundance of money can engender feelings of security and opportunity (Dyk, 2004).

People spend money when they are sad, happy, angry, excited, content, or depressed, and often they spend it *because* they are sad, happy, angry, excited, content, or depressed. Indeed, the media are very aware of the close connection between emotion and spending money, and millions of dollars are spent each year to exploit this connection. Their attempts to speak to who we are or who we would like to be, to get us to interact emotionally with their promotional advertisements, and to eventually convince us to purchase their products are their primary goals. For example, think about the latest movie you went to see, the last restaurant you ate at, or the newest technology toy you purchased. Can you pinpoint where you learned about them, what caused you to identify with them, and why you eventually chose to purchase them?

Many of us indulge in spending (or as I refer to it, *retail therapy*) to cope with stress, cure the blues, diffuse feelings of anger or frustration, ease boredom, or soothe ourselves after a bad day. While an occasional little pick-me-up is probably therapeutic to some extent, it's important not to underestimate how these impulsive purchases can create or perpetuate financial problems. Unfortunately, our emotional connection with money can lead to unmanageable debt.

DEALING WITH DEBT

Household debt is at an all-time high (Dew, 2008). In 2007, consumer debt reached 2.4 trillion dollars—double the rate from 1997—and the average American household consumer debt equals 20 percent of a consumer's yearly income (Federal Reserve Board, 2007; Maki, 2000). Debt is a significant topic when discussing families and work; money problems and economic hardship can lead to financial ruin, filing for bankruptcy, the breakup of relationships, and eventual divorce. In fact, two studies revealed that couples cited financial and economic problems as the fifth and sixth leading causes of their divorces (Johnson and others, 2000; Schramm, Marshall, Harris, & George, 2003). Among newlyweds' top relationship concerns were debt brought into marriage and financial decision making (Schramm, Marshall, Harris, & Lee, 2005). Another recent study of newly married couples found that consumer debt greatly inhibited these couples' attempts to form their new family system (Dew, 2008). Because of their high debt, couples have difficulty finding time together because they work greater hours in attempts to pay down their debt.

These findings are important to our understanding of family life and work. They provide insight for family practitioners who work with premarital couples, such as those who provide premarital education; through educational programs, these practitioners can sensitize couples to debt issues prior to their marriages. If couples learn about debt prior to marriage (Dew, 2008):

- They may decide to postpone their wedding until their debt is paid down or is paid off.
- They may decide to marry, but with the understanding that paying off their debt will yield higher levels of relationship satisfaction.
- They may decide not to acquire credit cards and incur debt, because they know that such debt creates declines in marital happiness.
- They are better able to construct effective plans to pay down their debt and to minimize conflict while doing so.

Of course, beyond learning about debt and its consequences, couples should take efforts to learn about financial management strategies, such as learning how to budget so that debt isn't a necessary way of life (Dew, 2008). Understanding money and its significance to married life is perhaps one of the ways in which young couples can best prepare for marriage.

A common type of debt many young married couples have today is student loan debt. Today, two-thirds of all students who complete a four-year undergraduate degree graduate with an average of $19,237 in student loan debt (National Postsecondary Student Aid Survey, 2005). Of course, this amount is significantly higher if a student obtains a higher degree or a professional degree.

Student loans are typically low-interest loans that students are responsible for paying back after graduation, leaving school, or dropping below half-time enrollment; typically, repayment begins within six to nine months (U.S. Department of Education, 2008). The U.S. Department of Education emphasizes that these are real loans with real consequences for not paying them back, such as negative impacts on a person's credit score. There are a number of repayment plans possible that provide flexibility in how and when the loans can be paid back.

Payment amounts are determined based on the size of the loan debt and the time allowed to pay the debt back. According to Federal Student Aid guidelines, daily interest on student loans is calculated using the following formula:

$$\text{Number of days since last payment} \times$$
$$\text{Principal Balance Outstanding} \times$$
$$\text{Interest Rate Factor} =$$
$$\text{Interest Amount}$$

Under some circumstances, student loans can be cancelled or even forgiven, as is the case for some public service employees. Loan consolidation, or combining all student loans into one outstanding debt and one overall payment, is also an option many students are choosing.

Saving for the future also takes discipline and planning. There are several principles that people intent on saving might want to consider (Evans, 2004):

1. Is this expenditure really necessary? (Or is it possible to get the same personal affect without using money or using less of it?)
2. Is this expenditure contributing to my wealth or taking from it?
3. Is this an impulse purchase or a planned purchase?
4. Am I being pressured to make an expenditure I'm not certain about?

All couples need to talk about money and its significance to their relationships. The best time to talk about it is all the time! Topics such as acquiring and managing debt, goal setting, distinguishing between wants and needs, and establishing and maintaining a monthly budget are just a few of the issues couples should address on a regular basis. How healthy are your money matters?

Family Life Education

Today, balancing the demands of work and family life is a challenging—but necessary—task for a significant number of American families. In this chapter, we spent some time looking at the differences in work experiences among various racial and ethnic groups, as well as the differing configurations (such as married or single parents) of working families. While a number of trends were presented, it's important to have an understanding of these trends because they give us a real picture of what's happening in our economic lives today, what a lot of families are up against, and what their day-to-day struggles are. Given the interrelated nature of family living, it's easy to see how what goes on at work can significantly impact a family's well-being, functioning, and overall health.

Managing complex, multifaceted work/family roles is also a reality for many Americans today. There are a number of ways in which families can ease the stress and strain associated with work, such as keeping their families a priority, managing time more effectively, and carving out time for one another. But today it's just as important to have realistic expectations about trying to balance work and family life. There will be times when things won't get done around the house—the carpet will be in desperate need of vacuuming, children will be able to drive their Hot Wheels cars through the dust on the furniture and become excited about the "road" they created, and sometimes it will just be easier to put dirty dishes in the dishwasher with the clean ones, and wash them all—again. There will be times when parents yell and fight and scream at one another because they're so overworked and overwhelmed, and just plain tired. That's the reality of balancing work and family. Much like a circus act where the performer is trying to keep a number of plates spinning in the air at the same time, sometimes in work and family life we can't keep all the plates going. And certainly today, money constraints due to the economic crisis make matters worse—as the man noted in the opening vignette of this chapter, money seems to be at the base of all of his worries and anxieties.

Can combining work and family really work today? We learned a number of strategies that families who effectively balance the two employ. But above all, it's necessary to keep in mind that we can't possibly control everything. If families keep a sense of humor about the neglected housework, if they're willing to revise plans and schedules as necessary to accommodate everyone's needs, and if they communicate often, they can minimize the stressors associated with work and family. Learning to let go of things that won't really matter in the long run is fairly easy to do. When confronted with work/family stressors, ask yourself: Is this going to make a difference in five years? If not, let it go and focus on the things that *will* make a difference a few years from now.

Is Love Enough to Overcome Financial Incompatibility?

Republican and Democrat. Dog lover and cat lover. Mountains and beach. Catholic and Muslim. A lot of people with opposite likes and beliefs are happy and content in their relationships. But can couples with polar opposite financial habits merge their spending and find a way to make it all work? Can love overcome financial incompatibility?

Her Side: Okay, here's the deal, the way I look at things. My parents are an upper-class family, and I admit I've been a bit spoiled my whole life. I had the privilege of going to private schools, I graduated from college without any student loan debt, and my parents bought me a car for my college graduation gift. I got my first credit card when I was in high school, and I admit that they have always paid the balance for me every month. I guess I'm not that worried about when we get married because, first of all, it's not like he or his parents have to help with the wedding or anything—yes, it's going to be lavish, but my parents are paying for it, so we won't have any debt from that. Also, my parents have said that they'll always be there to help us, so I'm not even worried about when we get married—money has never been anything to me, and I think that's the way things will continue after we get married.

His Side: I grew up on a farm in a rural area. Money was always tight. Always. We never went without, but I never remember a time when my mom bought name brands at the grocery store— she always bought the generic brands to save money, and from as long as I can remember, she clipped coupons out of the newspaper to help "find pennies" wherever she could. I'm worried because I don't think my fiancé has a realistic picture of what finances and household expenses really are. . . . To her, when she spends, it's like spending Monopoly money because she's never had to earn it or even touch it! It always just appears in her bank account, like it's magic or something. I've tried to talk to her about it, I want us to both be aware of our spending beliefs and styles. I *want* to have a financial plan in place before we're married. I *want* each of us to have a good understanding of personal finance. I *want* to establish a realistic spending plan. But I don't think it's possible. I love her to death, but I'm wondering if there's such a thing as financial incompatibility? Will it always be *the* issue we're struggling with in our marriage? I don't earn what her dad does— and I don't think I'll ever make that kind of money.

Your Side: Good communication is the key to any lasting relationship, and communicating about money is no exception. Given this couple's differences in their experiences with money,

1. Do you believe that compatibility in this area is too important to ignore?
2. If you were friends with this couple, or if you were working with them as their financial planner, how would you best advise them? Would you suggest they have joint bank accounts and credit cards, or separate ones? Why?
3. Will their marriage work? Why or why not?

Summary

Working Families: The Transformation of American Homes

- An important measure of family health and well-being is economic stability and the ability of families to meet their daily needs. The socioeconomic status of a family is the government's measure of the family's relative economic and social ranking within a community.

- Although gender equality has been the law of the land in the United States since the passing of the Civil Rights Act, women have continued to fight against bias, prejudice, discrimination, and sexual harassment in the workplace.

- There is also a disparity among women's earnings when viewed across the ethnic spectrum.

- *Dual-earner couples* are defined as marriages or relationships in which both partners work. Workforce participation among couples is influenced by factors such as education level, urban living, ethnicity, unemployment, and discrimination.

- Military families must not only deal with stressors that are common to all families but they must also navigate stressors associated with separation from family members. Responding to the deleterious effects of short-notice deployment, the military has revamped their pre-deployment support programs to better prepare families for these stressors, including helping military families improve their financial planning and well-being.

- Just as each single-parent family has its own unique starting point and its own unique developmental history, each type of single-parent family has a unique demographic presence in the workforce of the United States.

Couples and Work: Just Trying to Make Ends Meet

- Economic stability is an important measure of family well-being, and research indicates that a significant number of Americans today have difficulty meeting their family's economic needs.

- The way work hours are structured throughout the week greatly influences personal and family well-being. Working overtime is an additional stressor that resonates strongly throughout all family systems.

- Job loss and financial hardship rank among the more severe stressors that families can encounter, and aside from the financial constraints it puts on a family, there are multiple negative impacts on the family's emotional and physical health.

- Some mothers opt out of the workforce and choose instead to stay at home and nurture their children. This sort of household work is often a critical component of a successful home for dual-earner couples. Additionally, a growing number of men have decided to stay at home so they can care for their children while their wives work outside the home.

The Balancing Act: Juggling Family Life and Work

- After the birth or the adoption of a child, dual-earner couples often struggle to find a way to juggle the responsibilities associated with managing the multiple roles of mother/father, employee, and wife/husband.

- This juggling act often creates stressors such as interrole conflict, time-based conflict, strain-based conflict, or behavior-based conflict. In recognition of the multiple roles with which most U.S. families must now cope, the federal government enacted the Family and Medical Leave Act.

- Dual-earner couples are vulnerable to work/family conflict, as well as work/family spillover/crossover (when a spouse brings the emotional events and tensions of one environment to the other).

- Balance is the positive psychological state we achieve through regularly meeting our own, others', and work-related needs. Family health and family cohesion is greatly influenced by how well working couples are able to find balance between the demands of work and family life.

- While couples may marry with the intent to share household chores and childrearing, discrepancies between who does what often becomes a source of recurring conflict.

- Although the assignment of parenting duties and household chores is influenced by factors such as wage earnings and education, it often simply falls along traditional gender roles. The majority of mothers today work at least 30 hours a week outside the home, and the burden of taking on the dual responsibilities of wage earner and housekeeper can become a source of resentment.

- Contemporary parents must weigh options regarding childcare, whether it's rearranging work schedules, having extended family provide childcare, or opting to use a childcare center or preschool. Yet another option is shared care—a childcare arrangement in which parents share a babysitter or nanny.

- While the demands of balancing work and family can sometimes be draining on a family, research indicates that families who successfully juggle work and family obligations tend to employ similar strategies.

The Government's Role: Policies for Working Families

- Although understanding the full scope of poverty is difficult, the effects of poverty are so profound—particularly on children—that it is important to learn all we can.

- *Family policy* refers to governmental goals and/or programs that support and strengthen families through research, education, and civic involvement that centers on current social factors that often face contemporary families, such as work, health, education, or the community.

- Because poverty and lack of insurance has such an impact on the health of a population, many industrialized nations provide universal healthcare or guaranteed access to medical treatment. Because there is no universal health coverage in the United States, socioeconomic status is a primary determinant of the ability to access appropriate healthcare.

- To improve the living quality of the poor in the United States, numerous social welfare programs have been established, such as Head Start, Medicare, Medicaid, and Temporary Assistance for Needy Families.

Marriage and Money

- A couple's spending styles are directly related to financial personality styles, and these personality styles develop through past experiences with money. If a couple's individual financial personalities are not in sync, conflict can occur.

- No matter what income level, money is intricately connected with emotion.

- Household debt is at an all-time high, and debt is a significant topic when discussing families and work, because money problems and economic hardship can lead to financial ruin, filing for bankruptcy, the breakup of relationships, and eventual divorce.

- Understanding money and its significance to married life is one of the ways in which young couples can best prepare for marriage, and through premarital educational programs, family practitioners attempt to teach couples about debt issues so they can better plan for the future.

Key Concepts and Terms

socioeconomic status (SES), p. 388

Women's Liberation, p. 389

gender equality, p. 389

glass ceiling, p. 389

occupational sexism, p. 389

gender wage gap, p. 389

pink-collar phenomenon, p. 391

dual-earner couples, p. 391

blue-collar workers, p. 392

white-collar professional occupations, p. 392

basic budgets, p. 397

job status, p. 398

job complexity, p. 398

job autonomy, p. 399

family well-being, p. 399

shift work, p. 400

overtime, p. 401

household work, p. 402

opportunity cost method, p. 402

market alternative cost method, p. 402

stay-at-home dads, p. 403

interrole conflict, p. 404

time-based conflict, p. 404

strain-based conflict, p. 404

Family and Medical Leave Act (FMLA), p. 405

behavior-based conflict, p. 405

work–family spillover/crossover, p. 405

balance p. 406

family cohesion, p. 406

second shift, p. 407

residual tasks, p. 407

shared care, p. 409

poverty rate, p. 413

poverty line, p. 413

working poor, p. 413

universal healthcare, p. 414

social welfare, p. 414

Suggested Readings

Drago, R. W. *Striking a balance: Work, family, life* (Boston: Dollars & Sense, 2007).

Melskins, P., & Whalley, P. *Putting work in its place: A quiet revolution* (Ithaca, NY: Cornell University Press, 2002).

Neumark, D. *Sex differences in labor markets* (London: Routledge, 2004).

Pavlicin, K. M. *Surviving deployment: A guide for military families* (St. Paul, MN: Elva Resa Publishers, 2003).

Multiple-Choice Questions

1. _____ put forth the idea that women suffered oppression in patriarchal, male-dominated cultures such as that found in the United States.
   a. Gender equality
   b. Occupational sexism
   c. Women's Liberation
   d. Glass ceiling

2. When comparing women with other women in the workforce, the earnings gap is associated with _____ .
   a. age
   b. family background
   c. ethnicity
   d. education

3. In 2000, two-thirds of all U.S. working women were still crowded into 21 of the 500 occupational categories (The Wage Project, 2003). This is an example of the _____ .
   a. pink-collar phenomenon
   b. blue-collar phenomenon
   c. white-collar phenomenon
   d. red-collar phenomenon

4. More than half of married couples in the United States are _____ (U.S. Labor Department, 2007).
   a. white-collar workers
   b. blue-collar workers
   c. exposed to occupational sexism
   d. dual-earners

5. If paid, stay-at-home-moms would work approximately 50 hours a week and earn around _____ annually.
   a. $46,000
   b. $64,000
   c. $88,000
   d. $134,000

6. _____ occurs when the demands in one domain make it difficult to carry out effective role performance in another domain.
   a. Interrole conflict
   b. Time-based conflict
   c. Strain-based conflict
   d. Behavior-based conflict

7. The term *working poor* refers to _____ .
   a. people who are working, but who continue to remain below the poverty line for their family size
   b. anybody below the poverty line
   c. people who are unemployed and below the poverty line
   d. people who are below the poverty line and are employed or looking for work

8. Sociologist Arlie Hochschild (1989) referred to the burden of taking on the dual responsibilities of wage-earner and housekeeper as the _____ .
   a. residual role
   b. second shift
   c. dominant role
   d. third shift

Answers: 1. c; 2. c; 3. a; 4. d; 5. d; 6. c; 7. a; 8. b

Uncoupling: Relationship Deterioration and Divorce

13

My parents were married for almost 24 years when their marriage—and our lives—seemed to start coming apart. To this day I don't know what caused their marriage to end. The change in the family's atmosphere wasn't sudden, it wasn't drastic . . . it was very gradual. But there was a change.

My dad worked for a trucking company and had long working hours. I think at some point, Mom felt like she was a single parent. I remember one argument where my mom threw some of my dad's clothes down the steps and yelled, "If all you want is a roommate instead of a wife, go back to college. Go back to your buddies!" I saw the look of hurt on Dad's face. He just turned away and walked out of the house. After that episode, their arguments became more and more frequent, and more and more volatile. It seemed as though they couldn't be in the same room without putting each other down or saying hurtful things to one another.

I remember when Mom and Dad sat us all down to tell us that they were going to get a divorce. It didn't surprise me—in some ways I felt that they had already divorced one another, but just continued to live in the same house. But the arguing didn't stop after the divorce. Instead of arguing about Dad never being home and always working, the arguments turned to who got what furniture, about money, and about who "got" us kids. Instead of arguing in the home we once shared, they argued in the driveway when Dad came to pick us up. Not too long ago my mom died from leukemia, and the most tragic part of her death is that I don't think she and Dad ever found closure. I don't think they ever found a way to put the divorce behind them and grow beyond the destruction and the hurt they caused one another—and us.

Source: Author's files

FOR most couples, the decision to divorce is not brought about by one isolated event. Instead, relationship deterioration is the result of multiple factors that occur over a period of time.

How is it that couples who once vowed to love one another until death parted them, who vowed to stick together through thick and thin, end up with such disdain for one another? With the frequently (albeit inaccurate) reported divorce rates hovering between 40 and 50 percent in the United States, it is little wonder that many people today believe that to "love and cherish" one another until they are parted by death is unrealistic and unlikely. Like any other family process, marital separation and/or divorce do not happen overnight, but happen over time, through a series of changes and transitions within the marriage relationship, as the opening vignette illustrates. Because each marital relationship has its own set of unique circumstances, there is no universal, one-size-fits-all pathway to uncoupling or to marital dissolution. Nor is there is a single cause for marital or relationship distress.

No relationship is immune to problems. This chapter offers a perspective on relationship deterioration and uncoupling, describing current divorce trends and factors that may predict the likelihood of divorce. We'll focus our attention on the multidimensional processes that contribute to marital breakdown and/or uncoupling. By doing this, you will gain a firm understanding of those factors that put couples most at risk to divorce. Because of the uniqueness of each couple's intimate relationships, it is impossible to say that there is a way to divorce-proof relationships. But having this knowledge base certainly better equips us to recognize difficulties that lead to divorce—and to avoid them. In Chapter 14 we'll turn our attention to the outcomes of divorce, as well as the processes involved with rebuilding family life after divorce.

Uncoupling

Divorce is not a new social phenomenon—its occurrence throughout history is well documented. From biblical days, when a male spouse could simply utter the words "I divorce thee" to his wife if he was dissatisfied, to today's current climate of **no-fault divorce** (a divorce in which neither spouse blames the other for the breakdown of the marriage), **divorce** involves socially sanctioned methods that legally terminate the marriage. To get a sense of divorce in the United States, in the following section we will discuss the current trends in marital disruption/termination.

TODAY'S DIVORCE TRENDS

So what *is* the accurate picture of divorce in the United States? Determining a precise statistic for the number of annual divorces in the United States is difficult because some states, including California, Colorado, Indiana, and Louisiana, do not record these figures. The best we can do, therefore, is look at the available **raw numbers**, or the actual number of those who marry and divorce. For example, in the year 2006, slightly over 2 million people wed while approximately 1 million divorced (U.S. Census Bureau, 2008i). Using these figures, it appears that nearly 52 percent of these marriages ended in divorce; however, this figure is inaccurate, because the people who were *divorced* in that year are not necessarily the same people who were *married* in that year.

For a more accurate picture of the divorce rate, we can look at different age cohorts to see who is more likely to divorce. In general, divorce is largely among younger couples, with most divorces concentrated among individuals ages 24 to 44 years (Dickson, Christian, & Remmo, 2004). For example, the latest available data from the National Center for Health Statistics (2005) reports that the likelihood for divorce is highest for men under age 45, 50 percent of whom are getting divorces. This is in contrast to men aged 60 and older, who have the lowest rate, about 36 percent. Similarly, the likelihood for divorce is highest for women under age 45, who have a divorce rate of between 44 and 52 percent. Divorce rates are lowest for women aged 60, about 32 percent. The NCHS (2005) data further suggest that approximately one-third of marriages among young adults (those in their 20s) will end in divorce within 10 years, and 43 percent within 15 years.

Although using age cohorts to determine divorce rates does not provide an entirely accurate picture of divorce rates in the United States, we can see that as the percentage of aging adults increases proportionately, the number of divorces decreases. Thus, to get a more accurate understanding of the number of those divorcing, most countries use the crude divorce rate. The **crude divorce rate** is the number of divorces that occur per 1,000 population. The crude divorce rate allows us to compare trends over time, and it takes into account the size of the population we are studying. To view the actual number of divorces and the crude divorce rates in the United States since 1965, refer to Figure 13.1. This figure allows us to observe fluctuations and variations—the rise and fall—in the numbers marrying and divorcing. As you can see, the divorce rate has begun to level off; currently, the divorce rate is at its lowest rate since 1975, nearly matching the divorce rate of 1970 (before the no-fault divorce legislation).

FIGURE 13.1   Actual Number of Divorces and Crude Divorce Rates in the United States, 1965–2008

Since the beginning of the twenty-first century, marriage and divorce rates have remained relatively constant.

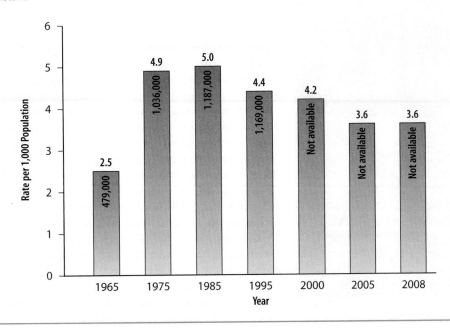

Source: U.S. Department of Health and Human Services (2008).

PREDICTORS OF DIVORCE: ARE SOME COUPLES MORE PRONE TO DIVORCE THAN OTHERS?

In Chapter 3 we learned about the different premarital and marital couples types (identified by Drs. John and Julie Gottman through their marital stability research) who may be prone to divorce. But while decades of empirical research have yet to isolate and determine precisely who will divorce and who will not, scientific study has identified **correlates of divorce**—certain social and socioeconomic characteristics that affect the longevity of a marriage and the probability that a marriage will end in divorce. These characteristics do not *cause* divorce, but their presence has been found to *strongly correlate* with those who do divorce.

Researchers have found that an individual's social and demographic characteristics, as well as certain lifecourse circumstances at the time of marriage are significant predictors of divorce; these make some couples more prone to divorce than others. These predictors include the couple's age, premarital pregnancy, parental separation, whether or not the couple cohabits before marriage, religiosity of the couple, and the socioeconomic background of the couple.

Age at Marriage The age of the partners when they marry has been found to be the most consistent predictor of divorce (Bramlett & Mosher, 2001; Heaton, 2002; Oropesa & Landale, 2004; Raley & Bumpass, 2003). For instance, research has revealed that about one-half of those who marry before age 18 divorce (Heaton, 2002). Furthermore, 40 percent of those who marry before they are 20 years of age are likely to divorce, and men who are at least five years older or five years younger than their spouses are also more likely to divorce (Heaton, Albrecht, & Martin, 1985; Heaton, 2002). In comparison, only about one-fourth of those who get married after the age of 25 get divorced (Heaton, 2002).

For teenagers in particular, it appears that lack of marital preparation, poor marital role performance, and lack of life coping skills contribute to marital breakup (Amato & Previti, 2004; Booth & Edwards, 1985; Hetherington, 2003). Emotional immaturity may also contribute to increased divorce rates among teens. Referred to as the **maturity effect,** young teenagers often have unrealistic expectations about marriage, and they are also more likely than those in their 20s to misjudge their mate's qualities and characteristics (Lehrer, 2006). Additionally, recent research that examined divorce among whites, African Americans, and Hispanic women found that marrying in the teens is a **destabilizing effect,** or a factor/factors that disrupts the stability of a marital relationship (Phillips & Sweeney, 2005).

Premarital Pregnancy The correlation between premarital childbearing and subsequent marital dissolution has long been established. Those who experience premarital pregnancy or premarital childbearing (either as an unmarried teenager or young adult, or as a cohabiting couple) have greater incidences of marital dissolution than those who do not have children prior to marriage, both in the United States and nations abroad (Heaton, 2002; Teachman, 2002; Phillips & Sweeney, 2005). For example, in addition to the United States, premarital pregnancy and childbearing is associated with high rates of divorce in Australia, Britain, Canada, and Sweden (Andersson, 1997; Balakrishnan and others, 1987; Berrington & Diamond, 1997; Bracher, Santow, Morgan, & Trussell, 1993). These findings suggest that the timing of childbearing has a significant influence on marital stability; other research suggests that a premarital pregnancy or birth increased the likelihood of divorce by 1.2 to 1.3 times (Kposowa, 1998).

PEOPLE who have children before they get married put their future marriage at risk. Premarital childbearing has a significant influence on a couple's marital stability.

Parental Separation Research has demonstrated that those who experience the end of their parents' marriage are more likely to divorce than those whose parents do not divorce (among many others, Hetherington, 2003; Kapinus, 2004, 2005). Many social scientists refer to this phenomenon as **intergenerational transmission** of divorce. The **socialization hypothesis** further explains this by putting forward the notion that because children of divorce have less experience with successful marital role models, their inability to adequately cope with the difficulties of marital living puts them at greater risk for divorce (Amato, 1996; Amato & DeBoer, 2001; Teachman, 2002). Other researchers suggest that divorce is a learned behavior in that the experience of parental divorce may reduce an individual's expectations for the longevity of his or her relationship or perhaps promote acceptance of marital dissolution (Axinn & Thornton, 1996; Thornton, 1991).

Because children and adolescents spend a great deal of time casually observing their parents' marriage, it is understandable how their attitudes about marriage can be shaped by these experiences. For instance, in a study of over 400 children who experienced the divorce of their parents, the researcher found that girls tend to adopt more pro-divorce attitudes than boys do (Kapinus, 2004). A newer study by the same investigator revealed that young adults who feel that their parents should divorce appear to hold more positive views of divorce (Kapinus, 2006). These studies help lend insight into how parents' marital quality facilitates the intergenerational transmission of attitudes.

Premarital Cohabitation Many couples view cohabitation as a trial marriage of sorts. Does this mean that couples who live together before marriage are less likely to divorce? The answer is *no*. Despite the fact that premarital cohabitation allows the couple to rehearse marital roles, these couples divorce *more frequently* than those who do not live together before marriage (Heaton, 2002; Wu & Penning, 1997). In fact, in the United States, over 50 percent of cohabiting relationships dissolve within five years (Milan, 2000). Researchers have repeated similar findings in other developed countries such as Australia, Britain, Canada, Germany, and Sweden (Bracher and others, 1993; DeMaris & MacDonald, 1993; Hall & Zhao, 1995; Lillard, Brien, & Waite, 1995).

THE popular MTV television show, *Engaged and Underage,* highlights the weddings of couples between the ages of 18 and 22. What the show fails to address is the high risk of divorce these couples face.

Researchers attribute the high risk of divorce among couples who cohabit before marriage to lesser commitment—while about 90 percent of cohabiters plan to marry, only 35 to 50 percent actually do (Teachman, 2002, 2003). Furthermore, cohabiters have higher levels of marital expectations (Brown & Booth, 1996). Since living together prior to marriage is thought to be a trial marriage and a time to work out differences, cohabiters have higher expectations of relationship quality when they actually marry.

Religiosity Religion and religiosity are other relevant factors in predicting who is most at risk to divorce. **Religiosity** refers to the religious beliefs a couple holds. Those couples who do not have a religious preference or who do not hold strong religious beliefs have higher divorce rates than those couples who do. Figure 13.2 shows us that of all adults polled who have ever been married, 73 percent of those who attend church weekly or more have not divorced (Pew Research Center, 2008).

A number of researchers in the United States have found that spouses who share religiosity in their marriage have higher levels of marital happiness and are at a lower risk for divorce (among many, Treas & Giesen, 2000; Brown, Orbuch, & Bauermeister, 2008). In one study that examined religious beliefs and marital stability among white and African American couples in the United States, the researchers discovered that, although blacks were more likely than whites to have lower incomes, longer periods of cohabitation prior to marriage, more premarital births, and divorced parents (all predictors of divorce), religiosity was predictive of marital stability (Brown and others, 2008). Also, the more frequently black and white wives attended religious services, the less likely the couple was to divorce.

Socioeconomic Background Substantial bodies of empirical evidence suggest that the risk of divorce is much greater among those from lower socioeconomic backgrounds and among those with lower levels of educational attainment (Greenstein, 1995; South, 1995; Teachman & Polonko, 1990; White & Rogers, 2000). This may be because those from lower socioeconomic backgrounds are more likely to marry at young ages (Kiernan, 1986). As we learned in the previous chapter, there are a significant number of stressors associated with household finances; thus, increased rates of divorce among those from lower SES backgrounds may also be due to the difficulties associated with living from paycheck to paycheck (White, 1991).

FIGURE 13.2   Who's Been Divorced, by Religion

People who attend church or temple regularly are less likely to divorce.

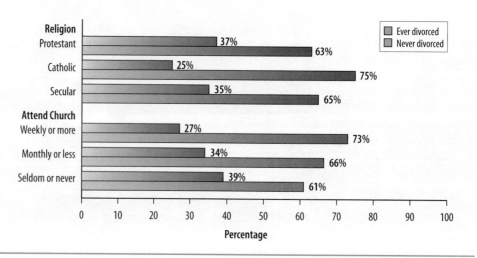

Source: Pew Research Center (2008).

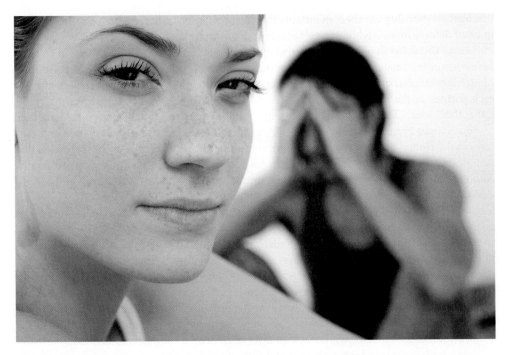

SOMETIMES the day-to-day pile-up of stressors, such as those associated with coursework when the couple is in college, can take its toll on marital satisfaction.

SOCIAL AND CULTURAL CAUSES OF DIVORCE

The reasons couples cite for divorce are many: abuse, financial difficulties, sex and sexuality difficulties, alcohol or other substance use or abuse, heightened conflict, one or both spouses feeling that their needs have not been met or fulfilled by the other spouse, adultery, "falling out of love," and irreconcilable differences. Gathering information describing precise reasons couples dissolve their marriages is difficult because these data are not collected from state to state.

According to sociologist Anne-Marie Ambert (2005), the reasons for marital discontentment that may eventually result in marital dissolution are culture-specific. Ambert suggests that a couple's social and cultural backgrounds provide a framework for the dissolution of marriage. For example, in cultures where there is an emphasis on individualism and individual gratification, such as in Western, individualistic societies, couples divorce because they are unhappy, "fall out of love," have sexual problems or communication problems, or have what they perceive as irreconcilable differences. On the other hand, in collectivist societies, where marriage is thought necessary to promote the well-being of the community, divorce on the basis of unhappiness would be considered thoughtless and trivial.

Still, the *reasons* people divorce are not the same as the *causes* of divorce. According to Ambert (2005), a number of interrelated cultural factors have contributed to the rise of divorce in the United States and other Western countries. For example, as the significance of religion in Western cultures lessened throughout the nineteenth century, divorce rates began to slowly rise. Ambert contends that because religion is increasingly absent in the institution of marriage, marriage has undergone a shift from a **covenant** (binding) union to a union of individual choice. This **desacralization of marriage** has been a significant factor in Western societies' accepting a temporary nature of marriage, as opposed to a "till death do us part" concept of marriage.

The sociocultural trends of the desacralization of marriage have led to more liberal divorce laws, such as the no-fault divorce laws in the 1970s. Since that time, divorce rates have increased and remain relatively high; since these laws were passed, many couples tend to view the institution of marriage with less significance and turn to divorce as an easy way out of a troubled relationship. Ambert maintains that divorce legislation perpetuates a "normalization" of divorce in society, making it socially and culturally accepted.

As we discussed in our study of dating and mate selection in Chapter 7, Western cultures have become increasingly individualistic over the past two centuries. As a result, the institution of marriage emphasizes *individuals'* needs and wants rather than the *mutual* responsibilities of each partner in the marital relationship. According to Ambert, marriage is based on rights rather than duties. This emphasis on individual fulfillment increases demands on the marriage.

Sociologist Frank Furstenberg (1994) agrees with Ambert when he notes that divorce patterns in the United States and other Western societies are directly related to the high value that Americans place on autonomy and independence, rather than on commitment to family. Although many couples manage to maintain mutual respect while satisfying individual needs, that mutual support is sometimes sacrificed for individual fulfillment. Simons and his colleagues (1996) note, "If the reason for marriage is mutual love and support, it is difficult for people to justify staying in a relationship where this is no longer present" (p. 219).

Because of the trends toward the secularization of marriage and the subsequent changes in divorce legislation, along with the increase of individualism, Western cultures have developed lower levels of tolerance when marriages do not meet individual expectations for fulfillment, contentment, happiness, and companionship. Ambert (2005) concludes that because couples today expect more from their partners and are unwilling to tolerate mutual sacrifices and challenges that accompany marital life, these unrealistic expectations contribute to the sociocultural factors that have given rise to divorce rates over the past half-century.

One body of research sheds additional light on the role of cultural forces on divorce trends. These very powerful and complex forces are interrelated (Fine & Fine, 1994). They include:

- Changes in popular opinion concerning divorce
- Lawmakers' desires to make divorce laws more consistent with the behaviors of those seeking divorce (such as, did the spouse really have an affair, or was this story fabricated in order to facilitate divorce?)
- Changes in the acceptance of divorce among religious denominations
- Recognition of the impact of special groups, such as fathers' rights and women's rights
- Desire among helping professionals (therapists, counselors, pastors, priests, social workers, family life educators) to make the processes of divorce less harmful and adversarial

Figure 13.3 illustrates that more Americans than ever before believe that divorce is morally acceptable; it shows us how attitudes have changed just since the turn of the century. Another recent poll of Americans indicates that the majority of adults today believe that divorce is preferable to staying in an unhappy marriage; these findings hold true across gender, race, and different age groups, and are presented in Figure 13.4 (Pew Research Center, 2007).

While the research identifies many reasons people seek divorce, it is more difficult to specify which reasons best reflect current divorce trends. Are the trends seen in divorce over the past 50 years or so due to changes in Western cultural values, as Ambert (2005) asserts? Or do the trends relate to changes in divorce laws, such as the no-fault divorce legislation of the 1970s? It is difficult to determine if the changes seen in divorce trends are due to legislative efforts that drive the changes in cultural values, or if it is instead the cultural values that push changes in divorce laws.

Whatever the role of cultural forces, the no-fault divorce legislation "clearly contributed to changed perceptions of marriage and divorce. As opposed to the belief

FIGURE 13.3   Opinion of Divorce

Cultural tolerance for divorce continues to grow.

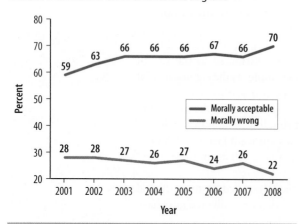

Source: Gallup Poll (2008).

FIGURE 13.4 Views about Divorce, by Gender, Race, and Age

The majority of adults polled believe that divorce is an acceptable alternative to staying in a bad marriage.

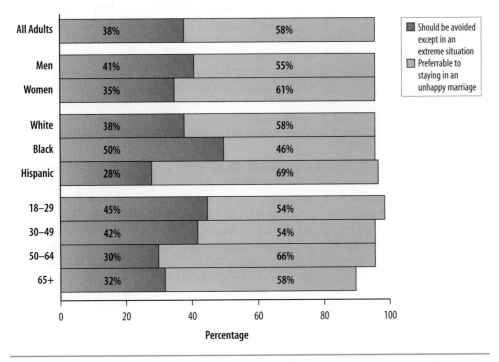

	Should be avoided except in an extreme situation	Preferrable to staying in an unhappy marriage
All Adults	38%	58%
Men	41%	55%
Women	35%	61%
White	38%	58%
Black	50%	46%
Hispanic	28%	69%
18–29	45%	54%
30–49	42%	54%
50–64	30%	66%
65+	32%	58%

Source: Pew Research Center (2007).

that marriage is a lifetime commitment that involves continuing responsibilities of each spouse to the other, the perception that marriage is a contract between equals that can be terminated at will by one spouse has become increasingly popular" (Fine & Fine, 1994, p. 261).

RACIAL AND ETHNIC DIFFERENCES IN DIVORCE

Are there racial and ethnic differences that make some couples more likely to divorce than others? African American couples are 1.5 to 2 times as likely to end their marriages than whites and Hispanics are (Raley, Durden, & Wildsmith, 2004; Sweeney & Phillips, 2004;

Starter Marriages?

Some people who enter marriage today do so with the belief that it is a temporary growth situation, and that if it doesn't fulfill their expectations, they will end it. As the name implies, **starter marriages** last five years or less and end before children enter the picture.

1. Do you think there are benefits in having a practice, or starter, marriage? What might some consequences of starter marriages be?

2. Would you marry someone who previously had a starter marriage? Why or why not?

Own It!

Bulanda & Brown, 2007). But what accounts for this trend? Scientific study helps provide some answers.

When trying to determine what puts some couples at greater risk to divorce than others, researchers have distinguished between *structural* factors and *cultural* factors .

Structural Factors **Structural factors** refer to the family's finances and its economic status; understandably, these factors are integral to the formation and maintenance of marriages and all types of other intimate relationships (Bulanda & Brown, 2007). For example, researchers have attributed poor marital quality/satisfaction (and thus, higher divorce rates) among couples to economic stability, which includes such things as employment, annual income, and educational attainment (Trent & South, 2003). Additionally, many men believe that they are not ready for marriage until they have established financial independence and stability (Smock, 2004).

Today, the economic disadvantages and financial burdens faced by Hispanics and blacks are great (Bulanda & Brown, 2007). As we saw in the previous chapter, when couples deal with economic stressors and instability, the quality and the stability of their marriages suffer (White & Rogers, 2000). Although blacks and Hispanics have similar economic and educational disadvantages, it appears that the economic circumstances are particularly uncertain and insecure for blacks, and that these factors are very closely tied to their marital quality. In a study that examined marital quality and divorce among 6,231 whites, blacks, and Hispanics, the researchers discovered that, in comparison to whites, when blacks are economically disadvantaged they exhibit lower marital happiness, lower levels of marital interaction, and higher levels of conflict; they also perceive their marriages to be more unstable than whites and Hispanics do (Bulanda & Brown, 2007). Although the economic picture for blacks and Hispanics is bleak, and although people from lower socioeconomic backgrounds are at a greater risk for divorce, this factor alone does not account for the divorce trends seen among these cohorts (Bulanda & Brown, 2007). Instead, it appears that certain cultural factors are more responsible than economic factors for the differences in divorce trends among African Americans and Hispanics.

Cultural Factors **Cultural factors** refer to whether the couple embraces an individualistic or collectivist social identity. In earlier chapters you discovered that among all races and ethnicities, African Americans are the least likely to marry, are the mostly likely to cohabit before and instead of marriage, and are the most likely to have children outside of marriage. African American couples are also more likely to have parents who divorced than other races and ethnicities (Teachman, 2002). As you've just seen, all of these cultural factors make African American couples more divorce-prone, and explain to a large extent why this racial group has a higher percentage of divorces than whites and Hispanics.

Interestingly, despite being more educationally and economically disadvantaged than African Americans, Hispanics tend to have relatively high levels of marital satisfaction and marital quality (Bulanda & Brown, 2007). Their economic picture does not seem to negatively impact their marriages (Raley and others, 2004; Phillips & Sweeney, 2005). Certain cultural factors appear to minimize Hispanic couples' risk of divorce.

For instance, as our study of marriage and intimate relationships has shown, family, or *familism*, is central to the lives of Hispanics. They are also a pro-marriage culture because of their religious beliefs, and they socialize their children to value marriage and family. As we have also learned, Hispanic cultures are collectivist cultures, wherein the needs of the culture are valued over individualistic needs. The high value Hispanics place on family partly explains why divorce rates among Hispanics are lower than among blacks, despite the fact that Hispanics are more educationally and economically disadvantaged (Umaña-Taylor & Fine, 2003). This phenomenon is referred to as the **paradox of Mexican American nuptiality**—their collectivist orientation may buffer against their disadvantaged economic situation, and help preserve their marital quality and stability (Oropesa & Gorman, 2000).

These research findings are interesting because they appear to support Ambert's (2005) belief that collectivist cultures have lower divorce rates than individualistic cultures. The

ESPECIALLY among black and Hispanic couples, marital quality and stability suffer due to economic stressors associated with low incomes.

Catholic religion is central in the lives of Hispanic families (Umana-Taylor & Fine, 2003), and as you have just seen, religion and religiosity also minimize divorce risk. What all of these studies tell us is that the combined cultural factors such as familism, a collectivist identity, and religiosity all work together to make these families less likely to divorce.

Recent events in the United States have put another group at greater risk to the experiences of divorce: service men and women. Prior to deployments to Iraq and Afghanistan, rates of marital dissolution were lower than the national average, around 2.1 for Army personnel, and about 3.0 among enlisted members in other branches of the military; this is in comparison to current national divorce rates of 3.6 (Teachman & Tedrow, 2008). Now, the strains of deployment on service men and women are evident.

DIVORCE AND MILITARY SERVICE

In the previous chapter we discovered that military personnel today face significant stressors, many of which are related to longer and more frequent deployments than service men and women have experienced in the past. In just the last few years, the divorce rate among enlisted members has significantly increased. In 2008, the U.S. Department of Defense noted that the military divorce rates continued to climb to unprecedented rates:

- *Army:* 3.9 percent
- *Air Force:* 4.1 percent
- *Navy:* 3.0 percent
- *Marine Corps:* 4.1 percent

The stressors associated with family living among those who have careers in the military are many, and most of these unprecedented strains are associated with deployment to the wars overseas: Spouses are left to be single parents to children and to take care of everything at home, finances are affected, marriages are disrupted, mental health is at risk, and often households are run differently when the military member is home than when he or she is away. Can

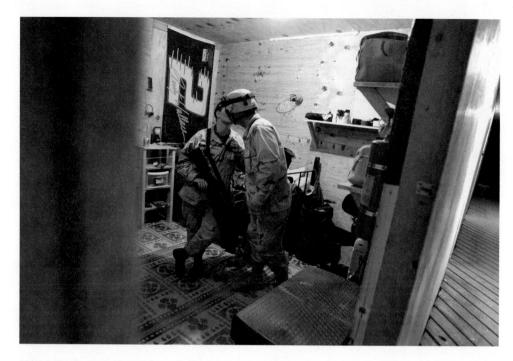

BEING deployed to Iraq or Afhganistan puts significant strains on service men and women, and today the divorce rates among military personnel reflect these unique stressors.

anything be done to preserve and to better protect these marriages? Although it is too early to determine the effectiveness of programs, all branches of the U.S. military have established and implemented support programs to help ease the family stressors associated with deployment. The goal of each of these programs is to help families navigate the difficult transitions and situations.

Sometimes, love turns sour to the point that ending the marriage appears to be the only solution to the turmoil and the angst. In Chapter 8 we discussed many marriage stressors that may ultimately culminate in the termination of the marital relationship. Divorce, however, is not simply a matter of signing a piece of paper; it is just as multifaceted and complex as the marriage it ultimately dissolves.

Emotionally Ending the Marriage

Many researchers have studied the processes involved in relationship deterioration and relationship end (for example, Knapp, 1978; Phillips & Wood, 1983; Wood, 1982), but one researcher in particular put forth a model of relationship deterioration that recognizes the processes involved in ending a marital relationship.

PROCESSES OF RELATIONSHIP DECLINE

Psychologist Steven Duck's (1982, 1984) model of relationship deterioration emphasizes both *intrapersonal dynamics,* which focus on the individual's intellectual and emotional roles in the relationship, and *interpersonal dynamics,* which focus on how spouses interact. Rather than focus on the end of a relationship as simply a process of a decline in intimacy (or the **de-escalation of intimacy**), Duck's model notes five phases of breakdown in the couple's relationship.

1. *Dyadic breakdown.* The **dyadic breakdown phase** refers to the breakdown of the couple's established relational patterns. During this first phase of decline, couples cannot identify precisely what is wrong with the relationship, yet they begin to sense that something is not right. Frequent disruptions—caused by these increased responsibilities such as childrearing and careers—in the everyday interactions between spouses eventually lead to dissatisfaction. The dissatisfaction eventually threatens the longevity of the relationship.

2. *Intrapsychic phase.* According to Duck, the second phase of relationship deterioration is the **intrapsychic phase**, or *individual cognition,* which refers to the point at which couples begin to focus on those aspects of the relationship with which they are dissatisfied or disappointed. Importantly, these feelings of distress are *rarely* mutual. The feelings of discontent are initially experienced as nagging thoughts that ebb and flow in strength, or may begin as feelings of depression (Anderson & Sabatelli, 2007).

During this phase of decline, conflict may escalate and one or both partners may begin to blame and criticize the other. Constance Ahrons (1999), one of the nation's leading researchers in the field of divorce and remarriage, describes this as a phase where couples "collect evidence" in order to justify leaving or ending the marriage. Duck (1992) notes similar findings when he observes that during this phase of relationship turmoil, couples adopt negative, pessimistic, or distrustful attitudes about their spouses or the marital relationship in general. He describes the attitude as one of *brooding.* In the beginning, spouses may keep their brooding to themselves as they may think of possible solutions or resolutions to the problem. At some point during this phase, however, the spouses can no longer keep the brooding to themselves and they begin to talk to others about the problems they are experiencing within their marriage. Duck contends that when spouses begin to complain to others about their dissatisfaction with their marriage, it is perhaps in an effort to test the waters, to see how their friends might react if they bring up the possibility of terminating the relationship. Sadly, children are often brought into the middle of the conflict and asked to choose sides (Ahrons, 1999).

3. *Dyadic phase.* According to Duck, the **dyadic phase** occurs when couples discuss their dissatisfaction with their marriage and attempt to find either a resolution or decide to end the relationship. Not all couples enter into discussions, however. Some simply become emotionally divorced, emotionally withdrawing from one another or from their marriage (Bowen, 1978). Others may choose to remain in a marriage with high levels of conflict, distress, and dissatisfaction.

In some instances, couples may intend to work together to solve the difficulties, yet in the end, they may determine that the marriage cannot be salvaged, as in the following scenario. As the husband explains,

> For me, it began with the deaths of my wife's father, and then my father about a year apart. Confrontation with the early deaths of parents led me to evaluate my own life. In the process, old issues surfaced that had to be dealt with—in retrospect, I don't think I did a very good job at it. There was depression, increasing conflict with my wife as I withdrew more and more, and failed attempts at counseling. We tried, but nothing worked. The question still remains today—did we try hard enough? (Welch, 2004)

Sometimes, unlike the husband above, spouses never communicate their marital dissatisfaction. Duck (1984, 1992) later modified his model to acknowledge that not only do some spouses not always communicate their dissatisfactions and disappointments with one another, but many may even make arrangements to leave

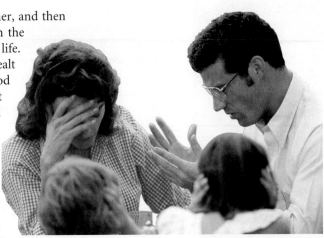

PARENTS should be attentive to their children's needs when sharing their decision to end the marriage.

the relationship without discussing the decision with their spouse. Many partners simply leave the relationship because it is too difficult to openly communicate about the relationship problems (Metts, Cupach, & Bejlovec, 1989).

4. *Social phase.* Once a couple decides that the relationship will be terminated, they then decide, either individually or jointly, how they will disclose the news of their breakup to family and friends. According to Duck, this public announcement constitutes the **social phase** of relationship deterioration. Ahrons (1994) refers to this transition as **family metacognition**, the phase in which the spouses begin to openly share with others the problems in their marriage and the possibility that it may come to an end. This is a time of much insecurity and imbalance within the family system, particularly for the spouse who did not initiate the divorce, as well as for the children (Lauer & Lauer, 1991; Sprenkle & Cyrus, 1983). During this time of destabilization, husbands and wives often begin to shift their roles to that of co-divorced parents and ex-spouses, even though they may not have made arrangements for one spouse to leave the family home or begin formal separation proceedings (Anderson & Sabatelli, 2007).

A Good Divorce?

The real issues in divorce aren't about child support payments, sharing parenting, and winning in court. Almost always, the real issues in divorce are hostility, rejection, pain, and depression, all leading to a conflict and more pain. The divorce often becomes a weapon of destruction for spouses to use against each other. By structuring problem solving in the divorce process, couples can avoid compounding the problems.

Divorce attorney Ed Sherman (2003) helps spouses legally end their marriage while they find ways to heal existing emotional wounds caused by the failed relationship. To keep the divorce as conflict-free as possible, he advises his couples to:

- **Get reliable legal information and advice.** Many couples can avoid the court process if they work toward mutual agreements that are in the best interests of their children and of themselves.
- **Prepare your case.** Each party should prepare the facts of his or her own case and gather the necessary information and the supporting documents before consulting a divorce attorney.
- **Prepare yourself.** Couples need to separate *legal* divorce issues from *real* divorce issues, and keep them separate throughout the divorce process. Entangling the two only prolongs the legal process.
- **Decide what you really want.** Is the settlement you want about your children's well-being, security, and peace of mind? Or is it about revenge, getting even, and getting every cent the other spouse has?
- **Don't make decisions until your emotions have leveled off.** Don't react—respond.

TALK ABOUT IT

1. Is it realistic to think that spouses can communicate about their divorce and their divorce settlement while setting their emotions aside? Why or why not?
2. Did you experience the divorce of your parents? How did they manage their divorce?

Source: Adapted from Sherman (2003).

Eventually the news of the breakup circulates among family and friends. During this phase of relationship end, the soon-to-be-divorced partners begin to provide either their joint account or individual account of what led to the deterioration of their marriage, which, according to Duck, is rarely the absolute truth! This process is termed **account-making**. At this point in the process, spouses openly criticize their partners (Duck, 1992) or disparage them to the point where family and friends often conclude that the end of the marriage is for the best (La Gapia, 1982). Once the news of the imminent divorce is made public, the final stage of relationship decline begins.

5. *Grave dressing.* Whenever we lose someone we love, we need a proper way to say goodbye. According to Duck (1992), the "death" of a marriage is no exception. In the **grave dressing phase** of relationship end, the couple must come to terms with the breakup of the marriage. This part of the process is similar to dealing with the death of a loved one, as couples who divorce begin to piece together a rational explanation that explains why the marriage "died." According to Duck, the grave dressing extends the account-making that couples engaged in during the social phase of relationship deterioration. But more importantly, grave dressing allows the dissolved couple to cope with the feelings that so often accompany divorce, such as depression, loneliness, guilt, remorse, confusion, and grief. Duck contends that the grave dressing phase completes the multifaceted process of relationship deterioration.

At this point, the many facets of the divorce process begin. As this section illustrates, relationship deterioration involves much more than a reversal or loss of intimacy in the relationship. It initially begins with one or both partners experiencing feelings of dissatisfaction or unease about something that is occurring in the marital relationship; this leads to an eventual breakdown in the interaction patterns in the marriage. The partners may discuss their difficulties and attempt to resolve their problems or move toward dissolving the marriage if they feel the marriage is beyond repair. During the final stages of relationship deterioration, couples make public among their various social networks their intent to end the marriage, and eventually grieve the loss of the relationship, giving it some sense of finality.

THE TRANSITION TO DIVORCE

Divorce seldom occurs because of a single, isolated event (such as an episode of marital infidelity), but instead involves a series of gradual transitions to marital end. According to Ahrons, the decision to divorce, the announcement of the impending divorce to family and friends, and the couple's separation are the "most grueling disruptions" that occur during the transition to divorce (1994, p. 77). She explains, "These first three turbulent transitions—the decision, the announcement, the separation—form the core of the **emotional divorce**" (p. 116). Following the *decision* during the intrapsyhic or individual cognition phase (as discussed earlier), and the *announcement* during the social phase or the family metacognition phase (also discussed earlier), at some point, the couple decides to *separate.*

"Separating" does not necessarily mean the same thing to every couple. To some, it may mean a cooling-off period; to others, it is the first step on the way to the divorce attorneys. Whatever the assigned meaning, the **separation period** is a time marked by a disruption in the norms of family relationships—**normlessness**—and ambiguity, in which spousal and parental roles may become unclear. As a result, the future of the family seems uncertain. Because there are no clear-cut rules about how couples should separate, many are faced with unfamiliar, ambivalent, and conflicting feelings. The angst felt by separating couples has much to do with the type of separation they experience (Ahrons, 1994).

Disorderly Separation A disorderly separation is characterized by its abruptness and is usually not the result of careful consideration. Consider the relationship of Allison and Patrick, the parents of four grown children. On the way home from their anniversary celebration with family and friends, Patrick unexpectedly announced to his wife of 28 years that he was in love with a colleague from work and that he wanted out of the marriage—immediately. This sudden announcement set the stage for a tumultuous, turbulent, and chaotic separation. Not only did it signal a sudden halt to a long-term relationship but it also launched the family into an immediate crisis that threatened the family dynamic. Ahrons (1994) notes that abrupt departures such as these create feelings of rejection, abandonment, confusion, helplessness, uncertainty, and rage. And, unfortunately, existing coping skills are seldom sufficient to aid in navigating this new crisis.

Orderly Separation Now consider the relationship of Shauna and Tony, the parents of three school-aged children. Over a period of about two years, Shauna became increasingly unhappy in her marriage. While she and Tony both willingly entered marriage counseling in hopes of saving their marriage, it became obvious to both of them that their marriage could not be salvaged. Before they told their children, Shauna and Tony spent several weeks discussing how to end their marriage. As part of this process, they discussed how, what, and when they would tell their children, their family, and their friends; how, what, and when they would divide their marital property; how their roles as parents and providers would change; and how they would continue to be divorced co-parents. As Shauna notes, "Our approach to this was that we were not getting divorced *from* one another, but that we were getting divorced *to* one another. We wanted to put as much thought and planning into our separation and divorce as we did into our marriage." As Ahrons observes, even though a separation may be orderly, it is still painful. In the case of Shauna and Tony, they noted that even though the planning did not prevent devastation and emotional hurt for them and their children, it allowed them to rebound much more quickly when the actual separation and divorce took place. Ahrons (1994) concludes that despite the fact that pain is unavoidable in any instance of marital breakup, when a separation is orderly, "at least the family [makes] the active choice to heal" (p. 112).

Legally Ending the Marriage: The Formal Divorce

Making the transition from married life to divorced life is not an easy process. We've discussed the difficulty of making the emotional transition, but the legal processes that must take place to formalize and finalize the divorce can further compound this stressful experience. Once the decision to divorce has been made, there is much to decide: child custody, community property settlement, child support, and spousal support.

In the United States, **family law** establishes policies and regulations to ensure that married or divorced couples fulfill their obligations to each other and to their children. Although specific family laws vary from state to state, these laws were enacted to protect the rights and well-being of all family members. There are contractual obligations of marital parties according to family laws. These marriage laws ensure that (Ventura & Reed, 1998):

- Each spouse financially supports one another, as is their obligation.
- After the death of a spouse, the deceased spouse's property must be shared with his or her spouse. In most states the minimum is one-third of the estate.
- Each spouse shares equal responsibility in all debts that are incurred while married.
- State property laws are void if spouses negotiate pre- or postnuptial agreements. *Pre-* or *postnuptial agreements* are legally binding agreements between spouses regarding the distribution of assets after divorce or the death of one or both spouses.

Like marriage laws, family laws that govern formal separation and divorce proceedings are also intended to ensure that ex-spouses' and children's rights are protected. While these laws do not lessen the emotional toll families endure post-divorce, they do provide a framework for the legal aspects of marital dissolution.

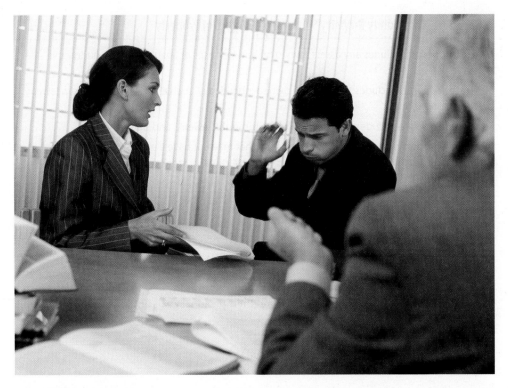

BECAUSE marriage is a legally binding agreement, couples must have their marriage legally dissolved if they wish to divorce one another. Family laws ensure that divorced couples take care of their children, and guide how property is settled.

COMMUNITY PROPERTY SETTLEMENT

If couples have not discussed it prior to the legal proceedings, dividing marital property and assets—and even debt—is a daunting task, particularly so if the marriage has been long. When dividing assets and debt, a number of types of property must be negotiated; these are displayed in Table 13.1 (page 440). Once these assets are determined, a dollar value must be assigned to each asset. Depending on the amount and value of the property, divorcing couples may be able to do this on their own (although they will require an attorney to finalize the distribution), or they may need to acquire the help of various appraisers (professional property valuators).

Each state has specific legal guidelines for dividing marital assets and debt. Family laws guiding property division take into account (Ventura & Reed, 1998):

- *Current and future earnings.* Judges often award a larger share of marital property to the spouse who earns the least and who has the lower earnings potential.
- *Current standard of living.* Judges often distribute the marital property and assets so that neither spouse suffers a dramatic decline in the lifestyle to which he or she had become accustomed. Nevertheless, women's lifestyles are more negatively impacted than men's are.
- *Individual contributions to the marriage.* Judges consider the unique contributions each spouse has brought to the marriage, whether an economic contribution or a less tangible contribution such as being a full-time parent or managing the household chores.
- *The length of the marriage.* The longer couples are married, the more difficult it is to determine separate property.
- *Age and health.* Spouses who are older or who are in poorer mental or physical health are usually awarded a larger share of marital property than healthier spouses.

Other factors that come into play when determining a property settlement include whether the divorcing couple lives in an *equitable distribution* state, wherein spouses receive

TABLE 13.1 Community Property Settlement—Types of Property

Marital property. Includes any assets owned by both spouses or acquired jointly during the marriage.

Separate property. Includes those assets owned individually, such as a piece of heirloom jewelry owned by one spouse.

Tangible property. Includes homes, cars, boats, furniture, jewelry, and pets.

Intangible property. Includes property or assets that may not have a market value but have inherent value, such as retirement benefits, bank certificates, or stocks.

their fair share of the marital property ("fair share" meaning whatever the judge determines!), or in a *community property state*, where there is a strict 50/50 split. Currently, only 9 states are community property states; Puerto Rico allows property to be owned as community property also. Figure 13.5 illustrates which states are equitable distribution states and which are community property states. When couples are dividing community property and trying to reach a property settlement, they should keep in mind their personal goals and financial needs for life after divorce (Ventura & Reed, 1998).

SPOUSAL SUPPORT

Historically, spousal support was absolutely essential. Because ex-wives were typically less educated than their husbands, had fewer employment opportunities, and had fewer job skills, women had very little means of supporting themselves and their children. To compensate, ex-husbands were responsible for paying **alimony** to their ex-spouses. Alimony, today more commonly referred to as **spousal support**, is a monetary payment, typically paid monthly, that one spouse pays to the other spouse during and after the divorce proceedings. A great misconception is that spousal support payments are mandatory by law. Not so! Family court judges determine whether or not alimony is to be paid, and their decisions are legally binding.

FIGURE 13.5 Community Property and Equitable Distribution States

Currently, only nine states and Puerto Rico are classified as community property states.

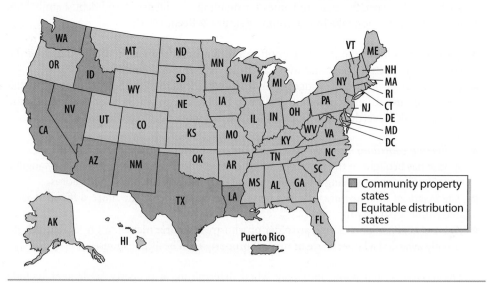

Spousal support payments are predicated on the assumption that most men and women can provide for themselves following divorce; thus, today's support payments are considered to be *rehabilitative* alimony payments, which are short-term in nature, rather than *permanent* alimony payments. Rehabilitative payments are based on such things as the length of the marriage, the number of children, and the needs of each ex-spouse (Ventura & Reed, 1998).

Divorce attorneys, family court judges, and divorce mediators help negotiate spousal support settlements. It is sometimes possible for a spouse to opt for a lump-sum alimony payment, rather than monthly payments. Spousal support can also be modified if spouses' circumstances change.

CHILD SUPPORT

Whether the parents are married or divorced, spouses have an obligation to provide for their children under 18 years old. Just as with spousal support payments following divorce, **child support** payments are typically paid out as fixed, monthly payments. They may be paid by one or the other spouse, or ex-spouses may split the costs associated with raising children, typically until the children reach their early 20s. The amount assigned to one or both spouses is determined largely by the custody arrangements, and though the child support guidelines (mathematical formulas) vary from state to state, these guidelines are typically percentages of the parents' income. Because of state-to-state variances in the mathematical formula, it is difficult to determine what an "average" monthly child support payment might be. For example, in Texas, child support awards are based on the parents' *gross income,* or the income before federal, state, and local income taxes are deducted. The court will generally follow these guidelines unless the parents agree to a different payment amount (Office of Child Support Enforcement, 2008):

- 20 percent, 1 child
- 25 percent, 2 children
- 30 percent, 3 children
- 35 percent, 4 children
- 40 percent, 5 children
- not less than 40 percent, 6 children

Special rules apply in cases of split or joint custody, or multiple children in different households. In addition, if the family court believes that the paying parent is not making as much money as he or she could (given the individual's past employment history or education level), the payment can be based on *earning potential,* the income the parent could potentially earn. This monthly payment is just for the "basics." If children require special education, have medical costs that exceed health insurance benefits, or are involved in extracurricular activities, parents are expected to share these costs equally.

How Much Child Support Is Paid Annually? According to the Office of Child Support Enforcement (OCSE, 2008), a division of the federal government that tracks child support payments, there were 15.8 million child support cases in 2007. In 2007, over $25 billion in child support payments were collected and distributed (OCSE, 2008).

Child support payments are collected in a variety of ways, including withholding wages, intercepting unemployment compensation, and intercepting federal income tax returns. Figure 13.6

FIGURE 13.6   Total Collections Received by Method of Collection, 2007

The majority of child support payments are collected through withholding wages.

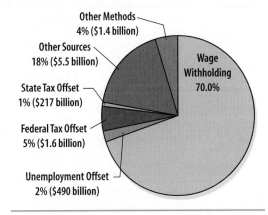

Other Methods 4% ($1.4 billion)
Other Sources 18% ($5.5 billion)
State Tax Offset 1% ($217 billion)
Federal Tax Offset 5% ($1.6 billion)
Unemployment Offset 2% ($490 billion)
Wage Withholding 70.0%

Source: Office of Child Support Enforcement (2008).

FIGURE 13.7 Total Current Support Due, 2008

Americans owe a staggering amount of back child support. In 2008, this figure amounted to $30 billion.

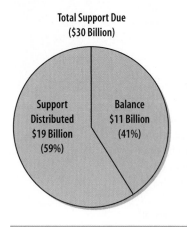

Total Support Due
($30 Billion)

Support Distributed $19 Billion (59%)

Balance $11 Billion (41%)

Source: Office of Child Support Enforcement (2008).

shows the methods of child support collection in 2007; 70 percent of all payments collected are through wage withholding. About one-third of custodial fathers are owed child support by their ex-wives (U.S. Census Bureau, 2008i).

Does Everyone Pay? Just because a family court issues a judgment does not mean that spouses pay the court-mandated amount. Some spouses may view child support payments as nothing more than spousal support in disguise. The spouses believe the money will go to support the ex-spouse's lifestyle, and not toward raising the children. Some ex-spouses feel that the amount designated for child support is too great and they subsequently pay an amount they feel is "fair." Conversely, custodial parents often feel that the amount awarded is too low, and may go back to family court, sometimes repeatedly, to request modification of the initial decision. Sometimes this is done out of anger or revenge; other times the request is made out of genuine need.

No matter the reason people do not pay child support, as of 2007, noncustodial parents owed a staggering $30 billion in late child support payments (OCSE, 2008; see Figure 13.7). Since the turn of this century, about 60 percent of those who owe back (late) child support continue to pay on the debt they owe (OCSE, 2008). As you will see in Chapter 14, the economic hardship of the noncustodial parent forces many divorced parents onto public assistance from the federal government.

CHILD CUSTODY

Perhaps one of the most grueling aspects associated with divorce is determining child custody arrangements. **Custody** refers to who is responsible for the children's financial, physical, and emotional well-being (Ahrons, 1994). **Legal custody** refers to which parent has the right to make decisions about how the child is reared, such as decisions concerning education or religion. It is common today for parents to be awarded **shared legal custody,** which means that both parents have an equal say in the child's upbringing. Family laws provide several custody options for divorced co-parents.

Joint Custody Parents who have **joint custody** of their children share in the decision making on behalf of their children. They may also share the physical custody of their children. This type of arrangement helps ensure that children receive the benefits of having both parents actively involved in their lives. Three types of joint custody are:

- *Joint legal custody.* Both parents share equally in decisions in childrearing, but the child resides primarily with one parent.
- *Joint physical custody.* Children spend close to equal time with each parent but one parent has primary legal custody.
- *Joint legal and physical custody.* Both parents share equally in decisions and physical custody.

Physical Custody When a parent is granted **physical custody,** he or she is granted the legal right to have the child live primarily with him or her, making this parent the *custodial parent.* The *noncustodial parent* is granted the right to have child visitations on a schedule determined by the parents, or by the courts if the co-parents cannot agree. Today, three out of every four mothers have physical custody (about 74 percent) of the children following divorce (U.S. Census Bureau, 2008i).

Sole Custody Just as the term implies, **sole custody** means that one parent is the primary parent—legally, physically, or both legally and physically. This type of custody arrangement was historically awarded to mothers because courts assumed they were the more nurturing parent, but today, more states have moved away from this arrangement because it tends to significantly minimize and limit the role of one parent. Even in the event that sole legal and physical custody is awarded to one parent, the other parent is often awarded visitation rights; however, if one parent is deemed unfit for reasons such as substance or alcohol abuse, or physical, sexual, or emotional abuse or neglect, he or she may only be awarded *supervised visitation*. In that event, the court requires supervision of the noncustodial parent's visitation by a third party, such as the custodial parent or a representative of a public or private supervisory agency. In extreme cases when a parent is determined by the court to pose a threat to the children, the parent may be denied all parental rights.

Bird's Nest This is an alternative to some of the more common custody arrangements just discussed. The *bird's nest custody* arrangement is joint legal and physical custody with a bit of a twist: Rather than have the children move between two different homes, the parents take turns going back and forth to their separate homes. This way, the children are able to remain in the family home. The core distinction of this arrangement is that each parent maintains a separate residence where they reside when it's not their turn to live in the "bird's nest." Sometimes one parent leaves right away when the other parent arrives, or sometimes the family shares a family dinner together or another activity. This is typically the most expensive type of child custody arrangement, because parents need to maintain three different residences—the bird's nest and each parent's separate residence. This is the type of custody arrangement TLC reality TV stars, Jon and Kate Gosselin (of *Jon and Kate Plus 8*) agreed on.

DIVORCE MEDIATION

Navigating through the legal processes of divorce can be an intimidating and overwhelming task, even in the best of circumstances. That ex-spouses are often hurt and angry only compounds the complexities associated with terminating a marriage. **Divorce mediation** is a process that helps ex-spouses resolve child support, child custody, and property settlements for themselves and for their children, rather than having a judge determine these issues for them. With the help of a **divorce mediator**, who is an objective third party to the divorce, the divorcing couple determines the terms of their divorce settlement, such as child support and visitation rights and schedules for the parent who does not receive custody. During the mediation process, a host of other parenting issues can also be settled, including who pays for health insurance benefits or/and dental care, and even who pays for dance lessons and music lessons. The only issue that is off limits to divorce mediators is family violence, because of its potential volatility.

No-Fault Divorce Laws: Is It Time for a Change?

Mark and Jan have been married for 13 years. If you ask Mark, that's long enough. Is Mark having an affair? No. Is Jan no longer a fit mother to their three children? Of course not, Mark insists, she's a great mom. Jan will tell you she loves Mark and very much wants to preserve their marriage. Mark's reason? "I'm ready for a change. I'm just not in love with her anymore."

Ever since no-fault divorce became the norm in the 1970s and 1980s, experts have debated its merits and faults. Have no-fault laws hurt marriage? Is it time for a change?

YES: According to opponents of no-fault divorce, divorce is too often seen as the best solution to a bad situation long before other options can be explored. According to no-fault divorce opponents, the problems with the legislation are many:

- **Divorce doesn't promise fulfillment.** Adults who were once in an unhappy marriage but are now divorced are no more likely to be happy and fulfilled than their counterparts who remained in a difficult marriage to work things out (Powell, 2005).
- **Divorce is rarely the decision of both partners.** Rather than promoting individual freedom within relationships, no-fault divorce enables one partner to impose his or her will over the other.
- **Divorce is a consequence to be avoided.** Many studies suggest that divorce leads to poorer health and shorter life expectancy (Powell, 2005).

NO: Divorce, fault or no-fault, is never a pleasant time for a couple and their children. Advocates of no-fault divorce legislation maintain that no-fault divorce legislation benefits each party of the divorce—including children—in the following ways:

- **It allows for cleaner divorce proceedings.** Current no-fault statutes allow for the dissolution of a marriage without one partner or the other being forced to make a legal case against the other for proof of irreconcilability.
- **It benefits children.** Children's post-divorce adjustment relies more on the visibility of their parents' conflict, post-divorce involvement with both parents in childrearing, and economic circumstances than on the divorce itself (Krauth, 2005).
- **It provides equity in divorce settlements.** Divorce legislation protects women and children and helps ensure that they receive equal and fair settlements as well as post-divorce support.

WHAT DO YOU THINK?

1. How easy do you think divorce should be? Is divorce something to be avoided or embraced? Why?
2. What kinds of incentives/disincentives should state governments include in their marriage laws? Should the government be involved in divorce matters? Why or why not?

Sources: Powell (2005); Krauth (2005).

To come to a settlement that is acceptable to both parties, divorce mediators first ask the ex-spouses to present the things they want in a divorce settlement. Then, using a structured format, the mediator helps the ex-partners find options and solutions to their disputes. He or she also guides ex-partners to a mutually agreed-on divorce settlement.

Does divorce mediation work? Overall, yes. Although both parties need to commit to the process for it to be successful, the clear winners in a mediated parenting agreement and divorce settlement are the children. By helping parents come to an agreement that is in the best interest of their children, mediation often reduces the emotions that accompany the divorce process, and it frequently reduces (or eliminates altogether) the need to go to court. There are fees associated with divorce mediation, which vary from mediator to mediator, but in most cases divorce mediation reduces the costs associated with divorce because it reduces court costs and other expenses associated with prolonged divorce settlements.

Ending a marriage causes strife and turmoil for all the parties involved. It is difficult for hurting, angry people to be effective parents. It is difficult for hurting, angry ex-spouses to be effective divorced partners. And too often, children are caught in the middle. As Ahrons (1994) concludes, "The interests of the children must come first . . . [and] they must feel as protected and secure as possible" (p. 175).

Not all marriages will survive. Not all marriages should survive. But a great many marriages *can* survive if both partners are committed to working on the underlying problems that precipitated the hurt and conflict, and the issues that led them to the divorce option.

Avoiding Divorce: Getting a Marriage Back on Track

Saving a marriage is not an easy task. It can take weeks, months, or even years, but if couples are willing to put work into the relationship, there is a wide range of resources available to them today. Marriage and family therapy or counseling are the most effective ways to help couples work through their difficulties, to help them increase their marital satisfaction and happiness, and to stop a divorce that seemed inevitable.

Couples in distress do not seek counseling: Only about 37 percent of divorcing couples report seeking any type of professional help for their marriage (Doss, Rhoades, Stanley, & Markman, 2009). Those who do go to counseling or therapy experience marriage problems for about six years before they turn to professionals for help. A number of couples attend marriage workshops and retreats, refer to self-help relationship books, or turn to Internet types of help-seeking before they turn to marriage counseling or therapy, despite the seriousness of their relationship troubles. It's important for couples to know that, although self-help books can provide meaningful information, therapy/counseling helps couples work together to settle issues without adding to the frustration, anger, and disappointment that are common among divorcing couples.

WHERE TO FIND HELP FOR TROUBLED MARRIAGES

Marriage and family therapists (MFTs) are mental health professionals who are trained and licensed to diagnose and treat a number of issues, including marital problems. The marriage and family therapy discipline is based on substantial bodies of empirical research that show family problems and marital problems are best treated within the context of relationships. To this end, MFTs use Family Systems theory to understand a couple's interaction and relational patterns. Introduced in Chapter 3, this is the theory we have used to understand the multitude of family processes we have studied together so far. Using what is referred to as **solution-focused treatments**, an MFT works with the couple to help them understand their marital problems as they exist now, and they focus on solutions and actions that help to resolve the problems. For example, in therapy sessions the couple and the MFT will explore the couple's roles, rules, and stages of their family's development. (Refer to Chapter 1 for a refresher on the lifecourse of families.) They will also determine the couple's interaction patterns (such as their communication skills and the ways in which they handle conflict), and find ways to improve on these. Sometimes one or both members of the couple will have a problem, such as depression or an addiction to alcohol or other substances. These problems, too, are addressed within the context of the couple's relationship, because in the practice of marriage and family therapy the unit of treatment is not the *person*—it is the relationships in which the person interacts on a daily basis.

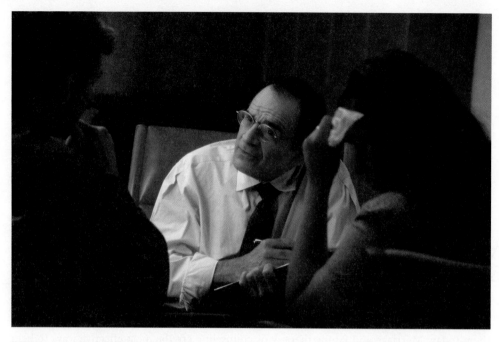

EVEN though it's difficult to bring a marriage back from the brink of divorce, marriage therapy with a licensed MFT can provide couples the skills they need to strengthen their ailing marriages.

Commonly, a couple's therapy will concentrate on various aspects of the relationship, such as communication, mutual respect, building trust, improving family balance, and honesty. In essence, marriage and family therapy can best be thought of as a skills-building process where couples develop or build on skills necessary for a successful marriage. Throughout this text, we have focused on strengthening a number of these skills, such as understanding the processes associated with intimacy, love, gender roles, communication, conflict resolution, and sexuality.

HEALING MARITAL RELATIONSHIPS

Today, more and more couples are realizing that marriage therapy/counseling is an effective tool to enhance their relationship, and to promote a healthy, lifelong marriage. Unfortunately, many couples wait until their problems seem insurmountable before they seek help. But with a trained therapist who can help them identify the issues that are affecting their relationship, couples are finding that it *is* possible to bring a marriage back from the brink of divorce. As Family Life Educator, Dr. Vic Harris, Instructor of Family Studies at Utah State University, observes, "Most relationships get stuck at some point and they need a little help (or sometimes a lot of help) to get unstuck. One of the best ways couples can [help themselves] is to overcome the stigma sometimes associated with seeking marital therapy. Couples [should be] proactive and seek therapy early—before the relationship falls apart" (Harris, 2009). Harris suggests a number of ways for couples to take the first steps toward healing their relationships:

- *Understand contexts and environments.* When struggling, it helps if couples can identify the settings or contexts in which the problems originate. Are the problems stemming from *personal* contexts, such as the degree of love a person experienced in his or her family of origin, or do the problems originate because of *relationship* contexts, such as chronically unresolved stress or conflict, or financial problems?
- *Understand individual traits.* Individual traits include such things as a person's personality, attitudes, and skills. For example, some people handle stress differently than others, and some people exhibit extreme anger while others hold their feelings inside.

- *Understand couple traits.* Couples can improve their troubled state by working to improve their cohesion (emotional closeness), control (increase give-and-take), and consensus (the level of agreement on issues).
- *Change yourself first.* Often when a couple is experiencing great distress, it's easy for them to focus on the problems with their spouse, and not on things they perhaps need to work on themselves. Harris provides three principles that can help a person who is considering divorce: (1) change his or her own behavior first, (2) change his or her attitude about the relationship/spouse, and (3) change his or her heart.

When we get married, the possibility of separation or divorce is probably the furthest thing from our minds. But as our study this term has showed us, there are a number of normative and non-normative stressors, as well as the challenges of living day-to-day, that can take their toll on even the strongest of couples. Sadly, marriages often take the brunt of the stress. If a marriage is in trouble, couples should never feel embarrassed about seeking help from a professional. Getting a marriage back on track is tough work, but the potential outcome makes it an avenue definitely worth exploring.

Family Life Education

Certainly, divorce is not a new social phenomenon, and as the divorce trends indicated, the United States has seen divorce rates fluctuate throughout its history. What remains unclear is whether the trends seen in divorce rates over the past 50 years or so are due to changing cultural values that, in turn, influence changes in divorce legislation, or whether the legislative efforts have been responsible for changes in cultural values.

The opening vignette of this chapter illustrates the gradual, progressive deterioration of the marriage of the parents of one of my students. In real life, *every* family fights. In real marriages, *every* couple has arguments and disagreements, and *every* couple will at one time or another have a verbal exchange that hurts one or the other partner.

The breakdown and subsequent termination of a marital relationship is not necessarily a result of the de-escalation of intimacy, but is instead, as Duck (1982, 1984) and Ahrons (1994) described, a process of dissatisfaction with a couple's relational patterns. This dissatisfaction, left unattended, eventually reaches a point at which marital partners emotionally divorce from one another long before the legal divorce takes place. When the divorce proceedings do begin, the transition from married family life to divorced family life is very difficult for parents and their children. As the author of the opening vignette described, "The arguments turned to who got what furniture, about money, and who 'got' us kids." Indeed, once the decision to divorce was made, the spouses then entered into the long-term legal process of divorce and had to come to agreement on issues such as community property settlement, child support, and child custody.

Despite our most blue-ribbon efforts, there are some relationships that we cannot prevent from coming unraveled—we cannot always prevent divorce. I leave the concluding comments to the student who wrote the opening vignette of this chapter:

> If I could title this paper the title would be "THE DECEPTION OF THE GRADUAL."
> You see, the changes that took place in our family took place slowly and gradually,
> bit by bit. And as each change occurred, my parents became comfortable and complacent with the changes. Rather than try to actively do something about what was
> happening, they let it go on, slowly but surely, letting the conflict and discontent
> progress to the point where there was no turning back. They let it progress to the
> point where there were too many hurt feelings, too many words hurled at one
> another to ever take back and start over. Gradual, ever so gradual.
> The deception of the gradual . . .

When a Marriage Is on the Verge of Divorce, Can It Be Saved?

When a couple is hurting and experiencing relationship difficulties, marital therapy can often help them mend their broken relationship. Today, couples look to marriage and family therapists to help them overcome their troubles from difficulties with emotional affection, communication problems, infidelity, high conflict levels, or concerns about separation or divorce (Doss and others, 2009). But when a marriage is on the verge of divorce, can it really be saved?

Her Side: The weight of this entire marriage is on me. I am the primary breadwinner, I pay all the bills, I am responsible for cleaning the house, taking care of the kids, the cars, the dogs, I'm responsible for planning every holiday, for everyone's health . . . I can't talk to him about anything, because as soon as I do I feel like he just shuts me down, shuts me out. I've read books and tried all sorts of things, but I feel like I'm trying all alone. Can this marriage ever work if *I* am the only one who wants to work on things? At this point, I'm not even sure I *want* it to work . . . it's just one more thing *I* have to do.

His Side: I have been very unhappy for a long time, and now I see that she is unhappy and depressed. In all honesty, I have been taking out my unhappiness on her—it's like I want her to feel as miserable as I do all the time, and I think deep down that's why I haven't even tried to lift a finger to help her out—I wanted her to hurt. This may be hard to believe, but I still want to give us a chance. I really do still love her. I'm willing to do anything to make this work. Both of our parents are divorced, and we promised each other a long time ago that we would never do that to our kids. And here we are. I'm willing to go to counseling or whatever it takes to turn this marriage around, to get it back where it used to be. But at this point, I'm not sure anyone can help us. I never thought she'd want to leave, but now that she's thinking about it, I realize I pushed her away.

Your Side: Looking at this couple's situation,

1. Do you believe there is hope for this couple's marriage? Why or why not?
2. Saving a marriage is not just about preventing a divorce but about rebuilding a relationship of trust, respect, and happiness. If you were this couple's counselor, what three things would you suggest they do first to take steps toward reconciliation?
3. Do you think that current divorce laws should mandate marriage counseling for all couples who are considering divorce? What would be the benefits of such legislation? The downfalls?

Summary

Uncoupling

- Uncoupling and the factors that lead to it are complex. Because each marital relationship has its own set of unique circumstances, there is no universal, one-size-fits-all pathway to uncoupling or to marital dissolution.

- Divorce involves socially sanctioned methods that legally terminate the marriage. Because some states do not record annual divorce statistics, the best way to determine the number of annual divorces in the United States is to look at the crude divorce rate—the number of divorces that occur per 1,000 population.

- Correlates of divorce are certain social and socioeconomic characteristics that affect the longevity of a marriage and the probability that a marriage will end in divorce. These predictors include the couple's age, premarital pregnancy, parental separation, whether the couple cohabits before marriage, religiosity of the couple, and the socioeconomic background of the couple.

- Reasons for marital discontentment that may eventually result in marital dissolution tend to be culture-specific. In cultures where there is an emphasis on individualism and individual gratification, couples divorce because they are unhappy or because of what they perceive as irreconcilable differences. In collectivist societies, where marriage is thought necessary to promote the health of the community, divorce on the basis of unhappiness is considered thoughtless and trivial.

- The reasons people divorce are not the same as the causes of divorce, and there are interrelated cultural factors that contribute to the rise of divorce in the United States and other Western countries. These factors include the desacralization of marriage, the liberalization of divorce laws, the trend toward individualism, unrealistic expectations, and other cultural forces, such as the legislation that created no-fault divorce.

- Racial and ethnic differences make some couples more likely to divorce. Economic factors and education influence higher divorce rates, but cultural factors have even more impact, especially among African Americans and Hispanics. Although many Hispanic families face great economic difficulties, cultural factors such as *familism,* a collectivist identity, and religiosity all work together to make divorce less likely. This is known as the *paradox of Mexican American nuptiality.*

- Service men and women experience higher-than-average rates of divorce, and women in the service experience twice the divorce rates as men in the service. Researchers believe the increase in divorce rates is due to the stressors associated with deployment to Iraq and Afghanistan.

Emotionally Ending the Marriage

- Divorce is not an isolated event in a family's life; rather, it involves a series of transitions that include both emotional and legal processes.

- Psychologist Steven Duck's model of relationship deterioration describes five phases of breakdown in the couple's relationship: the dyadic breakdown, the intrapsychic phase, the dyadic phase, the social phase, and the grave dressing phase.

- Divorce seldom occurs because of a single event; instead, it involves a series of transitions, which include the decision, the announcement, and the separation. These transitions form the core of the emotional divorce.

- The separation period tends to be a time of disruption in the norms of family relationships and a time of ambiguity in which spousal and parental roles may become unclear.

- The anxiety felt by separating couples depends on what type of separation they experience: orderly separation, characterized by planning (though still painful), or disorderly separation, characterized by abruptness and usually not the result of careful consideration.

Legally Ending the Marriage: The Formal Divorce

- After the emotional transition to divorce takes place, the legal processes that take place to formalize, and finalize, the divorce often intensify this stressful experience.

- In the United States, family law establishes policies and regulations to ensure that married or divorced couples fulfill their obligations to each other and to their children, and that ex-spouses' and children's rights are protected.

- Dividing marital property and assets can be a difficult task. When dividing assets and debt, marital property, separate property, tangible property, and intangible property all must be negotiated. Family laws guiding property division consider current and future earnings, current standards of living, individual contributions to the marriage, the length of the marriage, and the age and health of each ex-spouse.

- Spousal support payments are considered as short-term rehabilitative alimony payments, and are based on the needs and resources of each ex-spouse, the value of the property received in the settlement, the length of the marriage, the physical and emotional health of each spouse, and the number of children present in the home, among other factors.

- Whether married or divorced, parents have an obligation to provide for their children under age 18. Child support payments may be made by either spouse. Ex-spouses may split the costs associated with raising children, typically until the children reach their early 20s. The amount assigned to one or both spouses is determined by the custody arrangements.

- Custody refers to who is responsible for the children's financial, physical, and emotional well-being. A parent who has legal custody has the right to make decisions about how the child is reared, such as decisions concerning education or religion. With shared legal custody, both parents have an equal say in the child's upbringing. Family laws provide several custody options for divorced co-parents, including joint custody, physical custody, sole custody, and the bird's nest custody option.

- Divorce mediation helps ex-spouses resolve child support, child custody, and property settlements for themselves and for their children, rather than having a judge determine these issues for them. Mediation often reduces the anger and hurt that accompany the divorce process, and reduces or eliminates the need to go to court.

Avoiding Divorce: Getting a Marriage Back on Track

- Marriage and family therapy are effective ways that help couples work through their marital difficulties. However, only slightly more than one-third of couples in trouble seek any type of professional help for their marriages.

- Marriage and family therapists (MFTs) are trained and licensed professionals who treat a number of family and marital issues. Using the Family Systems theory, an MFT explores the couple's relational and interaction patterns with solution-focused goals in mind.

- There are a number of ways for couples to take steps toward healing their relationships. These include understanding the contexts and environments in which the problems originated, understanding individual and couple traits, and being willing to change oneself first.

Key Terms and Concepts

no-fault divorce, p. 424

divorce, p. 424

raw numbers, p. 424

crude divorce rate, p. 425

correlates of divorce, p. 426

maturity effect, p. 426

destabilizing effect, p. 426

intergenerational transmission, p. 427

socialization hypothesis, p. 427

religiosity, p. 428

covenant, p. 429

desacralization of marriage, p. 429

starter marriages, p. 431

structural factors, p. 432

cultural factors, p. 432

paradox of Mexican American nuptiality, p. 432

de-escalation of intimacy, p. 434

dyadic breakdown phase, p. 435

intrapsychic phase, p. 435

dyadic phase, p. 435

social phase, p. 436

family metacognition, p. 436

account-making, p. 437

grave dressing phase, p. 437

emotional divorce, p. 437

separation period, p. 437

normlessness, p. 437

family law, p. 438

alimony, p. 440

spousal support, p. 440

child support, p. 441

custody, p. 442

legal custody, p. 442

shared legal custody, p. 442

joint custody, p. 442

physical custody, p. 442

sole custody, p. 443

divorce mediation, p. 443

divorce mediator, p. 443

marriage and family therapist (MFT), p. 446

solution-focused treatments, p. 446

Suggested Readings

Ahrons, C. *The good divorce: Keeping your family together when your marriage comes apart* (New York, Harper-Collins, 1995).

Hetherington, M., and Kelly, J. *For better or for worse: Divorce reconsidered* (New York: W. W. Norton, 2002).

Walsh, F. *Strengthening family resilience* (New York: Guilford Press, 1999).

Multiple-Choice Questions

1. Referred to as the _____ , at young ages teenagers often have unrealistic expectations about marriage, and they are also more likely than those in their 20s to misjudge their mate's qualities and characteristics (Lehrer, 2006).
   a. age effect
   b. maturity effect
   c. immaturity effect
   d. destabilizing effect

2. In comparison to couples who do not live together before marriage, people who participate in premarital cohabitation, which allows the couple to rehearse marital roles, divorce _____ .
   a. less frequently
   b. at the same rate
   c. more frequently
   d. not enough data

3. During this first phase of decline in a couple's relationship, couples cannot identify precisely what is wrong with the relationship, yet they begin to sense that something is wrong.
   a. Dyadic breakdown
   b. Intrapsychic phase
   c. Dyadic phase
   d. Social phase

4. _____ , today more commonly referred to as *spousal support*, is a monetary payment, typically paid monthly, that one spouse pays to the other spouse during and after the divorce proceedings.
   a. Alimony
   b. Spousal alimony
   c. Spousal allowance
   d. Spousal maintanence

5. When a parent is granted _____ custody, he or she is granted the legal right to have the child live primarily with him or her, making this parent the *custodial parent.*
   a. joint
   b. physical
   c. shared legal
   d. domestic

6. The _____ is the number of divorces that occur per 1,000 population.
   a. raw divorce rate
   b. basic divorce rate
   c. simple divorce rate
   d. crude divorce rate

7. Which of the following is NOT a contractual obligation of marital parties according to family laws?
   a. After the death of a spouse, the deceased spouse's property must be shared with his or her spouse. In most states the minimum is one-half of the estate.
   b. Each spouse shares equal responsibility in all debts that are incurred while married.
   c. State property laws are void if spouses negotiate pre- or postnuptial agreements.
   d. Each spouse financially supports one another, as is their obligation.

8. _____ is a process that helps ex-spouses resolve child support, child custody, and property settlements for themselves and for their children, rather than having a judge determine these issues for them.
   a. Divorce resolution
   b. Divorce reconciliation
   c. Divorce mediation
   d. Divorce negotiation

Answers: 1. b; 2. c; 3. a; 4. a; 5. b; 6. d; 7. a; 8. c

Rebuilding: Family Life Following Divorce

14

I fell for it every time when I was younger. Every time my brothers asked, "Do you wanna play 52-pick-up?," I zealously jumped at the chance to "play cards" with them. I felt grown up and proud that I was included in their card game. It wasn't until I was 5 or 6 that I realized the game of 52-pick-up was only a game for them, because they had a lot of fun watching me pick up 52 cards that were scattered all over the floor!

When my parents divorced, and then when each of them remarried, a recurring thought I had was, "This is just like 52-pick-up." Our lives were a mess of scattered pieces, flipped upside down. Just like the cards in the game, our lives were disorganized and thrown all over the place. And someone had to pick them up and reorganize them again. It took time, but we all did eventually get all the pieces picked up, and got everything back in order—not in the same order, a different order. But it works for us.

Source: Author's files

THE experiences associated with divorce are so disrupting to families that divorce is ranked as one of the most stressful life events a family can encounter. The aftermath of divorce must be navigated well so that families can successfully rebuild themselves.

When parents go through a divorce, the entire family system is thrown into turmoil, with each family member feeling the disturbance in different ways. For those who are divorcing, the ramifications weigh heavily as family life undergoes reconstruction. The transitions associated with divorce, as outlined in the previous chapter, include (Ahrons, 1994; Duck, 1982):

1. *The Decision* to terminate the marriage.
2. *The Announcement* to children, family, and friends that the relationship is beyond repair and will be ending.
3. *The Separation,* whether orderly or disorderly, ultimately results in a period of time marked by multiple disruptions in the "normal" way of family living.
4. *The Formal Divorce* is a period of time during which grueling decisions relating to the division of property, spousal support, child support, and child custody must be made.

The events leading up to the family court's decree finalizing the divorce involves changes in all aspects of family life. At this point in your study of family life, you should have a clearer understanding of why divorce is ranked as one of the most stressful life events a family can experience, second only to the death of a loved one. You should also have a clearer understanding of how family stress and family crisis can affect the emotional and physical well-being of family members. Divorce is deeply intertwined with those areas of family crisis and stress (see Chapter 15).

Beyond the challenges, demands, and stressors associated with divorce, there is a final transition that must be traversed that we haven't yet discussed—the *aftermath* of divorce. It is during this transition that families re-establish their identities. Well after the decision to divorce is made public to family and friends, well after the separation takes place, and well after the legal divorce is finalized, the reconstruction continues. Just as there is no universal pathway to uncoupling, there is no universal pathway to rebuilding following divorce. In this chapter we will discuss the transitions and the ways in which families rebuild their new lives. Different families' structures bring them certain challenges, which we will explore in the context of binuclear families, single-parent families, and remarriage and stepfamilies.

The Aftermath of Divorce: Transitions

Just as the opening student comments illustrate, divorce ultimately results in a complex mix-up of existing family relationships. The transition of status from married to divorced often leads to upheaval and disorganization within the family system. To cope with these changes, families must take on the central task associated with the aftermath of divorce—the reorganization of the family. This requires reconstructing the single nuclear family into a *binuclear family*, a process that creates two family systems from one family of origin.

THE BINUCLEAR FAMILY

The term **binuclear family** refers to the separate, distinct households that form after marital separation or divorce. This dramatic change in family life reverberates throughout the entire family system, and this turn of events often brings the entire family to new levels of stress and crisis. The two subsystems that have been formed—the maternal (mother) and the paternal (father)—are now the child's family of origin. This restructuring from one central family into two accounts for much of the upheaval and confusion associated with divorce.

Constance Ahrons is a therapist and an internationally recognized lecturer and top professional in the area of divorce. She and her colleague, therapist Roy Rodgers (1987), believe that the major goal of family reorganization centers on establishing healthy patterns of relating within *all* areas of family life. This transformation involves replacing old patterns of interrelating with new patterns, and replacing existing family boundaries with new ones. *Over time, these changes help to redefine the family into a binuclear family.* As the former spouses navigate this rocky transition, they must find a way to establish their independence while continuing to fulfill their obligations to their children, their families, their friends, and their careers (Ahrons & Rodgers, 1987). According to anthropologist Paul Bohannan (1971), the co-parental divorce is the most painful, difficult, and complex aspect of the divorce. To better understand co-parenting in the aftermath of divorce, it helps to understand former spouse relationships.

WHEN parents divorce, a domino effect of numerous transitions begins, and these transitions often result in much turmoil for children and adolescents. Although parents can do a great deal to ease the rocky post-divorce road, counselors or therapists can help children and adolscents cope with many facets of their parents' divorce. If you experienced the divorce of your parents, were counseling services made available to you? If so, how did they help? If not, how do you think you could have benefited from such services?

FORMER SPOUSE RELATIONSHIPS

Despite the frequency of divorce in today's family life, the ongoing relationship between divorced partners is often marked by bitterness, anger, hurt, and hostility. Former spouse relationships are especially important to consider because the relationship between ex-spouses lays the groundwork and sets the emotional climate for the newly defined binuclear family (Ahrons & Rodgers, 1987). Research characterizes five former spouse relationship styles (Ahrons & Rodgers, 1987; Gold, 1992):

- **Perfect Pals.** These are divorced partners who remain friends after they divorce, and they try to accommodate their ex-partner's needs so that they can better focus on parenting. In most cases, these ex-spouses have joint legal custody of their children.
- **Cooperative Colleagues.** Following divorce, a considerable number of ex-spouses are able to cooperate as parents, but they do not feel that they are friends as do Perfect Pals. Even though they may still have disagreements and differences of opinion regarding childrearing and financial issues, they work diligently to keep the conflicts to a minimum so their children will not experience any additional trauma.
- **Angry Associates.** Anger is an integral part of this type of post-divorce relationship. Not only is the divorce experience marked with long, heated battles over property, custody, visitation, and other matters, the fighting continues for many years following the divorce. Effective co-parenting is not a goal of these divorced partners; consequently, children of Angry Associates are all too often caught in the middle of their parents' battles.
- **Fiery Foes.** These divorced couples are incapable of co-parenting. The anger is so intense that they will not allow the other to parent—the other parent represents the enemy. These divorces are marked by significant litigation, with the legal battles continuing for several years following the divorce, and children become pawns in their parents' ongoing battles.
- **Dissolved Duos.** After the divorce, these couples break off all contact with one another. In some instances, one partner (typically the man) literally "disappears," and thus leaves the mother with the entire burden and responsibility of reorganizing and redefining the family.

By any definition, the dissolution of a marriage is a stressful life event. There is no question that **primary divorce stressors,** such as custody arrangements, visitation, and child support, are demanding and that they exert a number of strains on the entire family. **Secondary divorce stressors** are those things that occur following the divorce. In essence, secondary stressors are the "fallout" associated with divorce. For example, hundreds of studies have revealed that divorced individuals experience more depression, are less happy, and are at greater risks for health problems than married individuals are (for a complete review, see Amato, 2000). But are there differences between how women and men experience divorce? Is there such a thing as his-and-her divorces?

DIVORCED MOMS

Divorced women—particularly those who have children—face a number of these experiences, including financial difficulties. In addition, they must contend with role overload when they assume the roles of both mother and father to their children. As you saw in Chapters 12 and 13, these financial limitations directly influence things such as housing, food, clothing, transportation, medical care, childcare, and the opportunities for recreational and/or leisure activities (Lynch & Kaplan, 2000).

Such difficulties not only have immediate negative impacts on women and their children but they may also have cumulative impacts on the single mother. First, the ongoing stressful conditions associated with divorce exert negative health effects on a person, causing such things as a lowered ability to fight infections and an increased risk to cancer (Wickrama and others, 2006). Second, the stressors and strains associated with divorce also affect emotional health, and oftentimes mothers experience increased levels of depression, anxiety, stress, self-doubt, and pessimism about the future. For example, after a divorce, mothers tend to stay angrier longer and are less likely to forgive than fathers (Hetherington & Kelly, 2002; Bonach, Sales, & Koeske, 2005). Furthermore, the adverse social conditions associated with divorced single motherhood expose mothers to disadvantaged social positions that include such things as long work weeks and single-handed parenting and childcare—that mothers are often solely responsible for their children's well-being is especially difficult for divorced moms (Wickrama and others, 2006; Braver, Shapiro, & Goodman, 2006).

In addition to these findings, research reveals another disturbing finding: The demands of single motherhood following divorce are so great that it appears to substantially increase the probability of alcohol abuse in mothers of young children (Williams & Dunne-Bryant, 2006). In a study of nearly 5,000 post-divorce women, the investigators found that among parents of preschool children, women reported greater consumption of alcohol than men did. The researchers attach some caution to these findings because they did not assess the mothers' and fathers' *pre-divorce* levels of alcohol use. However, they speculate that an increase in mothers' drinking may be the result of social drinking (such as attending more clubs or bars following their divorces), or the result of a decline in social support; feeling alone, the women turn to alcohol. Because of the ramification of these findings for children's well-being, family and social scientists need to explore whether mothers are at greater risk of abusing alcohol following divorce.

DIVORCED DADS

While mothers' difficulties following divorce are commonly due to financial worries and single-handed parenting, divorced dads' greatest stressors are associated with the decreased contact they have with their children (Braver and others, 2006). A number of recent studies show that fathers are more depressed, stressed, and disheartened than mothers after divorce because of their inability to be with their children, and because they miss their children so

DIVORCED moms often struggle with role overload because they typically assume the roles of both mother and father to their children. A recent research finding shows that divorced mothers abuse alcohol more than divorced fathers do. Why do you think this is? What can be done for single mothers to prevent this outcome?

THE greatest stressor divorced fathers face is the lack of contact with their children. This decreased involvement with children often leads to fathers taking on the role of friend, rather than parent, when they are with their children. This experience is referred to as "Disneyland Dads." What are some potential disadvantages to this type of parenting? Are there any advantages?

much (Baum, 2006; Bokker, Farley, & Denny, 2005; Stone, 2007; Hallman & Deinhart, 2007). Often, the father doesn't have control over how often he sees his children, because frequent contact with the children may be impeded or altogether prohibited by his former wife who continues to carry hostile, angry, or bitter feelings toward her ex-husband. For example, about one-third of divorced mothers move the kids 400 to 500 miles away from their fathers within the first two years following divorce; this drastically reduces the amount of time fathers can spend with their children (Bailey & Zvonkovic, 2006; Kelly, 2007). Other research also suggests that custodial moms discourage children's contact with their fathers by denying access to the children, by engaging in conflicts or confrontations at the time of picking up the children, and by cutting into the time fathers have with their kids by not having them ready when the father arrives to pick them up (Lehr & MacMillan, 2001; Leite & McKenry, 2002). Many times, fathers will reduce or greatly avoid contact with their children in an effort to keep away from the ongoing conflict with their former wives (Hetherington & Kelly, 2002). In addition, some mothers act as **gatekeepers** of their children, but too frequently mothers not only guard the gate—they lock it. A number of recent studies show that many mothers acknowledge that they deny visitation, make it difficult for fathers to see their children, and that they do not intend to share parenting with the father (Cookston, Braver, Griffin, deLusé, & Miles, 2007; Markham, Ganong, & Coleman, 2007; Henley & Pasley, 2007; Criddle & Scott, 2005).

Children's involvement with their fathers following divorce is important to their development. Studies show that children who experience a warm post-divorce relationship with their fathers have higher self-esteem, fewer behavioral problems, and better social, academic, and cognitive skills (Hetherington, 1991). This appears to be especially true for African American children (McLanahan & Sandefur, 1994). Fathers' involvement in the lives of their children matters, because children without fathers are more likely to drop out of high school, become dependent on alcohol or other substances, become delinquent, run away from home, end up in prison, or commit suicide (Parke & Brott, 1999; Finley, 2003).

Unfortunately, however, divorce often brings with it significant changes in the ways in which fathers parent, particularly the noncustodial father. For example, post-divorce noncustodial fathers are more likely to be permissive in their parenting and take on a recreational, companion role rather than the role of disciplinarian (Furstenberg & Cherlin, 1991). This phenomenon of fathers taking on the "friend" role following divorce is so common that some have labeled noncustodial fathers as "Disneyland Dads." While these fathers are happy to entertain their children, fathers who do not have custody tend to be less sensitive to their children's emotional needs and are less supportive of them in times of crisis and stress (Stewart, 1999). This inability to effectively parent may, in turn, contribute to the amount of contact a father seeks to have with his children following divorce. For instance, some research suggests that many newly divorced dads feel overwhelmed with their new parenting role because their experiences with their children before divorce were most often limited to day-to-day tasks and responsibilities (Pleck, 1997). Because of this lack of parenting skills, many fathers take on the "friend" role. Others may completely withdraw from their children rather than risk being inadequate.

Each year, 1 million children experience the divorce of their parents (U.S. Census Bureau, 2008i). Understandably, over the past several decades, much attention has been given to the effects of divorce on children, as divorce is one of the most common stressors experienced by today's children (Shaw & Ingoldsby, 1999). In the section that follows, we'll take a closer look at how divorce affects children and adolescents.

How Divorce Affects Children and Adolescents

A substantive body of research shows that divorce has detrimental impacts on both short- and long-term adjustment in children and adolescents. In some instances, divorce is beneficial to children, such as when there is physical, sexual, or emotional violence, but in most instances, divorce has some negative effects on children (Wallerstein & Lewis, 2004; Hetherington, 2003; Kelly & Emery, 2003; Cartwright, 2006).

THE NEGATIVE EFFECTS OF DIVORCE

An abundance of empirical research concludes that children who experience their parents' divorce are at increased risk for certain difficulties. Post-divorce effects on children and adolescents are broken down into three areas: acting out, emotional problems, and problems in school (Shaw & Ingoldsby, 1999). Children **externalize difficulties** through their behavior when they grapple with the inner turmoil, confusion, anger, and hurt they feel in the aftermath of their parents' divorce. Commonly known as **acting out,** children and adolescents externalize their feelings about the divorce, typically through aggressive misbehaviors, noncompliance, disobedience, delinquency, increased absences from school, and increased aggressiveness (Amato, 2000; Fincham, 2002; Hetherington & Kelly, 2002; Stanley & Fincham, 2002). Children of divorce are also more likely to become teenage parents and leave home earlier (Hetherington, 2003). It is not surprising that boys exhibit externalizing behaviors more frequently than girls. This may be due to boys' increased vulnerability to stressor experiences in general (Shaw, 1993). This also explains why boys experience greater post-divorce adjustment difficulties than girls do (Fincham, 2002).

Internalizing difficulties results in emotional problems such as worry, feelings of unhappiness, anxiety, depression, distress, guilt, and poor self-concept. When compared with children whose parents' marriages are intact, children of divorced families have been shown to have a lower concept of self, as well as a lower sense of well-being, and they also have less problem-solving skills (Gohm, Otshi, Darlington, & Diener, 1998; Parish & Wigle, 1985; Hetherington, 2003). Additionally, children of divorced parents report lower levels of intimacy with parents and friends and experience interpersonal relationship problems, including difficulty in trusting others (Fincham, 2002; King, 2002; Stanley & Fincham, 2002; Hetherington, 2003). The correlation between divorce and internalizing problems is especially high for girls (Fincham, 2002; Stanley & Fincham, 2002; Furstenberg & Allison, 1989).

Is Divorce Hazardous to Your Health?

From tobacco to sugar, the federal government has made it standard practice to warn us of impending danger. But what if you were to learn that there was something as hazardous to your health as a pack-a-day Marlboro habit? Would you consider this important information?

We have discussed the emotional impact, financial issues, and more—but what about physical health? What kind of impact does uncoupling have on our bodies?

According to research:

- Becoming single shortens a person's lifespan by seven years.
- Married men and women are half as likely as divorced men to die prematurely from heart disease.
- Divorced or separated adults are 4.5 times more likely to become addicted to alcohol than are those who are married.
- The risk of becoming seriously ill is 12 times greater for divorced and separated adults than it is for married adults.
- People going through a divorce or separation are at double the risk for being involved in an accident.

Interestingly, results such as these cross all racial and ethnic lines. Couples in Europe and Asia share similar statistics. Things like economic stability and emotional support, found commonly in marriages, allow for things such as better diet, safer living environments, fewer hours spent at work, and more hours spent on leisure activities.

People have only so much stress reserve, and indeed, experiencing a divorce is one of the greatest stressors an individual and a family can endure. To help minimize stress, therapists suggest:

- Set realistic goals and priorities—family reorganization takes time.
- Talk about your feelings with someone you trust, and cry when you need to.
- Eliminate blame, criticism, "should have," "could have," and "would have" from your vocabulary—none of these change the situation.
- Exercise and get plenty of rest.
- Let others help.

Source: Dilulio (1997).

In general, children who experience their parents' separation or divorce have more difficulties in the classroom and performing academically than children who have not had similar experiences (Carlson, 1995). In fact, children from established households headed by one parent or children who live in an established stepfamily perform better academically than those children who have recently experienced their parents' divorce.

Why is this so? To a large extent, the reasons children whose parents are divorcing demonstrate poor academic performance are intrinsically tied to the internalization problems encountered by children of divorced families. The emotional aspects of divorce, such as anxiety, depression, guilt, and possibly aggression, affect the children's ability to concentrate in school, negatively affecting their ability to meet scholastic expectations (Dacey & Travers, 2002). This emotional toll may also affect children's ability to interact socially with teachers and peers.

Shaw and Ingoldsby (1999) point to a body of research that speaks to the fact that children of divorced families often experience a subsequently lower socioeconomic status (SES), which has consistently been linked to poor school achievement. This tends to be the case especially among those children who reside in single-parent families that have little interaction with the other parent. Although some children experience great resilience after family dissolution, a significantly large number of children are not as fortunate.

CHILDREN'S AND ADOLESCENTS' ADAPTATION

In terms of those aspects that determine how children and adolescents adjust to family reorganization and redefinition, empirical evidence strongly suggests that it is not the divorce *per se* that ultimately influences post-divorce adaptation; rather, there appear to be mediating family process variables that account for children's responses to divorce. Shaw and Ingoldsby (1999) outline the interrelated family factors that affect children's and adolescents' long-term adjustment to divorce.

Separation from an Attachment Figure Recall from Chapter 6 that emotional attachment between a child and a caregiver is critical to a child's development. Central to the concept of attachment is the idea that as a result of this initial attachment, children develop a sense of security and trust, allowing for optimal development. When a child experiences the loss of a primary attachment figure, such as in the case of divorce, it may trigger difficulties in interpersonal relationships, including friendships and love relationships (Hannum & Dvorak, 2004; Hinderlie & Kenny, 2002; McIntyre, Heron, McIntyre, Burton, & Engler, 2003). Table 14.1 (page 462) shows us the common reactions children have to divorce, by age group. Shaw and Ingoldsby recognize that it is difficult to determine conclusively whether these relationship difficulties are due to the separation from the parent, or whether the problems are due to the multifaceted, multidimensional family processes associated with divorce and the resulting family reorganization.

The Passage of Time Is it true that time heals all wounds? The effects of **temporal influences,** such as the passage of time and the child's age at the time of divorce, may play a role in children's long-term adjustment to their parents' divorce, although there is conflicting evidence. For example, Shaw and Ingoldsby (1999) observe, "As time passes, many of the stressors associated with divorce are lessened in intensity as adults and children adapt to new living situations" (p. 350). Other research offers conflicting findings.

Psychologist Judith Wallerstein devoted more than two decades to studying the effects of divorce on children. In her landmark longitudinal study in the early 1970s of 131 children from dissolved families, she found that one-half to two-thirds of the children in her study carried with them feelings of vulnerability and fear, and noted that for children of divorce, growing up was harder every step of the way than it was for children whose parents did not divorce. In *The Unexpected Legacy of Divorce* (2000), Wallerstein, Lewis, and Blakeslee discuss a research finding that materialized some 30 years after her research had begun—that children carried with them these same feelings of vulnerability and fear well into adulthood. Notes Wallerstein, "When children of divorce become adults, they are badly frightened that their relationships will fail, just like the most important relationship in their parents' lives failed. Their decisions about whether or not to marry are shadowed by the experience of growing up in a home where their parents could not hold it together" (p. 8).

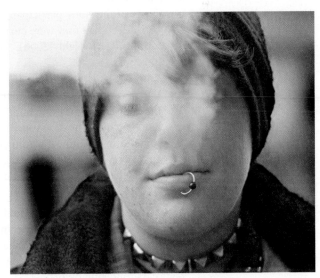

CHILDREN who are struggling with the breakup of their parents' marriage may exhibit external behaviors, such as rebellion, smoking or drinking, and skipping school. These behaviors are referred to as *acting out.*

TABLE 14.1   Children's Reaction to Divorce by Developmental Stage

Age	Reaction
Infants	Infants may react to their parents' distress by losing their appetites, changing their sleep patterns, or exhibiting changes in other routines, such as being fussy during play time. Parents should try to maintain a daily routine, and relate physically and emotionally to the infant.
Toddlers	Toddlers may react to the absence of the parent by crying more and becoming clingy. They may have trouble eating and sleeping, and they may regress to behaviors they had as infants, such as thumb sucking or needing diapers. Parents should reassure their toddler that they will always love her or him. Regular contact with both parents is essential.
Preschoolers	Preschoolers are often called the "forgotten mourners." They know something is wrong and they grieve the loss of the absent parent, but they do not know how to put their feelings into words. They often blame themselves for their parents' breakup. Parents should reassure them that the children did nothing to cause the divorce, and that they will always be loved. Regular contact with both parents is essential.
School-Aged	Children at this age understand that their parents don't love each other and that they can't live together. Children may fantasize about ways to reunite their parents. They feel a tremendous sense of loss and rejection, and they worry a lot about the future, about who will care for them and what will happen if their remaining parent dies. They may have physical symptoms such as headaches and stomach aches, and they may have problems sleeping. They may show signs of depression, such as withdrawing from friends and activities. Parents need to be good listeners and reassure children that the divorce is not the children's fault. They need to have predictable contact with the absent parent.
Preteens and Adolescents	Although children of this age understand the permanence of divorce, they don't like it, and they don't readily accept it. It is not uncommon for children of this age to act out and become rebellious. Parents need to talk about the adolescent's feelings and concerns, not about the problems the parents are having with their ex-spouses. Parents need to make sure the child's responsibilities are age appropriate and not so demanding that they have to grow up too soon.

Sources: DeBord (1997); Long & Forehand (2002).

Recent research appears to confirm Wallerstein's findings. Using data gathered from life-story interviews of 40 young adults, ages 19 to 29, the researcher discovered that although a majority of the study participants were positive about their parents' divorces, the majority also considered that they were currently experiencing negative effects related to their parents' separations (Cartwright, 2006). One study participant discussed her hesitancy to enter relationships:

> I've never really had any boyfriend from 14 onwards. . . . I don't [know] whether that's a reflection of me and not wanting to because of my parents breaking up. I kind of almost think, I've almost got a bad way of thinking. Like, I don't want to start something if I know it's going to be a waste of time, where it's not going to ever go anywhere, cuz then it's wasting my time, I kind of don't ever open up to anyone, so I think [their divorce] affected me. (p. 132)

The Relationship between the Custodial Parent and the Child   Without question, the greatest change to which children and adolescents need to adapt post-divorce is their relationship with their parents. These changes are so significant that researchers have coined the phrase **diminished parenting** to describe this new relationship that takes place during the first few years following divorce. Today, an estimated 13.6 million parents have custody of 21.2 million children under the age of 21 while the other parent lived somewhere else; this number represents 26 percent of all children in the United States (Grall, 2007). In 2007, 5 of every 6 custodial parents were mothers (84 percent), and 1 in 6 were fathers (16 percent). The racial and ethnic differences in custodial parenting are presented in Figure 14.1.

Research has revealed changes in the custodial parent's (most typically the mother) behavior, such as less frequent displays of showing affection, particularly to boys, and less nurturing behavior (Amato, 2000). One body of research shows that the conflict between the custodial parent and the children increases, and the ability to communicate with the children declines (Amato & Rezac, 1994). This study is of particular note because the researchers studied over 12,000 children in all types of single-parent homes. During the first year or so following divorce, many children assume more household responsibilities and often exhibit greater independence. Meanwhile, the custodial parent's parenting becomes more negative and less consistent. Some custodial mothers may become permissive in their parenting style and emotionally dependent on their children. But there are any number of family process variables (such as economic difficulties or support, the mother's emotional state, her extended family and social support) that contribute to disturbances in parenting.

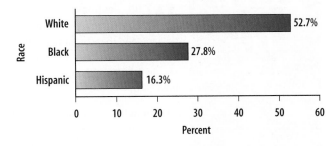

FIGURE 14.1 Custodial Mothers, by Race

Custodial mothers are more likely to be white.

Source: Grall (2007).

The Relationship between the Noncustodial Parent and the Child One of the single greatest adjustments required for family reorganization into a binuclear family is that of incorporating a noncustodial parent into the family dynamics. In the United States, it is more than likely that the nonresident parent is the father. The success or failure of this adjustment depends largely on the frequency of visitation the noncustodial parent has with his or her children. On average, about 32 percent of children of divorce have no contact or visitation with their fathers following divorce, but nearly one-fourth of nonresident fathers see their children at least once a week (U.S. Department of Health and Human Services, 2009). For those who do have visitation arrangements, the children spend significantly less time with the nonresidential parent than they did with that parent prior to the divorce. As the length of time increases following the divorce, the amount of time nonresident parents typically spend with their children decreases (Lehr & MacMillan, 2001).

But as with any parent–child relationship, the frequency of contact and the length of visitations are not as important as the quality of the interactions and the relationship between the child and the parent. A strong, intimate relationship with the noncustodial parent, then, bodes well for children's adjustment to a binuclear family, as it appears that good parent–child relationships cushion and shield against the adverse effects of divorce (Davis & Friel, 2001; Lehr & MacMillan, 2001; White & Gilbreth, 2001). One study indicated that as children of divorce became adults, 62 percent of those studied noted that their relationships with their fathers improved or stayed the same over the 20 years since their parents' divorce (Ahrons & Tanner, 2003).

Co-Parenting in Binuclear Families It has been said that it is difficult for suffering parents to be effective parents. Divorced parents understandably have many adjustments of their own to make following

STUDIES have shown that children who experience close relationships with their parents following the divorce are provided a cushion against the negative side-effects of divorce.

the dissolution of their marriage, such as adjusting to custody arrangements and binuclear family parenting, financial support, and relocation, but these do not lessen the parents' responsibilities in assuring the needs of their children are met.

Regardless of the custodial arrangements, the parents' post-divorce relationship—such as those detailed in Ahrons and Rodgers's couple relationship types—greatly influences how they fulfill their parental functions. A recent study supports this. For example, data drawn from the binuclear family study, a study that followed the lives of 98 pairs of spouses and their children for 20 years, revealed that over half of the participants indicated that their parents got along fairly well, now that the children were grown (Ahrons, 2007). Further, one-half of those surveyed reported that their parents were now Cooperative Colleagues, and another 10 percent believed their parents were Perfect Pals. Only 22 percent indicated that their parents were still Angry Associates or Fiery Foes. Several factors affect parenting following divorce:

- *Parents' education level.* Parents with higher education levels tend to engage in higher levels of co-parenting than do parents with lower education levels (Cooksey & Craig, 1998).
- *Income level.* Parents in higher SES brackets tend to co-parent more effectively than do parents in lower income brackets (Arditti, 1999).
- *Duration of the marriage.* Couples who were married longer are more likely to engage in more cooperative post-divorce parenting (Ahrons & Rodgers, 1987).
- *Time elapsed since the divorce.* If other variables, such as higher education levels and higher SES levels are present, divorced couples are more apt to effectively co-parent over time as "wounds begin to heal" (Furstenberg & Cherlin, 1991).
- *Remarriage of one or both spouses.* Remarriage often negatively impacts former spouses' ability to co-parent (Ahrons & Rodgers, 1987).
- *Who initiated the divorce.* Most commonly, the spouse who initiates the divorce is the more cooperative co-parent (Duran-Aydingtug, 1995).
- *The legal process of divorce.* If the divorce process involved hostility and conflict or was difficult and protracted, the father tends to be less involved with his children (Madden-Derdich & Arditti, 1999).

While more parents share joint custody of their children following divorce than in past decades, as you saw earlier, significantly more children live with their mothers following divorce than with their fathers (Grall, 2007). This distinction is important because family

Should Parents Stay Together for the Sake of the Kids?

Divorce is an icon of the American family experience. Even those who reach adulthood with an intact family have witnessed its effects on others in their circle of close relationships. To use a cliché, "What about the children?"

Should parents, for the children's sake, keep their dissolving marriages together?

YES: According to Judith Wallerstein, children do not need healthy, happy, and affirmed parents as much as they need their parents to stay together. With the exceptions of abuse and severe dysfunction, Wallerstein contends that a terrible marriage is better than a great divorce.

- **Divorce restricts dual parenting.** In many broken marriages today, the noncustodial parent (usually the father) becomes increasingly absent. Joint custody rarely occurs.
- **Children are not as adversely affected by marital stress.** It is often claimed that it is better for children for their parents to divorce than for them to be in a household of stress and discord. Evidence seems to suggest otherwise. Wallerstein's findings suggest that 90 percent of children felt more content pre-divorce than afterward.

NO: Mavis Hetherington, psychology professor at the University of Virginia and authority on divorce, states that although there is a pronounced relationship between divorce and childhood behavioral disorders, over 75 percent of children who have gone through divorce are eventually able to reason through their new lives and develop into normal, well-adjusted adults. Hetherington asserts:

- **Family dysfunction, not divorce, is the real culprit.** Typically, couples do not split over behaviors and traits acquired by their mates in the last weeks preceding the breakup. The dysfunction present at the time of the divorce is often an amplified image of the dysfunction that has been present in the marriage all along.
- **Situational complications are to blame.** Often, a child's post-split development hinges on the environmental complications. Healthy adjustment is very likely, so far as the children receive social support and adequate financial resources. Parental remarriage is also a strong help in maintaining a healthy recovery in children and adolescents.

WHAT DO YOU THINK?

1. Can you think of people who, although products of divorce, have successfully adjusted to life and have lived up to society's expectations of "success"? Describe them.
2. Can you think of people who experienced parental divorce and as a result have struggled to maintain normalcy in their daily living? Describe them.
3. Compare the people you described in questions 1 and 2. What are the factors that may have contributed to their respective outcomes?

Source: Hetherington (2003); Wallerstein (1991).

study researchers have determined that there are considerable differences between mothers and fathers and how they fulfill their parental duties and functions following divorce—for example, the majority of custodial mothers carry out their parenting responsibilities in the same way they parented before they divorced (Baum, 2003). And while some fathers also continue to parent in the same way as before they divorced, other fathers' parental involvement increases, and as we saw earlier, others' involvement decreases.

For the past several decades, social norms dictated that because mothers are the more "nurturing" parent, they should be awarded custody of the children following divorce. Yet because recent scientific studies have revealed that children fare better when both parents are involved in their growing up, legal and social policies have changed to accommodate the needs of the children. Family courts today are more likely than in the past to award joint custody (Emery, 1994).

LIVING, LOVING, AND PARENTING IN POST-DIVORCE FAMILIES

Decades of research indicate that, by and large, the picture of divorce for children isn't usually bright or optimistic. Emerging findings, however, show that Americans are finding newer and better ways to "live, love, and parent" in a divorce-saturated society. Hetherington and Kelly (2002) found, after studying 1,400 families, that the multiple processes of divorce can result in healing and ultimate fulfillment. Their research addresses past research findings:

- *Divorce only has two outcomes: Win or lose.* Hetherington and Kelly (2002) maintain that there are a number of different ways that people adjust to divorce. The process of divorce does *not* produce only winners or losers. Each of these patterns of adjusting are not permanent, and will change over time.
- *Children always lose out after a divorce.* Divorce is not a rosy experience for children, but *over time* children demonstrate their resiliency to their parents' divorce.
- *The pathways following divorce are fixed and unchanging.* According to the researchers, the effects of divorce are not irrevocable. A negative experience can be offset by later positive experiences.
- *Men are the big winners in divorce.* Although women experience greater economic losses following divorce, overall they do better emotionally following divorce than do men. Even though women frequently fall into poverty following divorce, this trend is changing as women become better educated, and as federal and state agencies become stricter about enforcing child support payments.
- *The absence of a father is the greatest risk to children.* Indeed, fathers matter. But it's not the mere *presence* of a father that makes a difference. The researchers discovered that involved, supportive mothers can counter the adverse effects of a father's absence.

Divorce presents many disruptions in children's and adolescents' lives. Some of these changes require coping and adaptation beyond their years, and clearly put the child at risk for short- and long-term developmental, academic, and interpersonal problems. The interconnected family and environmental variables influencing a youth's adjustment and adaptation to divorce point to the need for effective parenting and co-parenting when establishing a binuclear family. Reorganizing and redefining a family from one nuclear family into a binuclear family is a multifaceted transition that requires tremendous efforts of both parents to assure the best interests of the children are met. Former spouse relationships that promote collaborative, cooperative shared parenting foster positive parent–child relationships that benefit both the parents and the children. The divorce transition still involves many challenges, particularly for single mothers. In the next section we'll explore the difficulties faced by single mothers.

Challenges for Single Parents

Households headed by single parents include impoverished, never-married ethnic minority women or teenaged mothers, gay and lesbian parents whose unions are not legally recognized, never-married women who have adopted or borne a child, widows and widowers, and women and men who find themselves single after a marital breakup (Gottfried & Gottfried, 1994).

Additionally, many families instantly became single-parent families when a spouse is called to war, or when a spouse dies in combat.

Regardless of its makeup, each single-parent family has its own unique starting point and its own unique developmental history (Anderson & Sabatelli, 2007). Because mothers with children compose the largest segment of single-parent households, our discussion will center on the issues and challenges faced by single mothers.

As you have learned, family structure is a crucial determinant for the health and well-being of children and adults alike. While the majority of children who are brought up in single-parent homes fare well, there are risks associated with single-parent living. Children from single-parent homes are twice as likely to repeat a grade in school and/or to drop out of high school, and they are at much greater risk of being unemployed (McLanahan & Sandefur; 1994; Hetherington, 2003). And while every family structure is prone to its fair share of problems, single mothers face issues that magnify the stress of raising children. Anderson and Sabatelli (2006) identify the most significant challenges that face single-parent mothers following divorce: changes in financial status, changes in residence, changes in boundaries for children, changes in the emotional environment, and post-divorce dating.

CHANGES IN HOUSEHOLD FINANCES

Another interrelated family factor that affects children's and adolescents' long-term adjustment to divorce is the state of family economics before and after divorce. Economic hardship is a post-divorce reality for many families, particularly for women. Recall from Chapter 13 that part of the legal terms of a divorce is determining child support due the custodial parent. Even if the noncustodial parent (usually the father) faithfully pays child support, however, the amount is rarely sufficient to meet the living expenses of the mother and children.

The economic toll of divorce often translates into still more adjustments for children (Amato, 2000). These adjustments may require enduring potentially poorer quality of parenting as the custodial parent must take on more work, and coping with the effects of financial pressures and strains on the family. While some children are more fortunate and are able to remain living in the family home, the financial pressures may mean that they need to make other sacrifices such as forgoing music lessons and/or sports lessons in order to make ends meet.

When economic hardship afflicts single-parent households, other challenges arise for families already struggling to reorganize and redefine themselves following divorce. Because of the interrelated nature of family living, economic hardship then affects every other aspect of family life, including the challenges newly divorced families face.

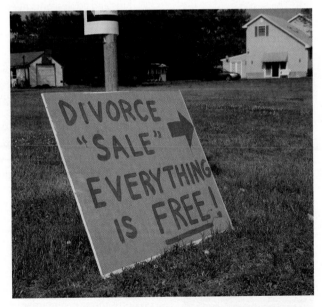

"NEW everything." That's what many people who experience divorce say is the result of divorce. A new home because the single parent can no longer afford the family home . . . a new school . . . new peers . . . new interactions with parents and stepparents. . . . All of these new experiences are what account for some of the stress and pain associated with divorce.

CHANGES IN RESIDENCE

A common expression in the realm of family life education is that divorce brings with it "new everythings"—a new family structure, a new way of interacting with parents, and perhaps at some point, a new family if one or both parents remarry. In many cases, these transitions include relocating to a new home. Unless the move is within the same neighborhood, a move to a new home introduces other "new everythings," for it also brings new neighborhoods, new peers, new schools, and new teachers.

The FAMILY *Table*

Helping Kids Cope with the Breakup of a Marriage

There is no concrete formula or recipe that guarantees that children will come out of divorce unscathed, but there are things that parents can do to help reduce the impact of their decision to end their marriage.

How to Tell Them

Child psychologists and family therapists recommend that, if possible, spouses should be together when they tell their children about their divorce.

- Parents should reaffirm their love and commitment to their children, and assure them they will always take care of them.
- Parents should assure children that they are not responsible for the divorce.
- Parents should speak honestly and simply, but they should leave out all the ugly details.

Keep the Kids Out of the Fight

How ex-spouses act toward each other and toward the children impacts children's adjustment.

- Children should never be forced to side with one parent over the other; they are not pawns or weapons to be used to hurt the other parent.
- Children should never be used as messengers, and parents should never speak badly about the other parent to the children.
- Child support issues should never be talked about in front of children.

Don't Spoil Them

Although it's tempting to spoil children or to lavish them with gifts to help absolve some of the guilt parents feel, child psychologists believe this only makes children feel more insecure.

- Don't relax the household rules or boundaries, and they should be similar for both parents.
- Kids and adolescents need stable routines and stable boundaries, even though they will push the limits.

Put the Children First

Angry, hurting, vengeful ex-spouses can make angry, hurting, vengeful parents. Even though it is understandable that ex-spouses want little interaction with each other, parents need to make co-parenting work for the sake of the children.

- Work on parenting goals together for the well-being of the children.
- Custody arrangements should be centered on what the children need, not what the parents need or want.
- Don't interfere with visitation arrangements.

TALK ABOUT IT

1. What are some ways divorcing families can preserve their shared identity? Acknowledge their history?
2. What are some ways that helping professionals, such as family life educators and social workers, can help families define their identities as they separate and form new family systems through remarriage?

Source: Mayo Clinic (2004).

Recently divorced single parents often find that because of the radical changes in their finances, they are no longer able to live in their pre-divorce home (Kelly & Emery, 2003). Quite frequently, in an effort to lessen the strain on the family budget that comes with transitioning to single-parent living, divorced women find that they are forced to sell their homes. Additionally, this transition involves not just an economic rebalancing but also an emotional rebalancing (Anderson & Sabatelli, 2006). When recently divorced single parents then move to a different neighborhood and into a less expensive home, they and their children are faced with the harsh reality of a new beginning that redefines the family system (Kelly & Emery, 2003). Perhaps Trisch, a divorced woman who is selling her home and moving forward, sums it up best:

> Goodbye to the home that I spent endless afternoons and weekends looking for—making sure it met all of the rigid requirements. I'll probably never find another house like that again. It was so much more than a house—it represented an achievement of a goal, a new beginning of the beginning. And now I've lost it all. Goodbye to the home we were making. Goodbye to the tulips planted in the fall but that we never saw together in the spring when it came time for them to bloom. (cited in Fisher & Alberti, 2000, p. 106)

CHANGES IN BOUNDARIES

Central to the challenges of post-divorce parenting is the issue of reworking parenting roles. And as Anderson and Sabatelli (2007) note, even for those parents who are willing, strongly desiring of, and firmly committed to parenting cooperatively, divorce is always accompanied by greater separateness and autonomy, along with a decline in interdependence—and this change in the relationship between parents and children adds to the other everyday, ordinary stresses associated with parenting.

In essence, the re-establishment of parenting roles ensures that what was once shared by both parents is now covered independently by each parent. Some tasks associated with establishing new parental roles following divorce include (Graham, 2005):

- Forming new relationships with children that do not include ongoing input, support, and the collaboration from the other parent. Even in the best of circumstances where both parents are actively involved in the children's lives, one parent is still absent from the home.
- Creating a working business relationship with the former spouse that ensures successful completion of childrearing tasks, such as helping children with homework, taking them to after-school activities, or taking them to doctor or dentist appointments.
- Establishing methods of discipline that do not rely on the other parent's input or aid.
- Developing a parenting plan. The parenting plan outlines the rights and responsibilities of each parent and establishes an appropriate working relationship between the parents (for issues regarding the children's health, education, and well-being).
- Communicating clearly and accurately to the other parent those things that are taking place in the child's life. At the forefront of such communication are the child's emotional stability and the protection of the child's best interests. Making these the priority of communication minimizes the children's exposure to ongoing parental conflict and minimizes the temptation to drag the child into the parents' battles.

It is beyond question that the exit of one member from the family system disrupts the balance of the entire system. However, if proper care and attention are given to the re-establishment of parental roles following divorce, over time the family will re-establish itself and find a new reorganized balance.

CHANGES IN THE EMOTIONAL ENVIRONMENT

There is no other way to state it: Divorce hurts! Managing the emotional climate of the binuclear family is just as important as managing finances and new parenting roles.

Single mothers' ability to become sole administrator of the home hinges on their ability to manage the emotional climate of their newly defined single-parent homes. In other words, the mother must assume all authority and responsibility, as well as provide love, understanding, and support. While many single mothers rely on their former spouses, daycare providers, or the children's grandparents to assist them, many others decide that if they are the custodial parent, they should have complete authority in whatever decisions are made (Anderson & Sabatelli, 2007; Graham, 2004). This shift in authority allows single mothers to separate from former spouses and gain autonomy. Without this authority, boundaries may not be clear and, all too often children, former spouses, and/or grandparents may undermine the mother's efforts and render her ineffective—thus ensuring that inconsistent, dysfunctional parenting roles are established.

According to Anderson and Sabatelli (2006), fathers also have difficulties in managing the emotional tasks of the post-divorce family. Divorced fathers tend to struggle with managing the emotional climate of the home because of a frequent inability to maintain a sense of home and family, even if he is the noncustodial parent. Typically, when the father is the nonresident parent, he experiences these feelings of loss and he may feel that he has lost control and influence over his children (Kruk, 1991). Fathers will often experience an even greater sense of loss and powerlessness if there remain high levels of conflict between the father and his former wife, if his ex-spouse limits his visitations to his children (in order to exert control over him or punish him), or if the custodial and visitation agreements are not strictly adhered to (Wallerstein, 1998).

DATING

When women and men experience being single after they divorce, many feel a mix of positive and negative emotions. Some choose to date because they simply do not like being alone. In fact, for some individuals, being single is particularly difficult if they never learned how to live as a single before their marriage, perhaps moving straight from their parents' homes to their marital homes (Fisher & Alberti, 2000). But many may find their newfound status to be liberating—a time to invest in themselves. As one newly divorced man explains:

> I've become aware that living as a single person is an affirmation of strength and self—not an embarrassing admission of failure. I'm more relaxed in the company of others. Postmarital guilt, self-doubts, and questions like "Will I ever love again?" are greatly diminished. I am happy as a single person—something I had not thought possible before. (p. 235)

Most people, however, are not disenchanted with marriage and are not content to remain single following their divorce. Indeed, it is not unusual for many men and women to rush into dating following their marital separation or divorce. For many of these individuals, dating helps them fill the void of their loss with a new, more intense love (Ahrons, 1994). The way men and women handle postmarital romance differs, however. According to Anderson and Sabatelli (2006):

- Post-divorce men initiate dating relationships sooner than do post-divorce women.
- Following divorce, men rely more on their dating partners for intimacy and support than do women.
- Women have stronger, more intimate social support networks than do men and turn to these rather than to a dating partner for intimacy and support.
- Men have greater financial resources to pursue a new partner.

- The demands of single parenting and economic pressures leave women with less energy to pursue a dating relationship.

There are further reasons why newly divorced individuals choose whether or not to date. Some may delay dating to protect themselves from being hurt; others may delay dating in an attempt to gain independence and autonomy; and still others may rush into dating and courtship in an effort to quickly remarry. Beyond not wanting to be "alone," some of these individuals may want to quickly re-establish "normalcy," or find supportive relationships that will help them redefine their identities. While the reasons for dating following divorce are complex and varied, creating new relationships helps restructure an individual's social network in a way that more closely meets the individual's changing needs (Anderson & Sabatelli, 2007).

Not all dating relationships end with another trip down the aisle, but about 60 percent of those who divorce will marry within 5 years, and today, an estimated one-third of all children in the United States will live in a stepparent home before they reach the age of 18 (U.S. Census Bureau, 2006 Parke, 2007). There are a number of transitions associated with repartnering following divorce.

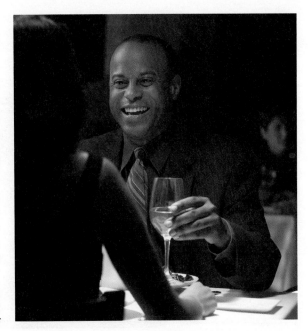

MEN are sooner to date following divorce than women are. This may be because they have greater financial freedom and because they commonly do not have physical custody of their children. If you are from a divorced family, was it difficult for you to see your parents date after their divorce? Why or why not?

Transitions to Repartnering

Stepfamilies are rapidly becoming the most common family structure in the United States (Grall, 2007). Although remarriages are common today, there remains a stereotypical view that these marriages are not as functional as "traditional" marriages (Ganong & Coleman, 2004). To better understand the transitions associated with forming a new family system following divorce, in the following section we'll examine the stages of the remarriage experience, remarriage stability, and the many characteristics of stepfamilies today.

REMARRIAGE

Transitioning to a new family structure involves a developmental process, just as with any other change encountered throughout the life cycle of the family. As you know, with the dissolution of the nuclear family system because of divorce, two separate family forms emerge, creating a binuclear family. When either one or both of the former spouses choose to remarry, a stepfamily is formed. Like many of the family processes we have discussed throughout this text, remarriage is also a process of different developmental stages. These stages include early remarriage, middle remarriage, and late remarriage.

Early Remarriage Psychologist Patricia Papernow (1984, 1993) has addressed the patterns commonly seen in the family life cycle development of remarried and stepfamilies. **Remarriage** refers to instances when either one or both of the spouses have been previously married. As its name implies, **early remarriage** refers to the early stages of the new relationship, and brings with it not only the developmental difficulties of a traditional marriage, but also carries with it difficulties unique to stepfamilies. When one or both of the married partners bring children from a previous relationship into the new marital relationship, the newly merged family is referred to as a **stepfamily.**

WHEN two families merge, it is common for each side to feel that the other is intruding into their family. These feelings often compound the interactions of stepfamilies, and significantly contribute to why it takes stepfamilies two to three years to adjust to stepfamily living.

When two families come together, histories, rituals, and family customs must be merged. As noted family scientist and psychologist Hara Marano (2000) explains, "culture clash" is built into any marriage because of the different histories brought to a marriage. This culture clash within a new family occurs because each of us has preferred patterns of interacting along with shared memories and shared histories—*each family of origin has its own shared identity.* When families merge, members from each family of origin may feel that new family members are intruding into their family, and in a very real sense, intruding into their identity. As Papernow points out, however, this is the starting point for every remarried or stepfamily. A lack of shared patterns of interacting and a lack of shared histories are expected and normal at this stage of remarriage. Because newly formed stepfamilies lack shared experiences, the two families interact primarily with their biological parents, siblings, grandparents, and other extended family members during the early remarriage stage (Anderson & Sabatelli, 2007). These interaction patterns may last for up to two to three years after remarriage or the formation of a stepfamily; thus, one of the central developmental tasks of remarriage is to allow time for the newly merged family system to grow and share new experiences together.

Middle Remarriage During the **middle remarriage** stage of development, which takes most families about three to five years to complete, the family becomes a more cohesive system and functions less along strictly biological lines. In order to successfully transition to this stage of remarried family life, the family needs to restructure family boundaries and identify family members' roles (Anderson & Sabatelli, 2007):

- Ensure that each family member's needs, expectations, and feelings are considered equally. This is accomplished through honest communication and shared empathy.
- Compromise between "old" and "new" ways of doing things such as homework or celebrating holidays. "Out with the old, in with the new" doesn't apply when it comes to remarried families.
- Clarify family boundaries and expectations with regard to the noncustodial parent, biological relatives, and steprelatives.

If the family makes this successful transition, the family will emerge as not only a more cohesive system with unambiguous boundaries but also as a family with a shared purpose and a shared family identity (Papernow, 1984).

Late Remarriage During **late remarriage**—approximately 6 to 10 (or more) years after the remarriage—the family's boundaries and roles are restructured to the point where there is a greater deal of "authenticity" in interactions and shared intimacy within the family system (Anderson & Sabatelli, 2007). If family members are flexible and successful in realigning their boundaries to accommodate the realities of remarried and/or stepfamily living, then closer, warmer, more endearing relationships are likely to form among stepfamily members. This doesn't mean that family living is sunshine and roses all of the time. As with any family, there will be times of conflict, anger, and hurt feelings. There will be times when one family member feels excluded or when another family member feels awkward including a nonbiological family member in decision making or family rituals. In some remarried families, members may simply agree to accept more distant, less involved relationships with one another (Anderson & Sabatelli, 2007). To be a successful remarried family not only requires a realization from the married partners that "there's a history of something that came before" (Marano, 2000) it also requires the belief that trust and understanding will grow as families share experiences over time.

REMARRIAGE STABILITY

In the case of remarriage, practice does not make perfect. Approximately 60 percent of remarriages end in divorce, with an average length of about seven years' duration (Kreider, 2005). The picture is even bleaker with third marriages, which typically end after about five years. Why is the future of remarriage so grim?

There are several reasons. For example, as we just discussed, when couples embark on a second marriage, they often do not have a firm understanding of their identity as a stepfamily, or what it means to merge two families (Gerlach, 2005). Many remarrying partners enter into a second marriage with unrealistic expectations and without a sound understanding of the complexities of stepfamily life. As a result, these couples lack the necessary coping skills to traverse many transitions as they rebuild their lives together. According to Peter Gerlach, a social worker and board member of the Stepfamily Association of America, remarried families also face greater differences than once-married families in the emotional, legal, social, and financial environments of their families. Gerlach explains that there are as many as 60 significant ways a second marriage differs from a first-marriage environment.

Other research suggests that instability in subsequent marriages is the result of a breakdown in the commitment, cohesion, and communication in first marriages (Ihinger-Tallman & Pasley, 1987). For example, some couples use divorce to resolve marital conflict, and others experience deep emotional wounds following divorce. These situations often result in partners who have difficulty making another commitment. Other couples have difficulties establishing cohesion, or the emotional ties that bind families together, because of the lack of a shared family history. Finally, unless remarrying couples address communication problems—near the top of the list of reasons why people seek divorce—they run the risk of carrying the same problems into a subsequent marriage.

According to Gerlach (2005), the essence of remarriage is not really different from first marriages: "The relationship objectives are the same—to lovingly help each other fulfill a set of core personal needs over time . . . while each partner evolves as a unique individual in a changing world. The shared [goals] needed to grow and keep a healthy, satisfying love relationship are the same in both cases." The key to establishing a successful subsequent marriage and family system is a joint commitment from both partners. This will help ensure that all members of the newly formed family system are met. Today, it is important to understand that stepfamilies are not one-size-fits-all in their characteristics.

Demonizing Divorce

Constance Ahrons (2004) believes that because the United States clings to the idealized image of the "perfect" traditional family and views divorce as a dragon that must be slain, when couples do divorce there are few safety nets of support—and this, in turn, is what accounts for the upheaval experienced in divorcing families' lives.

1. Is divorce the culprit of family breakdown in America today?

2. If Americans were more accepting of divorce, do you think that the stressors of divorce would be minimized? Why or why not?

STEPFAMILIES TODAY

Stepfamilies are very common in today's world, but there used to be negative undertones associated with the term *stepfamily,* such as the "evil" stepmother who is cruel to her stepchildren, so often portrayed in children's storybooks. Due to the increasing incidence of stepfamilies, there have been attempts over the years to soften the terminology and to use other terms that do not carry the negative connotation, such as "integrated family," "complicated family form," "merged family," or "reconstituted" or "combined family." The alternate term with which most of us are familiar is the term **blended families.** The Stepfamily Association of America (SAA, 2009), however, disagrees with the use this term, pointing out that when two family systems join together, they do not "blend." Notes the SAA, "A stepfamily does not *recreate* a first family (or, blend into something entirely new with all prior connections severed and the former existence obliterated)." Thus, according to the SAA, to "blend" a family would mean that children and spouses in stepfamilies must lose their identity, their individuality, and their active attachment to the absent parent, to the former first family. All other family forms are defined by the relationship that exists between the parent and child, such as foster, adoptive, single-parent, or biological. The SAA holds, then, that it is more accurate and preferred to use the term *stepfamily.* They also assert that implying that two distinct family systems can fold into one sets the new family structure up for unrealistic expectations and "doom" (SAA, 2009).

Stepfamily Types While the presence of children from a previous marriage defines a stepfamily, the composition of stepfamilies differs. In some instances, members of a stepfamily may or may not live full time within the stepfamily household; in many cases, children are members of *two* stepfamily households. Table 14.2 summarizes the different types of stepfamilies, each defined by the parent–child relationship. Also, in stepfamilies, children are described in different ways. For example, *siblings* share the same two biological parents, while *stepsiblings* are not biologically related, but have parents who are married to one another. A *mutual child* is the child (or children) who is born to the remarried couple. Some researchers refer to this as the "cement" child, as they are thought to cement the relationship.

Stepfamily Characteristics Many students often mistakenly assume that stepfamilies are no different than first families since there are two parents in the home who share in the everyday tasks of rearing children. While on the surface it may appear that there are not significant differences, the complex combination of roles and relationships makes stepfamily living very different from a nuclear family's, as Table 14.3 shows us. Certain characteristics distinguish stepfamilies from first families (Parziale & Parziale, 2002).

The Stepfamily Is Born of Loss. Every stepfamily has one thing in common: they have all faced loss (Wallerstein & Kelly, 1980). Unlike first marriages, a stepfamily is typically born of

TABLE 14.2 Types of Stepfamilies

Biological mother/stepfather	In this family structure, the household comprises the mother's biological children and her stepchildren (the children of the stepfather).
Biological father/stepmother	In this family form, the household comprises the father's biological children and his stepchildren (the children of the stepmother).
Complex stepfamily	In this type of stepfamily, both partners have children from previous relationships or marriage, although the children may reside in different households.
Joint biological-stepfamily	Within this household, the couple has at least one biological child that is the product of both married parents, and at least one biological child of either parent (meaning the other parent would be the stepparent).

Source: Stepfamily Association of America (2009).

TABLE 14.3 The Ways That Stepfamilies and Nuclear Families Differ

Structural Factor	Typical Stepfamily	Typical Nuclear Family
Number of co-parenting homes	Usually homes linked by legal documents, emotions, finances, genes and ancestry, shared history, responsibilities, and memories	Usually one home
Grandparents (living *and* dead)	Usually six or eight or more	Usually four
Physical and legal child custody	Sole, joint, or split; usually subject to legal decree(s) and often legally contested	Shared; no legal suits or decrees
Spouses' parenting values and styles (e.g., child discipline)	Preformed before remarrying and cohabiting; often needs compromising	Evolved together over years; differences are usually less stressful
Caregivers' legal parenting rights and responsibilities regarding minor kids' school/health/custody/etc. (varies by state)	Fewer and less clear rights (stepparents and stepgrandparents); responsibilities more confusing; a legal parenting agreement may exist, which excludes any stepparents	More and clearer rights (bio-parents and bio-grandparents); responsibilities far clearer; no legal documents to enforce or litigate
Last names	Re-wedded bio-mom's names may differ from their kids' names; without adoption, stepsibs have different last names	Adults and kids usually all have the same last name, so less chance of identity and loyalty (priority) confusions
Family-member loyalty, bonding, and cohesion	Initially, pseudo or little among merging families; may or may not improve with time; much more fragile	Generally much stronger throughout the family life cycle; they usually transcend traumas

Source: Adapted from Gerlach (2005).

loss—of a parent or family through death, through divorce, or through desertion. And because divorce is frequently accompanied by relocation, the members of a stepfamily may also be mourning the loss of other family members (such as a grandmother or grandfather, a favorite aunt or uncle), previous friends, their former home or school, their former neighborhood, or their dreams. The grief is exacerbated during holidays, birthdays, school events, and other special family times. According to the SAA (2009), adults and children each grieve over certain specific losses associated with divorce. For example, adults typically grieve over the loss of a partner and the loss of the marital relationship, while children grieve the loss of a parent and stability.

The Family Boundaries and Roles Are Ambiguous. The frequent entrances and exits of family members from the various stepfamily households, such as stepchildren/stepsiblings leaving for visitations or coming for visitations, may lead to indistinct or blurred boundaries. This ambiguity creates confusion and uncertainty as to who is "in" the family and who is not, and causes doubt about family affiliations. Further, the roles in stepfamilies have no clear, traditionally understood labels, no clear definitions, and no clear expectations (Parziale & Parziale, 2002). In a biological family, the role of Mom or Dad is typically well understood by the family, the community, and society. In a stepfamily, however, there is no how-to manual or job description for the roles of "stepparent" or "stepchild," and these roles are not clearly defined by society. Additionally, there are different roles depending on the composition of the stepfamily structure (such as biological mother, biological father, etc.). Further compounding the complexity of stepparenting relationships and heightening the ambiguity is that there is no legal relationship between stepparents and stepchildren: Stepparents cannot authorize emergency medical care, access the child's academic records, or sign legal documents relating to the child.

There Is a Disparity of Individual, Marital, and Family Life Cycles. When two family systems form a stepfamily, an obstacle that all family members face is the fact that they do not share a common history, common traditions, or common life experiences. Compounding these differences is that fact that there will be children with varying developmental needs. It is also quite likely that there will be differences in parenting styles, career aspirations, finances, retirement goals, and lifestyles. As Parziale and his colleague note, when developmental phases among family members are crossed, individual family members' needs may be out of sync with those of other family members, which adds to the stressors associated with role ambiguity.

There Are Several Loyalty Conflicts. Because children have strong emotional ties to their biological parents, their loyalty to the biological parents remains strong. The most common loyalty conflict involves the stepparent whenever children feel that their relationship with their biological parent(s) is threatened as a result of the stepparent joining the family system (Parziale & Parziale, 2002). Another common loyalty conflict exists among siblings. For example, what happens if one sibling *likes* the new stepparent and other siblings *do not?* Is it okay to "love" the new stepparent? Because of these types of loyalty conflicts, the cohesion of the stepfamily is seldom at the same level as the first family's.

IT'S understandable that children may sometimes feel loyalty conflicts when a parent remarries following divorce. Children often struggle with whether it's okay to love the stepparent—if they do, does that mean they no longer love their biological parent? Children need constant affirmation that there is enough love to go around for everyone.

Stepfamilies Experience More Stress Than Nuclear Families. Unlike first families, step-families sometimes face years of instability due to the inherent multiple changes. The first two years are often quite turbulent; it may take as long as eight years for the family to reorganize and adjust. All too often, stepparents and children are immediately thrust into conflicting multiple roles. Stepparents walk into a parenting role before emotional or attachment ties with the children have been established; meanwhile, children are expected to instantly love Mom or Dad's new spouse and to get along with their new stepsiblings. All of these changes and expectations are sources of great stress for all involved. Is it any wonder that stepfamily formation and stepfamily life is so challenging?

STEPFAMILY CHALLENGES

It takes a long time for stepfamily members to get used to the new roles each are being assigned, as well as the new relationships and boundaries intrinsic to new stepfamilies. Because of the inherent "relational overload" that accompanies the numerous and complex steprelationships, stepfamilies face many more challenges than do those in first-time families (Parziale & Parziale, 2002).

Common Challenges for Adults Even though remarriage is rapidly becoming the most common family form in the United States (Bramlett & Mosher, 2001), it still carries with it a stigma of sorts. In general, first-time marriages receive substantially more emotional and physical support from family and friends, as well as from their place of worship. When adults remarry, they inherit new responsibilities and obligations to their new family. These additional responsibilities may cause added strain, and may include:

- *Financial difficulties.* Financial strain is common in stepfamilies as stepfathers and step-mothers alike may be under a court order to pay child and/or spousal support to their former families (Mason, Fine, & Carnochan, 2001; Manning, Stewart, & Smock, 2003).
- *Adjusting to new parenting roles.* Stepping immediately into the role of stepparent is diffi-cult because it requires learning how to share parenting. Stepparents find that they must change existing parenting techniques, developing new techniques that fit the new fam-ily—and developing a new role with the children (Bray, 1999). Because children of divorce experience higher rates of emotional, behavioral, and academic problems than do children of never-divorced families, stepparents have a formidable task as they try to establish a sense of normalcy (Coleman, Ganong, & Fine, 2000).
- *Establishing discipline.* Exerting authority and discipline are two of the biggest obstacles associated with stepparenting. The SAA (2009) recommends that stepparents initially adopt a "friend" role with their stepchildren, rather than role of instant parent. Giving children time to get to know a new stepparent affords the stepfamily the opportunity to begin to build a shared history. Reassuring children that the stepparent is not trying to replace the child's biological parent also helps to ease the transition (Coleman and others, 2000).
- *Bonding as a couple.* It is essential that the couple take time to nurture one another and their relationship. This requires finding time to spend time alone together in order to affirm each other and to demonstrate affection (Kheshgi-Genovese & Genovese, 1997).
- *Grieving past losses.* Most divorced adults are wounded in some way and frequently expe-rience guilt, shame, fear, distrust, and a feeling of failure. Even if the individual is the one who initiated the divorce, he or she may experience deep feelings of loss—the loss of dreams, the loss of goals, the loss of security, or the loss of a fairytale type of love. The sense of loss is one of the most difficult obstacles to overcome.

Common Challenges for Children Children enter into a stepfamily with a history of loss that is beyond their control. They tend to respond to this transition with feelings of helpless-ness and anger. Too often, parents mistakenly assume that because children are young, they

IT may take as long as eight years for a stepfamily to reorganize and adjust to the new family system.

are oblivious to the changes that surround them, or they believe that because children are young, they will quickly "bounce back." As we have seen throughout this chapter, a child's ability to bounce back is largely dependent on how they are parented during the turbulent processes of transition—not only by their biological parents but also by their stepparents. To help children thrive as they transition to stepfamily living, adults must understand the common challenges children face as they enter into this new family system:

■ *Loss of power and control.* Children lose more than a parent when their nuclear family dissolves; because they have no choice in how the events unfold, they frequently feel a loss of power and control. This sense of powerlessness can be overwhelming for a child. To help children heal, it is imperative that they be given control over some aspect of their new life. For example, when children are allowed to make small decisions, such as how to spend their allowance or devising new stepfamily rules, this contributes to their feelings of control and minimizes their feelings of helplessness (Kalter, Alpern, Spence, & Plunkett, 1984; Robson, Cook, & Gilliland, 1995).

■ *Guilt.* Children often blame themselves for their parents' divorce. They may believe that they were "bad" or "naughty" and that their behavior drove the other parent away; they may believe that they are too "unlovable" or that they are too "expensive" for the parent to care for them; in the case of a deceased parent, they may have "wished" their parent was dead at some point in time. It is crucial that parents engage in honest communication with their children throughout the many processes of divorce and convey to the children that divorce or death is *never* the fault of the child. It is also of the utmost importance that parents assure their children that their parents love them under any circumstances (Warshak, 2000).

■ *Loyalty conflicts.* When a parent remarries, children often feel that if they become close to the new stepparent or if they "love" the stepparent, they are unfaithful and disloyal to their biological parent—they feel they have betrayed that parent. If divorced parents continue arguing in front of their children or use the children as pawns in the divorce process, this heightens these loyalty struggles. Thus, the rejection of a new stepparent or a new home may be more a reflection of their fear of abandoning their biological parent rather than dislike for the stepparent. It is vital that both parents and stepparents assure (again and again!) the children that it is possible to love many people at the same time and that having a relationship with a stepparent in no way means that they love their biological parent any less (Kheshgi-Genovese & Genovese, 1997).

■ *Anger.* It is normal for children to feel angry toward their parents following divorce and during the formation of a stepfamily. The anger may be due to the sense of powerlessness and lack of control they have in the situation, and it may be directed toward a parent who visits infrequently or fails to follow through on promises. The anger may also be a response to a move from the family home, neighborhood, or school. However the child's anger is expressed, it is essential that parents and stepparents reassure the children that it is normal to feel angry, and to feel whatever they have been feeling (Kelly & Emery, 2003; Strohschein, 2005).

Because stepfamilies are structurally and emotionally different from first families, both adults and children have difficulty adjusting and adapting to the changes swept in by divorce (Seymour, Francis, & Steffens, 2005). For adults, adjustment centers on their ability to maintain a close relationship with their new spouse. Children's ability to adapt is largely dependent on how sensitive parents and stepparents are to children's feelings and behaviors. "A little understanding [is] the right foundation for the beginning of a strong stepfamily relationship" (Seymour and others, 2005).

SUCCESSFUL STEPFAMILY LIVING

With all the added stressors and tensions so commonly experienced in stepfamily life, newly formed families may wonder if it is possible for family life to be high in happiness and satisfaction. Marriage and family therapists Emily Visher and John Visher (1993) provide key characteristics of those families who successfully adapt to the multifaceted changes associated with divorce and remarriage.

■ *They develop realistic expectations.* All members within the stepfamily understand that it will never be the same as the first family. They also understand that love and care do not develop instantly; these develop slowly, over time, as the family builds its own history, rituals, and traditions through shared experiences.

■ *They allow time for mourning.* Adults and children come to understand that they need time to mourn the loss of the family they once had. By allowing open, honest communication, and by sharing feelings of anger, fear, and guilt, the family begins healing.

■ *Remarried couples nurture a strong relationship.* Adults take time to nurture their relationship and pay close attention to their needs as a couple. It is difficult to be effective parents and stepparents when couples suffer in their own relationships.

■ *They accept that becoming a stepparent takes time.* While biological parents have time to evolve into their parenting roles, stepparents are instantly thrust into their roles. When stepparents do not force togetherness with their stepchildren, their relationships with their stepchildren have a better chance of thriving.

■ *Stepparents slowly develop the role of disciplinarian.* Not only does intimacy take time to be earned, so does the role of authoritarian. Discipline works better if the biological parent takes the lead until the relationship between the stepparent

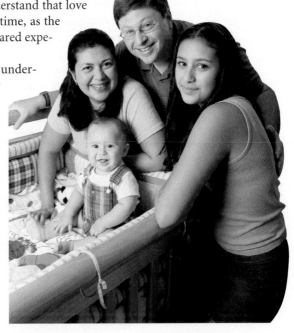

HAVING realistic expectations and acknowledging that love and care do not develop instantly are the foundations on which strong, successful stepfamilies are built and fostered.

and stepchild is stronger (Shoup Olsen, 1997). In successful stepfamilies, stepparents are able to vary their roles, particularly if they have biological children of their own (taking the lead parenting role with their own children but stepping aside to allow the parent and co-parent of stepchildren to discipline their children).

■ *They develop a stepfamily history.* For successful stepfamily living, flexibility is key! It is necessary to give each other permission to do things differently than they did in their first family, from establishing a new homework schedule than in the past, to doing household chores, to establishing new (and perhaps different) birthday and holiday rituals and traditions. Over time, as families share experiences, they weave together their own unique family history—and thus strengthen family ties.

■ *They work cooperatively with the absent parent.* Stepparents learn to make arrangements far in advance of events and visitations to ensure collaborative shared parenting. Stepfamilies who have flexible family boundaries that allow for multiple exits and entrances into and from the family system tend to experience more cooperative parenting, such as is common with African American and Hispanic families. Whether or not residual angry, hostile, or bitter feelings exist, communication is essential.

Those who are successful in transitioning their multiple family systems into a cohesive stepfamily system know that, just as with divorce, remarriage involves multiple, simultaneous processes and is accompanied by common struggles faced by both children and adults.

Family Life Education

Divorce hurts, and the transitions that take place in life after divorce are no less emotionally confusing or painful than is the process of divorce. As noted by the student in the opening of this chapter, divorce is a broken experience that requires time for family members to pick up all of the pieces, to reassemble, and to reorganize their lives. Feelings of despair, disappointment, and helplessness are not uncommon, as it takes years for family members to develop a new orientation to post-divorce life.

The transition to life following divorce involves many processes, which involve emotional, economic, parental, and legal ramifications. For children and adolescents whose parents divorce, there are many negative outcomes. There are also many variables associated with post-divorce outcomes, such as being separated from an important attachment figure, the relationship between the parents and their children, the family's economics, and whether one or both parents remarry. The most critical factor in determining outcomes, however, is the parents' ability to effectively co-parent or share parenting.

Although adapting to single-parent life is difficult for mothers, fathers, and children, the most dramatic changes in family life and family structure come about when parents remarry and form stepfamilies. Despite the fact that popular television shows often portray first families and remarried families as similar entities, the differences between the two are vast. Not only does the family structure vary, but so too do their histories, their experiences, and family members' roles. Becoming a stepfamily requires unique tasks for both adults and children—accepting these changes does not happen over night, but requires years to fully integrate as a family system. Realistic expectations—recognizing that the stepfamily will never be the same as the first family and that love and care do not develop instantly—is the foundation on which strong, successful stepfamilies are built and fostered.

Is there family life after divorce? This is a question that I've posed to many of my students taking my course. I often ask my students to draw a "picture" of divorce. Quite often, students draw a "broken" or "split" home of sorts, with the children residing with the mother while the father lives in another home. In many of these drawings, students draw tears or expressions of sadness on family members' faces. But one drawing in particular captured my attention. It was an illustration of a mature tree that had split, as if it had been struck by lightning or had been destroyed during a storm. In the midst of the split tree trunk was just a hint of new growth—a sprig of bright green, spring-like growth. That drawing captured the essence of divorce and remarriage, the transitions to stepfamily living. When a marriage breaks down and the nuclear family dissolves, the family feels as though it was struck by lightning or twisted apart by a storm. Left wounded, battered, broken, and damaged, many families feel that the family will never recover. Yet, slowly over time, new growth takes place—a new structure grows from the old.

The Reality of Remarriage

Many people mistakenly assume that a marriage is a marriage is a marriage. But when couples remarry, they need to understand that their second or subsequent marriages will be vastly different from their first marriage. As you learned in this chapter, first marriages differ from subsequent marriages in a number of ways. Is it any wonder that divorce rates are higher among remarriages than they are among first marriages? Does the following couple have realistic expectations about their remarriage?

Her Side: Experience counts! I know the mistakes I made the first time around, and I vowed never to repeat those mistakes. A family is a family. I don't think that his children with his first wife will come between us, and I don't think that my kids will come between us. We both *knew* what we were getting into when we started dating each other. My teenage daughter is having a little difficulty accepting him as her stepfather, but I believe that time heals all wounds, and that she'll eventually come around. I think my expectations are realistic. I know it will take time, but I think eventually we will all settle into a good pattern of relating to each other. If I were being honest, I'd have to say I'm more worried about his ex-wife coming between us than I am about his kids visiting us every weekend.

His Side: My concerns are the polar opposite of her concerns. I don't think my ex-wife will be as big a problem as the kids will be. I don't think she's being realistic about merging our two families. I know she wants it to work, and I know that she believes that if she is warm and honest and caring that my kids will respect her and love her—but it won't be as *automatic* as I think she expects it to be. Yes, time heals all wounds. But during that *time* is when the conflicts, the problems with loyalty, learning to parent different children, and learning to emotionally connect with every family member happens. I'm not saying we can't do it, or that we shouldn't do it. . . . I'm just saying that I think we have a rougher road ahead of us than either of us can imagine.

Your Side: Making a go of any marriage is tough work, but it's even tougher to make remarriages work. In considering the couple's comments:

1. What strengths does this couple possess that will help better navigate the transitions to remarried life? What are the couple's realistic expectations?
2. In your opinion, what are the primary unrealistic expectations of this couple? What can be done to help them forge new role expectations, new rules, and goals for a life together as a stepfamily?

Summary

The Aftermath of Divorce: Transitions

- Just as there is no universal pathway to uncoupling, there is no universal pathway to rebuilding following divorce.

- *Binuclear family* refers to the separate, distinct households that form after marital separation or divorce. Two subsystems—maternal and paternal—are now the child's family of origin, and this restructuring from one central family unit into two accounts for much of the upheaval and confusion associated with divorce.

- The relationship between ex-spouses during their marriage sets the emotional climate for the newly defined binuclear family.

- There are five former spouse relationship styles: Perfect Pals, Cooperative Colleagues, Angry Associates, Fiery Foes, and Dissolved Duos.

- Divorced women often face financial difficulties, and these have cumulative impacts on her and her children because the financial limitations influence housing, food, clothing, transportation, medical care, childcare, and the opportunities for recreation and/or leisure. Divorced moms are also at greater risk to abuse alcohol.

- Divorced dads' stressors are associated with the decreased contact they have with their children.

- Although parents have many adjustments to make following the dissolution of their marriage, these do not lessen the parents' responsibilities to meet the needs of their children. In addition to the parents' post-divorce relationship, parents' education level, income level, the duration of the marriage, the time elapsed since the divorce, whether or not one or both spouses remarry, who initiated the divorce, and whether the legal process of divorce was hostile or cooperative all affect their parenting.

- Mothers and fathers differ considerably in how they fulfill their parental duties and functions following divorce. While most custodial mothers carry out their parenting responsibilities in the same way they did before they divorced, custodial fathers are more likely to parent differently. Additionally, post-divorce noncustodial fathers are more likely to be more permissive in their parenting and take on a "friend" role following divorce, perhaps due to many fathers' lack of parenting skills or lack of understanding of child development.

How Divorce Affects Children and Adolescents

- Although divorce is sometimes beneficial to children, children of divorce are at increased risk for emotional difficulties, which they may externalize by "acting out," or internalize as anxiety, depression, and poor self-concept. Children who experience their parents' separation or divorce also have more difficulties in the classroom and performing academically than children who have not had similar experiences.

- The interrelated family factors that affect children's and adolescents' long-term adjustment to divorce include the separation of the child from an attachment figure, the passage of time, the age of the child when the divorce takes place, the relationship the child has with each parent post-divorce, whether or not one or both parents remarry after divorce, and the economic status of the binuclear family post-divorce.

- Although mothers have been awarded custody of the children following divorce for the past several decades, recent scientific studies have revealed that children fare better when both parents are involved in their growing up. Now legal and social policies have changed and family courts today are more likely to award joint custody.

Challenges for Single Parents

- Whether headed solely by mothers or solely by fathers, single-parent households are becoming more common and more diverse.

- Single-parent mothers face many significant challenges following divorce, including changes in financial status, residence, setting boundaries for children, and emotional environment, along with post-divorce dating.

- Recently divorced single women often find that they are forced to sell their homes and relocate to a more affordable home. Unless the move is within the same neighborhood, a move to a new home introduces other "new everythings" as well as the stressors that come with them.

■ Since the interdependence divorced parents once had with each other no longer exists, they have to re-establish their parenting roles to ensure that what was once shared by both parents is now covered independently by each parent.

■ Managing the emotional climate of the binuclear family is just as important as managing finances and new parenting roles. Single mothers' ability to become sole administrator of the home hinges on their ability to assume all authority and responsibility, as well as provide love, understanding, and support. Divorced fathers tend to struggle with managing the emotional climate of the home because of their frequent inability to maintain a sense of home and family.

■ After divorce, men and women often experience being single with a mix of positive and negative emotions. Some may struggle with loneliness and a lack of normalcy; others many may find their newfound status liberating.

■ Men and women handle postmarital dating differently. Post-divorce men tend to initiate dating relationships sooner, are more apt to redefine their identity through another love relationship, experience lesser degrees of work and role strain, and may date sooner after divorce. Post-divorce women redefine their identity through independence and autonomy, turn to social support networks for intimacy and support, and have less energy to pursue a dating relationship due to the demands of single parenting and economic pressures.

Transitions to Repartnering

■ When either one or both of the former spouses choose to remarry, a stepfamily is formed. The United States has the highest remarriage rate in the world, and stepfamilies are rapidly becoming the most common family structure.

■ Remarriage may be run as a process of early, middle, and late developmental stages.

■ Because members of a stepfamily bring into the newly formed family system their own unique, intimate histories, a central developmental task is to allow time for the newly merged family system to grow and share new experiences together. Additionally, the family's boundaries and roles must be restructured.

■ Many people use the alternate term *blended families* to refer to stepfamilies, but the Stepfamily Association of America (SAA) disagrees with this term and points out that to "blend" a family would mean that children and spouses in stepfamilies must lose their identity, their individuality, and their active attachment to the absent parent, to the former first family. Thus, the SAA prefers the term *stepfamily*.

■ The complex combination of roles and relationships makes stepfamily living very different from that of a nuclear family. First, all stepfamilies are born of loss, and the children are members of two (or more) households. Because of the difference in the individual, marital, and family life cycles of the various family members, the family boundaries and roles tend to be ambiguous. Second, there tend to be several loyalty conflicts. Finally, compounded by the fact that society promotes a widespread negative connotation of stepfamilies, stepfamilies tend to experience more stress than nuclear families.

■ It can take four years or more for a stepfamily to feel like an integrated family, and upward of two years for children to be friendly to their new stepparent and stepsiblings. For adults, adjustment centers on their ability to maintain a close relationship with their new spouse. Children's ability to adapt is largely dependent on how sensitive parents and stepparents are to their feelings and behaviors.

■ Parents who successfully adapt to the changes associated with divorce and remarriage develop realistic expectations, allow the family time for mourning the loss of the family they once had, take time to nurture their relationship and pay close attention to their needs as a couple, accept that becoming a stepparent takes time, slowly develop their roles as disciplinarians, develop a unique stepfamily history, and work cooperatively with the absent parent.

Key Terms and Concepts

binuclear family, p. 455

Perfect Pals, p. 456

Cooperative Colleagues, p. 456

Angry Associates, p. 456

Fiery Foes, p. 456

Dissolved Duos, p. 456

primary divorce stressors, p. 456

secondary divorce stressors, p. 456

gatekeepers, p. 458

externalizing difficulties, p. 459

acting out, p. 459

internalizing difficulties, p. 459

temporal influences, p. 461

diminished parenting, p. 462

remarriage, p. 471

early remarriage, p. 471

stepfamily, p. 471

middle remarriage, p. 472

late remarriage, p. 473

blended families, p. 474

Suggested Readings

Gottlieb, A. *Sons talk about their gay fathers: Life curves* (New York: Harrington Park Press, 2003).

Hetherington, M., and Kelly, J. *For better or for worse: Divorce reconsidered* (New York: W.W. Norton, 2002).

Orange, C. *Sing your own song: A guide for single moms* (Center City, MN: Hazelden, 2001).

Ricci, I. *Mom's house, dad's house: The complete guide for parents who are separated, divorced, or remarried* (New York: Simon & Schuster, 1997).

Multiple-Choice Questions

1. The term _____ refers to the separate, distinct households that form after marital separation or divorce.
   a. bilocal family
   b. duonuclear family
   c. multinuclear family
   d. binuclear family

2. After a divorce, these couples break off all contact with one another.
   a. Perfect Pals
   b. Dissolved Duos
   c. Cooperative Colleagues
   d. Angry Associates

3. This post-divorce effect on children and adolescents results in emotional problems such as worry, unhappiness, anxiety, depression, distress, guilt, and poor self-concept.

   a. Cognitive dissonance

   b. Intrapsychic turmoil

   c. Externalizing difficulties

   d. Internalizing difficulties

4. Which of the following is NOT true about the way men and women handle postmarital romance?

   a. Post-divorce women initiate dating relationships sooner than do post-divorce men.

   b. Following divorce, men rely more on their dating partners for intimacy and support than do women.

   c. Women have stronger, more intimate social support networks than do men.

   d. The demands of single parenting and economic pressures leave women with less energy to pursue a dating relationship.

5. During the _____ stage of development, which takes most families about three to five years to complete, the family becomes a more cohesive system and functions less along strictly biological lines.

   a. pre-marriage

   b. early remarriage

   c. middle remarriage

   d. late remarriage

6. Some researchers refer to this as the "cement" child because the child is thought to cement the relationship of a remarried couple.

   a. Stepchild

   b. Stepsibling

   c. Permanent child

   d. Mutual child

7. Common problems children face when transitioning to stepfamily living include all of the following except for

   _____ .

   a. loss of power and control

   b. grieving past losses

   c. guilt

   d. loyalty conflicts

8. The Stepfamily Association of America (SAA, 2009) disagrees with the use this term, which is used to soften the terminology and negative connotations associated with the term "stepfamily."

   a. Integrated family

   b. Complicated family form

   c. Blended family

   d. Merged family

Answers: 1. d; 2. b; 3. d; 4. a; 5. c; 6. d; 7. b; 8. c

Family Change: Stress, Crisis, and Transition

15

It was a typically bitter-cold, grey-blue day in January. The snow on the ground looked particularly bright with ice crystals blanketing the snow. "Diamonds," I said out loud. She didn't look over at me, but looking at nothing in particular out of her car window she nodded her head in agreement. I patted her knee, "Mom, let's not worry until we know the test results, okay?" A few hours later, traveling down the same highway and looking at the same snow-covered prairie, I heard myself thinking, "It's just a dream . . . I'll wake up tomorrow and all this will be just a horrible dream . . . there's no way she has terminal cancer, she's only 56 . . . this is all just a dream."

It was a typically bitter-cold, grey-blue day in December. The wind had a particular bite to it and there were snow crystals swirling in the air. "Maybe we'll get our first snow tonight?" he said out loud. I didn't look over at him, but I nodded silently in agreement. He put his arm around my shoulder, "Let's not worry about this until we hear what the doctor says, okay?" A few hours later, traveling down the highway in the first snowstorm of the winter, I heard myself thinking, "It's just a dream . . . I'll wake up tomorrow and all this will be just a horrible dream . . . there's no way I have cancer . . . I'm only 37, I have four small sons to raise, what will they do without me? . . . this is all just a dream."

This is all just a dream . . .

Source: Author's files

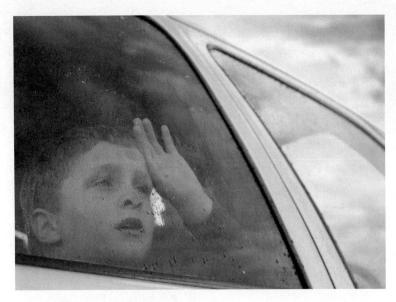

IN the U.S. economic crisis in 2008, 1 in 54 homeowners lost their homes because of rising unemployment rates. Is it possible for a family to rally against crises such as these?

No one can predict what tomorrow or the months and years ahead will bring for any given family. The very nature of the family life process involves countless complexities, and along with it, inevitable change. At this point in our study of marriage and the family, we have discussed that there are expected, or **normative**, changes that take place throughout the family life cycle. Some of these changes are considered "vulnerability points," such as getting married; starting a sexual relationship; having a baby; parenting a teenager (or four!); juggling dual careers, financial commitments and overcommitments; and caring for aging parents. **Non-normative** life events, or things we cannot predict or anticipate, or things that are not commonly experienced by most families, also bring much disruption to family living. These would include life events such as a child being diagnosed with cancer, unemployment, experiencing a natural disaster, mothers fighting in combat, or a teenager becoming pregnant.

Most people know and accept this fact of inevitable change in family life, so why is it that some families stay intact during times of change and crisis (even if they're hanging on only by a thread), while other families totally unravel in response to the slightest hint of change? While some families experience life's expected events, and even the unexpected events and circumstances as bumps in the road, other families are derailed and destabilized during stressful times and times of crisis.

My own experiences with cancer and the near loss of my own life was, without question, a personal life-altering experience. It was also life altering for every member of my family. As difficult as those years were, however, we came through it deeply enriched with a stronger sense of "who" we were as a family.

As we examine the family crisis studies throughout the following pages, we will discover that some families bind together during times of uncertainty, and other families do not "struggle well." For many families today, the pile-up of day-to-day stressors, change, and transition ultimately gives way to crisis—and signals the beginning of the end for the family. In the section that follows, we'll explore how stress affects family development and how it tends to change family roles and family rules. We'll then look at different types of family stress and crises, including the unique crisis of family violence. Finally, we'll examine the different ways families cope with and adapt to change.

Family Change

Family life never stays the same because *families always change.* Marriage and family therapist David Olson and his colleagues (Olson, Russell, & Sprenkel, 1983) delineate three specific types of stress that families experience: *family development stress, psychological stress* (stress within the individual), and *family stress and crisis.*

FAMILY DEVELOPMENT STRESS

As early as World War I and the Great Depression in the early part of the twentieth century, social and family scientists focused on how stress affects people and what techniques and strategies people use to cope with the stressors associated with significant personal challenges, such as experiencing the death of a loved one, or social, global, and economic events such as war or the Depression.

While there is no way to arrive at a generic, one-size-fits-all definition of *stress,* the author of the *Encyclopedia of Stress* describes stress as any stimulus that "affects the body in complex ways" and "evokes complex reactions in the various systems of the body" (McGuigan, 1999, p. 216). Along these same lines, anything that elicits a physiological and/or psychological response—a stress response—to any stimuli is termed a **stressor.** The stressor can either be "good stress" or "positive stress" or "productive stress" (termed **eustress**), or "bad stress" or "negative stress" or "harmful stress" (termed **distress**). Stressors are considered to be either **acute,** meaning that they last a relatively short period of time, or **chronic,** indicating that the stressor is usually longer in duration. Most common stressors fall within four primary categories: personal, social/family, work (school), and environmental (Cordon, 1997). These categories of stress allow us to use the assumption that different people can experience the same event and not necessarily be affected in the same way (Pearlin, 1982). Any number of things can cause "stress" to an individual or family—for instance, what is "stressful" to one family, such as planning a wedding, may be "challenging" or "exciting" to another family. Stress can be experienced as a physiological or mental response to certain stimuli, or it can be experienced as a result of certain life events.

Just as an individual grows up and faces stressors of life and stressors associated with developmental tasks, so too does the family. As you saw in Chapter 1, Evelyn Duvall's (1977) classic work viewed families as dynamic systems that are in constant growth-motion, and asserted that the best way to understand families is to understand the human development phases of the individual, as well as to get a grasp on the stages of development a family experiences. As the many tasks in Duvall's work illustrate, building and maintaining a family is hard work. Along with the transitions throughout the lifecourse of the family, many of these transitions often cause stress; sometimes this stress is experienced as a **family crisis.** As David Olson and his colleagues (1983) point out, using a family development framework allows us to see that families always change, and as a family system grows and changes, there is a call for the family to reorganize itself and to adapt and adjust to the changes. Specifically, according to Olson and others, family reorganization and adaptation involve the following characteristics.

Changes in Structure The structure of the family is dynamic and must therefore adapt to the ongoing entrances and exits within the family system. Family stress theorist Pauline Boss (2003) notes that stress is often the result of family members being added or subtracted from the family system, and that the stress will remain until the structure is reorganized. Babies are born. Adolescents grow up and leave the home. Young adults marry and have children of their own. Parents age and may require care. Spouses may die. And sometimes, children may die. All of these changes require reorganization in the family's structure.

Changes in Family Roles As the family structure changes, family roles change. Over the course of your life, for example, your roles will likely change from being a son or a daughter, to being part of a couple, perhaps to being mother or father, to being caregiver for your aging parents, mother-in-law or father-in-law, and perhaps grandparent. Boss (2003) points out that changing family roles perpetuates changes in previously established family boundaries. Like family structures, family boundaries are in a continuous state of change and growth.

ANTICIPATED and joyous family life events, such as the marriage of an adult child, can nonetheless be stressful experiences.

Changes in Family Rules As roles change, the rules of communication among family members also change. For instance, perhaps you found that as you grew from childhood to adolescence to young adult, you assumed more autonomy and independence. Your individual growth demands that, along with the change in family structure and family roles, your parents must now allow you to be a young adult. This requires that previously established rules give way to new rules that accommodate your newfound independence.

Understanding what is required of families to reorganize and adapt to change and transition is at the heart of family stress theories. Yet, before we get into the fundamentals of family stress and crisis, it is necessary to recall from our discussion about the nature of a family as a system (see Chapter 3) some of the assumptions of Family Systems theory and apply them to the family crisis context:

■ *The family is a system of interrelated components.* A "family" is not a whole entity, but rather a whole composed of interconnected parts. When examining family stress and crisis, then, we need to consider how we relate to and interact with others in interdependent relationships. Thus, if we experience psychological stress or distress in our own personal daily lives, we will most likely transfer this stress to our families. Similarly, if we experience psychological stress in our own individual development, we will most likely transfer this stress to our families as well. This helps explain why the *entire family* experiences the stress and/or crisis.

■ *Family members affect and are affected by each other.* What happens to one family member eventually affects (or happens to) others within the family system. Recall from Chapter 3 Virginia Satir's concept of the "hanging mobile," which illustrates the delicate balance among components that make up a family. Whether the disruption is a normative life event or non-normative, such events have an impact on every member of the family system.

■ *Each family must be viewed as a whole.* Because we affect and are affected by each member in our family, others outside of our family cannot fully understand the nature of a stressful event or a crisis without knowing more about our family of origin.

■ *Each family's goal is to maintain homeostasis, or balance.* As a family undergoes change, the disruption in balance can result in stress or crisis. Whenever a family is thrown off balance as a result of normative or non-normative disruptions either from within or outside the family, the system will do whatever it takes to bring it back to balance. Sometimes a family may erupt in arguments and disagreements, escalating family conflict. To restore equilibrium, families will often employ previously established interactions and behaviors. All too often, families find that attempts to restore equilibrium through conflict are ill suited to aid them through the change the family is experiencing.

Duvall's family development framework (see Table 15.1) helps us to see the changes and transitions associated with family living, and it also allows us to more fully understand that the *entire family system* experiences the ripple effects of the stressor(s).

Stress doesn't simply affect our mood or temperament; it also impacts our physical and mental health and overall well-being. In the following section, we explore the type of stress people experience at an individual level, *response-based stress.* We'll then examine *event-based stress,* the types of individual stress people experience within the context of family living.

RESPONSE-BASED STRESS

Whether we are experiencing eustress or distress, or chronic stress or acute stress, the demands to the human body are the same (Selye, 1982). Physician Hans Selye (1985) developed the three-stage **General Adaptation Syndrome** to describe the physiological responses to eustress and distress (see Figure 15.1 on page 492). Because stress can result from any number of sources and stimuli, Selye primarily focuses on the internal processes of stress. Understanding the effects of stress on individuals is important because most of us live our daily lives within the context of our family—and because of the nature of family as interconnecting members of a whole, our individual stress will ultimately be felt within the family.

TABLE 15.1   The Family Life Cycle and Associated Developmental Tasks

Family Life Cycle Stage	Developmental Task
Married Couple	■ Establish and maintain effective communication patterns. ■ Establish and maintain mutually satisfying intimacy levels and marital relationship. ■ Establish and maintain a mutually satisfying sexual relationship.
Childbearing and Preschool-Age Children	■ Adjust income to include new family member and the associated costs of childcare. ■ Realign marital roles to include the role of parents. ■ Allow for changes in emotional and physical needs.
School-Age Children	■ Establish and maintain effective family communication systems/patterns. ■ Find ways to enjoy privacy as a couple. ■ Support children's educational achievement.
Teenagers	■ Renegotiate parental roles to include more adult–almost adult communication/interaction with teens. ■ Establish balance of allowing teens freedom to become independent with mature responsibility. ■ Maintain financial security and anticipation of costs associated with postsecondary education.
Launching Young Adults	■ Release young adults into the world (college, the military, marriage, the workforce) while still maintaining a home to which they can *occasionally* return. ■ Adjust marital relationship to return to a two-member family system.
Middle-Aged Parents	■ Rebuild the pre-child intimacy levels in the marital relationship. ■ Assure financial security for later years. ■ Accept multiple entrances and exits from family system (children leaving, children marrying and becoming parents).
Later-in-Life Families	■ Adjust to retirement life. ■ Adjust to aging. ■ Cope with inevitable death of spouse and acknowledge one's own impending end of life.

Source: Adapted from Duvall (1977).

In the first stage of stress response, *Alarm Reaction,* the brain perceives the stressor and immediately signals the body to deal with it by neurological and physiological means. The body is innately programmed to react to the imminent threat. Because of our inborn **fight or flight** tendency—either to fight the stressor or run away from it—our normal state of homeostasis, or balance, in the mind and body is upset. The body responds by producing increased levels of corticosteroids (giving us that sense of "nervousness" and/or "anxiousness" when we perceive a stressor), and by increasing the metabolism (giving us that sense of anxious, "extra" energy).

During the second stage, the *Stage of Resistance,* the body continues to battle the stressor and remains in a continued state of elevated arousal. Because the immune system has remained on "high alert" for a prolonged period, it begins to weaken, placing the individual at a greater risk of becoming ill. For example, have you ever noticed that during finals week a great number of students in class or in the residence halls are coughing or sneezing, or have a runny nose, a sore throat, mono, or the flu? With a continuous state of arousal, such as the stress of preparing for finals, students' immune systems become weakened, putting them at a greater risk of becoming ill. If the stress continues, a person will enter stage three, *Exhaustion.* During this stage, the body has depleted every resource it has; often this results in long-term

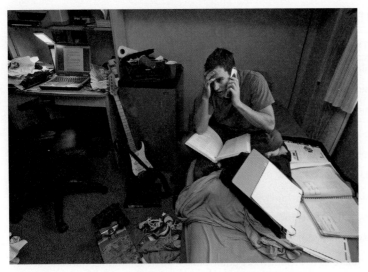

illnesses. People under too much stress may also experience such things as worry, stomach problems, frequent headaches, and the inability to sleep or to eat.

As professor of community health John Romas, and preventive medicine physician Manoj Sharma (2000) point out, though, psychological stress is not isolated to an individual's experience or perception; in order to fully understand an individual's response to stress, *situational* contexts in which the stress occurs, referred to as *event-based stress,* must also be taken into consideration.

WHEN you're stressed out to your max, what are your stress symptoms? Do you find that you are more susceptible to the flu or a sore throat during mid-term week or finals week?

EVENT-BASED STRESS

Any change, whether experienced at the individual level or the family level, can result in the physiological and psychological side effects of stress. Indeed, we all experience daily hassles, such as traffic, that can cause stress. A **life change event,** however, is typically an event that is forever life altering, and that requires significant social and psychological adjustment (Wheaton, 1994).

Social Readjustment Rating Scale To help us better understand the range of life change events and the impact they have on our health, physicians T. H. Holmes and R. H. Rahe (1967) studied 5,000 medical patient records in order to determine whether certain situational

FIGURE 15.1 Stages of Selye's General Adaptation Syndrome

The General Adaptation Syndrome describes the physical reactions we experience to eustress and distress.

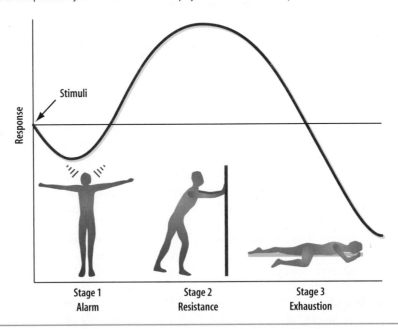

Source: "Stages of Selye's General Adaptation Syndrome," pg. 12 from PRACTICAL STRESS MANAGEMENT by John A. Romas and Manoj Sharma. Copyright © 2000 by Allyn & Bacon. Reprinted by permission of Pearson Education, Inc.

or life events (such as divorce, changing schools, or trouble with the in-laws) created enough stress to cause patients to experience stressors that eventually led to physical illness. To make this determination, these researchers created the **Social Readjustment Rating Scale (SRRS)**, which identified associations between life events and life transitions, and the impact of these events and transitions on individual physical health and well-being. They assigned numerical values to a range of life events, from the most severe to the least severe, such as the death of a spouse to changes in sleeping and eating habits.

In their classic study, Holmes and Rahe found that higher scores indicated anywhere from nearly a 40 percent chance to nearly an 80 percent chance of becoming ill within the next year. People who scored over 300 in the study were linked to heart attacks, diabetes, and depression; people with scores lower than 300 were one-half as likely to suffer from these illnesses. People who experienced daily hassles, such as those common to college students, were more likely to develop coughs and colds. But it is not necessary to come to a total "score" on the SRRS. It is simply used here as a guideline to illustrate the multitude of stressors present in our individual and family lives, and as an indicator of the relative impact of stressful life and situational events. We could probably add items to this list that the researchers did not include to make it more contemporary and more reflective of our lives today, such as cohabiting with someone, roommate difficulties, working while going to school, and single parenting.

As Romas and Sharma (2000) conclude, the SRRS allows us to see life events as stressors that have potential impact on the development of an individual and/or family. Very few major life events or situational stressors (or even individual stressors) are experienced in *isolation*, but are usually experienced within the context of family living. For example, if one member of the family experiences a very stressful event, a ripple effect reverberates throughout the entire family system, causing a temporary or long-term disruption in the balance of the family. As one of my students once commented succinctly, "Something is really yanking on our family mobile!"

If we view stress in this light, then, our definition of stress can be broadened to include the family and **family stress,** which is the result of an imbalance between the demands an event places on a family, and that family's ability—or inability—to meet them. Duvall (1971) describes family stress as "any situation for which the usual patterns of family living are inadequate." Although the demands brought on by family developmental changes or transitions are stressors, many families learn to cope with them. Other families, however, have a more difficult time adjusting. Some families "struggle well" and adapt to life's uncertainties, while other families unravel.

Transactional Model of Stress The **Transactional Model of Stress** is also called the *interactional model* of stress. Rather than focusing on the physiological/psychological effects, as the General Adaptation Syndrome does, or emphasizing specific life change events in the

---

"If One More Thing Goes Wrong . . ."

Traffic backs up, cars don't start, computers crash, financial aid offices lose paperwork and cause student loans to be delayed, boyfriends and girlfriends break up. Life, at times, can get messy.

1. List five daily hassles in your life (such as starting school, a change in your work schedule, and parking or speeding tickets), and five major stressors in your life (such as having an illness or injury, experiencing a pregnancy, or the death of a family member or close friend).

2. How do you deal with these stressors in your life—what are your coping strategies? Have you considered contacting your campus health center to talk to someone about the demands of your daily life?

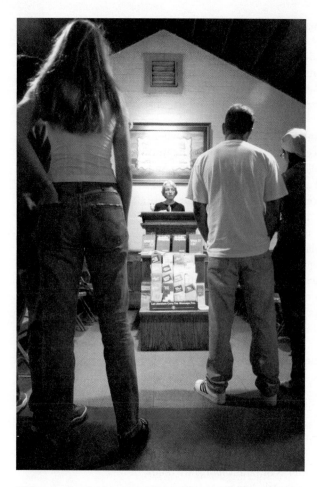

PEOPLE who take control over their situation, such as someone who attends an Alcoholics Anonymous meeting, are said to have an internal locus of control. Commonly, people who possess this type of control fare better in times of stress, transition, and change.

environment, as the SRRS does, other stress theorists instead consider stress to be the result of an *interaction* between the *person and his or her environment* (Antonovsky, 1979; Lazarus, 1966, 1984). More importantly, these bodies of research suggest that it doesn't matter *what* event causes the stress; what matters is the *meaning* we attach to the stressor (recall the Symbolic Interaction framework from Chapter 3). In other words, when we are exposed to a stressor, how do we perceive it? What meaning do we assign to it? How is the stimulus or stressor *interpreted*? What cultural and ethnic factors contribute to how we interpret our stressors?

According to the Transactional Model of Stress, the impact of the stressor is wholly dependent on our perception and appraisal of the stressor (Cohen, 1984; Lazarus & Cohen, 1977). Karen Glanz, a researcher for social and behavioral medicine, and her colleagues (Glanz, Rimer, & Lewis, 2002) provide the three key concepts of the Transactional Model of Stress and Coping:

- *Primary appraisal.* When a stressor occurs, we instinctively evaluate and assess the significance of it. Some of the questions that come to mind include: Is it a challenge? If so, then we probably have the personal and family resources needed to overcome it successfully. Is it a threat? If so, then our personal and family resources may not be sufficient to meet the demands of the stressor. Is it potentially life altering? Is it beyond our control? Is it anticipated? Is it manageable? Is it of little consequence? If so, we can ignore it.

- *Secondary appraisal.* In this appraisal of the stressor, we first assess how controllable the stressor is and then decide which resources we are going to use to enable us to cope. This is the "What can I do?" appraisal. **External locus of control** refers to the perceptio that we cannot control what happens in some aspects of our lives. For example, consider an alcoholic who blames her alcoholism on the fact that her abusive father was an alcoholic and her grandmother was an alcoholic as well. She may believe that she was predestined to a life of alcohol abuse. This woman perceives her circumstances as beyond her control. She blames her alcoholism, or her stressor, as external to her own behaviors. On the other hand, an **internal locus of control** refers to the perception that we are, to a large extent, in control of our destiny. For instance, if this same woman were to break the cycle of alcoholism in her family, seek treatment, and abstain from alcohol, she would have the ability to control her lifestyle. Research shows that people who possess an internal locus of control cope more effectively and efficiently with individual and family stress and family crisis (Bogenschultz, 2005; Gamm, Nussbaum, & Biesecker, 2004; Murray, Malcarne, & Goggin, 2003).

- *Coping efforts.* The coping efforts refer to those methods and strategies individuals and families use to bring order to, normalize, or regulate the stressor. Some individuals and families use **problem management** strategies. These strategies are aimed at directly attacking the stressor or changing the stressor. **Emotional regulation** strategies help individuals and families change their perception, interpretation, and the meaning of the stressor. In my own situation, for example, my husband and I chose to view my illness as a challenge, something that we would overcome together, instead of perceiving it as something that could ultimately take my life. We used **meaning-based coping** strategies, which are those coping techniques that produce positive emotion. By equipping ourselves with as much information about my illness and treatment plan as we could, we were choosing to remain optimistic (Glanz and others, 2002).

Ultimately, the coping efforts that individuals and families use largely determine the outcome of the stressor. If a stressor is perceived as being insurmountable, the stressor may lead to a personal and familial crisis. On the other hand, if the stressor is experienced as a temporary bump in the road on the relational journey, the outcome may be less detrimental.

Family Crisis

While it is a certainty that families grow, change, and experience many transitions, whether the family experiences these changes and transitions as family *stress* or family *crisis* largely depends on whether the family has the ability to adapt to these changes in the family environment.

Recall that in cases of family stress, there is an imbalance between the stressor(s) placed on the family and their ability to meet the demands of the stressor(s). If the family adapts to meet these demands, they will weather this significant, but temporary, period of family stress. If, however, they cannot make the adjustments necessary to cope with these inevitable changes, reorganizations, and disruptions, these stressors may develop into a family crisis. Table 15.2 describes four types of family crises: Dismemberment, Demoralization, Accession, and Demoralization Plus Dismemberment or Accession. *Dismemberment* family crisis depicts the separation or isolation of an individual from the rest of his or her family. *Demoralization* family crisis describes crises that tend to bring disgrace to a family system. *Accession* family crisis is when turbulence occurs due to the addition of a family member. *Demoralization Plus Dismemberment or Accession* occurs when a family is thought to be demoralized because of "embarrassing" stressors, such as the imprisonment or the suicide of a family member.

Like family stress situations, when a family crisis occurs, family members must use their problem-solving and coping skills to navigate the situation until balance is restored. Typically,

TABLE 15.2 Types of Family Crises

There are four categories of family stress, and each stressor places different demands on the family system. Family stress is said to occur when the demands of the stressor(s) outweigh the family's ability to meet these demands.

Dismemberment

Hospitalization
Loss of child
Loss of spouse
Orphanhood
Separation (military service, work, etc.)

Accession

Adoption
Birth (and possibly pregnancy)
Deserter returns
Relative moves in
Reunion after separation
Stepmother, stepfather marries

Demoralization

Disgrace (alcoholism, crime, delinquency, drug addiction, etc.)
Infidelity
Nonsupport
Progressive dissension

Demoralization Plus Dismemberment or Accession

Annulment
Desertion
Divorce
Illegitimacy
Imprisonment
Institutionalization
Runaway
Suicide or homicide

Source: Adapted from Evelyn Millis Duvall and Reuben Hill, *Being Married* (New York: Association Press; Boston: D. C. Heath and Company, 1960), pp. 298–299, from a classification originally suggested by T. D. Eliot.

however, because a crisis is almost always unexpected, families find themselves in unfamiliar territory, and their established repertoire of problem-solving strategies are not effective. This short change of coping and problem-solving skills increases fear, anger, guilt, and anxiety—and these feelings lead to an increased state of turbulence, or family crisis (Moos, 1987). The following foundational theoretical models will shed light on the "how" and "why" some families experience change as stress, while others experience it as crisis.

THE ABCs OF FAMILY CRISIS: THE FAMILY CRISIS MODEL

For decades, family researchers and social scientists have been intrigued with why some families who face a given stressor, such as the death of a spouse or child, or the serious illness or injury of a close family member, seem to adjust while others who face the same stressor do not. To examine this difference, family therapist Rueben Hill (1949) conducted research to understand the stressors that families experienced during times of war. From his early work that examined war separation and reunion, Hill put forth the **ABC-X Family Crisis Model,** still considered a major contribution to the area of family stress and family vulnerability research. Hill's model explains why families vary in the way they adapt and adjust to change, transition, and stress. Hill's ABC-X model views a family crisis situation as a combination of various factors: *A* factors are the initial crisis-causing events; *B* factors are the resources a family has at its disposal to meet the demands of the crisis; *C* factors are the meanings families ascribe to the event; and *X* factors are the outcomes of the event, the results of whether or not a family copes effectively with the crisis event. Figure 15.2 illustrates Hill's (1958) interactive ABC-X Family Crisis Model.

The *A* Factor The *A* factor is the event that initially causes the stress. This stressor can be a normative development in the family life cycle, such as the birth of a child or the marriage of an adult child. It can also be a non-normative event, such as the early death of a spouse, job loss, or winning the lottery. It is important to note that *A* factors can fall anywhere along the continuum of expected family developmental tasks noted earlier in this chapter, from individual developmental tasks, to catastrophic life events. *A* factors are *family-specific:* What one family perceives as a stressor or vulnerability, another family may not. Whatever the stressor, because of the interconnecting nature of the family, it provokes change within the *entire* family system—changes in such aspects as family boundaries, family roles, family communication, or family processes (Burr, 1973). When the change is significant, the stressor induces a disturbance in the family's routine way of functioning. According to Hill, then, it isn't just the nature of the stressor event that influences the depth of a person's reaction to the stressor.

FIGURE 15.2   Hill's ABC-X Model of Family Stress

Why do some families adapt and adjust to stress, and other families have difficulty doing so? The ABC-X model helps us understand the variances in family coping.

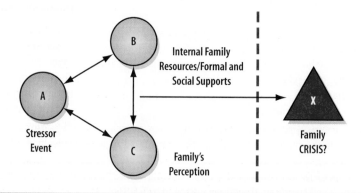

Whether "stress" becomes a "crisis" depends on the amount of disruption the stressor causes in the family system. The *A* factor then interacts with the *B* factor.

The *B* Factor The *B* factor refers to the number of family resources that will help the family meet the demands of the stressor or crisis. Some families possess particular strengths within the family system, such as effective communication skills and problem-solving or coping strategies. Other families are weaker in these areas. Some families have access to extended family and community resources. To illustrate, consider a family in which a parent has a serious illness. Sometimes family and friends may pitch in and prepare meals for the family for a period of weeks or months to get them through the most critical period. This community may also arrange for rides for the children to and from school, take in the children after school, and provide comfort to the individual who is ill as well as the spouse who is taking care of the house, the expenses, and the children. Having friends and family "pitching in" minimizes the disruption—and in turn, the vulnerability—a family may experience during a parent's illness. Hill theorized that the *A* and *B* factors then interact with the *C* factor.

The *C* Factor The *C* factor refers to the definition the family assigns to the change, transition, stressor, or disruption. *This is why* A *factors are said to be family-specific;* whether a family experiences a stressor as a crisis depends on their *perception* or *interpretation* of the event. According to Hill, the amount of change (such as changes in family boundaries, family roles, family rules, communication, and routine) that occurs and induces stress influences the severity of the crisis; thus, the family's vulnerability depends on how the family perceives these changes. Factors that come into play include how families answer questions such as: Are the changes serious? Are they minor? Are they short term? Ultimately, the definition the family assigns to the stressor event produces the *X* factor.

The *X* Factor The *X* factor can be thought of as the end product of the initiating event, the family's resources to cope with it, and the meaning they assign to it—the combination of the *A, B,* and *C* factors. The *X* factor could be a momentary bump in the family's life journey, or it could be a life-altering family crisis. Recall that each person processes and perceives stress in unique ways. Families operate with the same uniqueness and subjectivity, and the outcome—the *X* factor—is wholly dependent on the resources the family has to meet life's challenges, in tandem with their perception of the stressor or the definition they assign to the challenge.

At one time or another, we have all reached a point of complete exasperation and uttered the words, "If *one more thing* happens," or "This is the *last straw!*" We all have felt the effects of **pile-up.** Using Hill's ABC-X Model as the foundation, noted family researchers Hamilton McCubbin and Joan Patterson (1982) developed the **Double ABC-X Model** to understand the effects of the accumulation, or pile-up, of stressors and strains and how families adapt to them. Pile-up can result from either a single stressor that coincides with life events/changes, multiple stressors, or multiple stressors that coincide with life events/changes. Regardless of the nature of the pile-up, this model recognizes that the effects of prior stresses and strains are exacerbated and intensified when another stressor is added into the mix. Figure 15.3 illustrates the Double ABC-X Model.

We have now established that the stressors, or the life changes, aren't necessarily the key elements that lead to crisis. More important is the family's ability to make the necessary adaptations and adjustments in the family system to accommodate the change. When the appropriate adjustments are made, not only are families able to add to their repertoire of problem-solving and coping skills, but stressors and life crises can actually propel both individual and family to develop more intimate, satisfying levels of functioning. Nevertheless, in order to achieve those intimate levels of functioning—in order to survive a family crisis—the family must learn to complete a standard set of adaptive tasks demanded by life's many transitions, changes, and stressors.

FAMILY ADAPTIVE TASKS

Professor of psychiatry and behavioral sciences Rudolf Moos and research health scientist Jeanne Schaefer (1987) created a framework to help guide students of family life as well as professionals in the field of family studies to understand and appreciate those adaptive tasks and adjustments that families need to successfully navigate normative and non-normative life transitions and changes. Families facing change encounter five major adaptive tasks. To successfully adjust, families must:

1. *Establish the meaning and understand the personal significance of the situation.* When a stressor is introduced into the family system, the family as a collective system tries to make sense of what is happening. Charles Darwin once noted that "human beings cannot adapt to their environment alone; they are *interdependent* and must make collective efforts to survive." Sometimes the stressor is of such great magnitude, such as discovering that a spouse is having an extramarital affair or learning that parents are divorcing, that common initial reactions may include numbness, shock, confusion, and disbelief. A family member or members confronting a stressor may also have a keen sense that there is no reality or past experi-

FIGURE 15.3   McCubbin's Double ABC-X Model of Family Stress and Crisis: Pile-Up

The Double ABC-X model helps us understand the effects of pile-up stressors.

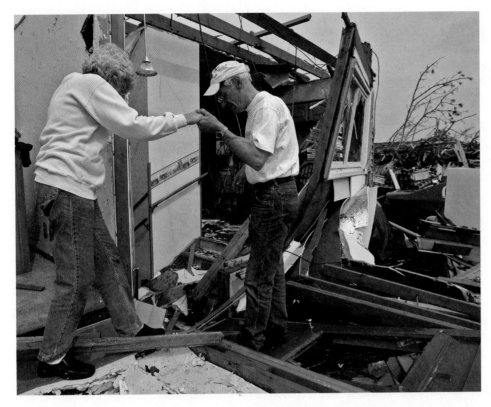

FAMILIES must adjust and adapt to come out successfully on the other side of change and crisis. During times of uncertainty, family and friends provide emotional support and reassurance and help struggling loved ones make decisions.

ence from which to draw to handle this stressful event. As disbelief gives way to reality, the life event becomes clearer and the family attempts to "wrap their minds around it," to cognitively grasp what is unfolding. Eventually, the family must acknowledge the reality of the circumstances; at this point individual family members and the family as a collective system assign significance to the situation. As Moos and Schaefer explain, it is important to understand that major life events are not "singular" in nature. Finding out that a spouse or an intimate partner has been cheating, for example, potentially involves other stressors, such as the realization that the marriage or the relationship is in trouble, the possibility of divorce, and contemplating the losses associated with a marital dissolution. The potential for this type of "domino" effect exists for many life changes. Consequently, establishing the meaning of transition and change is an ongoing process.

2. *Confront reality and respond to the requirements of the external situation.* Stressor events demand our attention: A loved one who dies must be buried and his or her personal items sorted through; a family who experiences violence must cope with not only the trauma of the physical violence but also the need to realign family roles and rules. Moos and Schaefer's point is that sometimes, in the midst of the confusion and shock associated with life change and crisis, families must still cope with the immediate needs of the situation.

3. *Sustain relationships with family members and friends as well as with other individuals who may be helpful in resolving the crisis and aftermath.* This is perhaps not as easy as it may seem. Many times people who experience change and crisis turn inward, becoming private in their grief as a result of their experiences. Whether a family opens up to other extended family members or friends depends on their cultural and ethnic backgrounds, as some cultures and ethnicities are more open and willing to share than are others. Culture and society are the sculptors that shape what events a particular family perceives as stressful (Pearlin, 1982), and culture also dictates which coping strategies and problem-solving skills are appropriate and

FAMILY LIFE NOW

Should Women Fight in Combat?

As you take a stroll through the tents and barracks of soldiers deployed in Afghanistan, Iraq, and Kuwait, you will notice the signs of a new era in the American family: Moms in combat. Should women be allowed to serve in combative military roles?

YES: Today, there are over 200,000 women serving in the United States military. That's roughly 15 percent of the U.S. armed forces. Beginning with the first woman who fired a missile in combat over Iraq in 1999, women are here to stay on the front lines and should be allowed to fight if they so desire:

- **Societal Factors Encouraging Female Participation in Combat.** An integration of women into the military is merely a reflection of current society. Gender segregation is not as prevalent today. Women are waiting longer to wed. It is illegal to discriminate against women in civilian society. All of these factors make gender integration in the military a given.
- **The Changing Face of War.** War today is less *Braveheart* and more *Matrix;* computer technology, miniaturization, and other new tactics make war less brawn and more brain. Women are not fighting bayonet to bayonet.
- **Lack of Recruits.** Recruiters are having more and more difficulty finding men to fill jobs as mechanics, analysts, and engineers, necessitating the use of more women in these and other roles.

NO: Motherhood is crucial to healthy children and the United States. Therefore, the military should not purposely place young women, especially mothers, in harm's way. This is because:

- **It's Against Common Understanding.** The protection of motherhood and of children is one of the oldest ideas in humanity; some argue that it is instinctual.
- **Children Need Moms at Home.** In the event of a child losing a mother, of course the best person to fill the motherly role is a healthy and loving father; however, the two are not interchangeable. Children especially need their mothers up through age 3. Separation due to military deployment, often lasting several months to a year or longer, widens the risks these children face in their development.
- **The United States Is Unique in Enlisting Women.** Taking the brutality and insensitivity of the Soviet military and the totalitarian notions of the Baathist Iraqi army into consideration, neither of these nations allow women into combat. Even Sweden and other egalitarian European nations will not let women serve in combat roles. The United States is at the cutting edge when it comes to socially damaging military policies.

WHAT DO YOU THINK?

1. How might the presence of women affect the job of the American military, or does it?
2. Imagine you are a single mother about to deploy into military action. How might you feel about your son or daughter not being with you for a year or more?
3. Discuss what unique values and skills women might bring to the battlefield. Can you think of ways that having women fighting for our country would be valuable?

Sources: Carlson (2003); Rivers (2003).

acceptable to use (Cordon, 1997). Moos and Schaefer suggest that these interpersonal relationships often "help individuals obtain information necessary to make wise decisions, find emotional support for them, and secure reassurance about the problems they face" (p. 12).

4. *Preserve a reasonable emotional balance by managing distressful feelings in response to the situation.* Life transitions and change are often accompanied by powerful, sometimes overwhelming, emotions. According to Moos and Schaefer, the feelings of anger, guilt, self-blame, resentment, fear, anxiety, worry, hopelessness, and helplessness may be overpowering. Being able to maintain some level of emotional balance is necessary in order for a family to adapt to the change and maintain a sense of hope, even when that hope is temporarily overshadowed by the circumstances.

5. *Preserve a satisfactory self-image and maintain a sense of competence and mastery.* It is important to maintain a sense of confidence in the family's ability to adapt to, adjust to, and overcome life's challenges; the family must have a sense of an internal locus of control. When families are able to recognize that *all* families face struggles and challenges, with sufficient support networks and time, *all* families can successfully navigate change.

No family is immune from stress, change, and transition. Perhaps now you have a better understanding of why some families weather the storms of crisis and change and come out stronger, and why other families can experience similar situations and circumstances, only to become weaker or dissolve altogether. You should now understand how the family's perception of the event and the ability of family members to face it head on, while making the necessary adjustments within the family system, help push the family toward adaptation. When lines of communication remain open among family members and friends, and when these individuals are able to simultaneously accept help and yet do what they can for themselves, they are able to avoid crisis and manage stress. According to family sociologist Ronald L. Pitzer (2004),

> In every life crisis [and change] there is danger and opportunity . . . a turning point for better or worse. Things will never be quite the same again. They may not necessarily be worse; perhaps they will be better, but they will definitely be different. Though not entirely masters of our fate, neither are we prisoners.

Family Coping and Resilience

Finding a way to cope with the pile-up of daily stressors and transcending profound life crises is possible. Yet, to overcome the stresses and crises many families experience, family members must have an awareness of those behaviors that promote coping and resiliency to help lessen the influence and impact of a quickly changing, demanding, difficult life circumstance.

FAMILY COPING

A family's ability to cope effectively in the face of adversity and change increases if the family possesses a variety of coping strategies. By using personal, family, and community resources, families are better able to make the necessary adaptations to reduce the impact of stressors. Rudolf Moos and Jeanne Schaefer (1987) provide an overview of the major types of **family coping skills** that families tend to use in times of change and crisis:

Appraisal-Focused Coping With **appraisal-focused coping,** families try to understand why the crisis occurred and to find meaning in the circumstances that caused the crisis. Skills needed include the ability to analyze the situation logically and to prepare mentally for certain events to unfold. **Cognitive redefinition** occurs when families attempt to reframe the life

IN an attempt to cope with the tragic murder of his daughter by a convicted sex offender, Mark Lunsford pushed for federal legislation—Jessica's Law—that would mandate that convicted sex offenders who have been released from prison wear electronic monitoring devices. This type of coping strategy following a tragedy is called *problem-focused coping*.

event or stressor in ways that are more favorable. If a spouse loses a job, for example, a family might reframe the situation by saying, "Well, at least she has her health." This type of coping mechanism appears to take the "sting" out of the reality/threat of the situation. **Cognitive avoidance** or **denial** is an attempt to deny the seriousness of the situation, saying, for example, "He isn't cheating on me—I'm sure there is a reasonable explanation as to why they were together."

Problem-Focused Coping The **problem-focused coping** strategy allows the family to confront the reality of the crisis head-on by seeking and obtaining information about the crisis, thereby allowing family members to regain a sense of control over their situation. Families who lose a child to a violent act, for example, might petition lawmakers to create legislation to protect other children from similar acts of violence, such as Mothers Against Drunk Driving (MADD). In cases such as these, families seek the support from the community as well from family members. Problem-solving actions are concrete, tangible ways of meeting the demands of the crisis that provide a sense of competence and that bolster the family's esteem.

Emotion-Focused Coping Family crises often evoke a wide range of feelings and emotions. In many cases, these feelings and emotions are so new that just experiencing them produces fear and anxiety. To manage their feelings, families might develop **emotion-focused coping** skills or capacities to maintain hope. One coping strategy families develop is **progressive desensitization,** where family members gradually allow themselves increasing exposure to the varying aspects of the stressor. This was evidenced after the attacks of September 11, 2001, when family members of those who lost their lives in the Twin Towers ventured to "Ground Zero." **Emotional discharge,** another coping skill, is just what the term implies—venting! Emotional discharge entails venting anger, frustration, confusion, disappointment, hatred, and despair in response to tragic or sudden and unexpected news. While some families tend to vent their emotions, other families use humor. All of these strategies have one goal—to reduce the tension produced by the stressor event. **Resigned acceptance** occurs when the family ultimately accepts the situation and recognizes that nothing will change the course their family life has taken.

FAMILY RESILIENCE

Family resilience refers to a family's ability to function in a healthy fashion during times of change, stress, adversity, crisis, and transition. Successful adaptation to periods of family stress and crisis involves resilience, and a certain "hardiness" that allows the family to "withstand and rebound from disruptive life changes" (Walsh, 2003, p. 1). Often, a crisis serves as a wake-up call to the family. Confronted with a crisis, family members often reevaluate their priorities and tend to invest more deeply in meaningful relationships and life pursuits. The crisis may even serve as a time of personal and relational growth, as the newfound personal exploration that accompanies crises can often help family members "discover or develop new insights and abilities . . . through weathering a crisis together, relationships [can be] enriched and more loving than they might otherwise have been" (Walsh, 2003).

KEY FAMILY RESILIENCE PROCESSES

Family resilience is reinforced by numerous family resilience processes that help guide families through the times of change and challenge. These processes also help foster a speedier recovery and help family members create deeper interpersonal relationships following the stressor or crisis event (Cowan, Cowan, & Schultz, 1996). By drawing from these family resiliency resources, the family system can "rally in times of crisis, buffer stress, reduce the risk of dysfunction, and support optimal adaptation—emerge stronger and more resourceful in meeting future challenges" (Walsh, 2003, p. 3). Professor of psychiatry and co-director of the University of Chicago's Center for Family Health, Froma Walsh (2003) refers to a number of empirical family stress/crisis research findings and delineates the key processes in family resilience:

Family Belief System and Spirituality A family's belief system has a powerful effect in how a stressor, such as the loss of a job, or a tragedy, such as the death of a child, is viewed. The belief system informs the meaning the family assigns to the event. It also determines if a family has a shared meaning or a shared reality. Walsh refers to empirical research, which suggests that family belief systems help families organize their family processes and their approaches to family crisis and change; this, in turn, fosters resiliency by promoting problem solving, healing, and growth.

In addition, medical studies consistently offer evidence that spiritual beliefs and the practice of faith, prayer, and other spiritual rituals not only help families frame their life changes and challenges with shared meaning and purpose but they also give meaning to situations that are "beyond ourselves." For example, we may be able to tap into resources to help empower us to leave an abusive relationship, but some of life's challenges are beyond us. Walsh further notes that cultural, ethnic, and religious beliefs and traditions help families find strength, comfort, and guidance, and ultimately facilitate passage through life's transitions.

Making Meaning of Adversity As we discussed earlier, the meaning a family attaches to family change and challenge greatly influences how families cope and adapt to the life event. Families who approach change as a *shared challenge,* as opposed to an individual's problem, have an enhanced ability to overcome adversity. Walsh notes that highly functioning and healthy functioning families understand that becoming a family entails continuous growth and motion across the family's life cycle. The family researcher notes,

> A family life-cycle orientation helps [family] members see disruptive transitions as *milestones* in their shared life passage. By normalizing and contextualizing distress,
>
> family members can enlarge their perspective to see their reactions and difficulties as understandable. . . . The tendency for blame [and] shame is reduced in viewing their complicated feelings and dilemmas as "normal," common, and *expectable* among families facing similar predicaments. (italics mine)

Highly functioning families also have a positive view of life. Even in the midst of the grimmest circumstances, these families remain optimistic and maintain a positive outlook rather than prematurely giving up and giving in. This "can-do" spirit promotes shared confidence and encouragement, bolsters courage and determination, and fuels shared initiative and perseverance—all "hallmarks" of family resilience (Walsh, 2003).

FOR many people, a spiritual belief system helps them cope through times of crisis. Research indicates that spirituality helps families to be more resilient to the effects of change or crisis.

Flexibility Walsh refers to this family process as the ability to "bounce forward," or to change whatever needs to be changed in the family system in order to accommodate new challenges. This reorganization of the family system allows families to reconstruct and recalibrate what is "normal," and allows members to adjust their interactions and behaviors to allow the current conditions to fit into the family's daily life. Flexibility and adaptability are key factors in family resilience.

The FAMILY *Table*

Young Families and Stress Management

Bryan and Misty have been married for almost 14 years and have four children under the age of 9. To them, life is very good. That's not to say, however, that there aren't challenges. Bryan works a full-time career as a campus chaplain, and Misty home-schools all of their children. The house needs repairs, the laundry needs washing, the bills need to be paid, the kids need time, and Bryan and Misty need . . . each other.

Stress takes its toll on all families, particularly young families. School competes with parenting competes with work competes with . . . and on it goes. Young families need to be intentional when dealing with stress.

Financial

- *Plan ahead for all spending activities.* Set aside a place in your budget for leisure and rest. Extravagance is not necessary—a simple trip to the zoo or a "date night" twice a month may do wonders for young couples and families.
- *Live within your means.* Spend no more than you earn, save no less than what you are able. Simplicity may be more elegant than you think.

Time

- *Set priorities.* Decide for your family a "pecking order" for time consumption. For example, when work activities and family needs conflict, make decisions based on the principles you and your spouse set ahead of time.
- *Keep "organized" activities to a minimum.* As children enter school, more and more activities compete against family time. Soccer, play practice, recitals, and the like can wear families down. Extracurricular activities are a wonderful tool for socialization for your children, but they will never take the place of quality family time.
- *Make reservations for romance.* Children are affected by the level of emotional intimacy shared by their parents. Make time for special times of togetherness, be they date nights on a regular basis or even one hour of quiet time together after the kids go to bed.

Relationships

- *Make friends.* Get to know some new neighbors. Invite someone over to dinner. Offer to babysit a friend's children for a night in exchange for another night when they can watch yours.
- *Connect with extended family.* E-mail and cell phones make it easier than ever to connect (or perhaps *re*-connect) with family and friends you haven't seen in awhile.

TALK
ABOUT IT

1. What are the main instigators of stress in your life right now? How can these be adjusted, limited, or prioritized?
2. Take time to prioritize the important things in your life. Where do things such as extended family, work, leisure, and school fit in?

Source: Managing Stress in Young Families (2008).

Communication In determining those factors that foster family resiliency, Walsh posits that the family communication processes of bringing clarity to the situation, encouraging open emotional expression by all family members, and promoting collaborative problem solving are each key elements. For example, *delivering clear messages* removes any ambiguity that might exist; this, in turn, helps to facilitate the meaning the family assigns to the situation and also promotes informed decision making and problem solving. Walsh notes that allowing *open emotional expression* promotes a family climate of trust, empathy, and tolerance. Further, when family members cannot or are not allowed to be open with their feelings, self-destructive behaviors may result. *Collaborative problem solving* helps facilitate "bouncing forward." Families who share in decision making and conflict resolution promote resiliency by setting clear goals and by taking the necessary steps toward meeting these goals.

Walsh's work presents for us an empirically based resiliency framework that allows us to see the importance of fostering a strong, healthy family system that helps families navigate the normative and non-normative twists and turns that naturally accompany family life and intimate relationships. This framework is based on the basic family system premise that takes into account the interconnections that exist between family members, and the idea that key family processes influence adaptation and adjustment for each family member. Furthermore, the resiliency framework supports families' efforts to "work well, play well, and love well." According to Walsh, understanding the importance of a shared perception of the situation, shared hope, shared resources, and a shared commitment to struggle together may ultimately result in personal growth, and surprisingly deep levels of intimacy. "In bouncing forward . . . each family must find its own pathways through adversity, fitting their situation, their cultural orientation, and their personal strengths and resources. Families build on small successes and use failures as learning experiences" (p. 15).

The Crisis of Family Violence

Divorce. Poverty. Suicide. Illness. Sexual violence. Mental illness. Family separation because of war. Bankruptcy. Foreclosure. Job loss. Families today are experiencing a wide variety of changes, transitions, and challenges, and are often called on to confront simultaneous challenges. Entire chapters could be written about dealing with each of these family crises, but an increasingly widespread social problem in the United States demands our attention: family violence. Today, in the United States alone, over 25,000 women will find refuge in a domestic violence shelter as the result of having been severely abused by their male intimate partner; slightly over 19,000 children will have witnessed the violence taking place in their homes (National Network to End Domestic Violence, 2007).

In this section, we'll take a close look at the number of family members who were battered in the United States over a five-year period. It is important to keep in mind that behind the numbers are countless lives that are, undeniably, forever changed because of the violence committed against them. We begin by considering the following experience of a college student (Welch, 2004).

Melanie is a 20-year-old university sophomore. She carries a pretty full class load, she juggles her academic load with her job responsibilities, and she tries to find time to be with her fiancé, friends, and family. She dreads finals week. But Melanie lives with past childhood experiences that make her day-to-day college life

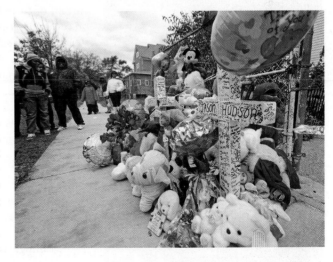

NO one is exempt from family violence. In 2008, *American Idol* contestant and Oscar winning star of *DreamGirls*, Jennifer Hudson, lost her mother, brother, and 7-year-old nephew as the result of domestic homicides. Hudson's former brother-in-law is charged with their murders.

tougher to handle than that of many students. From the age of 10, her stepfather repeatedly sexually assaulted her. She recalls:

> When I was in fourth grade, my step-dad one morning before work and after my mom had already left for work sexually molested me at least 30 or 40 times. [In my 7th-grade year] it was at least once or twice a week during that time period. . . . It was always after my mom went to bed . . . he came into my room and then. . . .
>
> Flashbacks still haunt me . . . where I wake up in the middle of the night, curled up in a ball because I'm scared and I can still, after all these years, feel him on my skin . . . it's like, you wake up and you know he's in the room with you. . . . Even though I'm in college now, there are some nights I can't sleep, and I'm still absolutely terrified of someone who is dead.
>
> I'm engaged and my wedding is less than a month away. [Aside from the normal fears of getting married] I also have to deal with, if Danny holds me a certain way, or touches me a certain way, I remember something that Alan did to me. . . . It's so unfair that Alan stole that part away from Danny, that there are some things that Danny can't do with me because Alan did them to me. I am absolutely terrified because of what happened to me when I was 10 and then when I was 14. Things like this stay with you. . . .

The effects are long lasting.

DOMESTIC VIOLENCE

Violence that takes place in the home is a prevalent, multifaceted social ailment in the United States. Contributing to these assaults are individual factors, such as family of origin patterns, psychopathology, mental illness, and genetic causes; community factors, such as poverty, educational levels, absent or inaccessible family services; and cultural factors, such as media influences.

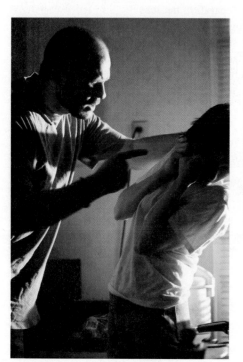

EACH year in the United States, over 3 million children witness their mothers being abused by her intimate partner.

Domestic violence, or **family violence,** is violence perpetrated against family members by an offender who is related to the victim either biologically or legally, such as by marriage or through adoption (U.S. Department of Justice, 2009). Although most people think of family violence as something that takes place between intimate partners and children, the people who carry out family violence—the **batterers**—include current or former spouses, parents or adoptive parents, legal guardians or foster parents, biological or adopted children, current or former stepchildren, a sibling, grandchildren, grandparents, in-laws, or other relatives, such as aunts, uncles, nephews, and nieces.

Domestic violence is an umbrella term that encompasses any behavior designed to intentionally inflict emotional, sexual, or physical harm. Acts of domestic or family violence may result in harming children, intimate partners (spouse, cohabiting partner, gay or lesbian partner), and/or elderly family members. There are three broad categories of domestic violence:

- *Physical violence* includes such acts as hitting, punching, pushing, slapping, biting, or throwing something at the victim.
- *Emotional violence* includes such acts as controlling the amount of contact a family member has with family and friends, name-calling, constant criticism, threats to leave the partner or throw him or her out, displays of intense jealousy/accusations that one is being unfaithful, controlling the spending and distribution of money, excessive rule-making, and threats of physical or sexual harm.

Know the Signs of an Abusive Partner

Becky lives in fear. She has been living with her boyfriend, Tony, for three years. They have a child together, and another one on the way. Instead of enjoying affection and security with her mate, Becky suffers emotional abuse and physical violence. Tragically, she is caught between her love for the way things used to be with Tony and the desire for her and her children to live free from abuse. She wants out, but Tony has threatened much more, even the unspeakable, if she leaves or if the authorities are brought in.

Everyone has a right not to be abused in a relationship. *Abuse is not inevitable,* and there are ways to minimize your risk of encountering abuse in your relationships.

Is Your Partner Abusive?

Following are signs that you may be in an abusive relationship. Pay attention to these signs—they don't go away, they don't get better. If he promises it will never happen again, just remember: IT WILL.

- **Overly protective mannerisms.** Your boyfriend berates your friends and tries to keep you from seeing them. He repeatedly asks for detailed descriptions of who you were with, where you went, and why you were with them.
- **Problems with anger.** Trivial and mundane things set him off. He has random and erratic mood swings, putting you at the mercy of his emotional states.
- **Rigidity and belligerence.** Instead of a balanced view of relationship roles, he insists on defining the relationship in his terms, and his terms only. He ignores your needs and forges ahead with his desires.
- **Highly critical.** He is always making comments about your appearance. Healthy relationships are affirming relationships.

If you are currently in an abusive relationship, it is important that you take measures to ensure your own safety and that of any children that are in the home. Finances, counseling, and possible reconciliation (if possible) are all details that can be worked out later. *It is imperative that you remove yourself from the abuse.*

- Put together a list of people you can call (family, friends, clergy, etc.) when faced with an abusive situation.
- Make known to your list of friends a clue, sign, or code word that will discreetly notify them that you are being abused and need assistance immediately.
- When an argument occurs, find a safe place to have it. Rooms with no exits, kitchens with knives, or rooms without phones are not good places to have an argument with an abusive partner.

Once you have left an abusive situation, seek help to ensure the abuse never happens again. In addition to counseling for you and any children that have been involved, you may want to contact your local law enforcement office for suggestions on personal safety after you have left a violent relationship.

Source: National Coalition Against Domestic Violence (2005).

- *Sexual violence* includes marital rape (unwanted, forcible sex by a person's marital partner), battering rape (rape along with other acts of physical violence), and forced sexual acts (such as forced oral or anal sex).

Demographers measure family violence in two ways: through survey interviews with the victims, and through statistics gathered by police.

The Battered Although no one is immune from abuse, there are specific factors that place some at greater risk for experiencing violence than others; for example, women who have less education (especially women who do not attend college), who come from lower socioeconomic status, or who are single parents or young teenage parents are more likely to be victims of violence. Also, women who have witnessed a parent being battered are at higher risk of being victims themselves. Generally, women who have low self-esteem, feel a sense of inferiority, are passive, or believe that they are responsible for the batterer's actions are more likely to be abused. When violence is perpetrated against a partner, it is referred to as **intimate partner violence (IPV).**

No gender or racial/ethnic group is immune from family violence, as the data in Figure 15.4 illustrate. While women are victimized more frequently than men, about 15 percent of all acts of IPV are perpetrated against men by women (National Coalition Against Domestic Violence, 2008). In addition, intimate partner violence and family violence cross every socioeconomic and educational level, and every family type, including married, single-parent, gay, straight, and cohabiting families. For example, each year there are over 6,500 incidents of intimate partner violence among gays, lesbians, bisexuals, and transgender people (Catalan, 2004). In the United States, one in four women and one in eight men suffers physical and/or emotional violence at the hands of an intimate partner (Centers for Disease Control, 2009). Females who are 20 to 24 years of age are at the greatest risk of intimate partner violence (U.S. Department of Justice, 2009); however, as shown in Figure 15.5, women in rural areas seek the services of domestic violence shelters more than those from suburban or urban areas do.

The statistics regarding violence perpetrated at the hands of an intimate partner or a family member are staggering (National Coalition Against Domestic Violence, 2008; U.S. Department of Justice, 2009; Durose and others, 2005):

■ *Domestic violence.* Marital rape accounts for nearly one-fourth of all rapes, and affects over 75,000 women each year; 22 percent of all nonfatal violent victimizations are IPV acts against females age 12 or older; 8 percent of all pregnant women in the United States are subjected to physical violence during their pregnancy; and each year between 3 and 10 million children witness some form of violence in their homes.

FIGURE 15.4   Domestic Partner Violence by Race/Ethnicity and Gender

No one is immune from family violence.

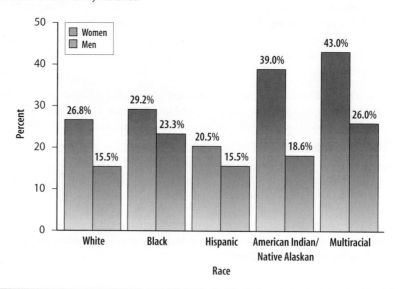

Source: Centers for Disease Control (2009).

- *Dating violence/Teen violence.* One in four teen girls in a relationship report being pressured into performing oral sex or having sex against their wishes, and one in five teens report having been hit, slapped, or pushed by a partner.
- *Domestic murders.* On average, every day in the United States four women are killed by their intimate partners, and IPV is the leading cause of death among pregnant women in the United States. Intimate partners are responsible for 30 percent of all female homicides each year and 5 percent of all male homicides.
- *Violence against children.* Physical abuse is the leading cause of death in infants under 4 years of age. A child is abused every 35 seconds in the United States, and each year 3.2 million children experience some type of maltreatment or abuse by a parent/caregiver; sadly, these numbers are believed to be vastly underreported. (See Figure 15.6.)

Indeed, these trends are alarming. But *why* do people batter? What are the characteristics of those who abuse their family members? We'll examine these questions in the following section.

The Batterer As the statistics reveal, men are more likely to abuse a family member more than are women. Those who abuse their partners or their children (see Figure 15.7 on page 510) share some common characteristics; for example, most batterers have low self-esteem and tend to blame everyone else for their behavior. They are also typically extremely jealous and often use sex as their weapon of aggression and ultimate instrument of control. Although violence is the way they express their anger or frustration, they underestimate or even deny that their behaviors are "really that violent" or harmful. Batterers have the need to control and dominate, and they become master manipulators—they can manipulate their partner's weaknesses and their strengths.

There is a common misconception that family violence results from an argument that "got out of hand," then escalated into physical blows. Most often, this is not the case. Many abused women note that the violence appeared to have no trigger or cause, and appeared to come out of

FIGURE 15.5 Primary Populations Served by Domestic Violence Shelters

Across the United States, local programs provide support to victims of domestic violence in a variety of communities.

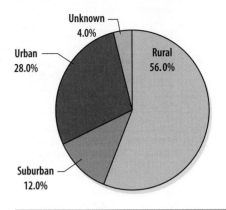

Source: National Network to End Domestic Violence (2007).

FIGURE 15.6 Types of Child Abuse and Neglect by Percent of Total Abuse

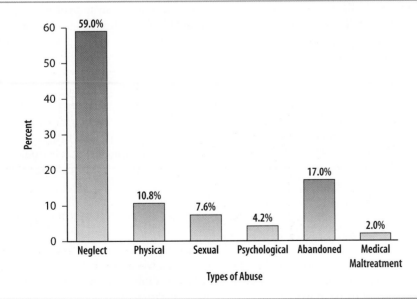

Source: U.S. Department of Health and Human Services (2009).

FIGURE 15.7 Who Abuses Children?

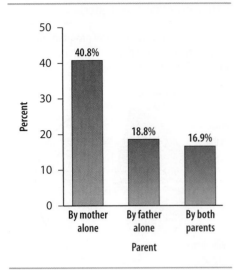

Source: U.S. Department of Health and Human Services (2009).

the blue. Another common misconception is that alcohol use or substance abuse are almost always associated with acts of family violence. In the 5.3 million cases of family violence in a five-year period in the United States, 52.2 percent of the victims indicated that there was no drug or alcohol use by the family offender (Durose and others, 2005). While on the surface, domestic violence appears to be acts of physical, emotional, or sexual aggression against a victim, the central issues in family violence are not the acts of aggression at all. Rather, the central issues of domestic violence are *control and domination*—and are commonly perpetuated by the strongest against the weakest (McGoldrick, Broken Nose, & Potenza, 1999).

Minnesota Program Development, Inc., is a nonprofit organization that works to eliminate violence against women and children. After interviewing hundreds of battered and sexually abused women to better understand how the men in their lives controlled them, and after interviewing the men who hurt them to better understand the tactics they used to maintain an environment of fear and control, the organization developed the **Power and Control Wheel.** Shown in Figure 15.8, the Power and Control Wheel depicts behaviors that batterers use to control and dominate their intimate partners and/or children.

As you can see, abusive and battering men use a whole host of tactics, ranging from degrading and humiliating comments, physical hits, punches, and kicks, false imprisonment, various forms of sexual abuse, threats and intimidation, economic exploitation, and murder to control and dominate.

Other researchers identify three categories of means that batterers use to control and dominate (Dalton & Schneider, 2001):

- *The ruler and the ruled.* Batterers often set stringent, unreasonable rules at home while also exerting extreme control in every facet of family life. For example, a husband might dictate which route the spouse must use when driving to the grocery store or taking the children to school. Any violation of the rules results in subsequent punishment.
- *Internalizing the rules.* Over time, batterers need to use less and less overt methods of control, and can rely on more subtle forms of control due to a *generalized climate of abuse.* This change is a result of the spouse and the children internalizing which behaviors result in abuse. Family members learn to suppress themselves in order to ensure the batterer is not "set off." For example, a mother may put the children to bed early so they are not present when the batterer comes home from work, or a woman may not voice her opinion—even over a trivial issue, such as where she would like to eat dinner—for fear of being hit.
- *Rules enforced by punishment.* According to Dalton and Schneider, batterers "cement" their enforcement of the rules through the use of fear, emotional abuse, and social isolation. As the Power and Control Wheel illustrates, batterers maintain an environment of control and fear through humiliation, criticism, financial abuse, sexual abuse, and emotional abuse. By cutting victims off from family and friends, a batterer's domination is enhanced (Dalton & Schneider, 2001). Furthermore, victims cannot leave if they do not have access to economic resources (Dalton & Schneider, 2001). As a battered wife for 17 years recounts, "When he wasn't hitting me, he was reminding me that he could. He was reminding me and getting me ready. Like the cat playing with the bird, letting it live a bit longer before he killed it" (p. 72).

THE CYCLE OF VIOLENCE

In 1979, a professor of psychological studies and victim advocate for battered women, Lenore Walker, pioneered research that resulted in her **Cycle of Violence** model. In her research, she examined lives of battered women and found that two-thirds of the 1,600 study respondents recounted similar patterns of intimate partner abuse. Not every abusive relationship experi-

FIGURE 15.8   The Power and Control Wheel

The Power and Control Wheel shows us the method by which batterers control and abuse their victims.

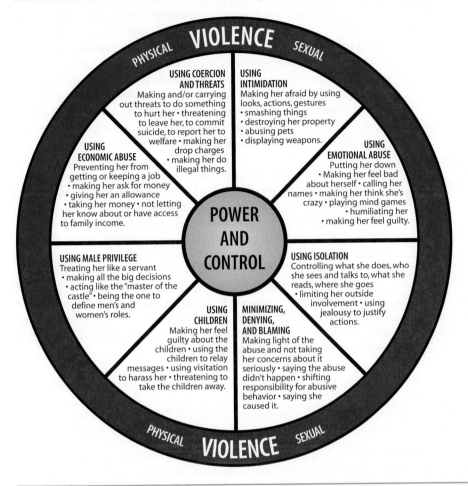

Source: Domestic Abuse Intervention Project, 202 E. Superior Street, Duluth, MN 55802, 218-722-2781, www .duluth-model.org.

ences every phase of this cycle every time, but Walker's research shows how abusive relationships are cyclical in nature.

The Cycle of Violence, shown in Figure 15.9 (page 512), illustrates three phases of violence commonly seen in abusive relationships: the *tension-building* phase, the *acute battering* or violent act, and the *respite* (nonviolent) phase.

Tension-Building   In this phase, the victim senses that an explosive, violent incident is about to take place. The batterer begins to isolate his partner, threaten her, slap her, pinch her, belittle her, destroy her property, and withdraw affection. As the victim begins to feel tension and fear, her fear builds, and in response, she tries to keep her partner calm and happy by being agreeable, nurturing, and kind. At this point, some women begin to withdraw from or isolate themselves from their family and friends. All of her efforts have one goal: to keep the batterer from becoming violent. According to Walker, the psychological anguish that accompanies this phase is the worst aspect of relationship violence. In fact, the psychological anguish may become so unbearable that many women antagonize or provoke the batterer in order to "just get it over with."

FIGURE 15.9 Lenore Walker's Cycle of Violence

The Cycle of Violence, created by Lenore Walker, illustrates the three phases of violence in abusive relationships: tension-building, acute battering, and the respite phase.

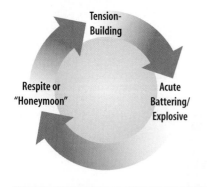

Source: Walker (1979).

Acute Battering Incident Savage. Destructive. Out of control. Brutal. This is how Walker describes the next phase of the Cycle of Violence. During this phase, the violence from the tension-building phase escalates into an acute battering incident, where the violence can become deadly. Along with degrading, humiliating verbal abuse, the batterer severely beats his partner, either by hitting, punching, and kicking, or by using a weapon. He may even rape her. The battered woman cannot control when the episode will end. According to Walker, the victim usually does not fight back, because she realizes doing so may only make it worse. Sometimes the victim may call the police, but typically she does not do so until several days after the incident. If she attempts to leave, she is at a greater risk of being killed by her partner.

Respite This phase is often called the loving phase or the "honeymoon" or "flower" phase. Walker terms this as a time of "illusion of bliss." During this time, the abuser apologizes profusely. He may cry, beg for forgiveness, and vow that he will never harm the victim again. He will often give her gifts to express his regret and lavish her with attention and love. In part, this may provide an answer to a common question: Why does she stay? Perhaps she stays because she has a sense of renewed hope that things are getting better. If a victim has filed charges against her abuser, her renewed sense of hope might cause her to drop the legal charges or to cancel appointments with mental health counselors or victims' advocates because she really believes he will change for good this time. Her renewed sense of hope leads her to believe that the violence won't happen again. *But it will.*

Family Life Education

Life is filled with irony, isn't it? When writing the first edition of this text, as I prepared to put the "finishing touches" on this chapter, my family received word that our son's closest friend was killed in an auto accident three days after her 20th birthday. At her funeral her older sister noted, "I keep hoping this is a bad dream and I'll wake up . . . but the stark reality is, we all now have to find a way to be a family without her. And I don't know how we're going to do that."

There are many predictable "vulnerability points" throughout the lifecourse of a family: Marriages begin; couples experience stress over finances, sex, in-laws, and daycare; babies are born; kids get ear infections and sometimes get hurt and need stitches; adolescents grow up, move out, fall in love, get married—and the cycle begins all over again. When the pressures associated with daily life in this quick-paced culture accompany these normative developmental changes, it is no wonder that families experience the pile-up effect of these stressors.

Many of us wish we didn't have to confront some of life's daily challenges, but these day-to-day events actually serve an important function. Just as we put money in the bank to have it available in times of need, our "routine" stressors allow our families to build coping strategies for when we need them. Normative changes, transitions, and stressors strengthen our resiliency. They help develop the identity of "who" the family is. They allow us to hone our coping skills, our communication skills, and our relational skills. With each life change, we add to this "bank account" of coping. As a result, when (not *if*) the inevitable life-altering event happens, we have resources on which to draw to help us make it through. The reality of family living is that change—sometimes agonizingly painful—is inevitable. As Duvall (1971) puts it, "Strong families are not without their problems, but use their resources to weather the storms that strike every family from time to time" (p. 516).

And that is how this young woman's family will continue to "be" a family without her presence. Like all families who find the capacity to cope, they will confront the reality of her death and respond to the tasks at hand. They will make the necessary choices that fit with their cultural and religious beliefs. They will continue to sustain the strong family and kinship ties that bound them together before this tragedy. They will rely on family and friends and accept help where and when it is needed, yet at the same time, they will do what they can for themselves. And, over time, the balance lost in their forever-changed family system will eventually find itself again.

Different . . . but not necessarily broken.

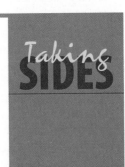

Are There Gender Differences in the Experiences of Stress?

College—homework, exams, relationship trials and triumphs, finances, trying to figure out future careers. Is it any wonder that college is considered to be one of the most trying, stressful developmental phases in a person's lifetime (Ross, Niebling, Bradley, & Heckert, 1999)? Over the past 10 years, researchers have sought to better understand the sources of stress among college students with regard to gender. Female students tend to be affected most by financial pressures, exam pressures, failing an exam, being rejected by someone, and relationship breakups (Frazier & Schauben, 1994). Males, on the other hand, have a greater number of stressors related to changes in their sleeping and eating habits, heavier workloads, increased and new responsibilities, and breaking up with a girlfriend (Ross and others, 1999). Both genders' experiences of stress are related to their self-esteem and overall health status (Hudd and others, 2000). But there's one more key player in how men and women respond to stress: sex hormones.

Her Side: Estrogen appears to heighten the effects of the stress hormone, oxytocin. Because of this, women tend to feel the effects of stress more than men. This isn't to say, however, that they react more strongly; to the contrary! Because of the way women are socialized (for instance, to be nurturing and relational), women "tend" to their stress by "befriending" other people. The "tend and befriend" tactic—turning to family and friends, talking to them, venting to them—appears to help women work through their stress in healthy, productive ways. They may stress out more often and get upset more frequently than men do, but they work through it much more quickly.

His Side: Testosterone appears to buffer the effects of the stress hormone, oxytocin. Because of this, men are somewhat immune from minor or day-to-day stressors. In cases of extreme stress, men are more apt to respond aggressively. Men, therefore, "fight" their stressors through aggression, or they ignore them by means of withdrawal or bottling up of emotions, by "flight." This "fight or flight" tactic appears to work against men. They may stress out less often than women, and ignore minor daily hassles better than women, but when bigger stressors hit, all of the pent-up frustrations are released.

Your Side: Think about your experiences with stress.

1. Do you believe that women and men are affected by different stressors, as the research suggests? Do your stressors fall in the categories that the research documents? How might they differ?
2. What is your reaction to the notion that estrogen and testosterone affect the feelings and reactions to stress?

Source: Taylor and others (2000).

Summary

Family Change

- Family life never stays the same because families always change.

- Stress is best viewed as the result of stimuli that evoke physiological and/or psychological responses, and anything that elicits these stress responses is a stressor. The stressor can either be eustress (positive stress) or distress (negative stress), and most fall within four primary categories: personal, social/family, work/school, and environmental.

- Like individuals, families face stress too. Family stress often occurs during lifecourse transitions, and sometimes this stress is experienced as a family crisis. As family systems confront stress, grow, and change, they must adjust to these changes, which involves making changes in family structure, making changes in family roles, and making changes in family rules.

- David Olson and colleagues outline three types of stress that families experience: family development stress, psychological stress (stress within the individual), and family stress and crisis.

- To fully understand the fundamentals of family stress and crisis and why the entire family system experiences the ripple effects of the stressor(s), it is necessary to view the family as a system and apply elements of Family Systems theory.

- The General Adaptation Syndrome model describes three stages of physiological responses to eustress and distress: alarm reaction, stage of resistance, and exhaustion.

- A life change event is typically life altering, requiring significant social and psychological adjustment. The Social Readjustment Rating Scale identifies associations between life events and life transitions, and the impact of these events and transitions on individual physical health and well-being. Few life change events are experienced in isolation; they often affect the entire family.

- Family stress is the result of an imbalance between the demands an event places on a family, and that family's ability or inability to meet them.

- The Transactional Model of Stress reflects the interaction between a person and his or her environment. Whatever event causes the stress, the impact of the stressor is wholly dependent on our perception and appraisal of the stressor. The model includes three key concepts: *Primary appraisal,* when people instinctively evaluate and assess the significance of the event; *secondary appraisal,* when people assess how controllable the stressor is and then decide which resources they will use to cope. External locus of control refers to the perception that we cannot control what happens in some aspects of our lives, while internal locus of control refers to the perception that we are in control of our destiny. Finally, *coping efforts* are those strategies individuals and families use to bring order to and regulate the stressor.

Family Crisis

- Whether a family experiences changes and transitions as family *stress* or family *crisis* depends largely on whether the family has the ability to adapt to these changes in the family environment.

- Typically, there are four types of family crises: *dismemberment,* the separation or isolation of an individual from the rest of his or her family; *demoralization,* crises that tend to bring disgrace to a family system; *accession,* when turbulence occurs due to the addition of a family member; and *demoralization plus dismemberment or accession,* when a family is thought to be demoralized because of embarrassing stressors.

- The ABC-X Family Crisis Model explains why families vary in the way they adapt and adjust to change, transition, and stress. This model views a family crisis situation as a combination of various factors: *A* factors are the initial crisis-causing events; *B* factors are the resources a family has at its disposal to meet the demands of the crisis; *C* factors are the meanings families ascribe to the event; and *X* factors are the outcomes of the event, the results of whether or not a family copes effectively with the crisis event. The Double ABC-X Model aims to identify the effects of the pile-up of stressors and how families adapt to them.

- There are adaptive tasks that families facing change must encounter. To successfully adjust, families must establish the meaning and understand the personal significance of the situation; confront reality and respond to the requirements of the external situation; sustain relationships with family members and friends as well as with other individuals who may be helpful in resolving the crisis and aftermath; preserve a reasonable emotional balance by managing distressful feelings in response to the situation; and preserve a satisfactory self-image and maintain a sense of competence and mastery.

Family Coping and Resilience

- By using personal, family, and community resources, families are better able to cope with stressors. The major types of family coping skills used in times of change and crisis are *appraisal-focused coping,* when families try to understand why the crisis occurred and to find meaning in the circumstances that caused the crisis; *problem-focused coping* allows the family to confront the reality of the crisis by obtaining information about the crisis; and *emotion-focused coping,* when families develop the capacity to maintain hope.

- Family resilience refers to a family's ability to function in a healthy fashion during times of change, stress, adversity, crisis, and transition. Confronted with a crisis, resilient families often re-evaluate their priorities and may invest more deeply in meaningful relationships as a result.

- Family resilience is reinforced by numerous family resilience processes that help guide families through the times of change and challenge: the family belief system, the ability to make meaning of adversity, having a positive outlook, and the presence of spirituality, flexibility, connectedness, and family communication skills.

The Crisis of Family Violence

- Domestic violence—violence perpetrated against family members by a person who is related to the victim either biologically or legally—crosses every socioeconomic and educational level, and every family type. Family of origin patterns, psychopathology, mental illness, and genetic causes; poverty, educational levels, absent or inaccessible family services; and cultural factors, such as media influences, all may contribute to domestic violence.

- There are three broad categories of domestic violence: *physical violence,* such as hitting, punching, or slapping; *emotional violence*—for example, controlling the amount of contact a family member has with family and friends, and showing intense displays of jealousy, or threats of physical or sexual harm; and *sexual violence,* which includes marital rape, battering rape, and forced sexual acts.

- Women with less education, of lower socioeconomic status, and who are single parents or young teenage parents are more likely to be victims of violence. Generally, women with low self-esteem, who are passive, or believe that they are responsible for the batterer's actions, are more likely to be abused.

- Batterers share some common characteristics, such as low self-esteem, the tendency to blame others for their behavior, a propensity for extreme jealousy, and the frequent use of sex as their weapon of aggression and their instrument of control. Batterers also tend to deny that their behaviors are harmful, and because they have the need to control and dominate, they become master manipulators.

- Most often, violence appears to have no trigger. At the root of domestic violence is the need for control and domination.

- The Power and Control Wheel depicts behaviors that batterers use to control and dominate their intimate partners and/or children, and shows that abusive and battering men use many tactics, including degrading and humiliating comments, physical attacks, imprisonment, various forms of sexual abuse, threats and intimidations, economic exploitation, and murder.

- The tactics batterers frequently use fall into three categories: the *Ruler and the Ruled,* wherein batterers set unreasonable rules at home while also exerting extreme control in every facet of family life; *Internalizing the Rules,* which describes how, over time, batterers need to use less overt methods of control, and can rely on more subtle forms of control due to a generalized climate of abuse; and *Rules Enforced by Punishment,* which is when batterers "cement" their enforcement of the rules through the use of fear, emotional abuse, and social isolation.

- Lenore Walker's Cycle of Violence model shows how abusive relationships are cyclical in nature, and describes three phases of violence commonly seen in abusive relationships: the *tension-building phase,* in which the victim senses that a violent incident is about to take place; the *acute battering,* when the violence from the tension-building phase escalates into a violent battering incident; and the *nonviolent respite phase,* when the abuser apologizes profusely, begs for forgiveness, and may vow that he will never harm her again.

Key Terms and Concepts

normative, p. 488

non-normative, p. 488

stressor, p. 489

eustress, p. 489

distress, p. 489

acute, p. 489

chronic, p. 489

family crisis, p. 489

General Adaptation Syndrome, p. 490

fight or flight, p. 491

life change event, p. 492

Social Readjustment Rating Scale (SRRS), p. 493

family stress, p. 493

Transactional Model of Stress, p. 493

external locus of control, p. 494

internal locus of control, p. 494

problem management, p. 494

emotional regulation, p. 494

meaning-based coping, p. 494

ABC-X Family Crisis Model, p. 496

A factor, p. 496

B factor, p. 497

C factor, p. 497

X factor, p. 497

pile-up, p. 497

Double ABC-X Model, p. 497

family coping skills, p. 501

appraisal-focused coping, p. 501

cognitive redefinition, p. 501

cognitive avoidance or denial, p. 502

problem-focused coping, p. 502

emotion-focused coping, p. 502

progressive desensitization, p. 502

emotional discharge, p. 502

resigned acceptance, p. 502

family resilience, p. 502

domestic violence or family violence, p. 506

batterer, p. 506

intimate partner violence (IPV), p. 508

Power and Control Wheel, p. 510

Cycle of Violence, p. 510

Suggested Readings

Boss, P. *Ambiguous loss: Learning to live with unresolved grief* (Cambridge, MA: Harvard University Press, 1999).

Ledray, L. *Recovering from rape* (New York: Henry Holt, 1994).

Loseke, D., Gelles, R., & Cavanaugh, M. *Current controversies in family violence* (Thousand Oaks, CA: Sage, 2005).

McKenry, P., & Price, S. *Families and change: Coping with stressful events and transitions* (Thousand Oaks, CA: Sage, 2005).

Multiple-Choice Questions

1. Which of the following is not one of Olson's three specific types of family stress?
   a. family developmental stress
   b. ssychological stress
   c. economic stress
   d. family stress and crisis

2. This stressor is also known as "bad stress," "negative stress," or "harmful stress."
   a. distress
   b. eustress
   c. acute
   d. chronic

3. In Hill's ABC-X Family Crisis Model, these factors refer to the number of family resources that will help them meet the demands of the stressor or crisis.
   a. *A* factors
   b. *B* factors
   c. *C* factors
   d. *X* factors

4. _____ occurs when families attempt to reframe the life event or stressor in ways that are more favorable.
   a. Cognitive avoidance or denial
   b. Appraisal-focused coping
   c. Cognitive redefinition
   d. Family coping

5. _____ is an umbrella term that encompasses any behavior designed to intentionally inflict emotional, sexual, or physical harm.
   a. Physical violence
   b. Emotional violence
   c. Sexual violence
   d. Domestic violence

6. _____ occurs when the family ultimately accepts the situation and recognizes that nothing will change the course their family life has taken.
   a. Progressive desensitization
   b. Emotional discharge
   c. Family resilience
   d. Resigned acceptance

7. A(n) _____ refers to the perception that we are, to a large extent, in control of our destiny.
   a. internal locus of control
   b. external locus of control
   c. extra-sensory locus of control
   d. psychic locus of control

8. _____ family crisis is when turbulence occurs due to the addition of a family member.
   a. Demoralization
   b. Dismemberment
   c. Accession
   d. Demoralization plus dismemberment or accession

Answers: 1. c; 2. a; 3. b; 4. c; 5. d; 6. d; 7. a; 8. c

Family Life and Aging 16

It was years ago, very early on a bitterly cold winter morning. My mother had been ill for some time and we were on our way to a cancer specialist, several hours' drive away. I helped her into the car and after she was situated I fastened her seatbelt. And then it happened.

Suddenly, for the first time, I noticed that she appeared so weak, and at that moment I knew: *she* needed *me*. This woman, the very pillar of strength who fought (and beat) cancer twice before, who single-handedly had raised her four children while her husband fought in the Vietnam war, this woman who had supported, encouraged, guided, and taught us, appeared so small and fragile and helpless beneath the blankets. Fighting back tears, I tucked the blanket around her legs, thinking, *"When did this happen? When did I become the parent and she the child?"*

Over the next few weeks she died by inches. I cared for her every day ... bathing her, feeding her, loving her. The stress was indescribable—I left my home every morning at 7:30, as soon as I got my children off to school, cared for her all day, got home in time to get the kids from school, work on homework with them, feed them, bathe them, tuck them into bed.... This was our routine for about 6 weeks, until she died. Although it was the most difficult thing I had ever done in my life, my relationship with my parents deepened to a level we had never experienced before.... In that situation, you're forced to talk about things you would otherwise never talk about.

My mother held me when I was first born, weak and unable, and I held her at the end, weak and unable. Together, we had traveled the arc of life.

Source: Author's files

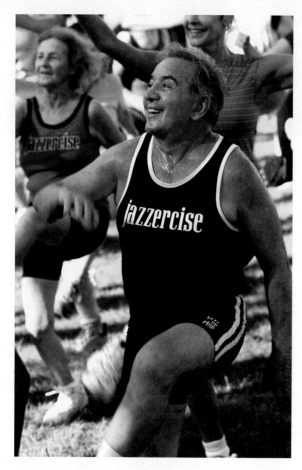

FROM Woodstock to Medicare? The drug, sex, and rock-and-roll generations of the 1960s and 1970s are today's aging population.

Our nation is moving into an unprecedented time in its history: By the year 2030, there will be 72 million people (roughly 20 percent of the population) over the age of 65 living in the United States—more than ever before (He, Sangupta, Velkoff, & DeBarros, 2005). What accounts for this surge in the aging population? Baby boomers are getting older. **Baby Boomers** are those people who were born between 1946 and 1964. During this time in American history, the birth rates rose sharply because of the economic prosperity following World War II. The first Baby Boomers will turn 65 years old in 2011. Is this country prepared for its aging population?

This entire generation, accustomed to living in a "youthful culture," is growing old. But do they know how? After the age of 40 or so, is it really downhill until we die? One hundred years ago, few people made it past the age of 70—the average **life expectancy** was 47. Today, the average life expectancy is anywhere from 68 to 80, depending on a person's race and gender (He and others, 2005). White females are expected to live to the age of 80, and African American women have a life expectancy of 74.8 (He and others, 2005). Similarly, white men have a life expectancy of 74.9, and African American men are expected to live until the age of 68.2. How will the aging live out the years that have been added to their lifespan?

In this chapter, we'll examine the demographics of America's aging. We'll also discusss the developmental forces involved in aging, such as the biological changes that take place, and family development through aging, including the aged's sexuality experiences and grandparenting. Finally, we'll look at the changes associated with aging lifestyles, such as retirement and caregiving.

Aging and the Aged

Understanding the aging population is important in our study of marriage, family, and intimate relationships because the increasing numbers of this population are challenging U.S. policy makers, healthcare providers, health and life insurance companies, businesses, and families (He and others, 2005). How will the nation meet the needs of the increasing numbers of the aging and the aged? How will families care for their aging loved ones?

America is turning gray. One hundred years ago, there were significantly more young people than older Americans. Today, there are significantly more aging Americans (those over the age of 65) than young people (those under the age of 65) with one in eight Americans 65 years or older, or about 39.5 million adults (U.S. Census Bureau, 2009, 1-Year Estimates). By 2030, it is estimated that one in six will be 65 years or older (Citron, 2003). Looking further into the future, from the years 2010 to 2050, the senior population is expected to more than double, from 35 million to nearly 87 million (He and others, 2005).

THE PORTRAIT OF AGE IN THE UNITED STATES

In the decade that spanned 1990 to 2000, baby boomers represented the most expansive generation of any before it. In Figure 16.1, the U.S. Census Bureau (2007) provides a current portrait of the age structure of the United States' older population.

FIGURE 16.1 Percent of the Total Population Who Are 65 Years and Over, 2007

Note: Estimate: 12.5 percent, margin of error: +/–0.1 percent.

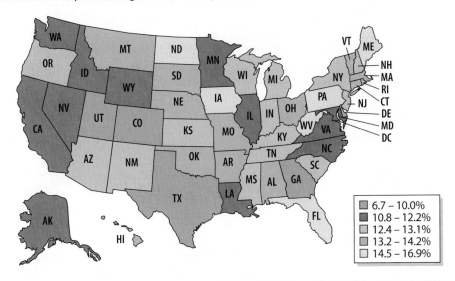

6.7 – 10.0%
10.8 – 12.2%
12.4 – 13.1%
13.2 – 14.2%
14.5 – 16.9%

Source: U.S. Census Bureau (2007). 2005–2007 American Community Survey.

- *Older population.* In 2010, there were slightly over 40 million older adults (those aged 65 and older) in the United States, representing slightly over 13 percent of its population. The median age of the elderly today is 75 years of age.
- *Gender.* Females outnumber males in the elderly population: 57 percent of those over 65 are female, while 43 percent are male.
- *Diversity.* Within the U.S. population, there is great diversity among older adults, as illustrated in Figure 16.2 (page 522). Compared with African American and white older adults, Hispanic Americans are experiencing significantly large increases. For example, by the year 2050, according to the U.S. Census Bureau (2005a), the percentage of older Hispanic Americans will nearly double.
- *Education.* In 2009, about 20 percent of those age 65 and over had a college degree. The U.S. Census Bureau projects that by the year 2030, as baby boomers age, 85 percent will have graduated from high school, and 75 percent will have a college degree.
- *Life expectancy.* Children born in 2001 will have an average life expectancy of 77.9 years (75.4 years for men, 80.4 years for women)—an all-time record. Those who reached the age of 65 in 2001 had an average life expectancy of 18 more years (16.4 years for men, 19.4 years for women).
- *Centenarians.* There were over 53,000 centenarians (those age 100 or over) in 2005. This age group makes up about .02 percent of the total population, an increase of 35 percent since 1990. Over 80 percent of centenarians are women, and the majority lives in metropolitan areas.

To be sure, the face of America is changing! As you can see, there are gender, racial, and ethnic differences in the life expectancies of people. What are the forces that influence their aging? Why do some people age well, and others do not?

DEVELOPMENTAL FORCES IN AGING

Multiple forces influence and affect how people age. **Gerontologists,** who are scientists who study aging, along with family sociologists, developmentalists, and family life educators, have developed perspectives that help them analyze these influences. The **lifespan perspective** of development emphasizes that from the cradle to the grave, human beings are in a constant,

FIGURE 16.2   U.S. Population Aged 65 and Over by Race, 2007, 2030, 2050

As the United States reaches the mid-century mark, the Hispanic and Asian aging populations will experience significant increases in their numbers.

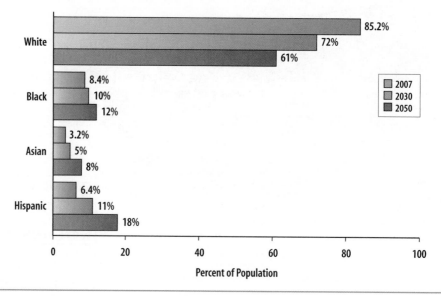

Source: He and others (2005); U.S. Census Bureau (2007).

continuous state of growth-motion. This perspective posits that simply because we age does not mean that we completed our intrapersonal and interpersonal developmental tasks and growth. In applying the lifespan perspective, those who study aging are interested in answering the larger question: Why and how do we age the way we do?

One ongoing controversy is the **nature-nurture debate:** Are the influences of aging determined by nature (your inborn, hereditary characteristics such as genetic influences) or by nurture (your environmental, experiential, societal, and cultural experiences across your lifespan)? For many years, most social scientists who studied aging focused on the nature side of the argument—that is, they believed that the influences of aging are biologically driven and as such, not much could be done to prevent certain, inevitable outcomes. Today, however, those who study human development and the aging process argue that aging is a process of *both* nature *and* nurture, and that the two forces interact to create a unique individual. In particular, there are four interactive forces of development:

1. *Biological forces.* These refer to all genetic and health-related factors. For example, is a person genetically predisposed to getting cancer? Also included in this area of development are lifestyle choices such as diet, exercise, smoking, and alcohol consumption. Race and ethnic differences are also included, because some races are more predisposed for certain illnesses such as high blood pressure and diabetes.
2. *Psychological forces.* These refer to all cognitive, emotional, and perceptual factors. Among the aging, things such as cognitive impairment due to certain diseases, and memory loss and retention are considered.

3. *Sociocultural forces.* These include cultural, ethnic, societal, relational, and interpersonal factors. In this area of development, family scientists consider employment, living arrangements, marital status, parenting and grandparenting, and caregiving.
4. *Lifecycle forces.* All of these forces interact and combine to create a person's unique, individual developmental experiences.

As you have seen, there are certain expected lifecourse events as well as those that we do not expect or anticipate. Paul Baltes, a psychologist who specializes in aging, and his research associates (Baltes, Lindenberger, & Staudinger, 1998) identify three varying sets of interacting lifecourse influences: *normative age-graded influences, normative history-graded influences,* and *non-normative influences.*

Normative age-graded influences are developmental changes that are caused by biological, psychological, and sociocultural forces. These age-graded influences are typically highly correlated to a person's chronological age, such as the start of menstruation, puberty growth spurts, menopause, hearing loss, vision loss, or the loss of memory skills. These biological developmental changes are significant because they often signal major transitions in people's lives. For example, a teenager who begins menstruating is now capable of bearing children; a woman who begins menopause can no longer bear children. In many cultures, there are rituals or rites of passage that mark progression into different stages of life, and these events correspond to certain ages. Among Israeli women in the Mideast, for instance, menopause is marked with a *croning ceremony.* This rite of passage is celebrated at the age of 50, and during this ceremony aging women are recognized as the embodiment of wisdom, healing, and teaching. Within this culture, *crones* are the ones who care for the dying and are the "spiritual midwives," the "knowers of all mysteries."

Every culture establishes norms associated with the timing of the events. This is the culture's **social clock,** and it includes rites of passage, such as graduating from high school or college, getting married, or retiring—all by a socially and culturally accepted age.

Normative history-graded influences are events or conditions that people in a given culture or society experience simultaneously. The history-related events may be *biological* in nature, such as the AIDS epidemic in Africa; *psychological* in nature, such as racism in this country that resulted in the Civil Rights Movement of the 1960s; or *sociocultural,* such as the Great Depression of the 1930s or the sexual revolution that took place throughout the 1960s and the 1970s. It is these history-graded influences that sometimes give certain generations their nicknames, such as those who grew up during the Great Depression era, the "baby boomers," or Generation X (those born after 1965). The impact and effect of history-graded influences is great. For example, most people in the United States remember where they were when they learned of the terrorist attacks on September 11, 2001. More recently, Americans experienced the catastrophic destruction caused by Hurricane Katrina in 2005; the images of the poor, packed into the convention center in New Orleans without food and water, will remain etched on our memories for quite some time.

Non-normative influences are things that most people do not experience—these influences are uncommon, rare, or unanticipated events. Some non-normative influences may be favorable, such as gaining a large, unexpected inheritance from a long-lost uncle, but most often these events are not favorable and cause disruption in individual and family life. While we expect that we will have to experience the death of our parents, for example, we do not expect that this will occur while we are in college. Similarly, we might expect that we ourselves will experience a serious illness as we enter mid- or later life, but we do not anticipate that we will experience a life-threatening illness in our teens or 20s—or that our children will at any point in their childhood. As we discussed in Chapter 15, such non-normative events are experienced as crises.

As you learned in Chapter 1, *we do not develop in isolation.* Throughout our lifespan, our development is multifaceted, shaped and reshaped by many interacting influences. Who we are and how we came to be the persons we are is a complex tapestry woven together from biological, psychological, social, and cultural influences. And how we age is no exception.

Aging Is . . .

Bifocals? Sore joints? Diminished memory? "Aging" means different things to different people. To Asian cultures, the aged are the foundation of wisdom and are highly revered and respected. In other cultures, such as America, the aged and the aging process are often feared.

1. Complete the following sentence: To me, aging is _____.

2. What frightens you most about aging? What intrigues you most about aging?

AGE Isn't just a number—it's an attitude! Does aging mean we have to be "old"?

WHAT IS AGING?

Most of us have heard the cliché, "You're as young as you feel!" But are we? Although I may feel as though I'm 25 or 30 in spirit, my uncooperative knees and my need for bifocal eyeglasses tell me that my 20s and 30s are history! So how do we characterize the aging process? Is it a pattern of intricate, genetically timed biological changes? Or is aging a mindset? Aging is not a uniform process for all; certainly there are universal aging processes, but individual coping and adaptation to lifecourse experiences all affect how we age (Crosnoe & Elder, 2002).

Primary Aging To better understand the aging process, it is necessary to examine biological, age-related declines. Researchers, gerontologists, and developmentalists alike distinguish between primary aging and secondary aging. **Primary aging** refers to the basic biological processes that are genetically programmed and that take place with the passage of time (Cavanaugh & Blanchard-Fields, 2002). These aging processes represent the core aspects of aging, and they are summarized in Table 16.1 (Cavanaugh & Blanchard-Fields, 2002).

According to biologist Leonard Hayflick (1994), every species in the animal kingdom has a maximum lifespan. For humans, it appears to be about 110 or 120 years. According to Hayflick, each species has a genetically programmed time limit, because at a certain point in time, cells lose their ability to replicate. This time limit, known as the **Hayflick limit**, is what accounts for the aging process and life expectancy. Hayflick proposed that there are three cellular factors that cause aging: the diminished capacity to adapt to stressors, a reduction in the speed of performance, and an increased susceptibility to disease (Hayflick, 1994). It appears, then, that there is little a person can do to prevent the inevitability of aging. Are there things we can do, however, to help us slow the aging process?

Secondary Aging While the characteristics associated with primary aging cannot be delayed inevitably, to a very large extent we have control over age-related declines that are associated with **secondary aging**—physiological declines that are the result of environmental and behavioral influences that significantly impact how we age. Among other things, secondary aging is influenced by lifestyle choices such as smoking, poor nutrition, lack of exercise, sun exposure, alcohol and/or substance use, and sexual behaviors.

It is often difficult to determine whether the declines associated with aging are due to primary or secondary influences. For example, smoking, which is associated with secondary age-

TABLE 16.1 Primary Aging: Biological Changes Associated with Aging

These changes are genetically programmed and take place over time, and all of the changes are irreversible. Eventually, the biological changes lead to death. Death by primary aging factors is referred to as "death by natural causes."

- **Age-related anatomical and functional changes.** These include changes in the immune system and the ability to fight infection or disease, changes in vision and hearing, changes in the function of joints, and changes in memory retention.
- **Progressive changes.** Starting at about age 30, we begin to lose brain neurons. By the age of 50, our brain size is reduced to 97 percent, and by the age of 70, our brain size is reduced to about 92 percent.
- **Inevitable changes.** This category includes declines in sensory functions. Hearing, vision, taste, and balance become less acute. Reaction times become slower because the speed of nerve impulses slows.
- **Universally experienced changes.** Regardless of society or culture, all primary aging changes are experienced by everyone.

Source: Adapted from Cavanaugh & Blanchard-Fields (2002).

related declines, accelerates the deterioration of the cardiovascular and respiratory systems: Yet it is sometimes difficult to determine whether it is the primary aging influences, such as being more susceptible to disease, or the behavior that causes the greater likelihood that an aged person will develop cancer. The easiest way, then, to determine whether physical deterioration is related to primary or secondary causes is to keep in mind that, as developmental psychologist Barbara Lemme (2005) observed, "primary aging is generally identifiable by its inevitability, universality, and irreversibility, while secondary aging appears only among a part of the population, is related to extrinsic factors such as behavior and socioeconomic status, and may . . . be prevented or perhaps reversed."

Ageism Ageism refers to the stereotypical attitudes people hold about the aging and the elderly. People who are **ageist** have a fixed and negative mindset about older people. As a result of these attitudes, the aging population is often subjected to bias and unfair treatment. The biggest problem associated with ageism is that it limits the things people can accomplish, and it denies them the respect and freedom that all people deserve (Lemme, 2005). Ageism may lead to unfair housing, unfair employment, and unfair educational opportunities. For example, a woman with 20 years of administrative office experience may be turned down for a job, or she may be denied a promotion over a younger employee with less experience. Ageism can also interfere with proper medical diagnoses, such as in instances of depression or anxiety in the aging and the elderly; too often these mental diagnoses are misinterpreted or diagnosed as physical conditions and are subsequently either mistreated or left untreated (Lemme, 2005).

While there are, indeed, losses associated with aging, there are also many inherent gains. For instance, in a study completed by the National Council on Aging (NCOA), nearly one-half of the older Americans surveyed considered themselves to be middle-aged or young. Only about 15 percent of those age 75 or older consider themselves to be "old" (Parkin, 2002). In another study, among

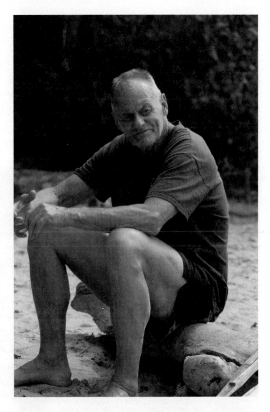

FORMER Navy Seal, 75 year-old Rudy Boesch, is the oldest participant who has appeared on the TV show, *Survivor*. He competed with people less than half his age for 6 weeks on the island of Borneo, where he came in third place.

those Americans ages 65 to 69, nearly one-half of those surveyed indicated that these were the best years of their lives (Parkin, 2001). In this same research endeavor, 44 percent of those in their 70s, and 33 percent of those in their 80s described the present as their best years. Of the older Hispanic study participants, 57 percent indicated the later years in life were their best years; similarly, 60 percent of older African American respondents said old age is the best phase of their lifespan.

So what does it mean to age successfully? In a biological sense, it might mean that as a person ages there is a minimal level of decline in physiological, cognitive, and social and emotional functioning. But for our purposes here, we must consider which life experiences allow some people to age more successfully than others—how do they manage their later years in life? With this in mind, we turn our attention to the effects of aging with regard to family relationships and family living in middle and old age.

Marriage Experiences through Aging

As life expectancies increase, so do issues concerning later-life family living, because as we age we experience a number of transitions, challenges, losses, and gains—in our health, and in our family relationships and lifestyles. Relationships are essential in later age because stable, intimate relationships throughout the life cycle protect us against various biological losses associated with aging and buffers us against the loss of social roles (Kulik, 1999; Lemon, Bengston, & Peterson, 1972; Lowenthal & Haven, 1968). In the following section, we'll explore family development among the aging, including marital satisfaction among aging couples, sexuality, and experiences with parenting and grandparenting.

THE MARRIAGE RELATIONSHIP: MARITAL SATISFACTION

When we view families from a developmental perspective, we can see the relatively predictable changes associated with family living (see Chapter 1). The Family Life Cycle model not only helps to define a family's current developmental stage but it also helps us to understand the organization of the family system, how it changes over time, and the significance and importance of these changes for each individual within the family system (Lemme, 2005). Just as individuals are in a constant state of growth-motion and must accomplish certain developmental tasks, families too must navigate the developmental tasks associated with the aging family. As Figure 16.3 illustrates, a family spends about 25 to 30-plus years from the time the last child leaves home, a period known as *the empty nest*, through retirement, until the death of both spouses. Indeed, the middle and later years of family life make up at least half of the family life cycle. As the family moves through time, many changes take place and responsibilities change. Relationships with others are a key aspect of adulthood and aging (Cavanaugh & Blanchard-Fields, 2002).

Have you ever wondered how couples stay married for 40, 50, or 60 years? With all of the changes across individual and family life cycles; with all of the challenges, transitions, and crises families confront; and with all of the environmental and non-normative events that can occur, what is the secret to marital success? As

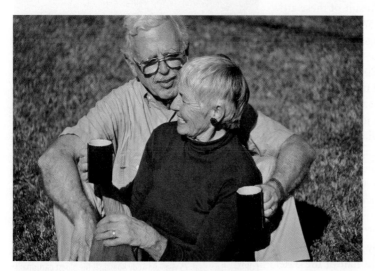

COUPLES who experienced high levels of intimacy and interdependence in their marriages typically have high levels of marital satisfaction as they age. Overall, older couples tend to be more positive in their communication and emotions.

you have seen through our study, marital satisfaction and happiness ebb and flow throughout the family life cycle and are affected by events such as childbirth and the launching of a child into early adulthood. As married couples age, their relationship continues to undergo changes, influencing their relationship quality. According to social psychologists Benjamin Karney and Thomas Bradbury (1995), marriages that are strong in reciprocity and interdependence remain high in intimacy and closeness, and continue to thrive through old age. On the other hand, marriages that demonstrate lower levels of interdependence and reciprocity are characterized by higher levels of stress and conflict during this phase of family development.

Researchers identify some specific characteristics that speak directly to the differences in relational quality between middle-aged and older married couples. For instance, two bodies of research discovered that as couples age, there are fewer sources of marital conflict and there is greater potential for pleasure than in middle adulthood (Carstensen, Gottman, & Levenson, 1995; Levenson, Carstensen, & Gottman; 1993). They also found that as couples age, there are fewer gender differences in those things each spouse finds pleasurable. Overall, researchers found couples to have more positive emotions. In comparison to younger couples, older couples tend to use more affectionate, positive language during times of conflict, and tend to be less emotionally negative toward their spouse. It should be noted, however, that if a couple is unhappy during the earlier years of their marriage, becoming older does not mean that they will suddenly find happiness! Younger, unhappy couples eventually age to become older, unhappy couples.

In middle-aged couples, sources of conflict tend to center on childrearing, money issues, communication, sex, and in-laws, whereas in older couples (age 65 and older), sources of conflict include communication, what the couple does for recreation, money issues, sex, and adult children (Levenson and others, 1993). In mid-life, things that bring couples pleasure include memories of past good times, children and grandchildren, spending time with friends, and vacations. Older couples enjoy the same things, except children and grandchildren are at the top of their list (Levenson and others, 1993).

FIGURE 16.3 Family Life Cycle by Length of Time in Each of the Eight Stages

As a family moves through time, a number of changes take place in family members' responsibilities and in their interpersonal relationships.

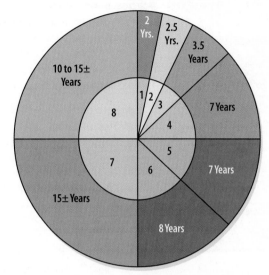

1. Married couples (without children)	5. Families with teenagers (oldest child, 13–20 years)
2. Childbearing families (oldest child, birth–30 months)	6. Families launching young adults (first child gone to last child leaving home)
3. Families with preschool children (oldest child, 30 months–6 years)	7. Middle-aged parents (empty nest to retirement)
4. Families with schoolchildren (oldest child, 6–13 years)	8. Aging family members (retirement to death of both spouses)

Source: From Duvall, Evelyn Millis & Miller, Brent C. *Marriages and Family Development 6/E* © 1985 Published by Allyn and Bacon, Boston, MA. Copyright © 1985 by Pearson Education. Reprinted by permission of the publisher.

THE SEXUAL RELATIONSHIP

Current knowledge suggests that sexual functioning and frequency decline with age, and that sex decreases in importance over time; these declines are largely associated with the physical changes and health declines that occur during aging (Lindau and others, 2007). Despite these declines, however, throughout adulthood and into later adulthood sexual activity plays an important role in intimate relationships. In fact, according to the National Council on Aging (NCOA, 1998a, 1998b), "an active sex life appears to be as normal a part of aging as retirement and having grandchildren." A 2004 survey of middle-aged and the elderly's sexual attitudes

The Keys to Great Sex in Later Life

Many of the health-related problems people commonly experience as they get older cause concern for older adults with regard to sexual activity. For instance, following a heart attack, men and women are often concerned that the physical demands of the sex act may place additional stress on their hearts; consequently, they avoid sexual activity. Throughout the Family Life Cycle, a healthy lifestyle is key to enjoying satisfying sexual relations. Indeed, what is good for a person's overall health is also good for their sexual health. Thus, to improve or maintain overall health throughout the lifecycle, adults should:

- Eat a nutritious, well-balanced diet.
- Stop smoking!
- Consume alcohol only in moderation.
- Engage in regular exercise, which lowers blood pressure (and thereby helps with erection health), helps control weight, and improves lung capacity.
- Receive regular medical checkups.
- Reduce stress (stress and anxiety decrease sexual arousal).

With good health, and equipped with a sound knowledge and realistic expectations about sexuality through aging, sexual fulfillment later in life is a healthy, positive, and attainable goal.

and behaviors, conducted by the American Association of Retired People (AARP), reveals that sexual activity is important in older peoples' lives—and that it is pleasurable. Recent research also shows that sex is still an important and positive aspect in the lives of 70-year-olds, even if sexual dysfunctions are present (Bechman, Waem, Gustafson, & Skoog 2008).

CONTRARY to popular belief, older adults enjoy rich, satisfying, pleasurable sex lives. Essential to later-life sexuality is a healthy lifestyle that includes good nutrition, exercise, and stress reduction.

Sexual studies among the aging are far and few between. However, one study undertaken by the NCOA found that 39 percent of the respondents indicated they were satisfied with the amount of sex they currently had, while 39 percent reported they wanted more frequent sex; only about 4 percent said they wanted sex less frequently (NCOA, 1998a, 1998b). The study also determined that only about 19 percent of widows and widowers were sexually active, compared to 60 percent of married men and women.

Clearly, older Americans are sexually active. But how do they rate the quality of their sexual experiences? Is sex better when we age? Worse? The same as when we are younger? How people experience their sexuality involves a complex interaction between mind, body, and emotions. As people get older, age-related changes (associated with both primary and secondary aging) influence the physical and psychological aspects of their sex life.

DIVORCE

Divorce is relatively infrequent among America's elderly population, although as baby boomers reach old age, divorce rates are rising. Figure 16.4 depicts the martial status of those over the age of 65. As you can see, slightly more than one-half are married, and about one-third are widowed; only about 10 percent are divorced or separated. The experi-

FIGURE 16.4   Marital Status of Those Age 65 and Older, 2010

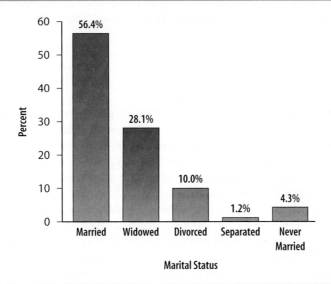

Source: U.S. Census Bureau (2010).

ence of separation and divorce in later life is similar to separation and divorce experienced earlier in the lifespan—there are psychological, social, and financial consequences of divorce for both younger and older adults. However, divorce in middle and later ages carries with it special characteristics and stressors unique to older adults. Unlike younger adults who divorce, people (particularly over age 50) were brought up in an era when marriage was considered to be a till-death-do-us-part commitment and divorce was less acceptable. Because of long-held beliefs and values, divorce later in life contributes to the stressors associated with marital breakup.

More Traumatic Because of the longer commitment and investment into each other's lives, divorce later in life is more traumatic (Uhlenberg, Cooney, & Boyd, 1990). Divorcing couples face losing longtime friendships and other social networks, further distinguishing later-in-life divorce from divorce earlier in the lifecourse (Gerstel, 2003). Because women obtain much of their identity and self-worth from their roles of wife and mother, divorce is even more traumatic.

Greater Financial Burdens Although the financial responsibilities associated with rearing children decrease over time, divorce in mid- and later life may limit the amount of support parents can provide to their children, particularly in areas such as college tuition or other areas of assistance (such as helping with a down payment for a home; Pasley, 1998). Because some older women lack education, skills, and employment experiences that affect their ability to either re-enter the paid labor force or to move up the ladder in their current positions, women who divorce in later life have significantly more limitations in their range of options following divorce than do younger women. Furthermore, retirement benefits, healthcare benefits, and Social Security benefits may also be negatively affected by divorce in later life.

Significant Impacts on Parent–Child Relationships When parents of adult children divorce, the parents' relationship with their children is significantly affected. Although issues such as child support and visitation do not affect the parent–child relationship as they do when younger parents divorce, there is less contact between parents and young adult children after parental divorce in later life (Aquilino, 1994; Furstenberg, Hoffman, & Shrestha, 1995). The father–child relationship tends to be particularly vulnerable, while the relationship between the mother and the children appears to remain intact (Cooney, 1994). Divorce in later life may be particularly difficult as it can weaken the kinship ties and intergenerational ties that are so important to successful aging (Furstenberg and others, 1995; Pasley & Ihinger-Tallman, 1994).

REMARRIAGE

Current trends indicate that older adults are less likely to remarry following divorce or the death of a spouse than are younger adults. Yet, when older adults do remarry, they face a unique set of obstacles. For instance, grown children are more likely to accept their parents' remarriage, while the aging adults' peers are less accepting (Vinick, 1978, 1986). Grown stepchildren, however, are frequently concerned about inheritance issues, which may influence their feelings about a parent's remarriage.

The marital relationship of remarried older adults differs as well. A study by professor of child and family studies Kay Pasley and her colleagues (1994) found that remarried older adults reported less frequent negative types of conflict, such as arguing, shouting, sulking, or brooding; and less frequent occurrences of abusive physical behavior, such as slapping or hitting. The researchers assert that the infrequent instances of negative conflict contribute to increased levels of marital happiness and satisfaction. In a similar study, aging psychologists Ruth Bograd and Bernard Spilka (1996) examined self-disclosure and its relationship to marital satisfaction in mid-life (ages 30 to 40) and late-life (ages 60 to 75) remarriages among 125 couples. Their overall findings suggest that couples who remarried in mid-life appear to develop more effective communication and interaction patterns that were missing in their first marriages. As a result, these newly developed communication skills contribute to higher levels of marital satisfaction.

As baby boomers begin to age and as the population of older age cohorts continues to grow, increasing attention will be given to the significance of the marital relationship throughout the later years in the lifecourse. What is known is that most long-term marriages are rich and rewarding, both emotionally and sexually.

Intergenerational Ties

Intergenerational ties refer to the relationships between family members across multiple generations, and these relationships are indeed important to the aging population. Women over the age of 65, for example, are three times more likely to be widowed than men (He and others, 2005). Figure 16.5 shows us the percentages of widows and widowers from the ages of 65. Thus, as adults grow older through later adulthood, their interpersonal relationships across generations become increasingly important, because these intergenerational ties provide the foundation for intimacy throughout the aging process (Fingerman, 2001).

In everyday language, the term *generation* describes people who were born during the relatively same time period (such as the "baby boomer" generation). When discussing intergenerational relationships, however, the term *generation* is used to describe family members who are "on the same rung of the family ladder," or who are related to one another either biologically or through adoption. Most intergenerational relationships are offshoots of the parent–child relationship, although biological ties are not a necessary prerequisite in order for someone to experience a sense of family, kinship, and intimacy (Fingerman, 2001). For example, sometimes after many years with a stepmother or stepfather, the "step" aspect of the relationship becomes less significant and the relationship becomes as meaningful as those between biological parents and their children.

Similarly, older African American adults frequently do not distinguish "kin" along biological lines; for instance, it is common for nieces, nephews, godchildren, or even younger

ADULTS' relationships with their parents are affected by their gender, geographic distance, their parents' marital status, and their culture.

adults who are not blood or otherwise related to fill the role of an adult child for older African American males (Johnson, 1999). **Fictive kin** are people who are not biologically related to someone, but who fulfill a family role. Among African American families, fictive kin are important sources of emotional support, as well as support in meeting the elderly's needs (MacRae, 1992). As African Americans age, they tend to enjoy warmer relationships with their brothers, sisters, children, and fictive kin than white aging Americans do (MacRae, 1992). Aging Hispanic and Asian families also experience extended kin and fictive kin relationships more often than white families do. Importantly, later in the developmental lifecourse, intimacy "may exist between individuals who *define themselves* as parent and offspring" (Fingerman, 2001, p. 23, italics mine). Of the many different and varying interpersonal intimate relationships we form throughout our lives, none is as important to some people as the relationship between parent and child.

FIGURE 16.5 Percentage of Widows and Widowers, Aged 65–85+

Because of their longer life expectancy, there are more widows (women who have lost their husbands to death) than there are widowers (men who have lost their wives).

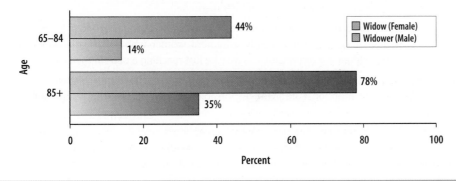

Source: He and others (2005).

PARENTING: ARE WE THERE YET?

Some parents look forward to launching their children, while others do so with much trepidation and doubt. Still others do not successfully manage the transition to an **empty nest**—the home with no children—well at all. Table 16.2 presents the changes that occur in the family system that accompany the empty nest. As you can see, significant changes take place in the family members' roles, as well as in the relationships with the now-grown children. While marriage and family courses emphasize the earlier years of parenting and the significance of the parent–child relationship during the early years, preschool years, and school years of a child's life, too often much is left unsaid about the importance of the parent–adult child relationship.

When a child enters into early adolescence, an important turning point is reached in the parent–child relationship. It is during this phase of development that parents and children alike establish intimacy levels that will, to a very large extent, define their subsequent *parent–adult child* relationship. This developmental stage of the family life cycle brings important questions to the forefront, such as: How do adolescent children affect the well-being of their parents? Because children come of age during this period of family development and eventually leave the nest (and perhaps return to the nest again and again), what impact does this have on mid-life parents?

In many families, children's entry into adolescence coincides with the parents' transition to mid-life. As young adolescents strive for increased independence and autonomy, they often begin to challenge their parents' authority. Meanwhile, parents are encountering their own developmental tasks associated with mid-life, such as caring for their aging parents and preparing for retirement. These normative lifecourse events introduce many challenges into the family system, as parents are forced to play simultaneous roles as caretaker and parent. But typically, marital satisfaction and stability increase as children enter into their adolescent years (Swensen, Eskew, & Kohlhepp, 1981; Veroff, Douvan, & Kulka, 1981; Wu & Penning, 1997). This increase is likely because conflicts over childrearing issues decline.

It is also during these middle years of the family life cycle that parents and children begin to renegotiate their relationship, and parents begin to reflect on their parenting experiences,

TABLE 16.2 Developmental Tasks Associated with the Empty Nest

As parents begin to empty the nest, there are common struggles that most couples encounter:

- **Change in roles/loss of roles.** When children leave, it's not uncommon for parents to feel a void once their parenting role is diminished or lost. Some parents try to fill this void with volunteer or other activities. Parents also need to shift to the role of parent of *adult* children.

- **Marital issues.** Raising children requires so much time, energy, and attention that sometimes children are a diversion that keeps parents from working on problems in their marriage. When children leave the nest, the diversion is no longer there. Parents need to re-examine their goals as a couple as they enter the second half of their marriage.

- **Career change.** Frequently, emptying the nest coincides with changes in one or both parents' careers. While men may be thinking of early retirement, women who entered the workforce later because of childrearing responsibilities may be just reaching a peak in their careers.

- **Caregiving shifts.** Typically, as children leave the home, parents find that their own parents need more care and attention. Caregiving responsibilities don't lessen—they simply shift to a different generation.

- **Relationships with children.** For many parents, accepting their children as adults is difficult; other parents accept that their children are adults and require less advice and support. What is more important to mid-life parents, however, is *how* children leave the nest: Are the parents and children on good terms?

and "accept their life choices, relate to their children, and adjust to 'how [the children] have turned out'" (Lemme, 2005, p. 274). These reflections about their success or failure as parents greatly affect the parents' purpose in life, their self-acceptance, and thus their well-being.

THE PARENT–ADULT CHILD RELATIONSHIP IN LATE ADULTHOOD

As parents age and begin to experience physiological and cognitive changes, their roles within the family change, also. The parent–adult child relationship is central to the lives of the elderly: Aside from having their adult children there to provide care when needed, having warm and close relationships with their children provide aging parents a sense of well-being (Pinquart & Soerensen, 2000). According to aging developmentalist Karen Fingerman (2001), four primary factors influence intimacy between older adults and their adult children: gender, geographic distance, a parent's marital status, and culture.

1. *Gender.* Gender plays a significant role in the intimacy levels of the elderly and their grown children. Women, for example, tend to express greater emotional intensity than do men in their intergenerational ties (Fingerman, 2001; Troll & Fingerman, 1996). Subsequently, elderly mothers and their adult daughters and daughters-in-law experience greater intimacy than do fathers and sons.
2. *Geographic distance.* One national survey indicated that 63 percent of elderly parents see at least one of their children weekly (Crimmins & Ingegneri, 1990). Of the 11,000 senior citizen respondents in the national study, only 20 percent noted that they see their children once per month (or less).
3. *Parent's marital status.* The older parent's marital status also influences the quality of intimacy between elderly parents and their children. Widowed or single older people (particularly women) frequently turn to their grown children or grandchildren for companionship and emotional support.
4. *Culture.* Culture and ethnicity are key determinants in how intergenerational relationships develop and how intimacy is fostered within these relationships. In the United States, for example, involvement in the aging parent's daily life is not supported by American culture, whereas in Japan and other Asian cultures such involvement is a dominant belief. These cultural differences may explain in part the discrepancies seen in the research as it relates to the impact of adult–child involvement in aging parents' lives, such as in India and among Mexican Americans. But clearly, while the "intimacy parents and offspring share in late life does not involve the close sense of oneness they could derive from a romantic partner" (Fingerman, 2001, p. 31), older adults take pleasure in these intergenerational ties.

Today, some of the most enjoyable, enriching intergenerational relationships the aging experience are with their grandchildren.

BECOMING A GRANDPARENT

I admit it—I look forward to the day I become a grandparent! I confess that I will in all likelihood be the type of grandparent who is armed and ready with photo albums in my purse, ready to spring them on unsuspecting victims.

IN Asian cultures, the elderly are revered for their wisdom and experiences, and they are cared for by their children and grandchildren. How do these experiences compare with how the aged are cared for in the U.S.? In America, do you think the elderly are valued? Why or why not?

Becoming a grandparent is an exciting time for most people (Somary & Stricker, 1998). As adults enter their middle years, they begin to take on several new roles, such as in-law, grandparent, and caregiver to their aging parents. In the United States, some parents become grandparents in their 30s (Szinovacz, 1998), but typically most do so while in their 40s (about one-third), and about one-half of women become grandparents while in their 50s. And, as you saw in Chapter 11, today a significant number of grandparents assume the parenting role. Figure 16.6 provides a snapshot of the percentage of grandparents who are responsible for their grandchildren, state by state.

Overall, the experience of grandparenting appears to be immensely satisfying; to be sure, 92 percent of survey respondents in one study expressed high levels of satisfaction with their grandparenting role (Kaufman & Elder, 2003; Segatto & Di Filippo, 2003). Studies have shown that grandparents wish to see their grandchildren on a frequent basis, and these relationships have positive outcomes on grandchildren's development (Adkins, 1999). Of course, there are many different ways that people grandparent.

STYLES OF GRANDPARENTING

Just as there are different parenting styles, there are different styles of grandparenting. In a classic study by a pioneer in the study of aging, Bernice Neugarten and her colleague K. K. Weinstein (1964) identified five primary styles of grandparenting: formal, fun seeker, remote, involved, and dispenser of wisdom.

In the **formal grandparenting** role, grandparents see their role along common, traditional lines. These grandparents babysit every now and then and indulge their grandchildren on occasion, but when it comes to childrearing and discipline, they play a "hands-off" role; they are content to leave that aspect of parenting to the parents. About one-third of the grandparents practiced this grandparenting style. One study surveyed a representative sample of grandparents and found that over one-half of their research participants had a **companionate relationship** with their grandchildren (Cherlin & Furstenberg, 1986). Similar to the formal relationship, companionate grandparents enjoy warm, loving, and nurturing relationships with their grandkids, although they are happy to send them home when it is time!

FIGURE 16.6   **Percent of Grandparents Responsible for their Grandchildren, 2007**

Note: Estimate: 40.6 percent, margin of error: +/–0.3 percent.

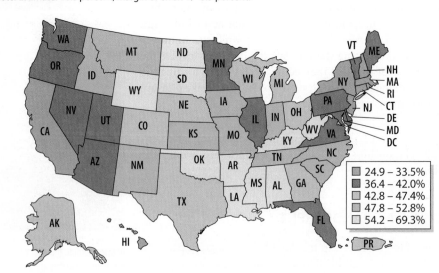

Source: U.S. Census Bureau (2007). 2005–2007 American Community Survey.

Another common style of grandparenting is the **fun seeker**. These grandparents have a relationship with their grandchildren that is characterized by an informal, spontaneous playfulness. On the other hand, the distant grandparent has little or no contact with grandchildren and is only involved on occasional holidays or birthdays. This grandparenting style is defined as a **remote relationship**.

As you know, many grandparents today assume the role of parent and are *surrogate* parents; this grandparenting style is described as an **involved relationship.** Overall, African Americans, Asian Americans, Italian Americans, and Hispanic Americans are more likely to be actively involved in their grandchildren's lives than are whites, because the sense of family is a core value among these cultures (Cavanaugh & Blanchard-Fields, 2002). Finally, the **dispenser of wisdom** grandparent offers information and advice to their grandchildren—often whether it is asked for or not.

To be sure, there are many changes that take place in family relationships as people age. Central to the lives of the aging are intergenerational relationships, whether they are with biological kin or with fictive kin. As you learned in Chapter 11, many couples today are forgoing parenting altogether; given the significance of intergenerational relationships in later life, it will be interesting to see the impact of childlessness on couples in the future.

As individuals and couples near the later years in life, there are other substantial changes that must be navigated. In the section that follows, we'll explore other factors associated with aging, including retirement and family caregiving.

Family Changes toward the End of Life

Throughout this text, we have discussed how marital and intimate relationship development and family development involve multiple processes that unfold over the life of the relationship. To fully understand family development, we must take into account the cultural and social contexts in which the family evolves and understand that each transition or milestone has both positive and negative ramifications.

SITTING in a rocker, dozing the entire afternoon? Or actively engaged in pursuing hobbies and volunteering? Today, a significant number of retirees have full, active days as they volunteer in their communities.

So far in this chapter we've discussed how marriages and other family relationships change as men and women age and enter the later years of their lifespans. But a discussion about family life through the maturing years would not be complete without examining other significant life transitions that also have significant impact on a person's later years. These are the changes that take place within a family's day-to-day living. External factors affect the daily lives of aging adults and their families, including retirement and caregiving.

RETIREMENT AND LEISURE

Contemporary themes of aging research focus on the successful adaptation to the later years by viewing aging as a series of multiple, interrelated processes (Crosnoe & Elder, 2002). Beyond the biological and physiological changes that people experience as they age are external factors that determine how people's later years will progress. If we consider "aging" as a holistic experience that involves changes not just in people's bodies but also in their marital and other interpersonal relationships, as well as in their ability to use their leisure time in productive and meaningful ways, we can reassess our view of the aging process. Let's expand our definition of aging, then, to an even broader view; that is, "successful aging" is a *pattern* of well-being and adaptation to the challenges of middle adulthood and later life (Rowe & Kahn, 1998). With this definition in mind, we consider later-in-life changes that significantly affect the later years in the lifecourse: retirement and family caregiving.

Retirement as a Developmental Process Retirement is not an isolated event but a developmental process requiring several adjustments and adaptations. It is also considered a life stage, because it spans many years of middle and late adulthood. Most of us will spend anywhere from 5 to over 20 years in the retirement stage of life. Although many adults diligently plan for financial security by the time they retire, such as preparing a financial portfolio, all too often they neglect their "psychological" portfolio and do not prepare themselves for the psychological aspects of retirement (American Psychological Association, 2005).

To address the transitional processes associated with permanently exiting the workforce, gerontologist Robert Atchley (2000) identified six phases associated with the processes of retirement as the result of numerous research studies. Atchley's phases provide a general framework of the steps associated with retirement, but keep in mind that retirement is experienced on an individual level that is influenced by a person's culture. Indeed, every phase iden-

FIGURE 16.7 The Phases of Retirement

Phase 1: Pre-retirement.

People start to consider retiring and begin preparing for the next stage, and they begin to disengage from the workplace.

Phase 2: Retirement.

People can take one of three possible routes to retirement:
- The *honeymoon* route is characterized by a "taking-it-easy" routine.
- The *immediate retirement routine* course is characterized by the ability to easily establish a busy yet comfortable schedule soon after retirement.
- The *rest and relaxation* route of retirement is a period characterized by low activity.

Phase 3: Disenchantment.

Instead of experiencing euphoria and relaxation, some experience a period of disappointment and uncertainty.

Source: Atchley, R. (2000).

tified by Atchley will not be experienced by everyone. The phases do provide a framework, however, with which to understand the multiple transitions necessary to navigate this normative change in the lifecourse. Figure 16.7 presents the six phases of retirement. As you can see, the retirement process typically unfolds gradually, from someone slowly disengaging from the workplace (sometimes this is referred to as *phased retirement*) to reorienting to establishing a daily routine that does not involve going to work. This stage in the lifespan ends when a person's health begins to decline and she or he can no longer live independently, or when a person's spouse or partner becomes dependent on the other for care. The important thing to keep in mind about retirement is that it is a unique experience for each person. How do relationships fare when someone retires?

Marital Life after Retirement A substantive body of research concludes that because social relationships and acquaintances that originate in the workplace dissolve after retirement (Bosse and others, 1990), pensioners tend to place greater emphasis on family life and will gain support, love, and friendship from these family relationships (Kulik, 1999). Because retirement is such a significant marker of transition and adaptation for the retiree and his or her family, one body of research examined the impacts of a number of factors on the lives of male retirees. In a sample of 137 men on the verge of retirement and a sample of 211 men who had already retired, empirical investigation revealed some significant findings among the two groups (Kulik, 1999).

First, both groups of men attached greater importance to their marriages than they did to their own health status, but there were significant differences between the two groups of men in their life orientation. **Life orientation** refers to the emphasis pre-retirees or retirees place on various aspects of life, such as family life and economic security. For instance, pre-retired men focused more on the economic factors, such as career, finances, and material possessions than did retired men. Retired men attached greater significance to their marital and family relationships than did the pre-retired men.

Second, there were also significant differences between the two groups' attitudes regarding gender role behaviors, particularly with respect to household labor. Retired husbands expressed more conservative, traditional values about gender roles than did pre-retired men. In both groups, husbands of working women expressed more liberal views regarding gender role behaviors than did the men whose wives did not work outside the home. Interestingly, gender role behaviors, such as the division of household labor, present in the early years of the marital relationship, are apparently central issues in marital interaction and family living in the later years of life, too.

Phase 4: Reorientation.

Reorientation is a period during which retirees assess their retirement experience and start making the necessary adjustments that will improve their lives, such as taking up new hobbies or volunteering.

Phase 5: Retirement Routine.

The ability to master a comfortable, rewarding, and satisfying retirement routine is the ultimate goal of retirement.

Phase 6: Termination of Retirement.

As people age and begin to decline physically, they either become dependent on their partner or spouse, or their partners become dependent on them for elder care.

FAMILY LIFE NOW

How Does America Pay for the Aging?

As people gain extra years in their life expectancies, the costs to help them stay alive are also increasing. Skyrocketing drug bills, costing the elderly hundreds—or even thousands—each month, have given rise to the number of senior citizens who may have to decide between life-saving drugs or other necessities, such as food, utilities, even needed hospital care. Aged Americans have support in Medicare, a federally administered system of health insurance available to people over the age of 65. The legislation is passed and the coverage is in place, but not all of America's aged are satisfied. Is Medicare a good thing?

YES: Medicare is an answer to years of support and positioning by aging advocates. The process of obtaining Medicare is involved but nonetheless worth doing. Once enrolled, seniors save money, and that is the bottom line.

- **Seniors support it.** Trained senior volunteers, in testimony before the U.S. Senate Special Committee on Aging, stated that Medicare saves money and is not overly confusing.
- **Personal interaction is necessary.** Most seniors find that if they take time to visit with the many experts who have volunteered to walk them through enrollment, their anxiety over the "confusing" elements of Medicare is relieved.
- **People already enrolled support it overwhelmingly.** Those asked said that the time and effort it required to review the various coverage plans was more than worth it. The bottom line? Medicare does what it sets out to do: It saves seniors money.

NO: Some aging Americans believe that the program is short on benefits, long on cost, and deeply rooted in political rhetoric.

- **Enrollment is too complicated.** The government has taken steps to make enrollment easy and accessible. However, because 72 percent of its potential customers have never been online, it's easy to understand the intimidation factor. Additionally, many seniors may be confused about the drugs they take, which makes phone enrollment a challenge as well.
- **Medicare is overpriced.** Research from the Congressional Budget Office estimates that the program will cost about $800 billion more than estimated over the next 10 years because of complications in enrollment.
- **Private companies are on the take.** The current Medicare bill as drafted ensures that private insurance companies are the ones primarily administrating (and profiting from) Medicare. Doing so establishes higher drug prices and added confusion to Medicare administration.

WHAT DO YOU THINK?

1. How important is drug coverage for U.S. seniors? Do you think we, as taxpayers, are responsible for covering these costs? Why or why not?
2. In what ways does the inclusion of private health insurers help or complicate prescription drug benefits?
3. It is said that seniors are having to go without drugs due to economics. Discuss the role and responsibility of government in this dilemma. What about drug companies? What about personal responsibility?

Sources: Friedman (2006); Ganz (2006).

Third, Kulik's research also looked at marital intimacy in the later years of life and found three distinct types of intimacy: *reciprocity*, in which both spouses confide in one another and self-disclose; *nonreciprocity*, in which one spouse confides and shares, but the other spouse has a confidant outside of the marriage; and *segregative*, in which neither spouse shares with the other, but instead shares with someone outside the marriage. The research revealed that among the study participants, reciprocity is the most commonly expressed type of intimacy (approximately 70 percent), and nonreciprocity is the least common type (11 percent).

In summary, certain aspects of marital life are characterized by change as men and women approach and enter their retirement years. It appears that both pre-retired men and retired men alike find their marital lives to be enjoyable and positive, although retired men report higher degrees of marital satisfaction. As men and women approach retirement and enter retirement, their families and family life become central to their lives (Kulik, 1999).

FAMILY CAREGIVING

Many people hold the common misconception that elderly people who can no longer "do" for themselves reside in a long-term care facility, such as a retirement home or a nursing home. On the contrary: For every one person who resides in a healthcare facility, there are at least two who live out their remaining years with the help of family caregivers (He and others, 2005). These family members provide the lion's share of medical and personal health assistance, in addition to emotional, spiritual, and financial support.

Today's longer lifespans present a new challenge to spouses and adult children alike, because providing care for aging spouses and parents extends the caregiving career by a number of years. In most cases, caregiving is not isolated to a single period in the family life cycle, but instead exists throughout the entire family life cycle. The **caregiving career** consists of those years that caregivers tend to dependent children, aging parents, and eventually, dependent husbands or wives (Brody, 1985). By the latter part of the human life cycle, it is often the spouse who provides the necessary help or assistance for her or his aging partner (Zarit, Birkel, & Malonebeach, 1989). If the spouse cannot provide the necessary care, the burden shifts to the adult children—most typically to the adult daughters (Lemme, 2005).

Characteristics of Caregivers There is great variability among caregivers and their experiences. Race, ethnicity, socioeconomic status, education level, marital status, and personality characteristics affect both the caregiver and the person receiving the care. In most cases, family members work together to decide who will help with what in providing various caregiving tasks (Ingersoll-Dayton, Neal, Ha, & Hammer, 2003). Research has shown that people who have launched all of their children, are not working outside of the home, and are not married are more likely to provide care for aging parents (Brody & Schoonover, 1986). According to the National Council on Aging (NCOA) (2005), there are other general characteristics of caregivers. For example, the caregiving landscape is dominated by women, making daughters and daughters-in-law the most common caregiver. In an examination of national health care trends, the National Council on Aging (2005) found that approximately 73 percent of all caregivers are women, with an average age of 46. Additionally, women are more likely than men to miss work or reduce their workload in

AS Americans live longer, the caregiving career has been extended by several years. While caring for a loved one is stressful, many adults find the experience rewarding.

Elder Abuse: An Aging Reality?

Elder abuse is conceptualized by family practitioners in broad, diverse terms, and includes physical abuse, sexual abuse, emotional abuse, psychological abuse, financial abuse, neglect, and abandonment. Today, the National Center on Elder Abuse estimates that 2.1 million elders are abused each year. Tragically, these numbers are vastly underreported: The U.S. Census Bureau estimates that for every case of elder abuse that is reported, five go unreported. Elder abuse, in any form, is never acceptable. Effective intervention can help put a stop to this alarming trend.

1. What kind of interventions can you think of that help stop or prevent elder abuse?

2. If you suspected that a family member was abusing an elderly person, would you say anything to the abuser? Would you turn them into the authorities? Why or why not?

order to care for a family member or an ailing spouse. Research in early 2000 indicated that nearly 90 percent of caregivers for people with Alzheimer's disease are women (Daire, 2004).

Why is it that women are the more likely caregivers for their aging parents? Developmentalists Denise Boyd and Helen Bee (2009) offer two suggestions. One factor may be that women experience greater emotional closeness to their parents, and consequently feel a greater need to care for them as they age. Another factor may be related to the ways in which women are socialized. As you learned in Chapter 4, women are typically socialized to be the nurturing parent to their own children; they simply transfer their nurturing to their aging parents.

Caring for aging parents or a dependent spouse involves multiple tasks (Gatz & Hurwicz, 1990):

- Emotional support
- Personal care (bathing, dressing, toileting, wound care, assisting with mobility or medications)
- Instrumental help (cooking, cleaning, grocery shopping, laundry, lawn care, and such)
- Financial management or financial assistance
- Making decisions about care and arranging any required care by physicians, nursing care, social services, hospice care, and the like.

Caregiving responsibilities exert physical and emotional wear and tear on caregivers. This is called **caregiver burden**.

Stressors Associated with Caregiving Providing care for aging loved ones is a stressful experience, both for the caregiver and for the entire family system. So stressful is caring for an aging loved one that depression rates for caregivers is between 30 and 50 percent (Lemme, 2005). The more stressful aspects of caregiving include (NCOA, 2005):

- *Transformation of a cherished relationship.* For many caregivers, it is difficult when an interdependent relationship is transformed to a dependent relationship. When the caregiver is a spouse, the caregiving role becomes the overarching aspect of the marital relationship.
- *Problematic physical behaviors.* Because the caregiver is responsible for helping a loved one with dressing, bathing, toileting, and communicating, many caregivers feel a great deal of stress from these perpetual responsibilities.
- *Cognitive impairments.* When caregivers are taking care of a cognitively impaired spouse or parent, such as those with dementia or Alzheimer's disease, emotional distress is felt greatly by both patient and caregiver.

A number of stressors and rewards are commonly reported by adult child caregivers. Psychologist Mary Ann Parris Stephens and several colleagues undertook numerous studies to determine the types of stressors caregivers experience when caring for a loved one (among many others, 2001, 2000, 1999, 1997). Some of the stressors include:

- Receiving complaints and criticisms from parents
- Uncooperative or demanding parents
- Agitated parents
- Forgetful or unresponsive parents
- Helping with personal care needs
- Managing a parent's financial or legal affairs
- Receiving little help from family or friends

Although caregiving is often difficult and demanding, it also provides many rewards. Stephens's multiple research studies show many rewards, including:

- Knowing the parent is well cared for
- Spending quality time with a parent
- Enjoying the parent's affection and appreciation
- Seeing a parent derive pleasure from small things
- Seeing a parent calm and content
- Experiencing a closer relationship with a parent

The stressors are not isolated to individual caregivers, however. As we have discussed throughout this text, any life event—anticipated or not—produces ripple effects that reverberate throughout the entire family system. When a parent or family member becomes a caregiver for a spouse or elderly parent, not only does it cause stress and strain on the caregiver, but these also radiate throughout the entire family system and, in turn, affect the family's balance. This stress causes increased family tensions, reduced time families have to spend together, role conflict and role strain, changes in individual and family lifestyles, and financial strain (Lemme, 2005). And according to Lemme, the tensions created by family caregiving can exacerbate previously existing strengths or weaknesses in the family system.

The Sandwich Generation Being in the middle of two generations—parenting adolescents or younger children while at the same time caring for aging parents—is known as the **sandwich generation**, and it presents many challenges to middle-aged adults, as the opening vignette illustrates for us. As Boyd and Bee (2009) observe, being squeezed between two generations is perhaps one of the greatest distinguishing features of families today compared to the family decades ago. Note the authors, "In middle adulthood . . . the family role involves not only giving assistance in both directions in the generational chain, but also shouldering the primary responsibility for maintaining affectional bonds. These responsibilities produce what is sometimes called the mid-life 'squeeze,' and those being squeezed form the sandwich generation" (p. 433).

When the tables turn and middle-aged adults begin to parent their parents, they are suddenly taking on conflicting roles. In negotiating these competing roles, many of these adults experience losses associated with providing care to their aging parent. Understanding these losses are key in understanding and coping with the feelings associated with parenting parents (Conway & Conway, 2000).

Parents' Losses and Needs As parents age and lose their independence, their children notice other gradual losses along the way. In addition to losing their financial stability, for example, aging parents also lose what was once an important social network, an important source of identity. As their aging friends begin to die, their social identity is further eroded. With the loss of their social network, losses associated with physical decline become that much more pronounced. With their vision, hearing, mobility, memory, strength, and independence in jeopardy, many older adults feel that they will lose their usefulness and their worth. Therefore, it is essential that aging parents are shown that they have continued dignity, and that they are still valued and useful to society. Older parents may also need to have their business needs

TODAY, a significant number of middle-aged adults are pulled in two directions as they provide care for their children and their elderly parents. While there are a number of stressors associated with being a part of the sandwich generation, can you think of any possible benefits or rewards?

met, such as helping them pay bills and care for their property. While caring for the parents, adult children also have needs and experience losses, too.

Adult Children's Losses and Needs The caregiver—the adult child—experiences losses, too. As we have discussed, middle-aged adults lose their time and freedom and take on a number of additional stressors that may affect their own personal health and intimate relationships. As they devote increasing amounts of time to their parents' needs, adult children are leaving less time to spend with their own spouses and children, or to furthering their careers. By and large, parents have been backups throughout life, providing for their children's every need. Thus, when they age, "not only are they weakening physically and shrinking physically in size, [they also] shrink in their capacity to help" (Conway & Conway, 2000). As we observe the gradual deterioration and decline in our parents, we realize (often quite suddenly, as in my experience) that our parents are mortal—and that death is an eventuality.

It is important to understand, then, that when adult children assume the role of caregiver for their aging parents, new needs and family challenges emerge (Conway & Conway, 2000). Being the "squeeze" generation often means that in the process of meeting the needs of two generations, the adult children's personal needs are squeezed out and forgotten. Consequently, it is important for sandwiched caregivers to nurture their marital and other intimate relationships by making time to spend with one another (Conway & Conway, 2000). It's also imperative that adult-children caregivers guard their own mental, emotional, and physical health. This may include learning coping techniques that help buffer the stress associated with caregiving, and doing things that nourish mental health and the physical body. Finally, middle-aged children caring for their parents need to be realistic. A parent may sometimes require "tough love," just as parenting a child does. It is necessary to balance being rational with sensitivity and compassion.

Managing the dual roles of parenting two generations simultaneously brings a variety of conflicting feelings. But if family members understand the legitimate needs of the family members and can make the adaptations and adjustments necessary to meet those needs, then parenting parents while parenting children can be a deeply rich and rewarding life experience. Yet there is one more lifecourse event with which family members must cope—death.

Death Is . . .

In American culture, oftentimes death is far removed from us: We die in hospitals, not in our family homes as in eras past; we have funeral directors and mortuaries prepare our loved one for burial and take care of the funeral services; at funeral services the family members are often curtained off in a private area. Most of us are uncomfortable around death, and some of us are uncomfortable talking about death. Take some time to fill out the following inventory about death and dying, and share your thoughts with a friend or a family member.

TALK ABOUT IT

1. Talking about death or thinking about death makes me feel _____ _____ .

2. What frightens me most about death is _____ _____ .

3. What intrigues me most about death is _____

4. Sometimes, I worry that I will die too soon. This makes me feel _____ _____ .

5. If I engaged in a conversation with a person who is dying, I would feel _____ _____ .

6. If I engaged in a conversation with a person who is dying, I would say _____ _____ .

7. If I touched someone who is dying, I would feel _____ _____ .

8. If someone asked me if I believed in an afterlife, I would have to say _____ _____ .

9. When I think about the possibility of life after death, I feel _____ _____ .

10. If I lost my mom to death, I would _____ _____ .

11. If I lost my dad to death, I would _____ _____ .

12. The following people in my life have died: _____ _____ .

13. I could see myself providing care for a dying person. This makes me feel _____ _____ .

14. In general, I would say America's attitudes about death are _____ _____ .

15. To die is to _____ _____ .

Dying and Death Experiences

Are you afraid of dying? When you think about people in your life who have died, which words would you use to describe your feelings? Would you avoid talking with someone who is dying?

It is difficult to think about death, especially the death of a family member. But death is as much a part of our life cycle development as is birth. None of us is immune to the gut-wrenching heartache and the feelings of despair that accompany losing someone we love. Death is not isolated to the later years in life; people lose friends, boyfriends, girlfriends, sexual partners, intimate cohabiting partners, fiancés, children, and young spouses to death at every point in the life cycle of family development. Because dying in old age is an expected lifecourse event, we study it here.

There is a seemingly endless list of topics associated with death and dying: the biomedical approach to death, the nature and meaning of death, suicide, murder, war, terrorism, euthanasia, the right to die, death in childhood, the funeral. All of these topics are worthy of study and discussion. But because acknowledging, accepting, and understanding death is important for the dying person as well as those the person is leaving behind, in this section we will examine those topics that are significant to the end of life—dying as a transition from life, the grief process, and losing a spouse in old age.

DYING: THE TRANSITION FROM LIFE

About three days before my mother died, she was somewhere between "life" and "death." She was alert, yet distant. What struck me the most was the intensity of her labor—the intensity of her death-work. About 48 hours before she took her final breath, I crawled into bed with her and cuddled with her. I wasn't sure I could ask the question that was burning in my heart to ask her. But I decided that throughout my entire life she encouraged her children to ask her anything, so I did. "What's it like to die?" I asked. She didn't answer right away, but I knew she heard me so I didn't pose the question again. After a while, she closed her eyes and gasping for each breath

IN the United States, some people choose to die at home, surrounded by their loved ones. If you had a choice, would you prefer to die at home or in the hospital? What shapes your choice?

she said, "You know honey . . . I thought it was hard work to bring you children into this world . . . but it is much harder to leave this world . . . you ask me what it's like to die . . . it's hard work . . . it's hard work." (Author's files)

Dying is but one of the countless transitions we make throughout our lifespan. Some transitions are hoped for and are long awaited; others, like death, are anticipated yet not necessarily welcome. What makes the transition from life to death so compelling? Robert Kastenbaum (2007), the author of the landmark text in death research and death education, explains some of the complexities of this transition:

> The transition from life is unique because the separation is so complete. However, the dying process does have aspects in common with other types of transitions: There are interactions that can either be upsetting or comforting, communications that can either inform or confuse, and self-evaluations that can either undermine or strengthen one's sense of identity. The transition from life is unique for every individual, [because] no two people bring the same thoughts, feelings, accomplishments, and illness-related experiences. Furthermore, no two people have the same set of human relationships. The quality of life during the final illness depends much on the quality of the individual's relationships with others and the availability of those who are most capable of providing comfort and support. (p. 115)

Dying When does "dying" begin? From the moment of birth? Is aging equivalent to dying? According to Kastenbaum (2007), dying does not necessarily begin as a biological or physiological process, but rather begins as a psychosocial event. In other words, *we* construct our personal conceptions of "dying" throughout our lifecourse, a definition drawn from our individual life experiences.

As death appears imminent, the medical community, the family, and friends adjust their mindset from preventing death to helping a loved one make the transition from life to death. For some, this can become a highly anxious time. The fear of death—whether our own death or the death of a loved one—can lead to death anxiety. **Death anxiety** refers to the tension, feelings of distress, and apprehension associated with discussions and thoughts of death (Kastenbaum, 2007). When death is an inevitability, individuals may attempt to avoid the painful tension associated with death anxiety by responding with *denial*, which rejects key features of the reality of the dying or death experience. So accustomed are people to suppressing their death anxieties and fears, Kastenbaum observes, empirical studies that attempt to measure death anxiety are of little use.

Pathways to Death Kastenbaum (2007) explains that all dying processes take time and all take a unique shape; however, there are three trajectories or pathways to death. These trajectories each have unique characteristics in how the dying are cared for.

The **lingering trajectory** of death is one in which the transition from life to death takes an extended period of time, such as with some types of cancer, diabetes, or other progressive illnesses or diseases. Caregivers do what they can to keep the patient or loved one comfortable, but recognize that they have done all that they can to preserve life. At this point in the process, it is quite unusual to see "dramatic rescue scenes" as the person inches closer to death. Kastenbaum notes that it is rare that a patient on a lingering pathway to death has much control over the management of his or her condition. In fact, "the slowly dying person seldom speaks of final things to family and friends—or to anybody" (p. 124). Sometimes it is difficult for family members to accept the finality of their loved one's condition and their imminent death. Conversely, sometimes family members become impatient when a loved one lingers well beyond expectations, because they need time to organize their emotions. According to Kastenbaum, the lingering trajectory is advantageous in that it allows both the dying person and the family time to get used to the idea of dying, work out any unresolved conflicts, and engage in meaningful life review.

While the lingering trajectory allows the dying person as well as family and friends a chance to prepare for the impending death, this is not the case with the **expected quick trajectory**, typically associated with an acute crisis or illness, such as a heart attack or vehicle accident. These types of events demand quick action to save a life. In expected quick trajectories of death, time is the critical factor. There are several types of expected quick trajectories:

- *Pointed.* The ill person may or may not be saved, and thus is exposed to any number of very high-risk procedures in an attempt to save the life.
- *Danger period.* The ill person may or may not be conscious. The family vigilantly waits by the bedside as the family member lingers between life and death, waiting for the danger period to subside (the danger period can last from several hours to several days).
- *Crisis.* The ill person is not in immediate danger of dying, but still runs the risk of dying suddenly, such as with an acute case of pneumonia.
- *Will probably die.* Nothing can be done to preserve the life of the ill person. Medical staff keep the person as comfortable as possible as family members wait for the death to occur.

The **unexpected quick trajectory** has the elements of time pressure and surprise. For example, a young girl may be admitted to the hospital for a routine case of pneumonia, but within days her case worsens drastically, and she dies in a week. In these cases, there is typically not enough time to save the life of the injured or ill person. Since their rapid decline in health is usually unexpected, there is no time allowed for friends and family to plan or to prepare themselves emotionally. This pathway to death is surrounded with resounding cries of confusion, sadness, and a sense of helplessness as family members wonder, "What's happening?" "What should we do?" and "What *can* we do?"

When an elderly loved one becomes ill and begins to die, any one of the aforementioned trajectories can be the pathway to death. Although many elderly patients die from lengthy terminal illnesses such as advanced cancers, progressive heart disease or diabetes, dementia or Alzheimer's disease, or Parkinson's disease, not all elderly people die from lengthy, prolonged illnesses. Ageism and stereotypes may cause us to forget that some elderly people live active, vibrant lives and may die as the result of a skiing accident, a fall, or a car accident. For example, a former nontraditional student of mine was 86 years old and was completing her first college degree at the time of her death. "Miss Mary" survived heart attacks and the amputation of her leg due to diabetes, yet she was killed suddenly in a car accident in which she was not the driver.

As dying people and their families follow different pathways toward death, those who are left take different pathways as they mourn the loss of someone they loved. Each of us responds to the death of a loved one in different ways.

RESPONSES TO LOSS

There is no singular, universal, "right" way to transition to the death of someone we love. In large part, our responses to death are determined by our cultural and ethnic backgrounds.

Mourning refers to the culturally prescribed expressions of the thoughts and feelings of a **bereaved person**—someone who suffers the loss of a loved one. In essence, mourning refers to how people display their grief. Most rituals associated with death are deeply rooted in the culture's religious beliefs. For example, among the Hmong, an ethnic group from the mountainous regions of southern China, the response to death is very elaborate and complex and includes a number of people to assure the deceased person's passage to the next life. With this death experience, those who serve as guides to the spirit world include coffin makers, warriors, food servers, drummers, and counselors to the dead. With Middle Eastern Muslim families, it is commonplace for women to be extreme in their expressions of sadness (screaming, pulling their hair) at the time of death and at the funeral, and to mourn the loss for a period of at least one year (Sharifzadeh, 1997). Among Latino families, death brings family members together, even though they may have been geographically or emotionally separated; the death experience strengthens family values and family ties (Cavanaugh & Blanchard-Fields, 2002).

Despite the cultural-specific ways in which we grieve, there are death-related experiences that are common to people and cultures throughout the world. Every culture expresses bereavement and grief. We are said to be bereaved when someone we love or someone we are close to dies. According to Kastenbaum (2007), "Bereavement conveys the idea of a tearing-apart, forcible separation that results in the loss of something we once had" (p. 350). **Bereavement** is active—it refers to a person's specific, unique reactions following the news that a loved one has died. While people can mourn and grieve over the loss of any number of things (such as the end of a marriage or intimate relationship or the loss of a job), bereavement is experienced only by people who lose someone to death.

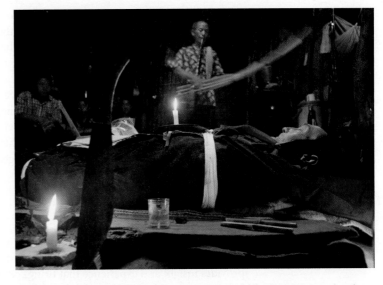

AMONG the Hmong people of Southeast Asia, death rituals are closely followed to ensure the safe passage of the deceased person's soul to the spirit world. Americans typically observe the death rituals of their heritage.

Grief is a response to the painful, forcible separation that takes place when we are faced with death. Grief can be expressed in many physiological forms: a feeling of tightness in the throat, shortness of breath, a need for sighing, an empty feeling in the abdomen, muscular weakness, tension, inability to sleep, changes in appetite, absent-mindedness or difficulty in concentrating, failures of memory, and the tendency to do the same things over and over. In addition to its physiological manifestations, grief is also characterized by three emotional and cognitive stages (Hooyman & Kiyak, 2002):

- *Initial phase.* Initial responses to death include shock, numbness, and disbelief, followed by overwhelming sorrow. Elderly spouses and caregivers can become ill quickly following the death of an intimate partner or family member.
- *Intermediate phase.* People idealize the deceased. Widows and widowers tend to regret every wrongdoing or misspoken word in their relationship. Some become angry at the deceased or displace their anger onto other family members or healthcare providers. The bereaved may experience anguish, disorganization, and despair, and may feel they have lost the motivation to carry on.
- *Final phase.* Recovery and reorganization occur but may take several years. Because the elderly may have diminished coping skills and lack the physical capacity required to do their "grief work," grieving may be a much more complex experience.

As Kastenbaum notes, grief affects every sphere of one's life. There are many different types of loss and grief (such as the death of a friend, the death of a parent, and the death of a child), and all require coping and rebuilding. As you learned in Chapter 15, the death of a spouse, however, is thought to be the greatest stressor one can experience. More women than men experience the death of a spouse because women's average life expectancy is longer than that of men.

Grief experiences also differ between widows and widowers. Older spouses tend to grieve for 30 months or more following the death of a spouse (Thompson, Itzen, & Abendstern, 1991), while younger widows and widowers mourn for significantly shorter periods of time. On the other hand, younger mourners tend to express more intense grief reactions than do older spouses. This may be partly because older adults anticipate, at least to some degree, that they will eventually lose a spouse to death.

Gender differences are also seen in how men and women respond as bereaved spouses. In general, men experience deeper levels of depression than do women. This may be attributable to women's larger social support networks (Diamond, Lund, & Caserta, 1987). Men, on the other hand, experience greater social isolation and loneliness following the death of a spouse. Some research suggests that this may be partly because men long for the emotional support they received from their wives. Since women have larger social support networks and thus can receive emotional support from sources other than a spouse, they tend to fare better than men following the death of their marriage partner (Bradsher, 1997). This difference in social support may account for the discrepancies observed between men and women's grieving.

According to one body of research, another difference in mental health may relate to the stresses and strains associated with the caregiving role for an ill or dependent spouse (Wilcox, 2003). Many women indicate that because they no longer experience the stress of caring for their ill husband, their mental health is stronger after his death.

Family Life Education

As we near the end of our study of family, intimate, and marital relationships, it is only fitting that we consider the last phase or chapter of life—aging and death. Miss Mabel, 108 years old, provides insight and experience that brings closure to our study (Welch, 2004):

> That is probably the worst part about aging—losing the people you love. Oh, I've grown accustomed to my vision and to my hearing. I've grown accustomed to having troubles when I stand . . . I've lost my husband and my children, and even two of my grandchildren. And you know, no matter how long you live, no matter how many people die, you never become accustomed to death. I miss them all. But death is a part of living. The sadness we encounter when a loved one dies is all related to the happiness we have when they are alive. You can't have one without the other. We lose. We mourn. We pick ourselves back up. And we go on. But you still miss them every day, you still think of them every day.

Summary

Aging and the Aged

- Baby boomers—those people who were born between 1946 and 1964—are getting older and life expectancies are increasing. The increasing number of this population challenges U.S. policy makers, healthcare providers, health and life insurance companies, businesses, and families.

- Gerontologists, family sociologists, developmentalists, and family life educators have developed perspectives that help them analyze the various influences on aging. One such model is the lifespan perspective of development, which emphasizes that just because one is older does not mean that one has completed one's intrapersonal and interpersonal developmental growth.

- For many years, most social scientists who studied aging focused on the biologically driven forces of aging. But today, social scientists believe that aging is a process of four interactive forces of development—biological forces, psychological forces, sociocultural forces, and life-cycle forces—and that all of the forces interact and combine to create a person's unique, individual developmental experiences. Furthermore, there are three varying sets of interacting lifecourse influences: normative age-graded influences, normative history-graded influences, and non-normative influences.

- *Primary aging* refers to the basic biological processes that take place over time. *Secondary aging* refers to physiological declines that are the result of environmental and behavioral influences.

- *Ageism* refers to the stereotypical attitudes people hold about the aging and the elderly.

Marriage Experiences through Aging

- Just as individuals must accomplish certain developmental tasks, families, too, must navigate the developmental tasks associated with the aging family.

- Maintaining stable intimate relationships throughout the life cycle protects against biological losses associated with aging and buffers against the loss of social roles. Marriages that are strong in reciprocity remain high in intimacy, while marriages that demonstrate lower levels of interdependence are prone to higher levels of stress and conflict.

- As couples age, there are often fewer sources of marital conflict and greater potential for marital satisfaction. Couples tend to find more pleasures in common in later marriage and to have more positive emotions.

- Sexual activity plays an active role in intimate relationships into later adulthood. While men's and women's desire for more frequent sex may differ, an active sex life is important to marital satisfaction in later life. Nearly three-fourths of sexually active older men and women said that they are as sexually satisfied or even more satisfied than they were in their 40s.

- With good health, and with sound knowledge and realistic expectations about sexuality through aging, sexual fulfillment later in life is a healthy, positive, and attainable goal.

- The experience of separation and divorce in later life is similar to that experienced earlier in the lifespan, but divorce in middle and later ages carries with it special characteristics and stressors unique to older adults. Because of long-held beliefs and values, divorce later in life contributes to the stressors associated with marital breakup.

- Remarried older adults experience less frequent negative types of conflict, and less frequent occurrences of abusive physical behavior than remarried younger couples. Consequently, remarried older adults experience increased levels of marital happiness and satisfaction. Additionally, couples remarried in mid-life appear to develop more effective communication and interaction patterns that were missing in their first marriages. These contribute to higher levels of marital satisfaction.

Intergenerational Ties

- As adults grow older through later adulthood, their interpersonal relationships across generations, or intergenerational ties, become increasingly important because they provide the foundation for intimacy throughout the aging process.

- In many families, children's entry into adolescence coincides with the parents' transition to mid-life. While young adolescents strive for independence and challenge their parents' authority, the parents are encountering their own mid-life developmental tasks such as caring for aging parents and preparing for retirement. These normative lifecourse events challenge the family system.

- Because most disagreements between parents and teens are commonly over insignificant matters, parents' marital satisfaction tends to increase as their children enter adolescence.

- During the middle years of the family life cycle, parents and children begin to renegotiate their relationship, and parents begin to reflect on their success or failure as parents. These reflections greatly affect the parents' purpose in life, self-acceptance, and thus their well-being.

- Mid-life couples commonly encounter struggles such as changing or losing roles, dealing with marital issues that often surface after the nest is emptied, changing careers, shifting their caregiving to a different generation, and maintaining strong relationships with their children who are adults themselves and require less advice and support.

- The parent–adult child relationship is central to the lives of the elderly. Four primary factors influence intimacy between older adults and their adult children: gender, geographic distance, parents' marital status, and culture.

- For many adults in their middle years, the experience of grandparenting is immensely satisfying. Grandparenting styles may be categorized as formal, fun-seeking, distant, surrogate, and dispenser of wisdom.

Family Changes toward the End of Life

- "Successful aging" is a pattern of well-being and adaptation to the challenges of middle adulthood and later life.

- *Life orientation* refers to the emphasis pre-retirees or retirees place on various aspects of life, such as family life and economic security. Because social relationships and acquaintances that originate in the workplace dissolve after retirement, retirees tend to place greater emphasis on family life.

- Research indicates there are three distinct types of marital intimacy in the later years of life: *reciprocity,* in which both spouses confide in one another and self-disclose; *nonreciprocity,* in which one spouse confides and shares, but the other spouse has a confidant outside of the marriage; and *segregative,* in which neither spouse shares with the other, but instead with someone outside the marriage.

- Contrary to popular belief, most older people don't reside in healthcare facilities, but live out their remaining years with the help of family caregivers. The *caregiving career* consists of those years that caregivers tend to dependent children, aging parents, and eventually, dependent husbands or wives.

- In most cases, family members work together to decide who will help with what in providing various caregiving tasks. People who have launched all of their children, are not working outside of the home, and are not married are more likely to provide care for aging parents. Daughters and daughters-in-law are the most common caregivers.

- *Caregiver burden* refers to the physical and emotional wear and tear caregiving responsibilities exert on the caregivers.

- The *sandwich generation* refers to those parents who are in the middle of two generations—parenting adolescent or younger children while caring for aging parents.

Dying and Death Experiences

- When death is an inevitability, individuals may attempt to avoid the painful tension associated with death anxiety by responding with denial. Additionally, they may experience death anxiety—the tension, feelings of distress, and apprehension associated with discussions and thoughts of death.

- There are three trajectories or pathways to death, each with its unique characteristics in how the dying are cared for: The *lingering trajectory* describes the transition from life to death over an extended period of time; the *expected quick trajectory* is typically associated with an acute crisis or illness; and the *unexpected quick trajectory* applies when there is typically not enough time to save the life of the injured or ill person. Since the rapid decline in health is usually unexpected in an unexpected quick trajectory, there is no time allowed for friends and family to plan or to prepare themselves emotionally.

- Responses to death are largely determined by one's cultural and ethnic background but there are death-related experiences common to people and cultures throughout the world. Every culture expresses bereavement and grief. *Mourning* refers to the culturally prescribed expressions of the thoughts and feelings of a bereaved person—someone who suffers the loss of a loved one. *Grief* is a response to the painful separation that takes place when we are faced with death, and is expressed physiologically, emotionally, and cognitively.

Key Terms and Concepts

Baby Boomer, p. 520

life expectancy, p. 520

gerontologists, p. 521

lifespan perspective, p. 522

nature-nurture debate, p. 522

normative age-graded influences, p. 523

social clock, p. 523

normative history-graded influences, p. 523

non-normative influences, p. 523

primary aging, p. 524

Hayflick limit, p. 524

secondary aging, p. 524

ageism, p. 525

ageist, p. 525

intergenerational ties, p. 530

fictive kin, p. 531

empty nest, p. 532

formal grandparenting, p. 534

companionate relationship, p. 534

fun seeker, p. 535

remote relationship, p. 535

involved relationship, p. 535

dispenser of wisdom, p. 535

life orientation, p. 537

caregiving career, p. 539

elder abuse, p. 540

caregiver burden, p. 540

elder abuse, p. 540

sandwich generation, p. 541

death anxiety, p. 545

lingering trajectory, p. 545

expected quick trajectory, p. 546

unexpected quick trajectory, p. 546

mourning, p. 546

bereaved person, p. 546

bereavement, p. 547

grief, p. 547

Suggested Readings

Boss, P. *Ambiguous loss: Learning to live with unresolved grief* (Cambridge, MA: Harvard University Press, 1999).

Doka, K., & Davidson, J. *Caregiving and loss: Family needs, professional responses* (Lakewood, NJ: Hospice Foundation of America, 2003).

Kastenbaum, R. *Death, society, and human experience* (9th ed.) (Boston: Allyn & Bacon, 2007).

Midlam, M. McWaters, G. & O'Donnell, J. *The retirement guide: A comprehensive handbook on aging, retirement, caregiving and health—How to plan and pay for it* (Toronto, ON: Insomniac Press, 2006).

Multiple-Choice Questions

1. Of the four interactive forces of development, lifecycle forces refer to _____ .
   a. all genetic and health-related factors
   b. all cognitive, emotional, and perceptual factors
   c. all forces that interact and combine to create a person's unique, individual developmental experiences
   d. forces that include cultural, ethnic, societal, relational, and interpersonal factors

2. When people hold stereotypical attitudes about the aging and the elderly, this is known as _____ .
   a. generational bias
   b. ageism
   c. sexism
   d. bigotry

3. When one is parenting adolescents or younger children while at the same time caring for aging parent, this is termed _____ .
   a. the in-between generation
   b. the sandwich generation
   c. the crushed generation
   d. the divided-attention generation

4. This type of expected quick trajectory occurs when an ill person may or may not be saved, and thus is exposed to any number of very high-risk procedures in an attempt to save the life.
   a. Pointed
   b. Danger period
   c. Crisis
   d. Will probably die

5. _____ is a response to the painful, forcible separation that takes place when we are faced with death.
   a. Grief
   b. Bereavement
   c. Mourning
   d. Anguish

6. This type of marital intimacy in later marriage is one in which neither spouse shares with the other, but instead shares with somebody outside of the marriage.
   a. Nonreciprocity
   b. Reciprocity
   c. Desegregative
   d. Segregative

7. Most of us will spend anywhere from _____ years in the retirement stage of life.
   a. 10 to 25
   b. 15 to 30
   c. 5 to over 20
   d. 0 to over 15

8. Among other things, _____ is influenced by lifestyle choices such as smoking, poor nutrition, lack of exercise, sun exposure, alcohol and/or substance use, and irresponsible sexual behaviors.
   a. secondary aging
   b. primary aging
   c. Hayflick aging
   d. generational aging

Answers: 1. c; 2. b; 3. b; 4. a; 5. a; 6. d; 7. c; 8. a

Glossary

A factor Part of Reuben Hill's ABC-X Family Crisis Model, these are the initial crisis-causing events.

ABC-X Family Crisis Model Reuben Hill's model that views a family crisis situation as a combination of various factors.

account-making Couples share with family and friends their individual accounts of what led to the deterioration of their marriage.

acting out A post-divorce effect in which children and adolescents externalize their feelings about the divorce, typically through aggressive misbehaviors, noncompliance, disobedience, delinquency, increased absences from school, and increased aggressiveness.

active listening When we actively listen, we become connected to another person so we not only hear what they are saying, but understand what they are feeling.

acute/chronic Stressors are considered to be either acute, meaning that they last a relatively short time, or chronic, meaning longer in duration.

agape (love) Self-sacrificing, spiritual love that looks out for the interests and well-being of others; a selfless, enduring, other-centered type of love that provides intrinsic satisfaction with no reciprocity expected or demanded.

ageism Stereotypical attitudes toward the aging and elderly.

ageist Ageists make predetermined, negative assumptions about older people.

age-related norms Socially approved and shaped pathways that determine the "right" time for certain life events, such as marriage or having children.

alimony A monetary payment, typically paid monthly, paid by one spouse to the other during and after the divorce proceedings.

altruistic love An unselfish, giving kind of love.

anal eroticism Sexual activity that includes anal intercourse, as well as oral stimulation of the anus, manually stroking the outside of the anus, and inserting one or more fingers into the anus.

anal intercourse The sexual activity of the male placing his penis into his partner's anus.

anal stage During the anal stage (ages 1 to 3), the focus of the sensual energy is associated with toilet training, particularly with respect to the anus.

Androgen Insensitivity Syndrome (AIS) A disorder characterized by an abnormality on the X sex chromosome, typically passed down from the mother; this results in prena-

tal development that differentiates as if no androgen at all was present.

androgens Testes produce androgens (testosterone), the masculinizing sex hormones.

androgynous In androgynous cultures there are no rigid gender roles guiding men and women's behaviors.

androgyny Without assigned gender value; when a person possesses traits, behaviors, or characteristics typically associated with the opposite gender.

angry associates Divorced couples whose anger is an integral part of the post-divorce relationship. Long, heated battles over property, custody, visitation, and other matters continue for many years following the divorce.

antinatalist An ideology that discourages childbearing.

anxious/ambivalent attachment types Insecurity is the hallmark of this attachment type. Fearing for the partner's love, anxious/ambivalent adults cling to the partner and push for commitment—often pushing the partner away.

appraisal-focused coping A coping style that attempts to understand why the crisis occurred and to find meaning in the circumstances. Skills needed include the ability to logically analyze the situation and mentally prepare for certain events to unfold.

artificial insemination The medical process by which donor sperm is placed by syringe into the woman's vagina, cervix, or uterus.

asexuality Having no sexual attraction to either gender.

Assisted Reproductive Technology (ART) Treatments that involve fertilization through the manipulation of the woman's ova and the male's sperm.

attachment Best described as an emotional or affectional bond that ties or binds the child to the parent or primary caregiver.

Attachment theory John Bowlby's Attachment theory describes enduring patterns of interpersonal relationships from cradle to grave. With the premise that all newborns must be nurtured in order to survive, Bowlby observed that they form a type of bond—an attachment—with their caregivers. From this close affectional and emotional bond, children derive a sense of security, a trusting sense that the world is a safe place to be.

authoritarian parents Parents who exert authority and control over their children, but without being responsive, warm, or affectionate, imposing rigid rules of behavior that must be obeyed without question. Parent–child communication is very low.

authoritative parents Parents who are responsive while expecting certain behavior of their children. Parents do not use shame, withdraw love, or impose guilt to control behavior. They set clear but flexible boundaries for their children's behavior, encourage parent–child communication, and use a balance of power and reason.

autonomy A person's desire to self-rule, or one's will.

autonomy granting Permissive parents allowing their children age-appropriate independence and self-governing.

avoidant attachment types Avoidant types report that they seldom find "real" love. They also show discomfort with intimacy and are hesitant to trust others.

B factor Part of Reuben Hill's ABC-X Family Crisis Model, *B* factors are the resources a family has at its disposal to meet the demands of the crisis.

baby boomers People who were born between 1946 and 1964.

balance In terms of work and family, the positive psychological state we achieve through regularly meeting our own, others', and work-related needs.

balance/homeostasis When an infection enters the body, various systems work together to bring it back into balance, or homeostasis. The same holds true for a family system when it experiences any departure from its usual state of balance (normal).

barrier contraceptive A contraceptive method that provides a chemical or physical barrier between the sperm and the ovum.

basic budgets The amount of money families need to manage at the most basic level; it must cover costs associated with housing, food, transportation, childcare, healthcare, clothing, personal care items, school materials, and taxes.

batterer A person who commits family violence.

Beginning of the Crowd Still same-sex in nature, peer groups toward the end of sixth grade/beginning of seventh grade begin to shift to crowds that consist of 10 or more core members. Crowd activities (dances, ball games, etc.) provide preadolescents the chance to "practice" interacting with the opposite sex.

behavior-based conflict Occurs when incompatibilities exist between the demands of the work role and the demands of the family role.

bereaved person Someone who suffers the loss of a loved one.

bereavement Refers to a person's specific, unique reactions following the news that a loved one has died.

bi-directional In the contexts of family living, not only is the individual influenced by the environment, but the environment is influenced by the individual. These influences are said to be bi-directional.

binuclear family The separate, distinct households that form after marital separation or divorce.

bisexuality Having erotic and amorous desires for people of either gender.

blended families The alternate term for the more familiar stepfamilies.

blue-collar workers Individuals holding jobs in the service sector, such as sales, office, production, and transportation.

booty call *See* Friends with benefits.

boundary Every system has some type of border, or boundary, between it and its environment. In a family, boundaries serve the purpose of affecting the flow of information within the system. They are essential because they are what separate us from our environment or from other family members.

breakup costs Emotional and financial costs of a breakup, and the search cost necessary to find another love.

breakup risk This is a relationship cost that includes determining the lover's future overall benefit with the individual, the lover's future net benefit with another lover, and the lover's current breakup costs. If these costs are considered high, the risk of being "dumped" is relatively low.

C factor Part of Reuben Hill's ABC-X Family Crisis Model, *C* factors are the meanings families ascribe to the event.

caregiver burden Caregiving responsibilities impose a burden of physical and emotional wear and tear on caregivers.

caregiving career Those years caregivers commit to tending to dependent children, aging parents, and eventually, dependent spouses.

case study This methodology involves study of either a single person or a small group of people.

cenogamy A form of marriage that is often referred to as group marriage. In cenogamous marriages, every man and woman is married to each other at the same time.

Certified Family Life Educator (CFLE) A person who has demonstrated knowledge (gained through work experience and college coursework) in the following content areas: families in society, family dynamics, human growth and development, human sexuality, interpersonal relationships, family resource management, parent education, family law and public policy, and ethics.

child language brokering Children in non–English-speaking homes are called on to be mediators and to speak or read, since in most cases the children are the first to acquire competence in a new language.

child support Whether married or divorced, parents must provide financially for any of their children under 18 years old.

childfree by choice Independent of social or physiological restrictions, some people make the choice to have no children.

childless/childfree Couples may consider themselves childless if they are unable to conceive or bear children of their own, or adopt children. Some couples remain childfree as a deliberate choice.

chlamydia The most common bacterial sexually transmitted infection reported in the United States; it is transmitted through vaginal and anal intercourse, and from a mother to her baby during birth.

chronosystem This system reflects the changes that happen over time, accounting for the collective historical precursors of current social attitudes (discrimination, definition of marriage, etc.).

Circumplex Model of Marital and Family Systems This model was created to address family cohesion, adaptability, and communication, providing the means to assess a family's level of functioning and health. According to David Olson's model, families who exhibit balance function more sufficiently and effectively over time than families who are more out of balance.

civil union   A legal term that speaks to the commitment, or the marriage contract, made by partners.

classical conditioning   John B. Watson's (1878–1958) theory that people make associations between two events. For example, babies open their mouths and smack their lips when their parent puts them in a highchair, or when their parent opens the jar of baby food.

closed boundaries   Forming one end of the boundary spectrum, closed boundaries prevent information from coming in or going out.

cognitive avoidance or denial   The attempt to deny the seriousness of a particular situation or events.

cognitive cue   If we discover that we want to spend more time with a person, we may then rely on cognitive cues. We get to know another's personality traits, beliefs, goals and aspirations, as well as the roles they play in life. At this point, after much self-disclosure and time, we decide to pursue a deeper relationship and enter into a committed partnership.

Cognitive Development theory   This theory holds that before social and environmental forces can influence a child's concept of gender, the child must first gain a certain awareness or understanding about gender.

cognitive redefinition   Cognitive redefinition occurs when families attempt to reframe the life event or stressor in ways that are seen as more favorable.

cognitive theories   Cognitive theories focus on how children think and how they understand their world.

cohabitation   To live together as if a married couple.

cohabitation effect   The negative effects that cohabitation has on first marriages such as lower marital satisfaction, higher divorce rates, lower levels of marital happiness, and less satisfying sexual relationships.

cohabiting   Cohabiting couples are unmarried partners who live together in a single household.

collectivist cultures   Cultures that define their identity in terms of the relationships individuals hold with others, which takes priority over individual needs; group membership is important.

commitment   This can mean different things to different people. For many, commitment is the until-death-do-us-part component of a couple's relationship. It speaks to relationship longevity, stability, quality, and satisfaction.

common law marriage   A relationship comprised of cohabiting heterosexual partners, but no legal marriage ceremony has taken place; however, the couple holds themselves out to the world that they are husband and wife.

communication   The process of making and sharing meanings.

companionate love   Deep, tender, mature, affectionate attachment bonds shared between two people; companionate love may or may not include feelings of physical arousal. This type of love combines the elements of intimacy and commitment, often beginning as romantic love, and then becoming companionate love as couples build intimacy.

companionate relationship   Companionate grandparents enjoy warm, loving, and nurturing relationships with their grandchildren, though they may be happy to send them home when it is time.

conceptualization   The process through which the researcher specifically denotes or indicates all of the concepts—or constructs—under investigation.

conditional forgiveness   The type of forgiveness used when people want relational repair, but they want to make it very clear that repeating certain behaviors will not be tolerated.

confidence gap   The phenomenon in which men and women have different confidence levels in their academic abilities—men tend to have more confidence in their academic abilities than women.

confirming messages or responses   Types of communication characterized by recognition of the other person, relevant dialogue, and acceptance; all of these show a willingness to be involved in the relationship.

conflict   Instances of stress or disagreements.

Conflict theory   Similar to structural-functionalism, Conflict theory concentrates primarily on social structures and their interrelationships. Like the functionalist view, this theory supports the notion that society has some bearing on and to some degree shapes individual behavior. It differs in its basic theme that human beings are prone to conflict.

confounding (rival) variable   Rival variables that are unrelated, unconnected, or not pertinent to the variables under investigation that can skew or affect the results of the study.

conjugal role   A culturally defined and assigned set of behaviors each marriage partner is expected to carry out.

construct   A concept referring to intangibles in the inquiry.

constructive conflict   Conflict that serves to build relationships and to foster loyalty, commitment, and intimacy.

consummate love   Considered by Sternberg to be total, whole, absolute, and all-inclusive, consummate love combines all three elements of love—intimacy, commitment, and passion.

contact hypothesis   The idea that negative stereotypes (prejudices) about other groups exist because of the lack of contact and interaction between groups.

contexts   Areas of individual and family development that play a role in the relationship between people and their environments. These multiple environments surround individuals from birth; a person is in constant interaction with these different contexts.

control group   In an experiment, the subjects in this group are treated exactly the same as those in the experimental group, except they are not exposed to the independent variable.

cool pose   A version of masculinity within black culture that "presents a powerful face to the world" while also entailing the expected cooperative behaviors of black culture.

cooperative colleagues   Divorced parents who put aside negative feelings toward the ex-spouse to cooperate in assuring the well-being of their children.

correlates of divorce   Certain social and socioeconomic characteristics that affect the longevity of a marriage and the probability that a marriage will end in divorce.

cost   The inverse or opposite of *reward*. Costs can be experienced as punishments (lost rewards) due to individuals engaging in one behavior over another.

courting/courtship   Socially prescribed forms of conduct that guide or groom young men and women toward matrimony.

covenant   A binding religious or spiritual union.

covenant marriage   In some traditions, marriage is viewed as a union bound together by more than legal ties or personal commitment, but divinely ordered and thus should not be entered lightly.

cross-sex friendships   Friendships between opposite-sex peers.

Crowd Disintegration   As adolescents mature into adulthood and take on adult responsibilities, such as a job, and as they become involved in serious intimate relationships, crowd-type friendship groups begin to disintegrate. Often the support of friends is replaced by an intimate partner with whom young adults now share and disclose.

Crowd in Transition   During the end of junior high and throughout high school, peer groups are seen as in transition. Smaller cliques are formed within the larger crowd.

crude birth rate   The number of childbirths per 1,000 women, per year.

crude divorce rate   The number of divorces that occur per 1,000 population.

cultural competence   Accepting and respecting the cultural differences of others.

cultural factors   In terms of divorce, this refers to whether the couple embraces an individualistic or collectivist social identity.

cultural scenarios   Sexual scripts that recognize influences such as our families of origin and our communities, mass media, educational systems, and religious beliefs.

cultural scripts   Common guidelines that provide instructions about what behaviors and emotions are expected in certain situations.

cunnilingus   The erotic, oral stimulation of the woman's external sex organs.

custody   Refers to who is responsible for the children's financial, physical, and emotional well-being.

cyber-stalking   Online stalking.

Cycle of Violence model   A model illustrating the three phases of violence commonly seen in abusive relationships: the tension-building phase, the acute battering or violent act, and the respite (nonviolent) phase.

data churning   Also known as "fishing," this refers to the practice of devising the purposes of the research or formulating a research hypothesis after the data are gathered and analyzed.

dating   Socializing for any number of reasons, such as for relaxation and escape from everyday responsibilities or to pursue a relationship to determine whether the partner is a potential spouse or a partner for a life-long relationship.

dating scripts   The models that guide our dating interactions.

dealing-with-problems focus   As early as the 1960s, a long list of social ills that affected family life began to direct education for family living, which became focused on or problems of sexuality, gender roles, marriage, and other social issues.

death anxiety   Tension, feelings of distress, and apprehension associated with discussions and thoughts of death.

decode   The interpretation of unspoken exchanges.

de-escalation of intimacy   A decline in intimacy.

Defense of Marriage Act (DOMA)   A law signed by President Bill Clinton confirming that marriage is a legal union of one man and one woman as husband and wife.

dependent love   A type of love that is seen in adult–infant/adult–child relationships, wherein adults meet and gratify the needs of their infant or child, without expectation of anything in return.

desacralization of marriage   The societal shift from marriage as a binding religious union to a union of individual choice.

destructive conflict   Destructive conflict can be either overt, which refers to obvious conflict, or covert, which is more subtle, but nonetheless hurtful. Whether it is overt or covert, destructive conflict is unhelpful and, at its very worst, deadly (as in the case of physical violence that escalates).

developing-family-potentials focus   Promoting goals ranging from building on family strengths to developing healthy, fulfilling, and responsible interpersonal relationships, family life education aims to build on positive aspects of family life and the family's potential to enhance personal life and family living.

developmental tasks   Developmental tasks entail achieving certain biological, physical, cognitive/intellectual, social, emotional, and spiritual tasks across the lifecourse.

diminished parenting   Refers to the new relationship between parents and children in the first few years following a divorce.

direct forgiveness   Family members or intimate partners clearly, plainly, and directly tell the offender that she or he is forgiven.

Dissolved Duos   After the divorce, dissolved duos break off any contact with one another.

distress   A stressor can be "bad stress," "negative stress," or "harmful stress."

distress reactions   Reactions to a breakup that include such things as physical and emotional pain, loss of interest in sex, and guilt.

diverse   In the United States, it refers to people's differences in age, gender, race, ethnicity, cultures, sexual orientation, and religion.

diversity   The broad spectrum of demographic and philosophical differences among groups within a culture.

divorce   Socially sanctioned actions to legally terminate marriage.

divorce mediation   The process involving an objective third party who helps ex-spouses resolve child support, child custody, and property settlements for themselves and for their children, rather than having a judge determine these issues for them.

divorce mediator   An objective third party to the divorce who aids the divorcing couple in determining the terms of their divorce settlement, such as child support and visitation rights and schedules for the parent who does not receive custody.

DOMA (The Defense of Marriage Act)   This legislation forbids any federal recognition of same-sex marriages.

domestic violence   Violence perpetrated against family members by a person who is related to the victim either biologically or legally, such as by marriage or through adoption.

Double ABC-X Model   Using Reuben Hill's ABC-X Model as the foundation, family researchers developed the Double ABC-X Model to better understand the effects of the accumulation, or pile-up, of stressors and strains and how families adapt to them.

doula   A professional provider of labor support (emotional, physical, and informational) to women and their companions.

dual-career couples Couples in which both partners are employed in professional or managerial positions.

dual-earner couples Couples in which both spouses are actively engaged in the workforce.

Duck's Relationship Filtering Model Similar to the filter model of mate selection, Stephen Duck proposed that when deciding whether to enter into or continue an interpersonal relationship, we have a set of filters through which we sort information: sociological or incidental cue, preinteraction cues, interaction cues, and cognitive cues.

dyadic breakdown phase The period during which a couple's established pattern of relationship breaks down.

dyadic phase According to Stephen Duck, the dyadic phase occurs when couples discuss their dissatisfaction with their marriage and attempt either to find a resolution or to end the relationship.

dyspareunia Sexual pain experienced by women as a result of sexual dysfunction.

early remarriage The early stages of the new relationship, when the developmental difficulties of a traditional marriage occur, along with difficulties unique to stepfamilies.

Ecological Model A theory developed by Russian-born Uri Bronfenbrenner that explains the multiple influences that affect individuals' and families' development over their lifetimes. The central concept is that people develop in a variety of interacting contexts.

ecosystem Also referred to as contexts (within the Ecological Model), these are areas of individual and family development that play a role in the relationship between people and their environments.

Eight Stages of Man Erik Erikson's theory that contends that social and emotional development is a lifelong process that takes place in eight stages.

elder abuse Physical, sexual, emotional, psychological, or financial abuse; neglect; and abandonment of an elder.

elopement Secret marriages between love partners that take place without parental approval and/or knowledge.

emergency contraception (EC) Made of the same hormones found in birth control pills, EC prevents pregnancy by interrupting the release of an egg.

emotional attachment Feelings that promote a sense of closeness, bonding with one another, and connection.

emotional communication The physical gestures and movements that convey our emotions. Also known as *nonverbal forms of communications.*

emotional discharge The act of giving vent to or expressing anger, frustration, confusion, disappointment, hatred, and despair in response to tragic or sudden/unexpected news.

emotional divorce Emotionally withdrawing from a marriage partner or from the marriage.

emotional needs Emotional needs encompass self-esteem, social and spiritual needs, and safety.

emotional regulation Strategies designed to help individuals and families change their perception, interpretation, and the meaning of the stressor.

emotional safety The high degree of trust required to self-disclose.

empty love This type of love is void of passion and intimacy. Commitment is the only element in the relationship.

empty nest The home with no children after children have grown and left.

endogamy Refers to marrying within one's same group, such as Muslims marrying Muslims, Catholics marrying Catholics, or Asians marrying Asians.

endometriosis A disease characterized by the buildup or migration of uterine tissue to other parts of the body (such as the ovaries or fallopian tubes).

entertainment needs Entertainment needs are considered by Vuong to be, by and large, social aspects of day-to-day living and family life (hobbies, interests, etc.).

erectile dysfunction Also known as *impotence,* this condition is marked by an inability to achieve an erection.

eros/erotic lovers Sensual or sexual love. Erotic lovers are passionate and romantic and seek out passionately expressive lovers.

estrogen The feminizing hormone.

ethics Refers to the principles or standards of people's conduct, or the principals of right and good. Research ethics are concerned with the relationship between the researcher and research subjects.

ethnicity This refers to a social construction that is used to identify groups of people (commonly races) who share common cultural traits, such as religion, customs, language, and dress.

eustress A stressor can be "good stress," "positive stress," or "productive stress."

Evolutionary theory The Evolutionary Theory for Mate Selection purports that we choose mates for the sole purpose of ensuring reproductive success—and thus the success of the species and society.

excitement phase The first of four distinct phases of sexual response.

exogamy A requirement to marry outside of a particular group. In the United States, for example, we cannot marry a sibling or, in some states, a first cousin.

exosystem The exosystem consists of the fabrics of society in which policies are made and influenced that ultimately have an impact on the elements of the microsystem and the individual.

expected quick trajectory A transition from life to death typically associated with an acute crisis or illness, such as a heart attack or vehicle accident. These types of events demand quick action to save a life.

experimental design Used to determine causal relationships among variables. In this mode, researchers control or hold constant certain variables being studied in order to determine which variable is effecting the change in the other variable.

experimental group The group that is exposed to the independent variables under question.

expressive roles These roles, described by Talcott Parsons, were given to the female as a compliment to the male. The wife-mother was the people-oriented mate responsible for enhancing emotional relationships among members of the family.

expressive schemas Patterns of behavior associated with femininity; having an interpersonal or relational orientation.

extended family The family unit where two or more generations of close family relatives live together in one household.

external locus of control Refers to the perception that we cannot control what happens in some aspects of our lives.

externalizing difficulties Commonly referred to as *acting out*, children and adolescents externalize their feelings about the divorce, typically through aggressive misbehaviors, noncompliance, disobedience, delinquency, increased absences from school, and increased aggressiveness.

extra relationship involvement (ERI) Any behavior that oversteps the expectations of exclusivity and expectations of monogamy.

extramarital sex (EMS) Occurs when a married person has a sexual relationship (any type of sexual activity, such as mutual masturbation, or oral, anal, or vaginal sex) with someone other than his or her spouse.

family A family consists of two or more people related by birth, marriage, or adoption residing in the same unit.

Family and Medical Leave Act Under the Family and Medical Leave Act (FMLA), federal and state employees and those who work for employers with 50 or more employees are able to take up to 12 weeks of unpaid leave to care for an ill child, parent, or spouse, or for one's own serious illness without fear of losing their job, benefits, or status.

family cohesion The extent to which family members feel emotionally close and bonded to one another.

family coping skills Skills that families tend to use in times of change and crisis.

family crisis Transitions throughout the lifecourse of the family often cause stress; sometimes this stress is experienced as a family crisis.

Family Deficit Model Promoted the idea that single-parent households were negative experiences for children for the sole reason that the family structure was not nuclear.

family law In the United States, family law establishes policies and regulations to protect the rights and well-being of all family members and ensure that married or divorced couples fulfill their obligations to each other and to their children. Specific family laws vary from state to state.

Family Life Cycle Comprised of multiple entrances and exits from the family of origin.

family life education Borrowing and adapting theoretical frameworks from the fields of sociology and psychology, this perspective provides organized, programmatic education to help families cope with change.

family meetings Formal or informal regular family discussions that provide structure and organization to the family system and allow for meaningful conversation.

family metacognition The phase in marriage deterioration in which the spouses begin to openly share with others the problems in their marriage and the possibility that it may come to an end.

family of origin The family into which we are born or brought into by adoption.

family of procreation The family unit that is formed when we marry and produce children.

family resiliency A family's ability to function effectively during times of change, stress, adversity, crisis, and transition.

family stress The result of an imbalance between the demands an event places on a family, and that family's ability or inability to meet them.

family system The family is a living, ever-changing, dynamic system that consists of various individuals and their interconnected, intergenerational patterns of interactions. In this context, a system's primary function is to bring together and arrange the various interrelated parts into a whole, organized entity.

Family Systems theory (FST) Developed by Murray Bowen, this theory views a family as a whole entity comprising interconnected parts seeking to maintain balance.

family values Usually refers to a society's paradigm or viewpoint that expects its members to adhere to perceived proper social roles, such as marrying and having children, remaining monogamous and faithful to the marriage partner, and opposing same-sex relationships, marriages, and parenting by gay or lesbian partners.

family violence A common term for domestic violence.

family well-being Includes psychological health; high levels of self-esteem, sense of power, and internal locus of control; good physical health; low behavior/conduct problems; good social support; high marital quality and stability; and good parent–child relationships.

fatuous A descriptive term referring to infatuation-based relationships.

fatuous love Combining passion and commitment, fatuous love relationships result in a sprint toward cohabitation or marriage. Because the relationship lacks intimacy and the time necessary for intimacy to grow and develop, and because passion will fade sooner or later, the only element remaining is commitment.

fellatio The oral stimulation of the male's external sex organs.

femininity The qualities, behaviors, and attitudes that are deemed by a particular culture to be ideally appropriate for girls and women; most often associated with nurturing and life-giving attributes such as kindness, gentleness, and patience.

Feminist theory A theory that embraces the conflict approach to understanding and analyzing the roles of women in terms of marriage and family in perpetuating inequalities in the male/female relationships.

fertility cues When seeking mates, men will select women who possess certain fertility cues, such as youth, attractiveness, and permissiveness.

fertility rate The average number of live births per woman, in a given population, per year.

fictive kin People who are not biologically related but who fulfill a family role.

field research Observation research taking place in a natural setting, such as at the family's own home or the child at a playground, instead of at a clinic.

Fiery Foes Ex-spouses who are incapable of co-parenting and who engage in legal battles for several years following the divorce.

fight or flight Because of our inborn "fight or flight" tendency, our normal state of homeostasis (balance) in the mind and body becomes upset when exposed to stress or stressors.

Filter Theory of Mate Selection This theory suggests that individuals use a filtering mechanism that helps them sort out a potential mate from the vast pool of candidates.

forgiveness   A deliberate process that transforms a strong desire for revenge into a positive response.

framework   A systematic structure for classifying families, their behaviors, or their experiences.

friends with benefits   A term used to describe one who has regular sex with another, but does not relate to that person as a boyfriend or girlfriend. Also described as a *booty call*.

fully developed crowd   A group of opposite-sex cliques; the same-sex friendship affiliations from elementary school and early years of junior high are no longer dominant.

functional communication   Communication that addresses only the ins and outs of daily life, leaving one feeling as though something is lacking in one's family connections.

gamete intrafallopian transfer (GIFT)   An Assisted Reproductive Technology process in which unfertilized eggs and a male's sperm are placed in a woman's fallopian tubes to foster natural fertilization.

gatekeepers   Divorced mothers who deny visitation, make it difficult for fathers to see their children, and intend not to share parenting with the fathers of their children.

gender   Encompasses characteristics such as gender role, gender identity, gender presentation, and gender stereotypes.

gender attribution   The process by which we encounter someone and reach an opinion of what his or her gender is.

gender conformity   The degree of pressure felt from one's environment to conform to gender stereotypes.

gender constancy   Between kindergarten and about second grade, children understand that acting like a girl if you are a boy doesn't make you a girl, and acting like a boy if you are a girl doesn't make you a boy. Children realize that sex is a permanent attribute.

gender contentedness   The degree of contentedness people feel toward their biologically assigned gender.

gender equality   Equality between men and women in the job place and economic equality.

gender identity   Our intuitive sense of our maleness or our femaleness; our internal feelings of what it is to be a man or a woman.

gender inequality   The obvious or hidden disparities or discrimination in opportunities or advancements among individuals, based solely on a person's gender.

gender polarization, bipolar gender   A model in which cultural viewpoints almost always emphasize the differences between men and women.

gender presentation   The way in which an individual presents his or her gender identity through personality, habits, and behaviors.

gender roles   The explicitly expressed and implicitly implied behaviors, feelings, attributes, and traits that society expects of the male or the female.

gender schemas   The way in which we internalize and incorporate specific gendered behaviors and expectations.

gender socialization   The specific messages and practices we receive from our culture concerning the nature of being a male or a female, of being feminine or masculine.

gender stability   Between the ages of 4 and 6, children reach the realization that their gender will always be the same—that they were a boy or a girl as a baby and will be a boy or a girl when they grow up.

gender stereotypes   Long-held assumptions or labels about male and female capabilities and limitations.

gender typing   The process of developing the behaviors, thoughts, and emotions associated with a particular gender.

gender wage gap   The disparity in men's and women's earnings in the United States.

General Adaptation syndrome   Physician Hans Selye (1975) developed the three-stage General Adaptation syndrome to describe the physiological responses to eustress and distress. The stages are alarm reaction, stage of resistance, and exhaustion.

General System theory (GST)   Encompassing areas of study from economics to biology to the intricacies of family life, this theory constitutes a worldview or a paradigm that keeps at the forefront the notion that objects do not exist in isolation, but instead are interconnected to parts of a larger whole.

genital stage   From ages 12 and beyond, or the genital stage, people develop mature sexual interests in the opposite sex, according to psychoanalytic theory.

genogram   A diagram with various figures that illustrate relationships between family members.

gerontologists   Scientists who study aging.

glass ceiling   Refers to discrimination against women in the workplace, specifically in situations where advancement in an organization is stopped because of occupational sexism.

gonorrhea   The second-most common sexually transmitted infection reported in the United States; sometimes referred to as *the clap* or *the drip*; it is transmitted through intercourse, oral sex, and anal sex, and it can also be transmitted from the mother to her baby during childbirth.

grave dressing phase   A divorcing couple comes to terms with the breakup of the marriage and they begin to piece together a rational, logical explanation that explains why the marriage "died."

grief   Physical and emotional responses to the painful, forcible separation that takes place when we are faced with death.

group context   The couple's social network of family, peers, and community.

gunnysacking   This refers to a spouse or a family member who holds in resentment, hurt, anger, frustration, and bitter feelings until that "last straw"—when the spouse or family member unloads all of the pent-up feelings in the midst of an argument.

Hayflick limit   According to Leonard Hayflick, each species has a genetically programmed time limit, because at a certain point in time, cells lose their ability to replicate. The Hayflick limit accounts for the aging process and life expectancy.

hegemonic masculinity   Each culture's ideal, dominant standard of masculinity to which men are to aim.

herpes   A sexually transmitted infection caused by the herpes simplex virus; it is transmitted through touching and kissing, and through vaginal, anal, or oral sex.

heterogamous   These relationships involve couples who are dissimilar in one or more dimensions, such as race, ethnic, and religious backgrounds, or dissimilar in age, political ideology, socioeconomic status, and values and beliefs.

heterogamy Refers to partners who are of different races, religions, or ethnicities.

heterosexuality Having erotic and amorous desires for people of the opposite gender.

homogamy Partnering with someone similar in ethnic and racial background, religious upbringing, age, education level, political ideology, socioeconomic status, and values and beliefs.

homosexuality Having erotic and amorous desires for people of the same gender.

homosocial play Children's preference for same-sex playmates; occurs from age 3 to age 11 or 12.

hooking up Physical or sexual interaction with the absence of commitment or affection.

hormone contraceptive Methods of contraception that use artificial hormones to prevent ovulation as well as thicken the cervical mucus, which inhibits sperm from traveling into the uterus.

household A household consists of all people who occupy a housing unit regardless of relationship.

household work The work associated with staying at home in order to nurture one's children.

human papilloma virus (HPV) A sexually transmitted infection; high-risk forms can lead to cancer of the cervix, vagina, anus, or penis; low-risk forms can lead to genital warts; it is spread through vaginal, oral, and anal intercourse as well as through skin-to-skin contact.

hypotheses testing An integral part of the sequential research process, taking place at a later point in the investigation. Based on evidence gathered, a researcher can either reject a hypothesis or fail to reject a hypothesis.

hypothesis A speculative statement about a variable or the relationship between variables in a study.

identity An individual's sense of who she or he is.

immediate context Factors influencing a couple's interaction, such as the physical setting, the couple's mood, and the couple's reason for talking.

immigrant Foreign-born people who have been granted the right to permanently live and work within the United States..

incompetent suitors A type of stalker; they have poor social and emotional skills, and have difficulty expressing themselves.

independent couple These couples value closeness, companionship, sharing, and self-disclosure (although they do not disclose quite as much as traditional couples). They are not as conventional in their beliefs as traditional couples.

indirect forgiveness Family members or intimate partners communicate this type of forgiveness by nonverbal displays (such as a hug, a smile, or eye contact) and by acting as though the transgression never happened.

individualistic cultures In these cultures, individual goals are more important than the goals of the group. Individuals define their identity or sense of self by way of personal attributes (wealth, social status, education level, marital status, etc.).

individuation Adolescents must form an identity separate from their family of origin (individuation).

infatuated love This type of love consists of passion only. "Hollywood" marriages are made of this, but not long-term marriages.

infatuation An intense, extravagant, and often short-lived passion for another person, often confused for love.

infertility The inability to conceive a baby after trying for a period of one year.

infidelity/cheating A breach of faith that occurs when there is a violation of the couple's mutually agreed-on rules or boundaries of a relationship.

Institutional Review Boards (IRBs) Research review committees established by academic and other research institutions that review and approve research plans for scholars and researchers, and ensure the ethical treatment of research subjects.

instrumental roles An element of Parsons's functionalist theory, instrumental roles were assigned to the male husband-father who, as the task-oriented mate, was assigned responsibility for being primary breadwinner and protector against imbalance or disequilibrium in the family.

instrumental schema Patterns associated with masculinity and focus on task-oriented behaviors and "getting the job done."

instrumental support The element of marriage in which husband and wife both boost the well-being, productivity, and career of their spouse.

intensive mothering Term coined by Sharon Hays to reflect the mothering roles and expectations that have been evolving since the 1980s, when women flooded the workplace.

intensive mothering ideology The Western cultural belief that a mother should give of herself unconditionally, and focus all of her time, energy, money, love, support, and every other resource she has, on raising her children.

interaction cue These cues allow us to assess whether we want to get to know a person any better. As we interact, we gain a better idea of the extent to which we may want to relate to a person.

interdependent love *See* Interdependent relationships.

interdependent relationships Certain cultures, such as Latino and Asian, value interdependent relationships, in which the opinions of family members and close friends figure importantly.

interfaith marriage This term refers to when people of different religious faiths marry.

intergenerational approach to family therapy An approach seeking to understand the transmission of relational behaviors from one generation to the next.

Intergenerational Family theory The theory that patterns of relational functioning (including intimacy) are passed down from generation to generation.

intergenerational ties The relationships between family members across multiple generations.

intergenerational transmission Research suggests that those who experience the end of their parents' marriage are more likely to divorce than those whose parents do not divorce. Many social scientists refer to this phenomenon as *intergenerational transmission of divorce.*

internal locus of control Referring to the perception that we are, to a large extent, in control of our destiny.

internalizing difficulties Internalizing difficulties result in emotional problems such as worry, feelings of unhappiness, anxiety, depression, distress, guilt, and poor self-concept.

Internet dating Usually through an Internet site, these electronic liaisons allow people to remain anonymous or to fully self-disclose personal information.

interpersonal scripts Sexual scripts that recognize how different people interact and relate to each other within specific social situations.

interracial Referring to romantic or marriage partners of differing races.

interrole conflict When we take on (or have assigned to us) many roles simultaneously, interrole conflict occurs.

intersexed/intersexual Refers to when a child's genitalia are ambiguous or indistinguishable.

intimacy Loving relationships characterized by feelings of closeness, connectedness, and bondedness.

intimacy seekers Stalkers; they desire to establish an intimate, loving relationship with their victim.

intimacy status The commitment and depth of the relationship.

intimate A person capable of experiencing closeness and forming a deep and enduring emotional attachment to another.

intimate partner violence (IPV) Violence perpetrated against a relationship partner.

intrafaith marriage Intrafaith marriages are between couples who share the same religion but have different beliefs or follow different traditions within that faith (such as a Baptist who marries a Presbyterian).

intrapsychic phase According to Stephen Duck, the second phase of relationship deterioration, also called *individual cognition,* when a couple begins to focus on aspects of the relationship with which they are dissatisfied or disappointed.

intrapsychic scripts Sexual scripts that account for individual desires, fantasies, emotions, and intentions while at the same time considering the interpersonal responses of others.

intrinsic rewards Intrinsic rewards, such as joy, satisfaction, contentment, pleasure, gratification, and so on, are the rewards of altruistic love. Most of us do not feel the need to reciprocate altruistic love because the rewards obtained are pleasurable in and of themselves.

in vitro fertilization (IVF) An Assisted Reproductive Technology process whereby a woman's eggs are surgically removed from her ovary and mixed with a man's sperm in a laboratory culture dish; if the eggs are fertilized and appear to be growing at a normal rate, the embryos are placed within the uterus.

involved relationship Some grandparents assume the role of parents as they are involved in the everyday rearing of their grandchildren.

isolates People who are socially withdrawn with no apparent need for social or close personal interactions.

jealousy An emotional reaction to the perception that a valued relationship is threatened because of a third party.

job autonomy Occurs when employees are allowed a high degree of independence and self-direction.

job complexity Occurs when jobs are challenging and stimulating at the same time.

job status Refers to a type or kind of job that offers some kind of prestige in an organization or community.

joint custody Parents share in the decision making on behalf of their children. They may also share the physical custody of their children.

kinship care A situation in which grandparents provide a living environment for their grandchildren.

Klinefelter's Syndrome A genetic disorder in which an extra X chromosome is present, resulting in an XXY chromosomal pattern. This disorder is considered to be one of the most common of all genetic abnormalities. While the internal reproductive organs and external genitalia develop normally, a male affected by Klinefelter's syndrome will have smaller-than-normal testes and will not produce sperm.

Knapp's Relationship Escalation Model Describes how relationships are initially formed and how they progress over time: initiation, experimenting/exploration, intensification, integrating, and bonding/intimacy.

late remarriage It takes approximately six to ten (or more) years after the remarriage for the family's boundaries and roles to be restructured to the point where there is a greater deal of "authenticity" in interactions and shared intimacy within the family system.

latency stage According to Freud, at about ages 7 to 11, the sensual energies subside for a time.

learning theories Theories that emphasize the role of the environment, such as the home, school, community, and peers, in shaping a child's development.

Learning theory The theory that traits and behaviors are not inborn, but learned.

legal custody Refers to which parent has the right to make decisions about how the child is reared, such as decisions concerning education or religion.

life change event Typically, a life-altering event that requires significant social and psychological adjustment.

life expectancy Based on statistical averages, the age at which adults are expected to die is anywhere from age 68 to 80, depending on a person's race and gender.

life transition Within psychology and family studies, a point at which people take on new roles and obligations, such as becoming a parent.

lifespan perspective Emphasizes that human beings are in a constant, continuous state of growth from the cradle to the grave.

liking Intimacy is the sole element in the relationship and is the stuff that great, long-lasting friendships are made of. There is typically no passion or commitment.

lingering trajectory A term that describes a lengthy transition from life to death, such as occurs with some types of cancer, diabetes, or other progressive illnesses or diseases.

Linus blanket relationship A type of relationship describing people (most typically females) who have a driving need to be "in love" with someone and who need the security of being cared for.

literature review An comprehensive search of existing research studies related to a particular topic of inquiry.

Love Economic Model Chau Vuong's Love Economic Model is based on the primary assumptions that people are rational decision makers and, as a result, are able to tally up both the benefits and costs of falling in love and being in love.

Vuong further contends that "sex and commitment are the only differences between friendship and love."

love maps   We carry a mental blueprint of the "ideal" love relationship, which is shaped by our experiences with love in infancy and early childhood and by our parents' and primary caregivers' attitudes toward love and sexuality.

love stories   Our unique, personal experiences with love.

ludus/ludic lovers   This refers to love that is playful, flirtatious, carefree, and casual. Ludic lovers don't care as much about commitment as they do about playing the sport or the game of love.

machismo   The attitude, common in Latin American cultures, that men are superior to women, and that men are socially and physically dominating.

macrosystem   The macrosystem recognizes that a society has a set of overarching cultural values and beliefs that affect individual development by establishing either implicit or explicit rules about what is or is not acceptable behavior.

maintenance costs   Maintenance costs are delineated as emotional costs and time costs involved in finding the right person.

manic/manic lovers   Jealousy, envy, protectiveness, and exclusivity are the hallmark traits of manic lovers. Manic love is frenzied, agitated, hectic, and chaotic all at the same time.

marianismo   The belief among Latin American cultures that women are semi-divine and are morally superior to and spiritually stronger than men.

market alternative cost method   Estimates the value of household labor by looking at what it would cost in the current market to pay someone to do the household labor the mother performs.

marriage and family therapist (MFT)   Mental health professionals who are trained and licensed to diagnose and treat a number of issues, including marital problems.

marriage models   Marriages we have seen or have experienced that influence and deeply affect our way of thinking about marriage.

Masculine Gender Roles Stress Theory (MGRS)   This theory maintains that there are stressors that may result from a man's fear that he is not measuring up to or meeting societal expectations for masculinity.

masculinity   A socially/culturally constructed set of beliefs, values, and opinions that shape manly character, or manliness

masturbation   Sexual self-stimulation.

matching hypothesis   The premise that most of us want a socially desirable person regardless of our own degree of social desirability.

materialistic needs   Those primary needs required for survival and happiness, including food, water, shelter, and transportation.

maternal gatekeeping   When women's socialization—and the inherent cultural notion that she will always be the better parent—makes it difficult for her to relinquish her traditional roles.

Maternal Role Attainment (MRA)   The process through which a woman, through pregnancy and after the birth of her child, continues to construct an "ideal" image of herself as mother, and adopts roles that support this ideal image.

maturity effect   The higher likelihood of teenagers to have unrealistic expectations about marriage and to misjudge their mate's qualities and characteristics.

meaning-based coping   Employing deliberate strategies to produce positive emotion, such as arming oneself with information about one's illness and treatment in order to remain optimistic.

meanings   In the context of family communication, the definition to which we assign to verbal and nonverbal interactions.

men's studies   Research and study of male/female inequality (conflict, antagonism, and tension) from the male perspective.

menopause   A period of time during which marked fluctuations of estrogen levels cause the cessation of a woman's monthly menstrual cycle.

merger status   When intimate partners in a relationship experience an equal balance of power, or merger.

mesosystem   This ecosystem shares all of the elements that are present in the microsystem, but with a focus on the interaction between the various elements rather than on the individual.

message   The obvious meaning of a communication.

metamessage   The underlying context in which a communication takes place.

microsystem   The developmental context nearest the individual and representing those interactions to which people are directly exposed. The elements composing this ecosystem are the individuals, groups, and agencies that have the earliest and most immediate influences on the individual.

middle remarriage   During the middle remarriage stage of development, which takes most families about three to five years to complete, the family becomes a more cohesive system and functions less along strictly biological lines.

miscarriage   Spontaneous abortion, or loss of a fetus or embryo before the 20th week of pregnancy.

miscegenation   The mixture of races, ethnicities, or religions who produce children together.

mixed co-parenting   A type of co-parenting in which one or both parents' responses are mixed—sometimes they support one another, sometimes they don't.

mixed couple   In this couple type, one spouse may have the expectations and characteristics of a traditional couple whereas the other spouse may have expectations typical of an individual couple type.

monogamism   The belief that monogamy is the only true, morally, and socially appropriate type of marriage or love relationship.

monogamy   A dyadic (two-person) form of marriage that involves the practice of having one sexual partner. The sex partner reciprocates this exclusivity to his or her marital partner.

moral commitment   Moral commitment refers to each person's value and belief systems. Before committing to or ending a relationship, individuals consciously weigh what is right and what is wrong, guided by their value/belief/religious framework.

morning after pill/Plan B   *See* Emergency contraception.

mothering   A process whereby someone performs the relational and logistical work of caring for others.

mourning   Culturally prescribed expressions of the thoughts, feelings, and behaviors of a bereaved person.

mutual dependency   A couple's reliance on one another for need fulfillment, such as socially and sexually.

myotonia   The involuntary head-to-toe muscle tension occurring during sexual response.

narcissistic entitlement   A sense of being entitled to, or deserving, only the good things in life; a pride-related barrier to forgiveness.

natalism   An ideology that embraces childbearing.

Native American/Alaska Native (NA/AN)   The aboriginal peoples of the United States and their descendants, and who maintain tribal affiliation or community attachment.

natural selection   The belief that nature selects the best adapted varieties of species to survive and reproduce.

nature vs. nurture debate   The ongoing debate between those people who feel the influences of aging determined by nature (your inborn, hereditary characteristics such as genetic influences) or by nurture (your environmental, experiential, societal, and cultural experiences across your lifespan).

near-peers   These couples or marriage partners believe in equality, although when children are born or the family's finances need to increase, the male may assume less responsibility for the children.

need for affiliation   The universal and innate drive to have relationships in our lives.

never-married singles   These are individuals who have not married. This does not mean, however, that they live alone or that they do not have an intimate partner.

no-fault divorce   A divorce in which neither spouse legally blames the other for the breakdown of the marriage.

noncoital   Sexual activities besides sexual intercourse, such as masturbation, oral-genital sex, and anal sex.

nonlove   The absence of intimacy, commitment, and passion. Nonlove may exist in a relationship where physical, emotional, or sexual violence is present.

non-normative influences   Uncommon, rare, or unanticipated events.

non-normative life events   Unexpected life events, such as the death of a loved one due to a terrorist attack or the loss of the family home because of a hurricane, that have an impact on a person's developmental lifecourse.

nonprobability sample   These nonrandom samples are used when the use of probability samples is impossible.

nonregulated couples   These couples have a difficult time bouncing back from arguments and disputes because the manner in which they handle the conflict only compounds the issues at hand.

nonrelational messages   Issues or topics concerning things outside of the relationship.

nonverbal communication   Nonverbal communication occurs with or without the spoken word. It includes facial expressions, motions of the body, eye contact, patterns of touch, expressive movements, hand gestures, the spatial arrangements in the physical environment, and emotions.

normative age-graded influences   Developmental changes caused by biological, psychological, and sociocultural forces.

normative history-graded influences   Events or conditions that people in a given culture or society experience simultaneously.

normlessness   A disruption in the norms of family relationships.

nuclear family   The nuclear family consists of a biological father, a biological mother, and their biological or adopted children.

nurturing communication   Interactions that convey intimacy, caring, recognition, and validation of family members.

observations   Sensory ascertainment that helps us understand and make sense of our world. More specifically, these observations help us gather data and reach conclusions in our research.

occupational sexism   Belief that the male gender is more capable of certain work-related tasks and professions than women are.

off-time events   Lifetime events not occurring at the typical, more common points in a person's life. For example, a pregnancy is considered off-time if it occurs during adolescence.

online dating   Using the Internet as a tool in the process of finding a mate.

on-time events   Normative events are often referred to as *on-time events* because of their relative predictability across the lifespan.

open boundaries   These are boundaries where the transfer of information is so unobstructed that family members within the systems lose their identities.

operant conditioning   B. F. Skinner (1904–1990) believed that children learn behaviors through a series of rewards and punishments called *operant conditioning*.

operational definition   Created by researchers at the outset of research to describe or characterize the constructs (concepts) that are being studied.

opportunity cost method   Attempts to value household work by asking "What would a person be paid in wage labor for one hour of household work?"

oral stage   During the oral stage (from birth to about age 1), the focus of sensual energy is the mouth and the tongue; the emphasis for personality development is thus centered on breastfeeding.

oral-genital sex   Oral-genital sex is practiced by all couple types: heterosexual, gay, lesbian, and bisexual.

orgasm phase   The third stage in Masters and Johnson's description of sexual response. Orgasm is a sudden release of the vasocongestion and myotonia that occurred during the excitement and plateau phases.

overtime   The hours a person works beyond her or his normal 40-hour per week schedule.

pair bond   A couple who is emotionally bonded to one another, which characterizes the couple's union.

paradox of Mexican American nuptuality   The phenomenon in which divorce rates among Mexican Americans are lower than among blacks, despite the fact that Mexican Americans are more educationally and economically disadvantaged.

passion   The physical attraction and romantic feelings that initially draw us to another person.

passionate love   A wildly powerful emotion experienced as intense longing for the selected love object, along with profound sexual arousal and confused feelings.

patriarchal family structure   This family form includes the father figure, his wife, and his children. Everyone in the family is considered to be under the authority of the patriarch, the father.

peer marriages   Peer couples collaborate not only in their love relationships, but in day-to-day household tasks, parenting, and managing family finances. Equity and fairness are hallmarks of peer marriages.

Pelvic Inflammatory Disease (PID)   Even when women are able to successfully ovulate, the fertilized ovum may have difficulty reaching the uterus due to blocked or scarred fallopian tubes. This disorder, pelvic inflammatory disease (PID), is caused by untreated sexually transmitted infections (i.e., gonorrhea and chlamydia).

Perfect Pals   Divorced partners who remain friends after they divorce.

permissive parents   Also referred to as *indulgent parents,* permissive parents demonstrate high levels of warmth, affection, and responsiveness toward their children, and also show adequate to high levels of parent–child communication. This parenting style does not place high demands on children, nor do parents attempt to control their children's behavior; children's behavior is mostly self-regulated.

personal context   Factors specific to each member of the couple, such as personality traits and the attitudes and beliefs about the overall status of the relationship; emotional reactions to intimacy; willingness to self-disclose; and each partner's intimacy needs, goals, and motives.

personality need fulfillment   An established pattern of mutual exchanges of support, sympathy, and decision making. Each person also satisfies his or her partner's deeper emotional and sexual needs.

phallic stage   According to Freud, during the phallic stage (ages 3 to 6), children are intensely interested in the physical differences between men and women.

philos   A term suggesting brotherly love, used to describe the affectionate feelings shared between friends and family.

physical custody   The legal right to have a child live primarily with one parent, who becomes the custodial parent.

pile-up   Pile-up can result from either a single stressor that coincides with life events/changes, multiple stressors, or multiple stressors that coincide with life events/changes.

pink-collar phenomenon   The tendency for women to be concentrated in certain occupational categories.

plateau phase   The second of four stages of sexual response as put forth by Masters and Johnson.

polyandry   The form of polygamy in which women have multiple husbands at the same time.

polygamy   The practice of having more than one marriage partner.

polygyny   The form of polygamy or plural marriage that involves the practice of a man having multiple wives at the same time.

pool of candidates   Eligible relationship partners.

population   The entire group of people who share a common experience or characteristic under academic examination.

poverty line   The estimated minimum income necessary for a family to meet basic needs, such as food, shelter, clothing, and other essentials.

poverty rate   The percentage of people with incomes below the published poverty line.

Power and Control Wheel   A model depicting behaviors batterers use to control and dominate their intimate partners and/or children.

pragma/pragma lovers   Practicality and logic guide the pragmatic lover. With pragma love, the costs and benefits associated with love are carefully weighed and considered before entering into a relationship.

Pre-Crowd Stage   From about kindergarten through fifth grade, isolated same-sex peer groups exist in the form of cliques, or small groups, of four to nine members. Spontaneous shared activities provide the opportunity to relate personally.

predatory stalkers   A type of stalker who spies on the victim in order to plan a sexual attack.

preinteraction cue   These cues provide at-a-glance information that helps us decide whether we would even consider wanting a date with a certain person. Outward attractiveness would be an example of a preinteraction cue.

preintimate   Capable and desirous of intimacy but unable to sustain a long-term relationship.

pre-term   A baby born before the 37th week of pregnancy is considered pre-term.

preventing-the-problems focus   Family life educator Richard Kerckhoff maintained that families faced with radical societal changes only need to be shown how to do the correct things to prevent family problems.

primary aging   Basic biological processes that are genetically programmed to occur over time.

primary divorce stressors   Provisions such as custody arrangements, visitation, and child support.

proactive discipline   Using techniques that encourage appropriate behavior and that discourage inappropriate behaviors.

probability sample   In a probability sample, each person has the same likelihood (probability) of being selected for the study.

problem management   Management strategies aimed at directly attacking the stressor or changing the stressor.

procreative consciousness   Awareness of our ability to create children; to procreate with another.

progressive desensitization   Occurs when family members gradually allow themselves increasing exposure to the varying aspects of the stressor.

pronatalism   An ideology that embraces childbearing.

propinquity   Refers to geographical closeness; one cannot interact with someone if one is not in the same geographic region.

protest reactions   Behaviors and feelings that attempt to reestablish a relationship, such as trying to reinvolve the ex-partner in sexual relations.

prototype   Researcher Beverly Fehr asked her study sample to freewrite various features or attributes they assigned to "love." The list provided a prototype or model of love.

provider/protector cues   Women tend to seek out a mate who possesses protector/provider cues, such as intelligence, physical strength, and ambition.

pseudointimate A person or relationship that appears to be intimate but lacks depth.

psychoanalytic theories Championed by Sigmund Freud, these theories focus on the personality development of children.

psychosexual stages In Freud's view, development takes place through a series of psychosexual stages, in which sensual energy or satisfaction is focused on one particular part of the body.

psychosocial The social and emotional aspects of development.

psychosocial development The social and emotional development of an individual.

punishment Used to decrease the likelihood that a behavior will be repeated.

Quiverfull movement A pronatalist belief in which couples are motivated to have many children because of a desire to be obedient to what they believe are commands in the Bible.

race Refers to a group of people who are distinguished from another group of people, typically by their skin color, ancestry, or genetics.

racial/ethnic socialization The way in which families teach children about the social meanings of their race/ethnicity.

racism A belief system which holds that race accounts for differences in human character and/or ability; it results in discrimination and prejudice based on someone's race or ethnic background.

rapid ejaculation (RE) Ejaculation that occurs before, on, or shortly after penetration with minimal sexual stimulation.

rapport A connection or bond we feel toward another person.

raw numbers Actual numbers; e.g., the actual number of people who marry and divorce.

reflective listening A form of active listening in which we pay close attention to a person's verbal and emotional messages, and respectfully acknowledge their perspective.

refractory period A period of time in which the male is incapable of achieving an erection.

reframe To view the issue from another perspective.

regulated couples Regulated couples use communication patterns and interpersonal behaviors that promote closeness and intimacy, such as using more positive comments than negative comments during times of tension.

Reiss's Wheel Theory of Love Sociologist Ira Reiss described love as a developmental process that unfolds over time, with four stages or processes: rapport, self-revelation, mutual dependency, and personality need fulfillment. Similar to a rolling wheel, these stages of love may be experienced many times, and in turn, deepen the love bonds between partners.

rejected stalkers A type of stalker who wants to reverse, correct, or avenge rejection of their affections, infatuation, or love.

rejection costs Rejection costs include, among other things, rejection sensitivity (anxiety, lowered self-esteem), immunity to rejection (frequency of past rejections), and the emotional cost of the rejection.

relational context Characteristics of the relationship and how the couple defines it. Factors such as companionship, trust, commitment level, intimacy needs, and type of conflict.

relational culture A framework of understandings—a private, unique, distinct language—that couples construct in private.

relational expectancies Couples enter marriage with certain expectations about their marriage and spouse, which have developed throughout the course of their lives. Relational expectancies are key factors in marital satisfaction and marriage longevity.

relational messages Messages that have something to do with the partner or relationship.

relational transgressions Hurtful words or actions that communicate a devaluation of the partner or the relationship.

religiosity An individual's preference for religious expression.

remarriage A marriage in which either one or both spouses have been previously married.

remote relationship Remote relationships are characterized by the distant grandparent who has little or no contact with grandchildren and is only involved on occasional holidays or birthdays.

representativeness The degree to which the characteristics of the population are represented by the sample.

research To study the family thoroughly through the process of scholarly or scientific inquiry.

research hypothesis The statement of the research problem.

research integrity Refers to the relationship between researchers and the truth in reporting their findings.

research question The research question, or research hypothesis, is the core of any valid project and takes into account a clear understanding of the problem to be addressed and a clear vision of the objective. With these addressed, the answer to this question is presented clearly and concisely.

resentful stalkers Stalkers who are out for vengeance because they believe they were wronged by their victim.

residual tasks Bill paying, yard work, and chauffeuring children.

resigned acceptance The ultimate acceptance of circumstances, as when family members recognize that nothing will change the course their family life has taken.

resolution phase The final stage of sexual response. During resolution the sexual response pattern is reversed as the heart rate, blood pressure, and respiration return to pre-excitement levels.

resource dilution hypothesis A theory that contends parents' finite resources become diluted when spread over a larger number of children.

response bias When using human beings as subjects, this is the risk whereby subjects' past and current experiences may affect their responses. This is a flaw that may occur when researchers rely on individuals' self-reports.

response rate The percentage of study subjects who respond to the survey.

responsiveness The verbal and/or nonverbal behavior that conveys support and affection to a partner.

rewards Used to reinforce behavior and increase the likelihood that the behavior will occur again; the benefits (the payback, profit, or compensations) exchanged in a social relationship. Offered consistently, relationship rewards such as nurture, appreciation, trust, and making/seeing the other person happy develop a strong sense of liking in a relationship. Essentially, whatever attributes a person has on her or his love prototype list are her or his perceived rewards in the relationship.

Risk and Protective Factor Model   Assumes that every family form has protective factors, which positively influence children, and risk factors, which have a potentially negative impact on families and children; the overall experience of the children is determined by whether the protective factors outweigh the risk factors or vice versa.

role   A key concept in Symbolic Interaction theory is that of role, or a "system of meanings." A woman may simultaneously have the role of wife, mother, sister, daughter, aunt, and so forth. She will take on the role of actor and follow the rules—the expectations—assigned to that role.

role conflict   Refers to the contradictory demands of the various roles individuals must perform, such as parent versus employee.

role strain   Occurs when there are competing demands from multiple roles.

romantic infatuation   A type of infatuation that is often referred to as *romantic love*. Defined in the *American Heritage Dictionary* (2000) as "a foolish, unreasoning, or extravagant passion or attraction," and "an object of extravagant short-lived passion," romantic infatuation involves a complicated, often overpowering, blend of emotion and sex.

romantic love   Intimacy and passion comprise romantic love. Because of the accompanying physical and/or sexual attraction and arousal, it is a more intense form of love than liking.

routine housework   House cleaning, meal preparation, grocery shopping, cleaning up after meals, and laundry.

rules   Communication rules govern what family members can and cannot discuss or share and how they are to interact with their own family members.

sacrament of marriage   Referring to marriage as a sacred act, dissolved only by the death of one partner.

sample   A group of people from which researchers collect survey responses.

sample size   The value (e.g., number, weight, etc.) of the sample. Sample size affects the degree to which the sample is considered to be representative.

sandwich generation   A term describing being in the middle of two generations—parenting adolescent or younger children while at the same time caring for aging parents.

scapegoating   An example of displacement, scapegoating occurs when anger and hostility are directed at one family member in particular who always bears the brunt of everyone's frustration.

scientific method   The process by which researchers formulate questions concerning social and individual phenomena and seek out answers.

script theory   The idea that individuals use scripts that help us organize the information in our environments.

search costs   Includes our attractiveness, or our ability to attract potential partners, along with social networking skills.

second shift   Sociologist Arlie Hochschild's (1989) term for the burden of the dual responsibilities of wage earner and housekeeper.

secondary aging   Physiological declines that are the result of environmental and behavioral influences, which significantly affect how we age.

secondary divorce stressors   The "fallout" associated with divorce, including depression and greater risks for health problems.

secure attachment types   Secure adults, like securely attached infants, have little difficulty seeking or maintaining closeness with another. They don't fear being abandoned or losing their partner.

self-disclosure   Voluntarily sharing things with someone else that are personal or private to us.

self-revelation   Refers to *self-disclosure*. When we feel comfortable in another person's presence, we feel more comfortable self-disclosing our personal hopes, dreams, fears, and goals.

self-righteousness   The inability to see one's own potential for doing wrong or hurting another person; a pride-related barrier to forgiveness.

separate couple   Individuals in this couple type are less willing to relinquish their autonomy than those in traditional and independent couple types. They report lower levels of self-disclosure and sharing, and, as a result, experience psychological distance. Separate couples do not share the levels of companionship as the other two couple types, and they tend to share less positive feelings about their spouse and about their relationship than the other couple types do.

separation period   A period marked by a disruption in the norms of family relationships. To some, it may mean a cooling off period; to others, it may mean the first step on the way to the divorce attorneys.

sex   biological traits that distinguish males from females, such as the internal and external reproductive anatomy, chromosomes, hormones, and other physiological characteristics.

sex hormones   Estrogen and testosterone, which influence the masculinizing or feminizing process in development.

sex reassignment surgery (SRS)/genital surgery   The surgical alteration to the body that transforms a person's gender from male to female, or female to male.

sexism   A prejudice or discrimination based on biological sex; a belief system that assumes a hierarchy of human worth based on the social construction of the differences between the sexes; an ideology of male supremacy, superiority, authority, and beliefs/behaviors that support and sustain this ideology.

sexual dysfunction   The inability to fully enjoy sex.

sexual harassment   Any unwelcome sexual or physical conduct by a person of either gender, directed to a person of either gender.

sexual orientation   The focus of a person's erotic desires or fantasies, or a person's affectionate or romantic feelings toward a particular gender.

sexual preference   The term used by people who believe that sexuality is fluid and is more a matter of choice than of biology.

sexual scripting framework   The notion that societal and cultural processes ultimately determine and proscribe what we perceive as "sexual" and how we behave sexually.

sexual scripts   The shared, gender-specific social and cultural expectations that guide our beliefs about sex, such as our beliefs about appropriate sexual partners and sexual behaviors.

sexual selection   A form of natural selection that happens in two ways: (1) members of one sex compete among themselves for opportunities to mate, thereby "out-reproducing" other competitors; and (2) a sex chooses to mate with a specific, more preferable person.

sexuality   Sociologist Ira Reiss defined sexuality as "the erotic arousal and genital responses resulting from following sexual scripts of that society."

sexually transmitted infections (STI)   Infectious diseases transmitted between partners through sexual contact.

shared care   A childcare arrangement in which parents share a babysitter or nanny.

shared legal custody   Both parents have an equal say in a child's upbringing.

shift work   Working nonstandard hours or working a schedule other than the typical Monday–Friday workweek.

simple infatuation   A physical attraction that is often accompanied by emotion-filled daydreams and fantasies about someone, perhaps an actor or actress, a pop star or singing idol, or even a teacher.

single-parent household   A household with one parent, with no parenting partner or spouse.

social clock   Culturally established norms associated with the timing of events. This social clock includes rites of passage, such as graduating from high school or college, getting married, or retiring—all by a socially and culturally accepted age.

social ecology   The perspective that recognizes that individual family members' experiences, as well as outside social factors and policies, significantly affect the quality and the nature of their relationships.

Social Exchange theory   This theory centers on the exchange of people's material or symbolic resources, asserting that individuals act out of self-interest to capitalize on the resources they possess.

Social Expectations model   Developed by psychologist Mary Levitt, this model illustrates how spouses' expectations of marital relationships are based on past relationship interactions with the spouse. This model also takes into account the influence of societal norms on spousal expectations.

social identity   Refers to whether the goals of a society/culture emphasize the advancement of the group's interests *(collectivist)* or individual interests *(individualistic)*.

Social Learning theory (SLT)   Albert Bandura's (1925–present) theory that children acquire behaviors and personality traits by observing others. An offshoot of the traditional Behaviorism theory, this theory addresses the roles of reward and punishment and it goes a step further to include an individual's realm of cognition—the role of observation—in the process of learning.

social phase   According to Stephen Duck, the public disclosure of a couple's decision to terminate the marriage, the announcement constitutes the social phase of relationship deterioration. Once a couple decides that the relationship will be terminated, they then decide, either individually or jointly, how they will disclose the news of their breakup to family and friends.

Social Readjustment Rating Scale (SRRS)   A scale identifying associations between life events and life transitions, and the impact of these events and transitions on individual physical health and well-being.

social science research   The examination of social and individual processes by engaging in and using methods beyond logic, common sense, intuition, or reason alone.

social union   The legal term that speaks to the commitment, or the marriage contract, partners make to one another.

socialization hypothesis   The hypothesis that because children of divorce have less experience with successful marital role models they are less able to cope with their own marital difficulties and are thus at greater risk for divorce.

socialization needs   Another base goal of parenting is to meet the socialization needs of children, which encompasses ensuring they become productive, contributing members of society.

sociocultural context   The norms, beliefs, and ideals of the culture and subcultures in which couples live and relate.

sociocultural theories   Theories maintaining that children's development does not occur by stages but through direct interaction with culture, which shapes their values, goals, and expectations.

socioeconomic status (SES)   The government's measure of a family's relative economic and social ranking within a community.

sociological/incidental cue   The first filter of Stephen Duck's system, this relates to the restrictions and limitations placed on one's ability to meet people. These cues speak to one's sociological location or position, or the places where one lives and works.

sole custody   One parent is the primary parent—legally, physically, or both legally and physically.

specialization   The element of marriage in which each spouse can take on tasks and concentrate on those things he or she does well.

speed dating   A quick meeting that allows people to meet each other face to face to decide if they share mutual interests and if they are interested in another, more extended, date.

sperm bank   Sperm for artificial insemination procedures is retrieved from donors and stored in sperm banks.

spousal support   Today, alimony is more commonly referred to as spousal support.

stability   The stability provided by marriage allows men to mature, making them more likely to find a job and think toward the future instead of engaging in risk-taking behaviors such as drug and alcohol abuse. Married men and women are also more likely to accept and maintain jobs that may not be as personally rewarding, but are in the couple/family's best economic interests.

stalking   The obsessive following, observing, or contacting of another person, or the obsessive attempt to engage in any of these activities.

starter marriages   Marriages that last less than five years and that end before children are born to a couple.

status   Employers tend to pay married men and women at a higher rate than single men and women. This discrimination toward unmarried men allows for great economic gain and greater economic opportunities for married men, thereby affording them and their families a certain status unmarried individuals do not have.

stepfamily A stepfamily is formed when, after the death, divorce, or separation of one parent, the other parent marries again. A stepfamily is also formed when a never-married parent marries.

sterility The absolute inability to reproduce, either because the woman has no uterus or ovaries, or the male has no testes or sperm production.

stillbirth The death of a fetus after the 20th week of pregnancy. Stillbirth occurs approximately once in every 115 births, or about 26,000 per year.

stonewalling Takes place when communication between marital partners completely shuts down. Either one or both spouses distance themselves by refusing to communicate, ignoring each other, and becoming remote.

storge/storgic lovers Storge love is best described as friendship love, or a type of affectionate love between companions. Storgic lovers typically come to love each other over time, as opposed to the instantaneous type of love found with eros lovers.

strain-based conflict Occurs when the demands in one domain make it difficult to perform effectively in another domain.

stressor Anything that elicits a physiological and/or psychological response to any stimuli.

structural commitment Those commitments bound by institutions such as marriage.

structural factors Refers to a family's finances and economic status; these factors are integral to the formation and maintenance of marriages and other intimate relationships.

Structural-Functionalist theory This theory, introduced by Talcott Parsons, maintains that gender-based role specialization is a necessary function in order to promote family (and hence, societal) equilibrium.

structures Patterns of role arrangement within a society.

subsystems The relational patterns and interactions among the separate individuals within a family.

supportive co-parenting Situation in which parents directly or indirectly agree by promoting the same general message to the child, or when one parent directly asks the other for assistance with an issue that involves the child.

surrogate mother A woman who carries the fetus of another couple.

survey A structured questionnaire comprising a list of questions.

survival needs The provision of food, shelter, safety, security, and love—a base goal of parenting.

Symbolic Interaction theory This approach to examining family life and family communication assumes that human behavior is a continuous dialogue where people watch the behaviors of people and then react to these behaviors.

symbols In an attempt to share meanings, each culture uses symbols, or codes. Some symbols are universal behaviors, such as the kiss, which represents affection, love, or a greeting.

syphilis A sexually transmitted bacterial infection caused by a microscopic organism; may be either congenital or acquired through sexual contact or contaminated needles.

system According to Rosenblatt, it means to "piece together" or to connect one entity to another.

testicular cancer A type of cancer that develops in the testicles, a part of the male reproductive system.

testosterone The masculinizing hormone produced by the testicles.

time-based conflict Takes place when demands from the work domain and the family domain vie for a parent's time and attention.

timing Refers to the age at which a transition takes place.

traditional family The traditional family is a middle-class nuclear family composed of a husband, wife, and biological or adopted children.

transactional The dynamic process whereby our exchanges with others simultaneously affect and are affected by our intimate relations.

Transactional Model of Stress According to this model, stress is the result of an interaction between the person and his or her environment.

transgender Refers to people who feel that their biologically assigned gender is a false or incomplete description of themselves.

transsexual A person whose sexual identity is opposite to assignment at birth.

transvestite/cross-dresser A person who dresses and acts as a person of the opposite gender from the one with which he or she was born.

Triangular Theory of Love Robert Sternberg's theory conceptualizes eight different types of love relationships. These relationships take into account that each individual will experience many types of love throughout their lifecourse.

trouble talk Talking about emotional and relationship problems.

Turner's syndrome Occurs when one of the two X sex chromosomes is completely or partially absent. Affecting only female infants, who are sometimes referred to as *XO babies* (meaning an X and a zero, or no other chromosome). The individual does not develop ovaries and is consequently sterile.

turning point A transition that entails a permanent, lasting shift in the direction of the lifecourse of a person's relationship.

unexpected quick trajectory A rapid transition from life to death with elements of time pressure and surprise, when there is typically not enough time to save the life of the injured or ill person and there is no time allowed for friends and family to plan or to prepare themselves emotionally.

uninvolved parents Parents who are typically low in responsiveness, warmth, and affection. They are also low in parental control or demands. Both parents reject and neglect their children.

unsupportive co-parenting Occurs when one parent undermines the other parent's efforts, interrupts the interactions of the other parent and child, is openly critical of the other's parenting styles or parenting activity, or ignores the other parent's request for assistance with a child's needs.

urban tribe Refers to mixed-gender circles of friends (typically in their twenties or thirties) who are the primary social support system for singles.

validity The extent to which a researcher is able to provide an empirical definition that reflects the true meaning of the construct being considered.

variable A characteristic that is measured in a study. The value of the characteristic varies among the people or group being studied, hence the name.

verbal communication Refers to exchanges of thoughts, messages, or information through the spoken word.

viral hepatitis An inflammation of the liver causing impairments in liver function; there are three types of viral hepatitis: Hepatitis A, Hepatitis B, and Hepatitis C.

wage gap The inequality between men's and women's wages in the United States.

white-collar occupations Professional occupations such as attorneys, bankers, and doctors.

Women's Liberation A feminist movement that put forth the idea that women suffered oppression in patriarchal, male-dominated cultures such as those in the United States.

work-family spillover/crossover Occurs when a spouse carries the emotional events and tensions of one environment to the other.

working poor Refers to those people who are working, but who continue to remain below the poverty threshold for their family size.

***X* factor** Part of Reuben Hill's ABC-X Family Crisis Model, *X* factors are the outcomes of the event, the results of whether or not a family copes effectively with the crisis event.

XX sex chromosomes This chromosome combination results in a "female" genetic blueprint for the developing embryo.

XY sex chromosomes This chromosome combination results in a "male" genetic blueprint for the developing embryo.

zygote intrafallopian transfer (ZIFT) An Assisted Reproductive Technology process in which an egg is fertilized outside of the body and then is placed immediately in the woman's fallopian tubes, allowing the conceptus to travel naturally to the uterus and implant.

A Campaign for Forgiveness Research. (2008). Available: www
.forgiving.org.htm [2008, September 26].

Acs, G., & Nelson, S. (2002). The kids are alright? Children's
well-being and the rise of cohabitation. *Assessing the new
federalism policy brief B-48.* Washington, DC: Urban Institute.

Acs, G., & Nelson, S. (2004). *What do "I do's" do? Potential benefits of marriage for cohabiting couples with children.* Available: www.urban.org/url.cfm?ID=31101 [2004, July 9].

Adamec, C. (2004). *The complete idiot's guide to adoption.* New
York: Penguin.

Adkins, V. (1999). Grandparents as a national asset: A brief note.
Activities, Adaptation, and Aging, 24, 13–18.

Adler, N. E., Boyce, T., Chesney, M. A., Cohen, S., Folkman, S.,
Kahn, R. L., et al. (1994). Socioeconomic status and health:
The challenge of the gradient. *American Psychologist, 49,*
15–24.

Administration on Aging. (2000). *Facts about older Americans.*
Available: www.aoa.gov/ [2005, April 27].

Afable-Munsuz, A., & Brindis, C.D. (2006). Acculturation and
the sexual reproductive health of Latino youth in the United States: A literature review. *Perspectives on Sexual and Reproductive Health, 38*(4), 208–220.

AFL-CIO. (2004). *Facts about working women.* Available: www
.aflcio.org/issues/politics/women [2004, August 108].

Agresti, A., & Finlay, B. (1997). *Statistical methods for the social
sciences* (3rd ed.). Upper Saddle River, NJ: Prentice Hall.

Agresti, A., & Finlay, B. (2008). *Statistical methods for the social
sciences* (4th ed.). Boston: Pearson Prentice Hall.

Ahlborg, T., Dahlof, L. G., & Strandmark, M. (2000). First-time
parents' sexual relationships. *Scandinavian Journal of Sex-
ology, 3,* 127–139.

Ahlborg, T., Lars-Gosta, D., & Hallberg, L. (2005). Quality of the
intimate and sexual relationship in first-time parents six
months after delivery. *The Journal of Sex Research, 42*(7),
167–174.

Ahnert, L., & Lamb, M. E. (2003). Shared care: Establishing a balance between home and childcare settings. *Child Development, 74*(4), 1044–1049.

Ahnert, L., & Lamb, M. E. (2004). Child care and its impact on
young children (2–5). In R. E. Tremblay, R. G. Barr, and R.
Peters (Eds.), *Encyclopedia of Early Childhood Development,*
1–6. Montreal, Quebec: Centre of Excellence for Early
Childhood Development. Available: www.excellence-early-
childhood.ca/documents/Ahnert-LambANGxp.pdf.

Ahrons, C. (1994). *The good divorce: Keeping your family together when your marriage comes apart.* New York: Harper-
Collins.

Ahrons, C. (1999). Divorce: An unscheduled family transition.
In B. Carter and M. McGoldrick (Eds.), *The expanded family life cycle: Individual, family, and social perspectives* (3rd
ed.) (pp. 381–398). Boston: Allyn & Bacon.

Ahrons, C. (2004). *We're still family: What grown children have to
say about their parents' divorce.* New York: Harper-Collins.

Ahrons, C. R. (2007). Family ties after divorce: Long-term implications for children. *Family Process, 46*(1), 53–65.

Ahrons, C., & Rodgers, R. H. (1987). *Divorced families: Meeting
the challenge of divorce and remarriage.* New York: Norton.

Ahrons, C., & Tanner, J. L. (2003). Adult children and their fathers: Relationship changes 20 years after parental divorce.
Family Relations, 52, 340–351.

Ainsworth, M. D. S., Blehar, M. C., Waters, E., & Wall, S. (1978).
*Patterns of attachment: A psychological study of the strange
situation.* Hillsdale, NJ: Erlbaum.

Alan Guttmacher Institute. (1997). *Risks and realities of early
childbearing worldwide.* Washington, DC: Alan Guttmacher Institute.

Alan Guttmacher Institute. (1998). *Into a new world.* Washington, DC: Alan Guttmacher Institute.

Alan Guttmacher Institute. (1999). *Overall trends and state-by-
state information.* Washington, DC: Alan Guttmacher Institute.

Alan Guttmacher Institute. (2001). *Five-country study points to
ways the United States could further decrease teenage pregnancy and STD rates.* Washington, DC: Alan Guttmacher
Institute.

Alan Guttmacher Institute. (2004). *U.S. teenage pregnancy statistics: Overall trends, trends by race and ethnicity, and state-
by-state information.* Washington, DC: Alan Guttmacher
Institute.

Albert, B. (2004). *With one voice 2004: America's adults and teens
sound off about teen pregnancy: An annual national survey.*
The National Campaign to Prevent Teen Pregnancy.
Available: www.teenpregnancy.org/resources/readings/pdf/
[2006, March 21].

Albert, B. (2007). America's adults and teens sound off about teen
pregnancy. The National Campaign to Prevent Teen Pregnancy. Available: www.thenationalcampaign.org/
resources/pdf/pubs/WOV2007_fulltext.pdf [2008, December 20].

Albert, B., Brown, S., & Flannigan, C. M., (2003). *14 and younger: The sexual behavior of young adolescents*. The National Campaign to Prevent Teen Pregnancy. Available: www.teenpregnancy.org/resources/reading/pdf/14summary.pdf [2006, March 17].

Alberts, M. (2002). *The ecological model of human development: The foundation for a family policy perspective*. The University of Minnesota Children, Youth, and Family Consortium. Available: www.cyfc.umn.edu/publications/connection/pubs/05summer/01-foundationfamilypolicy.html [2006, January 21].

Al-Fadhli, H. M., & Smith, J. C. (1996). Assessing the impact of violence on motivation for parenthood among blacks and whites. *Journal of Negro Education, 65*(4), 424–433.

Alford, S. (2001). *Transitions. Rights. Respect. Responsibility.* Available: www.advocatesforyouth.org [March 20, 2006].

Allegretto, S. (2005, September 1). Basic family budgets: Working families' incomes often fail to meet living expenses around the U.S. *Economic Policy Institute Briefing Paper #165*. Available: www.epi.org/content.cfm/bp165 [2005, October 5].

Allen, J. & Land, D. (1999). Attachment in adolescence. In J. Casidy and P. Shaver (Eds.), *Handbook of attachment* (pp. 319–335). New York: Guilford.

Allen, K. R. (1997). Lesbian and gay families. In T. Arendell (Ed.), *Contemporary parenting: Challenges and issues.* New York: Sage.

Allen, M., & Burrell, N. (1996). Comparing the impact of homosexual and heterosexual parents on children: Meta-analysis of existing research. *Journal of Homosexuality, 32*(2), 19–33.

Allen, S. M., & Hawkins, A. J. (1999). Maternal gatekeeping: Mothers' beliefs and behaviors that inhibit greater father involvement in family work. *Journal of Marriage and the Family, 61*(1), 199–212.

Allport, G. W. (1958). *The nature of prejudice.* Garden City, NY: Doubleday.

Amato, P. (1996). Explaining the intergenerational transmission of divorce. *Journal of Marriage and the Family, 58*, 628–640.

Amato, P. (2000). The consequences of divorce for adults and children. *Journal of Marriage and the Family, 62*(4), 1269–1287.

Amato, P., & DeBoer, D. B. (2001). The transmission of marital instability across generations: Relationship skills or commitment to marriage? *Journal of Marriage and Family, 63*, 1038–1051.

Amato, P., & Previti, D. (2004). People's reasons for divorcing: Gender, social class, the life course, and adjustment. *Journal of Family Issues, 24*, 602–606.

Amato, P. R., & Fowler, F. (2002). Parenting practices, child adjustment, and family diversity. *Journal of Marriage and Family, 64*(3), 703–716.

Amato, P. R., & Rezac, S. (1994). Contact with nonresident parents, interparental conflict, and children's behavior. *Journal of Family Issues, 15*, 191–207.

Amato, P. R., Johnson, D. R., Booth, A., & Rogers, S. J. (2003). Continuity and change in marital quality between 1980 and 2000. *Journal of Marriage and the Family, 65*(1), 1–22.

Ambert, A. (2005). *Divorce: Facts, causes and consequences.* Ottawa, ONT: Vanier Institute of the Family. Available: www.vifamily.ca/library/cft/divorce.html [2006, April 1].

American Academy of Pediatrics, Committee on Psychosocial Aspects of Child and Family Health. (2002). Coparent or second parent adoption by same-sex parents. *Pediatrics, 109*, 339–240.

American Academy of Pediatrics. (2001). Care of adolescent parents and their children. *Pediatrics, 107*(2), 429–434.

American Adoptions. (2009). *The steps to adoption.* Available: www.americanadoptions.com [2009, August 1].

American Association of Retired People. (2004). *Sexuality at midlife and beyond: 2004 update of attitudes and behaviors.* Available: http://assets.aarp.org/rgcenter/general/2004_sexuality.pdf [2009, February 28].

American Association of Retired Persons. (1999). *AARP/Modern Maturity sexuality study.* Atlanta, GA: NFO Research.

American Cancer Society. (2008). Testicular cancer: What are they key statistics for testicular cancer? Available: http://www.cancer.org/docroot/CRI/content/CRI_2_4_IX_What_are_the_key_statistics_for_testicular_cancer_41.asp?sitearea= [2009, August 1].

American College Health Association. (n.d.). Available: www.acha-ncha.org [2009, August 1].

American College of Obstetrics and Gynecology. (2006). Available: www.acog.org [2006, March 20].

American Medical Association. (2006, March 8). Sex and intoxication among women more common on spring break. Available: www.ama-assn.org/ama/pub/category/16083.html [2006, March 16].

American Psychological Association. (2005). *Controlling anger—before it controls you.* Available: www.apa.org/pubinfo/anger.html [2005, November 14].

American Religious Identity Survey. (2001). Available: www.gc.cuny.edu/faculty/research_briefs/aris/aris_index.htm [2005, September 10].

American Society for Aesthetic Plastic Surgery. (2002). *Older patients benefit from modified cosmetic plastic surgery techniques.* Available: www.surgery.org/news_releases/feb0102age65.html [2004, June 1].

American Society for Reproductive Medicine. (2008). *More than 50,000 babies born as result of ART in 2006.* Available: http://www.asrm.org/Patients/topics/ivf.html [2009, August 1].

American Society of Reproductive Medicine. (2006). *Infertility in women and in men.* Available: www.asrm.org/patients/faqs.html#Q2 [2006, March 18].

American Urological Association. (2008). *Introduction to premature ejaculation.* Available: www.PEhomepage.com [2008, October 17].

Andersen, B. L., & Cyranowski, J. M. (1995). Women's sexuality: Behaviors, responses, and individual differences. *Journal of Consulting and Clinical Psychology, 63*, 891–906.

Anderson, J. L., Crawford, C. B., Nadeau, J., & Lindberg, T. (1992). Was the Duchess of Windsor right? A cross-cultural review of the socioecology of ideals of female body shape. *Ethology and Sociobiology, 13*, 197–227.

Anderson, J. R., Doherty, W. J., & Van Ryzin, M. J. (2008, July 17–30). Developmental trajectories of marital happiness: Predictors and outcomes. Paper presented at the International Association for Relationship Research Conference, Providence, RI.

Anderson, R. N. (2002). Table 1: Deaths: Leading causes for 2000. *National Vital Statistics Reports, 50*(16).

Anderson, S. A., & Sabatelli, R. M. (2007). *Family interaction: A multigenerational developmental perspective* (4th ed.). Boston: Allyn & Bacon.

Anderson, S. A., Russell, S. R., & Schumm, W. R. (1983). Perceived marital quality and family life-cycle categories: A further analysis. *Journal of Marriage and the Family, 45,* 127–139.

Anderssen, N., Amlie, C., & Ytteroy, E. A. (2002). Outcomes for children with lesbian or gay parents: A review of studies from 1978 to 2000. *Scandinavian Journal of Psychology, 43,* 335–351.

Andersson, G. (1997). The impact of children on divorce risks of Swedish women. *European Journal of Population, 13,* 109–145.

Angelo, E. J. (1994). The negative impact of abortion on women and families: The many faces of abortion grief. In M. T. Mannion (Ed.), *Post abortion aftermath* (pp. 44–57). Kansas City, MO: Sheed & Ward.

Annie E. Casey Foundation (2009). *Children in poverty by race.* Available: http://datacenter.kidscount.org/data/acrossstates/Rankings.aspx?ind=44 [2009, July 27].

Anspaugh, D. J., & Ezell, G. (2004). *Teaching today's health* (7th ed.). San Franscisco: Pearson Benjamin Cummings.

Antonovsky, A. (1979). *Health, stress, and coping.* San Francisco: Jossey-Bass.

Aquilino, W. S. (1994). Later life parental divorce and widowhood: Impact on young adults' assessment of parent-child relations. *Journal of Marriage and the Family, 56,* 908–922.

Arab American Institute. (2007). *Arab Americans: Demographics.* Available: www.aaiusa.org/arab-americans/22/demographics [2009, February 1].

Arcus, M. E., Schvaneveldt, J. D., & Moss, J. J. (1993). The nature of family life education. In M. E. Arcus, J. D. Schvaneveldt, and J. J. Moss (Eds.), *Handbook of family life education: Foundations of family life education* (Vol. 1). Newbury Park, CA: Sage.

Arditti, J. (1999). Rethinking relationships between divorced mothers and their children: Capitalizing on family strengths. *Family Relations, 48*(2), 109–119.

Arendell, T. (2000). Conceiving and investigating motherhood: The decade's scholarship. *Journal of Marriage and the Family, 62,* 1192–1207.

Armstrong, F. (2005, June 23). Speed-date queen finds her perfect niche: Social singles keep entrepreneur busy making matches. *Business Edge, 1*(12).

Arnold, L. B. (2005). Don't you know what causes that? Advice, celebration, and justification in a large families bulletin board. *Communication Studies, 56*(4), 331–351.

Aron, A., Fisher, H. E., Mashek, D. J., Strong, G., Hai-Fang, L., & Brown, L. L. (2005). Reward, motivation, and emotion systems associated with early-stage intense romantic love, *Journal of Neurophysiology, 94*(1), 327–337.

Aron, A., Mashek, D. J., Fisher, H. E., Li, H., & Brown, L. L. (2005, July 16–20), Love really is "all in your head." Paper presented at the American Physiological Society Conference on Neurohypophyseal Hormones, Steamboat Springs, CO.

Artazcoz, L., Benach, J., Borrell, C., & Cortes, I. (2004). Unemployment and mental health: Understanding the interactions among gender, family roles, and social class. *American Journal of Public Health, 94*(1), 82–88.

Atchley, R. C. (2000). *Social forces and aging* (9th ed.). Belmont, CA: Wadsworth.

Atkins, D. C., Jacobson, N. S., & Baucom, D. H. (2001). Understanding infidelity: Correlates in a national random sample. *Journal of Family Psychology, 15,* 735–749.

Atwater, E. (1992). Peers. *Adolescence, 3,* 151–153.

Australian Relationships Survey. (2006). *Why do people get married?* Available: www.relationship.com/au/advice/faqs/FAQ220.faq/base_view [2008, July 14].

Axinn, W., & Thornton, A. (1996). The influence of parent's marital dissolutions on children's attitudes toward family formation. *Demography, 33,* 66–81.

Axmaker, L. W. (2004). What you need to know about child sexual abuse. Available: www.prevent-abuse-now.com/stats.htm [2004, October 4].

Babbie, E. (2006). *The practice of social research* (11th ed.). Belmont, CA: Wadsworth.

Baca Zinn, M., & Pok, A. Y. (2002). Tradition and transition in Mexican-origin families. In R. L. Taylor (Ed.), *Minority families in the United States: A multicultural perspective* (3rd ed.) (pp. 79–100). Upper Saddle River, NJ: Prentice Hall.

Bachman, G. F., & Guerrero, L. K. (2006). Relational quality and communicative responses following hurtful events in dating relationships: An expectancy violations analysis. *Journal of Social and Personal Relationships, 23*(6), 943–963.

Bachmann, G. A., & Phillips, N. A. (1998). Sexual dysfunction. In J. F. Steege, D. A. Metzger, and B. S. (Eds.), *Chronic pelvic pain: An integrated approach* (pp. 77–90). Philadelphia: Saunders.

Bagarozzi, D. A., & Anderson, S. A. (1989). *Personal, marital, and family myths: Theoretical formulations and clinical strategies.* New York: Norton.

Bailey, J. M., Bobrow, D., Wolfe, M., & Mikach, S. (1995). Sexual orientation of adult sons of gay father. *Developmental Psychology, 31*(1), 124–129.

Bailey, S., & Zvonkovic, A. (2003). Parenting after divorce. *Journal of Divorce and Remarriage, 39*(3/4), 59–80.

Baird, L. S., & Beccia, P. J. (1980). The potential misuse of overtime. *Personnel Psychology, 33,* 557–565.

Bajracharya, S., Sarvela, P., & Isberner, F. (1995). A retrospective study of first sexual intercourse experiences among undergraduates. *Journal of American College Health, 43,* 169–177.

Baker, A. (2007). *Adult children of parental alienation syndrome.* New York: Norton.

Baker, B., & Lightle, S. S. (2001). Cracks in the glass ceiling: An analysis of gender equity in the federal government career field. *The Journal of Government Financial Management, 1,* 18–26.

Balakrishnan, T., Vaninadha Rao, K., Lapierre-Adamcyk, E., & Krotki, K. (1987). A hazard model analysis of the covariates of marriage dissolution in Canada. *Demography, 24,* 395–406.

Baltes, P. B., Lindenberger, U., & Staudinger, U. M. (1998). Lifespan theory in developmental psychology. In R. M. Lerned (Ed.), *Handbook of child psychology: Vol 1. Theoretical models of human development* (5th ed) (pp. 1029–1143). New York: Wiley.

Bancroft, J., Carnes, J., Janssen, E., & Long, J. S. (2005). Erectile and ejaculatory problems in gay and heterosexual men. *Archives of Sexual Behavior, 24,* 285–297.

Bancroft, J., Loftus, J., & Long, J. S. (2003). Distress about sex: A national survey of women in heterosexual relationships. *Archives of Sexual Behavior, 322,* 193–208.

Banda, J. (2004, March). *Africa News Service.*

Bandura, A. (1977). *Social learning theory.* Englewood Cliffs, NJ: Prentice Hall.

Bandura, A. (1986). *Social foundations of thought and action: A social cognitive theory.* Englewood Cliffs, NJ: Prentice Hall.

Bandura, A., & Bussey, K. (1999). Social cognitive theory of gender development and differentiation. *Psychological Review, 106*(4), 676–713.

Banfield, S., & McCabe, M. P. (2001). Extra relationship involvement among women: Are they different from men? *Archives of Sexual Behavior, 30*(2), 119–143.

Bank, B. J., & Hansford, S. L. (2000). Gender and friendship: Whey are men's best same-sex friendships less intimate and supportive? *Journal of Social and Personal Relationships, 7,* 63–78.

Banks, J. A., & McGee-Banks, C. A. (2002). *Multicultural education: Issues and perspectives* (4th ed.). New York: Wiley.

Barbarin, O. A, & McCandies, T. (2003). African American families. In J. J. Ponzetti, Jr. (Ed.), *International encyclopedia of marriage and family* (2nd ed., Vol. 1.) (pp. 50–56). New York: Macmillan.

Barber, N. (1998). Secular changes in standards of bodily attractiveness in American women: Different masculine and feminine ideals. *Journal of Psychology, 132*(1), 87–95.

Barbor, C. (2001, Jan./Feb.). Finding real love. *Psychology Today.*

Barbour, C., Barbour, N. H., & Scully, P.A. (2005). *Families, schools, and communities: Building partnerships for educating children.* Upper Saddle River, NJ: Pearson.

Barnes, S. (1998, February). It's just a quarrel. *American Bar Association Journal, 24.*

Barnett, R. C., & Rivers, C. (1996). *She works, he works: How two-income families are happy, healthy, and thriving.* Cambridge, MA: Harvard University Press.

Barraket, J., & Henry-Waring, M. S. (2008). Getting it on(line). *Journal of Sociology, 44*(2), 149–165.

Barrett, A. (1999). Social support and life satisfaction among the never married. *Research on Aging, 21*(1), 46–72.

Barrett, A. (2004). Oral sex and teenagers: A sexual health educator's perspective. *Canadian Journal of Sexuality, 13,* 197–200.

Barrett, G., Pendry, E., Peacock, J., Victor, C., Thakar, R., & Manyonda, I. (2000). Women's sexual health after childbirth. *British Journal of Obstetrics and Gynecology, 107,* 186–195.

Bartels, A., & Zeki, S. (2000). The neural basis of romantic love. *Neuroreport, 11*(17), 3829–3834.

Bartholomew, K. (1990). Avoidance of intimacy: An attachment perspective. *Journal of Social and Personal Relationships, 7,* 147–178.

Bartoli, A. M., & Clark, M. D. (2006). The dating game: Similarities and differences in dating scripts among college students. *Sexuality and Culture, 10*(4), 54–80.

Basow, S. A., & Rubenfeld, K. (2003). Troubles talk. *Sex Roles: A Journal of Research, 48*(3/4), 183–188.

Basson, R. (2005). Women's sexual dysfunction: Revised and expanded definitions. *CMAJ, 172*(10), 1327–1333.

Basson, R. (2006). Sexual desire and arousal disorders in women. *New England Journal of Medicine, 354*(14), 1497–1506.

Baum, F. (1999). Cross-national trends in childlessness. Australian National University Research School of Social Sciences. *Working Papers in Demography, 73.*

Baum, N. (2003). Divorce process variables and the co-parental relationship and parental role fulfillment of divorced parents: Family and couple research. *Family Process, 42,* 117–131.

Baum, N. (2006). Post divorce paternal disengagement. *Journal of Marriage and Family Therapy, 32,* 245–254.

Baumeister, R. (2002). *Humility, egotism, forgiveness, and the victim role.* Available: www.forgiving.org.htm [2008, September 26].

Baumrind, D. (1991). The influence of parenting style on adolescent competence and substance use. *Journal of Early Adolescence, 11*(1), 56–95.

Baxter, J. (1993). *Work at home: The domestic division of labour.* Queensland, Australia: University of Queensland Press.

Baxter, J., Hewitt, B., & Haynes, M. (2008). Life course transitions and housework: Marriage, parenthood, and time on housework. *Journal of Marriage and Family, 70,* 259–272.

Beall, A. E., & Sternberg, R. J. (1995). The social construction of love. *Journal of Social and Personal Relationships, 12,* 417–438.

Bechman, N, Waem, M., Gustafson, D., & Skoog, I. (2008). Secular trends in self reported sexual activity and satisfaction in Swedish 70 year olds: Cross sectional survey of four populations, 1971–2001. *BMJ,* 10.1136/bmj.a279.

Becker, G. S. (1981). *A treatise on the family.* Cambridge, MA: Harvard University Press.

Bedard, M. E. (1992). *Breaking with tradition: Diversity, conflict, and change in contemporary families.* Dix Hills, NY: General Hall.

Bee, H., & Boyd, D. (2003). *Lifespan development* (3rd ed.). Boston: Allyn & Bacon.

Behnke, A. O., & MacDermid, S. M. (2004). Family well-being. *A Sloan Work and Family Encyclopedia* entry. Available: http://wfnetwork.bc.edu/encyclopedia_entry.php?id=235 [2009, August 11].

Belansky, E. S., & Boggiano, A. K. (1994). Predicting helping behaviors: The role of gender and instrumental/expressive self-schemata. *Sex Roles: A Journal of Research, 30*(9), 647–662.

Belsky, J. (1990). Children and marriage. In F. Fincham and T. Bradbury (Eds.), *The psychology of marriage: Basic issues and applications* (pp. 172–200). New York: Guilford.

Belsky, J. (2001). Developmental risks (still) associated with early childcare. *Journal of Child Psychology and Psychiatry and Allied Disciplines, 42,* 845–859.

Belsky, J., & Pensky, E. (1988). Marital change across the transition to parenthood. *Marriage and Family Review, 12,* 133–156.

Belsky, J., Woodworth, S., & Crnic, K. (1996). Trouble in the second year: Three questions about family interaction. *Child Development, 67,* 556–578.

Bem, S. L. (1974). The measurement of psychological androgyny. *Journal of Consulting and Clinical Psychology, 42*(2), 155–162.

Bem, S. L. (1981). Gender schema theory: A cognitive account of sex typing. *Psychological Review, 88,* 354–364.

Bem, S. L. (1993). *The lenses of gender: Transforming the debate on sexual inequality.* New Haven, CT: Yale University Press.

Bem, S. L. (1998). *An unconventional family.* New Haven, CT: Yale University Press.

Bennett, L. (2002). *Watch out, listen up! 2002 feminist primetime report.* National Organization for Women Foundation. Available: www.nowfoundation.org/watchout3/reportA.pdf [2005, July 17].

Benoit, D., & Parker, K. C. H. (1994). Stability and transmission of attachment across three generations. *Child Development, 65,* 1444–1456.

Beres, M. A., Herold, E., & Maitland, S. B. (2004). Sexual consent behaviors in same-sex relationships. *Archives of Sexual Behavior, 33*(5), 475–486.

Berkowitz, D., & Marsiglio, W. (2007). Gay men: Negotiating procreative, father, and family identities. *Journal of Marriage and Family, 69*(2), 366–381.

Bernardes, J. (2000). *Family studies: An introduction.* London: Routledge.

Berndt, T. S., & Savin-Williams, R. C. (1990). Friendship and peer relations. In S. S. Feldman & G. R. Elliot (Eds.), *At the threshold* (pp. 277–307). Cambridge, MA: Harvard University Press.

Bernhardt, E. (2004). Cohabitation and marriage among young adults in Sweden: Attitudes, expectations, and plans. *Scandinavian Population Studies, 13,* 157–170.

Berrington, A., & Diamond, I. (1997). Marital dissolution among the 1958 British birth cohort: The role of cohabitation. *Population Studies, 53,* 19–38.

Berrueta-Clement, J., Barnett, W., Schweinhart, L., Epstein, A., & Weikart, D. (1984). Changed lives: The effects of the Perry Preschool Project on youths through age 19. *Monographs of the High/Scope Educational Research Foundation, (8).* Ypsilanti, MI: High/Scope Press.

Berscheid, E. (1985). Interpersonal attraction. In G. Lindzey and E. Aronson (Eds.), *Handbook of social psychology* (3rd ed., vol. 2) (pp. 413–484). New York: Random House.

Bi, L., & D'agostino, F. (2004). The doctrine of filial piety: A philosophical analysis of the concealment case. *Journal of Chinese Philosophy, 31*(4), 451–467.

Bianchi, S. M. (2000). Maternal employment and time with children: Dramatic change or surprising continuity? *Demography, 37,* 401–414.

Bianchi, S. M., Subaiya, L., & Kahn, J. R. (1999, May). The gender gap in the economic well-being of nonresident fathers and custodial mothers. *Demography, 36,* 195–203.

Bigner, J. J., & Jacobsen, R. B. (1989). Parenting behaviors of homosexual and heterosexual fathers. *Journal of Homosexuality, 18*(1/2), 173–186.

Binstock, G. (2003). Separations, reconciliations, and living apart in cohabiting and marital unions. *Journal of Marriage and Family, 65,* 432–443.

Bippus, A. M. (2000). Humor usage in comforting messages: Factors predicting outcomes. *Western Journal of Communication, 64,* 359–384.

Bjorntorp, P. (1987). Fat cell distribution and metabolism. In R. J. Wurtman and J. J. Wurtman (Eds.), *Human obesity.* New York: New York Academy of Sciences.

Black, D., Sanders, S., & Taylor, L. (2007). The economics of lesbian and gay families. *Journal of Economic Perspectives, 21*(2), 53–70.

Blair, S. L., & Lichter, D. (1991). Measuring the division of household labor: Gender segregation of housework among American couples. *Journal of Family Issues, 12,* 91–113.

Blake, J. (1981). Family size and the quality of children. *Demography, 18,* 421–442.

Bland, J. (1998). *About gender: Social learning theory.* Available: www.gender.org.uk/about/02psycho/22_socln.htm [2005, July].

Blank, R. (2004). *Place matters: Addressing rural poverty.* Rural Poverty Research Center. Available: www.rprconline.org [2006, January 21].

Bleske-Rechek, A. L., & Buss, D. M. (2001). Opposite-sex friendship: Sex differences and similarities in initiation, selection, and dissolution. *Personality and Social Psychology Bulletin, 27,* 1310–1323.

Bleske-Rechek, A., & Buss, D. M. (2000). Can men and women just be friends? *Journal of Social and Personal Relationships, 7,* 131–151.

Bloir, K. (2005). Single, custodial fathers. *OSU Extension Factsheet, Family and Consumer Sciences.* Columbus: Ohio State University.

Blumer, H. (1969). *Symbolic interaction.* Englewood Cliffs, NJ: Prentice Hall.

Blumstein, P., & Schwartz, P. (1983). *American couples.* New York: William Morrow.

Boellstorff, T. (2005). Between religion and desire: Being Muslim and gay in Indonesia. *American Anthropologist 107*(4), 575–585.

Bogart, L. M., Cecil, H., & Wagstaff, D. A. (2000). Is it "sex"? College students' interpretations of sexual behavior terminology. *The Journal of Sex Research, 37*(2), 108–116.

Bogenschultz, M. P. (2005). Specialized 12-step programs and 12-step facilitation for the dually diagnosed. *Journal of Community and Mental Health, 41*(1), 7–20.

Bograd, R., & Spilka, B. (1996). Self-disclosure and marital satisfaction in mid-life and late-life remarriages. *International Journal of Aging and Human Development, 42*(3), 161–172.

Bohannan, P. (1971). *Divorce and after.* New York: Doubleday.

Bokker, P., Farley, R., & Denny, G. (2005). Emotional well-being among recently divorced fathers. *Journal of Divorce and Remarriage, 41,* 157–172.

Bonach, K., Sales, E., & Koeske, G. (2005). Gender differences in co-parenting quality. *Journal of Divorce and Remarriage, 42,* 1–28.

Bonkowski, S. (2003). Gay and lesbian parenting. *Family Law Advisor.* Available: www.divorcenet.com/il/ilart-15a.html [2004, August 12].

Booth, A., & Edwards, J. (1985). Age at marriage and marital stability. *Journal of Marriage and the Family, 47,* 67–75.

Booth, A., & Johnson, D. R. (1994). Declining health and marital quality. *Journal of Marriage and the Family, 47,* 67–74.

Booth, S. (2001, Nov. 1). Oral report: Are girls having oral sex to please the guys? *Teen People, 4,* 145.

Bos, H. M. W., van Balen, F., & van den Boom, D. C. (2004). Experience of parenthood, couple relationship, social support, and child-rearing goals in planned lesbian mother families. *Journal of Child Psychology and Psychiatry, 45,* 755–764.

Boss, P. (2003). *Family stress: Classic and contemporary readings.* Thousand Oaks, CA: Sage.

Boss, P. G., Doherty, W. J., LaRossa, R., Schumm, W. R., & Steinmetz, S. K. (1993). *Sourcebook of family theories and methods: A contextual approach.* New York: Plenum.

Bosse, R., Aldwin, C. M., Levinson, M. R., Workman-Daniels, K., & Ekerdt, D. J. (1990). Differences in social support among retirees and workers: Findings from the normative aging study. *Psychology of Aging, 5,* 41–47.

Bouhdiba, A. (2001). *Sexuality in Islam.* San Francisco: Saqi Books.

Bowen, M. (1966). The use of family theory in clinical practice. *Comprehensive Psychology, 7,* 345–374.

Bowen, M. (1974). Toward the differentiation of self in one's family of origin. In F. Andres and J. Lorio (Eds.), *Georgetown Family Symposium.* Washington, DC: Georgetown University Medical Center, Department of Psychiatry.

Bowen, M. (1978). *Family therapy in clinical practice.* New York: Jason Aronson.

Bower, B. (1995). Nice guys look better in women's eyes. *Science News, 147*(11), 165.

Bowlby, J. (1969/1973/1980). *Attachment and loss: Attachment* (Vols. 1–3). New York: Basic Books.

Bowlby, J. (1988). *A secure base.* London: Routledge.

Bowleg, L., Lucas, K. J, & Tschann, J. M. (2004). The ball was always in his court: An exploratory analysis of relationship scripts, sexual scripts, and condom use among African American women. *Psychology of Women Quarterly, 28*(1), 70–82.

Boyd, D., & Bee, H. (2006). *Lifespan development* (4th ed) Boston: Allyn & Bacon.

Boyd, D., & Bee, H. (2009). *Lifespan development* (5th ed.). Boston: Allyn & Bacon.

Boyse, C. (2008). *Media trends tracked.* Available: http://www.tvb .org/rcentral/MediaTrendsTrack/tvbasics/09TimeViewing Persons.asp [July 13, 2009].

Bracher, M., Santow, G., Morgan., S., & Trussell, J. (1993). Marriage dissolution in Australia: Models and explanations. *Population Studies, 47,* 403–425.

Bradsher, J. E. (1997). Older women and widowhood. In J. M. Coyle (Ed.), *Handbook on women and aging* (pp. 418–429). Westport, CT: Praeger.

Brady, S. S., & Halpern-Felsher, B. L. (2007). Adolescents' reported consequences of having oral sex versus vaginal sex. *Pediatrics, 119*(2), 229–237.

Bramlett, M. D., & Mosher, W. D. (2001). First marriage dissolution, divorce, and remarriage: United States. *Vital and Health Statistics, 323.* Hyattsville, MD: National Center for Health Statistics.

Bramlett, M. D., & Mosher, W. D. (2002). Cohabitation, marriage, divorce, and remarriage in the United States. *National Center for Health Statistics Vital Health Statistics, 23,* 22.

Brannon, R. (1976). The male sex role: Our culture's blueprint of manhood, and what it's done for us lately. In D. S. David and R. Brannon (Eds.), *The forty-nine percent majority: The male sex role.* Reading, MA: Addison-Wesley.

Brantley, A., Knox, D., & Zusman, M. E. (2002). When and why gender differences in saying "I love you" among college students. *College Student Journal, 36*(4), 614–616.

Braver, S., Shapiro, J. R., & Goodman, M. R. (2006). Consequences of divorce for parents. In M. A. Fine & J. H. Harvey (Eds.), *Handbook of divorce and relationship dissolution* (pp. 313–337). Mahwah, NJ: Erlbaum.

Bray, J. H. (1999). From marriage to remarriage and beyond. In E. M. Hetherington (Ed.), *Coping with divorce, single parenting, and remarriage* (pp. 253–271). Mahwah, NJ: Erlbaum.

Brem, S. S. (1992). *Intimate relationships.* New York: McGraw-Hill.

Brener, N., Lowry, R., Kann, L., Kolbe, L., Lehnherr, J., Janssen, R., & Jaffe, H. (2002). Trends in sexual risk behaviors among high school students: United States, 1991–2001. *Morbidity and Mortality Weekly Report, 51*(38), 856–859.

Brewaeys, A., & Van Hall, E. V. (1997). Lesbian motherhood: The impact on child development and family functioning. *Journal of Psychosomatic Obstetrics and Gynecology, 18,* 1–16.

Bridge, R., Judd, C., & Moock, P. (1979). *The determinants of educational outcomes: The impact of families, peers, teachers, and schools.* Cambridge, MA: Ballinger.

Briton, N. J., & Hall, J. A. (1999). Beliefs about female and male nonverbal communication. *Journal of Nonverbal Behavior, 23*(1), 91–100.

Brody, E., & Schoonover, C. (1986). Patterns of parent care when adult daughters work and when they do not. *The Gerontologist, 26,* 372–381.

Brody, E. M. (1985). Parent care as a normative family stress. *Gerontologist, 25,* 19–29.

Brody, G., Flor, D., & Neubaum, E. (1998). Coparenting processes and child competence among rural African-American families. In M. Lewis and C. Feiring (Eds.), *Families, risk, and competence.* Mahwah, NJ: Erlbaum.

Broman, C. L., Reckase, M. D., & Freedman-Doan, C. R. (2006). The role of parenting in drug use among black, Latino, and white adolescents. *Journal of Ethnicity in Substance Use, 5*(1), 39–50.

Bronfenbrenner, U. (1979). *The ecology of human development: Experiments by nature and design.* Cambridge, MA: Harvard University Press.

Brooks, R. (2002). Transitional friends? Young people's strategies to manage and maintain their friendships during a period of repositioning. *Journal of Youth Studies, 5,* 449–467.

Brooks-Gunn, J., & Markman, L.B. (2005). The contribution of parenting to ethnic and racial gaps in school readiness. *Future of Children, 15*(1), 139–168.

Brown, E., Orbuch, T. L, & Bauermeister, J. A. (2008). Religiosity and marital stability among Black American and white American couples. *Family Relations, 57,* 186–197.

Brown, P. J., & Konner, M. (1987). An anthropological perspective of obesity. *Annals of the New York Academy of Sciences, 499,* 29–46.

Brown, S. L., & Booth, A. (1996). Cohabitation versus marriage: A comparison of relationship quality. *Journal of Family Issues, 14*(2), 236–260.

Brown, S. L., Van Hook, J., & Glick, J. (2005, March 30–April 2). Generational differences in cohabitation and marriage in the U.S. Paper presented at the annual meeting of the Population Association of America, Philadelphia.

Brown, S., & Booth, A. (1996). Cohabitation versus marriage: A comparison of relationship quality. *Journal of Marriage and the Family, 58,* 668–678.

Brown, T. N., Tanner-Smith, E. E., Lesane-Brown, C. L., & Ezell, M. E. (2007). Child, parent, and situational correlates of familial ethnic/race socialization. *Journal of Marriage and Family, 69*(1), 14–26.

Browning, D. (2004). *Why marry?* Available: www.equalityin marriage.org/bmwhy.html [2004, July 8].

Bruckner, H., & Bearman, P. (2005). After the promise: The STD consequences of adolescent virginity pledges. *Journal of Adolescent Health, 36*(4), 271–278.

Brummen, H. J., Bruinse, H. W., van de Pol, G., Heintz, A. P. M., & van der Vaart, C. H. (2006). Which factors determine the sexual function 1 year after childbirth? *British Journal of Gynecology, 113,* 914–918.

Bryant, A. S. (1994). Relationship characteristics of American gay and lesbian couples: Findings from a national survey. In L. A. Kurdek (Ed.), *Social services for gay and lesbian couples* (pp. 101–117). New York: Haworth.

Bryant, A. S., & Demian (1994). Relationship characteristics of American gay and lesbian couples: Findings from a national survey. In L. A. Kurdek (Ed.), *Social services for gay and lesbian couples* (pp. 101–117). New York: Haworth.

Buchanan, C. M., Maccoby, E. E., & Dornbusch, S. M. (1991). Caught between parents: Adolescents' experience in divorced homes. *Child Development, 62,* 1008–1029.

Buckley, T. R, & Carter, R. T. (2005). Black adolescent girls: Do gender role and racial identity impact their self-esteem? *Sex Roles, 53*(9-10), 647–661.

Buehlman, K. T., Gottman, J. M., & Katz, L. F. (1992). How a couple views their past predicts their future: Predicting divorce from an oral history interview. *Journal of Family Psychology, 5,* 295–318.

Buhler, R. (2005). *Is it really 50 percent?* Available: www.family .org/married/youngcouples [2005, February 9].

Bulanda, J. R., & Brown, S. L. (2007). Race-ethnic differences in marital quality and divorce. *Social Science Research, 36,* 945–967.

Bumpass, L., Castro Martin, T., & Sweet, J. (1991). The impact of family background and early marital factors on marital disruption. *Journal of Family Issues, 12,* 22–42.

Bumpass, L., & Lu, H. H. (2000, March). Trends in cohabitation and implications for children's family contexts in the United States. *Population Studies, 54,* 29–41.

Bumpass, L., & Sweet, J. (1972). Differentials in marital instability: 1970. *American Sociological Review, 37,* 754–766.

Burleson, B. R. (1992). Taking communication seriously. *Communication Monographs, 59,* 79–86.

Burleson, B. R. (2003). The experience and effects of emotional support: What the study of cultural and gender differences can tell us about close relationships, emotion, and interpersonal communication. *Journal of Social and Personal Relationships, 10,* 1–23.

Burney, M. A. (2002). *Codependence: The dance of wounded souls.* Cambria, CA: Joy to You & Me Enterprises.

Burr, W. R. (1970). Satisfaction with various aspects of marriage over the life cycle: A random middle class sample. *Journal of Marriage and the Family, 32,* 29–37.

Burr, W. R. (1973). *Theory construction and the sociology of the family.* New York: Wiley.

Burrello, K. N. (2005). *What are the strengths of interracial families?* Diversity Dating Organization. Available: www .diversitydtg.com/articles/interracialfamilies.htm [2008, October 20].

Burton, L., Dilworth-Anderson, P., & Merriwether-de-Vries, C. (1995). Context of surrogate parenting among contemporary grandparents. *Marriage and Family Review, 20,* 349–366.

Buss, D. (1985). Human mate selection. *American Scientist, 73,* 47–51.

Buss, D. (1989). Sex difference in human mate preferences: Evolutionary hypotheses testing in 37 cultures. *Behavioral and Brain Sciences, 12,* 1–49.

Buss, D. (1999). *Evolutionary psychology. The new science of the mind.* Boston: Allyn & Bacon.

Buss, D., & Angleitner, A. (1989). Mate selection preferences in Germany and the United States. *Personality and Individual Differences, 10,* 269–1280.

Buss, D., & Barnes, M. (1986). Preferences in human mate selection. *Journal of Personality and Social Psychology, 50,* 559–570.

Buss, D. M. (1994). *The evolution of desire: Strategies of human mating.* New York: Basic Books.

Buss, D. M., & Schmitt, D. P. (1993). Sexual strategies theory: An evolutionary perspective on human dating. *Psychological Review, 100,* 204–232.

Bussey, K., & Bandura, A. (1984). Influence and gender constancy and social power on sex-linked modeling. *Journal of Personality and Social Psychology, 47,* 1292–1302.

Bussey, K., & Bandura, A. (1992). Self-regulatory mechanisms governing gender development. *Child Development, 63,* 1236–1250.

Bussey, K., & Bandura, A. (1999). Social cognitive theory of gender development and differentiation. *Psychological Review, 106,* 676–713.

Butler, R. N., & Lewis, M. I. (1986). *Midlife love life: How to deal with the physical and emotional changes of midlife and their effect on your sex life.* New York: Harper & Row.

Byers, E. S. (2005). Relationship satisfaction and sexual satisfaction: A longitudinal study of individuals in long-term relationships. *The Journal of Sex Research, 42,* 113–118.

Byers, S. E., Sears, H. A., & Weaver, A. D. (2008). Parents' reports of sexual communication with children in kindergarten to grade 8. *Journal of Marriage and Family, 70,* 86–96.

Byers, S. E., Sears, H. A., Voyer, S. D., Thurlow, T. L., Cohen, J. N., & Weaver, A. D. (2003). An adolescent perspective on sexual health education at school and at home: I. High school students. *Canadian Journal of Human Sexuality, 12,* 1–17.

Cahill, B. & Adams, E. (1997). An exploratory study of early childhood teachers' attitudes toward gender roles. *Sex Roles: A Journal of Research, 36*(7/8), 517–530.

Call, V., Sprecher, S., & Schwartz, P. (1995). The incidence and frequency of marital sex in a national sample. *Journal of Marriage and the Family, 57,* 639–4652.

Call, V. R. A., & Heaton, T. B. (1997). Religious influence on marital stability. *Journal for the Scientific Study of Religion, 36,* 382–392.

Campbell, F. A., Pungello, E. P., Miller-Johnson, S., Burchinal, M., & Ramey, C. T. (2001). The development of cognitive and academic abilities: Growth curves from an early childhood educational experiment. *Developmental Psychology, 37*(2), 231–242.

Campbell, F. A., Ramey, C. T., Pungello, E. P., Sparling, J., & Miller-Johnson, S. (2002). Early childhood education: Young adult outcomes from the Abecedarian Project. *Applied Developmental Science, 6,* 42–57.

Campbell, K. (2002, February 14). Today's courtship: White teeth, root beer, and e-mail? *Christian Science Monitor,* 1–4.

Campbell, N. (2003). *Be fruitful and multiply.* San Antonio, TX: Vision Forum.

Campbell, S. B., Cohn, J. F., Flanagan, C., Popper, S., et al. (1992). Course and correlates of postpartum depression during the transition to parenthood. *Development and Psychopathology, 4,* 29–47.

Campbell, T. L. (1993). Health promotion/disease prevention and the family. In B. Elliott (Ed.), *Vision 2010: Families and health care.* Minneapolis: National Council on Family Relations.

Campenni, C. E. (1999). Gender stereotyping of children's toys: A comparison of parents and nonparents. *Sex Roles, 40,* 121–138.

Canales, G. (2000). Gender as subculture: The first division of multicultural diversity. In I. Cuellar and F. A. Paniagua (Eds.), *Handbook of multicultural mental health: Assessment and treatment of diverse populations* (pp. 63–77). New York: Academic Press.

Canary, D. J., Cody, M. J., & Manusov, V. (2000). *Interpersonal communication: A goals-based approach* (2nd ed.). New York: Bedford/St. Martin's Press.

Cant, J. G. H. (1981). Hypothesis for the evolution of human breasts and buttocks. *American Naturalist, 117,* 199–204.

Caplan, G. (1976). The family as a support system. In G. Caplan & M. Killiea (Eds.), *Support systems and mutual help: Multidimensional explorations* (pp. 19–36). New York: Grune & Stratton.

Cardillo, M. (2005). *Intimate relationships: Personality development through interaction during early life.* Available: www .personalityresearch.org/papers/cardillo [2005, November 30].

Carlson, A. (2003). *Mothers at war: The American way?* (Aired April 25, 2003, CNN). Transcript retrieved April 1, 2006, from www.wnd.com/news/printer-friendly.asp?ARTICLE_ ID=31981.

Carlson, B. E. (1984). Children's observations of interpersonal violence. In A. R. Roberts (Ed.), *Battered women and their families* (pp. 147–167). New York: Springer.

Carlson, C. (1995). Working with single-parent and stepfamily systems. In A. Thomas and J. Grimes (Eds.), *Best practices in school psychology* (3rd ed.) (pp. 1097–1110). Washington, DC: National Association of School Psychologists.

Caron, S. L., & Moskey, E.G. (2002). Changes over time in teenage sexual relationships. *Adolescence, 37*(47), 15–27.

Carpenter, C., & Gates, G. J. (2008). Gay and lesbian partnership: Evidence form California. *Demography, 45*(3), 573–590.

Carranza, M. A., Gouveia, L., Cogua, J., & Ondracek-Sayers, K. (2002). The integration of the Hispanic/Latino immigrant workforce: Final project report. *Task Force on the Productive Integration of the Immigrant Workforce Population.* Available: http://lri.unl.edu/HLIWSREPORTfinal.pdf [2009, June 25].

Carroll, J. (2007, June). Americans: 2.5 children is "ideal" family size. *Gallup Poll Briefing,* 96–108.

Carstensen, L. L., Gottman, J. M., & Levenson, R. W. (1995). Emotional behavior in long-term marriage. *Psychology and Aging, 10,* 140–149.

Carter, B., & McGoldrick, M. (1999). *The expanded family life cycle: Individual, family, and social perspectives* (3rd ed.). Boston: Allyn & Bacon.

Carter, B., & McGoldrick, M. (2005). *The expanded family life cycle: Individual, family, and social perspectives* (4th ed.). Boston: Allyn & Bacon.

Carton, J. S., Kessler, E. A., & Pape, C. L. (1999). Nonverbal decoding skills and relationship well-being in adults. *Communication Monographs, 69*(1), 33–51.

Cartwright, C. (2006). You want to know how it affected me? Young adults' perceptions of the impact of parental divorce. *Journal of Divorce and Remarriage, 44*(3/4), 125–143.

Cartwright, R. (1999, Autumn). Childless or childfree? *Journal of Fertility Counseling.*

Carver, P. R., Yunger, J. L., & Perry, D. G. (2003). Gender identity and adjustment in middle childhood. *Sex Roles: A Journal of Research, 49,* 95–110.

Casper, L. M., & Bianchi, S. M. (2002). *Continuity and change in the American family.* Thousand Oaks, CA: Sage.

Cassidy, J., & Berlin, L. J. (1994). The insecure/ambivalent pattern of attachment: Theory and research. *Child Development, 65,* 971–991.

Casta-eda, D. M. (1993) The meaning of romantic love among Mexican-Americans. *Journal of Social Behavior and Personality, 8*(2), 257–272.

Catalan, S. (2004). *Criminal victimization, 2003.* Washington, DC: United States Department of Justice, Bureau of Justice Statistics. Available: http://222.ojp.usdoj.gov/bjs/abstract/ cv03.htm [2006, April 4].

Cate, R. M., & Lloyd, S. A. (1992). The history of courtship. In R. Cate & S. Lloyd (Eds.), *Courtship* (pp. 13–32). Newbury Park, CA: Sage.

Caughlin, J. P. (2002). The demand/withdraw pattern of communication as a predictor of marital satisfaction over time: Unresolved issues and future directions. *Human Communication Research, 28,* 49–85.

Cavanaugh, J. C., & Blanchard-Fields, F. (2002). *Adult development and aging* (4th ed.). Belmont, CA: Wadsworth.

Ceballo, R., & Hurd, N. (2008). Neighborhood context, SES, and parenting: Including a focus on acculturation among Latina mothers. *Applied Developmental Science, 12*(4), 176–180.

Ceballo, R., Chao, R. K., Hill, N. E., Le, H., Murry, V. M., & Pinderhughes, E. E. (2008). Excavating culture: Summary of results. *Applied Developmental Science, 12*(4), 220–226.

Ceballo, R., Lansford, J. E., Abbey, A., & Stewart, A. J. (2004). Gaining a child: Comparing the experiences of biological parents, adoptive parents, and stepparents. *Family Relations, 53*(1), 38–48.

Centers for Disease Control, National Center for Health Statistics. (2007, December 5). *National Vital Statistics Report, 56*(7).

Centers for Disease Control. (2008). Births, marriages, divorces, and deaths: Provisional data for July 2007. *National Vital Statistics Reports, 56,* 14.

Centers for Disease Control. (2009). Sexual and reproductive health of persons aged 10–24 years: United States, 2002–2007. *MMWR, 58*(SS06), 1–58. Available: http://www.cdc.gov/mmwr/preview/mmwrhtml/ss5806al.htm?s_cid=ss5806al_e [2009, August 1].

Centers for Disease Control. (2009, February 8). 1 in 4 women, 1 in 9 men suffer intimate partner violence. *Morbidity and Mortality Weekly Report.*

Centers for Disease Control and Prevention. (2004). *Genital HPV infection: CDC fact sheet.* Available: www.cdc.gov/std/HPV/STDFact-HPV.htm [2006, March 17].

Centers for Disease Control and Prevention. (2005a). *Sexually transmitted disease surveillance, 2004.* Available: www.cdc.gov/std/stats/04pdf/2004SurveillanceAll.pd [2006, March 17].

Centers for Disease Control and Prevention. (2005b). *Viral hepatitis: National Center for Infectious Diseases.* Available: www.cdc.gov/ncidod/diseases/hepatitis/ [2006, March 17].

Centers for Disease Control and Prevention. Division of Vital Statistics. (2005c). Births: Preliminary data for 2004. *National Vital Statistics Report, 54*(8). Available: www.cdc.gov/nchs/data/nvsr/nvsr54/nvsr54_08.pdf [2006, March 20].

Centers for Disease Control, and Prevention. (2008). Teen birth rate rises for the first time in 15 years. Available: www.cdc.gov/nchs/pressroom.html [2009, January 10].

Centers for Disease Control and Prevention. (2009). Division of STD Prevention (DSTDP). Available: www.cdc.gov/std/ [2009, January 10].

Cere, D. (2001, Spring). Courtship today: The view from academia. *Public Interest, 53.*

Cervera, N. (1994). Family change during an unwed teenage pregnancy. *Journal of Youth and Adolescence, 23*(1), 119–140.

Chafetz S. (1975). Masculine/feminine or human?? An overview of the sociology of sex roles. *Contemporary Sociology, 4*(3), 230–231.

Chamberlain, P., & Patterson, G. R. (1995). Discipline and child compliance in parenting. In M. H. Mornstein (Ed.), *Handbook of parenting. Vol 4: Applied and practical parenting.* Mahwah, NJ: Erlbaum.

Chambers, W. C. (2007). Oral sex: Varied behaviors and perceptions in a college population. *The Journal of Sex Research, 44*(1), 28–42.

Chandler, D. (2005). *Television and gender roles.* University of Wales. Available: www.aber.ac.uk/media/Modules/TF33120/gendertv [2005, August 25].

Chao, R., & Kanatsu, A. (2008). Beyond socio-economic: Explaining ethnic group differences in parenting through cultural and immigration processes. *Applied Developmental Science, 12*(4), 181–187.

Chapman, S. (2004). *Practical aspects of polygamy: The benefits polygamy has for women and the controls it places on men.* Available: www.polygamy.com/Practical/Practical-Aspects-of-Polygamy.html [2004, October 9].

Cheah, C. S. L., & Rubin, K. H. (2004). Comparison of European American and mainland Chinese mothers' responses to aggression and social withdrawal in preschoolers. *International Journal of Behavioral Development, 28,* 83–94.

Chen, A., & Kaplan, H. B. (2001). Intergenerational transmission of constructive parenting. *Journal of Marriage and Family, 63*(1), 17–31.

Chen, G.-M. (1995). Differences in self-disclosure patterns among Americans versus Chinese: A comparative study. *Journal of Cross-cultural Psychology, 26,* 84–91.

Cherlin, A. J. (1999, November). Going to extremes: Family structure, children's well-being, and social science. *Demography, 36,* 421–428.

Cherlin, A. J. (2004). The deinstitutionalization of American Marriage. *Journal of Marriage and Family, 66*(4), 848–861.

Cherlin, A. J., & Furstenberg, F. F. (1986). *The new American grandparent.* New York: Basic Books.

Cherlin, A. J., Furstenberg, F. F., Chase-Linsdale, L., Kiernan, K. E., Robins, P. K., Morrison, D. R., & Teitler, J. O. (1995). Longitudinal studies of effects of divorce on children in Great Britain and the United States. *Science, 252,* 1386–1389.

Chevret, M., Jaudinot, E., Sullivan, K., Marrel, A., & De Gendre, A. S. (2004). Quality of sexual life and satisfaction in female partners of men with ED: Psychometric validation of the index of sexual life (ISL) questionnaire. *Journal of Sex & Marital Therapy, 30,* 141–155.

Chewning, B., Douglas, J., Kokotailo, P. K., LaCourt, J., St. Clair, D., & Wilson, D. (2001). Protective factors associated with American Indian adolescents' safer sexual patterns. *Maternal and Child Health Journal, 5*(4), 273–280.

Chicago Tribune. (2002). *When a marriage can't make room for daddy* (January 19, 2005). Available: http://www.turnonyourinnerlight.com/ChicagoTribune01192005.htm [2009, June 25].

Child Trends. (2006). Oral sex. 2002: National Survey of Family Growth. Available: www.cdc.gov/nchs/nsfg [2007, August 20].

Child Trends. (2008). *Family structure.* Available: www.childtrendsdatabank.org/indicators/59FamilyStructure.cfm [2008, August 21].

Children's Defense Fund. (2002). *The state of children in America's union.* Available: www.childrensdefense.org/pdg/minigreenbook.pdf [2005, February 27].

Chiong, J. A. (1998). *Racial categorization of multiracial children in schools.* Westport, CT: Bergin & Garvey.

Christensen, A., & Shenk, J. L. (1991). Communication, conflict, and psychological distance in nondistressed, clinic, and divorcing couples. *Journal of Consulting and Clinical Psychology, 59,* 458–463.

Christopher, F. S., & Sprecher, S. (2000). Sexuality in marriage, dating, and other relationships: A decade review. *Journal of Marriage and the Family, 62*(4), 999–1017.

Christophersen, E. R. (1988). *Little people: Guidelines for common sense child rearing* (3rd ed.). Kansas City, MO: Westport.

Ciano-Boyce, C., & Shelley-Sireci, L. (2002). Who is Mommy tonight? Lesbian parenting issues. *Journal of Homosexuality, 43,* 1–13.

Citron, N. (2003, July 1). Demographics, health, and health services. *American Demographics.*

Clark, S. C. (1995). Advance report on final divorce statistics, 1989 and 1990. *Monthly Vital Statistics Report, 43*(9). Hyattsville, MD: National Center for Health Statistics.

Clarkberg, M., Stolzenberg, R. M., & Waite, L. J. (1996). Attitudes, values, and entrance into cohabitational unions. *Social Forces, 74.*

Clarke, L., & Berrington, A. (1998). *Socio-demographic predictors of divorce.* Available: www.oneplusone.org.uk/downloads/reviewpapers/1%20-%20Socio-demographic%20predictors%20of%20divorce.pdf [2005, January 15].

Clarke, L., Di Salvo, P., Joshi, H., & Wright, J. (1997). *Stability and instability in children's lives: Longitudinal evidence from Great Britain,* Research Paper 97-1. Centre for Population Studies, London School of Hygiene and Tropical Sciences.

Class, R. M. (1999). Silence about sexual problems can hurt relationships. *The Journal of the American Medical Association, 281*(6), 584.

Claxton, A., & Perry-Jenkins, M. (2008). No fun anymore: Leisure and marital quality across the transition to parenthood. *Journal of Marriage and Family, 70,* 28–43.

Clinebell, H. J., & Clinebell, C. H. (1970). *The intimate marriage.* New York: Harper & Row.

Coard, S. I., Foy-Watson, S., Zimmer, C., & Wallace, A. (2007). Considering culturally relevant parenting practices in intervention development and adaptation: A randomized controlled trial of the Black Parenting Strengths and Strategies (BPSS) Program. *The Counseling Psychologist, 35*(6), 797–820.

Cohan, C. I., & Kleinbaum, S. (2002). Toward a greater understanding of the cohabitation effect: Premarital cohabitation and marital communication. *Journal of Marriage and Family, 64,* 180–192.

Cohen, F. (1984). Coping. In J. D. Matarazzo, S. M. Weiss, J. A. Herd, N. E. Miller, and S. M. Weiss (Eds.), *Behavioral health: A handbook of health enhancement and disease prevention.* New York: Wiley.

Cohen, L., & Roth, S. (1984). Coping with abortion. *Journal of Human Stress, 10*(3), 140–145.

Cohen, T. F. (1993). What do fathers provide? Reconsidering the economic and nurturant dimensions of men as parents. In J. C. Hood (Ed.), *Men, work, and family* (pp. 1–22). Newbury Park, CA: Sage.

Coleman, M., & Ganong, L. H. (1991). Remarriage and stepfamily research in the 1980s. In A. Booth (Ed.), *Contemporary families: Looking forward, looking back* (pp. 192–207). Minneapolis: National Council on Family Relations.

Coleman, M., & Ganong, L. H. (Eds.). (2003). *Handbook of contemporary families: Considering the past, contemplating the future.* Thousand Oaks, CA: Sage.

Coleman, M., Ganong, L. H., & Fine, M. (2000). Reinvestigating remarriage: Another decade of progress. *Journal of Marriage and the Family, 62,* 1288–1307.

Coley, R. L. (2002). What mothers teach, what daughters learn: Gender mistrust and self-sufficiency among low-income women. In A. Booth and A. C. Crouter (Eds.), *Just living together: Implications of cohabitation on families* (pp. 97–106). Mahwah, NJ: Erlbaum.

Collins, P. H. (2004). *Black sexual politics: African Americans, gender and the new racism.* New York: Routledge.

Coltrane, S. (2000). Research on household labor: Modeling and measuring the social embeddedness of routine family work. *Journal of Marriage and the Family, 62,* 1208–1233.

Commonwealth Fund Commission. (1999, May). *Health concerns across a woman's health.* New York: Author.

Commonwealth Fund Commission. (2008). *Why not the best: Results from the National Scorecard on U.S. Health System Performance.* http://www.commonwealthfund.org/Content/Publications/Fund-Reports/2008/Jul/Why-Not-the-Best—Results-from-the-National-Scorecard-on-U-S—Health-System-Performance—2008.aspx [2009, August 11].

Congressional Caucus on Women's Issues. (2005). *Chutes & ladders: The search for solid ground for women in the workforce.* Available: http://www.womenwork.org/policy/chutes.htm [2009, August 11].

Congressional Research Service. (2007). *The cost of the Iraq, Afghanistan, and other Global War on Terror Operations since 9/11.* Washington, DC: Congressional Research Service.

Connell, C. M., & Prinz, R. J. (2002). The impact of childcare and parent-child interactions on school readiness and social skill development for low-income African American children. *Journal of School Psychology, 40*(2), 177–193.

Connell, R. W. (1987). *Gender and power: Society, the person, and sexual politics.* Stanford, CA: Stanford University Press.

Connolly, A., Thorp, J., & Pahel, L. (2005). Effects of pregnancy and childbirth on postpartum sexual function: A longitudinal prospective study. *International Urogynecological Journal of Pelvic Floor Dysfunction.* Available: www.ncibi.nlm.nih.gov/entrez/query.fcgi?cmd=retrieve&db=pubmed&dopt=Abstract&list_uids=15838587&query_hl=53 [2006, March 22].

Conway, J., & Conway, S. (2000). *Parenting your parents.* Available: www.midlife.com [2005, May].

Cooksey, E., & Craig, P. (1998). Parenting from a distance: The effects of parental characteristics on contact between nonresidential fathers and their children. *Demography, 35*(2), 187–200.

Cookston, J. T., Braver, S. L., Griffin, W., deLusé, S. R., & Miles, J. C. (2007). Effects of the Dads for Life intervention on interparental conflict and co-parenting in the two years after divorce. *Family Processes, 46*(1), 123–137.

Cooney, T. M. (1994). Young adults' relations with parents: The influence of recent parental divorce. *Journal of Marriage and the Family, 56,* 45–56.

Cooney, T. M., & Kurz, J. (1996). Mental health outcomes following recent parental divorce. *Journal of Family Issues, 17,* 495–513.

Cooney, T. M., Smyer, M. A., Hagstad, G. O., & Klock, R. (1986). Parental divorce in young adulthood: Some preliminary findings. *American Journal of Orthopsychiatry, 56,* 470–477.

Coontz, S. (1992). *The way we never were: American families and the nostalgia trap.* New York: Basic Books.

Coontz, S. (1999). *American families: A multicultural reader.* New York: Routledge.

Corbett, M. (2005). U.S. households led by single mothers and displaced homemakers on the rise. *Women's Work.* Available: www.womenwork.org [2009, February 7].

Cordon, I. M. (1997). *Stress.* Available: www.csun.edu/~vcpsy00h/students/stress.htm [2004, September 22].

Cowan, C. P., & Cowan, P. A. (2000). *When partners become parents: The big life change for couples.* Mahwah, NJ: Erlbaum.

Cowan, P., Cowan, C. P., & Schulz, M. (1996). Thinking about risk and resilience in families. In E. M. Hetherington and E. Blechman (Eds.), *Stress, coping, and resiliency in children and families* (pp. 1–38). Mahwah, NJ: Erlbaum.

Cowly, G. (1996). The biology of beauty. *Newsweek, 25,* 60–67.

Craft, C. (2004). The National Adoption Information Clearinghouse. Available: http://adoption.about.com/od/gaylesbian/f/problems.htm [2004, August 12].

Craig, R. S. (1992a). The effect of television day part on gender portrayals in television commercials: A content analysis. *Sex Roles, 26*(5/6), 197–211.

Craig, R. S. (1992b). Men's men and women's women: How TV commercials portray gender to different audiences. In R. Kemper (Ed.), *Issues and effects of mass communication: Other voices* (pp. 89–100). San Diego, CA: Capstone Publishers.

Crawford, J. (2005). *Making sense of census 2000.* National Association for Bilingual Education. Available: www.nabe.org/research/demography.html [2005, November 16].

Crawford, M., & Unger, R. (2000). *Women and gender: A feminist psychology* (3rd ed.). Boston: McGraw-Hill.

Criddle, M., & Scott, M. (2005). Mandatory divorce education and post divorce parental conflict. *Journal of Divorce and Remarriage, 62,* 99–111.

Crimmins, E. M., & Ingegneri, D. G. (1990). Interaction and living arrangements of older parents and their children. *Research on Aging, 12,* 3–35.

Crittenden, P. M., Partridge, M. F., & Claussen, A. H. (1991). Family patterns of relationship in normative and dysfunctional families. *Development and Psychopathology, 3,* 491–512.

Crockenberg, S. C., & Leerkes, E. M. (2003). Parental acceptance, postpartum depression, and maternal sensitivity: Mediating and moderating processes. *Journal of Family Psychology, 17,* 80–93.

Crosnoe, R., & Elder, G. H. (2002). Successful adaptation in the later years: A lifecourse approach to aging. *Social Psychology Quarterly, 65*(4), 309–328.

Crouter, A. C. (1995). Processes linking families and work: Implications for behavior and developing in both settings. In R. D. Parke and S. Kellam (Eds.), *Exploring family relationships with other social contexts* (pp. 55–79). Hillsdale, NJ: Erlbaum.

Crouter, A. C., Bumpus, M. F., Head, M. R., & McHale, S. M. (2001). Implications of overwork and overload for the quality of men's family relationships. *Journal of Marriage and Family, 63*(2), 404–416.

Cunningham, M. R. (1986). Measuring the physical in physical attractiveness: Quasi-experiments on the sociobiology of female facial beauty. *Journal of Personality and Social Psychology, 50,* 925–935.

Cunningham, M. R., Roberts, A. R., Barbee, A. P., Duren, P. B., & Wu, C. H. (1995). Their ideas of beauty are, on the whole, the same as ours: Consistency and variability in the cross-cultural perception of female physical attractiveness. *Journal of Personality and Social Psychology, 68,* 261–279.

Current Population Reports. (2008). *Fertility of American women: 2006.* Available: http://www.census.gov/prod/2008pubs/p20-558.pdf [2009, August 1].

Czaplewski, M. J., & Jorgensen, S. R. (1993). The professionalization of family life education. In M. E. Arcus, J. D. Schvaneveldt, and J. J. Moss (Eds.), *Handbook of family life education: Foundations of family life education* (pp. 51–75). Newbury Park, CA: Sage.

Dacey, J., & Travers, J. (2002). *Human development across the lifespan* (5th ed.). Boston: McGraw-Hill.

Daire, A. (2004). Investigating caregiver distress with the Parental Bonding Instrument (PBI). *Dementia: The International Journal of Social Research and Practice, 3,* 83–94.

Daley, S. P. (1993). Health experience of minority families. In B. Elliott (Ed.), *Vision 2010: Families and health care.* Minneapolis: National Council on Family Relations.

Dalton, C., & Schneider, E. M. (2001). *Battered women and the law.* New York: Foundation Press.

Darden, E. C., & Zimmerman, T. S. (1992). Blended families: A decade review, 1970–1990. *Family Therapy, 19,* 25–31.

Darling, C. A. (1987). Family life education. In M. B. Sussman and S. K. Steinmetz (Eds.), *Handbook of marriage and the family* (pp. 815–833). New York: Plenum.

Darling, C. A., & Steinberg, L. (1993). Parenting style as context: An integrative model. *Psychological Bulletin, 1*(13), 487–496.

Darwin, C. (1871). *The descent of man and selection in relation to sex.* London: Murray.

David, M. B. (2005). *From a woman's place: The case for polygamy.* Available: www.polygamy.com/practical/From-A-Woman-Place.htm [2006, January 2].

Davidson, J. K., Sr., & Darling, C. A. (1989). Self-perceived differences in the female orgasmic response. *Family Practice Research Journal, 8,* 75–84.

Davidson, J., Darling, C. A., & Norton, L.X. (1995). Religiosity and the sexuality of women: Sexual behavior and sexual satisfaction revisited. *Journal of Sex Research, 32,* 235–243.

Davies, M. F., (2001). Socially desirable responding and impression management in the endorsement of love styles. *Journal of Psychology, 135*(5), 562–570.

Davis, D. A., & Davis, S. S. (1993). Sexual values in a Moroccan town. In W. J. Lonner and R. S. Malpass (Eds.), *Psychology and culture* (pp. 225–230). Boston: Allyn & Bacon.

Davis, D., Shaver, P. R., & Vernon, M. L. (2003). Physical, emotional, and behavioral reactions to breaking up: The roles of gender, age, emotional involvement, and attachment style. *Personality and Social Psychology Bulletin, 29*(7), 871–884.

Davis, E. C., & Friel, L. V. (2001). Adolescent sexuality: Disentangling the effects of family structure and family contexts. *Journal of Marriage and Family, 63*(3), 669–681.

Davis, K. K., Crouter, A. C., & McHale, S. M. (2006). Implications of shift work for parent-adolescent relationships in dual-earner families. *Family Relations, 55,* 450–460.

Dawson, D. A. (1991). Family structure and children's health and well-being: Data from the 1988 National Health Interview Survey on Child Health. *Journal of Marriage and the Family, 53,* 573–584.

Day, R. (1992). The transition to first intercourse among racially and culturally diverse youth. *Journal of Marriage and the Family, 54,* 749–762.

Deaux, K., & Hanna, R. (1984). Courtship in the personals column: The influence of gender and sexual orientation. *Sex Roles, 11,* 363–375.

Deavers, K., & Brown, D. (1985). *Natural resource dependence, rural development, and rural poverty. Rural development research report no. 48.* Washington, DC: US Department of Agriculture Economic Research Services. ERIC Document Reproduction Service: ERIC Item: ED 358 775.

DeBartolo Cormak, S. (2000, April). Getting the word. *Family Tree Magazine,* 28–24.

DeBord, K. (1997). *Focus on kids: The effects of divorce on children.* North Carolina Cooperative Extension Service. Available: www.ces.ncsu.edu/depts/fcs/human/pubs/effectsdivorce.html [2009, August 12].

DeBord, K. (1997). *The effects of divorce on children.* GH 6600. Columbia: University of Missouri Cooperative Extension.

Defrain, J. (2000). *Creating a strong family: Qualities of strong families.* Lincoln: University of Nebraska Cooperative Extension, Institute of Agriculture and Natural Resources.

DeLamater, J. D., & Friedrich, W. N. (2002). Human sexual development. *The Journal of Sex Research, 39*(1), 10–15.

DeLamater, J. D., & Hyde, J. S. (1998). Essential versus social constructionism in the study of human sexuality. *The Journal of Sex Research, 35,* 10–18.

DeLuccie, M. F. (1995). Mothers as gatekeepers: A model of maternal mediators of father involvement. *The Journal of Genetic Psychology, 156*(1), 115–131.

DeMaris, A., & MacDonald, W. (1993). Premarital cohabitation and marital instability: A test of the unconventiality hypothesis. *Journal of Marriage and the Family, 55,* 399–407.

DeMaris, A., & Rao, V. (1992). Premarital cohabitation and subsequent marital stability in the United States. *Journal of Marriage and the Family, 54,* 178–190.

Demo, D. H. (1997). Family type and adolescent adjustment: Research findings. *Stepfamily Association of America.* Available: www.saafamilies.org [2005, November 25].

DeMulder, E. K., Denham, S., Schmidt, M., & Mitchell, J. (2000). Q-sort assessment of attachment security during the preschool years: Links from home to school. *Developmental Psychology, 36*(2), 274–282.

DeNavas-Walt, C. R, & Cleveland, R. (2002). Money income in the Unites States: 2001. *United States Census Bureau Current Population Reports* (pp. 60–218). Available: http://landview.census.gov/prod/2002pubs/p60-218.pdf [2005, September 30].

DeNavas-Walt, C., Proctor, B., & Mills, R. (2004). Income, poverty, and health insurance coverage in the United States: 2003. *Current Population Report P60-226.* Washington, DC: U.S. Census Bureau. Available: www.census.gov/prod/2004pubs/p60-226.pdf.

DeParle, J. (1991, January 27). Suffering in the cities persists as U.S. fights other battles. *New York Times,* p. 15.

Desrochers, S. (1995). What types of men are most attractive and most repulsive to women? *Sex Roles, 32,* 375–392.

DeSteno, D. (2004, May). New perspectives on jealousy: An integrative view of the most social of social emotions. Paper presented at the meeting of the American Psychological Society, Chicago.

DeSteno, D., Valdesolo, P., & Bartlett, M. Y. (2006). Jealousy and the threatened self: Getting to the heart of the green-eyed monster. *Journal of Personality and Social Psychology, 91*(4), 626–641.

Deutsch, F. M., Lozy, J. L, & Saxon, S. E. (1993). Taking credit: Couples' reports of contributions to childcare. *Journal of Family Issues, 14,* 421–437.

Dew, J. (2007). Two sides of the same coin? The differing roles of assets and consumer debt in marriage. *Journal of Family and Economic Issues, 28,* 89–104.

Dew, J. (2008). Debt change and marital satisfaction change in recently married couples. *Family Relations, 57,* 60–71.

Diamond, M., & Sigmundson, H. K. (1997, March). Sex reassignment at birth: A long term review and clinical implications. *Archives of Pediatrics and Adolescent Medicine, 151,* 298–304.

Diamond, M., Lund, D. A., & Caserta, M. S. (1987). The role of social support in the first two years of bereavement in an elderly sample. *The Gerontologist, 27,* 599–604.

Dickson, E. C., Christian, A., & Remmo, C. J. (2004). An exploration of marital and family issues among the later-life adult. In A. Vangelisti (Ed.), *Handbook of family communication.* Mahwah, NJ: Erlbaum.

Dilulio, J. J. (1997, April 7). Deadly divorce: Divorce can be hazardous to your health. *National Review.* Available: www.findarticles.com/p/articles.mi_m1282/is_n6_v49/ [2006, April 6].

Dillman, D. A. (1978/1999). *Mail and Internet surveys: The tailored design method.* New York: Wiley.

Dilorio, C., Dudley, W. N., Kelly, M., Soet, J. E., Mbwara, J., & Sharpe, J. (2001). Social cognitive correlates of sexual experience and condom use among 13- through 15-year-old adolescents. *Journal of Adolescent Health, 29*(3), 208–216.

Dimitrov, D. (2004). *Hepatitis: Questions and answers.* Planned Parenthood. Available: www.plannedparenthood.org/pp2/portal/files/portal/medicalinfo/sti/pub0hepatitis.xml [2006, March 17].

Dion, K. L., & Dion, K. K. (1993). Individualistic and collectivistic perspectives on gender and the cultural context of love and intimacy. *Journal of Social Issues, 49,* 53–69.

Dobson, J. (2005). *Courtship is an alternative to the dating model.* Available: www.uexpress.com/focusonthefamily/index.html?uc_full_date=20020428 [2005, October 20].

Dolich, C. (2005). *Male-female sex differences in cross-sex and same-sex adolescent friendships.* Available: http://students.haverford.edu/cdolich/final%20paper.htm [2005, November 27].

Donahoo, S. (2004). *Single parenting and children's academic achievement.* Available: http://library.adoption.com/pring.php?articleid=3341 [2004, August 14].

Donahue, P. (1991). Clinical management of intersex abnormalities. *Current Problems in Surgery, 28*(8), 513–570.

Donnelly, D. A. (1993). Sexually inactive marriages. *The Journal of Sex Research, 30,* 171–179.

Doosje, B., Rojahn, K., & Fischer, A. (1999). Partner preferences as a function of gender, age, political orientation and level of education. *Sex Roles, 40,* 45–60.

Doss, B. D., Rhoades, G. K., Stanley, S. M., & Markman, H. J. (2009). Marital therapy, retreats, and books: The who, what, when, and why of relationship help-seeking. *Journal of Marital and Family Therapy, 35*(1), 18–29.

Dreger, A. (1998). *Hermaphrodites and the medical invention of sex.* Cambridge, MA: Harvard University Press.

Drummet, A. R., Coleman, M., & Cable, S. (2003). Military families under stress: Implications for family life education. *Family Relations, 52,* 279–287.

Duck, S. W. (1982). A topography of relationship disengagement an dissolution. In S. W. Duck (Ed.), *Personal relationships, 4: Dissolving personal relationships* (pp. 1–30). New York: Academic Press.

Duck, S. W. (1984). A perspective on the repair of personal relationships: Repair of what? When? In S. W. Duck (Ed.), *Personal relationships, 5: Repairing personal relationships.* London: Academic Press.

Duck, S. W. (1985). Social and personal relationships. In M. L. Knapp and G. R. Miller (Eds.), *Handbook of interpersonal communication* (pp. 665–686). Beverly Hills, CA: Sage.

Duck, S. W. (1992). *Human relationships* (2nd ed.). Newbury Park, CA: Sage.

Duncan, G. J., Boisjoly, J., Levy, D. M., Kremer, M., & Eccles, J. (2003). *Empathy or antipathy? The consequences of racially and socially diverse peers on attitudes and behaviors.* Working Paper Series. Chicago, IL: Joint Center for Policy Research.

Duncan, G., & Rodgers, W. (1988). Longitudinal aspects of childhood poverty. *Journal of Marriage and the Family, 50,* 1007–1022.

Dunn, J. (2004). Understanding children's family worlds: Family transitions and children's outcome. *Merrill-Palmer Quarterly, 50*(3), 224–235.

Dunphy, D. C. (1963). The social structure of urban adolescent peer groups. *Sociometry, 26,* 230–246.

Duran-Aydingtug, C. (1995). Former spouse interaction: Normative guidelines and actual behavior. *Journal of Divorce and Remarriage, 22,* 147–161.

Durbin, M., DiClemente, R., Siegel, D., Krasnovsky, F., Lazarus, N., & Camacho, T. (1993). Factors associated with multiple sex partners among junior high school students. *Journal of Adolescent Health Care, 14,* 202–207.

Durex. (2007). *Global sex survey.* Available: www.about.com [2008, December 19].

Durose, M. R., Harlow, C. W., Langan, P. A., Motivans, M., Rantala, R. R., & Smith, E. L. (2005). *Family violence statistics: Including statistics on strangers and acquaintances.* Washington, DC: United States Department of Justice, Bureau of Justice Statistics. Available: www.ojp.usdoj.gov/bjs [2006, April 4].

Dutton, M. A. (1998, March/April). Cultural issues in trauma treatment. *Centering Newsletter, 3*(2).

Duvall, E. M. (1971). *Family development* (4th ed.). Philadelphia: Lippincott.

Duvall, E. M. (1977). *Marriage and family development* (5th ed.). Philadelphia: Lippincott.

Dye, J. L, (2005). Fertility of American women: June 2004. *United States Census Bureau Current Population Reports* (pp. 20–555). Washington, DC: United States Census Bureau.

Dyk, P. H. (2004). Complexity of family life among the low-income and working poor: Introduction to the special issue. *Family Relations, 53*(2), 122–126.

Eamon, M. K., & Mulder, C. (2005). Predicting antisocial behavior among Latino young adolescents: An ecological systems analysis. *American Journal of Orthopsychiatry, 75,* 117–127.

Early Child Care Research Network. (2003). Does amount of time spent in childcare predict socioemotional adjustment during the transition to kindergarten? *Child Development, 74,* 976–1005.

East, P. L, & Felice, M. E. (1990). Outcomes and parent-child relationships of former adolescent mothers and their 12-year-old children. *Journal of Developmental and Behavioral Pediatrics, 11,* 175–183.

Eccles, J. S., Jacobs, J. E., & Harold, R. E. (1990). Gender role stereotypes, expectancy effects, and parents' socialization of gender differences. *Journal of Social Issues, 46,* 183–201.

Edwards, J. N., & Booth, A. (1994). Sexuality, marriage, and wellbeing: The middle years. In A. S. Rossi (Ed.), *Sexuality across the life course* (pp. 233–259). Chicago: University of Chicago Press.

Edwards, R., & Hamilton, M. A. (2004). You need to understand my gender role: An empirical test of Tannen's model of gender and communication. *Sex Roles, 50,* 491–504.

Egan, S. K., & Perry, D. G. (2001). Gender identity: A multidimensional analysis with implications for psychosocial adjustment. *Developmental Psychology, 37,* 451–463.

Egeland, B., & Hiester, M. (1995). The long-term consequences of infant daycare and mother/infant attachments. *Child Development, 66,* 474–485.

Ehrle, J., Kortenkamp, K., & Stagner, M. (2003). Family structure and outcomes for children of long-term welfare recipients. Unpublished manuscript. Washington, DC: Urban Institute.

Eisler, R. M. (1995). The relationship between masculine gender role stress and men's health risk: The validation of a construct. In R. F. Levant and W. S. Pollack (Eds.), *A new psychology of men* (pp. 207–225). New York: Basic Books.

Eisler, R. M., & Skidmore, J. R. (1987). Masculine gender role stress: Scale development and component factors in the appraisal of stressful situations. *Behavior Modification, 11,* 123–136.

Elek, S. M., Hudson, D. B., & Bouffard, C. (2003). Marital and parenting satisfaction and infant care self-efficacy during the transition to parenthood: The effect of infant sex. *Issues in Comprehensive Pediatric Nursing, 26,* 45–57.

Elliot, A. J., & Reis, H. T. (2003). Attachment and exploration in adulthood. *Journal of Personality and Social Psychology, 85,* 317–331.

Elnashar, A. M., Ibrahim, M. E., El-Desoky, M. M., Ali, O. M., & Hassan, M. (2006). Female sexual dysfunction in lower Egypt. *British Journal of Obstetrics & Gynecology, 114,* 201–206.

Emery, R. E. (1994). *Renegotiating family relationships: Divorce, child custody and mediation.* New York: Guilford.

England, P., & Thomas, R. (2007). The decline of the date and the rise of the college hook up. In A. Skolnick and J. Skolnick (Eds.), *Family in transition* (14th ed.). Boston: Allyn & Bacon.

Equal Employment Opportunity Commission. (2004). *Federal sexual harassment policy.* Available: www.eeoc.gov/facts/fs-sex.html [2005, March].

Erber, R., & Erber, M. W. (2001). *Intimate relationships: Issues, theories, and research* (2nd ed.). Boston: Allyn & Bacon.

Erdwins, C. J. (2001). The relationship of woman's role strain to social support, role satisfaction, and self-efficacy, *Family Relations, 50*(3), 230–238.

Erikson, E. H. (1959). Identity and the life cycle. *Psychological Issues, 1,* 1–171.

Erikson, E. H. (1963). *Childhood and society* (2nd ed.). New York: Norton.

Erikson, E. H. (1974). *Dimensions of a new identity.* New York: Norton.

Erikson, E. H. (1986). *Vital Involvement in Old Age.* New York: Norton.

Ermisch, J., & Francesconi, M. (2002). The effect of parents' employment on children's educational attainment. ISER Working Paper No. 2002-21, University of Esses. Available: www.socserv2.mcmaster.ca/sedap/p/JErmisc.pdf [2005, October 17].

Eskridge, W. N., & Hunter, N. D. (1997). *Sexuality, gender, and the law.* Westbury, NY: Foundation Press.

Evangel. (2004, July). The weather will change. *Today's Pentecostal Evangel.*

Evans, B. A. (2004). *Androgen insensitivity syndrome (AIS).* Intersex Society of North America. Available: www.isna.org/html.

Evans, R. P. (2004). *The five lessons a millionaire taught me.* Salt Lake City, UT: Aurcadia Press.

Exline, J. J., Baumeister, R. F., Bushman, B. J., Campbell, W. K., & Finkel, E. J. (2004). Too proud to let go: Narcissistic entitlement as a barrier to forgiveness. *Journal of Personality and Social Psychology, 87,* 894–912.

Eyre, R., & Eyre, L. (2008, February, 29). *Balancing work and family.* Logan: Utah State University.

Fagan, P. F., & Hanks, D. B. (1997). *The child abuse crisis: The disintegration of marriage, family, and the American community.* Washington, DC: The Heritage Foundation.

Family Life Center. (2009). *Unemployment and marriage.* Available: www.support@familylife.co.za [2009, February 1].

Family Life. (2000). *Unmarried cohabitation: Why it's not a good idea.* Available: www.fol.org.au [2004, May 27].

Family Violence Prevention. (2006). *The facts on reproductive health and violence against women.* Available: www.endabuse.org/resources/facts/ReproductiveHealth.pdf [2009, August 1].

Faulkner, S. (2003). Good girl or flirt girl: Latinas' definitions of sex and sexual relationships. *Hispanic Journal of Behavioral Sciences, 25*(2), 174–200.

Fausto-Sterling, A. (2000). *Sexing the body: Gender politics and the construction of sexuality.* New York: Basic Books.

Federal Reserve Board. (2007). *Consumer credit.* Federal Reserve, G-19. Available: http://www.federalreserve.gov/releases/g19/ [2009, August 11].

Feeney, J. A., & Noller, P. (1990). Attachment style as a predictor of adult romantic relationships. *Journal of Personality and Social Psychology, 58,* 281–291.

Feeney, J. A., & Noller, P. (1991). Attachment style and verbal descriptions of romantic partners. *Journal of Social and Personal Relationships, 8*(2), 187–215.

Fehr, B. (1988). Prototype analysis of the concepts of love and commitment. *Journal of Personality and Social Psychology, 55,* 557–579.

Feingold, A. (1982). Do taller men have prettier girlfriends? *Psychological Reports,* 810.

Feingold, A. (1990). Gender differences in the effects of physical attractiveness on romantic attraction: A comparison across five research paradigms. *Journal of Personality and Social Psychology, 59,* 981–993.

Feingold, A. (1992). Gender differences in mate selection preferences: A test of the parental investment model. *Psychological Bulletin, 112,* 125–139.

Feldman, H. A., Johannes, C. B., Derby, C. A., Kleinman, K. P., Mohr, B. A., Araujo, A. B., & McKinlary, J. B. (2000). Erectile dysfunction and coronary risk factors: Prospective results from the Massachusetts male aging study. *Preventive Medicine, 30*(4), 328–338.

Fernandez, D. (2002). *Sexual attraction among humans.* Available: http://serendip.brynmawr.edu/biology/b103/f02/web1/dfernandez.html [2004, May 30].

Fernandez-Dols, J. M. (1999). Facial expression and emotion: A situationist view. In P. Philippot, R. S. Feldman, and E. J. Coats (Eds.), *The social context of nonverbal behavior* (2nd ed., Vol. 1) (pp. 242–261). Cambridge: Cambridge University Press.

Ferraro, T., & Smith, D. (2004). *Marriage license laws and requirements.* Available: www.smh.com.au/articles/2004/07/15/1089694492548 [2004, July 15].

Fetsch, R. (2009). *Suggestion for maintaining mental health during employment transitions.* Colorado State University, Human Development & Family Studies. Available: www.ext.colostate.edu [2009, February 8].

Field, T. (1996). Attachment and separation in young children. *Annual Review of Psychology, 47,* 541–562.

Fields, J. (2001). Living arrangements of children: 1996. *United States Census Bureau current population reports* (pp. 70–74). Available: www.census.gov/prod/2001pubs/p70-74.pdf [2005, September 30].

Fields, J. (2004). America's families and living arrangements: 2003. *United States Census Bureau current population reports* (pp. 20–553). Available: www.census.gov/prod/2004pubs/p20-553.pdf [2008, July 5].

Fields, J., & Casper, L. (2001). American's families and living arrangements: 2000. *United States Census Bureau current population reports* (pp. 20–537). Available: www.census.gov/prod/2001pubs/p20-537.pdf [2006, January 6].

Figueiredo, B., Field, T., Diego, M., Hernandez, Reif M., Deeds, O., & Ascenio, A. (2008). Partner relationships during the transition to parenthood. *Journal of Reproductive and Infant Psychology, 26*(2), 99–107.

Fincham, F. D. (2002). Divorce. In N. J. Salkind (Ed.), *Child development: Macmillan psychology reference series.* Farmington Hills, MI: Macmillan.

Fincham, F. D., Beach, S. R. H., & Davila, J. (2004). Forgiveness and conflict resolution in marriage. *Journal of Family Psychology, 18,* 72–81.

Fincham, F. D., Hall, J. H., & Beach, S. R. H. (2006). Forgiveness in marriage: Current status and future directions. *Family Relations, 55,* 415–427.

Fine, M. A., & Fine, D. R. (1994). An examination and evaluation of recent changes in divorce laws in five Western countries: The critical role of values. *Journal of Marriage and the Family, 56*(2), 249–263.

Fingerman, K. L. (2001). A distant closeness: Intimacy between parents and their children in later life. *Generations, 25*(2), 26–33.

Fink, B., & Penton-Voak, I. (2002). Evolutionary psychology of facial attractiveness. *Current Directions in Psychological Sciences, 11,* 154–158.

Finkel, E. J., Rusbult, C. E., Kumashiro, M., & Hannon, P. A. (2002). Dealing with betrayal in close relationships: Does commitment promote forgiveness? *Journal of Personality and Social Psychology, 82*(6), 956–974.

Finley, G. E. (2003). Father-child relationships following divorce. In J. R. Miller, R. M. Lerner, L. B. Schiamberg, & P. M. Anderson (Eds.), *Encyclopedia of human ecology, Volume 1: A–H.* (pp. 291–293). Santa Barbara, CA: ABC-CLIO.

Firestone, R. W., & Firestone, L. (2004). Methods for overcoming the fear of intimacy. In D. J. Mashek & A. P. Aron (Eds.), *Handbook of closeness and intimacy* (pp. 375–395). Mahwah, NJ: Erlbaum.

Firestone, R., & Catlett, J. (2000). *Fear of intimacy.* Santa Barbara, CA: Glendon.

Fischer, M. J. (2008). Does campus diversity promote friendship diversity? A look at interracial friendships in college. *Social Science Quarterly, 89*(3), 631–655.

Fisher, B., & Alberti, R. (2000). *Rebuilding: When your relationship ends* (3rd ed.). Atascadero, CA: Impact.

Fisher, H. E. (2004). *Why we love: The nature and chemistry of romantic love.* New York: Henry Holt.

Fitzpatrick, M. A. (1988). *Between husbands and wives.* Newbury Park, CA: Sage.

Fitzpatrick, M. A., & Best, P. (1979). Dyadic adjustment in relational types: Consensus, cohesion, affectional expression, and satisfaction in enduring relationships. *Communication Monographs, 46,* 167–178.

Flack, W. F., Daubman, K. A., Caron, M. L., Asadorian, J. A., D'Aureli, N. R., Gigliotti, S. N., et al. (2008). Risk factors and consequences of unwanted sex among university students: Hooking up, alcohol, and stress response. *Journal of Interpersonal Violence, 22*(2), 139–157.

Flaks, S., Ficher, I., Masterpaqsqua, F., & Joseph, G. (1995). Lesbians choosing motherhood: A comparative study of lesbian and heterosexual parents and their children. *Developmental Psychology, 31,* 104–114.

Flanders, L. (1997). *Real majority, media minority: The cost of sidelining women in reporting.* Monroe, ME: Common Courage Press.

Flanigan, C., Suellentrop, K., Albert, B., Smith, J., & Whitehead, M. (2005). *Science says #17: Teens and oral sex.* Available: www.teenpregnancy.org/works/pdf/ScienceSays_17_OralSex.pdf [2006, March 18].

Fleming, W. C. (2007). Getting past our myths and stereotypes about Native Americans. *The Educational Digest, 72*(7), 51–58.

Florsheim, P., Emi, S., McCann, C., Matthew, W., Ritsuko, F., & Trina, S., et al. (2003). The transition to parenthood among young African American and Latino couples: Relational predictors of risk for parental dysfunction. *Journal of Family Psychology, 17,* 65–79.

Flynn, N. (2004). *The historical evolution of dating in America.* Available: http://inside.ard.edu/academic/specialproj/darling/transition/group21/history.html [2004, May 27].

Fong, T. P. (2002). *The contemporary Asian American experience: Beyond the model minority* (2nd ed.). Upper Saddle River, NJ: Prentice Hall.

Forcey, L. R. (1994). Feminist perspectives on mothering and peace. In E. N. Glenn, G., Chang, and L. R. Forcey (Eds.), *Mothering: Ideology, experience, and agency,* (pp. 355–375). New York: Routledge.

Forum on Child and Family Statistics. (2005). *America's children: Key national indicators of well-being: 2005.* Table POP6.a. Available: www.childstats.gov/americaschildren/pop6.asp [2006, April 29].

Forward. (1989). Available: www.allaboutcounseling.com [2004, October 4].

Fowers, B. J., & Olson, D. H. (1986). Predicting marital success with PREPARE: A predictive validity study. *Journal of Marital and Family Therapy, 12,* 403–413.

Fowers, B. J., & Olson, D. H. (1993). ENRICH marital satisfaction scale: A brief research and clinical tool. *Journal of Family Psychology, 7*(2), 176–185.

Fowers, B. J., Montel, K. H., & Olson, D. H. (1996). Predicting marital success for premarital couple types based on PREPARE. *Journal of Marital and Family Therapy, 22*(1), 103–119.

Fox, R. C., Lidz, V., & Bershady, H. L. (2005). *After Parsons: A theory of social action for the twenty-first century.* New York: Russell Sage Foundation.

Frable, D. E. S. (1997). Gender, racial, ethnic, sexual, and class identities. *Annual Review of Psychology, 48,* 139–162.

Francese, P. (2004, April). Marriage drain's big cost. *American Demographics,* 40–42.

Franken, M. W. (1983). Sex role expectations in children's vocational aspirations and perceptions of occupations. *Psychology of Women Quarterly, 8,* 59–68.

Frazier, A. P., & Schauben, J. L. (1994). Stressful life events and psychological adjustment among female college students. *Measurement and Evaluation in Counseling and Development, 27*(1), 1–12.

Freeman, H. E., & Corey, C. R. (1993). Insurance status and access to health services among poor persons. *Health Services Research, 28,* 531–541.

Frey, K., & Hojjat, M. (1998). Are love styles related to sexual styles? *The Journal of Sex Research, 35*(3), 265–271.

Friedman, S. (2006). *Don't blame Medicare for Part D's problem.* Available: www.newsday.com/news/columnists/ny-bzsaul4692482apr08,0,7098705 [2006, April 5].

Frisch, R. E. (1990). Body fat, menarche, fitness and fertility. In R. E. Frisch (Ed.), *Adipose tissue and reproduction.* Basel, Switzerland: Karger.

Frisch, R. E., & McArthur, J. W. (1974). Menstrual cycles: Fatness as a determinant of minimum weight for height necessary for their maintenance. *Science, 185,* 548–556.

Fronczek, P. (2005). *Income, earnings, and poverty from the 2004 American community survey.* Washington, DC: United States Census Bureau.

Fu, X. (1999). An interracial study of marital disruption in Hawaii: 1983–1996. *Journal of Divorce and Remarriage, 32.*

Fu, X., Tora, H., & Kendall, J. (2001). Marital happiness and interracial marriage: A study in a multi-ethnic community in Hawaii. *Journal of Comparative Family Studies, 32*(1), 47–60.

Furstenberg, F. F. (1974). Work experience and family life. In J. O'Toole (Ed.), *Work and the quality of life.* Cambridge, MA: MIT Press.

Furstenberg, F. F. (1994). History and current status of divorce in the United States. *The Future of Children, 4,* 29–43.

Furstenberg, F. F., & Allison, P. D. (1989). How marital dissolution affects children: Variations by age and sex. *Developmental Psychology, 25,* 540–549.

Furstenberg, F. F., & Cherlin, A. J. (1991). *Divided families: What happens to children when parents part.* Cambridge, MA: Harvard University Press.

Furstenberg, F. F., Hoffman, S. D., & Shrestha, L. (1995). The effect of divorce on intergenerational transfers: New evidence. *Demography, 32,* 319–333.

Furukawa, T., Yokouchi, T., Hirai, T., Kitamura, T., & Takahashi, K. (1999). Parental loss in childhood and social support in adulthood among psychiatric patients. *Journal of Psychiatric Research, 22,* 165–169.

Gable, S., Crnic, K., & Belsky, J. (1994). Coparenting within the family system: Influences on children's development. *Family Relations, 43,* 380–386.

Gagnon, J. H., & Simon, W. (1973). *Sexual conduct: The social sources of human sexuality.* Chicago: Aldine.

Gajuwala, A. L. (2004). *The challenge of being different: A Christian-Hindu marriage.* Available: www.interchurchfamilies .org/journal/98su14.shtm [2004, July 21].

Gallup Poll. (2007). *Americans: 2.5 children is "ideal" family size.* Available: http://www.gallup.com/poll/27973/americans-25-children-ideal-family-size.aspx [2009, August 2].

Gallup Poll. (2008). *The cultural tolerance for divorce grows to 70%.* Available: http://www.gallup.com/poll/107380/cultural-tolerance-divorce-grows-70.aspx [2009, August 12].

Galvin, K. M., Bylund, C. L., & Brommel, B. J. (2008). *Family communication: Cohesion and change* (7th ed.). Boston: Pearson Allyn & Bacon.

Gamm, J. L., Nussbaum, R. L., & Biesecker, B. B. (2004). Genetics and alcoholism among at-risk relatives I: Perceptions of cause, risk, and control. *American Journal of Medicine and Genetics, 128*(2), 144–150.

Gangestad, S. W., & Simpson, J. A. (2000). The evolution of human mating: Trade-offs and strategic pluralism. *Behavioral and Brain Sciences, 23,* 573–644.

Gangestad, S. W., Thornhill, R., & Yeo, R. A. (1994). Facial attractiveness, developmental stability, and fluctuating asymmetry. *Ethology and Socialbiology, 15,* 73–85.

Ganong, L. H., & Coleman, H. (2004). *Stepfamily relationships: Development, dynamics, and interventions.* New York: Kluwer Academic/Plenum.

Ganz, M. (2006). *Plan D doesn't stand for disaster.* Available: http://seattlepi [2006, April 5].

Gass, M. S., Dunn, C. D., & Stys, S. J. (1986). Effect of episiotomy on the frequency of vaginal outlet lacerations. *Journal of Reproductive Medicine, 31*(4), 240–244.

Gates, G. J. (2006). Same-sex couples and the gay, lesbian, bisexual population: New estimates from the American Community Survey. *The Williams Institute on Sexual Orientation Law and Public Policy,* UCLA School of Law. Available: www.law.ucla.edu [2008, July 16].

Gatz, M., & Hurwicz, M. (1990). Are old people more depressed? Cross-sectional data on Center for Epidemiological Studies depression scale factors. *Psychology and Aging, 5,* 284–290.

Gazmararian, J. A., Petersen, R., Spitz, A. M., Goodwin, M. M., Saltzman, L. E., & Marks, J. S. (2000). Violence and reproductive health: Current knowledge and future research directions. *Maternal and Child Health Journal, 4*(2), 79–84.

Geary, D. C. (1998). Male, female: The evolution of human sex differences. *Current Directions in Psychological Science, 8,* 115–120.

Geary, D. C. (2000). Evolution and proximate expression of human paternal investment. *Psychological Bulletin, 126,* 55–77.

Geary, D. C., Vigil, C., & Byrd-Craven, J. (2004). Evolution of human mate choice. *Journal of Sex Research, 41,* 27–42.

Gee, C. B., Scott, R. L., Castellani, A. M., & Cordova, J. V. (2002). Predicting 2-year marital satisfaction from partners' discussion of the marriage check-up. *Journal of Marriage and Family, 28*(4), 399–407.

Geiger, B. (1996). *Fathers as primary caregivers.* Westport, CT: Greenwood.

Geis, F. L. (1993). Self-fulfilling prophecies: A social psychological view of gender. In A. E. Beall & R. J. Sternberg (Eds.), *The psychology of gender* (pp. 9–54). New York: Guilford.

Gentile, D. A., & Walsh, D. A. (2002). A normative study of family media habits. *Applied Developmental Psychology, 23,* 157–178.

George, R. M., & Lee, B. J. (1997). Abuse and neglect of children. In R. A. Maynard (Ed.), *Kids having kids: Economic costs and social consequences of teen pregnancy* (pp. 205–230). Washington, DC: Urban Institute.

Gerbner, G. (1993, June 15). Women and minorities on television: A study in casting and fate. The *American Federation of Radio and Television Artists,* 1–14.

Gerlach, P. K. (2004). *Bonding (attachment) wounds: Why some kids and adults can't love.* Available: http://sfhelp.org/01/bonding.htm [2000, April 4].

Gerlach, P. K. (2005). *Forge a healthy remarriage.* Available: www .saafamilies.org/faqs/fats.htm [2005, April 8].

German, K. (2002). *Effects of intimacy on adult development.* Available: www.oberlin.edu/faculty/darling [2005, November 30].

Gershoff, E. T. (2002). Parental corporal punishment and associated child behaviors and experiences: A meta-analytic and theoretical review. *Psychological Bulletin, 128*(4), 539–579.

Gerson, M. J. (1980). The lure of motherhood. *Psychology of Women Quarterly, 5*(2), 207–218.

Gerson, M. J. (1985). *Hard choices: How women decide about work, career, and motherhood.* Berkeley: University of California Press.

Gerson, M. J. (1986). The prospect of parenthood for women and men. *Psychology of Women Quarterly, 10,* 49–62.

Gerson, M. J., Posner, J. A., & Morris, A. M. (1991). The wish for a child in couples eager, disinterested, and conflicted about having children, *The American Journal of Family Therapy, 19*(4), 334–343.

Gerstel, N. (2003). Divorce. In W. Outhwaite (Ed.), *The Blackwell dictionary of twentieth century social thought.* Oxford: Basil Blackwell.

Gilford, R. (1984). Contrasts in marital satisfaction throughout old age: An exchange theory and analysis. *Journal of Gerontology, 39,* 325–333.

Gilligan, C. (1982). *In a different voice: Psychological theory and women's development.* Cambridge, MA: Harvard University Press.

Gilmore, D. (1990). *Manhood in the making: Cultural concepts of masculinity.* New Haven, CT: Yale University Press.

Ginther, D., & Pollak, R. (2003, April). *Does family structure affect children's educational outcomes?* Working Paper No. w9628. Cambridge, MA: National Bureau of Economic Research.

Glanz, K., Rimer, B. K., & Lewis, F. M. (2002). *Health behavior and health education: Theory, research, and practice.* San Francisco: Wiley & Sons.

Glass, J. C., & Hunneycutt, T. L. (2002). Grandparents parenting grandchildren: Extent of situation issues involved and educational implications. *Educational Gerontology, 28*(2), 139–161.

Glass, R. D., & Wallace, K. R. (1996). Challenging race and racism. In M. P. P. Root (Ed.), *The multicultural experience: Racial borders as the new frontier* (pp. 341–358). Thousand Oaks, CA: Sage.

Glendon Association, The. (2005). *Parent-child relationships.* Available: http://64.82.2.174/glendon_compass.html [2005, December 1].

Glenn, N., & Marquardt, E. (2001). *Hooking up, hanging out, and hoping for Mr. Right: College women on dating and mating today.* Institute for American Values. Available: www.americanvalues.org/Hooking_Up.pdf [2005, October 20].

Goer, H. (1995). *Obstetric myths versus research realties: A guide to the medical literature.* Wesport, CT: Bergin & Garvey.

Gohm, C. L., Oishi, S., Darlington, J., & Diener, E. (1998). Culture, parental conflict, parental marital status, and the subjective well-being of young adults. *Journal of Marriage and the Family, 60,* 319–314.

Gold, L. (1992). *Between love and hate: A guide to civilized divorce.* New York: Plenum.

Goldberg, H. (1976). *The hazards of being male: Surviving the myth of masculine privilege.* New York: Nash.

Goldstein, M. C. (1987/2002). When brothers share a wife. *Natural History, 96*(3), 109–112.

Golombok, S. (1983). Children in lesbian and single-parent households: Psychosexual and psychiatric appraisal. *Journal of Child Psychology, 24*(4), 551–572.

Golombok, S. (1999). Lesbian and gay families. In A. Bainham, S. Day Sclater, and M. Richards (Eds.), *What is a parent?* Oxford: Hart.

Golombok, S., & Hines, M. (2002) Sex differences in social behavior. In P. K. Smith and C. H. Hart (Eds.), *Blackwell handbook of childhood social development.* Oxford, England: Blackwell.

Golombok, S., Perry, B., Burson, A., Murray, C., Mooney-Somers, J., et al. (2003). Children with lesbian parents: A community study. *Developmental Psychology, 39*(1), 20–33.

Golombok, S., Spencer, A., & Rutter, M. (1983). Children in lesbian and single-parent households: Psychosexual and psychiatric appraisal. *Journal of Child Psychology and Psychiatry, 24,* 551–572.

Goode, W. (1966). Family disorganization. In R. Merton and R. Nisbet (Eds.), *Contemporary social problems* (2nd ed.) (pp. 493–522). New York: Harcourt.

Goodman, K. L. (1991). Racial and religious intermarriage. Unpublished work. Church of Latter Day Saints (LDS) Research Information Division.

Goodwin, R. (1990). Sex differences among partner preferences: Are they really very similar? *Sex Roles, 55,* 935–938.

Gordon, D. (2002). *Female sexual arousal disorder.* Female Sexual Medicine Center, UCLA Medical Center. Los Angeles, CA. Available: www.newshe.com [2009, August 1].

Gordon, D. (2003). Female sexual arousal disorder. *The Gale Encyclopedia of Medicine* (2nd ed.). Farmington Hills, MI: Gale Group.

Gordon, K. C., Baucom, D. H., & Snyder, D. K. (2004). An integrative intervention for promoting recovery from extramarital affairs. *Journal of Marital and Family Therapy, 30,* 213–232.

Gordon, L. H. (2001). Intimacy: The art of working out your relationships. In R. Manis (Ed.), *The marriage and family workbook: An interactive reader, text, and workbook* (pp. 101–110). Boston: Allyn & Bacon.

Gottfried, A. E., & Gottfried, A. W. (1994). *Redefining families: Implications for children's development.* New York: Plenum.

Gottman, J. M. (1979). *Marital interactions: Experimental investigations.* New York: Academic Press.

Gottman, J. M. (1994a). *What predicts divorce? The relationship between marital process and marital outcomes.* Hillsdale, NJ: Erlbaum.

Gottman, J. M. (1994b). *Why marriages succeed or fail.* New York: Simon & Schuster.

Gottman, J. M. (1999). *The marriage clinic: A scientifically based marital therapy.* New York: Norton.

Gottman, J. M., Markham, J. J., & Notarius, C. I. (1977). The topography of marital conflict: A sequential analysis of verbal and nonverbal behavior. *Journal of Marriage and the Family, 39,* 461–477.

Gottman, J. M., & Porterfield, A. (1981). Communicative competence in the nonverbal behavior of married couples. *Journal of Marriage and the Family, 43,* 817–824.

Gottman, J. M., Ryan, K. D., Carrere, S., & Erlye, A. M. (2002). Toward a scientifically based marital therapy. In H. A. Liddle, D. A. Santisteban, R. F. Levant, and J. H. Bray (Eds.), *Family psychology: Science-based interventions* (pp. 147–174). Washington, DC: American Psychological Association.

Gottman, J., & Gottman, J. (2007). *Ten lessons to transform your marriage.* New York: Three Rivers.

Graham, E., & Crossan, C. (1996, March 8). Too much to do, too little time. *Wall Street Journal,* R1–R2.

Graham, L. (2005). *Resource guide for parenting after divorce.* Manhattan, KS: Riley County District Court, State of Kansas.

Grall, T. (2003, October). Custodial mothers and fathers and their child support: 2001. *United States Census Bureau Current Population Reports* (pp. 60–225). Washington, DC: United States Census Bureau.

Grall, T. S. (2007). Custodial mothers and fathers and their child support: 2005. *Current Population Reports,* P60–234. Washington, DC: U.S. Government Printing Office.

Gramstad, D. (2004). *Androgyny and gender dialects.* Available: www.math.uio.no/~thomas/gnd/androgyny.html.

Gray, J. (1992). *Men are from Mars, women are from Venus.* New York: HarperCollins.

Graydon, S. (2003). *Made you look: How advertising works and why you should know.* Vancouver, BC: Annick.

Green, R. (1978). Sexual identity of 37 children raised by homosexual or transsexual parents. *American Journal of Psychiatry, 135,* 692–697.

Green, R., Mandel, J. B., Hotvedt, M. E., Gray, J., & Smith, L. (1986). Lesbian mothers and their children: A comparison with solo parent heterosexual mothers and their children. *Archives of Sexual Behavior, 15,* 167–184.

Greenhaus, J. H., & Beutell, N. J. (1985). Sources of conflict between work and family roles. *Academy of Management Review, 10,* 76–88.

Greenstein, T. N. (1995). Gender ideology, marital disruption, and the employment of married women. *Journal of Marriage and the Family, 57,* 31–42.

Grogan-Kaylor, A. (2005). Corporal punishment and the growth trajectory of children's antisocial behavior. *Child Maltreatment, 10,* 283–292.

Grosswald, B. (2004). The effects of shift work on family satisfaction. *Families in Society, 85*(3), 413–423.

Grunebaum, H. (2003). Thinking about romantic/erotic love. In M. Coleman and L. Ganong (Eds.), *Points and counterpoints* (pp. 88–91). Los Angeles: Roxbury.

Gruzen, L. (1990). *Raising your Jewish/Christian child.* New York: Newmarket Press.

Gullotta, T., Adams, G., & Montemayor, R. (1993). *Adolescent sexuality.* London: Sage.

Guo, B., & Huang, J. (2005). Marital and sexual satisfaction in Chinese families: Exploring the moderating effects. *Journal of Sex & Marital Therapy, 31,* 21–29.

Guralnik, D. B. (Ed.). (1982). *Webster's new world dictionary of the American language.* New York: Simon & Schuster.

Gurin, P. (1999). New research on the benefits of diversity in college and beyond: An empirical analysis. *Diversity Digest, 5*(15).

Gurman, T., & Borzekowski, D. L. G. (2004). Condom use among Latino college students. *Journal of American College Health, 52,* 169–178.

Guttman, H. A. (2002). The epigenesis of the family system as a context for individual development. *Family Process, 41,* 533–545.

Gutmann, M. C. (1997). Trafficking in men: The anthropology of masculinity. *Annual Review of Anthropology, 26,* 385–409.

Haavio-Mannila, E., & Kontula, O. (1997). Correlates of increased sexual satisfaction. *Archives of Sexual Behavior, 26,* 399–419.

Haddock, S. A., Zimmerman, T. S., Ziemba, S. J., & Current, L. R. (2001). Ten adaptive strategies for family and work balance: Advice from successful families. *Journal of Marital and Family Therapy, 27*(4), 445–458.

Hagestad, G. O. (1985). Continuity and connectedness. In V. L. Bengtson (Ed.), *Grandparenthood* (pp. 31–38). Beverly Hills, CA: Sage.

Hagestad, G. O., & Call, V. R. A. (2007). Pathways to childlessness: A life course perspective. *Journal of Family Issues, 28*(10), 1338–1361.

Hahn, B. (1993). Marital status and women's health: The effect of economic marital acquisitions. *Journal of Marriage and the Family, 55,* 495–504.

Halgunseth, L. (2003). Language brokering: Positive developmental outcomes. In M. Coleman and L. Ganong (Eds.), *Points*

and counterpoints: Controversial relationship and family issues in the 21st century (pp. 154–156). Los Angeles: Roxbury.

Hall, D. R., & Zhao, J. Z. (1995). Cohabitation and divorce in Canada: Testing the selectivity hypothesis. *Journal of Marriage and the Family, 57,* 421–427.

Hallman, M., & Deinhart, R. (2007). Father's experiences after separation and divorce. *Fathering, 5,* 4–24.

Halpern, C., Udry, J. R., & Suchindran, C. (2000). Adolescent males' willingness to report masturbation. *The Journal of Sex Research, 37*(4), 327–332.

Halpern-Felsher, B., Cornell, J. L., Kropp, R. Y., & Tschann, J. M. (2005). Oral versus vaginal sex among adolescents: Perceptions, attitudes, and behavior. *Pediatrics, 115*(4), 845–851.

Ham, B. (2004, February 26). One in four women report severe abuse in their lifetime. *Health Behavior Science News.* Available: www.hbns.org/news/lifetime02-26-04.cfm [2006, April 1].

Hammer, L., & Thompson, C. (2003). Work-family role conflict. *Sloan work and family encyclopedia.* Available: www.bc.edu/bc_org/avp/wfnetwork/rft/wfpedia/wfpWFRCent.html [2004, August 10].

Hammond, D., & Jablow, A. (1987). Gilgamesh and the Sundance Kid: The myth of male friendship. In H. Brod (Ed.), *The making of masculinities* (pp. 241–258). Boston: Allen & Unwin.

Hanisch, K. A. (1999). Job loss and unemployment research from 1994 to 1998: A review of and recommendations for research and intervention. *Journal of Vocational Behavior, 55,* 188–220.

Hannum, J. W., & Dvorak, D. M. (2004). Effects of family conflict, divorce, and attachment patterns on the psychological distress and social adjustment of college freshmen. *Journal of College Student Development, 45*(1), 27–42.

Hanson, S. L. (1992). Involving families in programs for pregnant teens: Consequences for teens and their families. *Family Relations, 41,* 303–311.

Hao, L. (1996). Family structure, private transfers, and the economic well-being of families with children. *Social Forces, 75,* 269–292.

Harley, W. F. (2001). *His needs, her needs: Building an affair-proof marriage.* Grand Rapids, MI: Fleming H. Revell.

Harper, M., & Schoeman, W. J. (2003). Influences of gender as a basic-level category in person perception on the gender belief system. *Sex Roles: A Journal of Research, 49*(9/10), 517–526.

Harris, C. R., & Christenfeld, N. (1996). Gender, jealousy, and reason. *Psychological Science, 7,* 364–366.

Harris, H. L. (2002, December). School counselors' perceptions of biracial children: A pilot study. *Professional School Counseling.*

Harris, V. W. (2008). The triangular theory of balancing work and family. Unpublished manuscript, Utah State University, Logan.

Harris, V. W. (2009). *Preparation for marriage: 10 things you'll wish you knew.* Utah Council on Family Relations. Available: www.usu.edu/fchd/htm/ [2009, February 10].

Harrison, T. W. (2003, March 1). Adolescent homosexual concerns regarding disclosure. *Journal of School Health.*

Hartill, L. (2001). Life with a supersized family. *The Christian Science Monitor*. Available: www.csmonitor.com/2001/0910/p15sl-lifp.html [2009, January 12].

Hartill, L. (2001, July 25). A brief history of interracial marriage. *The Christian Science Monitor*.

Hartup, W. W., & Moore, S. G. (1990). Early peer relations: Developmental significance and prognostic implications. *Early Childhood Research Quarterly, 59*(1), 1–17.

Harvard Family Research Project. (2006). *Family involvement makes a difference in school success*. Available: http://www.hfrp.org/ [2009, August 2].

Harwood, K., McLean, N., & Durkin, K. (2007). First-time mothers' expectations of parenthood: What happens when optimistic expectations are not matched by later experiences? *Developmental Psychology, 43*(1), 1–12.

Haskey, J. (1996). The proportion of married couples who divorce: Past patterns and current prospects. *Population Trends, 83*, 25–36.

Hassebrauck, M., & Fehr, B. (2002). Dimensions of relationship quality. *Personal Relationships, 9*, 253–270.

Hatcher, R., & Nelson, A. (2004). Combined hormonal contraceptive methods. In R. A. Hatcher et al. (Eds.), *Contraceptive technology* (pp. 361–460). New York: Irvington.

Hatfield, E. (1988). Passionate and companionate love. In R. L. Sternberg and M. L. Barns (Eds.), *The psychology of love* (pp. 191–217). New Haven, CT: Yale University Press.

Hatfield, E., & Rapson, R. (1987). Passionate love. New directions in research. In W. H. Jones and D. Perlman (Eds.), *Advances in interpersonal relations, 1* (pp. 109–139). Greenwich, CN: JAI Press.

Hatfield, E., & Rapson, R. (1993). Historical and cross-cultural perspectives on passionate love and sexual desire. *Annual Review of Sex Research, 4*, 67–97.

Hatfield, E., & Rapson, R. L. (1998). Emotional contagion and the communication of emotion. In M. T. Palmer & G. A. Barnett (Eds.), *Progress in communication sciences, Vol. 14*, 73–89.

Hatfield, E., & Rapson, R. L. (2007). Passionate love and sexual desire: Multidisciplinary perspectives. In J. P. Forgas (Ed.), *Personal relationships: Cognitive, affective, and motivational processes*. Tenth Symposium of Social Psychology, Sydney, Australia.

Hatfield, E., & Sprecher, S. (1986). Measuring passionate love in intimate relations. *Journal of Adolescence, 9*, 383–410.

Hatfield, E., & Sprecher, S. (1995). Men's and women's preferences in marital partners in the United States, Russia, and Japan. *Journal of Cross-Cultural Psychology, 26*, 728–750.

Hatfield, E., & Walster, G. W. (1978). *A new look at love*. Reading, MA: Addison-Wesley.

Hatfield, E., Brinton, C., & Cornelius, J. (1989). Passionate love and anxiety in young adolescents. *Motivation and Emotion, 13*, 271–289.

Hayen, A., Lincoln, D., Moore, H., & Thomas, M. (2002). Trends in potentially avoidable mortality in NSW. *NSW Public Health Bulletin, 13*(11/12), 226–236.

Hayflick, L. (1994). *How and why we age*. New York: Ballantine Books.

Hayford, S. R., & Morgan, S. P. (2008). Religiosity and fertility in the United States: The role of fertility intentions. *Social Forces, 86*(3), 1163–1189.

Hays, S. (1996). *The cultural contradictions of motherhood*. New Haven, CT: Yale University Press.

Hazan, C., & Shaver, P. (1987). Romantic love conceptualized as an attachment process. *Journal of Personality and Social Psychology, 52*, 511–524.

He, W., Sangupta, M., Velkoff, V. A., & DeBarros, K. A. (2005). 65+ in the United States: 2005. *United States Census Bureau Current Population Reports* (pp. 23–209). Available: www.census.gov/prod/2006pubs/p23-209.pdf [2006, April 12].

Heaton, T. B. (2002). Factors contributing to increased marital stability in the United States. *Journal of Family Issues, 23*(3), 392–409.

Heaton, T. B., Albrecht, S. L., & Martin, T. K. (1985). The timing of divorce. *Journal of Marriage and the Family, 47*, 631–639.

Hebert, S., & Popadiuk, N. (2008). University students' experiences of nonmarital breakups: A grounded theory. *Journal of College Student Development, 49*(1), 1–14.

Heine, S.J. (2001). Self as cultural product: An examination of East Asian and North American selves. *Journal of Personality, 69*, 881–906.

Heller, P., & Wood, B. (1998). The process of intimacy: Similarity, understanding, and gender. *Journal of Marital and Family Therapy, 24*(3), 273–288.

Heller, P., & Wood, B. (2000). The influence of religious and ethnic differences on marital intimacy: Intermarriage versus intramarriage. *Journal of Marital and Family Therapy, 26*(2), 241–252.

Hellerstedt, W. L., Peterson-Hickey, M., Rhodes, K. L., & Garwick, A. (2006). Environmental, social, and personal correlates of having ever had sexual intercourse among American Indian youths. *American Journal of Public Health, 96*(12), 2228–2234.

Helwig, A. A. (1998). Gender-role stereotyping: Testing theory with a longitudinal sample. *Sex Roles: A Journal of Research, 35*(5), 403–423.

Henderson-King, D. H., & Veroff, J. (1994). Sexual satisfaction and marital well-being in the first years of marriages. *Journal of Social and Personal Relationships, 11*, 509–534.

Hendren, H. & Atala, A. (1995). Repair of high vagina in girls with severely masculinized anatomy from the adrenogenital syndrome. *Journal of Pediatric Surgery, 30*(1), 91–94.

Hendrick, C., & Hendrick, S. (1986). A theory and method of love. *Journal of Personality and Social Psychology, 50*, 392–402.

Hendrick, C., & Hendrick, S. S. (1989). Research on love: Does it measure up? *Journal of Personality and Social Psychology, 56*, 784–794.

Hendrick, S., & Hendrick, C. (1983). *Liking, loving, and relating*. Monterey, CA: Brooks/Cole.

Hendrick, S., & Hendrick, C. (1992). *Romantic love*. Newbury Park, CA: Sage.

Henley, K., & Pasley, K. (2006). Coparenting following divorce. In M. Fine and J. Harvey (Eds.), *Handbook of divorce* (pp. 241–262). Mahwah, NJ: Erlbaum.

Henshaw, S. K. (2004). *U.S. teenage pregnancy statistics with comparative statistics for women aged 20–24*. New York: The Alan Guttmacher Institute.

Hensley, W. E. (1994). Height as a basis for interpersonal attraction. *Adolescence, 29*(114), 469–474.

Hesse-Biber, S. N., & Carter, G. L. (2005). *Working women in America.* New York: Oxford University Press.

Hester, D. (2003). Rhetoric of the medical management of intersexed children. *Genders Online Journal, 38.* Available: www.genders.org/g38/g38_hester.html [2005, March].

Hetherington, E. M. (1991). The role of individual differences and family relationships in children's coping with divorce and remarriage. In P. A. Cowan and E. M. Hetherington (Eds.), *Family transitions* (pp. 165–194). Hillsdale, NJ: Erlbaum.

Hetherington, E. M. (1999). *Coping with divorce, single parenting, and remarriage: A risk and resiliency perspective.* Mahwah, NJ: Erlbaum.

Hetherington, E. M. (2003). Intimate pathways: Changing patterns in close personal relationships across time. *Family Relations, 52,* 318–331.

Hetherington, E. M., Cox, M., & Cox, R. (1985). Long-term effects of divorce and remarriage on the adjustment of children. *Journal of the American Academy of Child Psychiatry, 24,* 518–530.

Hetherington, E. M., & Kelly, J. (2002). *For better or worse: Divorce reconsidered.* New York: Norton.

Hetherington, E. M., & Stanley-Hagan, M. M. (1997). The effects of divorce on fathers and their children. In M. E. Lamb (Ed.), *The role of the father* (3rd ed.) (pp. 191–211). New York: Wiley.

Hetherington, E. M., Stanley-Hagan, M. M., & Anderson, E. (1989). Marital transitions: A child's perspective. *American Psychologist, 44,* 303–312.

Hill, N. E., & Tyson, D. F. (2008). Excavating culture: Ethnicity and context as predictors of parenting behavior. *Applied Developmental Science, 12*(4), 188–197.

Hill, R. (1949). *Families under stress.* New York: Harper.

Hill, R. (1958). Generic features of families under stress. *Social Casework, 49,* 139–150.

Hinderlie, H. H., & Kenny, M. (2002). Attachment, social support, and college adjustment among Black students at predominantly White universities. *Journal of College Student Development, 43,* 327–340.

Hobbs, F., & Stoops, N. (2002). Demographic trends in the 20th century: 2000. *United States Census Bureau Special Reports, CENSR-4.* Available: www.census.gov/prod/2002pubs/censr-4.pdf [2006, January 6].

Hochschild, A. (1989). *The second shift.* New York: Avon.

Hodges, B. C., Leavy, J., Swift, R., & Gold, R. S. (1992). Gender and ethnic differences in adolescents' attitudes toward condom use. *Journal of School Health, 62*(3), 103–106.

Hoeffer, B. (1981). Children's acquisition of sex-role behavior in lesbian-mother families. *American Journal of Orthopsychiatry, 51,* 536–544.

Hoff, T., Green, L., & Davis, J. (2003). *National survey of adolescents and young adults: Sexual health knowledge, attitudes, and experiences.* Menlo Park, CA: The Henry J. Kaiser Family Foundation.

Hofferth, S. L. (2001). Race/ethnic differences in father involvement in two-parent families: Culture, context, or economy. Paper presented at the Urban Seminar on Fatherhood, Harvard University, Cambridge, MA, April 23–24, 1999.

Hoffman, C., & Hurst, N. (1990). Gender stereotypes: Perception or rationalization? *Journal of Personality and Social Psychology, 58,* 197–208.

Hoffman, L. W., & Hoffman, M. L. (1973). The value of children to parents. In J. T. Fawcett (Ed.), *Psychological perspectives on population* (pp. 19–76). New York: Basic Books.

Hofmeyr, G. J., & Sonnedecker, E. W. (1987). Elective episiotomy in perspective. *South African Medical Journal, 71*(6), 357–359.

Holland, J., Ramazanoglu, C., Scott, S., Sharpe, S., & Thomson, R. (1990). Sex, gender, and power: Young women's sexuality in the shadow of AIDS. *Sociology of Health and Illness, 12*(3), 336–350.

Hollander, D. (2003). Among young adults, use of the internet to find sexual partners is rising. *Journal of Sex Research, 40,* 129–133.

Holmes, T. H., & Rahe, R. H. (1967). The social readjustment rating scale. *Journal of Psychometric Research, 11,* 213–218.

Hook, M. K., Gerstein, L. H., Detterich, L., & Gridley, B. (2003). How close are we? Measuring intimacy and examining gender differences. *Journal of Counseling and Development, 81*(4), 462–472.

Hooyman, N., & Kiyak, H. A. (2002). *Social gerontology: A multidisciplinary perspective* (6th ed.). Boston: Allyn & Bacon.

Horon, I., & Cheng, D. (2001). Enhanced surveillance for pregnancy-associated mortality, Maryland, 1993–1998. *The Journal of the American Medical Association, (285)*11.

Howard, J. A., & Hollander, J. A. (1997). *Gendered situations, gendered sleeves: A gender lens on social psychology.* Newbury Park, CA: Sage.

Howe, D., Brandon, M., Hinings, D., & Schofield, G. (1999). *Attachment theory, child maltreatment and family support.* Mahwah, NJ: Erlbaum.

Hoyt, W. T., Fincham, F. D., McCullough, M. E., Maio, G. R., & Davila, J. (2005). Responses to interpersonal transgressions in families: Forgivingness, forgivability, and relationship-specific effects. *Journal of Personality and Social Psychology, 89,* 375–394.

Hu, Y., & Goldman, N. (1990). Mortality differentials by marital status: An international comparison. *Demography, 27,* 233–250.

Hudd, S. S., Dumlao, J., Erdmann-Sager, D., Murray, D., Phan, E., Soukas, N., & Yokozuka, N. (2000). Stress at college: Effects on health habits, health status, and self-esteem. *College Student Journal, 34*(2), 1–9.

Hudson, M. (2009). *Realistic expectations for great parenting.* Community Programs, Family Services of the North Shore. Available: www.familyservices.bc.ca [2009, January 26].

Huebner, A. (2000, March). Adolescent growth and development. *Virginia Cooperative Extension Publication Number 350-850.*

Hughes, D., Smith, E. P., Steven, H. C., Rodriquez, J., Johnson, D. J., & Spice, P. (2006). Parents' ethnic-racial socialization practices: A review of research and directions for future study. *Developmental Psychology, 42,* 747–770.

Hughes, K. (2005). The adult children of divorce: Pure relationships and family values? *The Australian Sociological Assocation, 41*(1), 69–86.

Huitt, W. (2003). A systems model of human behavior. *Educational Psychology Interactive.* Valdosta, GA: Valdosta State University.

Human Resources & Skills Development. (2005). *The work-family interface.* Available: www.hrsdc.gc.ca/en/lp/spila/wlb/vcswlb/40personal_strategies.html [2005, October 3].

Human Rights Campaign Foundation. (2004). *Answers to questions about marriage equality* (pp. 164–172). Washington, DC: Author.

Human Rights Campaign. (2008). *Taxation of domestic partner benefits.* Available: www.hrc.org/issues/workplace/benefits/4820.htm [2008, December 12].

Hunt, M. (1974). *Sexual behavior in the 1970s.* Chicago: Playboy Press.

Hunt, M. M. (1959). *The natural history of love.* New York: Funk and Wagnalls.

Hurlbert, D. F., Apt, C., & Rabehl, S. M. (1993). Key variables to understanding female sexual satisfaction: An examination of women in nondistressed marriages. *Journal of Sex and Marital Therapy, 12*(2), 134–165.

Huston, A. C. (1983). Sex typing. In P. H. Mussen & E. M. Hetherington (Eds.), *Handbook of child psychology: Socialization personality and social behavior.* New York: Wiley.

Huynh, V. W., & Fuligni, A. J. (2008). Ethnic socialization and the academic adjustment of adolescents from Mexican, Chinese, and European backgrounds. *Developmental Psychology, 44*(4), 1202–1208.

Hynie, M., Lyndon, J. E., Cote, S., & Wiener, S. (1998). Relational sexual scripts and women's condom use: The importance of internalized norms. *Journal of Sex Research, 35*(4), 370–380.

Ihinger-Tallman, M., & Pasley, K. (1987). *Remarriage.* Beverly Hills, CA: Sage.

Ingersoll-Dayton, B., Neal, M., Ha, J., & Hammer, J. (2003). Collaboration among siblings providing care for older parents. *Journal of Gerontological Social Work, 40,* 51–66.

Institute for Women's Policy Research. (2008). *The gender wage gap: 2007.* Publication IWPR No. C350. Available: www.iwpr.org/femstats/wocdata.ht [2009, January 31].

International Reading Association. (2005). *The power of language* (video). Available: www.reading.org/InformationFor/Parents.aspx.

IPARV (Intimate Partner Abuse and Relationship Violence). (2002). *Intimate partner abuse and relationship violence working group.* American Psychological Association. Available: www.apa.org/pi/iparv.pdf [2005, June].

Jaccard, J., Dittus, P. J., & Gordon, V. V. (2000). Parent-teen communication about premarital sex: Factors associated with the extent of communication. *Journal of Adolescent Research, 15,* 187–208.

Jaccard, J., Dodge, T., & Dittus, P. (2002). Parent-adolescent communication about sex and birth control: A conceptual framework. In S. S. Feldman and D. A. Rosenthal (Eds.), *Talking sexuality: Parent-adolescent communication* (pp. 9–41). San Francisco: Jossey-Bass.

Jackson, C. (2002). Disciplining gender? *World Development, 30*(3), 497–510.

Jackson, C., Henriksen, L., & Foshee, V. A. (1998). The authoritative parenting index: Predicting health risk behaviors among children and adolescents. *Health Education Behavior, 25*(3), 319–337.

Jandt, F., & Hundley, H. (2007). Intercultural dimensions of communicating masculinities. *Journal of Men's Studies, 15*(2), 216–231.

Janus, S. S., & Janus, C. L. (1993). *The Janus report on sexual behavior.* New York: Wiley.

Jenny, C., Roesler, T. A., & Poyer, K. L. (1994). Are children at risk for sexual abuse by homosexuals? *Pediatrics, 94,* 41–44.

Jerrome, D. (1990). Intimate relationships. In J. Bond and P. Coleman (Eds.), *Aging in society* (pp. 181–208). London: Sage.

Jhally, S. (2002). *Wrestling and manhood: Gender, race, and class in professional wrestling.* Northhampton, MA: Media Education Foundation.

Joanides, C., Mayhew, M., & Mamalakis, P. M. (2002). Investigating inter-Christian and intercultural couples associated with the Greek Orthodox Archdiocese of America: A qualitative research project. *The American Journal of Family Therapy, 30,* 373–383.

Johnsen, J. (2005). *Sexually transmitted infections: The facts.* Planned Parenthood. Available: www.plannedparenthood.org/pp2/portal/files/portal/medicalinfo/sti/pub-sti-facts-1.xml [2006, March 17].

Johnsen, J., & Davis, J. (2004). *Genital herpes: Questions and answers.* Planned Parenthood. Available: www.plannedparenthood.org/pp2/portal/files/portal/medicalinfo/sti/pub-sti-facts-1.xml [2006, March 17].

Johnson, A. (2008, October). Financial first aid. Paper presented at the Family Consumer Science Agent In-Service, St. George, UT.

Johnson, C. (1999a). Fictive kin among oldest old African Americans in the San Francisco Bay Area. *Journal of Gerontology: Psychological Sciences, 54B,* S368–S375.

Johnson, C. L. (1999b). Family life of older Black men. *Journal of Aging Studies, 13,* 145–160.

Johnson, D. R., White, L. K., Edwards, J. N., & Booth, A. (1986). Dimension of marital quality: Toward methodological and conceptual retirement. *Journal Family Issues, 7,* 31–45.

Johnson, F. L., & Airies, E. J. (1983). Conversational patterns among same-sex pairs of late-adolescent close friends. *The Journal of Genetic Psychology, 142,* 225–238.

Johnson, M. M. (1999, April 6). Housework inequity vs. maternal gatekeeping—get a load of this! *Detroit Free Press.*

Johnson, M. P. (1991). Commitment to personal relationships. *Advances in Personal Relationships, 3,* 117–143.

Johnson, N. J., Backlund, E., Sorlie, P. D., & Loveless, C. A. (2000): Marital status and mortality: The National Longitudinal Mortality Study. *Annual of Epidemiology, 10,* 224–238.

Johnson, S. M., & O'Connor, E. (2002). *The gay baby boom: The psychology of gay parenthood.* New York: New York University Press.

Johnson, T., Kulesa, P., Cho, Y., & Shavitt, S. (2005). The relation between culture and response styles: Evidence from 19 countries. *Journal of Cross-Cultural Psychology, 36,* 264–277.

Jones, A. C. (2003, April 1). Reconstructing the stepfamily: Old myths, new stories. *Social Work.* Available: www.highbeam.com/library/doc3.asp?docid=1G1:100767739 [2006, January 6].

Jones, J. M. (2002, August 16). *Public divided benefits of living together before marriage.* Gallup News Service. Available: www.gallup.com/poll/releases/pr02081.asp [2008, July 10].

Jordan, B. (1993). *Birth in four cultures: A crosscultural investigation of childbirth in Yucatan, Holland, Sweden, and the United States* (4th ed.). Prospect Heights, IL: Waveland.

Kachadourian, L. K., Fincham, F. D., & Davila, J. (2005). Attitudinal ambivalence, rumination, and forgiveness of partner transgressions in marriage. *Personality and Social Psychology Bulletin, 31,* 334–342.

Kaestle, C. E., & Tucker Halpern, C. (2007). What's love got to do with it? Sexual behaviors of opposite-sex couples through emerging adulthood. *Perspectives on Sexual and Reproductive Health, 39*(3), 134–141.

Kalter, N., Alpern, D., Spence, R., & Plunkett, J. W. (1984). Locus of control in children of divorce. *Journal of Personality Assessment, 48*(4), 410–414.

Kamp, C. M., Dush, M. G., Taylor, R., & Kroger, A. (2008). Marital happiness and psychological well-being across the life course. *Family Relations, 57,* 211–226.

Kapinus, C. A. (2004). The effect of parents' attitudes toward divorce on offspring's attitudes: Gender and parental divorce as mediating factors. *Journal of Family Issues, 25,* 112–135.

Kapinus, C. A. (2005). The effect of parental marital quality on young adults' attitudes toward divorce. *Sociological Perspectives, 48*(3), 319–335.

Kapinus, C. A., & Johnson, M. P. (2002). Personal, moral, and structural commitment to marriage: Gender and the effects of family life cycle stage. *Sociological Focus, 35,* 189–205.

Karney, B. R., & Bradbury, T. N. (1995). The longitudinal course of marital quality and stability: A review of theory, method, and research. *Psychological Bulletin, 118,* 3–34.

Karney, B. R., & Bradbury, T. N. (1997). Neuroticism, marital interaction, and the trajectory of marital satisfaction. *Journal of Personality and Social Psychology, 72,* 1075–1092.

Karney, B., & Crown, J. (2006). *Families under stress: An assessment of data, theory, and research on marriage and divorce in the military.* Santa Monica, CA: Rand Corporation.

Karremans, J. C., Van Lange, P. A. M., & Holland, R. W. (2005). Forgiveness and its associations with prosocial thinking, feelings, and doing beyond the relationship with the offender. *Journal of Personality and Social Psychology, 84,* 1011–1026.

Kass, L. R. (1997). The end of courtship. *Public Interest, 126,* 39–64.

Kastenbaum, R. J. (2004). *Death, society, and human experience.* Boston: Allyn & Bacon.

Kastenbaum, R. J. (2007). *Death, society, and human experience* (9th ed.). Boston: Pearson Education.

Katz, P. A. (1982). Development of children's racial awareness and intergroup attitudes. In L. Katz (Ed.), *Current topics in early childhood education.* New Jersey: Ablex.

Kaufman, G., & Elder, G. (2003). Grandparenting and age identity. *Journal of Aging Studies, 17,* 269–282.

Kelley, D. (1998). The communication of forgiveness. *Communication Studies, 49,* 255–271.

Kelley, D. L. (1999). Relational expectancy fulfillment as an explanatory variable for distinguishing couple types. *Human Communication Research, 25*(3), 420–442.

Kelley, D. L, & Burgoon, J. K. (1991). Understanding marital satisfaction and couple type as functions of relational expectations. *Human Communication Research, 18,* 40–69.

Kellogg, T. (1990*). Broken toys, broken dreams: Understanding and healing boundaries, codependence, compulsion, and family relationships.* Amherst, MA: BRAT.

Kelly, J. B. (2007). Children's living arrangements following divorce. *Family Process, 46,* 35–52.

Kelly, J. B., & Emery, R. E. (2003). Children's adjustment following divorce: Risk and resiliency perspectives. *Family Relations, 52*(4), 352–362.

Kennedy, S., & Bumpass, L. (2007). Cohabitation and children's living arrangements: New estimates from the United States. Unpublished manuscript. Madison: Center for Demography, University of Wisconsin.

Kenney, K. R. (2002). Counseling interracial couples and multiracial individuals: Applying a multicultural counseling competency framework. *Counseling and Human Development, 35*(14), 1–13.

Kenrick, D. T., Sadalla, E. K., Groth, G., & Trost, M. R. (1990). Evolution, traits, and the stages of human courtship: Qualifying the parental investment model. *Journal of Personality, 58,* 97–116.

Kerckhoff, R. K. (1964). Family life education in America. In H. T. Christensen (Ed.), *Handbook of marriage and the family* (pp. 881–911). Chicago: Rand McNally.

Kheshgi-Genovese, Z., & Genovese, T. A. (1997). Developing the spousal relationship within stepfamilies. *Families in Society, 78*(3), 255–264.

Kids Count. (2007). *Data snapshot: One out of five U.S. children is living in an immigrant family.* Available: www.aecf.org/KnowledgeCenter/Publications.aspx?pubuid={8661AE11-DBBC-4CBD-92A0-C37DC7AE6D93} [2008, August 21].

Kids Count. (2008). *Children in single-parent families by race.* Available: www.kidscount.org/datacenter/compare_results.jsp?i=722 [2008, August 29].

Kiernan, K. (1997). The legacy of parental divorce: Social, economic, and demographic experiences in adulthood. CASE Paper 1. Centre for the Analysis of Social Exclusion, London School of Economics.

Kiernan, K. E. (1986). Teenage marriage and marital breakdown: A longitudinal study. *Population Studies, 40*(1), 35–54.

Killian, K. D. (2001). Reconstituting racial histories and identities: The narratives of interracial couples. *Journal of Marital and Family Therapy, 27*(1), 27–42.

Kim, J. E., Hetherington, E. M., & Reiss, D. (1999). Associations among family relationships, antisocial peers, and adolescents' externalizing behaviors: Gender and family type differences. *Child Development, 70,* 1209–1230.

Kim, J., & Hatfield, E. (2004). Love types and subjective well-being. *Social Behavior and Personality: An International Journal, 32,* 173–182.

Kimlicka, T. A., Wakefield, J. A., & Goad, N. A. (1982). Sex roles of ideal opposite-sexed persons for college males and females. *Journal of Personality Assessment, 46,* 519–521.

Kimuna, S. R., & Kjamba, Y. K. (2005). Wealth and extramarital sex among men in Zambia. *International Family Planning Perspectives, 31,* 83–89.

King, V. (2002). Parental divorce and interpersonal trust in adult offspring. *Journal of Marriage and Family, 64*(3), 642–656.

King's Church, The. (2001). *Dating vs. courtship.* Available: www.tkc.com/resources/audio/datingaudio.html [2004, May 27].

Kinsey Institute, The. (2007). *HIV/AIDS by race.* Available: www.indiana.edu/~kinsey. [2007, November 10].

Kinsey, A. C., Pomeroy, W. B., Martin, C. E., & Gebhard, P. H. (1953). *Sexual behavior in the human female.* Philadelphia, PA: Saunders.

Kipilis, K. & Diamond, M. (1998). Pediatric ethics and the surgical assignment of sex. *Journal of Clinical Ethics, 9*(4), 398–410.

Kirby, J. S., Baucom, D. H., & Peterman, M. A. (2005). An investigation of unment intimacy needs in marital relationships. *Journal of Marital and Family Therapy, 31*(4), 313–325.

Klaus, M. H., Kennell, J. H., & Klaus, P. H. (1995). *Bonding: Building the foundations of secure attachment and independence.* Boston: Addison-Wesley.

Klerman, L. V. (2004). *Another chance: Preventing additional births to teen mothers.* Washington, DC: National Campaign to Prevent Teen Pregnancy.

Klinkenberg, D., & Rose, S. (1994). Dating scripts of gay men and lesbians. *Journal of Homosexuality, 26*(4), 23–35.

Kluwer, E. S., & Johnson, M. D. (2007). Conflict frequency and relationship quality across the transition to parenthood. *Journal of Marriage and Family, 69,* 1089–1106.

Knapp, M. (1978). *Social intercourse: From greeting to goodbye.* Boston: Allyn & Bacon.

Knapp, M. (1984). *Interpersonal communication and human relationships.* Boston: Allyn & Bacon.

Knox, D. (2002, March). College student attitudes toward interreligious marriage. *College Student Journal.*

Knox, D., Breed, R., & Zusman, M. (2007). College men and jealousy. *College Student Journal, 41*(2), 494–499.

Knox, D., Sturdivant, L., & Zusman, M. E. (2001). College student attitudes toward sexual intimacy. *College Student Journal, 35,* 241–243.

Knox, D., & Zusman, M. E. (2002). When and why gender differences in saying "I love you" among college students. *College Student Journal, 36,* 614–615.

Knox, D., Zusman, M. E., Bluffington, C., & Hemphill, G. (2000). Interracial dating attitudes among college students. *College Student Journal, 3,* 69–71.

Knox, D., Zusman, M., & McNeely, A. (2008). University student beliefs about sex: Men vs. women. *College Student Journal, 42*(1), 181–186.

Knutson, J., Enright, R., & Garbers, B. (2008). Validating the developmental pathway of forgiveness. *Journal of Counseling and Development, 86*(2), 193–199.

Koerner, A. F., & Fitzpatrick, M. A. (2002a). Nonverbal communication and marital adjustment and satisfaction: The role of decoding relationship relevant and relationship irrelevant affect. *Communication Monographs, 69,* 33–51.

Koerner, A. F., & Fitzpatrick, M. A. (2002b). Toward a theory of family communication. *Communication Theory, 12,* 70–91.

Koevecses, Z. (1988). *The language of love: The semantics of passion in conversational English.* Lewisburg, PA: Bucknell University Press.

Kohlberg, L. (1966). A cognitive developmental analysis of children's sex-role concepts and attitudes. In E. E. Maccoby (Ed.), *The development of sex differences* (pp. 82–173). Stanford, CA: Stanford University Press.

Korenman, S., & Miller, J. E. (1997). Effects of long-term poverty on physical health of children in the National Longitudinal Survey of Youth. In G. J. Duncan and J. Brooks-Gunn (Eds.), *Consequences of growing up poor.* New York: Russell Sage Foundation.

Kovacs, L. (1983). A conceptualization of marital development. *Family Therapy, 3,* 183–210.

Kposowa, A. J. (1998). The impact of race on divorce in the United States. *Journal of Comparative Family Studies, 29*(3), 529–548.

Krauth, L. D. (2005). The contentious debate about no-fault divorce: Who is most at risk? In E. Schroeder (Ed.), *Taking sides: Clashing views on controversial issues in family and personal relationships* (pp. 238–242). Dubuque, IA: McGraw-Hill.

Kreider, R. M. (2005). *Number, timing, and duration of marriages and divorces: 2001.* Current Population Reports, P70-97. Washington, DC: U.S. Census Bureau.

Kreider, R. M., & Fields, J. M. (2002). Number, timing, and duration of marriages and divorces: 1996. *United States Census Bureau Current Population Reports* (pp. 70–80). Available: www.census.gov/prod/2002pubs/p70-80.pdf [2005, February 27].

Kreider, R. M., & Fields, J. M. (2005, July). Living arrangements of children: 2001. *United States Census Bureau current population reports, P70–104* (p. 2). Available: www.census.gov/prod/2005pubs/p70-104.pdf [2006, January 6].

Kretchmar, M. D., & Jacobvitz, D. B. (2002). Observing mother-child relationships across generations: Boundary patterns, attachment, and the transmission of caregiving. *Family Process, 41,* 351–374.

Krieger, N. (2001). Critical perspectives on racial and ethnic differences in health and later life. *The National Academic Press,* Committee on Population. Available: www.darwin.nap.edu/books/0309092116.html.

Kruk, E. (1991). Discontinuity between pre-and post-divorce father-child relationships: New evidence regarding paternal disengagement. *Journal of Divorce and Remarriage, 16*(3/4), 195–227.

Kulik, L. (1999). Continuity and discontinuity in marital life after retirement: Life orientations, gender role ideology, intimacy, and satisfaction. *The Journal of Contemporary Human Services, 8*(3), 286–294.

Kupperbusch, C., Matsumoto, D., Kooken, K., Loewinger, S., Uchida, H., Wilson-Cohn, C., & Yrizarry, N. (1999). Cultural influences on nonverbal expressions of emotion. In P. Philippot, R. S. Feldman, and E. J. Coats (Eds.), *The social context of nonverbal behavior* (2nd ed., Vol. 1) (pp. 17–44). Cambridge: Cambridge University Press.

Kurdek, L. A. (1991). Sexuality in homosexual and heterosexual couples. In K. McKinney and S. Sprecher (Eds.), *Sexuality in close relationships* (pp. 177–191). Hillsdale, NJ: Erlbaum.

Kurdek, L. A. (1999). The nature and predictors of the trajectory of change in marital quality for husbands and wives over the first 10 years of marriage. *Developmental Psychology, 35*(5), 1283–1296.

Kurdek, L. A. (2005). What do we know about gay and lesbian couples? *Current Directions in Psychological Science, 14*(5), 251–254.

Kurgman, S. D., & Dubowitz, H. (2003). Failure to thrive. *American Family Physician, 68,* 879–884.

Kuttler, A. F., LaGreca, A. M., & Prinstein, M. J. (1999). Friendship qualities and social-emotional functioning of adolescents with close, cross-sex friendships. *Journal of Adolescent Research, 9*(3), 339–366.

La Gapia, J. J. (1982). Rituals of disengagement: In S. W. Duck (Ed.), *Personal relationships, 4: Dissolving personal relationships.* London: Academic Press.

Laan, E., & Both, S. (2008). What makes women experience desire? Feminism & *Psychology, 18*(4), 505–514.

Lamb, K. A., Lee, G. R., & DeMaris, A. (2003). Union formation and depression: Selection and relationship effects. *Journal of Marriage and Family, 65,* 953–962.

Lamb, M. E. (1987). *The father's role: Cross-cultural perspectives.* Hillsdale, NJ: Erlbaum.

Lamb, M. E. (2000). The effects of quality of care on child development. *Applied Developmental Science, 4*(3), 112–115.

Lamb-Parker, F., Boak, A. Y., Griffin, K. W., Ripple, C., & Peay, L. (1999). Parent-child relationship, home learning environment, and school readiness. *School Psychology Review, 28,* 413–425.

Lambert, S. (2005). Gay and lesbian families: What we know and where to go from here. *The Family Journal: Counseling and Therapy for Couples and Families, 13*(1), 43–51.

Lamberts, S. (1997). The endocrinology of aging. *Science, 278*(5337), 419–424.

Land, R. (2004). *How religion defines America: What the world thinks of God.* Available: www.news.bbc.co.uk/1/hi/programmes/wtwtgod/3518221.stm [2005, September 9].

Landis, D., & O'Shea, W. A., III. (2000). Cross-cultural aspects of passionate love: An individual differences analysis. *Journal of Cross-Cultural Psychology 31,* 752–777.

Landolt, M. A., Lalumiers, M. L., & Quinsey, V. L. (1995). Sex differences in intra-sex variations in human mating tactics: An evolutionary approach. *Ethology and Socialbiology, 16,* 3–23.

Laner, M. R., & Ventrone, N. A. (1998). Egalitarian daters/traditionalist dates. *Journal of Family Issues, 19,* 468–477.

Lang, K., & Zagorsky, J. L. (2001). Does growing up with a parent absent really hurt? *Journal of Human Resources, 36*(2), 253–273.

Langlois, J. H., Kalakanis, L., Rubenstein, A. J., Lavson, A., Hallam, M., & Smoot, M. (2000). Maxims or myths of beauty? A meta-analytic and theoretical review. *Psychological Bulletin, 126,* 390–423.

Lansford, J. E., Deater-Deckard, K., Dodge, K. A., Bates, J. E., & Pettit, G. S. (2004). Ethnic differences in the link between psychical discipline and alter adolescent externalizing behaviors. *Journal of Child Psychology and Psychiatry, 45,* 801–812.

Larsen, A. S., & Olson, D. H. (1989). Predicting marital satisfaction using PREPARE: A replication study. *Journal of Marital and Family Therapy, 15,* 311–322.

Larson, N. C. (2004). Parenting stress among adolescent mothers in the transition to adulthood. *Child and Adolescent Social Work Journal, 21*(5), 457–476.

Larson, P. J., & Olson, D. H. (2005). *Spiritual beliefs and marriage: A national survey based on ENRICH.* The Association of Marriage and Family Ministries. Available: www.amfmonline.com/featured/beliefsMarriage-LarsonOlson.asp [2005, October 1].

Larzelere, R. E., & Kuhn, B. R. (2005). Comparing child outcomes of physical punishment and alternative disciplinary tactics: A meta-analysis. *Clinical Child and Family Psychology Review, 8*(1), 1–37.

Lauer, R. H., & Lauer, J. C. (1991). The long-term relational consequences of problematic family backgrounds. *Family Relations, 40,* 286–290.

Laughlin, J. (2005). *Men's studies and fatherhood.* Available: www.akamaiuniversity.us/MensStudies [2005, June 15].

Laumann, E. O., Gagnon, J. H., Michael, R. T., & Michaels, S. (1994). *The social organization of sexuality: Sexual practices in the United States.* Chicago: University of Chicago Press.

Laumann, E. O., Nicolosi, A., Classer, D. B., et al. (2005) Sexual problems among women and men aged 40–80: Prevalence and correlates identified in the Global Study of Sexual Attitudes and Behaviors. *International Journal of Impotency Research, 17,* 39–57.

Laurenceau, J. P., Barrett, L. F., & Rovine, M. J. (2005). The Interpersonal Process Model of Intimacy in Marriage: A daily-diary and multilevel modeling approach. *Journal of Family Psychology, 19*(2), 314–323.

Lawler, K. A., Younger, J. W., Piferi, R. L., Jobe, R. L., Edmondson, K., & Jones, W. H. (2005). The unique effects of forgiveness on health: An exploration of pathways. *Journal of Behavioral Medicine, 28,* 157–167.

Lawler, K. A., Younger, K. W., Piferi, R. L., Billington, E., Jobe, R., Edmondson, K., & Jones, W. H. (2003). A change of heart: Cardiovascular correlates of forgiveness in response to interpersonal conflict. *Journal of Behavioral Medicine, 26*(5), 373–393.

Lawrance, K., & Byers, E. S. (1995). Sexual satisfaction in long-term heterosexual relationships: The interpersonal exchange model of sexual satisfaction. *Personal Relationships, 2,* 267–285.

Lawrence, R. H., Bennett, J. M., & Markides, K. S. (1992). Perceived intergenerational solidarity and psychological distress among older Mexican Americans. *Journals of Gerontology: Social Sciences, 47,* S55–S65.

Lawrence, R., Rothman, A. D., Cobb, R. J., Rothman, M. T., & Bradbury, T. N. (2008). Marital satisfaction across the transition to parenthood. *Journal of Family Psychology, 22*(1), 41–50.

Lawson, D., & Brossart, F. (2001). Intergenerational transmission: Individuation and intimacy across three generations. *Family Process, 40,* 429–442.

Lawson, K. (2004). Development and psychometric properties of the Perceptions of Parenting Inventory. *The Journal of Psychology, 138*(5), 433–455.

Lazarovici, L. (2005). *When working women head to the polls, jobs and health care will top their lists.* Available: http://www.aflcio.org/aboutus/thisistheaflcio/publications/magazine/0604_wwreport.cfm [2009, August 11].

Lazarus, R. S. (1966). *Psychological stress and the coping process.* New York: McGraw-Hill.

Lazarus, R. S. (1984). Puzzles in the study of daily hassles. *Journal of Behavioral Medicine, 7,* 375–389.

Lazarus, R. S., & Cohen, J. B. (1977). Environmental stress. In I. Altman and J. F. Wohlwill (Eds.), *Human behavior and environment* (Vol. 2). New York: Plenum.

Lazarus, R. S., & Folkman, S. (1984). *Stress, appraisal, and coping.* New York: Guilford.

Lee, J. A. (1973). *The color of love: An exploration of the ways of loving.* Don Mills, Ontario: New Press.

Lee, S. M., & Edmonston, B. (2005). New marriages, new families: U.S. racial and Hispanic intermarriage. *Population Bulletin, 60*(2).

Legal Information Institute. (2005). *Marriage laws of the fifty states.* Available: www.law.cornell.edu/topics/Table_Marriage.htm [2006, February 16].

Lehman, P. (2000). A validity study of the femininity ideology scale. Master's thesis, Florida Institute of Technology.

Lehr, R., & MacMillan, P. (2001). The psychological and emotional impact of divorce: The noncustodial fathers' perspective. *Families in Society, 82*(4), 373–382.

Lehrer, E. L. (2006). Religion and high school graduation: A comparative analysis of patterns for white and black young women. *Review of Economics of the Household, 4*(3), 277–293.

Lehrman, G. (2001). *The history of private life: Courtship in early America.* The Gilder Lehrman Institute of American History. Available: http://yalepress.yale.edu [2004, June 4].

Leichliter, J. S., Chandra, A., Kiddon, N., Fenton, K. A., & Aral, S. O. (2007). Prevalence and correlates of heterosexual anal and oral sex in adolescents and adults in the United States. *The Journal of Infectious Diseases, 196,* 1852–1859.

Leite, R. W., & McKenry, P. C. (2002). Aspects of father status and post-divorce father involvement with children. *Journal of Family Issues, 23,* 601–623.

Leitenberg, H., Detzer, M. J., & Srebnik, D. (1993). Gender differences in masturbation and the relation of masturbation experiences in preadolescence and/or early adolescence to sexual behavior and sexual adjustment in young adulthood. *Archives of Sexual Behavior, 22,* 87–98.

Lemme, B. (2006). *Development in adulthood* (4th ed). Boston: Pearson Education.

Lemme, B. H. (2002). *Development in adulthood* (3rd ed.). Boston: Allyn & Bacon.

Lemon, B. W., Bengston, V. L., & Peterson, J. A. (1972). An exploration of the activity theory of aging: Activity types and life satisfaction among in-movers to a retirement community. *Journal of Gerontology, 27,* 511–523.

Lempers, J. D., & Clark-Lempers, D. S. (1993). A functional comparison of same-sex and opposite-sex friendships during adolescence. *Journal of Adolescent Research, 8*(1), 89–108.

Lengermann, P. M., & Brantley, J. N. (1988). Feminist theory. In G. Ritzer (Ed.), *Sociological theory* (pp. 400–443). New York: Knopf.

Lenton, A. P., & Webber, L. (2006). Cross-sex friendships: Who has more? *Sex Roles: A Journal of Research, 54,* 809–820.

Lerman, R. A. (2002a, July). *How do marriage, cohabitation, and single parenthood affect the material hardships of families with children?* Washington, DC: Urban Institute.

Lerman, R. A. (2002b, July). *Impact of marital status and parental presence on the material hardship of families with children.* Washington, DC: Urban Institute.

Lerner, R. M. (1995). *American's youth in crisis: Challenges and options for programs and policies.* Thousand Oaks, CA: Sage.

Lerner, R. M., Castellino, D. R., Terry, P. A., Villarruel, F. A., & McKinney, M. H. (1995). A developmental contextual perspective on parenting. In M. H. Bornstein (Ed.), *Handbook of parenting: Biology and ecology of parenting* (Vol. 2) (pp. 285–309). Hillsdale, NJ: Erlbaum.

Lerner, R., Noh, E. R., & Wilson, C. (2004). *The parenting of adolescents and adolescents as parents: A developmental contextual perspective.* Available: http://parenthood.library.wisc.edu/Lerner/Lerner.html [2004, August 12].

Levant, R., Richmond, K., Cook, S., House, A. T., & Aupont, M. (2007). The Femininity Ideology Scale: Factor, structure, reliability, convergent and discriminate validity, and social contextual variation. *Sex Roles, 57,* 373–383.

Levchuck, C. M., Kosek, J. K., & Drohan, M. (2000). *Healthy living.* Farmington Hills, MI: UXL.

Levenson, R. W., Carstensen, L. L, & Gottman, J. M. (1993). Long-term marriage: Age, gender, and satisfaction. *Psychology and Aging, 8,* 301–313.

Lever, J. (1994, August 23). Sexual revelations. *The Advocate,* 17–24.

Lever, J. (1995, August 22). Lesbian sex survey. *The Advocate,* 21–30.

Leving, J. M. (2004). *Fathers' rights: Hard-hitting and fair advice for every father involved in a custody dispute.* New York: Basic Books.

Levinger, G. (1976). A social psychological perspective on marital dissolution. *Journal of Social Issues, 32,* 21–42.

Levinger, G. (1982, August). A systems perspective on the development of close relationships. Presented at the Annual American Psychological Association Meeting, Washington, DC.

Levitt, M. J. (1991). Attachment and close relationships: A life span perspective. In J. L. Gewirtz and W. F. Kurtines (Eds.), *Intersections with attachment* (pp. 183–206). Hillsdale, NJ: Erlbaum.

Lewis, M. (2003). *Sexual selection.* Available: www.as.wvu.edu/~kgarbutt/EvolutionPage/FinalPapers/Sex10.htm [2004, June 4].

Lewis, W. J. (1997). Factors associated with post abortion adjustment problems: Implications for triage. *Canadian Journal of Human Sexuality, 6*(1), 9–16.

Li, N. P., Bailey, L. M., Kenrick, D. T., & Linsenmeier, L. A. W. (2002). The necessities and luxuries of mate preferences: Testing the tradeoffs. *Journal of Personality and Social Psychology, 82,* 947–955.

Lief, H. I. (1980). Comments on current thinking on the orgasm experience. *Medical Aspects of Human Sexuality, 14*(7), 55, 59, 62.

Lillard, L., Brien, M., & Waite, L. (1995). Premarital cohabitation and subsequent marital dissolution: A matter of self selection? *Demography, 32,* 437–457.

Lillard, L., & Panis, C. (1996). Marital status and morality: The role of health. *Demography, 33,* 313–327.

Lillard, L., & Waite, L. (1995). 'Til death do us part: Marital disruption and mortality. *American Journal of Sociology, 100,* 1131–1156.

Lin, G., & Rogerson, P. A. (1995). Elder parents and the geographic availability of their adult children. *Research on Aging, 17,* 303–331.

Lin, J., & Bernstein, J. (2008, October). *What we need to get by.* Economic Policy Institute Briefing Paper #224.

Lindau, S. T., Schumm, L. P., Laumann, E. O., Levinson, W., O'Muircheartaigh, C. A., & Waite, I. J. (2007). A study of sexuality and health among older adults in the United States. *New England Journal of Medicine, 357,* 762–774.

Lindgren, H. G. (1998). *Listening with your heart as well as your words.* NebGuide 92-1092. Lincoln: University of Nebraska Cooperative Extension.

Lindley, L. L., Joshi, P., & Vincent, M. L. (2007, November 3–7). Personal and family factors associated with virginity among

African American male and female high school students. Paper presented at the 135th American Public Health Association Annual Meeting, San Diego, CA.

Lindlof, T. R., & Taylor, B. C. (2002). *Qualitative communication research methods* (2nd ed.). Thousand Oaks, CA: Sage.

Lino, M. (2005). *Expenditures on children by families, 2004.* U.S. Department of Agriculture, Center for Nutrition Policy and Promotion. Miscellaneous Publication N. 1528-2004.

Lips, H. M. (2001). Lessons learned in women's studies classrooms. *Psychology of Women Quarterly, 25,* 168.

Liu, C. (2000). A theory of marital sexual life. *Journal of Marriage and Family, 62,* 363–374.

Long, N., & Forehand, R. (2002). *Making divorce easier on your child: 50 effective ways to help children adjust.* New York: Contemporary Books.

Lott-Whitehead, L., & Tully, C. (1992). The family of lesbian mothers. *Smith College Studies in Social Work, 63,* 265–280.

Loudoun, R. (2008). Balancing shiftwork and life outside work: Do 12-hour shifts make a difference? *Applied Ergonomics, 39,* 572–579.

Low, B. S. (2000). *Why sex matters: A Darwinian look at human behavior.* Princeton, NJ: Princeton University Press.

Lowenthal, M. F., & Haven, C. (1968). Interaction and adaptation: Intimacy as a critical variable. *American Sociological Review, 33*(20), 20–30.

Lowrey, C. (2009). Parenting advice 101: Parents need more than a date night, they need adventure. Available: www.articlesbase.com/parenting-articles [2009, January 28].

Lu, L., Gilmour, R., & Kao, S. F. (2001). Cultural values and happiness: An East–West dialogue. *The Journal of Society Psychology, 141*(4), 477–493.

Lugaila, T., & Overturf, J. (2004). Children and the households they live in: 2000. *United States Census Bureau Special Reports, CENSR-14* (p. 9). Available: www.census.gov/prod/2004pubs/censr-14.pdf [2006, January 6].

Luhmann, N. (1986). *Love as passion: The codification of intimacy.* Cambridge, MA: Harvard University Press.

Lundqvist, L.-O. (2006). A Swedish adaptation of the Emotional Contagion Scale: Factor structure and psychometric properties. *Scandinavian Journal of Psychology, 47,* 263–272.

Luoma, J., & Pearson, J. (2002). Suicide and marital status in the United States, 1991–1996: Is widowhood a risk factor? *American Journal of Public Health, 92,* 1518–1522.

Luskin, F. (2003). *Forgive for good: A proven prescription for health and happiness.* San Francisco: Harper.

Lynch, J., & Kaplan, G. (2000). Socioeconomic position. In L. F. Berkman and I. Kawachi (Eds.), *Social epidemiology* (pp. 13–35). New York: Oxford University Press.

Maccoby, E. E. (1988). Gender as a social category. *Developmental Psychology, 24,* 755–765.

Macdonald, H. (2003). *Magazine advertising and gender: Representations of gender in magazine advertising.* Available: www.mediaed.org.uk/posted_documents/MagazineAdverts.htm [2008, November 12].

MacDonald, K. (1992). Warmth as a developmental construct: An evolutionary analysis. *Child Development, 63,* 753–773.

MacGeorge, E. L, Graves, A. R., Feng, B., & Gillihan, S. J. (2004). The myth of gender cultures: Similarities outweigh differences in men's and women's provision of and responses to supportive communication. *Sex Roles: A Journal of Sex Research, 50*(3–4), 143–175.

MacKay, H. (1994). *DINKs.* Lindfield, NSW: MacKay.

Mackey, R., Diemer, M., & O'Brien, A. (2000). Psychological intimacy in the lasting relationships of heterosexual and same-gender couples. *Sex Roles: A Journal of Research, 43*(4), 201–227.

Mackinnon, C.A. (2001). *Sex equality.* New York: Foundation Press.

MacNeil, S., & Byers, E. S. (2005). Dyadic assessment of sexual self-disclosure and sexual satisfaction. *Journal of Personal and Social Relationships, 22,* 193–205.

MacRae, H. (1992). Fictive kin as a component of the social networks of older people. *Research on Aging, 14,* 226–247.

Madden, M., & Lenhart, A. (2006). Online dating. *Pew Internet & American Life Project,* Washington, DC.

Madden-Derdich, D., & Arditti, J. (1999). The ties that bind: Attachment between former spouses. *Family Relations, 48*(3), 243–249.

Maher, B. (2004). *Abstinence until marriage: The best message for teens.* The Family Research Council. Available: www.frc.org [March 20, 2006].

Main, M., & Hesse, E. (1990). Parents' unresolved traumatic experiences are related to infant disorganized attachment status: Is frightened and/or frightening parental behavior the linking mechanism? In M. T. Greenberg, D. Cicchetti, and E. M. Cummings (Eds.), *Attachment in the preschool years: Theory, research, and intervention* (pp. 161–182). Chicago: University of Chicago Press.

Maio, G. R., Thomas, G., Fincham, F. D., & Carnelley, K. B. (2008). Unraveling the role of forgiveness in family relationships. *Journal of Personality and Social Psychology, 94*(2), 307–319.

Major, B., Cozzarelli, C., Cooper, M. L., Zubek, J., Richards, C., Wilhite, M., et al. (2000). Psychological responses of women after first trimester abortion. *Archives of General Psychiatry, 58,* 777–784.

Makes Marks, L. F. (2007). Great mysteries: Native North American religions and participatory visions. *ReVision, 29*(3), 29–37.

Maki, D. M. (2000, February 2). *The growth of consumer credit and the household debt service burden.* FEDS Working Paper No. 2000-12. Available: http://ssrn.com/abstract=221416 or DOI: 10.2139/ssrn.221416 [2009, August 11].

Maleki, M. (2000). *Intimacy difficulties.* Available: www.class.utoronto.ca/pamphlets/intimacy.htm [2005, November 30].

Malhotra, A. (2002). *Gender, caste, and religious identities: Restructuring class in colonial Punjab.* New York: Oxford University Press.

Managing stress in young families. (2008). Iowa State University Extension. Available: www.extension.iastate.edu/Publications/PM1660B.pdf [2009, February 28].

Mann, S. A., Grimes, M. D., Kemp, A. A., & Jenkins, P. J. (1997). Paradigm shifts in family sociology? Evidence from three decades of family textbooks. *Journal of Family Issues, 18*(3), 315–350.

Manning, W. D., & Brown, S. L. (2003). *Children's economic well-being in cohabitating parent families: An update and extension. Working paper series 03–05.* Bowling Green, OH: Bowling Green State University Center for Family and Demographic

Research. Available: www.bgsu.edu/organizations/cfdr/research/pdf/2003/2003_05.pdf [2006, May 25].

Manning, W. D., & Jones, A. J. (2006, March 30–April 1). Cohabitation and marital dissolution. Paper presented at the annual meeting of the Population Association of America, Los Angeles.

Manning, W. D., & Lichter, D. (1996). Parental cohabitation and children's economic well-being. *Journal of Marriage and the Family, 58,* 998–1010.

Manning, W. D., & Smock, P. J. (2003, May 3). Measuring and modeling cohabitation: New perspectives from quantitative data. Paper presented to the Population Association of America.

Manning, W. D., Stewart, S. D., & Smock, P. J. (2003). The complexity of fathers' parenting responsibilities and involvement with nonresident children. *Journal of Family Issues, 24*(5), 645–667.

Marano, H. E. (2000, March/April). Divorced? Don't even think of remarrying until you read this. *Psychology Today, 33*(2), 57–62.

March of Dimes. (2003). *Stillbirth: Pregnancy and newborn health education center.* Available: www.marchofdimes.com [2003, July 11].

Margolin, L. (1992). Child abuse by mothers' boyfriends: Why the overrepresentation? *Child Abuse and Neglect, 16,* 541–545.

Markeiwicz, D., Doyle, A. B., & Brendgen, M. (2001). The quality of adolescents' friendships: Associations with mothers' interpersonal relationships, attachments to parents and friends, and prosocial behaviors. *Journal of Adolescence, 24,* 429–445.

Markham, M., Ganong, L., & Coleman, M. (2007). Mothers' cooperation in coparental relationships. *Family Relations, 56,* 369–377.

Markman, H. J. (1984). The longitudinal study of couples' interaction: Implications for understanding and predicting the development of marital distress. In K. Hahlweg and N. S. Jacobson (Eds.), *Marital interaction: Analysis and modification* (pp. 253–281). New York: Guilford.

Markus, H., Crane, M., Bernstein, S., & Siladi, M. (1982). Self-schemas and gender. *Journal of Personality and Social Psychology, 42,* 563–574.

Marsden, M. (2007). Love and elopement in northern Pakistan. *Journal of the Royal Anthropological Institute, 13*(1), 91–108.

Marsh, H. W. (1990). Two-parent, stepparent, and single-parent families: Changes in achievement, attitudes, and behaviors during the last two years of high school. *Journal of Educational Psychology, 82*(2), 327–340.

Marshall, T. C. (2008). Cultural differences in intimacy: The influence of gender-role ideology and individualism-collectivism. *Journal of Social and Personal Relationships, 25*(1), 143–168.

Marsiglio, W., & Donnelly, D. (1991). Sexual intercourse in later life: A national study of married persons. *Journal of Gerontology, 46,* 338–344.

Martin, C. L. (1990). Attitudes and expectations about children with nontraditional and traditional gender roles. *Sex Roles, 22,* 151–165.

Martin, S. P. (2002). *Delayed marriage and childbearing: Implications and measurement of diverging trends in family timing.* College Park: University of Maryland Department of Sociology and Maryland Population Research Center.

Martinson, F. M. (1994). *The sexual life of children.* Westport, CT: Bergin and Garvey.

Mason, M. A., Fine, M. A., & Carnochan, S. (2001). Family law in the new millennium: For whose families? *Journal of Family Issues, 22*(7), 859–881.

Masters, W. H., & Johnson, V. E. (1966). *Human sexual response.* Boston: Little, Brown.

Masters, W. H., Johnson, V. E., & Kolodny, R. C. (1982). *Human sexuality.* Boston: Little, Brown.

Matthiesen, S., & Wenn, H. M. (2004). Summary of the recommendations on sexual development in females. *Journal of Sexual Medicine, 1,* 24–34.

Mauldon, J. (1992). Children's risks of experiencing divorce and remarriage: Do disabled children destabilize marriage? *Population Studies, 46,* 349–362.

Maushart, S. (2002). *Wifework: What marriage really means for women.* New York: Bloomsbury.

Mayer, E. (1987). *Love and tradition: Marriage between Jews and Christians.* New York: Schocken Books.

Mayo Clinic. (2003). *Sperm smarts: Otimizing fertilty.* Available:: www.mayoclinic.com [2003, July 8].

Mayo Clinic. (2004). Divorce: Helping your child cope with the breakup. *Children's Health.* Available: www.mayoclinic.com/health/divorce/HO00055 [2006, April 11].

Mazur, A., Mueller, U., Krause, W., & Booth, A. (2002). Causes of sexual decline in aging married men: Germany and American. *International Journal of Impotence Research, 14,* 101–106.

McAdams, D. P. (1989). *Intimacy: The need to be close.* New York: Doubleday.

McBride, B. A., & Mills, G. (1993). A comparison of mother and father involvement with their preschool age children. *Early Childhood Research Quarterly, 8,* 457–477.

McCandish, B. M. (1987). Against all odds: Lesbian mother family dynamics. In F. W. Bozett (Ed.), *Gay and lesbian parents* (pp. 23–36). New York: Praeger.

McCartney, K., & Haas, M. (2002). *Better caregiving training, smaller childcare classes lead to improved cognitive and social skills in children.* Cambridge, MA: Harvard Graduate School of Education. Available: www.gse.harvard.edu/news/features/mccartney05052002.html [2005, October 20].

McClun, L. A., & Merrell, K. W. (1998). Relationship of perceived parenting styles, locus of control orientation, and self-concept among junior high age students. *Psychology in the Schools, 35*(4), 381–390.

McCready, S., Harland, K., & Beattie, K. (2006, January). Violent victims? Young men as perpetrators and victims of violent crime. *Centre for Men's Studies, Research Update No. 1.* Available: www.incore.ulst.ac.uk/about/specialist/cyms/CYMS_ru1.pdf [2006, February 17].

McCreary, D. R., Newcomb, M. D., & Sadava, S. W. (1998). The relationship between masculine gender role stress and psychological adjustment: A question of construct validity? *Sex Roles, 39,* 81–95.

McCubbin, H. I., & Patterson, J. M. (1982). Family adaptation to crisis. In H. I. McCubbin, M. B. Sussman, and J. M. Patterson (Eds.), *Family stress, coping, and social support.* Springfield, IL: Thomas.

McDonald, P. F. (1990). The 1980s: Social and economic change affecting families. *Family Matters, 26,* 13–18.

McDonald, P. F. (2000). Low fertility in Australia: Evidence, causes, and policy responses. *People and Place, 8*(2), 6–21.

McGoldrick, M., & Carter, B. (1999). Remarried families. In B. Carter & M. McGoldrick (Eds.), *The expanded family life cycle* (3rd ed.)(pp. 417–435). New York: Guilford.

McGoldrick, M., Broken Nose, M. A., & Potenza, M. (1999). Violence and the family life cycle. In B. Carter and M. McGoldrick (Eds.), *The expanded family life cycle: Individual, family, and social perspectives* (pp. 470–491). Boston: Allyn & Bacon.

McGuigan, F. J. (1999). *Encyclopedia of stress.* Boston: Allyn & Bacon.

McHale, J., Rao, N., & Krasnow, A. (2000). Constructing family climates: Chinese mothers' reports of their coparenting behavior and preschoolers' adaptation. *International Journal of Behavioral Development, 24,* 111–118.

McIlrath, D., & Huitt, W. (1995, December). *The teaching-learning process: A discussion of models.* Valdosta, GA: Valdosta State University.

McIntyre, A., Heron, R. L., McIntyre, M. D., Burton, S. J., & Engler, J. N. (2003). College students from families of divorce: Keys to their resilience. *Journal of Applied Developmental Psychology, 24,* 17–31.

McKay, A. (2004). Oral sex among teenagers: Research, discourse, and education. *Canadian Journal of Human Sexuality, 13,* 201–203.

McLanahan, S., & Sandefur, G. (1994). *Growing up with a single parent: What hurts, what helps.* Cambridge, MA: Harvard University Press.

McLaughlin, I. G., Leonard, K. E., & Senchak, M. (1992). Prevalence and distribution of premarital aggression among couples applying for a marriage license. *Journal of Family Violence, 7,* 309–319.

McLaughlin, K. (2005). Exploring and sharing family stories. *International Reading Association.* Available: www.read writethink.org [2005, November 14].

McLeod, J. D., & Nonnemaker, J. M. (2000). Poverty and child emotional and behavioral problems: Racial/ethnic differences in processes and effects. *Journal of Health and Social Behavior, 41,* 137–161.

McMurray, A., & Blackmore, A. M. (1993). Influences on parent-child relationships in noncustodial fathers. *Australian Journal of Marriage and the Family, 14*(3), 151–159.

McNulty, J. K. (2008). Forgiveness in marriage: Putting the benefits into context. *Journal of Family Psychology, 22*(1), 171–175.

McQuillan, K. (2004). When does religion influence fertility? *Population and Development Review, 30*(1), 25–56.

McQuillen, J. S. (2003). The influence of technology on the initiation of interpersonal relationships. *Education, 123,* 616–623.

McWilliams, P. (1998). *Ain't nobody's business if you do: The absurdity of consensual crimes in a free country.* Los Angeles, CA: Prelude Press.

Mead, G. H. (1934). *Mind, self, and society* (C. Morris, Introduction and Ed.). Chicago: University of Chicago Press.

Media Watch. (2008). Available: http://citizenmediawatch.com/index.php/2008/10/ [July 13, 2009].

Medina, S., & Magnuson, S. (2009). Motherhood in the 21st century: Implications for counselors (Practice & Theory). *Journal of Counseling and Development, 87*(1), 90–98.

Medora, N. P., Larson, J. H., Hortacsu, N., & Dave, P. (2002). Perceived attitudes towards romanticism: A cross-cultural study of American, Asian-India, and Turkish young adults. *Journal of Comparative Family Studies, 33,* 155–179.

Melhuish, E. C. (1991). Research on daycare for young children in the United Kingdom. In E. C. Melhuish and P. Moss (Eds.), *Daycare for young children: International perspectives* (pp. 152–153). London: Tavistock/Routledge.

Mellan, O. (1994). *Money harmony.* New York: Walker and Company.

Mendelson, M. J., & Kay, A. C. (2003). Positive feelings in friendship: Does imbalance in the relationship matter? *Journal of Social and Personal Relationships, 20,* 101–116.

Mercer, C. H., Fenton, K. A., Johnson, A. M., et al. (2003). Sexual function problems and help seeking behaviour in Britain: National probability sample survey. *British Medical Journal, 327,* 4267.

Mercer, R. T. (1986). *First-time motherhood: Experiences from teens to forties.* New York: Springer.

Mercer, R. T. (2004). Becoming a mother versus maternal role attainment. *Journal of Nursing Scholarship, 36*(3), 226–232.

Merck Manual. (2003). *Complications of pregnancy: Women's health issues* (Section 22, Chapter 245). Available: www.merck.com/mrkshared/mmanual_home/sec22/245.jsp [2003, July 11].

Merlo, R., & Rowland, D. (2000). The prevalence of childlessness in Australia. *People and Place, 8*(2), 21–32.

Merolla, A. J. (2008). Communicating forgiveness in friendships and dating relationships. *Communication Studies, 59*(2), 114–130.

Merritt, J., & Shoup Olsen, C. (2002). *What happens now? The children are gone.* Kansas State University Agricultural Experiment Station and Cooperative Extension Service, Publication #MF-2554. Available: www.oznet.ksu.edu [2006, June 26].

Meschke, L. L., Bartholomae, S., & Zentall, S. R. (2002). Adolescent sexuality and parent-adolescent processes: Promoting healthy teen choices. *Journal of Adolescent Health, 31,* 264–269.

Metts, S., Cupach, W., & Bejlovec, R. A. (1989). "I love you too much to ever start liking you": Redefining romantic relationships. *Journal of Social and Personal Relationships, 6,* 259–274.

Meyer, D. R., & Bartfield, J. (1996). Compliance with child support orders in divorce cases. *Journal of Marriage and Family, 58*(1), 201–212.

Michael, R. T., Gagnon, J. H., Laumann, E. O., & Kolata, G. (1994). *Sex in America: A definitive study.* Boston: Little, Brown.

Michael, Y., Berkman, L., Colditz, G., & Kawachi, I. (2001). Living arrangements, social integration, and change in functional health status. *American Journal of Epidemiology, 153,* 123–131.

Michaud, S. L., & Warner, R. M. (1997). Gender differences in self-reported response in troubles talk. *Sex Roles: A Journal of Sex Research, 37,* 527–540.

Milan, A. (2000). One hundred years of families. *Canadian Social Trends, 56,* 1–13.

Milkie, M. A., Bianchi, S. M., Mattingly, M. J., & Robinson, J. P. (2002, July). Gendered division of childrearing: Ideals, realties, and the relationship to parental well-being. *Sex Roles: A Journal of Research,* 21–39.

Millbank, J. (2003). From here to maternity: A review of the research on lesbian and gay families. *Australian Journal of Social Issues, 38*(4), 541–599.

Miller, L. C., Berg, J. H., & Archer, R. L. (1983). Openers: Individuals who elicit intimate self-disclosure. *Journal of Personality and Social Psychology, 44,* 1234–1244.

Miller, R. B. (2001). Do children make a marriage unhappy? *Marriage and Families.* Available: http://marriageandfamilies.byu.edu/issues/2001/April/children.aspx [2006, March 29].

Miller, R. S., & Lefcourt, H. M. (1982). The assessment of intimacy. *Journal of Personality Assessment, 46,* 514–518.

Miscegenation. Wikipedia, Free Encyclopedia. Available: http://en.wikipedia.org/wiki/miscegenation [2004, July 19].

Moir, A., & Jessel, D. (1991). *Brain sex: The real difference between men and women.* New York: Doubleday.

Money, J. (2003). *Mate selection across cultures.* Newbury Park, CA: Sage.

Monsour, M. (2002). *Women and men as friends: Relationships across the lifespan in the 21st century.* Mahwah, NJ: Erlbaum.

Montefiore, S. S. (1993, March/April). Let the games begin: Sex and the not-thirtysomethings. *Psychology Today, 26*(2), 66–72.

Monthly Labor Review. (2004, June). *A visual essay: Blacks, Asians, and Hispanics in the civilian labor force.* Available: http://www.bis.gov/opub/mir/2004/06/ressum.pdf [2008, October 11].

Mooney, J. (1985). *The destroying angel: Sex, fitness, and food in the legacy of degeneracy theory, Graham Crackers, Kellogg's Corn Flakes and health history.* Buffalo, NY: Prometheus Books.

Moos, R. H. (1987). *Life transitions and crises: A conceptual overview.* New York: Plenum Press.

Moos, R. H., & Schaefer, J. A. (1987). Life transitions and crises: A conceptual overview. In R. H. Moos (Ed.), *Coping with life crises: An integrated approach* (pp. 3–28). New York: Plenum Press.

Morales, A., Heaton, J. P. W., & Carson, C. C. (2000). Andropause: A misnomer for a true clinical entity. *Journal of Urology, 163,* 705–712.

Morgan, E., & Kuykendall, C. (2000). Spiritual intimacy. *Marriage Partnership, 17*(2), 60.

Mosher, W. D., Chandra, A., & Jones, J. (2005). Sexual behavior and selected health measures: Men and women 15–44 years of age, United States 2002. *Advance Data, 352.*

Muehlenhard, C. L., Peterson, Z. D., Karwoski, L., Bryan, T. S., & Lee, R. S. (2003). Gender and sexuality: An introduction to the special issue. *Journal of Sex Research, 40*(1), 1–4.

Mullen, P. E., Pathe, M., & Purcell, R. (2000). *Stalkers and their victims.* Cambridge, MA: Cambridge University Press.

Munson, M. L., & Sutton, P. D. (2005). Births, marriages, divorces, and deaths: Provisional data for 2004. *National Vital Statistics Report, 53*(21). Hyattsville, MD: National Center for Health Statistics.

Murphy, M., Glaser, K., & Grundy, E. (1997). Marital status and long-term illness in Great Britain. *Journal of Marriage and the Family, 59,* 156–164.

Murray, J. (2000). Marital protection and marital selection: Evidence from a historical-prospective sample of American men. *Demography, 37,* 511–521.

Murray, M. A., Malcarne, V. L., & Goggin, K. (2003). Alcohol-related God/higher power control beliefs, locus of control, and recovery within the Alcoholics Anonymous paradigm. *Alcoholic Treatment Quarterly, 21*(3), 23–39.

Murry, V. M., Brody, G. H., Simons, R. L., Cutrona, C. E., & Gibbons, F. X. (2008). Disentangling ethnicity and context as predictors of parenting within rural African American families. *Applied Developmental Science, 12*(4), 202–210.

Muslim Public Affairs Council. (2006). Sexuality for women. Available: www.mpac.org.

Myers, D. G. (2004). *Social psychology.* New York: McGraw-Hill.

Myers, D. G. (2005). *Psychology* (8th ed.). New York: Worth.

Myers, D. G. (2008). *Social psychology* (9th ed.). New York: McGraw-Hill.

Nanda, S. (1990). *Neither man nor woman: The Hijras of India.* Belmont, CA: Wadsworth.

Natenshon, H. (1999). A day center for adolescents with eating disorders within Southern Health. Paper presented to the Butterfly-Southern Health Eating Disorder Conference, March 2004. Available: www.thebutterflyfoundation.org/au [2005, November].

National Academy of Sciences. (1991). *Diet and health.* Washington, DC: National Academy of Sciences Press.

National Academy of Sciences. (1995). *Research ethics.* Washington, DC: National Academy of Sciences Press. Available: www.nas.edu [2006, February 5].

National Association of Scholars. (2001). Junk mathematics in the service of race preferences. *Science Newslist, 6*(1).

National Campaign to Prevent Teen Pregnancy. (2008). *National data.* Available: http://www.thenationalcampaign.org/national-data/default.aspx [2009, August 2].

National Center for Children in Poverty. (1999). *Poverty and brain development.* Columbia University Mailman School of Public Health. Available: www.nccp.org/media/pbd99-text.pdf [2006, January 22].

National Center for Exploited and Missing Children. (2005). A family resource guide on parental kidnapping. Available: www.missingkids.com/en_US/publications/NC08.pdf. [2006, June 22].

National Center for Health Statistics. (2003). Births: Preliminary data for 2002. *NVSR, 51*(11), PHS 2003-1120. Available: www.cdc.gov/nchs/births.htm [2006, July 7].

National Center for Health Statistics. (2005). *Cohabitation, marriage, divorce, and remarriage in the United. States.* DHHS Publication No. (PHS) 2002-1998 (July 2002). Available: http://www.cdc.gov/nchs/data/series/sr_23/sr23_022.pdf [2009, August 12].

National Center for Health Statistics. (2005). *Marriages and divorces.* Available: www.cdc.gov/nchs [2005, December 27].

National Center for Health Statistics. (2007). *Teen birth rates rise for the first time in 15 years.* Available: www.cdc.gov/NCHS/pressroom/07newsreleases/teenbirth.htm [2009, January 10].

National Center for Health Statistics. (2008). *Unmarried and single Americans week.* Available: http://www.census.gov/

population/www/socdemo/hh-fam/cps2008.html [2009, July 22].

National Coalition Against Domestic Violence. (2005). *Safety plan.* Available: www.ncadv.org/protectyourself/SafetyPlan_130.html [2009, February 26].

National Coalition Against Domestic Violence. (2008). *Battered women.* Available: www.ncadv.org [2009, February 27].

National College Health Assessment. (2004). *American College Health Association.* Available: www.psu.edu/ATOD/nchaexec.html [2006, March 20].

National College Health Assessment. (2008). *Reference group data report.* Available: http://www.acha-ncha.org/reports_ACHA-NCHAoriginal.html [2009, August 1].

National Council for Adoption. (2008). *Adoption facts and statistics.* Available: http://www.adoptioncouncil.org/resources/facts_stats.html [2009, August 1].

National Council on Aging. (1998a). *Healthy sexuality and vital aging.* Available: www.ncoa.org/index [2005, February].

National Council on Aging. (1998b). *Sex after 60: A natural part of life.* Available: www.ncoa.org/index [2005, February].

National Council on Aging. (2005). *Caregiver research: The latest news.* Available: http://www.ncoa.org/content.cfm?sectionID=379&detail=2044 [2009, August 12].

National Council on Family Relations (NCFR). (2009). *NCFR—Providing skills and knowledge to enrich family life.* Available: http://www.ncfr.org/conf/current/annual.asp [2009, June 25].

National Gay and Lesbian Task Force. (2003). *Marriage and partnership recognition.* Available: www.thetaskforce.org/theissues/issue.cfm?issueID=14.html [2006, May 25].

National Guidelines Task Force. (1994). *Guidelines for comprehensive sexuality education.* New York: SIECUS.

National Institute of Child Health and Human Development. (2001a). *Female reproduction.* Available: www.nichd.nih.gov.er/lib.ksu.edu/about/cpr/rs/report/female_reproduction.htm [2003, July 8].

National Institute of Child Health and Human Development. (2001b). *Male reproduction.* Available: www.nichd.nih.gov.er/lib.ksu.edu/about/cpr/rs/report/male_reproduction.htm [2003, July 8].

National Institutes of Health. (2005). *Turner syndrome.* Available: http://rarediseases.info.nih.gov/GARD/Disease.aspx?diseaseID=7831.

National Issues Forum. (1996). Available: http://www.pbs.org/newshour/forum/january96/fishkin_1-19.html [2009, June 25].

National Marriage Project. (2005). *The state of our unions, 2005: The social health of marriage in America.* Available: www.marriage.rutgers,edu/Publications/SOOU/SOOU2005.pdf [2006, May 25].

National Network to End Domestic Violence. (2007). *National summary.* Available: www.nnedv.org [2009, February 27].

National Organization on Adolescent Pregnancy, Parenting, and Prevention. (2004). *Unique developmental needs of the children of adolescent parents.* Available: www.noappp.org [2004, August 12].

National Organization on Adolescent Pregnancy, Parenting, and Prevention. (2008). Available: www.healthyteennetwork.org [2009, January 1].

National Organization for Women. (2005). *Violence against women in the United States.* Available: www.now.org/issues/violence/stats.html [2006, May 13].

National Postsecondary Student Aid Survey. (2005). *Student aid survey data.* Available: http://www.ohe.state.mn.us/mPg.cfm?pageID=1570 [2009, August 11].

National Task Force to End Sexual and Domestic Abuse Against Women. (2005). Violence against women act, 2005. Available: www.hbns.org/news/lifetime02-26-04.cfm. [2006, June 22].

National Vital Statistics Report. (2008). Births, marriages, divorces, and deaths: Provisional data for June 2007. *NVSR, 56*(12).

National Vital Statistics Reports. (2003). Revised birth and fertility rates for the Unites States, 2000 and 2001. *NVSR, 51*(4).

National Vital Statistics Reports. (2004). *Births, marriages, divorces, and deaths: Preliminary data for 2004, Table A.* Available: www.cdc.gov/nchs/ [2006, January 15].

National Vital Statistics Reports. (2006, September 29). Births, marriages, and divorces. *National Vital Statistics Reports, 55*(1), Tables 1 & 32. Available: healthvermont.gov/research/stats/2004/documents/APPX_D.PDF - Similar — [2009, July 22].

Needham, L. B. (1999). *An investigation of exceptions to patterns of mate selection in evolutionary theory among resource dependent and independent females.* Available: http://mutans.astate.edu/dcline/Guide/Mate_selection.html [2004, May 27].

Nelson, J. N. (1978). Age and sex differences in the development of children's occupational reasoning. *Journal of Vocational Behavior, 13,* 287–297.

Neto, F. (1993). Love styles and self-representations. *Personality and Individual Differences, 14,* 795–803.

Neto, F. (1994). Love styles among Portuguese students. *Journal of Psychology, 128,* 613–616.

Neto, F. (2001). Love styles of three generations of women. *Marriage & Family Review, 33*(4), 19–30.

Neto, F. (2007). Forgiveness, personality and gratitude. *Personality and Individual Differences, 43,* 2313–2323.

Neto, F., Mullet, E., Deschamps, J., Barros, J., Benvindo, R., Camino, L., Palconi, A., Kagleanga, V., & Machado, M. (2000). Attitudes toward love. *Journal of Cross-Cultural Psychology, 31*(5), 626–636.

Nettles, E. J., & Loevinger, J. (1983). Sex role expectations and ego level in relation to problem marriages. *Journal of Personality and Social Psychology, 45,* 676–687.

Neugarten, B. L, & Weinstein, K. K. (1964). The changing American grandparent. *Journal of Marriage and the Family, 26,* 299–304.

Newcomb, M. D. (1983). Relationship qualities of those who live together. *Alternative Lifestyles, 6,* 78–102.

Newcomb, M. D., & Bentler, P. M. (1983). Dimension of subjective female orgasmic responsiveness. *Journal of Personal and Social Psychology, 44*(4), 862–873.

NICHD Early Child Care Research Network. (2000). The relation of child care to cognitive and language development. *Child Development, 71*(4), 960–980.

NICHD Early Child Care Research Network. (2003a). Do children's attention processes mediate the link between family predictors and school readiness? *Developmental Psychology, 39*(3), 581–593.

NICHD Early Child Care Research Network. (2003b). Does amount of time spent in childcare predict socioemotional adjustment during the transition to kindergarten? *Child Development, 74*(4), 976–1005.

Nichols, M. (2004). *Family therapy: Concepts and methods.* Boston: Allyn & Bacon.

Nichols, M. P., & Schwartz, R. C. (2004). *Family therapy: Concepts and methods* (6th ed.). Boston: Allyn & Bacon.

Nichols, M. P., & Schwartz, R. C. (2009). *The essentials of family therapy* (4th ed.). Boston: Allyn & Bacon.

Nielsen Media. (2008). *Nielsen media research on video, iPods: Additional analysis, what's your playmix ratio?* Available: http://www.nielsenmedia.com/nc/portal/site/Public/menuitem.55dc65b4a7d5adff3f65936147a062a0/?vgnextoid=27e6a153e [July 13, 2009].

Nielsen, L. (1999). Demeaning, demoralizing, and disenfranchising divorced dads: A review of the literature. *Journal of Divorce and Remarriage, 31*(3/4), 139–177.

Niemiec, R., Sikorski, M., & Walberg, H. (1999). Designing school volunteer programs. *NASSP Bulletin, 83,* 114–116.

Nock, S. L. (1995). A comparison of marriages and cohabiting relationships. *Journal of Family Issues, 16*(1), 53–76.

Noland, C. (2006). Listening to the sound of silence: Gender roles and communication about sex in Puerto Rico. *Sex Roles, 55*(5-6), 283–294.

Noller, P. (1993). Gender and emotional communication in marriage: Different cultures or differential social power? *Journal of Language and Social Psychology, 12,* 132–152.

Nord, W., & Haynes, C. (1998). *Taking religion seriously across the curriculum.* Alexandria, VA: Association for Supervision and Curriculum Development.

Notarius, C. I., Benson, P. R., Sloane, D., Vanzetti, N. A., & Hornyak, L. M. (1989). Exploring the interface between perception and behavior: An analysis of marital interaction in distressed and nondistressed couples. *Behavioral Assessment, 11,* 39–64.

Oakes, J. (1988). Tracking in mathematics and science education: A structural contribution to unequal schooling. In L. Weis (Ed.), *Class, race, & gender in American education,* (pp. 106–125). Albany, NY: State University of New York.

O'Connell, M., & Lofquist, D. (2009). Counting same-sex couples: Official estimates and unofficial guesses. Housing and Household Economic Statistics Division, U.S. Bureau of the Census. Available: http://www.census.gov/population/www/socdemo/files/counting-paper.pdf [2009, July 22].

Oda, R. (2001). Sexual dimorphic mate preference in Japan: An analysis of lonely hearts advertisements. *Human Nature, 12,* 191–206.

O'Donnell, L., Steuve, A., Wilson-Simmons, R., Dash, K., Agronick, G., & JeanBaptiste, V. (2006). Heterosexual risk behaviors among urban young adolescents. *The Journal of Early Adolescence, 26*(87), 87–109.

O'Donohue, W., & Crouch, J. L. (1996). Marital therapy and gender-linked factors in communication. *Journal of Marital and Family Therapy, 22,* 87–101.

Office of Child Support Enforcement. (2005, June). *Child support enforcement FY 2004: Preliminary report.* Available: www.acf.dhhs.gov/programs/cse/–20k [2006, April 1].

Office of Child Support Enforcement. (2008). Available: www.acf.hhs.gov/programs/cse/pubs/2008/preliminary_report_fy2007/Prelim2007.pdf [2009, February 14].

Ogata, K., & Miyashita, K. (2000). Exploring links between father's participation in family chores, child's empathy, family function, and father's identity development. *Japanese Journal of Family Psychology, 14,* 15–27.

Oggins, J., Leber, D., & Veroff, J. (1993). Race and gender differences in black and white newlyweds' perception of sexual and marital relations. *The Journal of Sex Research, 30,* 152–160.

O'Hare, W. (1988) *The rise of poverty in rural America.* Washington, DC: Population Reference Bureau. ERIC Document Reproduction Service: ERIC Item: ED 302 350.

Okazaki, S. (2002). Influences of culture on Asian Americans' sexuality. *Journal of Sex Research, 39,* 34–41.

O'Keefe, E. S. C., & Hyde, J. S. (1983). The development of occupational sex-role stereotypes: The effects of gender stability and age. *Sex Roles, 9,* 481–492.

Okun, B. F. (2002). *Effective helping: Interviewing and counseling techniques* (6th ed.). Monterey, CA: Brooks/Cole.

Oldstone-Moore, J. (2002). *Confucianism: Origins, beliefs, practices, holy texts, sacred place.* New York: Oxford University Press.

Olson, D. H., & McCubbin, H. I. (1983). *Families: What makes them work.* Beverly Hills, CA: Sage.

Olson, D. H., & Olson, A. K. (2000). *Empowering couples: Building on your strengths.* Minneapolis, MN: Life Innovations.

Olson, D. H., & Olson-Sigg, A. (2007). *Overview of cohabitation research.* PREPARE/ENRICH. Available: www.prepare-enrich.com [2008, July 10].

Olson, D. H., Russell, C. S., & Sprenkel, D. H. (1983). Circumplex model of marital and family systems: VI. Theoretical update. *Family Process, 22,* 69–83.

Olson, D. H., Russell, C. S., & Sprenkel, D. H. (1989). *Circumplex model: Systematic assessment and treatment of families.* New York: Haworth.

Olson, D. H., Sprenkel, D. H., & Russell, C. S. (1979). Circumplex model of marital and family systems: Cohesion and adaptability dimensions, family types, and clinical applications. *Family Process, 18,* 3–28.

Olson, T. (2004). *Don't die with your helmet on.* Calgary, Alberta, Canada. Available as eBook: www.dontdiewithyourhelmeton [2009, January 26].

Omarzu, J. (2000). A disclosure model: Determining how and when individuals will self-disclose. *Personality and Social Psychology Review, 4*(2), 174–185.

O'Neil, R. (2002, September). Experiments in living: The fatherless family. *CIVITAS.*

Ooms, T. (2002). Strengthening couples and marriage in low-income communities. In A. J. Hawkins, L. D. Wardle, and D. O. Coolidge (Eds.), *Revitalizing the institution of marriage for the twenty-first century* (pp. 79–100). Westport, CT: Praeger.

Openshaw, D. K. (1999). Resiliency. In C. A. Smith (Ed.), *The encyclopedia of parenting.* Westport, CT: Greenwood.

Openshaw, D. K. (2004). *The psychosocial development of adolescence: Intimacy.* Available: www.usu.edu/openshaw [2005, November 30].

Oppenheim, D., Sagi, A., & Lamb, M. E. (1988). Infant-adult attachment on the kibbutz and their relation to socioemotional development four years later. *Developmental Psychology, 24*(3), 427–433.

Oppenheimer, M. (2007). Recovering from an extramarital relationship from a non-systemic approach. *American Journal of Psychotherapy, 61*(2), 181–191.

Orbuch, T. L., House, J. S. Mero, R. P., & Webster, P. S. (1996). Marital quality over the life course. *Social Psychology Quarterly, 59,* 162–171.

Oregonian, The. (2003, October 25). Record number of childless women: The Census Bureau says a record 26.7 million women of childbearing age had no children in 2002, a 10% increase over 1990.

Orlofsky, J. L., Marcia, J. E., & Lesser, I. M. (1973). Ego identity status and the intimacy versus isolation crisis of young adulthood. *Journal of Personality and Social Psychology, 27,* 211–219.

Oropesa, R. S., & Gorman, B. K. (2000). Ethnicity, immigration, and beliefs about marriage as a "tie that binds." In L. J. Waite, C. Bachrach, M. Hindin, E. Thomson, & A. Thornton (Eds.), *The ties that bind: Perspectives on marriage and cohabitation* (pp. 188–211). New York: Aldine de Gruyter.

Oropesa, R. S., & Landale, N. S. (2004). The future of marriage and Hispanics. *Journal of Marriage and Family, 66,* 901–920.

Orthner, D. (2002). *Deployment and separation adjustment among Army civilian spouses. Survey report.* Available: www.armymwr.com/corporate/operations/planningsurveys.asp [2009, January 28].

Osteen, S. R., & Neal, R. A. (2009). Couples and money: Let's talk about it. Oklahoma Cooperative Extension Service, T-4201.

Oswald, D. L., & Clark, E. M. (2003). Best friends forever? High school best friendships and the transition to college. *Journal of Social and Personal Relationships, 10,* 187–196.

Pace, S. (2004). *Every 9 seconds.* Available: www.saidit.org/archives [2004, October 4].

Padgett, T., & Sikora, F. (2003, May). Color-blind love: Once considered taboo, interracial marriages are now on the rise—even in some unexpected places. *Time.*

Page, M. E. (2005). Understanding racial differences in the economic costs of growing up in a single-parent family. *Demography, 42*(1), 75–90.

Pan, S. (1993). Chinese wives: Psychological and behavioral factors underlying their orgasm frequency. Unpublished manuscript. Beijing: Renmin University.

Papernow, P. L. (1984). The stepfamily cycle: An experiential model for stepfamily development. *Family Relations, 33,* 355–363.

Papernow, P. L. (1993). *Becoming a stepfamily: Patterns of development in remarried families.* San Francisco: Jossey-Bass.

Papp, L. M., Cummings, E. M., & Goeke-Morey, M. C. (2009). For richer, for poorer: Money as a topic of marital conflict in the home. *Family Relations, 58,* 91–103.

Parish, T. S., & Wigle, S. E. (1985). A longitudinal study of the impact of parental divorce on adolescents' evaluations of self and parents. *Adolescence, 20,* 239–244.

Park, K. (2005). Choosing childlessness: Weber's typology of action and motives of the voluntarily childless. *Sociological Inquiry, 75*(3), 372–402.

Parke, M. (2007, May). Are married parents really better for children? What research says about the effects of family structure on child well-being. *Couples and Married Research and Policy Brief: Center for Law and Social Policy.*

Parke, R. D., & Brott, A. A. (1999). *Throwaway dads: The myths and barriers that keep men from being the fathers they want to be.* Boston: Houghton Mifflin.

Parke, R. D., & Brott, A. A. (2003). Throwaway dads. In M. Coleman and L. Ganong (Eds.), *Points and counterpoints: Controversial relationship and family issues in the twenty-first century* (pp. 3–13). Boston: Houghton Mifflin.

Parkin, S. (2001). Myths and realties of aging study. *National Council on Aging.* Available: www.ncoa.org/index [2005, February].

Parkin, S. (2002). American perceptions on aging in the 21st century. *National Council on Aging.* Available: www.ncoa.org/indes [2005, February].

Parmet, S. (2004, June 23–30). Male sexual dysfunction. *JAMA, 291*(24). Available: http://jama.ama-assn.org/cgi/content/full/291/24/3076 [2009, August 1].

Parsons, T. (1951). *The social system.* Glencoe, IL: Free Press.

Parziale, J., & Parziale, J. B. (2002). *The journey: A traveling guide to Christian stepfamilies.* Tucson, AZ: InStep Ministries.

Pasley, K. (1998). Divorce: Remarriage in later adulthood. *Stepfamily Association of America.* Available: www.saafamilies.org/faqs/findings/7.htm [2005, April 30].

Pasley, K., & Ihinger-Tallman, M. (1994). *Stepparenting: Issues in theory, research, & practice.* Westport, CT: Greenwood.

Patterson, C. J. (1996). Lesbian mothers and their children: Findings from the Bay area Families Study. In J. Laird and R. J. Green (Eds.), *Lesbians and gays in couples and families: A handbook for therapists* (pp. 420–437). San Francisco: Jossey-Bass.

Patterson, C. J. (2000). Family relationships of lesbians and gay men. *Journal of Marriage and Family, 62,* 1052–1069.

Patterson, C. J. (2002). Lesbian and gay parenthood. In M. H. Bornstein (Ed.), *Handbook of parenting, Volume 3: Status and social conditions of parenting* (pp. 255–274). Mahwah, NJ: Erlbaum.

Patterson, C. J. (2004). Lesbian and gay parents and their children: Summary of research findings. In *Lesbian and gay parenting: A resource for psychologists.* Washington, DC: American Psychological Association.

Patterson, C. J. (2006). Children of lesbian and gay parents. *Current Directions in Psychological Science, 15*(5), 241–244.

Patterson, C. J., & Chan, R. W. (1996). Gay fathers and their children. In R. P. Cabaj and T. S. Stein (Eds.), *Textbook of homosexuality and mental health.* Washington, DC: American Psychiatric Press.

Patterson, J., & Kim, P. (1991). *The day America told the truth: What people really believe about everything that really matters.* Englewood Cliffs, NJ: Prentice Hall.

Paul, E. L, & White, K. M. (1990, Summer). The development of intimate relationships during late adolescence. *Adolescence, 375*–400.

Paulozzi, L. J., Saltman, L. E., Thompson, M. P., & Holmgreen, P. (2001). *Surveillance for homicide among intimate partners: United States, 1981–1998.* Centers for Disease Control and Prevention. Available: www.cdc.gov/mmwr/PDF/SS/SS5003.pdf [2005, August 27].

Pearlin, L. I. (1982). The social contexts of stress. In L. Goldberger and S. Brenitz (Eds.), *Handbook of stress: Theoretical and clinical aspects.* New York: Free Press.

Pearson, K. (1911). *The grammar of science* (3rd ed.). London: Adam and Charles Black.

Pedhazur, E. J., & Schmelkin, L. P. (1991). *Measurement, design, and analysis: An integrated approach.* Hillsdale, NJ: Erlbaum.

Pennington, S. B. (1987). Children of lesbian mothers. In F. W. Bozett (Ed.), *Gay and lesbian parents* (pp. 58–174). New York: Praeger.

Peplau, L. A., & Fingerhut, A. D. (2007). The close relationships of lesbians and gay men. *Annual Reviews of Psychology, 58,* 405–424.

Peplau, L. A., & Spalding, L. R. (2000). The close relationships of lesbians, gay men, and bisexuals. In C. Hendrick and S. S. Hendrick (Eds.), *Close relationships: A sourcebook* (pp. 111–124). Thousand Oaks, CA: Sage.

Perlman, S. D., & Abramson, P. R. (1981). Sexual satisfaction in married and cohabiting individuals. In K. Kelley and D. Byrne, *Exploring human sexuality.* Englewood Cliffs, NJ: Prentice Hall.

Perrin, E. C. (2002). *Sexual orientation in child and adolescent health care.* New York: Kluwer Academic/Plenum.

Perry, D. G., & Bussey, K. (1984). *Social development.* Englewood Cliffs, NJ: Prentice Hall.

Perry-Jenkins, M., & Folk, K. 1994. Class, couples and conflict: Effects of the division of labor on assessments of marriage in dual-earner marriages. *Journal of Marriage and the Family, 56,* 165–180.

Perry-Jenkins, M., Repetti, R. L., & Crouter, A. C. (2001). Work and family in the 1990s. In R. Milardo (Ed.), *Understanding families into the new millennium: A decade in review* (pp. 200–217). Lawrence, KS: NCFR and Alliance Communications Group.

Peterson, C. (1999). Grandfathers' and grandmothers' satisfaction with the grandparenting role: Seeking new answers to old questions. *International Journal of Aging and Human Development, 49,* 61–78.

Peterson, R., & Green, S. (1999, June). Family first—keys to successful family functioning: Family communication. *Virginia Cooperative Extension Publication Number 350-092.* Available: ext.vt.edu/pubs/family/350-092/350-092.html [2005, October 19].

Pettigrew, T. F., & Tropp, L. R. (2006). A meta-analytic test of intergroup contact theory. *Journal of Personality and Social Psychology, 90,* 751–783.

Peven, D. A., & Shulman, B. H. (1999). The issue of intimacy in marriage. In J. Carlson and L. Sperry (Eds.), *The intimate couple* (pp. 276–283). New York: Bruner/Mazel.

Pew Forum on Religion & Public Life. (2008). *U.S. religious landscape survey.* Available: www.pewforum.org [2008, August 25].

Pew Research Center. (2007). *Purpose of marriage.* Available: www.pewsocialtrends.org/pubs/?chartid=447 [2008, July 14].

Pew Research Center. (2007). *Views about divorce.* Available: http://pewresearch.org/pubs/?ChartID=432 [2009, August 12].

Pew Research Center. (2008). *Current views about divorce.* Available: http://pewresearch.org/pubs/?ChartID=431 [2009, August 12].

Pew Research Forum. (2008). *Inside the middle class: Bad times hit the good life.* Available: pewsocialtrends.org/pubs/706/middle-class-poll [2008, April 9].

Phelan, P. (1995). Incest and its meaning: The perspective of fathers and daughters. *Child Abuse and Neglect, 19*(1), 7–24.

Phillips, D. I. W., Handelsman, D. J., Eriksson, J. G., Forsen, T., Osmond, C., & Barker, D. J. P. (2001). Prenatal growth and subsequent marital status: Longitudinal study. *British Medical Journal, 322,* 771.

Phillips, G. M., & Wood, J. T. (1983). *Communication and human relationships: The study of interpersonal communication.* New York: Macmillan.

Phillips, J. A., & Sweeney, M. M. (2005). Premarital cohabitation and marital disruption among White, Black, and Mexican American women. *Journal of Marriage and Family, 67*(2), 296–314.

Phillips, N. A. (2000). Female sexual dysfunction: Evaluation and treatment. *American Family Physician, 62,* 127–136.

Phuong-Mai, N., Terlouw, C., & Pilot, A. (2005). Cooperative learning vs. Confucian heritage culture's collectivism: Confrontation to reveal some cultural conflicts and mismatch. *Asia Europe Journal, 3*(3), 403–419.

Pickover, S. (2002). Breaking the cycle: A clinical example of disrupting an insecure attachment system. *Journal of Mental Health Counseling, 24,* 358–367.

Pierce, C. A. (1996). Body height and romantic attraction: A meta-analytic test of the male-taller norm. *Social Behavior and Personality, 24*(2), 143–150.

Pierrehumbert, B., Ramstein, T., Karmaniola, A., & Halfon, O. (1996). Child care in the preschool years: Attachment, behavior problems and cognitive development. *European Journal of Psychology of Education, 11*(2), 201–214.

Pimple, K. D. (2001). *Six domains of research ethics.* Bloomington: Indiana University Poynter Center for the Study of Ethics and American Institutions. Available: www.poynter.indiana.edu [2006, February 5].

Pinderhughes, E. E., Hurley, S., & The Conduct Problems Prevention Research Group (2008). Disentangling ethnic and contextual influences among parents raising youth in high-risk communities. *Applied Developmental Science, 12*(4), 211–219.

Pinel, J. P. (1997). *Biopsychology* (3rd ed.). Boston: Allyn & Bacon.

Pinquart, M., & Soerensen, S. (2000). Influences of socioeconomic status, social network, and competence on subjective well-being in later life: A meta-analysis. *Psychology and Aging, 15,* 187–224.

Pinquart, M., & Soerensen, S. (2004). Associations of caregiver stressors and uplifts with subjective well-being and depressive mood: A meta-analytic comparison. *Aging and Mental Health, 8,* 438–449.

Pinsof, W. M. (2002, June 22). The death of 'til death us do part: The transformation of pair-bonding in the twentieth century. *Family Process.* Available: www.highbeam.com/library/doc3.asp?DOCID=1G1:90301620 [2006, January 3].

Pittman, L. D., & Chase-Lansdale, P. L. (2001). African American adolescent girls in impoverished communities: Parenting style and adolescent outcomes. *Journal of Research on Adolescence, 11,* 199–224.

Pitts, J. R. (1964). The structural functional approach. In E. T. Christensen (Ed.), *Handbook of marriage and the family.* Chicago: Rand McNally.

Pitzer, R. L. (2004). *Change, crisis, and loss in our lives.* Available: www.extension.mn.edu/distribution/familydevelopment/DE2455.html [2004, September 22].

Planned Parenthood. (2006). *How to talk to your kids about sex.* Available: www.pamf.org/teen/parents/sex/talksex.html [2006, March 20].

Planned Parenthood. (2009). *Emergency contraception pill (morning after pill)*. Available: http://www.plannedparenthood .org/health-topics/emergency-contraception-morning- after-pill-4363.htm [2009, August 1].

Pleck, E. H., & Pleck, J. H. (1997). Fatherhood ideals in the United States: Historical dimensions. In M. Lamb (Ed.), *The roles of the father in child development.* New York: Wiley.

Pleck, J. H. (1997). Paternal involvement: Levels, sources, and consequences. In M. E. Lamb (Ed.), *The role of the father in child development* (pp. 66–103). New York: Wiley.

Plotnikoff, D. (1994, August 24). Sexism and bias pollute cyberspace. *Baltimore Sun*, p. 6D.

Pogrebin, L. C. (1980). *Growing up free: Raising your child in the 80s.* New York: McGraw-Hill.

Popenoe, D., & Whitehead, B. D. (2001). *The state of our unions: The social health of marriages in America.* New Brunswick, NJ: Rutgers University National Marriage Project.

Popenoe, D., & Whitehead, B. D. (2002). Why men won't commit: Exploring young men's attitudes about sex, dating, and marriage. *The National Marriage Project, Rutgers University.* Available: www.marriage.rutgers.edu [2002, December].

Popenoe, D., & Whitehead, B. D. (2005). *The state of our unions.* New Brunswick, NJ: National Marriage Project.

Powell, D. (2005). Divorce-on-demand: Forget about gay marriage—What about the state of regular marriage? In E. Schroeder (Ed.), *Taking sides: Clashing views on controversial issues in family and personal relationships* (pp. 243–246). Dubuque, IA: McGraw-Hill.

Powers, V. (2004). T & D. In K. R. Gilbert (Ed.), *Annual editions: The family, 06/07.* New York: McGraw-Hill.

Prager, K. J. (1995). *The psychology of intimacy.* New York: Guilford.

Prager, K. J. (1999). The multi-layered context of intimacy. In J. Carlson and L. Sperry (Eds.), *The intimate couple.* New York: Bruner/Mazel.

Prager, K. J., & Buhrmester, D. (1998). Intimacy and need fulfillment in couple relationships. *Journal of Social and Personal Relationships, 15*(4), 435–469.

Presser, H. B. (2003). *Working in a 24/7 economy: Challenges for American families.* New York: Russell Sage Foundation.

Price, S. (Ed.). (1993). *Vision 2010: Families and health care.* Minneapolis: National Council on Family Relations.

Pride, M. (1985). *The way home: Beyond feminism, back to reality.* Wheaton, IL: Good News Publishers.

Priel, B., & Besser, A. (2001). Bridging the gap between attachment and object relations theories: A study of the transition to motherhood. *British Journal of Medical Psychology, 74,* 85–100.

Prince, D. W., & Hoppe, M. H. (2000). Getting the message: How to feel your way with other cultures. *Leadership in Action, 20*(2), 1–4.

Purnine, D. M., Carey, M. P., & Jorgensen, R. S. (1994). Gender differences regarding preferences for specific heterosexual practices. *Journal of Sex and Marital Therapy, 20,* 271–287.

Qian, Z. (1999). Who intermarries? Education, nativity, region, and interracial marriage, 1980 and 1990. *Journal of Comparative Family Studies, 30,* 579–586.

Quilliam, S. (2005). *Staying together: From crisis to deeper commitment.* London: Vermillion.

Quillian, L., & Campbell, M. E. (2003). Beyond black and white: The present and future of multiracial friendship segregation. *American Sociological Review, 68:* 540–566.

Quinlivan, J. A., Tan, L. H., Steele, A., & Balck, K. (2004). Impact of demographic factors, early family relationships and depressive symptomatology in teenage pregnancy. *Australian and New Zealand Journal of Psychiatry, 38*(4), 197–208.

Radziszewska, B., Richardson, J. L., Dent, C. W., & Flay, B. R. (1996). Parenting style and adolescent depressive symptoms, smoking, and academic achievement: Ethnic, gender, and SES differences. *Journal of Behavioral Medicine, 19,* 289–305.

Rae, S. (1995). Party of one. *Men's Health, 10*(7), 72–75.

Raffaelli, M., Bogenschneider, K., & Flood, M. F. (1998). Parent-teen communication about sexual topics. *Journal of Family Issues, 19,* 315–333.

Raley, R. K., & Bumpass, L. (2003). The topography of the divorce plateau: Levels and trends in union stability in the United States after 1980. *Demographic Research, 8,* 245–259.

Raley, R. K., Durden, T. E., & Wildsmith, E. (2004). Understanding Mexican-American marriage patterns using a life-course approach. *Social Science Quarterly, 85,* 872–890.

Randall, H. E., & Byers, E. S. (2003). What is sex? Students' definitions of having sex, sexual partner, and unfaithful sexual behaviour. *The Canadian Journal of Human Sexuality, 12,* 87–96.

Rao, K. V., & DeMaris, A. (1995). Coital frequency among married and cohabiting couples in the U.S. *Journal of Biosocial Science, 27,* 135–150.

Raphel, S. (2008). Kinship care and the situation for grandparents. *Journal of Childhood and Adolescent Psychiatric Nursing, 21*(2), 118–120.

Rathus, S. A., & Nevid, J. S. (1992). *Adjustment and growth: The challenges of life* (5th ed.). Ft. Worth: Harcourt Brace Jovanovich.

Read, J. G. (2003). The sources of gender role attitudes among Christian and Muslim Arab-American women. *Sociology of Religion, 64*(2), 207–223.

Rector, R. E., Pardue, M. G., & Martin, S. (2004). What do parents want taught in sex education programs? The Heritage Foundation, Executive Summary #1722. Available: www .heritage.org/research/welfare/bg1722.cfm.

Reeder, H. M. (2003). The effect of gender role orientation on same- and cross-sex friendship formation. *Sex Roles: A Journal of Research, 49,* 143–152.

Regan, P. (2000). The role of sexual desire and sexual activity in dating relationships. *Social Behavior and Personality, 28*(1), 51–60.

Reid, J. (1990). *Education and rural development: A review of recent evidence.* Paper presented to the American Educational Research Association, Boston, MA.

Reiss, I. L. (1960, May). Toward a sociology of the heterosexual love relationship. *Marriage and Family Living, 22,* 139–145.

Reiss, I. L. (1971). *The family system in America.* New York: Holt, Rinehart, & Winston.

Reiss, I. L. (1989). Society and sexuality: A sociological explanation. In K. McKinney and S. Sprecher (Eds.), *Human sexuality: The societal and interpersonal context* (pp. 3–29). Norwood, NJ: Ablex.

Renaud, C., Byers, E. S., & Pan, S. (1997). Sexual and relationship satisfaction in mainland China. *The Journal of Sex Research, 34*(4), 399–411.

Rennison, C. M. (2003, February 23). *Intimate partner violence, 1993–2001.* Bureau of Justice Statistics Crime Data Brief. Available: www.ojp.usdoj.gov/bjs/pub/pdf/ipv01.pdf.

Retsinas, N. P., & Belsky, E. S. (Eds.). (2002). *Low-income homeownership: Examining the unexamined goal.* Washington, DC: Brookings Institution Press. Available: www.brookings.org/dybdocroot/savingsforthepoor.html [2006, January 2].

Reynolds, G. P., Wright, J. V., & Beale, B. (2003). The roles of grandparents in educating today's children. *Journal of Instructional Psychology, 30*(4), 316–325.

Ribar, D. C. (2003). *What do social scientists know about the benefits of marriage? A review of quantitative methodologies* (pp. 1–79). Washington, DC: George Washington University Department of Economics.

Rice, P. F. (1993). *Intimate relationships, marriage, and families.* Mountain View, CA: Mayfield.

Richardson, P. (1981). Women's perceptions of their important dyadic relationships during pregnancy. *Journal of Maternal and Child Nursing, 10*(3), 159–174.

Richardson, S., & McCabe, M. P. (2001). Parental divorce during adolescence and adjustment in early adulthood. *Adolescence, 36,* 467–489.

Richters, J., de Visser, R., Rissel, C., & Smith, A. (2006). Sexual practices at last heterosexual encounter and occurrence of orgasm in a national survey. *Journal of Sex Research, 43*(3), 217–226.

Ridley, C., Ogolsky, B., Payne, P., Totenhagen, C., & Cate, R. (2008). Sexual expression: Its emotional context in heterosexual, gay, and lesbian couples. *The Journal of Sex Research, 45*(3), 305–315.

Rivers, C. (2003). Critics aside, military moms are here to stay. *WeNews* (May 28). Retrieved April 1, 2006, from www.womensnews.org/article.cfm?aid=1345.

Robbins, C. A., & Streetman, L. G. (1994). Resolution of nonmarital adolescent pregnancy and the transition to adulthood: Educational attainment and financial well-being. *Review of Policy Research, 13*(1–2), 141–154.

Robson, M., Cook, P., & Gilliland, J. (1995). Helping children manage stress. *British Education Research Journal, 21*(2), 165–174.

Roche, K. M., Ensminger, M. E., & Cherlin, A. J. (2007). Variations in parenting and adolescent outcomes among African American and Latino families living in low-income, urban areas. *Journal of Family Issues, 28*(7), 882–909.

Roehling, P. V., & Moen, P. (2003). Dual-earner couples. *Sloan Work and Family Encyclopedia.* Available: www.bc.edu/bc_org/avp/wfnetwork/rft/wfpedia/wfpDECent.html [2004, August 10].

Rogers, S. J., & White, L. K. (1998). Satisfaction with parenting: The role of marital happiness, family structure, and parents' gender. *Journal of Marriage and the Family, 60*(2), 293–308.

Roloff, M. E., Soule, K. P., & Carey, C. M. (2001). Reasons for remaining in a relationship and responses to relational transgressions. *Journal of Social and Personal Relationships, 18,* 362–385.

Romas, J. A., & Sharma, M. (2000). *Practical stress management* (2nd ed.). Boston: Allyn & Bacon.

Rosario, M., Meyer-Bahlburg, H., Hunter, J., Exner, T., Swadz, M., & Keller, A. (1996). The psychosexual development of urban lesbian, gay and bisexual youths. *The Journal of Sex Research, 33,* 113–126.

Rose, S., & Frieze, I. H. (1989). Young singles' scripts for a first date. *Gender and Society,* 3, 258–268.

Rose, S., & Frieze, I. H. (1993). Young singles' contemporary dating scripts. *Sex Roles, 28,* 499–509.

Rosenblatt, P. C. (1994). *Metaphors of family systems theory: Toward new constructions.* New York: Guilford.

Rosenblum, K. E., & Travis, T.-M. C. (2003). *The meaning of difference: American constructions of race, sex and gender, social class, and sexual orientation.* Boston: McGraw-Hill.

Rosenlee, L. L. (2006). *Confucianism and women: A philosophical interpretation.* Albany: NW State University of New York.

Ross, C., Mirowsky, J., & Goldsteen, K. (1991). The impact of the family on health. In A. Booth (Ed.), *Contemporary families: Looking forward, looking back.* Minneapolis: National Council on Family Relations.

Ross, D. S., & Ross, R. R. (2004). *Interfaith weddings: An introduction.* Available: www.love-track.com/cc/cc_f_one_rabbirev.html [2004, July 21].

Ross, E. S., Niebling, C. B., Bradley, C., & Heckert, M. T. (1999). Sources of stress among college students. *College Student Journal, 33*(2), 1–5.

Rostosky, S. S., Riggle, E. D. B., Dudley, M. G., & Wright, M. L. (2006). Commitment in same-sex relationships: A qualitative analysis of couples' conversations. *Journal of Homosexuality, 51*(3), 199–223.

Rotundo, E. A. (1993). *American motherhood.* New York: Basic Books.

Rowe, J., & Kahn, R. (1998). *Successful aging.* New York: Random House.

Rubin, L. (1983). *Intimate strangers: Men and women together.* New York: Harper & Row.

Rubin, L., (1986). On men and friendship. *Psychoanalytic Review, 73,* 165–181.

Rubin, R. (1967). Attainment of the maternal role. Part 1. *Nursing Research, 16,* 237–245.

Rubin, Z. (1973). *Liking and loving: An invitation to social psychology.* New York: Holt, Rinehart, & Winston.

Rusbult, C. (2002). *Betrayal, forgiveness, and reconciliation in close relationships.* Available: www.forgiving.org.htm [2008, September 26].

Rusbult, C. E., & Buunk, B. P. (1993). Commitment processes in close relationships: Interdependence analysis. *Journal of Social and Personal Relationships, 10,* 175–204.

Russell, E. B., & Harton, H. C. (2005). The "other factors": Using individual and relationship characteristics to predict sexual and emotional jealousy. *Current Psychology: Developmental, Learning, Personality, Social, 24*(4), 242–257.

Russo, L. (2000). *Date rape: A hidden crime.* Australian Institute of Criminology, ISSN 0817-8542, Number 157.

Russo, N. F., & Zierk, K. I. (1992). Abortion, childrearing, and women's well-being. *Professional Psychology: Research and Practice, 23,* 269–280.

Rutledge, K. (2000). *Social learning theory.* Available: http://teachnet.edb.utexas.edu/~lynda_abbott/Social.html [2005, March].

Rybak, A., & McAndrew, F. T. (2006). How do we decide whom our friends are? Defining levels of friendship in Poland and the United States. *The Journal of Social Psychology, 146*(2), 147–163.

Ryder, V. (1990). *Contemporary living.* South Holland, IL: Goodheart-Wilcox.

Saad, F. M. (2002, July). *Marriage in Africa: Islam versus culture.* Paper presented to the Woman's World Congress, Makerere University, Kampala. Available: www.makerere.ac.ug/womenstudies/full%20papers/SAAD.htm [2004, October 10].

Sabatelli, R. M. (1988). Exploring relationship satisfaction: A social exchange perspective on the interdependence between theory, research, and practice. *Family Relations, 37,* 217–222.

Sacerdote, B., & Marmaros, D. (2005). *How do friendships form?* NBER Working Paper W11530. Available: www.ssrn.com/abstract=776569. [2008, November 1].

Sagarin, B. J. D., Becker, V., Guadango, R. E., Nicastle, L. D., & Millevoi, A. (2003). Sex differences (and similarities) in jealousy. *Evolution and Human Behavior, 24,* 17–23.

Salmela-Aro, K., Aunola, K., Saisto, T., Halmesmaki, E., & Nurmi, J. E. (2006). Couples share similar changes in depressive symptoms and marital satisfaction anticipating the birth of a child. *Journal of Social and Personal Relationships, 23*(5), 781–803.

Samaniego, R. Y., & Gonzales, N. A. (1999). Multiple mediators of the effects of acculturation status on delinquency for Mexican American adolescents. *American Journal of Community Psychology, 27,* 189–210.

Sanders, S. A., & Reinisch, J. M. (1999). Would you say you had sex if . . . ? *Journal of the American Medical Association, 281,* 275–277.

Sanger, M. (1914, March). The woman rebel. *The Aim, 1*(1).

Sarwer, D. B. (2001). Plastic surgery in children and adolescents. In J. Thompson and L. Smolak (Eds.), *Body image, eating disorders, and obesity in youth* (pp. 341–366). Washington, DC: American Psychological Association.

Sarwer, D. B. (2002). Awareness and identification of body dysmorphic disorder by aesthetic surgeons: Results of a survey of American Society for Plastic Surgery members. *Aesthetic Surgery Journal, 22,* 341.

Sarwer, D. B., Magee, L., & Clark, V. (2003). What is beauty? Physical appearance and cosmetic medical treatments: Psychological and socio-cultural influences. *Journal of Cosmetic Dermatology, 2*(1), 29.

Satir, V. (1972). *People making.* Palo Alto, CA: Science & Behavior.

Savin-Williams, R. C., & Esterberg, E. G. (2000). Lesbian, gay, and bisexual families. In D. H. Dmo, K. R. Allen, and M. A. Fine (Eds.), *Handbook of family diversity.* New York: Oxford University Press.

Sax, L. J. (2008). *The gender gap in college: Maximizing the developmental potential of women and men.* San Francisco: Jossey-Bass.

Scheib, J. E., Gangestad, S. W., & Thornhill, R. (1999). Facial attractiveness, symmetry, and cues of good genes. *Proceedings of the Royal Society of London B, 266,* 131–132.

Schenk, J., Pfrang, H., & Rausche, A. (1983). Personality traits versus the quality of the marital relationship as the determinant of marital sexuality. *Archives of Sexual Behavior, 12*(1), 31–42.

Schlosser, E. (2002, Sept./Oct.). Making it work. *Mother Jones,* 68–73.

Schmitt, D. P., & Buss, D. M. (2001). Human mate poaching: Tactics and temptations for infiltrating existing mateships. *Journal of Personality and Social Psychology, 80,* 894–917.

Schmitt, D. P., Shackelford, T., Duntley, J., Tooke, W., & Buss, D. M. (2001). The desire for sexual variety as a tool for understanding basic human mating strategies. *Personal Relationships, 8,* 425–455.

Schneller, D. P., & Arditti, J. A. (2004). After the break-up: Interpreting divorce and rethinking intimacy. *Journal of Divorce and Remarriage, 42,* 1–37.

Scholly, K., Katz, A. R., Gascoigne, J., & Holck, P. S. (2005). Using social norms theory to explain perceptions and sexual health behaviors of undergraduate college students: An exploratory study. *Journal of American Collegiate Health, 53*(4), 159–166.

Schoppe, S. J., Mangelsdorf, S. C., & Frosch, C. (2001). Coparenting, family process, and family structure: Implications for preschoolers' externalizing behavior problems. *Journal of Family Psychology, 15,* 526–545.

Schramm, D. G., Marshall, J. P., Harris, V. W., & George, A. (2003). *Marriage in Utah: 2003 baseline statewide survey on marriage and divorce.* Salt Lake City: Utah Department of Workforce Services.

Schramm, D. G., Marshall, J. P., Harris, V. W., & Lee, T. R. (2005). After "I do": The newlywed transition. *Marriage and Family Review, 38,* 45–67.

Schumm, W. R., Bell, B. D., & Gade, P. A. (2000). Effects of a military overseas peacekeeping deployment on marital quality, satisfaction, and stability. *Psychological Reports, 87,* 815–821.

Schwartz, M. A., & Scott, B. M. (2003). *Marriages and families: Diversity and change* (4th ed.). Upper Saddle River, NJ: Prentice Hall.

Schwartz, P. (1994). *Peer marriage: How love between equals really works.* New York: Free Press.

Schwartz, P. (2001). Peer marriage: What does it take to create a truly egalitarian relationship? In A. S. Skolnick and J. H. Skolnick (Eds.), *Families in transition* (11th ed.) (pp. 182–190). Boston: Allyn & Bacon.

Scott, C. F., & Sprecher, S. (2000). Sexuality in marriage, dating, and other relationships: A decade review. *Journal of Marriage and the Family, 62*(4), 999–1017.

Searcy, W. A. (1982). The evolution effects of mate selection. *Annual Review of Ecological Systems, 13,* 57–85.

Seccombe, K. (1991). Assessing the costs and benefits of children: Gender comparisons among childfree husbands and wives. *Journal of Marriage and the Family, 53,* 191–202.

Seeber, M., & Gorrell, C. (2001). The science of orgasm: Sex and your psyche. *Psychology Today, 34*(6), 48–59.

Seepersad, S., Choi, M-K, & Shin, N. (2008). How does culture influence the degree of romantic loneliness and closeness? *The Journal of Psychology, 142*(2), 209–217.

Segatto, B., & Di Filippo, L. (2003). Relationship and emotions in couples in the retirement and/or empty nest phase. Eta_Evolutiva, Giunti Firenze.

Segura, D. A., & Pierce, J. L. (1993, Autumn). Chicana/o family structure and gender personality: Chodorow, familism, and psychoanalytic sociology revisited. *Signs.*

Seifer, R., Sameroff, A. J., Baldwin, C. P., & Baldwin, A. (1992). Child and family factors that ameliorate risk between 4 and 13 years of age. *Journal of American Academy of Child and Adolescent Psychiatry, 31*(4), 893–903.

Seiffge-Krenke, I. (1993). Close friendship and imaginary companions in adolescence. In B. Laursen (Ed.), *Close friendships in adolescence* (pp. 73–87). San Francisco: Jossey-Bass.

Sellitz, C., Wrightsman, L. S., & Cook, S. W. (1976). *Research methods in social science* (3rd ed.). New York: Holt, Rinehart, & Winston.

Selvin, E., Burnett, A. L., & Platz, E. A. (2007). Prevalence of and risk factors for erectile dysfunction in U.S. Men. *American Journal of Medicine, 120*(2), 151–157.

Selye, H. (1982). History and present status of stress concept. In L. Goldberger and S. Breznit (Eds.), *Handbook of stress: Theoretical and clinical aspects* (pp. 7–17). New York: Free Press.

Selye, H. (1985). History and present status of the stress concept. In A. Monat and R. S. Lazarus (Eds.), *Stress and coping* (2nd ed.). New York: Columbia University.

Selzer, R. (1978). *Mortal lessons: Notes on the art of surgery* (pp. 45–46). Baltimore, MD: Johns Hopkins University Press.

Senecal, S., Murad, N., & Hess, U. (2003). Do you know what I feel? Predictors and judgments of each other's emotional reactions to emotion-eliciting situations. *Sex Roles, 48*(1/2), 21–37.

Sergios, P., & Cody, J. (1985). Importance of physical attractiveness and social assertiveness skills in male homosexual dating behavior and partner selection. *Journal of Homosexuality, 12,* 71–84.

Seymour, T., Francis, C., & Steffens, P. (1995). *Supporting stepfamilies: What do the children feel?* NF 95-223. Lincoln: University of Nebraska Cooperative Extension.

Sgoutas-Emch, S. A. (2005). *Health care options.* Poster presented at the 17th annual American Psychological Society conference, Los Angeles.

Shadish, W. (1993). Effects of family and marital psychotherapies: A meta-analysis. *Journal of Consulting and Clinical Psychology, 61*(6), 992–1002.

Sharifzadeh, V. S. (1997). Families with Middle Eastern roots. In E. W. Lynch and M. J. Hanson (Eds.), *Developing cross-cultural competence: A guide for working with children and families* (pp. 441–482). Baltimore, MD: Paul H. Brookes.

Sharp, E. A., & Ganong, L. H. (2000). Raising awareness about marital expectations: An unrealistic beliefs change by integrative teaching? *Family Relations, 49,* 71–76.

Shaver, P. R., Morgan, H. J., & Wu, S. (1996). Is love a basic emotion? *Personal Relationships, 3,* 81–96.

Shaw, D. S. (1993). Parental functioning and children's adjustment in families of divorce: A prospective study. *Journal of Abnormal Child Psychology, 21*(1), 119–143.

Shaw, D. S., & Ingoldsby, E. M. (1999). Children of divorce. In R. T. Ammerman, C. G. Last, and M. Hersen (Eds.), *Handbook of prescriptive treatments for children and adolescents* (2nd ed.) (pp. 346–363). Boston: Allyn & Bacon.

Sheehan, C. L. (2003). *Marriage and families* (2nd ed). Boston: Allyn & Bacon.

Sherman, E. (2003). *Divorce solutions: How to make any divorce better.* Santa Cruz, CA: Nolo Press Occidental.

Shore, R. (1997). *Rethinking the brain.* New York: Families and Work Institute.

Shoup Olsen, C. (1997). *Stepping stones for stepfamilies.* MF 2238. Manhattan, KS: Kansas State University Cooperative Extension.

Shucksmith, J., Leo, B., Hendry, L. B., & Glendinning, A. (1995). Models of parenting: Implications for adolescent well-being within different types of family contexts. *Journal of Adolescence, 18,* 253–270.

Sieburg, E. (1973). *Interpersonal confirmation: A paradigm for conceptualization and measurement.* Paper presented to the International Communication Association, Montreal, Quebec. ERIC Reproduction Service: ERIC Item: ED 098 634 1975.

SIECUS. (Winter, 2004). Sexuality and youth in communities of color fact sheet. *SIECUS Report, 32*(1).

Signorielli, N. (1992). Children, television, and conceptions about chores: Attitudes and behaviors. *Sex Roles, 27*(3/4), 157–170.

Silberman, S. (1995). The relationships among love, marital satisfaction, and duration of marriage. Unpublished dissertation, Arizona State University, Tempe, AZ.

Silverman, J. S. (2003). Fallacies about love and marriage. In M. Coleman and L. Ganong (Eds.), *Points and counterpoints* (pp. 91–93). Los Angeles: Roxbury.

Silverstein, B., Purdue, L., Peterson, B., & Kelly, E. (1986). The role of the mass media in promoting a thin standard of bodily attractiveness in women. *Sex Roles, 14*(9–10), 519–532.

Simanski, J. (2005). *Mapping trends in U.S. legal immigration: 1980–2003.* Available: www.census.gov/population/www/socdemo/immigration.html [2006, January 2].

Simmons, T., & Dye, J. L. (2004). *Grandparents living with children.* Washington, DC: U.S. Census Bureau. Retrieved June 26, 2006 from www.census.gov/prod/2003/pubs/c2kbr-31.pdf.

Simmons, T., & O'Connell, M. (2003). Married-couple and unmarried-partner households: 2000. *United States Census Bureau report.* Available: www.landview.census.gov/prod/2003pubs/censr-5.pdf [2008, July 3].

Simmons, T., & O'Neill, G. (2001). Households and families: 2000. *United States Census Bureau Brief, C2KBR/01-8* (p. 2). Available: www.census.gov/prod/2001pubs/c2kbr01-8.pdf [2006, January 2].

Simon, W., & Gagnon, G. (1986). Sexual scripts: Permanence and change. *Archives of Sexual Behavior, 15,* 97–120.

Simon, W., & Gagnon, J. H. (1984). Sexual scripts. *Society, 22,* 53–60.

Simons, R. L., et al. (Eds.). (1996). *Understanding differences between divorced and intact families.* Thousand Oaks, CA: Sage.

Singh, D. (1993a). Adaptive significance of female attractiveness: Role of the waist-to-hip ratio. *Journal of Personality and Social Psychology, 65,* 293–307.

Singh, D. (1993b). Body shape and women's attractiveness. The critical role of waist-to-hip ratio. *Human Nature, 4,* 297–321.

Singh, D. (1994). Is thin really beautiful and good? Relationship between waist-to-hip ratio (WHR) and female attractiveness. *Personality and Individual Differences, 16,* 123–132.

Singh, D. (2001). *Myself Mona Ahmed.* Zurich, Switzerland: Scalo Publishers.

Singh, D. (2002). Female mate value at a glance: Relationship of waist-to-hip ratio to health, fecundity, and attractiveness. *Neuroendocrinology Letters. Special Issue, 23,* 81–91.

Singh, D. (2004). Mating strategies of young women: Role of physical attractiveness. *Journal of Sex Research, 41*(1), 43–54.

Sjoberg, D. L. (2002). *How the family environment affects intimacy.* Available: www.oberlin.edu/faculty/ndarling/adint .htm#sjoberg.

Skelton, C., & Hall, E. (2001). *The development of gender roles in young children.* Department of Education, University of Newcastle, UK. Available: www.eoc.org.uk/research.html [2008, November 19].

Smetana, J. G. (1995). Parenting styles and conceptions of parental authority during adolescence. *Child Development, 66,* 299–316.

Smith, D. (2003). The older population in the United States: March 2002. *United States Census Bureau Current Population Reports* (pp. 20–546). Available: www.census.gov/prod/ 2003pubs/p20-546.pdf [2004, June 5].

Smith, D. E. (1993). The standard North American family. *Journal of Family Issues, 14,* 50–65.

Smith, D. M., & Gates, G. J. (2001, August 22). Gay and lesbian families in the United States: Same sex unmarried partner households: A preliminary analysis of 2000 United States census data. *Human Rights Campaign Report* (p. 2). Available: www.urban.org/UploadedPDF/1000491_gl_partner_ households.pdf [2006, January 3].

Smith, J. R., Brooks-Gunn, J., & Klebanov, P. K. (1997). Consequences of living in poverty for young children's cognitive and verbal ability and early school achievement. In G. J. Duncan and J. Brooks-Gunn (Eds.), *Consequences of growing up poor.* New York: Russell Sage Foundation.

Smith, K., & Waitzman, N. (1994). Double Jeopardy: Interaction effects of marital and poverty status on the risk of mortality. *Demography, 31,* 487–507.

Smith, K., & Zick, C. (1994). Linked lives, dependent demise? Survival analysis of husbands and wives. *Demography, 31,* 81–93.

Smith, P. K., & Drew, L. M. (2002). Grandparenthood. In M. Bornstein (Ed.), *Handbook of parenting* (2nd ed.) (pp. 141–172). Mahwah, NJ: Erlbaum.

Smith, S. (1995). Family theory and multicultural family studies. In B. B. Ingoldsby and S. Smith (Eds.), *Families in multicultural perspective* (pp. 5–35). New York: Guilford.

Smith, S. S. (2002, March 1). *NCHS dataline. Public health reports.* Available: www.highbeam.com/library/doc3.asp? docid=1G1:94042640 [2006, January 3].

Smith, T. W. (1994). *The demography of sexual behavior.* Menlo Park, CA: Kaiser Family Foundation.

Smith, T. W. (2001, October). *The emerging twenty-first century American family.* University of Chicago National Opinion Research Center. Available: www.norc.uchicago.edu/online/ emerge.pdf [1999 edition].

Smith, T. W. (2006). *American sexual behavior: Trends, sociodemographic differences, and risk behavior.* Chicago: National Opinion Research Center, GSS Topical Report No. 25. Available: www.norc.org [2007, November 11].

Smith, W. M., Jr. (1968). Family life education—Who needs it? *The Family Coordinator, 17,* 55–61.

Smock, P. J. (2004). The wax and wane of marriage: Prospects for marriage in the 21st century. *Journal of Marriage and Family, 66,* 966–973.

Smock, P. J., & Gupta, S. (2002). Cohabitation in contemporary North America. In A. Booth and A. C. Crouter (Eds.), *Just living together: Implications of cohabitation on families, children, and social policy* (pp. 53–84). Mahwah, NJ: Erlbaum.

Smock, P. J., Casper, L., & Wyse, J. (2008). Nonmarital cohabitation: Current knowledge and future directions for research. *Population Studies Center,* Report 08–648.

Smock, P., & Manning, W. (2004). Living together unmarried in the United States: Demographic perspectives and implications for family policy. *Law & Policy, 26*(1), 87–117.

Smock, W., Manning, W., & Porter, M. (2005). Everything's there except money: How money shapes decisions to marry among cohabitors. *Journal of Marriage and Family, 67*(3), 680–696.

Snarey, J., Son, L., Kuehne, V. S., Hauser, S., & Vaillant, G. (1987). The role of parenting in men's psychosocial development: A longitudinal study of early adulthood infertility and midlife generativity. *Developmental Psychology, 23,* 593–603.

Snyder, D. K., Gordon, K. C., & Baucom, D. H. (2004). Treating affair couples: Extending the written disclosure paradigm to relationship trauma. *Clinical Psychology: Science and Practice, 11*(2), 155–159.

Sokolow, J. A. (1983). *Eros and modernization: Sylvester Graham, health reform, and the origins of Victorian sexuality in America.* Rutherford, NJ: Farleigh Dickinson Press.

Solomon-Fears, C. (2008). Nonmarital childbearing: Trends, reasons, and public policy interventions. *CRS Report for Congress.* Order Code RL34756. Available: http://ftp.fas.org/ sgp/crs/misc/RL34756.pdf [2009, August 2].

Solot, D., & Miller, M. (2004). Affirmation of family diversity. *Alternatives to Marriage Project.* Available: www.unmarried .org/family.html [2004, October 10].

Somary, K., & Stricker, G. (1998). Becoming a grandparent: A longitudinal study of expectations and early experiences as a function of sex and lineage. *The Gerontologist, 38,* 53–61.

Sorgen, C. (2008). All about jealousy. Available: www.medicinenet .com [2008, November 6].

Soulliere, D. M. (2006). Wrestling with masculinity: Messages about manhood in the WWE. *Sex Roles, 55,* 1–12.

South, S. (1995). Do you need to shop around? Age at marriage, spousal alternatives, and marital dissolution. *Journal of Family Issues, 16,* 432–449.

Spence, J. T., & Helmreich, R. L. (1972). The attitudes toward women scale. *SAS Catalog of Selected Documents in Psychology, 2*(66).

Sprecher, S. (1989). The importance to males and females of physical attractiveness, earning potential, and expressiveness in initial attraction. *Sex Roles, 21,* 591–607.

Sprecher, S. (1998). Social exchange theories and sexuality. *The Journal of Sex Research, 35*(1), 32–44.

Sprecher, S. (2002). Sexual satisfaction in premarital relationships: Associations with satisfaction, love, commitment, and stability. *The Journal of Sex Research, 39*(13), 190–197.

Sprecher, S., & McKinney, K. (1993). *Sexuality.* Newbury Park, CA: Sage.

Sprecher, S., & Regan, P. (2000). Sexuality in a relational context. In C. Hendrick and S. S. Hendrick (Eds.), *Close relationships: A sourcebook* (pp. 217–227). Thousand Oaks, CA: Sage.

Sprecher, S., & Regan, P. (2002). Liking some things (in some people) more than others: Partner preferences in romantic relationships and friendships. *Journal of Social and Personal Relationships, 19,* 463–481.

Sprecher, S., Sullivan, Q., & Hatfield, E. (1994). Mate selection preferences: Gender differences examined in a national sample. *Journal of Personality and Social Psychology, 66,* 1074–1080.

Sprenkle, D. H., & Cyrus, C. (1983). Abandonment: The sudden stress of divorce. In C. R. Rigley and H. I. McCubbin (Eds.), *Stress and the family (Vol. 2): Coping with catastrophe* (pp. 53–75). New York: Bruner/Mazel.

Sprigg, P. (2004). Questions and answers: What's wrong with letting same-sex couples "marry"? (pp. 173–179). In E. Schroeder (Ed.), *Taking sides: Clashing views on controversial issues in family and personal relationships.* New York: McGraw-Hill.

Stacey, J., & Biblarz, T. J. (2001). (How) Does sexual orientation of parents matter? *American Sociological Review, 65,* 159–183.

Stack, P. F. (1998, September 20). Globally, polygamy is commonplace. *The Salt Lake Tribune.*

Stanley, S. M., & Fincham, F. D. (2002). The effects of divorce on children. *Couples Research and Therapy Newsletter, 8*(1), 7–10.

Starling, K. (2000, February). The joys and dangers of love on the internet. *Ebony.*

Starrels, M. E., Bould, S., & Nicholas, L. J. (1994). The feminization of poverty in the United States: Gender, race, ethnicity, and family factors. *Journal of Family Issues, 15,* 590–607.

Stein, P. (1981). *Single life: Unmarried adults in social context.* New York: St. Martin's Press.

Steinberg, L. (1998). Parent-child relationships. *Gale Encyclopedia of Childhood and Adolescence.* Farmington Hills, MI: Gale Group.

Steinberg, L., Lamborn, S. D., Darling, N., Mounts, N. S., & Dornbusch, S. M. (1994). Over-time changes in adjustment and competence among adolescents from authoritative, authoritarian, indulgent, and neglectful families. *Child Development, 65,* 754–770.

Steinberg, L., & Morris, A. S. (2001). Adolescent development. *Annual Review of Psychology, 52,* 83–110.

Steinberg, L., Mounts, N., Lamborn, S., & Dornbusch, S. (1991). Authoritative parenting and adolescent adjustment across various ecological niches. *Journal of Research on Adolescence, 1,* 19–36.

Stepfamily Association of America. (2009). What is a stepfamily? Available: www.saafamilies.org/faqs/fats.htm [2005, April 8].

Stephens, M. A. P., & Franks, M. M. (1999). Intergenerational relationships in later-life families: Adult daughters and sons as caregivers to aging parents. In J. C. Cavanaugh and S. K. Whitbourne (Eds.), *Gerontology: An interdisciplinary perspective* (pp. 329–354). New York: Oxford University Press.

Stephens, M. A. P., Franks, M. M., & Atienza, A. A. (1997). Where two roles intersect: Spillover between parent care and employment. *Psychology and Aging, 12,* 30–37.

Stephens, M. A. P., Townsend, A. L., Martire, L. M., & Druley, J. A. (2001). Balancing parent care with other roles: Interrole conflict of adult daughter caregivers. *Journal of Gerontology: Psychological Sciences, 56B,* P24–P34.

Sternberg, R. J. (1986). A triangular theory of love. *Psychological Review, 93,* 119–135.

Sternberg, R. J. (1988). *The psychology of love.* New Haven, CT: Yale University Press.

Stevens, D. P., Kiger, G., & Riley, P. J. (2006). His, hers, our ours? Work-to-family spillover, crossover, and family cohesion. *The Social Science Journal, 43,* 425–436.

Stewart, S. D. (1999). Disneyland dads, Disneyland moms? How nonresident parents spend time with their children. *Journal of Family Issues, 20,* 539–556.

Stone, G. (2007). Father post divorce well-being. *Journal of Divorce and Remarriage, 41,* 139–150.

Stoops, N. (2004). *Educational attainment in the United States: 2003.* Current Population Reports. Washington, DC: United States Census Bureau.

Straus, M. A. (1992). Children as witnesses to marital violence: A risk factor for lifelong problems among a nationally representative sample of American men and women. *Report of the twenty-third Ross roundtable.* Columbus, OH: Ross Laboratories.

Strohschein, L. (2005). Parental divorce and child mental health trajectories. *Journal of Marriage and Family, 67*(5), 1286–1300.

Strohschein, L., Gauthier, A. H., Campbell, R., & Kleparchuk, C. (2008). Parenting as a dynamic process: A test of the resource dilution hypothesis theory. *Journal of Marriage and Family, 70,* 670–683.

Stroup, A. L, & Pollock, G. E. (1999). Economic consequences of marital dissolution for Hispanics. *Journal of Divorce and Remarriage, 30*(1/2), 149–166.

Sue, D. W., & Sue, D. (2003). *Counseling the culturally different: Theory and practice* (2nd ed.). New York: Wiley.

Sullivan, H. S. (1953). *The interpersonal theory of psychiatry.* New York: Norton.

Sullivan, M. (2009). *Wage gap is wider for women of color.* Women's Policy Research. Available: www.iwpr.org [2009, February 5].

Survey of Army Families IV. (2001). Available: www.armymwr.com/corporate/docs/planning/SAFIVExutiveSummary.pdf [2009, January 28].

Sutton, P. D., & Munson, M. L. (2006). Births, marriages, divorces, and deaths: Provisional data for September 2005. *National Vital Statistics Reports, 54*(15), Hyattsville, MD: National Center for Health Statistics.

Sweeney, M. M., & Phillips, J. A. (2004). Understanding racial differences in marital disruption: Recent trends and explanations. *Journal of Marriage and Family, 66,* 239–250.

Swensen, C. H., Eskew, R. W., & Kohlhepp, K. A. (1981). Stage of family life cycle, ego development, and the marriage relationship. *Journal of Marriage and Family, 43,* 841–853.

Swenson, C. H., & Trahaug, G. (1985). Commitment in the long-term marriage relationship. *Journal of Marriage and the Family, 47*(4), 939–945.

Symons, D. (1979). *The evolution of human sexuality.* Oxford, England: Oxford University Press.

Szinovacz, M. E. (1998). Grandparents today: A demographic profile. *The Gerontologist, 38,* 37–52.

Taffel, R. (1994). *Why parents disagree: How men and women parent differently and how we can work together.* New York: William Morrow.

Tannen, D. (1990). *You just don't understand: Women and men in conversation.* New York: William Morrow.

Tanner, J. M. (1990). *Foetus into man: Physical growth from conception to maturity.* Cambridge, MA: Harvard University Press.

Taylor, R. (2002). *Minority families in the United States: A multicultural perspective.* Upper Saddle River, NJ: Prentice Hall.

Taylor, R. L. (2000). Diversity within African American families. In D. H. Demo, K. R. Allen, and M.A. Fine (Eds.), *Handbook of family diversity* (pp. 232–251). New York: Oxford.

Taylor, R. L., Yellowbird, M., & Snipp, C. M. (2002). Native American families in the United States: Part IV; American Indian Families: Chapter 12. In R. Taylor, *Minority families in the United States: A multicultural perspective* (pp. 225–249). Upper Saddle River, NJ: Prentice Hall.

Taylor, S. E., Klein, L. C., Lewis, B. P., Grunewald, T. L., Gurung, R. A., & Updegraff, J. A. (2000). Biobehavioral responses to stress in females: Tend-and-befriend, not fight-or-flight. *Psychology Review, 107*(3), 411–429.

Teachman, J. D. (2002). Childhood living arrangements and the intergenerational transmission of divorce. *Journal of Marriage and the Family, 64,* 717–729.

Teachman, J. D. (2003). Premarital sex, premarital cohabitation, and the risk of subsequent marital dissolution among women. *Journal of Marriage and Family, 65*(2), 444–455.

Teachman, J. D., & Polonko, K. (1990). Cohabitation and marital stability. *Social Forces, 69,* 207–220.

Teachman, J. D., & Tedrow, D. (2008). Divorce, race, and military service: More than equal pay and equal opportunity. *Journal of Marriage and Family, 70,* 1030–1044.

Teachman, J. D., Tedrow, L. M., & Crowder, K. D. (2000). The changing demography of America's families. *Journal of Marriage & Family, 62*(4), 1234–1246.

Tennov, D. (1979). *Love and limerence: The experience of being in love.* New York: Steing and Day.

Thacker, S. B., & Banta, H. D. (1983). Benefits and risks of episiotomy: An interpretive review of the English language literature. *Obstetrics and Gynecological Survey, 38*(6), 322–338.

Theisen, C. (2004). *The parent coach plan: Eight parenting responsibilities.* Available: www.parentcoachplan.com. [2006, March 26].

Thibaut, J. W., & Kelley, H. H. (1959). *The social psychology of groups.* New York: John Wiley.

Thomas, A., & Sawhill, I. (2005). For love *and* money? The impact of family structure on family income. *The Future of Children, 15*(2), 57–74.

Thomas-Hunt, M., & Phillips, K. W. (2004). When what you know is not enough: Expertise and gender dynamics in task groups. *Personality and Social Psychology Bulletin, 30*(12), 1585–1598.

Thompson, A. (1984). Emotional and sexual components of extramarital relations. *Journal of Marriage and the Family, 46,* 35–42.

Thompson, L. Y., Snyder, C. R., Hoffman, L., Michael, S. T., Rasmussen, H. N., Billings, L. S., et al. (2005). Dispositional forgiveness of self, others, and situations. *Journal of Personality, 73,* 313–359.

Thompson, P., Itzin, C., & Abendstern, M. (1991). *I don't feel old: The experience of later life.* New York: Oxford University Press.

Thorne, B. (1986). Girls and boys together … but mostly apart: Gender arrangements in elementary schools. In W. W. Hartup and Z. Rubin (Eds.), *Relationships and development* (pp. 167–184). Hillsdale, NJ: Erlbaum.

Thornhill, R., & Gangestad, S. W. (1993). Human facial beauty: Averageness, symmetry and parasite resistance. *Human Nature, 4,* 237–269.

Thornton, A. (1991). Influence of the marital history of parents on the marital and cohabitational experiences of children. *American Journal of Sociology, 96,* 868–894.

Thorp, J. M., & Bowes, W. A. (1989). Episiotomy: Can its routine use be defended? *American Journal of Obstetrics and Gynecology, 160,* 1027–1039.

Timmermann, G. M. (1991). A concept analysis of intimacy. *Issues of Mental Health Nursing, 12*(1), 19–30.

Tolson, T. F. J., & Wilson, M. N. (1990). Familial support in the black community. *Journal of Clinical Child Psychology, 19*(4), 347–355.

Tooman, C. (1970, April). It goes to bed with you, no matter what you are. *Marriage,* 28–31.

Torres, M. N. (1993, July). Cultural sensitivity. *ADVANCE for Nurse Practitioners,* 16–18.

Townsend, J. (1995). Sex without emotional involvement: An evolutionary interpretation of sex differences. *Archives of Sexual Behavior, 24,* 173–2005.

Townsend, J. M., & Levy, G. D. (1990). Effects of potential partners' physical attractiveness and socioeconomic status on sexuality and partner selection. *Archives of Sexual Behavior, 19,* 149–164.

Townsend, J. M., & Roberts, L. W. (1993). Gender differences in mate selection among law students: Divergence and convergence criteria. *Journal of Psychology, 29,* 507–528.

Trager, J. (2009). STDs and oral sex. *Sexual Health Communication.* Available: http://www.healthcentral.com/sexual-health/safesex-270837-5.html?ic=506016 [2009, August 1].

Trask, B. S., & Koivunen, J. M. (2006). Trends in marriage and cohabitation in culturally diverse families. In B. S. Trask and R. Hamon (Eds.), *Cultural diversity and families: Expanding perspectives* (pp. 121–136), Thousand Oaks, CA: Sage.

Treas, J., & Giesen, D. (2000). Sexual infidelity among married and cohabiting Americans. *Journal of Marriage and the Family, 64,* 48–60.

Trent, K., & South, S. J. (2003). Spousal alternatives and marital relations. *Journal of Family Issues, 24,* 787–810.

Triandis, H., & Suh, E. (2002). Cultural influences on personality. *Annual Review of Psychology. 53,* 133–160.

Troll, L., & Fingerman, K. L. (1996). Parent/child bonds in adulthood. In C. Malestesta-Magai and S. McFadden (Eds.), *Handbook of emotion, adult development and aging.* Orlando, FL: Academic Press.

Trybulski, J. (2005). The long-term phenomena of women's postabortion experiences. *Western Journal of Nursing Research, 27*(5), 559–576.

Tschann, J. (1988). Self-disclosure in adult friendship: Gender and marital status differences. *Journal of Social and Personal Relationships, 5,* 65–81.

Tsuda, T., Aoyama, H., & Froom, J. (1994). Primary health care in Japan and the United States. *Social Science and Medicine, 38*(4), 489–495.

Turner's Syndrome Society. (2009). Available: http://www.turner-syndrome-us.org/ [July 13, 2009].

Turner, L. H., & West, R. (2006). *Perspectives on family communication* (3rd ed.). Boston: McGraw-Hill.

Ubillos, S., Paez, D., & Gonzalez, J. L. (2000). Culture and sexual behavior. *Psiothema, 12,* 70–82.

Udry, J. R. (1988). Biological predispositions and social control in adolescent sexual behavior. *American Sociological Review, 53,* 709–722.

Uhlenberg, P., Cooney, T. M., & Boyd, R. (1990). Divorce for women after midlife. *Journal of Gerontology: Social Sciences, 45,* S3–S11.

Umaña-Taylor, A. J., & Fine, M. A. (2003). Predicting commitment to wed among Hispanic and Anglo partners. *Journal of Marriage and Family, 65,* 117–139.

Umberson, D. (1987). Family status and health behaviors: Social control as a dimension of social integration. *Journal of Health and Social Behavior, 28,* 306–319.

Umberson, D. (1992). Gender, marital status, and the social control of health behavior. *Social Science and Medicine, 35,* 907–917.

U.S. Bureau of Labor Statistics. (2005). http://www.census.gov/Press-Release/www/releases/archives/facts_for_features_special_editions/004109.html [2009, August 11].

U.S. Bureau of Labor Statistics. (2008). *Highlights of women's earnings in 2007.* BLS Report 1008.

U.S. Census Bureau. (2001). *Statistical abstract of unmarried partners living together.* Washington, DC: United States Census Bureau.

U.S. Census Bureau. (2002). *Diversity continues to grow in the U.S.* Available: www.factfinder.census.gov [2004, October 9].

U.S. Census Bureau. (2004a). *America's families and living arrangements: 2004. Table C-2.* Available: www.census.gov/population/www/socdemo/hhfam/cps2004.html [2006, January 21].

U.S. Census Bureau (2004b). *Average number of children per family. Table ST-F1-1990.* Available: www.census.gov/population/socdemo/hh-fam/tabST-F1-1990.pdf [2006, April 29].

U.S. Census Bureau. (2004c). *Current population survey: Families and living arrangements: Historical tables. Table CH-2: Living arrangements of White children under 18 years old: 1960 to present; Table CH-3: Living arrangements of Black children under 18 years old: 1960 to present; Table CH-4: Living arrangements of Hispanic children under 18 years old: 1970 to present.* Available: www.census.gov/population/www/socdemo/hh-fam.html#history [2006, January 21].

U.S. Census Bureau. (2004d). *Source and accuracy of estimates for income, poverty, and health insurance coverage in the United States: 2004.* Available: www.census.gov/hhes/www/income/p60_220sa.pdf [2006, April 29].

U.S. Census Bureau. (2004e). *U.S. interim projections by age, sex, race, and Hispanic origin.* Available: www.census.gov/ipc/www/usinterimproj/ [2006, January 21].

U.S. Census Bureau. (2005a). *Alternative income estimates in the United States: 2003.* Available: www.census.gov/prod/2003/p60-228.pdf.

U.S. Census Bureau. (2005b). Estimated median age at first marriage. *United States Census Bureau Current Population Survey: March and annual social and economic supplements, 2005 and earlier.* Available: www.census.gov/population/socdemo/h-fam/ms2.pdf [2006, May 26].

U.S. Census Bureau. (2005c). *Historical income tables: Families. Table F-7: Type of family (all races) by median and mean income: 1947 to 2001.* Available: www.census.gov/hhes/income/histinc/f07.html [2005, September 5].

U.S. Census Bureau. (2006). *How many mothers?* Available: www.cdc.gov/nchs/data/nvsr/nvsr54/nvsr54_02.pdf [2009, January 5].

U.S. Census Bureau. (2006). Marital status of the population by sex, race, and Hispanic origin: 1990–2006. *Current Population Reports,* P20-537. Available: www.census.gov/population/www/socdemo/hh-fam.html. [2008, July 12].

U.S. Census Bureau. (2006). *People 18 years old and over, by total money income in 2005, work experience in 2005, age, race, Hispanic origin, and sex.* Available: www.pubdb3.census.gov/macro/032006/perinc/new02_001.htm [2009, March 17].

U.S. Census Bureau. (2006). *Statistical abstract of the United States* (122nd ed.). Washington, DC: U.S. Government Printing Office.

U.S. Census Bureau. (2006a). *Annual estimates by race alone.* Available: www.census.gov/popest/states/asrh/tables/SC-EST2003-04.pdf [2008, September 6].

U.S. Census Bureau. (2006a). *Personal income distribution for females, 25+ according to educational attainment.* Available: http://pubdb3.census.gov/macro/032006/perinc/new03_128.htm [2008, November 12].

U.S. Census Bureau. (2006b). *Personal income distribution for males, 25+ according to educational attainment.* Available: http://pubdb3.census.gov/macro/032006/perinc/new03_128.htm [2008, November 12].

U.S. Census Bureau. (2006b). *Money income of households. Current Population Reports,* P60-231. Available: www.census.gov/hhes/www/income/histinc/h05.html [2008, August 20].

U.S. Census Bureau. (2007). *Asian/Pacific American Heritage Month.* CB07-FF.05, March 1, 2007. Available: http://www.for_features_special_editions/009714.html [2009, August 11].

U.S. Census Bureau. (2007). *Population 65 years and over in the United States.* S0103. Available: www.factfinder.census.gov [2009, February 28].

U.S. Census Bureau. (2007). *Single-parent households showed little variation since 1994.* CB07-46 (March 27). Available: http://www.census.gov/Press-Release/www/releases/archives/families_households/009842.html [2009, August 11].

U.S. Census Bureau. (2007). American Community Survey: Population 65 years and older in the United States, 2005–2007. S0103. Available: http://www.factdinfer.census.gov [2009, August 12].

U.S. Census Bureau. (2007a). *Income quintiles, 2007.* Available: www.pubdb3.census.gov/macro/032007/hhinc/new05_000.htm [2008, August 26].

U.S. Census Bureau. (2007b). *Minority population tops 100 million.* Available: www.census.gov/population/www/socdemo/compraceho.html [2008, September 1].

U.S. Census Bureau. (2008). *Facts for Features.* CB08-FF.02. Available: http://www.census.gov/Press-Release/www/

releases/archives/facts_for_features_special_editions/010968.html [2009, August 12].

U.S. Census Bureau. (2008a). *Facts for features.* Available: www.census.gov/Press-Release/www/releases/archives/facts_for_features_special_editions/010968.htm [2008, August 19].

U.S. Census Bureau. (2008b). *Current Population Survey, 2007 Annual Social and Economic Supplement.* Available: www.census.gov/population/www/socdemo/hh-fam.html [2008, August 20].

U.S. Census Bureau. (2008b). *Unmarried and single Americans.* CB08-FF.16 Available: www.census.gov/acs/www/Products/users_guide/index.htm [2009, January 25].

U.S. Census Bureau. (2008c). *Living arrangements of children: Household economic studies. Current Populations,* P70-114. Washington, DC: Author.

U.S. Census Bureau. (2008d). *Same-sex "marriage" will not be counted in 2010 U.S. Census.* Available: www.lifesitenews.com/ldn/2008/jul/08071803.htm [2008, August 23].

U.S. Census Bureau. (2008e). *State of the Union 2008: By the numbers.* Available: www.reuters.com/article/pressRelease/idUS155591+29-Jan-2008+PRN20080129.html [2008, August 23].

U.S. Census Bureau. (2008f). *Asian/Pacific American heritage month: May 2008.* Available: www.census.gov/Press-Release/www/releases/archives/facts_for_features_special_editions/011602.html.

U.S. Census Bureau. (2008g). *American and Alaska Native heritage month: November 2007.* Available: www.census.gov/Press_Release/www/releases/archives/facts_for_features_special_editions/010849.html [2008, September 2].

U.S. Census Bureau. (2008i). *Custodial mothers and fathers and their child support.* Available: www.census.gov/Press-Release/www/releases/archives/children/010634.html [2009, February 14].

U.S. Census Bureau (2008j). *Household income rises, poverty rate unchanged, number of uninsured down.* CB08-129. Available: www.census.gov/Press-Release/www/releases/archives/income_wealth/012528.html [2009, July 27].

U.S. Census Bureau (2008k). *American Indian and Alaska Native Heritage Month: November 2008.* CB08-FF.18. Available: www.census.gov/Press-Release/www/releases/archives/facts_for_features_special_editions/012782.html [2009, July 27].

U.S. Department of Agriculture. (2008). *The cost of raising children.* Available: www.usda.gov [2009, January 12].

U.S. Department of Defense. (2008). *Military divorce rate.* Available: www.defenselink.mil/ [2009, February 14].

U.S. Department of Education. (2008). *Federal student aid: Repaying your student loans.* Available: http://studentaid.ed.gov/PORTALSWebApp/students/english/repaying.jsp [2008, November 12].

U.S. Department of Health and Human Services (2005). *Administration on Children, Youth, and Families, Child Maltreatment 2003.* Washington, DC: U.S. Government Printing Office, 2005. Available: www.acf.hss.gov/programs/cb/publications/cm03/index.htm [2006, June 22].

U.S. Department of Health and Human Services. (2003). *Researchers identify a possible cause of infertility in some women with endometriosis.* National Institute of Child Health and Human Development, June 17, 2003. Available: http://www.nichd.nih.gov/news/releases/infertility.cfm [2009, August 1].

U.S. Department of Health and Human Services. (2006). *Fertility, family planning, and the health of U.S. women: Data from the 2002 National Survey of Family Growth.* Series 23–25. Hyattesville, MD: National Center for Health Statistics.

U.S. Department of Health and Human Services. (2006). *Seventh Annual Report to Congress* (Washington, DC: A-283). Available: www.acf.hhs.gov/programs/ofa/annualreport7/Appendix/TANF_7th_Report?Appendix.Pdf. [2009, February 2].

U.S. Department of Health and Human Services. (2009). *Noncustodial parents participation in their children's lives: Evidence from the survey of income and program participation.* Available: www.hhs.gov [2009, February 25].

U.S. Department of Health and Human Services, Administration on Children, Youth and Families. (2009). *Child maltreatment: 2007.* Washington, DC: U.S. Government Printing Office. Available: http://www.childwelfare.gov/faq.cfm [2009, August 14].

U.S. Department of Justice. (2003). *Sourcebook of criminal justice statistics.* Washington, DC: U.S. Government Printing Office.

U.S. Department of Justice. (2007). *Stalking and cyberstalking.* Available: http://www.ojp.usdoj.gov/nij/topics/crime/stalking/welcome.htm [2009, July 15].

U.S. Department of Justice. (2009). *Intimate partner violence in the United States: Bureau of Justice Statistics.* Available: www.ojp-usdoj.gov/bjs/ [2009, February 27].

U.S. Department of Labor. (2007). *In dual-earner couples, family roles are changing in U.S.* (March 21). Available: http://www.america.gov/st/washfile-english/2007/March/20070321162913berehellek0.6708338.html [2009, August 11].

U.S. Department of Labor. (2008). *Quick stats on women workers, 2008.* Available: www.dol.gov/wb/stats/main.htm [July 13, 2009].

U.S. Department of Labor, Bureau of Labor Statistics. (2003). *Employment status of the civilian population by sex and age.* Available: www.bld.gov/news.release/empsit.t01.htm [2005, May 30].

U.S. Department of Labor, Bureau of Labor Statistics. (2008). *Women's share of labor force.* Available: www.bls.gov [2008, September 11].

U.S. Economic Research Service. (2004). *Rural poverty at a glance.* Available: www.ers.usda.gov/briefing/IncomePovertyWelfare/htm [2006, January 21].

Urbaniak, G. C. (2003). Physical attractiveness and the "nice guy paradox": Do nice guys really finish last? *Sex Roles, 49,* 413–426.

van Ijzendoorn, M. H. (1995). Adult attachment representations, parental responsiveness, and infant attachment: A meta-analysis on the predictive validity of the Adult Attachment Interview. *Psychological Bulletin, 117,* 387–403.

Vandell, D. L., & Corsaniti, M. A. (1990). Childcare and the family: Complex contributors to child development. In K. McCartney (Ed.), *Childcare and maternal employment.* San Francisco: Jossey-Bass.

Vangelisti, A. L. (2001). Making sense of hurtful interactions in close relationships: When hurt feelings create distance. In V. Manusov and J. H. Harvey (Eds.), *Attribution, communication behavior, and close relationships: Advances in personal relations* (pp. 38–58). New York: Cambridge University Press.

Vangelisti, A. L. & Young, S. L. (2000). When words hurt: The effects of perceived intentionality on interpersonal relationships. *Journal of Social and Personal Relationships, 17,* 393–424.

Varcoe, K. P., Emper, N., & Lees, N. (2002). Working with military audiences to improve financial well-being. *JFCS(94)*1, 33–34.

Vaughan, P. (1999). Dealing with infidelity. *The Washington Post,* March 30.

Veevers, J. E. (1980). *Childless by choice.* Toronto: Butterworth.

Venkatraman, M. M. (1995). A cross-cultural study of the subjective well-being of married elderly persons in the United States and India. *Journals of Gerontology: Social Sciences, 50B,* S35–44.

Ventura, J., & Reed, M. (1998). *Divorce for dummies.* New York: Wiley.

Veroff, J., Douvan, E., & Kulka, R.A. (1981). *The inner American: A self-portrait from 1957 to 1976.* New York: Basic Books.

Villarruel, A. M. (1998). Cultural influences on the sexual attitudes, beliefs, and norms of young Latina adolescents. *Journal of the Society of Pediatric Nurses, 3*(2), 69–80.

Villarruel, A. M., & Rodriguez, D. (2003). Beyond stereotypes: Promoting safer sex behaviors among Latino adolescents. *Journal of Obstetric, Gynecologic, and Neonatal Nursing, 32*(2), 258–263.

Vinick, B. H. (1978). Remarriage in old age. *Journal of Geriatric Psychiatry, 11*(1), 75–77.

Vinick, B. H. (1986). Difficult task: Caring for an invalid wife. *Medical Aspects of Human Sexuality, 20,* 141–145.

Violata, C., & Russell, C. (1994). *Effects of non-maternal care on child development: A meta-analysis of published research.* Paper presented to the Canadian Psychological Association, Pentticton, British Columbia.

Visher, E. B., & Visher, J. S. (1993). *Stepfamilies: Myths and realities.* New York: Citadel Press.

Visher, E., & Visher, J. (1982). *How to win as a stepfamily.* New York: Dembner.

Visher, E., & Visher, J. (1996). *Therapy with stepfamilies.* New York: Bruner/Mazel.

Vobejda, B. (1993, June 24). Census Bureau says rapid changes in family size, style are slowing. *The Washington Post,* p. A21.

Vohs, D., Cantonese, K. R., & Baumeister, R. F. (2004). Sex in "his" versus "her" relationships. In J. H. Harvey, A. Wenzel, and S. Sprecher (Eds.), *Handbook of sexuality in close relationships* (pp. 455–474). Mahwah, NJ: Erlbaum.

von Sydow, K. (1999). Sexuality during pregnancy and after childbirth: A metacontent analysis of 59 studies. *Journal of Psychosomatic Research, 47,* 27–49.

Voydanoff, P. (1983). Unemployment: Family, strategies for adaptation. In C. R. Figley and H. I. McCubbin (Eds.), *Stress and the family, II—Coping with catastrophe* (pp. 90–102). New York: Brunner/Mazel.

Vuong, C. (2003). *The soulmate manifesto: Uniting all soulmate believers in an effort to solve dating.* San Francisco: Aluran.

Wade, L., Kremer, E., & Brown, J. (2005). The incidental orgasm: The presence of clitoral knowledge and the absence of orgasm for women. *Women and Health, 42*(1), 117–138.

Wade, N. G., Bailey, D. C., & Shaffer, P. (2005). Helping clients heal: Does forgiveness make a difference? *Professional Psychology: Research and Practice, 36*(6), 634–641.

Wage Project. (2009). *Men outearn women in almost all occupations.* National Council of Women's Organizations. Available: http://www.womensorganizations.org/index.php?option=com_content&task=view&id=208&Itemid=82 [2009, August 11].

Wainright, J. L., & Patterson, C. J. (2006). Delinquency, victimization, and substance use among adolescents with female same-sex parents. *Journal of Family Psychology, 20,* 526–530.

Waite, L. (1995). Does marriage matter? *Demography, 32,* 483–507.

Waite, L. J., & Gallagher, M. (2000). *The case for marriage: Why married people are happier, healthier, and better off financially.* New York: Doubleday.

Waite, L., & Gallagher, M. (2001). *The case for marriage: Why married people are happier, healthier, and better off financially.* New York: Random House.

Waite, L., & Gallagher, M. (2002). *The case for marriage.* New York: Doubleday.

Waite, L., & Joyner, K. (2001). Emotional satisfaction and physical pleasure in sexual unions: Time horizon, sexual behavior, and sexual exclusivity. *Journal of Marriage and Family, 63,* 247–264.

Walker, L. E. (1979). *The battered woman.* New York: Harper & Row.

Wallace, S. R., & Silverberg Koerner, S. (2003). Influence of child and family factors on judicial decisions in contested custody cases. *Family Relations, 52,* 180–188.

Wallerstein, J., & Kelly, J. (1980). *Surviving the break-up: How children actually cope with divorce.* New York: Basic.

Wallerstein, J., & Lewis, M. (2004). The unexpected legacy of divorce: Report of a 25-year study. *Psychoanalytic Psychology, 21,* 353–370.

Wallerstein, J. S. (1987). Children of divorce: Report of a ten-year follow-up of early latency-age children. *American Journal of Orthopsychiatry, 57,* 199–211.

Wallerstein, J. S. (1991). The long-term effects of divorce on children: A review. *Journal of the American Academy of Child and Adolescent Psychiatry, 30,* 349–360.

Wallerstein, J. S. (1998). Children of divorce: A society in search of policy. In M. A. Mason, A. Skolnick, and S. D. Sugarman (Eds.), *All our families: New policies for a new century* (pp. 66–94). New York: Oxford University Press.

Wallerstein, J. S., Lewis, J. M., & Blakeslee, S. (2000). *The unexpected legacy of divorce: A 25-year landmark study.* New York: Hyperion.

Walsh, F. (2003). Family resilience: A framework for clinical practice. *Family Process, 42,* 1–18.

Waring, E. M. (1984). The measurement of marital intimacy. *Journal of Marital and Family Therapy, 10,* 185–192.

Warshak, R. (2000). Remarriage as a trigger of parental alienation syndrome. *American Journal of Family Therapy, 28*(3), 229–241.

Waters, E. (2004). *Urban tribes: Are friends the new family?* New York: Bloombury Publishers.

Watkins, E. S. (2008). Conceiving the future: Pronatalism, reproduction, and the family in the United States, 1890–1938. *Journal of Interdisciplinary History, 39*(1), 144–145.

Waynforth, D. (2001). Mate-choice trade-offs and women's preference for physically attractive men. *Human Nature, 12*, 207–220.

Webster, B. H., Jr., & Bishaw, A. (2007). *Income, earnings, and poverty data from the 2006 American Community Survey*, 5. U.S. Census Bureau, American Community Survey Reports, ACS-08. Washington, DC: U.S. Government Printing Office. Available: http://www.census.gov/prod/2007pubs/acs-08.pdf. [2009, August 11].

Weeks, D. J. (2002). Sex for the mature adult: Health, self-esteem and countering ageist stereotypes. *Sexual and Relationship Therapy, 17*(3), 231–240.

Weiderman, M. W. (1993). Evolved gender differences in mate preferences: Evidence from personal advertisements. *Ethology and Sociobiology, 14*, 331–352.

Weill, S. (2005). *The real truth about teens and sex.* New York: Penguin.

Weinstein, E., & Rosen, E. (2006). *Teaching about human sexuality and family: A skills-based approach.* Belmont, CA: Wadsworth.

Weinstock, H., Berman, S., & Cates, W. (2004). Sexually transmitted diseases among American youth: Incidence and prevalence estimates. *Perspectives Sex Reproductive Health, 36*(1), 6–10.

Weiss, H. B. (1990). Beyond *parens patriae:* Building policies and programs to care for our own and others' children. *Children and Youth Services Review, 12*, 269–284.

Weiss, R. (1969). The fund of sociability. *Transaction, 6*(9), 36–43.

Weiss, R. S. (1982). Attachment in adult life. In C. M. Parkes and J. Stevenson-Hinde (Eds.), *The place of attachment in human behavior* (pp. 171–184). New York: Basic Books.

Weiten, W. (1997). *Psychology: Themes and variations, briefer version* (3rd ed.). Pacific Grove, CA: Brooks/Cole.

Welch, K. (2004). *Development: Journey through childhood and adolescence.* Boston: Allyn & Bacon.

Wells, G. (1986). *The meaning makers: Children learning language and using language to learn.* Portsmouth, NH: Heinemann.

Wells, K. R. (2001). Premature ejaculation. *The Gale Encyclopedia of Medicine* (2nd ed). Farmington Hills, MI: Gale Group.

West, L., Anderson, J., & Duck, S. (1996). Crossing the barriers to friendships between men and women. In J. T. Wood (Ed.), *Gendered relationships* (pp. 111–127). Mountain View, CA: Mayfield.

Wester, S. R., Vogel, D. L., Wei, M., & McLain, R. (2006). African American men, gender role conflict, and psychological distress: The role of racial identity. *Journal of Counseling and Development, 84*, 419–429.

Weston, R., & Qu, L. (2001, Autumn). Men's and women's reasons for not having children. *Family Matters.*

Wheaton, B. (1994). Sampling the stress universe. In W. R. Avison and I. H. Gotlib (Eds.), *Stress and mental health: Contemporary issues and prospects for the future.* New York: Plenum Press.

Whelan, R. (1993). *Broken homes and battered children: A study of the relationship between child abuse and family type.* London: Family Education Trust.

Whisman, M. A., Dixon, A. E., & Johnson, B. (1997). Therapists' perspectives of couple problems and treatment issues in couple therapy. *Journal of Family Psychology, 11*, 361–366.

Whitbourne, S. K., & Weinstock, C. (1979). *Adult development: The differentiation of experience.* New York: Holt, Rinehart & Winston.

White, G. L. (1981). A model of romantic Jealousy. *Motivation and Emotion, 5*, 295–310.

White, J. (2003, Sept./Oct.). Sex and gender confusion: Our sense of being manly or womanly. *Indian Life.*

White, J. M., & Klein, D. M. (2008). *Family theories:* An introduction (3rd ed.). Thousand Oaks, CA: Sage.

White, L, & Rogers, S. J. (2000). Economic circumstances and family outcomes: A review of the 1990s. *Journal of Marriage and Family, 52*, 904–12.

White, L. (1990). Determinants of divorce: A review of research in the eighties. *Journal of Marriage and the Family, 52*, 904–912.

White, L., & Gilbreth, J. G. (2001). When children have two fathers: Effects of relationships with stepfathers and noncustodial fathers on adolescent outcomes. *Journal of Marriage and Family, 63*, 155–167.

White, L. K. (1991). Divorce over the life course: The role of marital happiness. *Journal of Family Issues, 12*, 5–21.

White, L. K., & Rogers, S. J. (2000). Economic circumstances and family outcomes: A review of the 1990s. *Journal of Marriage and the Family, 62*, 1035–1051.

White, T. M., Townsend, A. L., & Stephens, M. A. P. (2000). Comparisons of African American and White women in the parent care role. *The Gerontologist, 40*, 718–728.

Whitehead, B. (2004, April 4). Testimony before the United States Senate Committee on Health Education, Labor and Pensions Subcommittee on Children and Families.

Wickrama K. A. S., Lorenz, F. O., Conger, R. D., & Elder, G. H. (2006). Changes in family financial circumstances and the physical health of married and recently divorced mothers. *Social Science and Medicine 63*, 123–136.

Wickrama, K. A. S., Lorenze, F., Wallace, L., Peiris, L., Conger, R., & Elder, G. (2001). Family influence on physical health during the middle years: The case of onset hypertension. *Journal of Marriage and the Family, 63*, 527–539.

Wiederman, M. W. (1997). Extramarital sex: Prevalence and correlates in a national survey. *Journal of Sex Research, 34*, 167–174.

Wiederman, M. W. (1999). Volunteer bias in sexuality research using college student participants. *The Journal of Sex Research, 36*, 59–66.

Wiederman, M. W. (2005). The gendered nature of sexual scripts. *The Family Journal: Counseling and Therapy for Couples and Families, 13*(4), 496–502.

Wilcox, S. (2003). The effects of widowhood on physical and mental health, health behaviors, and health outcomes: The women's health initiative. *Health Psychology, 22*(5), 1–9.

Wildermuth, S. M., & Vogl-Bauer, S. (2007). We met on the net: Exploring the perceptions of online romantic relationship participants. *Southern Communication Journal, 72*(3), 211–227.

Williams, D. G. (1985). Gender, masculinity-femininity, and emotional intimacy in same-sex friendships. *Sex Roles, 12*, 587–600.

Williams, G. B. (2000). Grief after elective abortions. *AWOHNN Lifelines, 4*(2), 37–40.

Williams, J. E., & Best, D. L. (1990). *Measuring sex stereotypes: A multination study.* Newbury Park, CA: Sage.

Williams, K., & Dunne-Bryant, A. (2006). Divorce and adult psychological well-being: Clarifying the role of gender and child age. *Journal of Marriage and Family, 68,* 1178–1196.

Wilmouth, J., & Koso, G. (2002). Does marital history matter? Marital status and wealth outcomes among pre-retirement adults. *Journal of Marriage and the Family, 64,* 254–268.

Wisconsin Department of Health and Family Services. (2003, May). *The Wisconsin plan to prevent adolescent pregnancy.* Madison: Wisconsin Department of Health and Family Services.

Witmer, D. (2005). *Dating violence.* Available: www.parentingteens.about.com/es/daterape [2005, October 29].

Witt, S. (1997). Parental influence on children's socialization to gender roles. *Adolescence, 32,* 253–258.

Wood, E., Desmarais, S., & Gugula, S. (2002). The impact of parenting experience on gender stereotyped toy play of children. *Sex Roles, 47,* 39–49.

Wood, J. T. (1982). Communication and relational culture: Bases for the study of human relationships. *Communication Quarterly, 30,* 75–84.

Wooden, M. (1999). Job insecurity and job instability: Getting the facts straight. *BCA Papers, 1*(1), 14–18.

World Factbook. (2006). *Crude birth rates and fertility rates.* Available: www.enwikipedia.org/The_World_Factbook#Sources [2006, March 18].

World Health Organization. (1985). Appropriate technology for birth. *Lancet, 2*(8452), 436–437.

Wu, Z. (2007, October 23). Shacked up: A demographic profile of non-marital cohabitation. Paper presented on the Breakfast on the Hill Seminar Series, Ottawa, Ontario.

Wu, Z., & Penning, M. J. (1997). Marital instability after midlife. *Journal of Family Issues, 18*(5), 459–478.

Wyckoff, S. C., Miller, K. S., Forehand, R., Bau, J. J., Fasula, A., Long, N., & Armistead, L. (2008). Patterns of sexuality communication between preadolescents and their mothers and fathers. *Journal of Child and Family Studies, 17,* 649–662.

Xu, Y., & Burleson, B. (2004). The association of experienced spousal support with marital satisfaction: Evaluating the moderating effects of sex, culture, and type of support. *Journal of Family Communication, 4*(2), 123–145.

Yamaguchi, K., & Fergusson, L. R. (1995). The stopping and spacing of childbirths and their birth history predictors: Rational choice theory and event history analysis. *American Sociological Review, 60,* 272–289.

Yeung, W. J., Sandberg, J., Davis-Kean P., & Hofferth, S. (2001). Children's time-use with fathers in intact families. *Journal of Marriage and the Family, 63*(1), 136–154.

Yim, J. Y., & Mahalingam, R. (2006). Culture, masculinity, and psychological well-being in Punjab, India. *Sex Roles, 55,* 715–724.

Young, M., Young, D., & Luquis, T. (2000). Sexual satisfaction among married women. *American Journal of Health Studies, 16*(2), 73–84.

Younger, J. W., Piferi, R. L., Jobe, R. L., & Lawler, J. A. (2004). Dimensions of forgiveness: The views of laypersons. *Journal of Social and Personal Relationships, 21,* 837–855.

Zahedi, A. (2007). Contested meanings of the veil and political ideologies of Iranian regimes. *Journal of Middle East Women's Studies, 3*(3), 75–99.

Zand, D., & Rose, S. (1992). Establishing lesbian relationships. Unpublished manuscript, University of Missouri, St. Louis.

Zarit, S. H., Birkel, R. C., & Malonebeach, E. (1989). Spouses as caregivers: Stresses and interventions. In M. Z. Goldstein (Ed.), *Family involvement in the treatment of the frail elderly.* Washington, DC: American Psychiatric Association.

Zhang, L., Li, X., Shah, I. H., Baldwin, W., & Stanton, B. (2007). Parent-adolescent sex communication in China. *The European Journal of Contraception and Reproductive Health Care, 12*(2), 138–147.

Zogby International. (2004, January 28). *Survey on parental opinions and character of relationship-based abstinence education vs. comprehensive (or abstinence-first, then condoms) sex education.*

Zweig, M. (2004). *What's class got to do with it? American society in the twenty-first century.* Ithaca, NY: Cornell University Press.

Name Index

Abendstern, M., 547
Adamec, C., 343
Adams, E., 120
Adkins, V., 534
Afable-Munsuz, A., 15, 112
Agresti, A., 39
Ahlborg, T., 336
Ahrons, C., 435, 436, 437, 438, 442, 445, 447, 454, 455, 456, 463, 464, 470
Ainsworth, M. D. S., 189, 190
Airies, E. J., 155, 157
Alan Guttmacher Institute, 321, 322
Albert, B., 283, 284
Alberti, R., 469, 470
Alberts, M., 21, 23
Albrecht, S. L., 426
Al-Fadhli, H. M., 323
Alford, S., 285
Ali, O. M., 311
Allegretto, S., 388, 397
Allen, J., 189
Allen, K. R., 375
Allen, M., 52
Allison, P. D., 459
Allport, G. W., 158
Alpern, D., 478
Amato, P., 426, 427, 456, 459, 463, 467
Amato, P. R., 362, 391, 401
Ambert, A., 429, 430, 432
American Academy of Pediatrics, 52
American Adoptions, 317, 342
American Association of Retired People (AARP), 528
American Cancer Society, 292
American Civil Liberties Union (ACLU), 343
American College Health Association, 296
American College of Obstetrics and Gynecology (ACOG), 336
American Medical Association (AMA), 297, 314
American Psychological Association, 92, 164, 536
American Society of Reproductive Medicine, 337, 338, 339

American Urological Association, 312
Amlie, C., 343
Andersen, B. L., 305
Anderson, J., 156
Anderson, J. R., 270
Anderson, S. A., 90, 91, 93, 260, 261, 269, 395, 435, 436, 467, 469, 470, 471, 472, 473
Anderssen, N., 343
Andersson, G., 426
Angelo, E. J., 347
Angleitner, A., 207
Annie E. Casey Foundation, 413
Antonovsky, A., 494
Aquilino, W. S., 529
Arab American Institute, 19, 393
Aral, S. O., 291, 306
Archer, R. L., 141
Arcus, M. E., 25, 26, 27
Arditti, J., 464
Arditti, J. A., 142
Arendell, T., 355, 356
Arnold, L. B., 331
Aron, A., 181, 309
Artazcoz, L., 401
Atala, A., 109
Atchley, R. C., 536, 537
Atkins, D. C., 308
Atwater, E., 152, 153
Aunola, K., 332
Aupont, M., 113
Axinn, W., 427

Babbie, E., 36, 38, 39, 41, 44
Bachman, G. F., 225
Bachmann, G. A., 310
Bagarozzi, D. A., 91
Bailey, D. C., 97
Bailey, J. M., 344
Bailey, J. M., 207
Bailey, S., 458
Baird, L. S., 401
Balakrishnan, T., 426
Balck, K., 321
Baldwin, A., 373
Baldwin, C. P., 373
Baldwin, W., 286
Baltes, P. B., 523
Bancroft, J., 311
Banda, J., 114, 115
Bandura, A., 111, 114, 119, 122, 123, 124, 125, 130, 368

Banfield, S., 307
Bank, B. J., 155
Banks, C. A. M., 7
Banks, J. A., 7
Barbarin, O. A., 14
Barber, N., 235
Barbor, C., 162
Barbour, C., 6, 10
Barbour, N. H., 6, 10
Barnett, R. C., 409
Barraket, J., 216, 217, 218
Barrett, A., 245, 246
Barrett, G., 336
Barrett, L. F., 144
Bartels, A., 309
Bartholomae, S., 284
Bartholomew, K., 190
Bartlett, M. Y., 182
Bartoli, A. M., 213, 214, 215
Basow, S. A., 155, 156
Basson, R., 311, 312
Bates, J. E., 362
Baucom, D. H., 142, 308
Bauermeister, J. A., 428
Baum, F., 328
Baum, N., 458, 465
Baumeister, R., 98
Baumeister, R. F., 304
Baumrind, D., 360, 361, 362, 383
Baxter, J., 369, 371, 407
Beach, S. R. M., 96
Beale, B., 374
Beall, A. E., 172, 174
Beattie, K., 55
Beccia, P. J., 401
Bechman, N., 528
Bedard, M. E., 246
Bee, H., 125, 127, 363, 539, 541
Behnke, A. O., 399
Bejlovec, R. A., 436
Belansky, E. S., 118
Belhar, M. C., 189
Bell, B. D., 38, 39
Belsky, J., 270, 359, 381, 408
Bem, S. L., 111, 116, 118, 119, 128
Benach, J., 401
Bengston, V. L., 526
Benoit, D., 190
Benson, P. R., 333
Berg, J. H., 141
Berkman, I., 258

Berkowitz, D., 325
Bernardes, J., 50
Berndt, T. S., 154
Bernhardt, E., 231, 233
Bernstein, J., 398, 399
Berrington, A., 426
Berscheid, E., 146
Bershady, H. L., 50
Besser, A., 357
Best, D. L., 112
Best, P., 268
Beutell, N. J., 115, 404
Bi, L., 114
Bianchi, S. M, 369
Biblarz, T. J., 126
Biesecker, B. B., 494
Bigner, J. J., 344
Binstock, G., 226
Bippus, A. M., 82
Birkel, R. C., 539
Bishaw, A., 413
Black, D., 227, 231
Blair, S. L., 370, 407
Blake, J., 330
Blakeslee, S., 461
Blanchard-Fields, F., 524, 525, 526, 535, 546
Bland, J., 122
Bleske-Rechek, A. L., 156
Bloir, K., 373
Blumer, H., 77
Blumstein, P., 293, 305, 306
Boak, A. Y., 363
Bobrow, D., 344
Boellstorff, T., 19, 289
Bogenschneider, K., 284
Bogenschultz, M. P., 494
Boggiano, A. K., 118
Bograd, R., 530
Bohannon, P., 455
Boisjoly, J., 158
Bokker, P., 458
Bonach, K., 457
Bonkowski, S., 344
Booth, A., 303, 304, 391, 426, 428
Booth, S., 291
Borrell, C., 401
Borzekowski, D. L. G., 288
Bos, H. M. W., 324, 344
Boss, P., 489
Boss, P. G., 50, 51, 69, 76, 208
Bosse, R., 536

Haavio-Mannila, E., 303
Haddock, S. A., 409
Hagestad, G. O., 325
Halgunseth, L., 78
Hall, D. R., 427
Hall, E., 128, 129
Hallberg, 336
Hallman, M., 458
Halmesmaki, E., 332
Halpern, C., 291
Halpern-Felsher, B. L., 294, 295
Hamilton, M. A., 82
Hammer, J., 539
Hammer, L., 404
Hanisch, K. A., 401
Hanks, D. B., 234
Hanna, R., 214
Hannum, J. W., 461
Hansford, S. L., 155
Hanson, S. L., 322
Harland, K., 55
Harley, W. F., 199
Harris, C. R., 308
Harris, V. W., 406, 416, 446, 447
Harrison, T. W., 293
Hartill, L., 331
Harton, H. C., 184
Hartup, W. W., 408
Harvard Family Research
    Project, 363
Harwood, K., 366
Hassebrauck, M., 142
Hasson, M., 311
Hatfield, E., 146, 172, 178, 179,
    180, 207
Haven, C., 526
Hayen, A., 413
Hayflick, L., 524
Hayford, S. R., 331
Haynes, C., 23
Haynes, M., 369
Hays, S., 356
Hazan, C., 190
He, W., 520, 522, 530, 531, 539
Head, M. R., 401
Heaton, T. B., 248, 426, 427
Hebert, S., 226
Heckert, M. T., 513
Heine, S. J., 145
Heintz, A. P., 336
Heller, P., 141, 145, 147
Hellerstedt, W. L., 18, 289
Helwig, A. A., 124
Henderson-King, D. H., 304
Hendren, H., 109
Hendrick, C., 179, 190, 193, 194
Hendrick, S., 190, 193, 194
Hendrick, S. S., 179
Hendry, L. B., 362
Henley, K., 458
Henriksen, L., 362
Henry-Waring, M. S., 216, 217,
    218
Heron, R. L., 461
Hesse, E., 190
Hesse-Biber, S. N., 116, 117

Hetherington, E. M., 362, 426,
    427, 457, 458, 459, 465,
    466, 467
Hewitt, B., 369
Hill, R., 495, 496, 497
Hinderlie, H. H., 461
Hines, M., 126
Hinings, D., 189
Hirai, T., 189
Hochschild, A., 370, 383, 406,
    421
Hodges, B. C., 288
Hoeffer, B., 344
Hofferth, S., 359
Hoffman, L. W., 323
Hoffman, M. L., 323
Hoffman, S. D., 529
Hojjat, M., 308, 309
Holland, J., 283
Hollander, D., 217
Hollander, J. A., 114
Holmes, T. H., 492, 493
Hook, M. K., 147
Hooyman, N., 547
Hoppe, M. H., 161
Hornyak, L. M., 333
Hortacsu, N., 173
Hotvedt, M. E., 344
House, A. T., 113
House, J. S., 269
Howard, J. A., 114
Howe, D., 189
Huang, J., 304
Hudd, S. S., 513
Hudson, M., 380, 381
Huebner, A., 154
Hughes, D., 377
Huitt, W., 21
Hundley, H., 111
Hunneycutt, T. L., 374
Hunt, M., 304
Hunt, M. M., 174
Hunter, N. D., 132, 257
Hurwicz, M., 539
Huston, A. C., 125
Huynh, V. W., 377
Hyde, J. S., 125, 282
Hynie, M., 283

Ibrahim, M. E., 311
Ihinger-Tallman, M., 473, 529
Ingegneri, D. G., 533
Ingersoll-Dayton, B., 539
Ingoldsby, E. M., 459, 460, 461
Institute for Women's Policy
    Research, 389, 390
International Council on
    Infertility Information
    Dissemination, 339
Itzen, C., 547

Jaccard, J., 284
Jackson, C., 362
Jacobson, N. S., 308
Jacobson, R. B., 344
Jacobvitz, D. B., 357

Jandt, F., 111
Janssen, E., 311
Janus, C. L., 291, 303
Janus, S. S., 291, 303
Jaudinot, E., 304
Jenny, C., 375
Jessel, D., 99
Jhally, S., 111
Jobe, R. L., 96
Johnsen, J., 299
Johnson, A., 415
Johnson, D. R., 391
Johnson, F. L., 155, 157
Johnson, M. D., 335, 336
Johnson, M. M., 531
Johnson, M. P., 223
Johnson, N. J., 416
Johnson, S. M., 344
Johnson, T., 20, 144
Johnson, V. E., 291
Jones, A. J., 11
Jones, J. M., 228
Jorgensen, R. S., 303
Jorgensen, S. R., 28
Joseph, G., 344
Joshi, P., 288
Joyner, K., 244, 245, 310

Kachadourian, L. K., 96
Kaestle, C. E., 309
Kahn, R., 536
Kalter, N., 478
Kamp, C. M., 40
Kapinus, C. A., 427
Kaplan, G., 456
Kaplan, H. B., 363
Karney, B. R., 269, 527
Karwoski, L., 106
Kass, L. R., 212
Kastenbaum, R. J., 545
Katz, L. F., 333
Kaufman, G., 534
Kawachi, I., 258
Kay, A. C., 153
Kelley, D., 97
Kelley, D. L., 268
Kelley, H. H., 209, 236
Kellogg, T., 74
Kelly, J., 457, 466, 474
Kelly, J. B., 458, 459, 469, 479
Kendall, J., 264
Kennedy, S., 227
Kennell, J. H., 189
Kenney, K. R., 265
Kenny, M., 461
Kenrick, D. T., 207
Kerckhoff, R. K., 25
Kessler, E. A., 85
Kheshgi-Genovese, Z., 477, 479
Kiddon, N., 291, 306
Kids Count, 16
Kiernan, K. E., 428
Kiger, G., 406
Killian, K. D., 157
Kim, J., 178
Kim, J. E., 362

Kimuna, S. R., 308
King, V., 459
Kinsey Institute, 288
Kipilis, K., 109
Kirby, J. S., 142
Kitamura, T., 189
Kiyak, H. A., 547
Kjamba, Y. K., 308
Klaus, M. H., 189
Klaus, P. H., 189
Klein, D. M., 49, 69, 70, 76, 208,
    209, 210
Kleinbaum, S., 234
Kleparchuk, C., 330
Klerman, L. V., 322
Klinkenberg, D., 213, 214, 215,
    216
Kluwer, E. S., 335, 336
Knapp, M., 221, 223, 236, 434
Knox, D., 182, 183, 184, 292, 310
Knutson, J., 97, 98
Koerner, A. F., 85
Koeske, G., 457
Kohlberg, L., 124
Kohlhepp, K. A., 532
Koivunen, J. M., 227, 229, 231
Kontula, O., 303
Kortenkamp, K., 259
Kovacs, L., 269
Kposowa, A. J., 426
Krasnovsky, F., 362
Krasnow, A., 360
Krause, W., 304
Krauth, L. D., 444
Kreider, R. M., 373, 473
Kremer, E., 305
Kremer, M., 158
Kretchmar, M. D., 357
Krieger, N., 388, 389
Kroeger, A., 40
Kruk, E., 470
Kuhn, B. R., 379
Kulik, L., 526, 536, 537, 539
Kulka, R. A., 532
Kupperbusch, C., 20, 144
Kurdek, L. A., 210, 270, 306
Kuttler, A. F., 155
Kuykendall, C., 147

La Gapia, J. J., 437
Laan, E., 290
LaGreca, A. M., 155
Lamb, M. E., 357, 408
Lamborn, S. D., 361
Lamb-Parker, F., 363
Land, D., 189
Landale, N. S., 426
Landis, D., 180
Laner, M. R., 214
Lang, K., 358
Lansford, J. E., 362
LaRossa, R., 50
Lars-Gosta, 336
Larson, A. S., 267
Larson, J. H., 173
Larson, N. C., 321

Larzelere, R. E., 379
Lauer, J. C., 436
Lauer, R. H., 436
Laughlin, J., 55
Laumann, E. O., 282, 302, 307, 311
Laurenceau, J. P., 144
Lawler, J. A., 96
Lawrance, K, 302, 303, 304
Lawrence, R., 365
Lawson, D., 162
Lawson, K., 323, 324
Lazarovici, L., 397
Lazarus, N., 362
Lazarus, R. S., 494
Leavy, J., 288
Leber, D., 304
Lee, J. A., 193, 194, 200, 201
Lee, R. S., 106
Lee, S. M., 157
Lee, T. R., 416
Leerkes, E. M., 357
Lees, N., 394
Lefcourt, H. M., 160
Lehman, P., 113
Lehr, R., 458, 463
Lehrer, E. L., 426, 451
Lehrman, G., 321
Leichliter, J. S., 291, 293, 306
Leite, R. W., 458
Leitenberg, H., 291
Lemme, B. H., 248, 525, 533, 539, 540, 541
Lemon, B. W., 526
Lempers, J. D., 155
Lengermann, P. M., 54
Lenhart, A., 216, 217, 218
Lenton, A. P., 156
Leo, B., 362
Lerman, R. A., 259
Lerner, R., 354, 355
Lesane-Brown, C. L., 377
Lesser, I. M., 147
Levant, R., 113, 114
Levenson, R. W., 527
Lever, J., 306
Levinger, G., 214
Levy, D. M., 158
Lewis, F. M., 494, 495
Lewis, J. M., 461
Lewis, M., 459
Lewis, W. J., 347
Li, H., 181
Li, N. P., 207
Li, X., 286
Lichter, D., 370, 407
Lidz, V., 50
Lillard, L. A., 427
Lin, J., 398, 399
Lincoln, D., 413
Lindau, S. T., 527
Lindenberger, U., 523
Lindgren, H. G., 88, 89, 90
Lindley, L. L., 288
Lindlof, T. R., 85
Linsenmeier, L. A. W., 207

Liu, C., 308
Lofquist, D., 247
Long, J. S., 311
Long, N., 462
Lott-Whitehead, L., 344
Loudoun, R., 400
Lowenthal, M. F., 526
Lowrey, C., 370
Lozy, J. L., 369
Lu, H. H., 231
Lucas, K. J., 282, 288
Luhmann, N., 175
Lund, D. A., 547
Lundqvist, L.-O., 178
Luquis, T., 304
Luskin, F., 97
Lynch, J., 456

MacDermid, S. M., 399
Macdonald, H., 131
MacDonald, W., 427
MacGeorge, E. L., 82
MacKay, H., 327
Mackey, R., 146
Mackinnon, C. A., 132
MacMillan, P., 458, 463
MacNeil, S., 304
MacRae, H., 531
Madden, M., 216, 217, 218
Madden-Derdich, D., 464
Magnuson, S., 356
Mahalingam, R., 112
Maher, B., 285
Main, M., 190
Maio, G. R., 96, 98
Major, B., 347
Makes Marks, L. F., 18
Maki, D. M., 416
Malcarne, V. L., 494
Maleki, M., 161
Malhotra, A., 112
Malonebeach, E., 539
Managing Stress in Young Families, 504
Mandel, J. B., 344
Mangelsdorf, S. C., 360
Manning, W. D., 11, 229, 231, 233, 477
Manusov, V., 87
Marano, H. E., 472, 473
March of Dimes, 340, 341
Marcia, J. E., 147
Markeiwicz, D., 189
Markham, J. J., 93
Markham, M., 458
Markman, H. J., 83, 445
Markman, L., 363
Marmaros, D., 158
Marquardt, E., 219, 220, 221
Marrel, A., 304
Marsden, M., 173, 174
Marsh, H. W., 373
Marshall, J. P., 416
Marshall, T. C., 141, 145
Marsiglio, W., 325
Martin, S. P., 329

Martin, T. K., 426
Mashek, D. J., 181
Mason, M. A., 477
Masterpasqua, F., 344
Masters, W. H., 291
Matthiesen, S., 311
Mattingly, M. J., 369
Mauldon, J., 259
Maushart, S., 258
Mayer, E., 266
Mayo Clinic, 468
Mazur, A., 304
McAdams, D. P., 151
McAndrew, F. T., 153
McBride, B. A., 369
McCabe, M. P., 307
McCandies, T., 14
McCandish, B. M., 344
McCartney, K., 408
McClunn, L. A., 362
McCready, S., 55
McCreary, D. R., 113
McCubbin, H. I., 497
McDonald, P. F., 327
McGoldrick, M., 56, 57, 58, 59, 61, 263, 381, 510
McGuigan, F. J., 489
McHale, J., 360
McHale, S. M., 400, 401
McIntyre, A., 461
McIntyre, M. D., 461
McKenry, P. C., 458
McKinney, K., 309
McLain, R., 112
McLanahan, S., 458, 467
McLean, N., 366
McLeod, J. D., 362
McNeely, A., 292
McNulty, J. K., 96
McQuillan, K., 331
McQuillen, J. S., 308
McWilliams, P. 8
Mead, G. H., 76
Media Watch, 131
Medina, S., 356
Medora, N. P., 173
Mellan, O., 415
Mendelson, M. J., 153
Mercer, C. H., 311
Mercer, R. T., 356
Merck Manual, 339, 340
Merlo, R., 327
Mero, R. P., 269
Merolla, A. J., 97
Merrell, K. W., 362
Merriwether-de-Vries, C., 375
Meschke, L. L., 284
Metts, S., 436
Michael, R. T., 282
Michael, Y., 258
Michaels, 356
Michaels, S., 282
Michaud, S. L., 81, 82
Mikach, S., 344
Milan, A., 427
Miles, J. C., 458

Milkie, M. A., 369
Millbank, J., 52
Miller, B. C., 527
Miller, L. C., 141
Miller, M., 11, 13, 25, 226
Miller, R. S., 160
Mills, G., 369
Minnesota Program Development, Inc., 510
Miyashita, K., 360
Moen, P., 405
Moir, A., 99
Money, J., 176
Monsour, M., 156
Montefiore, S. S., 302
Montel, K. H., 267
Monthly Labor Review, 392
Moore, H., 413
Moore, S. G., 408
Moos, R. H., 496, 498, 501
Morgan, E., 147
Morgan, P., 11
Morgan, S., 426
Morgan, S. P., 331
Morris, A. M., 324
Morris, A. S., 362
Mosher, W. D., 426, 477
Moss, J. J., 25, 26
Mounts, N. S., 361
Muehlenhard, C. L., 106
Mueller, U., 304
Mulder, C., 362
Mullen, P. E., 182
Murray, M. A., 494
Myers, D. G., 144, 212

Nanda, S., 119
Natenshon, H., 74
National Academy of Sciences (NAS), 48
National Association of Scholars, 158
National Campaign to Prevent Teen Pregnancy, 321
National Center for Health Statistics, 244, 245, 319, 425
National Coalition against Domestic Violence, 507, 508
National College Health Assessment (NCHA), 295, 296
National Council for Adoption, 342
National Council on Aging (NCOA), 525, 527, 528, 539, 540
National Council on Family Relations (NCFR), 27
National Guidelines Task Force, 285
National Infertility Association, 339
National Information Center for Children and Youth with Disabilities, 341
National Institutes of Health, 108

National Issues Forum (NIF), 9
National Network to End
    Domestic Violence, 505, 509
National Organization on
    Adolescent Pregnancy,
    Parenting, and Prevention,
    322
National Right to Life
    Campaign, 346
National Survey of Family
    Growth (NSFG), 11
National Vital Statistics Report,
    318
Neal, M., 539
Needham, L. B., 206, 207
Neighbour, R. H., 60
Nelson, J. N., 125
Neto, F., 20, 193, 194, 195
Neubaum, E., 360
Neugarten, B. L., 534
Nevid, J. S., 327
Newcomb, M. D., 113
Nichols, M. P., 69, 192
Niebling, C. B., 513
Nielsen Media, 132
Niemiec, R., 23
Noh, E. R., 354
Noland, C., 114
Noller, P., 85, 190
Nonnemaker, J. M., 362
Nord, W., 23
Norton, L. X., 309
Notarius, C. I., 93, 333
Nurmi, J. E., 332
Nussbaum, R. L., 494

O'Brien, A., 146
O'Connell, M., 227, 228, 229,
    230, 247
O'Conner, E., 344
Oda, R., 207
O'Donnell, L., 293
O'Donohue, W., 84
Office of Child Support
    Enforcement (OCSE), 441,
    442
Ogata, K., 360
Oggins, J., 304
Ogolsky, B., 302
Okazaki, S., 289
O'Keefe, E. S. C., 125
Okun, B. F., 84
Oldstone-Moore, J., 114
Olsen, C. S., 480
Olson, D. H., 39, 71, 72, 232,
    234, 267, 488, 489, 514
Olson, T., 378
Olson-Sigg, A., 232, 234
Omarzu, J., 88
Openshaw, D. K., 145, 154
Oppenheimer, M., 307
Orbuch, T. L., 269, 428
Orlofsky, J. L., 147, 149
Oropesa, R. S., 426, 432
O'Shea, W. A., III, 180
Oswald, D. L., 154

Otshi, S., 459

Padgett, T., 264
Paez, D., 283
Pan, S., 304, 305
Pape, C. L., 85
Papernow, P. L., 471, 472, 473
Papp, L. M., 388
Parish, T. S., 459
Park, K., 327
Parke, M., 471
Parke, R. D., 358, 458
Parker, K. C. H., 190
Parkin, S., 526
Parmet, S., 311
Parsons, T., 50, 62
Partridge, M. F., 190
Parziale, J., 474, 476, 477
Parziale, J. B., 474, 476, 477
Pasley, K., 458, 473, 529
Pathe, M., 182
Patterson, C. J., 52, 126, 343,
    375
Patterson, G. R., 380
Patterson, J. M., 497
Paul, E. L., 153
Payne, P., 302
Pearlin, L. I., 489, 499
Pearson, K., 37
Peay, L., 363
Pedhazur, E. J., 36, 39
Penning, M. J., 427, 532
Pennington, S. B., 344
Pensky, E., 381
Peplau, L. A., 211
Perrin, E. C., 343
Perry, D. G., 122, 130
Perry-Jenkins, M., 370, 398,
    399
Peterman, M. A., 142
Peterson, J. A., 526
Peterson, Z. D., 106
Peterson-Hickey, M., 18, 289
Pettigrew, T. F., 158
Pettit, G. S., 362
Peven, D. A., 146
Pew Research Center, 228, 229,
    231, 232, 249, 428, 430,
    431
Pew Research Forum, 88
Pfrang, H., 304
Phelan, P., 79
Phillips, G. M., 434
Phillips, J. A., 426
Phillips, K. W., 389
Phillips, N. A., 310
Philpot, 113
Phuong-Mai, N., 114
Piaget, J., 368
Pickover, S., 190
Pierce, J. L., 128
Piferi, R. L., 96
Pilot, A., 114
Pimple, K. D., 48
Pinel, J. P., 107
Pinquart, M., 533

Pittman, L. D., 361
Pitts, J. R., 51
Pitzer, R. L., 501
Planned Parenthood of
    America, 287, 345, 346, 347
Platz, E. A., 311
Pleck, E. H., 357
Pleck, J. H., 357, 359, 369, 459
Plunkett, J. W., 478
Pok, A. Y., 392
Pollak, R., 259
Polonko, K., 428
Popadiuk, N., 226
Popenoe, D., 4, 9, 11, 13
Porter, M., 229
Porterfield, A., 86
Posner, J. A., 324
Potenza, M., 510
Powell, D., 444
Powers, V., 412
Poyer, K. L., 375
Prager, K. J., 141, 143, 144, 145,
    151, 166
Presser, H. B., 400
Previti, D., 426
Priel, B., 357
Prince, D. W., 161
Prinstein, M. J., 155
Prinz, R. J., 363
Purcell, R., 182
Purnine, D. M., 303

Qian, Z., 264
Qu, L., 327
Quilliam, S., 268
Quillian, L., 158
Quinlivan, J. A., 321

Radziszewska, B., 361
Raffaelli, M., 284
Rahe, R. H., 492, 493
Raley, R. K., 426, 431, 432
Rao, N., 360
Raphel, S., 374
Rapson, R., 146, 172
Rapson, R. L., 179, 180
Rathus, S. A., 327
Rausche, A., 304
Read, J. G., 19
Reckase, M. D., 363
Reed, M., 438, 439, 440, 441
Reeder, H. M., 156
Regan, P., 309, 310
Reis, H. T., 189
Reiss, D., 362
Reiss, I. L., 193, 195, 201, 281
Remmo, C. J., 425
Renaud, C., 304
Repetti, R. L., 398, 399
Reynolds, G. P., 374
Rezac, S., 463
Rhoades, G. K., 445
Rhodes, K. L., 18, 289
Ribar, D. C., 258
Rice, P. F., 178
Richardson, J. L., 361

Richardson, P., 333
Richmond, K., 113
Richters, J., 304
Ridley, C., 302
Riggle, E. D. B., 224
Riley, P. J., 406
Rimer, B. K., 494, 495
Ripple, C., 363
Rissel, C., 304
Rivers, C., 409, 500
Robinson, J. P., 369
Robson, M., 478
Roche, K. M., 361
Rodgers, R. H., 455, 456, 464
Rodriguez, D., 112, 288
Roehling, P. V., 405
Roesler, T. A., 375
Rogers, S. J., 356, 391, 428, 432
Rojahn, K., 207
Roloff, M. E., 225
Romas, J. A., 492, 493
Rose, S., 211, 213, 214, 215, 216
Rosen, E., 293
Rosenblatt, P. C., 69
Rosenblum, K. E., 110
Ross, D. S., 265
Ross, E. S., 513
Ross, R. R., 265
Rostosky, S. S., 224
Roth, S., 347
Rothman, A. D., 365
Rothman, M. T., 365
Rotundo, E. A., 357
Rovine, M. J., 144
Rowe, J., 536
Rowland, D., 327
Rubenfeld, K., 155, 156
Rubin, K. H., 363
Rubin, L., 155
Rubin, R., 356
Rubin, Z., 178
Rusbult, C., 95
Rusbult, C. E., 223
Russell, C. S., 71, 72, 488
Russell, E. B., 184
Russell, S. R., 269
Russo, L., 218
Russo, N. F., 347
Rutledge, K., 119, 123
Rutter, M., 344
Ryan, K. D., 83
Rybak, A., 153

Saad, F. A., 4, 5
Sabatelli, R. M., 90, 91, 93, 260,
    261, 395, 435, 436, 467,
    469, 470, 471, 472, 473
Sacerdote, B., 158
Sagarin, B. J. D., 183
Saisto, T., 332
Salary.com, 402
Sales, E., 457
Salmela-Aro, K., 332, 333, 334
Samaniego, R. Y., 361
Sameroff, A. J., 373
Sandberg, J., 359

Subject Index

Dunphy, D. C. (stages of friendship development), 152–154
Dyadic phase of relationship decline, 435–436
Dying. *See* Death
Dyspareunia, 311

Ecological Model (Bronfenbrenner), 19, 21–24, 30, 49
  chronosystem, 24–25
  exosystem, 23–24
  macrosystem, 24
  mesosystem, 23
  microsystem, 22–23
  person, 22
Economic factors
  and child rearing, 327, 329, 332
  and conflict theory, 53
  contemporary families, impact on, 13
  and divorce, 432
  financial hardship post-divorce, 467, 469
  of marriage, 4, 250–251, 415–417
  unemployment, 401, 402
  working families, 388–415
Ecosystem, 22–23
Education
  and division of household chores, 371
  and earnings, 391
  family life, 25–29
  and income less than family budget, 399
  and parenting after divorce, 464
  and single mothers, 396
  student loan debt, 416–417
  teaching children about diversity, 16
Eight Stages of Man (Erikson), 149–151, 166
Elder abuse, 524
Elopement, 174
Emergency contraception (EC), 344
Emotional attachment, 145, 166
Emotional discharge, 502
Emotional divorce, 437, 449
Emotional environment, post-divorce, 470
Emotional needs, 196
Emotional regulation, 495
Emotional safety, 88
Emotion-focused coping, 502
Empathy, 82, 153
Empirical definitions, 39–40
Empty nest, 526, 532
Endogamy, 211
Endometriosis, 338
Entertainment needs, 196
Entitlement, sense of, 98
Equal Opportunity Commission, 132
Equity in the marital partnership, 91–92
Erectile dysfunction (ED), 311–312
Erikson, Erik, 149–150, 367
Eros, 193
Erotic lovers, 193
Estrogen, 107
Ethics, 48
Ethnicity
  definition of, 13
  and divorce, 431–433
  and parenting, differences in styles, 363–364

Eustress, 489
Event-based stress, 493–496
Evolutionary theory, 206–208, 236
Exclusivity and monogamous marriage, 5
Exhaustion in stress response, 492–493
Exogamy, 211
Exosystem (Ecological Model), 23–24, 30
Expectations of marriage, 261, 270–271, 274
Experimental design, 42–43
Experimental group, 43
Expressive roles, 50
Expressive schemas, 118–119
Expressiveness and intimacy, 146
Extended family, 10
  African Americans/Black Caribbeans, 14
Externalizing difficulties, 459
External locus of control, 495
Extramarital sex (EMS), 307
Extra Relationship Involvement (ERI), 307

Familism
  and Hispanics, 432, 433
  and Latinos, 15
Family and Medical Leave Act (FMLA), 405
Family cohesion, 406
Family coping skills, 501, 515
Family crisis, 489, 514
  ABC-X Family Crisis Model, 497–499
  types of, 496
Family Deficit Model, 372–373
Family/families
  adaptive tasks, 500–501
  African American/Black Caribbean, 14–15
  American, racial and ethnic composition, 14
  budget, 397–399
  caregiving, 539–542
  change, 488–495, 488–501, 514
  changing nature of, 9, 10–14, 55–56, 357, 359, 514
  childless/childfree, 11
  and children, 6, 12–13, 324–325
  cohabiting couples, 11–12
  communication. *See* Communication
  contemporary, 10–19, 359
  coping, 501–502, 515
  crisis model, 497
  in cultural contexts, 20–25
  definition of, 6
  developmental tasks, 260–261
  end-of-life changes, 535–542
  family life education, 25–29
  gay or lesbian, 12–13, 324–325
  versus household, 6
  intergenerational approach to therapy, 192
  Latino, 15–16
  post-divorce, 466
  resilience, 502–505, 515
  Satir's family as mobile, 70
  and shift work, 400
  single-parent, 10, 73, 418
  size of, 329–331
  social science research, 36–37
  stepfamilies, 11, 73, 471, 474–480, 483
  stress management, 504
  system, 69, 259, 491, 526

  "traditional," 7–9
  well-being, 400
  working, 388–414, 419–420
Family law, 438
Family Life Cycle, 59–60, 62, 259, 526–527
  developmental tasks, 492
  paradigm, 259–260, 274
Family life education, 25–29, 30, 61
  aging and death, 548
  balancing work and family, 417–418
  cohabitation and, 234, 236
  content areas, 28
  definition of, 26
  divorce and, 447, 480
  effective communication and, 98–100
  gender and, 133–134
  intimacy and, 164–165
  marriage and, 272–273
  parenthood and, 347–348
  parenting and, 381
  remarriage and, 480–481
  sex and sexuality, 312
  stress and, 512–513
  time line, 26–27
Family meetings, 87
Family metacognition, 436
Family of origin, 6, 29, 260, 472
Family of procreation, 6
Family policy, 411
Family projection process, 323
Family stress, 488–489, 494
Family Systems theory (FST), 68–75
  key concepts, 69–73
  Virginia Satir, 70
Family theories, 48–56
  Conflict theory, 49, 52–54
  Ecological Model, 19, 21–24, 30, 49
  Family Development theory, 49
  Feminist theory, 54
  introduction to, 49–50, 62
  men's studies, 55–56
  Social Exchange theory, 49–50
  Structural-Functionalism, 50–52
  Symbolic Interaction theory, 49
  Systems theory, 49
Family values, 7–8
Family violence. *See* Domestic violence
Family-work balance, 404–411
  strategies, 409–411
Fatherhood, 357–359. *See also* Parenthood
Fatherlessness, consequences of, 358
Fathers and childcare, 382
Fatuous relationships, 178, 180
Female-headed households
  and African American/Black Caribbean families, 14
  and poverty, 413
Female sexual selection, 207–208, 236
Femininity
  definition of, 113
  expressive schemas, 118–119
  intercultural, 114
  status of women, 114–115
Femininity Ideology Scale (FIS), 113
Feminist movement, 389
Feminist theory, 54, 62

Fertility cues, 207
Fertility rates, 11, 318–319
    Quiverfull movement, 331
Fictive (nonrelated) kin, 15, 531
Field research, 42
Fiery Foes, 456, 464
Fight or flight response, 492
Filter Theory of Mate Selection, 210–211, 236
Finances. *See* Economic factors; Money
Financial cost of love, 196
Financial incompatibility, 418
Findings, application of research, 44
Flexibility and resilience, 504
Food stamps, 414
Forced marriage, 4
Forgiveness, 95–98
    barriers to, 98
    definition of, 95
Formal divorce, 438–445, 449, 454
Formal grandparenting, 534
Framework, 49
    sexual scripting, 282
Frequency of sex, in intimate relationships,
    314
Freud, Sigmund, 366
Friendships
    and culture/ethnicity, 156–159
    stages of development, 151–154
    urban tribes, 246
Friend with benefits, 220
Functional communication, 86
Fun seeker, 535

Gamete intrafallopian transfer (GIFT), 339
Gardasil vaccine, 301
Gatekeepers, 458
Gays and lesbians
    and adoption, 343–344
    and cohabitation, 231
    communication within family, 73
    dating scripts, 214–215, 216
    demographics, 247, 273
    families, 3, 52
    federal census of 2010, 12–13
    mate selection, 210–211
    never-marrieds, 247–248
    parenthood, 324–325, 349, 375–376
    singlehood, 243
Gender
    aging and, 521
    biology of, 106–109, 134
    confidence gap, 118
    conflict in family roles, 115
    contemporary issues, 132–133, 135, 431
    culture of, 110–121, 135
    definition of, 106
    development, theories of, 121–124
    glass ceiling, 116–117
    inequality, 116–118
    infidelity and, 308
    learning from the media, 130–132
    learning from parents and peers, 125–127
    nature *versus* nurture, 106
    reassignment, 121
    roles, 110–111, 122, 127, 135, 261
    schemas, 118–121, 135

versus sex, 106–107, 134
    stability, 124, 125
    wage gap, 117–118, 389–390
Gender constancy, 124
Gender cues, 80
Gender differences
    in communication, 80–82
    dating scripts, 215
    in earnings, 389–390
    in emotional and affection needs, 199
    and experience of love, 194–195
    and experiences of stress, 513
    in friendships, 155–156
    and grief, 547–548
    and intimacy, 147
    in parent–adult child relationship, 533
    sex and love, views of, 310
    sexual desire, 290
    and sexual selection, 207–208
    and singlehood, 246
Gender equality, 389
Gender identity, 120–121, 124, 343–344
Gender-neutral children, 128
Gender polarization, 116
Gender typing, 155
General Adaptation Syndrome, 491, 493
General Systems theory (GST), 69
Genital herpes, 300–301
Genital phase of development, 366
Genital warts, 301
Genograms, 192–193, 200
Gerontologists, 521
Glass ceiling, 116–117, 389
Goal-oriented sexual activity, 305, 314
Gonorrhea, 298–299
Government policies for working families,
    411–415, 420
Grandparenting, styles of, 534–535
Grandparents
    becoming, 533–534
    children raised by, 534, 535
    parenting grandchildren, 374–375
Grave dressing phase of a relationship, 437
Grief, 547, 550
Group context, of intimacy, 144
Group marriage, 6
Group *versus* the individual, 20
Gunnysacking, 94

Harmonious couples, 267
Hayflick limit, 524
Head Start, 414
Health benefits of marriage, 258
Healthcare, 413–414
Hegemonic masculinity, 111
Herpes, 300–301
Heterogamy, 211, 263
Heterosexual couples, 3
    dating scripts, 214
Heterosexual orientation, 282
Hijras, 119–120
Hispanics
    aging and, 526, 531
    children in poverty, by family structure,
        395
    custodial mothers, 463

divorce and, 431, 432–433
    domestic partner violence, 508
    families, 10, 230
    marriage and, 250
    parenting styles, 363
    racial/ethnic identity, development of,
        376–377
    sexuality and, 298, 299, 300
    singlehood and, 245, 248
    teen birth rates, 319
    wage comparisons by sex, race, and
        ethnicity, 390–391, 392
Homeostasis, 50, 71, 491
Homogamy, 210
Homosexual orientation, 282
Homosocial play, 127
Hooking up, 219–221
Hormone contraceptive methods, 344
Hormone replacement therapy (HRT), 311
Household(s)
    chores, division of as source of conflict, 90,
        369, 371–372, 406, 407, 419
    configurations of, in the U.S., 7
    contemporary parents, 372, 373
    definition of, 6
    responsibilities, 261–262, 274, 369–372
Household work, 402
Housing assistance, 414
Human life cycle, 56–59
Human papillomavirus (HPV), 301
Humor, use of, 89–90
Hypothesis, 39
Hypotheses testing, 39

Ideal-actual gap, 369
"Ideal body" standard, 235
"Ideal" family size, 330
Identity, sense of, 154
    learning, 376–377
Immediate context, of intimacy, 143
Immigrants, 16
Impotence, 311–312
Incestuous relationships, 79–80
Incidental cue, 223
Independent couples, 268–269
Indians, 119, 120
Indirect forgiveness, 97
Individual identity, and intimacy, 146
Individualistic cultures
    definition of, 20–21
    intimacy and, 144, 166
    singlehood and, 242–243
Individuation, 154
Infancy as stage of human life cycle, 57, 58
Infanticization in television and film, 131
Infatuation, 177, 200
Infertility, 349
    definition of, 337
    psychological impact of, 339
    treatment of, 338–339
Infidelity, 306–308
Initiation, 221–222
Institute for Social and Behavioral Research,
    9
Institutional Animal Care and Use
    Committee (IACUC), 47

Institutional marriage, 250–252
Institutional Review Board (IRB), 47, 48
Instrumental roles, 50
Instrumental schemas, 118–119
Instrumental support and marriage, 258
Integration, 222
Intelligent design (ID), 24
Intensification, 222
Intensive mothering, 356
    ideology, 356, 382
Interactional model of stress, 494–495
Interaction cue, 223
Interconnecting, Family Systems theory and, 69–70, 74–75, 259
Intercultural masculinities, 112–113
Interdependent love, 188, 200
Interfaith marriage, 265–266
Intergenerational approach to family therapy, 192
Intergenerational Family theory, 162
Intergenerational ties, 530–535, 549
Intergenerational transmission, 427
Internalizing difficulties, 459
Internal locus of control, 495
Internet
    date-related activities, 216–219
    relationships, 308
Interpersonal relationships, 69–70, 74–75, 141–142
    attraction theories, 206–211
Interpersonal scripts, 213, 283
Interracial diversity, increase in, 13
Interracial intimacy, 157
Interracial marriage, 263–265
    demographics, 267
Interrole conflict, 404
Intersex Society of North America, 109
Intersexual conditions, 107–109
Intersexuals, 120
Intervention *versus* education, 25
Intimacy, 139–167, 198, 223
    as basic human need, 140–149, 166
    communication and, 164
    components of, 146–147
    contexts of, 143
    de-escalation of intimacy, 434
    definitions of, 141–142
    development of, 149–160, 166
    fear of, 162–163
    interracial, 157
    marital, in the later years, 538
    Miller Social Intimacy Scale (MSIS), 160
    obstacles to, 161–164, 166
    as process, 145, 166
    responsiveness, 141
    role of, in relationships, 142–145
    sexual, 155
    Sternberg's Triangular Theory of Love, 185
Intimacy status, 147
Intimate partner violence (IPV), 348, 508
Intimates, 147
Intrafaith marriage, 265–266
Intrapsychic phase of relationship decline, 435
Intrapsychic scripts, 213, 283

Intrinsic rewards, and altruistic love, 188
In vitro fertilization (IVF), 338–339
Involuntary caretaking, 374
Involuntary extramarital experiences, 306–308
Involved relationship, 535
Irrelevant sexualization in television and film, 131
Islamic Americans, 212
Isolates, 149

Japanese/Japanese Americans, 212
    communication skills and, 77
    love and, 180
Jealousy, 182–184, 200
Job autonomy, 399
Job complexity, 399
Job status, 398–399
Joint custody, 442

Kinship care, 374
Klinefelter's Syndrome, 108
Knapp's Relationship Escalation Model, 221–223, 236

Labor and birth, 335
Language brokers, children as, 78
Latency phase of development, 366
Latinas/Latinos, 229, 264, 287
    adolescents and sex, 293
    children in poverty, by family structure, 395
    collectivist culture, 20
    poverty and, 413
    uninvolved parenting styles, 361
    wage comparisons by sex, race, and ethnicity, 390–391, 392
Latino families, 15–16
    familism, high value of, 15
    sexual communication, 287–288
Learning theory, 122, 367–368
Legal custody, 442
Legal separation, 254
Legislation
    abortion, 13, 346
    Civil Rights Act, 13, 132, 389
    Communities of Color Teen Pregnancy Prevention Act of 2007, 322
    Equal Pay Act of 1963, 389
    Family and Medical Leave Act (FMLA), 405
    Lilly Ledbetter Fair Pay Act, 390
    and marriage, 4, 252–254, 264
    and same-sex parents, 52
    Welfare and Medicaid Reform Act of 1996, 414
Lesbian Feminist theory, 54
Liberal Feminist theory, 54
Life change event, 493, 542
Life expectancy, 520
Life orientation, 538, 549
Lifespan
    perspective, 522
    sexual development and, 280–281
Life transition, 325
Liking, 186, 187, 200
Lilly Ledbetter Fair Pay Act, 390

Listening
    active, 88
    reflective, 89
    styles, ineffective, 89
Literature review, 39, 44–47, 62
Long-distance relationships (LDRs), 163
Louisiana Covenant Marriage Act, 253
Love
    attachment and, 188–190
    benefits of, 196
    in collectivist cultures, 173–174, 179–180, 200
    companionate, 178, 184–187
    costs of, 196–197
    culture and, 172–174, 194, 200, 201
    definitions of, 176–180, 184–187, 200
    development of, 200
    first experiences, 187–188
    history of, 174–175, 200
    in individualist cultures, 173–174, 179–180, 200
    Lee's six types, 193–194
    marriage and, 175
    negative sides of, 180–184
    parenting style and, 364
    passionate, 177–180
    as prototype, 176–177
    science of, 180, 181
    sex and, 308–310
    Sternberg's love types, 186–187
    Sternberg's Triangular Theory of Love, 185–186
    stories, 191–192
    theories of, 193–197, 200–201
Love Economic Model (Vuong), 196–197, 201
Love maps, 176
Ludic lovers, 193

Machismo, 112
Macrosystem (Ecological Model), 24, 30
Maintenance costs of love, 196, 197
Male sexual selection, 207, 236
Manic lovers, 194
Marianismo, 114, 287–288
Marital conflict, 400
Marital couple types, 268–270, 274
Marital satisfaction, 269–270, 271, 274, 549
    aging and, 526–527, 529
    infidelity and, 308
    parenthood and, 366, 369
    sexual relationship and, 302–305
Market alternative cost method, 402
Marriage
    aging and, 526–527, 548–549
    average age for, 243
    children's benefits, 259
    as communicative reality, 252
    contemporary families and, 13
    couple types, 268–270
    courtship, goal of, 211–213
    as covenant, 429
    economic aspects, 4, 258
    gays and lesbians, 247–248
    health benefits of, 258
    institution of, 250–254

Marriage (*cont.*)
    interfaith, 265–266
    interracial, 263–265
    intrafaith, 265
    legal dimensions of, 3–4, 254–257
    love as basis for, 175
    money and, 415–418, 420
    as part of the family life cycle, 60
    reasons for, 250
    rights and privileges of, 257–258
    roles within, 261–262
    as sacrament, 4–5, 252, 274
    sadaqa, 4
    same-sex couples, 255, 256
    satisfaction and, 266–271
    social dimensions of, 2–4, 249–254
    transition to, challenges of, 259–266
    types of, 5–6
Marriage and family therapists (MFTs), 446, 450
Marriage Covenant Act, 252–254
Marriage license, 3
Marxist Feminist theory, 54
Masculine Gender Role Stress theory (MGRS), 113
Masculinity
    cultural standards, 111–113
    definition of, 111
    instrumental schemas, 118–119
    shifting definitions of, 55
Masturbation, 290–291
Matching hypothesis, 210
Materialistic needs, 196
Maternal gatekeeping, 369
Maternal Role Attainment (MRA), 356–357, 382
Mate selection, 207, 236
Matrilineal lines, 18
Maturity effect, 426
Meaning
    adversity and, 503
    communication of, 75–79, 83
    private couple meanings, 495–496
Meaning-based coping, 495–496
Media influence on gender, 130–132
Mediation, 443
Medicaid, 414
Medical abortion, 345–347
Medicare, 414, 537
Men
    and childcare, 382
    divorced fathers, 457–459
    fatherhood, 357–359
    infertility, 338
    as single parents, 373–374
    in the workforce, 396–397
Men's studies, 55–56, 62
Mesosystem (Ecological Model), 23, 30
Message, definition of, 81
Metamessage, definition of, 81
Mexican Americans and extended families, 10, 16
Microsystem (Ecological Model), 22–23, 30
Middle age as stage of human life cycle, 58–59
Military service, 419

deployment of women, 490
    divorce and, 433–434, 449
    working families in the, 393–394
Miller Social Intimacy Scale (MSIS), 160
Miscarriage, 339–340
Miscegenation, 264
Misoprostol, 345
Mixed couples, types of, 269
Money
    financial difficulties for deployed families, 394
    marriage and, 415–418, 420
    as source of marital conflict, 90, 388
Monogamism, 5
Monogamy, 5, 30, 303
Moral commitment, 224
Morning after pill, 344
Motherhood, 355–357. *See also* Parenthood
    historical role, 369
Mothering, definition of, 355
Mourning, 546, 550
Multigenerational family groups, 10
Multiracial individuals, 13
Muslim societies, experience of love in, 173–174
Mutual dependency, 195

Narcissistic entitlement, 98
Natalism, 330
National Coalition Against Domestic Violence, 507, 508
National Coalition of Free Men, 55
National Council on Aging (NCOA), 525–526, 527, 528, 539
National Council on Family Relations (NCFR), 27
National Marriage Project, 4, 9, 11
National Survey of Family Growth (NSFG), 11
National Transgender Advocacy Coalition (NTAC), 120, 121
Native Americans/Alaska Natives (NA/AI), 17–18
    racial/ethnic identity, development of, 376–377
    sexual scripts, 289
    singlehood and, 244, 245
    in the workforce, 393
Natural selection, 206
Nature-nurture debate, 106, 522
Needs
    for affiliation, 141
    fulfillment of, 196
Negative effects of divorce, 459–461
Neurotransmitters, 181
Never-married singles, 244–245, 246, 273
No-fault divorce, 424, 429, 430, 444
Noncoital sexual relations, 290–293
Nonfamily households, 6, 7, 243
Nonmarital sex
    cohabiting couples, 305–306
    gay and lesbian couples, 306
Non-normative influences, 523
Non-normative life events, 57, 62, 488, 505
Nonprobability samples, 43–44
Nonreciprocity, 538

Nonregulated couples, 94–95
Nonrelational messages, 85
Nonverbal communication, 84–86
Normative age-graded influences, 523
Normative developmental tasks, 56, 62
Normative history-graded influences, 523
Normative life events, 488, 505
Normlessness, 437
Norms, age-related, 325, 329
Nuclear family, 7–9
    communication within, 73
    definition of, 7
    stepfamilies, 475
Nurturing communication, 86

Observational research method, 41–42
Occupational sexism, 389
Off-time events, 57
Omiai, 212
Online dating, 216–219
On-time events, 56
Open boundaries, 70–71
Operant conditioning, 367
Operational definitions, 39–40
Opportunity cost method, 402
Oral-genital sex, 291, 294
Oral herpes, 300
Oral stage, of development, 366
Orderly separation, 438
Orgasmic response, 304–305, 314
Overtime, demands of, 401

Pair bonds, 211, 250
PAP test, 301
Paradox of Mexican American nuptuality, 432
Parental separation, as correlate of divorce, 427
Parenthood, 317–351, 354–384
    contemporary, 372–377
    co-parenting, 359–360
    delayed childbearing, 328–329, 348
    family size, 329–331
    fatherhood, 357–359, 383
    motherhood, 355–357, 382
    motives for having children, 322–325
    Perceptions of Parenting Inventory, 323, 324
    as process, 354–360, 382
    roles, division of, 369
    same-sex couples, 324–325, 349
    single parents, 372–374
    timing of, 325–326, 349
    transition to, 364–372, 383
Parenting
    best practices, 378–381, 384
    ethnic group differences, 363–364
    parents, 541–542
    sandwich generation, 541
    shift work and, 400
    styles of, 360–364, 383
Participatory caretaking, 374
Partner selection
    Social Exchange theory, 209–210
Passionate love, 177–180, 198, 309
    culture, influence of, 179–180
    definition of, 178

Roles, 76–77
  changes in, 489
  conflicting expectations, 91
  establishing marital, 261
  historical patterns, 369
  motherhood, 355–356
  parenthood, transition to, 364–366
Role strain, 77, 541
Romance
  history of, 174–175
  infatuation, 178–179
  parenthood and, 370
Romantic infatuation, 178–179
Romantic love, 173–174, 175, 178–179, 309
Routine housework, 370–371
Rules
  changes in, 489, 491
  creation of, 72–74
  domestic abuse and, 510

Sacrament of marriage, 4–5, 252
Sadaqa (charity marriages), 4
Same-sex partners, 3
  Adoption and, 343–344
  with children, 52, 375–376
  dating scripts, 214–215
  demographics, 247–248
  and the 2010 federal census, 12–13
  marriage, 132, 255, 256
  sexual satisfaction and, 306
Samples, 40, 43, 44
  convenience, 46
Sample size, 43
Sandwich generation, 541, 550
Satisfaction, 274, 306
  marital, 269–270, 302–305, 526–527, 529
  sexual, 314. *See also* Sexual satisfaction
  singlehood and, 246
Scientific method, 37–38, 62
Scripts, sexual, 281
Script theory, 213
Search cost of love, 196, 197
Secondary aging, 524–525
Secondary divorce stressors, 456
Second shift, 370, 407
Self-disclosure, 88, 145, 222
Self-revelation, 195
Self-righteousness, 98
Selye's General Adaptation Syndrome, 491, 493
Separate couples, 269
Separation period, 437–438, 454
Sex
  definition of, 106, 280–281
  differentiation of males and females, 108
  frequency of, in intimate relationships, 304
  hooking up, 219–221
  infidelity, 306–308
  love and, 308–310
  marital satisfaction and, 302–305
  noncoital, 291–293
  relationships and, 302–310, 314
  selection of, 109
  as source of marital conflict, 90
Sex assignment surgery (SRS), 121
Sex hormones, 107

Sexism, 116
Sexual arousal, 290
Sexual desire, 311
  and marriage, 252
Sexual development across the lifespan, 280–281
Sexual dyad, 305
Sexual dysfunction, 310–312, 314
Sexual harassment, 132–133
Sexual satisfaction
  after childbirth, 336
  aging and, 527–528
  love and, 310
Sexuality
  and adolescents, 155, 293–295
  after childbirth, 336, 349
  as component of intimacy, 146
  and culture, 281–289, 305
  and early adulthood, 295–297
  parents' influence on, 284
  relational aspects, 302–305
  versus sex, 280–281
Sexually transmitted infections (STIs), 297–302
Sexual orientation, 120, 282, 344
  and marriage, 255, 256
Sexual preference, 120
Sexual relations
  after testicular cancer, 292
  noncoital, 291–293
Sexual response, phases of, 291
Sexual scripting framework, 282
Sexual scripts, 281, 282–283, 313
Sexual selection, 206–208
Shared care, 409
Shared legal custody, 442
Shift work, 400–401
Simple infatuation, 177
Singlehood, 6, 7, 242–249, 273
  divorced singles, 248
  historical view, 243
  life satisfaction and, 246
  never-married singles, 244–246
  types of, 244
  urban tribes, 246
  widows and widowers, 248
Single-parent families, 10, 418
  communication within, 73
Single parents, 372–374, 383
  post-divorce challenges, 466–471, 482–483
  in the workforce, 395–397
Situational stress, 493
Social clock, 523
Social cognitive filter, 123
Social ecology, 21
Social Exchange theory, 208–210, 236
Social Expectations Model, 271
Social factors, impact on contemporary families, 13
Social identity, 144–145
Social institution, marriage as, 4
Social integration, 142
Socialization
  learning gender and, 125–132
  motherhood and, 355–356
  needs, 355

Socialization hypothesis, 427
Social Learning theory (SLT), 122–124, 368
Social phase of relationship decline, 436
Social Readjustment Rating Scale (SRRS), 493–494
Social science literature, reading/interpreting, 44–47
Social science research, 36–48, 61
  definition of, 36
Social union, 2–4
Social welfare, 414–415
Sociocultural context, of intimacy, 144
Sociocultural theories, 368
Sociocultural trends, 429–431
Socioeconomic status (SES), 388–389
  divorce and, 428
  healthcare and, 414
  poverty and, 413
Sociological cue, 223
Sole custody, 443
Solution-focused treatments, 446
Spanking, 379
Specialization, and marriage, 258
Speed dating, 215–216
Sperm banks, 338
Spirituality and resilience, 503
Spousal support, 440–441
  loss of, following death, 548
Stability and marriage, 258
Stage of Resistance, in stress response, 492
Stalking, 181–182, 200
Starter marriage, 431
Status and marriage, 258
Stay-at-home dads, 403–404
Stay-at-home moms, 402–403
Stepfamilies, 11
  adapting successfully, 479–480, 483
  challenges for adults and children, 477–479
  characteristics of, 474, 475–477
  communication within, 73
  definition of, 471
  types of, 474, 475
Stepfamily Association of America (SAA), 474, 476, 483
Stereotyped relationships, 149
Stereotypes and gender, 127, 128–130, 135
Sterility, 337
Stillbirth, 340–342, 349
Stonewalling, 95
Storgic lovers, 194
Storying, 86
Stress
  event-based, 493–496
  family development, 488–489, 491
  response-based, 491–493
  situational, 493
Stress management and young families, 504
Stressors, 489
  adaptive tasks, 500–501
  caregiving and, 540–541
Structural commitment, 224
Structural factors, 432
Structural Functionalism, 50–52, 62
Structural-Functionalist perspective (Talcott Parsons), 50, 62